ARTICLES on AMERICAN
and
BRITISH LITERATURE

an Index to Selected Periodicals, 1950-1977

ARTICLES on AMERICAN
and
BRITISH LITERATURE

an Index to Selected Periodicals, 1950-1977

compiled by

Larry B. Corse *and* Sandra Corse

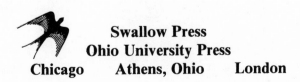

Swallow Press
Ohio University Press
Chicago   Athens, Ohio   London

Swallow Press Books
are Published by
Ohio University Press
Athens, Ohio

Library of Congress Cataloging in Publication Data

Corse, Larry B.
  Articles on American and British literature.

  ''Continuing bibliographies in the indexed
periodicals, 1950-1977'': p.
  1. American literature—History and criticism—
Bibliography. 2. English literature—History and
criticism—Bibliography. 3. American literature—
Periodicals—Indexes. 4. English literature—
Periodicals—Indexes. I. Corse, Sandra. II. Title.
Z1225.C67 [PS88]   016.820'9'0091   81-4010
ISBN 0-8040-0408-0   AACR2

TABLE OF CONTENTS

v

INSTRUCTIONS

The bibliography is organized by nationality, period, subject (author or topic), and author of article. The alphabetical listing of authors is preceded in each section by a listing of general articles on varying topics.

The subject headings are in capital letters. Each entry consists of the entry number, the author of the article, the title of the article enclosed in quotation marks, the abbreviation for the journal, the volume number, year of publication, and the page numbers:

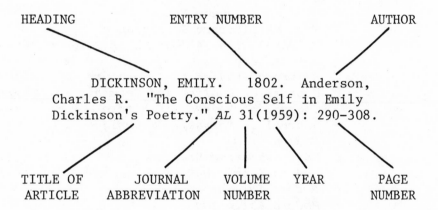

The table of abbreviations which follows provides the full name of each journal.

Preceding the main bibliography is a list of all bibliographies that are serialized in the indexed journals.

TABLE OF ABBREVIATIONS

AL	*American Literature*
ALR	*American Literary Realism, 1870-1910*
BALF	*Black American Literature Forum* [formerly *Negro American Literature Forum*]
CD	*Comparative Drama*
CLA	*College Language Association Journal*
Coll L	*College Literature*
Comp L	*Comparative Literature*
Con L	*Contemporary Literature* [formerly *Wisconsin Studies in Contemporary Literature*]
Crit	*Critique: Studies in Modern Fiction*
Criticism	*Criticism*
EAL	*Early American Literature*
EIC	*Essays in Criticism*
EL	*Essays in Literature* [Western Illinois Univ.]
ELH	*ELH*
ELN	*English Language Notes*
ELR	*English Literary Renaissance*
Ext	*Extrapolation: A Journal of Science Fiction and Fantasy*
HSL	*Hartford Studies in Literature*
JEGP	*Journal of English and Germanic Philology*
JML	*Journal of Modern Literature*
JNT	*Journal of Narrative Technique*
MD	*Modern Drama*
MFS	*Modern Fiction Studies*
MLR	*Modern Language Review*
MLQ	*Modern Language Quarterly*
MP	*Modern Philology*
NCF	*Nineteenth-Century Fiction*
NCL	*Notes on Contemporary Literature*
NEQ	*New England Quarterly*
Novel	*Novel: A Forum on Fiction*
PMLA	*PMLA*
PQ	*Philological Quarterly*
RD	*Renaissance Drama*
RES	*Review of English Studies*
SAF	*Studies in American Fiction*
SEL	*Studies in English Literature, 1500-1900*
SLI	*Studies in the Literary Imagination*
SLJ	*Southern Literary Journal*
SN	*Studies in the Novel*
SP	*Studies in Philology*
Speculum	*Speculum*
SR	*Studies in Romanticism*
SSF	*Studies in Short Fiction*
TCL	*Twentieth-Century Literature*
TSLL	*Texas Studies in Literature and Language*
VP	*Victorian Poetry*
WAL	*Western American Literature*
WC	*Wordsworth Circle*

CONTINUING BIBLIOGRAPHIES
IN THE INDEXED PERIODICALS, 1950-1977

"Anglo-German Literary Bibliography." *Journal of English and Germanic Philology* 49(1950)-60(1961).

"An Annual Bibliography of Afro-American, African, and Caribbean Literature." *College Language Association Journal* 20(1976-77)-21 (1977-78).

"Annual Bibliography of Studies in Western American Literature." *Western American Literature* 1(1966-67)-12(1977-78).

"Annual Review." [an annotated bibliography of studies of literature of the Modernist period] *Journal of Modern Literature* 1(1970-71)-6(1977).

"Bibliography." [of explications of short fiction] *Studies in Short Fiction* 1(1964)-14(1977).

"A Bibliography of Critical Arthurian Literature." *Modern Language Quarterly* 11(1950)-24(1963).

"A Bibliography of New England." *New England Quarterly* 23(1950)-39(1966).

"Bibliography on the Relations of Literature and the Other Arts." *Hartford Studies in Literature* 6(1974)-8(1976).

"Coleridge Scholarship." [bibliographic essay] *Wordsworth Circle* 3(1972)-8(1977).

"Current Bibliography." [an annotated bibliography of studies in twentieth-century literature] *Twentieth Century Literature* 1(]955-56)-23(1977).

"English Literature, 1660-1800: A Current Bibliography." [annotated] *Philological Quarterly* 29(1950)-49(1970). Bibliography continues as "The Eighteenth Century: A Current Bibliography." [annotated] *Philological Quarterly* 50(1971)-54(1975).

"Historical Novels." [review essay] *Speculum* 20(1950)-28(1953), 32(1957).

"Literature of the Renaissance." *Studies in Philology* 47(1950)-66(1969).

"Modern Drama: A Selective Bibliography of Works Published in English." *Modern Drama* 3(1960-61)-11(1968-69).

"Modern Drama Studies: An Annual Bibliography." *Modern Drama* 17 (1974)-20(1977).

"Recent Studies in Elizabethen and Jacobean Drama." [bibliographic essay] *Studies in English Literature, 1500-1900* 1(1961)-17(1977).

"Recent Studies in the English Renaissance." [bibliographic essay]
Studies in English Literature, 1500-1900 1(1961)-17(1977).

"Recent Studies in the Nineteenth Century." [bibliographic essay]
Studies in English Literature, 1500-1900 1(1961)-17(1977).

"Recent Studies in the Restoration and Eighteenth Century." [bibliographic essay] *Studies in English Literature, 1500-1900* 1(1961)-17(1977).

"The Romantic Movement: A Selective and Critical Bibliography."
Philological Quarterly 29(1950)-43(1964), *English Language Notes* 3(1965-66)-15(1977-78).

"A Selective and Critical Bibliography of Studies in Prose Fiction."
Journal of English and Germanic Philology 49(1950)-50(1951).

"Studies in Augustan Literature." [bibliographic essay] *Philological Quarterly* 55(1976)-56(1977).

"Studies in Eighteenth-Century Fiction." [bibliographic essay]
Philological Quarterly 55(1976)-56(1977).

"Studies in English Drama 1660-1800." [bibliographic essay] *Philological Quarterly* 55(1976)-56(1977).

"Studies in Restoration Literature." [bibliographic essay] *Philological Quarterly* 55(1976)-56(1977).

"Wordsworth Scholarship." [bibliographic essay] *Wordsworth Circle* 3(1972)-8(1977).

"The Year's Scholarship in Science Fiction and Fantasy." *Extrapolation* 17(1976)-18(1977).

"The Year's Work in Victorian Poetry." [bibliographic essay] *Victorian Poetry* 1(1963)-15(1977).

PREFACE

This cumulative bibliography was compliled to assist students using small college libraries with limited collections of literary periodicals. By selecting and indexing the periodicals most likely to be in these libraries over a period that includes the complete run of most of the journals, we hoped to provide them with a reference work that would greatly simplify access to the scholarly periodical material.

The bibliography should also prove useful to anyone who needs to locate periodical items quickly. Because it indexes forty-eight periodicals, including the major literary and many significant smaller journals, over a twenty-eight year period of intense literary scholarship, the bibliography provides in a single reference source a survey of a very large amount of this work.

Limitations of size and consideration of the value to the intended user, undergraduate students and others for whom completeness is not a primary concern, were factors in the choice of journals. We have not indexed journals whose articles while valuable to the professional scholar require, on the whole, a more specialized background than those in the indexed periodicals. Journals have not been indexed which are devoted to studies of a single author on the assumption that these journals can be easily searched and because inclusion of them would have greatly expanded this bibliography.

The selection has been further limited to those journals that are primarily devoted to scholarship on English-language literatures. We have, therefore, not indexed journals which publish large amounts of other material. There are some exceptions, notably *Speculum* and the *New England Quarterly*, which were included because of the significant material in certain areas, the omission of which would have weakened sections of the bibliography.

The rule we followed in the indexing was to list every item in the journals, excluding only book reviews, articles on foreign-language literatures, and articles on language and linguistics not directly related to literary matters. For those periodicals whose volume year does not coincide with the calendar year, those issues dated 1949 and 1978 were omitted.

We wish to acknowledge several people whose assistance made this work possible. Our son Theron spent hours sorting, alphabetizing, and running errands in libraries. Suzette Love, Barbara Fuller, Rosie Atkins, Winnie Thacker, and Penny Fort worked hard typing this difficult manuscript. We are especially grateful to June Woodard and Robert Harrell of Clayton Junior College's media services for instruction in preparation of camera-ready copy and the facilities for doing the work. And, finally, we wish to thank George Hendrick for his assistance, encouragement, and advice.

Larry B. Corse
Clayton Jr. College
Morrow, Georgia

Sandra Corse
Framingham State College
Framingham, Massachusetts

DRAMA. 1. Ashmore, Jerome. "Interdisciplinary Roots of the Theater of the Absurd." *MD* 14(1971): 72-83.

2. Barish, Jonas A. "Exhibitionism and the Antitheatrical Prejudice" *ELH* 36(1969): 1-29.

3. Blair, Herbert. "Language and Structure in Poetic Drama." *MLQ* 18(1957): 27-34.

4. Büdel, Oscar. "Contemporary Theater and Aesthetic Distance." *PMLA* 76(1961): 277-291.

5. Caine, Cindy S. A. M. "Structure in the One-Act Play." *MD* 12(1970): 390-398.

6. Caputi, Anthony. "The Shallows of Modern Serious Drama." *MD* 4(1961): 111-116.

7. Carlson, Marvin. "Modern Drama: A Selected Bibliography of Bibliographies." *MD* 8(1965): 112-118.

8. Carpenter, Charles A. "The New Bibliography of Modern Drama Studies." *MD* 12(1969) 49-56.

9. Cohn, Ruby. "Myth about Myths." *MD* 12(1969): 319-323.

10. "Commentary." [Esslin, Popovic, Tarn, Porubjak, Wirth, Hristic, Englch, Lasica, Czerwinski, Pronko] *CD* 3(1969): 219-229.

11. Dahlstrom, Carl E. W. L. "An Approach to Tragedy." *MD* 1(1958): 35-49.

12. ----------. "An Approach to Tragedy II: Aspects of the Tragic Vein." *MD* 1(1958): 71-83.

13. Eskin, Stanley G. "Theatricality in Avant-Garde Drama." *MD* 7(1964): 213-222.

14. Faber, M.D. "Analytic Prolegomena to the Study of Western Tragedy." *HSL* 5(1973): 31-60.

15. Fifield, Merle. "Quod quaeritis, O discipuli." *CD* 5(1971): 53-69.

16. Gassner, John. "Forms of Modern Drama." *Comp L* 7(1955): 129-143.

17. Gerstenberger, Donna. "Perspectives of Modern Verse Drama." *MD* 3(1960): 24-29.

18. Golden, Leon. "Aristotle, Frye, and the Theory of Tragedy." *Comp L* 27(1975): 47-58.

19. Grant, Thomas M. "American History in Drama: The Commemorative Tradition and Some Recent Revisions." *MD* 19(1976): 327-340.

20. Green, Gordon C. "The Propaganda Play." *MD* 4(1962): 429-430.

21. Groff, Edward. "Point of View in Modern Drama." *MD* 2(1959): 268-282.

22. Gutke, Karl S. "A Style for the Anti-Hero: Metaphysical Farce in the Modern Theater." *SLI* 9,#1(1976): 119-137.

23. Hanzeli, Victor E. "The Progeny of Atreus." *MD* 3(1960): 75-81.

24. Inglis, Fred. "Classicism and Poetic Drama." *EIC* 16(1966): 154-169.

25. Kaufman, R. J. "Epilogue." *CD* 3(1969): 230-235.

26. ----------. "On the Supersession of the Modern Classic Style." *MD* 2(1960): 358-369.

27. ----------. "Tragedy and Its Validating Conditions." *CD* 1(1967): 3-18.

28. Keyssar, Helene. "I Love You. Who Are You? The Strategy of Drama in Recognition Scenes." *PMLA* 92(1977): 297-306.

29. Knepler, Henry. "Translation and Adaptation in the Contemporary Drama." *MD* 4(1961): 31-41.

30. Kreutz, Irving. "Who's Holding the Mirror?" *CD* 4(1970): 79-88.

31. Kurman, George. "Entropy and the 'Death' of Tragedy: Notes for a Theory of Drama." *CD* 9 (1975): 283-304.

32. McGee, Timothy J. "The Role of the *Quem Quaeritis* Dialogue in the History of Western Drama." *RD* n.s. 7(1976): 177-192.

33. Mendelsohn, Leonard R. "The Player as Director: An Approach to Character." *CD* 6(1972): 115-124.

34. Norton, Elizabeth **Towne, and Robert P.** Shedd. "Modern Drama: A Selective Bibliography of Works Published in English in 1959." *MD* 3(1960): 143-161.

35. Parker, Gerald D. "The Modern Theatre as Autonomous Voice." *MD* 16(1973): 373-392.

36. Rockas, Leo. "The Subtext of Drama." *Coll L* 3(1976): 42-48.

37. Schwarz, Alfred. "Toward a Poetic of Modern Realistic Tragedy." *MD* 9(1966): 136-146.

38. Sellin, Eric. "Absurdity and the Modern Theatre." *CLA* 12(1969): 199-204.

39. Shedd, Robert G. "Modern Drama: A Selective Bibliography of Works Published in Enblish in 1960 and 1961." *MD* 5(1962): 223-244.

40. Sochatoff, A. Fred. "Four Variations on the Becket Theme in Modern Drama." *MD* 12(1969): 83-91.

41. Spanos, William V. "Modern Drama and the Aristotelian Tradition: The Formal Imperatives of Absurd Time." *Con L* 12(1971): 345-372.

42. Stein, Karen F. "Metaphysical Silence in Absurd Drama." *MD* 13(1970): 423-431.

43. Stroup, Thomas B. "Ritual and Ceremony in the Drama." *CD* 11(1977): 139-146.

44. Styan, J. L. "Drama as Ritual." *MLQ* 27 (1966): 323-331.

45. Thompson, Marjorie. "The Image of Youth in the Contemporary Theater." *MD* 7(1965): 433-445.

46. Usmiani, Renate. "A New Look at the Drama of 'Job'." *MD* 13(1970): 191-200.

47. Vowles, Richard B. "Psychology and Drama: A Selected Checklist." *Con L* 3,#1(1962): 35-48.

48. Weiss, Aureliu. "Mob Scenes: Their Generic Limitations." *CD* 1(1962): 254-265.

49. Wiessman, Philip. "A Lively Theater of Lives: Portraiture Versus Art." *MD* 2(1959): 263-267.

50. Witte, W. "The Mind's Construction: Characters at Cross Purposes." *MLR* 58(1963): 326-334.

51. Zilliacus, Clas. "Documentary Drama: Form and Content." *CD* 6(1972): 223-253.

FICTION. 52. Allott, Miriam. "The Temporal Mode: Four Kinds of Fiction." *EIC* 8(1958): 214-216.

53. Armstrong, Nancy. "Character, Closure, and Impressionist Fiction." *Criticism* 19(1977): 317-337.

54. Auerbach, Nina. "Incarnation of the Orphan." *ELH* 42(1975): 395-419.

55. Bickerton, Derek. "Modes of Interior Monologue: A Formal Definition." *MLQ* 28(1967): 229-239.

56. Bilan, R. P. "The Basic Concepts and Criteria of F. R. Leavis's Novel Criticism."

Novel 9(1976): 197-216.

57. Bjornson, Richard. "The Picaresque Novel in France, England, and Germany." *Comp L* 29)1977): 124-147.

58. Blanchard, Lydia. "Review - Essay: "Women and Fiction: The Limits of Criticism." *SN* 9(1977): 339-354.

59. Bland, D. S. "Endangering the Reader's Neck: Background Description in the Novel." *Criticism* 3(1961): 121-139.

60. Blissett, William. "Wagnerian Fiction in English." *Criticism* 5(1963): 239-260.

61. Bloom, Edward, ed. "In Defense of Authors and Readers." *Novel* 11(1977): 5-25.

62. Bonwit, Marianne. "Babel in Modern Fiction." *Comp L* 2(1950): 236-247.

63. Booth, Wayne C. "Distance and Point-of-View; An Essay in Classification." *EIC* 11(1961): 60-79.

64. ----------. *"The Rhetoric of Fiction and the Poetics of Fictions."* *Novel* 1(1968): 105-117.

65. Bowling, Lawrence Edward. "What Is The Stream of Consciousness Technique?" *PMLA* 65(1950): 333-345.

66. Bradbury, Malcolm. "Towards a Poetics of Fiction: (1) An Approach Through Structure." *Novel* 1(1967): 45-52.

67. Brantlinger, Patrick. "Romances, Novels, and Psychoanalysis." *Criticism* 17(1975): 15-40.

68. Buckeye, Robert. "The Anatomy of the Psychic Novel." *Crit* 9,#2(1967): 33-45.

69. Champagny, Robert. "Implicitness in Narrative Fiction." *PMLA* 85(1970): 988-991.

70. Clark, Priscilla P. "Newspapers and Novels: Some Common Functions and Themes." *SN* 7(1975): 166-180.

71. Cohn, Dorrit. "Narrated Monologue: Definition of a Fictional Style." *Comp L* 18(1966): 97-112.

72. Cox, James T., Margaret Putnam, and Marvin Williams. "Textual Studies in the Novel: A Selected Checklist, 1950-1974." *SN* 7(1975): 445-471.

73. Detweiler, Robert. "The Moment of Death in Modern Fiction." *Con L* 13(1972): 269-294.

74. Dodsworth, Martin. "The Truth of Fiction." *EIC* 9(1959): 443-446.

75. Fogel, Stanley. "'And All The Little Typologies': Notes on Language Theory in the Contemporary Experimental Novel." *MFS* 20(1974): 328-336.

76. Freedman, William. "The Literary Motif: A Definition and Evaluation." *Novel* 4(1971): 123-131.

77. Friedman, Norman. "Point of View in Fiction; The Development of a Critical Concept." *PMLA* 70(1955): 1160-1184.

78. Frohock, W. M. "The Failing Center: Recent Fiction and the Picaresque Tradition." *Novel* 3(1969): 62-69.

79. Gerstenberger, Donna. "Conceptions Literary and Otherwise: Women Writers and the Modern Imagination." *Novel* 9(1976): 141-150.

80. Gindin, James. "Review - Essay: Thwarted Expectations." *SN* 6(1974): 477-485.

81. Goldberg, M. A. "Chronology, Character, and the Human Condition: A Reappraisal of the Modern Novel." *Criticism* 5(1963): 1-12.

82. Grant, Douglas. "The Novel and Its Critical Terms." *EIC* 1(1951): 421-429.

83. Greenberg, Alvin. "Breakable Beginnings: The Fall into Reality in the Modern Novel." *TSLL* 10(1968): 134-142.

84. ----------. "The Death of the Psychic: A Way to the Self in the Contemporary Novel." *Criticism* 8(1966): 1-18.

85. ----------. "The Novel of Disintegration: Paradoxical Impossibility in Contemporary Fiction." *Con L* 7(1966): 103-124.

86. Greenman, Myron. "Understanding New Fiction." *MFS* 20(1974): 307-316.

87. Grella, George. "Murder and Manners: The Formal Detective Novel." *Novel* 4(1970): 30-48.

88. Gross, Beverly. "Narrative Time and the Open-Ended Novel." *Criticism* 8(1966): 362-376.

89. Guerard, Albert J. "The Illuminating Distortion." *Novel* 5(1972): 101-121.

90. Hardy, Barbara. "Towards a Poetics of Fiction: (3) An Approach Through Narrative." *Novel* 2(1968): 5-14.

91. Hardy, William. "Toward a Formalist Criticism of Fiction." *TSLL* 3(1961): 81-88.

92. Harold, Brent. "The Intrinsic Sociology in Fiction." *MFS* 23(1977): 593-599.

93. Harvey, W. J. "Work in Progress I: Character and the Context of Things." *EIC* 13(1963): 50-66.

94. Hernadi, Paul. "Dual Perspective: Free Indirect Discourse and Related Techniques." *Comp L* 24(1972): 32-43.

95. Hoffman, Frederick J. "The Moment of Violence: Ernst Jünger and the Literary Problem of Fact." *EIC* 10(1960): 405-421.

96. Honan, Park. "Realism, Reality, and the Novel (A Symposium)." *Novel* 2(1969): 197-211.

97. Humphrey, Robert. "'Stream of Consciousness': Technique or Genre?" *PQ* 30(1951): 434-347.

98. Hutchens, Eleanor N. "Towards a Poetics of Fiction: (5) The Novel as Chronomorph." *Novel* 3(1970): 215-224.

99. Johnson, James William. "The Adolescent Hero: A Trend in Modern Fiction." *TCL* 5(1959): 3-11.

100. Kagle, Stephen Earl. "The Societal Quest." *Ext* 12(1971): 79-85.

101. Kahler, Erich. "The Transformation of Modern Fiction." *Comp L* 7(1955): 121-128.

102. Kermode, Frank. "Novel, History and Type." *Novel* 1(1968): 231-238.

103. Kuehn, Robert E. "The Novel Now: Some Anxieties and Prescriptions." *Con L* 7(1966): 124-141.

104. Kumar, Shiv K. "Bergson's Theory of the Novel." *MFS* 6(1960): 337-344.

105. Lesser, Simon O. "The Attitude of Fiction." *MFS* 2(1956): 47-55.

106. Lodge, David. "Towards a Poetics of Fiction: (2) An Approach Through Language." *Novel* 1(1968): 158-169.

107. May, Derwent. "The Novelist as Moralist and Moralist as Critic." *EIC* 10(1960): 320-328.

108. Merivale, Patricia. "The Raven and the Bust of Pallas: Classical Artifacts and the Gothic Tale." *PMLA* 89(1974): 960-966.

109. Miller, J. Hillis. "Narrative and History." *ELH* 41(1974): 455-473.

110. Moss, Howard. "Notes on Fiction." *Con L* 7(1966): 1-20.

111. Ong, Walter, S.J. "Form, Theme, and Audience Is Always a Fiction." *PMLA* 90(1975): 9-21.

112. Paris, Bernard J. "Form, Theme, and Imitation in Realistic Fiction." *Novel* 1(1968): 140-149.

113. Parrinder, Patrick. "The Look of Sympathy: Communication and Moral Purpose in the Realistic Novel." *Novel* 5(1972): 135-147.

114. Pascal, Roy. "The Autobiographical Novel and the Autobiography." *EIC* 9(1959): 134-150.

115. ----------. "Narrative Fictions and Reality." *Novel* 11(1977): 40-50.

116. ----------. "Tense and Novel." *MLR* 57(1962): 1-11.

117. Pratt, Annis. "Women and Nature in Modern Fiction." *Con L* 13(1972): 476-490.

118. Reed, Walter L. "The Problems with a Poetics of the Novel." *Novel* 9(1976): 101-113.

119. Rodway, A. E. "The Truth of Fiction." *EIC* 8(1958): 405-417.

120. ----------. "The Truth of Fiction." *EIC* 9(1959): 447-449.

121. Ruthrof, H. G. "Aspects of a Phenomenological View of Narrative." *JNT* 5(1975): 87-99.

122. Ryf, Robert S. "Character and Imagination in the Experimental Novel." *MFS* 20(1974): 317-327.

123. Schickel, Richard. "The Old Critic and the New Novel." *Con L* 5(1964): 26-36.

124. Scholes, Robert. "The Contributions of Formalism and Structuralism to the Theory of Fiction." *Novel* 6(1973): 134-151.

125. ----------. "On Realism and Genre." *Novel* 2(1969): 269-271.

126. ----------. "Towards a Poetics of Fiction: (4) An Approach Through Genre." *Novel* 2(1969): 101-111.

127. Spacks, Patricia Meyer. "Taking Care: Some Women Novelists." *Novel* 6(1972): 36-51.

128. Spiegal, Alan. "Flaubert to Joyce: Evolution of a Cinematographic Form." *Novel* 6 (1973): 229-243.

129. Stevick, Philip. "Naive Narration: Classic to Post Modern." *MFS* 23(1977): 531-542.

130. ----------. "Novel and Anatomy: Notes Toward an Amplification of Frye." *Criticism* 10 (1968): 153-165.

131. Stoehr, Taylor. "Realism and Verisimilitude." *TSLL* 11(1969): 1269-1288.

132. Tanselle, G. Thomas. "Problems and Accomplishments in the Editing of the Novel." *SN* 7(1975): 323-360.

133. Todorov, Tzvetan. "Structural Analysis of Narrative." *Novel* 3(1969): 70-76.

134. Turner, Paul. "Novels, Ancient and Modern." *Novel* 2(1968): 15-24.

135. Visser, N. W. "Temporal Vantage Point in the Novel." *JNT* 7(1977): 81-93.

136. Wallace, Ronald. "Never Mind that the Nag's a Pile of Bones: The Modern Novel and the Comic Tradition." *TSLL* 19(1977): 1-23.

137. Watt, Ian. "Realism and the Novel." *EIC* 2(1952): 376-396.

138. ----------. "Second Thoughts Series: Serious Reflections on *The Rise of the Novel*." *Novel* 1(1968): 205-218.

139. Welsh, Alexander. "Realism as a Practical and Cosmic Joke." *Novel* 9(1975): 23-39.

140. West, Paul. "The Nature of Fiction." *EIC* 13(1963): 95-100.

141. Wicks, Ulrich. "The Nature of Picaresque: A Modal Approach." *PMLA* 89(1974): 240-249.

142. Yeazell, Ruth. "Fictional Heroines and Feminist Critics." *Novel* 8(1974): 29-38.

FICTION (SCIENCE FICTION). 143. Aldiss, Brian. "The Billion Year Spree: I. Origin of the Species." *Ext* 14(1973): 167-191.

144. Armytage, W. H. G. "Extrapolators and the Exegetes of Evolution." *Ext* 7(1965): 2-17.

145. Badami, Mary Kenny. "A Feminist Critique of Science Fiction." *Ext* 18(1976): 6-19.

146. Barthell, Robert J. "SF: A Literature of Ideas." *Ext* 13(1971): 56-63.

147. Canary, Robert H. "Science Fiction as Fictive History." *Ext* 16(1974): 81-96.

148. Clareson, Thomas D. "An Annotated Bibliography of Critical Writings Dealing with Science Fiction." *Ext* 11(1970): 56-83.

149. ----------. "An Annotated Bibliography of Critical Writings Dealing with Science Fiction." [Part II] *Ext* 12(1970): 35-59.

150. ----------. "An Annotated Bibliography of Material Dealing with Science Fiction." [Part III] *Ext* 12(1971): 109-145.

151. ----------. "Science Fiction: The New Mythology." *Ext* 10(1969): 69-115.

152. Clareson, Thomas D. and Edward S. Lanterbach. "A Checklist of Articles Dealing with Science Fiction." *Ext* 1(1960): 29-34.

153. Clarke, I. F. *Voices Prophesying War*: Problems in Research." *Ext* 9(1968): 26-32.

154. Fergus, George. "A Checklist of SF Novels with Femal Protogomists." *Ext* 18(1976): 20-27.

155. Friend, Beverly. "Virgin Territory: Women and Sex in Science Fiction." *Ext* 14 (1972): 49-58.

156. Hall, H. W. "The Bibliographic Control of Science Fiction." *Ext* 15(1973): 42-50.

157. Hammilton, John B. "Notes Toward a Definition of Science Fiction." *Ext* 4(1962): 2-14.

158. Hillegas, Mark R. "The Clarkson Collection of Science Fiction at Harvard." *Ext* 5 (1963): 2-14.

159. ----------. "Science Fiction and the Idea of Progress." *Ext* 1(1960): 25-28.

160. ----------. "Science Fiction as Cultural Phenomenon: A Re-evaluation." *Ext* 4(1963): 26-33.

161. Johnson, William B. "A Checklist on the Martian 'Canal' Controversy." *Ext* 5(1964): 40-48.

162. Johnson, William B. and Thomas D. Clareson. "The Interplay of Science and Fiction: The Canals of Mars." *Ext* 5(1964): 37-39.

163. Kaufman, V. Mils. "Brave New Improbable Worlds: Critical Notes on 'Extrapolation' as Mimetic Technique in Science Fiction." *Ext*

5(1963): 17-24.

164. Kroitor, Harry P. "The Special Demands of Point of View in Science Fiction." *Ext* 17(1976): 153-159.

165. McClintock, Michael W. "Some Preliminaries to the Criticism of Science Fiction." *Ext* 15(1973): 17-24.

166. Merril, Judith. "What Do You Mean - Science? Fiction?" [Part I] *Ext* 7(1966): 30-46.

167. ----------. "What Do You Mean - Science? Fiction?" [Part II] *Ext* 8(1966): 2-19.

168. Michaelson, L. W. "Science Fiction and Social Change." *Ext* 11(1969): 25-27.

169. Mitchell, Stephen O. "Alien Vision: The Techniques of Science Fiction." *MFS* 4(1958): 346-356.

170. Mobley, Jane. "Toward a Definition of Fantasy Fiction." *Ext* 15(1974): 117-128.

171. Mumper, Mark. "*SF*: A Literature of Humanity." *Ext* 14(1972): 90-93.

172. Munson, Ronald. "*SF*: The Literature of Possibility." *Ext* 15(1973): 35-41.

173. Newell, Kenneth B. "Science Fiction and the Merging of Realism." *Ext* 14(1972): 6-12.

174. Newman, John. "America at War: Horror Stories for a Society." [bibliography] *Ext* 16(1974): 33-41.

175. ----------. "America at War: Horror Stories for a Society." [bibliography] [Part II] *Ext* 16(1975): 164-191.

176. Pfeiffer, John. "Black American Speculative Literature: A Checklist." *Ext* 17 (1975): 35-43.

177. Russ, Joanna. "Dream Literature and Science Fiction." *Ext* 11(1969): 6-14.

178. ----------. "The Subjuctivity of Science Fiction." *Ext* 15(1973): 51-59.

179. Samuelson, David N. "The Spinning Galaxy: A Shift in Perspective on Magazine *SF*" *Ext* 17(1975): 44-48.

180. Stevenson, Lionel. "The Artistic Problem: Science Fiction as Romance." *Ext* 4(1963): 17-22.

181. Suvin, Darko. "*SF* Theory: Internal and External Delimination and Utopia." *Ext* 19 (1977): 13-15.

182. Teitler, Stuart A. "By the World Forgot." [bibliography] *Ext* 12(1970): 106-108.

183. Weinkauf, Mary S. "Theme for SF: Aesthetics and Overpopulation." *Ext* 13(1972): 152-164.

184. Wilson, Robert H. "Some Recurrent Symbols in Science Fiction." *Ext* 2(1960): 2-4.

185. Wolfe, Gary K. "The Limits of Science Fiction." *Ext* 14(1972): 30-38.

186. Wolf, Jack C. "Science Fiction and the Fallacy of Hope." *Ext* 17(1976): 151-152.

187. Wymer, Thomas L. "Perception and Value in Science Fiction." *Ext* 16(1975): 103-112.

FICTION (SHORT FICTION). 188. Baldeshwiler, Eileen. "The Lyric Short Story: The Sketch of a History." *SSF* 6(1969): 443-453.

189. Burns, Landon C. "A Cross-Reference Index of Short Story Anthologies and Author - Title Listing." *SSF* 7(1970): 1-218.

190. ----------. "A Cross-Referenced Index of Short Fiction Anthologies and Author - Title Listing." *SSF* 13(1976): 113-276.

191. Burns, Landon C. and Janet P. Alwang. "A Third Supplement to a Cross-Referenced Index of Short Fiction Anthologies and Author-Title Listings." *SSF* 14(1977): 203-232.

192. Fitzgerald, Gregory. "The 'Satiric Short Story': A Definition." *SSF* 5(1968): 349-354.

193. Friedman, Norman. "What Makes a Short Story Short?" *MFS* 4(1958): 103-117.

194. Good, Graham. "Notes on the Novella." *Novel* 10(1977): 197-211.

195. Gullason, Thomas A. "The Short Story: An Underrated Art." *SSF* 2(1964): 13-31.

196. May, Charles E. "The Unique Effect of the Short Story: A Reconsideration and An Example." *SSF* 13(1976): 289-297.

197. Williams, Phillip G. "Teaching the Short Story in the Community College." *Coll L* 4(1977): 165-175.

FICTION (UTOPIAN AND ANTI-UTOPIAN). 198. Beauchamp, Gorman. "Cultural Primitivism as Norm in the Dystopian Novel." *Ext* 19(1977): 88-96.

199. Bowman, Sylvia E. "Utopian Views of Man and the Machine." *SLI* 6,#2(1973): 105-120.

200. Ketterer, David. "Utopian Fantasy as Millennial Motive and Science-Fictional Motif." *SLI* 6,#2(1973): 79-103.

201. Lewis, Arthur O., Jr. "The Anti-Utopian Novel: Preliminary Notes and a Checklist." *Ext* 2(1961): 27-32.

202. Patrick, J. Max. "Inside Utopia." *Ext* 8(1966): 20-24.

203. Rhodes, Carolyn H. "Intelligence Testing in Utopia." *Ext* 13(1971): 25-47.

204. Rose, Steven. "The Fear of Utopia." *EIC* 24(1978): 55-70.

205. Sargent, Lyman Tower. "Opportunities for Research on Utopian Literature to 1900." *Ext* 19(1977): 16-26.

206. ----------. "Utopia - The Problem of Definition." *Ext* 16(1975): 137-148.

207. Stevick, Philip. "The Limits of Anti-Utopia." *Criticism* 6(1964): 233-245.

208. Suvin, Darko. "Defining the Literary Genre of Utopia: Some Historical Semantics, Some Geneology, A Proposal and a Plea." *SLI* 6,#2(1973): 121-145.

209. Wager, W. Warren. "Utopian Studies and Utopian Thought: Definitions and Horizons." *Ext* 19(1977): 4-12.

210. Walsh, Chad. "Attitudes Toward Science in the Modern 'Inverted Utopias.'" *Ext* 2(1961): 23-26.

211. Weinkauf, Mary S. "Edenic Motifs in Utopian Fiction." *Ext* 11(1969): 15-22.

FILM. 212. Daniel, Wendell. "A Researcher's Guide and Selected Checklist to Film as Literature and Language." *JML* 3(1973): 323-350.

213. Horman, Sidney R. "The Uses of Silence: The Elizabethan Dumb Shows and the Silent Cinema." *CD* 2(1968): 213-228.

214. Rogers, Ivor. "Redemption of Physical Reality in SF Films." *Ext* 13(1972): 85-91.

215. Silverstein, Norman. "Film and Language, Film and Literature." *JML* 2(1971): 154-160.

216. Smith, Julian. "Short Fiction on Film: A Selected Filmography." *SSF* 10(1973): 397-409.

FOLKLORE. 217. Abrahams, Roger. "Folklore in Culture: Notes toward an Analytic Method." *TSLL* 5(1963): 98-110.

218. ----------. "The Literary Study of the Riddle." *TSLL* 14(1972): 177-197.

219. Leach, MacEdward. "Problems of Collecting Oral Literature." *PMLA* 77(1962): 335-340.

220. Paredes, Americo. "Some Aspects of Folk Poetry." *TSLL* 6(1964): 213-225.

221. Thompson, Stitch. "The Challenge of Folklore." *PMLA* 79(1964): 357-365.

LANGUAGE. 222. Brown, James. "Eight Types of Puns." *PMLA* 71(1956): 14-26.

223. Cioffari, Vincenzo. "The Printed Word-The Language of Thought." *CLA* 7(1963): 170-173.

224. Delany, Samuel R. "About Five Thousand One Hundred and Seventy-five Words." *Ext* 10(1969): 52-66.

225. Farrison, W. Edward. "Dialectology Versus Negro Dialect." *CLA* 13(1969): 21-26.

226. French, Warren. *"Texas Studies in English*: A Bibliographical Momento." *TCL* 6(1960): 33-35.

227. Hill, Archibald A. "Principles Governing Semantic Parallels." *TSLL* 1(1959): 356-365.

228. Hulme, Hilda. "The English Language as a Medium of Literary Expression." *EIC* 8(1958): 68-76.

229. Jones, Kirkland C. "The Language of the Black 'In-Crowd': Some Observations of Intra-Group Communication." *CLA* 15(1971): 80-89.

230. Kemp, Lorena E. "Linguistics and Grammatical Rules." *CLA* 7(1964): 263-268.

231. Levin, Samuel R. "On Automatic Production of Poetic Sequences." *TSLL* 5(1963): 138-146.

232. Levy, Raphael. "The Etymology of English Bawd and Cognate Terms." *PQ* 32(1953): 83-89.

233. McCarles, Michael. "The Literal and the Metaphorical: Dialectic or Interchange." *PMLA* 91 (1976): 279-290.

234. Morgan, Raleigh, Jr. "African Linguistic Features in Creolized Languages." *CLA* 14(1970): 42-56.

235. ----------. "Factors in Speech Variation and Change." *CLA* 8(1964): 13-20.

236. Palmer, R. Roderick. "The Marriage of Linguistics and Syntax." *CLA* 9(1965): 83-90.

237. Roberts, Thomas J. "Literary - Linguistics: A Bibliography, 1946-1961." *TSLL* 4(1963): 625-629.

238. Sommerfelt, Alf. "The Interrelationship of Language and Culture." *TSLL* 1(1960): 449-456.

239. Waters, Frank. "Words." *WAL* 3(1968): 227-234.

240. Williamson, Juanita V. "Selected Features of Speech: Black and White." *CLA* 13(1970): 420-433.

241. Zanger, Jules. "'Guinea': Dialect and Stereotype." *CLA* 18(1975): 553-562.

LITERARY CRITICISM. 242. Abrams, M. H. "A Note on Wittgenstein and Literary Criticism." *ELH* 41(1974): 541-554.

243. Adams, Robert M. "Transparency and Opaqueness." *Novel* 7(1974): 197-209.

244. Altieri, Charles F. "Northrup Frye and the Problem of Spiritual Authority." *PMLA* 87(1972): 964-975.

245. Amis, Kingsley. "'Emily-coloured primulas.'" *EIC* 2(1952): 342-345.

246. Armstrong, J. H. Scobell. "A Note on 'Persuasive Definitions.'" *EIC* 6(1956): 111-113.

247. Bateson, F. W. "Abstract and Concrete Imagery." *EIC* 4(1954): 206-211.

248. ----------. "Catharsis: An Excision from the Dictionary of Critical Terms." *EIC* 8(1958): 119-120.

249. ----------. "Contributions to a Dictionary of Critical Terms: I. 'Comedy of Manners.'" *EIC* 1(1951): 89-94.

250. ----------. "Contributions to a Dictionary of Critical Terms: II. 'Dissociation of Sensibility.'" *EIC* 1(1951): 302-312.

251. ----------. "Criticism and the Public." *EIC* 3(1953): 468-470.

252. ----------. "Criticism for Criticism's Sake." *EIC* 4(1954): 337-339.

253. ----------. "Dissociation of Sensibility." *EIC* 2(1952): 213-214.

254. ----------. "The Function of Criticism at the Present Time." *EIC* 3(1953): 1-27.

255. ----------. "How to Teach Reading." *EIC* 7(1957): 468-470.

256. ----------. "Language and Literature." *EIC* 8(1958): 335-336.

257. ----------. "Language and Literature." *EIC* 18(1969): 176-182.

258. ----------. "Literature and Linguistics." *EIC* 17(1967): 335-347.

259. ----------. "A Note on 'Persuasive Definitions.'" *EIC* 6(1956): 116.

260. ----------. "The Object of Literary Criticism." *EIC* 14(1964): 436-437.

261. ----------. "Organs of Critical Opinion. II. *The Review of English Studies*." *EIC* 6(1956): 190-201.

262. ----------. "Organs of Critical Opinion. IV. *The Times Literary Supplement*." *EIC* 7(1957): 349-362.

263. ----------. "The Review of English Studies." *EIC* 6(1956): 478-480.

264. ----------. "The School of Knight." *EIC* 4(1954): 222-224.

265. ----------. "Textual Criticism and its Problems." *EIC* 17(1967): 385-391.

266. ----------. "Textual Criticism and its Problems." *EIC* 18(1968): 96-100, 460--.

267. ----------. "Tragedy and 'Tragedy.'" *EIC* 5(1955): 287-289.

268. Beebe, Maurice. "Introduction: What Modernism Was." [with bibliography] *JML* 3(1974): 1065-1084.

269. Bilsky, Manuel. "I. A. Richards' Theory of Metaphor." *MP* 50(1952): 130-137.

270. Bloom, Edward A. "The Allegorical Principle." *ELH* 18(1951): 163-190.

271. ----------. "The Vatic Temper in Literary Criticism." *Criticism* 5(1963): 297-315.

272. Bloom, Edward A. and Lillian D. "The Satiric Mode of Feeling: A Theory of Intention." *Criticism* 11(1969): 115-139.

273. Bloomfield, Morton W. "A Grammatical Approach to Personification Allegory." *MP* 60(1962): 161-171.

274. Bogerhoff, E. B. O. "'Mannerism' and 'Baroque': A Simple Plea." *Comp L* 5(1953): 323-331.

275. Bowers, Fredson. "Established Texts and Definitive Editions." *PQ* 41(1962): 1-17.

276. Breitkreuz, Hartmut. "Motif and Literary Genesis." *ELN* 8(1971): 267-269.

277. Browne, Robert M. "Grammar and Rhetoric in Criticism." *TSLL* 3(1961): 144-157.

278. Butt, John. "The Review of English Studies." *EIC* 6(1956): 475-478.

279. Cary, Norman Reed. "An Apologetic for Christian Criticism: A Comment on 'The Vatic Temper in Literary Criticism.'" *Criticism* 6(1964): 266-272.

280. Collie, M. J. "Information vs. Persuasion: A Note on Critical Method." *EIC* 6(1956): 241-245.

281. ----------. "Social Security in Literary Criticism." *EIC* 9(1959): 151-158.

282. Crane, R. S. "Literature, Philosophy, and the History of Ideas." *MP* 52(1954): 73-83.

283. Crompton, Donald W. "The New Criticism: A Caveat." *EIC* 10(1960): 359-364.

284. Crutwell, Patrick. "The State of Criticism." *EIC* 3(1953): 365-367.

285. Culler, Jonathan. "Beyond Interpretation: the Prospects of Contemporary Criticism." *Comp L* 28(1976): 244-256.

286. Curtis, James M. "Bergson and Russian Formalism." *Comp L* 28(1976): 109-121.

287. Davie, Donald. "Second Thoughts: III - F. R. Leavis's 'How to Teach Reading.'" *EIC* 7(1957): 232-241.

288. Davis, Robert Murray. "On Editing Modern Texts: Who Should Do What, and to Whom?" *JML* 3(1974): 1012-1020.

289. Dawson, S. W. "'Provincial' - A Modern Literary Term." *EIC* 5(1955): 275-280.

290. Dembo, L. S. "Introduction and Perspective." *Con L* 9(1968): 277-289.

291. DeNeef, A. Leigh. "On the Teaching of Literary Criticism." *Coll L* 2(1975): 85-96.

292. Dollerup, Cay, and F. W. Bateson. "The Mode of Existence of the Criticism of Literature: An Argument." *EIC* 19(1969): 420-433.

293. Douglas, Wallace W. "The Meanings of 'Myth' in Modern Criticism." *MP* 50(1953): 232-242.

294. Edgley, R. "The Object of Literary Criticism." *EIC* 14(1964): 221-236.

295. Eliot, T. S. "The Three Provincialities (1922). With a Postscript (1950)." *EIC* 1(1951): 38-41.

296. Empson, William. "Answers to Comments." *EIC* 3(1953): 114-120.

297. ----------. "The Intentional Fallacy, Again." *EIC* 23(1973): 435.

298. ----------. "Yes and No." *EIC* 5(1955): 88-90.

299. Enright, D. J. "Criticism for Criticism's Sake." *EIC* 4(1954): 333-337.

300. ----------. "Literature and/or Belief." *EIC* 7(1957): 112-113.

301. ----------. "Literature and/or Belief: A Progress Report." *EIC* 6(1956): 60-69.

302. Erlich, Victor. "Limits of the Biographical Approach." *Comp L* 6(1954): 130-137.

303. Evans, Ellis. "Mr. R. A. Sayce on Meaning." *EIC* 8(1958): 111-113.

304. Farley-Hills, D. L. "Dr. Leavis' Critical Apologia." *Criticism* 3(1961): 95-100.

305. Fife, Robert Herdon. "The Basis of Literary History." *PMLA* 66,#1(1951): 11-20.

306. Foster, Richard. "Criticism as Poetry." *Criticism* 1(1959): 100-122.

307. Fowler, Roger. "Language and Literature." *EIC* 18(1968): 164-176.

308. ----------. "Literature and Linguistics." *EIC* 17(1967): 322-335.

309. Frazer, Ray. "The Origin of the Term *Image*." *ELH* 27(1960): 149-162.

310. French, A. L. "Purposive Imitation: A Skirmish with Literary Theory." *EIC* 22(1972): 109-130.

311. French, Warren. "Six Years of *New World Writing*: As Bibliographical Guide." *TCL* 3(1958): 190-196.

312. Frye, Northrup. "On Value Judgments." *Con L* 9(1968): 311-318.

313. Garg, T. M. "Intention." *EIC* 7(1957): 175-186.

314. Garard, Albert. "On the Logic of Romanticism." *EIC* 7(1957): 262-273.

315. Gifford, Henry. "Criticism and the Public." *EIC* 3(1953): 463-468.

316. Gilman, E. "Literary and Moral Values." *EIC* 21(1971): 180-194.

317. Gleckner, Robert F. "Romanticism and the Self-Annihilation of Language." *Criticism* 18(1976): 173-189.

318. Gray, James. "Abstract and Concrete Imagery." *EIC* 4(1954): 198-206, 211-212.

319. Gray, J. M. "Aristotle's Poetics and Elder Olson." *Comp L* 15(1963): 164-175.

320. Greenwood, E. B. "Language and Literature." *EIC* 18(1968): 477-478.

321. Grossvogel, David. "Perception as a Form of Phenomological Criticism." *HSL* 1(1969): 83-88.

322. Guillén, Claudio. "Poetics as a System." *Comp L* 22(1970): 193-222.

323. Haas, W. "Language and Literature." *EIC* 8(1958): 325-327.

324. Hagopian, John V. "Symbol and Metaphor in the Transformation of Reality into Art." *Comp L* 20(1968): 45-54.

325. Hardy, Barbara. "Formal Analysis and Common Sense." *EIC* 11(1961): 112-115.

326. Harland, Richard. "Intention and Critical Judgement." *EIC* 25(1975): 215-225.

327. Hartman, Geoffrey. "Crossing Over: Literary Commentary and Literature." *Comp L* 28(1976): 257-276.

328. Harvey, W. J. "The Temporal Mode." *EIC* 7(1957): 471.

329. Hasley, Louis. "The Interpretation of Beliefs in Literature." *CLA* 5(1961): 95-106.

330. Hawkins, Harriett. "As we Read the Living?" *EIC* 24(1974): 97-100.

331. Hayman, Ronald. "How to Teach Reading." *EIC* 7(1957): 465-468.

332. ----------. "Organs of Critical Opinion. II. Reviewing in *The New Statesman and The Spectator*." *EIC* 6(1956): 434-445.

333. Hill, D. M. "Catharsis: Am Excision From the Dictionary of Critical Terms." *EIC* 8(1958): 113-119.

334. Hiroch, E. D. "Faulty Perspectives." *EIC* 25(1975): 154-168.

335. ----------. "Literary Evaluation as Knowledge." *Con L* 9(1968): 319-331.

336. ----------. "Objective Interpretation." *PMLA* 75(1960): 463-479.

337. Hoffman, Frederick J. "The Scholar-Critic: Trends in Contemporary British and American Literary Study." *MLQ* 26(1965): 1-15.

338. Holland, Norman N. "Transactive Criticism: Re-creation Through Identity." *Criticism* 18(1976): 334-352.

339. Holloway, John. "The New and Newer Critics." *EIC* 5(1955): 365-381.

340. ----------. "The Temporal Mode." *EIC* 7(1957): 470-471.

341. James, G. Ingli. "The Unexplored Romanticism." *Criticism* 1(1959): 62-71.

342. Jameson, Fredric. "Metacommentary." *PMLA* 86(1971): 9-18.

343. Jarrett-Kerr, Martin. "The State of Criticism." *EIC* 3(1953): 363-364.

344. Killham, John. "My Quarrel with Booth." *Novel* 1(1968): 267-272.

345. Knight, G. Wilson. "The New Interpretation." *EIC* 3(1953): 382-395.

346. ----------. "The School of Knight." *EIC* 4(1954): 217-222, 430-431.

347. Knox, Norman. "On the Classification of Ironies." *MP* 70(1972): 53-62.

348. Kridl, Manfred. "The Integral Method of Literary Scholarship: Theses for Discussion." *Comp L* 3(1951): 18-31.

349. Krieger, Murray. "The Existential Basis of Contextual Criticism." *Criticism* 8(1966): 305-317.

350. ----------. "Literary Analysis and Evaluation—— And the Ambidextrous Critic." *Con L* 9(1968): 290-310.

351. Larrissy, Edward. "'The Intentional Fallacy'." *EIC* 23(1973): 212-215.

352. Leakey, F. W. "Intention in Metaphor." *EIC* 4(1954): 191-198.

353. Leavis, F. R. "The State of Criticism." *EIC* 3(1953): 364-365.

354. Lee, Brian and Allan Rodway. "Coming to Terms." *EIC* 14(1964): 109-125.

355. Leech, Clifford. "The Presuppositions of Tragedy." *EIC* 5(1955): 178-181.

356. Lerner, Laurence D. "Cliché and Commonplace." *EIC* 6(1956): 249-265.

357. LeRoy, Gaylord, and Ursula Beitz. "The Marxist Approach to Modernism." *JML* 3(1974): 1158-1174.

358. Levin, Harry. "Criticism in Crisis." *Comp L* 7(1955): 144-155.

359. ----------. "What Is Realism?" *Comp L* 3(1951): 193-199.

360. Madden, William. "The Divided Tradition of English Criticism." *PMLA* 73(1958): 69-80.

361. Malone, Kemp. "British and American." *MLR* 53(1958): 405-408.

362. Marsh, Robert. "The 'Fallacy' of Universal Intention." *MP* 55(1958): 263-275.

363. Martin, Wallace. "The Hermeneutic Circle and the Art of Interpretation." *Comp L* 24(1972): 97-117.

364. Massey, Irving. "Two Types of Visual Metaphor." *Criticism* 19(1977): 285-295.

365. Maxwell, J. C. "The Presuppositions of Tragedy." *EIC* 5(1955): 175-178.

366. ----------. "Textual Criticism and its Problems." *EIC* 17(1967): 383-385.

367. ----------. "Textual Criticism and its Problems." *EIC* 18(1968): 87-88, 237-239, 459-460.

368. Mayoux, Jean-Jacques. "At the Sources of Symbolism." *Criticism* 1(1959): 279-297.

369. McArthur, Herbert. "Tragic and Comic Modes." *Criticism* 3(1961): 36-45.

370. McNulty, J. Bard. "Literature as a Form of Order." *Coll L* 3(1976): 1-16.

371. Michel, Laurence. "The Emperor's Clothes (again) or, Is Criticism Possible? (again)." *EIC* 15(1965): 239-243.

372. ----------. "Yardsticks for Tragedy." *EIC* 5(1955): 81-88.

373. Morrell, Roy. "The Psychology of Tragic Pleasure." *EIC* 6(1956): 22-37.

374. Muir, Kenneth. "Criticism: Practical and Impractical." *EIC* 8(1958): 340-345.

375. Nelson, Cary. "Reading Criticism." *PMLA* 91(1976): 801-815.

376. Nokes, Geoffrey, "'Emily-coloured primulas.'" *EIC* 2(1952): 338-342.

377. Noland, Richard. "The Future of Psychological Criticism." *HSL* 5(1973): 88-105.

378. Norman, Liane. "Risk and Redundancy." *PMLA* 90(1975): 285-291.

379. O'Connor, Gerard W. "The Many Ways to Read an 'Old' Book." *Ext* 15(1973): 72-74.

380. Ong, Walter J., S. J. "A Dialectic of Aural and Objective Correlatives." *EIC* 8(1958): 166-181.

381. ----------. "The Jinnee in the Well-Wrought Urn." *EIC* 4(1954): 309-320.

382. ----------. "The Jinnee in the Well-Wrought Urn." *EIC* 5(1955): 195.

383. Orsini, G. N. G. "The Organic Concepts in Aesthetics." *Comp L* 21(1969): 1-30.

384. Oxenhandler, Neal. "Ontological Criticism in America and France." *MLR* 55(1960): 17-23.

385. **Palomo**, Dolores. "Scholes, Barthes, and Structural Criticism." *MLQ* 36(1975): 193-206.

386. Peter, John. "Symbol and Implication: Notes Apropos of a Dictum of Coleridge's." *EIC* 4(1954): 145-167.

387. Pittock, Malcolm. "How to Teach Reading." *EIC* 7(1957): 462-465.

388. Raleigh, John Henry. "The New Criticism as an Historical Phenomenon." *Comp L* 11(1959): 21-28.

389. Ramsey, Paul. "A Question of Judgement: Wimsatt on Intent." *EIC* 22(1972): 408-416.

390. Richards, Bernard. "Memorability as a Critical Criterion." *EIC* 26(1976): 42-49.

391. Roberts, Mark. "Organs of Critical Opinion. III. Reviewing in the *London Magazine* and some other Monthlies." *EIC* 7(1957): 144-162.

392. Rodway, Allan. "Intention and Purport." *EIC* 25(1975): 477.

393. Rodway, A. E. and G. Salgado. "The School of Knight." *EIC* 4(1954): 212-217.

394. Rogers, Robert. "A Gathering of Roses - An Essay on the Limits of Context." *HSL* 5(1973): 61-76.

395. Salmon, Vivian. "Language and Literature." *EIC* 8(1958): 327-334.

396. Sanders, Scott. "The Left-handedness

of Modern Literature." *TCL* 23(1977): 417-436.

396a. Sayce, R. A. "Literature and Language." *EIC* 7(1957): 119-133.

397. Scher, Steven Paul. "Notes toward a Theory of Verbal Music." *Comp L* 22(1970): 147-156.

398. Schwartz, Elias. "The Problem of Literary Genres." *Criticism* 13(1971): 113-130.

399. Selden, Raman. "Objectivity, and Theory in Literary Criticism." *EIC* 23(1973): 283-297.

400. Sewall, Richard B. "The Tragic Form." *EIC* 4(1954): 345-358.

401. Shumaker, Wayne. "A Modest Proposal for Critics." *Con L* 9(1968): 332-348.

402. Sleight, Richard. "Mr. Empson's Complex Words." *EIC* 2(1952): 325-337.

403. Smith, Constance I. "A Comment on *Essays in Criticism*." *EIC* 7(1957): 345-346.

404. Spencer, Benjamin T. "Criticism: Centrifugal and Centripetal." *Criticism* 8(1966): 139-154.

405. Spilka, Mark. "The Necessary Stylist: A New Critical Revision." *MFS* 6(1960): 283-297.

406. Staff, Antonia. "Intention and Purport." *EIC* 26(1976): 97-98.

407. Stein, Walter. "Literature and/or Belief: A Progress Report." *EIC* 6(1956): 344-347.

408. Stark, Richard. "The Emperor's Clothes Again." *EIC* 15(1965): 471-473.

409. Stedmon, John. "Literature and Language." *EIC* 7(1957): 475-477.

410. Steiner, F. George. "Contributions to a Dictionary of Critical Terms. 'Egoism' and 'Egotism.'" *EIC* 2(1952): 444-452.

411. Steinmann, Martin, Jr. "A Note on 'Persuasive Definitions.'" *EIC* 6(1956): 113-116.

412. ----------. "Tragedy or 'Tragedy .'" *EIC* 5(1955): 281-287.

413. Storch, R. F. "The Jinnee in the Well-Wrought Urn." *EIC* 5(1955): 193-195.

414. Sutherland, Raymond Carter. "Theological Notes on the Origin of Types, 'Shadows of Things to Be.'" *SLI* 8,#1(1975): 1-13.

415. Thompson, Eric. "'Dissociation of Sensibility.'" *EIC* 2(1952): 207-213.

416. Thorpe, James. "The Aesthetics of Textual Criticism." *PMLA* 80(1965): 465-482.

417. Turner, Darwin T. "A Primer for Critics." *CLA* 8(1965): 217-224.

418. Vivas, Eliseo. "Mr. Wimsatt on the Theory of Literature." *Comp L* 7(1955): 344-361.

419. ----------. "Reply to Some Criticism." *Criticism* 9(1967): 123-131.

420. Von Hendy, Andrew. "A Poetics for Demogorgon: Northrop Frye and Contemporary Criticism." *Criticism* 8(1966): 318-335.

421. Waggoner, Hyatt H. "The Current Revolt Against the New Criticism." *Criticism* 1(1959): 211-225.

422. Wasiolek, Edward. "Anglo-American Empiricism and Literary Theory." *MP* 62(1965): 247-250.

423. ----------. "Croce and Contextualist Criticism." *MP* 57(1959): 44-54.

424. Wasson, Richard. "From Priest to Prometheus: Culture and Criticism in the Post-Modernist Period." *JML* 3(1974): 1188-1202.

425. Watson, George C. "Contributions to a Dictionary of Critical Terms: *Imagination* and

Fancy." *EIC* 3(1953): 201-214.

426. Wellek, René. "Hippolyte Taine's Literary Theory and Criticism." *Criticism* 1(1959): 1-18.

427. ----------. "Hippolyte Taine's Literary Theory and Criticism." (conclusion) *Criticism* 1 (1959): 123-138.

428. ----------. "Poetics, Interpretation, and Criticism." *MLR* 69(1974): xxi-xxxi.

429. White, David A. "Northrup Frye: Value and System." *Criticism* 15(1973): 189-211.

430. Wick, Warner. "Aesthetics and Ordinary Language." *MP* 53(1956): 187-198.

431. Wimsatt, W. K., Jr. "Croce and Art for Art's Sake." *EIC* 6(1956): 358-361.

432. ----------. "History and Criticism." *PMLA* 66,#1(1951): 21-31.

433. ----------. "Horses of Wrath: Recent Critical Lessons." *EIC* 12(1962): 1-17.

434. Zomberg, Paul G. "Textual Criticism and its Problems." *EIC* 18(1968): 88-96, 457-460.

MISCELLANEOUS. 435. Bell, Robert. "Metamorphoses of Spiritual Autobiography." *ELH* 44 (1977): 108-126.

436. Bluefarb, Sam. "The Middle-Aged Man in Contemporary Literature." *CLA* 20(1976): 1-13.

437. Boswell, Jackson Campbell. "Another Generation of Vipers." *ELN* 14(1976): 124-131.

438. Bowers, Fredson. "Current Theories of Copy-Text, with an Illustration from Dryden." *MP* 48(1950): 12-20.

439. Brown, Calvin S. "The Relations between Music and Literature as a Field of Study." *Comp L* 20(1970): 97-107.

440. Burke, Kenneth. "Thanatopsis for Critics: A Brief Thesaurus of Deaths and Dyings." *EIC* 2(1952): 369-375.

441. Cohn, Jan and Thomas H. Miles. "The Sublime: In Alchemy, Aesthetics, and Psychoanalysis." *MP* 74(1977): 289-304.

442. Duffey, Bernard. "Some Questions of Methods." *ELH* 31(1964): 318-329.

443. Elliott, Robert C. "The Satirist and Society." *ELH* 21(1954): 237-248.

444. Engstrom, Alfred G. "The Single Tear: A Stereotype of Literary Sensibility." *PQ* 42(1963): 106-109.

445. Farrison, W. Edward. "A Dictionary Editor's *Via Media*." *CLA* 10(1967): 209-216.

446. Garber, Frederick. "Self, Society, Value, and the Romantic Hero." *Comp L* 19(1967): 321-333.

447. Greenwood, E. B. "Literature and Philosophy." *EIC* 20(1970): 5-17.

448. Gregory, Horace. "Second Thoughts on the Teaching of Contemporary Literatur." *Con L* 5(1964): 18-25.

449. Guttmann, Allen. "The Conversion of the Jews." *Con L* 6(1965): 161-176.

450. Hodgart, M. J. C. "Misquotation as Re-creation." *EIC* 3(1953): 28-38.

451. Holland, Norman N. "UNITY IDENTITY TEXT SELF." *PMLA* 90(1975): 813-822.

452. Hutchens, Eleanor H. "The Identification of Irony." *ELH* 27(1960): 352-363.

453. Irwin, W. R. "The Survival of Pan." *PMLA* 76(1961): 159-167.

454. **Jackson, Irene Dobbs.** "*Negritude* in Full Bloom: A Study in Outline." *CLA* 7(1963):

77-83.

455. Johnston, Walter E. "The Shepherdess in the City." *Comp L* 26(1974): 124-141.

456. Kahler, Erich. "Doctor Faustus from Adam to Sartre." *CD* 1(1967): 75-92.

457. Kellman, Steven G. "Dropping Names: The Poetics of Titles." *Criticism* 17(1975): 152-167.

458. Korg, Jacob. "Language Change and Experimental Magazines, 1910-1930." *Con L* 13 (1972): 144-161.

459. Kroeber, Karl. "The Relevance and Irrelevance of Romanticism." *SR* 9(1970): 297-306.

460. Kurman, George. "Negative Comparison in Literary Epic Narrative." *Comp L* 21(1969): 337-347.

461. Lamont, Rosette C. "From Hero to Anti-Hero." *SLI* 9,#1(1976): 1-22.

462. Lerner, Lawrence. "Love and Gossip: or, How Moral is Literature." *EIC* 14(1964): 126-147.

463. Levin, Harry. "The Title as Literary Genre." *MLR* 72(1977): xxiii-xxxvi.

464. Lillyman, W. J. "The Blue Sky: A Recurrent Symbol." *Comp L* 21(1969): 116-124.

465. Mansell, Darrel. "Unsettling the Colonel's Hash: 'Fact' in Autobiography." *MLQ* 37 (1976): 115-132.

466. Meidnes, Olga McDonald. "Literature and Philosophy." *EIC* 20(1970): 385-390.

467. Morse, J. Mitchell. "The Artist as Savior." *MFS* 5(1959): 103-107.

468. Panshin, Alexei and Cory. "First Chapter: The World Beyond the Hill." *Ext* 13 (1972): 133-145.

469. Peckham, Morse. "Towards a Theory of of Romanticism." *PMLA* 66(1951): 5-23.

470. Peterson, R. G. "Critical Calculations: Measure and Symmetry in Literature." *PMLA* 91(1976): 367-375.

471. Pickering, Sam, Jr. "The First Part-Issue of New Fiction." *ELN* 13(1975): 124-127.

472. Pike, Burton. "Time in Autobiography." *Comp L* 28(1976): 326-342.

473. Praz, Mario. "Literary History." *Comp L* 2(1950): 97-106.

474. Richmond, Hugh M. "Personal Identity and Literary Personal: A Study in Historical Psychology." *PMLA* 90(1975): 209-221.

475. Silverstein, Theodore. "Allegory and Literary Form." *PMLA* 82(1967): 28-32.

476. Smith, J. Allen. "Aspects of Law and Literature: The Revival and the Search for Doctrine." *HSL* 9(1977): 213-222.

477. Starkey, Margaret M. "The History of Ideas and Literary Studies." *MLQ* 13(1952): 264-267.

478. Weintraub, Wiktor. "The Problem of Improvization in Romantic Literature." *Comp L* 16 (1964): 119-137.

479. Weisgerber, Jean. "The Use of Quotations in Recent Literature." *Comp L* 22(1970): 36-45.

480. Wellek, René. "Comparative Literature Today." *Comp L* 17(1965): 325-337.

481. Williams, Raymond. "The Idea of Culture." *EIC* 3(1953): 239-266.

482. Wimsatt, W. K., Jr. "Verbal Style: Logical and Counterlogical." *PMLA* 65(1950): 5-20.

483. Ziolkowski, Theodore. "The Telltale Teeth. Psychodontia to Sociodontia." *PMLA* 91(1976): 9-22.

POETRY. 484. Adams, Percy G. "The Historical Importance of Assonance to Poets." *PMLA* 88 (1973): 8-18.

485. Adler, Alfred. "In What Sense Can Poetic Meaning Be Verified?" *EIC* 2(1952): 196-206.

486. ----------. "The Verification of Poetic Meaning." *EIC* 3(1953): 109.

487. Allen, Dick. "What Rough Beast: SF-Oriented Poetry." *Ext* 17(1975): 8-17.

488. Alteiri, Charles. "Objective Image and Act of Mind in Modern Poetry." *PMLA* 91(1976): 101-114.

489. Balliet, Conrad A. "The History and Rhetoric of the Triplet." *PMLA* 80(1965): 528-534.

490. Bateson, F. W. "Immediacy in Poetry." *EIC* 2(1952): 460-462.

491. ----------. "The Matter of Metre." *EIC* 14(1964): 104-106.

492. ----------. "Poetry and the Positivists." *EIC* 7(1957): 474-475.

493. Bayley, John. "Immediacy in Poetry: A Romantic Plea." *EIC* 2(1952): 453-460.

494. Berland, Alwyn. "Some Techniques of Fiction in Poetry." *EIC* 4(1954): 372-385.

495. Boosleter, Paul C., Warren Creel, and George S. Hastings, Jr. "Perception and English Poetic Meter." *PMLA* 88(1973): 200-208.

496. Brown, Calvin S. "Monosyllables in English Verse." *SEL* 3(1963): 473-491.

497. Bruns, Gerald L. "Poetry as Reality: The Orpheus Myth and Its Modern Counterparts." *ELH* 37(1970): 263-286.

498. Cable, Thomas. "Timers, Stressers, Linguists: Contention and Compromise." *MLQ* 33 (1972): 227-239.

499. Cecil, Lord David. "Immediacy in Poetry." *EIC* 2(1952): 462-465.

500. Childs, Barney. "Articulation in Sound Structures: Some Notes Toward an Analytic." *TSLL* 8(1966): 423-445.

501. Cooper, Helen. "The Goat and the Eclogue." *PQ* 53(1974): 368-379.

502. Cotton, John. "These Be Your Gods, O Israel." *EIC* 5(1955): 296-297.

503. Cummings, D. W., and John Herum. "Metrical Boundaries and Rhythm-Phrases." *MLQ* 28(1969): 405-412.

504. Cunningham, J. V. "Logic and Lyric." *MP* 51(1953): 33-41.

505. Davis, C. W. "These Be Your Gods, O Israel." *EIC* 5(1955): 293-296.

506. Emma, Joan. "The Ethic of Disentegration: A Recent Case in Poetics." *Con L* 6(1965): 106-113.

507. Finney, Gretchen. "A World of Instruments." *ELH* 20(1953):87-120.

508. Fowler, A. D. S. "Rhythm and Meaning." *EIC* 6(1956): 352-357.

509. Fowler, Rowena. "Comparative Metrics and Comparative Literature." *Comp L* 29(1977): 289-299.

510. Gang, T. M. "Poetry and the Positivists." *EIC* 7(1957): 473-474.

511. Gaunt, David M. "The Creation-Theme in Epic Poetry." *Comp L* 29(1977): 213-220.

512. Gibbon, F. P. "Poetry and the Positi-

vists." *EIC* 7(1957): 472-473.

513. Gilbert, Sandra M. "'My Name is Darkness': The Poetry of Self-Definition." *Con L* 18 (1977): 443-457.

514. Graves, Robert. "These Be Your Gods, O Israel!" *EIC* 5(1955): 129-150.

515. Greene, Thomas. "The Norms of Epic." *Comp L* 13(1961): 193-207.

516. Greenfield, Stanley. "Ellipsis and Meaning in Poetry." *TSLL* 13(1971): 137-147.

517. ----------. "Grammar and Meaning in Poetry." *PMLA* 82(1967): 377-387.

518. Greenwood, E. B. "Poetry and Paradise: A Study in Thematics." *EIC* 17(1967): 6-25.

519. Hainsworth, J. D. "Poets and Brutes." *EIC* 12(1962): 98-104.

520. Halpern, Martin. "On the Two Chief Metrical Modes in English." *PMLA* 77(1962): 177-186.

521. Hamm, Victor M. "Meter and Meaning." *PMLA* 69(1954): 695-710.

522. Hendren, Joseph W. "A Word for Rhythm and a Word for Meter." *PMLA* 76(1961): 300-308.

523. Kneiger, Bernard. "Five Years of *The Explicator*: A Bibliographical Guide." *TCL* 6(1960): 136-144.

524. Kramer, Lawrence. "The Wodwo Watches the Water Clock: Language in Postmodern British and American Poetry." *Con L* 18(1977): 319-342.

525. Kurman, George. "Ecphrasis in Epic Poetry." *Comp L* 26(1974): 1-13.

526. Lerner, Laurence. "An Essay on Pastoral." *EIC* 20(1970): 271-297.

527. Mahoney, John L. "Some Antiquarian and Literary Influences of Percy's *Reliques*." *CLA* 7(1964): 240-246.

528. Malof, Joseph. "Meter as Organic Form." *MLQ* 27(1966): 3-17.

529. ----------. "The Native Rhythm of English Meters." *TSLL* 5(1964): 580-594.

530. Matthews, G. M. "Sex and the Sonnet." *EIC* 2(1952): 119-137.

531. McKeon, Richard. "Semantics, Science, and Poetry." *MP* 49(1952): 145-159.

532. Morgan, Bayard Quincy. "Compulsive Patterns in Poetry." *PMLA* 75(1960): 634-635.

533. Naremore, James. "The Imagists and the French 'Generation of 1900.'" *Con L* 11(1970): 354-374.

534. Nuttall, A. D. "Fishes in the Trees." *EIC* 24(1974): 20-38.

535. Olson, Elder. "William Empson, Contemporary Criticism and Poetic Diction." *MP* 47(1950): 222-252.

536. Pace, George B. "The Two Domains: Meter and Rhythm." *PMLA* 76(1961): 413-419.

537. Parker, Patricia. "The Progress of Phaedria's Bower: Spenser to Coleridge." *ELH* 40 (1973): 372-397.

538. Perloff, Marjorie. "The Two Poetries: An Introduction." *Con L* 18(1977): 263-278.

539. Perry, John Oliver. "The Relationship between Rhythm and Meaning." *Criticism* 7(1965): 373-378.

540. ----------. "The Relationships of Disparate Voices in Poems." *EIC* 15(1965): 49-64.

541. Ramsey, Paul. "Free Verse: Some Steps Toward Definition." *SP* 65(1968): 98-108.

542. Ridland, J. M. "The Matter of Metre." *EIC* 14(1964): 102-104.

543. Rodway, A. E. "The Verification of Poetic Meaning." *EIC* 3(1953): 105-108.

544. Rogers, Robert. "The Dynamics of Metaphor: Modes of Mentation in Poetry." *HSL* 3 (1971): 157-190.

545. Rosenthal, M. L. "Modern British and American Poetic Sequences." *Con L* 18(1977): 416-421.

546. Saunders, J. W. "Poetry in the Managerial Age." *EIC* 4(1954): 243-281.

547. Schwartz, Elias. "Rhythm and Meaning in English Verse." *Criticism* 6(1964): 246-255.

548. Schwartz, Elias, W. K. Wimsatt, Jr., and Monroe C. Beardsley. "Rhythm and 'Exercise in Abstraction.'" *PMLA* 77(1962): 668-674.

549. Siegel, Paul N. "Sex and the Sonnet." *EIC* 2(1952): 465-468.

550. Sims, D. L. "Rhythm and Meaning." *EIC* 6(1956): 347-352.

551. Soldatic, Joseph A. "Functions of Color in Poetry." *EL* 4(1977): 49-58.

552. Sullivan, Nancy. "Perspective and the Poetic Process." *Con L* 6(1965): 114-131.

553. Towne, Frank. "Logic, Lyric and Drama." *MP* 51(1954): 265-268.

554. Vigee, Claude. "Metamorphoses of Modern Poetry." *Comp L* 7(1959): 97-120.

555. West, Paul. "Symbol and Equivalent: The Poetry of Industrialism." *EIC* 9(1959): 61-71.

556. Wimsatt, W. K., Jr., and Monroe C. Beardsley. "A Word for Rhythm and a Word for Meter." *PMLA* 76(1961): 300-308.

557. ----------. "The Concept of Meter: An Exercise in Abstraction." *PMLA* 74(1959): 585-598.

558. Wright, George T. "The Lyric Present: Simple Present Verbs in English Poems." *PMLA* 89 (1974): 563-579.

GENERAL AND MISCELLANEOUS. 559. Abrahams, Roger D. "Creativity, Individuality, and the Traditional Singer." *SLI* 3,#1(1970): 5-34.

560. Banta, Martha. "American Apocalypses: Excrement and Ennui." *SLI* 7,#1(1974): 1-30.

561. Bluestein, Gene. "The Brotherhood of Sinners: Literary Calvinism." *NEQ* 50(1977): 195-213.

562. Brown, Lloyd W. "The West Indian as as Ethnic Stereotype in Black American Literature." *BALF* 5(1971): 8-14.

563. Carey, George A. "'And Everyone of Them's Gone But Me': Another Look at Tangier Island's Oldest Inhabitant." *SLI* 3,#1(1970): 73-87.

564. Carpenter, Frederic I. "'The American Myth': Paradise (To Be) Regained." *PMLA* 74(1959): 599-606.

565. Cawelti, John. "God's Country, Las Vegas and the Gunfighter: Differing Visions of the West." *WAL* 9(1975): 273-283.

566. ----------. "Prolegomena to the Western." *WAL* 4(1970): 259-271.

567. ----------. "The Writer as Celebrity: Some Aspects of American Literature as Popular Culture." *SAF* 5(1977): 161-174.

568. Cope, Jackson, and others. "Addenda to *Articles on American Literature Appearing in Current Periodicals, 1920-1945.*" *AL* 22(1950): 61-74.

569. Curnow, Wystan. "Romanticism and Modern American Criticism." *SR* 12(1973): 777-799.

570. Dance, Daryl C. "Tuning in the Boiler Room and the Cotton Patch: New Directions in the Study of Afro-American Folklore." *CLA* 20(1977): 547-553.

571. French, Warren. "West as Myth: Status Report and Call for Action." *WAL* 1(1966): 55-58.

572. Puttmann, Allen. "Images of Value and the Sense of the Past." *NEQ* 35(1962): 3-26.

573. Haslam, Gerald. "Literature of *The People:* Native American Voices." *CLA* 15(1971): 153-170.

574. Hill, A. A. "Three Examples of Unexpectedly Accurate Indian Lore." *TSLL* 6(1964): 80-83.

575. Holmes, J. Welfred. "Three Uncommon Records of the Commonplace." *CLA* 9(1966): 215-224.

576. Horgan, Paul. "The Pleasure and Perils of Regionalism" *WAL* 8(1974): 167-171.

577. Jones, Harry L. "An Essay on the Blues." *CLA* 13(1963): 62-67.

578. Jones, Iva G. "Research in Afro-American Literature." *CLA* 15(1971): 240-244.

579. McGhee, Nancy B. "The Folk Sermon: A Facet of the Black Literary Heritage." *CLA* 13(1969): 51-61.

580. Miller, Perry. "The Shaping of the American Character." *NEQ* 28(1955): 435-454.

581. Nower, Joyce. "The Traditions of Negro Literature in the United States." *BALF* 3(1969): 5-12.

582. Rickels, Milton. "The Humorists of the Old Southwest in the London *Bentleys* Miscellany." *AL* 27(1956): 557-560.

583. Rosenberg, Neil V. "The Communication of Attitudes: White Folklore about Negroes." *BALF* 3(1969): 88-90.

584. Siegel, Roslyn. "The Black Man and the Macabre in American Literature." *BALF* 10(1976): 133-136.

585. Twining, Mary Arnold. "An Anthropological Look at Afro-American Folk Narrative." *CLA* 14(1970): 57-61.

586. Twining, Mary A. and William C. Saunders. "'One of These Days': The Function of Two Singers in the Sea Island Community." *SLI* 3, #1(1970): 65-71.

587. VanDerBeets, Richard. "The Indian Captivity Narrative as Ritual." *AL* 43(1972): 548-562.

588. Walker, Don D. "Philosophical and Literary Implications in the Historiography of the Fur Trade." *WAL* 9(1974): 79-104.

589. Ward, William S. "American Authors and British Reviewers 1798-1826." *AL* 49(1977): 1-21.

590. Westbrook, Max. "The Practical Spirit: Sacrality and the American West." *WAL* 3(1968): 193-205.

591. Whicher, Stephen E. "Swedish Knowledge of American Literature, 1920-1952: A Supplementary Bibliography." *JEGP* 58(1959): 666-671.

592. Williams, Ora. "A Bibliography of Works Written by American Black Women." *CLA* 15(1972): 354-377.

DRAMA. 593. Stratman, Carl J., C.S.U. "American Dramatic Periodicals with Only One Issue, 1798-1959." *AL* 39(1967): 180-190.

594. Twining, Mary Arnold. "*Heaven Bound* or *The Devil Play:* A Note on Dichotomous Predicates." *CLA* 19(1976): 347-351.

FICTION. 595. Attebury, Louie W. "The American West and the Archetypal Orphan." *WAL* 5(1970): 205-217.

596. Bell, Bernard W. "Literary Sources of the Early Afro-American Novel." *CLA* 18(1974): 29-44.

597. Bennett, Stephen B. and William W. Nichols. "Violence in Afro-American Fiction: An Hypothesis." *MFS* 17(1971): 221-228.

598. Bowron, Bernard R., Jr. "Realism in America." *Comp L* 3(1951): 268-285.

599. Brightfield, Myron F. "American and the Americans, 1840-1860, as Depicted in English Novels of the Period." *AL* 31(1959): 309-324.

600. Buell, Lawrence. "New Views of American Narrative: A Review-Essay." *TSLL* 19(1977): 234-246.

601. Butler, Michael. D. "Sons of Oliver Edwards; or, The Other American Hero." *WAL* 12 (1977): 53-66.

602. Byrd, James W. "Stereotypes of White Characters in Early Negro Novels." *CLA* 1(1957): 28-35.

602a. Cardwell, Guy A. "The Plantation House: An Analogical Image." *SLJ* 2,#1(1969): 3-21.

603. Clareson, Thomas D. "An Annotated Checklist of American Science Fiction, 1880-1915." *Ext* 1(1959): 5-20.

604. Farrison, W. Edward. "Much Ado about Negro Fiction: A Review Essay." *CLA* 19(1975): 90-100.

605. Hansen, Arlen J. "The Celebration of Solipsism: A New Trend in American Fiction." *MFS*

19(1973): 5-16.

606. Harwell, Richard B. "Essay Review: Gone with Miss Ravenel's Courage, or Bugles Blow so Red: A Note on the Civil War Novel." *NEQ* 35 (1962): 253-261.

607. Jackson, Blyden. "A Golden Mean For The Negro Novel." *CLA* 3(1959): 81-87.

608. Jackson, Blyden. "The Negro's Image of the Universe as Reflected in His Fiction." *CLA* 4(1960): 22-31.

609. Lee, Hector H. "Tales and Legends in Western American Literature." *WAL* 9(1975): 239-254.

610. Male, Roy R. "The Story of the Mysterious Strangers in American Fiction." *Criticism* 3(1961): 281-294.

611. Meier, August. "Some Reflections on the Negro Novel." *CLA* 2(1959): 168-177.

612. Mills, Nicolaus. "American Fiction and the Genre Critics." *Novel* 2(1969): 112-122.

613. Nagel, James. "An Annotated Bibliography of Selected Recent Books on American Fiction." *SAF* 1(1973): 76-91.

614. Ramsey, Jarold W. "The Wife Who Goes Out like a Man, Comes Back as a Hero: The Art of Two Oregon Indian Narratives." *PMLA* 92(1977): 9-18.

615. Todd, Edgeley W. "A Note on 'The Mountain Man as Literary Hero'." *WAL* 1(1966): 219-221.

616. Turner, Darwin T. "*The Negro Novel in America:* In Rebuttal." *CLA* 10(1966): 122-134.

617. Walker, Don D. "The Mountain Man as Literary Hero." *WAL* 1(1966): 15-25.

618. Winner, Viola Hopkins. "The American Pictorial Vision: Objects and Ideas in Hawthorne, James, and Hemingway." *SAF* 5(1977): 143-159.

POETRY. 619. Barsness, John. "The Dying Cowboy Song." *WAL* 2(1967): 50-57.

620. Dippie, Brian W. "Bards of the Little Big Horn." *WAL* 1(1966): 175-195.

621. Haslam, Gerald. "American Indians: Poets of the Cosmos." *WAL* 5(1970): 15-29.

622. Hull, Gloria T. "Black Women Poets from Wheatley to Walker." *BALF* 9(1975): 91-96.

623. Lovell, John, Jr. "Reflections on the Origins of the Negro Spiritual." *BALF* 3(1969): 91-97.

624. Ross, Morton L. "Alan Swallow and Modern, Western American Poetry." *WAL* 1(1966): 95-104.

SEVENTEETH AND
EIGHTEENTH CENTURIES

GENERAL AND MISCELLANEOUS. 625. Andrews, William F. "The Literature of the 1727 New England Earthquake." *EAL* 7,#3(1973): 281-294.

626. Arner, Robert D. "The Death of Major André: Some Eighteenth-Century Views." *EAL* 11 (1976): 52-67.

627. ----------. "The Short, Happy Life of the Virginia 'Moniter'." *EAL* 7,#2(1972): 130-147.

628. Baker, Houston A., Jr. "Balancing the Perspective: A Look at Early Black American Literary Artistry." *BALF* 6(1972): 65-70.

629. Bercovitch, Sacvan. "Selective Checklist on Typology." *EAL* 5,#1 part 2(1970): 1-80.

630. ----------. "Selective Checklist on Typology: Part II." *EAL* 6(1972): Supplement, 1-80.

631. Boswell, Jackson Cambell. "A Check List of Americana in a *Short-Title Catalogue of Books Printed in England, Scotland, and Ireland and of English Books Printed Abroad 1475-1640.*" *EAL* 9,#2(1974): Supplement.

632. Bullough, Vern L. "An Early American Sex Manual or, Aristotle Who?" *EAL* 7,#3(1973): 236-246.

633. Cantor, Milton. "The Image of the Negro in Colonial Literature." *NEQ* 36(1963): 452-477.

634. Cutting, Rose Marie. "America Discovers Its Literary Past: Early American Literature in Nineteenth-Century Anthologies." *EAL* 9,#3 (1975): 226-251.

635. Davis, Richard Beale. "Southern Writing of the Revolutionary Period, c. 1760-1790." *EAL* 12(1977): 107-120.

636. Davis, Thomas M. "The Exegetical Traditions of Puritan Typology." *EAL* 5,#1 part 1 (1970): 11-50.

637. Granger, Bruce. "From Silence Dogood to Launcelot Langstaff." *EAL* 3,#1(1968): 11-16.

638. ----------. "Hudibras in the American Revolution." *AL* 27(1955): 499-508.

639. Hedges, William L. "Towards a Theory of American Literature, 1765-1800." *EAL* 4,#1(1969): 5-14.

640. Heimart, Alan. "Puritanism, the Wilderness, and the Frontier." *NEQ* 26(1953): 361-382.

641. Hook, Andrew D. "Scottish Contributions to the American Enlightenment." *TSLL* 8(1967): 519-532.

642. Jones, Phyllis. "Biblical Rhetoric and the Pulpit Literature of New England." *EAL* 11 (1977): 245-258.

643. Leary, Lewis. "Literature in New York, 1775." *EAL* 11(1976): 4-21.

644. Lemay, J. A. Leo. "Review Essay: Recent Bibliographies in Early American Literature." *EAL* 8,#1(1973): 66-77.

645. Manning, Stephen. "Typology and the Literary Critic." *EAL* 5,#1, part 1 (1970): 51-73.

646. Martin, Wendy. "Women and the American Revolution." *EAL* 11(1977): 322-335.

647. McAlexander, Patricia Jewell. "The Creation of the American Eve: The Cultural Dialogue on the Nature and Role of Women in Late Eighteenth-Century America." *EAL* 9,#3(1975): 252-266.

648. Modlin, Charles E. "Aristocracy in the Early Republic." *EAL* 6,#3(1972): 252-257.

649. Moore, Jack B. "Black Humor in An Early American Short Story." *EAL* 1,#2(1966): 7-8.

650. Mühlenfels, Astrid A. Von. "A Bibliography of German Scholarship on Early American Literature: 1850-." *EAL* 2,#2(1967): 32-35.

651. Murdock, Kenneth B. "Clio in the Wilderness: History and Biography in Puritan New England." *EAL* 6,#3(1972): 201-219.

652. Parker, David L. "Petrus Ramus and the Puritans: The 'Logic of Preparationist Conversion Doctrine'." *EAL* 8,#2(1973): 140-162.

653. Rees, Robert A. "Seeds of the Enlightenment: Pulbic Testamony in the New England Congregational Churches, 1630-1750."
EAL 3,#1(1968): 22-29.

654. Seigel, Jules Paul. "Puritan Light
Reading." *NEQ* 37(1964): 185-199.

655. Simpson, Lewis P. "Federalism and
the Crisis of Literary Order." *AL* 32(1960): 253-
266.

656. Stein, Roger B. "Seascape and the
American Imagination: The Puritan Seventeenth
Century." *EAL* 7,#1(1972): 17-37.

657. Stein, Stephen J. "An Apocalystic
Rationale for the American Revolution." *EAL* 9,
#3(1975): 211-225.

658. Stowell, Marion Barber. "American
Almanacs and Feuds." *EAL* 9,#3(1975): 276-285.

659. Strauch, Carl P. "Review Essay:
Typology and the American Renaissance." *EAL*
6,#2(1971): 167-178.

660. Tichi, Cecelia. "The American Revolution and the New Earth." *EAL* 11(1976): 202-
210.

661. ----------. "The Puritan Historians
and their New Jerusalem." *EAL* 6,#2(1971): 143-
155.

662. West, Paul. "Literature and Politics
II. Tocqueville on the Literature of Democracies."
EIC 12(1962): 254-272.

663. White, Eugene E. "Decline of the
Great Awakening in New England." *NEQ* 24(1951):
35-52.

664. Wilson, Joan Hoff. "Dancing Dogs of
the Colonial Period: Women Scientists." *EAL* 7,
#3(1973): 225-235.

665. Ziff, Lazar. "The Literary Consequences of Puritanism." *ELH* 30(1963): 293-305.

PROSE.   666. Galinsky, Hans. "Exploring
the Exploration Report." *EAL* 12(1977): 5-24.

667. Granger, Bruce. "The Addisonian Essay
in the American Revolution." *SLI* 9,#2(1976): 43-52.

668. Hankins, Richard. "Puritans, Patriots,
and Panegyric: The Beginnings of American Biography." *SLI* 9,#2(1976): 95-109.

669. Minter, David L. "By Dens of Lions:
Notes on Stylization in Early Puritan Captivity
Narratives." *AL* 45(1973): 335-347.

670. Wardenaar, Leslie A. "Humor in the
Colonial Promotional Tract: Topics and Techniques." *EAL* 9,#3(1975): 286-300.

FICTION.   671. Moore, Jack B. "'The Captain's Wife': A Native Short-Story Before Irving." *SSF* 1(1964): 103-106.

672. Sanderlein, R. Reed. "A Variant Version of 'The Child of Snow'." *EAL* 2,#2(1967): 22-
26.

673. Stein, Roger. "Pulled Out of the Bay:
American Fiction in the Eighteenth Century." *SAF*
2(1974): 13-36.

674. Tanselle, G. Thomas. "Review Essay:
Two Editions of Eighteenth Century Fiction."
EAL 6,#3(1972): 274-283.

675. Winans, Robert B. "The Growth of a
Novel-Reading Public in Late-Eighteenth-Century
America." *EAL* 9,#3(1975): 267-275.

POETRY.   676. Crawford, Richard. "Watts
for Singing. Metrical Poetry in American Sacred
Tunebooks, 1761-1785." *EAL* 11(1976): 139-146.

677. Daly, Robert. "Puritan Poetics: The
World, the Flesh, and God." *EAL* 12(1977): 136-162.

678. Henson, Robert. "Form and Content of
the Puritan Funeral Elegy." *AL* 32(1960): 11-27.

679. Kaiser, Leo M. "On the Latin in the
Meserole Anthology." *EAL* 6,#2(1971): 165-167.

680. Lemay, J. A. Leo. "Additions to
'Seventeenth-Century American Poetry: A Bibliography of the Scholarship, 1943-1966.'" *EAL* 1,#3
(1967): 14-15.

681. ----------. "Francis Knapp: A Red
Herring in Colonial Poetry." *NEQ* 39(1966): 233-237.

682. ----------. "Seventeenth-Century American Poetry: A Bibliography of the
Scholarship, 1943-1966." *EAL* 1,#1(1966): 9-18.

683. Pecora, Madeline. "The Date of 'The
Plain Case Stated'." *EAL* 6,#2(1971): 185-186.

684. Putnam, Michael C. J. "The Story of
the Storm." *NEQ* 33(1960): 489-501.

685. Wages, Jack D. "Elegy and Moch Elegy
in Colonial Virginia." *SLI* 9,#2(1976): 79-93.

686. Waggoner, Hyatt H. "Puritan Poetry."
Criticism 6(1964): 291-313.

DRAMA.   687. Mates, Julian. "The Dramatic
Anchor: Research Opportunities in the American
Drama Before 1800." *EAL* 5,#3(1971): 76-79.

688. Teunissen, John J. "Blockheadism
and the Propaganda Plays of the American Revolution." *EAL* 7,#2(1972): 148-162.

689. Tichi, Cecelia. "Thespis and the
'Carnall Hipocrite': A Puritan Motive for Aver-
sion to Drama." *EAL* 4,#2(1969): 86-103.

690. Zipes, Jack. "Dunlap, Kotzebue, and
the Shaping of American Theater: A Reevaluation
from a Marxist Perspective." *EAL* 8,#3(1974): 272-
284.

ADAMS, JOHN QUINCY. 691. Berry, Roger B.
"John Adams: Two Further Contributions to the
Boston Gazzette, 1766-1768." *NEQ* 31(1958): 90-99.

692. Kagle, Steven Earl. "The Diary of
John Adams and Motive of 'Achievement.'" *HSL* 3
(1971): 93-107.

693. Lewis, Robert G., and Walter J. Morris.
"John Quincy Adams' Verse Translation of Jean-
Baptiste Rouseau's *Ode à la Fortune.*" *NEQ* 44(1971):
444-458.

694. Rothman, Irving N. "Two Juvenalian
Satires by John Quincy Adams." *EAL* 6,#3(1972):
234-251.

695. Simpson, Lewis P. "John Adams and
Hawthorne: The Fiction of the Real American Revolution." *SLI* 9,#2(1976): 1-17.

ALLEN, JAMES.   696. Meserole, Harrison T.
"'Come dry-Brained Marble eyed Porticks': James
Allen and Francis Quarles." *EAL* I,#3(1967): 6-7.

ALSOP, RICHARD.   697. Fucilla, Joseph G.
"An Early American Translation of the Count Ugo-
lino Episode." *MLQ* 11(1950): 480-487.

AMES, FISHER.   698. Simpson, Lewis P.
"Federalism and the Crisis of Literary Order."
AL 32(1960): 253-266.

BARLOW, JOEL.   699. Arner, Robert D.
"The Smooth and Emblematic Song: Joel Barlow's
The Hasty Pudding." *EAL* 7,#1(1972): 76-91.

700. Christensen, Merton A. "Deism in Joel
Barlow's Early Work: Heterodox Passages in *The
Vision of Columbus.*" *AL* 27(1956): 509-520.

701. Egan, Clifford L. "On the Fringe of the Napoleonic Catastrophe: Joel Barlow's Letters from Central and Eastern Europe, 1812." *EAL* 10,#3(1976): 251-272.

702. Erdman, David V. "William Blake's Debt to Joel Barlow." *AL* 26(1954): 94-98.

703. Gimmestad, Victor. E. "Joel Barlow's Editing of John Trumbull's *M'Fingal*." *AL* 47 (1975): 97-102.

704. Griffith, John. "'The Columbiad' and 'Greenfield Hill': History, Poetry, and Ideology in the Late Eighteenth Century." *EAL* 10,#3 (1976): 235-250.

See also 686, 14655.

BARTRAM, WILLIAM. 705. Lee, Berta Grattan. "William Bartram: Naturalist or 'Poet'?" *EAL* 7,#2(1972): 124-129.

BAY PSALM BOOK. 706. Dorenkamp, J. H. "*The Bay Psalm Book* and the Ainsworth Psalter." *EAL* 7,#1(1972): 3-16.

707. Turner, Maxine. "Three Eighteenth-Century Revisions of the *Bay Psalm Book*." *NEQ* 45(1972): 270-277.

BEVERLEY, ROBERT. 708. Arner, Robert D. "The Quest for Freedom: Style and Meaning in Robert Beverley's *History and Present State of Virginia*." *SLJ* 8,#2(1976): 79-98.

BILLINGS, WILLIAM. 709. Barbow, J. Murray. "The Texts of Billings' Church Music." *Criticism* 1(1959): 49-61.

BLAIR, JAMES. 710. Bain, Robert A. "The Composition and Publication of *The Present State of Virginia, and the College*." *EAL* 6,#1(1971): 31-54.

711. -----------. "A Note on James Blair and the Southern Plain Style." *SLJ* 4,#1(1971): 68-73.

BOLLING, ROBERT. 712. Lemay, J. A. Leo. "Robert Bolling and the Bailment of Colonial Chiswell." *EAL* 6,#2(1971): 99-142.

BOWDOIN, JAMES. 713. Walett, Francis G. "James Bowdoin, Patriot Propagandist." *NEQ* 23 (1950): 320-338.

BRACKENRIDGE, HUGH HENRY. 714. Bush, Sargent, Jr. "*Modern Chivalry* and 'Young's Magazine.'" *AL* 44(1972): 292-299.

715. Haims, Lynn. "Of Indians and Irishmen: A Note on Brackenridge's Use of Sources for Satire in *Modern Chivalry*." *EAL* 10,#1(1975): 88-92.

716. Harkey, Joseph H. "The *Don Quixote* of the Frontier: Brackenridge's *Modern Chivalry*." *EAL* 8,#2(1973): 193-203.

717. Martin, Wendy. "The Rogue and the Rational Man: Hugh Henry Brackenridge's Study of a Con Man in *Modern Chivalry*." *EAL* 8,#2(1973): 179-192.

718. Nance, William L. "Satiric Elements in Brackenridge's *Modern Chivalry*." *TSLL* 9(1967): 381-389.

719. Smeall, J. F. S. "The Evidence that Hugh Brackenridge Wrote 'The Cornwalliad'." *PMLA* 80(1965): 542-548.

720. Whittle, Amberys R. "*Modern Chivalry*: The Frontier as Crucible." *EAL* 6,#3(1972): 263-270.

BRADFORD, WILLIAM. 721. Brumm, Ursula. "Did the Pilgrims Fall Upon Their Knees When They Arrived in the New World?" *EAL* 12(1977): 25-35.

722. Daly, Robert. "William Bradford's Vision of History." *AL* 44(1973): 525-537.

723. Hovey, Kenneth Alan. "The Theology of History in *Of Plymouth Plantation* and Its Predecessors." *EAL* 10,#1(1975): 47-66.

724. Major, Minor W. "William Bradford Versus Thomas Morton." *EAL* 5,#2(1970): 1-13.

BRADSTREET, ANNE. 725. Eberwein, Jane Donahue. "The 'Unrefined ore' of Anne Bradstreet's Quaternions." *EAL* 9,#1(1974): 19-26.

726. Hensley, Jeannine. "The Editor of Anne Bradstreet's Several Poems." *AL* 35(1964): 502-504.

727. Hildebrand, Anne. "Anne Bradstreet's Quaternions and 'Contemplations'." *EAL* 8,#2(1973): 117-125.

728. Irvin, William J. "Allegory and Typology 'Imbrace and Greet': Anne Bradstreet's 'Contemplations.'" *EAL* 10,#1(1975): 30-46.

729. Johnston, Thomas E. Jr., "A Note on the Voices of Anne Bradstreet, Edward Taylor, Roger Williams, and Philip Pain." *EAL* 3,#2(1968): 125-126.

730. Laughlin, Rosemary M. "Anne Bradstreet: Poet in Search of Form." *AL* 42(1970): 1-17.

731. "McMahon, Helen. "Anne Bradstreet, Jean Bertault, and Dr. Crooke." *EAL* 3,#2(1968): 118-123.

732, Requa. Kenneth A. "Anne Bradstreet's Poetic Voices." *EAL* 9,#1(1974): 3-18.

733. Richardson, Robert D., Jr. "The Puritan Poetry of Anne Bradstreet." *TSLL* 9(1967): 317-331.

734. Rosenfeld, Alvin H. "Anne Bradstreet's 'Contemplations': Patterns of Form and Meaning." *NEQ* 43(1970): 79-96.

735. Rosenmeir, Rosamund. "Divine Translation: A Contribution to the Study of Anne Bradstreet's Method in the Marriage Poems." *EAL* 12 (1977): 121-135.

736. Stanford, Ann. "Anne Bradstreet: An Annotated Checklist." *EAL* 3,#3(1969): 217-228.

737. ----------. "Anne Bradstreet: Dogmatist and Rebel." *NEQ* 39(1966): 373-389.

738. ----------. "Anne Bradstreet's Portrait of Sir Philip Sidney." *EAL* 1,#3(1967): 11-13.

See also 686, 4710.

BREWER, LUCY. 739. Medlicott, Alexander, Jr. "The Legend of Lucy Brewer: An Early American Novel." *NEQ* 39(1966): 461-473.

BROWN, CHARLES BROCKDEN. 740. Aldridge, A. Owen. "Charles Brockden Brown's Poem on Benjamin Franklin." *AL* 38(1966): 230-235.

741. Bell, Michael Davitt. "'The Double-Tongued Deceiver': Sincerity and Duplicity in the Novels of Charles Brockden Brown." *EAL* 9,#2(1974): 143-163.

742. Bennett, Charles E. "Charles Brockden Brown's 'Portrait of an Emigrant'." *CLA* 14(1970): 87-90.

743. Bernard, Kenneth. "*Arthur Mervyn*: The Ordeal of Innocence." *TSLL* 6,(1965): 441-459.

744. Berthoff, W. B. "'A Lesson on Concealment': Brockden Brown's Method in Fiction." *PQ* 37(1958): 45-57.

745. ----------. "Charles Brockden Brown's Historical 'Sketches': A Consideration." *AL* 28

(1956): 147-154.

746. Brancaccio, Patrick. "Studied Ambiguities: *Arthur Mervyn* and the Problem of the Unreliable Narrator." *AL* 42(1970): 18-27.

747. Bredahl, A. Carl. "Transformation in *Wieland*." *EAL* 12(1977): 177-192.

748. Butler, Michael D. "Charles Brockden Brown's *Wieland*: Method and Meaning." *SAF* 4(1976): 127-142.

749. Cleman, John. "Ambiguous Evil: A Study of Villains and Heroes in Charles Brockden Brown's Major Novels." *EAL* 10,#2(1975): 190-219.

750. Davies, Rosemary Reeves. "Charles Brockden Brown's *Ormond*: A Possible Influence upon Shelley's Conduct." *PQ* 43(1964): 133-137.

751. Franklin, Wayne. "Tragedy and Comedy in Brown's *Wieland*." *Novel* 8(1975): 147-163.

752. Gilmore, Michael T. "Calvinism and Gothicism: The Example of Brown's *Wieland*." *SN* 9(1977): 107-118.

753. Greiner, Donald J. "Brown's Use of the Narrator in *Wieland*: An Indirect Plea for the Acceptance of Fiction." *CLA* 13(1969): 131-136.

754. Hedges, William L. "Benjamin Rush, Charles Brockden Brown, and the American Plague Year." *EAL* 7,#3(1973): 295-311.

755. Hedges, William L. "Charles Brockden Brown and the Culture of Contradictions." *EAL* 9,#2 (1974): 107-142.

756. Hemenway, Robert. "Brockden Brown's Twice Told Insanity Tale." *AL* 40(1968): 211-215.

757. ----------. "Charles Brockden Brown's Law Study: Some New Documents." *AL* 39(1967): 199-204.

758. Hobson, Robert W. "Voices of Carwin and other Mysteries in Charles Brockden Brown's *Wieland*." *EAL* 10,#3(1976): 307-309.

759. Hughes, Philip Russell. "Archetypal Patterns in *Edgar Huntley*." *SN* 5(1973): 176-190.

760. Kimball, Arthur G. "Savages and Savagism: Brockden Brown's Dramatic Irony." *SR* 6 (1967): 214-225.

761. Krause, Sydney J. "*Ormond*: Seduction in a New Key." *AL* 44(1973): 570-574.

762. Lyttle, David. "The Case Against Carwin." *NCF* 26(1971): 257-269.

763. Manly, William M. "The Importance of Point of View in Brockden Brown's *Wieland*." *AL* 35 (1963): 311-321.

764. McAlexander, Patricia Jewell. "*Arthur Mervyn* and the Sentimental Love Tradition." *SLI* 9,#2(1976): 31-41.

765. Nelson, Carl. "A Just Reading of Charles Brockden Brown's *Dimond*." *EAL* 8,#2(1973): 163-178.

766. Reid, S. W. "Brockden Brown in England: Notes on Henry Colburn's 1822 Editions of his Novels." *EAL* 9,#2(1974): 188-195.

767. Schulz, Dieter. "Edgar Huntley as Quest Romance." *AL* 43(1971): 323-335.

768. Tichi, Cecelia. "Charles Brockden Brown, Translator." *AL* 44(1972): 1-12.

769. Tilton, Eleanor M. "'The Sorrows' of Charles Brockden Brown." *PMLA* 69(1954): 1304-1308.

770. Witherinton, Paul. "Benevolence and the 'Utmost Stretch': Charles Brockden Brown's Narrative Dilemma." *Criticism* 14(1972): 175-191.

771. Witherington, Paul. "Brockden Brown's Other Novels: *Clara Howard* and *Jane Talbot*." *NCF* 29(1974): 257-272.

772. ----------. "Charles Brockden Brown: A Bibliographical Essay." *EAL* 9,#2(1974): 164-187.

773. ----------. "Charles Brockden Brown's *Ormond*: The American Artist and His Masquerades." *SAF* 4(1976): 111-119.

774. Ziff, Lazar. "A Reading of *Wieland*." *PMLA* 77(1962): 51-57.

BROWN, WILLIAM HILL. 775. Arner, Robert D. "Sentiment and Sensibility: The Role of Emotion and William Hill Brown's *The Power of Sympathy*." *SAF* 1(1973): 121-132.

776. Byers, John R., Jr. "Further Verification of the Authorship of *The Power of Sympathy*." *AL* 43(1971): 421-427.

777. Davidson, Cathy N. "*The Power of Sympathy* Reconsidered: William Hill Brown as Literary Craftsman." *EAL* 10,#1(1975): 14-29.

778. Martin, Terence. "William Hill Brown's *Ira and Isabella*." *NEQ* 32(1959): 238-242.

779. Walser, Richard. "More About the First American Novel." *AL* 24(1952): 352-357.

BYRD, WILLIAM. 780. Adams, Percy G. "The Real Author of *William Byrd's Natural History of Virginia*." *AL* 28(1956): 211-220.

781. Arner, Robert D. "Westover and the Wilderness: William Byrd's Images of Virginia." *SLJ* 7,#2(1975): 105-123.

782. Dolmetsch, Carl R. "Response" to Maureen Sullivan, *EAL* 8,#1, 88-89 . *EAL* 8,#1(1973): 89-90.

783. ----------. "William Byrd II: Comic Dramatist?" *EAL* 6,#1(1971): 18-30.

784. ----------. "William Byrd of Westover as an Augustan Poet." *SLI* 9,#2(1976): 69-77.

785. Simpson, Lewis P. "Review Essay: William Byrd and the South." *EAL* 7,#2(1972): 187-195.

786. Siebert, Donald T. "William Byrd's *Histories of the Line*: The Fashioning of a Hero." *AL* 47(1976): 535-551.

787. Smith, David. "William Byrd Surveys America." *EAL* 11(1977): 296-310.

788. Sullivan, Maureen. "To the Editor." ["William Byrd II: Comic Dramatist?" *EAL* 6,#1, 18-33.] *EAL* 8,#1(1973): 88-89.

CHILTON, EDWARD. 789. Bain, Robert A. "The Composition and Publication of *The Present State of Virginia, and the College*." *EAL* 6,#1 (1971): 31-54.

CHURCH, BENJAMIN. 790. Bowden, Edwin T. "Benjamin Church's *Choice* and American Colonial Poetry." *NEQ* 32(1959): 170-184.

COLMAN, BENJAMIN. 791. Kaiser, Leo M. "Benjamin Colman's 'Hymn of Praise': Text and Comments." *EAL* 2,#2(1967): 27-31.

COOKE, EBENEZER. 792. Arner, Robert D. "Clio's *Rhimes*: History and Satire in Ebenezer Cooke's 'History of Bacon's Rebellion'." *SLJ* 1,#2 (1974): 91-106.

793. ----------. "*The Sot-Weed Factor*: The Structure of Satire." *SLJ* 4,#1(1971): 33-47.

794. Cohen, Edward T. "The Elegies of Ebenezer Cooke." *EAL* 4,#2(1969): 49-72.

See also 4618.

COTTLE, JABEZ.   795. McLoughlin, William G. "The Life of Elder Jabez Cottle (1747-1820): A Spiritual Autobiography in Verse." *NEQ* 38(1965): 375-386.

COTTEN, JOHN.   796. Etulain, Richard W. "John Cotten: A Checklist." *EAL* 4,#1(1969): 64-69.

797. Grabo, Normas S. "John Cotten's Aesthetics: A Sketch." *EAL* 3,#1(1968): 4-10.

798. Habegger, Alfred. "Preparing the Soul for Christ: The Contrasting Forms of John Cotten and Thomas Hooker." *AL* 41(1969): 342-354.

799. Schorer, C. E. "'One Cotten, of Acquia Creek, Husband of Ann Cotten.'" *AL* 22 (1950): 342-345.

CREVECOEUR, MICHEL-GUILLAUME JEAN DE. 800. Adams, Percy G. "The Historical Value of Crèvecoeur's *Voyage dans la haute Penslvanie et dans la New York.*" *AL* 25(1953): 152-168.

801. Beranger, Jean F. "The Desire for Communication: Narrator and Narratee in *Letters from an American* Farmer." *EAL* 12(1977): 73-85.

802. Kehler, Joel R. "Crèvecoeur's Farmer James: A Reappraisal." *EL* 3(1976): 206-213.

803. Kulungian, Harold. "The Aestheticism of Crevecoeur's American Farmer." *EAL* 12 (1977): 197-201.

804. Philbrick, Thomas. "Crevecoeur as New Yorker." *EAL* 11(1976): 22-30.

DICKENSON, JOHN.   805. Aldridge, A. Owen. "Paine and Dickenson." *EAL* 11(1976): 125-138.

806. Marambaud, Pierre. "Dickinson's *Letters from a Farmer in Pennsylvania.*" *EAL* 12 (1977): 63-72.

807. Soler, William G. "John Dickinson's 'Ode, on the French Revolution'." *AL* 25(1953): 287-292.

DIGGES, THOMAS.   808. Elias, Robert H., and Michael N. Stanton. "Thomas Atwood Digges and *Adventures of Alonzo:* Evidence from Robert Southey." *AL* 44(1972): 118-122.

DUNLAP, WILLIAM.   809. Leary, Lewis. "Unrecorded Early Verse by William Dunlap." *AL* 39(1967): 87-88.

810. Moramarco, Fred. "The Early Drama Criticism of William Dunlap." *AL* 40(1968): 9-14.

811. Pickering, James H. "*Satanstoe:* Cooper's Debt to William Dunlap." *AL* 38(1967): 468-477.

812. Zipes, Jack. "Dunlap, Kotzebue, and the Shaping of American Theater: A Reevaluation from a Marxist Perspective." *EAL* 8,#3(1974): 272-284.

DWIGHT, TIMOTHY.   813. Aldridge, Alfred Owen. "Timothy Dwight's Poshumous Gift to British Theology." *AL* 21(1950): 479-481.

814. Freimarck, Vincent. "Timothy Dwight's Brief Lives in *Travels in New England and New York.*" *EAL* 8,#1(1973): 44-58.

815. ----------. "Timothy Dewight's *Dissertation* on the Bible." *AL* 24(1952): 73-77.

816. Griffith, John. "'The Columbiad' and 'Greenfield Hill': History, Poetry, and Ideology in the Late Eighteenth Century." *EAL* 10,#3(1976): 235-250.

817. Lee, Robert Edson. "Timothy Dwight and the Boston *Palladium.*" *NEQ* 35(1962): 229-239.

818. Ravitz, Abe C. "Timothy Dwight: Professor of Rhetoric." *NEQ* 29(1956): 63-72.

819. Sears, John F. "Timothy Dwight and the American Landscape." *EAL* 11(1977): 311-321.

See also 14655.

EDWARDS, JONATHAN.   820. Baumgartner, Paul R. "Jonathan Edwards: The Theory behind his Use of Figurative Language." *PMLA* 78(1963): 321-325.

821. Clark, George Peirce. "An Unpublished Letter by Jonathan Edwards." *NEQ* 29(1956): 228-236.

822. Davidson, Clifford. "Jonathan Edwards and Mysticism." *CLA* 11(1967): 149-156.

823. Griffith, John. "Jonathan Edwards as a Literary Artist." *Criticism* 15(1973): 156-173.

824. Howard, Leon. "The Creative Imagination of a College Rebel: Jonathan Edwards' Undergraduate Writings." *EAL* 5,#3(1971): 50-56.

825. Kimnach, Wilson H. "Jonathan Edwards' Sermon Mill." *EAL* 10,#2(1975): 167-178.

826, Kolodny, Annette. "Imagery in the Sermons of Jonathan Edwards." *EAL* 7,#2(1972): 172-182.

827. Loewinsohn, Ron. "Jonathan Edwards' Opticks: Images and Metaphors of Light in Some of his Major Works." *EAL* 8,#1(1973): 21-32.

828. Lowance, Mason I. "Images or Shadows of Divine Things: The Typology of Jonathan Edwards." *EAL* 5,#1, part 1 (1970): 141-181.

829. Lyttle, David. "Jonathan Edwards on Personal Identity." *EAL* 7,#2(1972): 163-171.

830. Martin, Jean-Pierre. "Edwards' Epistomology and the New Science." *EAL* 7,#3(1973): 247-264.

831. Morris, William S. "Essay Review: The Reappraisal of Edwards." *NEQ* 30(1957): 515-525.

832. Parker, Gail Thain. "Jonathan Edwards and Melancholy." *NEQ* 41(1968): 193-212.

833. Pierce, David C. "Jonathan Edwards and the 'New Sense' of Glory." *NEQ* 41(1968): 82-95.

834. Shafer, Thomas A. "Manuscript Problems in the Yale Edition of Jonathan Edwards." *EAL* 3,#3(1969): 159-171.

835. Shea, Daniel B. Jr. "The Art and Instruction of Jonathan Edward's *Personal Narrative.*" *AL* 37(1965): 17-32.

836. Stein, Stephen J. "Jonathan Edwards and the Rainbow: Biblical Exegesis and Poetic Imagination." *NEQ* 47(1974): 440-456.

837. Stuart, Robert Lee. "Jonathan Edwards at Enfield: 'And Oh The Cheerfulness and Pleasantness . . ..'" *AL* 48(1976): 46-59.

838. Tomas, Vincent. "The Modernity of Jonathan Edwards." *NEQ* 25(1952): 60-84.

839. Watts, Emily Stipes. "The Neoplatonic Basis of Jonathan Edwards. 'True Virtue'." *EAL* 10,#2(1975): 179-189.

See also 2211.

ELLIOT, JAMES.   840. Huddleston, Eugene L. "Indians and Literature of the Federalist Era: The Case of James Elliot." *NEQ* 44(1971): 221-237.

FISKE, JOHN.   841. Bray, James. "John Fiske: Puritan Precursor of Edward Taylor." *EAL* 9,#1(1974): 27-38.

842. Muhlenfels, Astrid Schmitt-v. "John Fiske's Funeral Elegy on John Cotten." *EAL* 12 (1977): 49-62.

FRANKLIN, BENJAMIN.   843. Aldridge, Alfred

Owen. "Benjamin Franklin and Philosophical Necessity." *MLQ* #12(1951): 292-309.

844. ----------. "Charles Brockden Brown's Poem on Benjamin Franklin." *AL* 38(1966): 230-235.

845. ----------. "Franklin's Essay on Daylight Saving." *AL* 28(1956): 23-29.

846. ----------. "A Religious Hoax by Benjamin Franklin." *AL* 36(1964): 204-209.

847. ----------. "The Sources of Franklin's 'The Ephemera'." *NEQ* 27(1954): 388-391.

848. Amacher, Richard E. "A New Franklin Satire." *EAL* 7,#2(1972): 103-110.

849. Baender, Paul. "The Basis of Franklin's Duplicative Satires." *AL* 32(1960): 267-279.

850. Barnes, Jack C. "A Moral Epistle: A Probable Addition to the Franklin Canon." *NEQ* 30 (1957): 73-84.

851. Davidson, Edward H. "Franklin and Brownrigg." *AL* 23(1951): 38-56.

852. Grenander, M. E. "Benjamin Franklin's String Quartet." *EAL* 7,#2(1972): 183-186.

853. Griffith, John. "The Rhetoric of Franklin's *Autobiography*." *Criticism* 13(1971): 77-94.

854. Kushen, Betty. "Three Earliest Published Lives of Benjamin Franklin, 1790-93: The *Autiobiography* and its Continuations." *EAL* 9,#1 (1974): 39-52.

855. Larson, David M. "Franklin on the Nature of Man and the Possibility of Virtue." *EAL* 10,#2(1975): 111-120.

856. Lemay, J. A. Leo. "Franklin's Suppressed 'Busy-Body.'" *AL* 37(1965): 307-311.

857. Meister, Charles W. "Franklin as a Proverb Stylist." *AL* 24(1952): 157-166.

858. Newcomb, Robert. "Franklin and Richardson." *JEGP* 57(1958): 27-35.

859. ----------. "Poor Richard and the English Epigram." *PQ* 40(1961): 270-280.

860. ----------. "Poor Richard's Debt to Lord Halifax." *PMLA* 70(1955): 535-539.

861. Phillips, William L. "Franklins Version of the 'Lord's Prayer': A Restoration of the Text." *AL* 22(1950): 338-341.

862. Sappenfield, James A. "The Bizarre Death of Daniel Rees and the Continuity of Franklin Criticism." *EAL* 4,#2(1969): 73-85.

863. Sayre, Robert Freeman. "The Worldly Franklin and the Provincial Critics." *TSLL* 4 (1963): 512-524.

864. Schiller, Andrew. "Franklin as Music Critic." *NEQ* 31(1958): 505-514.

865. Simson, George. "Legal Sources for Franklin's 'Edict'." *AL* 32(1960): 152-157.

866. Sokolow, Jayme A. "'Arriving at Moral Perfection': Benjamin Franklin and Leo Tolstoy." *AL* 47(1975): 427-432.

867. Tatham, Campbell. "Benjamin Franklin, Cotton Mather, and the Outward State." *EAL* 6,#3 (1972): 223-233.

See also 949.

FRENEAU, PHILIP. 868. Andrews, William L. "Freneau's 'A Political Litany': A Note on Interpretation." *EAL* 12(1977): 193-196.

869. ----------. "Goldsmith and Freneau in 'The American Village'." *EAL* 5,#2(1970): 14-23.

870. Arnen, Robert D. "Neoclassicism and Romanticism: A Reading of Freneau's 'The Wild

Honey Suckle.'" *EAL* 9,#1(1974): 53-61.

871. Batten, Charles L., Jr. "A Newly Discovered Poem by Philip Freneau on the Death of General Moreau." *AL* 44(1972): 457-459.

872. Collins, John F. "Two Last Poems of Freneau." *EAL* 7,#2(1972): 111-119.

873. Itzkowitz, Martin E. "Freneau's 'Indian Burying Ground' and Keats' 'Grecian Urn.'" *EAL* 6,#3(1972): 258-262.

874. Kyle, Carol A. "That Poet Freneau: A Study of the Imagistic Success of *The Pictures of Columbus*." *EAL* 9,#1(1974): 62-70.

875. Marsh, Philip. "Freneau's Last Published Poem." *AL* 30(1958): 103-106.

876. Mason, Julian. "Madison's August 1791 Letter Praising Freneau." *EAL* 9,#3(1975): 325-327.

HAMMON, BRITON. 877. Foster, Frances S. "Briton Hammon's *Narrative:* Some Insights into Beginnings." *CLA* 21(1977): 179-186.

HAMMON, JUPITER. 878. Palmer, R. Roderick. "Jupiter Hammon's Poetic Exhortations." *CLA* 18(1974): 22-28.

See also 628.

HAMMOND, JOHN. 879. Arner, Robert D. "A Note on John Hammond's *Leah and Rachel*." *SLJ* 6,#1 (1973): 77-80.

HARTWELL, HENRY. 880. Bain, Robert A. "The Composition and Publication of *The Present State of Virginia, and the College*." *EAL* 6,#1(1971): 31-54.

HILL, FRANCIS BAYLOR. 881. Bottorff, William K., and Roy C. Flanagan, eds. "*The Diary of Frances Baylor Hill* of 'Hillsborough' King and Queen County, Virginia (1977)." *EAL* 2,#3(1968): 4-53.

HOOKER, THOMAS. 882. Bush, Sargent. "The Growth of Thomas Hooker's *The Poor Doubting Christian*." *EAL* 8,#1(1973): 3-20.

883. Emerson, Everett H. "Notes on the Thomas Hooker Canon." *AL* 27(1956): 554-555.

884. ----------. "Thomas Hooker Materials at the Connecticut Historical Society." *EAL* 6,#2 (1971): 187-188.

885. Frederick, John T. "Literary Art in Thomas Hooker's *The Poor Doubting Christian*." *AL* 40(1968): 1-8.

886. Habegger, Alfred. "Preparing the Soul for Christ: The Contrasting Sermon Forms of John Cotton and Thomas Hooker." *AL* 41(1969): 342-354.

887. Pettit, Norman. "Hooker's Doctrine of Assurance: A Critical Phase in New England Spiritual Thought." *NEQ* 47(1974): 518-534.

888. Rossiter, Clinton. "Thomas Hooker." *NEQ* 25(1952): 459-488.

889. Shuffelton, Frank C. "Thomas Prince and His Edition of Thomas Hooker's *Poor Doubting Christian*." *EAL* 5,#3(1971): 68-75.

HOPKINS, SAMUEL. See 668.

HUMPHREYS, DAVID. 890. Bottorff, William K. "Humphreys' 'Ode to Laura': A Lost Satire." *EAL* 2,#2(1967): 36-38.

HUTCHINSON, THOMAS. 891. Shaw, Peter. "Their Kinsman, Thomas Hutchinson: The Boston Patriots and His Majesty's Royal Governor." *EAL* 11(1976): 183-190.

JEFFERSON, THOMAS. 892. Gittleman, Edwin. "Jefferson's 'Slave Narrative': The Declaration of Independence as a Literary Text." *EAL* 8,#3(1974):

239-256.

893. Levin, David. "Cotton Mathers' Declaration of Gentlemen and Thomas Jefferson's Declaration of Independence." *NEQ* 50(1977): 509-514.

894. Sensabaugh, George F. "Jefferson's Use of Milton in the Ecclesiastical Controversies of 1776." *AL* 26(1955): 552-559.

JOHNSON, EDWARD. 895. Gallagher, Edward J. "An Overview of Edward Johnson's *Wonder-Working Providence*." *EAL* 5,#3(1971): 30-49.

896. ----------. "*The Wonder-Working Providence* as Spiritual Biography." *EAL* 10,#1(1975): 75-87.

See also 668.

KNIGHT, SARAH KEMBLE. 897. Stephens, Robert O. "The Odyssey of Sarah Kemble Knight." *CLA* 7(1964): 247-255.

898. Thorpe, Peter. "Sarah Kemble Knight and the Picaresque Tradition." *CLA* 10(1966): 114-121.

LEWIS, RICHARD. 899. Lemay, J. A. Leo. "Richard Lewis and Augustan American Poetry." *PMLA* 83(1968): 80-101.

MARSHALL, JOHN. See 668.

MARTIN, ALEXANDER. 900. Lemay, J. A. Leo. "A Note on the Canon of Alexander Martin." *EAL* 7, #1(1972): 92.

901. Walser, Richard. "Alexander Martin, Poet." *EAL* 6,#1(1971): 55-62.

MATHER, COTTON. 902. Andrews, William D. "The Printed Funeral Sermons of Cotton Mather." *EAL* 5,#2(1970): 24-44.

903. Bercovitch, Sacvan. "Cotton Mather Against Rhyme: Milton and the Psalterium Americanum." *AL* 39(1967): 191-193.

904. ----------. "'Nehemias Americanus': Cotton Mather and the Concept of the Representative American." *EAL* 8,#3(1974): 220-238.

905. ----------. "New England Epic: Cotton Mather's *Magnalia Christi Americana*." *ELH* 33(1966): 337-350.

906. Bernhard, Virginia. "Cotton Mather and the Doing of Good: A Puritan Gospel of Wealth." *NEQ* 49(1976): 225-241.

907. Cromphout, Gustaaf Van. "Cotton Mather as Plutarchan Biographer." *AL* 46(1975): 465-481.

908. Eberwein, Donahue. "'In a book, as in a glass': Literary Sorcery in Mather's Life of Phips." *EAL* 10,#3(1976): 289-300.

909. Gay, Carol. "The Fettered Tongue: A Study of the Speech Defect of Cotton Mather." *AL* 46(1975): 451-464.

910. Gura, Philip F. "Cotton Mather's *Life of Phips*: 'A Vice with the Vizard of Vertue Upon It.'" *NEQ* 50(1977): 440-457.

911. Isani, Mukhtar Ali. "Cotton Mather and the Orient." *NEQ* 43(1970): 46-58.

912. Johnston, Thomas E. "A Translation of Cotton Mather's Spanish Works: *La Fe del Christiano* and *La Religion Pura*." *EAL* 2,#2(1967): 7-21.

913. Kaiser, Leo M. "On Mather's *Christian Philosopher*." *EAL* 11(1977): 280.

914. ----------. "On the Latin Verse in Cotton Mather's *Magnalia Christi Americana*." *EAL* 10,#3 (1976): 301-306.

915. Levin, David. "Cotton Mather's Declaration of Gentlemen and Thomas Jefferson's Declaration of Independence." *NEQ* 50(1977): 509-514.

916. ----------. "The Hazing of Cotton Mather." *NEQ* 36(1963): 147-171.

917. Lowance, Mason I., Jr. "Typology and the New England Way: Cotton Mather and the Exegesis of Biblical Types." *EAL* 4,#1(1969): 15-37.

918. Manierre, William Reid. "Some Characteristic Mather Redactions." *NEQ* 31(1958): 496-505.

919. McKay, David P. "Cotton Mather's Unpublished Singing Sermon." *NEQ* 48(1975): 410-422.

920. Silverman, Kenneth. "Cotton Mather's Foreign Correspondence." *EAL* 3,#3(1969): 172-185.

921. Tatham, Campbell. "Benjamin Franklin Cotton Mather, and The Outward State." *EAL* 6,#3 (1972): 223-233.

922. Van Cromphout, Gustaaf. "Cotton Mather: The Puritan Historian as Renaissance Humanist." *AL* 49(1977): 327-337.

923. Vartanian, Pershing. "Cotton Mather and the Puritan Transition into the Enlightenment." *EAL* 7,#3(1973): 213-224.

924. Woody, Kennerly M. "Bibliographical Notes to Cotton Mather's *Manuductio Ad Ministerium*." *EAL* 4,#1(1969): Supplement.

925. ----------. "Cotton Mather's *Manuductio Ad Theologiam*: The 'More Quiet and Hopeful Way.'" *EAL* 4,#2(1969): 3-48.

See also 668.

MATHER, INCREASE. 926. Országh, Ladislas. "A Seventeenth-Century Hungarian Translation of a Work by Increase Mather." *AL* 34(1962): 94-96.

MATHER, RICHARD. 927. Scheick, William J. "Anonymity and Art in *The Life and Death of That Reverend Man of God, Mr. Richard Mather*." *AL* 42 (1971): 457-467.

MATILDA. 928. Huddleston, Eugene L. "Matilda's 'On Reading the Poems of Phillis Wheatley, the African Poetess'." *EAL* 5,#3(1971): 57-67.

MORTON, THOMAS. 929. Arner, Robert D. "Mythology and the Magpole of Merrymount: Notes on Thomas Morton's 'Rise Oedipus'." *EAL* 6,#2(1971): 156-164.

930. ----------. "Pastoral Celebration and Satire in Thomas Morton's 'New English Canaan.'" *Criticism* 16(1974): 217-231.

931. Major, Minor W. "William Bradford Versus Thomas Morton." *EAL* 5,#2(1970): 1-13.

MOXON, GEORGE. 932. Kaiser, Leo M. "Three Hymns Attributed to George Moxon." *EAL* 8,#2(1973): 104-110.

MURRAY, WILLIAM VANS. 933. Mason, Julian. "William Vans Murray; The Fancy of a Poet," *EAL* 6,#1(1971): 63-68.

OAKES, URIAN. 934. Hahn, T. G. "Urian Oakes's *Elegie* on Thomas Shepard and Puritan Politics. *AL* 45(1973): 163-181.

935. Lemay, J. A. Leo. "Jonson and Milton: Two Influences in Oakes's *Elgie*." *NEQ* 38(1965): 90-92.

936. Scheick, William J. "Standing in the Gap: Urian Oakes' Elegy on Thomas Shepard." *EAL* 9,#3(1975): 301-306.

PAIN, PHILIP. 937. Johnston, Thomas E., Jr. "A Note on the Voices of Anne Bradstreet, Edward Taylor, Roger Williams, and Philip Pain." *EAL* 3,#2(1968): 125-126.

938. Stanford, Donald E. "The Imagination of Death in the Poetry of Philip Pain, Edward Taylor, and George Herbert." *SLI* 9,#2(1976): 53-67.

See also 686.

PAINE, THOMAS. 939. Aldridge, A. Owen. "Paine and Dickinson." *EAL* 11(1976): 125-138.

940. Aldridge, Alfred O. "Thomas Paine in Latin-America." *EAL* 3,#3(1969): 139-147.

941. Boulton, James B. "Literature and Politics I. Tom Paine and the Vulgar Style." *EIC* 12(1962): 18-33.

942. Cordasco, Francesco. "Thomas Paine and the History of 'Junius'" A Forgotten *Cause Célèbre*." *JEGP* 52(1953): 226-228.

943. Leary, Lewis. "The First Published Poem of Thomas Paine of Boston: A Note on the Generation Gap in 1786." *NEQ* 43(1970): 130-134.

944. Macgregor-Hastie, Roy. "Stop Press." *EIC* 12(1962): 229-230.

945. Purdy, Strother B. "A Note on the Burke-Paine Controversy." *AL* 39(1967): 373-375.

PARKS, WILLIAM. 946. Joost, Nicholas. "'Plain Dealer' and *Free Thinker:* A Revaluation." *AL* 23(1951): 31-37.

PERCY, GEORGE. 947. Barbour, Philip L. "The Honorable George Percy: Premier Chronicler of the First Virginia Voyage." *EAL* 6,#1(1971): 7-17.

PRIME, BENJAMIN. 948. Wheelock, C. Webster. "The Poet Benjamin Prime (1733-1791)." *AL* 40(1969): 459-471.

RALPH, JAMES. 949. McKillop, Alan D. "James Ralph in Berkshire." *SEL* 1,#3(1961): 43-51.

950. Shipley, John B. "James Ralph's Place and Date of Birth." *AL* 36(1964): 343-346.

ROGERS, ROBERT. See 13579.

ROWLANDSON, MARY. 951. Leach, Douglas Edward. "The 'Whens' of Mary Rowlandson's Captivity." *NEQ* 34(1961): 352-363.

ROWSON, SUSANNA. 952. Parker, Patricia, L. "*Charlotte Temple:* America's First Best Seller." *SSF* 13(1976): 518-520.

See also 4397.

RUSH, BENJAMIN. 953. Hedges, William L. "Benjamin Rush, Charles Brockden Brown, and the American Plague Year." *EAL* 7,#3(1973): 295-311.

SAFFIN, JOHN. 954. Coffee, Jessie A. "Arcadia to America: Sir Philip Sidney and John Saffin." *AL* 35(1973): 100-104.

955. Sands, Alice B. "Establishing John Saffin's Birthdate: A Biographical and Historical Problem." *EAL* 2,#1(1967): 12-17.

956. Weber, Brom. "A Puritan Poem Regenerated: John Saffin's 'Sayle Gentle Pinnance'." *EAL* 3,#2(1968): 65-71.

SEWALL, SAMUEL. 957. Clark, William Bedford. "*Caveat Emptor!:* Judge Sewall vs. Slavery." *SLI* 9,#2(1976): 19-30.

958. Isani, Mukhtar Ali. "The Growth of Sewall's *Phaenomena Quaedam Apocalyptica*." *EAL* 7,#1 (1972): 64-75.

959. Kaiser, Leo M. "On Sewall's Diary." *EAL* 11(1977): 279.

960. Thompson, W. Lawrence. "Classical Echoes in Sewall's Diaries (1674-1729)." *NEQ* 24(1951): 8-10.

SHIPPEN, JOHN. 961. Free, William J. "A Lost American Critical Document." *EAL* 1,#3(1967): 8-10.

962. Goldberg, J. Philip. "Some Conjecture upon John Shippen's 'Observations on Novel-Reading'." *EAL* 2,#1(1967): 6-11.

SMITH, EBENEZER. 963. McLoughlin, William G., ed. "Ebenezer Smith's Ballad of the Ashfield Baptists, 1772." *NEQ* 47(1974): 95-108.

SMITH, JOHN. 964. Emerson, Everett. "Captain John Smith, Autobiographer." *EAL* 2,#1(1967): 18-23.

SMITH, WILLIAM. 965. Andrews, William D. "William Smith and the Rising Glory of America." *EAL* 8,#1(1973): 33-43.

STEWART, JOHN. See 14655.

STODDARD, SOLOMON. 966. Grabo, Norman S. "The Poet to the Pope: Edward Taylor to Solomon Stoddard." *AL* 32(1960): 197-201.

TAYLOR, EDWARD. 967. Alexis, Gerhard T. "A Keen Nose for Taylor's Syntax." *EAL* 4,#3(1970): 97-101.

968. Arner, Robert D. "Edward Taylor's Gaming Imagery: Meditation 1.40." *EAL* 4,#1(1969): 38-40.

969. Bales, Kent and William J. Aull. "Touching Taylor Overly: A Note on 'Meditation Six.'" *EAL* 5,#2(1970): 57-59.

970. Ball, Kenneth R. "Rhetoric in Edward Taylor's *Preparatory Meditations*." *EAL* 4,#3(1970): 79-88.

971. Barbour, James W. "The Prose Context of Edward Taylor's Anti-Stoddard Meditations." *EAL* 10,#2(1975): 144-157.

972. Benton, Robert M. "Edward Taylor's Use of His Text." *AL* 39(1967): 31-42.

973. Black, Mindele. "Edward Taylor: Heavens Sugar Cake." *NEQ* 29(1956): 159-181.

974. Blake, Kathleen. "Edward Taylor's Protestant Poetic: Nontransubstantuating Metaphor." *AL* 43(1971): 1-24.

975. Blau, Herbert. "Heaven's Sugar Cake: Theology and Imagery in the Poetry of Edward Taylor." *NEQ* 26(1953): 337-360.

976. Boll, Robert N., and Thomas M. Davis. "Sainte Augustine and Edward Taylor's Meditation 138 (2)." *ELN* 8(1971): 183-185.

977. Bottorff, William K. "Edward Taylor: An Explication: 'Another Meditation at the Same Time.'" *EAL* 3,#1(1968): 17-21.

978. Brumm, Ursula. "The 'Tree of Life' in Edward Taylor's Meditations." *EAL* 3,#2(1968): 72-87.

979. Bush, Sargent, Jr. "Paradox Puritanism, and Taylor's *God's Determinations*." *EAL* 4,#3(1970): 48-66.

980. Callow, James T. "Edward Taylor Obeys Saint Paul." *EAL* 4,#3(1970): 89-96.

981. Colacurcio, Michael J. "God's Determinations Touching Half-Way Membership: Occasion and Audience in Edward Taylor." *AL* 39(1967): 298-314.

982. Davis, Thomas M. "Edward Taylor and the Traditions of Puritan Typology." *EAL* 4,#3(1970): 27-47.

983. ----------. "Edward Taylor's Elegies on the Mathers." *EAL* 11(1977): 231-244.

984. ----------. "Edward Taylor's 'Ocassional Meditations.'" *EAL* 5,#3(1971): 17-29.

985. ----------. "Edward Taylor's 'Valedictory' Poems." *EAL* 7,#1(1972): 38-63.

986. Davis, Thomas M. and Virginia L. Davis. "Edward Taylor on the Day of Judgement." *AL* 43 (1972): 525-547.

987. ----------. "Edward Taylor's Library: Another Note." *EAL* 6,#3(1972): 271-273.

988. ----------. "Edward Taylor's Metrical Paraphrases of the Psalms." *AL* 48(1977): 455-470.

989. Doepke, Dale. "A Suggestion for Reading Edward Taylor's 'The Preface.'" *EAL* 5,#3(1971): 80-82.

990. Duke, Maurice. "John Taylor of Caroline, 1753-1824: Notes Toward a Bibliography." *EAL* 6,#1(1971): 69-72.

991. Elkins, Mary Jane. "Edward Taylor: A Checklist." *EAL* 4,#1(1969): 56-63.

992. Fender, Stephen. "Edward Taylor and 'The Application of Redemption.'" *MLR* 59(1964): 331-334.

993. Garrison, Joseph M., Jr. "The 'Worship Mould': A Note on Edward Taylor's *Preparatory Meditations.*" *EAL* 3,#2(1968): 127-131.

994. Gatta, John, Jr. "The Comic Design of *God's Determinations Touching his Elect.*" *EAL* 10, #2(1975): 121-143.

995. Goodman, William B. "Edward Taylor Writes His Love." *NEQ* 27(1954): 510-515.

996. Grabo, Norman S. "'The Appeale Tried': Another Edward Taylor Manuscript." *AL* 34(1962): 394-400.

997. ----------. "Edward Taylor's Spiritual Huswifery." *PMLA* 79(1964): 554-560.

998. ----------. "The Poet to the Pope: Edward Taylor to Solomon Stoddard." *AL* 32(1960): 197-201.

999. Griffin, Edward M. "The Structure and Language of Edward Taylor's Meditation 2.112." *EAL* 3,#3(1969): 205-208.

1000. Griffith, Clark. "Edward Taylor and the Momentum of Metaphor." *ELH* 33(1966): 448-460.

1001. Halbert, Cecelia L. "Tree of Life Imagery in the Poetry of Edward Taylor." *AL* 38 (1966): 22-34.

1002. Hammond, Jeff, and Thomas M. Davis. "Edward Taylor: A Note on Visual Imagery." *EAL* 8,#2(1973): 126-131.

1003. Hodges, Robert R. "Edward Taylor's 'Artificiall Man.'" *AL* 31(1959): 76-77.

1004. Howard, Alan B. "The World as Emblem: Language and Vision in the Poetry of Edward Taylor." *AL* 44(1972): 359-384.

1005. Isani, Mukhtar Ali. "Edward Taylor and Ovid's *Art of Love:* The Text of a Newly Discovered Manuscript." *EAL* 10,#1(1975): 67-74.

1006. ----------. "Edward Taylor and the 'Turks.'" *EAL* 7,#2(1972): 120-123.

1007. Johnston, Thomas E., Jr. "Edward Taylor: An American Emblematist." *EAL* 3,#3(1969): 186-198.

1008. ----------. "A Note on the Voices of Anne Bradstreet, Edward Taylor, Roger Williams and Philip Pain." *EAL* 3,#2(1968): 125-126.

1009. Jones, Jesse C. "A Note on the Number of Edward Taylor's *Preparatory Meditations.*" *EAL* 9,#1(1974): 81-82.

1010. Junkins, Donald. "Edward Taylor's Creative Process." *EAL* 4,#3(1970): 67-78.

1011. ----------. "Edward Taylor's Revisions." *AL* 37(1965): 135-152.

1012. ----------. "'Should Stars Wooe Lobster Claws?' A Study of Edward Taylor's Poetic Practice and Theory." *EAL* 3,#2(1968): 88-117.

1013. "Kehler, Joel R. "Physiology and Metaphor in Edward Taylor's 'Meditation. Can. 1.3.'" *EAL* 9,#3(1975): 315-320.

1014. Keller, Karl. "The Example of Edward Taylor." *EAL* 4,#3(1970): 5-26.

1015. ----------. "A Modern Version of Edward Taylor." *EAL* 9,#3(1975): 321-324.

1016. ----------. "The Rev. Mr. Edward Taylor's Bawdry." *NEQ* 43(1970): 382-406.

1017. ----------. "'The World Slickt up in Types': Edward Taylor as a Version of Emerson." *EAL* 5,#1 part 1 (1970): 124-140.

1018. Medlicott, Alexander, Jr. "Notes on Edward Taylor from the Diaries of Stephen Williams." *AL* 34(1962): 270-274.

1019. Mignon, Charles W. "Edward Taylor's *Preparatory Meditations:* A Decorum of Imperfection." *PMLA* 83(1968): 1423-1428.

1020. ----------. "A Principle of Order in Edward Taylor's *Preparatory Meditations.*" *EAL* 4, #3(1970): 110-116.

1021. Murphey, Francis E. X. "An Edward Taylor Manuscript Book." *AL* 31(1959): 188-189.

1022. ----------. "Edward Taylor's Attitude Toward Publication: A Question Concerning Authority." *AL* 34(1962): 393-394.

1023. ----------. "A Letter on Edward Taylor's Bible." *EAL* 6,#1(1971): 91.

1024. Parker, David L. "Edward Taylor's Preparationism: A New Perspective on the Taylor-Stoddard Controversy." *EAL* 11(1977): 259-278.

1025. Pearce, Roy Harvey. "Edward Taylor: The Poet as Puritan." *NEQ* 23(1950): 31-46.

1026. Penner, Allen Richard. "Edward Taylor's Meditation One." *AL* 39(1967): 193-199.

1027. Pierpont, Phillip E. "Edward Taylor Checklist, III: Addenda, Corrections, and Clarifications." *EAL* 5,#3(1971): 91-94.

1028. Prosser, Evan. "Edward Taylor's Poetry." *NEQ* 40(1967): 375-398.

1029. Reed, Michael D. "Edward Taylor's Poetry: Puritan Structure and Form." *AL* 46(1974): 304-312.

1030. Reiter, Robert. "Poetry and Typology: Edward Taylor's *Preparatory Meditations,* Second Series, Numbers 1-30." *EAL* 5,#1, part 1 (1970): 111-123.

1031. [Requa, Kenneth A., and Karl Keller]. "Additions to the Edward Taylor Checklist." *EAL* 4,#3(1970): 117-119.

1032. Russell, Gene. "Dialectal and Phonetic Feactures of Edward Taylor's Rhymes." *AL* 43(1971): 165-180.

1033. Rowe, Karen E. "A Biblical Illumination of Taylorian Art." *AL* 40(1968): 370-374.

1034. ----------. "Sacred or Profane? Edward Taylor's Meditations on Canticles." *MP* 72 (1974): 123-138.

1035. Scheick, William J. "'The Inward Tacles and the Outward Traces': Edward Taylor's Elusive Transitions." *EAL* 12(1977): 163-176.

1036. ----------. "More Additions to the Edward Taylor Checklist." *EAL* 5,#2(1970): 62.

1037. ----------. "Nonsense from a Lisping Child: Edward Taylor on the Word as Piety." *TSLL* 13(1971): 39-53.

1038. ----------. "Typology and Allegory: A Comparative Study of George Herbert and Edward Taylor." *EL* 2(1975): 76-86.

1039. ----------. "A Viper's Nest, the Featherbed of Faith: Edward Taylor on the Will." *EAL* 5,#2(1970): 45-56.

1040. Shepherd, Emmy. "Edward Taylor's Injunction Against Publication." *AL* 33(1962): 512-513.

1041. Siebel, Kathy and Thomas M. Davis. "Edward Taylor and the Cleansing of *Aqua Vitae*." *EAL* 4,#3(1970): 102-109.

1042. Slethaug, Gordon E. "Edward Taylor's Copy of Thomas Taylor's *Types*: A New Taylor Document." *EAL* 8,#2(1973): 132-139.

1043. Sluder, Lawrence Lan. "God in the Background: Edward Taylor as Naturalist." *EAL* 7,#3(1973): 265-271.

1044. Sowd, David. "Edward Taylor's Answer to a 'Popish Pamphlet.'" *EAL* 9,#3(1975): 307-314.

1045. Stanford, Donald E. "The Earliest Poems of Edward Taylor." *AL* 32(1960): 136-151.

1046. ----------. "Edward Taylor and the 'Hermophrodite' Poems of John Cleveland." *EAL* 8,#1(1973): 59-61.

1047. ----------. "Edward Taylor and the Lord's Supper." *AL* 27(1955): 172-178.

1048. ----------. "Edward Taylor's Metrical History of Christianity." *AL* 33(1961): 279-295.

1049. ----------. "Edward Taylor's 'Spiritual Relation'." *AL* 35(1964): 467-475.

1050. ----------. "Edward Taylor versus the 'Young Cockerill' Benjamin Ruggles: A Hitherto Unpublished Episode from the Annals of Early New England Church History." *NEQ* 44(1971): 459-468.

1051. ----------. "The Imagination of Death in the Poetry of Philip Pain, Edward Taylor, and George Herbert." *SLI* 9,#2(1976): 53-67.

1052. ----------. "Nineteen Unpublished Poems by Edward Taylor." *AL* 29(1957): 18-46.

1053. ----------. "The Parentage of Edward Taylor." *AL* 33(1961): 215-221.

1054. ----------. "Two Notes on Edward Taylor." *EAL* 6,#1(1971): 89-90.

1055. Thomas, Jean L. "Drama and Doctrine in *God's Determinations*." *AL* 36(1965): 452-462.

1056. Thorpe, Peter. "Edward Taylor as Poet." *NEQ* 39(1966): 356-372.

1057. Weathers, Willie T. "Edward Taylor and the Cambridge Platonists." *AL* 26(1954): 1-31.

1058. Werge, Thomas. "The Tree of Life in Edward Taylor's Poetry: The Sources of a Puritan Image." *EAL* 3,#3(1969): 199-204.

See also 686.

TERRY, LUCY.   See 628.

TOMPSON, BENJAMIN.   1059. Eckstein, Neil T. "The Pastoral and the Primitive in Benjamin Tompson's 'Address to Lord Bellamont.'" *EAL* 8,#2(1973): 111-116.

1060. Fussell, Edwin S. "Benjamin Tompson, Public Poet." *NEQ* 26(1953): 494-511.

TRUMBULL, JOHN.   1061. Gimmestad, Victor E. "Joel Barlow's Editing of John Trumbull's *M' Fingal*." *AL* 47(1975): 97-102.

1062. ----------. "John Trumbull's Original Epithalamion." *EAL* 10,#2(1975): 158-166.

1063. Granger, Bruce Ingham. "John Trumbull and Religion." *AL* 23(1951): 57-79.

1064. ----------. "John Trumbull, Essayist." *EAL* 10,#3(1976): 273-288.

1065. Jaffe, Irma B. "Contemporary Words and Pictures: Drawings (1782-1810) by John Trumbull." *EAL* 11(1976): 31-51.

TYLER, ROYALL.   1066. Dennis, Larry R. "Legitimizing the Novels: Royall Tyler's *The Algerine Captive*." *EAL* 9,#1(1974): 71-80.

1067. Lauber, John. "*The Contrast*: A Study in the Concept of Innocence." *ELN* 1(1963): 33-37.

1068. Péladeau, Marious B. "Royall Tyler's *Other Plays*." *NEQ* 40(1967): 48-60.

1069. Stein, Roger B. "Royall Tyler and the Question of Our Speech." *NEQ* 38(1965): 454-474.

1070. Tanselle, G. Thomas. "Review Essay: The Editing of Royall Tyler." *EAL* 9,#1(1974): 83-95.

1071. ----------. "Royall Tyler, Judith Sargent Murray, and *The Medium*." *NEQ* 41(1968): 115-117.

WALTER, NEHEMIAH.   1072. Arner, Robert D. "Nehemiah Walter: Milton's Earliest American Disciple?" *EHL* 8,#1(1973): 62-65.

WARD, NATHANIEL.   1073. Arner, Robert D. "*The Simple Cobbler of Aggawam*: Nathaniel Ward and the Rhetoric of Satire." *EAL* 5,#3(1971): 3-16.

1074. Scheick, William J. "Nathaniel Ward's Cobbler as: 'Shoem-Aker.'" *ELN* 9(1971): 100-102.

1075. ----------. "The Widower Narrator in Nathaniel Ward's *The Simple Cobbler of Aggawam in America*." *NEQ* 47(1974): 87-96.

WARREN, MERCY.   1076. Hayes, Edmund M. "Mercy Otis Warren: *The Defeat*." *NEQ* 49(1976): 440-458.

WHEATLEY, PHILLIS.   1077. Applegate, Anne. "Phillis Wheatley: Her Critics and Her Contribution." *BALF* 9(1975): 123-126.

1078. Bridenbaugh, Carl. "The Earlist-Published Poem of Phillis Wheatley." *NEQ* 42(1969): 583-584.

1079. Huddleston, Eugene L. "Matilda's 'On Reading the Poems of Phillis Wheatley, the African Poetess'." *EAL* 5,#3(1971): 57-67.

1080. Isani, Mukhtar Ali. "The First Proposed Edition of *Poems on Various Subjects* and the Phillis Wheatley Canon." *AL* 49(1977): 97-103.

1081. Kuncio, Robert C. "Some Unpublished Poems of Phillis Wheatley." *NEQ* 43(1970): 287-297.

1082. Lapsansky, Phil. "*Deism* - An Unpublished Poem by Phillis Wheatley." *NEQ* 50(1977): 517-520.

1083. Rawley, James A. "The World of Phillis Wheatley." *NEQ* 50(1977): 666-677.

1084. Rigsby, Gregory. "Form and Content in Phillis Wheatley's Elegies." *CLA* 19(1975): 248-258.

1085. Robinson, William H. "Phillis Wheatley: Colonial Quandry." *CLA* 9(1965): 25-38.

1086. ----------. "Phillis Wheatley in London." *CLA* 21(1977): 187-201.

1087. Silverman, Kenneth. "Four New Letters by Phillis Wheatley." *EAL* 8,#3(1974): 257-271.

See also 622, 628.

WIGGLESWORTH, MICHAEL.   1088. Alexis, Gerhard T. "Wigglesworth's 'Easiest Room.'" *NEQ* 42(1969): 573-583.

1089. Strange, Arthur. "Michael Wigglesworth Reads the Poets." *AL* 31(1959): 325-326.

See also 686.

WILLIAMS, ROGER.   1090. Davis, Jack L. "Roger Williams Among the Narragansett Indians." *NEQ* 43(1970): 593-604.

1091. Guggisberg, Hans R. "Religious Freedom and the History of the Christian World in Roger Williams." *EAL* 12(1977): 36-48.

1092. Johnston, Thomas E., Jr. "A Note on the Voices of Anne Bradstreet, Edward Taylor, Roger Williams, and Philip Pain." *EAL* 3,#2(1968): 125-126.

1093. Reinitz, Richard. "The Typologoical Argument for Religious Toleration: The Separatist Tradition and Roger Williams." *EAL* 5,#1, part 1 (1970): 74-110.

1094. Teunissen, John J., and Evelyn J. Hinz. "Roger Williams, Thomas More and the Narrangansett Utopia." *EAL* 11(1977): 281-295.

WILLIAMS, STEPHEN. 1095. Medlicott, Alexander, Jr. "Notes on Edward Taylor from the Diaries of Stephen Williams." *AL* 34(1962): 270-274.

WINTHROP, JOHN. 1096. Benton, Robert M. "The John Winthrops and Developing Scientific Thought in New England." *EAL* 7,#3(1973): 272-280.

WISE, JOHN. 1097. Johnston, Thomas E., Jr. "John Wise: Early American Political Thinker." *EAL* 3,#1(1968): 30-40.

WOOLMAN, JOHN. 1098. Davis, Marianna W. "The Connatural Ground of John Woolman's Triangle." *CLA* 9(1965): 132-139.

NINETEENTH CENTURY

GENERAL AND MISCELLANEOUS. 1099. Adams, Richard P. "Permutations of American Romanticism." *SR* 9(1970): 249-268.

1100. Adams, R. P. "Romanticism and the American Renaissance." *AL* 23(1952): 419-432.

1101. Brubaker, B. R. "Spoils Appointments of American Writers." *NEQ* 48(1975): 556-564.

1102. Budd, Louis. "The Hungry Bear of American Realism." *ALR* 5(1972): 485-486.

1103. Butterfield, Stephen T. The Use of Language in the Slave Narratives." *BALF* 6(1972): 72-78.

1104. Cohn, Jan. "Women as Superflous Characters in American Realism and Naturalism." *SAF* 1(1973): 154-162.

1105. Dew, Marjorie. "Realistic Innocence: Cady's Footnote to a Definition of American Literary Realism." *ALR* 5(1972): 487-481.

1106. Eells, Walter Crosby. "American Doctural Dissertations on English Written by Women in the Nineteenth Century." *CLA* 2(1958): 25-33.

1107. Erisman, Fred. "American Regional Juvenile Literature, 1870-1910: An Annotated Bibliography." *ALR* 6(1973): 109-122.

1108. Fraiberg, Louis. "The *Westminister Review* and American Literature, 1824-1885." *AL* 24(1952): 310-329.

1109. Graham, D. B. "Aesthetic Experience in Realism." *ALR* 8(1975): 289-290.

1110. Griffith, Clark. "Caves and Cave Dwellers: The Study of a Romantic Image." *JEGP* 62 (1963): 551-568.

1111. ----------. "'Emersonianism and Poeism': Some Versions of the Romantic Sensibility." *MLQ* 22(1961): 125-134.

1112. Ives, Edward D. "Larry Gorman and the Cante Fable." *NEQ* 32(1959): 226-237.

1113. Katz, Joseph. "Bibliography and the Rise of American Realism." *SAF* 2(1974): 75-88.

1114. ----------. "Eroticism in American Literary Realism." *SAF* 5(1977): 35-50.

1115. Kelly, R. Gordon. "American Biographies for Children, 1870-1900." *ALR* 6(1973): 123-136.

1116. ----------. "American Children's Literature: An Historiographical Review. *ALR* 6 (1973): 89-108.

1117. Klein, Christa Ressmeyer. "Literature for America's Roman Catholic Children (1865-1895): An Annotated Bibliography." *ALR* 6(1973): 137-152.

1118. Kolb, Harold. "In Search of Definition: American Literary Realism and the Cliches." *ALR* 2(1969): 165-173.

1119. Linneman, William R. "Satires of American Realism, 1880-1900." *ALR* 34(1962): 80-93.

1120. Lutwack, Leonard. "The Iron Madonna and American Criticism in the Central Era." *MLQ* 15(1954): 343-348.

1121. ----------. "The New England Hierarchy." *NEQ* 28(1955): 164-185.

1122. Mulqueen, James E. "Conservatism and Criticism: The Literary Standards of American Whigs, 1845-1853." *AL* 41(1969): 355-372.

1123. Pauly, Thomas H. "The Literary Sketch in Nineteenth-Century America." *TSLL* 17(1975): 489-503.

1124. Pizer, Donald. "Late Nineteenth-Century American Realism: An Essay in Definition." *NCF* 16(1961): 263-269.

1125. Polk, Noel. "Guide to Dissertations on American Literary Figures, 1870-1910: Part One." *ALR* 8(1975): 177-280.

1126. ----------. "Guide to Dissertations on American Literary Figures, 1870-1910: Part Two." *ALR* 8(1975): 291-348.

1127. Rathbun, John W. "The Historical Sense in American Associationist Literary Criticism." *PQ* 40(1961): 553-568.

1128. Roemer, Kenneth M. "American Utopian Literature (1888-1900): An Annotated Bibliography." *ALR* 4(1971): 227-254.

1129. Roemer, Kenneth. "Utopia Made Practical: Compulsive Realism." *ALR* 7(1974): 273-275.

1130. Roth, George L. "American Theory of Satire, 1790-1820." *AL* 29(1958): 399-407.

1131. Shilling, Hanna-Beate. "The Role of the Brothers Schlegel in American Literary Criticism as Found in Selected Periodicals, 1812-1833: A Critical Bibliography." *AL* 43(1972): 563-579.

1132. Steele, Thomas J., S. J. "'Goodby to Sambo': The Contribution of Black Slave Narrative to the Abolition Movement." *BALF* 6(1972): 79-84.

1133. Ward, Robert S. "The American System in Literature." *NEQ* 38(1965): 363-374.

1134. Wilson, John B. "Grimm's Law and the Brahmins." *NEQ* 38(1965): 234-239.

1135. Yoder, R. A. "The Equilibrist Perspective: Toward a Theory of American Romanticism." *SR* 12(1973): 705-740.

1136. ----------. "The First Romantics and the Last Revolution." *SR* 15(1976): 493-530.

DRAMA. 1137. Dunkel, Wilbur D. "Ellen Kean's Appraisal of American Playgoers." *AL* 22 (1950): 163-166.

1138. Earnhart, Phyllis. "The First American Play in England?" *AL* 31(1959): 326-329.

1139. Farrison, W. Edward. *"The Kidnapped Clergyman* and Brown's *Experience."* *CLA* 18(1975): 507-515.

1140. Pizer, Donald. "The Radical Drama in Boston 1889-1891." *NEQ* 31(1958): 361-374.

1141. Shafer, Yvonne. "Black Authors in the Nineteenth-Century American Theatre." *CLA* 20(1977): 387-400.

See also 4057, 18231.

FICTION. 1142. Canaday, Nicholas, Jr. "The Antislavery Novel Prior to 1852 and Hildreth's *The Slave* (1836)." *CLA* 17(1973): 175-191.

1143. Cohn, Jan. "The Negro Character in Northern Magazine Fiction of the 1860's." *NEQ* 43(1970): 572-592.

1144. Doughty, Nanelia. "Realistic Negro Characterization in Postbellum Fiction." *BALF* 3 (1969): 57-62.

1145. Duus, Louise. "'Neither Saint nor Sinner': Women in Late Nineteenth-Century Fiction." *ALR* 7(1974): 276-277.

1146. Fine, David. "Immigrant Fiction, 1885-1918: An Annotated Bibliography." *ALR* 6 (1973): 169-196.

1147. Fleming, Robert E. "Humor in the Early Black Novel." *CLA* 17(1973): 250-262.

1148. Frederick, John T. "Hawthorne's 'Scribbling Women.'" *NEQ* 48(1975): 231-240.

1149. Fuson, Ben. "Three Kansas Utopian Novels of 1980." *Ext* 12(1970): 7-24.

1150. Gohdes, Clarence. "The Earliest Description of 'Western' Fiction." *AL* 37(1965): 70-71.

1151. Habegger, Alfred. "Nineteenth-Century American Humor: Easy going Males, Anxious Ladies, and Penelope Lapham." *PMLA* 91(1976): 884-899.

1152. Marler, Robert F. "From Tale to Short Story: The Emergence of a New Genre in the 1850's." *AL* 46(1974): 153-169.

1153. Musgrave, Marian E. "Patterns of Violence and Non-Violence in Pro-Slavery and Anti-Slavery Fiction." *CLA* 16(1973): 426-437.

1154. Pickering, Sam. "A Boy's Own War." *NEQ* 48(1975): 362-377.

1155. Ringe, Donald. "The American Revolution in American Romance." *AL* 49(1977): 352-365.

1156. Schmitz, Neil. "Tall Tale, Tall Talk: Pursuing the Lie in Jacksonian Literature." *AL* 48(1977): 471-491.

1157. Spingarn, Lawrence P. "The Yankee in Early American Fiction." *NEQ* 31(1958): 484-495.

1158. Stern, Milton R. "American Values and Romantic Fiction." *SAF* 5(1977): 13-33.

1159. Wasserstrom, William. "The Genteel Tradition and the Antipodes of Love." *ELH* 23(1956): 299-316.

1160. Wegelin, Christof. "The Rise of the International Novel." *PMLA* 77(1962): 305-310.

1161. Wilson, James D. "Incest and American Romantic Fiction." *SLI* 7,#1(1974): 30-50.

PERIODICALS. 1162. Blackburn, Charles F. "Some New Light on the *Western Messenger.*" *AL* 26(1954): 320-336.

1163. Burks, Mary Fair. "The First Black Literary Magazine in American Letters." *CLA* 19(1976): 318-321.

1164. Calhoun, Richard J. "The Ante-Bellum Literary Twilight: *Russell's Magazine.*" *SLJ* 3,#1 (1970): 89-110.

1165. Guilds, John C. "Simms as Editor and Prophet: The Flowering and Early Death of the *Southern Magnolia.*" *SLJ* 4,#2(1972): 69-92.

1166. Jacobs, Robert D. "Campaign For A Southern Literature. The *Southern Literary Messenger.*" *SLJ* 2,#1(1969): 66-98.

1167. Marovitz, Sanford E. "Romance or Realism? Western Periodical Literature: 1893-1902." *WAL* 10(1975): 45-58.

1168. Moore, Rayburn S. "'A Distinctively Southern Magazine': The *Southern Bivouac.*" *SLJ* 2,#2(1970): 51-65.

1169. Simpson, Lewis P. "A Literary Adventure of the Early Republic: The Anthology Society and the *Monthly Anthology.*" *NEQ* 27(1954): 168-190.

1170. Tomlinson, David. *"Simms's Monthly Magazine: The Southern and Western Monthly Magazine and Review."* *SLJ* 8,#1(1975): 95-102.

1171. Welsh, John R. "An Early Pioneer: Legaré's *Southern Review.*" *SLJ* 3,#2(1971): 2.

POETRY. 1172. Browne, Ray B. "American Poets in the Nineteenth-Century 'Popular' Songbooks." *AL* 30(1959): 503-522.

1173. Foerster, Donald M. "Homer, Milton, and the American Revolt Agains Epic Poetry: 1812-1860." *SP* 53(1956): 75-100.

1174. Patterson, Cecil L. "A Different Drum: The Image of the Negro in the Nineteenth-Century Songster." *CLA* 8(1964): 44-50.

1175. Rhode, Robert D. "America's 'Medium' Poets." *MLQ* 13(1952): 259-263.

1176. Roth, George L. "New England Satire on Religion, 1790-1820." *NEQ* 28(1955): 246-254.

1177. Sloane, David. "In Search of a Realistic Poetic Tradition." *ALR* 5(1972): 489-491.

TRANSCENDENTALISM. 1178. Albanese, Catherine. "The Kinetic Revolution: Transformation in the Language of the Transcendentalists." *NEQ* 48(1975): 319-340.

1179. Albrecht, Robert C. "The Theological Response of the Transcendentalists to the Civil War." *NEQ* 38(1965): 21-34.

1180. Bier, Jesse. "Weberism, Franklin, and the Transcendental Style." *NEQ* 43(1970): 179-192.

1181. Fogarty, Robert S. "A Utopian Literary Canon." *NEQ* 38(1965): 386-391.

1182. Hennessy, Helen. "The *Dial:* Its Poetry and Poetic Criticism." *NEQ* 31(1958): 66-87.

1183. Myerson, Joel. "A Calendar of Transcendental Club Meetings." *AL* 44(1972): 197-207.

1184. Myerson, Joel. "Two Unpublished Reminiscences of Brook Farm." *NEQ* 48(1975): 253-260.

1185. Porter, Lawrence C. "Transcendentalism: A Self-Potrait." *NEQ* 35(1962): 71-92.

1186. Thompson, Cameron. "John Locke and New England Transcendentalism." *NEQ* 35(1962): 435-457.

1187. Wilson, John B. "A Fallen Idol of the Transcendentalists: Baron de Gérando." *Comp L* 19 (1967): 334-340.

ADAMS, HENRY. 1188. Barber, David S. "Henry Adams' *Esther:* The Nature of Individuality and Immortality." *NEQ* 45(1972): 227-240.

1189. Bell, Millicent. "Adams' *Esther:* The Morality of Taste." *NEQ* 35(1962): 147-161.

1190. Bromé, Joseph A. "Henry Adams Silenced by the Cotton Famine." *NEQ* 33(1960): 237-240.

1191. Burns, Florence M. "Henry Adams's Appreciation of Nature." *NEQ* 26(1953): 237-243.

1192. Crowley, John W. "The Suicide of the Artist: Henry Adams' Life of *George Cabot Lodge*." *NEQ* 46(1973): 189-204.

1193. Edenbaum, Robert I. "The Novels of Henry Adams: Why Man Failed." *TSLL* 8(1966): 245-255.

1194. Folsom, James K. "Mutation as Metaphor in *The Education of Henry Adams*." *ELH* 30 (1963): 162-172.

1195. Harbert, Earl N. "*The Education of Henry Adams*: The Confessional Mode as Heuristic Experiment." *JNT* 4(1974): 3-18.

1196. Koretz, Gene H. "Augustines' *Confessions* and *The Education of Henry Adams*." *Comp L* 12(1960): 193-206.

1197. Maud, Ralph. "Henry Adams: Irony and Impasse." *EIC* 8(1958): 381-392.

1198. McIntyre, John P., S. J. "Henry Adams and the Unity of *Chartres*." *TCL* 7(1962): 159-171.

1199. Morison, Samuel Eliot. "A Letter and a Few Reminiscences of Henry Adams." *NEQ* 27(1954): 95-97.

1200. Munford, Howard M. "Henry Adams and the Tendency of History." *NEQ* 32(1959): 79-90.

1201. Page, Evelyn. "'The Man Around the Corner': An Episode in the Career of Henry Adams." *NEQ* 23(1950): 401-403.

1202. Roelofs, Gerrit H. "Henry Adams: Pessimism and the Intelligent Use of Doom." *ELH* 17(1950): 214-239.

1203. Scheyer, Ernst. "The Aesthete Henry Adams." *Criticism* 4(1962): 313-327.

1204. Shaw, Peter. "Blood is Thicker than Irony: Henry Adams' *History*." *NEQ* 40(1967): 163-187.

1205. Stark, Cruce. "The Historical Irrelevance of Heroes: Henry Adams's Andrew Jackson." *AL* 46(1974): 170-181.

1206. Taylor, Gordon O. "Of Adams and Aquarius." *AL* 46(1975): 68-82.

1207. Vandersee, Charles. "Henry Adams (1838-1918)." [bibliography] *ALR* 2(1969): 89-120.

1208. ----------. "Henry Adams (1838-1918)." [bibliography] *ALR* 8(1975): 13-34.

1209. ----------. "Henry Adams' Education of Martha Cameron: Letters, 1888-1916." [with text] *TSLL* 10(1968): 233-293.

1210. ----------. "The Mutual Awareness of Mark Twain and Henry Adams." *ELN* 5(1968): 285-292.

1211. Wagner, Vern. "The Lotus of Henry Adams." *NEQ* 27(1954): 75-94.

1212. Wasser, Henry. "The Thought of Henry Adams." *NEQ* 24(1951): 495-509.

1213. Wolfe, Patrick. "The Revealing Fiction of Henry Adams." *NEQ* 49(1976): 399-426.

See also 1145, 5724.

ADAMS, JOHN QUINCY. 1214. Jaffee, Adrian. "An Exchange of Poems by John Quincy Adams at Ghent." *AL* 40(1968): 67-70.

1215. Mason, Julian. "William Vans Murray: The Fancy of a Poet." *EAL* 6,#1(1971): 63-68.

1216. Wasser, Henry. "John Quincy Adams on the Opening Lines of Milton's *Paradise Lost*." *AL*

42(1970): 373-375.

ALCOTT, BRONSON. 1217. Broderick, John C. "Bronson Alcott's 'Concord Book.'" *NEQ* 29(1956): 365-380.

1218. Carson, Barbara Harrell. "*Proclus' Sunflower* and *The Dial*." *ELN* 11(1974): 200-202.

1219. Myerson, Joel. "Additions to Bronson Alcott's Bibliography: Letters and 'Orphic Sayings' in the *Plain Speaker*." *NEQ* 49(1976): 283-292.

1220. ----------. "'In the Transcendental Emporium': Bronson Alcott's 'Orphic Sayings' in the *Dial*." *ELN* 10(1972): 31-38.

1221. Stern, Madeleine B. "Mrs. Alcott of Concord to Mrs. Adams of Dubuque." *NEQ* 50(1977): 331-340.

See also 1223.

ALCOTT, LOUISA MAY. 1222. Auerbach, Nina. "Austen and Alcott on Matriarchy: New Women or New Wives." *Novel* 10(1976): 6-26.

1223. Gay, Carol. "The Philosopher and His Daughter: Amos Bronson Alcott and Louisa." *EL* 2 (1975): 181-191.

1224. Payne, Alma. "Duty's Child: Louisa May Alcott." *ALR* 6(1973): 261-262.

1225. ----------. "Louisa May Alcott (1832-1888)." [bibliography] *ALR* 6(1973): 27-44.

1226. Smith, Grover, Jr. "The Doll-Burners: D. H. Lawrence and Louisa Alcott." *MLQ* 19(1958): 28-32.

1227. Stern, Madeleine B. "Louisa's *Wonder Book*: A Newly Discovered Alcott Juvenile." *AL* 26 (1954): 384-390.

ALCOTT, WILLIAM ANDRUS. 1228. Salomon, Louis B. "The Least-Remembered Alcott." *NEQ* 34 (1961): 87-93.

ALLEN, JAMES. 1229. Bottorff, William K. "James Lane Allen (1849-1925) bibliography ." *ALR* 2(1969): 121-124.

AMES, NATHANIEL. 1230. Lang, Hans-Joachim, and Benjamin Lee. "The Authorship of *Symzonia*: The Case for Nathaniel Ames." *NEQ* 48(1975): 241-252.

1231. Walker, Warren S. "A Note on Nathaniel Ames." *AL* 26(1954): 239-241.

BAILEY, GAMALIEL. 1232. Holmes, J. Welfred. "Some Antislavery Editors at Work: Lundy, Bailey, Douglass." *CLA* 7(1963): 48-55.

BANCROFT, GEORGE. 1233. Schiller, Andrew. "A Letter From George Bancroft." *NEQ* 33(1960): 225-232.

BANGS, JOHN KENDRICK. 1234. Stronks, James. B. "John Kendrick Bangs Criticizes Norris's Borrowings in *Blix*." *AL* 42(1970): 380-386.

BEAUCHAMP, JEREBOAM. 1235. Justus, James H. "Warren's *World Enough and Time* and Beauchamp's *Confession*." *AL* 33(1962): 500-511.

BEECHER, HENRY WARD. 1236. Felcheim, Marvin. "Two Views of the Stage; or, the Theory and Practice of Henry Ward Beecher." *NEQ* 25(1952): 314-326.

BELASCO, DAVID. 1237. White, Lynn, Jr. "The Legacy of The Middle Ages in the American Wild West." *Speculum* 40(1965): 191-202.

BELLAMY, EDWARD. 1238. Beachamp, Gorman. "*The Iron Heel* and *Looking Backward*: Two Paths to Utopia." *ALR* 9(1976): 307-314.

1239. Bowman, Sylvia E. "Bellamy's Missing Chapter." *NEQ* 31(1958): 47-65.

1240. ----------. "Edward Bellamy (1850-1898)." [bibliography] *ALR* 1,#1(1967): 7-12.

1241. Fuson, Ben W. "A Poetic Precursor of

Bellamy's 'Looking Backward.'" [Contains text of Paxton's "A Century Hence"] *Ext* 5(1964): 31-36.

1242. Ketterer, David. "Utopian Fantasy as Millennial Motive and Science - Fictional Motif." *SLI* 6,#2(1973): 79-103.

1243. Schiffman, Joseph. "Edward Bellamy's Religious Thought." *PMLA* 68(1953): 716-732.

1244. Towers, Tom H. "The Insomnia of Julian West." *AL* 47(1975): 52-63.

See also 211, 4380.).

BIERCE, AMBROSE. 1245. Andrews, William. "Some New Ambrose Bierce Fables." *ALR* 8(1975): 349-352.

1246. Crane, John Kenny. "Crossing the Bar Twice: Post-Mortem Consciousness in Bierce, Hemingway, and Golding." *SSF* 6(1969): 361-376.

1247. Fatout, Paul. "Ambrose Bierce (1842-1914)." [bibliography] *ALR* 1,#1(1967): 13-19.

1248. ----------. "Ambrose Bierce, Civil War Topographer." *AL* 26(1954): 391-400.

1249. Fortenberry, George E. "Ambrose Bierce (1842-1914?): A Critical Bibliography of Secondary Comment." *ALR* 4(1971): 11-59.

1250. Logan, F. J. "The Wry Seriousness of 'Owl Creek Bridge.'" *ALR* 10(1977): 101-113.

1251. O'Brien, Matthew C. "Ambrose Bierce and the Civil War: 1865." *AL* 48(1976): 377-381.

1252. Roth, Russell. "Ambrose Bierce's 'Detestable Creature.'" *WAL* 9(1974): 169-176.

1253. Wiggins, Robert. "Ambrose Bierce: A Romantic in an Age of Realism." *ALR* 4(1971): 1-10.

BIRD, ROBERT MONTGOMERY. 1254. Bronson, Daniel R. "A Note on Robert Montgomery Bird's *Oralloosa*." *ELN* 9(1971): 46-49.

1255. Bryant, James C. "The Fallen World in *Nick of the Woods*." *AL* 38(1966): 352-364.

1256. Hall, Joan Joffee. "*Nick of the Woods*: An Interpretation of the American Wilderness." *AL* 35(1963): 173-182.

See also 157.

BLACK ELK. 1257. Neihardt, John. "The Book that Would Not Die." *WAL* 6(1972): 227-230.

BOKER, GEORGE HENRY. 1258. Shuman, R. Baird. "A Note on George Boker's *Francesca da Rimini*." *AL* 31(1960): 480-482.

BONNER, SHERWOOD. 1259. Biglane, Jean. "Sherwood Bonner: A Bibliography of Primary and Secondary Materials." *ALR* 5(1972): 39-60.

BRIGGS, CHARLES F. 1260. Ehrlich, Heyward. "Charles Frederick Briggs and Lowell's *Fable for Critics*." *MLQ* 28(1967): 329-341.

BROWN, ALICE. 1261. Toth, Susan. "Alice Brown (1857-1948)." [bibliography] *ALR* 5(1972): 134-144.

BROWN, WILLIAM WELLS. 1262. Farrison, W. Edward. "Brown's First Drama." *CLA* 2(1958):104-110.

1263. ----------. "Clotel, Thomas Jefferson, and Sally Hemings." *CLA* 17(1973): 147-174.

1264. ----------. "*The Kidnapped Clergyman* and Brown's *Experience*." *CLA* 18(1975): 507-515.

1265. ----------. "One Ephemera after Another." *CLA* 13(1969): 192-197.

See also 1147, 1161, 4391.

BROWNE, CHARLES FARRAR. 1266. Austin, James. "Charles Farrar Browne (1834-1867)." [bibliography] *ALR* 5(1972): 151-166.

1267. Dahl, Curtis. "Artemus Ward: Comic Panoramist." *NEQ* 32(1959): 476-485.

1268. Reed, John Q. "Artemus Ward's First Lecture." *AL* 32(1960): 317-319.

1269. ----------. "Artemus Ward's First Lecture Tour." *AL* 34(1963): 571-573.

1270. Rodgers, Paul C., Jr. "Artemus Ward and Mark Twain's 'Jumping Frog.'" *NCF* 28(1973): 273-286.

1271. Rowlette, Robert. "Mark Ward on Artemus Twain: Twain's Literary Debt to Ward." *ALR* 6(1973): 13-26.

1272. Temple, Wayne C. "Aetemus Ward's First Article." *AL* 34(1962): 403-405.

BROWNSON, ORESTES. 1273. Barnes, Daniel R. "Orestes Brownson and Hawthorne's Holgrave." *AL* 45(1973): 271-278.

1274. Fussell, Edwin. "*Leaves of Grass* and Brownson." *AL* 31(1959): 77-78.

BRYANT, WILLIAM CULLEN. 1275. Adler, Jacob H. "A Milton-Bryant Parallel." *NEQ* 24(1951): 377-380.

1276. Birdsall, Richard D. "William Cullen Bryant and Catharine Sedgwick." *NEQ* 28(1955): 349-371.

1277. Bryant, William Cullen, II. "The Waterfowl in Retrospect." *NEQ* 30(1957): 181-189.

1278. Dahl, Curtis. "Mound-Builders, Mormons, and William Cullen Bryant." *NEQ* 34(1961): 178-190.

1279. Donovan, Alan B. "William Cullen Bryant: 'Father of American Song.'" *NEQ* 41(1968): 505-520.

1280. Free, William J. "William Cullen Bryant on Nationalism, Imitation, and Originality in Poetry." *SP* 66(1969): 672-687.

1281. Glicksberg, Charles I. "William Cullen Bryant and Nineteenth-Century Science." *NEQ* 23(1950): 91-96.

1282. McLean, Albert, Jr. "Bryant's Thanatopsis: A Sermon in Stone." *AL* 31(1960): 474-479.

1283. Murray, Donald M. "Dr. Peter Bryant: Preceptor in Poetry to William Cullen Bryant." *NEQ* 33(1960): 513-522.

1284. Peck, Richard E. "Two Lost Bryant Poems: Evidence of Thompson's Influence." *AL* 39 (1967): 88-94.

1285. Ringe, Donald A. "William Cullen Bryant and the Science of Geology." *AL* 26(1955): 507-514.

1286. Sanford, Charles L. "The Concept of the Sublime in the Works of Thomas Cole and William Cullen Bryant." *AL* 28(1957): 434-448.

1287. Scheick, William J. "Bryant's River Imagery." *CLA* 20(1976): 205-209.

1288. Stimson, F. S. and Robert Bininger. "Studies of Bryant as Hispanophile: Another Translation." *AL* 31(1959): 189-191.

BUNNER, H. C. 1289. Stronks, James B. "Frank Norris's *McTeague*: A Possible Source in H. C. Bunner." *NCF* 25(1971): 474-478.

BURNETT, FRANCES HODGSON. 1290. Molson, Francis. "Frances Hodgson Burnett (1848-1942)." [bibliography] *ALR* 8(1975): 35-42.

BURROUGHS, JOHN. 1291. Coleman, Rufus A. "Trowbridge and Burroughs." *MLQ* 14(1953): 154-162.

CABLE, GEORGE WASHINGTON. 1292. Butcher, Philip. "Cable to Boyesen on *The Grandissimes*." *AL* 40(1968): 391-394.

1293. ----------. "George Washington Cable (1844-1925)." [bibliography] *ALR* 1,#1(1967): 20-25.

1294. ----------. "The Godfathership of *A Connecticut Yankee*." *CLA* 12(1969): 189-198.

1295. ----------. "Mutual Appreciation: Dunbar and Cable." *CLA* 1(1958): 101-102.

1296. ----------. "Two Early Southern Realists in Revival." *CLA* 14(1970): 91-95.

1297. Cardwell, Guy A. "George W. Cable Becomes a Professional Reader." *AL* 23(1952): 467-470.

1298. Cleman, John. "The Art of Local Color in Cable's *The Grandissimes*." *AL* 47(1975): 396-410.

1299. Eaton, Richard Bozman. "George W. Cable and the Historical Romance." *SLJ* 8,#1(1975): 82-94.

1300. Lorch, Fred W. "Cable and His Reading Tour with Mark Twain in 1884-1885." *AL* 23(1952): 471-486.

1301. Moore, Rayburn S. "'Don Joaquin,' A Forgotten Story by George W. Cable." *AL* 26(1954): 418-421.

1302. Ringe, Donald A. "The 'Double Center': Character and Meaning in Cable's Early Novels." *SN* 5(1973): 52-62.

1303. Rubin, Louis D., Jr. "The Divisions of the Heart: Cable's *The Grandissimes*." *SLJ* 1, #2(1969): 27-47.

1304. Turner, Arlin. "Mark Twain, Cable, and 'A Professional Newspaper Liar.'" *NEQ* 28(1955): 18-33.

See also 1144, 1399.

CARTER, ROBERT. 1305. Hoeltje, Hubert H. "Benjamin Disraeli's Letters to Robert Carter." *PQ* 31(1952): 17-26.

CHANNING, WILLIAM ELLERY. 1306. Berthoff, Warner. "Renan on W. E. Channing and American Unitarianism." *NEQ* 35(1962): 71-92.

1307. Edgell, David P. "A Note on a Transcendental Friendship." *NEQ* 24(1951): 528-532.

1308. Pommer, Henry F. "A Sermon by William Ellery Channing." *NEQ* 36(1963): 77-79.

1309. Puknat, Siegfried B. "Auerback and Channing." *PMLA* 72(1957): 962-976.

1310. Reinhardt, John E. "The Evolution of William Ellery Channing's Sociopolitical Ideas." *AL* 26(1954): 154-165.

1311. Virtanan, Reino. "Tocqueville and William Ellery Channing." *AL* 22(1950): 21-28.

See also 1906.

CHESNUTT, CHARLES W. 1312. Andrews, William L. "'Baxter's Procrustes': Some More Light on the Biographical Connection." *BALF* 11(1977): 75-78.

1313. ----------. "Chestnutt's Patesville: The Presence and Influence of the Past in *The House Behind the Cedars*." *CLA* 15(1972): 284-294.

1314. ----------. "A Reconsideration of Charles Waddell Chesnutt: Pioneer of the Color Line." *CLA* 19(1975): 136-151.

1315. ----------. "Significance of Charles W. Chesnutt's 'Conjure Stories.'" *SLJ* 7,#1(1974): 78-99.

1316. ----------. "William Dean Howells and Charles W. Chesnutt: Criticism and Race Fiction in the Age of Booker T. Washington." *AL* 48(1976): 327-339.

1317. Baldwin, Richard E. "The Art of *The Conjure Woman*." *AL* 43(1971): 385-398.

1318. Britt, David D. "Chesnutt's Conjure Tales: What You See Is What You Get." *CLA* 15(1972): 269-283.

1319. Cunningham, Joan. "The Uncollected Short Stories of Charles Waddell Chesnutt." *BALF* 9(1975): 57-58.

1320. Dixon, Melvin. "The Teller as Folk Trickster in Chesnutt's *The Conjure Woman*." *CLA* 18(1974): 186-197.

1321. Haslam, Gerald. "'The Sheriff's Children': Chesnutt's Tragic Racial Parable." *BALF* 2(1968): 21-25.

1322. Hemenway, Robert. "'Baxter's Procrustes': Irony and Protest." *CLA* 18(1974): 172-185.

1323. ----------. "Gothic Sociology: Charles Chesnutt and the Gothic Mode." *SLI* 7,#1 (1974): 101-119.

1324. Hovet, Theodore R. "Chesnutt's 'The Goophered Grapevine' as Social Criticism." *BALF* 7(1973): 85-88.

1325. Jackson, Wendell. "Charles W. Chesnutt's Outrageous Fortune." *CLA* 20(1976): 195-204.

1326. Keller, Dean. "Charles Waddell Chesnutt (1858-1932)." [bibliography] *ALR* 1,#3 (1968): 1-4.

1327. Render, Sylvia Lyons. "Tar Heelia in Chesnutt." *CLA* 9(1965): 39-50.

1328. Sedlack, Robert P. "The Evolution of Charles Chesnutt's *The House behind the Cedars*." *CLA* 19(1975): 125-135.

1329. Smith, Robert A. "A Note on the Folktales of Charles W. Chestnutt." *CLA* 5(1962): 229-232.

1330. Socken, Jane. "Charles Waddell Chesnutt and the Solution to the Race Problem." *BALF* 3(1969): 52-56.

1331. Taxel, Joel. "Charles Waddell Chesnutt's Sambo: Myth and Reality." *BALF* 9(1975): 105-108.

1332. Walcott, Ronald. "Chesnutt's 'The Sheriff's Children' as Parable." *BALF* 7(1973): 83-85.

See also 1147, 4391.

CHILD, FRANCIS JAMES. 1333. Howe, M. A. DeWolfe. "'Il Pesceballo': The Fishball Operetta of Francis James Child." *NEQ* 23(1950): 187-199.

1334. Reppert, James D. "William Macmath and F. J. Child." *PMLA* 71(1956): 510-520.

CHILD, LYDIA M. 1335. Edwards, Herbert. "Lydia M. Child's *The Frugal Housewife*." *NEQ* 26 (1953): 243-249.

1336. Swennes, Robert H. "Lydia Maria Child: Holographs of 'The Hero's Heart' and 'Brackett's Bust of John Brown.'" *AL* 40(1969): 539-542.

1337. Taylor, Lloyd C., Jr. "Lydia Maria Child: Biographer." *NEQ* 34(1961): 211-227.

See also 2040.

CHIVERS, THOMAS H. 1338. Davis, Richard Beale. "Thomas Holley Chivers and the Kentucky Tragedy." *TSLL* 1(1959): 281-288.

CHOPIN, KATE. 1339. Bender, Bert. "Kate Chopin's Lyric Short Stories." *SSF* 11(1974): 257-266.

1340. Bonner, Thomas, Jr. "Kate Chopin's European Consciousness." *ALR* 8(1975): 281-283.

1341. Butcher, Philip. "Two Early Southern Realists in Revival." *CLA* 14(1970): 91-95.

1342. Koloski, Bernard J. "The Structure of Kate Chopin's *At Fault*." *SAF* 3(1975): 89-94.

1343. ----------. "The Swinburn Lines in *The Awakening*." *AL* 45(1974): 608-610.

1344. Leary, Lewis. "Kate Chopin's Other Novel." *SLJ* 1,#1(1968): 60-74.

1345. Ringe, Donald A. "Cane River World: Kate Chopin's *At Fault* and Related Stories." *SAF* 3(1975): 157-166.

1346. ----------. "Romantic Imagery in Kate Chopin's *The Awakening*." *AL* 43(1972): 580-588.

1347. Seyersted, Per. "Kate Chopin (1851-1904)." [bibliography] *ALR* 3(1970): 153-159.

1348. Spangler, George M. "Kate Chopin's *The Awakening:* A Partial Dissent." *Novel* 3(1970): 249-255.

1349. Sullivan, Ruth, and Stewart Smith. "Narrative Stance in Kate Chopin's *The Awakening*." *SAF* 1(1973): 62-75.

CLARK, LEWIS GAYLORD. 1350. Moss, Sidney P. "Poe and His Nemesis -- Lewis Gaylord Clark." *AL* 28(1956): 30-49.

CLEMENS, SAMUEL. 1351. Allen, Gerald. "Mark Twain's Yankee." *NEQ* 39(1966): 435-446.

1352. Alsen, Eberhard. "Pudd'inhead Wilson's Fight for Popularity and Power." *WAL* 7 (1972): 135-143.

1353. Altenbernd, Lynn. "Huck Finn, Emancipator." *Criticism* 1(1950): 219-307.

1354. Ashmead, John. "A Possible Hannibal Source for Mark Twain's Dauphin." *AL* 34(1962): 105-107.

1355. Aspiz, Harold. "Mark Twain and 'Doctor' Newton." *AL* 44(1972): 130-136.

1356. Babcock, C. Merton. "Mark Twain's Chuck-Wagon Specialties." *WAL* 5(1970): 147-151.

1357. Baender, Paul. "Alias Macfarlane: A Revision of Mark Twain Biography." *AL* 38(1966): 187-197.

1358. ----------. "The Date of Mark Twain's 'The Lowest Animal.'" *AL* 36(1964): 174-179.

1359. ----------. "The 'Jumping Frog' as a Comedian's First Virtue." *MP* 60(1963): 192-200.

1360. ----------. Mark Twain and the Byron Scandal." *AL* 30(1959): 467-485.

1361. ----------. "Review Article: Two Books on Mark Twain." *PQ* 47(1968): 117-135.

1362. Baetzhold, Howard G. "'The Autobiography of Sir Robert Smith of Camelot': Mark Twain's Original Plan for *A Connecticut Yankee*." *AL* 32(1961): 456-461.

1363. ----------. "The Course of Composition of *A Connecticut Yankee:* A Reinterpretation." *AL* 33(1961): 195-214.

1364. ----------. "Found: Mark Twain's 'Last Sweetheart.'" *AL* 44(1972): 414-429.

1365. ----------. "Mark Twain: England's Advocate." *AL* 28(1956): 328-346.

1366. Baldanza, Frank. "The Structure of *Huckleberry Finn*." *AL* 27(1955): 347-355.

1367. Banta, Martha. "Escape and Entry in *Huckleberry Finn*." *MFS* 14(1968): 79-91.

1368. ----------. "Rebirth or Revenge: The Endings of *Huckleberry Finn* and *The American*." *MFS* 15(1969): 191-207.

1369. Bates, Allan. "Sam Clemens, Pilot-Humorist of a Tramp Steamboat." *AL* 39(1967): 102-109.

1370. ----------. "The Quintus Curtius Snodgrass Letters: A Clarification of the Mark Twain Cannon." *AL* 36(1964): 31-37.

1371. Beebe, Maurice and John Feaster. "Criticism of Mark Twain: A Selected Checklist." *MFS* 14(1968): 93-139.

1372. Beidler, Peter G. "The Raft Episode in *Huckleberry Finn*." *MFS* 14(1968): 11-20.

1373. Bickley, R. Bruce, Jr. 'Humorous Portraiture in Twain's News Writing." *ALR* 3(1970): 395-398.

1374. Blair, Walter. "The French Revolution and *Huckleberry Finn*." *MP* 55(1957): 21-35.

1375. ----------. "When was *Huckleberry Finn* Written." *AL* 30(1958): 1-25.

1376. Blues, Thomas. "The Strategy of Compromise in Mark Twain's 'Boy Books.'" *MFS* 14(1968): 21-31.

1377. Boggan, J. R. "That Slap, Huck, Did It Hurt? *ELN* 1(1964): 212-215.

1378. Booth, Bradford A. "Mark Twain's Comments on Bret Harte's Stories." *AL* 25(1954): 492-495.

1379. ----------. "Mark Twain's Comments on Holmes's *Autocrat*." *AL* 21(1950): 456-463.

1380. Branch, Edgar M. "Major Perry and the Monitor *Camanche*. An Early Mark Twain Speech." *AL* 39(1967): 170-179.

1381. ----------. "'My voice is still for Setchell': A Background Study of 'Jim Smiley and His Jumping Frog.'" *PMLA* 82(1967): 591-601.

1382. ----------. "Samuel Clemens: Learning to Venture a Miracle." *ALR* 8(1975): 91-100.

1383. Brand, John M. "The Incipient Wilderness: A Study of *Pudd'nhead Wilson*." *WAL* 7(1972): 125-134.

1384. Brodwin, Stanley. "Blackness and the Adamic Myth in Mark Twain's *Pudd'nhead Wilson*." *TSLL* 15(1973): 167-176.

1385. ----------. "The Humor of the Absurd: Mark Twain's Adamic Diaries." *Criticism* 14(1972): 49-64.

1386. ----------. "Mark Twain's Masks of Satan: The Final Phase." *AL* 45(1973): 206-227.

1387. Browne, Ray B. "Mark Twain and Captain Wakeman." *AL* 33(1961): 320-329.

1388. Budd, Louis. "A Listing of and Selection from Newspapar and Magazine Interviews with Samuel L. Clemens 1874-1910." *ALR* 10(1977): 1-100.

1389. ----------. "Twain, Howells, and the Boston Nihilists." *NEQ* 32(1959): 351-371.

1390. Burg, David F. "Another View of *Huckleberry Finn*." *NCF* 29(1974): 299-319.

1391. Burhans, Clinton S., Jr. "The Sober Affirmation of Mark Twain's Hadleyburg." *AL* 34 (1962): 375-384.

1392. Burns, Stuart L. "St. Petersburg Re-Visited: Helen Eustis and Mark Twain." *WAL* 5(1970): 65-112.

1393. Bush, Robert. "Grace King and Mark Twain." *AL* 44(1972): 31-51.

1394. Butcher, Philip. "'The Godfathership' of *A Connecticut Yankee*." *CLA* 12(1969): 189-198.

1395. ----------. "Mark Twain Sells Roxy down the River." *CLA* 8(1965): 225-233.

1396. ----------. "Mark Twain's Installment on the National Debt." *SLJ* 1,#2(1969): 48-55.

1397. Byers, John R., Jr. "Miss Emmeline Grangerford's Hymm Book." *AL* 43(1971): 259-263.

1398. Cardwell, Guy A. "Mark Twain, James R. Osgood, and Those 'Suppressed' Passages." *NEQ* 46(1973): 163-188.

1399. ----------. "Mark Twain's 'Row' with

George Cable." *MLQ* 13(1952): 363-371.

1400. ----------. "Samuel Clemens' Magical Pseudonym." *NEQ* 48(1975): 175-193.

1401. Carter, Paul J., Jr. "Mark Twain and the American Labor Movement." *NEQ* 30(1957): 382-389.

1402. ----------. "Mark Twain Describes a San Francisco Earthquake." *PMLA* 72(1957): 997-1004.

1403. ----------. "Olivia Clemens Edits *Following the Equator*." *AL* 30(1958): 194-209.

1404. Cecil, L. Moffitt. "Tom Sawyer: Missouri Robin Hood." *WAL* 4(1969): 125-131.

1405. Clark, George Peirce. "Mark Twain on Bret Harte: Selections from Two Unpublished Letters." *JEGP* 57(1958): 208-210.

1406. Clerc, Charles. "Sunrise on the River: 'The Whole World' of *Huckleberry Finn*." *MFS* 14 (1968): 67-78.

1407. Coburn, Mark D. "'Training is everything': Communal Opinion and the Individual in *Pudd'nhead Wilson*." *MLQ* 31(1970): 209-219.

1408. Collins, Billy J. "Huckleberry Finn: A Mississippi Moses." *JNT* 5(1975): 86-104.

1409. Colwell, James L. "Huckleberries and Humans: On the Naming of Huckleberry Finn." *PMLA* 86(1971): 70-76.

1410. Crowley, John W. "A Note on *The Gilded Age*." *ELN* 10(1972): 116-118.

1411. Cummings, Sherwood. "Science and Mark Twain's Theory of Fiction." *PQ* 37(1958): 26-33.

1412. da Ponte, Durant. "*Life* Reviews *Huckleberry Finn*." *AL* 31(1959): 78-81.

1413. ----------. "Some Evasions of Censorship in *Following the Equator*." *AL* 29(1957): 92-95.

1414. Delaney, Paul. "The Dissolving Self: The Narrators of Mark Twain's *Mysterious Stranger* Fragments." *JNT* 6(1976): 51-65.

1415. ----------. "You Can't Go Back to the Raft Ag'in Huck Honey! Mark Twain's Western Sequel to Huckleberry Finn." *WAL* 11(1976): 215-229.

1416. Doyno, Victor A. "Over Twain's Shoulder: The Composition and Structure of *Huckleberry Finn*." *MFS* 14(1968): 3-9.

1417. Eby, E. H. "Mark Twain's Testament." *MLQ* 23(1962): 254-262.

1418. Ensor, Allison. "The Contributions of Charles Webster and Albert Bigelow Paine to *Huckleberry Finn*." *AL* 40(1968): 222-227.

1419. ----------. "Mark Twain's 'The War Prayer': Its Ties to Howells and to Hymmology." *MFS* 16(1970): 535-539.

1420. Eppard, Philip B. "Mark Twain Dissects an Overrated Book." *AL* 49(1977): 430-440.

1421. Fatout, Paul. "Mark Twain, Litigant." *AL* 31(1959): 30-45.

1422. ----------. "Mark Twain's Nom de Plume." *AL* 34(1962): 1-7.

1423. Fender, Stephen. "'The Prodigal in a Far Country Chawing of Husks': Mark Twain's Search for a Style in the West." *MLR* 71(1976): 737-756.

1424. Fetterley, Judith. "Disenchantment: Tom Sawyer in *Huckleberry Finn*." *PMLA* 87(1972): 69-74.

1425. ----------. "The Sanctioned Rebel." *SN* 3(1971): 293-304.

1426. ----------. "Yankee Showman and Reformer: The Character of Mark Twain's Hank Morgan." *TSLL* 14(1973): 667-679.

1427. Fox, Maynard. "Two Primitives: Huck Finn and Tom Outland." *WAL* 1(1966): 26-33.

1428. Frantz, Ray W., Jr. "The Role of Folklore in *Huckleberry Finn*." *AL* 28(1956): 314-327.

1429. French, Bryant Morey. "James Hammond Trumbull's Alternative Chapter: Mottoes for *The Gilded Age*." *PQ* 50(1971): 271-280.

1430. Fussell, E. S. "The Structural Problem of *The Mysterious Stranger*." *SP* 49(1952): 95-104.

1431. Ganzel, Dewey. "Clemens, Mrs. Fairbanks, and *Innocents Abroad*." *MP* 63(1965): 128-140.

1432. ----------. "Samuel Clemens, Sub Rosa Correspondent." *ELN* 1(1964): 270-273.

1433. ----------. "Twain, Travel Books, and *Life on the Mississippi*." *AL* 34(1962): 40-55.

1434. Gardner, Joseph H. "Gaffer Hexam and Pap Finn." *MP* 66(1968): 155-156.

1435. ----------. "Mark Twain and Dickens." *PMLA* 84(1969): 90-101.

1436. Gerber, John C. "Mark Twain's Use of the Comic Pose." *PMLA* 77(1962): 297-304.

1437. Goold, Edgar H., Jr. "Mark Twain on the Writing of Fiction." *AL* 26(1954): 141-153.

1438. Graves, Wallace. "Mark Twain's 'Burning Shame.'" *NCF* 23(1968): 93-98.

1439. Gribben, Alan. "Anatole France and Mark Twain's Satan." *AL* 47(1976): 634-635.

1440. ----------. "'Good Books and A Sleepy Conscience': Mark Twain's Reading Habits." *ALR* 9 (1976): 295-306.

1441. ----------. "How Tom Sawyer Played Robin Hood 'By the Book.'" *ELN* 13(1976): 201-204.

1442. ----------. "'I Kind of Love Small Game': Mark Twain's Library of Literary Hogwash." *ALR* 9(1976): 65-76.

1443. Griffith, Clark. "Merlin's Grin: From 'Tom' to 'Huck' in *A Connecticut Yankee*." *NEQ* 48(1975): 28-46.

1444. ----------. "Pudd'nhead Wilson as Dark Comedy." *ELH* 43(1976): 209-226.

1445. Griska, Joseph M., Jr. "Two New Joel Chandler Harris Reviews of Mark Twain." *AL* 48(1977): 584-589.

1446. Gullason, Thomas Arthur. "The 'Fatal' Ending of *Huckleberry Finn*." *AL* 29(1957): 86-91.

1447. Guttmann, Allen. "Mark Twain's *Connecticut Yankee*: Affirmation of the Vernacular Tradition." *NEQ* 33(1960): 232-237.

1448. Hansen, Chadwick. "The Once and Future Boss: Mark Twain's Yankee." *NCF* 28(1973): 62-73.

1449. Harris, Helen L. "Mark Twain's Response to the Native American." *AL* 46(1975): 495-505.

1450. Hart, John E. "Heroes and Houses: The Progress of Huck Finn." *MFS* 14(1968): 39-46.

1451. Hill, Hamlin. "The Composition and Structure of *Tom Sawyer*." *AL* 32(1960): 379-392.

1452. ----------. "Mark Twain's 'Brace of Brief Lectures on Science.'" *NEQ* 34(1961): 228-239.

1453. ----------. "Mark Twain's Quarrels with Elisha Bliss.: *AL* 33(1962): 442-456.

1454. ----------. "Two Twain 'Heresies'." *MLQ* 26(1956): 327-333.

1455. ----------. "Who Killed Mark Twain?" *ALR* 7(1974): 119-124.

1456. Hoffman, Daniel G. "Jim's Magic: Black or White? *AL* 32(1960): 47-54.

1457. Jefferies, William B. "The Montesquiou Murder Case: A Possible Source for Some Incidents in *Pudd'nhead Wilson*." *AL* 31(1960): 488-490.

1458. Jones, Alexander E. "Mark Twain and Freemasonry." *AL* 26(1954): 363-373.

1459. ----------. "Mark Twain and Sexuality." *PMLA* 71(1956): 595-616.

1460. ----------. "Mark Twain and the Determinism of *What is Man?*" *AL* 29(1957): 1-17.

1461. ----------. "Mark Twain and the 'Many Citizens' Letter." *AL* 26(1954): 421-425.

1462. Jones, Daryl. "The *Hornet* Disaster: Twain's Adaptation in 'The Great Dark.'" *ALR* 9 (1976): 243-248.

1463. Jones, Joseph. "Mark Twain's *Connecticut Yankee* and Australian Nationalism." *AL* 40 (1968): 227-232.

1464. Kendall, Lyle H. "The Walter Scott Episode in *Huckleberry Finn*." *NCF* 16(1961): 279-281.

1465. Ketterer, David. "Epoch-Eclipse and Apocalypse: Special 'Effects' in *A Connecticut Yankee*." *PMLA* 88(1973): 1104-1114.

1466. Kimball, William J. "Samuel Clemens as a Confederate Soldier: Some Observations about 'The Private History of a Campaign that Failed.'" *SSF* 5(1968): 382-384.

1467. Kitzhaber, Albert R. "Mark Twain's Use of the Pomeroy Case in *The Gilded Age*." *MLQ* 15(1954): 42-56.

1468. Klass, Philip. "An Innocent in Time: Mark Twain in King Arthur's Court." *Ext* 16(1974): 17-32.

1469. Krause, Sydney J. "Cooper's Literary Offenses: Mark Twain in Wonderland." *NEQ* 38(1965): 291-311.

1470. ----------. "Olivia Clemens's 'Editing' Reviewed." *AL* 39(1967): 325-351.

1471. ----------. "Twain and Scott: Experience versus Adventures." *MP* 62(1965): 227-236.

1472. ----------. "Twain's Method and Theory of Composition." *MP* 56(1959): 167-177.

1473. Kruse, Horst H. "Annie and Huck: A Note on *The Adventures of Huckleberry Finn*." *AL* 39(1967): 207-214.

1474. Leary, Lewis. "More Letters from the *Quaker City*." *AL* 42(1970): 197-202.

1475. ----------. "Troubles with Mark Twain: Some Considerations on Consistency." *SAF* 2(1974): 89-103.

1476. Lease, Benjamin. "Mark Twain and the Publication of *Life on the Mississippi*: An Unpublished Letter." *AL* 26(1954): 248-250.

1477. Lindborg, Henry J. "A Cosmic Tramp: Samuel Clemens's *Three Thousand Years Among the Microbes*." *AL* 44(1973): 652-657.

1478. Linneman, William R. "*Punch* and *Huckleberry Finn*." *ELN* 2(1965): 293.

1479. Levy, Leo B. "Society and Conscience in *Huckleberry Finn*." *NCF* 18(1964): 383-391.

1480. Lorch, Fred W. "Cable and His Reading Tour with Mark Twain in 1884-1885." *AL* 23(1952): 471-486.

1481. ----------. "Hawaiian Feudalism and Mark Twain's *A Connecticut Yankee in King Arthur's Court*." *AL* 30(1958): 50-66.

1482. ----------. "A Note on Mark Twain's Lectures on the Far West." *AL* 24(1952): 377-379.

1483. ----------. "Mark Twain's 'Artemus Ward' Lecture on the Tour of 1871-1872." *NEQ* 25 (1952): 327-343.

1484. ----------. "Mark Twain's Lecture from *Roughing It*." *AL* 22(1950): 290-307.

1485. ----------. "Mark Twain's Lecture Tour of 1868-1869: 'The American Vandal Abroad'." *AL* 26(1955): 515-527.

1486. ----------. "Mark Twain's 'Morals' Lecture During the American Phase of His World Tour in 1895-1896." *AL* 26(1954): 52-66.

1487. ----------. "Mark Twain's Public Lectures in England in 1873." *AL* 29(1957): 297-304.

1488. ----------. "Mark Twain's 'Sandwich Islands' Lecture and the Failure at Jamestown, New York, in 1869." *AL* 25(1953): 314-325.

1489. ----------. "Reply to Mr. Alexander E. Jones." *AL* 26(1954): 426-427.

1490. Mannierre, William R. "Huck Finn: Empiricist Member of Society." *MFS* 14(1968): 57-66.

1491. ----------. "'No Money For to Buy the Outfit': *Huckleberry Finn* Again." *MFS* 10(1964): 341-348.

1492. ----------. "On Keeping the Raftsman's Passage in *Huckleberry Finn*." *ELN* 6(1968): 118-122.

1493. Marx, Leo. "The Pilot and the Passenger: Landscape Conventions and the Style of *Huckleberry Finn*." *AL* 28(1956): 129-146.

1494. May, John R. "The Gospel According to Philip Traum: Structural Unity in 'The Mysterious Stranger.'" *SSF* 8(1971): 411-422.

1495. McCloskey, John C. "Mark Twain as Critic in *The Innocents Abroad*." *AL* 25(1953): 139-151.

1496. McCullough, Joseph. "A Listing of Mark Twain's Contributions to the Buffalo *Express* 1869-1871." *ALR* 5(1972): 61-66.

1497. ----------. "Mark Twain and the Hy Slocum-Carl Byng Controversy." *AL* 43(1971): 42-59.

1498. McIntyre, James P. "Three Practical Jokes: A Key to Huck's Changing Attitude Toward Jim." *MFS* 14(1968): 31-37.

1499. McKee, John DeWitt. "*Roughing It* as Retrospective Reporting." *WAL* 5(1970): 113-119.

1500. McKeithan, D. M. "Madame de Laszowska Meets Mark Twain." *TSLL* 1(1959): 62-65.

1501. ----------. "Mark Twain's Letters of Thomas Jefferson Snodgrass." *PQ* 32(1953): 353-365.

1502. ----------. "The Morgan Manuscript of *The Man That Corrupted Hadleyburg*." *TSLL* 2(1961): 476-480.

1503. Meserve, Walter. "*Colonel Sellers As A Scientist*: A Play by S. L. Clemens and W. D. Howells." *MD* 1(1958): 151-156.

1504. Michelson, Bruse. "Mark Twain the Tourist: The Form of *The Innocents Abroad*." *AL* 49(1977): 385-398.

1505. Miller, William C. "Mark Twain's Source of 'The Latest Sensation Hoax'." *AL* 32(1960): 75-78.

1506. Moyne, Ernest J. "Mark Twain and Baroness Alexandria Gripenberg." *AL* 45(1973): 370-378.

1507. Nebeker, Helen E. "The Great Corruptor Satan Rehabilitated." *SSF* 8(1971): 635-637.

1508. Park, Martha M. "Mark Twain's Hadleyburg: A House Built on Sand." *CLA* 16(1973): 508-513.

1509. Parsons, Coleman O. "The Background of *The Mysterious Stranger*." *AL* 32(1960): 55-74.

1510. ----------. "Mark Twain: Clubman in South Africa." *NEQ* 50(1977): 234-254.

1511. Pearce, Roy Harvey. "'The End. Yours Truly, Huck Finn': Postscript." *MLQ* 24(1963): 253-256.

1512. Pettit, Arthur G. "Mark Twain, the Blood-Feud and the South." *SLJ* 4,#1(1971): 20-32.

1513. Pommer, Henry F. "Mark Twain's 'Commissioner of the United States.'" *AL* 34(1962): 385-392.

1514. Reese, Robert A., and Richard Dilworth Rust. "Mark Twain's 'The Turning Point of My Life.'" *AL* 40(1969): 524-535.

1515. Ridland, J. M. "Huck, Pip, and Plot." *NCF* 20(1965): 286-290.

1516. Rodgers, Paul C., Jr. "Artemus Ward and Mark Twain's 'Jumping Frog.'" *NCF* 28(1973): 273-286.

1517. Rodon, Stewart. "*The Adventures of Huckleberry Finn* and *Invisible Man*: Thematic and Structural Comparisons." *BALF* 4(1970): 45-50.

1518. Roemer, Kenneth M. "The Yankee(s) in Noahville." *AL* 45(1973): 434-437.

1519. Rogers, Franklin R. "Mark Twain and Daudet: A Tramp Abroad and *Tartarin sur les Alpes*." *Comp L* 16(1964): 254-263.

1520. Rogers, Rodney O. "Twain, Taine, and Lecky: The Genesis of a Passage in *A Connecticut Yankee*." *MLQ* 34(1973): 436-447.

1521. Ross, Michael L. "Mark Twain's *Pudd'nhead Wilson*: Dawson's Landing and the Ladder of Nobility." *Novel* 6(1973): 244-256.

1522. Rowlette, Robert. "'Mark Ward on Artemus Twain': Twain's Literary Debt to Ward." *ALR* 6(1973): 13-26.

1523. Rucker, Mary E. "Moralism and Determinism in 'The Man That Corrupted Hadleyburg.'" *SSF* 14(1977): 49-54.

1524. Salomon, Roger B. "Escape from History: Mark Twain's *Joan of Arc*." *PQ* 40(1961): 77-90.

1525. San Juan, Pastora. "A Source for *Tom Sawyer*." *AL* 38(1966): 101-102.

1526. Schmidt, Paul. "River vs. Town: Mark Twain's *Old Times on the Mississippi*." *NCF* 15(1960): 95-111.

1527. Schmitz, Neil. "The Paradox of Liberation in *Huckleberry Finn*." *TSLL* 13(1971): 125-136.

1528. Schorer, C. E. "Mark Twain's Criticism of *The Story of a Country Town*." *AL* 27(1955): 109-112.

1529. Schwartz, Thomas O. "Mark Twain and Robert Ingersoll: The Freethought Connection." *AL* 48(1976): 183-193.

1530. Scott, Arthur L. "The *Century Magazine* Edits *Huckleberry Finn*, 1884-1885." *AL* 27 (1955): 356-362.

1531. ----------. "*The Innocents Adrift* Edited by Mark Twain's Official Biographer." *PMLA* 78(1963): 230-237.

1532. ----------. "Mark Twain Revises *Old Times on the Mississippi*, 1875-1883." *JEGP* 54 (1955): 634-638.

1533. ----------. "Mark Twain's Revisions of *The Innocents Abroad* for the British Edition of 1872." *AL* 25(1953): 43-61.

1534. Shain, Charles E. "The Journal of the *Quaker City* Captain." *NEQ* 28(1955): 388-394.

1535. Spangler, George M. "*Puddn'head Wilson*: A Parable of Property." *AL* 42(1970): 28-37.

1536. Stern, Madeleine B. "Mark Twain Had His Head Examined." *AL* 41(1969): 207-218.

1537. Stone, Albert E., Jr. "Mark Twain's *Joan of Arc*: The Child as Goddess." *AL* 31(1959): 1-20.

1538. Strong, Leah A. "Mark Twain on Spelling." *AL* 23(1951): 357-359.

1539. Stronks, James B. "Mark Twain's Boston Stage Debut as seen by Hamlin Garland." *NEQ* 36(1963): 85-86.

1540. Tanner, Tony. "The Literary Children of James and Clemens." *NCF* 16(1961): 205-218.

1541. Tatham, Campbell. "'Dismal and Lonesome': A New Look at *Huckleberry Finn*." *MFS* 14 (1968): 47-55.

1542. Tenney, Thomas. "Mark Twain: A Reference Guide—First Annual Supplement." *ALR* 10 (1977): 327-412.

1543. Towers, Tom H. "'Hateful Reality': The Failure of the Territory in *Roughing It*." *WAL* 9(1974): 3-15.

1544. ----------. "'I Never Thought We Might Want to Come Back': Strategies of Transcendence in *Tom Sawyer*." *MFS* 21(1975): 509-520.

1545. Tuckey, John S. "Hannibal, Weggis, and Mark Twain's Eseldorf." *AL* 42(1970): 235-240.

1546. ----------. "Mark Twain's Later Dialogue: The 'Me' and the Machine." *AL* 41(1970): 532-542.

1547. Turner, Arlin. "Mark Twain, Cable, and 'A Professional Newspaper Liar'." *NEQ* 28(1955): 18-33.

1548. Tuttleton, James W. "Twain's Use of Theatrical Traditions in the Old Southwest." *CLA* 8(1964): 190-197.

1549. Vales, Robert L. "Thief and Theft in *Huckleberry Finn*." *AL* 37(1966): 420-429.

1550. Vandersee, Charles. "The Mutual Awareness of Mark Twain and Henry Adams." *ELN* 5 (1968): 285-292.

1551. Vogelback, Arthur L. "Mark Twain and the Fight for Control of the *Tribune*." *AL* 26(1954): 374-383.

1552. ----------. "Mark Twain and the Tammany Ring." *PMLA* 70(1955): 69-77.

1553. Wermuth, Paul C. "Santayana and *Huckleberry Finn*." *NEQ* 36(1963): 79-82.

1554. Wexman, Virginia. "The Role of Structure in 'Tom Sawyer' and 'Huckleberry Finn.'" *ALR* 6(1973): 1-12.

1555. White, William. "Mark Twain to the President of Indiana University." *AL* 32(1961): 461-463.

1556. Wigger, Anne P. "The Composition of Mark Twain's *Pudd'nhead Wilson and Those Extraordinary Twins*: Chronology and Development." *MP* 55(1957): 93-102.

1557. ----------. "The Source of Fingerprint Material in Mark Twain's *Pudd'nhead Wilson and Those Extraordinary Twins*." *AL* 28(1957): 517-520.

1558. Wiggins, Robert A. "Mark Twain and the Drama." *AL* 25(1953): 279-286.

1559. ----------. "The Original of Mark Twain's *Those Extraordinary Twins*." *AL* 23(1951): 355-357.

1560. Williams, James D. "Revision and Intention in Mark Twain's *A Connecticut Yankee*." *AL* 36(1964): 288-297.

1561. ----------. The Use of History in Mark Twain's *A Connecticut Yankee*." *PMLA* 80(1965): 102-110.

1562. Wilson, Mark K. "Mr. Clemens and Madame Blanc: Mark Twain's First French Critic." *AL* 45(1974): 537-556.

1563. Wuliger, Robert. "Mark Twain on *King Leopold's Soliloquy*." *AL* 25(1953): 234-235.

1564. Yates, Norris W. "The 'Counter-Conversion' of Huckleberry Finn." *AL* 32(1960): 1-10.

1565. Zwahlen, Christine. "Of Hell or of Hannibal?" *AL* 42(1971): 562-563.

See also 584, 590, 595, 602a, 610, 1144, 1151, 2567, 7671.

CLYMAN, JAMES.   1566. Zochert, Donald. "'A View of the Sublime Awful': The Language of a Pioneer." *WAL* 6(1972): 251-257.

COOKE, ROSE TERRY.   1567. Downey, Jean. "Three Unpublished Letters: Howells-Cooke." *AL* 32(1961): 463-465.

1568. Toth, Susan. "Rose Terry Cooke (1827-1892)." *ALR* 4(1971): 170-176.

See also 3231.

COOLBRITH, INA.   1569. Hubbard, George U. "Ina Coolbrith's Friendship with John Greenleaf Whittier." *NEQ* 45(1972): 109-118.

COOPER, JAMES FENIMORE.   1570. Abcarian, Richard. "Cooper's Critics and the Realistic Novel." *TSLL* 8(1966): 33-41.

1571. Aldridge, A. Owen. "Fenimore Cooper and the Picaresque Tradition." *NCF* 27(1972): 283-292.

1572. Beard, James Franklin. "Cooper and the Revolutionary Mythos." *EAL* 11(1976): 84-104.

1573. Bewley, Marius. "Fenimore Cooper and the Economic Age." *AL* 26(1954): 166-195.

1574. Bier, Jesse. "The Bisection of Cooper: Satanstoe as Prime Example." *TSLL* 9(1968): 511-521.

1575. ----------. "Lapsarians on *The Prairie*: Cooper's Novel." *TSLL* 4(1962): 49-57.

1576. Brenner, Gerry. "Cooper's 'Composite Order': *The Pioneers* as Structured Art." *SN* 2 (1970): 264-275.

1577. Bush, Sargent, Jr. "Charles Cap of *The Pathfinder*: A Foil to Cooper's Views on the American Character in the 1840's." *NCF* 20(1965): 267-273.

1578. Butler, Michael D. "Narrative Structure and Historical Process in *The Last of the Mohicans*." *AL* 48(1976): 117-139.

1579. Collins, Frank M. "Cooper and the American Dream." *PMLA* 81(1966): 79-94.

1580. Darnell, Donald. "Uncas as Hero: The *Ubi Sunt* Formula in *The Last of the Mohicans*." *AL* 37(1965): 259-266.

1581. Davie, Donald. "The Legacy of Fenimore Cooper." *EIC* 9(1959): 222-238.

1582. Denne, Constance Ayers. "Cooper's Artistry in *The Headsman*." *NCF* 29(1974): 77-92.

1583. Diemer, James S. "A Model for Harvey Birch." *AL* 26(1954): 242-247.

1584. Dryden, Edgar A. "History and Progress: Some Implications of Form in Cooper's Littlepage Novels." *NCF* 26(1971): 49-64.

1585. Frederick, John T. "Cooper's Eloquent Indians." *PMLA* 71(1956): 1004-1017.

1586. French, David P. "James Fenimore Cooper and Fort William Henry." *AL* 32(1960): 28-38.

1587. Gates, W. B. "Cooper's Indebtedness to Shakespeare." *PMLA* 67(1952): 716-731.

1588. ----------. "Cooper's *The Crater* and Two Explorers." *AL* 23(1951): 243-246.

1589. ----------. "Cooper's *The Sea Lions* and Wilkes' *Narrative*." *PMLA* 65(1950): 1069-1075.

1590. ----------. "A Neglected Satire on James Fenimore Cooper's *Home As Found*." *AL* 35(1963): 13-21.

1591. Griffin, Max L. "Cooper's Attitude Toward the South." *SP* 48(1951): 67-76.

1592. Kasson, Joy S. "Templeton Revisited: Social Criticism in *The Pioneers* and *Home as Found*." *SN* 9(1977): 54-64.

1593. Kay, Donald. "Major Character Types in *Home as Found*: Cooper's Search for American Principles and Dignity." *CLA* 14(1971): 432-439.

1594. Kaye, Frances W. "Cooper, Sarmiento, Wister, and Hernandez: The Search for a New World Literary Hero." *CLA* 19(1976): 404-411.

1595. Kehler, Joel R. "Architectural Dialecticism in Cooper's *The Pioneers*." *TSLL* 18(1976): 124-134.

1596. Kligerman, Jack. "Notes on Cooper's Debt to John Jay." *AL* 41(1969): 415-419.

1597. ----------. "Style and Form in James Fenimore Cooper's *Homeward Bound* and *Home as Found*." *JNT* 4(1974): 45-61.

1598. Lewis, Merrill. "Lost and Found—In the Wilderness: The Desert Metaphor in Cooper's *The Prairie*." *WAL* 5(1970): 195-204.

1599. Martin, Terence. "From the Ruins of History: *The Last of the Mohicans*." *Novel* 2(1969): 221-229.

1600. McAleer, John J. "Biblical Analogy in the Leatherstocking Tales." *NCF* 17(1962): 217-235.

1601. McCloskey, John C. "Cooper's Political Views in *The Crater*." *MP* 53(1955): 113-116.

1602. McWilliams, John P., Jr. "*The Crater* and the Constitution." *TSLL* 12(1971): 631-645.

1603. Mills, Gordon. "The Symbolic Wilderness: Cooper and London." *NCF* 13(1959): 329-340.

1604. O'Donnell, Charles. "The Moral Basis of Civilization: Cooper's Home Novels." *NCF* 17 (1962): 265-273.

1605. Parker, Hershel. "The Metaphysics of Indian-Hating." *NCF* 18(1963): 165-173.

1606. Paul, Jay S. "The Education of Elizabeth Temple." *SN* 9(1977): 187-194.

1607. ----------. "Home as Cherished: The Theme of Family in Fenimore Cooper." *SN* 5(1973): 39-51.

1608. Peck, H. Daniel. "A Repossession of America: The Revolution in Cooper's Trilogy of Nautical Romances." *SR* 15(1976): 589-606.

1609. Philbrick, Thomas. "Cooper's *The Pioneers*: Origins and Structure." *PMLA* 79(1964): 579-593.

1610. ----------. "*The Last of the Mohicans* and the Sounds of Discord." *AL* 43(1971): 25-41.

1611. ----------. "The Sources of Cooper's Knowledge of Fort William Henry." *AL* 36(1964): 209-214.

1612. Pickering, James H. "*Satanstoe*: Cooper's Debt to William Dunlap." *AL* 38(1967): 468-477.

1613. Ringe, Donald. "The American Revolution in American Romance." *AL* 49(1977): 352-365.

1614. ----------. "Chiaroscuro as an Artistic Device in Cooper's Fiction." *PMLA* 78(1963): 349-357.

1615. ----------. "Cooper's Last Novels, 1847-1850." *PMLA* 75(1960): 583-590.

1616. ----------. "Cooper's Littlepage Novels: Change and Stability in American Society." *AL* 32(1960): 280-290.

1617. ----------. "James Fenimore Cooper and Thomas Cole: An Analogous Technique." *AL* 30(1958): 26-36.

1618. ----------. "Man and Nature in Cooper's *The Prairie*." *NCF* 15(1961): 313-323.

1619. Robinson, E. Arthur. "Conservation in Cooper's *The Pioneers*." *PMLA* 82(1967): 564-578.

1620. Ross, Morton L. "Captain Truck and Captain Boomer." *AL* 37(1965): 316.

1621. Rucker, Mary E. "Natural, Tribal, and Civil Law in Cooper's *The Prairie*." *WAL* 12(1977): 215-222.

1622. Smith, Henry Nash. "Consciousness and Social Order: The Theme of Rranscendence in The Leatherstocking Tales." *WAL* 5(1970): 177-194.

1623. Stallman, R. W. "Stephen Crane and Cooper's Uncas." *AL* 39(1967): 392-396.

1624. Steinbrink, Jeffrey. "Cooper's Romance of the Revolution: *Lionel Lincoln* and the Lessons of Failure." *EAL* 11(1977): 336-343.

1625. Sundquist, Eric J. "Incest and Imitation in Cooper's *Home as Found*." *NCF* 32(1977): 261-284.

1626. Taft, Kendall B. "The Nationality of Cooper's 'Traveling Bachelor.'" *AL* 28(1956): 368-370.

1627. Tanner, James E. "A Possible Source for *The Prairie*." *AL* 47(1975): 102-104.

1628. Vance, William L. "'Man and Beast': The Meaning Cooper's *The Prairie*." *PMLA* 89(1974): 323-331.

1629. Vanderbeets, Richard. "Cooper and the 'Semblance of Reality': A Source for *The Deerslayer*." *AL* 42(1971): 544-546.

1630. Vandiver, Edward P., Jr. "Cooper's *The Prairie* and Shakespeare." *PMLA* 69(1954): 1302-1304.

1631. Walker, Warren S. "A 'Scottish Cooper' for an 'American Scott.'" *AL* 40(1969): 536-537.

1632. Zoellner, Robert H. "Conceptual Ambivalence in Cooper's Leatherstocking." *AL* 31 (1960): 397-420.

See also 584, 595, 601, 1158, 1469, 4019.

COZZENS, JAMES GOULD. 1633. Bracher, Frederick. "James Gould Cozzens: Humanist." *Crit* 1,#3(1958): 10-29.

1634. Coxe, Louis O. "The Complex World of James Gould Cozzens." *AL* 27(1955): 157-171.

1635. Coxe, Louis O., and others. "Comments on Cozzens." *Crit* 1,#3(1958): 48-56.

1636. Fowler, Alastair. "Isolation and Its Discontents." *TCL* 6(1960): 51-64.

1637. Garrett, George. "*By Love Possessed*: The Pattern and the Hero." *Crit* 1,#3(1958): 41-47.

1638. Long, Richard. "The Image of Man in James Gould Cozzens." *CLA* 10(1967): 299-307.

1639. Ludwig, Richard M. "James Gould Cozzens: A Review of Research and Criticism." *TSLL* 1(1959): 123-136.

1640. Lydenberg, John. "Cozzens and the Conservatives." *Crit* 1,#3(1958): 3-9.

1641. Meriwether, James B. "A James Gould Cozzens Checklist." *Crit* 1,#3(1958): 57-63.

1642. Shepherd, Allen. "'The New Aquist of True Incredible Experience': Point of View and Theme in James Gould Cozzen's 'Eyes to See.'" *SSF* 13(1976): 378-381.

1643. Weimer, David R. "The Breath of Chaos in *The Just and the Unjust*." *Crit* 1,#3(1958): 30-40.

CRANCH, CHRISTOPHER. 1644. Levenson, J. C. "Christopher Pearse Cranch: The Case History of a Minor Artist in America." *AL* 21(1950): 415-426.

1645. Myerson, Joel. "Transcendentalism and Unitarianism in 1840: A New Letter by C.P. Cranch." *CLA* 16(1973): 366-368.

CRANE, JONATHAN T. 1646. Gullason, Thomas A. "The Fiction of the Reverend Jonathan Townley Crane, D.D." *AL* 43(1971): 263-273.

CRANE, STEPHEN. 1647. Anderson, Warren D. "Homer and Stephen Crane." *NCF* 19(1964): 77-86.

1648. Andrews, William L. "A New Stephen Crane Fable." *AL* 47(1975): 113-114.

1649. Ayers, Robert W. "W. D. Howells and Stephen Crane: Some Unpublished Letters." *AL* 28 (1957): 469-477.

1650. Bassan, Maurice. "The Design of Stephen Crane's Bowery Experiment." *SSF* 1(1964): 129-132.

1651. ----------. "An Early Draft of *George's Mother*." *AL* 36(1965): 518-522.

1652. ----------. "Stephen Crane and 'The Eternal Mystery of Social Condition.'" *NCF* 19 (1965): 387-394.

1653. Beebe, Maurice and Thomas A. Gullason. "Criticism of Stephen Crane: A Selected Checklist with an Index of Separate Works." *MFS* 5(1959): 282-291.

1654. Brennan, Joseph X. "The Imagery and Art of *George's Mother*." *CLA* 4(1960): 106-115.

1655. ----------. "Ironic and Symbolic Structure in Crane's *Maggie*." *NCF* 16(1962): 303-315.

1656. ----------. "Stephen Crane and the Limits of Irony." *Criticism* 11(1969): 183-200.

1657. Buitenhuis, Peter. "The Essentials of Life: 'The Open Boat' as Existentialist Fiction." *MFS* 5(1959): 243-250.

1658. Burns, Landon C., Jr. "On 'The Open Boat.'" *SSF* 3(1966): 455-457.

1659. Cady, Edwin Harrison. "Stephen Crane and The Strenuous Life." *ELH* 28(1961): 376-382.

1660. Colvert, James B. "Structure and Theme in Stephen Crane's Fiction." *MFS* 5(1959): 199-208.

1661. Cook, Robert G. "Stephen Crane's 'The Bride Comes to Yellow Sky.'" *SSF* 2(1965): 368-369.

1662. Cox, James M. "*The Pilgrim's Progress* as Source for Stephen Crane's *The Black Riders*." *AL* 28(1957): 478-487.

1663. Cox, James Trammell. "The Imagery of *The Red Badge of Courage*." *MFS* 5(1959): 209-219.

1664. ----------. "Stephen Crane as Symbolic Naturalist: An Analysis of 'The Blue Hotel.'" *MFS* 3(1953): 147-158.

1665. Davison, Richard Allan. "Crane's 'Blue Hotel' Revisited: The Illusion of Fate." *MFS* 15 (1969): 537-539.

1666. Deamer, Robert Glen. "Stephen Crane and the Western Myth." *WAL* 7(1972): 111-123.

1667. Dean, James. "The Wests of Howells and Crane." *ALR* 10(1977): 254-266.

1668. Dendinger, Lloyd N. "Stephen Crane's Inverted Use of Key Images of 'The Rime of the Ancient Mariner.'"

1669. Dillingham, William B. "'The Blue Hotel': and the Gentle Reader." *SSF* 1(1964): 224-226.

1670. Eby, Cecil D. "The Source of Crane's Metaphor, 'Red Badge of Courage.'" *AL* 32(1960): 204-207.

1671. ----------. "Stephen Crane's 'Fierce Red Wafer.'" *ELN* 1(1963): 128-130.

1672. Ellis, James. "The Game of High-Five in 'The Blue Hotel.'" *AL* 49(1977): 440-442.

1673. Fraser, John. "Crime and Forgiveness: 'The Red Badge' in Time of War." *Criticism* 9(1967): 243-256.

1674. Free, William Joseph. "Smoke Imagery in *The Red Badge of Courage.*" *CLA* 7(1963): 148-152.

1675. Gerstenberger, Donna L. "'The Open Boat': Additional Perspective." *MFS* 17(1971): 557-561.

1676. Gibson, Donald B. "'The Blue Hotel' and the Ideal of Human Courage." *TSLL* 6(1964): 388-397.

1677. Gilkes, Lillian Bernard. "The London Newsletters of Stephen and Cora Crane: A Collaboration." *SAF* 4(1976): 173-201.

1678. ----------. "A New Stephen Crane Item." *SAF* 5(1977): 255-257.

1679. ----------. "No Hoax: A Reply to Mr. Stallman." *SSF* 2(1964): 77-83.

1680. ----------. "Stephen and Cora Crane: Some Corrections and a 'Millionaire' Named Sharefe." *AL* 41(1969): 270-277.

1681. ----------. "Stephen Crane and the Biographical Fallacy: The Cora Influence." *MFS* 16(1970): 441-461.

1682. ----------. "Stephen Crane's 'Dan Emmonds': A Pig in a Storm." *SSF* 2(1964): 66-71.

1683. Gleckner, Robert F. "Stephen Crane and the Wonder of Man's Conceit." *MFS* 5(1959): 271-281.

1684. Greenfield, Stanley B. "The Unmistakable Stephen Crane." *PMLA* 73(1958): 562-572.

1685. Grenberg, Bruce L. "Metaphysic of Despair: Stephen Crane's 'The Blue Hotel.'" *MFS* 14(1968): 203-213.

1686. Griffith, Benjamin W. "Robinson Jeffers' 'The Blood Sire' and Stephen Crane's 'War is Kind.'" *NCL* 3(Jan., 1973): 14-15.

1687. Griffith, Clark. "Stephen Crane and the Ironic Last Word." *PQ* 47(1968): 83-91.

1688. Gullason, Thomas A. "Additions to the Canon of Stephen Crane." *NCF* 12(1957): 157-160.

1689. ----------. "The Cranes at Pennington Seminary." *AL* 39(1968): 530-541.

1690. ----------. "The First Known Review of Stephen Crane's 1893 *Maggie.*" *ELN* 5(1968): 300-302.

1691. ----------. "The Last Will and Testament of Mrs. Mary Helen Peck Crane." *AL* 40 (1968): 232-235.

1692. ----------. "The Letters of Stephen Crane: Additions and Corrections." *AL* 41(1969): 104-106.

1693. ----------. "New Light on the Crane-Howells Relationship." *NEQ* 30(1957): 389-392.

1694. ----------. "The Significance of 'Wounds in the Rain'." *MFS* 5(1959): 235-242.

1695. ----------. "The Sources of Stephen Crane's *Maggie.*" *PQ* 38(1959): 497-502.

1696. ----------. "Stephen Crane: Anti-Imperialist." *AL* 30(1958): 237-241.

1697. ----------. "Stephen Crane's Sister: New Biographical Facts." *AL* 49(1977): 234-238.

1698. ----------. "Thematic Patterns in Stephen Crane's Early Novels." *NCF* 16(1961): 59-67.

1699. Hafer, Carol B. "The Red Badge of Absurdity: Irony in *The Red Badge of Courage.*" *CLA* 14(1971): 440-443.

1700. Hagemann, E. R. "'Correspondents Three' in the Graeco-Turkish War: Some Parodies." *AL* 30 (1958): 339-344.

1701. Hoffman, Daniel G. "Crane's Decoration Day Article and *The Red Badge of Courage.*" *NCF* 14 (1959): 78-80.

1702. Hough, Robert L. "Crane and Goethe: A Forgotten Relationship." *NCF* 17(1962): 135-148.

1703. Hungerford, Harold R. "'That was at Chancellorsville': The Factual Framework of *The Red Badge of Courage.*" *AL* 34(1963): 520-531.

1704. Johnson, George W. "Stephen Crane's Metaphor of Decorum." *PMLA* 78(1963): 250-256.

1705. Johnson, Glen M. "Stephen Crane's 'One Dash—Horses': A Model of Realistic Irony." *MFS* 23(1977): 571-578.

1706. Katz, Joseph. "The *Maggie* Nobody Knows." *MFS* 12(1966): 200-212.

1707. ----------. "Stephen Crane, 'Samuel Carlton,' and a Recovered Letter." *NCF* 23(1968): 220-225.

1708. Klotz, Marvin. "Romance or Realism? Plot, Theme, and Character in *The Red Badge of Courage.*" *CLA* 6(1962): 98-106.

1709. Knapp, Daniel. "Son of Thunder: Stephen Crane and the Fourth Evangelist." *NCF* 24 (1969): 253-291.

Kwait, Joseph J. "The Newspaper Experience: Crane, Norris and Dreiser." *NCF* 8(1953): 99-117.

1711. LaFrance, Marston. "A Few Facts About Stephen Crane and 'Holland.'" *AL* 37(1965): 195-202.

1712. ----------. "The Ironic Parallel in Stephen Crane's 1892 Newspaper Correspondence." *SSF* 6(1968): 101-103.

1713. ----------. "Stephen Crane Scholarship Today and Tomorrow." *ALR* 7(1974): 125-136.

1714. Linder, Lyle. "Applications from Social Science to Literary Biography: The Family World of Stephen Crane." *ALR* 7(1974): 280-282.

1715. Linneman, William R. "Stephen Crane's Contributions to *Truth.*" *AL* 31(1959): 196-197.

1716. Lorch, Thomas M. "The Cyclical Structure of *The Red Badge of Courage.*" *CLA* 10(1967): 229-238.

1717. Maclean, Hugh N. "The Two Worlds of 'The Blue Hotel.'" *MFS* 5(1959): 260-270.

1718. Mangum, Bryant. "Crane's Red Badge and Zola's." *ALR* 9(1976): 279.

1719. Marcus, Mordecai. "Structure and Irony in Stephen Crane's 'War Is Kind.'" *CLA* 9(1966): 274-278.

1720. ----------. "The Three-Fold View of Nature in 'The Open Boat.'" *PQ* 41(1962): 511-515.

1721. Marlow, Jean G. "Crane's Wafer Image: Reference to an Artillery Primer?" *AL* 43(1972): 645-

647.

1722. May, Charles E. "The Unique Effect of the Short Story: A Reconsideration and an Example." *SSF* 13(1976): 289-297.

1723. McDermott, John J. "Symbolism and Psychological Realism in *The Red Badge of Courage*." *NCF* 23(1968): 324-331.

1724. Morace, Robert. "A 'New' Review of 'The Red Badge of Courage.'" *ALR* 8(1975): 163-165.

1725. Nagel, James. "Structure and Theme in Crane's 'An Experiment in Misery.'" *SSF* 10(1973): 169-174.

1726. Nelson, Harland S. "Stephen Crane's Achievement as a Poet." *TSLL* 4(1963): 564-582.

1727. O'Donnell, Thomas F. "Charles Dudley Warner on *The Red Badge of Courage*." *AL* 25(1953): 363-365.

1728. ----------. "DeForest, Van Petten, and Stephen Crane." *AL* 27(1956): 578-580.

1729. ----------. "John B. Van Petten: Stephen Crane's History Teacher." *AL* 27(1955): 196-202.

1730. ----------. "A Note on the Reception of Crane's *The Black Riders*." *AL* 24(1952): 233-235.

1731. Osborne, Scott C. "The 'Rivalry-Chivalry' of Richard Harding Davis and Stephen Crane." *AL* 28(1956): 50-61.

1732. ----------. "Stephen Crane and Cora Taylor: Some Corrections." *AL* 26(1954): 416-418.

1733. ----------. "Stephen Crane's Imagery: 'Pasted Like a Wafer.'" *AL* 23(1951): 362.

1734. Paredes, Raymund A. "Stephen Crane and the Mexican." *WAL* 6(1971): 31-38.

1735. Parks, Edd Winfield. "Crane's 'The Open Boat.'" *NCF* 8(1953): 77.

1736. Peck, Richard E. "Stephen Crane and Baudelaire: A Direct Link." *AL* 37(1965): 202-204.

1737. Pilgrim, Tim A. "Repetition as a Nihilist Device in Stephen Crane's 'The Blue Hotel.'" *SSF* 11(1974): 125-129.

1738. Pizer, Donald. "Stephen Crane's *Maggie* and American Naturalism." *Criticism* 7(1965): 168-175.

1739. Randel, William. "The Cook in 'The Open Boat.'" *AL* 34(1962): 405-411.

1740. ----------. "From Slate to Emerald Green: More Light on Crane's Jacksonville Visit." *NCF* 19(1965): 357-368.

1741. Rechmitz, Robert M. "Depersonalization and the Dream in *The Red Badge of Courage*." *SN* 6 (1974): 76-87.

1742. Rogers, Rodney D. "Stephen Crane and Impressionism." *NCF* 24(1969): 292-304.

1743. Sadler, Frank. "Crane's 'Fleming': Appellation for Coward or Hero?" *AL* 48(1976): 372-376.

1744. Satterwhite, Joseph N. "Stephen Crane's 'The Blue Hotel': The Failure of Understanding." *MFS* 2(1956): 238-241.

1745. Simoneaux, Katherine G. "Color Imagery in Crane's *George's Mother*." *CLA* 14(1971): 410-419.

1746. ----------. "Color Imagery in Crane's *Maggie: A Girl of the Streets*." *CLA* 18(1974): 91-100.

1747. Solomon, Eric. "Another Analogue for *The Red Badge of Courage*." *NCF* 13(1958): 63-67.

1748. ----------. "Stephen Crane's War Stories." *TSLL* 3(1961): 67-80.

1749. ----------. "The Structure of *The Red Badge of Courage*." *MFS* 5(1959): 220-234.

1750. ----------. "Yet Another Source for *The Red Badge of Courage*." *ELN* 2(1965): 215-217.

1751. Stallman, R. W. "Crane's '*Maggie*': A Reassessment." *MFS* 5(1959): 251-259.

1752. ----------. "How Stephen Crane Got to Crete." *AL* 44(1972): 308-313.

1753. ----------. "New Short Fiction by Stephen Crane: I." *SSF* 1(1963): 1-7.

1754. ----------. "New Short Fiction by Stephen Crane: II." *SSF* 1(1964): 147-152.

1755. ----------. "Stephen Crane and Cooper's Uncas." *AL* 39(1967): 392-396.

1756. ----------. "Stephen Crane's Revisions of *Maggie: A Girl of the Streets*." *AL* 26(1955): 528-536.

1757. ----------. "Was Crane's Sketch of the Fleet Off Crete A Journalistic Hoax? A Reply to Miss Gilkes." *SSF* 2(1964): 72-76.

1758. Stone, Edward. "Crane and Zola." *ELN* 1(1963): 46-47.

1759. ----------. "Crane's 'Soldier of the Legion.'" *AL* 30(1958): 242-244.

1760. ----------. "The Many Suns of *The Red Badge of Courage*." *AL* 29(1957): 322-326.

1761. Stronks, James B. "Garland's Private View of Crane in 1898 (with a Postscript)." *ALR* 6(1973): 249-251.

1762. Tenenbaum, Ruth Betsy. "The Artful Monstrosity of Crane's *Monster*." *SSF* 14(1977): 403-405.

1763. Tuttleton, James W. "The Imagery of *The Red Badge of Courage*." *MFS* 8(1962): 410-415.

1764. VanDerBeets, Richard. "Character as Structure: Ironic Parallel and Transformation in 'The Blue Hotel.'" *SSF* 5(1968): 294-295.

1765. Vanderbilt, Kermit, and Daniel Weiss. "From Rifleman to Flagbearer: Henry Fleming's Separate Peace in *The Red Badge of Courage*." *MFS* 11(1965): 371-380.

1766. Vorpahl, Ben Merchant. "Murder by the Minute: Old and New in 'The Birde Comes to Yellow Sky.'" *NCF* 26(1971): 196-218.

1767. Weatherford, Richard M. "A New Stephen Crane Letter." *AL* 48(1976): 79-81.

1768. ----------. "Stephen Crane and O. Henry: A Correction." *AL* 44(1973): 666.

1769. Weeks, Robert P. "The Power of the Tacit in Crane and Hemingway." *MFS* 8(1962): 415-418.

1770. Wertheim, Stanley. "*The Red Badge of Courage* and Personal Narratives of the Civil War." *ALR* 6(1973): 61-65.

1771. ----------. "Stephen Crane Remembered." *SAF* 4(1976): 46-64.

1772. West, Ray B., Jr. "Stephen Crane: Author in Transition." *AL* 34(1962): 215-229.

1773. Westbrook, Max. "Stephen Crand and the Personal Universal." *MFS* 8(1962): 351-360.

1774. ----------. "Stephen Crane: The Pattern of Affirmation." *NCF* 14(1959): 219-229.

1775. Wogan, Claudia C. "Crane's Use of Color in *The Red Badge of Courage*." *MFS* 6(1960): 168-172.

See also 1114, 1646.

CRAWFORD, FRANCIS M. 1776. Pilkington, John, Jr. "Francis Marion Crawford (1854-1909)." *ALR* 4 (1971): 177-182.

DANA, RICHARD H., JR. 1777. Coyle, William. "The Friendship of Anthony Trollope and Richard Henry Dana, Jr." *NEQ* 25(1952): 255-262.

1778. Hill, Douglas B., Jr. "Richard Henry Dana, Jr., and 'Two Years Before the Mast.'" *Criticism* 9(1967): 312-325.

1779. Lucid, Robert F. "The Influence of *Two Years Before the Mast* on Herman Melville." *AL* 31(1959): 243-256.

DANA, RICHARD H. SR. 1780. Hunter, Doreen. "America's First Romantics: Richard Henry Dana, Sr., and Washington Allston." *NEQ* 45(1972): 3-30.

DAVIS, REBECCA HARDING. 1781. Hesford, Walter. "Literary Contexts in 'Life in the Iron-Mills'." *AL* 49(1977): 70-85.

See also 598, 1145.

DAVIS, RICHARD HARDING. 1782. Eichelberger, Clayton, and Ann McDonald. "Richard Harding Davis (1864-1916): A Check List of Secondary Comment." *ALR* 4(1971): 313-390.

1783. Hagemann, E. R. "'Correspondents Three' in the Graeco-Turkish War: Some Parodies." *AL* 30(1958): 339-344.

1784. Holman, Harriet R. "Interlude: Scenes from John Fox's Courtship of Fritzi Scheff, as Reported by Richard Harding Davis." *SLJ* 7,#2 (1975): 77-87.

1785. Osborne, Scott C. "The 'Rivalry-Chivalry' of Richard Harding Davis and Stephen Crane." *AL* 28(1956): 50-61.

1786. Solensten, John. "The Gibson Boy: A Reassessment." *ALR* 4(1971): 303-312.

1787. ----------. "Richard Harding Davis (1864-1916)." [bibliography] *ALR* 3(1970): 160-165.

1788. ----------. "Richard Harding Davis, Owen Wister, and *The Virginian:* Unpublished Letters and a Commentary." *ALR* 5(1972): 123-133.

DEFOREST, JOHN WILLIAM. 1789. Alsen, Eberhard. "Marx and DeForest: The Idea of Class Struggle in *Miss Ravenal's Conversion.*" *AL* 48 (1976): 223-228.

1790. Bergmann, Frank. "DeForest in Germany." *ALR* 1,#4(1968): 80-81.

1791. Gargano, James W. "A DeForest Interview." *AL* 29(1957): 320-322.

1792. ----------. "John W. DeForest and the Critics." *ALR* 1,#4(1968): 57-64.

1793. Hagemann, E. R. "A Checklist of Critical Comments in *The Nation* on John William DeForest." *ALR* 1,#4(1968): 76-79.

1794. ----------. "John William De Forest Faces 'The Nation.'" *ALR* 1,#4(1968): 65-75.

1795. ----------. "A John William DeForest Supplement, 1970." *ALR* 3(1970): 148-152.

1796. "John William De Forest (1826-1906): A Critical Bibliography of Secondary Comment." *ALR* 1,#4(1968): 1-56.

1797. Levy, Leo B. "Naturalism in the Making: De Forest's *Honest John Vane.*" *NEQ* 37(1964): 89-98.

1798. Light, James. "John William De Forest (1826-1906)." [bibliography] *ALR* 1,#1(1967): 32-35.

1799. O'Donnell, Thomas F. "De Forest, Van Petten, and Stephen Crane." *AL* 27(1956): 578-580.

1800. Robillard, Douglas. "De Forest Literary Manuscripts in the Yale Library." *ALR* 1, #4(1968): 81-83.

1801. Sessler, Harvey. "A Test for Realism in De Forest's 'Kate Beaumont.'" *ALR* 2(1969): 274-275.

See also 1114, 1144.

DICKINSON, EMILY. 1802. Anderson, Charles R. "The Conscious Self in Emily Dickinson's Poetry." *AL* 31(1959): 290-308.

1803. ----------. "From a Window in Amherst: Emily Dickinson Looks at the American Scene." *NEQ* 31(1958): 147-171.

1804. ----------. "The Trap of Time in Emily Dickinson's Poetry." *ELH* 26(1959): 402-424.

1805. Banzer, Judith. "'Compound Manner': Emily Dickinson and the Metaphysical Poets." *AL* 32 (1961): 417-433.

1806. Bingham, Millicent Todd, ed. "Prose Fragments of Emily Dickinson." *NEQ* 28(1955): 291-318.

1807. Birdsall, Virginia O. "Emily Dickinson's Intruder in the Soul." *AL* 37(1965): 54-64.

1808. Childs, Herbert E. "Emily Dickinson and Sir Thomas Browne." *AL* 22(1951): 455-465.

1809. Cody, John. "Metamorphosis of a Malady: Summary of a Psychoanalytic Study of Emily Dickinson." *HSL* 2(1970): 113-132.

1810. D'Avanzo, Mario L. "'Under the White Creator': The Snow of Dickinson and Emerson." *NEQ* 45(1972): 278-280.

1811. Diehl, Joanne Feit. "Emerson, Dickinson, and the Abyss." *ELH* 44(1977): 683-700.

1812. Donaldson, Scott. "Minding Emily Dickinson's Business." *NEQ* 41(1968): 574-582.

1813. Dorinson, Zahava Karl. "'I Taste a Liquor Never Brewed': A Problem in Editing." *AL* 35(1963): 363-365.

1814. Doyle, Connie M. "Emily Dickinson's 'The Wind Drew Off.'" *ELN* 12(1975): 182-184.

1815. Eby, Cecil D. "'I Taste a Liquor Never Brewed': A Variant Reading." *AL* 36(1965): 516-518.

1816. Emblem, D. L. "A Comment on 'Structural Patterns in the Poetry of Emily Dickinson.'" *AL* 37(1965): 64-65.

1817. Faris, Paul. "Eroticism in Emily Dickenson's 'Wild Nights!'" *NEQ* 40(1967): 269-274.

1818. Folsom, L. Edwin. "'The Souls That Snow': Winter in the Poetry of Emily Dickinson." *AL* 47(1975): 361-376.

1819. Ford, Thomas W. "Thoreau's Cosmic Mosquito and Dickinson's Terrestrial Fly." *NEQ* 48 (1975): 487-504.

1820. Garrison, Joseph M., Jr. "Emily Dickinson: From Ballerina to Gymnast." *ELH* 42 (1975): 107-124.

1821. Garrow, A. Scott. "A Note on Manzanilla." *AL* 35(1963): 366.

1822. Gillespie, Robert. "A Circumference of Emily Dickinson." *NEQ* 46(1973): 250-271.

1823. Grover, Dorys C. "Garland's 'Emily Dickinson' -- A Case of Mistaken Identity." *AL* 46(1974): 219-220.

1824. Gullans, Charles, and John Espey. "Emily Dickinson: Two Uncollected Poems." *AL* 44 (1972): 306-307.

1825. Higgins, David. "Twenty-five Poems by Emily Dickinson: Unpublished Variant Versions." *AL* 38(1966): 1-21.

1826. Hill, Archibald A. "Figurative Structure and Meaning: Two Poems by Emily Dickinson." *TSLL* 16(1974): 195-209.

1827. Hoepfner, Theodore C. "'Because I Could not Stop for Death.'" *AL* 29(1957): 96.

1828. Howard, William. "Emily Dickinson's Poetic Vocabulary." *PMLA* 72(1957): 225-248.

1829. Kennedy, Joyce Deveau. "O'Neill's Lavinia Mannon and the Dickinson Legend." *AL* 49 (1977): 108-113.

1830. Lind, Sidney E. "Emily Dickinson's 'Further in Summer than the Birds' and Nathaniel Hawthorne's 'The Old Manse.'" *AL* 39(1967): 163-169.

1831. Manierre, William R. "E. D.: Visions and Revisions." *TSLL* 5(1963): 5-16.

1832. Matchett, William H. "Dickinson;s Revision of 'Two Butterflies went out at Noon.'" *PMLA* 77(1962): 436-441.

1833. McCall, Dan. "'I Felt a Funeral in My Brain' and 'The Hollow of the Three Hills.'" *NEQ* 42(1969): 432-435.

1834. Merideth, Robert. "Emily Dickinson and the Acquisitive Society." *NEQ* 37(1964): 435-452.

1835. Miller, F. DeWolfe. "Emily Dickinson: Self-Potrait in the Third Person." *NEQ* 46 (1973): 119-134.

1836. Molson, Francis J. "Emily Dickinson's Rejection of the Heavenly Father." *NEQ* 47(1974): 404-426.

1837. Monteiro, George. "The One and Many Emily Dickinsons." *ALR* 7(1974): 137-142.

1838. Monteiro, George, and Barton L. St. Armand. "Garland's 'Emily' Dickenson—Identified." *AL* 47(1976): 632-633.

1839. Morse, Jonathan. "Emily Dickinson and the Spasmodic School: A Note on Thomas Wentworth Higginson's Esthetics." *NEQ* 50(1977): 505-509.

1840. O'Donnell, Patrick. "Zones of the Soul: Emily Dickinson's Geographical Imagery." *CLA* 21(1977): 62-73.

1841. Patterson, Rebecca. "Emily Dickinson's Jewel Imagery." *AL* 42(1971): 495-520.

1842. Pollak, Vivian R. "Emily Dickinson's Literary Allusions." *EL* 1(1974): 54-68.

1843. ----------. "'That fine Prosperity': Economic Metaphors in Emily Dickinson's Poetry." *MLQ* 34(1973): 161-179.

1844. Rogers, B. J. "The Truth Told Slant: Emily Dickinson's Poetic Mode." *TSLL* 14(1972): 329-336.

1845. Sandeen, Ernest. "Delight Deterred by Retrospect: Emily Dickinson's Late-Summer Poems." *NEQ* 40(1967): 483-500.

1846. Sewall, Richard B. "Emily Dickinson: New Looks and Fresh Starts." *MLQ* 29(1968): 84-90.

1847. Stephenson, William E. "Emily Dickinson and Watts's Songs for Children." *ELN* 3(1966): 278-281.

1848. Thomas, Owen. "Father and Daughter: Edward and Emily Dickinson." *AL* 40(1969): 510-523.

1849. Waggoner, Hyatt H. "Emily Dickinson: The Transcendent Self." *Criticism* 7(1965): 297-334.

1850. Wheatcroft, J. S. "Emily Dickinson's White Robes." *Criticism* 5(1963): 135-147.

1851. Wilner, Eleanor. "The Poetics of Emily Dickinson." *ELH* 38(1971): 126-154.

1852. Wilson, Suzanne M. "Emily Dickinson and Twentieth-Century Poetry of Sensibility." *AL* 36 (1964): 349-358.

1853. ----------. "Structural Patterns in the Poetry of Emily Dickinson." *AL* 35(1963): 53-59.

1854. Yetman, Michael G. "Emily Dickinson and the English Romantic Tradition." *TSLL* 15(1973): 129-147.

1855. Zacharias, Thundyil. "Circumstance, Circumference, and Center: Immanence and Transcendence in Emily Dickinson's Poems of Extreme Situations." *HSL* 3(1971): 73-92.

See also 404.

DOUGLASS, FREDERICK. 1856. Clasby, Nancy T. "Frederick Douglass's *Narrative:* A Content Analysis." *CLA* 14(1971): 242-250.

1857. Holmes, J. Welfred. "Some Antislavery Editors at Work: Lundy, Baily, Douglass." *CLA* 7 (1963): 48-55.

1858. Nichols, William W. "Individualism and Autobiographical Art: Frederick Douglass and Henry Thoreau." *CLA* 16(1972): 145-188.

1859. Perry, Patsy Brewington. "The Literary Content of *Frederick Douglass's Paper* through 1860." *CLA* 17(1973): 214-229.

1860. Stone, Albert E. "Identity and Art in Frederick Douglass's *Narrative." CLA* 17(1973): 192-213.

DRAKE, JOSEPH RODMAN. 1861. Slater, Joseph. "The Case of Drake and Halleck." *EAL* 8,#3(1974): 285-297.

DUYCKINCH, EVERT. 1862. Kay, Donald. "Herman Melville's Literary Relationship with Evert Duychkinch." *CLA* 18(1975): 393-403.

DWIGHT, JOHN S. 1863. Fertig, Walter L. "John Sullivan Dwight's Pre-Publication Notice of *Walden." NEQ* 30(1957): 84-90.

1864. Thomas, J. Wesley. "John Sullivan Dwight: A Translation of German Romanticism." *AL* 21(1950): 427-441.

EASTON, WILLIAM E. 1865. Fehrenback, Robert J. "William Edgar Easton's *Dessalines*: A Nineteenth-Century Drama of Black Pride." *CLA* 19 (1975): 75-89.

EDWARDS, ELISHA JAY. 1866. LaFrance, Marston. "A Few Facts about Stephen Crane and 'Holland.'" *AL* 37(1965): 195-202.

EGGLESTON, EDWARD. 1867. Randel, William. "Edward Eggleston (1837-1902)." [bibliography] *ALR* 1,#1(1967): 36-38.

1868. Wilson, Jack H. "Eggleston's Indebtedness to George Eliot in *Roxy." AL* 42(1970): 38-49.

EMERSON, RALPH WALDO. 1869. Adams, Richard P. "Emerson and the Organic Metaphor." *PMLA* 69 (1954): 117-130.

1870. Arms, George. "The Dramatic Movement in Emerson's 'Each and All'." *ELN* 1(1964): 207-211.

1871. Barbow, Brian M. "Emerson's 'Poetic' Prose." *MLQ* 35(1974): 157-172.

1872. Baumgartner, A. M. "'The Lyceum is My Pulpit': Homiletics in Emerson's Early Lectures." *AL* 34(1963): 477-486.

1873. Baym, Nina. "From Metaphysics to Metaphor: The Image of Water in Emerson and Thoreau." *SR* 5(1966): 230-243.

1874. Benoit, Ray. "Emerson on Plato: The Fire's Center." *AL* 34(1963): 487-498.

1875. Birdsall, Richard D. "Emerson and the Church of Rome." *AL* 31(1959): 273-281.

1876. Bloom, Robert. "Irving Babbitt's Emerson." *NEQ* 30(1957): 448-473.

1877. Bluestein, Gene. "Emerson's Epiphanies." *NEQ* 39(1966): 447-460.

1878. Braham, Lionel. "Emerson and Boehme: A Comparative Study in Mystical Ideas." *MLQ* 20 (1959): 30-35.

1879. Bridges, William E. "Transcendentalism and Psychotherapy: Another Look at Emerson." *AL* 41(1969): 157-177.

1880. Broderick, John C. "Emerson and Moorfield Storey: A Lost Journal Found." *AL* 38(1966): 177-186.

1881. Cameron, Kenneth Walter. "Coleridge and the Genesis of Emerson's 'Uriel.'" *PQ* 30(1951): 212-217.

1882. ----------. "An Early Prose Work of Emerson." *AL* 22(1950): 332-338.

1883. ----------. "Emerson, Thoreau, and the Society of Natural History." *AL* 24(1952): 21-30.

1884. ----------. "The Potent Song in Emerson's Merlin Poems." *PQ* 32(1953): 22-28.

1885. ----------. "A Sheaf of Emerson Letters." *AL* 24(1953): 476-480.

1886. Campbell, Harry Modean. "Emerson and Whitehead." *PMLA* 75(1960): 577-582.

1887. Carpenter, Hazen C. "Emerson and Christopher Pearse Cranch." *NEQ* 37(1964): 18-42.

1888. ----------. "Emerson, Eliot, and the Elective System." *NEQ* 24(1951): 13-34.

1889. Chandrasekharan, K. R. "Emerson's *Brahma*: An Indian Interpretation." *NEQ* 33(1960): 506-512.

1890. Chittick, V. L. O. "Emerson's 'Frolic Health.'" *NEQ* 30(1957): 209-234.

1891. Clendenning, John. "Emerson and Bayle." *PQ* 43(1964): 79-86.

1892. Cohen, Bernard. "Emerson's 'The Young American' and Hawthorne's 'The Intelligence Office.'" *AL* 26(1954): 32-43.

1893. Cohen, B. Bernard, and Lucian A. Cohen. "A Penny Paper's Review of Emerson's *Essays* (1841)." *NEQ* 29(1956): 516-521.

1894. Cook, Reginald L. "Emerson and Frost: A Parallel of Seers." *NEQ* 31(1958): 200-217.

1895. Cook, Robert G. "Emerson's 'Self-Reliance,' Sweeney, and Prufrock." *AL* 42(1970): 221-226.

1896. Cronkhite, G. Ferris. "The Transcendental Railroad." *NEQ* 24(1951): 306-328.

1897. Cummins, Roger William. "Unpublished Emerson Letters to Louis Prang and Whittier." *AL* 43(1971): 257-259.

1898. D'Avanzo, Mario L. "Emerson and Shakespeare in Stevens' 'Bantams in Pine-Woods.'" *AL* 49 (1977): 103-107.

1899. ----------. "'Under the White Creator': The Snow of Dickinson and Emerson." *NEQ* 45(1972): 278-280.

1900. Dedmond, Francis B. "'Croaking at booksellers': An Unpublished Emerson Letter." *AL* 49(1977): 414-417.

1901. Detweiler, Robert. "The Over-Rated 'Over-Soul.'" *AL* 36(1964): 65-68.

1902. Deutsch, Leonard J. "Ralph Waldo Ellison and Ralph Waldo Emerson: A Shared Moral Vision." *CLA* 16(1972): 159-178.

1903. Diehl, Joanne Feit. "Emerson, Dickinson, and the Abyss." *ELH* 44(1977): 683-700.

1904. Doherty, Joseph F. "Emerson and the Loneliness of the Gods." *TSLL* 16(1974): 65-75.

1905. Duffy, Charles. "Material Relating to R. W. Emerson in the Grimm *Nachlass*." *AL* 30(1959): 523-528.

1906. Edrich, Mary Worden. "The Rhetoric of Apostasy." *TSLL* 8(1967): 547-560.

1907. Englekirk, John E. "Notes on Emerson in Latin America." *PMLA* 76(1961): 227-232.

1908. Feuer, Lewis S. "Ralph Waldo Emerson's Reference to Karl Marx." *NEQ* 33(1960): 378-379.

1909. Fish, Howard M., Jr. "Five Emerson Letters." *AL* 27(1955): 25-30.

1910. Francis, Richard Lee. "Archangel in the Pleached Garden: Emerson's Poetry." *ELH* 33(1966): 461-472.

1911. Free, William J. "E. A. Robinson's Use of Emerson." *AL* 38(1966): 69-84.

1912. Friedrich, Gerhard. "A Note on Emerson's *Parnassus*." *NEQ* 27(1954): 397-399.

1913. Green, Eugene. "Reading Local History: Shattuck's *History*, Emerson's *Discourse*, and Thoreau's *Walden*." *NEQ* 50(1977): 303-314.

1914. Haig, Robert L. "Emerson and the 'Elective Word' of John Hunter." *NEQ* 28(1955): 394-397.

1915. ----------. "Emerson and William Hunter's Museum." *NEQ* 26(1953): 255-257.

1916. Haugrud, Raychel A. "Tyndall's Interest in Emerson." *AL* 41(1970): 507-517.

1917. Haviland, Thomas P. "Two Emerson Letters." *AL* 23(1951): 127-128.

1918. Holman, C. Hugh. "Hemingway and Emerson: Notes on the Continuity of an Aesthetic Tradition." *MFS* 1,#3(1955): 12-16.

1919. Hopkins, Vivian C. "Emerson and Bacon." *AL* 29(1958): 408-430.

1920. ----------. "Emerson and Cudworth: Plastic Nature and Transcendental Art." *AL* 23(1951): 80-98.

1921. ----------. "Two Unpublished Emerson Letters." *NEQ* 33(1960): 502-506.

1922. Jackson, Paul R. "Henry Miller, Emerson and the Divided Self." *AL* 43(1971): 231-241.

1923. Jaffe, Adrian. "An Earlier French Estimate of Emerson." *NEQ* 26(1953): 100-102.

1924. Jamieson, Paul F. "A Note on Emerson's 'Adirondacs.'" *NEQ* 31(1958): 88-90.

1925. Keller, Karl. "From Christianity to Transcendentalism: A Note on Emerson's Use of the Conceit." *AL* 39(1967): 94-98.

1926. Kloeckner, Alfred J. "Intellect and Moral Sentiment in Emerson's Opinions of 'The Meaner Kinds' of Men." *AL* 30(1958): 322-338.

1927. LaRosa, Ralph C. "Bacon and the 'Organic Method' of Emerson's Early Lectures." *ELN* 8 (1970): 107-114.

1928. ----------. "Emerson's Search for Literary Form: The Early Journals." *MP* 69(1971): 25-35.

1929. ----------. "Invention and Imitation in Emerson's Early Literatures." *AL* 44(1972): 13-30.

1930. Lauter, Paul. "Emerson's Revisions of *Essays* (First Series)." *AL* 33(1961): 143-158.

1931. ----------. "Truth and Nature: Emerson's Use of Two Complex Words." *ELH* 27(1960): 66-86.

1932. Lee, Roland F. "Emerson's 'Compensation' as Argument and as Art." *NEQ* 37(1964): 291-305.

1933. ----------. "Through Kierkegaard: Toward a Definition of Emerson's Theory of Communication." *ELH* 24(1957): 229-248.

1934. Lewis, R. W. B. "The Emerson Cause." *MLQ* 26(1965): 601-605.

1935. Liebman, Sheldon W. "The Development of Emerson's Theory of Rhetoric." *AL* 41(1969): 178-206.

1936. ----------. "Emerson's Transformation in the 1820's." *AL* 40(1968): 133-154.

1937. ----------. "The Origins of Emerson's Early Poetics: His Reading in the Scottish Common Sense Critics." *AL* 45(1973): 23-33.

1938. McCormick, John O. "Emerson's Theory of Human Greatness." *NEQ* 26(1953): 291-314.

1939. McDonald, John J. "Emerson and John Brown." *NEQ* 44(1971): 377-396.

1940. McElderry, B. R., Jr. "Wolfe and Emerson on 'Flow.'" *MFS* 2(1956): 77-78.

1941. McLean, Andrew M. "Emerson's *Brahma* as an Expression of Brahman." *NEQ* 42(1969): 115-122.

1942. Meese, Elizabeth A. "Transcendentalism: The Metaphysics of the Theme." *AL* 47(1975): 1-20.

1943. Miller, Norman. "Emerson's 'Each and All' Concept: A Reexamination." *NEQ* 41(1968): 381-392.

1944. Miller, Perry. "Emersonian Genius and the American Democracy." *NEQ* 26(1953): 27-44.

1945. Moss, William M. "'So Many Promising Youths': Emersons Disappointing Discoveries of New England Poet-Seers." *NEQ* 49(1976): 46-64.

1946. Murphy, Walter H. "A Letter by Emerson." *AL* 36(1964): 64-65.

1947. Murray, Donald M. "Emerson's 'Language as Fossil Poetry': An Analogy from Chinese." *NEQ* 29(1956): 204-213.

1948. Neufeldt, Leonard. "Emerson and the Civil War." *JEGP* 71(1972): 502-513.

1949. ----------. "The Vital Mind: Emerson's Epistemology." *PQ* 50(1971): 253-270.

1950. Newman, Franklin B. "Emerson and Buonarroti." *NEQ* 25(1952): 524-535.

1951. Obuchowski, Peter A. "Emerson's Science: An Analysis." *PQ* 54(1975): 624-632.

1952. O'Daniel, Thermon B. "Emerson is Literary Critic." *CLA* 8(1964-65): 21-43, 157-189, 246-276.

1953. ----------. "Emerson as Literary Critic [II]." *CLA* 8(1964): 157-189.

1954. Paris, Bernard J. "Emerson's "Bacchus.'" *MLQ* 23(1962): 150-159.

1955. Park, Martha M. "How Far From Emerson's Man of One Idea to Anderson's Grotesques?" *CLA* 20(1977): 374-379.

1956. Pommer, Henry F. "The Contents and Basis of Emerson's Belief in Compensation." *PMLA* 77(1962): 248-253.

1957. Porte, Joel. "Emerson, Thoreau, and the Double Consciousness." *NEQ* 41(1968): 40-50.

1958. ----------. "Nature as Symbol: Emerson's Noble Doubt." *NEQ* 37(1964): 453-476.

1959. Quinn, Patrick F. "Emerson and Mysticism." *AL* 21(1950): 397-414.

1960. Robinson, David B. "Children of Fire: Charles Ives on Emerson and Art." *AL* 48(1977): 564-576.

1961. Rose, E. J. "Melville, Emerson, and the Sphinx." *NEQ* 36(1963): 249-258.

1962. Ruchames, Louis. "Emerson's Second West India Emancipation Address." *NEQ* 28(1955): 383-388.

1963. ----------. "Two Forgotten Addresses by Ralph Waldo Emerson." *AL* 28(1957): 425-433.

1964. Schorer, C. E. "Emerson and the Wisconsin Lyceum." *AL* 24(1953): 462-475.

1965. Schriber, Mary Sue. "Emerson, Hawthorne, and 'The Artist of the Beautiful.'" *SSF* 8(1971): 607-616.

1966. Sealto, Merton M., Jr. "Emerson on the Scholar, 1833-1837." *PMLA* 85(1970): 185-195.

1967. Slater, Joseph. "Emerson's Praedials." *AL* 38(1966): 235-236.

1968. Sowder, William J. "Emerson's Early Impact on England: A Study in British Periodicals." *PMLA* 77(1962): 561-576.

1969. ----------. "Emerson's Rationalist Champions: A Study in British Periodicals." *NEQ* 37(1964): 147-170.

1970. Spiller, Robert E. "Emerson and Humboldt." *AL* 42(1971): 546-548.

1971. Stafford, William T. "Emerson and the James Family." *AL* 24(1953): 433-461.

1972. Strauch, Carl F. "The Date of Emerson's *Terminus*." *PMLA* 65(1950): 360-370.

1973. ----------. "Emerson and the Doctrine of Sympathy." *SR* 6(1967): 152-174.

1974. ----------. "Emerson's Phi Beta Kappa Poem." *NEQ* 23(1950): 65-90.

1975. ----------. "Emerson's Sacred Science." *PMLA* 73(1958): 237-250.

1976. ----------. "Hatred's Swift Repulsions: Emerson, Margaret Fuller, and Others." *SR* 7(1968): 65-103.

1977. ----------. "The MS Relationship of Emerson's 'Days.'" *PQ* 29(1950): 199-208.

1978. ----------. "The Year of Emerson's Poetic Maturity: 1834." *PQ* 34(1955): 353-377.

1979. Super, R. H. "Emerson and Arnold's Poetry." *PQ* 33(1954): 396-403.

1980. Taft, Kendall B. "The Byronic Background of Emerson's 'Good-Bye.'" *NEQ* 27(1954): 525-527.

1981. Tuerk, Richard. "Los Angeles' Reaction to Emerson's Visit to San Francisco." *NEQ* 44(1971): 477-482.

1982. Van Cromphout, Gustaaf. "Emerson and the Dialectics of History." *PMLA* 91(1976): 54-65.

1983. Ward, J. A. "Emerson and 'The Educated Will': Notes on the Process of Conversion." *ELH* 34(1967): 495-517.

1984. Whitaker, Thomas R. "The Riddle of Emerson's 'Sphinx .'" *AL* 27(1955): 179-195.

1985. White, William. "Thirty-three Unpublished Letters of Ralph Waldo Emerson." *AL* 33(1961): 159-178.

1986. ----------. "Two Unpublished Emerson Letters." *AL* 31(1959): 334-336.

1987. Wilson, John B. "Emerson and the 'Rochester Rappings.'" *NEQ* 41(1968): 248-258.

1988. Whitemeyer, Hugh H. "'Line' and 'Round' in Emerson's 'Uriel.'" *PMLA* 82(1967): 98-103.

1989. Wood, Barry. "The Growth of the Soul: Coleridge's Dialectical Method and the Strategy of Emerson's *Nature*." *PMLA* 91(1976): 385-397.

1990. Wyatt, David M.."Spelling Time: The Reader in Emerson's 'Circles " *AL* 48(1976): 140-151.

1991. Yoder, R. A. "Emerson's Dialectic." *Criticism* 11(1969): 313-238.

1992. ----------. "Toward the 'Titmouse Dimension': The Development of Emerson's Poetic Style." *PMLA* 87(1972): 255-270.

See also 598, 1110, 2510, 3307, 3642, 4224, 4567, 15286.

EMMONS, RICHARD. 1993. Rothwell, Kenneth S. "Another View of *The Fredoniad*: A Plea for Method." *AL* 33(1961): 373-378.

1994. Squier, Charles L. "Dulness in America: A Study in Epic Badness: *The Fredoniad*." *AL* 32(1961): 446-454.

ENGLISH, THOMAS DUNN. 1995. Moore, Rayburn S. "Thomas Dunn English: A Forgotten Contributor to The Development of Negro Dialect Verse in the 1870's." *AL* 33(1961): 72-75.

EWING, SAMUEL. 1996. Rothman, Irving N. "Structure and Theme in Samuel Ewing's Satire, the 'American Miracle.'" *AL* 40(1968): 294-308.

FERN, FANNY. 1997. Schlesinger, Elizabeth Bancroft. "Proper Bostonian as Seen by Fanny Fern." *NEQ* 27(1954): 97-102.

FIELD, EUGENE. 1998. Day, Robert A. "The Birth and Death of a Satirist: Eugene Field and Chicago's Growing Pains." *AL* 22(1951): 466-478.

FLINT, TIMOTHY. 1999. Hamilton, John A. "Timothy Flint's 'Lost Novel.'" *AL* 22(1950): 54-56.

2000. Vorpahl, Ben Merchant. "The Eden Theme and Three Novels by Timothy Flint." *SR* 10 (1971): 105-129.

FLOWER, BENJAMIN. 2001. Fairfield, Roy P. "Benjamin Orange Flower: Father of the Muckrakers." *AL* 22(1950): 272-282.

FREDERICK, HAROLD. 2002. Bigsby, C. W. E. "The 'Christian Science Case': An Account of the Death of Harold Frederic andthe Subsequent Inquest and Court Proceedings." *ALR* 1,#2(1968): 77-83.

2003. Blackall, Jean Frantz. "Perspectives on Harold Frederic's *Market-Place*." *PMLA* 86(1971): 388-405.

2004. Bredahl, A. Carl, Jr. "The Artist in *The Damnation of Theron Ware*." *SN* 4(1972): 432-441.

2005. Coale, Samuel. "Frederick and Hawthrone: The Romantic Roots of Naturalism." *AL* 48 (1976): 29-45.

2006. Crowley, John W. "The Nude and the Madonna in *The Damnation of Theron Ware*." *AL* 45 (1973): 379-389.

2007. Donaldson, Scott. "The Seduction of Theron Ware." *NCF* 29(1975): 441-452.

2008. Garner, Stanton. "Harold Frederick and Swinburn's *Locrine*: A Matter of Clubs, Copyrights, and Character." *AL* 45(1973): 285-292.

2009. ----------. "More Notes on Harold Frederick in Ireland." *AL* 39(1968): 560-562.

2010. ----------. "Some Notes on Harold Frederick in Ireland." *AL* 39(1967): 60-74.

2011. Graham, Don. "'A Degenerate Methodist': A New Review of *The Damnation of Theron Ware*." *ALR* 9(1976): 280-284.

2012. "Harold Frederic (1856-1898): A Critical Bibliography of Secondary Comment." *ALR* 1, #2(1968): 1-70.

2013. Johnson, George W. "Harold Frederic's Young Goodman Ware: The Ambiguities of a Realistic Romance." *MFS* 8(1962): 361-374.

2014. LeClair, Thomas. The Ascendant Eye: A Reading of *The Damnation of Theron Ware*." *SAF* 3(1975): 95-102.

2015. Luedtke, Luther S. "Harold Frederic's Satanic Soulsby: Interpretation and Sources." *NCF* 30(1975): 82-104.

2016. Milne, W. Gordon. "Frederic's 'Free' Woman." *ALR* 6(1973): 258-260.

2017. Monteiro, George, and Philip Eppard. "Harold Frederic's Earliest Publications." *ALR* 10 (1977): 168-190.

2018. O'Donnell, Thomas. "Harold Frederic (1856-1898)." [bibliography] *ALR* 1,#1(1967): 39-44.

2019. ----------. "Theron Ware, the Irish Picnic, and *Comus*." *AL* 46(1975): 528-536.

2020. Raleigh, John Henry. "The Damnation of Theron Ware." *AL* 30(1958): 210-227.

2021. Sage, Howard. "Harold Frederic's Narrative Essays: A Realistic-Journalistic Genre." *ALR* 3(1970): 388-392.

2022. Stein, Allen F. "Evasions of an American Adam: Structure and Theme in *The Damnation of Theron Ware*." *ALR* 5(1972): 23-38.

2023. VanDerBeets, Richard. "The Ending of *The Damnation of Theron Ware*." *AL* 36(1964): 358-359.

2024. ----------. "Harold Frederick and Comic Realism: The 'Drama Proper' of *Seth's Brother's Wife*." *AL* 39(1968): 553-560.

2025. Woodward, Robert. "Frederic's Collection of Reviews: Supplement to the Checklist of Contemporary Reviews of Frederic's Writings." *ALR* 1,#2(1968): 84-89.

2026. ----------. "Harold Frederic: Supplemental Critical Bibliography of Secondary Comment." *ALR* 3(1970): 95-147.

2027. ----------. "Illusion and Moral Ambivalence in *Seth's Brother's Wife*." *ALR* 2(1969): 281-282.

2028. ----------. "A Selection of Harold Frederic's Early Literary Criticism, 1877-1881. *ALR* 5(1972): 1-22.

2029. ----------. "Some Sources for Harold Frederic's *The Damnation of Theron Ware*." *AL* 33 (1961): 46-51.

2030. Woodward, Robert and Stanton Garner. "Frederic's Short Fiction: A Checklist." *ALR* 1, #2(1968): 73-76.

See also 1114.

FREEMAN, MARY WILKINS. 2031. Hirsch, David H. "Subdued Meaning in 'A New England Nun.'" *SSF* 2(1965): 124-136.

2032. Toth, Susan Allen. "Defiant Light: A Positive View of Mary Wilkins Freeman." *NEQ* 46 (1973): 82-93.

2033. ----------. "Mary Wilkins Freeman's Parable of Wasted Life." *AL* 42(1971): 564-567.

2034. Westbrook, Perry. "Mary E. Wilkins Freeman (1852-1930)." *ALR* 2(1969): 139-142.

See also 3231.

FULLER, HENRY BLAKE. 2035. Abel, Darrel. "Expatriation and Realism in American Fiction in the 1880's: Henry Blake Fuller." *ALR* 3(1970): 245-247.

2036. ----------. "'Howells or James': An Essay by Henry Blake Fuller." *MFS* 3(1957): 159-164.

2037. Fuller, Henry Blake. "The American School of Fiction." *ALR* 3(1970): 248-257.

2038. Swanson, Jeffrey. "A Checklist of the Writings of Henry Blake Fuller (1857-1929)." *ALR* 7(1974): 211-244.

2039. ----------. "'Flesh, Fish or Fowl': Henry Blake Fuller's Attitudes Toward Realism and Romanticism." *ALR* 7(1974): 195-210.

2040. Williams, Kenny. "Henry Blake Fuller (1857-1929)." [bibliography] *ALR* 1,#3(1968): 9-13. See also 598.

FULLER, MARGARET. 2041. Baer, Helene G. "Mrs. Childs and Miss Fuller." *NEQ* 26(1953): 249-255.

2042. Colville, Derek. "The Transcendental Friends: Clarke and Margaret Fuller." *NEQ* 30 (1957): 378-382.

2043. Hoyt, Edward A., and Loriman S. Brigham. "Glimpses of Margaret Fuller: The Green Street School and Florence." *NEQ* 29(1956): 87-98.

2044. Rosenthal, Bernard. *"The Dial,* Transcendentalism and Margaret Fuller." *ELN* 8(1970): 28-36.

2045. Strauch, Carl F. "Hatred's Swift Repulsions: Emerson, Margaret Fuller, and Others." *SR* 7(1968): 65-103. See also 3906.

GARLAND, HAMLIN. 2046. Alsen, Eberhard. "Hamlin Garland's First Novel: *A Spoil of Office.*" *WAL* 4(1969): 91-105.

2047. Bryer, Jackson, and Eugene Harding. "Hamlin Garland (1860-1940): A Bibliography of Secondary Comment." *ALR* 3(1970): 290-387.

2048. ----------. "Hamlin Garland: Reviews and Notices of His Work." *ALR* 4(1971): 103-156.

2049. Carter, Joseph. "Hamlin Garland's Liberated Woman." *ALR* 6(1973): 255-257.

2050. Duffey, Bernard. "Hamlin Garland's 'Decline' from Realism." *AL* 25(1953): 69-74.

2051. ----------. "Mr. Koerner's Reply Considered." *AL* 26(1954): 432-435.

2052. Edwards, Herbert. "Herne, Garland and Henry George." *AL* 28(1956): 359-367.

2053. Flanagon, John T. "Hamlin Garland Writes to His Chicago Publisher." *AL* 23(1952): 447-457.

2054. French, Warren. "What Shall We Do About Hamlin Garland?" *ALR* 3(1970): 283-289.

2055. Grover, Dorys C. "Garland's 'Emily Dickenson—A Case of Mistaken Identity." *AL* 46(1974): 219-220.

2056. Harrison, Stanley R. "Hamlin Garland and the Double Vision of Naturalism." *SSF* 6(1969): 548-556.

2057. Henson, Clyde E. "Joseph Kirkland's Influence on Hamlin Garland." *AL* 23(1952): 458-563.

2058. Irsfeld, John H. "The Use of Military Language in Hamlin Garland's 'The Return of a Private.'" *WAL* 7(1972): 145-147.

2059. Koerner, James D. "Comment on 'Hamlin Garland's 'Decline' from 'Realism.'" *AL* 26(1954): 427-432.

2060. Martinec, Barbara. "Hamlin Garland's Revisions of *Main-Travelled Roads.*" *ALR* 5(1972): 167-172.

2061. McCullough, Joseph. "Hamlin Garland's Letters to James Whitcomb Riley." *ALR* 9(1976): 249-260.

2062. ----------. "Hamlin Garland's Quarrel with 'The Dial.'" *ALR* 9(1976): 77-80.

2063. McElderry, B. R., Jr. "Hamlin Garland and Henry James." *AL* 23(1952): 433-446.

2064. Meyer, Roy W. "Hamlin Garland and The American Indian." *WAL* 2(1967): 109-125.

2065. Miller, Charles T. "Hamlin Garland's Retreat from Realism." *WAL* 1(1966): 119-129.

2066. Monteiro, George and Barton L. St. Armand. "Garland's 'Emily' Dickenson—Identified." *AL* 47(1976): 632-633.

2067. Pizer, Donald. "Hamlin Garland (1860-1940)." [bibliography] *ALR* 1,#1(1967): 45-51.

2068. ----------. "Hamlin Garland in the *Standard.*" *AL* 26(1954): 401-415.

2069. ----------. "'John Boyle's Conclusion': An Unpublished Middle Border Story by Hamlin Garland." *AL* 31(1959): 59-75.

2070. ----------. "The Radical Drama in Boston 1889-1891." *NEQ* 31(1958): 361-374.

2071. Schorer, C. E. "Hamlin Garland's First Published Story." *AL* 25(1953): 89-92.

2072. Silet, Charles, and Robert Welch. "Further Additions to *Hamlin Garland and the Critics.*" *ALR* 9(1976): 268-275.

2073. Stronks, James B. "Mark Twain's Boston Stage Debut as seen by Hamlin Garland." *NEQ* 36(1963): 85-86.

2074. ----------. "A Realist Experiments with Impressionism: Hamlin Garland's 'Chicago Studies.'" *AL* 36(1964): 38-52.

2075. ----------. "A Supplement to Bryer and Harding's *Hamlin Garland and the Critics: An Annotated Bibliography.*" *ALR* 9(1976): 261-267.

2076. Williams, John Joseph. "Hamlin Garland's 'Sidney Lanier.'" *ELN* 3(1966): 282-283. See also 598.

GARRISON, WILLIAM L. 2077. Merrill, Walter McIntosh. "A Passionate Attachment: William Lloyd Garrison's Courtship of Helen Eliza Benson." *NEQ* 29(1956): 182-302.

GILDER, RICHARD W. 2078. Scott, Arthur L. "The *Century Magazine* Edits *Huckleberry Finn,* 1884-1885." *AL* 27(1955): 356-362.

2079. Sloane, David. "Censoring for *The Century Magazine:* R. W. Gilder to John Hay on *The Bread Winners.*" *ALR* 4(1971): 255-267.

GILMAN, CAROLINE HOWARD. 2080. MacPike, Loralee. "Environment as Psychopathological Symbolism in 'The Yellow Wallpaper.'" *ALR* 8(1975): 286-288.

2081. Schopp-Schilling, Beate. "'The Yellow Wallpaper': A Rediscovered 'Realistic' Story." *ALR* 8(1975): 284-285.

GRISWOLD, RUFUS. 2082. Cohen, B. Bernard, and Lucian A. Cohen. "Poe and Griswald Once More." *AL* 34(1962): 97-101.

GUNN, THOMAS B. 2083. McDermott, John Francis. "Whitman and the Partons: Glimpses from the Diary of Thomas Butler Gunn." *AL* 29(1957): 316-319.

HALL, HAZEL. 2084. Saul, George Brandon. "Hazel Hall: A Chronological List of Acknowledged Verse in the Periodicals." *TCL* 1(1955): 34-36.

HALLECK, FITZ-GREENE. 2084a. Slater, Joseph. "The Case of Drake and Halleck." *EAL* 8,#3(1974): 285-297.

HARRIGAN, EDWARD. 2085. Moody, Richard. "Edward Harrigan." *MD* 19(1976): 319-326.

HARRIS, GEORGE WASHINGTON. 2086. Current-Garcia, Eugene. "Sut Lovingood's Rare Ripe Southern Garden." *SSF* 9(1972): 117-129.

2087. McClary, Ben Harris. "The Real Sut." *AL* 27(1955): 105-106.

2088. Rickels, Milton. "The Imagery of George Washington Harris." *AL* 31(1959): 173-187.

2089. Ross, Stephen M. "Jason Compsen and Sut Lovingood: Southwestern Humor as Stream of Consciousness." *SN* 8(1976): 278-290.

HARRIS, JOEL CHANDLER. 2090. David, Beverly. "Visions of the South: Joel Chandler Harris and His Illustrators." *ALR* 9(1976): 189-206.

2091. Griska, Joseph M., Jr. "Two New Joel Chandler Harris Reviews of Mark Twain." *AL* 48 (1977): 584-589.

2092. Ives, Sumner. "Dialect Differentiation in the Stories of Joel Chandler Harris." *AL* 27(1955): 88-96.

2093. Light, Kathleen. "Uncle Remus and the Folklorists." *SLJ* 7,#2(1975): 88-104.

2094. Strickland, William. "A Check List of the Periodical Contributions of Joel Chandler Harris (1848-1908)." *ALR* 9(1976): 207-230.

2095. Turner, Arlin. "Joel Chandler Harris (1848-1908)." [bibliography] *ALR* 1,#3(1968): 18-23.

2096. Turner, Darwin T. "Daddy Joel Harris and His Old-Time Darkies." *SLJ* 1,#1(1968): 20-41.

See also 584.

HARTE, BRET. 2097. Barnett, Linda D. "Bret Harte: An Annotated Bibliography of Secondary Comment, Part 1." *ALR* 5(1972): 189-320.

2098. ----------. "Bret Harte: An Annotated Bibliography of Secondary Comment, Part 2." *ALR* 5(1972): 331-484.

2099. Boggan, J. R. "The Regeneration of 'Roaring Camp.'" *NCF* 22(1967): 271-280.

2100. Booth, Bradford A. "Mark Twain's Comments on Bret Harte's Stories." *AL* 25(1954): 492-495.

2101. Buckland, Roscoe L. "Jack Hamlin: Bret Harte's Romantic Rogue." *WAL* 8(1973): 111-112.

2102. Duckett, Margaret. "Bret Harte's Portrayal of Half-Breeds." *AL* 25(1953): 193-212.

2103. ----------. "Plain Language from Bret Harte." *NCF* 11(1957): 260.

2104. Glover, Donald E. "A Reconsideration of Bret Harte's Later Work." *WAL* 8(1973): 143-151.

2105. Hudson, Roy F. "The Contributions of Bret Harte to America Oratory." *WAL* 2(1967): 213-222.

2106. Lauterbach, Edward S. "Tom Hood Discovers Bret Harte." *AL* 34(1962): 285-287.

2107. May, Ernest R. "Bret Harte and The *Overland Monthly*." *AL* 22(1950): 260-271.

2108. Morrow, Patrick. "Bret Harte (1836-1902)." *ALR* 3(1970): 167-177.

2109. ----------. "Bret Harte, Popular Fiction, and the Local Color Movement." *WAL* 8(1973): 123-131.

2110. ----------. "The Predicament of Bret Harte." *ALR* 5(1972): 181-188.

2111. Scheick, William. "William Dean Howells to Bret Harte: A Missing Letter." *ALR* 9 (1976): 276-278.

2112. Sherting, Jack. "Bret Harte's Civil War Poems: Voice of the Majority." *WAL* 8(1973): 133-142.

2113. Thomas, Jeffrey E. "Bret Harte and the Power of Sex." *WAL* 8(1973): 91-109.

See also 610, 1167, 1454.

HAWTHORNE, JULIAN. 2114. Park, Martha Mayes. "*Archibald Malmaison*: Julian Hawthorne's Contribution to Gothic Fiction." *Ext* 15(1974): 103-116.

HAWTHORNE, NATHANIEL. 2115. Abcarian, Richard. "The Ending of 'Young Goodman Brown.'" *SSF* 3(1966): 343-345.

2116. Abel, Darrel. "Black Glove and Pink Ribbon: Hawthorne's Metonymic Symbols." *NEQ* 42 (1969): 163-180.

2117. ----------. "The Devil in Boston." *PQ* 32(1953): 366-381.

2118. ----------. "Giving Lustre to Gray Shadows: Hawthornes' Potent Art." *AL* 41(1969): 373-388.

2119. ----------. "Hawthorne's Dimmesdale: Fugitive from Wrath." *NCF* 11(1956): 81-105.

2120. ----------. "Hawthorne's Pearl: Symbol and Character." *ELH* 18(1951): 50-66.

2121. ----------. "Immortality vs. Mortality in *Septimus Felton*: Some Possible Sources." *AL* 27(1956): 566-570.

2122. ----------. "'This Troublesome Morality': Hawthorne's Marbles and Bubbles." *SR* 8 (1969): 193-197.

2123. ----------. "'A Vast Deal of Human Sympathy': Idea and Device in Hawthorne's 'The Snow-Image.'" *Criticism* 12(1970): 316-332.

2124. ----------. "Who Wrote Hawthorne's Autobiography?" *AL* 28(1956): 73-77.

2125. Adams, John F. "Hawthorne's Symbolic Gardens." *TSLL* 5(1963): 242-254.

2126. Adams, Richard P. "Hawthorne's *Provincial Tales*." *NEQ* 30(1957): 39-57.

2127. Allen, Margaret V. "Imagination and History in Hawthorne's 'Legends of the Province House.'" *AL* 43(1971): 432-437.

2128. Allen, Mary. "Smiles and Laughter in Hawthorne." *PQ* 52(1973): 119-128.

2129. Allison, Alexander W. "The Literary Contexts of 'My Kinsman, Major Molineux.'" *NCF* 23 (1968): 304-311.

2130. Alsen, Eberhard. "The Ambitious Experiment of Dr. Rappaccini." *AL* 43(1971): 430-431.

2131. Anderson, D. K. "Hawthorne's Crowds." *NCF* 7(1952): 39-50.

2132. Anderson, Norman A. "'Rappaccini's Daughter': A Keatsian Analogue." *PMLA* 83(1968): 271-283.

2133. Arner, Robert D. "Hawthorne and Jones Very: Two Dimensions of Satire in 'Egotism; or, the Bosom Serpent.'" *NEQ* 42(1969): 267-275.

2134. Askew, Melvin W. "Hawthorne, the Fall, and the Psychology of Maturity." *AL* 34(1962): 335-343.

2135. Asquino, Mark L. "Hawthorne's Village Uncle and Melville's *Moby Dick*." *SSF* 10(1973): 413-414.

2136. Austin, Allen. "Satire and Theme in *The Scarlet Letter*." *PQ* 41(1962): 508-511.

2137. Autry, Max L. "Flower Imagery in Hawthorne's Posthumous Fiction." *SN* 7(1975): 215-226.

2138. Bales, Kent. "The Allegory and the Radical Romantic Ethic of *The Blithedale Romance*." *AL* 46(1974): 41-53.

2139. Barnes, Daniel R. "Faulkner's Miss Emily and Hawthorne's Old Maid." *SSF* 9(1972): 373-377.

2140. ----------. "Orestes Brownson and Hawthorne's Holgrave." *AL* 45(1973): 271-278.

2141. ----------. "'Physical Fact' and Folklore: Hawthorne's 'Egotism; or the Bosom Serpent.'" *AL* 43(1971): 117-121.

2142. ----------. "Two Reviews of *The Scarlet Letter* in *Holden's Dollar Magazine*." *AL* 44(1973): 648-652.

2143. Barnett, Gene A. "Hawthorne's Italian Towers." *SR* 3(1964): 252-256.

2144. Bassan, Maurice. "A New Account of Hawthorne's Last Days, Death, and Funeral." *AL* 27(1956): 561-565.

2145. Battaglia, Francis Joseph. "*The House of Seven Gables*: New Light on Old Problems." *PMLA* 82(1967): 579-590.

2146. Battaglia, Frank. "*The* (Unmeretricious) *House of Seven Gables*." *SN* 2(1970): 468-473.

2147. Baughman, Ernest W. "Public Confession and *The Scarlet Letter*." *NEQ* 40(1967): 532-550.

2148. Baxter, Annette K. "Independence vs. Isolation: Hawthorne and James on the Problem of the Artist." *NCF* 10(1955): 225-231.

2149. Baym, Nina. "*The Blithedale Romance*: A Radical Reading." *JEGP* 67(1968): 545-569.

2150. ----------. "Hawthorne's Holgrave: The Failure of the Artist-Hero." *JEGP* 69(1970): 584-598.

2151. ----------. "Hawthorne's Myths for Children: The Author Versus His Audience." *SSF* 10(1973): 35-46.

2152. ----------. "The Head, The Heart, and the Unpardonable Sin." *NEQ* 40(1967): 31-47.

2153. ----------. "*The Marble Faun*: Hawthorne's Elegy for Art." *NEQ* 44(1971): 355-376.

2154. ----------. "Passion and Authority in *The Scarlet Letter*." *NEQ* 43(1970): 209-230.

2155. Beebe, Maurice. "The Fall of the House of Pyncheon." *NCF* 11(1956): 1-17.

2156. Beebe, Maurice, and Jack Hardie. "Hawthorne Checklist." *SN* 2(1970): 519-587.

2157. Bell, Millicent. "Hawthorne's 'Fire Worship': Interpretation and Source." *AL* 24 (1952): 31-39.

2158. Benoit, Raymond. "Hawthorne's Psychology of Death: 'The Minister's Black Veil '" *SSF* 8(1971): 553-560.

2159. Bercovitch, Sacvan. "Diabolus in Salem." *ELN* 6(1969): 280-285.

2160. ----------. "Endicott's Breastplate: Symbolism and Typology in 'Endicott and the Red Cross.'" *SSF* 4(1967): 289-299.

2161. ----------. "Hilda's 'Seven-Branched Allegory,' An Echo from Cotton Mather in *The Marble Faun*." *EAL* 1,#2(1966): 5-6.

2162. ----------. "Of Wise and Foolish Virgins: Hilda *versus* Miriam in Hawthorne's *Marble Faun*." *NEQ* 41(1968): 281-286.

2163. Bier, Jesse. "Hawthorne on the Romance: His Prefaces Related and Examined." *MP* 53(1955): 17-24.

2164. Birdsall, Virginia Ogden. "Hawthorne's Fair-Haired Maidens: The Fading Light." *PMLA* 75 (1960): 250-256.

2165. ----------. "Hawthorne's Oak Tree Image." *NCF* 15(1960): 181-185.

2166. Blow, Suzanne. "Pre-Raphaelite Allegory in *The Marble Faun*." *AL* 44(1972): 122-127.

2167. Bochner, Joy. "Life in a Picture Gallery: Things in *The Potrait of a Lady* and *The Marble Faun*." *TSLL* 11(1969): 761-777.

2168. Boewe, Charles. "Rappaccini's Garden." *AL* 30(1958): 37-49.

2169. Boewe, Charles and Murray G. Murphey. "Hester Prynne in History." *AL* 32(1960): 202-204.

2170. Boswell, Jackson Campbell. "Bosom Serpents Before Hawthorne: Origin of a Symbol." *ELN* 12(1975): 279-287.

2171. Brant, Robert L. "Hawthorne and Marvell." *AL* 30(1958): 366.

2172. Brenzo, Richard. "Beatrice Rappaccini: A Victim of Male Love and Horror." *AL* 48(1976): 152-164.

2173. Bridgman, Richard. "As Hester Prynne Lay Dying." *ELN* 2(1965): 294-296.

2174. Brill, Lesley W. "Conflict and Accomodation in Hawthorne's 'The Artist of the Beautiful.'" *SSF* 12(1975): 381-386.

2175. Brodsky, Patricia Pollock. "Fertile Fields and Poisoned Gardens: Sologub's Debt to Hoffman, Pushkin, and Hawthorne." *EL* 1(1974): 96-108.

2176. Brodtkorb, Paul, Jr. "Art Allegory in *The Marble Faun*." *PMLA* 77(1962): 254-267.

2177. Broes, Arthur T. "Journey into Moral Darkness: 'My Kinsman, Major Molineux'." *NCF* 19 (1964): 171-184.

2178. Brown, Merle E. "The Structure of *The Marble Faun*." *AL* 28(1956): 302-313.

2179. Budz, Judith Kaufman. "Cherubs and Humblebees: Nathaniel Hawthorne and the Visual Arts." *Criticism* 17(1975): 168-181.

2180. Buitenhuis, Peter. "Henry James on Hawthorne." *NEQ* 32(1959): 207-225.

2181. Bunge, Nancy L. "Unreliable Artist-Narrators in Hawthorne's Short Stories." *SSF* 14 (1977): 145-150.

2182. Burhans, Clinton S., Jr. "Hawthorne's Mind and Art in 'The Hollow of the Three Hills.'" *JEGP* 60(1961): 286-295.

2183. Burns, Rex S. "Hawthorne's Romance of Traditional Success." *TSLL* 12(1970): 443-455.

2184. Bush, Sargent, Jr. "Bosom Serpents before Hawthorne: The Origins of a Symbol." *AL* 43(1971): 181-199.

2185. Byers, John R., Jr. "*The House of Seven Gables* and 'The Daughters of Dr. Byles.'" *PMLA* 89(1974): 174-177.

2186. Cannaday, Nicholas, Jr. "Hawthorne's Minister and the Veiling Deceptions of Self." *SSF* 4(1967): 135-144.

2187. Carnochan, W. B. "'The Minister's Black Veil': Symbol, Meaning, and the Context of Hawthorne's Art." *NCF* 24(1969): 182-192.

2188. Carpenter, Richard C. "Hawthorne's Polar Explorations: 'Young Goodman Brown' and 'My Kinsman, Major Molineux.'" *NCF* 24(1969): 45-56.

2189. Charney, Maurice. "Hawthorne and the Gothic Style." *NEQ* 34(1961): 36-49.

2190. Clark, C. E. Frazer, Jr. "Postumous Papers of a Decapitated Surveyor: *The Scarlet Letter* in the Salem Press." *SN* 2(1970): 395-419.

2191. Clay, Edward M. "The 'Dominating' Symbol in Hawthorne's Last Phase." *AL* 39(1968): 506-516.

2192. Clayton, Lawrence. "'Lady Eleonore's Mantle': A Metaphorical Key to Hawthorne's 'Legends of the Province House.'" *ELN* 9(1971): 49-51.

2193. Coale, Samuel. "Frederick and Hawthorne: The Romantic Roots of Naturalism." *AL* 48(1976): 29-45.

2194. Cohen, Bernard. "Edward Everett and Hawthorne's Removal from the Salem Custom." *AL* 27(1955): 245-249.

2195. ----------. "Emerson's 'The Young American' and Hawthorne's 'The Intelligence Office.'" *AL* 26(1954): 32-43.

2196. ----------. "Hawthorne's 'Mrs. Bullfrog' and *The Rambler*." *PQ* 32(1953): 382-387.

2197. Colacurcio, Michael J. "Footsteps of Ann Hutchinson: the Context of *The Scarlet Letter*." *ELH* 39(1972): 459-494.

2197a. Connolly, Thomas E. "Hawthorne's 'Young Goodman Brown': An Attack on Puritanic Calvanism." *AL* 28(1956): 370-375.

2198. Cook, Reginald. "The Forest of Goodman Brown's Night: A Reading of Hawthorne's 'Young Goodman Brown.'" *NEQ* 43(1970): 473-481.

2199. Crews, Frederick C. "The Logic of Compulsion in 'Roger Malvin's Burial.'" *PMLA* 79(1964): 457-465.

2200. ----------. "A New Reading of *The Blithedale Romance*." *AL* 29(1957): 147-170.

2201. ----------. "The Ruined Wall: Unconscious Motivation in *The Scarlet Letter*." *NEQ* 38(1965): 312-330.

2202. Cronin, Morton. "Hawthorne and Romantic Love and the Status of Women." *PMLA* 69(1954): 89-98.

2203. Cronkhite, G. Ferris. "The Transcendental Railroad." *NEQ* 24(1951): 306-328.

2204. Crowley, J. Donald. "The Design of Hawthorne's *Twice-Told Tales*." *SAF* 1(1973): 35-61.

2205. ----------. "Hawthorne Criticism and the Return to History." *SN* 6(1974): 98-105.

2206. Curran, Ronald T. "Irony: Another Thematic Dimension to 'The Artist of the Beautiful.'" *SR* 6(1966): 34-45.

2207. ----------. "'Yankee Gothic'; Hawthorne's 'Castle of Pyncheon.'" *SN* 8(1976): 69-80.

2208. Daly, Robert. "Fideism and the Allusive Mode in 'Rappaccini's Daughter.'" *NCF* 28(1973): 25-37.

2209. Darnell, Donald G. "'Doctrine by Ensample': The Emblem and *The Marble Faun*." *TSLL* 15(1973): 301-310.

2210. Dauner, Louise. "The 'Case' of Tobias Pearson: Hawthorne and the Ambiguities." *AL* 21(1950): 464-472.

2211. D'Avanzo, Mario L. "The Ambitious Guest in the Hands of An Angry God." *ELN* 14(1976): 38-42.

2212. ----------. "The Literary Sources of 'My Kinsman, Major Molineux': Shakespeare, Coleridge, and Milton." *SSF* 10(1973): 121-136.

2213. Davidson, Edward H. "Dimmesdale's Fall." *NEQ* 36(1963): 358-370.

2214. ----------. "Hawthorne and the Pathetic Fallacy." *JEGP* 54(1955): 486-497.

2215. Davidson, Frank. "Toward a Re-evaluation of *The Blithdale Romance*." *NEQ* 25(1952): 374-383.

2216. Davis, Joe. "The Myth of the Garden: Nathaniel Hawthorne's 'Rappaccini's Daughter.'" *SLI* 2,#1(1969): 3-12.

2217. Davis, Richard Allan. "The Villagers and 'Ethan Brand.'" *SSF* 4(1967): 260-262.

2218. Dennis, Carl. "*The Blithedale Romance* and the Problem of Self-Integration." *TSLL* 15(1973): 93-110.

2219. Dettlaff, Shirley M. "The Concept of Beauty in 'The Artist of the Beautiful': and Hugh Blair's Rhetoric." *SSF* 13(1976): 512-515.

2220. Deusen, Marshall Van. "Narrative Tone in 'The Custom House' and *The Scarlet Letter*." *NCF* 21(1966): 61-71.

2221. Dichmann, Mary E. "Hawthorne's Prophetic Pictures." *AL* 23(1951): 188-202.

2222. Dillingham, William B. "Arthur Dimmesdule's Confession." *SLI* 2,#1(1969): 21-26.

2223. ----------. "Structure and Theme in *The House of the Seven Gables*." *NCF* 14(1959): 59-70.

2224. Dobbs, Jeannine. "Hawthorne's Dr. Rappaccini and Father George Rapp." *AL* 43(1971): 427-430.

2225. Donohue, Agnes McNeill. "'From whose Bourn No Traveller Returns': A Reading of 'Roger Malvin's Burial.'" *NCF* 18(1963): 1-19.

2226. Doubleday, Neal F. "Hawthorne's Estimate of His Early Work." *AL* 37(1966): 403-409.

2227. Dryden, Edgar A. "Hawthorne's Castle in the Air: Form and Theme in *The House of Seven Gables*." *ELH* 38(1971): 294-317.

2228. Duban, James. "The Sceptical Context of Hawthorne's 'Mr. Higginbotham's Catastrophe.'" *AL* 48(1976): 292-301.

2229. Durr, Robert Allen. "Hawthorne's Ironic Mode." *NEQ* 30(1957): 486-495.

2230. Dusenbery, Robert. "Hawthorne's Merry Company: The Anatomy of Laughter in the Tales and Short Stories." *PMLA* 82(1967): 285-288.

2231. Dwight, Sheila. "Hawthorne and the Unpardonable Sin." *SN* 2(1970): 449-458.

2232. Eagle, Nancy L. "An Unpublished Hawthorne Letter." *AL* 23(1951): 360-362.

2233. Eakin, Paul John. "Hawthorne's Imagination and the Structure of 'The Custom-House.'" *AL* 43(1971): 346-358.

2234. Edgren, C. Hobart. "Hawthorne's 'The Ambitious Guest.'" *NCF* 10(1955): 151-156.

2235. Eisinger, Chester E. "Hawthorne as Champion of the Middle Way." *NEQ* 27(1954): 27-52.

2236. Emry, Hazel T. "Two Houses of Pride: Spenser's and Hawthorne's." *PQ* 33(1954): 91-94.

2236a. Ensor, Allison. "'Whispers of the Bad Angel': A *Scarlet Letter* Passage as a Commentary on Hawthorne's 'Young Goodman Brown.'" *SSF* 7(1970): 467-469.

2237. Erlich, Gloria Chasson. "Deadly Innocence: Hawthorne's Dark Women." *NEQ* 41(1968): 163-179.

2238. ----------. "Guilt and Expiation in 'Roger Malvin's Burial.'" *NCF* 26(1972): 377-389.

2239. Estrin, Mark W. "Narrative Ambivalence in Hawthorne's 'Feathertop.'" *JNT* 5(1975):

164-173.

2240. Evans, Oliver. "Allegory and Incest in 'Rappaccini's Daughter.'" *NCF* 19(1964): 185-195.

2241. Fairbanks, Henry G. "Hawthorne and the Machine Age." *AL* 28(1956): 155-163.

2242. ----------. "Sin, Free Will, and 'Pessimism' in Hawthorne." *PMLA* 71(1956): 975-989.

2243. Fass, Barbara. "Rejection of Paternalism: Hawthorne's 'My Kinsman, Major Molineaux' and Ellison's *Invisible Man*." *CLA* 14(1971): 317-323.

2244. Feeney, Joseph J., S. J. "The Structure in Hawthorne's 'The Maypole of Merry Mount.'" *SAF* 3(1975): 211-216.

2245. Fishman, Burton J. "Imagined Redemption in 'Roger Malvin's Burial.'" *SAF* 5(1977): 257-262.

2246. Flanagan, John T. "The Durable Hawthorne." *JEGP* 49(1950): 88-96.

2247. Flint, Allen. "Hawthorne and the Slavery Crisis." *NEQ* 41(1968): 393-408.

2248. Fogle, Richard H. "Hawthorne and Coleridge on Credibility." *Criticism* 13(1971): 234-241.

2249. Fossum, Robert H. "The Summons of the Past: Hawthorne's 'Alice Doane's Appeal.'" *NCF* 23(1968): 294-303.

2250. ----------. "Time and the Artist in 'Legends of the Province House.'" *NCF* 21(1967): 337-348.

2251. Franklin, H. Bruce. "Science Fiction as an Index to Popular Attitudes toward Science: A Danger, Some Problems, and Two Possible Paths." *Ext* 6(1965): 23-31.

2252. Freehafer, John. "*The Marble Faun* and the Editing of Nineteenth-Century Texts." *SN* 2 (1970): 487-503.

2253. Gallagher, Edward J. "The Concluding Paragraph of 'Young Goodman Brown.'" *SSF* 12(1975): 29-30.

2254. Gallagher, Kathleen. "The Art of Snake Handling: *Lamia, Elsie Venner,* and 'Rappaccini's Daughter.'" *SAF* 3(1975): 51-64.

2255. Gamble, Richard H. "Reflections of the Hawthorne-Melville Relationship in *Pierre*." *AL* 47(1976): 629-632.

2256. Gargano, James W. "Hawthorne's *The Artist of the Beautiful*." *AL* 35(1963): 225-230.

2257. Garlitz, Barbara. "Pearl: 1850-1955." *PMLA* 72(1957): 689-699.

2258. Gautreau, Henry W., Jr. "A Note on Hawthorne's 'The Man of Adamant.'" *PQ* 52(1973): 315-317.

2259. Granger, Bruce Ingham. "Arthur Dimmesdale as Tragic Hero." *NCF* 19(1964): 197-203.

2260. Greenwood, Douglas. "The Heraldic Device in *The Scarlet Letter*: Hawthorne's Symbolical Use of the Past." *AL* 46(1974): 207-210.

2261. Griffith, Clark. "Substance and Shadow: Language and Meaning in *The House of the Seven Gables*." *MP* 51(1954): 187-195.

2262. Griffith, Kelley, Jr. "Form in the Blithedale Romance." *AL* 40(1968): 15-26.

2263. Gross, Robert Eugene. "Hawthorne's First Novel: The Future of a Style." *PMLA* 78 (1963): 60-68.

2264. Gross, Seymour L. "Hawthorne and the Shakers." *AL* 29(1958): 457-463.

2265. ----------. "Hawthorne's 'Alice Doane's Appeal.'" *NCF* 10(1955): 232-236.

2266. ----------. "Hawthorne's 'Lady Eleanore's Mantle' as History." *JEGP* 54(1955): 549-554.

2267. ----------. "Hawthorne's 'My Kinsman, Major Moleneaux': History as Moral Adventure." *NCF* 12(1957): 97-109.

2268. ----------. "Hawthorne's Revision of 'The Gentle Boy.'" *AL* 26(1954): 196-208.

2269. ----------. "Hawthorne's 'Vision of the Fountain' as a Parody." *AL* 27(1955): 101-105.

2270. ----------. "'Solitude, and Love, and Anguish': The Tragic Design of *The Scarlet Letter*." *CLA* 3(1960): 154-165.

2271. Gupta, R. K. "Hawthorne's Theory of Art." *AL* 40(1968): 309-324.

2272. ----------. "Hawthorne's Treatment of the Artist." *NEQ* 45(1972): 65-80.

2273. Gwynn, Frederick L. "Hawthorne's 'Rappaccini's Daughter.'" *NCF* 7(1952): 217-219.

2274. Hall, Spencer. "Beatrice Cenci: Symbol and Vision in *The Marble Faun*." *NCF* 25(1970): 85-95.

2275. Halligan, John. "Hawthorne on Democracy: 'Endicott and the Red Cross.'" *SSF* 8(1971): 301-307.

2276. Hansen, Elaine Tuttle. "Ambiguity and the Narrator in *The Scarlet Letter*." *JNT* 5(1975): 147-163.

2277. Harding, Walter. "Another Source for Hawthorne's 'Egotism, or, the Bosom Serpent.'" *AL* 40(1969): 537-538.

2278. Hart, James D. "Hawthorne's Italian Diary." *AL* 34(1963): 562-567.

2279. Hart, John E. "'The Scarlet Letter' One Hundred Years After." *NEQ* 23(1950): 381-395.

2280. Hedges, William L. "Hawthorne's *Blithedale*: The Fountain of the Narrator." *NCF* 14(1960): 303-316.

2281. Herndon, Jerry A. "Hawthorne's Dream Imagery." *AL* 46(1975): 538-545.

2282. Hijiya, James A. "Nathaniel Hawthorne's *Our Old Home*." *AL* 46(1974): 363-373.

2283. Hilton, Earl. "Hawthorne, the Hippie, and the Square." *SN* 2(1970): 425-439.

2284. Hirsh, John C. "The Politics of Blithedale: The Dilemma of the Self." *SR* 11(1972): 138-146.

2285. Hoeltje, Hubert H. "A Forgotten Hawthorne Silhouette." *AL* 28(1957): 510-511.

2286. ----------. "Hawthorne, Melville, and 'Blackness.'" *AL* 37(1965): 41-51.

2287. ----------. "Hawthorne's Review of *Evangeline*." *NEQ* 23(1950): 232-242.

2288. ----------. "The Writing of *The Scarlet Letter*." *NEQ* 27(1954): 326-346.

2289. Holaday, Clayton A. "A Re-examination of Feathertop and RLR." *NEQ* 27(1954): 103-105.

2290. Holmes, Edward M. "Hawthorne and Romanticism." *NEQ* 33(1960): 476-488.

2291. Horne, Lewis B. "Place, Time, and Moral Growth in *The House of Seven Gables*." *SN* 2 (1970): 459-467.

2292. Howard, Leon. "Hawthorne's Fiction." *NCF* 7(1953): 237-250.

2293. Hurley, Paul J. "Young Goodman Brown's 'Heart of Darkness.'" *AL* 37(1966): 410-419.

2294. Isani, Mukhtar Ali. "Hawthorne and the Branding of William Prynne." *NEQ* 45(1972): 182-195.

2295. Jarrett, David W. "Hawthorne and Hardy as Modern Romancers." *NCF* 28(1974): 458-471.

2296. Jenkins, R. B. "A New Look at an Old Tombstone." *NEQ* 45(1972): 417-421.

2297. Johnson, Claudia D. "Hawthorne and Nineteenth-Century Perfectionism." *AL* 44(1973): 685-695.

2298. ----------. "'Young Goodman Brown' and Puritan Justification." *SSF* 11(1974): 200-203.

2299. Johnson, W. Stacy. "Hawthorne and *The Pilgrim's Progress.*" *JEGP* 50(1951): 156-166.

2300. Jones, Buford. "'The Hall of Fantasy' and the Early Hawthorne-Thoreau Relationship." *PMLA* 83(1968): 1429-1438.

2301. ----------. "Hawthorne's Coverdale and Spenser's Allegory of Mutability." *AL* 39 (1967): 215-219.

2302. ----------. "Hawthorne Studies: The Seventies." *SN* 2(1970): 504-518.

2303. Jones, Wayne Allen. "Hawthorne's First Published Review." *AL* 48(1977): 492-500.

2304. Jordan, Gretchen Graf. "Hawthorne's 'Bell': Historical Evolution through Symbol." *NCF* 19(1964): 123-139.

2305. Joseph, Brother. "Art and Event in 'Ethan Brand.'" *NCF* 15(1960): 249-259.

2306. Justus, James H. "Hawthorne's Coverdale: Character and Art in *The Blithedale Romance.*" *AL* 47(1975): 21-36.

2307. Kane, Patricia. "The Fallen Woman as Free-Thinker in *The French Lieutenant's Woman* and *The Scarlet Letter.*" *NCL* 2(Jan., 1972): 8-10.

2308. Katz, Seymour. "'Character,' 'Nature,' and Allegory in *The Scarlet Letter.*" *NCF* 23(1968): 3-17.

2309. Kern, Alexander C. "A Note on Hawthorne's Juveniles." *PQ* 39(1960): 242-246.

2310. Kesterson, David B. "Hawthorne and Nature: Thoreavian Influence?" *ELN* 4(1967): 200-206.

2311. Klinkowitz, Jerome. "Ending the *Seven Gables:* Old Light on a New Problem." *SN* 4(1972): 396-401.

2312. Kloeckner, Alfred J. "The Flower and the Fountain: Hawthorne's Chief Symbols in 'Rappaccini's Daughter.'" *AL* 38(1966): 323-336.

2313. Knox, George. "The Hawthorne-Lowell Affair." *NEQ* 29(1956): 493-502.

2314. Laser, Marvin. "'Head,' 'Heart,' and 'Will' in Hawthorne's Psychology." *NCF* 10(1955): 130-140.

2315. Lauber, John. "Hawthorne's Shaker Tales." *NCF* 18(1963): 82-86.

2316. Lease, Benjamin. "Salem vs. Hawthorne: An Early Review of *The Scarlet Letter.*" *NEQ* 44 (1971): 110-117.

2317. ----------. "'The Whole is a Prose Poem': An Early Review of *The Scarlet Letter.*" *AL* 44(1972): 128-130.

2318. Lefcowitz, Allan and Barbara. "Some Rents in the Veil: New Light on Priscilla and Zenobia in *The Blithedale Romance.*" *NCF* 21(1966): 263-276.

2319. Leibowitz, Herbert A. "Hawthorne and Spenser: Two Sources." *AL* 30(1959): 459-466.

2320. Lentz, Vern B., and Allen F. Stein. "The Black Flower of Necessity: Structure in *The Blithedale Romance.*" *EL* 3(1976): 86-97.

2321. Levin, David. "Shadows of Doubt: Specter Evidence in Hawthorne's 'Young Goodman Brown.'" *AL* 34(1962): 344-352.

2322. Levy, Alfred J. "*The House of Seven Gables:* The Religion of Love." *NCF* 16(1961): 189-203.

2323. Levy, Leo B. "*The Blithedale Romance:* Hawthorne's 'Voyage Through Chaos.'" *SR* 8(1968): 1-15.

2324. ----------. "*Fanshawe:* Hawthorne's World of Images." *SN* 2(1970): 440-448.

2325. ----------. "Hawthorne and the Sublime." *AL* 37(1966): 391-402.

2326. ----------. "Hawthorne, Melville, and the *Monitor.*" *AL* 37(1965): 33-40.

2327. ----------. "Hawthorne's 'Middle Ground'." *SSF* 2(1964): 56-60.

2328. ----------. "The Landscape Modes of *The Scarlet Letter.*" *NCF* 23(1969): 377-392.

2329. ----------. "*The Marble Faun:* Hawthorne's Landscape of the Fall." *AL* 42(1970): 139-156.

2330. ----------. "The Mermaid and the Mirror: Hawthorne's 'The Village Uncle.'" *NCF* 19(1964): 205-211.

2331. ----------. "Picturesque Style in *The House of Seven Gables.*" *NEQ* 39(1966): 147-160.

2332. ----------. "The Problem of Faith in 'Young Goodman Brown.'" *JEGP* 74(1975): 375-387.

2333. ----------. "The Temple and the Tomb: Hawthorne's 'The Lily's Quest.'" *SSF* 3(1966): 334-342.

2334. Lewis, Paul. "Victor Frankenstein and Owen Warland: The Artist as Satan as God." *SSF* 14 (1977): 279-282.

2335. Liebman, Sheldon W. "The Design of *The Marble Faun.*" *NEQ* 40(1967): 61-78.

2336. ----------. "Hawthorne and Milton: The Second Fall in 'Rappaccini's Daughter.'" *NEQ* 41(1968): 521-535.

2337. ----------. "Hawthorne's *Comus:* A Miltonic Source for 'The Maypole of Merry Mount.'" *NCF* 29(1972): 345-351.

2338. ----------. "Moral Choice in 'The Maypole of Merry Mount'." *SSF* 11(1974): 173-180.

2339. ----------. "Robert's Conversion: The Design of 'My Kinsman Major Molieneux.'" *SSF* 8(1971): 443-457.

2340. ----------. "'Roger Malvin's Burial': Hawthorne's Allegory of the Heart." *SSF* 12(1975): 253-260.

2341. Lind, Sidney E. "Emily Dickenson's 'Further in Summer than the Birds' and Nathaniel Hawthorne's *The Old Manse.*" *AL* 39(1967): 163-169.

2342. Long, Robert Emmet. "Henry James's Apprenticeship—The Hawthorne Aspect. *AL* 48 (1976): 194-216.

2343. ----------. "James's *Roderick Hudson:* The End of the Apprenticeship—Hawthorne and Turgenev." *AL* 48(1976): 312-326.

2344. ----------. "The Society and the Masks: *The Blithedale Romance* and *The Bostonians.*" *NCF* 19(1964): 105-122.

2345. ----------. "Transformations: *The Blithedale Romance* to Howells and James." *AL* 47

(1976): 552-571.

2346. Lovejoy, David S. "Lovewell's Fight and Hawthorne's 'Roger Malvin's Burial.'" NEQ 27(1954): 527-531.

2347. Lucke, Jessie Ryon. "Hawthorne's Madonna Image in The Scarlet Letter." NEQ 38 (1965): 391-392.

2348. Luecke, Sister Jane Marie, O. S. B. "Villains and Non-Villains in Hawthorne's Fiction." PMLA 78(1963): 551-558.

2349. Lynch, James J. "Structure and Allegory in 'The Great Stone Face'." NCF 15(1960): 137-146.

2350. Lyttle, David. "Giovanni! My Poor Giovanni." ["Rappaccini's Daughter"] SSF 9(1972): 147-156.

2351. Maclean, Hugh N. "Hawthorne's Scarlet Letter: The Dark Problem of This Life." AL 27(1955): 12-24.

2352. MacShane, Frank. "The House of the Dead." NEQ 35(1962): 93-101.

2353. Male, Roy R. "Criticism of Bell's 'Hawthorne's Fire-Worship: Interputation and Source.'" AL 25(1953): 84-87.

2354. ----------. "The Dual Aspects of Evil in 'Rappaccini's Daughter.'" PMLA 69(1954): 99-109.

2355. ----------. "'From the Innermost Germ': The Organic Principle in Hawthorne's Fiction." ELH 20(1953): 218-236.

2356. ----------. "Hawthorne and the Concept of Sympathy." PMLA 68(1953): 138-149.

2357. Manierre, William R. "The Role of Sympathy in The Scarlet Letter." TSLL 13(1971): 497-507.

2358. Marks, Alfred H. "Two Rodericks and Two Worms: 'Egotism; or, The Bosom Serpent' as Personal Satire." PMLA 74(1959): 607-612.

2359. ----------. "Who Killed Judge Pyncheon? The Role of the Imagination in The House of Seven Gables." PMLA 71(1956): 355-369.

2360. Marks, Barry A. "The Origin of Original Sin in Hawthorne's Fiction." NCF 14(1960): 359-362.

2361. Martin, Terence. "Adam Blair and Arthur Dimmesdale: A Lesson From the Master." AL 34(1962): 274-279.

2362. ----------. "Hawthorne's Public Decade and the Values of Home." AL 46(1974): 141-152.

2363. Marx, Leo. "The Machine in the Garden." NEQ 29(1956): 27-42.

2364. Mathews, James W. "Antinimianism in 'Young Goodman Brown.'" SSF 3(1965): 73-75.

2365. ----------. "Hawthorne and the Chain of Being." MLQ 18(1957): 282-294.

2366. Matlack, James H. "Hawthorne and Elizabeth Barstow Stoddard." NEQ 50(1977): 278-302.

2367. McCall, Dan. "The Design of Hawthorne's 'Custom-House.'" NCF 21(1967): 349-358.

2368. ----------. "Hawthorne's 'Familiar Kind of Preface.'" ELH 35(1968): 422-439.

2369. ----------. "'I Felt a Funeral in My Brain' and 'The Hollow of the Three Hills.'" NEQ 42(1949): 432-435.

2370. McCullen, Joseph T., and John C. Guilds. "The Unpardonable Sin in Hawthorne: A Re-examination." NCF 15(1960): 221-237.

2371. McDonald, John J. "Longfellow in Hawthorne's 'The Antique Ring.'" NEQ 46(1973): 622-626.

2372. ----------. "'The Old Manse' and Its Mosses: The Inception and Development of Mosses from an Old Manse." TSLL 16(1974): 77-108.

2373. McElroy, John. "The Brand Metaphor in 'Ethan Brand.'" AL 43(1972): 633-637.

2374. McHaney, Thomas L. "The Textual Editions of Hawthorne and Melville." SLI 2,#1(1969): 27-41.

2375. McNamara, Anne Marie. "The Character of Flame: The Function of Pearl in The Scarlet Letter." AL 27(1956): 537-533.

2376. McPherson, Hugo. "Hawthorne's Major Source for His Mythological Tales." AL 30(1958): 364-365.

2377. McWilliams, John P., Jr. "'Thorough-Going Democrat' and 'Modern Tory': Hawthorne and the Puritan Revolution of 1776." SR 15(1976): 549-572.

2378. Miller, James E., Jr. "Hawthorne and Melville: The Unpardonable Sin." PMLA 70(1955): 91-114.

2379. Miller, Paul W. "Hawthorne's 'Young Goodman Brown': Cynicism or Meliorism?" NCF 14 (1959): 255-264.

2380. Monteiro, George. "First Printing for a Hawthorne Letter." AL 36(1964): 346.

2381. ----------. "Hawthorne, James, and the Destructive Self." TSLL 4(1962): 58-71.

2382. ----------. "A Nonliterary Source for Hawthorne's 'Egotism; or the Bosom Serpent.'" AL 41(1970): 575-577.

2383. Moore, L. Hugh, Jr. "Hawthorne's Ideal Artist as Presumptuous Intellectual." SSF 2(1965): 278-283.

2384. Morrow, Patrick. "A Writer's Workshop: Hawthorne's 'The Great Carbuncle.'" SSF 6(1969): 157-164.

2385. Morsberger, Robert E. "'The Minister's Black Veil': 'Shrouded in a Blackness, Ten Times Black.'" NEQ 46(1973): 454-463.

2386. Moss, Shirley P. "The Problem of Theme in The Marble Faun." NCF 18(1964): 393-399.

2387. Moss, Sidney P. "A Reading of 'Rappaccini's Daughter.'" SSF 2(1965): 145-156.

2388. ----------. "The Symbolism of the Italian Background in The Marble Faun." NCF 23(1968): 332-336.

2389. Moyer, Patricia. "Time and the Artist in Kafka and Hawthorne." MFS 4(1958): 295-306.

2390. Murray, Peter B. "Mythopoesis in The Blithedale Romance." PMLA 75(1960): 591-596.

2391. Nevius, Blake R. "The Hawthorne Centenary." NCF 19(1964): 103-104.

2392. Newberry, Frederick. "'The Gray Champion': Hawthorne's Ironic Criticism of Puritan Rebellion." SSF 13(1976): 363-370.

2393. Nolte, William H. "Hawthorne's Dimmesdale: A Small Man Gone Wrong." NEQ 38(1965): 168-186.

2394. O'Donnell, Charles R. "Hawthorne and Dimmesdale: The Search for the Realm of Quiet." NCF 14(1960): 317-332.

2395. Orel, Harold. "The Double Symbol." AL 23(1951): 1-6.

2396. Pattison, Joseph C. "Point of View in Hawthorne." PMLA 82(1967): 363-369.

2397. Paulits, Walter J. "Ambivalence in 'Young Goodman Brown.'" *AL* 41(1970): 577-584.

2398. Pauly, Thomas H. "Hawthorne's Houses of Fiction." *AL* 48(1976): 271-291.

2399. Pearce, Roy Harvey. "Hawthorne and the Sense of the Past." *ELH* 21(1954): 327-349.

2400. ----------. "Robin Molineux on the Analyst's Couch: A Note on the Limits of Psychoanalytic Criticism." *Criticism* 1(1959): 83-90.

2401. Pederson, Glenn. "Blake's Urizen as Hawthorne's Ethan Brand." *NCF* 12(1958): 304-314.

2402. Perkins, George. "Howells and Hawthorne." *NCF* 15(1960): 259-262.

2403. Person, Leland, Jr. "Aesthetic Headaches and European Women in *The Marble Faun* and *The American*." *SAF* 4(1976): 65-79.

2404. Plank, Robert. "Heart Transplant Fiction." *HSL* 2(1972): 102-112.

2405. Price, Sherwood R. "The Heart, the Head, and 'Rappaccini's Daughter.'" *NEQ* 27(1954): 399-403.

2406. Quick, Jonathan R. "*Silas Marner* as Romance: The Example of Hawthorne." *NCF* 29(1974): 287-298.

2407. Ragan, James F. "Hawthorne's Bulky Puritans." *PMLA* 75(1960): 420-423.

2408. ----------. "The Irony in Hawthorne's Blithedale." *NEQ* 35(1962): 239-246.

2409. Reed, P. L. "The Telling Frame of Hawthorne's 'Legends of the Province House.'" *SAF* 4(1976): 105-111.

2410. Rees, John O. "Elizabeth Peabody and 'The Very A B C': A Note on *The House of Seven Gables*." *AL* 38(1967): 537-540.

2411. ----------. "Hawthorne's Concept of Allegory: A Reconsideration." *PQ* 54(1975): 494-510.

2412. Regan, Robert. "Hawthorne's 'Plagiary': Poe's Duplicity." *NCF* 25(1970): 281-298.

2413. Reid, Alfred S. "Hawthorne's Humanism: 'The Birthmark' and Sir Kenelm Digby." *AL* 38(1966): 337-351.

2414. Reilly, Cyril A. "On the Dog's Chasing His Own Tail in 'Ethan Brand.'" *PMLA* 68(1953): 975-981.

2415. Ringe, Donald A. "Hawthorne's Psychology of the Head and Heart." *PMLA* 65(1950): 120-132.

2416. Robinson, E. Arthur. "The Vision of Goodman Brown: A Source and Interpretation." *AL* 35(1963): 218-225.

2417. Rohrberger, Mary. "Hawthorne's Literary Theory and the Nature of His Short Stories." *SSF* 3(1965): 23-30.

2418. Rosenberry, Edward H. "Hawthorne's Allegory of Science: 'Rappaccini's Daughter.'" *AL* 32(1960): 38-46.

2419. Ross, Donald. "Dreams and Sexual Repression in The *Blithedale Romance*." *PMLA* 86 (1971): 1014-1017.

2420. Ross, Morton L. "What Happens in 'Rappaccini's Daughter.'" *AL* 43(1971): 336-345.

2421. Russell, John. "Allegory and 'My Kinsman, Major Molineux.'" *NEQ* 40(1967): 432-440.

2422. Ryskamp, Charles. "The New England Sources of *The Scarlet Letter*." *AL* 31(1959): 257-272.

2423. Sampson, Edward C. "Motivation in *The Scarlet Letter*." *AL* 28(1957): 511-513.

2424. ----------. "Three Unpublished Letters by Hawthorne to Epes Sargent." *AL* 34(1962): 102-105.

2425. Sandeen, Ernest. "*The Scarlet Letter* as a Love Story." *PMLA* 77(1962): 425-435.

2426. Sanders, Charles. "A Note on Metamorphosis in Hawthorne's 'The Artist of the Beautiful.'" *SSF* 4(1966): 82-83.

2427. Scanlon, Lawrence. "The Heart of *The Scarlet Letter*." *TSLL* 4(1962): 198-213.

2428. ----------. "That Very Singular Man, Dr. Heidegger." *NCF* 17(1962): 253-263.

2429. Schechter, Harold. "Death and Resurrection of the King: Elements of Primitive Mythology and Ritual in 'Roger Malvin's Burial.'" *ELN* 8(1971): 201-205.

2430. Schneider, Daniel J. "The Allegory and Symbolism of Hawthorne's *The Marble Faun*." *SN* 1 (1969): 38-50.

2431. Schriber, Mary Sue. "Emerson, Hawthorne, and 'The Artist of the Beautiful.'" *SSF* 8(1971): 607-616.

2432. Schulz, Dieter. "Imagination and Self-Improvement: The Ending of 'Roger Malvin's Burial.'" *SSF* 10(1973): 183-186.

2433. Schwartz, Joseph. "Three Aspects of Hawthorne's Puritanism." *NEQ* 36(1963): 192-208.

2434. Scrimgeour, Gary J. "The Marble Faun: Hawthorne's Faery Land." *AL* 36(1964): 271-287.

2435. Shaw, Peter. "Fathers, Sons, and the Ambiguities of Revolution in 'My Kinsman, Major Molineux.'" *NEQ* 49(1976): 559-576.

2436. ----------. "Their Kinsman, Thomas Hutchinson: The Boston Patriots and His Majesty's Royal Governor." *EAL* 11(1976): 183-190.

2436a. Sherbo, Arthur. "Albert Brisbane and Hawthorne's Holgrave and Hollingsworth." *NEQ* 27 (1954): 531-534.

2437. Sherman, William. "Henry Bright in New England: His First Meeting with Hawthorne." *NEQ* 46(1973): 124-126.

2438. Sherting, Jack. "The Upas Tree in Dr. Rappaccini's Garden: New Light on Hawthorne's Tale." *SAF* 1(1973): 203-207.

2439. Shroeder, John W. "Hawthorne's 'Egotism; or, the Boston Serpent' and Its Source." *AL* 31(1959): 150-162.

2440. ----------. "Hawthorne's 'The Man of Adamant': A Spenserian Source-Study." *PQ* 41(1962): 744-756.

2441. ----------. "'That Inward Sphere': Notes on Hawthorne's Heart Imagery and Symbolism." *PMLA* 65(1950): 106-119.

2442. Shulman, Robert. "Hawthorne's Quiet Conflict." *PQ* 47(1968): 216-236.

2443. Simpson, Lewis P. "John Adams and Hawthorne: The Fiction of the Real American Revolution." *SLI* 9,#2(1976): 1-17.

2444. Singer, David. "Hawthorne and the Wild Irish: A Note." *NEQ* 42(1969): 425-432.

2445. Smith, Julian. "Hawthorne's *Legends of the Province House*." *NCF* 24(1969): 31-44.

2446. ----------. "Historical Ambiguity in 'My Kinsman, Major Moleneux.'" *ELN* 8(1970): 115-120.

2447. ----------. "Why Does Zenobia Kill Herself?" *ELN* 6(1968): 37-39.

2448. Sprague, Claire. "Dream and Disguise in *The Blithedale Romance*." *PMLA* 84(1969): 596-597.

2449. Stanton, Robert. "Hawthorne, Bunyan, and the American Romances." *PMLA* 71(1956): 155-165.

2450. ----------. *"The Scarlet Letter* as Dialectic of Temperament and Idea." *SN* 2(1970): 474-486.

2451. ----------. "The Trial of Nature: An Analysis of *The Blithedale Romance*." *PMLA* 76 (1961): 528-538.

2452. St. Armand, Barton Levi. "Hawthorne's 'Haunted Mind': A Subterranean Drama of the Self." *Criticism* 13(1971): 1-25.

2453. Stein, William Bysshe. "The Parable of the Antichrist in 'The Minister's Black Veil.'" *AL* 27(1955): 386-392.

2454. Stibitz, E. Earle. "Ironic Unity in Hawthorne's 'The Minister's Black Veil.'" *AL* 34(1962): 182-190.

2455. Stock, Ely. "The Biblical Context of 'Ethan Brand.'" *AL* 37(1965): 115-134.

2456. Stoehr, Taylor. "'Young Goodman Brown' and Hawthorne's Theory of Mimesis." *NCF* 23(1969): 393-412.

2457. Stone, Edward. "The Antique Gentility of Hester Prynne." *PQ* 36(1957): 90-96.

2458. ----------. "Chillingworth and His 'Dark Necessity.'" *Coll L* 4(1977): 136-143.

2459. ----------. "Two More Glimpses of Hawthorne." *ELN* 3(1965): 52-55.

2460. Strandberg, Victor. "The Artist's Black Veil." *NEQ* 41(1968): 567-574.

2461. Strout, Cushing. "Hawthorne's International Novel." *NCF* 24(1969): 169-181.

2462. Stubbs, John C. "Hawthorne's *The Scarlet Letter*: The Theory of the Romance and the Use of the New England Situation." *PMLA* 83(1968): 1439-1447.

2463. Tanselle, G. Thomas. "A Note on the Structure of *The Scarlet Letter*." *NCF* 17(1962): 283-285.

2464. Ten Harmsel, Henrietta. "'Young Goodman Brown' and 'The Enormous Radio.'" *SSF* 9(1972): 407-408.

2465. Thompson, W. R. "The Biblical Sources of Hawthorne's 'Roger Malvin's Burial.'" *PMLA* 77 (1962): 92-96.

2466. Thorslev, Peter L., Jr. "Hawthorne's Determinism: An Analysis." *NCF* 19(1964): 141-157.

2467. Todd, Robert E. "The Magna Mater Archetype in *The Scarlet Letter*." *NEQ* 45(1972): 421-429.

2468. Travis, Mildred K. "A Note on 'Wakefield' and 'Old Mr. Marblehall.'" *NCL* 4(May)(1974): 9-10.

2469. ----------. "Of Hawthorne's 'The Artist of the Beautiful' and Spenser's 'Muiopotmos.'" *PQ* 54(1975): 537.

2470. Turner, Frederick W., III. "Hawthorne's Black Veil." *SSF* 5(1968): 186-187.

2471. Uroff, M. D. "The Doctors in 'Rappaccini's Daughter.'" *NCF* 27(1972): 61-70.

2472. Vance, William L. "The Comic Element in Hawthorne's Sketches." *SR* 3(1964): 144-160.

2473. Vanderbilt, Kermit. "From Passion to Impasse: The Structure of a Dark Romantic Theme in Hawthorne, Howells, and Barth." *SN* 8(1976): 419-429.

2474. Vickery, John B. "The Golden Bough at Merry Mount." *NCF* 12(1957): 203-214.

2475. Vogel, Dan. "Roger Chillingworth: The Satanic Paradox in *The Scarlet Letter*." *Criticism* 5(1963): 272-280.

2476. Waggoner, Hyatt. "Hawthorne and Melville Acquaint the Reader with Their Abodes." *SN* 2(1970): 420-424.

2477. ----------. "A Hawthorne Discovery: The Lost Notebook, 1835-1841." *NEQ* 49(1976): 618-626.

2478. Walcutt, Charles Child. *"The Scarlet Letter* and Its Modern Critics." *NCF* 7(1953): 251-264.

2479. Wallins, Roger P. "Robin and the Narrator in 'My Kinsman, Major Molineux.'" *SSF* 12 (1975): 173-179.

2480. Walsh, Thomas F., Jr. "The Bedevling of Young Goodman Brown." *MLQ* 19(1958): 331-336.

2481. Waterman, Arthur E. "Dramatic Structure in *The House of Seven Gables*." *SLI* 2,#1(1969): 13-19.

2482. Watson, Charles N., Jr. "The Estrangement of Hawthorne and Melville." *NEQ* 46(1973): 380-402.

2483. Weldon, Roberta F. "Wakefield's Second Journey." *SSF* 14(1977): 69-74.

2484. West, Harry C. "Hawthorne's Editorial Pose." *AL* 44(1972): 208-221.

2485. ----------. "Hawthorne's Magic Circle: The Artist as Magician." *Criticism* 16(1974): 311-325.

2486. ----------. "The Sources for Hawthorne's 'The Artist of the Beautiful.'" *NCF* 30 (1975): 105-110.

2487. Wheeler, Otis B. "Hawthorne and the Fiction of Sensibility." *NCF* 19(1964): 159-170.

2488. Whelan, Robert Emmet, Jr. "The Blithedale Romance: The Holy War in Hawthorne's Mansoul." *TSLL* 13(1971): 91-109.

2489. ----------. "Hester Prynne's Little Pearl: Sacred and Profane Love." *AL* 39(1968): 488-505.

2490. White, William M. "Hawthorne's Eighteen-Year Cycle: Ethan Brand and Reuben Bourne." *SSF* 6(1969): 215-218.

2491. Willoughby, John C. "'The Old Manse' Revisited: Some Analogues for Art." *NEQ* 46(1973): 45-61.

2492. Winslow, Joan D. "New Light on Hawthorne's Miles Coverdale." *JNT* 7(1977): 189-199.

2493. Yates, Norris. "An Instance of Parallel Imagery in Hawthorne, Melville, and Frost." *PQ* 36(1957): 276-280.

2494. ----------. "Ritual and Reality: Mask and Dance Motifs in Hawthorne's Fiction." *PQ* 34(1955): 56-70.

2495. Yoder, R. A. "Hawthorne and His Artist." *SR* 7(1968): 193-206.

2496. Zivley, Shirley. "Hawthorne's 'The Artist of the Beautiful' and Spenser's 'Muiopotmos.'" *PQ* 48(1969): 134-137.

See also 105, 108, 404, 598, 610, 618, 1110, 1114, 1123, 1158, 1161, 2933, 2954, 5418, 6313.

HAY JOHN. 2497. Monteiro, Gerald M. "John Hay's Short Fiction." *SSF* 8(1971): 543-552.

2498. Sloane, David. "Censoring for *The Century Magazine:* R. W. Gilder to John Hay on *The Bread-Winners.*" *ALR* 4(1971): 255-267.

2499. ----------. "John Hay (1838-1905)." *ALR* 3(1970): 178-188.

2500. ----------. "John Hay's *The Bread-Winners* as Literary Realsim." *ALR* 2(1969): 276-280.

2501. Vandersee, Charles. "The Great Literary Mystery of the Gilded Age." *ALR* 7(1974): 245-272.

See also 620.

HAYNE, PAUL H.   2502. Harwell, Richard Barksdale. "A Confederate View of the Southern Poets." *AL* 24(1952): 51-61.

2503. Moore, Rayburn S. "The Literary World Gone Mad: Hayne on Whitman." *SLJ* 10,#1(1977): 75-83.

2504. ----------. "The Old South and the New: Paul Hamilton Hayne and Muarice Thompson." *SLJ* 5,#1(1972): 108-122.

HEARN, LAFCADIO.   2505. Frost, O. W. "The Birth of Lafcadio Hearn." *AL* 24(1952): 372-377.

2506. Salvan, Albert. "Lafcadio Hearn's Views on the Realism of Zola." *PMLA* 67(1952): 1163-1167.

2507. Yu, Beongcheon. "Lafcadio Hearn (or Kiozumi Yakumo) (1850-1904)." [bibliography] *ALR* 1,#1 (1967): 52-55.

2508. ----------. "Lafcadio Hearn's Twice-Told Legends Reconsidered." *AL* 34(1962): 56-71.

HEDGE, F. H.   2509. Wilson, John B. "Phrenology and the Transcendentalists." *AL* 28 (1956): 220-225.

HENRI, ROBERT.   2510. Kwiat, Joseph J. "Robert Henri and the Emerson-Whitman Tradition." *PMLA* 71(1956): 617-636.

HENSON, JOSIAH.   2511. Doyle, Sister Mary Ellen, S. C. N. "Josiah Henson's Narrative: Before and After." *BALF* 8(1974): 176-182.

HENTZ, CAROLINE.   2512. Ellison, Rhoda Coleman. "Mrs. Hentz and the Green-Eyed Monster." *AL* 22(1950): 345-350.

HERNE, JAMES A.   2513. Edwards, Herbert. "Herne, Garland and Henry George." *AL* 28(1956): 359-367.

2514. Pizer, Donald. "An 1890 Account of *Margaret Fleming.*" *AL* 27(1955): 264-267.

2515. Quinn, Arthur H. and Julie Hern. "Act III of *Griffith Davenport.*" *AL* 24(1952): 330-351.

2516. Tallman, Richard S. "James A. Herne and Lamoine, Maine." *NEQ* 46(1973): 94-105.

HILDRETH, RICHARD.   2517. Canaday, Nicholas, Jr. "The Antislavery Novel Prior to 1852 and Hildreth's *The Slave* (1836)." *CLA* 17(1973): 175-191.

HOEHE, ALEX F.   2518. Pike, Robert E. "A Lost Book: *Hunt of the Buffaloes.*" *AL* 24(1952): 89-90.

HOLLEY, MARIETTA. See 1151.

HOLMES, OLIVER WENDELL.   2519. Boewe, Charles. "A Medicated Poem by Oliver Wendell Holmes." *NEQ* 31(1958): 392-401.

2520. ----------. "Reflex Action in the Novels of Oliver Wendell Holmes." *AL* 26(1954): 303-319.

2521. Flanagan, John T. "Dr. Holmes Selects American Verse for an Anthology." *JEGP* 51(1952): 192-195.

2522. Hamilton, John B. "Notes toward a Definition of Science Fiction." *Ext* 4(1962): 2-14.

2523. Hubbell, Jay B. "Oliver Wendell Holmes, Rev. Joseph Cook, and the *University Quarterly.*" *NEQ* 31(1958): 401-410.

2524. Lease, Benjamin. "Dr. Holmes Advises a Young Literary Aspirant: An Unpublished Letter." *NEQ* 28(1955): 96-98.

2525. Mattson, J. Stanley. "Oliver Wendell Holmes and 'The Deacon's Masterpiece': A Logical Story?" *NEQ* 41(1968): 104-114.

2526. Shoemaker, Neille. "The Contemporaneous Medical Reputation of Oliver Wendell Holmes." *NEQ* 26(1953): 477-493.

2527. Small, Miriam R. "Holmes Did Not Hear Lincoln at Gettysburg." *AL* 27(1955): 257-259.

2528. Tilton, Eleanor M. "Holmes and His Critic Motley." *AL* 36(1965): 463-474.

2529. Wentersdorf, Karl P. The Underground Workshop of Oliver Wendell Holmes." *AL* 35(1963): 1-12.

See also 2251, 2254.

HORTON, GEORGE M.   2530. Farrison, W. Edward. "George Moses Horton: Poet for Freedom." *CLA* 14(1971): 227-241.

2531. Walser, Richard. "Newly Discovered Acrostic by George Moses Horton." *CLA* 19(1975): 258-260.

HOWARD, BRONSON.   2532. Felheim, Marvin. "Bronson Howard, 'Literary Attache .'" *ALR* 2(1969): 174-179.

HOWARD, JAMES.   See 1147.

HOWE, EDGAR W.   2533. "Edgar Watson Howe (1853-1937): A Critical Bibliography of Secondary Comment." *ALR* 2(1969): 1-50.

2534. Eichelberger, Clayton L. "Edgar Watson Howe and Joseph Kirkland: More Critical Secondary Comment." *ALR* 4(1971): 279-290.

2535. Mayer, Charles W. "Realizing 'A Whole Order of Things': E. W. Howe's *The Story of a Country Town.*" *WAL* 11(1976): 23-36.

2536. Pickett, Calder M. "Edgar Watson Howe: Legend and Truth." *ALR* 2(1969): 70-73.

2537. Stronks, James B. "William Dean Howells, Ed Howe, and *The Story of a Country Town.*" *AL* 29(1958): 473-478.

HOWE, JULIA W.   2538. Snyder, Edward D. "The Biblical Battleground of the 'Battle Hymm of the Republic'." *NEQ* 24(1951): 231-238.

HOWELLS, WILLIAM DEAN.   2539. Aaron, Daniel. "Howells' 'Maggie'." *NEQ* 38(1965): 85-90.

2540. Abel, Darrell, ed. "'Howells or James?' An Essay by Henry Blake Fuller." *MFS* 3 (1957): 159-164.

2541. Adrian, Arthur A. "Augustus Hoppin to William Dean Howells." *NEQ* 24(1951): 84-89.

2542. Amacher, Anne Ward. "The Genteel Primitivist and the Semi-Tragic Octoroon." *NEQ* 29 (1956): 216-227.

2543. Andrews, William L. "William Dean Howells and Charles W. Chesnutt: Criticism and Race Fiction in the Age of Booker T. Washington." *AL* 48(1976): 327-339.

2544. Arms, George. "Howells' English Travel Books: Problems in Technique." *PMLA* 82(1967): 104-116.

2545. Ayers, Robert W. "W. D. Howells and Stephen Crane: Some Unpublished Letters." *AL* 28 (1957): 469-477.

2546. Beebe, Maurice. "Criticism of William Dean Howells: A Selected Checklist." *MFS* 16(1970): 395-419.

2547. Boardman, Arthur. "Howellsian Sex." *SN* 2(1970): 52-61.

2548. ----------. "Social Point of View in the Novels of William Dean Howells." *AL* 39(1967): 42-59.

2549. Bogardus, Ralph. "A Literary Realist and the Camera: W. D. Howells and the Uses of Photography." *ALR* 10(1977): 231-241.

2550. Bremer, Sidney H. "Invalids and Actresses: Howells's Duplex Imagery for American Women." *AL* 47(1976): 599-614.

2551. Brenner, Jack. "Howells and Ade." *AL* 38(1966): 198-207.

2552. Budd, Louis. "Annie Kilburn." *ALR* 1, #4(1968): 84-87.

2553. ----------. "Howells, the Atlantic Monthly, and Republicanism." *AL* 24(1952): 139-156.

2554. ----------. "Twain, Howells, and the Boston Nihilists." *NEQ* 32(1959): 351-371.

2555. ----------. "W. D. Howells' Defense of the Romance." *PMLA* 67(1952): 32-42.

2556. Campbell, Charles L. "Realism and Romance of Real Life: Multiple Fictional Worlds in Howell's Novels." *MFS* 16(1970): 289-302.

2557. Cargill, Oscar. "Henry James's 'Moral Policeman': William Dean Howells." *AL* 29(1958): 371-398.

2558. Carrington, George, Jr. "Howell's Christmas Sketches: The Uses of Allegory." *ALR* 10(1977): 242-253.

2559. Carter, Paul. "A Howells' Letter." *NEQ* 28(1955): 93-96.

2560. Cohn, Jan. "The Houses of Fiction: Domestic Architecture in Howells and Edith Wharton." *TSLL* 15(1973): 537-549.

2561. Cooley, Thomas. "The Wilderness Within: Howells's *A Boy's Town.*" *AL* 47(1976): 583-598.

2562. Cronkhite, G. Ferris. "Howells Turns to the Inner Life." *NEQ* 30(1957): 474-485.

2563. Crowley, John W. "'A Completer Verity': The Ending of W. D. Howells' *A Foregone Conclusion.*" *ELN* 14(1977): 192-197.

2564. ----------. "An Interoceanic Episode: *The Lady of Aroostook.*" *AL* 49(1977): 180-191.

2565. ----------. "The Length of Howells' *Shadow of a Dream.*" *NCF* 27(1972): 182-196.

2566. ----------. "The Oedipal Theme in Howells's Fennel and Rue." *SN* 5(1973): 104-109.

2567. ----------. "The Sacerdotal Cult and the Sealskin Coat: W. D. Howells in *My Mark Twain.*" *ELN* 11(1974): 287-292.

2568. Cumpiano, Marion W. "The Dark Side of *Their Wedding Journey.*" *AL* 40(1969): 472-486.

2569. ----------. "Howells' Bridge: A Study of the Artistry of *Indian Summer.*" *MFS* 16(1970): 363-382.

2570. Dean, James. "The Wests of Howells and Crane." *ALR* 10(1977): 254-266.

2571. Downey, Jean. "Three Unpublished Letters: Howells-Cooke." *AL* 32(1961): 463-465.

2572. Duffy, Charles. "An Unpublished Letter: Stedman to Howells." *AL* 30(1958): 369-370.

2573. Edwards, Herbert. "The Dramatization of *The Rise of Silas Lapham.*" *NEQ* 30(1957): 235-243.

2574. ----------. "Howells and Herne." *AL* 22(1951): 434-441.

2575. Ekstrom, William F. "The Equalitarian Principle in the Fiction of William Dean Howells." *AL* 24(1952): 40-50.

2576. Ellis, James. "William Dean Howells and the Family Home." *CLA* 8(1965): 240-245.

2577. Ellison, Jerome. "When Howells' Pipedream Came True." *NEQ* 42(1969): 253-260.

2578. Fertig, Walter L. "Maurice Thompson and *A Modern Instance.*" *AL* 38(1966): 103-111.

2579. Fischer, William C., Jr. "William Dean Howells: Reverie and the Nonsymbolic Aesthetic." *NCF* 25(1970): 1-30.

2580. Ford, Thomas W. "Howells and the American Negro." *TSLL* 5(1964): 530-537.

2581. Foster, Richard. "The Contemporaneity of Howells." *NEQ* 32(1959): 54-78.

2582. Fox, Arnold B. "Howells as a Religious Critic." *NEQ* 25(1952): 199-216.

2583. ----------. "Howells' Doctrine of Complicity." *MLQ* 13(1952): 56-60.

2584. Frazier, David. "Howells' Symbolic Houses: The Plutocrats and Palaces." *ALR* 10(1977): 267-279.

2585. ----------. *"Their Wedding Journey:* Howells' Fictional Craft." *NEQ* 42(1969): 323-349.

2586. Free, William J. "Howells' 'Editha' and Pragmatic Belief." *SSF* 3(1966): 285-292.

2587. Gardner, Joseph H. "Howells: The 'Realist' as Dickensian." *MFS* 16(1970): 323-344.

2588. Gargano, James W. "*A Modern Instance:* The Twin Evils of Society." *TSLL* 4(1962): 399-407.

2589. Giannone, Richard. "Howells' *A Foregone Conclusion:* Theme and Structure." *CLA* 6(1963): 216-220.

2590. Goldman, Laurel T. "A Different View of the Iron Madonna: William Dean Howells and His Magazine Readers." *NEQ* 50(1977): 563-586.

2591. Graham, D. B. "A Note on Howells, Williams, and the Matter of Sam Patch." *NCL* 4 (March, 1974): 10-13.

2592. Gullason, Thomas Arthur. "New Light on the Crane-Howells Relationship." *NEQ* 30(1957): 389-392.

2593. Habegger, Alfred. "The Autistic Tyrant: Howells' Self-Sacrificial Women and Jamesian Renunciation." *Novel* 10(1976): 27-40.

2594. Halfmann, Ulrich, ed. "Interviews with William Dean Howells." *ALR* 6(1973): 277-416.

2595. Halfmann, Ulrich, and Don R. Smith. "William Dean Howells: A Revised and Annotated Bibliography of Secondary Comment in Periodicals and Newspapers, 1868-1919." *ALR* 5(1972): 91-122.

2596. Hart, John E. "The Commonplace as Heroic in *The Rise of Silas Lapham.*" *MFS* 8(1962): 375-383.

2597. Hedges, Elain R. "*Cesar Birotteau* and *The Rise of Silas Lapham:* A Study in Parallels." *NCF* 17(1962): 163-174.

2598. Hedges, Elaine. "Howells on a Hawthornesque Theme." *TSLL* 3(1961): 129-143.

2599. Hilton, Earl. "Howells's *The Shadow of a Dream.*" *AL* 46(1974): 220-222.

2600. Hirsch, David H. "William Dean Howells and Daisy Miller." *ELN* 1(1963): 123-128.

2601. Hunt, Gary A. "'A Reality That Can't Be Quite Definitely Spoken': Sexuality in *Their Wedding Journey.*" *SN* 9(1977): 17-32.

2602. J. P. "*A Hazard of New Fortunes:* More About Some Old Friends." *ALR* 5(1972): 74-78.

2603. Kirk, Clara M. "Reality and Actuality in the March Family Narratives of W. D. Howells." *PMLA* 74(1959): 137-152.

2604. ----------. "Toward a Theory of Art: A Dialogue between W. D. Howells and C. E. Norton." *NEQ* 36(1963): 291-321.

2605. Kirk, Clara and Rudolf. "Howells and the Church of the Carpenter." *NEQ* 32(1959): 185-206.

2606. ----------. "Howells' Guidebook to Venice." *AL* 33(1961): 221-224.

2607. ----------. "William Dean Howells, George William Curtis, and the 'Haymarket Affair.'" *AL* 40(1969): 487-498.

2607a. Klinkowitz, Jerome. "Ethic and Aesthetic: The Basil and Isabel March Stories of William Dean Howells." *MFS* 16(1970): 303-322.

2608. Long, Robert Emmet. "Transformations: The *Blithedale Romance* to Howells and James." *AL* 47(1976): 552-571.

2609. Kutwack, Leonard. "William Dean Howells and the 'Editor's Study.'" *AL* 24(1952): 195-207.

2610. Lydenberg, John, and Edwin H. Cady. "Essay Review: The Howells Revival: Rounds Two and Three." *NEQ* 32(1959): 394-407.

2611. Marler, Robert F., Jr. "'A Dream': Howells' Early Contribution to the American Short Story." *JNT* 4(1974): 75-85.

2612. Marovitz, Sanford E. "Howells and the Ghetto: 'The Mystery of Misery.'" *MFS* 16(1970): 345-362.

2613. Mathews, James W. "Another Possible Origin of Howells' *The Shadow of a Dream*." *AL* 42(1971): 558-562.

2614. McMurray, William. "The Concept of Complicity in Howells' Fiction." *NEQ* 35(1962): 489-498.

2615. ----------. "Moral Law and Justice in Howells' Fiction." *ALR* 10(1977): 280-288.

2616. ----------. "Point of View in Howells's *The Landlord at Lion's Head*." *AL* 34(1962): 207-214.

2617. Meserve, Walter. "*Colonel Sellers As A Scientist*: A Play by S. L. Clemens and W. D. Howells." *MD* 1(1958): 151-156.

2618. ----------. "Truth, Morality, and Swedenborg in Howells' Theory of Realism." *NEQ* 27(1954): 252-257.

2619. Monteiro, George. "Howells on Lowell: An Unsigned Review." *NEQ* 38(1965): 508-509.

2620. ----------. "William Dean Howells and the *American Hebrew*." *NEQ* 50(1977): 515-516.

2621. Munford, Howard M. "The Disciple Proves Independent: Howells and Lowell." *PMLA* 74(1959): 484-487.

2622. Murphy, Rosalie and Seymour Gross. "Commonplace Reality and Romantic Phantoms: Howells' *A Modern Instance* and The Rise of Silas Lapham." *SAF* 4(1976): 1-14.

2623. Palmer, Erwin. "A Letter to Howells." *ALR* 9(1976): 81-82.

2624. Parker, Barbara L. "Howells Oresteia: The Union of Theme and Structure in *The Shadow of a Dream*." *AL* 49(1977): 57-69.

2625. Perkins, George. "Howells and Hawthorne." *NCF* 15(1960): 259-262.

2626. ----------. "*A Modern Instance*: Howells' Transition to Artistic Maturity." *NEQ* 47(1974): 427-439.

2627. Pizer, Donald. "The Ethical Unity of *The Rise of Silas Lapham*." *AL* 32(1960): 322-327.

2628. ----------. "The Evolutionary Foundation of W. D. Howells's *Criticism and Fiction*." *PQ* 40(1961): 91-103.

2629. ----------. "Evolutionary Literary Criticism and the Defense of Howellsian Realism." *JEGP* 61(1962): 296-304.

2630. Ratner, Marc L. "Howells and Boyesen: Two Views of Realism." *NEQ* 35(1962): 376-390.

2631. Reeves, John K. "The Limited Realism of Howells' *Their Wedding Journey*." *PMLA* 77(1962): 617-628.

2632. ----------. "The Way of a Realist: A Study of Howells' Use of the Saratoga Scene." *PMLA* 65(1950): 1035-1053.

2633. Rowlette, Robert. "Addenda to Halfmann and Smith: More New Howells' Items." *ALR* 9(1976): 43-56.

2634. ----------. "Addenda to Halfman: Six New Howells Interviews." *ALR* 8(1975): 101-108.

2635. ----------. "More Addenda to Halfmann: Nine New Howells Interviews." *ALR* 9(1976): 33-42.

2636. ----------. "William D. Howells' 1899 Midwest Lecture Tour." *ALR* 9(1976): 1-32.

2637. ----------. "William D. Howells' 1899 Midwest Lecture." *ALR* 10(1977): 125-167.

2638. Scharnhorst, Gary. "Maurice Thompson's Regional Critique of William D. Howells." *ALR* 9(1976): 57-64.

2639. Scheick, William. "William Dean Howells to Bret Harte: A Missing Letter." *ALR* 9(1976): 276-278.

2640. See, Fred G. "The Demystification of Style: Metaphoric and Metonymic Language in *A Modern Instance*." *NCF* 28(1974): 379-403.

2641. Seib, Kenneth. "Uneasiness at Niagara: Howells' *Their Wedding Journey*." *SAF* 4(1976): 15-25.

2642. Shuman, R. Baird. " The Howells-Lowell Correspondence: A New Item." *AL* 31(1959): 338-340.

2643. Simon, Myron. "Howells on Romantic Fiction." *SSF* 2(1965): 241-246.

2644. Solomon, Eric. "Howells, Houses and Realism." *ALR* 1,#4(1968): 89-93.

2645. Spangler, George M. "Moral Anxiety in *A Modern Instance*." *NEQ* 46(1973): 236-249.

2646. Stein, Allen F. "Marriage in Howells's Novels." *AL* 48(1977): 501-524.

2647. Stronks, James B. "An Early Autobiographical Letter by William Dean Howells." *NEQ* 33(1960): 240-242.

2648. ----------. "A Modern Instance." *ALR* 1,#4(1968): 87-89.

2649. ----------. "William Dean Howells, Ed Howe, and *The Story of a Country Town*." *AL* 29(1958): 473-478.

2650. Sullivan, Sister Mary Petrus. "The Function of Setting in Howells' *The Landlord at Lion's Head*." *AL* 35(1963): 38-52.

2651. Sweeney, Gerard M. "The *Medea* Howells Saw." *AL* 42(1970): 83-89.

2652. Tanselle, G. Thomas. "The Architecture of *The Rise of Silas Lapham*." *AL* 37(1966): 430-457.

2653. ----------. "The Boston Seasons of Silas Lapham." *SN* 1(1969): 60-66.

2654. Towers, Tom H. "'The Only Life We've Got': Myth and Morality in *The Kentons.*" *MFS* 16 (1970): 383-394.

2655. ----------. "Savagery and Civilization: The Moral Dimensions of Howells's *A Boy's Town.*" *AL* 40(1969): 499-509.

2656. Tuttleton, James W. "Howells and the Manners of The Good Heart." *MFS* 16(1970): 271-287.

2657. Vanderbilt, Kermit. "The Conscious Realism of Howells' *April Hopes.*" *ALR* 3(1970): 53-66.

2658. ----------. "From Passion to Impasse: The Structure of a Dark Romantic Theme in Hawthorne, Howells, and Barth." *SN* 8(1976): 419-429.

2659. ----------. "Howells Among the Brahmins: Why 'The Bottom Dropped Out' During *The Rise of Silas Lapham.*" *NEQ* 35(1962): 291-317.

2660. ----------. "Howells and Norton: Some Frustrations of the Biographer." *NEQ* 37(1964): 84-89.

2661. ----------. "Howells Studies: Past, or Passing, or to Come." *ALR* 7(1974): 143-154.

2662. ----------. "Marcia Gaylord's Electra Complex: A Footnote to Sex in Howells." *AL* 34 (1962): 365-374.

2663. ----------. "The Perception and Art of *Literary Friends and Acquaintances.*" *ALR* 10 (1977): 289-306.

2664. Ward, John W. "Another Howells Anarchist Letter." *AL* 22(1951): 489-490.

2665. Wasserstrom, William. "William Dean Howells: The Indelible Stain." *NEQ* 32(1959): 486-495.

2666. Wilson, Jack H. "Howells' Use of George Eliot's *Romola* in *April Hopes.*" *PMLA* 84 (1969): 1620-1627.

2667. Woodress, James. "Four Decades of Howells Scholarship." *TSLL* 2(1960): 115-123.

2668. ----------. "An Interview with Howells." *ALR* 3(1970): 71-75.

2669. ----------. :The Lowell-Howells Friendship: Some Unpublished Letters." *NEQ* 26 (1953): 523-528.

2670. Woodress, James, and Stanley P. Anderson. "A Bibliography of Writing About William Dean Howells." *ALR* 2(1969): Special Number, 1-132.

2671. Woodward, Robert. "'Punch' on Howells and James." *ALR* 3(1970): 76-77.

See also 598, 610, 1114, 1151, 1419, 2954, 15771.

INGERSOLL, ROBERT. 2672. Schwartz, Thomas D. "Mark Twain and Robert Ingersoll: The Freethought Connection." *AL* 48(1976): 183-193.

INGRAHAM, JOSEPH HOLT. 2673. French, Warren G. "A 'Lost' American Novel." *AL* 21(1950): 477-478.

IRVING, WASHINGTON. 2674. Adams, Thomas R. "Washington Irving—Another Letter From Spain." *AL* 25(1953): 354-358.

2675. Black, Michael L. "Bibliographical Problems in Washington Irving's Early Works." *EAL* 3,#3(1969): 148-158.

2676. Bowden, Mary Weatherspoon. "Knickerbocker's *History* and the 'Enlightened' Men of New York City." *AL* 47(1975): 159-172.

2677. Brooks, Elmer L. "A Note on Irving's Sources." *AL* 25(1953): 229-230.

2678. ----------. "A Note on the Source of 'Rip Van Winkle.'" *AL* 25(1954): 495-496.

2679. Clark, William Bedford. "A Tale of Two Chiefs: William Faulkner's Ikkemotubbe and Washington Irving's Blackbird." *WAL* 12(1977): 223-225.

2680. Conley, Patrick T. "The Real Ichabod Crane." *AL* 40(1968): 70-71.

2681. Couser, G. Thomas. "The Ruined Garden of Wolfert Webber." *SSF* 12(1975): 23-28.

2682. Current-Garcia, E. "Irving Sets the Pattern: Notes on Professionalism and the Art of the Short Story." *SSF* 10(1973): 327-341.

2683. Dula, Martha. "Audience Response to *A Tour on the Praries* in 1835." *WAL* 8(1973): 67-74.

2684. Durant, David. "Aeolism in *Knickerbocker's A History of New York.*" *AL* 41(1970): 493-506.

2685. Emerson, Everett H. and Katherine. "Some Letters of Washington Irving: 1833-1843." *AL* 35(1963): 156-172.

2686. Evans, James E. "The English Lineage of Diedrich Knickerbocker." *EAL* 10,#1(1975): 3-13.

2687. Fiske, John C. "The Soviet Controversy over Pushkin and Washington Irving." *Comp L* 7(1955): 25-31.

2688. Gates, W. B. "Shakespearean Elements in Irving's *Sketch Book.*" *AL* 30(1959): 450-458.

2689. Griffith, Ben W. "An Experiment on the American Bookseller: Two Letters from Irving to Godwin." *NCF* 12(1957): 237-239.

2690. Guttmann, Allen. "Washington Irving and the Conservative Imagination." *AL* 36(1964): 165-173.

2691. Hoffman, Daniel G. "Irving's Use of American Folklore in 'The Legend of Sleepy Hollow.'" *PMLA* 68(1953): 425-435.

2692. Kime, Wayne R. "The Completeness of Washington Irving's *A Tour on the Prairies.*" *WAL* 8(1973): 55-65.

2693. ----------. "Pierre M. Irving's Account of Peter Irving, Washington Irving, and the *Corrector.*" *AL* 43(1971): 108-114.

2694. ----------. "Poe's Use of Irving's *Astoria* in 'The Journal of Julius Rodman.'" *AL* 40 (1968): 215-222.

2695. ----------. "Washington Irving and *The Empire of the West.*" *WAL* 5(1971): 277-285.

2696. ----------. "Washington Irving's Revision of the *Tonquin* Episode in *Astoria.*" *WAL* 4 (1969): 51-59.

2697. Larrabee, Stephen A. "Some Printings of Irving in Finland Before 1900." *AL* 30(1958): 358-359.

2698. Lease, Benjamin. "*John Bull* Versus Washington Irving: More on the Shakespeare Committee Controversy." *ELN* 9(1972): 272-277.

2699. Lyon, Thomas J. "Washington Irving's Wilderness." *WAL* 1(1966): 167-174.

2700. Martin, Terence. "Rip, Ichabod, and the American Imagination." *AL* 31(1959): 137-149.

2701. McClary, Ben Harris. "A Bracebridge-Hall Christmas for Van Buren: An Unpublished Irving Letter." *ELN* 8(1970): 18-22.

2702. ----------. "Irving's Literary Midwifery: Five Unpublished Letters from British Repositories." *PQ* 46(1967): 277-283.

2703. ----------. "Mr. Irving of the Shakespear Committee: A Bit of Anglo-American Jealousy."

AL 41(1969): 92-95.

2704. ----------. "Two of Washington Irving's Friends Identified." *AL* 37(1966): 471-473.

2705. McLendon, Will I. "A Problem in Plagiarism: Washington Irving and Cousen de Courchamps." *Comp L* 30(1968): 157-169.

2706. Myers, Andrew. "The New York Years in Irving's *The Life of George Washington*." *EAL* 11(1976): 68-83.

2707. Peck, Richard E. "An Unpublished Poem by Washington Irving." *AL* 39(1967): 204-207.

2708. Proffer, Carl R. "Washington Irving in Russia: Pushkin, Gogol, Marlinsky." *Comp L* 20(1968): 329-342.

2709. Reed, Kenneth T. "Washington Irving and the Negro." *BALF* 4(1970): 43-44.

2710. Reichart, Walter A. "Washington Irving's Influence in German Literature." *MLR* 52 (1957): 537-553.

2711. Ringe, Donald A. "Irving's Use of The Gothic Mode." *SLI* 7,#1(1974): 51-65.

2712. ----------. "New York and New England: Irving's Criticism of American Society." *AL* 38 (1967): 455-467.

2713. Roth, Martin. "The Final Chapter of Knickerbocker's New York." *MP* 66(1969): 248-255.

2714. Shaw, Catherine M. "The Dramatic Vision of Washington Irving." *TSLL* 13(1971): 461-474.

2715. Sloane, David E. E. "Washington Irving's 'Insuperable Diffidence.'" *AL* 43(1971): 114-115.

2716. Spaulding, K. A. "A Note on *Astoria*: Irving's Use of the Robert Stuart Manuscript." *AL* 22(1950): 150-157.

2717. Watts, Charles H., II. "Poe, Irving, and the *Southern Literary Messenger*." *AL* 27(1955): 249-251.

2718. Weatherspoon, M. A. "1815-1819: Prelude to Irving's *Sketch Book*." *AL* 41(1970): 566-571.

2719. Wright, Nathalia. "Irvings Use of His Italian Experiences in *Tales of a Traveller*: The Beginning of an American Tradition." *AL* 31(1959): 191-196.

See also 1123.

JACKSON, HELEN HUNT. 2720. Byers, John, Jr. "Helen Hunt Jackson (1830-1885)." [bibliography] *ALR* 2(1969): 143-148.

2721. Byers, John, Jr., and Elizabeth Byers. "Helen Hunt Jackson (1830-1885): A Critical Bibliography of Secondary Comment." *ALR* 6(1973): 197-242.

JAMES, HENRY. 2722. Abel, Darrel, ed. "'Howells or James': An Essay by Henry Blake Fuller." *MFS* 3(1957): 159-164.

2723. Aldrich, C. Knight. "Another Twist to *The Turn of the Screw*." *MFS* 13(1967): 167-178.

2724. Allott, Miriam. "Symbol and Image in the Later Work of Henry James." *EIC* 3(1953): 321-336.

2725. Anderson, Charles R. "James's Portrait of the Southerner." *AL* 27(1955): 309-331.

2726. Andreach, Robert J. "Henry James's *The Sacred Fount*: The Existential Predicament." *NCF* 17(1962): 197-216.

2727. Aswell, E. Duncan. "James's *In the Cage*: The Telegraphist as Artist." *TSLL* 8(1966):

375-384.

2728. ----------. "James's Treatment of Artistic Collaboration." *Criticism* 8(1966): 180-195.

2729. ----------. "Reflections of a Governess: Image and Distortion in *The Turn of the Screw*." *NCF* 23(1968): 49-63.

2730. Aziz, Maqbool. "*Four Meetings*: A Caveat for James Critics." *EIC* 18(1968): 258-274.

2731. ----------. "Revisiting *The Pension Beaurepas*: the Tale and its Texts." *EIC* 23(1973): 268-282.

2732. Baker, Robert S. "Gabriel Nash's 'House of Strange Idols': Aestheticism in *The Tragic Muse*." *TSLL* 15(1973): 149-166.

2733. Banta, Martha. "Henry James and 'The Others.'" *NEQ* 37(1964): 171-184.

2734. ----------. "The Quality of Experience in *What Maisie Knew*." *NEQ* 42(1969): 483-510.

2735. ----------. "Rebirth or Revenge: The Endings of *Huckleberry Finn* and *The American*." *MFS* 15(1969): 191-207.

2736. Bargainnier, Earl F. "Browning, James, and 'The Private Life.'" *SSF* 14(1977): 151-158.

2737. Bass, Eben. "Dramatic Scene and *The Awkward Age*." *PMLA* 79(1964): 148-157.

2738. ----------. "Lemon-Colored Volumes and Henry James." *SSF* 1(1964): 113-122.

2739. Baxter, Annette K. "Independence vs. Isolation: Hawthorne and James on the Problem of the Artist." *NCF* 10(1955): 225-231.

2740. Baym, Nina. "Fleda Vetch and the Plot of *The Spoils of Poynton*." *PMLA* 84(1969): 102-111.

2741. ----------. "Revision and Thematic Change in *The Potrait of a Lady*." *MFS* 22(1976): 183-200.

2742. Bazzanella, Dominic J. "The Conclusion to *The Portrait of a Lady* Re-examined." *AL* 41(1969): 55-63.

2743. Beams, David W. "Consciousness in James's *The Sense of the Past*." *Criticism* 5 (1963): 148-172.

2744. Beauchamp, Andrea Roberts. "'Isabel Archer': A Possible Source for *The Portrait of a Lady*." *AL* 49(1977): 267-271.

2745. Beebe, Maurice, and William T. Stafford. "Criticism of Henry James: A Selected Checklist." *MFS* 12(1966): 117-177.

2746. ----------. "Criticism of Henry James: A Selected Checklist with an Index to Studies of Separate Works." *MFS* 3(1957): 73-96.

2747. Bell, Millicant. "Edith Wharton and Henry James: The Literary Relation." *PMLA* 74 (1959): 619-637.

2748. Bellman, Samuel Irving. "Henry James's 'The Tree of Knowledge': A Biblical Parallel." *SSF* 1(1964): 226-228.

2749. Bellringer, Alan W. "'The Sacred Fount': the Scientific Method." *EIC* 22(1972): 244-264.

2750. ----------. "*The Spoils of Poynton*: James's Intentions." *EIC* 17(1967): 238-243.

2751. ----------. "*The Spoils of Poynton*: James's Unintended Involvement." *EIC* 16(1966): 185-200.

2752. ----------. "*The Spoils of Poynton:* The 'Facts.'" *EIC* 18(1968): 357-359.

2753. Bercovitch, Sacvan. "The Revision of Rowland Mallett." *NCF* 24(1969): 210-221.

2754. Bersani, Leo. "The Narrator as Center in *The Wings of the Dove*." *MFS* 6(1960): 131-144.

2755. Bishop, Ferman. "Henry James Criticizes *The Tory Lover*." *AL* 27(1955): 262-264.

2756. Blackall, Jean Frantz. "*The Sacred Fount* as a Comedy of the Limited Observer." *PMLA* 78(1963): 384-393.

2757. Blasing, Mutlu. "Double Focus in *The American*." *NCF* 28(1973): 74-84.

2758. Boardman, Arthur. "Mrs. Grose's Reading of *The Turn of the Screw*." *SEL* 14(1974): 619-635.

2759. Bochner, Jay. "Life in a Picture Gallery: Things in *The Potrait of a Lady* and *The Marble Faun*." *TSLL* 11(1969): 761-777.

2760. Bode, Carl. "Henry James and Owen Wister." *AL* 26(1954): 250-252.

2761. Bontly, Thomas J. "Henry James's 'General Vision of Evil' in *The Turn of the Screw*." *SEL* 9(1969): 721-735.

2762. Booth, Bradford A. "Henry James and the Economic Motif." *NCF* 8(1953): 141-150.

2763. Borklund, Elmer. "Howard Sturgis, Henry James, and *Belchamber*." *MP* 58(1961): 255-269.

2764. Bouraoui, H. A. "Henry James and the French Mind: The International Theme in 'Madame de Mauves.'" *Novel* 4(1970): 69-76.

2765. Bowden, Edwin T. "Henry James and International Copyright Again." *AL* 25(1954): 499-500.

2766. ----------. "Henry James and the Struggle for International Copyright: An Unnoticed Item in the James Bibliography." *AL* 24(1953): 537-539.

2767. Broderick, John C. "Nature, Art and Imagination in *The Spoils of Poynton*." *NCF* 13 (1959): 295-312.

2768. Buitenhuis, Peter. "Henry James on Hawthorne." *NEQ* 32(1959): 207-225.

2769. Burde, Edgar J. "*The Ambassadors* and the Double Vision of James." *EL* 4(1977): 59-77.

2770. Burns, Landon. "Henry James's Mysterious Fount." *TSLL* 2(1961): 520-528.

2771. Byrd, Scott. "Crystal in *Middlemarch* and *The Golden Bowl*." *MFS* 18(1972): 551-554.

2772. ----------. "The Spoils of Venice: Henry James's 'Two Old Houses and Three Young Women' and *The Golden Bowl*." *AL* 43(1971): 371-384.

2773. Cambon, Glauco. "The Negative Gesture in Henry James." *NCF* 15(1961): 335-343.

2774. Canavan, Thomas L. "The Economics of Disease in James's 'The Pupil.'" *Criticism* 15 (1973): 253-264.

2775. Cargill, Oscar. "*The Ambassadors:* A New View." *PMLA* 75(1960): 439-452.

2776. ----------. "The First International Novel." *PMLA* 73(1958): 418-425.

2777. ----------. "Gabriel Nash--Somewhat Less Than Angel?" *NCF* 14(1959): 231-239.

2778. ----------. "Henry James's 'Moral Policeman': William Dean Howells." *AL* 29(1958): 371-398.

2779. ----------. Mr. James's Aesthetic Mr. Nash." *NCF* 12(1957): 177-187.

2780. ----------. "*The Portrait of a Lady:* A Critical Reappraisal." *MFS* 3(1957): 11-32.

2781. ----------. "*The Princess Casamassima:* A Critical Reappraisal." *PMLA* 71(1956): 97-117.

2782. ----------. "*The Turn of the Screw* and Alice James." *PMLA* 78(1963): 238-249.

2783. Clair, John A. "*The American:* A Reinterpretation." *PMLA* 74(1959): 613-618.

2784. Collins, Martha. "The Center of Consciousness on Stage: Henry James's *Confidence*." *SAF* 3(1975): 39-50.

2785. ----------. "The Narrator, the Satelites, and Isabel Archer: Point of View in *The Portrait of a Lady*." *SN* 8(1976): 142-157.

2786. Conn, Peter J. "*Roderick Hudson:* The Role of the Observer." *NCF* 26(1971): 65-82.

2787. ----------. "Seeing and Blindness in 'The Beast in the Jungle.'" *SSF* 7(1970): 472-475.

2788. Cook, David A. "James and Flaubert: The Evolution of Perception." *Comp L* 25(1973): 289-307.

2789. Coursen, Herbert R., Jr. "The Mirror of Allusion: *The Ambassadors*." *NEQ* 34(1961): 382-384.

2790. Cox, C. B. "The Golden Bowl." *EIC* 5 (1955): 190-193.

2791. Cranfill, Thomas M., and Robert L. Clark, Jr. "Cast in James's *The Turn of the Screw*." *TSLL* 5(1963): 189-198.

2792. ----------. "James's Revisions of *The Turn of the Screw*." *NCF* 19(1965): 394-398.

2793. ----------. "The Provocativeness of *The Turn of the Screw*." *TSLL* 12(1970): 93-100.

2794. Cromer, Viris. "James and Ibsen." *Comp L* 25(1973): 114-127.

2795. Crowl, Susan. "Aesthetic Allegory in 'The Turn of the Screw'." *Novel* 4(1971): 107-122.

2796. Davidson, Arnold E. "James's Dramatic Method in *The Awkward Age*." *NCF* 29(1974): 320-335.

2797. Diehl, Joanne Feit. "'One Life Within Us and Abroad': The Subverted Realist in *The Sacred Fount*." *JNT* 6(1976): 92-100.

2798. Dooley, D. J. "The Hourglass Pattern in *The Ambassadors*." *NEQ* 41(1968): 273-281.

2799. Dove, John Roland. "The Tragic Sense in Henry James." *TSLL* 2(1960): 303-314.

2800. Draper, R. P. "Death of a Hero? Winterbourne and Daisy Miller." *SSF* 6(1969): 601-608.

2801. Dubler, Walter. "The Princess Casamassima: Its Place in the James Canon." *MFS* 12 (1966): 44-60.

2802. Dunbar, Viola R. "Addenda to 'Biographical and Critical Studies of Henry James, 1941-1948.'" *AL* 22(1950): 56-61.

2803. Dunn, Albert A. "The Articulation of Time in *The Ambassadors*." *Criticism* 14(1972): 137-150.

2804. Durkin, Sister Mary Brian. "Henry James's Revisions of the Style of *The Reverberator*." *AL* 33(1961): 330-349.

2805. Durr, Robert A. "The Night Journey in *The Ambassadors*." *PQ* 35(1956): 24-38.

2806. Edel, Leon. "The Architecture of Henry James's 'New York Edition.'" *NEQ* 24(1951): 169-178.

2807. ----------. "A Further Note on 'An Error in *The Ambassadors*.'" *AL* 23(1951): 128-130.

2808. ----------. "Henry James and Vernon Lee." *PMLA* 69(1954): 677-678.

2809. ----------. "A Letter to the Editors." *AL* 24(1952): 370-372.

2810. ----------. "The Literary Conviction of Henry James." *MFS* 3(1957): 3-10.

2811. ----------. "To the Poet of Prose." *MFS* 12(1956): 3-6.

2812. ----------. "Who *Was* Gilbert Osmond?" *MFS* 6(1960): 164.

2813. Edelstein, Arnold. "'The Tangled Life': Levels of Meaning in *The Spoils of Poynton*." *HSL* 2(1970): 133-150.

2814. Edwards, Herbert. "Henry James and Ibsen." *AL* 24(1952): 208-223.

2815. Engleberg, Edward. "James and Arnold: Conscience and Consciousness in a Victorian 'Kunstlerroman.'" *Criticism* 10(1968): 93-114.

2816. Enn, C. M. "Commitment and Identity in 'The Ambassadors.'" *MLR* 66(1971): 522-531.

2817. Falk, Robert P. "Henry James and the 'Age of Innocence.'" *NCF* 7(1952): 171-188.

2818. Ferguson, Alfred R. "The Triple Quest of Henry James: Fame, Art, and Fortune." *AL* 27(1956): 475-498.

2819. Feurlicht, Ignace. "'Erlkönig' and *The Turn of the Screw*." *JEGP* 58(1959): 68-74.

2820. Fiderer, Gerald. "Henry James's 'Discriminating Occasion.'" *Crit* 11,#2(1969): 56-69.

2821. Field, Mary. "Henry James's Criticism of French Literature: A Bibliography and a Checklist." *ALR* 7(1974): 379-394.

2822. Finch, G. A. "A Retreading of James' Carpet." *TCL* 14(1968): 98-101.

2823. Firebaugh, Joseph J. "Inadequacy of Eden: Knowledge in *The Turn of the Screw*." *MFS* 3(1957): 57-63.

2824. ----------. "A Schopenhauerian Novel; James's *The Princess Casamassima*." *NCF* 13(1958): 177-197.

2825. ----------. "The Ververs." *EIC* 4(1954): 400-410.

2826. Fish, Charles K. "Description in Henry James's 'A light Man.'" *ELN* 2(1965): 211-215.

2827. ----------. "Form and Revision: The Example of *Watch and Ward*." *NCF* 22(1967): 173-190.

2828. ----------. "Indirection, Irony, and the Two Endings of James's 'The Story of a Masterpiece.'" *MP* 62(1965): 241-243.

2829. Folsom, James K. "Archimago's Well: An Interpretation of *The Sacred Fount*." *MFS* 7(1961): 136-145.

2830. Freedman, William A. "Universality in 'The Jolly Corner.'" *TSLL* 4(1962): 12-15.

2831. Friend, Joseph H. "The Structure of *The Portrait of a Lady*." *NCF* 20(1965): 85-95.

2832. Furbank, P. N. "Henry James: The Novelist as Actor." *EIC* 1(1951): 404-420.

2833. Gabbay, Lydia Rivlin. "The Four Square Coterie: A Comparison of Ford Maddox Ford and Henry James." *SN* 6(1974): 439-453.

2834. Gale, Robert L. "The Abasement of Mrs. Warren Hope." *PMLA* 78(1963): 98-102.

2835. ----------. "Art Imagery in Henry James's Fiction." *AL* 29(1957): 47-63.

2836. ----------. "H. J.'s J. H. in 'The Real Thing'." *SSF* 14(1977): 396-398.

2837. ----------. "Henry James and Italy." *NCF* 14(1959): 157-170.

2838. ----------. "A Note on Henry James's 'The Real Thing.'" *SSF* 1(1963): 65-66.

2839. ----------. "'Pandora' and Her President." *SSF* 1(1964): 222-224.

2840. ----------. "Religion Imagery in Henry James's Fiction." *MFS* 3(1957): 64-72.

2841. Gardner, Burdett. "An Apology for Henry James's 'Tiger-Cat.'" *PMLA* 68(1953): 688-695.

2842. Gargano, James W. "'The Aspern Papers': The Untold Story." *SSF* 10(1973): 1-10.

2843. ----------. "The Theme of 'Salvation' in *The Awkward Age*." *TSLL* 9(1967): 273-287.

2844. ----------. "*Washington Square*: A Study in the Growth of an Inner Self." *SSF* 13(1976): 355-362.

2845. ----------. "*What Maisie Knew*: The Evolution of a 'Moral Sense.'" *NCF* 16(1961): 33-46.

2846. Garis, Robert E. "The Two Lambert Strethers: A New Reading of *The Ambassadors*." *MFS* 7(1961): 305-316.

2847. Gegenheimer, Albert Frank. "Early and Late Revisions in Henry James's 'A Passionate Pilgrim.'" *AL* 23(1951): 233-242.

2848. Geismar, Maxwell. "Henry James: 'The Beast in the Jungle.'" *NCF* 18(1963): 35-42.

2849. Gibson, Priscilla. "The Uses of James's Imagery: Drama through Metaphor." *PMLA* 69(1954): 1076-1084.

2850. Gibson, William M. "Metaphor in the Plot of 'The Ambassadors.'" *NEQ* 24(1951): 291-305.

2851. Gillen, Francis. "The Dramatist in His Drama: Theory vs. Effect in *The Awkward Age*." *TSLL* 12(1971): 663-674.

2852. Girling, H. K. "The Function of Slang in the Dramatic Poetry of *The Golden Bowl*." *NCF* 11(1956): 130-147.

2853. ----------. "'Wonder' and 'Beauty' in *The Awkward Age*." *EIC* 8(1958): 370-380.

2854. Goddard, Harold C. "A Pre-Freudian Reading of *The Turn of the Screw* (with a Prefatory Note by Leon Edel)." *NCF* 12(1957): 1-36.

2855. Goldsmith, Arnold L. "Henry James's Reconciliation of Free Will and Fatalism." *NCF* 13(1958): 109-126.

2856. Goodman, Charlotte. "Henry James's *Roderick Hudson* and Nathaniel Parker Willis's *Paul Fane*." *AL* 43(1972): 642-645.

2867. Grant, William E. "'Daisy Miller': A Study of a Study." *SSF* 11(1974): 17-25.

2858. Greene, Mildred S. "*Les Liasons Dangereuses* and *The Golden Bowl*: Maggie's 'Loving Reason.'" *MFS* 19(1973): 531-540.

2859. Greene, Philip L. "Point of View in *The Spoils of Poynton*." *NCF* 21(1967): 359-368.

2860. Greenstein, Susan N. *"The Ambassadors:* The Man of Imagination Engaged and Provided For." *SN* 9(1977): 137-153.

2861. Grenander, M. E. "Henry James's *Capricciosa:* Christina Light in *Roderick Hudson* and *The Princess Cassamassima." PMLA* 75(1960): 309-319.

2862. Grenander, M. E., Beverly J. Rahn, and Francine Valvo. "The Time-Scheme in *The Portrait of a Lady." AL* 32(1960): 127-135.

2863. Griffith, John. "James's 'The Pupil' as Whodunit: The Question of Moral Responsibility." *SSF* 9(1972): 257-268.

2864. Grover, P. R. "Mérimée's Influence on Henry James." *MLR* 63(1968): 810-817.

2865. ----------. "Two Modes of Possessing—Conquest and Appreciation: 'The Princess Casamassima' and 'L'Education sentimental'." *MLR* 66(1971): 760-771.

2866. Gurko, Leo. "The Missing Word in Henry James's 'Four Meetings'." *SSF* 7(1970): 298-307.

2867. Habegger, Alfred. "The Disunity of *The Bostonians." NCF* 24(1969): 193-209.

2868. ----------. "Reciprocity and the Market Place in *The Wings of the Dove and What Maisie Know." NCF* 25(1971): 455-473.

2869. ----------. "'The Seige of London': Henry James and the *Pièce Bien Faite." MFS* 15 (1969): 219-230.

2870. Hagan, John. "A Note on a Symbolic Pattern in *The Wings of the Dove." CLA* 10(1967): 256-262.

2871. Hagopian, John V. "Seeing Through 'The Pupil' Again." *MFS* 5(1959): 169-171.

2872. Hall, William F. "The Continuing Relevance of James' 'The American Scene.'" *Criticism* 13(1971): 151-156.

2873. ----------. "Gabriel Nash: 'Famous Centre' of *The Tragic Muse." NCF* 21(1966): 167-184.

2874. ----------. "James's Conception of Society in *The Awkward Age." NCF* 23(1968): 28-48.

2875. ----------. "The Meaning of *The Sacred Fount:* 'Its own little law of composition.'" *MLQ* 37(1976): 168-178.

2876. Halliburton, D. G. "Self and Secularization in *The Princess Casamassima." MFS* 11(1965): 116-128.

2877. Harris, Marie P. "Henry James, Lecturer." *AL* 23(1951): 302-314.

2878. Hartsock, Mildred E. "Biography. The Treacherous Art." *JML* 1(1970): 116-119.

2879. ----------. "The Conceivable Child: James and the Poet." *SSF* 8(1971): 569-574.

2880. ----------. "The Dizzying Crest: Strether as Moral Man." *MLQ* 26(1965): 414-425.

2881. ----------. "Dizzying Summit: James's 'The Altar of the Dead.'" *SSF* 11(1974): 371-378.

2882. ----------. "Henry James and the Cities of the Plain." *MLQ* 29(1968): 297-311.

2883. ----------. "The Most Valuable Thing: James on Death." *MFS* 22(1976): 507-524.

2884. ----------. *"The Princess Casamassima:* The Politics of Power." *SN* 1(1969): 297-309.

2885. ----------. "Unintentional Fallacy: Critics and *The Golden Bowl." MLQ* 35(1974): 272-288.

2886. ----------. "Unweeded Garden: A View of *The Aspern Papers." SSF* 5(1967): 60-68.

2887. Hatcher, Joe B. "Shaw the Reviewer and James's *Guy Domville." MD* 14(1971): 311-334.

2888. Havens, Raymond D. "Henry James on One of His Early Stories." *AL* 23(1951): 131-133.

2889. Heilman, Robert B. "The Lure of the Demonic: James and Dürrenmatt." *Comp L* 13(1961): 346-357.

2890. Hinchliffe, Arnold P. "Henry James's *The Sacred Fount." TSLL* 2(1960): 88-94.

2891. Hirsch, David H. "William Dean Howells and Daisy Miller." *ELN* 1(1963): 123-128.

2892. Hoag, Gerald. "The Death of the Paper Lion." *SSF* 12(1975): 163-172.

2893. Holder, Alan. "The Lesson of the Master: Ezra Pound and Henry James." *AL* 35(1963): 71-79.

2894. ----------. "T. S. Eliot on Henry James." *PMLA* 79(1964): 490-497.

2895. Holland, Laurence B. *"The Wings of the Dove." ELH* 26(1959): 549-574.

2896. Hopkins, Viola. "Gloriana and the Tides of Taste." *NCF* 18(1963): 65-71.

2897. ----------. "Visual Art Devices and Parallels in the Fiction of Henry James." *PMLA* 76(1961): 561-574.

2898. Horowitz, Floyd R. "The Christian Time Sequence in Henry James's *The American." CLA* 9 (1966): 234-245.

2899. Horrell, Joyce Taylor. "A 'Shade of a Special Sense': Henry James and the Art of Naming." *AL* 42(1970): 203-220.

2900. Hudspeth, Robert N. "The Definition of Innocence: James's *The Ambassadors." TSLL* 6 (1964): 354-360.

2901. ----------. "A Hard, Shining Sonnet: The Art of Short Fiction in James's 'Europe.'" *SSF* 12(1975): 387-395.

2902. Hutchinson, Stuart. "James's Medal: Options in *The Wings of the Dove." EIC* 27(1977): 315-335.

2903. Hynes, Joseph A. "The Middle Way of Miss Farange: A Study of James's *Maisie." ELH* 32 (1965): 528-552.

2904. ----------. "The Transparent Shroud: Henry James and William Story." *AL* 46(1975): 506-527.

2905. Ives, C. B. "James's Ghosts in *The Turn of the Screw." NCF* 18(1963): 183-189.

2906. Izsak, Emily K. "The Composition of *The Spoils of Poynton." TSLL* 6(1965): 460-471.

2907. Jacobs, Edward Craney. "James's 'Amiable Auditress': An Ironic Pun." *SN* 9(1977): 311.

2908. Jacobson, Marcia. "Convention and Innovation in *The Princess Casamassima." JEGP* 76(1977): 238-254.

2909. ----------. "Literary Convention and Social Criticism in Henry James's *The Awkward Age." PQ* 54(1975): 633-646.

2910. ----------. "Popular Fiction and Henry James's Unpopular *Bostonians." MP* 73(1976): 264-275.

2911. James, Henry. "'A Tragedy of Error': James's First Story, With a Prefatory Note by Leon Edel." [with text] *NEQ* 29(1956): 291-317.

2912. Johnson, Courtney. "John Marcher and the Paradox of the Unfortunate Fall." *SSF* 6(1969): 121-135.

2913. Johnson, Lee Ann. "James's Mrs. Wix: The 'Dim, Crooked Reflector.'" *NCF* 29(1974): 164-172.

2914. ----------. "The Psychology of Characterization: James's Portraits of Verena Tarrant and Olive Chancellor." *SN* 6(1974): 295-303.

2915. Jones, Alexander E. "Point of View in *The Turn of the Screw*." *PMLA* 74(1959): 112-122.

2916. Jones, Granville H. "Henry James's 'Georgina's Reasons': The Under Side of Washington Square." *SSF* 11(1974): 189-194.

2917. Kaston, Carren Osna. "Houses of Fiction in 'What Maisie Knew.'" *Criticism* 18(1976): 27-42.

2918. Kau, Joseph. "Henry James and the Garden: A Symbolic Setting for 'The Beast in the Jungle.'" *SSF* 10(1973): 187-198.

2919. Kaye, Julian B. "*The Awkward Age, The Sacred Fount, and The Ambassadors*." *NCF* 17 (1963): 339-351.

2920. Kimbal, Jean. "The Abyss and the Wings of the Dove: The Image as a Revelation." *NCF* 10(1956): 281-300.

2921. ----------. "Henry James's Last Portrait of a Lady: Charlotte Stant in *The Golden Bowl*." *AL* 28(1957): 449-468.

2922. Kimmey, John L. "*The Bostonians* and *The Princess Casamassima*." *TSLL* 9(1968): 537-546.

2923. ----------. "*The Princess Casamassima* and the Quality of Bewilderment." *NCF* 22(1967): 47-62.

2924. ----------. "*The Tragic Muse* and Its Forerunners." *AL* 41(1970): 518-531.

2925. King, Kimball. "Theory and Practice in the Plays of Henry James." *MD* 10(1967): 24-33.

2926. King, Mary Jane. "The Touch of the Earth: A Word and a Theme in *The Portrait of a Lady*." *NCF* 29(1974): 345-348.

2927. Kinney, William. "The Death of Morgan in James's 'The Pupil.'" *SSF* 8(1971): 317-322.

2928. Knieger, Bernard. "James's 'Paste.'" *SSF* 8(1971): 468-469.

2929. Knoepflmacher, U. C. "'O rare for Strether!': *Antony and Cleopatra* and *The Ambassadors*." *NCF* 19(1965): 333-344.

2930. Koch, Stephen. "Transcendence in *The Wings of the Dove*." *MFS* 12(1966): 93-102.

2931. Korenman, Joan S. "Henry James and the Murderous Mind." *EL* 4(1977): 198-211.

2932. Kornfeld, Milton. "Villainy and Responsibility in *The Wings of the Dove*." *TSLL* 14 (1972): 337-346.

2933. Kraft, Quentin G. "The Central Problem of James's Fictional Thought: From *The Scarlet Letter* to *Roderick Hudson*." *ELH* 36(1969): 440-454.

2934. ----------. "Life Against Death in Venice." *Criticism* 7(1965): 217-223.

2935. Krause, Sydney J. "James's Revisions of the Style of *The Portrait of a Lady*." *AL* 30 (1958): 67-88.

2936. Kretsch, Robert W. "Political Passion in Balzac and Henry James." *NCF* 14(1959): 265-270.

2937. Labrie, Ross. "Henry James's Idea of Consciousness." *AL* 39(1968): 517-529.

2938. Lainoff, Seymour. "A Note on James's 'The Pupil." *NCF* 14(1959): 75-77.

2939. Lebowitz, Naomi. "*The Sacred Fount*: An Author in Search of His Characters." *Criticism* 4(1962): 148-159.

2940. Lemco, Gary. "Henry James and Richard Wagner: *The American*." *HSL* 6(1974): 147-158.

2941. Lerner, Daniel, and Oscar Cargill. "Henry James at the Grecian Urn." *PMLA* 66(1951): 316-331.

2942. Levine, George. "Isabel, Gwendolen, and Dorothea." *ELH* 30(1963): 244-257.

2943. Levy, Leo B. "Henry James's *Confidence* and the Development of the Idea of the Unconscious." *AL* 28(1956): 347-358.

2944. ----------. "A Reading of 'The Figure in the Carpet.'" *AL* 33(1961): 457-465.

2945. Lewis, R. W. B. "The Vision of Grace: James's *The Wings of the Dove*." *MFS* 3(1957): 33-40.

2946. Leyburn, Ellen Douglas. "Virginia Woolf's Judgment of Henry James." *MFS* 5(1959): 166-168.

2947. Lind, Ilse Dusoir. "The Inadequate Vulgarity of Henry James." *PMLA* 66(1951): 886-910.

2948. Lind, Sidney E. "James's 'The Private Life' and Browning." *AL* 23(1951): 315-322.

2949. ----------. "Some Comments on B. R. McElderry's 'The Uncollected Stories of Henry James.'" *AL* 23(1951): 130-131.

2950. Ling, Amy. "The Pagoda Image in Henry James's *The Golden Bowl*." *AL* 46(1974): 383-388.

2951. Lockridge, Ernest H. "A Vision of Art: Henry James's *The Tragic Muse*." *MFS* 12(1966): 83-92.

2952. Lohmann, Christopher K. "Jamesian Irony and the American Sense of Mission." *TSLL* 16(1974): 329-347.

2953. Long, Robert. "Adaptations of Henry James's Fiction for Drama, Opera, and Films; With a Checklist of New York Theatre Critics' Reviews." *ALR* 4(1971): 268-278.

2954. Long, Robert Emmet. "'The Ambassadors' and the Genteel Tradition: James's Correction of Hawthorne and Howells." *NEQ* 42(1969): 44-64.

2955. ----------. "Henry James's Apprenticeship—the Hawthorne Aspect." *AL* 48(1976): 194-216.

2956. ----------. "James's *Roderick Hudson*: The End of the Apprenticeship—Hawthorne and Turgenev." *AL* 48(1976): 312-326.

2957. ----------. "The Society and the Masks: *The Blithedale Romance* and *The Bostonians*." *NCF* 19(1964): 105-122.

2958. ----------. "A Source for Dr. Mary Prance in *The Bostonians*." *NCF* 19(1964): 87-88.

2959. ----------. "Transformations: *The Blithedale Romance* to Howells and James." *AL* 47 (1976): 552-571.

2960. Lucas, John. "*The Spoils of Poynton*." *EIC* 18(1968): 107-111.

2961. ----------. "*The Spoils of Poynton*: James's Intended Uninvolvement." *EIC* 16(1966): 482-489.

2962. Lucke, Jessie Ryon. "The Inception of 'The Beast in the Jungle.'" *NEQ* 26(1953): 529-532.

2963. Luecke, Sister Jane Marie, O.S.B. "*The Princess Casamassima*: Hyacinth's Fallible Consciousness." *MP* 60(1963): 274-280.

2964. Lycette, Ronald L. "Perceptual Touchstones for the Jamesian Artist-Hero." *SSF* 14(1977): 55-62.

2965. Lydenberg, John. "The Governess Turns the Screws." *NCF* 12(1957): 37-38.

2966. MacKenzie, Manfred. "Communities of Knowledge: Secret Society in Henry James." *ELH* 39(1972): 147-168.

2967. ----------. "Henry James: Serialist Early and Late." *PQ* 41(1962): 492-499.

2968. ----------. "Ironic Melodrama in *The Portrait of a Lady*." *MFS* 12(1966): 7-23.

2969. ----------. "*The Turn of the Screw*: Jamesian Gothic." *EIC* 12(1962): 34-38.

2970. Mackle, Elliott. "Two Mistakes by Henry James in 'The American Scene.'" *ALR* 10 (1977): 211-212.

2971. Macnaughton, W. R. "Maisie's Grace Under Pressure: Some Thoughts on James and Hemingway." *MFS* 22(1976): 153-164.

2972. ----------. "The First-Person Narrators of Henry James." *SAF* 2(1974): 145-164.

2973. Maguire, C. E. "James and Dumas, *fils*." *MD* 10(1967): 34-42.

2974. Maixner, Paul. "James on D'Annunzio— 'A High Example of Exclusive Estheticism.'" *Criticism* 13(1971): 291-311.

2975. Mariani, Umberto. "The Italian Experience of Henry James." *NCF* 19(1964): 237-254.

2976. Marovitz, Sanford E. "*Roderick Hudson*: James's *Marble Faun*." *TSLL* 11(1970): 1427-1443.

2977. Martin, Robert K. "Henry James and the Harvard College Library." *AL* 41(1969): 95-103.

2978. Martin, Terence. "Adam Blair and Arthur Dimmesdale: A Lesson from the Master." *AL* 34(1962): 274-279.

2979. ----------. "James's 'The Pupil': The Art of Seeing Through." *MFS* 4(1958): 335-345.

2980. Martineau, Barbara. "Portraits Are Murdered in the Short Fiction of Henry James." *JNT* 2(1972): 16-25.

2981. Maxwell, J. C. "Henry James's 'Poor Wantons': An Unnoticed Version." *NCF* 19(1964): 301-302.

2982. ----------. "The Text of *The Ambassadors*." *EIC* 11(1961): 116, 370.

2983. Mayer, Charles W. "Henry James's 'Indespensible Centre': The Search for Compositional Unity." *EL* 3(1976): 98-105.

2984. Mays, Milton A. "Down-Town with Henry James." *TSLL* 14(1972): 107-122.

2985. ----------. "Henry James, or, The Beast in the Palace of Art." *AL* 39(1968): 467-487.

2986. McCarthy, Harold. "Henry James and the American Aristocracy." *ALR* 4(1971): 61-72.

2987. McClary, Ben Harris. "'In Abject Terror of Rising': An Unpublished Henry James Letter." *ELN* 3(1966): 208-211.

2988. McCloskey, John C. "What Maisie Knows: A Study of Childhood and Adolescence." *AL* 36(1965): 485-513.

2989. McDonald, Walter R. "The Inconsistencies in Henry James's Aesthetics." *TSLL* 10(1969): 585-597.

2990. McElderry, B. R., Jr. "Hamlin Garland and Henry James." *AL* 23(1952): 433-446.

2991. ----------. "The 'Shy, Incongruous Charm' of 'Daisy Miller.'" *NCF* 10(1955): 162-165.

2992. McLean, Robert C. "The Completed Vision: A Study of *Madame de Mauves* and *The Ambassadors*." *MLQ* 28(1967): 446-461.

2993. ----------. "The Subjective Adventure of Fleda Vetch." *AL* 36(1964): 12-30.

2994. McMaster, Juliet. "'The Full Image of a Repetition' in *The Turn of the Screw*." *SSF* 6 (1969): 377-382.

2995. ----------. "The Portrait of Isabel Archer." *AL* 45(1973): 50-66.

2996. McMurray, William. "Pragmatic Realism in *The Bostonians*." *NCF* 16(1962): 339-344.

2997. ----------. "Reality in James's 'The Great Good Place.'" *SSF* 14(1977): 82-83.

2998. Mendelsohn, Michael J. "'Drop a Tear . . .': Henry James Dramatizes *Daisy Miller*." *MD* 7(1964): 60-64.

2999. Menikoff, Barry. "A House Divided: A New Reading of *The Bostonians*." *CLA* 20(1977): 459-474.

3000. Mercer, Caroline G. "Adam Verver, Yankee Businessman." *NCF* 22(1967): 251-269.

3001. Miller, J. Hillis. "Narrative and History." *ELH* 41(1974): 455-473.

3002. Mills, A. R. "*The Portrait of a Lady* and Dr. Leavis." *EIC* 14(1964): 380-387.

3003. Miner, Earl Roy. "Henry James's Metaphysical Romances." *NCF* 9(1954): 1-21.

3004. Mogen, David. "Agonies of Innocence: The Governess and Maggie Verver." *ALR* 9(1976): 231-242.

3005. Monteiro, George. "Another Princess." *PQ* 41(1962): 517-518.

3006. ----------. "A Contemporary View of Henry James and Oscar Wilde, 1882." *AL* 35(1964): 528-530.

3007. ----------. "Hawthorne, James, and the Destructive Self." *TSLL* 4(1962): 58-71.

3008. ----------. "Henry James and Scott Fitzgerald: A Source." *NCL* 6(March, 1976): 4-6.

3009. ----------. Henry James and the American Academy of Arts and Letters." *NEQ* 36(1963): 82-84.

3010. ----------. "Some Unpublished Letters of Henry James to John Hay." [with text] *TSLL* 4 (1963): 639-695.

3011. Mooney, Stephen. "James, Keats, and the Religion of Consciousness." *MLQ* 22(1961): 399-401.

3012. Moore, John Robert. "An Imperfection in the Art of Henry James." *NCF* 13(1959): 351-358.

3013. Morgan, Alice. "Henry James: Money and Morality." *TSLL* 12(1970): 75-92.

3014. Morris, R. A. "Classical Vision and the American City: Henry James's *The Bostonians*." *NEQ* 46(1973): 543-557.

3015. Morrison, Sister Kristen. "James's and Lubbock's Differing Points of View." *NCF* 16 (1961): 245-255.

3016. Muecke, D. C. "The Dove's Flight." *NCF* 9(1954): 76-78.

3017. Murray, Donald W. "Henry James and the English Reviewers, 1882-1890." *AL* 24(1952): 1-20.

3018. Nance, William. "'The Beast in the Jungle': Two Versions of Oedipus." *SSF* 13(1976): 433-440.

3019. ----------. *What Maisie Knew:* The Myth of the Artist." *SN* 8(1976): 88-102.

3020. Nash, Christopher. "Henry James as Puppetmaster: The Narrative Status of Maria Gostrey, Susan Stringham, and Fanny Assingham as *Ficelles*." *SN* 9(1977): 297-310.

3021. Nettels, Elsa. "*The Ambassadors* and the Sense of the Past." *MLQ* 31(1970): 220-235.

3022. ----------. "James and Conrad on the Art of Fiction." *TSLL* 14(1972): 529-543.

3023. Nicholas, Charles A. "A Second Glance at Henry James's 'The Death of the Lion'." *SSF* 9(1972): 143-146.

3024. Nicoloff, Philip L. "At the Bottom of Things in Henry James's 'Louisa Pallant'." *SSF* 7(1970): 409-420.

3025. Niemtzow, Annette. "Marriage and the New Woman in *The Portrait of a Lady*." *AL* 47(1975): 377-395.

3026. O'Grady, Walter. "On Plot in Modern Fiction: Hardy, James, and Conrad." *MFS* 11(1965): 107-115.

3027. Ohmann, Carol. "*Daisy Miller:* A Study of Changing Intentions." *AL* 36(1964): 1-11.

3028. Owen, Elizabeth. "The 'Given Appearance' of Charlotte Verver." *EIC* 13(1963): 364-374.

3029. Page, Philip. "The Curious Narration of *The Bostonians*." *AL* 46(1974): 374-383.

3030. Parker, Hershel. "An Error in the Text of James's *The American*." *AL* 37(1965): 316-318.

3031. Paterson, John. "The Language of 'Adventure' in Henry James." *AL* 32(1960): 291-301.

3032. Pearce, Howard. "Henry James's Pastoral Fallacy." *PMLA* 90(1975): 834-847.

3033. ----------. "Witchcraft Imagery and Allusion in James's *Bostonians*." *SN* 6(1974): 236-247.

3034. Perloff, Marjorie. "Cinderalla Becomes the Wicked Stepmother: *The Portrait of a Lady* as Ironic Fairy Tale." *NCF* 23(1969): 413-433.

3035. Perrin, Edwin N. "'The Golden Bowl.'" *EIC* 5(1955): 189-190.

3036. Person, Leland, Jr. "Aesthetic Headaches and American Women in *The Marble Faun* and *The American*." *SAF* 4(1976): 65-79.

3037. Phillips, Norma. "*The Sacred Fount:* The Narrator and the Vampires." *PMLA* 76(1961): 407-412.

3038. Popkin, Henry. "The Two Theatres of Henry James." *NEQ* 24(1951): 69-83.

3039. Powers, Lyall H. "Henry James and the Ethics of the Artist." *TSLL* 3(1961): 360-368.

3040. ----------. "James's Debt to Alphonse Daudet." *Comp L* 24(1972): 150-162.

3041. ----------. "James's *The Tragic Muse*—Ave atque Vale." *PMLA* 73(1958): 270-274.

3042. ----------. "Mr. James's Aesthetic Mr. Nash—Again." *NCF* 13(1959): 341-349.

3043. ----------. "*The Portrait of a Lady:* 'The Eternal Mystery of Things.'" *NCF* 14(1959): 143-155.

3044. ----------. "A Reperusal of James's 'The Figure in the Carpet.'" *AL* 33(1961): 224-228.

3045. Purdy, Strother B. "Conversation and Awareness in Henry James's 'A Round of Visits.'" *SSF* 6(1969): 421-432.

3046. ----------. "Henry James and the Sacred Thrill." *PQ* 48(1969): 247-260.

3047. Raleigh, John Henry. "Henry James: The Poetics of Empiricism." *PMLA* 66(1951): 107-123.

3048. Ranald, Ralph A. "*The Sacred Fount:* James's Portrait of the Artist Manqué." *NCF* 15 (1960): 239-249.

3049. Recchia, Edward. "James's 'The Figure in the Carpet': The Quality of Fictional Experience." *SSF* 10(1973): 357-365.

3050. Reid, Stephen. "Moral Passion in *The Portrait of a Lady* and *The Spoils of Poynton*." *MFS* 12(1960): 24-43.

3051. Reilly, Robert J. "Henry James and the Morality of Fiction." *AL* 39(1967): 1-30.

3052. Reiman, Donald H. "The Inevitable Imitation: The Narrator in 'The Author of *Beltraffio*.'" *TSLL* 3(1962): 503-509.

3053. Reynolds, Larry J. "Henry James's New Christopher Newman." *SN* 5(1973): 457-468.

3054. Riddel, Joseph N. "F. Scott Fitzgerald, the Jamesian Inheritance, and the Morality of Fiction." *MFS* 11(1965): 331-350.

3055. Rodenbeck, John. "The Bolted Door in James's *Portrait of a Lady*." *MFS* 10(1964): 330-340.

3056. Roper, Alan H. "The Moral and Metaphorical Meaning of *The Spoils of Poynton*." *AL* 32 (1960): 182-196.

3057. Rose, Alan. "The Spatial Form of *The Golden Bowl*." *MFS* 12(1966): 103-116.

3058. Rose, Shirley. "Waymarsh's 'Sombre Glow' and der Fliegende Holländer." *AL* 45(1973): 438-441.

3059. Rosenbaum, S. P. "Henry James and Creativity: 'The Logic of the Particular Case'." *Criticism* 8(1966): 44-52.

3060. ----------. "Letters to the Pell-Clarkes from Their 'Old Cousin and Friend' Henry James." *AL* 31(1959): 46-58.

3061. ----------. "Two Henry James Letters on *The American* and *Watch and Ward*." *AL* 30(1959): 533-537.

3062. Rosenblatt, Jason P. "Bridegroom and Bride in 'The Jolly Corner.'" *SSF* 14(1977): 282-284.

3063. Ross, Morton L. "James's 'The Birthplace': A Double Turn of the Narrative Screw." *SSF* 3(1966): 321-328.

3064. Rountree, Benjamin C. "James's Madame de Mauves and Madame de La Fayette's Princess de Clèves." *SSF* 1(1964): 264-271.

3065. Rouse, H. Blair. "Charles Dickens and Henry James: Two Approaches to the Art of Fiction." *NCF* 5(1950): 151-157.

3066. Routh, Michael. "Isabel Archer's 'Inconsequence': A Motif Analysis of *The Portrait of a Lady*." *JNT* 7(1977): 128-141.

3067. Rowe, John Carlos. "The Authority of the Sign in Henry James's 'The Sacred Fount.'" *Criticism* 19(1977): 223-241.

3068. ----------. "The Symbolization of Milly Theale: Henry James's *The Wings of the Dove*." *ELH* 40(1973): 131-164.

3069. Rubin, Louis D., Jr. "One More Turn of the Screw." *MFS* 9(1963): 314-328.

3070. Ruthrof, H. G. "A Note on Henry James's Psychological Realism and the Concept of Brevity." *SSF* 12(1975): 369-373.

3071. Rypins, Harold L., ed. by Leon Edel. "Henry James in Harley Street." *AL* 24(1953): 481-492.

3072. Sabiston, Elizabeth. "The Prison of Womanhood." *Comp L* 25(1973): 336-351.

3073. Sacks, Sheldon. "Novelists as Story-tellers." *MP* 73(1976): S97-S109.

3074. Samuels, Charles Thomas. "At the Bottom of the *Fount.*" *Novel* 2(1968): 46-54.

3075. Sandeen, Ernest. *The Wings of the Dove* and *The Portrait of a Lady:* A Study of Henry James's Later Phase." *PMLA* 69(1954): 1060-1075.

3076. Schecter, Harold. "The Unpardonable Sin in 'Washington Square.'" *SSF* 10(1973): 137-141.

3077. Schneider, Daniel J. "The Divided Self in the Fiction of Henry James." *PMLA* 90 (1975): 447-460.

3078. ----------. "The Ironic Imagery and Symbolism of James's *The Ambassadors.*" *Criticism* 9(1967): 174-196.

3079. ----------. "The Unreliable Narrator: James' *The Aspern Papers.*" *SSF* 13(1976): 43-49.

3080. Schneider, Sister Lucy, C.S.J. "Osculation and Integration: Isabel Archer in the One-Kiss Novel." *CLA* 10(1966): 149-161.

3081. Schrero, Elliot M. "The Narrator's Palace of Thought in *The Sacred Fount.*" *MP* 68 (1971): 269-288.

3082. Schriber, Mary S. "Isabel Archer and Victorian Manners." *SN* 8(1976): 441-457.

3083. Schulz, Max F. "The Bellegardes' Feud with Christopher Newman: A Study of Henry James's Revision of *The Americans.*" *AL* 27(1955): 42-55.

3084. Scoggins, James. "'The Author of *Beltraffio*': A Reapportionment of Guilt." *TSLL* 5(1963): 265-270.

3085. Sebouhian, George. "Henry James's Transcendental Imagination." *EL* 3(1976): 214-226.

3086. Secor, Robert. "Christopher Newman: How Innocent is James's American?" *SAF* 1(1973): 141-153.

3087. Segal, Ora. *The Liar:* A Lesson in Devotion." *RES* 16(1965): 272-281.

3088. ----------. "The Weak Wings of Pride: An Interpretation of James's 'The Bench of Desolation.'" *NCF* 20(1965): 145-154.

3089. Segnitz, T. M. "The Actual Genesis of Henry James's 'Paste.'" *AL* 36(1964): 216-219.

3090. Selig, Robert. "The Red Haired Lady Orator: Parallel Passages in *The Bostonians* and *Adam Bede.*" *NCF* 16(1961): 164-169.

3091. Sharp, Robert L. "Stevenson and James's Childhood." *NCF* 8(1953): 236-237.

3092. Shelden, Pamela Jacobs. "James Gothicism: The Haunted Castle of the Mind." *SLI* 7,#1 (1974): 121-134.

3093. Short, R. W. "Henry James's World of Images." *PMLA* 68(1953): 943-960.

3094. ----------. "Some Critical Terms of Henry James." *PMLA* 65(1950): 667-680.

3095. Shroeder, John W. "The Mothers of Henry James." *AL* 22(1951): 424-431.

3096. Shulman, Robert. "Henry James and the Modern Comedy of Knowledge." *Criticism* 10(1968): 41-53.

3097. Silver, John. "A Note on the Freudian Reading of 'The Turn of the Screw.'" *AL* 29(1957): 207-211.

3098. Silverstein, Henry. "The Utopia of Henry James." *NEQ* 35(1962): 458-468.

3099. Slabey, Robert M. "Henry James and 'The Most Impressive Convention in All History.'" *AL* 30(1958): 89-102.

3100. ----------. "'The Turn of the Screw': Grammar and Optics." *CLA* 9(1965): 68-72.

3101. Smith, Carl S. "James's Travels, Travel Writings, and the Development of His Art." *MLQ* 38(1977): 367-380.

3102. Smith, Charles R. "'The Lesson of the Master': An Interpretative Note." *SSF* 6(1969): 654-658.

3103. Smith, J. Oates. "Henry James and Virginia Woolf: The Art of Relationships." *TCL* 10(1964): 119-129.

3104. Snow, Lotus. "The Disconcerting Poetry of Mary Temple: A Comparison of the Imagery of *The Portrait of a Lady* and *The Wings of the Dove.*" *NEQ* 31(1958): 312-339.

3105. ----------. "'The Prose and the Modesty of the Matter': James's Imagery for the Artist in *Roderick Hudson* and *The Tragic Muse.*" *MFS* 12(1966): 61-82.

3106. ----------. "'A Story of Cabinets and Chairs and Tables': Images of Morality in 'The Spoils of Poynton' and 'The Golden Bowl'." *ELH* 30 (1963): 413-435.

3107. Spanos, Bebe. "The Real Princess Christina." *PQ* 38(1959): 488-496.

3108. Sparshott, F. E. "An Aspect of Literary Portraiture." *EIC* 15(1965): 359-360.

3109. Speck, Paul S. "A Structural Analysis of James's *Roderick Hudson.*" *SN* 2(1970): 292-304.

3110. Spencer, James L. "Symbolism in James's *The Golden Bowl.*" *MFS* 3(1957): 333-334.

3111. Spilka, Mark. "Henry James and Walter Besant: The 'Art of Fiction' Controversy." *Novel* 6(1973): 101-119.

3112. Stafford, William T. "The Ending of James's *The American:* A Defense of the Early Version." *NCF* 18(1963): 86-89.

3113. ----------. "Henry James the American: Some Views of His Contemporaries." *TCL* 1(1955): 69-76.

3114. ----------. "James Examines Shakespeare: Notes on the Nature of Genius." *PMLA* 73 (1958): 123-135.

3115. ----------. "Literary Allusions in James's Prefaces." *AL* 35(1963): 60-70.

3116. ----------. "Lowell 'Edits' James: Some Revisions in *French Poets and Novelists.*" *NEQ* 32(1959): 92-98.

3117. ----------. "A Whale, An Heiress, and a Southern Demigod: Three Symbolic Americans." *Coll L* 1(1974): 100-112.

3118. Stallman, R. W. "'The Sacred Rage': The Time-Theme in *The Ambassadors.*" *MFS* 3(1957): 41-56.

3119. ----------. "Who was Gilbert Osmond?" *MFS* 4(1958): 127-135.

3120. Stambaugh, Sara. "The Aesthetic Movement and *The Portrait of a Lady*." *NCF* 30 (1976): 495-510.

3121. Stein, Allen F. "The Beast in 'The Jolly Corner': Spencer Brydon's Ironic Rebirth." *SSF* 11(1974): 61-66.

3122. ----------. "The Hack's Progress: A Reading of James's 'The Velvet Glove.'" *EL* 1 (1974): 219-226.

3123. Stein, William Bysshe. "*The Aspern Papers*: A Comedy of Masks." *NCF* 14(1959): 172-178.

3124. ----------. "The Method at the Heart of Madness: *The Spoils of Poynton*." *MFS* 14(1968): 187-202.

3125. ----------. "'The Sacred Fount': The Poetics of Nothing." *Criticism* 14(1972): 373-389.

3126. Stevens, A. Wilbur. "Henry James' *The American Scene*: The Vision of Value." *TCL* 1(1955): 27-33.

3127. Stoehr, Taylor. "Words and Deeds in *The Princess Casamassima*." *ELH* 37(1970): 95-135.

3128. Stone, Edward. "Edition Architecture and 'The Turn of the Screw.'" *SSF* 13(1976): 9-16.

3129. ----------. "From Henry James to John Balderston: Relativity and the '20's.'" *MFS* 1,#2(1955): 2-11.

3130. ----------. "A Further Note on *Daisy Miller* and Cherbuliez." *PQ* 29(1950): 213-216.

3131. Stone, William. "On the Background of James's 'In the Cage.'" *ALR* 6(1973): 243-248.

3132. Stovall, Floyd. "Henry James's 'The Jolly Corner.'" *NCF* 12(1957): 72-84.

3133. Tanner, Tony. "The Literary Children of James and Clemens." *NCF* 16(1961): 205-218.

3134. Tartella, Vincent. "James's 'Four Meetings': Two Texts Compared." *NCF* 15(1960): 17-28.

3135. Terrie, Henry L., Jr. "Henry James and the 'Explosive Principle.'" *NCF* 15(1961): 283-299.

3136. Theobald, John R. "New Reflections on *The Golden Bowl*." *TCL* 3(1957): 20-26.

3137. Thomas, William B. "The Author's Voice in *The Ambassadors*." *JNT* 1(1971): 108-121.

3138. Thorberg, Raymond. "*Germaine*, James's *Notebooks*, and *The Wings of the Dove*." *Comp L* 22(1970): 254-264.

3139. Tick, Stanley. "Henry James's *The American*: *Voyons*." *SN* 2(1970): 276-291.

3140. Tilford, John E., Jr. "James the Old Intruder." *MFS* 4(1958): 157-164.

3141. Tintner, Adeline R. "Autobiography as Fiction: 'The Usurping Consciousness' as Hero of James's Memoirs." *TCL* 23(1977): 239-260.

3142. ----------. "Balzac's 'Madame Firmaini' and James's *The Ambassadors*." *Comp L* 25 (1973): 128-135.

3143. ----------. "Balzac's Two Maries and James's *The Ambassadors*." *ELN* 9(1972): 284-287.

3144. ----------. "The Countess and Scholastica: Henry James's 'L'Allegro' and 'Il Penseroso.'" *SSF* 11(1974): 267-276.

3145. ----------. "Henry James Criticism: A Current Perspective." *ALR* 7(1974): 155-168.

3146. ----------. "Hyacinth at the Play: the Play within the Play as a Novelistic Device in James." *JNT* 2(1972): 171-185.

3147. ----------. "Iconic Analogy in 'The Lesson of the Master': Henry James's Legend of Saint George and the Dragon." *JNT* 5(1975): 116-127.

3148. ----------. "The Influence of Balzac's 'L'Envers de I'Histoire Contemporaine' on James's 'The Great Good Place.'" *SSF* 9(1972): 343-351.

3149. ----------. "Isabel's Carriage-Image and Emma's Daydream." *MFS* 22(1976): 227-231.

3150. ----------. "James and Balzac: *The Bostonians* and 'La Fille aux yeux d'or.'" *Comp L* 29(1977): 241-254.

3151. ----------. "James's Mock Epic: 'The Velvet Glove', Edith Wharton, and Other Late Tales." *MFS* 17(1971): 483-499.

3152. ----------. "Keats and James and *The Princess Casamassima*." *NCF* 28(1973): 179-193.

3153. ----------. "The Metamorphoses of Edith Wharton in Henry James's *The Finer Grain*." *TCL* 21(1975): 355-380.

3154. ----------. "'The Old Things': Balzac's *Le Cure de Tours* and James's *The Spoils of Poynton*." *NCF* 26(1972): 436-455.

3155. ----------. "Review Essay: A Portrait of the Novelist as a Young Man. The Letters of Henry James." *SN* 8(1976): 121-128.

3156. ----------. "Review-Essay: Eight Ways of Looking at James." *SN* 9(1977): 73-94.

3157. ----------. "Why James Quoted Gibbon in 'Glasses.'" *SSF* 14(1977): 287-288.

3158. Todasco, Ruth Taylor. "Theme and Imagery in *The Golden Bowl*." *TSLL* 4(1962): 228-240.

3159. Tompkins, James P. "'The Beast in the Jungle': An Analysis of James's Late Style." *MFS* 16(1970): 185-191.

3160. Tompkins, Jane P. "The Redemption of Time in *Notes of a Son and Brother*." *TSLL* 14 (1973): 681-690.

3161. Trachtenberg, Stanley. "The Return of the Screw." *MFS* 11(1965): 180-182.

3162. Traschen, Isadore. "An American in Paris." *AL* 26(1954): 67-77.

3163. ----------. "Henry James and The Art of Revision." *PQ* 35(1956): 39-47.

3164. ----------. "James's Revision of the Love Affair in *The American*." *NEQ* 29(1956): 43-62.

3165. Tribble, Joseph L. "Cherbuliez's *Le Roman d'une Honnête Femme*: Another Source of James's *The Portrait of a Lady*." *AL* 40(1968): 279-293.

3166. Tuveson, Ernest. "'The Jolly Corner': A Fable of Redemption." *SSF* 12(1975): 271-280.

3167. ----------. "*The Turn of the Screw*: A Palimpsest." *SEL* 12(1972): 783-800.

3168. Tyler, Parker. "*The Sacred Fount*: 'The Actuality Pretentious and Vain' vs. 'The Case Rich and Edifying.'" *MFS* 9(1963): 127-138.

3169. Uroff, M. D. "Perception in James's 'The Real Thing.'" *SSF* 9(1972): 41-46.

3170. Veeder, William. "Strether and the Transcendence of Language." *MP* 69(1971): 116-132.

3171. Vincec, Sister Stephanie. "A Significant Revision in *The Wings of the Dove*." RES 23(1972): 58-61.

3172. Volpe, Edmond L. "James's Theory of Sex in Fiction." NCF 13(1958): 36-47.

3173. Waldron, Randall H. "Prefiguration in 'The Beast in the Jungle.'" SAF 1(1973): 101-104.

3174. Wallace, Ronald. "Gabriel Nash: Henry James's Comic Spirit." NCF 28(1973): 220-224.

3175. Ward, J. A. "*The Ambassadors*: Strether's Vision of Evil." NCF 14(1959): 45-58.

3176. ----------. "The Double Structure of *Watch and Ward*." TSLL 4(1963): 613-624.

3177. ----------. "Henry James and the Nature of Evil." TCL 6(1960): 65-69.

3178. ----------. "The Ineffectual Heroes of James's Middle Period." TSLL 2(1960): 315-327.

3179. ----------. "James's Idea of Structure." PMLA 80(1965): 419-426.

3180. ----------. "James's *The Europeans* and the Structure of Comedy." NCF 19(1964): 1-16.

3181. ----------. "Social Disintegration in *The Wings of the Dove*." Criticism 2(1960): 190-203.

3182. ----------. "Structural Irony in *Madame de Mauves*." SSF 2(1965): 170-182.

3183. Ward, Susan P. "Painting and Europe in *The American*." AL 46(1975): 566-573.

3184. Warner, John N. "'In View of Other Matters': The Religious Dimension of *The Ambassadors*." EL 4(1977): 78-94.

3185. Wasiolek, Edward. "Tolstoy's *The Death of Ivan Ilych* and Jamesian Fictional Imperatives." MFS 6(1960): 314-324.

3186. Watanabe, Hisayoshi. "Past Perfect Retrospection in the Style of Henry James." AL 34(1962): 165-181.

3187. Watkins, Floyd C. "Christopher Newman's Final Instinct." NCF 12(1957): 85-88.

3188. Watt, Ian. "The First Paragraph of *The Ambassadors*: An Explication." EIC 10(1960): 250-274.

3189. ----------. "The Text of *The Ambassadors*." EIC 11(1961): 116-119.

3190. Weber, Carl J. "Henry James and His Tiger-Cat." PMLA 68(1953): 672-687.

3191. Wegelin, Christof. "The 'Internationalism' of *The Golden Bowl*." NCF 11(1956): 161-181.

3192. ----------. "Jamesian Biography." NCF 19(1963): 283-287.

3193. Wellek, René. "Henry James's Literary Theory and Criticism." AL 30(1958): 293-321.

3194. West, Muriel. "The Death of Miles in *The Turn of the Screw*." PMLA 79(1964): 283-288.

3195. Westbrook, Perry D. "The Supersubtle Fry." NCF 8(1953): 134-140.

3196. White, William. "Unpublished Henry James on Whitman." RES 20(1969): 321-322.

3197. Wilkins, M. S. "A Note on *The Princess Casamassima*." NCF 12(1957): 88.

3198. Wilson, James D. "The Gospel According to Christopher Newman." SAF 3(1975): 83-88.

3199. Wilt, Judith. "A Right Issue from the Tight Place: Henry James and Maria Gostrey." JNT 6(1976): 77-91.

3200. Winner, Viola Hopkins. "The Artist and The Man in 'The Author of Beltraffio.'" PMLA 83(1968): 102-108.

3201. ----------. "Pictoralism in Henry James's Theory of the Novel." Criticism 9(1967): 1-21.

3202. Wood, Carl. "Frederich Winterbourne, James's Prisoner of Chillon." SN 9(1977): 33-45.

3203. Woodward, Robert. "*Punch* on Howells and James." ALR 3(1970): 76-77.

3204. Worden, Ward S. "A Cut Version of *What Masie Knew*." AL 24(1953): 493-504.

3205. ----------. "Henry James's *What Masie Knew*: A Comparison with the Plans in *The Notebooks*." PMLA 68(1953): 371-383.

3206. Wright, Walter. "Maggie Verver: Neither Saint nor Witch." NCF 12(1957): 59-71.

3207. Yeazell, Ruth. "The 'New Arithmetic' of Henry James." Criticism 16(1974): 109-119.

3208. ----------. "Talking in James." PMLA 91(1976): 66-77.

3209. Young, Robert E. "An Error in *The Ambassadors*." AL 22(1950): 244-253.

3210. ----------. "A Final Note on *The Ambassadors*." AL 23(1952): 487-490.

3211. Zietlow, Edward R. "A Flaw in *The American*." CLA 9(1966): 246-254.

3212. Zimmerman, Everett. "Literary Tradition and 'The Turn of the Screw.'" SSF 7(1970): 634-637.

See also 80, 93, 108, 436, 618, 1123, 3288, 4404, 6223, 7554, 19126, 19650.

JAMES, WILLIAM. 3213. Franklin, Phyllis. "The Influence of William James on Robert Herrick's Early Fiction." ALR 7(1974): 395-402.

3214. LeClair, Robert C. "William James to Theodore Flournoy of Geneva: Some Unpublished Letters." NEQ 26(1953): 512-523.

3215. Hoffman, Frederick J. "William James and the Modern Literary Consciousness." Criticism 4(1962): 1-13.

3216. Hull, Byron D. "'Henderson the Rain King' and William James." Criticism 13(1971): 402-414.

3217. Stafford, William T. "Emerson and the James Family." AL 24(1953): 433-461.

JEWETT, SARAH ORNE. 3218. Berthoff, Warner. "The Art of Jewett's *Pointed Firs*." NEQ 32(1959): 31-53.

3219. Bishop, Ferman. "Henry James Criticizes *The Tory Lover*." AL 27(1955): 262-264.

3220. ----------. "Sarah Orne Jewett's Ideas of Race." NEQ 30(1957): 243-249.

3221. Cary, Richard. "The Other Face of Jewett's Coin." ALR 2(1969): 263-270.

3222. ----------. "Sarah Orne Jewett (1849-1909)." [bibliography] ALR 1,#1(1967): 61-65.

3223. Eakin, Paul John. "Sarah Orne Jewett and the Meaning of Country Life." AL 38(1967): 508-531.

3224. Eichelberger, Clayton L. "Sarah Orne Jewett (1849-1909): A Critical Bibliography of Secondary Comment." ALR 2(1969): 189-262.

3225. Fike, Francis. "An Interpretation of *Pointed Firs*." *NEQ* 34(1961): 478-492.

3226. Humma, John B. "The Art and Meaning of Sarah Orne Jewett's 'The Courting of Sister Wisby'." *SSF* 10(1973): 85-91.

3227. Magowan, Robin. "Fromentin and Jewett: Pastoral Narrative in the Nineteenth Century." *Comp L* 16(1964): 331-337.

3228. ----------. "Pastoral and the Art of Landscape in the Country of the Pointed Firs." *NEQ* 36(1963): 229-240.

3229. Parker, John Austin. "Sarah Orne Jewett's 'Boat Song.'" *AL* 23(1951): 133-136.

3230. Smith, Eleanor M. "The Literary Relationship of Sarah Orne Jewett and Willa Sibert Cather." *NEQ* 29(1956): 472-492.

3231. Toth, Susan Allen. "Sarah Orne Jewett and Friends: A Community of Interest." *SSF* 9(1972): 233-241.

3232. ---------. "The Value of Age in the Fiction of Sarah Orne Jewett." *SSF* 8(1971: 433-441.

3232a. Waggoner, Hyatt H. "The Unity of *The Country of the Pointed Firs*." *TCL* 5(1959): 67-73.

See also 598.

KENNEDY, JOHN P. 3233. Eby, Cecil D., Jr. "John Pendleton Kennedy Was Not 'X.M.C.'." *AL* 31(1959): 332-334.

3234. Ellison, Rhoda Coleman. "An Interview with Horse-Shoe Robinson." *AL* 31(1959): 329-332.

3235. Osborne, William S. "'The Swiss Traveler' Essays: Earlist Literary Writings of John Pendleton Kennedy." *AL* 30(1958): 228-233.

3236. Ringe, Donald. "The American Revolution in American Romance." *AL* 49(1977): 352-365.

See also 602a.

KENNEDY, WILLIAM SLOAN. 3237. Hendrick, George. "Unpublished Notes on Whitman in William Sloan Kennedy's Diary." *AL* 34(1962): 279-285.

KING, GRACE. 3238. Bush, Robert. "Charles Gayarré and Grace King: Letters of a Louisiana Friendship." *SLJ* 7,#1(1974): 100-131.

3239. ----------. "Grace King (1852-1932)." *ALR* 8(1975): 43-52.

3240. ----------. "Grace King and Mark Twain." *AL* 44(1972): 31-51.

KIRKLAND, JOSEPH. 3241. Eichelberger, Clayton. "Edgar Watson Howe and Joseph Kirkland: More Critical Secondary Comment." *ALR* 4 (1971): 279-290.

3242. Henson, Clyde. "Joseph Kirkland (1830-1894)." [bibliography] *ALR* 1,#1(1967): 67-70.

3243. ----------. "Joseph Kirkland's Influence on Hamlin Garland." *AL* 23(1952): 458-463.

3244. Holaday, Clayton A. "Kirkland's *Captain of Company K*: A Twice Told Tale." *AL* 25 (1953): 62-68.

3245. ----------. "A Note on Kirkland's Autobiographical Writing." *ALR* 2(1969): 75-77.

3246. "Joseph Kirkland (1830-1893): A Critical Bibliography of Secondary Comment." *ALR* 2(1969): 51-69.

3247. Lease, Benjamin. "The Joseph Kirkland Papers." *ALR* 2(1969): 73-75.

3248. ----------. "Realism and Joseph Kirkland's *Zury*." *AL* 23(1952): 464-466.

3249. Monteiro, George. "A Note on the Realism of Joseph Kirkland." *ALR* 2(1969): 77-78.

3250. Roberts, Audrey. "Two Additions to the Joseph Kirkland Canon." *ALR* 6(1973): 252-254.

3251. Roberts, Audrey J. "'Word-Murder': An Early Joseph Kirkland Essay Published Anonymously." *ALR* 6(1973): 73-79.

See also 598.

KNAPP, SAMUEL. 3252. Loomis, Emerson Robert. "The Godwins in *The Letters of Shahcoolen*." *NCF* 17(1962): 78-80.

3253. McClary, Ben Harris. "A Note on *Letters of Shahcoolen*." *NCF* 17(1962): 288.

LANIER, SIDNEY. 3254. Antippas, A. P., and Carol Flake. "Sidney Lanier's Letters to Clare deGraffenreid." *AL* 45(1973): 182-206.

3255. Beavor, Joseph. "Lanier's Use of Science for Poetic Imagery." *AL* 24(1953): 520-533.

3256. Parks, Edd Winfield. "Lanier's 'Night and Day.'" *AL* 30(1958): 117-118.

3257. Ross, Robert H. "'The Marshes of Glynn': A Study in Symbolic Obscurity." *AL* 32 (1961): 403-416.

3258. Suendsen, Kester. "Lanier's Cone of Night: An Early Poetic Commonplace." *AL* 26(1954): 93-94.

See also 2706.

LEGARÉ, HUGH SWINTON. 3259. Kibler, James. Legaré's First Poems and His Early Career." *SLJ* 6,#1(1973): 70-76.

3260. Welsh, John R. "An Early Pioneer: Legaré's *Southern Review*." *SLJ* 3,#2(1971): 79-97.

LESLIE, ELIZA. See 2185.

LEWIS, HENRY CLAY. 3261. Rose, Alan H. "The Image of the Negro in the Writings of Henry Clay Lewis." *AL* 41(1969): 255-263.

LIPPARD, GEORGE. 3262. Ridgely, J. V. "George Lippard's *The Quaker City*: The World of American Porno-Gothic." *SLI* 7,#1(1974): 77-94.

LOCKE, DAVID ROSS. 3263. Austin, James. "David Ross Locke (1833-1888, pseud. Petroleum V. Nasby)." *ALR* 4(1971): 192-200.

LOCKHART, JOHN G. 3264. Martin, Terence. "Adam Blair and Arthur Dimmesdale: A Lesson from the Master." *AL* 34(1962): 274-279.

LODGE, GEORGE CABOT. 3265. Crowley, John W. "George Cabot Lodge (1873-1909)." [bibliography] *ALR* 6(1973): 45-50.

3266. Riggs, Thomas, Jr. "Prometheus 1900." *AL* 22(1951): 399-423.

See also 1192.

LONGFELLOW, HENRY WADSWORTH. 3267. Allaback, Steven. "Longfellow's 'Galgano.'" *AL* 46 (1974): 210-219.

3268. Austin, James C. "J. T. Fields and the Revision of Longfellow's Poems: Unpublished Correspondence." *NEQ* 24(1951): 239-250.

3269. Cox, James M. "Longfellow and Cross of Snow." *PMLA* 75(1960): 97-100.

3270. Elmen, Paul. "A New Longfellow Letter." *AL* 25(1954): 498-499.

3271. Golden, Samuel A. "Longfellow, Potgieter, and Pijnappel." *AL* 37(1965): 312-315.

3272. Griffith, John. "Longfellow and Herder and the Sense of History." *TSLL* 13(1971): 249-265.

3273. Hart, Loring E. "The Beginnings of Longfellow's Fame." *NEQ* 36(1963): 63-76.

3274. Hilen, Andrew. "Longfellow's 'A Lay of Courage.'" *PMLA* 67(1952): 949-959.

3275. Johnson, Harvey L. "Longfellow and Portuguese Language and Literature." *Comp L* 17 (1965): 225-233.

3276. Morrison, Robert Haywood. "An Apparent Influence of Thomas Moore on Longfellow." *PQ* 35(1956): 198-200.

3277. Moyne, Ernest J. and Tauno F. Mustanoja. "Longfellow's *Song of Hiawatha* and *Kalevala*." *AL* 25(1953): 87-89.

3278. Nyland, Waino. "*Kalevala* as a Reputed Source of Longfellow's *Song of Hiawatha*." *AL* 22(1950): 1-20.

3279. Pauly, Thomas H. "*Outre-Mer* and Longfellow's Quest for a Career." *NEQ* 50(1977): 30-52.

3280. Sears, Donald A. "Folk Poetry in Longfellow's Boyhood." *NEQ* 45(1972): 96-105.

3281. Shuman, R. Baird. "Longfellow, Poe, and *The Waif*." *PMLA* 76(1961): 155-156.

3282. Tichi, Cecelia. "Longfellow's Motives for the Structure of 'Hiawatha.'" *AL* 42 (1971): 548-553.

3283. Tryon, W. S. "Nationalism and International Copyright: Tennyson and Longfellow in America." *AL* 24(1952): 301-309.

3284. Von Abele, Rudolph. "A Note on Longfellow's Poetic." *AL* 24(1952): 77-83.

3285. Ward, Robert Stafford. "Longfellow's Roots in Yankee Soil." *NEQ* 41(1968): 180-192.

3286. Zimmerman, Michael. "War and Peace: Longfellow's 'The Occultation of Orion.'" *AL* 38(1967): 540-546.

See also 460, 620, 2287, 2371.

LOOMIS, CHARLES B.   3287. Hagemann, E. R. "'Correspondents Three' in the Graeco-Turkish War: Some Parodies." *AL* 30(1958): 339-344.

LOWELL, JAMES RUSSELL.   3288. Allott, Miriam. "James Russell Lowell: A Link Between Tennyson and Henry James." *RES* 6(1955): 399-401.

3289. Anderson, John Q. "Lowell's 'The Washers of the Shroud' and the Celtic Legend of the Washer of the Ford." *AL* 35(1963): 361-363.

3290. Bandy, W. T. "James Russell Lowell Saint-Beuve, and the *Atlantic Monthly*." *Comp L* 11(1959): 229-232.

3291. Broderick, John C. "Lowell's 'Sunthin' in the Pastoral Line'." *AL* 31(1959): 163-172.

3292. Brooks, Roger L. "A Matthew Arnold Letter to James Russell Lowell: The Reason for the American Lecture Tour." *AL* 31(1959): 336-338.

3293. Cauthen, I. B., Jr. "Lowell on Poe: An Unpublished Comment, 1879." *AL* 24(1952): 230-233.

3294. Clark, George Pierce. "Lowell's Part in the Harvard Exhibition of 1837." *AL* 22(1951): 497-500.

3295. ----------. "A Note on the Published Version of James Russell Lowell's Class Book Autobiography." *NEQ* 27(1954): 102-103.

3296. Duberman, Martin B. "Twenty-Seven Poems by James Russell Lowell." *AL* 35(1963): 322-351.

3297. Duffy, Charles. "A Correction: 'Peschiera.'" *AL* 23(1951): 363.

3298. Ehrlich, Heyward. "Charles Frederick Briggs and Lowell's *Fable for Critics*." *MLQ* 28 (1967): 329-341.

3299. ----------. "The Origin of Lowell's 'Miss Fooler.'" *AL* 37(1966): 473-475.

3300. Enkvist, Nils Erick. "The Biglow Papers in Nineteenth-Century England." *NEQ* 26 (1953): 219-236.

3301. Graham, Philip. "Some Lowell Letters." [with text] *TSLL* 3(1962): 557-582.

3302. Knox, George. "The Hawthorne-Lowell Affair." *NEQ* 29(1956): 493-502.

3303. Mendel, Sydney. "A Note on Lowell's 'Ode Recited at the Harvard Commemoration.'" *NEQ* 35(1962): 102-103.

3304. Miller, F. DeWolfe. "Lowell the Author of Bayard Taylor's Review of *Laus Veneris*." *AL* 27(1955): 106-107.

3305. Monteiro, George. "Howells on Lowell: An Unsigned Review." *NEQ* 38(1965): 508-509.

3306. Munford, Howard M. "The Disciple Proves Independent: Howells and Lowell." *PMLA* 74(1959): 484-487.

3307. Myerson, Joel. "Lowell on Emerson: A New Letter from Concord in 1838." *NEQ* 44(1971): 649-652.

3308. Pritchard, John Paul. "A Glance at Lowell's Classical Reading." *AL* 21(1950): 442-455.

3309. Rooney, Charles J., Jr. "A New Letter by Lowell." *AL* 36(1964): 214-215.

3310. Shuman, R. Baird. "The Howells-Lowell Correspondence: A New Item." *AL* 31(1959): 338-340.

3311. Stafford, William T. "Lowell 'Edits' James: Some Revisions in *French Poets and Novelists*." *NEQ* 32(1959): 92-98.

3312. Voss, Arthur. "Backgrounds of Lowell's Satire in 'The Biglow Papers.'" *NEQ* 23(1950): 47-64.

3313. ----------. "An Uncollected Letter of Lowell's Parson Wilbur." *NEQ* 26(1953): 396-402.

3314. Woodress, James L., Jr. "The Lowell-Howells Friendship: Some Unpublished Letters." *NEQ* 26(1953): 523-528.

MABIE, HAMILTON W.   3315. Rife, David. "Hamilton Wright Mabie: An Annotated Bibliography of Primary and Secondary Materials." *ALR* 9(1976): 315-380.

MAYO, WILLIAM S.   3316. Eby, Cecil D., Jr. "William Starbuck Mayo and Herman Melville." *NEQ* 35(1962): 515-520.

McGAFFEY, ERNEST.   See 620.

MELVILLE, HERMAN.   3317. Abcarian, Richard. "The World of Love and the Spheres of Fright: Melvilles 'Bartleby the Scrivener.'" *SSF* 1(1964): 207-215.

3318. Adler, Joyce Sparer. "*Billy Budd* and Melville's Philosophy of War." *PMLA* 91(1976): 266-278.

3319. Albrecht, Robert C. "The Thematic Unity of Melville's 'The Encantadas.'" *TSLL* 14 (1972): 463-477.

3320. ----------. "White Jacket's Intentional Fall." *SN* 4(1972): 17-26.

3321. Altschuler, Glenn C. "Whose Foot on Whose Throat? A Re-examination of Melville's *Benito Cereno*." *CLA* 18(1975): 383-392.

3322. Aspiz, Harold. "Phrenologizing the Whale." *NCF* 23(1968): 18-27.

3323. Asquino, Mark L. "Hawthorne's Village Uncle and Melville's *Moby Dick*." *SSF* 10(1973): 413-414.

3324. Ausband, Stephen C. "The Whale and the Machine: An Approach to *Moby Dick*." *AL* 47(1975): 197-211.

3325. Bach, Bert C. "Melville's Theatrical Mask: The Role of Narrative Perspective in His Short Fiction." *SLI* 2,#1(1969): 43-55.

3326. Barber, Patricia. "Herman Melville's House in Brooklyn." *AL* 45(1973): 433-434.

3327. ----------. "Two New Melville Letters." *AL* 49(1977): 418-421.

3328. Barbour, James. "The Composition of *Moby-Dick*." *AL* 47(1975): 343-360.

3329. Barbour, James, and Leon Howard. "Carlyle and the Conclusion of *Moby-Dick*." *NEQ* 49(1976): 214-224.

3330. Barnet, Sylvan. "The Execution in *Billy Budd*." *AL* 33(1962): 517-519.

3331. Barnett, Louise K. "Bartleby as Alienated Worker." *SSF* 11(1974): 379-385.

3332. Barrett, Laurence. "The Differences in Melville's Poetry." *PMLA* 70(1955): 606-623.

3333. Battenfeld, David H. "The Source for the Hymn in *Moby-Dick*." *AL* 27(1955): 393-396.

3334. Baym, Nina. "The Erotic Motif in Melville's *Clarel*." *TSLL* 16(1974): 315-328.

3335. Beebe, Maurice, Harrison Hayford, and Gordon Roper. "Criticism of Herman Melville: A Selected Checklist." *MFS* 8(1962): 312-346.

3336. Bell, Michael D. "The Glendinning Heritage: Melville's Literary Borrowings in *Pierre*." *SR* 12(1973): 741-762.

3337. ----------. "Melville's *Redburn*: Initiation and Authority." *NEQ* 46(1973): 558-572.

3338. Bell, Millicent. "Pierre Bayle and *Moby Dick*." *PMLA* 66(1951): 626-648.

3339. Bercovitch, Sacvan. "Melville's Search for National Identity: Son and Father in *Redburn, Pierre,* and 'Billy Budd.'" *CLA* 10(1967): 217-228.

3340. Bergmann, Johannes Dietrich. "'Bartleby' and *The Lawyer's Story*." *AL* 47(1975): 432-436.

3341. Bergstrom, Robert F. "The Topmost Grief: Rejection of Ahab's Faith." *EL* 2(1975): 171-180.

3342. Bernstein, John. "*Benito Cereno* and the Spanish Inquisition." *NCF* 16(1962): 345-350.

3343. Berthoff, Warner. "'Certain Phenomenal Men': The Example of *Billy Budd*." *ELH* 27 (1960): 334-351.

3344. Bezanson, Walter E. "Melville's *Clarel*: The Complex Passion." *ELH* 21(1954): 146-159.

3345. ----------. "Melville's Reading of Arnold's Poetry." *PMLA* 69(1954): 365-391.

3346. Bigelow, Gordon E. "The Problem of Symbolist Form in Melville's 'Bartleby the Scrivener.'" *MLQ* 31(1970): 345-359.

3347. Bois, J. J. "*The Whale* Without Epilogue." *MLQ* 24(1963): 172-176.

3348. Booth, Thornton. "*Moby Dick*: Standing Up to God." *NCF* 17(1962): 33-43.

3349. Bowen, James K. "Alienation and Withdrawal are not the Absurd: Renunciation and Preference in 'Bartleby the Scrivener.'" *SSF* 8(1971): 633-635.

3350. Bowen, Merlin. "*Redburn* and the Angle of Vision." *MP* 52(1954): 100-109.

3351. ----------. "Tactics of Indirection in Melville's *The Confidence-Man*." *SN* 1(1969): 401-420.

3352. Branch, Watson G. "The Genesis, Composition, and Structure of *The Confidence Man*." *NCF* 27(1973): 424-448.

3353. Braswell, William. "The Early Love Scenes in Melville's *Pierre*." *AL* 22(1950): 283-289.

3354. ----------. "Melville's *Billy Budd* as 'An Inside Narrative.'" *AL* 29(1957): 133-146.

3355. ----------. "Melville's Opinion of *Pierre*." *AL* 23(1951): 246-250.

3356. Breining, Helmbrecht. "The Destruction of Fairyland: Melville's 'Piazza' in the Tradition of the American Imagination." *ELH* 35(1968): 254-283.

3357. Bridgman, Richard. "Melville's Roses." *TSLL* 8(1966): 235-244.

3358. Brodtkorb, Paul, Jr. "*The Confidence-Man*: The Con-Man as Hero." *SN* 1(1969): 421-435.

3359. ----------. "The Definitive *Billy Budd*: 'But aren't it all sham?'" *PMLA* 82(1967): 602-612.

3360. Brodwin, Stanley. "Herman Melville's *Clarel*: An Existential Gospel." *PMLA* 86(1971): 375-387.

3361. Browne, Ray B. "*Billy Budd*: Gospel of Democracy." *NCF* 17(1963): 321-337.

3362. Busch, Frederick. "Thoreau and Melville as Cellmates." *MFS* 23(1977): 239-242.

3363. ----------. "The Whale as Shaggy Dog: Melville and 'The Man Who Studied Yoga.'" *MFS* 19 (1973): 193-206.

3364. Carlisle, E. F. "Captain Amasa Delano: Melville's American Fool." *Criticism* 7(1965): 349-362.

3365. Carothers, Robert, and John L. Marsh. "The Whale and the Panorama." *NCF* 26(1971): 319-328.

3366. Cawelti, John G. "Some Notes on The Structure of *The Confidence-Man*." *AL* 29(1957): 278-288.

3367. Chaffee, Patricia. "The Kedron in Melville's *Clarel*." *CLA* 18(1975): 374-382.

3368. Chandler, Alice. "Captain Vere and the 'Tragedies of the Palace.'" *MFS* 13(1967): 259-261.

3369. ----------. "The Name Symbolism of Captain Vere." *NCF* 22(1967): 86-89.

3370. Cifelli, Edward M. "*Billy Budd*: Boggy Ground to Build On." *SSF* 13(1976): 463-469.

3371. Clark, Marden J. "Blending Cadences: Rhythm and Structure in *Moby Dick*." *SN* 8(1976): 158-171.

3372. Cochran, Robert. "Babo's name in 'Benito Cereno': An Unnecessary Controversy?" *AL* 48(1976): 217-219.

3373. Cohen, Hennig. "Melville's Tomahawk Pipe: Artifact and Symbol." *SN* 1(1969): 397-400.

3374. ----------. "New Melville Letters." *AL* 38(1967): 556-559.

3375. ----------. "Melville's Surgeon Cuticle and Surgeon Cutbush." *SN* 5(1973): 251-253.

3376. ----------. "Melville to Mrs. Gifford, 1888." *Coll L* 2(1975): 229.

3377. Conarroe, Joel O. "Melville's Bartleby and Charles Lamb." *SSF* 5(1968): 113-118.

3378. Connolly, Thomas E. "A Note on Name-Symbolism in Melville." *AL* 25(1954): 489-490.

3379. Cowan, S. A. "In Praise of Self-Reliance: The Role of Bulkington in *Moby-Dick*." *AL* 38(1967): 547-556.

3380. Cross, Richard K. "*Moby-Dick* and *Under the Volcano:* Poetry from the Abyss." *MFS* 20(1974): 149-156.

3381. Dahl, Curtis. "Moby Dick's Cousin Behemoth." *AL* 31(1959): 21-29.

3382. D'Avanzo, Mario. "Melville's 'Bartleby' and John Jacob Astor." *NEQ* 41(1968): 259-264.

3383. Davidson, Frank. "Melville, Thoreau, and 'The Apple-Tree Table.'" *AL* 25(1953): 479-488.

3384. Day, A. Grove. "Hawaiian Echoes in Melville's *Mardi*." *MLQ* 18(1957): 3-8.

3385. Dichman, Mary E. "Absolutism in Melville's *Pierre*." *PMLA* 67(1952): 702-715.

3386. Dillingham, William B. "Melville's Long Ghost and Smollett's Count Fathom." *AL* 42 (1970): 232-235.

3387. Donaldson, Scott. "Damned Dollars and a Blessed Company: Financial Imagery in *Moby-Dick*." *NEQ* 46(1973): 279-283.

3388. ----------. "The Dark Truth of *The Piazza Tales*." *PMLA* 85(1970): 1082-1086.

3389. Donow, Herbert S. "Herman Melville and the Craft of Fiction." *MLQ* 25(1964): 181-186.

3390. Doubleday, Neal F. "Jack Easy and Billy Budd." *ELN* 2(1964): 39-42.

3391. Drew, Philip. "Appearance and Reality in Melville's *The Confidence-Man*." *ELH* 31(1964): 418-442.

3392. Dubler, Walter. "Theme and Structure in Melville's *The Confidence-Man*." *AL* 33(1961): 307-319.

3393. Duerksen, Roland A. "*Caleb Williams, Political Justice* and *Billy Budd*." *AL* 38(1966): 372-376.

3394. ----------. "The Deep Quandry in *Billy Budd*." *NEQ* 41(1968): 51-66.

3395. Eberwein, Robert T. "The Impure Fiction of *Billy Budd*." *SN* 6(1974): 318-326.

3396. Eby, Cecil D., Jr. "Another Breaching of 'Mocha Dick'." *ELN* 4(1967): 277-279.

3397. ----------. "William Starbuck Mayo and Herman Melville." *NEQ* 35(1962): 515-520.

3398. Eddy, D. Mathis. "Melville's Response to Beaumont and Fletcher: A New Source for *The Encantadas*." *AL* 40(1968): 374-380.

3399. ----------. "Melville's Sicilian Moralist." *ELN* 8(1971): 191-200.

3400. Eigner, Edwin M. "The Romantic Unity of Melville's *Omoo*." *PQ* 46(1967): 95-108.

3401. Eldridge, Herbert G. "'Careful Disorder': The Structure of *Moby-Dick*." *AL* 39(1967): 145-162.

3402. Ellen, Sister Mary, I. H. M. "Duplicate Imagery in *Moby-Dick*." *MFS* 8(1962): 252-264.

3403. ----------. "Parallels in Contrast: A Study of Melville's Imagery in *Moby Dick* and *Billy Budd*." *SSF* 2(1965): 284-290.

3404. Ellis, Theodore R., III. "Another Broadside into *Mardi*." *AL* 41(1969): 419-422.

3405. Emery, Allan Moore. "The Alternatives of Melville's 'Bartleby.'" *NCF* 31(1976): 170-187.

3406. Estrin, Mark W. "Robert Lowell's *Benito Cereno*." *MD* 15(1973): 411-426.

3407. Evans, William A. "The Boy and the Shadow: The Role of Pip and Fedallah in *Moby-Dick*." *SLI* 2,#1(1969): 77-81.

3408. Fabricant, Carole. "*Tristram Shandy* and *Moby Dick:* A Cock and Bull Story and a Tale of a Tub." *JNT* 7(1977): 57-69.

3409. Fenton, Charles A. "'The Bell-Tower': Melville and Technology." *AL* 23(1951): 219-232.

3410. Fiess, Edward. "Byron's Dark Blue Ocean and Melville's Rolling Sea." *ELN* 3(1966): 274-278.

3411. ----------. "Melville as a Reader and Student of Byron." *AL* 24(1952): 186-194.

3412. Firchow, Peter E. "*Bartleby:* Man and Metaphor." *SSF* 5(1968): 342-348.

3413. Firebaugh, Joseph J. "Humorist as Rebel: The Melville of *Typee*." *NCF* 9(1954): 108-120.

3414. Fisher, Marvin. "Bug and Humbug in Melville's 'Apple-Tree Table.'" *SSF* 8(1971): 459-466.

3415. ----------. "'The Lightning-Rod Man': Melville's Testament of Rejection." *SSF* 7(1970): 433-438.

3416. ----------. "Melville's 'Jimmy Rose': Truly Risen?" *SSF* 4(1966): 1-11.

3417. ----------. "Melville's 'The Fiddler': Succumbing to the Drummer." *SSF* 11(1974): 153-160.

3418. ----------. "Prospect and Perspective in Melville's 'Piazza.'" *Criticism* 16(1974): 203-216.

3419. Fiske, John C. "Herman Melville in Soviet Criticism." *Comp L* 5(1953): 30-39.

3420. Fite, Oliver L. "Billy Budd, Claggart, and Schopenhauer." *NCF* 23(1968): 336-343.

3421. Flanaghan, John T. "*The Spirit of the Times* Reviews Melville." *JEGP* 64(1965): 57-64.

3422. Fogle, Richard Harter. "*Billy Budd:* The Ordeal of the Fall." *NCF* 15(1960): 189-205.

3423. ----------. "The Unity of Melville's *The Encantadas*." *NCF* 10(1955): 34-52.

3424. Foster, Charles H. "Something in Emblems: A Reinterpretation of *Moby-Dick*." *NEQ* 34 (1961): 3-35.

3425. Foster, Elizabeth S. "Another Note on Melville and Geology." *AL* 22(1951): 479-487.

3426. Franklin, Bruce. "Redburn's Wicked End." *NCF* 20(1965): 190-194.

3427. ----------. "'Apparent Symbol of Despotic Command': Melville's *Benito Cereno*." *NEQ* 34 (1961): 462-477.

3428. Frederick, John T. "Melville's Early Acquaintance with Bayle." *AL* 39(1968): 545-547.

3429. ----------. "Symbol and Theme in Melville's *Israel Potter*." *MFS* 8(1962): 265-275.

3430. Fussell, Mary Everett Burton. "*Billy Budd:* Melville's Happy Ending." *SR* 15(1976): 43-58.

3431. Galloway, David D. "Herman Melville's *Benito Cereno:* An Anatomy." *TSLL* 9(1967): 239-252.

3432. Gardner, John. "*Bartleby:* Art and Social Commitment." *PQ* 43(1964): 87-98.

3433. Garner, Stanton. "Melville and Thomas Campbell: The 'Deadly Space Between.'" *ELN* 14 (1977): 289-290.

3434. Garrison, Daniel H. "Melville's Doubloon and the Shield of Achilles." *NCF* 26(1971):

171-184.

3435. Geiger, Don. "Melville's Black God:
Contrary Evidence in 'The Town-Ho's Story.'" *AL*
25(1954): 464-471.

3436. Giddings, T. H. "Melville, the Colt-
Adams Murder and 'Bartleby.'" *SAF* 2(1974): 123-
132.

3437. Gindin, James. "Review-Essay: Lots
of Cotton Wool." *SN* 9(1977): 312-325.

3438. Giovanni, G. "Melville and Dante."
PMLA 65(1950): 329.

3439. Glenn, Barbara. "Melville and the
Sublime in *Moby-Dick*." *AL* 48(1976): 165-182.

3440. Glick, Wendell. "Expediency and Absolute Morality in *Billy Budd*." *PMLA* 68(1953):
103-110.

3441. Goldsmith, Arnold L. "The 'Discovery
Scene' in *Billy Budd*." *MD* 3(1961): 339-342.

3442. Golemba, Henry L. "The Shape of
Moby-Dick." *SN* 5(1973): 197-210.

3443. Gollin, Richard and Rita. "Justice
in an Earlier Treatment of the *Billy Budd* 'Theme'."
AL 28(1957): 513-515.

3444. Gollin, Rita. "*Pierre's* Metamorphosis
of Dante's *Inferno*." *AL* 39(1968): 542-545.

3445. ---------. "The Quondam Sailor and
Melville's *Omoo*." *AL* 48(1976): 75-79.

3446. Green, Jesse D. "Diabolism, Pessimism,
and Democracy: Notes on Melville and Conrad." *MFS*
8(1962): 287-305.

3447. Grdseloff, Dorothee. "A Note on the
Origin of Fedallah in *Moby-Dick*." *AL* 27(1955):
396-403.

3448. Gross, Seymour L. "Mungo Park and
Ledyard in Melville's *Benito Cereno*." *ELN* 3
(1965): 122-123.

3449. Gupta, R. K. "Hautboy and Plinlimmon:
A Reinterpretation of Melville's 'The Fiddler.'"
AL 43(1971): 437-442.

3450. Guttman, Allen. "From *Typee* to *Moby-
Dick*: Melville's Allusive Art." *MLQ* 24(1963): 237-
244.

3451. Haber, Tom Burns. "A Note on Melville's
Benito Cereno." *NCF* 6(1951): 146-147.

3452. Haberstroh, Charles, Jr. "Melville,
Marriage, and Mardi." *SN* 9(1977): 247-260.

3453. ---------. "*Redburn*: The Psychological Pattern." *SAF* 2(1974): 133-144.

3454. Hands, Charles B. "The Comic Entrance
to Moby-Dick." *Coll L* 2(1975): 182-191.

3455. Harding, Walter. "A Note on the Title
'Moby-Dick.'" *AL* 22(1951): 500-501.

3456. Hauser, Helen A. "Spinozan Philosophy
in *Pierre*." *AL* 49(1977): 49-56.

3457. Hayford, Harrison. "Melville's Freudian Slip." *AL* 30(1958): 366-368.

3458. ----------. "Poe in *The Confidence-
Man*." *NCF* 14(1959): 207-218.

3459. Hayman, Allen. "The Real and the Original: Herman Melville's Theory of Prose Fiction."
MFS 8(1962): 211-232.

3460. Heffernan, Thomas F. "Melville and
Wordsworth." *AL* 49(1977): 338-351.

3461. Herbert, T. Walter, Jr. "Calvinism
and Cosmic Evil in *Moby-Dick*." *PMLA* 84(1969):
1613-1619.

3462. Hetherington, Hugh W. "A Tribute to
the Late Hiram Melville." *MLQ* 16(1955): 325-331.

3463. Higgins, Brian. "Plinlimmon and the
Pamphlet Again." *SN* 4(1972): 27-38.

3464. Hillway, Tyrus. "Melville as Amateur
Zoologist." *MLQ* 12(1951): 159-164.

3465. ----------. "Melville's Education in
Science." *TSLL* 16(1974): 411-425.

3466. Hirsch, David H. "The Dilemma of the
Liberal Intellectual: Melville's Ishmael." *TSLL*
5(1963): 169-188.

3467. Hitt, Ralph E. "Melville's Poems of
Civil War Controversy." *SLI* 2,#1(1969): 57-68.

3468. Hoeltje, Hubert H. "Hawthorne, Melville, and 'Blackness.'" *AL* 37(1965): 41-51.

3469. Hoffman, Dan G. "Melville's 'Story of
China Aster.'" *AL* 22(1950): 137-149.

3470. Horsford, Howard C. "The Design of the
Argument in *Moby-Dick*." *MFS* 8(1962): 233-251.

3471. ----------. "Evidence of Melville's
Plans for a Sequel to *The Confidence-Man*." *AL* 24
(1952): 85-89.

3472. Howington, Don S. "Melville's 'The
Encantadas': Imagery and Meaning." *SLI* 2,#1(1969):
69-75.

3473. Humma, John B. "Melville's *Billy Budd*
and Lawrence's 'The Prussian Officer': Old Adams
and New." *EL* 1(1974): 83-88.

3474. Hunsberger, Claude. "Vectors in Recent *Moby-Dick* Criticism." *Coll L* 2(1975): 230-245.

3475. Huntress, Keith. "Melville, Henry
Cheever, and 'The Lee Shore.'" *NEQ* 44(1971): 468-
475.

3476. Husni, Khalil. "The Whiteness of the
Whale: A Survey of Interpretations, 1851-1970."
CLA 20(1976): 210-221.

3477. Hutchinson, William H. "A Definitive
Edition of *Moby-Dick*." *AL* 25(1954): 472-478.

3478. Isani, Mukhtar A. "Melville's Use of
John and Awnsham Churchill's *Collection of Voyages
and Travels*." *SN* 4(1972): 390-395.

3479. ----------. "The Naming of Fedallah
in *Moby-Dick*." *AL* 40(1968): 380-385.

3480. ----------. "Zoroastrianism and the
Fire Symbolism in *Moby-Dick*." *AL* 44(1972): 385-
397.

3481. Ives, C. B. "*Billy Budd* and the Articles of War." *AL* 34(1962): 31-39.

3482. Jackson, Arlene M. "Technique and
Discovery in Melville's *Encantadas*." *SAF* 1
(1973): 133-140.

3483. Jackson, Kenny. "*Israel Potter*:
Melville's 'Fourth of July Story.'" *CLA* 6(1963):
194-204.

3484. Jackson, Margaret Y. "Melville's Use
of a Real Slave Muting in 'Benito Cereno.'" *CLA*
4(1960): 79-93.

3485. Jaffé, David. "Some Origins of *Moby-
Dick*: New Finds in an Old Source." *AL* 29(1957):
263-277.

3486. Jerman, Bernard R. "'With Real Admiration': More Correspondence between Melville
and Bentley." *AL* 25(1953): 307-313.

3487. Jones, Buford. "Melville's Buccaneers
and Crébillon's Sofa." *ELN* 2(1964): 122-126.

3488. Joswick, Thomas P. "'Typee': The
Quest for Origin." *Criticism* 17(1975): 335-354.

3489. Kaplan, Sidney. "Herman Melville and
the Whaling Enderbys." *AL* 24(1952): 224-230.

3490. Karcher, Carolyn Lury. "The Story of

Charlemont: A Dramatization of Melville's Concepts
of Fiction in *The Confidence-Man: His Masquerade*."
NCF 21(1966): 73-84.

3491. Kay, Donald. "Herman Melville's Literary Relationship with Evert Duyckinck." *CLA*
18(1975): 393-403.

3492. Keller, Clinton. "Melville's Delano:
Our Cheerful Axiologist." *CLA* 10(1966): 49-55.

3493. Kelly, Michael J. "Claggart's 'Equivocal Words' and Lamb's 'Popular Fallacies.'" *SSF*
9(1972): 183-186.

3494. Kennedy, Frederick J. "Herman Melville's
Lecture in Montreal." *NEQ* 50(1977): 125-137.

3495. Keyser, Elizabeth. "'Quite an Original':
The Composition in *The Confidence Man*." *TSLL* 15
(1973): 279-300.

3496. Kilbourne, W. G., Jr. "Montaigne and
Captain Vere." *AL* 33(1962): 514-517.

3497. Kissane, James. "Imagery, Myth and
Melville's *Pierre*." *AL* 26(1955): 564-572.

3498. Ledbetter, Kenneth. "The Ambiguity
of Billy Budd." *TSLL* 4(1962): 130-134.

3499. Leiter, Louis. "Queequeg's Coffin."
NCF 13(1958): 249-254.

3500. Lemon, Lee T. "*Billy Budd*: The Plot
Against the Story." *SSF* 2(1964): 32-43.

3501. Levy, Leo B. "Hawthorne, Melville,
and the Monitor." *AL* 37(1965): 33-40.

3502. Lewis, R. W. B. "Melville on Homer."
AL 22(1950): 166-176.

3503. Leyda, Jay. "Another Friendly Critic
for Melville." *NEQ* 27(1954): 243-252.

3504. Lish, Terrence G. "Melville's *Redburn*: A Study in Dualism." *ELN* 5(1967): 113-120.

3505. London, Philip W. "The Military Necessity: *Billy Budd* and *Vigny*." *Comp L* 14(1962):
176-186.

3506. Longenecker, Marlene. "Captain Vere
and the Form of Truth." *SSF* 14(1977): 337-343.

3507. Loving, Jerome M. "Melville's Par-
donable Sin." *NEQ* 47(1974): 262-278.

3508. Lucas, Thomas Edward. "Herman Melville: The Purpose of the Novel." *TSLL* 13(1972):
641-661.

3509. Lucid, Robert F. "The Influence of
Two Years Before the Mast on Human Melville." *AL*
31(1959): 243-256.

3510. Lynde, Richard D. "Melville's Success
in 'The Happy Failure: A Story of the River Hudson.'" *CLA* 13(1969): 119-130.

3511. MacShane, Frank. "Conrad on Melville."
AL 29(1958): 463-464.

3512. Mandel, Ruth B. "The Two Mystery Stories in *Benito Cereno*." *TSLL* 14(1973): 631-642.

3513. Margolies, Edward. "Melville and
Blacks." *CLA* 18(1975): 364-373.

3514. Markels, Julian. "Melville's Markings
in Shakespeare's Plays." *AL* 49(1977): 34-48.

3515. Matriano, Mary A. "Melville's 'The
Lightning-Rod Man.'" *SSF* 14(1977): 29-33.

3516. McCarthy, Paul. "Elements of Anatomy
in Melville's Fiction." *SN* 6(1974): 38-61.

3517. McDermott, John Francis. "The *Spirit
of the Times Reviews Moby Dick*." *NEQ* 30(1957):
392-395.

3518. McElderry, B. R., Jr. "Three Earlier
Treatments of the *Billy Budd* Theme." *AL* 27(1955):
251-257.

3519. McElroy, John Harmon. "Cannibalism in
Melville's *Benito Cereno*." *EL* 1(1974): 206-218.

3520. McHaney, Thomas L. "*The Confidence-
Man* and Satan's Disguises in *Paradise Lost*." *NCF*
30(1975): 200-205.

3521. ----------. "The Textual Editions of
Hawthorne and Melville." *SLI* 2,#1(1969): 27-41.

3522. Meldrun, Barbara. "The Artist in Melville's *Mardi*." *SN* 1(1969): 459-467.

3523. Merrill, Robert. "The Narrative Voice
in *Billy Budd*." *MLQ* 34(1973): 283-291.

3524. Milder, Robert. "Melville's 'Intentions' in *Pierre*." *SN* 6(1974): 186-199.

3525. Miller, James E., Jr. "*The Confidence-
Man: His Guises*." *PMLA* 74(1959): 102-111.

3526. ----------. "Hawthorne and Melville.
The Unpardonable Sin." *PMLA* 70(1955): 91-114.

3527. ----------. "The Many Masks of *Mardi*."
JEGP 58(1959): 400-413.

3528. ----------. "Redburn and *White Jacket*:
Initiation and Baptism." *NCF* 13(1959): 273-293.

3529. Miller, Paul W. "Sun and Fire in Melville's *Moby Dick*." *NCF* 13(1958): 139-144.

3530. Mills, Nicolaus C. "The Discovery of
Nil in *Pierre* and *Jude the Obscure*." *TSLL* 12
(1970): 249-262.

3531. Mitchell, Edward. "From Action to
Essence: Some Notes on the Structure of Melville's
The Confidence-Man." *AL* 40(1968): 27-37.

3532. Monteiro, George. "Melville's 'Timothy
Quicksand' and the Dead-Letter Office." *SSF* 9(1972):
198-201.

3533. Moore, Jack B. "Ahab and Bartleby:
Energy and Indolence." *SSF* 1(1964): 291-294.

3534. Moore, Richard S. "A New Review by
Melville." *AL* 47(1975): 265-270.

3535. Moorman, Charles. "Melville's *Pierre*
and the Fortunate Fall." *AL* 25(1953): 13-30.

3536. ----------. "Melville's Pierre in the
City." *AL* 27(1956): 571-577.

3537. Morseberger, Robert E. "Melville's
'The Bell-Tower' and Benvenuto Cellini." *AL* 44
(1972): 459-462.

3538. Moses, Carole. "Melville's Use of
Spenser in 'The Piazza.'" *CLA* 20(1976): 222-231.

3539. Moss, Sidney P. "'Cock-A-Doodle-Doo!'
and Some Legends in Melville Scholarship." *AL*
40(1968): 192-210.

3540. Murray, Henry A. "In Nomine Diabli."
NEQ 24(1951): 435-452.

3541. Naugle, Helen H. "The Name 'Bildad.'"
MFS 22(1976): 591-594.

3542. Nechas, James W. "Ambiguity of Word
and Whale: The Negative Affix in *Moby Dick*." *Coll
L* 2(1975): 198-225.

3543. Newbery, I. "'The Encantadas': Melville's *Inferno*." *AL* 38(1966): 49-68.

3544. Nichol, John W. "Melville and the Midwest." *PMLA* 66(1951): 613-625.

3545. Noone, John B. "*Billy Budd*: Two Concepts of Nature." *AL* 29(1957): 249-262.

3546. Norman, Liane. "Bartleby and the Reader." *NEQ* 44(1971): 22-39.

3547. Oates, J. C. "Melville and the Mani-
chean Illusion." *TSLL* 4(1962): 117-129.

3548. O'Daniel, Therman B. "Herman Melville
as a Writer of Journals." *CLA* 4(1960): 94-105.

3549. ----------. "An Interpretation of the Relation of the Chapter Entitled 'The Symphony' to *Moby Dick* as a Whole." *CLA* 2(1958): 55-57.

3550. Osbourn, R. V. "The White Whale and the Absolute." *EIC* 6(1956): 160-170.

3551. Packard, Hyland. "*Mardi*: The Role of Melville's Search for Expression." *AL* 49(1977): 241-253.

3552. Parke, John. "Seven Moby-Dicks." *NEQ* 28(1955): 319-338.

3553. Parker, Hershel. "Being Professional in Working on *Moby Dick*." *Coll L* 2(1975): 192-197.

3554. ----------. "'Benito Cereno' and *Cloister Life*: A Re-Scruting of a 'Source.'" *SSF* 9(1972): 221-232.

3555. ----------. "Evidences for 'Late Insertions' in Melville's Works." *SN* 7(1975): 407-321.

3556. ----------. "Five Reviews Not in *MOBY DICK as Doubloon*." *ELN* 9(1972): 182-185.

3557. ----------. "Melville's Salesman Story." *SSF* 1(1964): 154-158.

3558. ----------. "A Reexamination of *Melville's Reviewers*." *AL* 42(1970): 226-232.

3559. ----------. "Three Melville Reviews in the London *Weekly Chronicle*." *AL* 41(1970): 584-589.

3560. ----------. "Trafficking in Melville." *MLQ* 33(1972): 54-66.

3561. ----------. "Why *Pierre* Went Wrong." *SN* 8(1976): 7-23.

3562. Patrick, Walton R. "Melville's 'Bartleby' and the Doctrine of Necessity." *AL* 41(1969): 39-54.

3563. Pearce, Howard D. "The Narrator of 'Norfolk Isle and the Chola Widow.'" *SSF* 3(1965): 56-62.

3564. Pearce, Roy Harvey. "Melville's Indian-hater: A Note on a Meaning of *The Confidence-Man*." *PMLA* 67(1952): 942-948.

3565. Phelps, Leland R. "*Moby Dick* in Germany." *Comp L* 10(1958): 349-355.

3566. Philbrick, Thomas L. "Another Source for *White-Jacket*." *AL* 29(1958): 431-439.

3567. ----------. "Melville's 'Best Authorities.'" *NCF* 15(1960): 171-179.

3568. Phillips, Barry. "'The Good Captain': A Reading of *Benito Cereno*." *TSLL* 4(1962): 188-197.

3569. Pilkington, William T. "'Benito Cereno' and the 'Valor-Ruined Man' of *Moby-Dick*." *TSLL* 7(1965): 201-207.

3570. ----------. "Melville's *Benito Cereno*: Source and Technique." *SSF* 2(1965): 247-255.

3571. Pinkser, Sanford. "'Bartleby the Scrivener': Language as Wall." *Coll L* 2(1975): 17-27.

3572. Procter, Page S., Jr. "A Source for the Flogging Incident in *White-Jacket*." *AL* 22(1950): 176-177.

3573. Putzel, Max. "The Source and the Symbols of Melville's 'Benito Cereno.'" *Al* 34(1962): 191-206.

3574. Quirk, Tom. "Saint Paul's Types of the Faithful and Melville's Confidence Man." *NCF* 28(1974): 472-477.

3575. Rathbun, John W. "*Billy Budd* and the Limits of Perception." *NCF* 20(1965): 19-34.

3576. Reed, Walter L. "The Measured Forms of Captain Vere." *MFS* 23(1977): 227-235.

3577. Regan, Charles L. "Melville's Horned Woman." *ELN* 5(1967): 34-39.

3578. Reynolds, Larry J. "Antidemocratic Emphasis in *White-Jacket*." *AL* 48(1976): 13-28.

3579. Reynolds, Michael S. "The Prototype for Melville's Confidence-Man." *PMLA* 86(1971): 1009-1013.

3580. Robillard, Douglas. "Theme and Structure in Melville's *John Marr and Other Sailors*." *ELN* 6(1969): 187-192.

3581. Rockwell, Frederick S. "DeQuincey and the Ending of *Moby Dick*." *NCF* 9(1954): 161-168.

3582. Rose, Edward J. "Annihilation and Ambiguity: *Moby Dick* and 'The Town-Ho's Story.'" *NEQ* 45(1972): 541-558.

3583. ----------. "Melville, Emerson, and the Sphinx." *NEQ* 36(1963): 249-258.

3584. Rosenberry, Edward H. "Essay Review: Awash in Melvilliana." *NEQ* 33(1960): 523-528.

3585. ----------. "Melville's Ship of Fools." *PMLA* 75(1960): 604-608.

3586. ----------. "*Moby-Dick*, Epic Romance." *Coll L* 2(1975): 155-170.

3587. ----------. "The Problem of *Billy Budd*." *PMLA* 80(1965): 489-498.

3588. ----------. "Queequeg's Coffin-Canoe: Made in Typee." *AL* 30(1959): 529-530.

3589. Rosenfeld, William. "Uncertain Faith: Queequeg's Coffin and Melville's Use of the Bible." *TSLL* 7(1966): 317-327.

3590. Rosenthal, Bernard. "Elegy for Jack Chase." *SR* 10(1971): 213-229.

3591. ----------. "Melville, Marryat, and the Evil-Eyed Villian." *NCF* 25(1970): 221-224.

3592. ----------. "Melville's Island." *SSF* 11(1974): 1-9.

3593. Ross, Morton L. "Captain Truck and Captain Boomer." *AL* 37(1965): 316.

3594. ----------. "*Moby-Dick* as an Education." *SN* 6(1974): 62-75.

3595. Roundy, Nancy. "Fancies, Reflections and Things: the Imagination as Perception in 'The Piazza.'" *CLA* 20(1977): 539-546.

3596. Rowland, Beryl. "Grace Church and Melville's Story of 'The Two Temples.'" *NCF* 28(1973): 339-346.

3597. ----------. "Melville's Bachelors and Maids: Interpretation through Symbol and Metaphor." *AL* 41(1969): 389-405.

3598. ----------. "Melville's Waterloo in 'Rich Man's Crumbs.'" *NCF* 25(1970): 216-221.

3599. Ruland, Richard. "Melville and the Fortunate Fall: Typee as Eden." *NCF* 23(1968): 312-323.

3600. Russell, Jack. "*Israel Potter* and 'Song of Myself.'" *AL* 40(1968): 72-77.

3601. Sale, Arthur. "The Glass Ship: A Recurrent Image in Melville." *MLQ* 17(1956): 118-127.

3602. Samson, Joan P. "The Ambiguity of Ambergris in *Moby-Dick*." *Coll L* 2(1975): 226-228.

3603. Sattelmeyer, Robert, and James Barbour. "A Possible Source and Model for 'The Story of

China Aster' in Melville's *The Confidence-Man.*"
AL 48(1977): 577-583.

3604. Schiffman, Joseph. "Critical Problems in Melville's 'Benito Cereno.'" *MLQ* 11
(1950): 317-324.

3605. ----------. "Melville's Final Stage,
Irony: A Re-Examination of *Billy Budd* Criticism."
AL 22(1950): 128-136.

3606. Scholnick, Robert J. "Politics and
Poetics: The Reception of Melville's *Battle-
Pieces and Aspects of the War.*" *AL* 49(1977):
422-430.

3607. Schroeter, James. "*Redburn* and the
Failure of Mythic Criticism." *AL* 39(1967): 279-
297.

3608. Sealts, Merton M., Jr. "Did Melville Write 'October Mountain'?" *AL* 22(1950):
178-182.

3609. ----------. "The Ghost of Major Melville." *NEQ* 30(1957): 291-306.

3609a. ----------. "Melville and Richard
Henry Stoddard." *AL* 43(1971): 359-370.

3610. Seelye, John D. "The Golden Novel:
The Cabalism of Ahab's Doubloon." *NCF* 14(1960):
350-355.

3611. ----------. "'Spontaneous Impress of
Truth': Melville's Jack Chase: A Source, An
Analogue, A Conjecture." *NCF* 20(1966): 367-376.

3612. ----------. "Timothy Flint's
'Wicked River' and *The Confidence-Man.*" *PMLA* 78
(1963): 75-79.

3613. ----------. "'Ungraspable Phantom':
Reflections of Hawthorne in *Pierre* and *The
Confidence-Man.*" *SN* 1(1969): 436-443.

3614. Seltzer, W. H. "Camus's Absurd and
the World of Melville's *Confidence-Man.*" *PMLA*
82(1967): 14-27.

3615. Sewall, Richard B. "Ahab's Quenchless Feud: The Tragic Vision in Shakespeare and
Melville." *CD* 1(1967): 207-218.

3616. Shattuck, Roger. "Two Inside Narratives: *Billy Budd* and *L'Etranger.*" *TSLL* 4
(1962): 314-320.

3617. Sherbo, Arthur. "Melville's 'Portuguese Catholic Priest.'" *AL* 26(1955): 563-564.

3618. Sherwood, John C. "Vere as Colling-
wood: A Key to *Billy Budd.*" *AL* 35(1964): 476-484.

3619. Shroeder, John W. "Sources and Symbols for Melville's *Confidence-Man.*" *PMLA* 66
(1951): 363-380.

3620. Shulman, Robert. "Melville's Thomas
Fuller: An Outline for Starbuck and an Instance
of the Creator as Critic." *MLQ* 23(1962): 337-352.

3621. ----------. "Melville's 'Timoleon':
From Plutarch to the Early Stages of *Billy Budd.*"
Comp L 19(1967): 351-361.

3622. ----------. "Montaigne and the Techniques and Tragedy of Melville's *Billy Budd.*"
Comp L 16(1964): 322-330.

3623. ----------. "The Serious Functions
of Melville's Phallic Jokes." *AL* 33(1961): 179-
194.

3624. Shusterman, Alan. "Melville's 'The
Lightning-Rod Man': A Reading." *SSF* 9(1972):
165-174.

3625. Shusterman, David. "The 'Reader
Fallacy' and 'Bartleby the Scrivener.'" *NEQ* 45

(1972): 118-124.

3626. Simboli, David. "'Benito Cereno' as
Pedagogy." *CLA* 9(1965): 159-170.

3627. Simpson, Eleanor E. "Melville and the
Negro: From *Typee* to *Benito Cereno.*" *AL* 41(1969):
19-38.

3628. Slater, Judith. "The Domestic Adventurer in Melville's Tales." *AL* 37(1965): 267-279.

3629. Smith, Paul. "*The Confidence-Man* and
the Literary World of New York." *NCF* 16(1962):
329-337.

3630. Spector, Donald. "Melville's 'Bartleby' and the Absurd." *NCF* 16(1961): 175-177.

3631. Spofford, William K. "Melville's
Ambiguities: A Re-evaluation of 'The Town-Ho's
Story.'" *AL* 41(1969): 264-270.

3632. Springer, Norman. "Bartleby and the
Terror of Limitation." *PMLA* 80(1965): 410-418.

3633. Stafford, William T. "The New *Billy
Budd* and the Novelistic Fallacy: An Essay-Review."
MFS 8(1962): 306-311.

3634. ----------. "A Whale, An Heiress, and
A Southern Demigod: Three Symbolic Americas.
Coll L 1(1974): 100-112.

3635. Stanonik, Janez. "Did Melville Ever
See an Albino?" *AL* 43(1972): 637-638.

3636. Stark, John. "'The Cassock' Chapter
in *Moby-Dick* and the Theme of Literary Creativity."
SAF 1(1973): 105-111.

3637. Stavrou, C. N. "Ahab and Dick Again."
TSLL 3(1961): 309-320.

3638. Stein, William Bysshe. "*Billy Budd:*
The Nightmare of History." *Criticism* 3(1961):
237-250.

3639. ----------. "Melville's Comedy of
Faith." *ELH* 27(1960): 315-333.

3640. ----------. "Melville's Eros." *TSLL*
3(1961): 297-308.

3641. ----------. "The Old Man and the Triple Goddess: Melville's 'The Haglets.'" *ELH* 25
(1958): 43-59.

3642. Sten, Christopher W. "Bartleby the
Transcendentalist: Melville's Dead Letter to
Emerson." *MLQ* 35(1974): 30-44.

3643. ----------. "The Dialogue of Crisis
in *The Confidence-Man:* Melville's New Novel."
SN 6(1974): 165-185.

3644. ----------. "Vere's Use of the 'Forms':
Means and Ends in *Billy Budd.*" *AL* 47(1975): 37-51.

3645. Stern, Milton. "Some Techniques of
Melville's Perception." *PMLA* 73(1958): 251-259.

3646. Stewart, George R. "The Two Moby-
Dicks." *AL* 25(1954): 417-448.

3647. Stone, Albert E. "A New Version of
American Innocence: Robert Lowell's *Benito
Cereno.*" *NEQ* 45(1972): 467-483.

3648. Stone, Edward. "Bartleby and Miss
Norman." *SSF* 9(1972): 271-274.

3649. ----------. "The Buried Book: *Moby-
Dick* a Century Ago." *SN* 7(1975): 552-562.

3650. ----------. "The Function of the
Gams in *Moby-Dick.*" *Coll L* 2(1975): 171-181.

3651. ----------. "Melville's Late Pale
Usher." *ELN* 9(1971): 51-53.

3652. ----------. "Melville's Pip and Coleridge's Servant Girl." *AL* 25(1953): 358-360.

3653. ----------. "The Whiteness of 'The Whale.'" *CLA* 18(1975): 348-363.

3654. Stout, Janis P. "The Encroaching Sodom: Melville's Urban Fiction." *TSLL* 17(1975): 157-173.

3655. ----------. "Melville's Use of the Book of Job." *NCF* 25(1970): 69-84.

3656. Straugh, Carl F. "Ishmael: Time and Personality in *Moby-Dick*." *SN* 1(1969): 468-483.

3657. Strandberg, Victor H. "God and the Critics of Melville." *TSLL* 6(1964): 322-333.

3658. Strickland, Carol Colclough. "Coherence and Ambivalence in Melville's *Pierre*." *AL* 48(1976): 302-311.

3659. Stempel, Daniel, and Bruce Stillians. "*Bartleby the Scrivener*: A Parable of Pessimism." *NCF* 27(1972): 268-282.

3660. Suits, Bernard. "*Billy Budd* and Historical Evidence." A Rejoinder." *NCF* 18(1963): 288-291.

3661. Sullivan, Sister Mary Petrus. "*Moby Dick*: Chapter CXXIX, 'The Cabin.'" *NCF* 20 (1965): 188-190.

3662. Sutton, Walter. "Melville's 'Pleasure Party' and the Art of Concealment." *PQ* 30(1951): 316-327.

3663. Sweeney, Gerard M. "Melville's Hawthornian Bell-Tower: A Fairy-Tale Source." *AL* 45(1973): 279-285.

3664. Tanselle, G. Thomas. "Bibliographical Problems in Melville." *SAF* 2(1974): 57-74.

3665. ----------. "The First Review of *Typee*." *AL* 34(1963): 567-571.

3666. ----------. "A Further Note on 'Whiteness' in Melville and Others." *PMLA* 81(1966): 604.

3667. ----------. "Melville Writers to the New Bedford Lyceum." *AL* 39(1967): 391-392.

3668. Thomas, Joel J. "Melville's Use of Mysticism." *PQ* 53(1974): 413-424.

3669. Thompson, W. R. "Melville's 'The Fiddler': A Study in Dissolution." *TSLL* 2(1961): 492-500.

3670. Tichi, Cecelia. "Melville's Craft and Theme of Language Debased in *The Confidence-Man*." *ELH* 39(1972): 639-658.

3671. Trimpi, Helen P. "Harlequin-Confidence-Man: The Satirical Tradition of Commedia Dell' Arte and Pantomine in Melville's *The Confidence-Man*." *TSLL* 16(1974): 147-193.

3672. Tucker, Harry, Jr. "A Glance at 'Whiteness' in Melville and Camus." *PMLA* 80 (1965): 605.

3673. Tuerk, Richard. "Melville's 'Bartleby' and Isaac D'Israeli's *Curiosities of Literature, Second Series*." *SSF* 7(1970): 647-649.

3674. Turner, Darwin T. "Smoke from Melville's Chimney." *CLA* 7(1963): 107-113.

3675. ----------. "A View of Melville's 'Piazza.'" *CLA* 7(1963): 56-62.

3676. Tuveson, Ernest. "The Creed of *The Confidence-Man*." *ELH* 33(1966): 247-270.

3677. Vanderhaar, Margaret. "A Re-examination of 'Benito Cereno.'" *AL* 40(1968): 179-191.

3678. Vann, J. Don. "A Checklist of Melville Criticism, 1958-1968." *SN* 1(1969): 507-535.

3679. Vargish, Thomas. "Gnostic *Mythos* in *Moby-Dick*." *PMLA* 8(1966): 272-277.

3680. Vernon, John. "Melville's 'The Bell-Tower.'" *SSF* 7(1970): 264-275.

3681. Vessella, Carmella M. "Melville on Christmas Day, 1840." *AL* 49(1977): 107-108.

3682. Vogel, Dan. "The Dramatic Chapters in *Moby-Dick*." *NCF* 13(1958): 239-247.

3683. Wadlington, Warwick. "Ishmael's Godly Gamesomeness: Selftaste and Rhetoric in *Moby-Dick*." *ELH* 39(1972): 309-331.

3684. Waggoner, Hyatt. "Hawthorne and Melville Acquaint the Reader with Their Abodes." *SN* 2(1970): 420-424.

3685. Waite, Robert. "Melville's *Momento Mori*." *SAF* 5(1977): 187-197.

3686. Wallace, Robert K. "*Billy Budd* and the Haymarket Hangings." *AL* 47(1975): 108-113.

3687. Walser, Richard. "Another Early Review of *Typee*." *AL* 36(1965): 515-516.

3688. Ward, J. A. "The Function of the Cetological Chapters in *Moby-Dick*." *AL* 28(1956): 165-183.

3689. Watkins, Floyd C., and Ward Pafford. "*Benito Cereno*: A Note in Rebuttal." *NCF* 7(1952): 68-71.

3690. Watson, Charles N., Jr. "The Estrangement of Hawthorne and Melville." *NEQ* 46(1973): 380-402.

3691. ----------. "Melville and the Theme of Timonism: *Pierre* to *The Confidence-Man*." *AL* 44(1972): 398-413.

3692. ----------. "Melville's Agatha and Hunilla: A Literary Reincarnation." *ELN* 6(1968): 114-118.

3693. ----------. "Melville's *Israel Potter*: Fathers and Sons." *SN* 7(1975): 563-568.

3694. ----------. "Premature Burial in *Arthur Gordon Pym* and *Israel Potter*." *AL* 47(1975): 105-107.

3695. Weathers, Willie T. "*Moby-Dick* and the Nineteenth-Century Scene." *TSLL* 1(1960): 477-501.

3696. Welsh, Howard. "The Politics of Race in 'Benito Cereno.'" *AL* 46(1975): 556-566.

3697. Werge, Thomas. "*Moby-Dick* and the Calvinist Tradition." *SN* 1(1969): 484-506.

3698. Wheeler, Otis. "Humor in *Moby-Dick*: Two Problems." *AL* 29(1957): 203-206.

3699. Widmer, Kinglsey. "Melville's Radical Resistance: The Method and Meaning of *Bartleby*." *SN* 1(1969): 444-458.

3700. ----------. "The Negative Affirmation: Melville's 'Bartleby.'" *MFS* 8(1962): 276-286.

3701. ----------. "The Perplexed Myths of Melville: *Billy Budd*." *Novel* 2(1968): 25-35.

3702. ----------. "The Perplexity of Melville: *Benito Cereno*." *SSF* 5(1968): 225-238.

3703. ----------. "Review-Essay: The Learned Try-Works: A Review of Recent Scholarly Criticism of Melville." *SN* 5(1973): 117-124.

3704. Willett, Ralph W. "Nelson and Vere: Hero and Victim in *Billy Budd, Sailor*." *PMLA* 82 (1967): 370-376.

3705. Williams, David Park. "Hook and Ahab: Barrie's Strange Satire on Melville." *PMLA* 80 (1965): 483-488.

3706. Williams, Mentor L. "Some Notes and Reviews of Melville's Novels in American Religious

Periodicals, 1846-1849." *AL* 22(1950): 119-127.

3707. ----------. "Two Hawaiian-Americans Visit Herman Melville." *NEQ* 23(1950): 97-99.

3708. Wilson, G. R., Jr. "*Billy Budd* and Melville's Use of Dramatic Technique." *SSF* 4 (1967): 105-111.

3709. Withim, Phil. "*Billy Budd:* Testament of Resistance." *MLQ* 20(1959): 115-127.

3710. Woodruff, Stuart C. "Melville and His Chimney." *PMLA* 75(1960): 283-292.

3711. Woodson, Thomas. "Ahab's Greatness: Prometheus as Narcissus." *ELH* 33(1966): 351-369.

3712. Wright, Nathalia. "Form as Function in Melville." *PMLA* 67(1952): 330-340.

3713. ----------. "The Head and the Heart in Melville's *Mardi*." *PMLA* 66(1951): 351-362.

3714. ----------. "Moby-Dick: Jonah's or Job's Whale?" *AL* 37(1965): 190-195.

3715. ----------. "A Note on Melville's Use of Spenser: Hautia and the Bower of Bliss." *AL* 24(1952): 83-85.

3716. ----------. "*Pierre:* Herman Melville's *Inferno*." *AL* 32(1960): 167-181.

3717. Yannella, Donald. "Review-Essay: Some Recent Melville Studies." *SN* 8(1976): 214-222.

3718. Yarina, Margaret. "The Dualistic Vision of Herman Melville's 'The Encantadas.'" *JNT* 3(1973): 141-148.

3719. Yates, Norris. "An Instance of Parallel Imagery in Hawthorne, Melville, and Frost." *PQ* 36(1957): 276-280.

3720. Young, James Dean. "The Nine Gams of the *Pequod*." *AL* 25(1954): 449-463.

3721. Yu, Beongcheon. "Ishmael's Equal Eye: The Source of Balance in *Moby-Dick*." *ELH* 32(1965): 110-125.

3722. Zaller, Robert. "Melville and the Myth of Revolution." *SR* 15(1976): 607-622.

See also 610, 1110, 1158, 1161, 2363, 3793, 5594, 7590, 20235.

MILLER, JOAQUIN.   3723. Duckett, Margaret. "Carlyle, 'Columbus,' and Joaquin Miller." *PQ* 35(1956): 443-447.

3724. Dunbar, John Raine. "Some Letters of Joaquin Miller to Frederick Locker." *MLQ* 11(1950): 438-444.

3725. Rosenus, A. H. "Joaquin Miller and His 'Shadow.'" *WAL* 11(1976): 51-59.

MITHCELL, S. WEIR.   3726. Griffith, Kelley, Jr. "Weir Mitchell and the Genteel Romance." *AL* 44(1972): 247-261.

3727. Hayne, Barrie. "S. Weir Mitchell (1829-1914)." [bibliography] *ALR* 2(1969): 149-155.
See also 157.

MITCHELL, JOHN A.   3728. "A Most Unusual Country." [illustrations for Mitchell's *Drowsey* by Angus Peter Macdonnel] *Ext* 12(1971): 99-105.

MORRELL, BENJAMIN.   See 3931.

MOSES, GEORGE.   See 628.

MOTLEY, JOHN L.   3729. Tilton, Eleanor. "Holmes and His Critic Motley." *AL* 36(1965): 463-474.

MUIR, JOHN.   3730. Cohen, Michael P. "John Muir's Public Voice." *WAL* 10(1975): 177-187.

MURFREE, MARY N.   3731. Carleton, Reese.

"Mary Noailles Murfree (1851-1922): An Annotated Bibliography." *ALR* 7(1974): 293-378.

3732. Cary, Richard. "Mary Noailles Murfree (1850-1922)." *ALR* 1,#1(1967): 79-83.

NASBY, PETROLEUM V.   See DAVID ROSS LOCKE.

NEAL, JOHN.   3733. King, Peter J. "John Neal as a Benthamite." *NEQ* 39(1966): 47-65.

3734. Lease, Benjamin. "John Neal's Quarrel with the *Westminister Review*." *AL* 26(1954): 86-88.

3735. ----------. "Yankee Poetics: John Neal's Theory of Poetry and Fiction." *AL* 24(1953): 505-519.

3736. Martin, Harold C. "The Colloquial Tradition in the Novel: John Neal." *NEQ* 32(1959): 455-475.

3737. Ringe, Donald. "The American Revolution in American Romance." *AL* 49(1977): 352-365.

3738. Scheick, William J. "Power, Authority, and Revolutionary Impulse in John Neal's *Rachel Dyer*." *SAF* 4(1976): 143-155.

NEAL, JOSEPH C.   See 1151.

NEWBERRY, JULIA.   See 575.

NORRIS, FRANK.   3739. Astro, Richard. "*Vandover and the Brute* and *The Beautiful and Damned:* A Search for Thematic and Stylistic Reinterpretation." *MFS* 14(1968): 397-413.

3740. Burns, Stuart L. "The Rapist in Frank Norris's *The Octopus*." *AL* 42(1971): 567-569.

3741. Cooperman, Stanley. "Frank Norris and the Werewolf of Guilt." *MLQ* 20(1959): 252-258.

3742. Crow, Charles L. "The Real Vanamee and His Influence on Frank Norris' *The Octopus*." *WAL* 9(1974): 131-139.

3743. Davidson, Richard, ed. "The Remaining Seven of Frank Norris' 'Weekly Letters.'" *ALR* 1, #3(1968): 47-66.

3744. Davison, Richard Allan. " An Undiscovered Early Review of Norris' *Octopus*." *WAL* 3 (1968): 147-151.

3745. Dillingham, William B. "The Old Folks of *McTeague*." *NCF* 16(1961): 169-173.

3746. Folsom, James K. "Social Darwinism or Social Protest? The 'Philosophy' of *The Octopus*." *MFS* 8(1962): 393-400.

3747. French, Warren. "Frank Norris (1870-1902)." [bibliography] *ALR* 1,#1(1967): 84-89.

3748. Gardner, Joseph H. "Dickens, Romance, and *McTeague:* A Study in Mutual Interpretation." *EL* 1(1974): 69-82.

3749. Giles, James R. "Beneficial Atavism in Frank Norris and Jack London." *WAL* 4(1969): 15-27.

3750. Goldman, Suzy Bernstein. "*McTeague:* The Imagistic Network." *WAL* 7(1972): 83-99.

3751. Graham, D. B. "Art in *McTeague*." *SAF* 3(1975): 143-155.

3752. ----------. "Studio Art in *The Octopus*." *AL* 44(1973): 657-666.

3753. Hill, John S. "The Influence of Cesare Lombroso on Frank Norris's Early Fiction." *AL* 42(1970): 89-91.

3754. Johnson, George W. "Frank Norris and Romance." *AL* 33(1961): 52-63.

3755. Johnson, Lee. "Western Literary Realism: The California Tales of Norris and Austin." *ALR* 7(1974): 278-279.

3756. Kaplan, Charles. "Norris's Use of Sources in *The Pit*." *AL* 25(1953): 75-84.

3757. Katz, Joseph. "Frank Norris and 'The Newspaper Experience.'" *ALR* 4(1971): 73-77.

3758. Kwiat, Joseph J. "The Newspaper Experience: Crane, Norris and Dreiser." *NCF* 8(1953): 99-117.

3759. Love, Glen A. "Frank Norris's Western Metropolitans." *WAL* 11(1976): 3-22.

3760. McCluskey, John E. "Frank Norris' Literary Terminology: A Note on Historical Context." *WAL* 7(1972): 148-150.

3761. McElrath, Joseph, Jr. "The Erratic Design of Frank Norris's *Moran of the Lady Letty*." *ALR* (1977): 114-124.

3762. ----------. "Frank Norris's *Vandover and the Brute*: Narrative Technique and the Socio-Critical Viewpoint." *SAF* 4(1976): 27-43.

3763. ----------. "Norris' Return from Cuba." *ALR* 6(1973): 251-252.

3764. Pizer, Donald. "Another Look at *The Octopus*." *NCF* 10(1955): 217-224.

3765. ----------. "Evolutionary Ethical Dualism in Frank Norris' *Vandover and the Brute* and *McTeague*." *PMLA* 76(1961): 552-560.

3766. ----------. Frank Norris' Definition of Naturalism." *MFS* 8(1962): 408-410.

3767. ----------. "The Masculine-Feminine Ethic in Frank Norris' Popular Novels." *TSLL* 6 (1964): 84-91.

3768. ----------. "Synthetic Criticism and Frank Norris; Or, Mr. Marx, Mr. Taylor, and *The Octopus*." *AL* 34(1963): 532-541.

3769. Sheppard, Keith S. "A New Note for McTeague's Canary." *WAL* 9(1974): 217-218.

3770. Sherwood, John C. "Norris and the *Jeannette*." *PQ* 37(1958): 245-252.

3771. Stronks, James B. "Frank Norris's *McTeague*: A Possible Source in H. C. Bunner." *NCF* 25(1971): 474-478.

3772. ----------. "John Kendrick Bangs Criticizes Norris's Borrowings in *Blix*." *AL* 42 (1970): 380-386.

3773. Swensson, John. "'The Great Corner in Hannibal and St. Jo.': A Previously Unpublished Short Story by Frank Norris." *ALR* 4 (1971): 205-226.

3774. Walker, Don D. "The Western Naturalism of Frank Norris." *WAL* 2(1967): 14-29.

3775. Watson, Charles. "A Source for the Ending of *McTeague*." *ALR* 5(1972): 173-174.

3776. Westbrook, Wayne. "'The Great Corner in Hannibal and St.Jo'—Another Look." *ALR* 10 (1977): 213-214.

See also 1114, 6597.

NORTH, FRANKLIN. 3777. Roemer, Kenneth M. "The Yankee(s) in Noahville." *AL* 45(1973): 434-437.

NORTON, CHARLES ELIOT. 3778. Kirk, Clara M. "Toward a Theory of Art: A Dialogue Between W. D. Howells and C. E. Norton." *NEQ* 36(1963): 291-321.

3779. Marsden, Malcolm M. "Discriminating Sympathy: Charles Eliot Norton's Unique Gift." *NEQ* 31(1958): 463-483.

3780. Morison, Samuel Eliot. "Reminiscences of Charles Eliot Norton." *NEQ* 33(1960): 364-368.

3781. Rollins, Hyder E. "Charles Eliot Norton and Froude." *JEGP* 57(1958): 651-664.

3782. Vanderbilt, Kermit. "Howells and Norton: Some Frustrations of the Biographer." *NEQ* 37(1964): 84-89.

O'CONNER, WILLIAM DOUGLAS. 3783. Coleman, Rufus A. "Trowbridge and O'Conner: Unpublished Correspondence with Special Reference to Walt Whitman." *AL* 23(1951): 323-331.

3784. Loving, Jerome. "Genesis of *The Good Gray Poet*." *TSLL* 19(1977): 227-233.

3785. Milne, W. Gordon. "William Douglas O'Conner and the Authorship of *The Good Gray Poet*." *AL* 25(1953): 31-42.

O.HENRY. See WILLIAM SIDNEY PORTER.

OLMSTED, FREDERICK. 3786. Roper, Laura Wood. "'Mr. Law' and *Putnam's Monthly Magazine*: A Note on a Phase in the Career of Frederick Law Olmsted." *AL* 26(1954): 88-93.

OSGOOD, FRANCES SARGENT. See 3828.

PAGE, THOMAS N. 3787. Gross, Theodore. "Thomas Nelson Page (1853-1922)." [bibliography] *ALR* 1,#1(1967): 90-92.

3788. Holman, Harriet R. "Attempt and Failure: Thomas Nelson Page as Playwright." *SLJ* 3,#1 (1970): 72-82.

3789. Rubin, Louis D., Jr. "The Other Side of Slavery: Thomas Nelson Page's 'No Haid Pawn.'" *SLI* 7,#1(1974): 95-99.

See also 602a.

PARKER, THEODORE. 3790. Smith, H. Shelton. "Was Theodore Parker a Transcendentalist?" *NEQ* 23 (1950): 351-364.

PARKMAN, FRANCIS. 3791. Jacobs, Wilbur R. "Some of Parkman's Literary Devices." *NEQ* 31(1958): 244-252.

3792. Moore, L. Hugh. "Francis Parkman on the Oregon Trail: A Study in Cultural Prejudice." *WAL* 12(1977): 185-197.

3793. Powers, William. "Bulkington as Henry Chatillon." *WAL* 3(1968): 153-155.

PARTON, JAMES. 3794. McDermott, John Francis. "Whitman and the Partons: Glimpses from the Diary of Thomas Butler Gunn, 1856-1860." *AL* 29 (1957): 316-319.

PAULDING, JAMES K. 3795. Aderman, Ralph M. "James Kirke Paulding on Literature and the West." *AL* 27(1955): 97-101.

3796. ----------. "A Paulding Pamphlet Identified." *AL* 29(1957): 305-306.

PEABODY, ELIZABETH. 3797. Wilson, John B. "A Transcendental Minority Report." *NEQ* 29(1956): 147-158.

PERRY, THOMAS S. 3798. Pizer, Donald. "Evolution and Criticism: Thomas Sergeant Perry." *TSLL* 3(1961): 348-359.

PHELPS, ELIZABETH STUART. See 1151.

PHILLIPS, DAVID GRAHAM. 3799. Ravitz, Abe. "David Graham Phillips (1867-1911):" [bibliography] *ALR* 1,#3(1968): 24-29.

3800. Sloane, David E. E. "David Graham Phillips, Jack London, and Others on Contemporary Reviewers and Critics." *ALR* 3(1970): 67-71.

3801. Stallings, Frank L. "David Graham Phillips: A Critical Bibliography of Secondary Comment." *ALR* 3(1970): 1-35.

POE, EDGAR ALLAN. 3802. Autrey, Max L.

Edgar Allan Poe's Satiric View of Evolution." *Ext* 18(1977): 186-199.

3803. Bailey, J. O. "What Happens in 'The Fall of the House of Usher'?" *AL* 35(1964): 445-466.

3804. Bandy, W. T. "New Light on a Source of Poe's 'A Descent into the Maelstrom.'" *AL* 24(1953): 534-537.

3805. ----------. "Poe's Solution of 'Frailey Land Office Cipher.'" *PMLA* 68(1953): 1240-1241.

3806. ----------. "Were the Russians the First to Translate Poe?" *AL* 31(1960): 479-480.

3807. ----------. "Who Was Monsieur Dupin?" *PMLA* 79(1964): 509-510.

3808. Belgion, Montgomery. "The Mystery of Poe's Poetry." *EIC* 1(1951): 51-66.

3809. Benton, Richard P. "Is Poe's 'The Assisgnation' a Hoax?" *NCF* 18(1963): 193-197.

3810. ----------. "'The Mystery of Marie Roget'-A Defense." *SSF* 6(1969): 144-151.

3811. ----------. "Platonic Allegory in Poe's 'Eleonora.'" *NCF* 22(1967): 293-297.

3812. ----------. "Poe's 'Lionizing': A Quiz on Willis and Lady Blessington." *SSF* 5 (1968): 239-244.

3813. ----------. "Reply to Professor Thompson." *SSF* 6(1968): 97.

3814. ----------. "The Works of N. P. Willis as a Catalyst of Poe's Criticism." *AL* 39 (1967): 315-324.

3815. Braddy, Haldeen. "Poe's Flight from Reality." *TSLL* 1(1959): 394-400.

3816. Broderick, John C. "Poe's Revisions of 'Lenore.'" *AL* 35(1964): 504-510.

3817. Budick, E. Miller. "The Fall of the House: A Reappraisal of Poe's Attitudes toward Life and Death." *SLJ* 9,#2(1977): 30-50.

3818. ----------. "Poe's Gothic Idea: The Comic Geniture of Horror." *EL* 3(1976): 73-85.

3819. Burch, Francis F. "Clement Mansfield Ingleby on Poe's 'The Raven': An Unpublished British Criticism." *AL* 35(1963): 81-82.

3820. Butler, David W. "Usher's Hypochondriasis: Mental Alienation and Romantic Idealism in Poe's Gothic Tales." *AL* 48(1976): 1-12.

3821. Caputi, Anthony. "The Refrain in Poe's Poetry." *AL* 25(1953): 169-178.

3822. Carley, C. V. "A Source for Poe's 'Oblong Box.'" *AL* 29(1957): 310-312.

3823. Carlson, Eric W. "Symbol and Sense in Poe's 'Ulalume.'" *AL* 35(1963): 22-37.

3824. Carringer, Robert L. "Circumscription of Space and the Form of Poe's *Arthur Gordon Pym.*" *PMLA* 89(1974): 506-516.

3825. Carson, David L. "Ortolans and Geese: The Origin of Poe's *Duc De L'Omelette.*" *CLA* 8 (1965): 277-283.

3826. Cary, Richard. "'The Masque of the Red Death' Again." *NCF* 17(1962): 76-78.

3827. ----------. "Poe and the Great Debate." *TSLL* 3(1961): 223-233.

3828. ----------. "Poe and the Literary Ladies." *TSLL* 9(1967): 91-101.

3829. Casale, Ottavio M. "The Battle of Boston: A Revaluation of Poe's Lyceum Appearance." *AL* 45(1973): 423-428.

3830. Cauthen, I. B., Jr. "Lowell on Poe: An Unpublished Comment, 1879." *AL* 24(1952): 230-233.

3831. Cecil, L. Moffit. "Poe's 'Arabesque.'" *Comp L* 18(1966): 55-70.

3832. ----------. "Poe's Tsalal and the Virginia Springs." *NCF* 19(1965): 398-402.

3833. ----------. **"The Two Narratives of** Arthur Gordon Pyn." *TSLL* 5(1963): 232-241.

3834. Cohen, B. Bernard, and Lucian Cohen. "Poe and Griswald Once More." *AL* 34(1962): 97-101.

3835. Cohen, Hening. "Roderick Usher's Tragic Struggle." *NCF* 14(1959): 270-272.

3836. Cooney, James F. "'The Cask of Amontillado': Some Further Ironies." *SSF* 11(1974): 195-196.

3837. Coskren, Robert. "'William Wilson' and the Disintegration of Self." *SSF* 12(1975): 155-162.

3838. Dedmond, Francis P. "'The Cask of Amontillado' and the War of the Literati." *MLQ* 15 (1954): 137-146.

3839. DeFalco, Joseph M. "The Source of Terror in Poe's 'Shadow-A Parable.'" *SSF* 6(1969): 643-648.

3840. Delaney, Joan. "Poe's 'The Gold-Bug' in Russia: A Note on First Impressions." *AL* 42 (1970): 375-379.

3841. Dowell, Richard W. "The Ironic History of Poe's 'Life in Death': A Literary Skeleton in the Closet." *AL* 42(1971): 478-486.

3842. Doxey, William S. "Concerning Fortunato's 'Courtesy.'" *SSF* 4(1967): 266.

3843. Eakin, Paul John. "Poe's Sense of an Ending." *AL* 45(1973): 1-22.

3844. Eaves, T. C. Duncan. "Poe's Last Visit to Philadelphia." *AL* 26(1954): 44-51.

3845. Evans, Walter. "'The Fall of the House of Usher' and Poe's Theory of the Tale." *SSF* 14(1977): 137-144.

3846. Falk, Doris V. "Poe and the Power of Animal Magnetism." *PMLA* 84(1969): 536-546.

3847. Fisher, Benjamin F. "Poe's 'Metzengerstein': Not a Hoax." *AL* 42(1971): 487-494.

3848. Fraiberg, Louis. "Poe's Intimations of Mortality." *HSL* 5(1973): 106-125.

3849. Freeman, Fred B., Jr. "The Identity of Poe's 'Miss B.'" *AL* 39(1967): 389-391.

3850. ----------. "A Note on Poe's 'Miss B.'" *AL* 43(1971): 115-117.

3851. Furrow, Sharon. "Psyche and Setting: Poe's Picturesque Landscapes." *Criticism* 15(1973): 16-27.

3852. Fussell, Edwin. "Poe's 'Raven': Or, How to Concoct a Popular Poem from Almost Nothing at All." *ELN* 2(1964): 36-39.

3853. Gargano, James W. "'The Black Cat': Perverseness Reconsidered." *TSLL* 2(1960): 172-179.

3854. ----------. "'The Cask of Amontillado': A Masquerade of Motive and Identity." *SSF* 4(1967): 119-126.

3855. ----------. "Poe's 'Morella': A Note on Her Name." *AL* 47(1975): 259-264.

3856. ----------. "The Theme of Time in 'The Tell-Tale Heart.'" *SSF* 5(1968): 378-382.

3857. Gerber, Gerald E. "Additional Sources for 'The Masque of the Red Death.'" *AL* 37 (1965): 52-54.

3858. ----------. "Poe's Odd Angel." *NCF* 23(1968): 88-93.

3859. Girgus, Sam B. "Poe and R. D. Laing: The Transcendent Self." *SSF* 13(1976): 299-309.

3860. Goodwin, K. L. "Roderick Usher's Overrated Knowledge." *NCF* 16(1961): 173-175.

3861. Graveley, William H. "Christopher North and the Genesis of *The Raven*." *PMLA* 66 (1951): 149-161.

3862. Grubb, Gerald G. "The Personal and Literary Relationships of Dickens and Poe." *NCF* 5(1950): 1-22, 101-120, 209-221.

3863. Hagemann, E. R. "Two 'Lost' Letters by Poe, with Notes and Commentary." *AL* 28(1957): 507-510.

3864. Harbert, Earl N. "A New Poe Letter." *AL* 35(1963): 80-81.

3865. Harris, Kathryn Montgomery. "Ironic Revenge in Poe's 'The Cask of Amontillado.'" *SSF* 6(1969): 333-335.

3866. Hartley, Lodwick. "From Crazy House to The House of Usher: A Note Toward a Source." *SSF* 2(1965): 256-261.

3867. Hassell, J. Woodrow, Jr. "The Problem of Realism in 'The Gold Bug.'" *AL* 25(1953): 179-192.

3868. Hatvary, George Egon. "Poe's Borrowings from H. B. Wallace." *AL* 38(1966): 365-372.

3869. Haviland, Thomas P. "How Well Did Poe Know Milton?" *PMLA* 69(1954): 841-860.

3870. Helms, Randel. "Another Source for Poe's *Arthur Gordon Pym*." *AL* 41(1970): 572-575.

3871. Hinden, Michael. "Poe's Debt to Wordsworth: A Reading of 'Stanzas.'" *SR* 8(1960): 109-120.

3872. Hinz, Evelyn J. and John J. Teunissen. "Poe, *Pym*, and Primitivism." *SSF* 14(1977): 13-20.

3873. Hirsch, David H. "Another Source for Poe's 'The Duc De L'Omelette.'" *AL* 38(1967): 532-536.

3874. Hoffman, Michael J. "The House of Usher and Negative Romanticism." *SR* 4(1965): 158-168.

3875. Holt, Palmer C. "Poe and H. N. Coleridge's *Greek Classic Poets*: 'Pinakidia,' 'Politian,' and 'Morella' Sources." *AL* 34(1962): 8-30.

3876. Hubbell, Jay B. "Charles Chauncey Burr: Friend of Poe." *PMLA* 69(1954): 833-840.

3877. ----------. "The Literary Apprenticeship of Edgar Allan Poe." *SLJ* 1,#1(1968): 60-74.

3878. ----------. "Poe and the Southern Literary Tradition." *TSLL* 2(1960): 151-171.

3879. Jones, Buford, and Kent Ljungquist. "Monsieur Dupin: Further Details On the Reality Behind the Legend." *SLJ* 9,#1(1976): 70-77.

3880. Jones, Joseph. "'The Raven' and 'The Raven': Another Source of Poe's Poem." *AL* 30(1958): 185-193.

3881. Joseph, Gerhard. "Poe and Tennyson." *PMLA* 88(1973): 418-428.

3882. Kehler, Joel R. "New Light on the Genesis and Progress of Poe's Landscape Fiction." *AL* 47(1975): 173-183.

3883. Kelly, George. "Poe's Theory of Beauty." *AL* 27(1956): 521-536.

3884. ----------. "Poe's Theory of Unity." *PQ* 37(1958): 34-44.

3885. Kennedy, J. Gerald. "The Limits of Reason: Poe's Deluded Detectives." *AL* 47(1975): 184-196.

3886. ----------. "The Preface as a Key to the Satire in *Pym*." *SN* 5(1973): 191-196.

3887. Ketterer, David. "Poe's Usage of the Hoax and the Unity of 'Hans Phaall.'" *Criticism* 13(1971): 377-385.

3888. Kime, Wayne R. "Poe's Use of Irving's *Astoria* in 'The Journal of Julius Rodman.'" *AL* 40(1968): 215-222.

3889. Lauber, John. "'Ligeia' and Its Critics: A Plea for Literalism." *SSF* 4(1966): 28-32.

3890. Leary, Lewis. "Edgar Allan Poe: The Adolescent As Confidence Man." *SLJ* 4,#2(1972): 3-21.

3891. LeClair, Thomas. "Poe's *Pym* and Nabokov's *Pale Fire*." *NCL* 3(March, 1973): 2-3.

3892. Lee, Grace Farrell. "The Quest of Arthur Gordon Pym." *SLJ* 4,#2(1972): 22-33.

3893. Liebman, Sheldon. "Poe's Tales and His Theory of the Poetic Experience." *SSF* 7 (1970): 582-596.

3894. Lippit, Noriko Mizuta. "Tanizaki and Poe: The Grotesque and the Quest for Supernal Beauty." *Comp L* 29(1977): 221-240.

3895. Ljungquist, Kent. "Poe and the Sublime: His Two Short Sea Tales in the Context of an Aesthetic Tradition." *Criticism* 17(1975): 131-151.

3896. ----------. "Poe's Nubian Geographer." *AL* 48(1976): 73-75.

3897. ----------. "Poe's 'The Island of the Fay': The Passing of Fairyland." *SSF* 14(1977): 265-271.

3898. Lubbers, Klaus. "Poe's 'The Conqueror Worm.'" *AL* 39(1967): 375-379.

3899. Lubell, Albert J. "Poe and A. W. Schlegel." *JEGP* 52(1953): 1-12.

3900. Maddison, Carol Hopkins. "Poe's Eureka." *TSLL* 2(1960): 350-367.

3901. Marks, Alfred H. "Two Rodericks and Two Worms: 'Egotism; or, The Bosom Serpent' as Personal Satire." *PMLA* 74(1959): 607-612.

3902. Marks, Emerson R. "Poe as Literary Theorist: A Reappraisal." *AL* 33(1961): 296-306.

3903. Martin, Bruce K. "Poe's 'Hop-Frog' and the Retreat from Comedy." *SSF* 10(1973): 288-290.

3904. Mazow, Julia Wolf. "The Survial Theme in Selected Tales of Edgar Allan Poe." *SAF* 3(1975): 216-223.

3905. McCorison, Marcus Allen. "An Unpublished Poe Letter." *AL* 32(1961): 455-456.

3906. McNeal, Thomas H. "Poe's *Zenobia*: An Early Satire on Margaret Fuller." *MLQ* 11(1950): 205-216.

3907. Miller, James E., Jr. "'Ululume' Resurrected." *PQ* 34(1955): 197-205.

3908. Miller, John C. "A Poe Letter Re-Presented." *AL* 35(1964): 359-361.

3909. ----------. "An Unpublished Poe Letter." *AL* 26(1955): 560-561.

3910. Moldenhauer, Joseph J. "Beyond the Tamarid Tree: A New Poe Letter." *AL* 42(1971): 468-477.

3911. ----------. "Imagination and Perversity in *The Narrative of Arthur Gordon Pym*." *TSLL* 13(1971): 267-280.

3912. ----------. "Murder as a Fine Art: Basic Connections between Poe's Aesthetics, Psychology, and Moral Vision." *PMLA* 83(1968): 284-297.

3913. Monteiro, George. "Edgar Poe and the New Knowledge." *SLJ* 4,#2(1972): 34-40.

3914. Mooney, Stephen L. "The Comic in Poe's Fiction." *AL* 33(1962): 433-441.

3915. Moore, John Robert. "Poe's Reading of *Anne of Geierstein*." *AL* 22(1951): 493-496.

3916. Moore, Rayburn S. "A Note on Poe and the Sons of Temperance." *AL* 30(1958): 359-361.

3917. Morrison, Claudia C. "Poe's 'Ligeia': An Analysis." *SSF* 4(1967): 234-244.

3918. Moss, Sidney P. "A Conjecture Concerning the Writing of 'Arthur Gordon Pym.'" *SSF* 4(1966): 83-85.

3919. ----------. "Poe and His Nemesis--Lewis Gaylord Clark." *AL* 28(1956): 30-49.

3920. ----------. "Poe and the *Norman Leslie* Incident." *AL* 25(1953): 293-306.

3921. Nisbet, Ada B. "New Light on the Dickens-Poe Relationship." *NCF* 5(1951): 295-302.

3922. ----------. "Poe and Dickens." *NCF* 9(1955): 313-314.

3923. Obuchowski, Peter. "Unity of Effect in Poe's 'The Fall of the House of Usher.'" *SSF* 12(1975): 407-412.

3924. O'Donnell, Charles. "From Earth to Ether: Poe's Flight into Space." *PMLA* 77(1962): 85-91.

3925. Ostrom, John. "Fourth Supplement to *The Letters of Poe*." *AL* 45(1974): 513-536.

3926. ----------. "Second Supplement to the Letters of Poe." *AL* 29(1957): 79-86.

3927. ----------. "Supplement to *The Letters of Poe*." *AL* 24(1952): 358-366.

3928. Panek, LeRoy L. "'Maelzel's Chess-Player,' Poe's First Detective Mistake." *AL* 48 (1976): 370-372.

3929. Pauly, Thomas H. "'Hop-Frog—Is the Last Laugh Best?" *SSF* 11(1974): 307-309.

3930. Peters, H. F. "Ernest Jünger's Concern with E. A. Poe." *Comp L* 10(1958): 144-149.

3931. Pollin, Burton R. "The *Narrative* of Benjamin Morrel: Out of 'The Bucket' and into Poe's *Pym*." *SAF* 4(1976): 157-172.

3932. ----------. "Poe and Godwin." *NCF* 20 (1965): 237-253.

3933. ----------. "Poe and the *Boston Notion*." *ELN* 8(1970): 23-28.

3934. ----------. "Poe as Probable Author of 'Harper's Ferry.'" *AL* 40(1968): 164-178.

3935. ----------. "Poe, Freeman Hunt, and Four Unrecorded Reviews of Poe's Works." [with text] *TSLL* 16(1976): 305-313.

3936. ----------. "Poe in the *Boston Notion*." *NEQ* 42(1969): 585-589.

3937. ----------. "Poe's 'Diddling': The Source of Title and Tale." *SLJ* 2,#1(1969): 106-111.

3938. ----------. "Poe's Dr. Ollapod." *AL* 42(1970): 80-82.

3939. ----------. "Poe's *Narrative of Arthur Gordon Pym* and the Contemporary Reviewers." *SAF* 2(1974): 37-56.

3940. ----------. "Poe's 'Shadow' as a Source of His 'The Masque of the Red Death.'" *SSF* 6(1968): 104-106.

3941. ----------. "Politics and History in Poe's 'Mellonta Tauta': Two Allusions Explained." *SSF* 8(1971): 627-631.

3942. ----------. "Southey's *Curse of Kehama* in Poe's 'City in the Sea.'" *WC* 7(1976): 101-106.

3943. ----------. "'The Spectacles' of Poe—Sources and Significance." *AL* 37(1965): 185-190.

3944. ----------. "*Undine* in the Works of Poe." *SR* 14(1975): 59-74.

3945. Purdy, S. B. "Poe and Dostoyevsky." *SSF* 4(1967): 169-171.

3946. Rea, J. "In Defense of Fortunato's Courtesy." *SSF* 4(1967): 267-268.

3947. ----------. "Poe's 'The Cask of Amontillado.'" *SSF* 4(1966): 57-69.

3948. Reece, James B. "A Reexamination of a Poe Date: Mrs. Ellet's Letters." *AL* 42(1970): 157-164.

3949. Rein, David M. "Poe and Mrs. Shelton." *AL* 28(1956): 225-227.

3950. Reiss, Edmund. "The Comic Setting of 'Hans Pfaall.'" *AL* 29(1957): 305-309.

3951. Richmond, Lee J. "Edgar Allan Poe's 'Morella': Vampire of Volition." *SSF* 9(1972): 93-94.

3952. Ridgely, J. V. and Iola S. Haverstick. "Chartless Voyage: The Many Narratives of Arthur Gordon Pym" *TSLL* 8(1966): 63-80.

3953. Robinson, E. Arthur. "Order and Sentience in 'The Fall of the House of Usher.'" *PMLA* 76(1961): 68-81.

3954. ----------. "Poe's 'The Tell Tale Heart.'" *NCF* 19(1965): 369-378.

3955. Rosenfeld, Alvin. "Description in Poe's 'Landor's Cottage.'" *SSF* 4(1967): 264-266.

3956. Samuel, Dorothy J. "Poe and Baudelaire: Parallels in Form and Symbol." *CLA* 3(1959): 88-105.

3957. Schroeter, James. "A Misreading of Poe's 'Ligeia.'" *PMLA* 76(1961): 397-406.

3958. Schroeter, James, and Roy B. Pasler. "Poe's 'Ligeia.'" *PMLA* 77(1962): 675.

3959. Shulman, Robert. "Poe and the Powers of the Mind." *ELH* 37(1970): 245-262.

3960. Sippel, Erich W. "Bolting the Whole Shebang Together: Poe's Predicament." *Criticism* 15(1973): 289-308.

3961. Smith, Herbert F. "Usher's Madness and Poe's Organicism: A Source." *AL* 39(1967): 379-389.

3962. Spitzer, Leo. "A Reinterpretation of 'The Fall of the House of Usher.'" *Comp L* 4(1952): 351-363.

3963. Stauffer, Donald Barlow. "Style and Meaning in 'Ligeia' and 'William Wilson.'" *SSF* 2 (1965): 316-330.

3964. Stepp, Walter. "The Ironic Double in Poe's 'The Cask of Amontillado.'" *SSF* 13(1976): 447-453.

3965. Stern, Madeleine B. "Poe: 'The Mental Temperament' for Phrenologists." *AL* 40(1968): 155-163.

3966. Stovall, Floyd. "An Unpublished Poe Letter." *AL* 36(1965): 514-515.

3967. Stroupe, John H. "Poe's Imaginary Voyage: Pym as Hero." *SSF* 4(1967): 315-321.

3968. Sullivan, Ruth. "William Wilson's Double." *SR* 15(1976): 253-264.

3969. Sweet, Charles A., Jr. "'Ligeia' and the Warlock." *SSF* 13(1976): 85-88.

3970. Taft, Kendall B. "The Identity of Poe's Martin Van Buren Mavis." *AL* 26(1955): 562-563.

3971. Teunissen, John J., and Evelyn J. Hinz. "Poe's *Journal of Julius Rodman* as Parody." *NCF* 27(1972): 317-338.

3972. Thompson, G. R. "Dramatic Irony in 'The Oval Portrait': A Reconsideration of Poe's Revisions." *ELN* 6(1968): 107-114.

3973. ----------. "Is Poe's 'A Tale of the Ragged Mountains' a Hoax?" *SSF* 6(1969): 454-460.

3974. ----------. "On the Nose—Further Speculations on the Source and Meaning of Poe's 'Lionizing.'" *SSF* 6(1968): 94-96.

3975. ----------. "Poe's Readings of *Pelham*: Another Source for 'Tintinnabulation' and other Piquant Expressions." *AL* 41(1969): 251-255.

3976. ----------. "Unity, Death, and No-thingness-Poe's 'Romantic Skepticism.'" *PMLA* 85 (1970): 297-301.

3977. Twitchell, James. "Poe's 'The Oval Portrait' and the Vampire Motif." *SSF* 14(1977): 387-393.

3978. Vanderbilt, Kermit. "Art and Nature in 'The Masque of the Red Death.'" *NCF* 22(1968): 379-389.

3979. Walker, I. M. "The 'Legitimate Sources' of Terror in 'The Fall of House of Usher.'" *MLR* 61(1966): 585-593.

3980. Watson, Charles N., Jr. "Premature Burial in *Arthur Gordon Pym* and *Israel Potter*." *AL* 47(1975): 105-107.

3981. Watts, Charles H., II. "Poe, Irving, and *The Southern Literary Messenger*." *AL* 27 (1955): 249-251.

3982. Webb, Howard W., Jr. "A Further Note on the Dickens-Poe Relationship." *NCF* 15(1960): 80-82.

3983. West, Muriel. "Poe's 'Ligeia' and Issac D'Israeli." *Comp L* 16(1964): 19-28.

3984. Wetherill, P. M. "Edgar Allan Poe and Madame Sabatier." *MLQ* 20(1959): 344-354.

3985. Whipple, William. "Poe, Clark, and 'Thingum Bob.'" *AL* 29(1957): 312-316.

3986. ----------. "Poe's Two-edged Satiric Tale." *NCF* 9(1954): 121-133.

3987. Wilkinson, Ronald Sterne. "Poe's 'Balloon-Hoax' Once More." *AL* 32(1960): 313-317.

3988. Wimsatt, W. K., Jr. "A Further Note on Poe's 'Balloon Hoax.'" *AL* 22(1951): 491-492.

3989. ----------. "Mary Rogers, John Anderson, and Others." *AL* 21(1950): 482-484.

3990. Young, Philip. "The Earlier Psychologists and Poe." *AL* 22(1951): 442-445.

See also 108, 177, 483, 1158, 1161, 1166, 3281, 3458, 5723.

PORTER, WILLIAM SYDNEY. 3991. Barban, Arnold M. "The Discovery of an O.Henry *Rolling Stone*." *AL* 31(1959): 340-341.

3992. Current-Garcia, Eugene. "'Mr. Spirit' and *The Big Bear of Arkansas*: A Note on the Genesis of Southwestern Sporting and Humor Literature." *AL* 27(1955): 332-346.

3993. ----------. "O.Henry's Southern Heritage." *SSF* 2(1964): 1-12.

3994. Long, E. Hudson. "O.Henry (William Sidney Porter) (1862-1910)." [bibliography] *ALR* 1,#1(1967): 93-99.

3995. Marks, Patricia. "O.Henry and Dickens: Elsie in the Bleak House of Moral Decay." *ELN* 12 (1974): 35-37.

3996. McLean, Malcolm. "O.Henry in Honduras." *ALR* 1,#3(1968): 39-46.

3997. Weatherford, Richard M. "Stephen Crane and O.Henry: A Correction." *AL* 44(1973): 666.

PRESCOTT, W. H. 3998. Brotherston, Gordon J. "An Indian Farewell in Prescott's *The Conquest of Mexico*." *AL* 45(1973): 348-356.

REMINGTON, FREDERIC. See 1167.

RICKETSON, DANIEL. 3999. Dias, Earl J. "Daniel Ricketson and Henry Thoreau." *NEQ* 26(1953): 388-396.

RILEY, JAMES WHITCOMB. See 2061.

ROBINSON, ROWLAND E. 4000. Baker, Ronald. "Rowland E. Robinson (1833-1900)." [bibliography] *ALR* 2(1969): 156-159.

RUFFIN, EDMOND. 4001. Hobson, Fred. *"Anticipations of the Future;* or The Wish-Fulfillment of Edmund Ruffin." *SLJ* 10,#1(1977): 84-92.

RUSH, REBECCA. 4002. Meserole, Harrison T. "Some Notes on Early American Fiction: Kelroy Was There." *SAF* 5(1977): 1-12.

SANBORN, F. B. 4003. Harding, Walter. "Two F. B. Sanborn Letters." *AL* 25(1953): 230-234.

SANBORN, KATE. See 1151.

SANDERS, WILBUR EDGERTON. See 620.

SCHINDLER, SOLOMON. 4004. Segal, Howard P. *"Young West*: The Psyche of Technological Utopianism." *Ext* 19(1977): 50-58.

SCOTT, WILLIAM H. 4005. Cansler, Loman D. "He Hewed His Own Path: William Henry Scott, Ozark Songmaker." *SLI* 3,#1(1970): 37-63.

SEDGWICK, CATHERINE. 4006. Birdsall, Richard D. "William Cullen Bryant and Catherine Sedgwick." *NEQ* 28(1955): 349-371.

SIGOURNEY, LYDIA. 4007. Green, David Bonnell. "William Worsworth and Lydia Huntley Sigourney." *NEQ* 37(1964): 527-531.

4008. Wood, Ann Douglas. "Mrs. Sigourney and the Sensibility of the Inner Space." *NEQ* 45 (1972): 163-181.

SILL, EDWARD. 4009. Ferguson, A. R. "Frost, Sill and 'A Wishing Well.'" *AL* 33(1961): 370-373.

SIMMS, WILLIAM GILMORE. 4010. Bresnahan, Roger J. "William Gilmore Simms's Revolutionary War: A Romantic View of Southern History." *SR* 15 (1976): 573-588.

4011. "Cecil, L. Moffitt. "Simms's Porgy as National Hero." *AL* 36(1965): 475-484.

4012. ----------. "Symbolic Pattern in *The Yemassee*." *AL* 35(1964): 510-514.

4013. Duvall, S. P. C. "W. G. Simms's Review of Mrs. Stowe." *AL* 30(1958): 107-117.

4014. Eaves, T. C. Duncan. "An Early American Admirer of Keats." *PMLA* 67(1952): 895-898.

4015. Gates, W. B. "William Gilmore Simms and the Kentucky Tragedy." *AL* 32(1960): 158-166.

4016. Gendron, Dennis. "A Source for Simms's *The Yemassee*." *AL* 48(1976): 368-370.

4017. Guilds, John C. "Simms as Editor and Prophet: The Flowering and Early Death of the *Southern Magnolia*." *SLJ* 4,#2(1972): 69-92.

4018. Hoge, James O. "Byron's Influence on the Poetry of William Gilmore Simms." *EL* 2 (1975): 87-96.

4019. Holman, C. Hugh. "The Influence of Scott and Cooper on Simms." *AL* 23(1951): 203-218.

4020. ----------. "Simms and the British Dramatists." *PMLA* 65(1950): 346-359.

4021. Kibler, James E., Jr. "A New Letter of Simms to Richard Henry Wilde: On the Advancement of Sectional Literature." *AL* 44(1973): 667-669.

4022. ----------. "Simms' Indebtedness to Folk Tradition in 'Sharp Snaffles.'" *SLJ* 4,#2 (1972): 55-68.

4023. Kolodny, Annette. "The Unchanging Landscape: The Pastoral Impulse in Simms's Revolutionary War Romances." *SLJ* 5,#1(1972): 46-67.

4024. Ridgely, Joseph V. "*Woodcraft*: Simms' First Answer to *Uncle Tom's Cabin*." *AL* 31(1960): 421-433.

4025. Ringe, Donald. "The American Revolution in American Romance." *AL* 49(1977): 352-365.

4026. Shillingsburg, Miriam J. "From Notes to Novel: Simms's Creative Method." *SLJ* 5,#1 (1972): 89-107.

4027. Tomlinson, David. "*Simms's Monthly Magazine: The Southern and Western Monthly Magazine and Review*." *SLJ* 8,#1(1975): 95-102.

4028. Vauthier, Simone. "Of Time and the South: The Fiction of William Gilmore Simms." *SLJ* 5,#1(1972): 3-45.

4029. Watson, Charles S. "Simms's Answer to *Uncle Tom's Cabin*: Criticism of the South in *Woodcraft*." *SLJ* 9,#1(1976): 78-90.

4030. ----------. "Simms's Review of *Uncle Tom's Cabin*." *AL* 48(1976): 365-368.

4031. Wimsatt, Mary Ann. "Simms as Novelist of Manners: *Katherine Walton*." *SLJ* 5,#1 (1972): 68-88.

See also 602a.

SIRINGO, CHARLES A.   4032. Sawey, Orlan. "Charlie Siringo: Reluctant Propagandist." *WAL* 7(1972): 203-210.

STEDMAN, EDMUND C.   4033. Duffy, Charles. "An Unpublished Letter: Stedman to Howells." *AL* 30(1958): 369-370.

STICKNEY, TRUMBULL.   4034. Griffing, A. H. "The Achievement of Trumball Stickney." *NEQ* 46 (1973): 106-112.

4035. Murfin, Ross C. "The Poetry of Trumbull Stickney." *NEQ* 48(1975): 540-555.

4036. Myers, J. Wm. "A Complete Stickney Bibliography." *TCL* 9(1964): 209-212.

4037. Riggs, Thomas, Jr. "Prometheus 1900." *AL* 22(1951): 399-423.

STODDARD, ELIZABETH.   4038. Matlock, James H. "Hawthorne and Elizabeth Barstow Stoddard." *NEQ* 50(1977): 278-302.

4039. Weir, Sybil. "*The Morgesons*: A Neglected Feminist *Bildungsroman*." *NEQ* 49(1976): 427-439.

STODDARD, RICHARD HENRY.   4040. Sealts, Merton M., Jr. "Melville and Richard Henry Stoddard." *AL* 43(1971): 359-370.

STONE, JOHN A.   4041. Moody, Richard. "Lost and New Found: The Fourth Act of *Metamora*." *AL* 34(1962): 353-364.

STOWE, HARRIET BEECHER.   4042. Adams, John. "Harriet Beecher Stowe (1811-1896)." [bibliography] *ALR* 2(1969): 160-164.

4043. Ammons, Elizabeth. "Heroines in *Uncle Tom's Cabin*." *AL* 49(1977): 161-179.

4044. Cassara, Ernest. "The Rehabilitation of Uncle Tom: Significant Themes in Mrs. Stowe's Antislavery Novel." *CLA* 17(1973): 230-240.

4045. Duvall, Severn. "*Uncle Tom's Cabin*: The Sinister Side of the Patriarchy." *NEQ* 36 (1963): 3-22.

4046. ----------. "W. G. Simms's Review of Mrs. Stowe." *AL* 30(1958): 107-117.

4047. Graham, Thomas. "Harriet Beecher Stowe and the Question of Race." *NEQ* 46(1973): 614-621.

4048. Hovet, Theodore R. "Christian Revolution: Harriet Beecher Stowe's Response to Slavery." *NEQ* 47(1974): 535-549.

4049. Lebedun, Jean. "Harriet Beecher Stowe's Interest in Sojourner Truth, Black Feminist." *AL* 46(1974): 359-363.

4050. Levin, David. "American Fiction as Historical Evidence: Reflections on *Uncle Tom's Cabin*." *BALF* 5(1971): 132-136, 154.

4051. Lombard, Charles M. "Harriet Beecher Stowe's Attitude Towards French Romanticism." *CLA* 11(1968): 236-240.

4052. Meserve, Ruth I. "*Uncle Tom's Cabin* and Modern Chinese Drama." *MD* 17(1974): 57-66.

4053. Pickens, Donald K. "Uncle Tom Becomes Nat Turner: A Commentary on Two American Heroes." *BALF* 3(1969): 45-48.

4054. Reed, Kenneth T. "*Uncle Tom's Cabin* and the Heavenly City." *CLA* 12(1968): 150-154.

4055. Ridgely, Joseph V. "*Woodcraft*: Simms' First Answer to *Uncle Tom's Cabin*." *AL* 31(1960): 421-433.

4056. Roppolo, Joseph P. "Harriet Beecher Stowe and New Orleans: A Study in Hate." *NEQ* 30(1957): 346-362.

4057. ----------. "Uncle Tom in New Orleans: Three Lost Plays." *NEQ* 27(1954): 213-226.

4058. Steele, Thomas J., S. J. "Tom and Eva: Mrs. Stowe's Two Dying Christs." *BALF* 6 (1972): 85-90.

4059. Stone, Harry. "Charles Dickens and Harriet Beecher Stowe." *NCF* 12(1957): 188-202.

4060. Wyman, Margaret. "Harriet Beecher Stowe's Topical Novel on Woman Sufferage." *NEQ* 25(1952): 383-391.

See also 598.

SWINTON, JOHN.   4061. White, William. "Whitman and Swinton: Some Unpublished Correspondence." *AL* 39(1968): 547-553.

SWINTON, WILLIAM.   4062. Hollis, C. Carroll. "Whitman and William Swinton: A Co-operative Friendship." *AL* 30(1959): 425-449.

THOMPSON, MAURICE.   4063. Fertig, Walter L. "Maurice Thompson and *A Modern Instance*." *AL* 38 (1966): 103-111.

4064. Moore, Rayburn S. "The Old South and the New: Paul Hamilton Hayne and Maurice Thompson." *SLJ* 5,#1(1972): 108-122.

THOREAU, HENRY DAVID. 4065. Adams, Raymond. "Thoreau's Mock-Heroics and the American Natural History Writers." *SP* 52(1955): 86-97.

4066. Albrecht, Robert C. "Thoreau and His Audience." 'A Plea for Captain John Brown.'" *AL* 32(1961): 393-402.

4067. Allaback, Steven. "Oak Hall in American Literature." *AL* 46(1975): 545-549.

4068. Baym, Nina. "From Metaphysics to Metaphor: The Image of Water in Emerson and Thoreau." *SR* 5(1966): 230-243.

4069. Benoit, Raymond. "Walden as God's Drop." *AL* 43(1971): 122-124.

4070. Bishop, Jonathan. "The Experience of the Sacred in Thoreau's *Week*." *ELH* 33(1966): 66-91.

4071. Blasing, Mutlu. "The Economies of *Walden*." *TSLL* 17(1976): 759-775.

4072. Bode, Carl. "Thoreau and His Last Publishers." *NEQ* 26(1953): 383-388.

4073. ----------. "Thoreau, with Advice." *AL* 28(1956): 77-78.

4074. Boewe, Charles. "Thoreau's 1854 Lecture in Philadelphia." *ELN* 2(1964): 115-122.

4075. Bonner, Willard Hallam. "Captain Thoreau: Gubernator to a Piece of Wood." *NEQ* 39(1966): 26-46.

4076. ----------. "Mariners and Terreners: Some Aspects of Nautical Imagery in Thoreau." *AL* 34(1963): 507-519.

4077. Boudreau, Gordon V. "H. D. Thoreau, William Gilpin, and the Metaphysical Ground of the Picturesque." *AL* 45(1973): 357-369.

4078. Bradford, Robert W. "Thoreau and Therien." *AL* 34(1963): 499-506.

4079. Broderick, John C. "The Movement of Thoreau's Prose." *AL* 33(1961): 133-142.

4080. ----------. "Thoreau, Alcott, and the Poll Tax." *SP* 53(1956): 612-626.

4081. Brown, Theodore M. "Thoreau's Prophetic Architectural Program." *NEQ* 38(1965): 3-20.

4082. Busch, Frederick. "Thoreau and Melville as Cellmates." *MFS* 23(1977): 239-242.

4083. Cady, Lyman V. "Thoreau's Quotations from the Confucian Books in *Walden*." *AL* 33(1961): 20-32.

4084. Cameron, Kenneth Walter. "Emerson, Thoreau, and the Society of Natural History." *AL* 24(1952): 21-30.

4085. Colyer, Richard. "Thoreau's Color Symbols." *PMLA* 86(1971): 999-1008.

4086. Cronkhite, G. Ferris. "The Transcendental Railroad." *NEQ* 24(1951): 306-328.

4087. D'Avanzo, Mario L. "Thoreau's Brick Pillow." *NEQ* 50(1977): 664-666.

4088. Davidson, Frank. "Melville, Thoreau and 'The Apple-Tree Table.'" *AL* 25(1954): 479-488.

4089. ----------. "Thoreau's Hound, Bay Horse, and Turtle-Dove." *NEQ* 27(1954): 521-524.

4090. Duvall, S. P. C. "Robert Frost's 'Directive out of *Walden*.'" *AL* 31(1960): 482-488.

4091. Fertig, Walter L. "John Sullivan Dwight's Pre-Publication Notice of *Walden*." *NEQ* 30(1957): 84-90.

4092. Flanagan, John T. "Henry Salt and His Life of Thoreau." *NEQ* 28(1955): 237-246.

4093. Ford, Thomas W. "Thoreau's Cosmic Mosquito and Dickinson's Terrestrial Fly." *NEQ* 48 (1975): 487-504.

4094. Foster, Leslie D. "'Walden' and its Audiences: Troubled Sleep, and Religious and Other Awakenings." *MLR* 67(1972): 756-762.

4095. Glick, Wendell. "Thoreau's Use of His Sources." *NEQ* 44(1971): 101-109.

4096. Green, Eugene. "Reading Local History: Shattuck's *History*, Emerson's *Discourse*, and Thoreau's *Walden*." *NEQ* 50(1977): 303-314.

4097. Griffin, William J. "Thoreau's Reactions to Horatio Greenough." *NEQ* 30(1957): 508-512.

4098. Gura, Philip F. "Thoreau and John Josselyn." *NEQ* 48(1975): 505-518.

4099. ----------. "Thoreau's Maine Woods Indians: More Representative Men." *AL* 49(1977): 366-384.

4100. Harmon, Roger J. "Thoreau to His Publisher." *AL* 25(1954): 496-497.

4101. Harding, Walter. "Thoreau and Kate Brady." *AL* 36(1964): 347-349.

4102. ----------. "Thoreau and the Kalmucks: A Newly Discovered Manuscript." *NEQ* 32(1959): 91-92.

4103. ----------. "Thoreau on the Lecture Platform." *NEQ* 24(1951): 365-374.

4104. ----------. "Thoreau's Feminine Foe." *PMLA* 69(1954): 110-116.

4105. ----------. "Two F. B. Sanborn Letters." *AL* 25(1953): 230-234.

4106. Hendrick, George. "Henry S. Salt, The Late Victorian Socialists, and Thoreau." *NEQ* 50(1977): 409-422.

4107. ----------. The Influence of Thoreau's 'Civil Disobedience' on Gandhi's *Satyagraha*." *NEQ* 29(1956): 462-472.

4108. Hesford, Walter. "'Incessant Tragedies': A Reading of *A Week on the Concord and Merrimack Rivers*." *ELH* 44(1977): 515-525.

4109. Himelick, Raymond. "Thoreau and Samuel Daniel." *AL* 24(1952): 177-185.

4110. Hoagland, Clayton. "The Diary of Thoreau's 'Gentle Boy.'" *NEQ* 28(1955): 473-489.

4111. Hoeltje, Hubert H. "Misconceptions in Current Thoreau Criticism." *PQ* 47(1968): 563-570.

4112. Hovde, Carl F. "Literary Materials in Thoreau's *A Week*." *PMLA* 80(1965): 76-83.

4113. ----------. "Nature into Act: Thoreau's Use of His Journals in *A Week*." *AL* 30 Art: (1958): 165-184.

4114. Jaques, John F. "An Enthusiastic Newspaper Account of Thoreau's Second Lecture in Portland, Maine, January 15, 1851." *AL* 40(1968): 385-391.

4115. Johnson, Paul David. "Thoreau's Redemptive *Week*." *AL* 49(1977): 161-179.

4116. Jones, Buford. "'The Hall of Fantasy' and the Early Hawthorne-Thoreau Relationship." *PMLA* 83(1968): 1429-1438.

4117. Lane, Lauriat, Jr. "*Walden*, the Second Year." *SR* 8(1969): 183-192.

4118. Leary, Lewis. "Beyond the Brink of Fear: Thoreau's Wilderness." *SLI* 7,#1(1974): 67-76.

4119. ----------. "Walden Goes Wandering: The Transit of Good Intentions." *NEQ* 32(1959): 3-30.

4120. Lyon, Melvin E. "Walden Pond as a Symbol." *PMLA* 82(1967): 289-300.

4121. MacShane, Frank. "*Walden* and Yoga." *NEQ* 37(1964): 322-342.

4122. Miller, Perry. "Thoreau in the Context of International Romanticism." *NEQ* 34(1961): 147-159.

4123. Moldenhauer, Joseph J. "Images of Circularity in Thoreau's Prose." *TSLL* 1(1959): 245-263.

4124. ----------. "Thoreau to Blake: Four Letters Re-Edited." *TSLL* 8(1966): 43-62.

4125. Monteiro, George. "Birches in Winter: Notes on Thoreau and Frost." *CLA* 12(1968): 129-133.

4126. Myerson, Joel. "More Apropos of John Thoreau." *AL* 45(1973): 104-106.

4127. Nichols, William W. "Individualism and Autobiographical Art: Frederick Douglass and Henry Thoreau." *CLA* 16(1972): 145-158.

4128. Noverr, Douglas A. "A Note on Wendell Glick's 'Thoreau's Use of His Sources.'" *NEQ* 44 (1971): 475-477.

4129. Paul, Sherman. "Thoreau's 'The Landlord': 'Sublimely Trivial for the Good of Men.'" *JEGP* 54(1955): 587-590.

4130. Pederson, Lee A. "Americanisms in Thoreau's *Journal*." *AL* 37(1965): 167-184.

4131. Porte, Joel. "Emerson, Thoreau, and the Double Consciousness." *NEQ* 41(1968): 40-50.

4132. Reger, William. "Beyond Metaphor." *Criticism* 12(1970): 333-344.

4133. Rhoads, Kenneth W. "Thoreau: The Ear and the Music." *AL* 46(1974): 313-328.

4134. Robinson, E. Arthur. "Thoreau's Buried Short Story." *SSF* 1(1963): 16-25.

4135. Schiller, Andrew. "Thoreau and Whitman: The Record of a Pilgrimage." *NEQ* 28(1955): 186-197.

4136. Schwaber, Paul. "Thoreau's Development in *Walden*." *Criticism* 5(1963): 64-77.

4137. Shanley, J. Lyndon. "Thoreau's Geese and Yeats's Swans." *AL* 30(1958): 361-364.

4138. Skwire, David. "A Checklist of Wordplays in Walden." *AL* 31(1959): 282-289.

4139. Stein, William Bysshe. "The Hindu Matrix of *Walden:* The King's Son." *Comp L* 22 (1970): 303-318.

4140. ----------. Walden: The Wisdom of the Centaur." *ELH* 25(1958): 194-215.

4141. ----------. "The Yoga of Reading in *Walden*." *TSLL* 13(1971): 481-495.

4142. Stoller, Loe. "Thoreau's Doctrine of Simplicity." *NEQ* 29(1956): 443-461.

4143. Tanner, Stephen L. "Current Motions in Thoreau's *A Week*." *SR* 12(1973): 763-776.

4144. West, Michael. "Scatology and Eschatology: The Heroic Dimensions." *PMLA* 89(1974): 1043-1064.

4145. White, William. "Three Unpublished Thoreau Letters." *NEQ* 33(1960): 372-374.

4146. ----------. "An Unpublished Thoreau Poem." *AL* 34(1962): 119-121.

4147. Whitford, Kathryn. "Thoreau and the Woodlots of Concord." *NEQ* 23(1950): 291-306.

4148. Williams, Paul O. "The Concept of Inspiration in Thoreau's Poetry." *PMLA* 79(1964): 466-472.

4149. Woodson, Thomas. "Notes for the Annotation of *Walden*." *AL* 46(1975): 550-555.

4150. ----------. "Thoreau on Poverty and Magnaminity." *PMLA* 85(1970): 21-34.

4151. ----------. "The Two Beginnings of *Walden:* A Distinction of Styles." *ELH* 35(1968): 440-473.

See also 1110, 2310, 3999, 6712.

THORPE, THOMAS B. 4152. Lemay, J. A. Leo. "The Text, Tradition, and Themes of 'The Big Bear of Arkansas.'" *AL* 47(1975): 321-342.

4152a. Rickels, Milton. "A Bibliography of the Writings of Thomas Bangs Thorpe." *AL* 29 (1957): 171-179.

TICKNOR, GEORGE. 4153. Hart, Thomas R., Jr. "George Ticknor's *History of Spanish Literature:* The New England Background." *PMLA* 69(1954): 76-88.

4154. Lyon, Judson Stanley. "Wordsworth and Ticknor." *PMLA* 66(1951): 432-440.

4155. Ryder, Frank G. George Ticknor and Goethe—Boston and Göttingen." *PMLA* 67(1952): 960-972.

4156. ----------. "George Ticknor and Harvard." *MLQ* 14(1953): 413-424.

TOURGEE, ALBION W. 4157. Ealy, Marguerite, and Sanford Marovitz. "Albion Winegar Tourgee (1838-1905)." [bibliography] *ALR* 8(1975): 53-80.

TROWBRIDGE, JOHN T. 4158. Coleman, Rufus A. "Trowbridge and O'Conner: Unpublished Correspondence, with Special Reference to Walt Whitman." *AL* 23(1951): 323-331.

TUCKER, NATHANIEL. 4159. Wrobel, Arthur. "'Romantic Realism': Nathaniel Beverly Tucker." *AL* 42(1970): 325-335.

TUCKERMAN, FREDERICK. 4160. Golden, Samuel A. "Frederick Goddard Tuckerman: A Neglected Poet." *NEQ* 29(1956): 381-393.

TWAIN, MARK. See SAMUEL CLEMENS.

VERY, JONES. 4161. Arner, Robert D. "Hawthorne and Jones Very: Two Dimensions of Satire in 'Egotism; or, the Bosom Serpent.'" *NEQ* 42(1969): 267-275.

4162. Dennis, Carl. "Correspondence in Very's Nature Poetry." *NEQ* 43(1970): 250-273.

4163. Herbold, Anthony. "Nature as Concept and Tenchique in the Poetry of Jones Very." *NEQ* 40(1967): 244-259.

4164. Jones, Harry L. "The Very Madness: A New Manuscript." *CLA* 10(1967): 196-200.

WALLACE, HORACE B. 4165. Hatvary, George Egon. "Poe's Borrowings from H. B. Wallace." *AL* 38(1966): 365-372.

WARD, ARTEMUS. See CHARLES FARRAR BROWNE.

WARD, SAMUEL. 4166. Stafford, John. "Samuel Ward's Defense of Balzac's 'Objective' Fiction." *AL* 24(1952): 167-176.

WARE, WILLIAM. 4167. Dahl, Curtis. "New England Unitarianism in Fictional Antiquity: The Romances of William Ware." *NEQ* 48(1975): 104-115.

WARNER, CHARLES DUDLEY. 4168. Crowley, John W. "A Note on *The Gilded Age*." *ELN* 10(1972): 116-118.

4169. O'Donnell, Thomas F. "Charles Dudley Warner on *The Red Badge of Courage*." *AL* 25(1953): 363-365.

WASHINGTON, BOOKER T. 4170. Aaman, Clarence. "Three Negro Classics: An Estimate." *BALF* 4(1970): 113-119.

WASSON, DAVID A. 4171. Spence, Robert. "D. A. Wasson, Forgotten Transcendalist." *AL* 27 (1955): 31-41.

WEBB, FRANK. 4172. Davis, Arthur P. *"The Garies and Their Friends*: A Neglected Pioneer Novel." *CLA* 13(1969): 27-34.

4173. DeVries, James H. "The Tradition of the Sentimental Novel in *The Garies and Their Friends*." *CLA* 17(1973): 241-249.

See also 1147.

WEBB, LAURA S. See 620.

WHITCHER, FRANCES. See 1151.

WHITMAN, ALBERY ALLSON. 4174. Marshall, Carl L. "Two Protest Poems by Albery A. Whitman." *CLA* 19(1975): 50-56.

4175. Sherman, Joan R. "Albery Allson Whitman: Poet of Beauty and Manliness." [includes bibliography] *CLA* 15(1971): 126-143.

WHITMAN, SARAH HELEN. See 3828.

WHITMAN, WALT. 4176. Abrams, Robert E. "The Function of Dreams and Dream-Logic in Whitman's Poetry." *TSLL* 17(1975): 599-616.

4177. Adams, Richard P. "Whitman's 'Lilacs' and the Tradition of Pastoral Elegy." *PMLA* 72(1957): 479-487.

4178. Allen, Gay Wilson. "Regarding the Publication of the First *Leaves of Grass*." *AL* 28 (1956): 78-79.

4179. ----------. "Whitman and Michelet—Continued." *AL* 45(1973): 428-432.

4180. Andrews, Thomas F. "Walt Whitman and Slavery: A Reconsideration of One Aspect of His Concept of the American Common Man." *CLA* 9(1966): 225-233.

4181. "Baylen, Joseph, and Robert Holland. Whiteman, W. T. Stead, and the *Pall Mall Gazette*." *AL* 33(1961): 68-72.

4182. Bergman, Herbert. "Ezra Pound and Walt Whitman." *AL* 27(1955): 56-61.

4183. ----------. "The Influence of Whitman's Journalism on 'Leaves of Grass.'" *ALR* 3 (1970): 399-404.

4184. ----------. "Whitman and Tennyson." *SP* 51(1954): 492-504.

4185. Black, Stephen A. "Radical Utterances from the Soul's Abysms: Toward A New Sense of Whitman." *PMLA* 88(1973): 100-111.

4186. Bowers, Fredson. "The Manuscript of Walt Whitman's 'A Carol of Harvest, for 1867.'" *MP* 52(1954): 29-51.

4187. ----------. "The Manuscript of Whitman's 'Passage to India.'" *MP* 51(1953): 102-117.

4188. Broderick, John C. "An Unpublished Whitman Letter and Other Manuscripts." *AL* 37 (1966): 475-478.

4189. ----------. "Whitman's Earliest Known Notebook: A Clarification." *PMLA* 84(1969): 1657-1659.

4190. Buell, Lawrence. "Transcendentalist Catalogue Rhetoric: Vision Versus Form." *AL* 40 (1968): 325-339.

4191. Brown, Clarence A. "Walt Whitman and the 'New Poetry.'" *AL* 33(1961): 33-45.

4192. Carlile, Robert Emerson. "Leitmotif and Whitman's 'When Lilacs Last in the Dooryard Bloom'd.'" *Criticism* 13(1971): 329-339.

4193. Carlisle, E. F. "Walt Whitman: The Drama of Identity." *Criticism* 10(1968): 259-276.

4194. Clark, George Peirce. "'Saerasmid,' an Early Promoter of Walt Whitman." *AL* 27(1955): 259-262.

4195. Coffman, Stanley K., Jr. "'Crossing Brooklyn Ferry': A Note on the Catalogue Technique in Whitman's Poetry." *MP* 51(1954): 225-232.

4196. ----------. "Form and Meaning in Whitman's 'Passage to India.'" *PMLA* 70(1955): 337-349.

4197. Coleman, Rufus A. "Trowbridge and O'Conner: Unpublished Correspondence, with Special Reference to Walt Whitman." *AL* 23(1951): 323-331.

4198. Couser, G. Thomas. "Of Time and Identity: Walt Whitman and Gertrude Stein as Autobiographers." *TSLL* 17(1976): 787-804.

4199. Davis, Charles T. "Walt Whitman and the Problem of an American Tradition." *CLA* 5 (1961): 1-16.

4200. Eby, E. H. "Did Whitman Write *The Good Gray Poet?*" *MLQ* 11(1950): 445-449.

4201. Farzan, Massud. "Whitman and Sufism: Towards 'A Persian Lesson.'" *AL* 47(1976): 572-582.

4202. Finkel, William L. "Sources of Walt Whitman's Manuscript of Notes on Physique." *AL* 22(1950): 308-331.

4203. ----------. "Walt Whitman's Manuscript Notes on Oratory." *AL* 22(1950): 29-53.

4204. Ford, Thomas W. "Whitman's 'Excelsior': The Poem as Microcosm." *TSLL* 17(1976): 777-785.

4205. Foster, Steven. "Bergson's 'Intuition' and Whitman's 'Song of Myself.'" *TSLL* 6 (1964): 376-387.

4206. Francis, K. H. "Walt Whitman's French." *MLR* 51(1956): 493-506.

4207. Gargano, James W. "Technique in 'Crossing Brookly Ferry': The Everlasting Moment." *JEGP* 62(1963): 262-269.

4208. Geffen, Arthur. "Walt Whitman and Jules Michelet—One More Time." *AL* 45(1973): 107-114.

4209. Gohdes, Clarence. "Whitman and the 'Good Old Cause.'" *AL* 34(1962): 400-403.

4210. Golden, Arthur. "Passage to Less than India: Structure and Meaning in Whitman's 'Passage to India.'" *PMLA* 88(1973): 1095-1103.

4211. Graham, Mary-Emma. "Politics in Black and White: A View of Walt Whitman's Career as a Political Journalist." *CLA* 17(1973): 263-270.

4212. Grier, Edward F. "Walt Whitman's Earliest Known Notebook." *PMLA* 83(1968): 1453-1457.

4213. ----------. "Walt Whitman, the *Galaxy*, and *Democratic Vistas*." *AL* 23(1951): 332-350.

4214. Griffith, Clark. "Sex and Death: The Significance of Whitman's *Calamus* Themes." *PQ* 39(1960): 18-38.

4215. Hagenbüchle, Roland. "Whitman's Unfinished Quest for an American Identity." *ELH* 40 (1973): 428-478.

4216. Hendrick, George. "Unpublished Notes on Whitman in William Sloane Kennedy's Diary." *AL* 34(1962): 279-285.

4217. Hoeltje, Hubert H. "Whitman's Letter to Robert Carter." *AL* 25(1953): 360-362.

4218. Hollis, C. Carroll. "Whitman and William Swinton: A Co-operative Friendship." *AL* 30(1959): 425-449.

4219. Holloway, Emory. "More Temprance Tales by Whitman." *AL* 27(1956): 577-578.

4220. ----------. "Whitman Pursued." *AL* 27 (1955): 1-11.

4221. ----------. "Whitman's Last Words." *AL* 24(1952): 367-369.

4222. Hoople, Robin P. "'Chants Democratic and Native American': A Neglected Sequence in the Growth of *Leaves of Grass.*" *AL* 42(1970): 181-196.

4223. Hughson, Lois. "In Search of the True America: Dos Passos' Debt to Whitman in *U.S.A.*" *MFS* 19(1973): 179-192.

4224. Hunt, Joel A. "Mann and Whitman: Humaniores Litterae." *Comp L* 14(1962): 266-271.

4225. Hunt, Russell A. "Whitman's Poetics and the Unity of 'Calamus.'" *AL* 46(1975): 482-494.

4226. Johnson, Jane. "Whitman's Changing Attitude Toward Emerson." *PMLA* 73(1958): 452.

4227. Kahn, Sholom J. "Whitman's 'Black Lucifer': Some Possible Sources." *PMLA* 71(1956): 932-944.

4228. Kanes, Martin. "Whitman, Gide, and Bazalgette: An International Encounter." *Comp L* 14(1962): 341-355.

4229. Krause, Sydney J. "Whitman, Music, and *Proud Music of the Storm.*" *PMLA* 72(1957): 705-721.

4230. Little, William A. "Walt Whitman and the *Nibelungleid.*" *PMLA* 80(1965): 562-570.

4231. Livingston, James L. "Walt Whitman's Epistle to the Americans." *AL* 40(1969): 542-544.

4232. Lovell, John, Jr. "Appreciating Whitman: 'Passage to India.'" *MLQ* 21(1960): 131-141.

4233. Loving, Jerome M. "Whitman and Harlan: New Evidence." *AL* 48(1976): 219-222.

4234. Lozynsky, Artem. "Whitman's Death Bed: Two Nurses' Reports." *AL* 47(1975): 270-273.

4235. Mabbott, Thomas Ollive. "Walt Whitman Edits the *Sunday Times:* July, 1842-June, 1843." *AL* 39(1967): 99-102.

4236. Marks, Alfred H. "Whitman's Triadic Imagery." *AL* 23(1951): 99-126.

4237. Mason, John B. "Walt Whitman's Catalogues: Rhetorical Means for Two Journeys in 'Song of Myself.'" *AL* 45(1973): 34-49.

4238. McDermott, John Francis. "Whitman and the Partons: Glimpses from the Diary of Thomas Butler Gunn, 1856-1860." *AL* 29(1957): 316-319.

4239. McElderry, B. P., Jr. "The Inception of 'Passage to India.'" *PMLA* 71(1956): 837-839.

4240. Miller, Edwin H. "Walt Whitman and Ellen Eyre." *AL* 33(1961): 64-68.

4241. Miller, James E., Jr. "'Song of Myself' as Inverted Mystical Experience." *PMLA* 70 (1955): 636-661.

4242. ----------. "Whitman's 'Calamus': The Leaf and the Root." *PMLA* 72(1957): 249-271.

4243. Miner, Earl Roy. "The Background, Date, and Composition of Whitman's 'A Broadway Pageant.'" *AL* 27(1955): 403-405.

4244. Mitchell, Roger. "A Prosody for Whitman." *PMLA* 84(1969): 1606-1612.

4245. Moore, Rayburn S. "The Literary World Gone Mad: Hayne on Whitman." *SLJ* 10,#1(1977): 75-83.

4246. Pulos, C. E. "Whitman and Epictetus: The Stoical Element in *Leaves of Grass.*" *JEGP* 55 (1956): 75-84.

4247. Reiss Edmund. "Whitman's Debt to Animal Magnetism." *PMLA* 78(1963): 80-88.

4248. Reynolds, Michael S. "Whitman's Early Prose and 'The Sleepers.'" *AL* 41(1969): 405-414.

4249. Rosenthal, P. Z. "The Language of Measurement in Whitman's Early Writing." *TSLL* 15 (1973): 461-470.

4250. Rountree, Thomas J. "Whitman's Indirect Expression and Its Application to 'Song of Myself.'" *PMLA* 73(1958): 549-555.

4251. Russell, Jack. "*Israel Potter* and 'Song of Myself.'" *AL* 40(1968): 72-77.

4252. Schiller, Andrew. "Thoreau and Whitman: The Record of a Pilgrimage." *NEQ* 28(1955): 186-197.

4253. Scholnick, Robert. "Whitman and the Magazines: Some Documentary Evidence." *AL* 44 (1972): 222-246.

4254. Schwab, Arnold T. "James Huneker on Whitman: A Newly Discovered Essay." *AL* 38(1966): 208-218.

4255. Sewall, Richard H. "Walt Whitman, John P. Hale, and the Free Democracy: An Unpublished Letter." *NEQ* 34(1961): 239-242.

4256. Shephard, Esther. "A Fact Which Should Have Been Included in 'Whitman's Earliest Known Notebook: A Clarification' by John C. Broderick." *PMLA* 86(1971): 266.

4257. ----------. "An Inquiry into Whitman's Method of Turning Prose into Poetry." *MLQ* 14(1953): 43-59.

4258. ----------. "The Inside Front and Back Covers of Whitman's Earliest Known Notebook: Some Observations on the Photocopy and Verbal Descriptions." *PMLA* 87(1972): 1119-1122.

4259. ----------. "The Photo-duplicates of Whitman's Cardboard Butterfly." *PMLA* 70(1955): 876.

4260. ----------. "Possible Sources of Some of Whitman's Ideas and Symbols in *Hermes Mercurius Trismegistus* and Other Works." *MLQ* 14(1953): 60-81.

4261. ----------. "Walt Whitman's Whereabouts in the Winter of 1842-1843." *AL* 29(1957): 289-296.

4262. Stovall, Floyd. "Notes on Whitman's Reading." *AL* 26(1954): 337-362.

4263. ----------. "Walt Whitman and the Dramatic Stage in New York." *SP* 50(1953): 515-539.

4264. ----------. "Whitman, Shakespeare, and Democracy." *JEGP* 51(1952): 457-472.

4265. ----------. "Whitman, Shakespeare, and the Baconians." *PQ* 31(1952): 27-38.

4266. ----------. "Whitman's Knowledge of Shakespeare." *SP* 49(1952): 643-669.

4267. Stevenson, Lionel. "An English Admirer of Walt Whitman." *AL* 29(1958): 470-473.

4268. Summerhayes, Don. "Joyce's *Ulysses* and Whitman's 'Self': A Query." *Con L* 4(1963): 216-224.

4269. Tannenbaum, Earl. "Pattern in Whitman's 'Song of Myself': A Summary and a Supplement." *CLA* 6(1962): 44-49.

4270. Templeman, William Darby. "On Whitman's 'Apple-Peelings.'" *PQ* 35(1956): 200-202.

4271. Templin, Lawrence. "The Quaker Influence on Walt Whitman." *AL* 42(1970): 165-180.

4272. Whicher, Stephen E. "Whitman's Awakening to Death." *SR* 1(1961): 9-28.

4273. White, William. "An Unpublished Whitman Notebook for 'Lilacs'." *MLQ* 24(1963): 177-180.

4274. ----------. "More About the 'Publication' of the First *Leaves of Grass*." *AL* 28 (1957); 516-517.

4275. ----------. "A Tribute to William Hartshorne: Unrecorded Whitman." *AL* 42(1971): 554-558.

4276. ----------. "Walt Whitman on New England Writers: An Uncollected Fragment." *NEQ* 27(1954): 395-396.

4277. ----------. "Whitman and John Swinton: Some Unpublished Correspondence." *AL* 39 (1968): 547-553.

4278. ----------. "Whitman on American Poets: An Uncollected Piece." *ELN* 1(1963): 42-43.

4279. ----------. "Whitman's First 'Literary' Letter." *AL* 35(1963): 83-85.

4280. Wrobel, Arthur. "Whitman and the Phrenologists: The Divine Body and the Sensuous Soul." *PMLA* 89(1974): 17-23.

See also 590, 1274, 2510, 3784, 4893, 5064, 6866, 7607, 17313.

WHITTAKER, FREDERICK. See 620.

WHITTIER, JOHN GREENLEAF. 4281. Cary, Richard. "Whittier Regained." *NEQ* 34(1961): 370-375.

4282. Cummins, Roger William. "Unpublished Emerson Letters to Louis Prang and Whittier." *AL* 43(1971): 257-259.

4283. Eby, Cecil D., Jr. "Whittier's 'Brown of Ossawatomie.'" *NEQ* 33(1960): 452-461.

4284. Ernest, Joseph M., Jr. "Whittier and the 'Feminine Fifties.'" *AL* 28(1956): 184-196.

4285. Fabian, R. Craig. "Some Uncollected Letters of John Greenleaf Whittier to Gerrit Smith." *AL* 22(1950): 158-163.

4286. Hepler, John C. "'Gordon'—A New Whittier Poem." *NEQ* 34(1961): 93-95.

4287. Holmes, J. Welfred. "Whittier and Sumner: A Political Friendship." *NEQ* 30(1957): 58-72.

4288. Hubbard, George U. "Ina Coolbrith's Friendship with John Greenleaf Whittier." *NEQ* 45(1972): 109-118.

4289. Kimball, William J. "Two Views of History." *SSF* 8(1971): 637-639.

4290. Pickard, John B. "John Greenleaf

Whittier and Mary Emerson Smith." *AL* 38(1967): 478-497.

4291. ----------. "John Greenleaf Whittier and the Abolitionist Schism of 1840." *NEQ* 37 (1964): 250-254.

4292. Stillinger, Jack. "Whittier's Early Imitation of Thomas Campbell." *PQ* 38(1959): 502-504.

4293. Thaler, Alwin. "Whittier and the English Poets." *NEQ* 24(1951): 53-68.

4294. Trawick, Leonard M. "Whittier's *Snow-Bound*: A Poem about the Imagination." *EL* 1(1974): 46-53.

4295. Zanger, Jules. "A Note on Skipper Iresons' Ride." *NEQ* 29(1956): 236-238.

See also 620.

WIGGIN, KATE D. 4296. Erisman, Fred. "Transcendentalism for American Youth: The Children's Books of Kate Douglas Wiggin." *NEQ* 41 (1968): 238-247.

WILDE, RICHARD HENRY. 4297. Kibler, James E., Jr. "A New Letter of Simms to Richard Henry Wilde: On the Advancement of Sectional Literature." *AL* 44(1973): 667-669.

4298. Wright, Nathalia. "Richard Henry Wilde on Greenough's Washington." *AL* 27(1956): 556-557.

WILKES, CHARLES. 4299. Gates, W. B. "Cooper's *The Sea Lions* and Wilkes' *Narrative*." *PMLA* 65(1950): 1069-1075.

WILLIS, NATHANIEL P. 4300. Goodman, Charlotte. "Henry James's *Roderick Hudson* and Nathaniel Parker Willis's *Paul Fane*." *AL* 43(1972): 642-645.

WIRT, WILLIAM. See 668.

WOODBERRY, G. E. 4301. Hovey, R. B. "George Edward Woodberry: Genteel Exile." *NEQ* 23(1950): 504-526.

4302. Shackford, Martha Hale. "George Edward Woodberry as Critic." *NEQ* 24(1951): 510-527.

WOOLSON, CONSTANCE. 4303. Moore, Rayburn. "Constance Fenimore Woolson (1840-1894)." [bibliography] *ALR* 1,#3(1968): 36-38.

TWENTIETH CENTURY

GENERAL AND MISCELLANEOUS. 4304. Angoff, Allan. "Protest in American Literature since the End of World War II." *CLA* 5(1961): 31-40.

4305. Bebb, Bruce, and others. "American Authors: A Forum on Its Editions and Practices." *SN* 7(1975): 389-406.

4306. Brignano, Russell C. "Autobiographical Books by Black Americans: A Bibliography of Works Written Since the Civil War." *BALF* 7(1973): 148-156.

4307. Bigsby, C. W. E. "The White Critic in a Black World." *BALF* 6(1972): 39-45.

4308. Brooks, A. Russell. "The Comic Spirit and the Negro's New Look." *CLA* 6(1962): 35-43.

4309. Butcher, Philip. "The Younger Novelists and the Urban Negro." *CLA* 4(1961): 196-203.

4310. Chapman, Abraham. "The Harlem Renaissance in Literary History." *CLA* 11(1967): 38-58.

4311. Dance, Darrell. "Contemporary Militant Black Humor." *BALF* 8(1974): 217-222.

4312. Dow, Eddy. "Van Wyck Brooks and Lewis Mumford: A Confluence in the 'Twenties." *AL* 45 (1973): 407-422.

4313. Enck, John. "Campop." *Con L* 7(1966): 168-182.

4314. Farrison, W. Edward. "What American Negro Literature Exists and Who Should Teach It?" *CLA* 13(1970): 374-381.

4315. Fenderson, Lewis H. "The New Breed of Black Writers and Their Jaundiced View of Tradition." *CLA* 15(1971): 18-24.

4316. Feuser, W. F. "Afro-American Literature and Negritude." *Comp L* 28(1976): 289-308.

4317. Fisher, Vardis. "The Western Writer and the Eastern Establishment." *WAL* 1(1967): 244-259.

4318. Ford, Newell F. "Kenneth Burke and Robert Penn Warren: Criticism by Obsessive Metaphor." *JEGP* 53(1954): 172-177.

4319. Frey, John R. "Postwar German Reactions to American Literature." *JEGP* 54(1955): 173-194.

4320. Friedman, Norman. "Anglo-American Fiction Theory 1947-1962." *SN* 8(1976): 199-209.

4321. Gilenson, Boris. "Afro-American Literature in the Soviet Union." *BALF* 9(1975): 25, 28-29.

4322. Hart, Robert C. "Black-White Literary Relations in the Harlem Renaissance." *AL* 44(1973): 612-628.

4323. Haslam, Gerald. "Predators in Literature." *WAL* 12(1977): 123-131.

4324. Hubbell, Jay B. "1922: A Turning Point in American Literary History." *TSLL* 12 (1970): 481-492.

4325. Hunter, J. Paul. *"Forum:* The First Five Years." *TCL* 7(1961): 121-124.

4326. Jones, Howard Mumford. "Patterns of Writing and the Middle Class." *AL* 22(1951): 293-301.

4327. Josephy, Alvin M., Jr. "Publisher's Interests in Western Writing." *WAL* 1(1967): 260-266.

4328. Keller, Joseph. "Black Writing and Editorial Unbelief." *BALF* 3(1969): 35-38.

4329. Lehan, Richard. "French and American Philosphical and Literary Existentialism: A Selected Checklist." *Con L* 1,#3(1960): 74-88.

4330. Levin, David. "Essay Review: Salem Witchcraft in Recent Fiction and Drama." *NEQ* 28(1955): 537-546.

4331. Mason, Julian. "Some Thoughts on Literary Stereotyping." *BALF* 6(1972): 63-64,70.

4332. McDowell, Frederick P. W. "Stuart P. Sherman: The Evolution of His Critical Philosophy and Method." *SP* 50(1953): 540-557.

4333. McDowell, Robert E., and George Fortenberry. "A Checklist of Books and Essays About American Negro Novelists." *SN* 3(1971): 219-236.

4334. Montesi, Albert J. "Huey Long and *The Southern Review.*" *JML* 3(1973): 63-74.

4335. Musgrave, Marian E. "Triangles in Black and White: Interracial Sex and Hostility in Black Literature." *CLA* 14(1971): 444-451.

4336. Myers, Carol. "A Selected Bibliography of Recent Afro-American Writers." *CLA* 16(1973): 377-382.

4337. Oster, Harry. "The Afro-American Folktale in Memphis: Theme and Function." *BALF* 3(1969): 83-87.

4338. Scruggs, Charles. "'All Dressed Up and No Place to Go': The Black Writer and His Audience During the Harlem Renaissance." *AL* 48 (1977): 543-563.

4339. Shockley, Martin Staples. "Folklorists of Texas." *WAL* 7(1972): 221-223.

4340. Spencer, Benjamin T. "Nationality During the Interregnum (1892-1912)." *AL* 32(1961): 434-445.

4341. Steloff, Frances. "In Touch with Genius." *JML* 4(1975): 749-882.

4342. Stephens, Alan. "A Bibliographical Guide to *Spectrum.*" *TCL* 6(1960): 133-135.

4343. Susman, Warren I. "A Second Country: The Expatriate Image." *TSLL* 3(1961): 171-183.

4344. Thorp, Willard. "Exodus: Four Decades of American Literary Scholarship." *MLQ* 26 (1965): 40-61.

4345. Walker, Don D. "The Rise and Fall of Barney Tullus." *WAL* 3(1968): 93-102.

4346. Weinberg, Bernard. "Scholarship and the Southern Renaissance: A Victory for History." *MLQ* 26(1965): 184-202.

4347. Whitlow, Roger. "The Harlem Renaissance and After: A Checklist of Black Literature of the Twenties and Thirties." *BALF* 7(1973): 143-146.

4348. Winsatt, W. K., Jr. "The Chicago Critics." *Comp L* 5(1953): 50-74.

4349. ----------. "Criticism Today: A Report from America." *EIC* 6(1956): 1-21.

DRAMA. 4350. Brown, Lloyd W. "The Cultural Revolution in Black Theatre." *BALF* 8(1974): 159-164.

4351. Dodson, Owen. "Who Has Seen the Wind? Playwrights and the Black Experience." *BALF* 11(1971): 108-116.

4352. Dusenbury, Winifred L. "Myth in American Drama Between the Wars." *MD* 6(1963): 294-308.

4353. Flanagan, John T. "The Folk Hero in Modern American Drama." *MD* 6(1964): 402-416.

4354. Gerstenberger, Donna. "Verse Drama In America: 1916-1939." *MD* 6(1963): 309-322.

4355. Goldstein, Malcolm. "Body and Soul on Broadway." *MD* 7(1965): 411-421.

4356. Himelstein, Morgan Y. "Theory and Performance in the Depression Theater." *MD* 14 (1972): 426-435.

4357. Hunter, Frederick, J. "The Dramatic Critic Faces a Dilemma." *TCL* 2(1956): 140-147.

4358. Lago, Mary M. "Irish Poetic Drama in St. Louis." *TCL* 23(1977): 180-194.

4359. Lecky, Eleazer. *"New Theatre."* *MD* 6(1963): 267-276.

4360. McDermott, Douglas. "The Living Newspaper as a Dramatic Form." *MD* 8(1965): 82-94.

4361. ----------. "Propaganda and Art: Dramatic Theory and the American Depression." *MD* 11(1968): 73-81.

4362. Mendelsoh, Michael J. "The Social Critics on Stage." *MD* 6(1963): 277-285.

4363. Miller, Jeanne-Marie A. "Images of Black Women in Plays by Black Playwrights." *CLA* 20(1977): 494–507.

4364. Nardin, James T. "The Renaissance of American Drama." *MD* 1(1958): 115–124.

4365. Randel, William. "American Plays in Finland." *AL* 24(1952): 291–300.

4366. Taylor, William Pulliam. "The Reversal of the Tainted Blood Theme in the Works of Writers of the Black Revolutionary Theatre." *BALF* 10(1976): 88–91.

4367. Turner, Darwin T. "Dreams and Hallucinations in the Drama of the Twenties." *CLA* 3(1960): 166–172.

4368. ----------. "The Negro Dramatist's Image of the Universe, 1920–1960." *CLA* 5(1961): 106–120.

4369. ----------. "Negro Playwrights and the Urban Negro." *CLA* 12(1968): 19–25.

4370. ----------. "Past and Present in Negro American Drama." *BALF* 2(1968): 26–27.

4371. Turpin, Waters E. "The Contemporary American Negro Playwright." *CLA* 9(1965): 12–24.

4372. Valgemae, Mardi. "Expressionism and the New American Drama." *TCL* 17(1971): 227–234.

4373. Weales, Gerald. "What *Garrick Gaities?* A Note on Reference and Source Materials." *MD* 8(1965): 198–203.

4374. Wentz, John C. "American Regional Drama, 1920–1940: Frustration and Fulfillment." *MD* 6(1963): 286–293.

4375. Willis, Robert J. "Anger and the Contemporary Black Theatre." *BALF* 8(1974): 213–215.

FICTION. 4376. Aaron, Daniel. "The Occasional Novel: American Fiction and the Man of the Letters." *SAF* 5(1977): 127–141.

4377. Allen, Walter. "Thirties Fiction: A View from the 70's." *TCL* 20(1974): 245–251.

4378. Banks, Ann. "Symposium Sidelights." *Novel* 3(1970): 208–211.

4379. Barksdale, Richard K. "Alienation and the Anti-Hero in Recent American Fiction." *CLA* 10(1966): 1–10.

4380. Clareson, Thomas D. "The Scientist as Hero in American Science-Fiction 1880–1920." *Ext* 7(1965): 18–28.

4381. Cook, Sylvia. "Gastonia: The Literary Reverberations of the Strike." *SLJ* 7, #1 (1974): 49–66.

4382. Cosgrove, William. "Modern Black Writers: The Divided Self." *BALF* 7(1973): 120–122.

4383. Couch, William, Jr. "The Image of the Black Soldier in Selected American Novels." *CLA* 20(1976): 176–184.

4384. Crane, Maurice. "Impaled on a Horn: The Jazz Trumpeter as Tragic Hero." *Crit* 1,#2 (1957): 64–72.

4385. Detweiler, Robert. "Games and Play in Modern American Fiction." *Con L* 17(1976): 44–62.

4386. Durham, Frank. "The Reputed Demises of Uncle Tom; or, The Treatment of the Negro in Fiction by Southern Authors in the 1920's." *SLJ* 2,#2(1970): 26–50.

4387. Ellison, Ralph, and others. "The Uses of Fiction in History: A Discussion." *SLJ* 1,#2 (1969): 57–90.

4388. Fiedler, Leslie. "Second Thoughts on *Love and Death in the American Novel:* My First Gothic Novel." *Novel* 1(1967): 8–11.

4389. ----------. "The War Against the Academy." [See Also 'A Correction" vol.5, p. 180.] *Con L* 5(1964): 5–17.

4390. Flanagan, John T. "A Half-Century of Middlewestern Fiction." *Crit* 2,#3(1959): 16–34.

4391. Fleming, Robert E. "Roots of the White Liberal Stereotype in Black Fiction." *BALF* 9(1975): 17–19.

4392. Friedman, Melvin J. "Dislocations of Setting and Word: Notes on American Fiction since 1950." *SAF* 5(1977): 79–98.

4393. ----------. "The Schlemiel: Jew and Non-Jew." *SLI* 9,#1(1976): 139–153.

4394. Galloway, David D. "Clown and Saint: The Hero in Current American Fiction." *Crit* 7, #3(1965): 46–65.

4395. Garvin, Harry R. "Camus and the American Novel." *Comp L* 8(1956): 194–204.

4396. Gibson, Donald B. "Individualism and Community in Black History and Fiction." *BALF* 11 (1977): 123–129.

4397. Ginsberg, Elaine. "The Female Initiation Theme in American Fiction." *SAF* 3(1975): 27–37.

4398. Harper, Howard. "General Studies of Recent American Fiction: A Selected Checklist." *MFS* 19(1973): 127–135.

4399. Henkle, Roger. "Symposium Highlights: Wrestling (American Style) with Proteus." *Novel* 3(1970): 197–207.

4400. Lehan, Richard. "Existentialism in Recent American Fiction." *TSLL* 1(1959): 181–202.

4401. Lomax, Michael L. "Fantasies of Affirmation: The 1920's Novel of Negro Life." *CLA* 16(1972): 232–246.

4402. Long, Richard A. "The Outer Reaches: The White Writer and Blacks in the Twenties." *SLI* 7,#2(1974): 65–71.

4403. Milton, John R. "The American West: A Challenge to the Literary Imagination." *WAL* 1(1967): 267–284.

4404. O'Conner, William Van. "The Novel of Experience." *Crit* 1,#1(1956): 37–44.

4405. Peavy, Charles D. "The Black Revolutionary Novel: 1899–1969." *SN* 3(1971): 180–189.

4406. Peden, William. "The American Short Story During the Twenties." *SSF* 10(1973): 367–371.

4407. ----------. "The Black Explosion." *SSF* 12(1975): 231–241.

4408. ----------. "Publishers, Publishing, and the Recent American Short Story." *SSF* 1(1963): 33–44.

4409. Peterson, Levi S. "The Primitive and the Civilized in Western Fiction." *WAL* 1(1966): 197–207.

4410. Pilkington, William T. "Aspects of the Western Comic Novel." *WAL* 1(1966): 209–217.

4411. Poger, Sidney. "American Jewish Fiction: Local Color Movement of the Fifties." *CLA* 18(1975): 404–411.

4412. Prigozy, Ruth. "The Liberal Novelist in the McCarthy Era." *TCL* 21(1975): 253-264.

4413. Russell, Charles. "The Vault of Language: Self Reflective Artifice in Contemporary American Fiction." *MFS* 20(1974): 349-359.

4414. Samet, Tom. "Rickie's Cow: Makers and Shapers in Contemporary Fiction." *Novel* 9 (1975): 66-73.

4415. Schatt, Stanley. "You Must Go Home Again: Today's Afro-American Expatriate Writers." *BALF* 7(1973): 79-82.

4416. Sellin, Eric. "Neo-African and Afro-American Literatures." *JML* 1(1970): 249-253.

4417. Solotaroff, Theodore. "Some Random Thoughts on Contemporary Writing." *TCL* 20(1974): 270-276.

4418. Sonnichsen, C. L. "The Ambivalent Apache." *WAL* 10(1975): 99-114.

4419. Sukenick, Ronald. "Fiction in the Seventies: Ten Digressions on Ten Digressions." *SAF* 5(1977): 99-108.

4420. Swallow, Alan. "The Mavericks." *Crit* 2,#3(1959): 74-92.

4421. Thody, Philip. "A Note on Camus and the American Novel." *Comp L* 9(1957): 243-249.

4422. Tischler, Nancy M. "The Negro in Modern Southern Fiction: Sterotype to Archetype." *BALF* 2(1968): 3-6.

4423. Trachtenberg, Stanley. "The Hero in Stasis." *Crit* 7,#2(1964): 5-17.

4424. Turner, Darwin T. "Black Fiction: History and Myth." *SAF* 5(1977): 109-126.

4425. Turpin, Waters E. "Four Short Fiction Writers of the Harleem Renaissance—Their Legacy of Achievement." *CLA* 11(1967): 59-72.

4426. Vanderwerken, David L. "English 4503: Sports in Modern American Literature." *Coll L* 3(1976): 130-138.

4427. Wagner, Linda W. "Tension and Technique: The Years of Greatness." *SAF* 5(1977): 65-77.

4428. Waldmeir, Joseph J. "Only an Occasional Rutabaga: American Fiction Since 1945." *MFS* 15(1969): 467-481.

4429. Walker, Don D. "Criticism of the Cowboy Novel: Retrospect and Reflections." *WAL* 11 (1977): 275-296.

4430. Wedeman, John. "Defining the Black Voice in Fiction." *BALF* 11(1977): 79-82.

4431. West, B. June. "The 'New Woman.'" *TCL* 1(1955): 55-68.

FILM. 4432. Bourget, Jean-Loup. "Social Implications in the Hollywood Genres." *JML* 3(1973): 191-200.

4433. Clurman, Stuart. "An Archaeology of Contextual Space." *JML* 3(1973): 309-322.

4434. Cripps, Thomas R. "Negroes in Movies: Some Reconsiderations." *BALF* 2(1968): 6-7.

4435. Fleischer, Stefan. "A Study Through Stills of *My Darling Clementine*." *JML* 3(1973): 241-252.

4436. Folsom, James K. "'Western' Themes and Western Films." *WAL* 2(1967): 195-203.

4437. Nolley, Kenneth S. "The Western as Jidai-Geki." *WAL* 11(1976): 231-238.

4438. Pasquier, Sylvain du. "Buster Keaton's Gags." *JML* 3(1973): 269-291.

POETRY. 4439. Barksdale, Richard K. "Urban Crisis and the Black Poetic Avant-Garde." *BALF* 3(1969): 40-43.

4440. Bell, Bernard W. "New Black Poetry: A Double-Edged Sword." *CLA* 15(1971): 37-43.

4441. Bree, Germaine. "'New' Poetry and Poets in France and the United States." *Con L* 2, #2(1961): 5-11.

4442. Brooks, A. Russell. "The Motif of Dynamic Change in Black Revolutionary Poetry." *CLA* 15(1971): 7-17.

4443. Davis, Arthur P. "The New Poetry of Black Hate." *CLA* 13(1970): 382-391.

4444. Emanuel, James A. "A Note on the Future of Negro Poetry." *BALF* 1,#1(1967): [2-3].

4445. Fleischman, Wolgang Bernard. "Calme Bloc: Encyclopedia of Poetry and Poetics." *Con L* 7(1966): 194-200.

4446. Govan, Sandra. "The Poetry of Black Experience as Counterpoint to the Poetry of the Black Aesthetic." *BALF* 8(1974): 288-295.

4447. Molesworth, Charles. "'With Your Own Face On': The Origins and Consequences of Confessional Poetry." *TCL* 22(1976): 163-178.

4448. Noll, Bink. "'Quaker Hero, Burning'; Of Poetry and Power: A Poem and Comment." *Con L* 7(1966): 183-193.

4449. Novak, Estelle. "The Dynamo School of Poets." *Con L* 11(1970): 526-539.

4450. Poulin, A. J. "Center and Circumference: Personalism in Criticism." *JML* 1(1970): 109-115.

4451. Ransom, John Crowe. "The Poetry of 1900-1950." *ELH* 18(1951): 155-162.

4452. Rosenthal, M. L. "Dynamics of Form and Motive in Some Representative Twentieth-Century Lyric Poems." *ELH* 37(1970): 136-151.

4453. Schneidau, Herbert N. "The Age of Interpretation and the Moment of Immediacy: Contemporary Art vs. History." *ELH* 37(1970): 287-313.

4454. Smitherman, Geneva. "The Power of the Rap: The Black Idiom and the New Black Poetry." *TCL* 19(1973): 259-274.

4455. Tomlinson, Charles. "Some American Poets: A Personal Record." *Con L* 18(1977): 279-304.

4456. Whittemore, Reed. "The Two Rooms: Humor in Modern American Verse." *Con L* 5(1964): 185-191.

ABBEY, EDWARD. 4457. Pilkington, Tom. "Edward Abbey: Western Philosopher, or How to be a 'Happy Hopi Hippi.'" *WAL* 9(1974): 17-31.
See also 4409.

ADAMS, ANDY. 4458. Quissell, Barbara. "Andy Adams and the Real West." *WAL* 7(1972): 211-219.

ADAMS, SAMUEL HOPKINS. See 4380.

ADE, GEORGE. 4459. Brenner, Jack. "Howells and Ade." *AL* 38(1966): 198-207.

4460. Kolb, Harold. "George Ade (1866-1944)." [bibliography] *ALR* 4(1971): 157-169.

4461. Slazman, Jack. "Dreiser and Ade: A Note on the Text of *Sister Carrie*." *AL* 40(1969): 544-548.

AGEE, JAMES. 4462. Chesnick, Eugene. "The Plot Against Fiction: *Let Us Now Praise Famous Men*." *SLJ* 4,#1(1971): 48-67.

4463. Perry, J. Douglas, Jr. "Thematic Counterpoint in *A Death in the Family*: The Function of the Six Extra Scenes." *Novel* 5(1972): 234-

241.

4464. Ramsey, Roger. "The Double Structure of *The Morning Watch*." *SN* 4(1972): 494-503.

4465. Roe, Michael Morris, Jr. "A Point of Focus in James Agee's *A Death In the Family*." *TCL* 12(1966): 149-153.

AIKEN, CONRAD. 4466. Beach, Joseph Warren. "Conrad Aiken and T. S. Eliot: Echoes and Overtones." *PMLA* 69(1954): 753-762.

4467. Gossman, Ann. "'Silent Snow, Secret Snow': The Child as Artist." *SSF* 1(1964): 123-128.

4468. Gwyn, Frederick L. "The Functional Allusions in Conrad Aiken's 'Mr. Arcularis.'" *TCL* 2(1956): 21-25.

4469. Handa, Carolyn. "'Impulse': Calculated Artistry in Conrad's Short Stories." *SSF* 12(1975): 375-380.

4470. Tabachnick, Stephen E. "The Great Circle Voyage of Conrad Aiken's *Mr. Arcularis*." *AL* 45(1974): 590-607.

See also 19982.

ALBEE, EDWARD. 4471. Bennett, Robert B. "Tragic Vision in *The Zoo Story*." *MD* 20(1977): 55-66.

4472. Bierhaus, E. G., Jr. "Strangers in a Room: *A Delicate Balance* Revisited." *MD* 17 (1974): 199-206.

4473. Bigsby, C. W. E. "Curiouser and Curiouser: Edward Albee and the Great God Reality." *MD* 10(1967): 258-266.

4474. ----------. "Edward Albee's Georgia Ballad." *TCL* 13(1968): 229-236.

4475. ----------. "The Strategy of Madness: An Analysis of Edward Albee's *A Delicate Balance*." *Con L* 9(1968): 223-235.

4476. Campbell, Mary E. "Temptors in Albee's *Tiny Alice*." *MD* 13(1970): 22-33.

4477. Coe, Richard M. "Beyond Absurdity: Albee's Awareness of Audience in *Tiny Alice*." *MD* 18(1975): 371-384.

4478. Cohn, Ruby. "Albee's Box and Ours." *MD* 14(1971): 137-143.

4479. Cole, Douglas. "Albee's *Virginia Woolf* and Steele's *Tatler*." *AL* 40(1968): 81-82.

4480. Daniel, Walter C. "Absurdity in *The Death of Bessie Smith*." *CLA* 8(1964): 76-80.

4481. Davison, Richard Alan. "Edward Albee's *Tiny Alice*: A Note of Re-examination." *MD* 11 (1968): 54-60.

4482. Dozier, Richard. "Adultery and Disappointment in *Who's Afraid of Virginia Woolf?*" *MD* 11(1969): 432-436.

4483. Falk, Eugene H. "*No Exit* and *Who's Agraid of Virginia Woolf*: A Thematic Comparison." *SP* 67(1970): 406-417.

4484. Flasch, Mrs. Harold A. "Games People Play in *Who's Afraid of Virginia Woolf?*" *MD* 10 (1967): 280-288.

4485. Gabbard, Lucina P. "At the Zoo: From O'Neill to Albee." *MD* 19(1976): 365-374.

4486. Hopkins, Anthony. "Conventional Albee: *Box* and *Chairman Mao*." *MD* 16(1973): 141-148.

4487. Irwin, Robert. "The 'Teaching Emotion' in the Ending of *The Zoo Story*." *NCL* 6(September, 1976): 6-8.

4488. Knepler, Henry. "Conflict of Traditions in Edward Albee." *MD* 10(1967): 274-279.

4489. Levine, Mordecai H. "Albee's Liebestod." *CLA* 10(1967): 252-255.

4490. Mandanis, Alice. "Symbol and Substance in *Tiny Alice*." *MD* 12(1969): 92-98.

4491. Moses, Robbie Odom. "Death as a Mirror of Life: Edward Albee's *All Over*." *MD* 19 (1976): 67-78.

4492. Nilan, Mary M. "Albee's *The Zoo Story*: Alienated Man and the Nature of Love." *MD* 16(1973): 55-60.

4493. Otten, Terry. "Ibsen and Albee's Spurious Children." *CD* 2(1968): 83-93.

4494. Post, Robert M. "Fear Itself: Edward Albee's *A Delicate Balance*." *CLA* 13(1969): 163-171.

4495. Ramsey, Roger. "Jerry's Northerly Madness." *NCL* 1(September, 1971): 7-8.

4496. Rule, Margaret W. "An Edward Albee Bibliography." *TCL* 14(1968): 35-44.

4497. Valgemae, Mardi. "Albee's Great God Alice." *MD* 10(1967): 267-273.

4498. Von Szeliski, John J. "Albee: A Rare *Balance*." *TCL* 16(1970): 123-130.

4499. Wallace, Robert S. "*The Zoo Story*: Albee's Attack on Fiction." *MD* 16(1973): 49-54.

4500. White, James E. "An Early Play by Edward Albee." *AL* 42(1970): 98-99.

4501. ----------. "'Santayanian finesse' in Albee's *Tiny Alice*." *NCL* 3(November, 1973): 12-13.

4502. Willeford, William E. "The Mouse in the Model." *MD* 12(1969): 135-145.

4503. Witherington, Paul. "Albee's Gothic: The Resonances of Cliché." *CD* 4(1970): 151-165.

4504. ----------. "Language of Movement in Albee's *The Death of Bessie Smith*." *TCL* 13(1967): 84-88.

4505. Zimbardo, Rose A. "Symbolism and Naturalism in Edward Albee's *The Zoo Story*." *TCL* 8(1962): 10-17.

See also 6715.

ALGREN, NELSON. 4506. Studing, Richard. A Nelson Algren Checklist." *TCL* 19(1973): 27-39.

ALLEN, WOODY. See 4393.

AMMONS, A. R. 4507. Harmon, William. "'How Does One Come Home': A. R. Ammons' *Tape For the Turn of the Year*." *SLJ* 7,#2(1975): 3-32.

ANDERSON, MAXWELL. 4508. Abernethy, Francis E. "*Winterset*: A Modern Revenge Tragedy." *MD* 7(1964): 185-189.

4509. Avery, Laurence G. "Maxwell Anderson: A Changing Attitude Toward Love." *MD* 10(1967): 241-248.

4510. Belli, Angela. "Lenormand's *Asie* and Anderson's The *Wingless Victory*." *Comp L* 19(1967): 226-240.

4511. Gilbert, Veder M. "The Career of Maxwell Anderson: A Check List of Books and Articles." *MD* 2(1960): 386-394.

4512. Pearce, Howard D. "Job in Anderson's *Winterset*." *MD* 6(1963): 32-41.

4513. Tees, Arthur Thomas. "*Winterset*: Four Influences on Mio." *MD* 14(1972): 408-412.

ANDERSON, SHERWOOD. 4514. Anderson, David D. "Sherwood Anderson: A Photographic Gallery." *TCL* 23(1977): 17-39.

4515. Anderson, Sherwood. "Being a Writer."
TCL 23(1977): 1-16.

4516. Babb, Howard S. "A Reading of Sherwood Anderson's 'The Man Who Became a Woman'."
PMLA 80(1965): 432-436.

4517. Budd, Louis J. "The Grotesques of
Anderson and Wolfe." *MFS* 5(1954): 304-310.

4518. Chapman, Arnold. "Sherwood Anderson
and Eduardo Mallea." *PMLA* 69(1954): 34-45.

4519. Cianco, Ralph. "'The Sweetness of
Twisted Apples': Unity of Vision in *Winesburg,
Ohio*." *PMLA* 87(1972): 994-1006.

4520. Dickerson, Mary Jane. "Sherwood
Anderson and Jean Toomer: A Literary Relationship." *SAF* 1(1973): 163-175.

4521. Ditsky, John. "Sherwood Anderson's
Marching Men: Unnatural Disorder and the Art of
Force." *TCL* 23(1977): 102-114.

4522. Fanning, Michael. "Black Mystics,
French Cynics, Sherwood Anderson." *BALF* 11(1977):
49-53.

4523. Fussell, Edwin. "*Winesburg, Ohio*:
Art and Isolation." *MFS* 6(1960): 106-114.

4524. Helbling, Mark. "Sherwood Anderson
and Jean Toomer." *BALF* 9(1975): 35-39.

4525. Joselyn, Sister M., O. S. B. "Some
Artistic Dimensions of Sherwood Anderson's 'Death
in the Woods.'" *SSF* 4(1967): 252-259.

4526. Joseph, Gerhard. "The American Triumph of the Egg: Anderson's 'The Egg' and Fitzgerald's *The Great Gatsby*." *Criticism* 7(1965):
131-140.

4527. Klein, Mia. "Sherwood Anderson: The
Artist's Struggle for Self-Respect." *TCL* 23(1977):
40-52.

4528. Laughlin, Rosemary M. "Godliness and
the American Dream in Winesburg, Ohio." *TCL* 13
(1967): 97-103.

4529. Lawry, Jon S. "The Arts of Winesburg
and Bidwell, Ohio." *TCL* 23(1977): 53-66.

4530. ----------. "'Death in the Woods'
and the Artist's Self in Sherwood Anderson." *PMLA*
74(1959): 306-311.

4531. Lorch, Thomas M. "The Choreographic
Structure of *Winesburg, Ohio*." *CLA* 12(1968): 56-
65.

4532. Love, Glen A. "*Winesburg, Ohio* and
the Rhetoric of Silence." *AL* 40(1968): 38-57.

4533. Lucow, Ben. "Mature Identity in
Sherwood Anderson's 'The Sad Horn-Blowers.'" *SSF*
2(1965): 291-293.

4534. Luedtke, Luther. "Sherwood Anderson,
Thomas Hardy, and 'Tandy.'" *MFS* 20(1974): 531-
540.

4535. Maresca, Carol J. "Gestures as Meaning in Sherwood Anderson's *Winesburg, Ohio*." *CLA*
9(1976): 279-283.

4536. Mellard, James M. "Narrative Forms
in *Winesburg, Ohio*." *PMLA* 83(1968): 1304-1312.

4537. Murphy, George D. "The Theme of
Sublimation in Anderson's *Winesburg, Ohio*." *MFS*
13(1967): 237-246.

4538. Ohashi, Kichinosuki. "Sherwood Anderson in Japan: The Early Years." *TCL* 23(1977):
115-139.

4539. O'Neill, John P. "Anderson Writ
Large: 'Godliness' in *Winesburg, Ohio*." *TCL*
23(1977): 67-83.

4540. Park, Martha M. "How Far from Emerson's Man of One Idea to Anderson's Grotesques?"
CLA 20(1977): 374-379.

4541. Phillips, William L. "How Sherwood
Anderson Wrote *Winesburg, Ohio*." *AL* 23(1951): 7-30.

4542. Richardson, H. Edward. "Anderson and
Faulkner." *AL* 36(1964): 298-314.

4543. ----------. "Faulkner, Anderson, and
Their Tall Tale." *AL* 34(1962): 287-291.

4544. Rideout, Walter B., and James Meriwether. "On the Collaboration of Faulkner and
Anderson." *AL* 35(1963): 85-87.

4545. Ringe, Donald A. "Point of View and
Theme in 'I Want to Know Why.'" *Crit* 3,#1(1959):
24-29.

4546. San Juan, Epifanio, Jr. "Vision and
Reality: A Reconsideration of Sherwood Anderson's
Winesburg, Ohio." *AL* 35(1963): 137-155.

4547. Scafidel, J. R. "Sexuality in *Windy
McPherson's Son*." *TCL* 23(1977): 94-101.

4548. Schevill, James. "Notes on the Grotesque: Anderson, Brecht, and Williams." *TCL*
23(1977): 229-238.

4549. Schieck, William J. "Compulsion Toward Repetition: Sherwood Anderson's 'Death in
the Woods.'" *SSF* 11(1974): 141-146.

4550. Schriber, Mary Sue. "Sherwood Anderson in France: 1919-1939." *TCL* 23(1977): 140-156.

4551. Somers, Paul P., Jr. "Sherwood Anderson's Mastery of Narrative Distance." *TCL* 23(1977):
84-93.

4552. Spencer, Benjamin T. "Sherwood Anderson: American Mythopoeist." *AL* 41(1969): 1-18.

4553. Stewart, Maaja A. "Scepticism and Belief in Checkov and Anderson." *SSF* 9(1972): 29-40.

4554. Stouck, David. "*Winesburg, Ohio* and
the Failure of Art." *TCL* 15(1969): 145-152.

4555. ----------. "*Winesburg, Ohio*, As a
Dance of Death." *AL* 48(1977): 525-542.

4556. Tanselle, G. T. "Realist or Dreamer:
Letters of Sherwood Anderson and Floyd Dell."
MLR 58(1963): 532-537.

4557. Turner, Darwin T. "An Intersection
of Paths: Correspondence between Jean Tomer
and Sherwood Anderson." *CLA* 17(1974): 455-467.

4558. Wentz, John C. "Anderson's *Winesburg*
and the Hedgerow Theatre." *MD* 3(1960): 42-51.

4559. White, Ray Lewis. "Sherwood Anderson,
Ben Hecht, and *Eric Dorn*." *AL* 49(1977): 238-241.

4560. Winther, S. K. "The Aura of Loneliness in Sherwood Anderson." *MFS* 5(1959): 145-152.

4561. Zlotnick, Joan. "Dubliners in Winesburg, Ohio: A Note on Joyce's 'The Sisters' and
Anderson's 'The Philosophers.'" *SSF* 12(1975): 405-
407.

See also 4381, 5505, 5959, 6993.
ANGELOU, MAYA. 4562. Arensberg, Liliane K.
"Death as Metaphor of Self in *I Know Why the
Caged Bird Sings*." *CLA* 20(1976): 273-292.

4563. Hiers, John T. "Fatalism in Maya
Angelou's *I Know Why the Caged Bird Sings*." *NCL*
6(January, 1976): 5-7.

See also 4396.
ASHBERRY, JOHN. 4564. Moramarco, Fred.
"John Ashbery and Frank O'Hara: The Painterly
Poets." *JML* 5(1976): 436-442.

4565. Schulman, Grace. "To Create the Self." *TCL* 23(1977): 299-313.

ASHMEAD, JOHN. 4566. Muste, John L. "Better to Die Laughing: The War Novels of Joseph Heller and John Ashmead." *Crit* 5,#2(1962): 16-27.

ASIMOV, ISAAC. 4567. Stanton, Michael N. The Startled Muse: Emerson and Science Fiction." *Ext* 16(1974): 64-66.

ATHERTON, GERTRUDE. 4568. Atherton, Gertrude. "Poems." *ALR* 9(1976): 163-170.

4569. McClure, Charlotte. "A Checklist of the Writings of and About Gertrude Atherton." [Errata: Vol 10, p. 431] *ALR* 9(1976): 103-162.

4570. ----------. "Gertrude Atherton (1857-1948)." [bibliography] *ALR* 9(1976): 95-102.

ATTAWAY, WILLIAM. 4571. Klotman, Phyllis R. "An Examination of Whiteness in *Blood on the Forge*." *CLA* 15(1972): 459-464.

4572. Waldron, Edward E. "William Attaway's *Blood on the Forge*: The Death of the Blues." *BALF* 10(1976): 58-60.

AUCHINCLOSS, LOUIS. 4573. Kane, Patricia. "Lawyers at the Top: The Fiction of Louis Auchincloss." *Crit* 7,#2(1964): 36-46.

4574. Tuttleton, James W. "Louis Auchincloss: The Image of Lost Elegance and Virtue." *AL* 43 (1972): 616-632.

AUSTIN, MARY HUNTER. 4575. Berry, J. Wilkes. "Mary Hunter Austin (1868-1934)." *ALR* 2(1969): 125-131.

4576. Ford, Thomas W. *"The American Rhythm:* Mary Austin's Poetic Principle." *WAL* 5(1970): 3-14.

4577. Johnson, Lee. "Western Literary Realism: The California Tales of Norris and Austin." *ALR* 7(1974): 278-279.

BAKER, DOROTHY. 4578. Johnson, S. F. "Identities of Cassandra." *Novel* 1(1967): 71-74.

BALDERSTON, JOHN. 4579. Stone, Edward. "From Henry James to John Balderston: Relativity and the '20's.'" *MFS* 1,#2(1955): 2-11.

BALDWIN, JAMES. 4580. Allen, Shirley S. "Religious Symbolism and Physic Reality in Baldwin's *Go Tell It on the Mountain*." *CLA* 19(1975): 173-199.

4581. Anderson, Mary Louise. "Black Matriarchy: Portrayals of Women in Three Plays." *BALF* 10(1976): 93-95.

4582. Dance, Daryl C. "You Can't Go Home Again: James Baldwin and the South." *CLA* 18 (1974): 81-90.

4583. Bell, George E. "The Dilemma of Love in *Go Tell It on the Mountain* and *Giovanni's Room*." *CLA* 17(1974): 397-406.

4584. Bigsby, C. W. E. "The Committed Writer: James Baldwin as Dramatist." *TCL* 13(1967): 39-48.

4585. Bluefarb, Sam. "James Baldwin's 'Previous Condition': A Problem of Identification." *BALF* 3(1969): 26-29.

4586. Burks, Mary Fair. "James Baldwin's Protest Novel: *If Beale Street Could Talk*." *BALF* 10(1976): 83-87, 95.

4587. Gayle, Addison, Jr. "A Defense of James Baldwin." *CLA* 10(1967): 201-208.

4588. Gérard, Albert. "The Sons of Ham." *SN* 3(1971): 148-164.

4589. Goldman, Suzy Bernstein. "James Baldwin's 'Sonny's Blues': A Message in Music." *BALF* 8(1974): 231-233.

4590. Graves, Wallace. "The Question of Moral Energy in James Baldwin's *Go Tell It on the Mountain*." *CLA* 7(1964): 215-223.

4591. Gross, Barry. "The 'Uninhabitable Darkness' of Baldwin's *Another Country*: Image and Theme." *BALF* 6(1972): 113-121.

4592. Gross, Theodore. "The World of James Baldwin." *Crit* 7,#2(1964): 139-149.

4593. Hagopian, John V. "James Baldwin: The Black and the Red-White-and-Blue." *CLA* 7 (1963): 133-140.

4594. Inge, M. Thomas. "James Baldwin's Blues." *NCL* 2(September, 1972): 8-11.

4595. Kent, George E. "Baldwin and the Problem of Being." *CLA* 7(1964): 202-214.

4596. Kim, Kichung. "Wright, the Protest Novel, and Baldwin's Faith." *CLA* 17(1974): 387-396.

4597. Lash, John S. "Baldwin beside Himself: A Study in Modern Phallicism." *CLA* 8(1964): 132-140.

4598. Lee, Robert A. "James Baldwin and Matthew Arnold: Thoughts on 'Relevance.'" *CLA* 14(1971): 324-330.

4599. Murray, Donald C. "James Baldwin's 'Sonny's Blues': Complicated and Simple." *SSF* 14(1977): 353-357.

4600. O'Daniel, Therman B. "James Baldwin: An Interpretive Study." *CLA* 7(1963): 37-47.

4601. Pratt, Louis H. "James Baldwin and 'The Literary Ghetto.'" *CLA* 20(1976): 262-272.

4602. Reilly, John N. "'Sonny's Blues': James Baldwin's Image of Black Community." *BALF* 4(1970): 56-60.

4603. Standley, Fred L. *"Another Country,* Another Time." *SN* 4(1972): 513-521.

4604. Weixlmann, Joe. "Staged Segregation: Baldwin's *Blues for Mister Charlie* and O'Neill's *All God's Children Got Wings*." *BALF* 11(1977): 35-36.

4605. Willis, Antony A. "The Use of Coincidence in 'Notes of a Native Son.'" *BALF* 8(1974): 234-235.

See also 4316, 4351, 4371, 4382, 4396, 4407, 4415.

BARAKA, IMAMU AMIRI. See LEROI JONES.

BARKER, ELLIOTT. 4606. Noland, Richard W. "Lunacy and Poetry: Elliott Barker's *A Fine Madness*." *Crit* 8,#3(1966): 71-78.

BARNES, DJUNA. 4607. Baxter, Charles. "A Self-Consuming Light: *Nightwood* and the Crisis of Modernism." *JML* 3(1974): 1175-1187.

4608. Gunn, Edward. "Myth and Style in Djuna Barnes's *Nightwood*." *MFS* 19(1974): 545-555.

4609. Hipkiss, Robert A. "Djuna Barnes (1892-   )—a Bibliography." *TCL* 14(1968): 161-163.

4610. Pochoda, Elizabeth. "Style's Hoax: A Reading of Djuna Barnes' *Nightwood*." *TCL* 22(1976): 179-191.

4611. Williamson, Alan. "The Divided Image: The Quest for Identity in the Works of Djuna Barnes." *Crit* 7,#1(1964): 58-74.

BARRY, PHILIP. 4612. Meserve, Walter J. "Philip Barry: A Dramatist's Search." *MD* 13(1970): 93-99.

BARTH, JOHN.   4613. Antush, John V. "Allotropic Doubles in Barth's *Sot-Weed Factor*." *Coll L* 4(1977): 71-79.

4614. Bienstock, Beverly Gray. "Lingering on the Autognostic Verge: John Barth's *Lost in the Funhouse*." *MFS* 19(1973): 69-78.

4615. Bryer, Jackson R. "John Hawkes and John Barth: Two Bibliographies." *Crit* 6,#2(1963): 86-94.

4616. David, Jack. "The Trojan Horse at the End of the Road." *Coll L* 4(1977): 159-164.

4617. Davis, Cynthia. "'The Key to the Treasure': Narrative Movements and Effects in *Chimera*." *JNT* 5(1975): 105-115.

4618. Diser, Philip E. "The Historical Ebenezer Cooke." *Crit* 10,#3(1968): 48-59.

4619. Ewell, Barbara C. "John Barth: The Artist of History." *SLJ* 5,#2(1973): 32-46.

4620. Gillespie, Gerald. "Barth's 'Lost in the Funhouse': Short Story Text in its Cyclic Context." *SSF* 12(1975): 223-230.

4621. Harris, Charles B. "George's Illumination: Unity in *Giles Goat-Boy*." *SN* 8(1976): 172-184.

4622. Hinden, Michael. "*Lost in the Funhouse*: Barth's Use of the Recent Past." *TCL* 19 (1973): 107-118.

4623. "John Barth: An Interview." *Con L* 6(1965): 3-14.

4624. Jones, D. Allan. "John Barth's 'Anonymiad.'" *SSF* 11(1974): 361-366.

4625. Kiernan, Robert F. "John Barth's Artist in the Fun House." *SSF* 10(1973): 373-380.

4626. Knapp, Edgar H. "Found in the Barthouse: Novelist as Savior." *MFS* 14(1968): 446-451.

4627. Koelb, Clayton. "John Barth's 'Glossolalia.'" *Comp L* 26(1974): 334-345.

4628. LeClair, Thomas. "John Barth's *The Floating Opera*: Death and the Craft of Fiction." *TSLL* 14(1973): 711-730.

4629. Majdiak, Daniel. "Barth and the Representation of Life." *Criticism* 12(1970): 51-67.

4630. McKenzie, James. "Introduction to Polevaulting in Top Hats: A Public Conversation with John Barth, William Gass, and Ishmael Reed." *MFS* 22(1976): 131-152.

4631. Mercer, Peter. "The Rhetoric of *Giles Goat-Boy*." *Novel* 4(1971): 147-158.

4632. Miller, Russell H. "*The Sot-Weed Factor*: A Contemporary Mock-Epic." *Crit* 8,#2 (1965): 88-100.

4632a. Noland, Richard W. "John Barth and the Novel of Comic Nihilism." *Con L* 7(1966): 239-257.

4633. Puetz, Manfred. "John Barth's *The Sot-Weed Factor*: The Pitfalls of Mythopoesis." *TCL* 22(1976): 454-466.

4634. Rodriques, Eusebio L. "The Living Sakhyan in Barth's *Giles Goat-Boy*." *NCL* 2(September, 1972): 7-8.

4635. Rovit, Earl. "The Novel as Parody: John Barth." *Crit* 6,#2(1963): 77-85.

4636. Schickel, Richard. "*The Floating Opera*." *Crit* 6,#2(1963): 53-67.

4637. Smith, Herbert F. "Barth's Endless Road." *Crit* 6,#2(1963): 68-76.

4638. Strehle, Susan. "John Barth's Narrative Guile in 'Glossolalia.'" *NCL* 6(March, 1976): 13-15.

4639. Stubbs, John C. "John Barth as a Novelist of Ideas: The Themes of Value and Identity." *Crit* 8,#2(1965): 101-116.

4640. Tatham, Campbell. "John Barth and the Aesthetics of Artifice." *Con L* 12(1971): 60-73.

4641. Trachtenberg, Alan. "Barth and Hawkes: Two Fabulists." *Crit* 6,#2(1963): 4-18.

4642. Vanderbilt, Kermit. "From Passion to Impasse: The Structure of a Dark Romantic Theme in Hawthorne, Howells, and Barth." *SN* 8(1976): 419-429.

4643. Vitanza, Victor J. "The Novelist as Topologist: John Barth's *Lost in the Funhouse*." *TSLL* 19(1977): 83-97.

4644. Walter, James F. "A Psychronology of Lust in the Menippean Tradition: *Giles Goat-Boy*." *TCL* 21(1975): 394-410.

4645. Weixlmann, Joseph. "*Giles Goat-Boy* and J. B." *NCL* 7(May, 1977): 6.

BARTHELME, DONALD.   4646. Doxey, W. S. "Donald Barthelme's 'Views of My Father Weeping.'" *NCL* 3(March, 1973): 14-15.

4647. Gillen, Francis. "Donald Barthelme's City: A Guide." *TCL* 18(1972): 37-44.

4648. Longleigh, Peter J., Jr. "Donald Barthelme's *Snow White*." *Crit* 11,#3(1969): 30-34.

BASS, GEORGE.   See 4369.

BATES, ARTHENIA.   4649. Rowell, Charles H. "'He Was Nodding When He Did the Job': A Review Essay." *CLA* 17(1973): 279-286.

BEACH, JOSEPH WARREN.   4650. Simmons, Michael K. "A Look into *The Glass Mountain*." *AL* 41(1969): 422-425.

BELLOW, SAUL.   4651. Axelrod, Steven Gould. "The Jewishness of Bellow's Henderson." *AL* 47(1975): 439-443.

4652. Baker, Sheridan. "Saul Bellow's Bout with Chivalry." *Criticism* 9(1967): 109-122.

4653. Baruch, Franklin R. "Bellow and Milton: Professor Herzog in His Garden." *Crit* 9,#3 (1967): 74-83.

4654. Bolling, Douglass. "Intellectual and Aesthetic Dimensions of *Mr. Sammler's Planet*." *JNT* 4(1974): 188-203.

4655. Campbell, Jeff H. "Bellow's Intimations of Immortality: *Henderson the Rain King*." *SN* 1(1969): 323-333.

4656. Chapman, Abraham. "The Image of Man as Portrayed by Saul Bellow." *CLA* 10(1967): 285-298.

4657. Cohen, Sarah Blacher. "Sex: Saul Bellow's Hedonistic Joke." *SAF* 2(1974): 223-229.

4658. Crozier, Robert D., S. J. "Theme in *Augie March*." *Crit* 7,#3(1965): 18-32.

4659. Cushman, Keith. "Mr. Bellow's *Sammler*: The Evolution of a Contemporary Text." *SN* 7(1975): 425-444.

4660. Demarest, David P., Jr. "The Theme of Discontinuity in Saul Bellow's Fiction: 'Looking for Mr. Green' and 'A Father-to-Be.'" *SSF* 6 (1969): 175-186.

4661. Detweiler, Robert. "Patterns of Rebirth in *Henderson the Rain King*." *MFS* 12(1966):

405-414.

4662. Freedman, Ralph. "Saul Bellow: The Illusion of Environment." *Con L* 1,#1(1960): 50-65.

4663. Fuchs, Daniel. "Saul Bellow and the Modern Tradition." *Con L* 15(1974): 67-89.

4664. Galloway, David D. "The Absurd Man as Picaro: The Novels of Saul Bellow." *TSLL* 6(1964): 226-254.

4665. ----------. "*Mr. Sammler's Planet:* Bellow's Failure of Nerve." *MFS* 19(1973): 17-28.

4666. Goldberg, Gerald Jay. "Life's Customer, Augie March." *Crit* 3,#3(1960): 15-27.

4667. Guttman, Allen. "Bellow's *Henderson.*" *Crit* 7,#3(1965): 33-42.

4668. ----------. "Saul Bellow's Mr. Sammler." *Con L* 14(1973): 157-168.

4669. Handy, William J. "Saul Bellow and the Naturalistic Hero." *TSLL* 5(1964): 538-545.

4670. Harris, James Neil. "One Critical Approach to *Mr. Sammler's Planet.*" *TCL* 18(1972): 235-250.

4671. Hassan, Ihab H. "Saul Bellow: Five Faces of a Hero." *Crit* 3,#3(1960): 28-36.

4672. Hughes, Daniel J. "Reality and the Hero: *Lolita* and *Henderson The Rain King.*" *MFS* 6(1960): 345-364.

4673. Hull, Byron D. "'Henderson the Rain King' and William James." *Criticism* 13(1971): 402-414.

4674. Jefchak, Andrew. "Family Struggles in 'Seize the Day.'" *SSF* 11(1974): 297-302.

4675. Levenson, J. C. "Bellow's Dangling Men." *Crit* 3,#3(1960): 3-14.

4676. Lippit, Noriko. "A Perennial Survivor: Saul Bellow's Heroine in the Desert." *SSF* 12(1975): 281-283.

4677. Markos, Donald W. "Life against Death in *Henderson Rain King.*" *MFS* 17(1971): 193-205.

4678. Mathis, James C. "The Theme of *Seize the Day.*" *Crit* 7,#3(1965): 43-45.

4679. Meyers, Jeffrey. "Brueghel and *Augie March.*" *AL* 49(1977): 113-119.

4680. Overbeck, Pat Trefzger. "The Women in *Augie March.*" *TSLL* 10(1968): 471-484.

4681. Pearson, Carol. "Bellow's *Henderson the Rain King* and the Myth of the King, the Fool, and the Hero." *NCL* 5(November, 1975): 8-11.

4682. Richmond, Lee J. "The Maladroit, the Medico, and the Magician: Saul Bellow's *Seize the Day.*" *TCL* 19(1973): 15-26.

4683. Rodriques, Eusebio L. "Bellow's Africa." *AL* 43(1971): 242-265.

4684. ----------. "Bellow's Confidence Man." *NCL* 3(January, 1973): 6-8.

4685. ----------. "Koheleth in Chicago: The Quest for the Real in 'Looking for Mr. Green.'" *SSF* 11(1974): 387-393.

4686. ----------. "Reichianism in 'Henderson the Rain King.'" *Criticism* 15(1973): 212-233.

4687. Rooke, Constance. "Saul Bellow's 'Leaving the Yellow House': The Trouble with Women." *SSF* 14(1977): 184-187.

4688. Russell, Mariann. "White Man's Black Man: Three Views." *CLA* 17(1973): 93-100.

4689. "Saul Bellow: An Interview." *Con L* 6(1965): 156-160.

4690. Schneider, Harold W. "Two Bibliographies: Saul Bellow, William Styron." *Crit* 3,#3 (1960): 71-91.

4691. Schueler, Mary D. "The Figure of Madeleine in *Herzog.*" *NCL* 1(May, 1971): 5-7.

4692. Shulman, Robert. "The Style of Bellow's Comedy." *PMLA* 83(1968): 109-117.

4693. Toth, Susan Allen. "*Henderson the Rain King,* Eliot and Browning." *NCL* 1(November, 1971): 5-7.

4694. Trachtenberg, Stanley. "Bellow's *Luftmenschen:* The Compromise with Reality." *Crit* 9,#3(1967): 37-61.

4695. Trowbridge, Clinton W. "Water Imagery in *Seize the Day.*" *Crit* 9,#3(1967): 62-73.

4696. Young, James Dean. "Bellow's View of the Heart." *Crit* 7,#3(1965): 5-17.

See also 84, 94, 436, 483, 4400, 19703.

BENET, STEPHEN VINCENT. 4697. Griffith, John. "Narrative Technique and the Meaning of History in Benet and MacLeish." *JNT* 3(1973): 3-19.

4698. Saunders, Alexander. "The Identity of Benet's the Reverend John Smeet." *AL* 22(1951): 501-502.

4699. Wood, Frank. "Three Poems on Whitman." *Comp L* 4(1952): 44-53.

BERGER, THOMAS. 4700. Dippie, Brian W. "Jack Crabb and the Sole Survivors of Custer's Last Stand." *WAL* 4(1969): 189-202.

4701. Fetrow, Fred M. "The Function of the External Narrator in Thomas Berger's *Little Big Man.*" *JNT* 5(1975): 57-65.

4702. Gurian, Jay. "Style in the Literary Desert: *Little Big Man.*" *WAL* 3(1969): 285-296.

4703. Hassan, Ihab. "Conscience and Incongruity: The Fiction of Thomas Berger." *Crit* 5, #2(1962): 4-15.

4704. Oliva, Leo E. "Thomas Berger's *Little Big Man* as History." *WAL* 8(1973): 33-54.

4705. Wylder, Delbert E. "Thomas Berger's *Little Big Man.*" *WAL* 3(1969): 273-284.

See also 4410.

BERRIGAN, TED. See 621.

BERRYMAN, JOHN. 4706. Barbera, Jack V. "John Berryman: R. I. P." *JML* 2(1972): 547-553.

4707. ----------. "Shape and Flow in *The Dream Songs.*" *TCL* 22(1976): 146-162.

4708. Evans, Arthur and Catherine. "Pieter Bruegel and John Berryman: Two Winter Landscapes." *TSLL* 5(1963): 309-318.

4709. Haffenden, John. "A Year on the East Coast: John Berryman 1962-63." *TCL* 22(1976): 129-145.

4710. Johnson, Carol. "John Berryman and Mistress Bradstreet: A Relation of Reason." *EIC* 14(1964): 388-396.

4711. Meredith, William. "Henry Tasting All the Secret Bits of Life: Berryman's Dream Songs." *Con L* 6(1965): 27-33.

4712. Wilson, R. Patrick. "The Ironic Title of Berryman's *Love and Fame.*" *NCL* 5(September, 1975): 10-12.

See also 4447.

BESTER, ALFRED. 4713. Godshalk, William L. "Alfred Bester: Science Fiction or Fantasy?" *Ext* 16(1975): 149-155.

BETTS, DORIS. 4714. Evans, Elizabeth.

"The Mandarin and the Lady: Doris Betts' Debt to
Amy Lowell." *NCL* 6(November, 1976): 2-5.

BISHOP, ELIZABETH.   4715. McNally, Nancy L.
"Checklist of Elizabeth Bishop's Published Writings." *TCL* 11(1966): 201.

4716. ----------. "Elizabeth Bishop: The
Discipline of Description." *TCL* 11(1966): 189-200.

BISHOP, JOHN PEALE.   4717. Elby, Cecil D.,
Jr. "The Fiction of John Peale Bishop." *TCL* 7
(1961): 3-8.

4718. Fleissner, Robert F. "Bishop's 'No
More the Senator' Once More." *NCL* 2(January, 1972):
11-14.

4719. Moore, S. C. "The Criticism of John
Peale Bishop." *TCL* 12(1966): 66-77.

4720. Vauthier, Simone. "The Meaning of
Structure: Toward a New Reading of John Peale
Bishop's *Act of Darkness*." *SLJ* 7,#2(1975): 50-76.

BLACKBURN, PAUL.   4721. "An Interview with
Paul Blackburn." *Con L* 13(1972): 133-143.

BLAND, ALDEN.   4722. Fleming, Robert E.
"Overshadowed by Richard Wright: Three Black
Chicago Novelists." *BALF* 7(1973): 75-79.

BLISH, JAMES.   4723. Aldiss, Brian. "In
Memoriam: James Blish." *Ext* 17(1975): 5-7.

4724. Bradham, Jo Allen. "The Case in
James Blish's *A Case of Conscience*." *Ext* 16
(1974): 67-80.

4725. Reilly, Robert. "The Discerning
Conscience." *Ext* 18(1977): 176-180.

BOGAN, LOUISE.   4726. Perlmutter, Elizabeth F. "A Doll's Heart: The Girl in the Poetry
of Edna St. Vincent Millay and Louise Bogan." *TCL*
23(1977): 157-179.

BONTEMPS, ARNA.   4727. Conroy, Jack.
"Memories of Arna Bontemps, Friend and Collaborator." *BALF* 10(1976): 53-57.

BOOTH, PHILIP.   4728. Stern, Milton R.
"Halfway House: The Poems of Philip Booth." *TCL*
4(1959): 148-153.

BOWLES, JANE.   4729. Kraft, James. "Jane
Bowles as Serious Lady." *Novel* 1(1968): 271-277.

BOWLES, PAUL.   4730. Evans, Oliver. "Paul
Bowles and the 'Natural' Man." *Crit* 3,#1(1959):
43-59.

See also 4400.

BOYLE, KAY.   4731. Carpenter, Richard C.
"Kay Boyle: The Figure in the Carpet." *Crit* 7,
#2(1964): 65-78.

BRADBURY, RAY.   4732. Reilly, Robert.
"The Artistry of Ray Bradbury." *Ext* 13(1971):
64-74.

4733. Watt, Donald J. "Hearth or Salaman-
der: Uses of Fire in Bradbury's *Fahrenheit 451*."
NCL 1(March, 1971): 13-14.

BRAGG, LINDA.   4734. Smith, Virginia, and
Brian J. Benson. "An Interview with Linda Ann
Bragg." *CLA* 20(1976): 75-87.

BRAITHWAITE, WILLIAM.   4735. Butcher,
Philip. "William Stanley Braithwaite's Southern
Exposure: Rescue and Revelation." *SLJ* 3,#2
(1970): 49-61.

4736. Clairmonte, Glenn. "The Cup-Bearer:
William Stanley Braithwaite of Boston." *CLA* 17
(1973): 101-108.

BRALY, MALCOLM.   4737. Franklin, H. Bruce.
"Malcolm Braly: Novelist of the American Prison."
Con L 18(1977): 217-240.

BRAUTIGAN, RICHARD.   4738. Schmitz, Neil.
"Richard Brautigan and the Modern Pastoral." *MFS*
19(1973): 109-126.

BRAWLEY, BENJAMIN.   4739. Parker, John W.
"Toward an Appraisal of Benjamin Brawley's Poetry."
CLA 6(1962): 50-56.

BROOKS, GWENDOLYN.   4740. Baker, Houston A.,
Jr. "The Achievement of Gwendolyn Brooks." *CLA*
16(1972): 23-31.

4741. Davis, Arthur P. "The Black-and-Tan
Motif in the Poetry of Gwendolyn Brooks." *CLA* 6
(1962): 90-97.

4742. ----------. "Gwendolyn Brooks: Poet
of the Unheroic." *CLA* 7(1963): 114-125.

4743. Furman, Marva Riley. "Gwendolyn
Brooks: The 'Unconditioned' Poet." *CLA* 17(1973):
1-10.

4744. Hansell, William H. "Aestheticism
Versus Political Militancy in Gwendolyn Brooks's
'The Chicago Picasso' and 'The Wall.'" *CLA* 17
(1973): 11-15.

4745. ----------. "Essences, Unifyings, and
Black Militancy: Major Themes in Gewndolyn Brooks's
Family Pictures and *Beckonings*." *BALF* 11(1977):
63-66.

4746. ----------. "Gwendolyn Brooks's 'In
the Mecca': A Rebirth into Blackness." *BALF* 8
(1974): 199-207.

4747. Hudson, Clenora F. "Racial Themes in
the Poetry of Gwendolyn Brooks." *CLA* 17(1973): 16-
20.

4748. Hull, Gloria T. "A Note on the Poetic
Technique of Gwendolyn Brooks." *CLA* 19(1975): 280-
285.

4749. Hull, Gloria T., and Posey Gallagher.
"Update on *Part One*: An Interview with Gwendolyn
Brooks." *CLA* 21(1977): 19-40.

4750. Loff, Jon N. "Gwendolyn Brooks: A
Bibliography." *CLA* 17(1973): 21-32.

4751. Mahoney, Heidi. "Selected Checklist
of Material by and about Gwendolyn Brooks." *BALF*
8(1974): 210-211.

4752. Park, Sue S. "A Study in Tension:
Gwendolyn Brooks's 'The *Chicago Defender* Sends a
Man to Little Rock;'" *BALF* 11(1977): 32-34.

4753. Stavros, George. "An Interview with
Gwendolyn Brooks." *Con L* 11(1970): 1-20.

BROWN, FRANK L.   4754. Fleming, Robert E.
"Overshadowed by Richard Wright: Three Black
Chicago Novelists." *BALF* 7(1973): 75-79.

See also 4309.

BROWN, KENNETH.   4755. Bigsby C. W. E.
"The Violent Image: The Significance of Kenneth
Brown's *The Brig*." *Con L* 8(1967): 421-430.

BROWN, STERLING.   4756. O'Meally, Robert G.
"An Annotated Bibliography of the Works of Sterling A. Brown." *CLA* 19(1975): 268-279.

4757. Rowell, Charles H. "Sterling A. Brown
and the Afro-American Folk Tradition." *SLI* 7,#2
(1974): 131-152.

BRUNNER, JOHN.   4758. Brunner, John. "The
Genesis of 'Stand on Zanzibar' and Digressions."
Ext 11(1970): 34-43.

4759. Samuelson, David. "A Comparative
Study of Novels by Brunner and Delany." *Ext* 15
(1973): 75-96.

See also 147.

BULLINS, ED. 4760. Jackson, Kennell, Jr. "Notes on the Works of Ed Bullins and *The Hungered One*." *CLA* 18(1974): 293-299.

4761. Jeffers, Lance. "Bullins, Baraka, and Elder: The Dawn of Granduer in Black Drama." *CLA* 16(1972): 32-48.

4762. O'Brien, John. "Interview with Ed Bullins." *BALF* 7(1973): 108-112.

4763. Tener, Robert L. "Pandora's Box: A Study of Ed Bullins' Dramas." *CLA* 19(1976): 533-544.

4764. True, Warren R. "Ed Bullins, Anton Chekov, and the 'Drama of Mood.'" *CLA* 20(1977): 521-532.

See also 4350, 4351, 4363, 4407.

BURROUGHS, WILLIAM. 4765. Hassan, Ihab. "The Subtracting Machine: The Work of William Burroughs." *Crit* 6,#1(1963): 4-23.

4766. Roselanetz, Richard. "From Nightmare to Serendipity: A Restrospective Look at William Burroughs." *TCL* 11(1965): 123-130.

4766. Peterson, R. G. "A Picture Is a Fact: Wittgenstein and *The Naked Lunch*." *TCL* 12(1966): 8-86.

See also 83.

CABELL, JAMES BRANCH. 4767. Blish, James. "The Long Night of a Virginia Author." *JML* 2 (1971): 393-405.

4768. Duke, Maurice. "Letters of George Sterling to James Branch Cabell." *AL* 44(1972): 146-153.

4769. Godshalk, William Leigh. "Cabell's *Cream of the Jest* and Recent American Fiction." *SLJ* 5,#2(1973): 18-31.

4770. Himelick, Raymond. "Figures of Cabell." *MFS* 2(1956): 214-220.

4771. MacDonald, Edgar E. "Cabell's Hero: Cosmic Rebel." *SLJ* 2,#1(1969): 22-42.

4772. ----------. "Cabell's Richmond Trial." *SLJ* 3,#1(1970): 47-71.

4773. ----------. "The Glasgow-Cabell Entente." *AL* 41(1969): 76-91.

4774. Parks, Edd Winfield. "Cabell's *Cream of the Jest*." *MFS* 2(1956): 68-70.

4775. Schlegel, Dorothy B. "James Branch Cabell: A Latter-Day Enlightener." *CLA* 12(1969): 223-236.

4776. Warner, Richard. "The Illusion of Diabolism in the Cabellian Hero." *Novel* 8(1975): 241-245.

CAHAN, ABRAHAM. 4777. Marovitz, Sanford. "'Yekl': The Ghetto Realism of Abraham Cahan." *ALR* 2(1969): 271-273.

4778. Marovitz, Sanford, and Lewis Fried. "Abraham Cahan (1860-1951): An Annotated Bibliography." *ALR* 3(1970): 197-244.

CALDWELL, BEN. 4779. Potter, Vilma R. "New Politics, New Mothers." *CLA* 16(1972): 247-255.

See also 584, 4311.

CALDWELL, ERSKINE. 4780. Gray, R. J. "Southwestern Humor, Erskine Caldwell, and the Comedy of Frustration." *SLJ* 8,#1(1975): 3-26.

4781. MacDonald, Scott. "Repetition as Technique in the Short Stories of Erskine Caldwell." *SAF* 5(1977): 213-225.

4782. Sale, Richard B. "An Interview in Florida with Erskine Caldwell." *SN* 3(1971): 316-331.

CALISHER, HORTENSE. 4783. Hahn, Emily. "In Appreciation of Hortense Calisher." *Con L* 6(1965): 243-249.

CAMPBELL, JOHN. 4784. Stover, Leon. "Science Fiction, the Research Revolution, and John Campbell." *Ext* 14(1973): 129-148.

CAPOTE, TRUMAN. 4785. Hassan, Ihab H. "The Daydream and Nightmare of Narcissus." *Con L* 1,#2(1960): 5-21.

4786. Perry, J. Douglas, Jr. "Gothic as Vortex: The Form of Horror in Capote, Faulkner, and Styron." *MFS* 19(1973): 153-168.

4787. Pizer, Donald. "Documentary as Art: William Manchester and Truman Capote." *JML* 2 (1971): 105-118.

4788. Zacharias, Lee. "Living the American Dream: 'Children on Their Birthdays.'" *SSF* 12 (1975): 343-350.

CARROLL, PAUL VINCENT. 4789. Pallette, Drew B. "Paul Vincent Carroll—Since *The White Steed*." *MD* 7(1965): 375-381.

CARTER, STEVE. See 4351.

CASSILL, R. V. 4790. Roberts, David. "The Short Fiction of R. V. Cassill." *Crit* 9,#1(1966): 56-70.

CATHER, WILLA. 4791. Andes, Cynthia J. "The Bohemian Folk Practice in 'Neighbor Rosicky.'" *WAL* 2(1972): 63-64.

4792. Baker, Bruce, II. "Nebraska Regionalism in Selected Works of Willa Cather." *WAL* 3 (1968): 19-35.

4793. Bloom, Edward A. and Lillian D. Bloom. "The Genesis of *Death Comes to the Archbishop*." *AL* 26(1954): 479-506.

4794. ----------. "*Shadows on the Rock*: Notes on the Composition of a Novel." *TCL* 2(1956): 70-85.

4795. Bradford, Curtis. "Willa Cather's Uncollected Short Stories." *AL* 26(1955): 537-551.

4796. Bush, Sargent, Jr. "'The Best Years': Willa Cather's Last Story and Its Relation to Her Canon." *SSF* 5(1968): 269-274.

4797. Charles, Sister Peter Damian, O. P. "Love and Death in Willa Cather's *O Pioneers!*" *CLA* 9(1965): 140-150.

4798. ----------. "*My Ántonia*: A Dark Dimension." *WAL* 2(1967): 91-108.

4799. Dahl, Curtis. "An American Georgic: Willa Cather's *My Ántonia*." *Comp L* 7(1955): 43-51.

4800. Dinn, James M. "A Novelist's Miracle: Structure and Myth in *Death Comes for the Archbishop*." *WAL* 7(1972): 39-46.

4801. Fox, Maynard. "Proponents of Order: Tom Outland and Bishop Latour." *WAL* 4(1969): 107-115.

4802. ----------. "Symbolic Representation in Willa Cather's *O Pioneers*." *WAL* 9(1974): 187-196.

4803. ----------. "Two Primitives: Huck Finn and Tom Outland." *WAL* 1(1966): 26-33.

4804. Gelfant, Blanche H. "The Forgotten Reaping-Hook: Sex in *My Ántonia*." *AL* 43(1971): 60-82.

4805. George, Benjamin. "The French-Canadian Connection: Willa Cather as a Canadian Writer." *WAL* 11(1976): 249-261.

4806. Hart, Clive. "'The Professor's House': A Shapely Story." *MLR* 67(1972): 271-281.

4807. Hinz, Evelyn. "Willa Cather's Technique and the Ideology of Populism." *WAL* 7(1972): 47-61.

4808. Hinz, John. "The Hand of the Artist in *Shadow on the Rock*." *SAF* 5(1977): 263-268.

4809. ----------. "The Real Alexander's Bridge." *AL* 21(1950): 473-476.

4810. Kraus, Joe W. "Willa Cather's First Published Story." *AL* 23(1952): 493-494.

4811. Martin, Terence. "The Drama of Memory in *My Ántonia*." *PMLA* 84(1969): 304-311.

4812. Rosowski, Susan J. "Willa Cather's *A Lost Lady*: The Paradoxes of Change." *Novel* 11 (1977): 51-62.

4813. Rubin, Larry. "The Homosexual Motif in Willa Cather's 'Paul's Case.'" *SSF* 12(1975): 127-131.

4814. Schneider, Sister Lucy, C. S. J. "Artistry and Instinct: Willa Cather's 'Land-Philosophy.'" *CLA* 16(1973): 485-504.

4815. Smith, Eleanor M. "The Literary Relationship of Sara Orne Jewett and Willa Cather." *NEQ* 29(1956): 472-492.

4816. Stouck, David. "Perspective as Structure and Theme in *My Ántonia*." *TSLL* 12(1970): 285-294.

4817. ----------. "Willa Cather and the Indian Heritage." *TCL* 22(1976): 433-443.

4818. ----------. "Willa Cather and *The Professor's House*: 'Letting Go with the Heart.'" *WAL* 7(1972): 13-24.

4819. ----------. "Willa Cather's Last Four Books." *Novel* 7(1973): 41-53.

4820. Stuckey, William J. "*My Ántonia*: A Rose for Miss Cather." *SN* 4(1972): 473-483.

4821. Sullivan, Patrick J. "Willa Cather's Southwest." *WAL* 7(1972): 25-37.

4822. Thorberg, Raymond. "Willa Cather: From *Alexander's Bridge* to *My Ántonia*." *TCL* 7 (1962): 147-158.

4824. Walker, Don D. "The Western Humanism of Willa Cather." *WAL* 1(1966): 75-90.

4825. Yongue, Patricia Lee. "*A Lost Lady*: The End of the First Cycle." *WAL* 7(1972): 3-12.

See also 60, 4404.

CHANDLER, RAYMOND. 4826. Kaye, Howard. "Raymond Chandler's Sentimental Novel." *WAL* 10 (1975): 135-145.

CHEEVER, JOHN. 4827. Bracher, Frederick. "John Cheever and Comedy." *Crit* 6,#1(1963): 66-77.

4828. Burhans, Clinton S., Jr. "John Cheever and the Grave of Social Coherence." *TCL* 14 (1969): 187-198.

4829. Chesnick, Eugene. "The Domesticated Stroke of John Cheever." *NEQ* 44(1971): 531-552.

4830. Graves, Nora. "The Dominant Color in John Cheever's 'The Swimmer.'" *NCL* 4(March, 1974): 4-5.

4831. Kendle, Burton. "Cheever's Use of Mythology in 'The Enormous Radio.'" *SSF* 4(1967): 262-264.

4832. Sizemore, Christine W. "The Sweeney Allusion in John Cheever's 'Enormous Radio.'" *NCL* 7(September, 1977): 9.

4833. Ten Harmsel, Henrietta. "'Young Goodman Brown' and 'The Enormous Radio.'" *SSF* 9(1972): 407-408.

CHILDRESS, ALICE. 4834. Anderson, Mary Louise. "Black Matriarchy: Portrayals of Women in Three Plays." *BALF* 10(1976): 93-95.

See also 4363.

CHURCHILL, WINSTON. 4835. Blodgett, Geoffrey. "Winston Churchill: The Novelist as Reformer." *NEQ* 47(1974): 495-517.

4836. Titus, Warren. "Winston Churchill (1871-1947)." [bibliography] *ALR* 1,#1(1967): 26-31.

CLARK, WALTER V. T. 4837. Andersen, Kenneth. "Character Portrayal in *The Ox-Bow Incident*." *WAL* 4(1970): 287-298.

4838. Bates, Barclay W. "Clark's Man for All Seasons: The Achievement of Wholeness in *The Ox-Bow Incident*." *WAL* 3(1968): 39-49.

4839. Cochran, Robert W. "Nature and the Nature of Man in *The Ox-Bow Incident*." *WAL* 5(1971): 253-264.

4840. Houghton, Donald E. "Man and Animals in 'The Indian Well.'" *WAL* 6(1971): 215-218.

4841. Milton, John R. "The Western Attitude: Walter Van Tilburg Clark." *Crit* 2,#3(1959): 57-73.

4842. Peterson, Levi S. "Tragedy and Western American Literature." *WAL* 6(1972): 243-249.

4843. Stein, Paul. "Cowboys and Unicorns: The Novels of Walter Van Tilburg Clark." *WAL* 5 (1971): 265-275.

4844. Westbrook, Max. "The Archetypal Ethic of *The Ox-Bow Incident*." *WAL* 1(1966): 103-118.

4845. ----------. "Internal Debate as Discipline: Clark's *The Watchful Gods*." *WAL* 1(1966): 153-165.

See also 4403, 4409, 4420.

CLEAVER, ELDRIDGE. 4846. Felgar, Robert. "*Soul on Ice* and *Native Son*." *BALF* 8(1974): 235.

4847. Miller, E. S. "Cleaver and Juminer: Black Man and White Woman." *BALF* 11(1977): 25-31.

4848. Nower, Joyce. "Cleaver's Vision of America and the New White Radical: A Legacy of Malcolm X." *BALF* 4(1970): 21.

See also 4382.

COLLINS, THOMAS A. 4849. Collins, Thomas A. "From *Bringing in the Sheaves*, by Windsor Drake with a Foreword by John Steinbeck." *JML* 5(1976): 211-232.

COLTER, CYRUS. See 4407.

CONDON, RICHARD. 4850. Smith, Julian. "The Infernal Comedy of Richard Condon." *TCL* 14(1969): 221-230.

See also 4410.

CONNELL, EVAN S., JR. 4851. Shepherd, Allen. "Mr. Bridge in *Mrs. Bridge*." *NCL* 3(May, 1973): 7-11.

CONROY, FRANK. 4852. Ramsey, Roger. "The Illusion of Fiction in Frank Conroy's *Stop-Time*." *MFS* 20(1974): 391-399.

COOLIDGE, DAN. See 4410.

COOVER, ROBERT. 4853. Hansen, Arlen J. "The Dice of God: Einstein, Heisenberg, and Robert Coover." *Novel* 10(1976): 49-58.

4854. Heckard, Margaret. "Robert Coover, Metafiction, and Freedom." *TCL* 22(1976): 210-227.

4855. Hertzel, Leo J. "An Interview with Robert Coover." *Crit* 11,#3(1969): 25-29.

4856. ----------. "What's Wrong with the Christians." *Crit* 11,#3(1969): 11-24.

4857. Perkins, James Ashbrook. "Robert Coover and John Gardner: What Can We Do With the Poets?" *NCL* 6(March, 1976): 2-4.

4858. Rosa, Alfred F. "Mrs. Grundy Finally Appears in Robert Coover's 'The Pedestrian Accident.'" *NCL* 2(November, 1972): 2-3.

4859. Schmitz, Neil. "Robert Coover and the Hazards of Metafiction." *Novel* 7(1974): 210-219.

4860. Woodward, Robert H. "An Ancestor of Robert Coover's Mrs. Grundy." *NCL* 3(January, 1973): 11-12.

COTTER, JOSEPH S.   4861. Shockley, Ann Allen. "Joseph S. Cotter, Sr.: Biographical Sketch of a Black Louisville Bard." *CLA* 18 (1975): 327-340.

COURNOS, JOHN.   4862. Satterthwaite, Alfred. "John Cournos and H. D." *TCL* 22(1976): 394-410.

CRANE, HART.   4863. Arpad, Joseph J. "Hart Crane's Platonic Myth: The Brooklyn Bridge." *AL* 39(1967): 75-86.

4864. Baker, John. "Commerical Sources for Hart Crane's *The River*." *Con L* 6(1965): 45-55.

4865. Bryant, J. A., Jr. "Hart Crane, Poet of the Sixties." *JML* 1(1970): 283-288.

4866. Clark, David R. "Hart Crane's Technique." *TSLL* 5(1963): 389-397.

4867. Coffman, Stanley K. "Symbolism in *The Bridge*." *PMLA* 66(1951): 65-77.

4868. Cowan, James C. "The Theory of Relativity and *The Bridge*." *HSL* 3(1971): 108-115.

4869. Davison, Richard Allan. "Hart Crane, Louis Untermeyer, and T. S. Eliot: A New Crane Letter." *AL* 44(1972): 143-146.

4870. Day, Robert A. "Image and Idea in 'Voyages II.'" *Criticism* 7(1965): 224-234.

4871. Dembo, L. S. "Hart Crane and Samuel Greenberg: What is Plagiarism?" *AL* 32(1960): 319-321.

4872. ----------. "Hart Crane's 'Verticalist' Poem." *AL* 40(1968): 77-81.

4873. ----------. "The Unfractured Idiom of Hart Crane's *The Bridge*." *AL* 27(1955): 203-224.

4874. Grigsby, Gordon K. "The Photographs in the First Edition of *The Bridge*." *TSLL* 4(1962): 5-11.

4875. Hendrick, George. "Hart Crane Aboard the Ship of Fools: Some Speculations." *TCL* 9 (1963): 3-9.

4876. Hinz, Evelyn J. "Hart Crane's 'Voyages' Reconsidered." *Con L* 13(1972): 315-333.

4877. Holton, Milne. "'A Baudelairesque Thing': the Directions of Hart Crane's 'Black Tamborine.'" *Criticism* 9(1967): 215-228.

4878. Kahn, Sy. "Hart Crane and Harry Crosby: A Transit of Poets." *JML* 1(1970): 45-56.

4879. Knox, George. "Crane and Stella: Conjunction of Painterly and Poetic Worlds." *TSLL* 12(1971): 689-707.

4880. Kramer, Maurice. "Hart Crane's 'Reflexes.'" *TCL* 13(1967): 131-138.

4881. Kramer, Victor A. "The 'Mid-Kingdom' of Crane's 'Black Tamborine' and Toomer's *Cane*." *CLA* 17(1974): 486-497.

4882. Richman, Sidney. "Hart Crane's Voyages II: An Experiment." *Con L* 3,#2(1962): 65-78.

4883. Riddel, Joseph. "Hart Crane's Poetics of Failure." *ELH* 33(1966): 473-496.

4884. Rowe, H. D. "Hart Crane: A Bibliography." *TCL* 1(1955): 94-113.

4885. Simon, Marc. "Hart Crane and Samuel B. Greenberg: An Emblematic Interlude." *Con L* 12(1971): 166-172.

4886. ----------. "Hart Crane's 'Greenberg Mss' and the Launching of 'Voyages II.'" *JML* 5 (1976): 522-529.

4887. Slate, Joseph E. "William Carlos Williams, Hart Crane, and 'The Virtue of History.'" *TSLL* 6(1965): 486-511.

4888. Sundquist, Eric J. "Bringing Home the Word: Magic, Lies, and Silence in Hart Crane." *ELH* 44(1977): 376-399.

4889. Unterecker, John. "The Architecture of *The Bridge*." *Con L* 3,#2(1962): 5-19.

4890. Uroff, M. D. "Hart Crane's 'Voyages VI', Stanza 6." *ELN* 8(1970): 46-48.

4891. ----------. "The Imagery of Violence in Hart Crane's Poetry." *AL* 43(1971): 200-216.

4892. Willingham, John R. "'Three Songs' of Hart Crane's *The Bridge*: A Reconsideration." *AL* 27(1955): 62-68.

4893. Wood, Frank. "Three Poems on Whitman." *Comp L* 4(1952): 44-53.

4894. Yannella, Philip R. "'Inventive Dust': The Metamorphoses of 'For the Marriage of Faustus and Helen.'" *Con L* 15(1974): 102-122.

4895. ----------. "Towards Apotheosis: Hart Crane's Visionary Lyrics." *Criticism* 10(1968): 313-333.

4896. Zeck, Gregory R. "The Logic of Metaphor: 'At Melville's Tomb.'" *TSLL* 17(1975): 673-686.

CREELEY, ROBERT.   4897. Altieri, Charles. "The Unsure Egoist: Robert Creeley and the Theme of Nothingness." *Con L* 13(1972): 162-185.

4898. Johnson, Lee Ann. "Robert Creeley: A Checklist (1946-1970)." *TCL* 17(1971): 181-198.

4899. Leed, Jacob. "Robert Creeley and *The Lititz Review*: A Recollection with Letters." *JML* 5(1976): 243-259.

CROSBY, HARRY.   4900. Kahn, Sy. "Hart Crane and Harry Crosby: A Transit of Poets." *JML* 1(1970): 45-56.

4901. Reed, Victor. "Reading a 'Sound Poem' by Harry Crosby." *ELN* 6(1969): 192-196.

CULLEN, COUNTEE.   4902. Collier, Eugenia W. "I Do Not Marvel, Countee Cullin." *CLA* 11 (1967): 73-87.

4903. Copeland, Catherine H. "The Unifying Effect of Coupling in Countee Cullen's 'Yet Do I Marvel.'" *CLA* 18(1974): 258-261.

4904. Daniel, Walter C. "Countee Cullin as Literary Critic." *CLA* 14(1971): 281-290.

4905. Dorsey, David F. "Countee Cullen's Use of Greek Mythology." *CLA* 13(1969): 68-77.

4906. Jones, Norma Ramsay. "Africa, as Imaged by Cullen and Co." *BALF* 8(1974): 263-267.

4907. Larson, Charles R. "Three Harlem Novels of the Jazz Age." *Crit* 11,#3(1969): 66-78.

4908. Lomax, Michael L. "Countee Cullen: A Key to the Puzzle." *SLI* 7,#2(1974): 39-48.

CUMMINGS, E. E.   4909. Davis, William V. "E. E. Cumming's 'Except in Your.'" *ELN* 11(1974): 294-296.

4910. Engle, Wilson F. III. "Pilgrim as Prisoner: Cummings and Vonnegut." *NCL* 7(January, 1977): 13-14.

4911. Friedman, Norman. "Diction, Voice, and Tone: The Poetic Language of E. E. Cummings." *PMLA* 72(1957): 1036-1059.

4912. ----------. "E. E. Cummings and His Critics." *Criticism* 6(1964): 114-133.

4913. Kidder, Rushworth M. "'Author of Pictures': A Study of Cummings' Line Drawings in *The Dial*." *Con L* 17(1976): 470-505.

4914. Perrine, Laurence. "In Heavenly Realms of Hellas." *NCL* 1(January, 1971): 2-4.

4915. Sickels, Eleanor M. "The Unworld of E. E. Cummings." *AL* 26(1954): 223-246.

4916. Smelstor, Marjorie, S. C. "'Damn Everything but the Circus': Popular Art in the Twenties and *him*." *MD* 17(1974): 43-56.

4917. Smith, David E. "*The Enormous Room* and *The Pilgrim's Progress*." *TCL* 11(1965): 67-76.

4918. Smith, James F., Jr. "A Stereotyped Archetype: E. E. Cummings' Jean Le Negre." *SAF* 1(1973): 24-34.

4919. Tal-Mason, Patricia Buchanan. "The Whole E. E. Cummings." *TCL* 14(1968): 90-97.

4920. Von Abele, Rudolph. "'Only to Grow': Change in the Poetry of E. E. Cummings." *PMLA* 70 (1955): 913-933.

4921. Widmer, Kingsley. "Timeless Prose." *TCL* 4(1958): 3-8.

See also 4341.

CUNNINGHAM, EUGENE.   4922. Pike, Donald G. Eugene Cunningham: Realism and the Action Novel." *WAL* 7(1972): 224-229.

CUNNINGHAM, J. V.   4923. Winters, Yvor. "The Poetry of J. V. Cunningham." *TCL* 6(1961): 159-171.

DAHLBERG, EDWARD.   4924. Porter, Roger J. "Emptying His Sack of Woe: Edward Dahlberg's *Because I Was Flesh*." *Con L* 18(1977): 141-159.

4925. Spencer, Benjamin T. "American Literature as Black Mass: Edward Dahlberg." *TCL* 21(1975): 381-393.

DAVIS, FRANK M.   4926. Kloder, Helena. "The Film and Canvas of Frank Marshall Davis." *CLA* 15(1971): 59-63.

DAVIS, H. L.   4927. Brunvand, Jan Harold. "*Honey in the Horn* and 'Acres of Clams': The Regional Fiction of H. L. Davis." *WAL* 2(1967): 135-145.

4928. Bryant, Paul T. "H. L. Davis: Viable Uses for the Past." *WAL* 3(1968): 3-18.

4929. Etulain, Richard W. "H. L. Davis: A Bibliographical Addendum." *WAL* 5(1970): 129-135.

4930. Kellogg, George. "H. L. Davis, 1896-1960: A Bibliography." *TSLL* 5(1963): 294-303.

DAVIS, OSSIE.   See 4425.

DAWSON, WARRINGTON.   4931. Schwab, Arnold T. "Joseph Conrad and Warrington Dawson." *MP* 68(1971): 364-374.

DEAN, PHILIP HAYES.   See 4351.

DELANY, SAMUEL R.   4932. Gardiner, H. Jane. "Images of *The Waste Land* in *The Einstein Intersection*." *Ext* 18(1977): 116-123.

4933. Miesel, Sandra. "Samuel R. Delaney's Use of Myth in *Nova*." *Ext* 12(1971): 86-93.

4934. Sameulson, David. "A Comparative Study of Novels by Brunner and Delany." *Ext* 15(1973): 75-96.

See also 147.

DELL, FLOYD.   4935. Flanagan, John T. "A Letter from Floyd Dell." *AL* 45(1973): 441-452.

4936. Tanselle, G. Thomas. "Sinclair Lewis and Floyd Dell: Two Views of the Midwest." *TCL* 9 (1964): 175-184.

DELORIE, VINE, JR.   See 621.

DEMBY, WILLIAM.   4937. Connelly, Joseph. "William Demby's Fiction." *BALF* 10(1976): 100-103.

DEVOTO, BERNARD.   4938. Butterfield, L. H. "Bernard DeVoto in the Easy Chair: 1935-1955." *NEQ* 29(1956): 435-442.

4939. Sawey, Orlan. "Bernard DeVoto's Western Novels." *WAL* 2(1967): 171-182.

See also 588, 4429.

DEVRIES, PETER.   4940. Bowden, Edwin T. "Peter DeVries—The First Thirty Years: A Bibliography, 1934-1964." *TSLL* 6(1965): 545-570.

4941. Sale, Richard B. "An Interview in New York with Peter DeVries." *SN* 1(1969): 364-369.

DICK, PHILIP K.   See 147.

DICKEY, JAMES.   4942. Arnett, David L. "An Interview with James Dickey." *Con L* 16(1975): 286-300.

4943. Carnes, Bruce. "Deliverance in James Dickey's 'On the Coosawattee' and *Deliverance*." *NCL* 7(March, 1977): 2-3.

4944. Coulthard, Ron. "From Manuscript to Movie Script: James Dickey's *Deliverance*." *NCL* 3(November, 1973): 11-12.

4945. ----------. "Reflections upon a Golden Eye: A Note on James Dickey's Deliverance." *NCL* 3(September, 1973): 13-15.

4946. Davis, Charles E. "The Wilderness Revisited: Irony in James Dickey's *Deliverance*." *SAF* 4(1976): 223-230.

4947. Edwards, C. Hines, Jr. "A Foggy Scene in *Deliverance*." *NCL* 2(Nov., 1972): 7-9.

4948. Glancy, Eileen K. "James Dickey: A Bibliography." *TCL* 15(1969): 45-62.

4949. Guillory, Daniel L. "Myth and Meaning in Dickey's *Deliverance*." *Coll L* 3(1976): 56-62.

4950. ----------. "Water Magic in the Poetry of James Dickey." *ELN* 8(1970): 131-137.

4951. Italia, Paul G. "Love and Lust in James Dickey's *Deliverance*." *MFS* 21(1975): 203-213.

4952. Lindborg, Henry J. "James Dickey's *Deliverance*: The Ritual of Art." *SLJ* 6,#2(1974): 83-90.

4953. Longen, Eugene M. "Dickey's *Deliverance*: Sex and the Great Outdoors." *SLJ* 9,#2 (1977): 137-149.

4954. Shepherd, Allen. "Counter-Monster Comes Home: The Last Chapter of James Dickey's *Deliverance*." *NCL* 3(March, 1973): 8-12.

4955. Verburg, T. Larry. "Water Imagery in James Dickey's *Deliverance*." *NCL* 4(November, 1974): 11-13.

4956. Willig, Charles L. "Ed's Transformation: A Note on *Deliverance*." *NCL* 3(March, 1973): 4-5.

DONLEAVY, J. P. 4957. LeClair, Thomas. "A Case of Death: The Fiction of J. P. Donleavy." *Con L* 12(1971): 329-344.

4958. LeClair, Thomas. "*The Onion Eaters* and the Rhetoric of Donleavy's Comedy." *TCL* 18 (1972): 167-174.

4959. Sherman, William David. "J. P. Donleavy: Anarchic Man as Dying Dionysian." *TCL* 13 (1968): 216-228.

DOOLITTLE, HILDA. 4960. Bryer, Jackson. "H. D.: A Note on Her Critical Reputation." *Con L* 10(1969): 627-631.

4961. Bryer, Jackson R., and Pamela Roblyer. "H. D.: A Preliminary Checklist." *Con L* 10(1969): 632-675.

4962. Dembo, L. S. "Introduction." *Con L* 10(1969): 433-434.

4963. ----------. "Norman Holmes Pearson on H. D.: An Interview." *Con L* 10(1969): 435-446.

4964. Engel, Bernard F. "H. D.: Poems that Matter and Dilutations." *Con L* 10(1969): 507-522.

4965. Greenwood, E. B. "H. D. and the Problem of Escapism." *EIC* 21(1971): 365-376.

4966. Holland, Norman N. "H. D. and the 'Blameless Physician.'" *Con L* 10(1969): 474-506.

4967. Newlin, Margaret. "'Unhelpful Hymen!': Marrianne Moore and Hilda Doolittle." *EIC* 27 (1977): 216-230.

4968. Pearson, Norman Holmes. "Introduction: A Selection of Poetry and Prose." *Con L* 10(1969): 587-588.

4969. Pondrom, Cyrena N., ed. "Selected Unpublished Letters from H. D. to F. S. Flint: A Commentary on the Imagist Period." *Con L* 10(1969): 557-586.

4970. Quinn, Vincent. "H. D.'s 'Hermetic Definition': The Poet as Archetypal Mother." *Con L* 18(1977): 51-61.

4971. Riddel, Joseph N. "H. D. and the Poetics of 'Spiritual Realism.'" *Con L* 10(1969): 447-473.

4972. Satterthwaite, Alfred. "John Cournos and 'H. D..'" *TCL* 22(1976): 394-410.

4973. Wagner, Linda W. "*Helen in Egypt*: A Culmination." *Con L* 10(1969): 523-536.

4974. Weatherhead, A. Kingsley. "Style in H. D.'s Novels." *Con L* 10(1969): 537-556.

DORN, EDWARD. 4975. Okada, Roy. "An Interview with Edward Dorn." *Con L* 15(1974): 297-314.

DOS PASSOS, JOHN. 4976. Bernardin, Charles W. "John Dos Passos' Harvard Years." *NEQ* 27(1954): 3-26.

4977. Brown, Deming. "Dos Passos in Soviet Criticism." *Comp L* 5(1953): 332-350.

4978. Carver, Craig. "The Newspaper and Other Sources of Manhattan Transfer." *SAF* 3(1975): 167-179.

4979. Diggins, John P. "Visions of Chaos and Visions of Order: Dos Passos as Historian." *AL* 46(1974): 329-346.

4980. Gelfant, Blanche H. "The Search for Identity in the Novels of John Dos Passos." *PMLA* 76(1961): 133-149.

4981. Hughson, Lois. "In Search of the True America: Dos Passos' Debt to Whitman in *U. S. A.*" *MFS* 19(1973): 179-192.

4982. ----------. "Narration in the Making of *Manhattan Transfer*." *SN* 8(1976): 185-198.

4983. Kallich, Martin. "John Dos Passos—Fellow-Traveler: A Dossier with Commentary." *TCL* 1(1956): 173-190.

4984. Knox, George. "Dos Passos and Painting." *TSLL* 6(1964): 22-38.

4985. ----------. "Voice in the U. S. A. Biographies." *TSLL* 4(1962): 109-116.

4986. Lowry, E. D. "The Lively Art of *Manhattan Transfer*." *PMLA* 84(1969): 1628-1638.

4987. Ludington, Townsend. "The Ordering of the Camera Eye in *U. S. A.*" *AL* 49(1977): 443-446.

4988. McIlvaine, Robert M. "Dos Passos's Reading of Thorstein Veblen." *AL* 44(1972): 471-474.

4989. Morse, Jonathan. "Dos Passo's *U. S. A.* and the Illusions of Memory." *MFS* 23(1977): 543-555.

4990. Muste, John M. "Norman Mailer and John Dos Passos: The Question of Influence." *MFS* 17(1971): 361-374.

4991. Reinhart, Virginia S. "John Dos Passos Bibliography: 1950-1966." *TCL* 13(1967): 167-178.

4992. Ruoff, Gene. "Social Mobility and the Artist in *Manhattan Transfer* and *The Music of Time*." *Con L* 5(1964): 64-76.

4993. Stoltzfus, Ben. "John Dos Passos and the French." *Comp L* 15(1963): 146-163.

4994. Titche, Leon L., Jr. "Döblin and Dos Passos: Aspects of the City Novel." *MFS* 17(1971): 125-135.

4995. Vanderwerken, David L. "*Manhattan Transfer*: Dos Passos' Babel Story." *AL* 49(1977): 253-267.

4996. ----------. "*U. S. A.*: Dos Passos and the 'Old Words.'" *TCL* 23(1977): 195-228.

4997. Westerhoven, James N. "Autobiographical Elements in the Camera Eye." *AL* 48(1976): 340-364.

DOWNING, J. HYATT. 4998. Walden, Anthony J. "Late to the Harvest: The Fiction of J. Hyatt Downing." *WAL* 6(1971): 203-214.

DREISER, THEODORE. 4999. Becker, George J. "Theodore Dreiser: The Realist as Social Critic." *TCL* 1(1955): 117-127.

5000. Bucco, Martin. "The East-West Theme in Dreiser's *An American Tragedy*." *WAL* 12(1977): 177-183.

5001. Burgan, Mary E. "'Sister Carrie' and the Pathos of Naturalism." *Criticism* 15(1973): 336-349.

5002. Campbell, Charles L. "*An American Tragedy*: Or, Death in the Woods." *MFS* 15(1969): 251-259.

5003. Cohen, Lester H. "Locating One's Self: The Problematics of Dreiser's Social World." *MFS* 23(1977): 355-368.

5004. Dance, Daryl C. "Sentimentalism in Dreiser's Heroines Carrie and Jennie." *CLA* 14 70): 127-142.

5005. Davidson, Cathy N. and Arnold E. "Carrie's Sisters: The Popular Prototypes for Dreiser's Heroine." *MFS* 23(1977): 395-407.

5006. Dowell, Richard W. "You Will Not Like Me Im Sure: Dreiser to Miss Emma Rector November 28, 1893 to April 4, 1894. *ALR* 3(1970): 259-270.

5007. Durham, Frank. "Mencken as Missionary." *AL* 29(1958): 478-483.

5008. Fisher, Philip. "Looking Around to See Who I Am: Dreiser's Territory of the Self." *ELH* 44(1977): 728-748.

5009. Flanagan, John T. "Dreiser's Style in *An American Tragedy*." *TSLL* 7(1965): 285-294.

5010. Forrey, Robert. "Theodore Dreiser: Oedipus Redivivus." *MFS* 23(1977): 341-354.

5011. Freedman, William A. "A Look at Dreiser as Artist: The Motif of Circularity in *Sister Carrie*." *MFS* 8(1962): 384-392.

5012. Friedrich, Gerhard. "A Major Influence on Theodore Dreiser's *The Bulwark*." *AL* 29(1957): 180-193.

5013. Graham, D. B. "'The Cruise of the Idlewild': Dreiser's Revisions of a 'Rather Light' Story." *ALR* 8(1975): 1-12.

5014. ----------. "Dresier's Ant Tragedy: The Revision of 'The Shining Slave Makers.'" *SSF* 14(1977): 41-48.

5015. ----------. "Dreiser's Maggie." *ALR* 7(1974): 169-170.

5016. Gerber, Philip L. "The Alabaster Protégé: Dreiser and Bernice Fleming." *AL* 43 (1971): 217-230.

5017. ----------. "Dreiser's Financier: A Genesis." *JML* 1(1971): 354-374.

5018. ----------. "The Financier Himself: Dreiser and C. T. Yerkes." *PMLA* 88(1973): 112-122.

5019. ----------. "Frank Cowpoerwood: Boy Financier." *SAF* 2(1974): 165-174.

5020. Hakutani, Yoshinofu. "Dreiser and French Realism." *TSLL* 6(1964): 200-212.

5021. ----------. "Sister Carrie and the Problem of Literary Naturalism." *TCL* 13(1967): 3-17.

5022. Handy, William J. "A Re-Examination of Dreiser's *Sister Carrie*." *TSLL* 1(1959): 380-393.

5023. Heim, William J. "Letters from Young Dreiser." *ALR* 8(1975): 158-163.

5024. Hirsh, John. "The Printed Ephemera of Sister Carrie." *ALR* 7(1974): 171-172.

5025. Hoffman, Frederick J. "The Scene of Violence: Dostoevsky and Dreiser." *MFS* 6(1960): 91-105.

5026. Hovey, Richard B., and Ruth S. Ralph. "Dreiser's *The 'Genius'*: Motivation and Structure." *HSL* 2(1970): 169-183.

5027. Hussman, Lawrence. "Thomas Edison and *Sister Carrie*: A Source for Character and Theme." *ALR* 8(1975): 155-158.

5028. Jurnak, Sheila Hope. "Popular Art Forms in *Sister Carrie*." *TSLL* 13(1971): 313-320.

5029. Katope, Christopher G. "*Sister Carrie* and Spencer's *First Principles*." *AL* 41(1969): 64-

75.

5030. Klopf, Dorothy. "Theodore Dreiser's *The 'Genius'*: Much Matter and More Art." *MFS* 23 (1977): 441-448.

5031. Kwiat, Joseph J. "The 'Genius' and Everett Shinn, The 'Ash-Can' Painter." *PMLA* 67 (1952): 15-31.

5032. ----------. "The Newspaper Experience: Crane, Norris and Dreiser." *NCF* 8(1953): 99-117.

5033. Lane, Lauriat, Jr. "The Double in *An American Tragedy*." *MFS* 12(1966): 213-220.

5034. Lindborg, Mary Anne. "Dreiser's Sentimental Heroine, Aileen Butler." *AL* 48(1977): 590-596.

5035. Moers, Ellen. "The Survivors: Into the Twentieth Century." *TCL* 20(1974): 1-10.

5036. Moers, Ellen, and Sandy Petrey. "Dreiser's Wisdom. . . or Stylistic Discontinuities." *Novel* 11(1977): 66-69.

5037. Mookerjee, R. N. "Dreiser's Use of Hindu Thought in *The Stoic*." *AL* 43(1971): 273-278.

5038. O'Neill, John. "The Disproportion of Sadness: Dreiser's *The Financier* and *The Titan*." *MFS* 23(1977): 409-422.

5039. Orlov, Paul A. "The Subversion of the Self: Anti-Naturalistic Crux in *An American Tragedy*." *MFS* 23(1977): 457-472.

5040. Petrey, Sandy. "The Language of Realism, The Language of False Consciousness: A Reading of *Sister Carrie*." *Novel* 10(1977): 101-113.

5041. Phillips, William L. "The Imagery of Dreiser's Novels." *PMLA* 78(1963): 572-585.

5042. Pizer, Donald. "American Literary Naturalism: The Example of Dreiser." *SAF* 5(1977): 51-63.

5043. ----------. "Theodore Dreiser's 'Nigger Jeff': The Development of an Aesthete." *AL* 41(1969): 331-341.

5044. Purdy, Strother B. "*An American Tragedy* and *L'Etranger*." *Comp L* 19(1967): 252-268.

5045. Putzel, Max. "Dreiser, Reedy, and 'DeMaupassant, Junior.'" *AL* 33(1962): 466-484.

5046. Richman, Sidney. "Theodore Dreiser's *The Bulwark*: A Final Resolution." *AL* 34(1962): 229-245.

5047. Riggio, Thomas P. "Another Two Dreisers: The Artist as 'Genius.'" *SN* 9(1977): 119-136.

5048. ----------. "Europe without Baedeker: The Omitted Hanscha Jower Story—from *A Traveler at Forty*." *MFS* 23(1977): 423-440.

5049. ----------. "Review-Essay: The Divided Stream of Dreiser Studies." *SN* 9(1977): 211-216.

5050. Rusch, Frederic E. "Dreiser's Other Tragedy." *MFS* 23(1977): 449-456.

5051. Salzman, Jack. "Criticism of Theodore Dreiser: A Selected Checklist." *MFS* 23(1977): 473-486.

5052. ----------. "Dreiser and Ade: A Note on the Text of *Sister Carrie*." *AL* 40(1969): 544-548.

5053. ----------. "Dreiser Then and Now." *JML* 1(1971): 421-430.

5054. ----------. "Theodore Dreiser (1871-1945)." *ALR* 2(1969): 132-138.

5055. Seltzer, Leon F. "*Sister Carrie* and the Hidden Longing for Love: Sublimation or Subterfuge?" *TCL* 22(1976): 192-209.

5056. Stein, Allen. "*Sister Carrie*: A Possible Source for the Title." *ALR* 7(1974): 173-174.

5057. Steinbrecher, George, Jr. "Inaccurate Accounts of *Sister Carrie*." *AL* 23(1952): 490-493.

5058. Szuberla, Guy. "Dreiser at the World's Fair: The City without Limits." *MFS* 23(1977): 369-379.

5059. Vance, William L. "Dreiserian Tragedy." *SN* 4(1972): 39-51.

5060. Von Szeliski, John J. "Dreiser's Experiment with Tragic Form." *TCL* 12(1966): 31-39.

5061. Watson, Charles N., Jr. "The 'Accidental' Drownings in *Daniel Deronda* and *An American Tragedy*." *ELN* 13(1976): 288-291.

5062. Wentz, John C. "*An American Tragedy* as Epic Theater: The Piscator Dramatization." *MD* 4(1962): 365-376.

5063. Westbrook, Max. "Dreiser's Defense of Carrie Meeber." *MFS* 23(1977): 381-395.

5064. White, William. "Dreiser on Hardy, Henley, and Whitman: An Unpublished Letter." *ELN* 6(1968): 122-124.

5065. Williams, Edward Mercur. "Edmund Clarence Stedman at Home." *NEQ* 25(1952): 242-255.

5066. Williams, Philip. "The Chapter Titles of *Sister Carrie*." *AL* 36(1964): 359-365.

5067. Wittemeyer, Hugh. "Gaslight and Magic Lamp in *Sister Carrie*." *PMLA* 86(1971): 236-240.

5068. Wycherley, H. Alan. "Mechanism and Vitalism in Dreiser's Nonfiction." *TSLL* 11(1969): 1039-1049.

See also 436.

DUBOIS, W. E. B. 5069. Amann, Clarence A. "Three Negro Classics: An Estimate." *BALF* 4(1970): 113-119.

5070. Gibson, Lovie N. "W. E. B. DuBois as a Propaganda Novelist." *BALF* 10(1976): 75-77,79-83.

5071. Green, Dan S. "Bibliography of Writings about W. E. B. DuBois." *CLA* 20(1977); 410-421.

5072. Moses, Wilson J. "The Poetics of Ethiopianism: W. E. B. DuBois and Literary Black Nationalism." *AL* 47(1975): 411-426.

5073. Savory, Jerold J. "The Rending of the Veil in W. E. B. DuBois's *The Souls of Black Folk*." *CLA* 15(1972): 334-337.

5074. Turner, Darwin T. "W. E. B. DuBois and the Theory of a Black Aesthetic." *SLI* 7,#2 (1974): 1-21.

5075. Walden, Daniel. "DuBois' Pan-Americanism: A Reconsideration." *BALF* 8(1974): 260-262.

5076. Yellin, Jean Fayan. "An Index of Literary Materials in *The Crisis*, 1910-1934: Articles, Belles Lettres, and Book Reviews." *CLA* 14(1971): 452-465; 15(1971): 197-234.

See also 4316, 4391, 4401.

DUNBAR, PAUL LAURENCE. 5078. Butcher, Philip. "Mutual Appreciation: Dunbar and Cable." *CLA* 1(1958): 101-102.

5079. Candela, Gregory L. "We Wear the Mask: Irony in Dunbar's *The Sport of the Gods*." *AL* 48(1976): 60-72.

5080. Lee, A. Robert. "The Fiction of Paul Laurence Dunbar." *BALF* 8(1974): 166-172.

5081. Turner, Darwin T. "Paul Laurence Dunbar: the Poet and the Myths." *CLA* 18(1974): 155-171.

See also 4396.

DUNBAR-NELSON, ALICE. 5082. Williams, Ora. "Works by and About Alice Ruth (Moore) Dunbar-Nelson: A Bibliography." *CLA* 19(1976): 322-326.

See also 622.

DUNCAN, ROBERT. 5083. Weatherhead, A. K. "Robert Duncan and the Lyric." *Con L* 16(1975): 163-174.

EDWARDS, HARRY S. 5084. Bond, Adrienne. "*Eneas Africanus* and Faulkner's Fabulous Racehorse." *SLJ* 9,#2(1977): 3-15.

EFFINGER, GEORGE A. 5085. Sklepowich, Edward A. "The Fictive Quest: Effinger's *What Entropy Means to Me*." *Ext* 18(1977): 107-115.

EISELEY, LOREN. 5086. Ramsey, Roger. "Eiseley's Art: A Note." *NCL* 3(November, 1973): 9-11.

ELDER, LONNE. 5087. Jeffers, Lance. "Bullins, Baraka, and Elder: The Dawn of Grandeur in Black Drama." *CLA* 16(1972): 33-48.

5088. Lee, Dorothy. "Three Black Plays: Alienation and Paths to Recovery." *MD* 19(1976): 397-404.

ELIOT, T. S. 5089. Abel, Richard. "The Influence of St.-John Perse on T. S. Eliot." *Con L* 14(1973): 213-239.

5090. Adams, John F. "The Fourth Temptation in *Murder in the Cathedral*." *MD* 5(1963): 381-388.

5091. Anthony, Mother Mary. "Verbal Patterns in 'Burnt Norton I.'" *Criticism* 2(1960): 81-89.

5092. Austin, Allen. "T. S. Eliot's Theory of Personal Expression." *PMLA* 81(1966): 303-307.

5093. Banerjee, Ron D. K. "Dante through the Looking Glass: Rossetti, Pound, and Eliot." *Comp L* 24(1972): 136-149.

5094. Bartlett, Phyllis. "Other Countries, Other Wenches." *MFS* 3(1957): 345-349.

5095. Bates, Ronald. "A Topic in *The Waste Land*: Traditional Rhetoric and Eliot's Individual Talent." *Con L.* 5(1964): 85-104.

5096. Bateson, F. W. "Contributions to a Dictionary of Critical Terms: II. "Dissociation of Sensibility." *EIC* 1(1951): 302-312.

5097. ----------. "A Cooking Egg.'" *EIC* 3 (1953): 353-357.

5098. ----------. "'A Cooking Egg': Final Scramble." *EIC* 4(1954): 106-108.

5099. ----------. "Dissociation of Sensibility." *EIC* 2(1952): 213-214.

5100. Beach, Joseph Warren. "Conrad Aiken and T. S. Eliot: Echoes and Overtones." *PMLA* 69 (1954): 753-762.

5101. Behar, Jack. "Eliot and the Language of Gesture: The Early Poems." *TCL* 23(1977): 487-497.

5102. Bergonzi, Bernard. "Allusion in *The Waste Land*." *EIC* 20(1970): 382-385.

5103. Berry, Francis. "Allusion in *The Waste Land*." *EIC* 20(1970): 380-382.

5104. Boardman, Gwenn R. "T. S. Eliot and the Mystery of Fanny Marlow." *MFS* 7(1961): 99-105.

5105. Boyd, John Douglas. "T. S. Eliot as Critic and Rehtorician: The Essay on Jonson." *Criticism* 11(1969): 167-182.

5106. Bridges, Jean Bolen. "Similarities Between 'The Waste Land' and *The Sound and the Fury*." *NCL* 7(January, 1977): 10-13.

5107. Caldwell, James R. "States of Mind: States of Consciousness." *EIC* 4(1954): 168-179.

5108. Cargill, Oscar. "Death in a Handful of Dust." *Criticism* 11(1969): 275-296.

5109. Carnell, Corbin S. "Creation's Lonely Flesh: T. S. Eliot and Christopher Fry on the Life of the Senses." *MD* 6(1963): 141-149.

5110. Christian, Henry. "Thematic Development in T. S. Eliot's 'Hysteria.'" *TCL* 6(1960): 76-80.

5111. Cleophas, Sister M., R. S. M. "*Ash Wednesday*: The *Purgaterio* in Modern Mode." *Comp L* 11(1959): 329-339.

5112. Clubb, Merrel D., Jr. "The Heraclitean Element in Eliot's *Four Quartets*." *PQ* 40 (1961): 19-33.

5113. Colby, Robert A. "Orpheus in the Counting House: *The Confidential Clerk*." *PMLA* 72(1957): 791-802.

5114. Cook, Robert G. "Emerson's 'Self-Reliance', Sweeney, and Prufrock." *AL* 42(1970): 221-226.

5115. Cowley, V. J. E. "A Source for T. S. Eliot's 'Objective Correlative.'" *RES* 26(1975): 320-321.

5116. Cunningham, Gilbert F. "A Cooking Egg." *EIC* 3(1953): 347-350.

5117. Cunningsworth, A. J. "T. S. Eliot, Francis Vielé-Griffin, and the 'Objective Correlative.'" *ELN* 8(1971): 208-211.

5118. Cutts, John P. "Evidence for Ambivalence of Motives in *Murder in the Cathedral*." *CD* 8(1974): 199-210.

5119. Dallas, Elizabeth S. "Canon Cancrizans and the *Four Quartets*." *Comp L* 17(1965): 193-208.

5120. Davenport, Gary T. "Eliot's *The Cocktail Party*: Comic Perspective as Salvation." *MD* 17(1974): 301-306.

5121. Davison, Richard Allan. "Hart Crane, Louis Untermeyer, and T. S. Eliot: A New Crane Letter." *AL* 44(1972): 143-146.

5122. Day, Robert A. "The 'City Man' in *The Waste Land*: The Geography of Reminiscence." *PMLA* 80(1965): 285-291.

5123. DeLaura, David J. "Echoes of Butler, Browning, Conrad, and Pater in the Poetry of T. S. Eliot." *ELN* 3(1966): 211-221.

5124. ----------. "Pater and Eliot: The Origin of the 'Objective Correlative.'" *MLQ* 26 (1965): 426-431.

5125. Donker, Marjorie. "*The Waste Land* and the *Aeneid*." *PMLA* 89(1974): 164-173.

5126. Donnelly, Mabel C. "The Failure of Act III of Eliot's *The Cocktail Party*." *CLA* 21 (1977): 58-61.

5127. Dorris, George E. "Two Allusions in the Poetry of T. S. Eliot." *ELN* 2(1964): 54-57.

5128. Drew, Elizabeth. "A Cooking Egg." *EIC* 3(1953): 353.

5129. Duffey, Bernard I. "The Experimental Lyric in Modern Poetry: Eliot, Pound, Williams." *JML* 3(1974): 1085-1103.

5130. Duffy, John J. "T. S. Eliot's Objective Correlative: A New England Commonplace." *NEQ* 42(1969): 108-115.

5131. Eliot, T. S. "The Three Provincialities (1922). With a Postscript (1950)." *EIC* 1 (1951): 38-41.

5132. Ellis, P. G. "The Development of T. S. Eliot's Historical Sense." *RES* 23(1972): 291-301.

5133. Empson, William. "Mr. Empson and the Fire Sermon." *EIC* 6(1956): 481-482.

5134. Espey, John J. "The Epigraph to T. S. Eliot's 'Burbank with a Baedeker: Bleistein with a Cigar.'" *AL* 29(1958): 483-484.

5135. Fleissner, Robert F. "'Prufrock', Pater, and Richard II: Retracing a Denial of Princeship." *AL* 38(1966): 120-123.

5136. Fleming, Rudd. "*The Elder Statesman* and Eliot's 'Programme for the Metier of Poetry.'" *Con L* 2,#1(1961): 54-64.

5137. Florsheimer, Stephen. "*The Family Reunion*. A Reply to Mr. Murray." *EIC* 1(1951): 298-301.

5138. Foster, Steven. "Relativity and *The Waste Land*." *TSLL* 7(1965): 77-95.

5139. Franklin, Rosemary. "Death or the Heat of Life in the Handful of Dust." *AL* 41(1969): 277-279.

5140. French, A. L. "Death by Allusion?" *EIC* 20(1970): 269-271.

5141. Fussell, B. H. "Structural Methods in *Four Quartets*." *ELH* 22(1955): 212-242.

5142. Fussell, Paul, Jr. "The Gestic Symbolism of T. S. Eliot." *ELH* 22(1955): 194-211.

5143. Gaskell, Ronald. "'The Family Reunion.'" *EIC* 12(1962): 292-301.

5144. ----------. "*The Family Reunion*." *EIC* 13(1963): 106.

5145. Gerstenberger, Donna. "The Saint and the Circle: The Dramatic Potential of an Image." *Criticism* 2(1960): 336-341.

5146. Giannone, Richard J. "Eliot's 'Portrait of a Lady' and Pound's Portrait D'une Femme.'" *TCL* 5(1959): 131-134.

5147. Gibbons, Tom. "*The Waste Land* Tarot Identified." *JML* 2(1972): 560-565.

5148. Gibson, William M. "Sonnets in T. S. Eliot's *The Waste Land*." *AL* 32(1961): 465-466.

5149. Gillis, Everett A. "Hope for Eliot's Hollow Men?" *PMLA* 75(1960): 635-637.

5150. ----------. "The Spiritual Status of T. S. Eliot's Hollow Men." *TSLL* 2(1961): 464-475.

5151. Glasheen, Adaline E. and others. "'A Cooking Egg': Three Postscripts." *EIC* 3 (1953): 476-477.

5152. Gordon, Lyndall. "*The Waste Land* Manuscript." *AL* 45(1974): 557-570.

5153. Gross, Harvey. "*Gerontion* and the Meaning of History." *PMLA* 73(1958): 299-304.

5154. Hamalian, Leo. "The Figures in the Window: Design in T. S. Eliot's *The Family Reunion*." *Coll L* 4(1977): 107-121.

5155. Hanzo, Thomas. "Eliot and Kier-krgaard: 'The Meaning of Happening' in *The Cocktail Party*." *MD* 3(1960): 52-59.

5156. Harmon, William. "T. S. Eliot's Raids on the Inarticulate." *PMLA* 91(1976): 450-549.

5157. Hays, Peter L. "Commerce in 'The Waste Land.'" *ELN* 11(1974): 292-294.

5158. Helman, Robert B. "*Alcestis* and *The Cocktail Party*." *Comp L* 5(1953): 105-116.

5159. Heywood, Christopher. "*Lady Audley's Secret*: a T. S. Eliot Source?" *RES* 27(1976): 182-188.

5160. Holbrook, David. "Mr. Eliot's Chinese Wall." *EIC* 5(1955): 418-426.

5161. Holder, Alan. "T. S. Eliot on Henry James." *PMLA* 79(1964): 490-497.

5162. Hollahan, Eugene. "A Structural Dantean Parallel in Eliot's 'The Love Song of J. Alfred Prufrock.'" *AL* 42(1970): 91-93.

5163. Holt, Charles L. "On Structure and *Sweeney Agonistes*." *MD* 10(1967): 43-47.

5164. Howarth, Herbert. "Eliot, Beethoven, and J. W. N. Sullivan." *Comp L* 9(1957): 322-332.

5165. ----------. "T. S. Eliot's *Criterion*: The Editor and His Contributors." *Comp L* 11(1959): 97-110.

5166. Huffman, Claire. "T. S. Eliot, Eugenio Montale, and the Vageries of Influence." *Comp L* 27(1975): 193-207.

5167. Isani, Mukhtar Ali. "The Wisdom of the Thunder in Eliot's *The Waste Land*." *ELN* 10 (1973): 217-220.

5168. Jayne, Sears. "Mr. Eliot's Agon." *PQ* 34(1955): 395-414.

5169. Jones, Florence. "T. S. Eliot Among the Prophets." *AL* 38(1966): 285-302.

5170. Kantra, Robert A. "Satiric Theme and Structure in *Murder in the Cathedral*." *MD* 10(1968): 387-393.

5171. Keeley, Edmund. "T. S. Eliot and the Poetry of George Seferis." *Comp L* 8(1956): 214-226.

5172. Knieger, Bernard. "The Dramatic Achievement of T. S. Eliot." *MD* 3(1961): 387-392.

5173. Knox, George A. "Quest for the Word in Eliot's *Four Quartets*." *ELH* 18(1951): 310-321.

5174. Knust, Herbert. "What's the Matter with One-Eyed Riley?" *Comp L* 17(1965): 289-298.

5175. Krause, Sydney J. "Hollow Men and False Horses." *TSLL* 2(1960): 368-377.

5176. Kuna, F. M. "T. S. Eliot's Dissociation of Sensibility and the Critics of Metaphysical Poetry." *EIC* 13(1963): 241-252.

5177. Laurentia, Sister M., C. S. J. "Structural Balance and Symbolism in T. S. Eliot's 'Portrait of a Lady.'" *AL* 27(1955): 409-417.

5178. Leach, Elsie. "'Gerontion' and Marvell's 'The Garden.'" *ELN* 13(1975): 45-81.

5179. Le Brun, Philip. "T. S. Eliot and Henri Bergson." *RES* 18(1967): 149-161, 274-286.

5180. Levý, Jiri. "Synthesis of Antithesis in the Poetry of T. S. Eliot." *EIC* 2(1952): 434-443.

5181. Lightfoot, Marjorie J. "*Purgatory* and *The Family Reunion*: In Pursuit of Prosodic Description." *MD* 7(1964): 256-266.

5182. ----------. "The Uncommon Cocktail Party." *MD* 11(1969): 382-395.

5183. Litz, A. Walton. "*The Waste Land* Fifty Years After." *JML* 2(1972): 455-471.

5184. Lorch, Thomas M. "The Relationship between *Ulysses* and *The Waste Land*." *TSLL* 6 (1964): 123-133.

5185. Lucas, John. "*The Waste Land* Today." *EIC* 20(1970): 497-500.

5186. Lucas, John, and William Meyers. "*The Waste Land* Today." *EIC* 19(1969): 193-209.

5187. Marcus, Phillip L. "T. S. Eliot and Shakespeare." *Criticism* 9(1967): 22-41.

5188. Marsh, Florence. "The Ocean Desert: *The Ancient Mariner* and *The Waste Land*." *EIC* 9 (1959): 107-133.

5189. Matlaw, Myron. "Eliot the Dramtist." *CLA* 12(1968): 116-122.

5190. McConnell, Daniel J. "'The Heart of Darkness' in T. S. Eliot's *The Hollow Men*." *TSLL* 4(1962): 141-153.

5191. McGann, Mary E. "*The Waste Land* and *The Sound and the Fury*: To Apprehend the Human Process Moving in Time." *SLJ* 9,#1(1976): 13-21.

5192. McLauchlan, Juiet. "Allusion in *The Waste Land*." *EIC* 19(1969): 454-460.

5193. Mendilow, A. A. "T. S. Eliot's 'Long Unlovely Street.'" *MLR* 63(1968): 320-331.

5194. Miller, Milton. "What the Thunder Meant." *ELH* 36(1969): 440-454.

5195. Morrissette, Bruce A. "T. S. Eliot and Guillaume Apollinaire." *Comp L* 5(1953): 262-268.

5196. Motola, Gabriel. "The Mountain of *The Waste Land*." *EIC* 19(1969): 67-69.

5197. Mudford, P. G. "'Sweeney among the Nightingales.'" *EIC* 19(1969): 285-291.

5198. Murray, J. Middleton. "A Note on the 'Family Reunion.'" *EIC* 1(1951): 67-73.

5199. Myers, William. "Allusion in *The Waste Land*." *EIC* 20(1970): 120-122.

5200. Naples, Dianne. "Eliot's 'Tradition' and *The Sound and the Fury*." *MFS* 20(1974): 214-217.

5201. Oakes, Elizabeth. "Prufrock and King Arthur." *NCL* 7(May, 1977): 11.

5202. Oberg, Arthur K. "*The Cocktail Party* and the Illusion of Autonomy." *MD* 11(1968): 187-194.

5203. Ong, Walter J. "'Burnt Norton' in St. Louis." *AL* 33(1962): 522-526.

5204. Palmer, Richard E. "Existentialism in T. S. Eliot's *The Family Reunion*." *MD* 5(1962): 174-186.

5205. Perkins, David. "Rose Garden to Midwinter Spring: Achieved Faith in the *Four Quartets*." *MLQ* 23(1962): 41-45.

5206. Perrett, Marion. "Eliot, the Naked Lady, and the Missing Link." *AL* 46(1974): 289-303.

5207. Peter, John. "A New Interpretation of *The Waste Land*." *EIC* 2(1952): 242-266.

5208. ----------. "A New Interpretation of *The Waste Land* (1952). With Postscript (1969)." *EIC* 19(1969): 140-175.

5209. Pratt, Linda Ray. "The Holy Grail: Subversion and Revival of a Tradition in Tennyson and T. S. Eliot." *VP* 11(1973): 307-322.

5210. Preston, Priscilla. "A Note on T. S. Eliot and Sherlock Holmes." *MLR* 54(1959): 397-399.

5211. Pritchard, William H. "Reading *The Waste Land* Today." *EIC* 19(1969): 176-192.

5212. Puckett, Harry. "T. S. Eliot on Knowing: The Word Unheard." *NEQ* 44(1971): 179-196.

5213. Puhvel, Martin. "Reminiscent Bells in *The Waste Land*." *ELN* 2(1965): 286-287.

5214. Rahme, Mary. "T. S. Eliot and the 'Histrionic Sensibility.'" *Criticism* 10(1968): 126-137.

5215. Raina, M. L. "T. S. Eliot as Thinker." *JML* 3(1973): 134-142.

5216. Ramsey, Jarold. "*The Waste Land* and Shakleton on South Georgia." *ELN* 8(1970): 42-45.

5217. Randall, Dale B. J. "The 'Seer' and 'Seen' Themes in *Gatsby* and Some of Their Parallels in Eliot and Wright." *TCL* 10(1964): 51-63.

5218. Rayan, Krishna. "Suggestiveness and Suggestion." *EIC* 19(1969): 309-319.

5219. Reckford, Kenneth J. "Heracles and Mr. Eliot." *Comp L* 16(1964): 1-18.

5220. Richards, I. A. "'A Cooking Egg': Final Scramble." *EIC* 4(1954): 103-105.

5221. Ricks, Christopher. "A Note on *Little Gidding*." *EIC* 25(1975): 145-153.

5222. Rillie, John A. M. "Melodramatic Device in T. S. Eliot." *RES* 13(1962): 267-281.

5223. Rodgers, Audrey T. "Dance Imagery in the Poetry of T. S. Eliot." *Criticism* 16(1974): 23-38.

5224. ----------. "'He Do the Police in Different Voices': The Design of *The Waste Land*." *Coll L* 1(1974): 49-64.

5225. Rother, James. "Modernism and the Nonsense Style." *Con L* 15(1974): 187-202.

5226. Roy, Emil. "The Becket Plays: Eliot, Fry, and Anouilh." *MD* 8(1965): 268-276.

5227. Ryan, Lawrence V., and Frederick V. Strothman. "Hope for T. S. Eliot's 'Empty Men.'" *PMLA* 73(1958): 426-432.

5228. ----------. "Hope for Eliot's Hollow Men?" *PMLA* 75(1960): 637-638.

5229. Salamon, Linda Bradley. "A Gloss on 'Daunsinge': Sir Thomas Elyot and T. S. Eliot's *Four Quartets*." *ELH* 40(1973): 584-605.

5230. Schanzer, Ernest. "Mr. Eliot's Sunday Morning Service." *EIC* 5(1955): 152-158.

5231. Schneider, Elisabeth. "Prufrock and After: The Theme of Change." *PMLA* 87(1972): 1103-1118.

5232. Schuchard, Ronald. "Eliot and Hulme in 1916: Toward a Revaluation of Eliot's Critical and Spiritual Development." *PMLA* 88(1973): 1083-1094.

5233. ----------. "'First-Rate Blasphemy': Baudelaire and the Revised Christian Idiom of T. S. Eliot's Moral Criticism." *ELH* 42(1974): 276-295.

5234. ----------. "T. S. Eliot as an Extension Lecturer, 1916-1919." *RES* 25(1974): 163-173, 292-304.

5235. Schwartz, Edward. "Eliot's *Cocktail Party* and the New Humanism." *PQ* 32(1953): 58-68.

5236. Scrimgeour, C. A. "The Family Reunion." *EIC* 13(1963): 104-106.

5237. Sena, Vinod. "The Ambivalence of *The Cocktail Party*." *MD* 14(1972): 392-404.

5238. Sexton, James P. "*Four Quartets* and the Christian Calendar." *AL* 43(1971): 279-281.

5239. Shanahan, C. M. "Irony in Laforgue, Corbiere, and Eliot." *MP* 53(1955): 117-128.

5240. Sharoni, Edna G. "'Peace' and 'Unbar the Door': T. S. Eliot's *Murder in the Cathedral* and Some Stoic Forebears." *CD* 6(1972): 135-153.

5241. Shulman, Robert. "Myth, Mr. Eliot, and the Comic Novel." *MFS* 12(1966): 395-404.

5242. Smith, Grover. "Charles-Louis Phillipe and T. S. Eliot." *AL* 22(1950): 254-259.

5243. The Fortuneteller in Eliot's *Waste Land*." *AL* 25(1954): 490-492.

5244. Smith, James. "Notes on the Criticism of T. S. Eliot." *EIC* 22(1972): 333-361.

5245. Soldo, John J. "The American Foreground of T. S. Eliot." *NEQ* 45(1972): 355-372.

5246. ----------. "Knowledge and Experience in the Criticism of T. S. Eliot." *ELH* 35(1968): 284-308.

5247. Spanos, William V. "'Wanna Go Home, Baby?': *Sweeney Agonistes* as Drama of the Absurd." *PMLA* 85(1970): 8-20.

5248. Srivastava, Narsingh. "The Ideas of the *Bagavad Gita* in *Four Quartets*." *Comp L* 29 (1977): 97-108.

5249. Stanford, Donald L. "Two Notes on T. S. Eliot." *TCL* 1(1955): 133-134.

5250. Stein, Walter. "After the Cocktails." *EIC* 3(1953): 85-104.

5251. Stinton, T. C. W. and I. R. Browning. "'A Cooking Egg.'" *EIC* 3(1953): 350-353.

5252. Storm, Leo. "J. M. Roberton and T. S. Eliot." *JML* 5(1976): 315-321.

5253. Sugiyama, Yoko. "*The Waste Land* and Contemporary Japanese Poetry." *Comp L* 13(1961): 254-262.

5254. Sutton, Walter. "*Mauberley, The Waste Land,* and the Problem of Unified Form." *Con L* 9 (1968): 15-35.

5255. Tamplin, Ronald. "*The Tempest* and *The Waste Land*." *AL* 39(1967): 352-372.

5256. Tanner, Stephen L. "T. S. Eliot and Paul Elmer More on Tradition." *ELN* 8(1971): 211-215.

5257. Thale, Mary. "T. S. Eliot and Mrs. Browning on the Metaphysical Poets." *CLA* 11(1968): 255-258.

5258. Thompson, Eric. "Dissociation of Sensibility." *EIC* 2(1952): 207-213.

5259. Thrash, Lois G. "A Source for the Redemption Theme in *The Cocktail Party*." *TSLL* 9 (1968): 547-553.

5260. Tillyard, E. M. W. "'A Cooking Egg.'" *EIC* 3(1953): 345-347.

5261. Torrens, James, S. J. "Charles Maurras and Eliot's 'New Life.'" *PMLA* 89(1974): 312-322.

5262. ----------. "T. S. Eliot and the Austere Poetics of Valéry." *Comp L* 23(1971): 1-17.

5263. Virsis, Rasma. "The Christian Concept in *Murder in the Cathedral*." *MD* 14(1972): 405-407.

5264. Wagner, Linda W. "'O O O O That Shakespearian Rag.'" *Coll L* 3(1976): 139-143.

5265. Wagner, Robert D. "The Meaning of Eliot's Rose-Garden." *PMLA* 69(1954): 22-33.

5266. Ward, David E. "The Cult of Impersonality: Eliot, St. Augustine, and Flaubert." *EIC* 17(1967): 169-182.

5267. ----------. "Eliot, Murray, Homer, and the Idea of Tradition." *EIC* 18(1968): 47-59.

5268. Wasson, Richard. "T. S. Eliot's Antihumanism and Anitpragmatism." *TSLL* 10(1968): 445-455.

5269. Watkins, Floyd C. "T. S. Eliot's Painter of the Umbrian School." *AL* 36(1964): 72-75.

5270. Watts, C. T. "The Astonishing 'Objective Correlative.'" *EIC* 23(1973): 328-331.

5271. Weatherhead, A. Kingsley. "Baudelaire in Eliot's *Ash Wednesday* IV." *ELN* 2(1965): 288-289.

5272. ----------. "*Four Quartets:* Setting Love in Order." *Con L* 3,#2(1962): 32-49.

5273. Webster, Grant T. "T. S. Eliot as Critic: The Man Behind the Masks." *Criticism* 8(1966): 336-348.

5274. Whiteside, George. "T. S. Eliot's Dissertation." *ELH* 34(1967): 400-424.

5275. Williams, Raymond. "Second Thoughts I. T. S. Eliot and Culture." *EIC* 6(1956): 302-318.

5276. Williamson, George. "The Structure of The Waste Land." *MP* 47(1950): 191-206.

5277. Winter, Jack. "Prufrockism' in *The Cocktail Party*." *MLQ* 22(1961): 135-148.

5278. Wright, George T. "Eliot Written in a Country Churchyard." *ELH* 43(1976): 227-243.

5279. Wright, Keith. "Word-Repetition in T. S. Eliot's Early Verse." *EIC* 16(1966): 201-206.

5280. Wright, Nathalia. "A Source for Eliot's 'Objective Correlative.'" *AL* 41(1970): 589-591.

5281. Wyman, Linda. "*Murder in the Cathedral:* The Plot of Diction." *MD* 19(1976): 135-146.

See also 436, 488, 494, 504, 514, 6838, 7727, 18921.

ELKIN, STANLEY. 5282. LeClair, Thomas. "The Obsessional Fiction of Stanley Elkin." *Con L* 16(1975): 146-162.

5283. Sanders. Scott. "An Interview with Stanley Elkin." *Con L* 16(1975): 131-145.

ELLISON, HARLAN. 5284. Erlich, Richard, and John Crow. "Mythic Patterns in Ellison's *A Boy and His Dog.*" *Ext* 18(1977): 162-166.

ELLISON, RALPH. 5285. Baumbach, Jonathan. "Nightmare of a Native Son: Ralph Ellison's *Invisible Man*." *Crit* 6,#1(1963): 48-65.

5286. Bucco, Martin. "Ellison's **Invisible** West." *WAL* 10(1975): 237-238.

5287. Brown, Lloyd W. "Ralph Ellison's Exhorters: The Role in Rhetoric in *Invisible Man*." *CLA* 13(1970): 289-303.

5288. Callahan, John F. "Chaos, Complexity, and Possiblity: The Historical Frequencies of Ralph Waldo Ellison." *BALF* 11(1977): 130-138.

5289. Carson, David L. "Ralph Ellison Twenty Years After." *SAF* 1(1973): 1-23.

5290. Cash, Earl A. "The Narrators in *Invisible Man* and *Notes from Underground:* Brothers in the Spirit." *CLA* 16(1973): 505-507.

5291. Chafee, Patricia. "Slippery Round: Ralph Ellison's Bingo Player." *BALF* 10(1976): 23-24.

5292. Cheshire, Ardner, R., Jr. "*Invisible Man* and the Life of Dialogue." *CLA* 20(1976): 19-34.

5293. Clipper, Lawrence. J. "Folkloric and Mythic Elements in *Invisible Man.*" *CLA* 13(1970): 229-241.

5294. Covo, Jacqueline. "Ralph Ellison in France: Bibliographic Essays and Checklist of French Criticism, 1954-1971." *CLA* 16(1973): 519-526.

5295. ----------. "Ralph Waldo Ellison: Bibliographic Essays and Finding List of American Criticism, 1952-1964." *CLA* 15(1971): 171-196.

5296. Deutsch, Leonard J. "Ellison's Early Fiction." *BALF* 7(1973): 53-59.

5297. ----------. "Ralph Waldo Ellison and Ralph Waldo Emerson: A Shared Moral Vision." *CLA* 16(1972): 159-178.

5298. ----------. "*The Waste Land* in Ellison's *Invisible Man.*" *NCL* 7(September, 1977): 5-6.

5299. Doyle, Mary Ellen, S. C. N. "In Need of Folk: The Alienated Protagonists of Ralph Ellison's Short Fiction." *CLA* 19(1975): 165-172.

5300. Ehlers, Leigh A. "'Give Me the Ocular Proof!': *Othello* and Ralph Ellison's *Invisible Man.*" *NCL* 6(November, 1976): 10-11.

5301. Fass, Barbara. "Rejection of Paternalism: Hawthorne's 'My Kinsman, Major Molineaux' and Ellison's *Invisible Man.*" *CLA* 14(1971): 317-323.

5302. Fischer, Russell G. "*Invisible Man* as History." *CLA* 17(1974): 338-367.

5303. Goede, William. "On Lower Frequencies: The Buried Men in Wright and Ellison." *MFS* 15(1969): 483-501.

5304. Griffin, Edward M. "Notes from a Clean, Well-Lighted Place: Ralph Ellison's *Invisible Man.*" *TCL* 15(1969): 129-144.

5305. Guereschi, Edward. "Anticipations of *Invisible Man:* Ralph Ellison's 'King of the Bingo Game.'" *BALF* 6(1972): 122-124.

5306. Horowitz, Floyd Ross. "The Enigma of Ellison's Intellectual Man." *CLA* 7(1963): 126-132.

5307. ----------. "An Experimental Confession from a Reader of *Invisible Man.*" *CLA* 13(1970): 304-314.

5308. Howard, David C. "Points in Defense of Ellison's *Invisible Man.*" *NCL* 1(January, 1971): 13-14.

5309. Kent, George E. "Ralph Ellison and Afro-American Folk and Cultural Tradition." *CLA* 13(1970): 265-276.

5310. Klotman, Phyllis. "The Running Man as Metaphor in Ellison's *Invisible Man.*" *CLA* 13(1970): 277-288.

5311. Lane, James B. "Underground to Manhood: Ralph Ellison's *Invisible Man.*" *BALF* 7(1973): 64-72.

5312. Lee, A. Robert. "Sight and Mask: Ralph Ellison's *Invisible Man.*" *BALF* 4(1970): 22-33.

5313. Lieberman, Marcia R. "Moral Innocents: Ellison's *Invisible Man* and *Candide.*" *CLA* 15(1971): 64-79.

5314. Mitchell, Louis D. "Invisibility-Permanent or Resurrective." *CLA* 17(1974): 379-386.

5315. Moore, Robert H., ed. "On Initiation Rites and Power: Ralph Ellison Speaks at West Point." *Con L* 15(1974): 165-186.

5316. O'Daniel Therman B. "The Image of Man as Portrayed by Ralph Ellison." *CLA* 10(1967): 277-284.

5317. Olderman, Raymond M. "Ralph Ellison's Blues and *Invisible Man*." *Con L* 7(1966): 142-159.

5318. Overmyer, Janet. "The Invisible Man and White Women." *NCL* 6(May, 1976): 13-15.

5319. Pryse, Marjorie. "Ralph Ellison's Heroic Fugitive." *AL* 46(1974): 1-15.

5320. Rodon, Stewart. "*The Adventures of Huckleberry Finn* and *Invisible Man*: Thematic and Structural Comparisons." *BALF* 4(1970): 45-50.

5321. ----------. "Ralph Ellison's *Invisible Man*: Six Tentative Approaches." *CLA* 12 (1969): 244-256.

5322. Rovit, Earl H. "Ralph Ellison and the American Comic Tradition." *Con L* 1,#3(1960): 34-42.

5323. Sanders, Archie D. "Odysseus in Black: An Analysis of the Structure of *Invisible Man*." *CLA* 13(1970): 217-228.

5324. Saunders, Pearl I. "Symbolism in Ralph Ellison's 'King of the Bingo Game'." *CLA* 20(1976): 35-39.

5325. Schafer, William. "Ralph Ellison and the Birth of the Anit-Hero." *Crit* 10,#2(1968): 81-93.

5326. Scruggs, Charles W. "Ralph Ellison's Use of *The Aeneid* in *Invisible Man*." *CLA* 17(1974): 368-378.

5327. Selke, Hartmut K. "An Allusion to Sartre's *The Flies* in Ralph Ellison's *Invisible Man*." *NCL* 4(May, 1974): 3-4.

5328. ----------. "'The Education at College of Fools': References to Emerson's 'Self-Reliance' in *Invisible Man*." *NCL* 4(January, 1974): 13-15.

5329. Stark, John. "*Invisible Man*: Ellison's Black Odyssey." *BALF* 7(1973): 60-63.

5330. Staufenberg, Henry J., and Louis D. Mitchell. "Ellison's B. P. Rhinehart: 'Spiritual Technologist'." *BALF* 9(1975): 51-52.

5331. Sylvander, Carolyn W. "Ralph Ellison's *Invisible Man* and Female Stereotypes." *BALF* 9 (1975): 77-79.

5332. Tischler, Nancy M. "Negro Literature and Classic Form." *Con L* 10(1969): 352-365.

5333. Trimmer, Joseph F. "Ralph Ellison's 'Flying Home'." *SSF* 9(1972): 175-182.

5334. Turner, Darwin. "Sight in *Invisible Man*." *CLA* 13(1970): 258-264.

5335. Wasserman, Jerry. "Embracing the Negative: *Native Son* and *Invisible Man*." *SAF* 4 (1976): 93-104.

5336. Wilner, Eleanor R. "The Invisible Black Thread: Identity and Nonentity in *Invisible Man*." *CLA* 13(1970): 242-257.

See also 4382, 4387, 4396, 4400, 7743.

ENGLAND, GEORGE ALLAN.   See 4380.

EUSTIS, HELEN.   5337. Burns, Stuart L. "St. Petersburg Re-Visited: Helen Eustis and Mark Twain." *WAL* 5(1970): 65-112.

EVANS, MARI.   5338. Sedlack, Robert P. "Mari Evans: Consciousness and Craft." *CLA* 15 (1972): 465-476.

See also 4442.

EVERSON, WILLIAM.   See 6146.

FAIR, RONALD.   5339. Fleming, Robert E. "The Novels of Ronald L. Fair." *CLA* 15(1972): 477-487.

FARMER, PHILIP J.   5340. Jannone, Claudia. "*Venus on the Half Shell* as Structuralist Activity." *Ext* 17(1976): 110-117.

5341. Letson, Russell. "The Worlds of Phillip José Farmer." *Ext* 18(1977): 124-130.

5342. Wymer, Thomas. "Speculative Fiction, Bibliographies, and **Philip José Farmer**." *Ext* 18(1976): 59-96.

FARRELL, JAMES T.   5343. Berkow, Ira. "Farrell and Sports." *TCL* 22(1976): 105-110.

5344. Branch, Edgar M. "James T. Farrell: Four Decades after *Studs Lonigan*." *TCL* 22(1976): 28-35.

5345. Callaghan, Morley. "James T. Farrell: A Tribute." *TCL* 22(1976): 26-27.

5346. Chametzky, Jules. "James T. Farrell's Literary Criticism." *TCL* 22(1976): 80-89.

5347. Farrell, James T. "Farrell Looks at His Writing." *TCL* 22(1976): 11-18.

5348. ----------. "Relevance in Literature." *TCL* 22(1976): 19-25.

5349. Flynn, Dennis, and Jack Salzman. "An Interview with James T. Farrell." *TCL* 22(1976): 1-10.

5350. Fried, Lewis. "Bernard Carr and *His* Trials of the Mind." *TCL* 22(1976): 52-67.

5351. O'Connell, Barry. "The Lost World of James T. Farrell's Short Stories." *TCL* 22(1976): 36-51.

5352. Slade, Joseph W. "'Bare-Assed and Alone': Time and Banality in Farrell's *A Universe of Time*." *TCL* 22(1976): 68-79.

5353. Wald, Alan. "Farrell and Trotskyism." *TCL* 22(1976): 90-104.

See also 7757.

FAULKNER, WILLIAM.   5354. Ackerman, R. D. "The Immolation of Isaac McCaslin." *TSLL* 16(1974): 557-565.

5355. Adamowski, Thomas H. "Dombey and Son and Sutpen and Son." *SN* 4(1972): 378-389.

5356. ----------. "Joe Christmas: The Tyranny of Childhood." *Novel* 4(1971): 240-251.

5357. Adams, Percy G. "Humor as Structure and Theme in Faulkner's Trilogy." *Con L* 5(1964): 205-212.

5358. Alsen, Eberhard. "An Existentialist Reading of Faulkner's **'Pantaloon in Black.'**" *SSF* 14(1977): 169-178.

5359. Atkins, Anselm. "The Matched Halves of *Absalom, Absalom!*" *MFS* 15(1969): 264-265.

5360. Auer, Michael J. "Caddy, Benjy, and the Arts of the Apostoles: A Note on *The Sound and the Fury*." *SN* 6(1974): 475-476.

5361. Backman, Melvin. "Faulkner's Sick Heroes: Bayard Sartoris and Quentin Compson." *MFS* 2(1956): 95-109.

5362. ----------. "Sutpen and the South: A Study of *Absalom, Absalom!*" *PMLA* 80(1965): 596-604.

5363. ----------. "The Wilderness and the Negro in Faulkner's 'The **Bear**.'" *PMLA* 76(1961): 595-600.

5364. Baldanza, Frank. "The Structure of *Light in August*." *MFS* 13(1967): 67-78.

5365. Barnes, Daniel R. "Faulkner's Miss Emily and Hawthorne's Old Maid." *SSF* 9(1972): 373-377.

5366. Bassan, Maurice. "Benjy at the Monument." *ELN* 2(1964): 46-50.

5367. Baum, Catherine B. "'The Beautiful One': Caddy Compson as Heroine of *The Sound and the Fury*." *MFS* 13(1967): 33-44.

5368. Bedient, Calvin. "Pride and **Nakedness**: *As I Lay Dying*." *MLQ* 29(1968): 61-76.

5369. Beebe, Maurice. "Criticism of William Faulkner: A Selected Checklist." *MFS* 13(1967): 151-161.

5370. ----------. "Criticism of William Faulkner: A Selected Checklist with an Index to Separate Works." *MFS* 2(1956): 150-164.

5371. Behrens, Ralph. "Collapse of Dynasty: The Thematic Center of *Absalom, Absalom!*" *PMLA* 89(1974): 24-33.

5372. Beidler, Peter G. "A Darwinian Source for Faulkner's Indians in 'Red Leaves.'" *SSF* 10 (1973): 421-423.

5373. Benson, Jackson J. "Quentin Compson: Self-Portrait of a Young Artist's Emotions." *TCL* 17(1971): 143-159.

5374. Berland, Alwyn. *Light in August: The Calvinism of William Faulkner*." *MFS* 8(1962): 159-170.

5375. Björk, Lennart. "Ancient Myths and the Moral Framework of Faulkner's *Absalom, Absalom!*" *AL* 35(1963): 196-204.

5376. Blanchard, Margaret. "The Rhetoric of Communion: Voice in *The Sound and the Fury*." *AL* 41(1970): 555-565.

5377. Blotner, Joseph L. "*As I Lay Dying*: Christian Lore and Irony." *TCL* 3(1957): 14-19.

5378. Bond, Adrienne. "*Eneas Africanus* and Faulkner's Fabulous Racehorse." *SLJ* 9,#2(1977): 3-15.

5379. Bouvard, Loïc. "Conversation with William Faulkner (trans. Henry Dan Piper)." *MFS* 5(1959): 361-364.

5380. Bowling, Lawrence. "Faulkner: The Themes of Pride in *The Sound and the Fury*." *MFS* 11(1965): 129-139.

5381. Bradford, M. E. "Faulkner's 'Tomorrow' and the Plain People." *SSF* 2(1965): 235-240.

5382. Branch, Watson G. "Darl Bundren's 'Cubistic' Vision." *TSLL* 19(1977): 42-59.

5383. Bridgeman, Richard. "As Hester Prynne Lay Dying." *ELN* 2(1965): 294-296.

5384. Bridges, Jean Bolen. "Similarities Between 'The Waste Land' and *The Sound and the Fury*." *NCL* 7(January, 1977): 10-13.

5385. Brogunier, Joseph. "**A Housman Source** in *The Sound and the Fury*." *MFS* 18(1972): 220-225.

5386. ----------. "A Source for the Commissary Entries in *Go Down, Moses*." *TSLL* 14(1972): 545-554.

5387. Brooks, Cleanth. "Faulkner as Poet." *SLJ* 1,#1(1968): 5-19.

5388. ----------. "A Note on Faulkner's Early Attempts at the Short Story." *SSF* 10(1973): 381-388.

5389. ----------. "When Did Joanna Burden Die?: A Note." *SLJ* 6,#1(1973): 43-46.

5390. Brown, Calvin S. "Faulkner's Geography and Topography." *PMLA* 77(1962): 652-659.

5391. ----------. "Faulkner's Idiot Boy: The Source of a Simile in *Sartoris*." *AL* 44(1972): 474-476.

5392. ----------. "Faulkner's Three-in-One Bridge in *The Reivers*." *NCL* 1(March, 1971): 8-10.

5393. Brown, William R. "Faulkner's Paradox in Pathology and Salvation: *Sanctuary, Light in August, Requiem for a Nun*." *TSLL* 9(1967): 429-449.

5394. Buckley, G. T. "Is Oxford the Original of Jefferson in William Faulkner's Novels?" *PMLA* 76(1961): 447-454.

5395. Burroughs, Franklin G., Jr. "God the Father and Motherless Children: *Light in August*." *TCL* 19(1973): 189-202.

5396. Cecil, L. Moffitt. "Rhetoric for Benjy." *SLJ* 3,#1(1970): 32-46.

5397. Chapman, Arnold. "Pampas and Big Woods: Heroic Initiation in Güiraldes and Faulkner." *Comp L* 11(1959): 61-77.

5398. Clark, Edward D., Sr. "Private Truth in *The Sound and the Fury*." *CLA* 19(1976): 513-524.

5399. Clark, William Bedford. "A Tale of Two Chiefs: William **Faulkner's Ikkemotubbe and** Washington Irving's Blackbird." *WAL* 12(1977): 223-225.

5400. Collins, Carvel. "Miss Quentin's Paternity Again." *TSLL* 2(1960): 253-260.

5401. Conley, Timothy K. "Beardsley and Faulkner." *JML* 5(1976): 339-356.

5402. Connolly, Thomas E. "The Three Plots of *A Fable*." *TCL* 6(1960): 70-75.

5403. Cook, Richard M. "Popeye, Flem, and Sutpen: The Faulknerian Villain as Grotesque." *SAF* 3(1975): 3-14.

5404. Cooley, Thomas W. Jr. "Faulkner Draws the Long Bow." *TCL* 16(1970): 268-277.

5405. Cottrell, Beekman W. "Christian Symbols in *Light in August*." *MFS* 2(1956): 207-213.

5406. Crane, John Kenny. "The Jefferson Courthouse: An *Axis Exsecrabilis Mundi*." *TCL* 15(1969): 19-24.

5407. Creighton, Joanne Vanish. "Faulkner's 'The Fire and the Hearth.'" *SSF* 11(1974): 161-172.

5408. ----------. "Revision and Craftsmanship in the Hunting Trilogy of *Go Down Moses*." *TSLL* 15(1973): 577-592.

5409. ----------. "Self-Destructive Evil in *Sanctuary*." *TCL* 18(1972): 259-270.

5410. Cross, Barbara M. "Apocalypse and Comedy in *As I Lay Dying*." *TSLL* 3(1961): 251-258.

5411. Cross, Richard K. "The Humor of *The Hamlet*." *TCL* 12(1967): 203-215.

5412. Dahl, James. "A Faulkner Reminiscence: Conversations with Mrs. Maud Falkner." *JML* 3(1974): 1026-1030.

5413. Davis, Thadious M. "The Other Family and Luster in *The Sound and the Fury*." *CLA* 20 (1976): 245-261.

5414. Davis, William V. "*The Sound and the Fury:* A Note on Benjy's Name." *SN* 4(1972): 60-62.

5415. Devlin, Albert J. "Sartoris: Re-reading the MacCallum Episode." *TCL* 17(1971): 83-90.

5416. Dillon, Richard T. "Some Sources for Faulkner's Version of the First Air War." *AL* 44 (1973): 629-637.

5417. Doody, Terrence. "Shreve McCannon and the Confessions of *Absalom! Absalom!*" *SN* 6 (1974): 454-469.

5418. Edwards, C. H. "A Hawthorne Echo in Faulkner's Nobel Prize Acceptance Speech." *NCL* 1(March, 1971): 4-5.

5419. Eitner, Walter H. "The Aristoi of Yoknapatawpha County." *NCL* 7(September, 1977): 10-11.

5420. Esslinger, Pat M. "No Spinach in *Sanctuary.*" *MFS* 18(1972): 555-558.

5421. Farmer, Norman, Jr. "The Love Theme: A Principal Source of Thematic Unity in Faulkner's Snopes Trilogy." *TCL* 8(1962): 111-123.

5422. Faulkner, Howard. "The Stricken World of 'Dry September.'" *SSF* 10(1973): 47-50.

5423. Feaster, John. "Faulkner's *Old Man:* A Psychoanalystic Approach." *MFS* 13(1967): 89-93.

5424. Flynn, Robert. "The Dialectic of *Sanctuary.*" *MFS* 2(1956): 109-113.

5425. Forrer, Richard. "*Absalom, Absalom!:* Story-Telling as a Mode of Transcendence." *SLJ* 9,#1(1976): 22-46.

5426. Franklin, R. W. "Narrative Management in *As I Lay Dying.*" *MFS* 13(1967): 57-65.

5427. Frazier, David L. "Gothicism in *Sanctuary:* The Black Pall and the Crap Table." *MFS* 2(1956): 114-124.

5428. Galharn, Carl. "Faulkner's Faith: Roots from *The Wild Palms.*" *TCL* 1(1955): 139-160.

5429. Garrett, George. "Faulkner's Early Literary Criticism." *TSLL* 1(1959): 3-10.

5430. Garrison, Joseph M., Jr. "The Past and Present in 'That Evening Sun.'" *SSF* 13(1976): 371-373.

5431. Geffen, Arthur. "Profane Time, Sacred Time, and Confederate Time in *The Sound and the Fury.*" *SAF* 2(1974): 175-198.

5432. Gelfant, Blanche F. "Faulkner and Keats: The Ideality of Art in 'The Bear.'" *SLJ* 2,#1(1969): 43-65.

5433. Gold, Joseph. "Delusion and Redemption in Faulkner's *A Fable.*" *MFS* 7(1961): 145-156.

5434. ----------. "The 'Normality' of Snopesism: Universal Themes in Faulkner's *The Hamlet.*" *Con L* 3,#1(1962): 25-34.

5435. ----------. "William Faulkner's 'One Compact Thing.'" *TCL* 8(1962): 3-9.

5436. Grant, William E. "Benjy's Branch: Symbolic Method in Part I of *The Sound and the Fury.*" *TSLL* 13(1972): 705-710.

5437. Greene, Theodore M. "The Philosophy of Life Implicit in Faulkner's *The Mansion.*" *TSLL* 2(1961): 401-418.

5438. Greet, T. Y. "The Theme and Structure of Faulkner's *The Hamlet.*" *PMLA* 72(1957): 775-790.

5439. Gresset, Michel. "Faulkner's 'The Hill.'" *SLJ* 6,#2(1974): 3-18.

5440. Groden, Michael. "Criticism in New

Composition: Ulysses and *The Sound and the Fury.*" *TCL* 21(1975): 265-277.

5441. Gross, Beverly. "Form and Fulfillment in *The Sound and the Fury.*" *MLQ* 29(1968): 439-449.

5442. Grossman, Joel M. "The Source of Faulkner's 'Less Oft is Peace.'" *AL* 47(1975): 436-438.

5443. Gwynn, Frederick L. "Faulkner's Prufrock—And Other Observations." *JEGP* 52(1953): 63-70.

5444. ----------. "Faulkner's Raskolnikov." *MFS* 4(1958): 169-172.

5445. Hagopian, John V. "*Absalom, Absalom!* and the Negro Question." *MFS* 19(1973): 207-210.

5446. ----------. "Nihilism in Faulkner's *The Sound and the Fury.*" *MFS* 13(1967): 45-55.

5447. Harold, Brent. "The Value and Limitations of Faulkner's Fictional Method." *AL* 47(1975): 212-229.

5448. Harter, Carol Clancey. "Recent Faulkner Scholarship: Five More Turns of the Screw." *JML* 4(1974): 139-145.

5449. ----------. "The Winter of Isaac McCaslin: Revisions and Irony in Faulkner's 'Delta Autum.'" *JML* 1(1970): 209-225.

5450. Hemenway, Robert. "Enigmas of Being in *As I Lay Dying.*" *MFS* 16(1970): 133-146.

5451. Hepburn, Kenneth Wm. "Faulkner's *Mosquitoes:* A Poetic Turning Point." *TCL* 17(1971): 19-28.

5452. Hermann, John. "Faulkner's Heart's Darling in 'That Evening Sun.'" *SSF* 7(1970): 320-323.

5453. Hiers, John T. "Faulkner's Lord-to-God Bird in 'The Bear.'" *AL* 47(1976): 636-637.

5454. Hlavsa, Virginia V. "The Vision of the Advocate in *Absalom, Absalom!*" *Novel* 8(1974): 51-70.

5455. Hodgson, John A. "'Logical Sequence and Continuity': Some Observations on the Typographical and Structural Consistency of *Absalom, Absalom!*" *AL* 43(1971): 97-107.

5456. Hogan, Patrick G., Jr. "Faulkner's 'Female Line': 'Callina' McCaslin." *SSF* 1(1963): 63-65.

5457. Hogan, Patrick G., Jr. Dale A. Myers, and John E. Turner. "Muste's 'Failure of Love' in Faulkner's *Go Down, Moses.*" *MFS* 12(1966): 267-270.

5458. Holland, Norman. "Fantasy and Defense in Faulkner's 'A Rose for Emily.'" *HSL* 4(1972): 1-31.

5459. Holman, C. Hugh. "The Unity of Faulkner's *Light in August.*" *PMLA* 73(1958): 155-166.

5460. Howell, Elmo. "Faulkner's Enveloping Sense of History: A Note on 'Tomorrow.'" *NCL* 3 (March, 1973): 5-6.

5461. ----------. "Inversion and the 'Female' Principle: William Faulkner's 'A Courtship.'" *SSF* 4(1967): 308-314.

5462. ----------. "William Faulkner and the Chicksaw Funeral." *AL* 36(1965): 523-525.

5463. Hunt, Joel A. "Thomas Mann and Faulkner: Protrait of a Magician." *Con L* 8(1967): 431-436.

5464. ----------. "William Faulkner and Rabelais: The Dog Story." *Con L* 10(1969): 383-388.

5465. Hutten, Robert W. "A Major Revision in Faulkner's *A Fable*." AL 45(1973): 297-299.

5466. Jarrett, David W. "Eustacia Vye and Eula Varner, Olympians: The Worlds of Thomas Hardy and William Faulkner." *Novel* 6(1973): 163-174.

5467. Jensen, Eric G. "The Play Element in Faulkner's 'The Bear.'" TSLL 6(1964): 170-187.

5468. Jewkes, W. T. "Counterpoint in Faulkner's *The Wild Palms*." Con L 2,#1(1961): 39-53.

Johnston, Kenneth G. "Time of Decline: Pickett's Charge and the Broken Clock in Faulkner's 'Barn Burning.'" SSF 11(1974): 434-436.

5470. ----------. "The Year of Jubilee: Faulkner's 'That Evening Sun.'" AL 46(1974): 93-100.

5471. Jordan, Robert M. "The Limits of Illusion: Faulkner, Fielding, and Chaucer." *Criticism* 2(1960): 278-305.

5472. Justus, James H. "The Epic Design of *Absalom! Absalom!*" TSLL 4(1962): 157-166.

5473. Kane, Patricia. "Adaptable and Free: Faulkner's Ratliff." NCL 1(May, 1971): 9-11.

5474. ----------. "The Narcissa Benbow of Faulkner's *Flags in the Dust*." NCL 4(September, 1974): 2-3.

5475. ----------. "Only Too Rhetorical Rhetoric: A Reading of *Intruder in the Dust*." NCL 4(May, 1974): 2-3.

5476. Kartiganer, Donald M. "Faulkner's *Absalom, Absalom!*: The Discovery of Values." AL 37(1965): 291-306.

5477. ----------. "The Role of Myth in *Absalom, Absalom!*" MFS 9(1963): 357-369.

5478. ----------. "*The Sound and the Fury* and Faulkner's Quest for Form." ELH 37(1970): 613-639.

5479. Keefer, T. Frederick. "William Faulkner's *Sanctuary*: A Myth Examined." TCL 15(1969): 97-104.

5480. Kerr, Elizabeth M. "*As I Lay Dying* as Ironic Quest." Con L 3,#1(1962): 5-19.

5481. ----------. "*The Reivers*: The Golden Book of Yoknapatawpha County." MFS 13(1967): 95-113.

5482. ----------. "Snopes." Con L 1,#2 (1960): 66-84.

5483. King, Roma A., Jr. "Everyman's Warfare: A Study of Faulkner's *Fable*." MFS 2(1956): 132-138.

5484. Kinney, Arthur F. "Faulkner and Flaubert." JML 6(1977): 222-247.

5485. Klinkowitz, Jerome. "The Thematic Unity of *Knight's Gambit*." Crit 11,#2(1969): 81-100.

5486. Klotz, Marvin. "Procrustean Revision in Faulkner's *Go Down, Moses*." AL 37(1965): 1-16.

5487. Knight, Karl F. "'Spintrius' in Faulkner's 'The Bear.'" SSF 12(1975): 31-32.

5488. Korenman, Joan S. "Faulkner and 'That Undying Mark.'" SAF 4(1976): 81-91.

5489. ----------. "Faulkner's Grecian Urn." SLJ 7,#1(1974): 3-23.

5490. Lamont, William H. F. "The Chronology of *Light in August*." MFS 3(1957): 360-361.

5491. Larsen, Eric E. "The Barrier of Language: The Irony of Language in Faulkner." MFS 13(1967): 19-31.

5492. Leaver, Florence. "The Structure of *The Hamlet*." TCL 1(1955): 77-84.

5493. Levins, Lynn Gartrell. "The Four Narrative Perspectives in *Absalom, Absalom!*" PMLA 85 (1970): 35-47.

5494. Lily, Paul R., Jr. "Caddie and Addie: Speakers of Faulkner's Impeccable Language." JNT 3(1973): 170-182.

5495. Lind, Ilse Dusoir. "Apocalyptic Vision as Key to *Light in August*." SAF 3(1975): 133-141.

5496. ----------. "The Calvinistic Burden of *Light in August*." NEQ 30(1957): 307-329.

5497. ----------. "The Design and Meaning of *Absalom! Absalom!*" PMLA 70(1955): 887-912.

5498. Lydenberg, John. "Nature Myth in Faulkner's 'The Bear.'" AL 24(1952): 62-72.

5499. Manglaviti, Leo M. J. "Faulkner's 'That Evening Sun' and Mencken's 'Best Editorial Judgment.'" AL 43(1972): 649-654.

5500. Markvic, Vida. "Interview with Faulkner." TSLL 5(1964): 463-466.

5501. McAlexander, Hubert, Jr. "William Faulkner—The Young Poet in Stark Young's *The Torches Flare*." AL 43(1972): 647-649.

5502. McCarron, William E. "Shakespeare, Faulkner and Ned William McCaslin." NCL 7(December, 1977): 8-9.

5503. McGann, Mary E. "*The Waste Land* and *The Sound and the Fury*: To Apprehend the Human Process Moving in Time." SLJ 9,#1(1976): 13-21.

5504. McGlynn, Paul D. "The Chronology of 'A Rose for Emily.'" SSF 6(1969): 461-462.

5505. McHaney, Thomas L. "Anderson, Hemingway, and Faulkner's *The Wild Palms*." PMLA 87(1972): 465-474.

5506. Mellard, James M. "Calaban as Prospero: Benjy and *The Sound and the Fury*." *Novel* 3(1970): 233-248.

5507. ----------. "*The Sound and the Fury*: Quentin Compson and Faulkner's 'Tragedy of Passion.'" SN 2(1970): 62-75.

5508. Meriwether, James B. "The Novel Faulkner Never Wrote: His *Golden Book* or *Doomsday Book*." AL 42(1970): 93-96.

5509. ----------. "A Prefatory Note by Faulkner for the Compson Appendix." AL 43(1971): 281-284.

5510. ----------. "The Text of Faulkner's Books: An Introduction and Some Notes." MFS 9 (1963): 159-170.

5511. Messerli, Douglas. "The Problem of Time in *The Sound and the Fury*: A Critical Reassessment and Reinterpretation." SLJ 6,#2(1974): 19-41.

5512. Middleton, David. "Faulkner's Folklore in *As I Lay Dying*: An Old Motif in a New Manner." SN 9(1977): 46-53.

5513. Miller, David. "Faulkner's Women." MFS 13(1967): 3-17.

5514. Milum, Richard A. "Faulkner and the Cavalier Tradition: The French Bequest." AL 45 (1974): 580-589.

5515. ----------. "Ikkemotubbe and the Spanish Conspiracy." AL 46(1974): 389-391.

5516. Mitchell, Charles. "The Wounded Will of Faulkner's Barn Burner." MFS 11(1965): 185-189.

5517. Momberger, Philip. "A Reading of Faulkner's 'The Hill.'" *SLJ* 9,#2(1977): 16-29.

5518. Monoghan, David M. "The Single Narrator of *As I Lay Dying*." *MFS* 18(1972): 213-220.

5519. Monteiro, George. "Bankruptcy in Time: A Reading of William Faulkner's *Pylon*." *TCL* 4(1958): 9-20.

5520. ----------. "The Limits of Professionalism: A Sociological Approach to Faulkner, Fitzgerald, and Hemingway." *Criticism* 15(1973): 145-155.

5521. Morrison, Sister Kirstin. "Faulkner's Joe Christmas: Character through Voice." *TSLL* 2 (1961): 419-443.

5522. Moses, W. R. "The Unity of *Wild Palms*." *MFS* 2(1956): 125-131.

5523. Muir, E. A. "A Footnote on *Sartoris* and Some Speculation." *JML* 1(1971): 389-393.

5524. Muller, Gilbert H. "The Descent of the Gods: Faulkner's 'Red Leaves' and the Garden of the South." *SSF* 11(1974): 243-249.

5525. Muste, John M. "The Failure of Love in *Go Down, Moses*." *MFS* 10(1964): 366-378.

5526. Naples, Dianne. "Eliot's 'Tradition' and *The Sound and the Fury*." *MFS* 20(1974): 214-217.

5527. Nash, H. C. "Faulkner's 'Furniture Repairer and Dealer': Knitting up *Light in August*." *MFS* 16(1970): 529-531.

5528. Nebeker, Helen E. "Chronology Revised." *SSF* 8(1971): 471-473.

5529. Nestrick, William V. "The Function of Form in 'The Bear', Section IV." *TCL* 12(1966): 131-137.

5530. Payne, Ladell. "The Trilogy: Faulkner's Comic Epic in Prose." *SN* 1(1969): 27-37.

5531. Pearce, Richard. "Faulkner's One Ring Circus." *Con L* 7(1966): 270-283.

5532. ----------. "'Pylon,' 'Awake and Sing!' and the Apocalyptic Imagination of the 30's." *Criticism* 13(1971): 131-141.

5533. Peavy, Charles D. "An Early Casting of Benjy: Faulkner's 'The Kingdom of God.'" *SSF* 3(1966): 347-348.

5534. ----------. "Faulkner and the Howe Interview." *CLA* 11(1967): 117-123.

5535. ----------. "Jason Compson's Paranoid Pseudocommunity." *HSL* 2(1970): 151-156.

5536. ----------. "A Note on the 'Suicide Pact' in *The Sound and the Fury*." *ELN* 5(1968): 207-209.

5537. Perry, J. Douglas, Jr. "Gothic as Vortex: The Form of Horror in Capote, Faulkner, and Styron." *MFS* 19(1973): 153-168.

5538. Pitavy, François A. "A Forgotten Faulkner Story: 'Miss Zilphia Gant.'" *SSF* 9 (1972): 131-142.

5539. Polk, Noel. "Review-Essay: Some Recent Books on Faulkner." *SN* 9(1977): 201-210.

5540. Pommer, Henry F. "*Light in August*: A Letter by Faulkner." *ELN* 4(1966): 47-48.

5541. Poresky, Louise A. "Joe Christmas: His Tragedy as Victim." *HSL* 8(1976): 209-222.

5542. Pryse, Marjorie L. "Race: Faulkner's 'Red Leaves.'" *SSF* 12(1975): 133-138.

5543. Putzel, Max. "Evolution of Two Characters in Faulkner's Unpublished Fiction." *SLJ* 5,#2(1973): 47-63.

5544. ----------. "What Is Gothic About *Absalom, Absalom!*" *SLJ* 4,#1(1971): 3-19.

5545. Ramsey, R. "Light Imagery in *The Sound and the Fury*." *JNT* 6(1976): 41-50.

5546. Rea, J. "Faulkner's Spotted Horses." *HSL* 2(1970): 157-164.

5547. Reed, Richard. "The Role of Chronology in Faulkner's Yoknapatawpha Fiction." *SLJ* 7,#1 (1974): 24-48.

5548. Richardson, H. Edward. "Anderson and Faulkner." *AL* 36(1964): 298-314.

5549. ----------. "Faulkner, Anderson, and Their Tall Tale." *AL* 34(1962): 287-291.

5550. ----------. "The 'Hemingwaves' in Faulkner's *Wild Palms*." *MFS* 4(1958): 357-360.

5551. Rideout, Walter, and James Meriwether. "On the Collaboration of Faulkner and Anderson." *AL* 35(1963): 85-87.

5552. Rinaldi, Nicholas M. "Game Imagery and Game-Consciousness in Faulkner's Fiction." *TCL* 10(1964): 108-118.

5553. Ringold, Francine. "The Metaphysics of Yoknapatawpha County: 'Airy Space and Scope for Your Delirium.'" *HSL* 8(1976): 223-240.

5554. Rosenman, John B. "A Note on William Faulkner's *As I Lay Dying*." *SAF* 1(1973): 104-105.

5555. ----------. "Physical-Spatial Symbolism in *As I Lay Dying*." *Coll L* 4(1977): 176.

5556. Ross, Stephen M. "Conrad's Influence

5556. Ross, Stephen. "Conrad's Influence on Faulkner's *Absalom! Absalom!*" *SAF* 2(1974): 199-210.

5557. ----------. "Jason Compsen and Sut Lovingood: Southwestern Humor as Stream of Consciousness." *SN* 8(1976): 278-290.

5558. ----------. "The 'Loud World' of Quentin Compson." *SN* 7(1975): 245-257.

5559. ----------. "Shapes of Time and Consciousness in *As I Lay Dying*." *TSLL* 16(1975): 723-737.

5560. Rossky, William. "*As I Lay Dying*: The Insane World." *TSLL* 4(1962): 87-95.

5561. ----------. "The Pattern of Nightmare in *Sanctuary*; or, Miss Reba's Dogs." *MFS* 15(1969): 503-515.

5562. Sadler, David F. "The Second Mrs. Bundren: Another Look at the Ending of *As I Lay Dying*." *AL* 37(1965): 65-69.

5563. Sanders, Barry. "Faulkner's Fire Imagery in 'That Evening Sun.'" *SSF* 5(1967): 69-71.

5564. Schamberger, J. Edward. "Renaming Percival Brownlee in Faulkner's *Bear*." *Coll L* 4(1977): 92-94.

5565. Sidney, George. "An Addition to the Faulkner Canon: The Hollywood Writings." *TCL* 6 (1961): 172-174.

5566. Simon, John K. "Faulkner and Sartre: Metamorphosis and the Obscene." *Comp L* 15(1963): 216-225.

5567. ----------. "The Scene and the Imagery of Metamorphosis in *As I Lay Dying*." *Criticism* 7(1965): 1-22.

5568. Slabey, Robert M. "Myth and Ritual in *Light in August*." *TSLL* 2(1960): 328-349.

5569. ----------. "Quentin Compson's 'Lost Childhood.'" *SSF* 1(1963): 173-183.

5570. Slatoff, Walter J. "The Edge of Order: The Pattern of Faulkner's Rhetoric." *TCL* 3(1957): 107-127.

5571. Sleeth, Irene Lynn. "William Faulkner: A Bibliography of Criticism." *TCL* 8(1962): 18-43.

5572. Smith, Julian. "A Source for Faulkner's *A Fable*." *AL* 40(1968): 394-397.

5573. Smithey, Robert A. "Faulkner and the Status Quo." *CLA* 11(1967): 109-116.

5574. Sowder, William J. "Colonel Thomas Sutpen as Existentialist Hero." *AL* 33(1962): 485-499.

5575. ----------. "Faulkner and Existentialism: A Note on the **Genaralissimo**." *Con L* 4(1963): 163-171.

5576. Spilka, Mark. "Quentin Compson's Universal Grief." *Con L* 11(1970): 451-469.

5577. Spivey, Herman E. "Faulkner and the Adamic Myth: Faulkner's Moral Vision." *MFS* 19 (1973): 497-505.

5578. Stafford, T. J. "Tobe's Significance in 'A Rose for Emily.'" *MFS* 14(1968): 451-453.

5579. Stafford, William T. "A Whale, An Heiress, and A Southern Demigod: Three Symbolic Americas." *Coll L* 1(1974): 100-112.

5580. Steinberg, Aaron. "*Absalom, Absalom:* The Irretrievable Bon." *CLA* 9(1965): 61-67.

5581. Stewart, David H. "The Purpose of Faulkner's Ike." *Criticism* 3(1961): 333-342.

5582. Stewart, George, and Joseph Backus. "'Each in its Ordered Place': Structure and Narrative in 'Benjy's Section' of *The Sound and the Fury*." *AL* 29(1958): 440-456.

5583. Stewart, Jack F. "Apotheosis and Apocalypse in Faulkner's 'Wash.'" *SSF* 6(1969): 586-600.

5584. Stone, William B. "Ike McCaslin and the Grecian Urn." *SSF* 10(1973): 93-94.

5585. Stoneback, H. R. "Faulkner's Blues: 'Pantaloon in Black.'" *MFS* 21(1975): 241-245.

5586. Strandberg, Victor. "Between Truth and Fact: Faulkner's Symbols of Identity." *MFS* 21(1975): 445-457.

5587. Sullivan, Ruth. "The Narrator in 'A Rose for Emily.'" *JNT* 1(1971): 159-178.

5588. Sultan, Stanley. "Call Me Ishmael: The Hagiography of Isaac McCaslin." *TSLL* 3(1961): 50-66.

5589. Swiggart, Peter. "Time in Faulkner's Novels." *MFS* 1,#2(1955): 25-29.

5590. Taylor, Walter. "Faulkner's Pantaloon: The Negro Anomaly at the Heart of *Go Down, Moses*." *AL* 44(1972): 430-444.

5591. Thornton, Weldon. "The Source of Faulkner's Jason." *SN* 1(1969): 370-372.

5592. Tobin, Patricia. "The Time of Myth and History in *Absalom, Absalom!*" *AL* 45(1973): 252-270.

5593. Torchiana, Donald T. "Faulkner's *Pylon* and the Structure of Modernity." *MFS* 3 (1957): 291-308.

5594. Travis, Mildred K. "Echoes of *Pierre* in *The Reivers*." *NCL* 3(September, 1973): 11-13.

5595. Trimmer, Joseph. "V. K. Ratliff: A Portrait of the Artist in Motion." *MFS* 20(1974): 454-467.

5596. Tritschler, Donald. "The Unity of Faulkner's Shaping Vision." *MFS* 5(1959): 337-343.

5597. Tucker, Edward L. "Faulkner's Drusilla and Ibsen's Hedda." *MD* 16(1973): 157-162.

5598. Turaj, Frank. "The Dialect in Faulkner's *A Fable*." *TSLL* 8(1966): 93-102.

5599. Underwood, Henry J., Jr. "Satre on *The Sound and the Fury*: Some Errors." *MFS* 12 (1966): 477-478.

5600. Vickery, Olga W. "*The Sound and the Fury*: A Study in Perspective." *PMLA* 69(1954): 1017-1037.

5601. Vinson, Audrey L. "Miscegenation and Its Meaning in *Go Down, Moses*." *CLA* 14(1970): 143-155.

5602. Volpe, Edmond L. "Faulkner's 'Red Leaves': The Deciduation of Nature." *SAF* 3 (1975): 121-131.

5603. Vorpahl, Ben Merchant. "Moonlight at Ballenbaugh's: Time and Imagination in *The Reivers*." *SLJ* 1,#2(1969): 3-26.

5604. Waggoner, Hyatt H. "The Historical Novel and the Southern Past: The Case of *Absalom, Absalom!*" *SLJ* 2,#2(1970): 69-85.

5605. Wagner, Linda W. "*As I Lay Dying*: Faulkner's 'All in the Family.'" *Coll L* 1(1974): 73-82.

5606. ----------. "Faulkner's Fiction: Studies in Organic Form." *JNT* 1(1971): 1-14.

5607. Wall, Carey. "Drama and Technique in Faulkner's *The Hamlet*." *TCL* 14(1968): 17-23.

5608. Wasiolek, Edward. "*As I Lay Dying*: Distortion in the Slow Eddy of Current Opinion." *Crit* 3,#1(1959): 15-23.

5609. Watkins, Floyd C. "Faulkner and His Critics." *TSLL* 10(1968): 317-329.

5610. ----------. "What Happens in *Absalom, Absalom!*" *MFS* 13(1967): 79-87.

5611. Watkins, Floyd, and Thomas Young. "Revisions of Style in Faulkner's *The Hamlet*." *MFS* 5(1959): 327-336.

5612. Watkins, Floyd C., and William B. Dillingham. "The Mind of Vardaman Bundren." *PQ* 39(1960): 247-251.

5613. Watson, James G. "If *Was* Existed: Faulkner's Prophets and the Patterns of History." *MFS* 21(1975): 499-507.

5614. West, Ray B., Jr. "Faulkner's *Light in August*: A View of Tragedy." *Con L* 1,#1(1960): 5-12.

5615. Wheeler, Otis B. "Faulkner's Wilderness." *AL* 31(1959): 127-136.

5616. Wheeler, Sally Padgett. "Chronology in *Light in August*." *SLJ* 6,#1(1973): 20-42.

5617. Whicher, Stephen E. "The Compson's Nancies—A Note on *The Sound and the Fury* and 'That Evening Sun.'" *AL* 26(1954): 252-255.

5618. Williams, John S. "'The Final Copper Light of Afternoon': Hightower's Redemption." *TCL* 13(1968): 205-215.

5619. Winn, James A. "Faulkner's Revisions: A Stylist at Work." *AL* 41(1969): 231-250.

5620. Winslow, Joan D. "Language and Destruction in Faulkner's 'Dry September.'" *CLA* 20 (1977): 380-386.

5621. Wolfe, Ralph **Haven, and Edgar Dan-**iels. "Beneath the Dust of 'Dry September.'" *SSF* 1(1964): 158-159.

5622. Zender, Karl F. "A Hand of Poker: Game and Ritual in Faulkner's 'Was.'" *SSF* 11(1974): 53-60.

5623. Zink, Karl E. "Faulkner's Garden: Women and the Immemorial Earth." *MFS* 2(1956): 139-149.

5624. ----------. "Flux and Frozen Moment: The Imagery of Stasis in Faulkner's Prose." *PMLA* 71(1956): 285-301.

5625. Zoellner, Robert H. "Faulkner's Prose Style in *Absalom, Absalom!*" *AL* 30(1959): 486-502.

See also 455, 584, 602a, 5908, 15335.

FAUSET, JESSIE.   5626. Feeny, Joseph J., S. J. "Greek Tragic Patterns in a Black Novel: Jessie Fauset's *The Chinaberry Tree*." *CLA* 18 (1974): 211-215.

See also 4401.

FENNER, LANON A.   See 4311.

FERLINGHETTI, LAWRENCE.   5627. Ianni, L. A. "Lawrence Ferlinghetti's Fourth Person Singular and the Theory of Relativity." *Con L* 8(1967): 392-406.

See also 590.

FERRIL, THOMAS H.   5628. Richards, Robert F. "Thomas Hornsby Ferril: A Biographical Sketch." *WAL* 9(1974): 205-214.

5629. Scherting, Jack. "An Approach to the Western Poetry of Thomas Hornsby Ferril." *WAL* 7 (1972): 179-190.

FIEDLER, LESLIE.   5630. Bluefarb, Sam. "Pictures of the Anti-Stereotype: Leslie Fiedler's Triptych: *The Last Jew in America*." *CLA* 18(1975): 412-421.

5631. Curran, Ronald. "'Fallen King' as Scapegoat in Fielder's 'Nude Croquet.'" *NCL* 4 (January , 1974): 8-13.

5632. Feinstein, Herbert. "Contemporary American Fiction: Harvey Swados and Leslie Fiedler (Interview)." *Con L* 2,#1(1961): 79-98.

5633. Fielder, Leslie. "Love and Death in the American Novel: My First Gothic Novel." *Novel* 1(1967): 8-11.

5634. Schulz, Max F. "Leslie A. Fiedler and the Hieroglyph of Life." *TCL* 14(1968): 24-34.

FISHER, RUDOLPH.   See 4425.

FISHER, VARDIS.   5635. Flora, Joseph M. "Vardis Fisher and Wallace Stegner: Teacher and Student." *WAL* 5(1970): 121-128.

5636. Kellogg, George. "Vardis Fisher: A Bibliography." *WAL* 5(1970): 45-64.

5637. Taber, Ronald W. "Vardis Fisher: New Directions for the Historical Novel." *WAL* 1 (1967): 285-296.

See also 595, 4403, 4420.

FITZGERALD, F. SCOTT.   5638. Alderman, Taylor. "The Begetting of Gatsby." *MFS* 19(1973): 563-565.

5639. Astro, Richard. "*Vandover and the Brute* and *The Beautiful and Damned*: A Search for Thematic and Stylistic Reinterpretation." *MFS* 14(1968): 397-413.

5640. Babb, Howard. "*The Great Gatsby* and the Grotesque." *Criticism* 5(1963): 336-348.

5641. Battista, Maria di. "The Aesthetic of Forbearance: Fitzgerald's *Tender is the Night*." *Novel* 11(1977): 26-39.

5642. Beebe, Muarice, and Jackson R. Bryer. "Criticism of F. Scott Fitzgerald: A Selected Checklist." *MFS* 7(1961): 82-94.

5643. Bettina, Sister M., SSND. "The Artifact in Imagery: Fitzgerald's *The Great Gatsby*." *TCL* 9(1963): 140-142.

5644. Bruccoli, Matthew J. "*Tender is the Night* and the Reviewers." *MFS* 7(1961): 49-54.

5645. Bryer, Jackson R. "F. Scott Fitzgerald and the State of American Letters in 1921." *MFS* 12(1966): 265-266.

5646. ----------. "F. Scott Fitzgerald: A Review of Research and Scholarship." *TSLL* 5(1963): 147-163.

5647. Bufkin, E. C. "A Pattern of Parallel and Double: The Function of Myrtle in *The Great Gatsby*." *MFS* 15(1969): 517-524.

5648. Buntain, Lucy M. "A Note on the Editions of *Tender in the Night*." *SAF* 1(1973): 208-213.

5649. Burhans, Clinton S., Jr. "'Magnificently Attune to Life': The Value of 'Winter Dreams.'" *SSF* 6(1969): 401-412.

5650. ----------. "Structure and Theme in *This Side of Paradise*." *JEGP* 68(1969): 605-624.

5651. Burton, Mary E. "The Counter-Transference of Dr. Diver." *ELH* 38(1971): 459-471.

5652. Casty, Alan. "'I and It' in the Stories of F. Scott Fitzgerald." *SSF* 9(1972): 47-58.

5653. Coleman, Tom C., III. "Nicole Warren Diver and Scott Fitzgerald: The Girl and the Egotist." *SN* 3(1971): 34-43.

5654. Ditsky, John. "F. Scott Fitzgerald and the Jacob's Ladder." *JNT* 7(1977): 226-228.

5655. Donaldson, Scott. "Scott Fitzgerald's Romance with the South." *SLJ* 5,#2(1972): 3-17.

5656. Doyno, Victor A. "Patterns in *The Great Gatsby*." *MFS* 12(1966): 415-426.

5657. Dudley, Juanita W. "Dr. Diver, Vivisectionist." *Coll L* 2(1975): 128-136.

5658. Dyson, A. E. "*The Great Gatsby*: Thirty-Six Years After." *MFS* 7(1961): 37-48.

5659. Eble, Kenneth. "The Craft of Revision: *The Great Gatsby*." *AL* 36(1964): 315-326.

5660. ----------. "*The Great Gatsby*." *Coll L* 1(1974): 35-48.

5661. Ellis, James. "The 'Stoddard Lectures' in *The Great Gatsby*." *AL* 44(1972): 470-471.

5662. Fraser, John. "Dust and Dreams and *The Great Gatsby*." *ELH* 32(1965): 553-564.

5663. Fussell, Edwin S. "Fitzgerald's Brave New World." *ELH* 19(1952): 291-306.

5664. Gindin, James. "Gods and Fathers in F. Scott Fitzgerald's Novels." *MLQ* 30(1969): 64-85.

5665. Griffith, Richard R. "A New Note on Fitzgerald's 'Babylon Revisited.'" *AL* 35(1963): 236-239.

5666. Gross, Barry. "Back West: Time and Place in *The Great Gatsby*." *WAL* 8(1973): 3-13.

5667. ----------. "Fitzgerald in the Fifties." *SN* 5(1973): 324-335.

5668. ----------. "*This Side of Paradise:* The Dominating Intention." *SN* 1(1969): 51-59.

5669. Hampton, Riley U. "Owl Eyes in *The Great Gatsby.*" *AL* 48(1976): 229.

5670. Hanzo, Thomas A. "The Theme and the Narrator of *The Great Gatsby.*" *MFS* 2(1956): 183-190.

5671. Hart, John E. "Fitzgerald's *The Last Tycoon:* A Search for Identity." *MFS* 7(1961): 63-70.

5672. Hausermann, H. W. "Fitzgerald's Religious Sense: Note and Query." *MFS* 2(1956): 81-82.

5673. Ingrisano, Michael W. "A Note on a Critique of F. Scott Fitzgerald." *AL* 24(1953): 539-540.

5674. Irish, Carol. "The Myth of Success in Fitzgerald's Boyhood." *SAF* 1(1973): 176-187.

5675. Joseph, Gerhard. "The American Triumph of the Egg: Anderson's 'The Egg' and Fitzgerald's *The Great Gatsby.*" *Citicism* 7(1965): 131-140.

5676. Kane, Patricia. "Place of Abomination: A Reading of Fitzgerald's 'Valley of Ashes.'" *ELN* 1(1964): 291-295.

5677. Korenman, Joan S. "'Only Her Hairdresser . . . ': Another Look at Daisy Buchanan." *AL* 46(1975): 574-578.

5678. Kreuter, Kent and Gretchen. "The Moralism of the Later Fitzgerald." *MFS* 7(1961): 71-80.

5679. Kruse, Horst H. "'Gatsby' and 'Gadsby.'" *MFS* 15(1969): 539-541.

5680. Kuehl, John. "Scott Fitzgerald: Romantic and Realist." *TSLL* 1(1959): 412-426.

5681. ----------. "Scott Fitzgerald's Critical Opinions." *MFS* 7(1961): 3-18.

5682. LaHurd, Ryan. "'Absolution': Gatsby's Forgotten Front Door." *Coll L* 3(1976): 113-123.

5683. Lauter, Paul. Plato's Stepchildren, Gatsby and Cohn." *MFS* 9(1963): 338-346.

5684. Lisca, Peter. "Nick Carraway and the Imagery of Disorder." *TCL* 13(1967): 18-28.

5685. Long, Robert Emmet. "*The Great Gatsby* and the Tradition of Joseph Conrad. Part I." *TSLL* 8(1966): 257-276.

5686. ----------. "*The Great Gatsby* and the Tradition of Joseph Conrad. Part II." *TSLL* 8 (1966): 407-422.

5687. MacPhee, Laurence E. "*The Great Gatsby's* 'Romance of Motoring': Nick Carraway and Jordan Baker." *MFS* 18(1972): 207-212.

5688. Male, Roy R. "'Babylon Revisited': A Story of the Exile's Return." *SSF* 2(1965): 270-277.

5689. Martin, Robert A. "The Hot Madness of Four O'Clock in Fitzgerald's 'Absolution' and Gatsby." *SAF* 2(1974): 230-238.

5690. Mazzella, Anthony J. "The Tension of Opposites in Fitzgerald's 'May Day.'" *SSF* 14(1977): 379-385.

5691. McCall, Dan. "'The Self-Same Song that Found a Path': Keats and *The Great Gatsby.*" *AL* 42(1971): 521-530.

5692. McDonnell, Robert F. "Eggs and Eyes in *The Great Gatsby.*" *MFS* 7(1961): 32-36.

5693. McNicholas, Sister Mary Verity, O. P. "Fitzgerald's Women in *Tender Is the Night.*" *Coll L* 4(1977): 40-70.

5694. Miller, Linda Patterson. "'As a Friend You Have Never Failed Me': The Fitzgerald -Murphy Correspondence." *JML* 5(1976): 357-382.

5695. Millgate, Michael. "Scott Fitzgerald as Social Novelist: Statement and Technique in 'The Great Gatsby.'" *MLR* 57(1962): 335-339.

5696. Monteiro, George. "Henry James and Scott Fitzgerald: A Source." *NCL* 6(March, 1976): 4-6.

5697. ----------. "The Limits of Professionalism: A Sociological Approach to Faulkner, Fitzgerald, and Hemingway." *Criticism* 15(1973): 145-155.

5698. Moses, Edwin. "Tragic Inevitability in *The Great Gatsby.*" *CLA* 21(1977): 51-59.

5699. Moyer, Kermit W. "Fitzgerald's Two Unfinished Novels: The Count and the Tycoon in Spenglerian Perspective." *Con L* 15(1974): 238-256.

5700. Murphy, George D. "The Unconscious Dimension of *Tender Is the Night.*" *SN* 5(1973): 314-323.

5701. Osborne, William R. "The Wounds of Charlie Wales in Fitzgerald's 'Babylon Revisited.'" *SSF* 2(1964): 86-87.

5702. Pinkser, Sanford. "Seeing *The Great Gatsby* Eye to Eye." *Coll L* 3(1976): 69-71.

5703. Porter, Bernard H. "The First Publications of F. Scott Fitzgerald." *TCL* 5(1960): 176-182.

5704. Prigozy, Ruth. "The Unpublished Stories: Fitzgerald in His Final Stage." *TCL* 20 (1974): 69-90.

5705. Qualls, Barry V. "Physician in the Counting House: The Religious Motif in *Tender Is the Night.*" *EL* 2(1975): 192-208.

5706. Randall, Dale B. J. "The 'Seer' and 'Seen' Themes in *Gatsby* and Some of Their Parallels in Eliot and Wright." *TCL* 10(1964): 51-63.

5707. Randall, John H., III. "Jay Gatsby's Hidden Source of Wealth." *MFS* 13(1967): 247-257.

5708. Riddel, Joseph N. "F. Scott Fitzgerald, the Jamesian Inheritance, and the Morality of Fiction." *MFS* 11(1965): 331-350.

5709. Robbins, J. Albert. "Fitzgerald and the Simple, Inarticulate Farmer." *MFS* 7(1961): 365-369.

5710. Scrimgeour, Gary J. "Against 'The Great Gatsby.'" *Criticism* 8(1966): 75-86.

5711. Slater, Peter Gregg. "Ethnicity in *The Great Gatsby.*" *TCL* 19(1973): 53-62.

5712. Speer, Roderick S. "*The Great Gatsby's* 'Romance of Motoring' and 'The Cruise of the Rolling Junk.'" *MFS* 20(1974): 540-543.

5713. Staley, Thomas F. "Time and Structure in Fitzgerald's 'Babylon Revisited.'" *MFS* 10(1964): 386-388.

5714. Stallman, Robert Wooster. "Conrad and *The Great Gatsby.*" *TCL* 1(1955): 5-12.

5715. ----------. "Gatsby and the Hole in Time." *MFS* 1,#4(1955): 2-16.

5716. ----------. "Two New Fitzgerald Letters." *MFS* 11(1965): 189-191.

5717. Stanton, Robert. "'Daddy's Girl': Symbol and Theme in *Tender is the Night.*" *MFS* 4 (1958): 136-142.

5718. Stephens, Robert O., and James Ellis. "Hemingway, Fitzgerald and the Riddle of 'Henry's

Bicycle.'" *ELN* 5(1967): 46-49.

5719.   Stewart, Laurence D.   "Scott Fitz-gerald D'Invilliers." *AL* 29(1957): 212-213.

5720.   Tamke, Alexander.   "The 'Gat' in Gatsby: Neglected Aspect of a Novel." *MFS* 14 (1968): 443-445.

5721.   Thale, Jerome.   "The Narrator as Hero." *TCL* 3(1957): 69-73.

5722.   Turlish, Lewis A.   "*The Rising Tide of Color:*   A Note on the Historicism of *The Great Gatsby.*" *AL* 43(1971): 442-444.

5723.   Tuttleton, James W.   "The Presence of Poe in *This Side of Paradise.*" *ELN* 3(1966): 284-289.

5724.   Wasserstrom, William.   "The Good of Guilt: Henry Adams, Scott and Zelda." *JML* 6 (1977): 289-310.

5725.   Westbrook, J. S.   "Nature and Optics in *The Great Gatsby.*" *AL* 32(1960): 78-84.

5726.   White, Eugene.   "The 'Intricate Des-tiny' of Dick Diver." *MFS* 7(1961): 55-62.

5727.   Wycherly, H. Alan.   "Fitzgerald Revisited." *TSLL* 8(1966): 277-283.

5728.   Yates, Donald A.   "The Road to 'Para-dise':   Fitzgerald's Literary Apprenticeship." *MFS* 7(1961): 19-31.

5729.   Young, Philip.   "Scott Fitzgerald on His Thirtieth Birthday Sends a Small Gift to Er-nest Hemingway." *MFS* 14(1968): 229-230.

See also 5241, 6221, 6344.

FLETCHER, JOHN GOULD.   5730.   Behrens, Ralph.   "John Gould Fletcher and Rimbaud's 'Al-chimie du verbe.'" *Comp L* 8(1956): 46-62.

FOOTE, MARY H.   5731.   Etulian, Richard. "Mary Hallock Foote (1847-1938)." *ALR* 5(1972): 145-150.

5732.   ----------.   Mary Hallock Foote: A Checklist." *WAL* 10(1975): 59-65.

FOX, JOHN, JR.   5733.   Holman, Harriet R. "Appraisal and Self-Appraisal."[includes text of Fox's "Personal Sketch" (1980)] *SLJ* 3,#2(1971): 18-38.

5734.   Titus, Warren.   "John Fox, Jr. (1862-1919)." [bibliography] *ALR* 1,#3(1968): 5-8.

FRANKLIN, J. E.   See 4363.

FRIEDMAN, BRUCE JAY.   5735.   Lewis, Stuart. "Myth and Ritual in the Short Fiction of Bruce Jay Friedman." *SSF* 10(1973): 415-416.

5736.   Lewis, Stuart A.   "Rootlessness and Alienation in the Novels of Bruce Jay Friedman." *CLA* 18(1975): 422-433.

5737.   Schulz, M. F.   "Wallent and Friedman: The Glory and the Agony of Love." *Crit* 10,#3 (1968): 31-47.

See also 4393.

FROST, ROBERT.   5738.   Allen, Ward.   "Rob-ert Frost's 'Iota Subscript.'" *ELN* 6(1969): 285-287.

5739.   Bass, Eben.   "Frost's Poetry of Fear." *AL* 43(1972): 603-615.

5740.   Berger, Harry, Jr.   "Poetry as Re-vision: Interpreting Robert Frost." *Criticism* 10(1968): 1-22.

5741.   Borroff, Marie.   "Robert Frost's New Testament: Language and the Poem." *MP* 69(1971): 36-56.

5742.   Bowen, James K.   "Propositional and

Emotional Knowledge in Robert Frost's 'The Death of the Hired Man,' 'The Fear,' and 'Home Burial.'" *CLA* 12(1968): 155-160.

5743.   Carlson, Eric W.   "Robert Frost on Vocal Imagination, the Merger of Form and Content." *AL* 33(1962): 519-522.

5744.   Cohen, Edward H.   "Robert Frost in Eng-land: An Unpublished Letter." *NEQ* 43(1970): 285-287.

5745.   Cook, Marjorie.   "The Completion of Boundaries: 'Trespess' by Robert Frost." *NCL* 5 (January, 1975): 2-5.

5746.   Cooke, Reginald L.   "Emerson and Frost: A Parallel of Seers." *NEQ* 31(1958): 200-217.

5747.   ----------.   "Frost on Frost: The Making of Poems." *AL* 28(1956): 62-72.

5748.   ----------.   "Frost the Diversionist." *NEQ* 40(1967): 323-338.

5749.   Duvall, S. P. C.   "Robert Frost's 'Di-rective' out of *Walden.*" *AL* 31(1960): 482-488.

5750.   Ferguson, A. R.   "Frost, Sill, and "A Wishing Well.'" *AL* 33(1961): 370-373.

5751.   Fleissner, Robert F.   "Frost and Ra-cism: The Evidence." *BALF* 9(1977): 118-119.

5752.   ----------.   "Frost's and Yevtushenko's 'Irreverant' Poems." *NCL* 6(January, 1976): 14-15.

5753.   Foster, Richard.   "Leaves Compared with Flowers: A Reading in Robert Frost's Poems." *NEQ* 46(1973): 403-423.

5754.   Geyer, C.   "A Poulterer's Measure: Rob-ert Frost as Prose Humorist." *SSF* 8(1971): 589-599.

5755.   Greenberg, Robert A.   "Frost in England: A Publishing Incident." *NEQ* 34(1961): 375-379.

5756.   Grieder, Josaphine.   "Robert Frost on Ezra Pound, 1913:   Manuscript Corrections of 'Por-trait d'une Femme.'" *NEQ* 44(1971): 301-305.

5757.   Haynes, Donald T.   "The Narrative Unity of *A Boy's Will.*" *PMLA* 87(1972): 452-464.

5758.   Hearn, Thomas K., Jr.   "Making Sweet-breads Do: Robert Frost and Moral Empiricism." *NEQ* 49(1976): 65-81.

5759.   Hepburn, James G.   "Robert Frost and His Critics." *NEQ* 35(1962): 367-376.

5760.   Irwin, W. R.   "Robert Frost and the Comic Spirit." *AL* 35(1963): 299-310.

5761.   ----------.   "The Unity of Frost's Masques." *AL* 32(1960): 302-312.

5762.   Juhnke, Anna K.   "Religion in Robert Frost's Poetry: The Play for Self-Possession." *AL* 36(1964): 153-164.

5763.   Lentricchia, Frank.   "Robert Frost: The Aesthetics of Voice and the Theory of Poetry." *Criticism* 15(1973): 28-42.

5764.   Leyburn, Ellen Douglas.   "A Note on Frost's *A Masque of Reason.*" *MD* 4(1962): 426-428.

5765.   Lieber, Todd M.   "Robert Frost and Wallace Stevens: 'What to Make of a Diminished Thing.'" *AL* 47(1975): 63-83.

5766.   Marcus, Mordecai.   "Motivation of Robert Frost's Hired Man." *Coll L* 3(1976): 63-68.

5767.   Miller, Lewis H., Jr.   "The Poet as Swinger: Fact and Fancy in Robert Frost." *Criti-cism* 16(1974): 58-72.

5768.   Monteiro, George.   "Birches in Winter: Notes on Thoreau and Frost." *CLA* 12(1968): 129-133.

5769.   ----------.   Frost's Quest for the 'Purple-Fringed.'" *ELN* 13(1976): 204-206.

5770. ----------. "Robert Frost's Linked Analogies." *NEQ* 46(1973): 463-468.

5771. ----------. "Robert Frost's Solitary Singer." *NEQ* 44(1971): 134-140.

5772. Perrine, Laurence. "The Tone of Frost's 'The Literate Farmer and the Planet Venus.'" *NCL* 5(March, 1975): 10-13.

5773. ----------. "'Two Tramps in Mud Time' and the Critics." *AL* 44(1973): 671-676.

5774. Poss, Stanley. "Low Skies, Some Clearing, Local Frost." *NEQ* 41(1968): 438-442.

5775. Sasso, Laurence J., Jr. "Robert Frost: Love's Question." *NEQ* 42(1969): 95-107.

5776. Schutz, Fred C. "Frost's 'The Literate Farmer and the Planet Venus': Why 1926?" *NCL* 4(November, 1974): 8-11.

5777. Sears, John F. "William James, Henri Bergson, and the Poetics of Robert Frost." *NEQ* 48(1975): 341-360.

5778. Sheffey, Ruthe T. "From Delight to Wisdom: Thematic Progression in the Poetry of Robert Frost." *CLA* 8(1964): 51-59.

5779. Shurr, William H. "Once More to the 'Woods': A New Point of Entry into Frost's Most Famous Poem." *NEQ* 47(1974): 584-594.

5780. Sokol, B. J. "What Went Wrong between Robert Frost and Ezra Pound." *NEQ* 49(1976): 521-541.

5781. Stock, Ely. "*A Masque of Reason* and *J. B.*: Two Treatments of the Book of Job." *MD* 3(1961): 378-386.

5782. Swennes, Robert H. "Man and Wife: The Dialogue of Contraries in Robert Frost's Poetry." *AL* 42(1970): 363-372.

5783. Taylor, Anya. "A Frost Debt to Beddoes." *ELN* 13(1976): 291-292.

5784. Townsend, R. C. "In Defense of Form: A Letter from Robert Frost to Sylvester Baxter, 1923." *NEQ* 36(1963): 241-249.

5785. Utley, Francis Lee. "Robert Frost's Virgilian Monster." *ELN* 10(1973): 221-223.

5786. Vail, Dennis. "Frost's 'Mowing': Work and Poetry." *NCL* 4(January, 1974): 4-8.

5787. ----------. "Point of View in Frost's 'The Peaceful Shepherd.'" *NCL* 4(November, 1974): 2-4.

5788. ----------. "Tree Imagery in Frost's 'Mending Wall.'" *NCL* 3(September, 1973): 9-11.

5789. Vander Ven, Tom. "Robert Frost's Dramatic Principle of 'Oversound.'" *AL* 45(1973): 238-251.

5790. Van Dore, Wade. "Robert Frost: A Memoir and a Remonstrance." *JML* 2(1972): 554-560.

5791. Vitelli, James R. "Robert Frost: The Contrarieties of Talent and Tradition." *NEQ* 47(1974): 351-367.

5792. Watson, Charles N., Jr. "Frost's Wall: The View from the Other Side." *NEQ* 44(1971): 653-656.

5793. Watts, Harold H. "Robert Frost and the Interrupted Dialogue." *AL* 27(1955): 69-87.

5794. Yates, Norris. "An Instance of Parallel Imagery in Hawthorne, Melville, and Frost." *PQ* 36(1957): 276-280.

See also 526.

GADDIS, WILLIAM. 5795. Benstock, Bernard. "On William Gaddis: In Recognition of James Joyce." *Con L* 6(1965): 177-189.

5796. Koening, Peter William. "Recognizing Gaddis' *Recognitions*." *Con L* 16(1975): 61-72.

5797. Salemi, Joseph S. "To Soar in Atonement: Art as Expiation in Gaddis' *The Recognitions*." *Novel* 10(1977): 127-136.

GAINES, ERNEST. 5798. Andrews, William L. "'We Ain't Going Back There': The Idea of Progress in *The Autobiography of Miss Jane Pittman*." *BALF* 11(1977): 146-149.

5799. Burke, William. "*Bloodline*: A Black Man's South." *CLA* 19(1976): 545-558.

5800. Hicks, Jack. "To Make These Bones Live: History and Community in Ernest Gaines's Fiction." *BALF* 11(1977): 9-19.

5801. McDonald, Walter. "'You Not a Bum, You a Man': Ernest J. Gaines's *Bloodline*." *BALF* 9(1975): 47-49.

5802. Shelton, Frank W. "Ambiguous Manhood in Ernest J. Gaines's *Bloodline*." *CLA* 19(1975): 200-209.

5803. Stoelting, Winifred L. "Human Dignity and Pride in the Novels of Ernest Gaines." *CLA* 14(1971): 340-358.

See also 4407.

GALE, ZONA. 5804. Monteiro, George. "Zona Gale and Ridgely Torrence." *ALR* 3(1970): 77-79.

5805. Simonson, Harold. "Zona Gale (1874-1938)." [bibliography] *ALR* 1,#3(1968): 14-17.

GARDNER, JOHN. 5806. Fitzpatrick, W. P. "Down and Down I Go: A Note on Shelley's *Prometheus Unbound* and Gardner's *Grendel*." *NCL* 9(January, 1977): 2-5.

5807. Perkins, James Ashbrook. "Robert Coover and John Gardner: What Can We Do With the Poets?" *NCL* 6(March, 1976): 2-4.

GARRETT, JIMMY. See 4350, 4366, 4375.

GARRIGUE, JEAN. 5808. Schulman, Grace. "To Create the Self." *TCL* 23(1977): 299-313.

GASS, WILLIAM. 5809. Busch, Frederick. "But This is What it is to Live in Hell: William Gass's 'In the Heart of the Heart of the Country.'" *MFS* 19(1973): 97-108.

5810. Kane, Patricia. "A Point of Law in William Gass's 'Icicles.'" *NCL* 1(March, 1971): 7-8.

5811. McKenzie, James. "Introduction to Polevaulting in Top Hats: A Public Conversation with John Barth, William Gass, and Ishmael Reed." *MFS* 22(1976): 131-152.

5812. Merrill, Reed B. "The Grotesque as Structure: 'Willie Masters' Lonesome Wife.'" *Criticism* 18(1976): 305-316.

GATES, LEWIS. 5813. Coolidge, John S. "Lewis E. Gates: The Permutations of Romanticism." *NEQ* 30(1957): 23-38.

GERNSBACK, HUGO. 5814. Williamson, Jack. "As I Knew Hugo." *Ext* 11(1970): 53-55.

GINSBERG, ALLEN. 5815. Hunsberger, Bruce. "Kit Smart's *Howl*." *Con L* 6(1965): 34-44.

GIOVANNI, NIKKI. 5816. Palmer, R. Roderick. "The Poetry of Three Revolutionists: Don L. Lee, Sonia Sanchez, and Nikki Giovanni." *CLA* 15(1971): 25-36.

GLASGOW, ELLEN. 5817. Becker, Allen W. "Ellen Glasgow and the Southern Literary Tradition." *MFS* 5(1959): 295-303.

5818. Day, Douglas. "Ellen Glasgow's Letters to the Saxtons." *AL* 35(1963): 230-236.

5819. Gore, Luther Y., ed. "'Literary Realism or Nominalism' by Ellen Glasgow: An Unpublished Essay." *AL* 34(1962): 72-79.

5820. MacDonald, Edgar E. "The Glasgow-Cabell Entente." *AL* 41(1969): 76-91.

5821. Marshall, George O. "Hardy's *Tess* and Ellen Glasgow's *Barren Ground*." *TSLL* 1(1960): 517-521.

5822. McDowell, Frederick P. W. "Ellen Glasgow and the Art of the Novel." *PQ* 30(1951): 328-347.

5823. ----------. "'The Old Pagan Scorn of Everlasting Mercy'—Ellen Glasgow's *The Deliverance*." *TCL* 4(1959): 135-142.

5824. ----------. "Theme and Artistry in Glasgow's *The Sheltered Life*." *TSLL* 1(1960): 502-517.

5825. Murr, Judy Smith. "History in *Barren Ground* and *Vein of Iron*." *SLJ* 8,#1(1975): 39-54.

5826. Patterson, Daniel W. "Ellen Glasgow's Plan for a Social History of Virginia." *MFS* 5 (1959): 353-360.

5827. Raper, J. R. "Glasgow's Psychology of Deceptions and *The Sheltered Life*." *SLJ* 8,#1 (1975): 27-38.

5828. ----------. "Invisible Things: The Short Stories of Ellen Glasgow." *SLJ* 9,#2(1977): 66-90.

5829. Steele, Oliver L. "Ellen Glasgow, Social History, and the 'Virginia Edition.'" *MFS* 7(1961): 173-176.

5830. ----------. "Gertrude Stein and Ellen Glasgow: Memoir of a Meeting." *AL* 33(1961): 76-77.

GLASPELL, SUSAN. 5831. Bach, Gerhard. "Susan Glaspell: Supplementary Notes." *ALR* 5 (1972): 67-73.

5832. Waterman, Arthur. "Susan Glaspell (1882?-1948)." *ALR* 4(1971): 183-191.

5833. ----------. "Susan Glaspell and the Provincetown Players." *MD* 7(1964): 174-184.

GODWIN, GAIL. 5834. Gardiner, Judith K. "'A Sorrowful Woman': Gail Godwin's Feminist Parable." *SSF* 12(1975): 286-290.

GORDON, CAROLINE. 5835. Blum, Morgan. "The Shifting Point of View: Joyce's 'The Dead' and Gordon's 'Old Red.'" *Crit* 1,#1(1956): 45-66.

5836. Cowan, Louise. "Nature and Grace in Caroline Gordon." *Crit* 1,#1(1956): 11-28.

5837. Griscom, Joan. "Bibliography of Caroline Gordon." *Crit* 1,#1(1956): 74-78.

5838. Hoffman, Frederick J. "Caroline Gordon: The Special Yield." *Crit* 1,#1(1956): 29-36.

5839. Lytle, Andrew. "The Forest of the South." *Crit* 1,#1(1956): 3-10.

5840. Ross, Danforth. "Caroline Gordon's Golden Ball." *Crit* 1,#1(1956): 67-73.

5841. Rubin, Larry. "Christian Allegory in Caroline Gordon's 'The Captive.'" *SSF* 5(1968): 283-289.

See also 4404.

GORDONE, CHARLES. 5842. Lee, Dorothy. "Three Black Plays: Alienation and Paths to Recovery." *MD* 19(1976): 397-404.

GOYEN, WILLIAM. 5843. Phillips, Robert. "Samuel and Samson: Theme and Legend in 'The White Rooster.'" *SSF* 6(1969): 331-333.

GRAU, SHIRLEY ANN. 5844. Berland, Alwyn. "The Fiction of Shirley Ann Grau." *Crit* 6,#1(1963): 78-84.

GREEN, PAUL. 5845. Pearce, Howard D. "From Folklore to Mythology: Paul Green's *Roll, Sweet Chariot*." *SLJ* 3,#2(1970): 62-70.

GREENBERG, SAMUEL. 5846. Dembo, L. S. "Hart Crane and Samuel Greenberg: What is Plagiarism?" *AL* 32(1960): 319-321.

5847. Simon, Marc. "Hart Crane and Samuel B. Greenberg: An Emblematic Interlude." *Con L* 12 (1971): 166-172.

GREGOR, ARTHUR. 5848. Schulman, Grace. "To Create the Self." *TCL* 23(1977): 299-313.

GREY, ZANE. 5849. Arrington, Leonard, and Jon Haupt. "Community and Isolation: Some Aspects of 'Mormon Westerns.'" *WAL* 8(1973): 15-31. See also 601.

GUTHRIE, A. B. 5850. Astro, Richard. "*The Big Sky* and the Limits of Wilderness Fiction." *WAL* 9(1974): 105-114.

5851. Cracroft, Richard H. "*The Big Sky*: A. B. Guthrie's Use of Historical Sources." *WAL* 6(1971): 163-176.

5852. Etulain, Richard W. "A. B. Guthrie: A Bibliography." *WAL* 4(1969): 133-138.

5853. Guthrie, A. B., Jr. "Why Write about the West?" *WAL* 7(1972): 163-169.

5854. Peterson, Levi S. "Tragedy and Western American Literature." *WAL* 6(1972): 243-249.

5855. Stineback, David C. "On History and Its Consequences: A. B. Guthrie's *The Thousand Hills*." *WAL* 6(1976): 177-189. See also 595, 4403, 4409.

HALBERSTAM, DAVID. 5856. Shepherd, Allen. "Functions of the Flashback in David Halberstam's *One Very Hot Day*." *NCL* 6(March, 1976): 11-13.

HALPER, ALBERT. 5857. Hart, John E. "Albert Harper's World of the Thirties." *TCL* 9 (1964): 185-195.

HAMILTON, DONALD. 5858. Erisman, Fred. "Western Motifs in the Thrillers of Donald Hamilton." *WAL* 10(1976): 283-292. See also 4351, 4363, 4369, 4375, 4425.

HANSBERRY, LORRAINE. 5859. Anderson, Mary Louise. "Black Matriarchy: Portrayal of Women in Three Plays." *BALF* 10(1976): 93-95.

5860. Farrison, W. Edward. "Lorraine Hansberry's Last Dramas." *CLA* 16(1972): 188-197.

5861. Potter, Vilma R. "New Politics, New Mothers." *CLA* 16(1972): 247-255.

5862. Powell, Bertie J. "The Black Experience in Margaret Walker's *Jubilee* and Lorraine Hansberry's *The Drinking Gourd*." *CLA* 21(1977): 304-312.

HANSON, JOSEPH M. 5863. White, John I. "A Ballad in Search of Its Author." [with text] *WAL* 2(1967): 58-62.

HARRINGTON, ALAN. 5864. Richey, Clarence W. "Rebirth from the Womb: A Note Upon an Analogue for the Concluding Episode in Alan Harrington's *The Secret Swinger*." *NCL* 1(September, 1971): 12-14.

HARRIS, MARK. 5865. "Mark Harris: An Interview." *Con L* 6(1965): 15-26.

See also 4393.

HARTLEY, MARSDEN. 5866. Burlingame, Robert. "Marsden Hartley's *Androscoggin:* Return to Place." *NEQ* 31(1958): 447-462.

HARTMANN, SADAKICHI. 5867. Haslam, Gerald W. "Three Exotics: Yone Nuguchi, Sheisei Tsueneishi, and Sadakichi Hartmann." *CLA* 19(1976): 362-373.

HAWKES, JOHN. 5868. Bischoff, Joan. "John Hawkes' Horses of the Apocalypse." *NCL* 6(September, 1976): 12-14.

5869. Bryer, Jackson R. "John Hawkes and John Barth: Two Bibliographies." *Crit* 6,#2(1963): 86-94.

5870. Cuddy, Lois A. "Functional Pastoralism in *The Blood Oranges.*" *SAF* 3(1975): 15-25.

5871. Greiner, Donald J. "The Thematic Use of Color in John Hawkes' *Second Skin.*" *Con L* 11 (1970): 389-400.

5872. Guerard, Albert J. "The Prose Style of John Hawkes." *Crit* 6,#2(1963): 19-29.

5873. "John Hawkes: An Interview." *Con L* 6(1965): 141-155.

5874. Lavers, Norman. "The Structure of *Second Skin.*" *Novel* 5(1972): 208-214.

5875. LeClair, Thomas. "John Hawkes's 'Death of an Airman' and *Second Skin.*" *NCL* 4 (January, 1974): 2-3.

5876. ----------. "The Unreliability of Innocence: John Hawkes' *Second Skin.*" *JNT* 3 (1973): 32-39.

5877. Matthew, Charles. "The Destructive Vision of John Hawkes." *Crit* 6,#2(1963): 38-52.

5878. Reutlinger, D. P. "*The Cannibal:* The Reality of Victim." *Crit* 6,#2(1963): 30-37.

5879. Rife, David J. "John Hawke's Starfish." *NCL* 7(January, 1977): 15.

5880. Rovit, Earl. "The Fiction of John Hawkes: An Introductory View." *MFS* 10(1964): 150-162.

5881. Scholes, Robert. "A Conversation on *The Blood Oranges.*" *Novel* 5(1972): 197-207.

5882. Shepherd, Allen. "Illumination Through (Anti) Climax: John Hawkes' *The Lime Twig.*" *NCL* 2(March, 1972): 11-13.

5883. Trachtenberg, Alan. "Barth and Hawkes: Two Fabulists." *Crit* 6,#2(1963): 4-18.

5884. Wallace, Ronald. "The Rarer Action: Comedy in John Hawkes's *Second Skin.*" *SN* 9(1977): 169-186.

5885. Warner, John M. "The 'Internalized Quest Romance' in Hawkes' *The Lime Twig.*" *MFS* 19 (1973): 89-96.

HAYDEN, ROBERT. 5886. Faulkner, Howard. "'Transformed by Steeps of Flight': The Poetry of Robert Hayden." *CLA* 21(1977): 282-291.

5887. Fetrow, Fred. "Robert Hayden's 'Frederick Douglass': Form and Meaning in a Modern Sonnet." *CLA* 17(1973): 79-84.

5888. Lewis, Richard O. "A Literary-Psychoanalytic Interpretation of Robert Hayden's 'Market.'" *BALF* 9(1975): 21-24.

5889. O'Sullivan, Maurice J., Jr. "The Mask of Allusion in Robert Hayden's 'The Diver.'" *CLA* 17(1973): 85-92.

5890. Post, Constance J. "Image and Idea in the Poetry of Robert Hayden." *CLA* 20(1976): 164-175.

HECHT, BEN. 5891. White, Ray Lewis. "Sherwood Anderson, Ben Hecht, *Eric Dorn.*" *AL* 49(1977): 238-241.

HEINLEIN, ROBERT. 5892. Perkins, James Ashbrook. "MYCROFTXX Is Alive and Well: The Ambiguous Ending of *The Moon Is a Harsh Mistress.*" *NCL* 5(January, 1975): 13-15.

5893. Schuman, Samuel. "Vladimer Nabokov's *Invitation to a Beheading* and Robert Heinlein's 'They.'" *TCL* 19(1973): 99-106.

5894. Showalter, Dennis E. "An Exercise in Rehabilitation." *Ext* 16(1975): 113-124.

5895. Speer, Diane Parkin. "Heinlein's *The Door into Summer* and *Roderick Random.*" *Ext* 12 (1970): 30-34.

HELLER, JOSEPH. 5896. Blues, Thomas. "The Moral Structure of *Catch-22.*" *SN* 3(1971): 64-79.

5897. Bronson, Daniel Ross. "'Man On a String' *Catch-22.*" *NCL* 7(March, 1977): 8.

5898. Burhans, Clinton S. "Spindrift and the Sea: Structural Patterns and Unifying Elements in *Catch-22.*" *TCL* 19(1973): 239-250.

5899. Doskow, Minna. "The Light Journey Episode in *Catch-22.*" *TCL* 12(1967): 186-193.

5900. Muste, John J. "Better to Die Laughing: The War Novels of Joseph Heller and John Ashmead." *Crit* 5,#2(1962): 16-27.

5901. Nagel, James. "The *Catch-22* Note Cards." *SN* 8(1976): 394-405.

5902. ----------. "Two Brief Manuscript Sketches: Heller's *Catch-22.*" *MFS* 20(1974): 221-224.

5903. Orr, Richard W. "Flat Characters in *Catch-22.*" *NCL* 1(January, 1971): 4.

5904. Pinsker, Sanford. "Heller's *Catch-22:* The Protest of a *Puer Eternis.*" *Crit* 7,#2(1964): 150-162.

5905. Proffitt, Edward. "Slocum's Accident: An American Tragedy." *NCL* 7(May, 1977): 7-8.

5906. Sale, Richard B. "An Interview in New York with Joseph Heller." *SN* 4(1972): 63-74.

5907. Sniderman, Stephen L. "'It Was All Yossaarian's Fault': Power and Responsibility in *Catch-22.*" *TCL* 19(1973): 251-258.

5908. Solomon, Eric. "From Christ in Flanders to *Catch-22:* An Approach to War Fiction." *TSLL* 11(1969): 851-866.

5909. Solomon, Jan. "The Structure of Joseph Heller's *Catch-22.*" *Crit* 9,#2(1967): 46-57.

5910. Stern, J. P. "War and the Comic Muse: *The Good Soldier, Schweik* and *Catch-22.*" *Comp L* 20(1968): 193-216.

5911. Strehle, Susan. "Slocum's Parenthetical Tic: Style as Metaphor in *Something Happened.*" *NCL* 7(December, 1977): 9-10.

5912. Thomas, W. K. "The Mythic Dimension of *Catch-22.*" *TSLL* 15(1973): 189-198.

5913. Waldmeir, Joseph J. "Two Novelists of the Absurd: Heller and Kesey." *Con L* 5(1964): 192-204.

HELLMAN, LILLIAN. 5914. Felheim, Marvin. "*The Autumn Garden:* Mechanics and Dialectics." *MD* 3(1960): 191-195.

5915. Knepler, Henry W. "*The Lark:* Translation vs. Adaptation: A Case History." MD 1 (1958): 15-28.

HEMINGWAY, ERNEST.   5916. Adair, William. "Death the Hunter: A Note on *Across the River and Into the Trees.*" NCL 7(January, 1977): 6-8.

5917. ----------. "*A Farewell to Arms:* A Dream Book.*" JNT 5(1975): 40-56.

5918. ----------. "Landscapes of the Mind: 'Big Two-Hearted River.'" Coll L 4(1977): 144-151.

5919. Allen, Michael J. B. "The Unspanish War in *For Whom the Bell Tolls.*" Con L 13(1972): 204-212.

5920. Anderson, Paul Victor. "Nick's Story in Hemingway's 'Big Two-Hearted River.'" SSF 7 (1970): 564-572.

5921. Armistead, Myra. "Hemingway's 'An Alpine Idyll.'" SSF 11(1977): 255-258.

5922. Atkins, Anselm. "Ironic Action in 'After the Storm.'" SSF 5(1968): 189-192.

5923. Backman, Melvin. "Hemingway: The Matador and the Crucified." MFS 1,#3(1955): 2-11.

5924. Baker, Carlos. "The Slopes of Kilimanjaro: A Biographical Perspective." *Novel* 1 (1967): 19-23.

5925. Barbour, James. "'The Light of the World': Hemingway's Comedy of Errors." NCL 7 (December, 1977): 5-8.

5926. ----------. "'The Light of the World': The Real Ketchel and the Real Light." SSF 13 (1976): 17-23.

5927. Beck, Warren. "The Shorter Happy Life of Mrs. Macomber." MFS 1,#4(1955): 28-37.

5928. ----------. "The Shorter Happy Life of Mrs. Macomber—1955, 1957." MFS 21(1975): 363-385.

5929. Beebe, Maurice. "Criticism of Ernest Hemingway: A Selected Checklist with an Index to Studies of Separate Works." MFS 1,#3(1955): 36-45.

5930. Beebe, Maurice, and John Feaster. "Criticism of Ernest Hemingway: A Selected Checklist." MFS 14(1968): 337-369.

5931. Benert, Annette. "Survival through Irony: Hemingway's 'A Clean, Well-Lighted Place.'" SSF 11(1974): 181-187.

5932. Bennett, Warren. "Character, Irony, and Resolution in 'A Clean, Well-Lighted Place.'" AL 42(1970): 70-79.

5933. Bernard, Kenneth. "Hemingway's 'Indian Camp.'" SSF 2(1965): 291.

5934. Brenner, Gerry. "Epic Machinery in Hemingway's *For Whom the Bell Tolls.*" MFS 16 (1970): 491-504.

5935. Burhans, Clinton S., Jr. "The Complex Unity of *In Our Time.*" MFS 14(1967): 313-328.

5936. ----------. "Hemingway and Vonnegut: Diminishing Vision in a Dying Age." MFS 21(1975): 173-191.

5937. ----------. "*The Old Man and the Sea:* Hemingway's Tragic Vision of Man." AL 31(1960): 446-455.

5938. Burnam, Tom. "Primitivism and Masculinity in the Work of Hemingway." MFS 1,#3(1955): 20-24.

5939. Canady, Nicholas, Jr. "Is There Any Light in Hemingway's 'The Light of the World.'"

SSF 3(1965): 75-76.

5940. Carlisle, E. Fred. "The Triple Vision of Nick Carraway." MFS 11(1965): 351-360.

5941. Carpenter, Frederic I. "Hemingway Achieves the Fifth Dimension." PMLA 69(1954): 711-718.

5942. Clendenning, John. "Hemingway's Gods, Dead and Alive." TSLL 3(1962): 489-502.

5943. Cochran, Robert W. "Circularity in *The Sun Also Rises.*" MFS 14(1968): 297-305.

5944. Colvert, James B. "Ernest Hemingway's Morality in Action." AL 27(1955): 372-385.

5945. Cooperman, Stanley. "Hemingway's Blue-eyed Boy: Robert Jordan and 'Purging Ecstasy.'" *Criticism* 8(1966): 87-96.

5946. Crane, John Kenny. "Crossing the Bar Twice." Post-Mortem Consciousness in Bierce, Hemingway, and Golding." SSF 6(1969): 361-376.

5947. Davies, Phillips G. and Rosemary R. "Hemingway's 'Fifty Grand' and the Jack Britton-Mickey Walker Prize Fight." AL 37(1965): 251-258.

5948. Davis, Robert Murray. "'If you did not go forward': Process and Stasis in *A Farewell to Arms.*" SN 2(1970): 305-311.

5949. Davidson, Arnold E. "The Dantean Perspective in Hemingway's *A Farewell to Arms.*" JNT 3(1973): 121-130.

5950. Davison, Richard A. "Carelessness and the Cincinnati Reds in *The Old Man and the Sea.*" NCL 1(January, 1971): 11-12.

5951. Donaldson, Scott. "Hemingway's Morality of Compensation." AL 43(1971): 399-420.

5952. Doody, Terrence. "Hemingway's Style and Jake's Narration." JNT 4(1974): 212-225.

5953. Dussinger, Gloria R. "'The Snows of Kilimanjaro': Harry's Second Chance." SSF 5(1967): 54-59.

5954. Eby, Cecil D. "The Real Robert Jordan." AL 38(1966): 380-386.

5955. Evans, Oliver. "The Arrow Wounds of Count Mippipopoulos." PMLA 77(1962): 175.

5956. ----------. "'The Snows of Kilimanjaro': A Revaluation." PMLA 76(1961): 601-607.

5957. Evans, Robert. "Hemingway and the Pale Cast of Thought." AL 38(1966): 161-176.

5958. Farquhar, Robin H. "Dramatic Structure in the Novels of Ernest Hemingway." MFS 14(1968): 271-282.

5959. Flanagan, John T. "Hemingway's Debt to Sherwood Anderson." JEGP 54(1955): 507-520.

5960. Flora, Joseph M. "Biblical Allusion in 'The Old Man and the Sea.'" SSF 10(1973): 143-147.

5961. ----------. "A Closer Look at the Young Nick Adams and His Father." SSF 14(1977): 75-78.

5962. ----------. "Hemingway's 'Up in Michigan.'" SSF 6(1969): 465-466.

5963. Freedman, Richard. "Hemingway's Spanish Civil War Dispatches." TSLL 1(1959): 171-180.

5964. Fuchs, Daniel. "Ernest Hemingway: Literary Critic." AL 36(1965): 431-451.

5965. Gelfant, Blanche. "Language as a Moral Code in *A Farewell to Arms.*" MFS 9(1963): 173-176.

5966. Glifford, William. "Ernest Hemingway: The Monsters and the Critics." MFS 14(1968): 255-

270.

5967. Graham, John. "Ernest Hemingway: The Meaning of Style." *MFS* 6(1960): 298-313.

5968. Green, James L. "Symbolic Sentences in 'Big Two Hearted River.'" *MFS* 14(1968): 307-312.

5969. Grimes, Larry. "Night Terror and Morning Calm: A Reading of Hemingway's 'Indian Camp' as Sequel to 'Three Shots.'" *SSF* 12(1975): 413-415.

5970. Groseclose, Barbara S. "Hemingway's 'The Revolutionist': An Aid to Interpretation." *MFS* 17(1971): 565-570.

5971. Hagopian, John V. "Tidying Up Hemingway's 'Clean, Well-Lighted Place.'" *SSF* 1(1964): 140-146.

5972. Halliday, E. M. "Hemingway's Ambiguity: Symbolism and Irony." *AL* 28(1956): 1-22.

5973. Halverson, John. "Christian Resonance in *The Old Man and the Sea*." *ELN* 2(1964): 50-54.

5974. Hattam, Edward. "Hemingway's 'An Alpine Idyll.'" *MFS* 12(1966): 261-264.

5975. Hayes, Curtis W. "A Study in Prose Styles: Edward Gibbon and Ernest Hemingway." *TSLL* 7(1966): 371-386.

5976. Hipkiss, Robert. "Ernest Hemingway's *The Things That I Know*." *TCL* 19(1973): 275-282.

5977. Hoffman, Frederick J. "No Beginning and No End: Hemingway and Death." *EIC* 3(1953): 73-84.

5978. Holder, Alan. "The Other Hemingway." *TCL* 9(1963): 153-157.

5979. Holland, Robert B. "Macomber and the Critics." *SSF* 5(1968): 171-178.

5980. Holman, C. Hugh. "Hemingway and Emerson: Notes on the Continuity of an Aesthetic Tradition." *MFS* 1,#3(1955): 12-16.

5981. Howell, John M. "Hemingway's Riddle and Kilimanjaro's Reusch." *SSF* 8(1971): 469-471.

5982. ----------. "The Macomber Case." *SSF* 4(1967): 171-172.

5983. Hurley, C. Harold. "The Attribution of the Waiter's Second Speech in Hemingway's 'A Clean, Well-Lighted Place.'" *SSF* 13(1976): 81-85.

5984. Hurwitz, Harold M. "Hemingway's Tutor, Ezra Pound." *MFS* 17(1971): 469-482.

5985. Inglis, David L. "Morley Callaghan and the Hemingway Boxing Legend." *NCL* 4(September, 1974): 4-7.

5986. Johnson, Robert D. "Hemingway's 'How Do You Like It Now, Gentlemen?': A Possible Source." *AL* 45(1973): 114-117.

5987. Johnston, Kenneth G. "Hemingway and Mantegna: The Bitter Nail Holes." *JNT* 1(1971): 86-94.

5988. ----------. "Hemingway's 'Wine of Wyoming': Disappointment in Americas." *WAL* 9(1974): 159-167.

5989. ----------. "The Star in Hemingway's *The Old Man and the Sea*." *AL* 42(1970): 388-391.

5990. Kerrigan, William. "Something Funny About Hemingway's Count." *AL* 46(1974): 87-93.

5991. Kinnamon, Keneth. "Hemingway, the *Corrida*, and Spain." *TSLL* 1(1959): 44-61.

5992. Knieger, Bernard. "The Concept of Maturity in Hemingway's Short Stories." *CLA* 8(1964): 149-156.

5993. Kobler, J. F. "Confused Chronology in *The Sun Also Rises*." *MFS* 13(1967): 517-520.

5994. Kruse, Horst H. "Ernest Hemingway's 'The End of Something': Its Independence as a Short Story and Its Place in the 'Education of Nick Adams.'" *SSF* 4(1967): 152-166.

5995. Kvam, Wayne. "Zuckmayer, Hilbert, and Hemingway." *PMLA* 91(1976): 194-205.

5996. Lair, Robert L. "Hemingway and Cezanne: An Indebtedness." *MFS* 6(1960): 165-168.

5997. Lauter, Paul. "Plato's Stepchildren: Gatsby and Cohn." *MFS* 9(1963): 338-346.

5998. Lehan, Richard. "Camus and Hemingway." *Con L* 1,#2(1960): 37-48.

5999. Leigh, David J., S. J. "'In Our Time': The Interchapters as Structural Guides to a Psychological Pattern." *SSF* 12(1975): 1-8.

6000. Leiter, Louis H. "Neural Projections in Hemingway's 'On the Quai at Smyrna.'" *SSF* 5(1968): 384-386.

6001. Lewis, Robert W., Jr. "The Survival of Hemingway." *JML* 1(1971): 446-453.

6002. Lid, R. W. "Hemingway and the Need for Speech." *MFS* 8(1962): 401-407.

6003. Light, James F. "The Religion of Death in *A Farewell to Arms*." *MFS* 7(1961): 169-172.

6004. Lisca, Peter. "The Structure of Hemingway's *Across the River and Into the Trees*." *MFS* 12(1966): 232-250.

6005. Lodge, David. "Hemingway's Clean, Well-Lighted, Puzzling Place." *EIC* 21(1971): 33-56.

6006. Longmire, Samuel E. "Hemingway's Praise of Dick Sisler in *The Old Man and the Sea*." *AL* 42(1970): 96-98.

6007. MacDonald, Scott. "The Confusing Dialogue in Hemingway's 'A Clean, Well-Lighted Place': A Final Word?" *SAF* 1(1973): 93-101.

6008. ----------. "Hemingway's 'The Snows of Kilimanjaro': Three Critical Problems." *SSF* 11(1974): 67-74.

6009. ----------. "Implications of Narrative Perspective in Hemingway's 'Now I Lay Me.'" *SAF* 1(1973): 213-220.

6010. ----------. "Implications of Narrative Perspective in Hemingway's 'The Undefeated.'" *JNT* 2(1972): 1-15.

6011. Macnaughton, W. R. "Maisie's Grace Under Pressure: Some Thoughts on James and Hemingway." *MFS* 22(1976): 153-164.

6012. Martine, James J. "Hemingway's 'Fifty Grand': The Other Fight(s)." *JML* 2(1971): 123-127.

6013. ----------. "A Little Light on Hemingway's 'The Light of the World.'" *SSF* 7(1970): 465-467.

6014. May, Charles E. "Is Hemingway's 'Well-Lighted Place' Really Clean Now?" *SSF* 8(1971): 326-330.

6015. McIlvaine, Robert M. "A Literary Source for the Caesarean Section in *A Farewell to Arms*." *AL* 43(1971): 444-447.

6016. Merrill, Robert. "Tragic Form in *A Farewell to Arms*." *AL* 45(1974): 571-579.

6017. Monteiro, George. "The Limits of Professionalism: A Sociological Approach to Faulkner, Fitzgerald, and Hemingway." *Criticism* 15(1973): 145-155.

6018. ----------. "The Reds, the White Sox, and *The Old Man and the Sea*." *NCL* 4(May, 1974): 7-9.

6019. Moore, L. Hugh. "Mrs. Hirsch and Mrs. Bell in Hemingway's 'The Killers.'" *MFS* 11(1965): 427-428.

6020. Moses, W. R. "Water, Water Everywhere: *Old Man* and *A Farewell to Arms*." *MFS* 5(1959): 172-174.

6021. Motola, Gabriel. "Hemingway's Code: Literature and Life." *MFS* 10(1964): 319-329.

6022. Oldsey, Bernard. "The Genesis of *A Farewell to Arms*." *SAF* 5(1977): 175-185.

6023. ----------. "Hemingway's Old Men." *MFS* 1,#3(1955): 31-35.

6024. ----------. "Of Hemingway's *Arms* and the Man." *Coll L* 1(1974): 174-189.

6025. ----------. "The Sense of an Ending in *A Farewell to Arms*." *MFS* 23(1977): 491-510.

6026. ----------. "The Snows of Ernest Hemingway." *Con L* 4(1963): 172-198.

6027. Parker, Stephen Jan. "Hemingway's Revival in the Soviet Union: 1955-1962." *AL* 35(1964): 485-501.

6028. Prizel, Yuri. "Hemingway in Soviet Literary Criticism." *AL* 44(1972): 445-456.

6029. Reynolds, Michael J. "Two Hemingway Sources for 'In Our Time.'" *SSF* 9(1972): 81-86.

6030. Richardson, H. Edward. "The 'Hemingwaves' in Faulkner's *Wild Palms*." *MFS* 4(1958): 357-360.

6031. Roberts, John J. "In Defense of Krebs." *SSF* 13(1976): 515-518.

6032. Rodgers, Paul C., Jr. "Levels of Irony in Hemingway's 'The Gambler, the Nun, and the Radio.'" *SSF* 7(1970): 439-449.

6033. Ross, Morton L. "Bill Gorton, the Preacher in *The Sun Also Rises*." *MFS* 18(1972): 517-527.

6034. Rouch, John S. "Jake Barnes as Narrator." *MFS* 11(1965): 361-370.

6035. Russell, H. K. "The Catharsis in *A Farewell to Arms*." *MFS* 1,#3(1955): 25-30.

6036. Ryan, William James. "Uses of Irony in *To Have and Have Not*." *MFS* 14(1968): 329-336.

6037. Schneider, Daniel J. "Hemingway's *A Farewell to Arms*: The Novel as Pure Poetry." *MFS* 14(1968): 283-296.

6038. Shelton, Frank W. "The Family in Hemingway's Nick Adams Stories." *SSF* 11(1974): 303-305.

6039. Shepherd, Allen. "Hudson's Cats in Hemingway's *Islands in the Stream*." *NCL* 2(September, 1972): 3-6.

6040. Slatoff, Walter J. "The 'Great Sin' in *For Whom the Bell Tolls*." *JNT* 7(1977): 142-148.

6041. Smith, Julian. "'A Canary for One': Hemingway in the Wasteland." *SSF* 5(1968): 355-361.

6042. ----------. "Hemingway and the Thing Left Out." *JML* 1(1970): 169-182.

6043. ----------. "More Products of the Hemingway Industry." *SSF* 7(1970): 638-646.

6044. Stein, William Bysshe. "Love and Lust in Hemingway's Short Stories." *TSLL* 3(1961): 234-242.

6045. ----------. "Ritual in Hemingway's 'Big Two-Hearted River.'" *TSLL* 1(1960): 555-561.

6046. Stephens, Robert O. "Hemingway and Stendahl: The Matrix of *A Farewell to Arms*." *PMLA* 88(1973): 271-280.

6047. ----------. "Hemingway's Old Man and the Iceberg." *MFS* 7(1961): 295-304.

6048. ----------. "Hemingway's Riddle of Kilimanjaro: Idea and Image." *AL* 32(1960): 84-87.

6049. ----------. "Language Magic and Reality in *For Whom the Bell Tolls*." *Criticism* 14(1972): 151-164.

6050. Stephens, Robert O., and James Ellis. "Hemingway, Fitzgerald and the Riddle of 'Henry's Bicycle.'" *ELN* 5(1967): 46-49.

6051. Stone, Edward. "Hemingway's Mr. Frazer: From Revolution to Radio." *JML* 1(1971): 375-388.

6052. ----------. "Some Questions About Hemingway's 'The Killers.'" *SSF* 5(1967): 12-17.

6053. Stuckey, W. J. "'The Killers' as Experience." *JNT* 5(1975): 128-135.

6054. ----------. "*The Sun Also Rises* on Its Own Ground." *JNT* 6(1976): 224-232.

6055. Sylvester, Bickford. "Hemingway's Extended Vision: *The Old Man and the Sea*." *PMLA* 81(1966): 130-138.

6056. ----------. "'They Went Through this Fiction Every Day': Informed Illusion in *The Old Man and the Sea*." *MFS* 12(1966): 473-476.

6057. Tomaneck, Jurgen, K. A. "Hemingway's Riddle of Kilimanjaro." *SSF* 7(1970): 326-327.

6058. Twitchell, James. "The Swamp in Hemingway's 'Big Two-Hearted River.'" *SSF* 9(1972): 275-276.

6059. Vanderbilt, Kermit. "*The Sun Also Rises*: Time Uncertain." *TCL* 15(1969): 153-154.

6060. Wagner, Linda W. "Juxtaposition in Hemingway's 'In Our Time.'" *SSF* 12(1975): 243-252.

6061. ----------. "The Marinating of *For Whom the Bell Tolls*." *JML* 2(1972): 533-546.

6062. ----------. "The Poem of Santiago and Manolin." *MFS* 19(1973): 517-529.

6063. ----------. "*The Sun Also Rises*: One Debt to Imagism." *JNT* 2(1972): 88-98.

6064. Walker, Robert G. "Anselmo, Atonement, and Hemingway's *For Whom the Bell Tolls*." *NCL* 7(March, 1977): 7-8.

6065. ----------. "Irony and Allusion in Hemingway's 'After the Storm.'" *SSF* 13(1976): 374-376.

6066. Weeks, Louis E., Jr. "Two Types of Tension: Art vs. Campcraft in Hemingway's 'Big Two-Hearted River.'" *SSF* 11(1974): 433-434.

6067. Weeks, Robert P. "The Power of the Tacit in Crane and Hemingway." *MFS* 8(1962): 415-418.

6068. White, Ray Lewis. "Hemingway's Private Explanation of *The Torrents of Spring*." *MFS* 13(1967): 261-263.

6069. White, William. "Hemingway as Translator: Kiki's Grandmother." *ELN* 4(1966): 128-132.

6070. Wilson, G. R., Jr. "Incarnation and Redemption in *The Old Man and the Sea*." *SSF* 14(1977): 369-373.

6071. Wyrick, Green D. "Hemingway and Bergson: The *Elan Vital*." *MFS* 1,#3(1955): 17-19.

6072. Yokelson, Joseph B. "A Dante-Parallel in Hemingway's 'A Way You'll Never Be.'" *AL* 41 (1969): 270-280.

6073. Young, Philip. "'Big World Out There': The Nick Adams Stories." *Novel* 6(1972): 5-19.

6074. ----------. "Hemingway's Manuscripts: The Vault Reconsidered." *SAF* 2(1974): 3-12.

6075. ----------. "Scott Fitzgerald on His Thirtieth Birthday Sends a Small Gift to Ernest Hemingway." *MFS* 14(1968): 229-230.

See also 111, 436, 618, 5505.

HERBERT, FRANK. 6076. Ower, John. "Idea and Imagery in Herbert's *Dune.*" *Ext* 15(1974): 129-139.

6077. Parkinson, Robert C. "*Dune*—An Unfinished Tetralogy." *Ext* 13(1971): 16-24.

6078. Stover, Leon E. "Is Jaspers Beer Good for You? Mass Society and Counter Culture in Herbert's *Santaroga Barrier.*" *Ext* 17(1976): 160-167.

HERGESHEIMER, JOSEPH. 6079. Napier, James J. "Letters of Sinclair Lewis to Joseph Hergesheimer, 1915-1992." *AL* 38(1966): 236-246.

HERLIHY, JAMES, LEO. 6080. Griffith, Benjamin W. "Midnight Cowboys and Edwardian Narrators: James Leo Herlihy's Contrasting Voices." *NCL* 2(January, 1972): 6-8.

HERRICK, ROBERT. 6081. Carlson, Doulgas O. "Robert Herrick: An Addendum." *ALR* 1,#3(1968): 67-68.

6082. Franklin, Phylis. "A Handlist of the Robert Herrick Papers of the University of Chicago." *ALR* 8(1975): 109-154.

6083. ----------. "The Influence of William James on Robert Herrick's Early Fiction." *ALR* 7 (L974): 395-402.

6084. ----------. "Robert Herrick as Novelist and Journalist." *ALR* 3(1970): 393-394.

6085. Genthe, Charles V. "Robert Herrick (1868-1938)." [bibliography] *ALR* 1,#1(1967): 56-60.

6086. Horlacher, Friedrich. "An Annotated Checklist of Robert Herrick's Contributions to the *Chicago Tribune.*" *ALR* 10(1977): 191-210.

6087. Taylor, Walter Fuller. "The Humanism of Robert Herrick." *AL* 28(1956): 287-301.

HERSEY, JOHN. 6088. Haltresht, Michael. "Dreams as a Characterization Device in Hersey's *White Lotus.*" *NCL* 1(May, 1971): 4-5.

6089. ----------. "*The Wall:* John Hersey's Interpretation of the Ghetto Experience." *NCL* 2 (January, 1972): 10-11.

6090. Plank, Robert. "*The Child Buyer:* A Review." *Ext* 2(1961): 40-41.

6091. Reising, R. W. "The Setting of Hersey's *Too Far to Walk.*" *NCL* 1(September, 1971): 10-11.

See also 203.

HEYWARD, DUBOSE. 6092. Durham, Frank. "Dubose Heyward's 'Lost' Short Stories." *SSF* 2 (1965): 157-163.

6093. ----------. "The Reputed Demises of Uncle Tom; or, The Treatment of the Negro in Fiction by Southern Authors in the 1920's." *SLJ* 2, #2(1970): 26-50.

6094. Slavick, William H. "Going to School to DuBose Heyward." *SLI* 7,#2(1974): 105-129.

See also 4402.

HIMES, CHESTER. 6095. Lee, A. Robert. "Real and Imagined Violence in the Novels of Chester Himes." *BALF* 10(1976): 13-22.

6096. Margolies, Edward. "Experience of the Black Expatriate Writer: Chester Himes." *CLA* 15(1972): 421-427.

6097. Reckley, Ralph. "The Oedipal Complex and Intraracial Conflict in Chester Himes' *The Third Generation.*" *CLA* 21(1977): 275-281.

6098. ----------. "The Use of the Doppelganger or Double in Chester Himes' *Lonely Crusade.*" *CLA* 20(1977): 448-458.

See also 4335, 4407, 6531.

HOAGLAND, EDWARD. 6099. Fontana, Ernest L. "The Territory of the Past in Hoagland's *Notes form the Century Before.*" *WAL* 9(1974): 45-51.

HOUGH, EMERSON. 6100. Wylder, Delbert E. "Emerson Hough as Conservationist and Muckraker." *WAL* 12(1977): 93-109.

6101. ----------. "Emerson Hough's *Heart's Desire:* Revisit to Eden." *WAL* 1(1966): 44-54.

HOWARD, SIDNEY. 6102. Meserve, Walter J. "Sidney Howard and the Social Drama of the Twenties." *MD* 6(1963): 256-266.

HROGAN, PAUL. 6103. McConnell, Richard M. M. and Susan Frey. "Paul Horgan: A Bibliography." *WAL* 6(1971): 137-150.

HUGHES, LANDSTON. 6104. Bontemps, Arra. "Memories of Langston Hughes." *BALF* 1,#2(1967): 12-13.

6105. Cobb, Martha K. "Concepts of Blackness in the Poetry of Nicolás Guillén, Jacques Roumain and Langston Hughes." *CLA* 18(1974): 262-272.

6106. Dandridge, Rita B. "The Black Woman as a Freedom Fighter in Langston Hughes' *Simple's Uncle Sam.*" *CLA* 18(1974): 273-283.

6107. Davis, Arthur P. "Langston Hughes: Cool Poet." *CLA* 11(1968): 280-296.

6108. Dickinson, Donald. "Working with Langston Hughes." *BALF* 1,#2(1967): 13-15.

6109. Emanuel, James A. "The Literary Experiments of Langston Hughes." *CLA* 11(1968): 335-334.

6110. Farrison, W. Edward. "Langston Hughes: Poet of the Negro Renaissance." *CLA* 15(1972): 401-410.

6111. Garber, Earlene D. "Form as a Complement to Content in Three of Langston Hughes' Poems." *BALF* 5(1971): 137-139.

6112. Hudson, Theodore R. "Langston Hughes' Last Volume of Verse." *CLA* 11(1968): 345-348.

6113. Jackson, Blyden. "A Word About Simple." *CLA* 11(1968): 310-318.

6114. Jones, Harry L. "A Danish Tribute to Langston Hughes." *CLA* 11(1968): 331-334.

6115. Klotman, Phyllis. "Jesse B. Semple and the Narrative Art of Langston Hughes." *JNT* 3 (1973): 66-75.

6116. Mathews, John F. "Langston Hughes as Translator." *CLA* 11(1968): 319-330.

6117. Miller, R. Baxter. "'Even After I Was Dead': *The Big Sea*—Paradox, Preservation, and Holistic Time." *BALF* 11(1977): 39-45.

6118. ----------. "'No Crystal Stair': Unity, Archetype, and Symbol in Langston Hughes's Poems on Women." *BALF* 9(1975): 109-114.

6119. O'Daniel, Therman B. "Langston Hughes: A Selected Classified Bibliography." *CLA* 11(1968): 349-366.

6120. Presley, James. "Langston Hughes, War Correspondent." *JML* 5(1976): 481-491.

6121. Schatt, Stanley. "Langston Hughes: The Minstrel as Artificer." *JML* 4(1974): 115-120.

6122. Smith, Raymond. "Langston Hughes: Evolution of the Poetic Persona." *SLI* 7,#2(1974): 49-64.

6123. Turner, Darwin T. "Langston Hughes as Playwright." *CLA* 11(1968): 297-309.

6124. Waldron, Edward. "The Blues Poetry of Langston Hughes." *BALF* 5(1971): 140-149.

6125. Williams, Melvin G. "The Gospel According to Semple." *BALF* 11(1977): 46-48.

6126. ----------. "Langston Hughes's Jesse B. Semple: A Black Walter Mitty." *BALF* 10(1976): 66-69.

See also 4316, 4351, 4369, 4407, 4425.

HUGO, RICHARD. 6127. Garber, Frederick. "Large Man in the Mountains: The Recent Work of Richard Hugo." *WAL* 10(1975): 205-218.

HUNEKER, JAMES G. 6128. Rottenberg, Annette T. "Aesthete in America: The Short Stories of James Gibbons Huneker." *SSF* 2(1965): 358-366.

6129. Schwab, Arnold T. "Huneker's Hidden Birthdate." *AL* 23(1951): 351-354.

6130. ----------. "Irish Author and American Critic: George Moore and James Huneker." *NCF* 8(1954): 256-271; and 9(1955): 22-37.

6131. ----------. "James Huneker on Whitman: A Newly Discovered Essay." *AL* 38(1966): 208-218.

6132. ----------. "James Huneker's Criticism of American Literature." *AL* 29(1957): 64-78.

6133. ----------. "Joseph Conrad's American Friend: Correspondence with James Huneker." *MP* 52(1955): 222-232.

HURST, FANNIE. See 6134.

HURSTON, ZORA NEALE. 6134. Burke, Virginia M. "Zora Neale Hurston and Fannie Hurst as They Saw Each Other." *CLA* 20(1977): 435-447.

6135. Giles, James R. "The Significance of Time in Zora Neale Hurston's *Their Eyes Were Watching God*." *BALF* 6(1972): 52-53, 60.

6136. Howard, Lillie P. "Marriage: Zora Neale Hurston's System of Values." *CLA* 21(1977): 256-268.

6137. Rayson, Ann L. *"Dust Tracks on a Road:* Zora Neale Hurston and the Form of Black Autobiography." *BALF* 7(1973): 39-45.

6138. Schwalbenberg, Peter. "Time as Point of View in Zora Neale Hurston's *Their Eyes Were Watching God*." *BALF* 10(1976): 104-105, 107-108.

6139. Walker, S. Jay. "Zora Neale Hurston's *Their Eyes Were Watching God*: Black Novel of Sexism." *MFS* 20(1974): 519-527.

See also 4430.

INGE, WILLIAM. 6140. Armato, Philip M. "The Bum as Scapegoat in William Inge's *Picnic*." *WAL* 10(1976): 273-282.

JACKSON, SHIRLEY. 6141. Hoffman, Steven K. "Individuation and Character Development in the Fiction of Shirley Jackson." *HSL* 8(1976): 190-208.

6142. Nebeker, Helen E. "'The Lottery': Symbolic Tour de Force." *AL* 46(1974): 100-107.

JARRELL, RANDALL. 6143. Quinn, Sister Bernetta, O. S. F. "Warren and Jarrell: The Remembered Child." *SLJ* 8,#2(1976): 24-40.

JEFFERS, ROBINSON. 6144. Bluestone, Stephen. "Robinson Jeffers and the Prophets: On *The Book of Jeremiah* and 'The Inhumanist.'" *NCL* 5(September, 1975): 2-3.

6145. Brophy, Robert J. "Jeffers' 'Cawdor' and the Hippolytus Story." *WAL* 7(1972): 171-178.

6146. Carpenter, Frederic I. "'Post Mortem': 'The Poet in Dead.'" *WAL* 12(1977): 3-10.

6147. Carpenter, Frederic L. "Robinson Jeffers Today: Beyond Good and Beneath Evil." *AL* 49(1977): 86-96.

6148. Griffith, Benjamin W. "Robinson Jeffers' 'The Blook Sire' and Stephen Crane's 'War is Kind.'" *NCL* 3(January, 1973): 14-15.

6149. Keller, Karl. "California, Yankees, and the Death of God: The Allegory in Jeffers' *Roan Stallion*." *TSLL* 12(1970): 111-120.

6150. Lockard, E. N. "A Visit to Robinson Jeffers in 1945." *ELN* 12(1974): 120-123.

6151. Nickerson, Edward. "Robinson Jeffers and the Paeon." *WAL* 10(1975): 189-193.

6152. ----------. "Robinson Jeffers: Apocalypse and His 'Inevitable Place.'" *WAL* 12(1977): 111-122.

JOHNSON, GEORGIA DOULGAS. See 622.

JOHNSON, HELENE. See 622.

JOHNSON, JAMES WELDON. 6153. Amann, Clarence A. "Three Negro Classics: An Estimate." *BALF* 4(1970): 113-119.

6154. Fleming, Robert E. "Irony as a Key to Johnson's *Autobiography of an Ex-Coloured Man*." *AL* 43(1971): 83-96.

6155. Kostelanetz, Richard. "The Politics of Passing: The Fiction of James Weldon Johnson." *BALF* 3(1969): 22-24.

6156. Larson, Charles R. "Contemporary Themes in Johnson's *Autobiography of an Ex-Coloured Man*." *BALF* 4(1970): 120-126.

6157. Ross, Stephen M. "Audience and Irony in Johnson's *The Autobiography of an Ex-Coloured Man*." *CLA* 18(1974): 198-210.

See also 4335, 4391, 4396, 4401.

JONG, ERICA. 6158. Jong, Erica. "Writing a First Novel." *TCL* 20(1974): 262-269.

JONES, GAYL. See 4430.

JONES, LEROI. 6159. Adams, George R. "'My Christ' in *Dutchman*." *CLA* 15(1971): 54-58.

6160. Bradey, Owen E. "Baraka's *Experimental Death Unit #1*: Plan for (R)Evolution." *BALF* 9 (1975): 59-61.

6161. Brown, Lloyd W. "LeRoi Jones as Novelist: Theme and Structure in *The System of Dante's Hell*." *BALF* 7(1973): 132-142.

6162. Ferguson, John. "*Dutchman* and *The Slave*." *MD* 13(1970): 398-405.

6163. Hagopian, John V. "Another Ride on Jones's Subway." *CLA* 21(1977): 269-274.

6164. Jackson, Esther M. "LeRoi Jones (Imamu Amiri Baraka): Form and the Progression of Consciousness." *CLA* 17(1973): 33-56.

6165. Jeffers, Lance. "Bullins, Baraka, and Elder: The Dawn of Grandeur in Black Drama." *CLA* 16(1972): 33-48.

6166. Klinkowitz, Jerome. "LeRoi Jones' *Dutchman* as Drama." *BALF* 7(1973): 123-126.

6167. Martin, Thaddeus. "*Dutchman* Reconsidered." *BALF* 11(1977): 62.

6168. Menchise, Don N. "LeRoi Jones and A Case of Shifting Identies." *CLA* 20(1976): 232-234.

6169. Miller, Jeanne-Marie A. "The Plays of LeRoi Jones." *CLA* 14(1971): 331-339.

6170. Munro, C. Lynn. "LeRoi Jones: A Man in Transition." *CLA* 17(1973): 57-78.

6171. O'Brien, John. "Racial Nightmare and the Search for Self: An Explication of LeRoi Jones' 'A Chase (Aligheri's Dream).'" *BALF* 7(1973): 89-90.

6172. Rice, Julian C. "LeRoi Jones' *Dutchman*: A Reading." *Con L* 12(1971): 42-59.

6173. Taylor, Willene P. "The Fall of Man Theme in Imamu Amiri Baraka's Dutchman." *BALF* 7 (1973): 127-130.

6174. Tener, Robert L. "The Corrupted Warrior Heroes: Amiri Baraka's *The Toilet*." *MD* 17 (1974): 207-215.

6175. Witherington, Paul. "Exorcism and Baptism in LeRoi Jones's *The Toilet*." *MD* 15(1972): 159-163.

See also 4311, 4335, 4442, 4350, 4351, 4363, 4366, 4369, 4371, 4375.

JONES, MADISON. 6176. Heirs, John T. "Buried Graveyards: Warren's *Flood* and Jones' *A Buried Land*." *EL* 2(1975): 97-104.

JONES, RUFUS. 6177. Friedrich, Gerhard. "A Major Influence on Theodore Dreiser's *The Bulwark*." *AL* 29(1957): 180-193.

KAUFMAN, GEORGE. 6178. Freedley, George. "George S. Kaufman: 1889-1962." *MD* 6(1963): 241-244.

KELLEY, WILLIAM M. 6179. Faulkner, Howard. "The Uses of Tradition: William Melvin Kelley's *A Different Drummer*." *MFS* 21(1975): 535-542.

6180. Klotman, Phyllis R. "An Examination of the Black Confidence Man in Two Black Novels: *The Man Who Cried I Am* and *dem*." *AL* 44(1973): 596-611.

6181. Weyant, Jill. "The Kelley Saga: Violence in America." *CLA* 19(1975): 210-220.

6182. Williams, Gladys M. "Technique as Evaluation of Subject in *A Different Drummer*." *CLA* 19(1975): 221-237.

See also 4335, 4415.

KELLY, GEORGE. 6183. Wills, Arthur. "The Kelly Play." *MD* 6(1963): 245-255.

KENNEDY, ADRIENNE. 6184. Benston, Kimberly W. "*Cities in Bezique*: Adrienne Kennedy's Expressionistic Vision." *CLA* 20(1976): 235-244.

6185. Brown, Lorraine. "'For the Characters Are Myself': Adrienne Kennedy's Funnyhouse of a Negro." *BALF* 9(1975): 86-88.

See also 4351, 4363, 4372.

KENNEDY, JOHN F. 6186. Bradley, Pearl G. "A Rhetorical Analysis of John F. Kennedy's Civil Rights Speech." *CLA* 9(1965): 171-176.

KEROUAC, JACK. 6187. Dardess, George. "The Delicate Dynamics of Friendship: A Reconsideration of Kerouac's *On The Road*." *AL* 46(1974): 200-206.

6188. Hull, Keith N. "A Dharma Bum Goes West to Meet the East." *WAL* 11(1977): 321-329.

6189. Leer, Norman. "Three American Novels and Contemporary Society: A Search for Commitment." *Con L* 3,#3(1962): 67-86.

KESEY, KEN. 6190. Atkinson, Michael. "One Flew Over the Fiction Course." *Coll L* 2(1975): 120-127.

6191. Forrey, Robert. "Ken Kesey's Psychopathic Savior: A Rejoinder." *MFS* 21(1975): 222-230.

6192. Foster, John Wilson. "Hustling to Some Purpose: Kesey's *One Flew Over the Cuckoo's Nest*." *WAL* 9(1974): 115-129.

6193. Kunz, Don R. "Mechanistic and Totemistic Symbolization in Kesey's *One Flew Over the Cuckoo's Nest*." *SAF* 3(1975): 65-82.

6194. Martin, Terence. "*One Flew Over the Cuckoo's Nest* and the High Cost of Living." *MFS* 19(1973): 43-56.

6195. Waldmeir, Joseph J. "Two Novelists of the Absurd: Heller and Kesey." *Con L* 5(1964): 192-204.

6196. Weixlman, Joseph. "Ken Kesey: A Bibliography." *WAL* 10(1975): 219-231.

KILLENS, JOHN OLIVER. 6197. Lehman, Paul. "The Development of a Black Psyche: An Interview with John Oliver Killens." *BALF* 11(1977): 83-89.

See also 4383.

KINNELL, GALWAY. 6198. Davis, William V. "'The Rank Flavor of Blood': Galway Kinnell's 'The Bear.'" *NCL* 7(March, 1977): 4-6.

KNOWLES, JOHN. 6199. Halio, Jay L. "John Knowles's Short Novels." *SSF* 1(1964): 107-112.

6200. Kennedy, Ian. "Dual Perspective Narrative and the Character of Phineas in *A Separate Peace*." *SSF* 11(1974): 353-359.

6201. Mellard, James M. "Counterpoint and 'Double Vision' in *A Separate Peace*." *SSF* 4(1967): 127-134.

6202. Travis, Mildred K. "Mirror Images in *A Separate Peace* and *Cat and Mouse*." *NCL* 5(September, 1975): 12-15.

6203. Weber, Ronald. "Narrative Method in *A Separate Peace*." *SSF* 3(1965): 63-72.

KORNBLUTH, CYRIL M. 6204. Pohl, Frederick. "Reminiscence: Cyril M. Kornbluth." *Ext* 17(1976): 120-109.

KOSINSKI, JERZY. 6205. Cahill, Daniel J. "Jerzy Kosinski: Retreat from Violence." *TCL* 18 (1972): 121-132.

6206. Coale, Samuel. "The Cinematic Self of Jerzy Kosinski." *MFS* 20(1974): 359-370.

6207. Gogol, John M. "Kosinski's Chance: McLuhan Age Narcissus." *NCL* 1(September, 1971): 8-10.

6208. Hirschberg, Stuart. "Becoming an Object: The Function of Mirrors and Photographs in Kosinski's *The Devil Tree*." *NCL* 4(March, 1974): 14-15.

6209. Richey, Clarence W. "'Being There' and Dasein: A Note on the Philosophical Presupposition Underlying the Novels of Jerzy Kosinski." *NCL* 2(September, 1972): 13-15.

6210. Richter, David H. "The Three Denouements of Jerzy Kosinski's *The Painted Bird*." *Con L* 15(1974): 370-385.

6211. Spendal, R. J. "The Structure of *The Painted Bird*." *JNT* 6(1976): 132-136.

KUBRICK, STANLEY.   6212. Brody, Alan. "*2001*." *HSL* 1(1969): 7-19.

6213. Doyno, Victor A. "'*2001*': Years and Shapes." *HSL* 1(1969): 131-132.

6214. Fenichel, Robert. "Comments on *2001* Symposium." *HSL* 1(1969): 133-135.

6215. Holland, Norman. "*2001*." *HSL* 1(1969): 20-25.

6216. Plank, Robert. "*2001*." *HSL* 1(1969): 26-33.

6217. Rogers, Robert. "*2001*." *HSL* 1(1969): 34-36.

6218. Stacy, Paul. "Cinematic Thought." *HSL* 1(1969): 124-130.

KUNITZ, STANLEY.   6219. Davis, Cynthia. "An Interview with Stanley Kunitz." *Con L* 15 (1974): 1-14.

LAMMING, GEORGE.   6220. Pouchet-Paquet, Sandra. "The Politics of George Lamming's *Natives of My Person*." *CLA* 17(1973): 109-116.

LARDNER, RING.   6221. Lease, Benjamin. "An Evening at the Scott Fitzgeralds': An Unpublished Letter of Ring Lardner." *ELN* 8(1970): 40-42.

6222. Webb, Howard W., Jr. "The Meaning of Ring Lardner's Fiction: A Re-evaluation." *AL* 31 (1960): 434-445.

LARSEN, NELLA.   6223. Lay, Mary M. "Parallels: Henry James's *The Portrait of a Lady* and Nella Larsen's *Quicksand*." *CLA* 20(1977): 475-486.

6224. Thorton, Hortense E. "Sexism as Quagmire: Nella Larsen's *Quicksand*." *CLA* 16 (1973): 285-301.

6225. Youman, Mary Mabel. "Nella Larsen's *Passing*: A Study in Irony." *CLA* 18(1974): 235-241.

LEE, DON L.   6226. Palmer, R. Roderick. "The Poetry of Three Revolutionists: Don L. Lee, Sonia Sanchez, and Nikki Giovanni." *CLA* 15(1971): 25-36.

See also 4311, 4442.

LEE, HARPER.   See 135.

LEE, LESLIE.   See 4351.

LE GUIN, URSULA.   6227. Cogell, Elizabeth Cummins. "Setting as Analogue to Characterization in Ursula Le Guin." *Ext* 18(1977): 131-141.

6228. Remington, Thomas J. "A Touch of Difference, A Touch of Love: Theme in Three Stories by Ursual K. Le Guin." *Ext* 18(1976): 28-41.

LE MAY, ALAN.   See 4410.

LEVERTOV, DENISE.   6229. Duddy, Thomas A. "To Celebrate: A Reading of Denise Levertov." *Criticism* 10(1968): 138-152.

6230. Morrow, Patrick. "Denise Levertov's 'The Five Day Rain.'" *NCL* 2(January, 1972): 4-6.

LEVIN, IRA.   6231. Lima, Robert. "The Satanic Rape of Catholicism in *Rosemary's Baby*." *SAF* 2(1974): 211-222.

LEWIS, JANET.   6232. Inglis, Fred C. "The Novels of Janet Lewis." *Crit* 7,#2(1964): 47-64.

LEWIS, SINCLAIR.   6233. Batchelor, Helen. "A Sinclair Lewis Portfolio of Maps: Zenith to Winnemac." *MLQ* 32(1971): 401-408.

6234. Brown, Deming. "Sinclair Lewis: The Russian View." *AL* 25(1953): 1-12.

6235. Bucco, Martin. "The Serialized Novels of Sinclair Lewis." *WAL* 4(1969): 29-37.

6236. Conroy, Stephen S. "Sinclair Lewis's Sociological Imagination." *AL* 42(1970): 348-362.

6237. Couch, William, Jr. "Sinclair Lewis: Crisis in the American Dream." *CLA* 7(1964): 224-234.

6238. Fife, Jim L. "Two Views of the American West." *WAL* 1(1966): 34-43.

6239. Grebstein, Sheldon. "Sinclair Lewis at Yale." *NEQ* 28(1955): 372-382.

6240. ----------. "Sinclair Lewis's Unwritten Novel." *PQ* 37(1958): 399-409.

6241. Lockerbie, D. Bruce. "Sinclair Lewis and William Ridgway." *AL* 36(1964): 68-72.

6242. Moodie, Clara L. "The Short Stories and Sinclair Lewis' Literary Development." *SSF* 12 (1975): 99-107.

6243. Napier, James J. "Letters of Sinclair Lewis to Joseph Hergesheimer, 1915-1922." *AL* 38 (1966): 236-246.

6244. Richardson, Lyon N. "*Arrowsmith*: Genesis, Development, Versions." *AL* 27(1955): 225-244.

6245. ----------. "Revision in Sinclair Lewis's *The Man Who Knew Coolidge*." *AL* 25(1953): 326-333.

6246. Rowlette, Robert. "A Sinclair Lewis Letter to the Indianapolis *News*." *ELN* 9(1972): 193-195.

6247. Tanselle, G. Thomas. "Sinclair Lewis and Floyd Dell: Two Views of the Midwest." *TCL* 9(1964): 175-184.

See also 7403.

LINEBARGER, PAUL MYRON ANTHONY.   6248. Wymer, Thomas L. "Cordwainer Smith: Satirist or Male Chauvinist." *Ext* 14(1973): 157-162.

LOCKE, ALAIN.   6249. Holmes, Eugene. "Alain Locke and the New Negro Movement." *BALF* 2 (1968): 60-68.

See also 4401.

LOMAX, JOHN.   See 619.

LONDON, JACK.   6250. Ahearn, Marie L. "*The People of the Abyss*: Jack London as New Journalist." *MFS* 22(1976): 73-84.

6251. Baskett, Sam S. "A Brace for London Criticism: An Essay Review." *MFS* 22(1976): 101-106.

6252. ----------. "Jack London on the Oakland Waterfront." *AL* 27(1955): 363-371.

6253. ----------. "*Martin Eden*: Jack London's Poem of the Mind." *MFS* 22(1976): 23-36.

6254. ----------. "*Martin Eden*: Jack London's 'Splendid Dream.'" *WAL* 12(1977): 199-214.

6255. ----------. "A Source of *The Iron Heel*." *AL* 27(1955): 268-270.

6256. Beauchamp, Gorman. "*The Iron Heel* and *Looking Backward*: Two Paths to Utopia." *ALR* 9(1976): 307-314.

6257. Bowen, James K. "Jack London's 'To Build a Fire': Epistemology and the White Wilderness." *WAL* 5(1971): 287-289.

6258. Ellis, James. "A New Reading of *The Sea Wolf*." *WAL* 2(1967): 127-134.

6259. Etulain, Richard. "The Lives of Jack London." *WAL* 11(1976): 149-164.

6260. Forrey, Robert. "Jack London: The

Cult and the Legend." *MFS* 22(1976): 595-599.

6261. Giles, James R. "Beneficial Atavism in Frank Norr's and Jack London." *WAL* 4(1969): 15-27.

6262. Gurian, Jay. "The Romantic Necessity in Literary Naturalism: Jack London." *AL* 38(1966): 112-120.

6263. Labor, Earle. "Jack London, 1876-1976: A Centennial Recognition." *MFS* 22(1976): 3-7.

6264. ----------. "Jack London: An Addendum." *ALR* 1,#2(1968): 91-93.

6265. ----------. "Jack London's Agrarian Vision." *WAL* 11(1976): 83-101.

6266. ----------. "Jack London's Symbolic Wilderness: Four Versions." *NCF* 17(1962): 149-161.

6267. ----------. "London and the 'Jackobites': A Modest Demurral." *MFS* 22(1976): 599-602.

6268. Labor, Earle, and King Hendricks. "Jack London's Twice-Told Tale." *SSF* 4(1967): 334-349.

6269. Lachtman, Howard. "Criticism of Jack London: A Selected Checklist." *MFS* 22(1976): 107-126.

6270. ----------. "Man and Superwoman in Jack London's 'The Kanaka Surf.'" *WAL* 7(1972): 101-110.

6271. Isani, Mukhtar Ali. "Jack London on Norris' *The Octopus*." *ALR* 6(1973): 66-69.

6272. McClintock, James I. "Jack London's Use of Carl Jung's *Psychology of the Unconscious*." *AL* 42(1970): 336-347.

6273. Mills, Gordon. "The Symbolic Wilderness Cooper and London." *NCF* 13(1959): 329-340.

6274. ----------. "The Transformation of Material in a Mimetic Fiction." *MFS* 22(1976): 9-22.

6275. Pankake, Jon. "Jack London's Wild Man: The Broken Myths of *Before Adam*." *MFS* 22 (1976): 37-50.

6276. Pearsall, Robert Brainard. "Elizabeth Barrett Meets Wolf Larsen." *WAL* 4(1969): 3-13.

6277. Schriber, Mary. "London in France, 1905-1939." *ALR* 9(1976): 171-178.

6278. Sloane, David E. E. "David Graham Phillips, Jack London, and Others on Contemporary Reviewers and Critics." *ALR* 3(1970): 67-71.

6279. ----------. "Jack London on Reviewing: An Addendum." *ALR* 6(1973): 70-72.

6280. Stasz, Clarice. "Androgyny in the Novels of Jack London." *WAL* 11(1976): 121-133.

6281. ----------. "The Social Construction of Biography: The Case of Jack London." *MFS* 22 (1976): 51-72.

6282. Teich, Nathaniel. "Marxist Dialectics in Content, Form, Point of View: Structures in Jack London's *The Iron Heel*." *MFS* 22(1976): 85-100.

6283. Vanderbeets, Richard. "Nietzche of the North: Heredity and Race in London's *The Son of the Wolf*." *WAL* 2(1967): 229-233.

6284. Walker, Dale. "Jack London (1876-1916)." *ALR* 1,#1(1967): 71-78.

6285. Warner, Richard H. "A Contemporary Sketch of Jack London." *AL* 38(1966): 376-380.

6286. Watson, Charles N., Jr. "Sexual Conflict in *The Sea-Wolf*: Further Notes on London's Reading of Kipling and Norris." *WAL* 11(1976): 239-248.

6287. Willson, Carolyn. "'Rattling the Bones': Jack London, Socialist Evangelist." *WAL* 11(1976): 135-148.

6288. Yoder, Jon. "Jack London as Wolf Barleycorn." *WAL* 11(1976): 103-119.

See also 144.

LOOMIS, EDWARD. 6289. Gallagher, Edward J. "Edward Loomis's 'Wounds.'" *SSF* 9(1972): 247-256.

See also 4420.

LOVECRAFT, HOWARD PHILLIPS. 6290. Emmons, Winfred S., Jr. "H. P. Lovecraft as a Mythmaker." *Ext* 1(1960): 35-37.

6291. ----------. "A Bibliography of H. P. Lovecraft." *Ext* 3(1961): 2-30.

LOWELL, AMY. 6292. Gerber, Philip L. "Dear Harriet . . . Dear Amy." *JML* 5(1976): 233-242.

6293. Healey, Claire. "Amy Lowell Visits London." *NEQ* 46(1973): 439-453.

6294. ----------. "Some Imagist Essays: Amy Lowell." *NEQ* 43(1970): 134-138.

6295. Overmyer, Janet. "Which Broken Pattern—A Note on Amy Lowell's 'Patterns.'" *NCL* 1(September, 1971): 14-15.

6296. Self, Robert T. "The Correspondence of Amy Lowell and Barrett Wendell, 1915-1919. *NEQ* 47(1974): 65-86.

See also 4714.

LOWELL, ROBERT. 6297. Axelrod, Steven. "Baudelaire and the Poetry of Robert Lowell." *TCL* 17(1971): 257-273.

6298. ----------. "Lowell's *The Dolphin* as a 'Book of Life.'" *Con L* 18(1977): 458-474.

6299. ----------. "Robert Lowell and the New York Intellectuals." *ELN* 11(1974): 206-209.

6300. Bowen, Roger. "Confession and Equilibrium: Robert Lowell's Poetic Development." *Criticism* 11(1969): 78-93.

6301. Branscomb, Jack. "Robert Lowell's Painters: Two Sources." *ELN* 15(1977): 119-122.

6302. Brumlove, Sister Eric Marie, S. S. N. D. "Permanence and Change in the Poetry of Robert Lowell." *TSLL* 10(1968): 143-153.

6303. Chadwick, C. "Meaning and Tone." *EIC* 13(1963): 432-435.

6304. Eddins, Dwight. "Poet and State in the Verse of Robert Lowell." *TSLL* 15(1973): 371-386.

6305. Estrin, Mark W. "Robert Lowell's *Benito Cereno*." *MD* 15(1973): 411-426.

6306. Eulbert, Donld. "Robert Lowell and W. C. Williams: Sterility in 'Central Park.'" *ELN* 5(1967): 129-135.

6307. Fein, Richard J. "*Lord Weary's Castle* Revisited." *PMLA* 89(1974): 34-41.

6308. Freimark, Vincent. "Another Holmes in Robert Lowell's 'Hawthorne.'" *ELN* 8(1970): 48-49.

6309. Furia, Philip. "'IS, the Whited Monster': Lowell's Quaker Graveyard Revisited." *TSLL* 17(1976): 837-854.

6310. Holder, Alan. "The Flintlocks of the Fathers: Robert Lowell's Treatment of the American Past." *NEQ* 44(1971): 40-65.

124 AMERICAN LITERATURE. TWENTIETH CENTURY

6311. Mazzaro, Jerome. "The Classicism of Robert Lowell's *Phaedra*." *CD* 7(1973): 87-106.

6312. ----------. "*Prometheus Bound*: Robert Lowell and Aeschylus." *CD* 7(1973): 278-290.

6313. McCall, Dan. "Robert Lowell's 'Hawthorne.'" *NEQ* 39(1966): 237-239.

6314. McFadden, George. "'Life Studies'—Robert Lowell's Comic Breaktrhough." *PMLA* 90 (1975): 96-106.

6315. Nelson, Rudolph L. "A Note on the Evolution of Robert Lowell's 'The Public Garden.'" *AL* 41(1969): 106-110.

6316. Perloff, Marjorie. "Death by Water: The Winslow Elegies of Robert Lowell." *ELH* 34 (1967): 116-140.

6317. ----------. "Realism and the Confessional Mode of Robert Lowell." *Con L* 11(1970): 470-487.

6318. Stone, Albert E. "A New Version of American Innocence: Robert Lowell's *Benito Cereno*." *NEQ* 45(1972): 467-483.

6319. Weatherhead, A. Kingsley. "Imagination and Fancy: Robert Lowell and Marianne Moore." *TSLL* 6(1964): 188-199.

6320. Wiebe, Dallas E. "Mr. Lowell and Mr. Edwards." *Con L* 3,#2(1962): 21-31.

LOY, MINA. 6321. Morse, Samuel French. "The Rediscovery of Mina Loy and the Avant Garde." *Con L* 2,#2(1961): 12-19.

LUMPKIN, GRACE. See 4381.

LYON, HARRIS MERTON. 6322. Eichelberger, Clayton, and Zoe Lyon. "Partial Listing of the Published Works of Harris Merton Lyon." *ALR* 3 (1970): 41-52.

6323. Lyon, Harris Merton. "The Riding Beggar: What Happened to the Great Rich Man After He Had Died." [Text] *SSF* 10(1973): 11-23.

6324. Lyon, Zoe. "Harris Merton Lyon (1883-1916)." *ALR* 3(1970): 36-40.

6325. ----------. "Harris Merton Lyon: Early American Realist." *SSF* 5(1968): 368-377.

6326. ----------. "A Brief Analysis of 'The Riding Beggar.'" *SSF* 10(1973): 25-26.

6327. Putzel Max. "Dreiser, Reedy, and 'De Maupassant, Junior.'" *AL* 33(1962): 466-484.

LYTLE, ANDREW. 6328. Bellis, Jack de. "Andrew Lytle's *A Name for Evil*: A Transformation of *The Turn of the Screw*." *Crit* 8,#3(1966): 26-40.

6329. Joyner, Nancy. "The Myth of the Matriarch in Andrew Lytle's Fiction." *SLJ* 7,#1 (1974): 67-77.

6330. Trowbridge, Clinton. "The Word Made Flesh: Andrew Lytle's *The Velvet Horn*." *Crit* 10,#2(1968): 53-68.

MACDONALD, ROSS. 6331. Pry, Elmer R. "Ross McDonald's Violent California: Imagery Patterns in *The Underground Man*." *WAL* 9(1974): 197-203.

MacKAYE, PERCY. 6332. Brock, D. Heyward, and James M. Welsh. "Percy MacKaye: Community Drama and the Masque Tradition." *CD* 6(1972): 68-84.

MacLEISH, ARCHIBALD. 6333. Gottesman, Lillian. "The *Hamlet* of A. MacLeish." *CLA* 11 (1967): 157-162.

6334. Griffith, John. "Narrative Technique and the Meaning of History in Benet and MacLeish."

JNT 3(1973): 3-19.

6335. MacLeish, Andrew. "*J. B.* and the Critics."' *MD* 2(1959): 224-230.

6336. Montgomery, Marion. "On First Looking Into MacLeish's *J. B.*" *MD* 2(1959): 231-242.

6337. Sickels, Eleanor M. "MacLeish and the Fortunate Fall." *AL* 35(1963): 205-217.

6338. Siegel, Ben. "Miracle on Broadway: and the Box-Office Magic of the *Bible*." *MD* 2 (1959): 45-46.

6339. Stock, Ely. "*A Masque of Reason* and *J. B.*: Two Treatments of the Book of Job." *MD* 3 (1961): 378-386.

MAILOR, NORMAN. 6340. Adams, Laura. "Criticism of Norman Mailer: A Selected Cheklist." *MFS* 17(1971): 455-463.

6341. Burg, David F. "The Hero of *The Naked and the Dead*." *MFS* 17(1971): 387-401.

6342. Busch, Frederick. "The Whale as Shaggy Dog: Melville and 'The Man Who Studied Yoga.'" *MFS* 19(1973): 193-206.

6343. Finholt, Richard D. "'Otherwise How Explain?' Norman Mailer's New Cosmology." *MFS* 17 (1971): 375-386.

6344. Foster, Richard. "Mailer and the Fitzgerald Tradition." *Novel* 1(1968): 219-230.

6345. Glicksberg, Charles I. "Norman Mailer: The Angry Young Novelist in America." *Con L* 1,#1 (1960): 25-34.

6346. Hoffman, Frederick J. "Norman Mailer and the Revolt of the Ego: Some Observations on Recent American Literature." *Con L* 1,#3(1960): 5-12.

6347. Kaufman, Donald L. "Catch 23: The Mystery of Fact." *TCL* 17(1971): 247-256.

6348. ----------. "The Long Happy Life of Norman Mailer." *MFS* 17(1971): 347-359.

6349. ----------. "Mailer's Lunar Bits and Pieces." *MFS* 17(1971): 451-454.

6350. Langbaum, Robert. "Mailer's New Style." *Novel* 2(1968): 69-78.

6351. Lennon, J. Michael. "Mailer's Radical Bridge." *JNT* 7(1977): 170-188.

6352. ----------. "Mailer's Sarcophagus: The Artist, The Media, and the 'Wad.'" *MFS* 23 (1977): 179-187.

6353. Merideth, Robert. "The 45-Second Piss: A Left Critique of Norman Mailer and *The Armies of the Night*." *MFS* 17(1971): 433-449.

6354. Muste, John M. "Norman Mailer and John Dos Passos: The Question of Influence." *MFS* 17(1971): 361-374.

6355. Pearce, Richard. "Norman Mailer's *Why Are We In Vietnam?* A Radical Critique of Frontier Values." *MFS* 17(1971): 409-414.

6356. Rabinovitz, Rubin. "Myth and Animism in *Why Are We In Vietman?*" *TCL* 20(1974): 298-305.

6357. Ramsey, Roger. "Current and Recurrent: The Vietnam Novel." *MFS* 17(1971): 415-431.

6358. Schulz, Max F. "Mailer's Divine Comedy." *Con L* 9(1968): 36-57.

6359. Seib, Kenneth A. "Mailer's March: The Epic Structure of *The Armies of the Night*." *EL* 1(1974): 89-95.

6360. Siegel, Paul N. "The Malign Deity of *The Naked and the Dead*." *TCL* 20(1974): 291-297.

6361. Stark, John. "*Barbary Shore:* The Basis of Mailer's Best Work." *MFS* 17(1971): 403-408.

6362. Taylor, Gordon D. "Of Adams and A-quarius." *AL* 46(1974): 68-82.

6363. Witt, Grace. "The Bad Man as Hipster: Norman Mailer's Use of Frontier Metaphor." *WAL* 4(1969): 203-217.

6364. Wagenheim, Allen J. "Square's Progress: *An American Dream.*" *Crit* 10,#1(1967): 45-68.

6365. Waldmeir, Joseph J. "Running with Mailer." *JML* 1(1971): 454-457.

6366. Waldron, Randall H. "The Naked, the Dead, and the Machine: A New Look at Norman Mailer's First Novel." *PMLA* 87(1972): 271-277.

MALAMUD, BERNARD. 6367. Barsness, John A. "*A New Life:* The Frontier Myth in Perspective." *WAL* 3(1969): 297-302.

6368. Bellman, Samuel I. "Women, Children, and Idiots First." *Crit* 7,#2(1964): 123-138.

6369. Fiedler, Leslie A. "Malamud's Travesty Western." *Novel* 10(1977): 212-219.

6370. Goldman, Mark. "Bernard Malamud's Comic Vision and the Theme of Identity." *Crit* 7,#2(1964): 92-109.

6371. Kellman, Stephen G. "*The Tenants* in the House of Fiction." *SN* 8(1976): 458-467.

6372. Leer, Norman. "Three American Novels and Contemporary Society: A Search for Commitment." *Con L* 3,#3(1962): 67-86.

6373. Leff, Leonard J. "Malamud's Ferris Wheel." *NCL* 1(January, 1971): 14-15.

6374. Mandel, Ruth B. "Bernard Malamud's *The Assistant* and *A New Life:* Ironic Affirmation." *Crit* 7,#2(1964): 110-122.

6375. May, Charles E. "Bernard Malamud's 'A Summer Reading.'" *NCL* 2(September, 1972): 11-13.

6376. ----------. "The Bread of Tears: Malamud's 'The Loan.'" *SSF* 7(1970): 652-654.

6377. Mellard, James M. "Malamud's Novels: Four Versionsof Pastoral." *Crit* 9,#2(1967): 5-19.

6378. ----------. "Malamud's *The Assistant:* The City Novel as Pastoral." *SSF* 5(1967): 1-11.

6379. Mesher, David R. "The Remembrance of Things Unknown: Malamud's 'The Last Mohican.'" *SSF* 12(1975): 397-404.

6380. Perrine, Laurence. "Malamud's 'Take Pity.'" *SSF* 2(1964): 84-86.

6381. Pinsker, Sanford. "A Note on Bernard Malamud's 'Take Pity.'" *SSF* 6(1969): 212-213.

6382. Reynolds, Richard. "'The Magic Barrel': Pinye Salzman's Kadish." *SSF* 10(1973): 100-102.

6383. Richey, Clarence W. "'The Woman in the Dunes': A Note on Bernard Malamud's *The Tenents.*" *NCL* 3(January, 1973): 4-5.

6384. Rovit, Earl H. "Bernard Malamud and the Jewish Literary Tradition." *Crit* 3,#2(1960): 3-10.

6385. Russell, Mariann. "White Man's Black Man: Three Views." *CLA* 17(1973): 93-100.

6386. Sweet, Charles A., Jr. "Unlocking the Door: Malamud's 'Behold the Key.'" *NCL* 5 (November, 1975): 11-12.

6387. Turner, Frederick W., III. "Myth Inside and Out: Malamud's *The Natural.*" *Novel* 1(1968): 133-139.

6388. Wegelin, Christof. "The American Schmlemiel Abroad: Malamud's Italian Stories and the End of American Innocence." *TCL* 19(1973): 77-88.

6389. Winn, H. Harbour, III. "Malamud's Uncas: 'Last Mohican.'" *NCL* 5(March, 1975): 13-14.

6390. Witherington, Paul. "Malamud's Allusive Design in A New Life." *WAL* 10(1975): 115-123.
See also 5241.

MALCOM X. 6391. Demarest, David P., Jr. "*The Autobiography of Malcom X:* Beyond Didacticism." *CLA* 16(1972): 179-187.

6392. Eakin, Paul John. "Malcom X and the Limits of Autobiography." *Criticism* 18(1976): 230-242.

6393. Hoyt, Charles A. "The Five Faces of Malcom X." *BALF* 4(1970): 107-112.
See also 4382.

MANCHESTER, WILLIAM. 6394. Pizer, Donald. "Documentary Narrative as Art: William Manchester and Truman Capote." *JML* 2(1971): 105-118.

MANFRED, FREDERICK. 6395. Austin, James C. "Legend, Myth, and Symbol in Frederick Manfred's *Lord Grizzly.*" *Crit* 6,#3(1963): 122-130.

6396. Kellog, George. "Frederick Manfred: A Bibliography." *TCL* 11(1965): 30-35.

6397. Lee, James W. "An Interview in Minnesota with Frederick Manfred." *SN* 5(1973): 358-382.

6398. Milton, John R. "*Lord Grizzly:* Rhythm, Form and Meaning in the Western Novel." *WAL* 1(1966): 6-14.

6399. "West of the Mississippi: An Interview with Frederick Manfred." *Crit* 2,#3(1959): 35-56.

6400. Westbrook, Max. "Riders of Judgement: An Exercise in Ontological Criticism." *WAL* 12(1977): 41-51.
See also 590, 4420.

MARCH, WILLIAM. 6401. Simmonds, Roy S. "William March's *Company K:* A Short Textual Study." *SAF* 2(1974): 105-113.

MARKHAM, EDWIN. 6402. Eschholz, Paul A. "Edwin Markham's 'The Ballad of the Gallows-Bird' and His Proposed *Collected Poems:* An Unpublished Letter." *ELN* 12(1975): 187-188.

MARSHALL, PAULE. 6403. Benston, Kimberly W. "Architectural Imagery and Unity in Paule Marshall's *Brown Girl, Brownstones.*" *BALF* 9(1975): 67-70.

6404. Brown, Lloyd W. "The Rhythms of Power in Paule Marshall's Fiction." *Novel* 7(1974): 159-167.

6405. Kapai, Leela. "Dominant Themes and Technique in Paule Marshall's Fiction." *CLA* 16 (1972): 49-59.

6406. Keizs, Marcia. "Themes and Style in the Works of Paule Marshall." *BALF* 9(1975): 67, 71-76.

6407. Stoeling, Winifred L. "Time Past and Time Present: The Search for Viable Links in *The Chosen Place, The Timeless People* by Paule Marshall." *CLA* 16(1972): 60-71.
See also 4309.

MARKFIELD, WALLACE. See 4393.

MASTERS, EDGAR LEE. 6408. Putzel, Max. "Masters' 'Maltravers': Ernest McGaffey." *AL* 31 (1960): 491-493.

6409. Russell, Herb. "Edgar Lee Masters'
Final Years in the Midwest." *EL* 4(1977): 212-220.

MATHEWS, JOHN F.   6410. Mathews, John F.
"*Ouanga*: My Venture in Libretto Creation." *CLA*
15(1972): 428-440.

See also 621.

MAYFIELD, JULIAN.   See 4309.

McCORD, DAVID. 6411. Davis, Roy. "The
Poetry of David McCord." *NEQ* 25(1952): 233-242.

McCOY, HORACE. 6412. Richmond, Lee J.
"A Time to Mourn and a Time to Dance: Horace Mc-
Coy's *They Shoot Horses, Don't They?*" *TCL* 17(1971):
91-100.

McCULLERS, CARSON. 6413. Broughton, Panthea Reid. "Rejection of the Feminine in Carson
McCullers' *The Ballad of the Sad Cafe*." *TCL* 20
(1974): 34-43.

6414. Edmonds, Dale. "'Correspondence':
A 'Forgotten' Carson McCullers Short Story." *SSF*
9(1972): 89-92.

6415. Emerson, Donald. "The Ambiguities of
Clock Without Hands." *Con L* 3,#3(1962): 15-28.

6416. Grinnel, James W. "Delving 'A Domestic Dilemma.'" *SSF* 9(1972): 270-271.

6417. Hassan, Ihab H. "Carson McCullers:
The Alchemy of Love and the Aesthetics of Pain."
MFS 5(1959): 311-326.

6418. Millichap, Joseph R. "The Realistic
Structure of *The Heart Is a Lonely Hunter*." *TCL*
17(1971): 11-17.

6419. Moore, Jack B. "Carson McCullers:
The Heart Is a Timeless Hunter." *TCL* 11(1965):
76-81.

6420. Perrine, Laurence. "Restoring 'A
Domestic Dilemma.'" *SSF* 11(1974): 101-104.

6421. Phillips, Robert S. "Dinesen's 'Money'
and McCullers' 'Ballad': A Study in Literary
Affinity." *SSF* 1(1964): 184-190.

6422. Rich, Nancy B. "The 'Ironic Parable
of Fascism' in *The Heart is a Lonely Hunter*." *SLJ*
9,#2(1977): 108-123.

6423. Vickery, John B. "Carson McCullers:
A Map of Love." *Con L* 1,#1(1960): 13-24.

See also 4397.

McKAY, CLAUDE.   6424. Barksdale, Richard K.
"Symbolism and Irony in McKay's *Home to Harlem*."
CLA 15(1972): 338-344.

6425. Collier, Eugenia W. "The Four-Way
Delimma of Claude McKay." *CLA* 15(1972): 345-353.

6426. Conroy, Sister Mary. "The Vagabond
Motif in the Writings of Claude McKay." *BALF* 5
(1971): 15-23.

6427. Helbling, Mark. "Claude McKay: Art
and Politics." *BALF* 7(1973): 49-52.

6428. Kent, George E. "Claude McKay's *Banana Bottom* Reappraised." *CLA* 18(1974): 222-234.

6429. Lang, Phyllis Martin. "Claude McKay:
Evidence of a Magic Pilgrimage." *CLA* 16(1973):
475-484.

6430. Larson, Charles R. "Three Harlem
Novels of the Jazz Age." *Crit* 11,#3(1969): 66-78.

6431. Lawrence, Leota S. "Three West Indian
Heroines: An Analysis." *CLA* 21(1977): 238-250.

6432. Lee, Robert A. "On Claude McKay's
'If We Must Die.'" *CLA* 18(1974): 216-221.

6433. Pyne-Timothy, Helen. "Perceptions of
the Black Woman in the Work of Claude McKay." *CLA*

19(1975): 152-164.

6434. Van Mol, Kay R. "Primitivism and Intellect in Toomer's *Cane* and McKay's *Banana Bottom*:
The Need for an Integrated Consciousness." *BALF*
10(1976): 48-52.

See also 4316, 4383, 4425.

McMURTRY, LARRY. 6435. Peavy, Charles D.
"Coming of Age in Texas: The Novels of Larry
McMurtry." *WAL* 4(1969): 171-188.

6436. ----------. "Larry McMurtry and Black
Humor: A Note on *The Last Picture Show*." *WAL* 2
(1967): 223-227.

6437. ----------. "A Larry McMurtry Bibliography." *WAL* 3(1968): 235-248.

6438. Stout, Janis P. "Journeying as a
Metaphor for Cultural Loss in the Novels of Larry
McMurtry." *WAL* 11(1976): 37-50.

McNICHOLS, CHARLES. 6439. Berner, Robert L.
"Charles L. McNichols and *Crazy Weather*: A Reconsideration." *WAL* 6(1971): 39-51.

McPHERSON, JAMES A. 6440. Laughlin, Rosemary M. "Attention, American Folklore: Doc Craft
Comes Marching In." *SAF* 1(1973): 220-227.

See also 4407.

MENCKEN, H. L. 6441. Durham, Frank. "Mencken as Missionary." *AL* 29(1958): 478-483.

6442. Manglaviti, Leo M. J. "Faulkner's
'That Evening Sun' and Mencken's 'Best Editorial
Judgment.'" *AL* 43(1972): 649-654.

6443. Martin, Edward A. "H. L. Mencken's
Poetry." *TSLL* 6(1964): 346-353.

6444. Morrison, Joseph L. "Colonel H. L.
Mencken, C. S. A." *SLJ* 1,#1(1968): 42-54.

6445. Nolte, William. "Criticism with
Vine Leaves." *TSLL* 3(1961): 16-39.

6446. Porter, Bernard H. "H. L. Mencken:
A Bibliography." *TCL* 4(1958): 100-107.

6447. Stenerson, Douglas C. "Mencken's Early
Newspaper Experience: The Genesis of a Style."
AL 37(1965): 153-166.

See also 4341.

MERIWETHER, LOUISE. 6448. Dandridge, Rita
B. "From Economic Insecurity to Disintegration:
A Study of Character in Louise Meriwether's *Daddy
Was a Number Runner*." *BALF* 9(1975): 82-85.

MERRILL, JAMES. 6449. Eaves, Morris. "Decision and Revision in James Merrill's *(Diblos)
Notebook*." *Con L* 12(1971): 156-165.

6450. Sheehan, David. "An Interview with
James Merrill." *Con L* 9(1968): 1-14.

MERTON, THOMAS. 6451. Sutton, Walter.
"Thomas Merton and the American Epic Tradition:
The Last Poems." *Con L* 14(1973): 49-57.

MERWIN, W. S. 6452. Anderson, Kenneth.
"The Poetry of W. S. Merwin." *TCL* 16(1970): 278-
286.

6453. Frawley, William. "Merwin's Unpunc-
tuated Verse." *NCL* 7(September, 1977): 2-3.

6454. Libby, Anthony. "W. S. Merwin and the
Nothing That Is." *Con L* 16(1975): 19-40.

MEWSHAW, MICHAEL. 6455. Hoge, James D.
"The Interrelation of Good and Evil in Mewshaw's
Waking Slow." *NCL* 2(September, 1972): 2-3.

MILLAY, EDNA ST. VINCENT. 6456. McKee,
Mary J. "Millay's *Aria Da Capo*: Form and Meaning." *MD* 9(1966): 165-169.

6457. Minot, Walter S. "Millay's 'Ungrafted Tree': The Problem of the Artist as Woman." *NEQ* 48(1975): 260-269.

6458. Perlmutter, Elizabeth F. "A Doll's Heart: The Girl in the Poetry of Edna St. Vincent Millay and Louise Bogan." *TCL* 23(1977): 157-179.

MILLER, ARTHUR. 6459. Barksdale, Richard K. "Social Background in the Plays of Miller and Williams." *CLA* 6(1963): 161-169.

6460. Bates, Barclay W. "The Lost Past in *Death of a Salesman*." *MD* 11(1968): 164-172.

6461. Bettina, Sister M., S. S. N. D. "Willy Loman's Brother Ben: Tragic Insight in *Death of a Salesman*." *MD* 4(1962): 409-412.

6462. Bigby, C. W. E. "The Fall and After—Arthur Miller's Confession." *MD* 10(1967): 124-136.

6463. ----------. "What Price Arthur Miller? An Analysis of *The Price*." *TCL* 16(1970): 16-25.

6464. Bliquez, Guerin. "Linda's Role in *Death of a Salesman*." *MD* 10(1968): 383-386.

6465. Bronsen, David. "*An Enemy of the People*: A Key to Arthur Miller's Art and Ethics." *CD* 2(1968): 229-247.

6466. Cook, Larry W. "The Function of Ben and Dave Singleman in *Death of a Salesman*." *NCL* 5(January, 1975): 7-9.

6467. Corrigan, Robert W. "The Achievement of Arthur Miller." *CD* 2(1968): 141-160.

6468. Eissenstat, Martha Turnquist. "Arthur Miller: A Bibliography." *MD* 5(1962): 93-106.

6469. Epstein, Arthur D. "A Look at *A View from the Bridge*." *TSLL* 7(1965): 109-122.

6470. Field, B. S., Jr. "Hamartia in *Death of a Salesman*." *TCL* 18(1972): 19-24.

6471. Gross, Barry. "*All My Sons* and the Larger Context." *MD* 18(1975): 15-28.

6472. ----------. "Peddler and Pioneer in *Death of a Salesman*." *MD* 7(1965): 405-410.

6473. Hagopian, John V. "Arthur Miller: The *Salesman's* Two Cases." *MD* 6(1963): 117-125.

6474. Hays, Peter L. "Arthur Miller and Tennessee Williams." *EL* 4(1977): 239-249.

6475. Heaton, C. P. "Arthur Miller on *Death of a Salesman*." *NCL* 1(January, 1971): 5.

6476. Hill, Philip G. "*The Crucible*: A Structural View." *MD* 10(1967): 312-317.

6477. Jackson, Esther Merle. "*Death of a Salesman*: Tragic Myth in the Modern Theatre." *CLA* 7(1963): 63-76.

6478. Jacobsen, Irving. "Family Dreams in *Death of a Salesman*." *AL* 47(1975): 247-258.

6479. ----------. "The Vestigial Jews on Mont Sant Angelo." *SSF* 13(1976): 507-512.

6480. Koppenhaver, Allen J. "*The Fall* and After: Albert Camus and Arthur Miller." *MD* 9(1966): 206-209.

6481. Lowenthal, Lawrence D. "Arthur Miller's *Incident at Vicky*: A Sartrean Interpretation." *MD* 18(1975): 29-42.

6482. Martin, Robert A. "Arthur Miller and the Meaning of Tragedy." *MD* 13(1970): 34-39.

6483. ----------. "Arthur Miller's *The Crucible*: Background and Sources." *MD* 20(1977): 279-292.

6484. Martin, Robert A., and Richard Meyer. "Arthur Miller on Plays and Playwriting." *MD* 19 (1976): 375-384.

6485. McAnany, Emile G., S. J. "The Tragic Commitment: Some Notes on Arthur Miller." *MD* 5 (1962): 11-20.

6486. Miller, Jeanne-Marie A. "Odets, Miller and Communism." *CLA* 19(1976): 484-493.

6487. Moss, Leonard. "Arthur Miller and the Common Man's Language." *MD* 7(1964): 52-59.

6488. Murray, Edward. "Point of View in *After the Fall*." *CLA* 10(1966): 135-142.

6489. Oberg, Arthur K. "'Death of a Salesman' and Arthur Miller's Search for Style." *Criticism* 9(1967): 303-311.

6490. Overland, Orm. "The Action and Its Significance: Arthur Miller's Struggle with Dramatic Form." *MD* 18(1975): 1-14.

6491. Reno, Raymond H. "Arthur Miller and the Death of God." *TSLL* 11(1969): 1069-1087.

6492. Rothenberg, Albert, and Eugene Shapiro. "The Defense of Psychoanalysis in Literature: *Long Day's Journey Into Night* and *A View from the Bridge*." *CD* 7(1973): 51-67.

6493. Stinson, John J. "Structure in *After the Fall*: The Relevance of the Maggie Episodes to the Main Themes and the Christian Symbolism." *MD* 10(1967): 233-240.

6494. Trowbridge, Clinton W. "Arthur Miller: Between Pathos and Tragedy." *MD* 10(1967): 221-232.

6495. Wells, Arvin R. "The Living and the Dead in *All My Sons*." *MD* 7(1964): 46-51.

See also 6715.

MILLER, HENRY. 6496. Foster, Steven. "A Critical Appraisal of Henry Miller's *Tropic of Cancer*." *TCL* 9(1964): 196-208.

6497. Jackson, Paul R. "Henry Miller, Emerson, and the Divided Self." *AL* 43(1972): 649-654.

6498. Levitt, Morton P. "Art and Correspondences: Durrell, Miller, and *The Alexandria Quartet*." *MFS* 13(1967): 299-318.

6499. Mitchell, Edward B. "Artists and Artists: The 'Aesthetics' of Henry Miller." *TSLL* 8(1966): 103-115.

6500. Renken, Maxine. "Bibliography of Henry Miller: 1945-1961." *TCL* 7(1962): 180-190.

See also 4341.

MILLER, VASSAR. 6501. Owen, Guy. "Vassar Miller: A Southern Metaphysical." *SLJ* 3,#1(1970): 83-88.

MILLER, WALTER. 6502. Griffin, Russell M. "Medievalism in *A Canticle for Leibowitz*." *Ext* 14(1973): 112-125.

MILLER, WARREN. 6503. Love, Glen A. "Warren Miller: White Novelist in a Black World." *BALF* 9(1975): 3, 11-16.

MILLETT, KATE. 6504. Kolodney, Annette. "The Lady's Not for Spurning: Kate Millett and the Critics." *Con L* 17(1976): 541-562.

MITCHELL, MARGARET. 6505. Watkins, Floyd C. "*Gone With the Wind* As Vulgar Literature." *SLJ* 2,#2(1969): 86-103.

See also 18412.

MOMADAY, N. SCOTT. 6506. Evers, Lawrence J. "Words and Place: A Reading of *House Made of Dawn*." *WAL* 11(1977): 297-320.

See also 621.

MOODY, WILLIAM VAUGHN.   6507. Brown, Maurice F. "William Vaughn Moody (1869-1910)." [bibliography]*ALR* 6(1973): 51-60.

6508. Fussell, Edwin S. "Robinson to Moody: Ten Unpublished Letters." *AL* 23(1951): 173-187.

6509. Pickering, Jerry V. "William Vaughn Moody: The Dramatist as Social Philosopher." *MD* 14(1971): 93-103.

6510. Riggs, Thomas, Jr. "Prometheus 1900." *AL* 22(1951): 399-423.

MOORE, MARIANNE. 6511. Brumbaugh, Thomas B. Concerning Marianne Moore's Museum." *TCL* 1(1956): 191-195.

6512. Newlin, Margaret. "'Unhelpful Hymen!': Marianne Moore and Hilda Doolittle." *EIC* 27(1977): 216-230.

6513. Parkin, Rebecca Price. "Certain Difficulties in Reading Marianne Moore: Exemplified in her 'Apparition of Splendor.'" *PMLA* 81(1966): 167-172.

6514. Replogle, Justin. "Marianne Moore and the Art of Intonation." *Con L* 12(1971): 1-17.

6515. Weatherhead, A. Kingsley. "Imagination and Fancy: Robert Lowell and Marianne Moore." *TSLL* 6(1964): 188-199.

6516. ----------. "Two Kinds of Vision in Marianne Moore." *ELH* 31(1964): 482-496.

See also 4341.

MORE, PAUL ELMER. 6517. Duggan, Francis X. "Paul Elmer More and the New England Tradition." *AL* 34(1963): 542-561.

6518. Tanner, Stephen L. "Paul Elmer More: Literary Criticism as the History of Ideas." *AL* 45(1973): 390-406.

MORRIS, WRIGHT. 6519. Baumbach, Jonathan. "Wake Before the Bomb: *Ceremony in Lone Tree*." *Crit* 4,#3(1961): 56-71.

6520. Harper, Robert D. "Wright Morris's *Ceremony in Lone Tree*: A Picture of Life in Middle America." *WAL* 11(1976): 199-213.

6521. Hunt, John W., Jr. "The Journey Back: The Early Novels of Wright Morris." *Crit* 5,#1 (1962): 41-60.

6522. Leer, Norman. "Three American Novels and Contemporary Society: A Search for Commitment." *Con L* 3,#3(1962): 67-86.

6523. Linden, Stanton J., and David Madden. "A Wright Morris Bibliography." *Crit* 4,#3(1961): 77-87.

6524. Madden, David. "The Great Plains in the Novels of Wright Morris." *Crit* 4,#3(1961): 5-23.

6525. ----------. "Wright Morris' *In Orbit*: An Unbroken Series of Poetic Gestures." *Crit* 10,#2(1968): 102-119.

6526. Morris, Wright. "National Book Award Address, March 12, 1957." *Crit* 4,#3(1961): 72-76.

6527. Richey, Clarence W. "'The Riverrun': A Note Upon a Joycean Quotation in Wright Morris' *In Orbit*." *NCL* 2(January, 1972): 14-15.

6528. Trachtenberg, Alan. "The Craft of Vision." *Crit* 4,#3(1961): 41-55.

6529. Waterman, Arthur E. "The Novels of Wright Morris: An Escape from Nostalgia." *Crit* 4,#3(1961): 23-40.

See also 4404.

MOTLEY, WILLARD.   6530. Bayliss, John F.

"Nick Romano: Father and Son." *BALF* 3(1969): 18-21.

6531. Giles, James R., and Jerome Klinkowitz. "The Emergence of Willard Motley in Black American Literature." *BALF* 6(1972): 31-34.

6532. Giles, James R., and N. Jill Weyant. "The Short Fiction of Willard Motley." *BALF* 9 (1975): 3-10.

6533. Grenander, M. E. "Criminal Responsibility in *Native Son* and *Knock on Any Door*." *AL* 49(1977): 221-233.

6534. Rayson, Ann L. "Prototypes for Nick Romano of *Knock on Any Door*: From the Diaries in the Collected Manuscripts of the Willard Motley Estate." *BALF* 8(1974): 248-251.

6535. Weyant, N. Jill. "Lyrical Experimentation in Willard Motley's Mexican Novel: *Let Noon Be Fair*." *BALF* 10(1976): 95-99.

6536. ----------. "Willard Motley's Pivotal Novel: *Let No Man Write My Epitaph*." *BALF* 11 (1977): 56-61.

6537. Wood, Charles. "The *Adventure* Manuscript: New Light on Willard Motley." *BALF* 6 (1972): 35-38.

MURO, AMADO JESUS.   See CHESTER SELTZER.

NABOKOV, VLADIMIR.   6538. Aldridge, A. Owen. "*Lolita* and *Les Liasons Dangereuses*." *Con L* 2,#3 (1961): 20-26.

6539. Appel, Alfred, Jr. "Conversation with Nabokov." *Novel* 4(1971): 209-222.

6540. ----------. "An Interview with Vladimir Nabokov." *Con L* 8(1967): 127-152.

6541. ----------. "*Lolita*: The Springboard of Parody." *Con L* 8(1967): 204-241.

6542. ----------. "The Road to *Lolita*, or the Americanization of an Emigré." *JML* 4(1974): 3-31.

6543. Bell, Michael. "*Lolita* and Pure Art." *EIC* 24(1974): 169-184.

6544. Brown, Clarence. "Nabokov's Pushkin and Nabokov's Nabokov." *Con L* 8(1967): 280-293.

6545. Bruffee, K. A. "Form and Meaning in Nabokov's *Real Life of Sebastian Knight*: An Example of Elegiac Romance." *MLQ* 34(1973): 180-190.

6546. Bryer, Jackson R. "Vladimir Nabokov's Critical Reputation in English: A Note and a Checklist." *Con L* 8(1967): 312-315.

6547. Bryer, Jackson R., and Thomas J. Bergin, Jr. "A Checklist of Nabokov Criticism in English." *Con L* 8(1967): 316-364.

6548. Ciancio, Ralph A. "Nabokov and the Verbal Mode of the Grotesque." *Con L* 18(1977): 509-533.

6549. Dembo, L. S. "Vladimir Nabokov, An Introduction." *Con L* 8(1967): 111-126.

6550. Field, Andrew. "The Artist as Failure in Nabokov's Early Prose." *Con L* 8(1967): 165-173.

6551. Flower, Timothy F. "The Scientific Art of Nabokov's 'Pale Fire.'" *Criticism* 17(1975): 223-233.

6552. Fromberg, Susan. "The Unwritten Chapters in *The Real Life of Sebastian Knight*." *MFS* 13(1967): 427-442.

6553. Gerschenkron, Alexander. "A Manufactured Monument?" *MP* 63(1966): 336-347.

6554. Godshalk, William Leigh. "Nabokov's Byronic *Ada*: A Note." *NCL* 2(March, 1972): 2-4.

6555. Grosshans, Henry. "Vladimir Nabokob and the Dream of Old Russia." *TSLL* 7(1966): 401-409.

6556. Hughes, Daniel. "Nabokov: Spiral and Glass (Review Essay)." *Novel* 1(1968): 178-185.

6557. ----------. "Reality and the Hero: Lolita and *Henderson the Rain King*." *MFS* 6(1960): 345-364.

6558. Joyce, James. "Lolita in Humberland." *SN* 6(1974): 339-348.

6559. Kaplan, Fred. "Victorian Modernists: Fowles and Nabokov." *JNT* 3(1973): 108-120.

6560. Karlinsky, Simon. "Illusion, Reality, and Parody in Nabokov's Plays." *Con L* 8(1967): 268-279.

6561. LeClair, Thomas. "Poe's *Pym* and Nabokob's *Pale Fire*." *NCL* 3(March, 1973): 2-3.

6562. Lee, L. L. "*Bend Sinister*: Nabokov's Political Dream." *Con L* 8(1967): 193-203.

6563. ----------. "Duplexity in V. Nabokov's Short Stories." *SSF* 2(1965): 307-315.

6564. Levine, Robert T. "*Lolita* and the Originality of Style." *EL* 4(1977): 110-121.

6565. Lyons, John D. "*Pale Fire* and the Fine Art of Annotation." *Con L* 8(1967): 242-249.

6566. McDonald, James L. "John Ray, Jr., Critic and Artist: The Foreward to *Lolita*." *SN* 5(1973): 352-357.

6567. Merivale, Patricia. "The Flaunting of Artifice in Vladimir Nabokov and Jorge Luis Borges." *Con L* 8(1967): 294-309.

6568. Miles, Thomas H. "Lolita: Humbert's Playful Goddess." *NCL* 6(November, 1976): 5-7.

6569. Mitchell, Charles. "Mythic Seriousness in *Lolita*." *TSLL* 5(1963): 329-343.

6570. Moynahan, Julian. "A Russian Preface for Nabokov's *Beheading*." *Novel* 1(1967): 12-18.

6571. Nicol, Charles. "Pnin's History." *Novel* 4(1971): 197-208.

6572. Patteson, Richard F. "Nabokov's *Bend Sinister*: The Narrator as God." *SAF* 5(1977): 241-253.

6573. ----------. "Nabokov's *Transparent Things*: Narration by the Mind's Eyewitness." *Coll L* 3(1976): 102-112.

6574. Prioleau, Elizabeth. "Humbert Humbert Through the *Looking Glass*." *TCL* 21(1975): 428-437.

6575. Proffitt, Edward. "A Clue to John Ray, Jr." *MFS* 20(1974): 551-552.

6576. Purdy, Strother B. "Solus Rex: Nabokov and the Chess Novel." *MFS* 14(1968): 379-395.

6577. Rosenfield, Claire. "*Despair* and the Lust for Immortality." *Con L* 8(1967): 174-192.

6578. Roth, Phyllis A. "A In Search of Aesthetic Bliss: A Rereading of *Lolita*." *Coll L* 2(1975): 28-49.

6579. ----------. "The Psychology of the Double in Nabokov's *Pale Fire*." *EL* 2(1975): 209-229.

6580. Schuman, Samuel. "Vladimir Nabokov's *Invitation to a Beheading* and Robert Heinlein's 'They.'" *TCL* 19(1973): 99-106.

6581. Seiden, Melvin. "Nabokov and Dostoevsky." *Con L* 13(1972): 423-444.

6582. "Selected Bibliography of Nabokov's Work." *Con L* 8(1967): 310-311.

6583. Stark, John. "Borges' 'Tlön, Uqbar, Orbis Tertius' and Nabokov's *Pale Fire*: Literature of Exhaustion." *TSLL* 14(1972): 139-145.

6584. Struve, Gleb. "Notes on Nabokov as a Russian Writer." *Con L* 8(1967): 153-164.

6585. Stuart, Dabney. "The Novelist's Composure: *Speak, Memory* as Fiction." *MLQ* 36(1975): 177-192.

6586. ----------. "*The Real Life of Sebastian Knight*: Angles of Perception." *MLQ* 29 (1968): 312-328.

6587. Uphaus, Robert W. "Nabakov's Kunstlerroman: Portrait of the Artist as a Dying Man." *TCL* 13(1967): 104-110.

6588. Walker, David. "The Viewer and the View: Chance and Choice in *Pale Fire*." *SAF* 4 (1976): 203-221.

6589. Williams, Carol T. "Nabokov's Dialectical Structure." *Con L* 8(1967): 250-267.

6590. ----------. "Nabokov's Dozen Short Stories: His World in Microcosm." *SSF* 12(1975): 213-222.

6591. ----------. "Web of Sense: *Pale Fire* in the Nabokov Canon." *Crit* 6,#3(1963): 29-45.

6592. Winston, Mathew. "*Lolita* and the Dangers of Fiction." *TCL* 21(1975): 421-427.

NEAL, LARRY. See 4442.

NEIHARDT, JOHN G. 6593. Black, W. E. "Ethic and Metaphysic: A Study of John G. Neihardt." *WAL* 2(1967): 205-212.

6594. McCluskey, Sally. "*Black Elk Speaks*: and So Does John Neihardt." *WAL* 6(1972): 231-242. See also 620, 1167, 1257.

NIN, ANAÏS. 6595. McBrien, William. "Anaïs Nin: An Interview." *TCL* 20(1974): 277-290. See also 4341.

NOGUCHI, YONE. 6596. Haslam, Gerald W. "Three Exotics: Yone Noguchi, Shiesei Tsuneishi, and Sadakichi Hartmann." *CLA* 19(1976): 362-373.

NORRIS, CHARLES. 6597. Goldsmith, Arnold L. "Charles and Frank Norris." *WAL* 2(1967): 30-49.

OATES, JOYCE CAROL. 6598. Catron, Douglas M. "A Contribution to A Bibliography of Works by and about Joyce Carol Oates." *AL* 49(1977): 399-314.

6599. Evans, Elizabeth. "Joyce Carol Oates' 'Patient Griselda.'" *NCL* 6(September, 1976): 2-5.

6600. Fossum, Robert H. "Only Control: The Novels of Joyce Carol Oates." *SN* 7(1975): 285-297.

6601. Keller, Karl. "A Modern Version of Edward Taylor." *EAL* 9,#3(1975): 321-324.

6602. McCormick, Lucienne P. "A Bibliography of Works by and About Joyce Carol Oates." *AL* 43(1971): 124-132.

6603. Park, Sue Simpson. "A Study in Counterpoint: Joyce Carol Oate's 'How I Contemplated the World from the Detroit House of Correction and Began My Life Over Again.'" *MFS* 22(1976): 213-224.

6604. Wegs, Joyce. "'Dont you know who I am?': The Grotesque in Oates's 'Where Are You Going, Where Have You Been?'" *JNT* 5(1975): 66-72.

O'BRIEN, EDWARD J. 6605. Joselyn, Sister M., O. S. B. "Edward Joseph O'Brien and the American Short Story." *SSF* 3(1965): 1-15.

O'CONNER, EDWIN.   6606. Rank, Hugh. "O'Conner's Image of the Priest." *NEQ* 41(1968): 3-29.

O'CONNER, FLANNERY.   6607. Abbot, Louise Hardeman. "Remembering Flannery O'Conner." *SLJ* 2,#2(1970): 3-25.

6608. Asals, Frederick. "The Mythic Dimensions of Flannery O'Connor's Greenleaf." *SSF* 5(1968): 317-330.

6609. Browning, Preston M. "Flannery O'Conner and the Demonic." *MFS* 19(1973): 29-42.

6610. ----------. "'Parker's Back': Flannery O'Conner's Iconography of Salvation by Profanity." *SSF* 6(1969): 525-535.

6611. Burns, Stuart L. "The Evolution of *Wise Blood.*" *MFS* 16(1970): 147-162.

6612. ----------. "'torn by the Lord's eye': Flannery O'Conner's Use of Sun Imagery." *TCL* 13 (1967): 154-166.

6613. Doxey, William S. "A Dissenting Opinion of Flannery O'Conner's 'A Good Man is Hard to Find.'" *SSF* 10(1973): 199-204.

6614. Drake, Robert. "The Paradigm of Flannery O'Connor's True Country." *SSF* 6(1969): 433-442.

6615. Edelstein, Mark G. "Flannery O'Conner and the Problem of Modern Satire." *SSF* 12(1975): 139-144.

6616. Evans, Elizabeth. "Three Notes on Flannery O'Conner." *NCL* 3(May, 1973): 11-15.

6617. Ferris, Sumner J. "The Outside and the Inside: Flannery O'Conner's *The Violent Bear It Away.*" *Crit* 3,#2(1960): 11-19.

6618. Friedman, Melvin J. "By and About Flannery O'Conner." *JML* 1(1970): 288-292.

6619. Gordon, Caroline. "Flannery O'Conner's *Wise Blood.*" *Crit* 2,#2(1958): 3-10.

6620. Gossett, Thomas F. "Flannery O'Conner's Opinions of Other Writers: Some Unpublished Comments." *SLJ* 6,#2(1974): 70-82.

6621. Green, James L. "Enoch Emery and His Biblical Namesakes in 'Wise Blood.'" *SSF* 10(1973): 417-419.

6622. Griffith, Albert J. "Flannery O'Conner's Salvation Road." *SSF* 3(1966): 329-333.

6623. Harrison, Margaret. "Hazel Motes Transit: A Comparison of Two Versions of Flannery O'Conner's 'The Train' with Chapter I of 'Wise Blood.'" *SSF* 8(1971): 287-293.

6624. Hays, Peter L. "Dante, Tobit, and 'The Aritificial Nigger.'" *SSF* 5(1968): 263-268.

6625. Hegarty, Charles M., S. J. "A Note on Flannery O'Conner." *SSF* 9(1972): 409-410.

6626. Joselyn, Sister M., O. S. B. "Thematic Centers in 'The Displaced Person.'" *SSF* 1(1964): 85-92.

6627. Katz, Claire. "Flannery O'Conner's Rage of Vision." *AL* 46(1974): 54-67.

6628. Klevar, Harvey. "Image and Imagination: Flannery O'Conner's Front Page Fiction." *JML* 4(1974): 121-132.

6629. Lorch, Thomas. "Flannery O'Conner: Christian Allegorist." *Crit* 10,#2(1968): 69-80.

6630. Maida, Patricia Dinneen. "'Convergence' in Flannery O'Conner's 'Everything that Rises Must Converge.'" *SSF* 7(1970): 549-555.

6631. ----------. "Light and Enlightenment in Flannery O'Conner's Fiction." *SSF* 13(1976): 31-36.

6632. Male, Roy R. "The Two Versions of 'The Displaced Person.'" *SSF* 7(1970): 450-457.

6633. Marks, W. S., III. "Advertisements for Grace: Flannery O'Conner's 'A Good Man is Hard to Find.'" *SSF* 4(1966): 19-27.

6634. Mayer, David R. "Apologia for the Imagination: Flannery O'Conner's 'A Temple of the Holy Ghost.'" *SSF* 11(1974): 147-152.

6635. Millichap, Joseph R. "The Pauline Old Man in Flannery O'Conner's 'The Comforts of Home.'" *SSF* 11(1974): 96-99.

6636. Montgomery, Marion. "Flannery O'Conner's Territorial Center." *Crit* 11,#3(1969): 5-10.

6637. Quinn, Sister M. Bernetta, O. S. F. "View from a Rock: The Fiction of Flannery O'Conner and J. F. Powers." *Crit* 2,#2(1958): 19-27.

6638. Rubin, Louis D., Jr. "Flannery O'Conner: A Note on Literary Fashions." *Crit* 2,#2 (1958): 11-18.

6639. Shinn, Thelma J. "Flannery O'Conner and the Violence of Grace." *Con L* 9(1968): 58-73.

6640. Soonenfield, Albert. "Flannery O'Conner: The Catholic Writer as Baptist." *Con L* 13 (1972): 445-457.

6641. Spivey, Ted R. "Flannery O'Conner's View of God and Man." *SSF* 1(1964): 200-206.

6642. Walden, Daniel, and Jane Salvia. "Flannery O'Conner's Dragon: Vision in 'A Temple of the Holy Ghost.'" *SAF* 4(1976): 230-235.

6643. Wedge, George F. "Two Bibliographies: Flannery O'Conner, J. F. Powers." *Crit* 2,#2(1958): 59-70.

6644. Williams, Melvin G. "Black and White: A Study in Flannery O'Conner's Characters." *BALF* 10(1976): 130-132.

6645. Woodward, Robert H. "A Good Route is Hard to Find: Place Names and Setting in O'Conner's 'A Good Man is Hard to Find.'" *NCL* 3(November, 1973): 2-6.

6646. Wynne, Judith F. "The Sacramental Irony of Flannery O'Conner." *SLJ* 7,#2(1975): 33-49.

ODETS, CLIFFORD.   6647. Dozier, Richard J. "Odets and 'Little Lefty.'" *AL* 48(1977): 597-598.

6648. Miller, Jeanne-Marie A. "Odets, Miller and Communism." *CLA* 19(1976): 484-493.

6649. Pearce, Richard. "'Pylon,' 'Awake and Sing!' and the Apocalyptic Imagination of the 30's." *Criticism* 13(1971): 131-141.

ODUM, HOWARD.   See 4383.

O'HARA, FRANK.   6650. Donaldson, Scott. "Appointment with the Dentist: O'Hara's Naturalistic Novel." *MFS* 14(1968): 435-442.

6651. Libby, Anthony. "O'Hara on the Silver Range." *Con L* 17(1976): 240-262.

6652. Moramarco, Fred. "John Ashberry and Frank O'Hara: The Painterly Poets." *JML* 5(1976): 436-462.

O'HARA, JOHN.   6653. McCormick, Bernard. "A John O'Hara Geography." *JML* 1(1970): 151-168.

6654. Shawen, Edgar. "Social Interaction in John O'Hara's 'The Gangster.'" *SSF* 11(1974): 367-370.

OLSEN, TILLIE.   6655. O'Connor, William Van. "The Short Stories of Tillie Olsen." *SSF* 1(1963): 21-25.

OLSON, CHARLES. 6656. Ballew, Steve. "History as Animated Metaphor in the *Maximus Poems*." *NEQ* 47(1974): 51-64.

6657. Dembo, L. S. "Charles Olson and the Moral History of Cape Ann." *Criticism* 14(1972): 165-174.

6658. Halberg, Robert van. "Olson's Relation to Pound and Williams." *Con L* 15(1974): 15-48.

6659. Merrill, Thomas F. "'The Kingfishers': Charles Olson's 'Marvelous Maneuver.'" *Con L* 17 (1976): 506-528.

6660. Perloff, Marjorie G. "Charles Olson and the 'Inferior Predecessors': 'Projected Verse' Revisited." *ELH* 40(1973): 285-306.

6661. Waldrop, Ronmarie. "Charles Olson: Process and Relationship." *TCL* 23(1977): 467-486.

OPPEN, GEORGE. 6662. Dembo, L. S. "The 'Objectivist' Poet: Four Interviews." *Con L* 10 (1969): 155-219.

O'NEILL, EUGENE. 6663. Adler, Jacob H. "The Worth of *Ah, Wilderness*." *MD* 3(1960): 280-288.

6664. Alexander, Doris. "Eugene O'Neill and Charles Lever." *MD* 5(1963): 415-420.

6665. ----------. "Eugene O'Neill and *Light on the Path*." *MD* 3(1960): 260-267.

6666. ----------. "Eugene O'Neill, 'The Hound of Heaven,' and the 'Hell Hole.'" *MLQ* 20 (1959): 307-314.

6667. ----------. "*Lazarus Laughed* and Buddha." *MLQ* 17(1956): 357-365.

6668. ----------. "Psychological Fate in *Mourning Becomes Electra*." *PMLA* 68(1953): 923-934.

6669. ----------. "*Strange Interlude* and Schopenhauer." *AL* 25(1953): 213-228.

6670. Andreach, Robert J. "O'Neill's Use of Dante in *The Fountain* and *The Hairy Ape*." *MD* 10(1967): 48-56.

6671. Asselineau, Roger. "*Mourning Becomes Electra* As a Tragedy." *MD* 1(1958): 143-150.

6672. Baum, Bernard. "*Tempest* and *Hairy Ape*: The Literary Incarnation of Mythos." *MLQ* 14 (1953): 258-273.

6673. Bowling, Charis Crosse. "The Touch of Poetry: A Study of the Role of Poetry in Three O'Neill Plays." *CLA* 12(1968): 43-55.

6674. Brashear, William R. "O'Neill and Shaw: the Play as Will and Idea." *Criticism* 8 (1966): 155-169.

6675. ----------. "O'Neill's Schopenhauer Interlude." *Criticism* 6(1964): 256-265.

6676. ----------. "The Wisdom of Silenus in O'Neill's *Iceman*." *AL* 36(1964): 180-188.

6677. Bryer, Jackson R. "Forty Years of O'Neill Criticism: A Selected Bibliography." *MD* 4(1961): 196-216.

6678. Chabrowe, Leonard. "Dionysus in *The Iceman Cometh*." *MD* 4(1962): 377-388.

6679. Chaitin, Norman. "O'Neill: The Power of Daring." *MD* 3(1960): 231-241.

6680. Chen, David Y. "Two Chinese Adaptations of Eugene O'Neill's *The Emporor Jones*." *MD* 9(1966): 431-439.

6681. Clark, Marden J. "Tragic Effect in *The Hairy Ape*." *MD* 10(1968): 372-382.

6682. Cohn, Ruby. "Absurdity in English: Joyce and O'Neill." *CD* 3(1969): 156-161.

6683. Conlin, Matthew T., O. F. M. "The Tragic Effect in *Autumn Fire* and *Desire Under the Elms*." *MD* 1(1959): 228-235.

6684. Cooley, John R. "*The Emperor Jones* and the Harlem Renaissance." *SL I* 7,#2(1974): 73-83.

6685. Dahlstrom, Carl E. W. L. "*Dynamo* and *Lazarus Laughed*: Some Limitations." *MD* 3(1960): 224-230.

6686. Day, Cyrus. "*Amor Fati*: O'Neill's Lazarus as Superman and Savior." *MD* 3(1960): 297-305.

6687. ----------. "The Iceman and the Bridegroom." *MD* 1(1958): 3-9.

6688. Engel, Edwin A. "O'Neill, 1960." *MD* 3(1960): 219-223.

6689. Falk, Doris V. "That Paradox, O'Neill." *MD* 6(1963): 221-238.

6690. Falk, Signi. "Dialogue in the Plays of Eugene O'Neill." *MD* 3(1960): 314-325.

6691. Fitzgerald, John J. "The Bitter Harvest of O'Neill's Projected Cycle." *NEQ* 40(1967): 364-374.

6692. Flory, Claude R. "Notes on the Antecedents of *Anna Christie*." *PMLA* 86(1971): 77-83.

6693. Frazer, Winifred L. "Chris and Poseidon: Man versus God in *Anna Christie*." *MD* 12 (1969): 279-285.

6694. ----------. "King Lear and Hickey: Bridegroom and Iceman." *MD* 15(1972): 267-278.

6695. ----------. "O'Neill's Iceman—Not Ice Man." *AL* 44(1973): 677-678.

6696. Frenz, Horst. "Notes on Eugene O'Neill in Japan." *MD* 3(1960): 306-313.

6697. ----------, and Frederick Fleisher. "Eugene O'Neill and the Royal Dramatic Theatre of Stockholm." *MD* 10(1967): 300-311.

6698. ----------, and Martin Mueller. "More Shakespeare and Less Aeschylus in Eugene O'Neill's *Mourning Becomes Electra*." *AL* 38(1966): 85-100.

6699. Gabbard, Lucina P. "At the Zoo: From O'Neill to Albee." *MD* 19(1976): 365-374.

6700. Gillett, Peter J. "O'Neill and the Racial Myths." *TCL* 18(1972): 111-120.

6701. Goldhurst, William. "A Literary Source for O'Neill's 'In the Zone.'" *AL* 35(1964): 530-534.

6702. Hartman, Murray. "*Desire Under the Elms* in the Light of Strindberg's Influence." *AL* 33(1961): 360-369.

6703. Hays, Peter L. "Biblical Perversions in *Desire Under the Elms*." *MD* 11(1969): 423-428.

6704. Herbert, Edward T. "Eugene O'Neill: An Evaluation by Fellow Playwrights." *MD* 6(1963): 239-240.

6705. Highsmith, James Milton. "The Cornell Letters: Eugene O'Neill on His Craftsmanship to George Jean Nathan." *MD* 15(1972): 68-88.

6706. ----------. "A Description of the Cornell Collection of Eugene O'Neill's Letters to George Jean Nathan." *MD* 14(1972): 420-425.

6707. Hinden, Michael. "*The Birth of Tragedy* and *The Great God Brown*." *MD* 16(1973): 129-140.

6708. Kennedy, Joyce Deveau. "O'Neill's Lavinia Mannon and the Dickinson Legend." *AL* 49 (1977): 108-113.

6709. Klavsons, Janis. "O'Neill's Dreamer: Success and Failure." MD 3(1960): 268-272.

6710. Lee, Robert C. "Evangelism and Anarchy in The Iceman Cometh." MD 12(1969): 173-186.

6711. ----------. "The Lonely Dream." MD 9(1966): 127-135.

6712. Marcus, Mordecai. "Eugene O'Neill's Debt to Thoreau in A Touch of the Poet." JEGP 62 (1963): 270-279.

6713. McAleer, John J. "Christ Symbolism in Anna Christie." MD 4(1962): 389-396.

6714. Metzger, Deena P. "Variations on a Theme: A Study of Exiles by James Joyce and The Great God Brown by Eugene O'Neill." MD 8(1965): 174-184.

6715. Miller, Jordan Y. "Myth and the American Dream: O'Neill to Albee." MD 7(1964): 190-198.

6716. Muchnic, Helen. "Circe's Swine: Plays by Gorky and O'Neill." Comp L 3(1951): 119-128.

6717. Nethercot, Arthur H. "Madness in the Plays of Eugene O'Neill." MD 18(1975): 259-280.

6718. ----------. "The Psychoanalyzing of Eugene O'Neill." MD 3(1960): 242-256, 357-372.

6719. ----------. "The Psychoanalyzing of Eugene O'Neill: Postscript." MD 8(1965): 150-155.

6720. ----------. "The Psychoanalyzing of Eugene O'Neill: P. P. S." MD 16(1973): 35-48.

6721. O'Neill, Joseph P., S. J. "The Tragic Theory of Eugene O'Neill." TSLL 4(1963): 481-498.

6722. Pallette, Drew B. "O'Neill and the Comic Spirit." MD 3(1960): 273-279.

6723. Pommer, Henry F. "The Mysticism of Eugene O'Neill." MD 9(1966): 26-39.

6724. Presley, Delma Eugene. "O'Neill's Iceman: Another Meaning." AL 42(1970): 387-388.

6725. Racey, Edgar F., Jr. "Myth as Tragic Structure in Desire Under the Elms." MD 5(1962): 42-46.

6726. Real, Jere. "The Brothel in O'Neill's Mansion." MD 12(1970): 383-389.

6727. Reardon, William R. "O'Neill Since World War II: Critical Reception in New York." MD 10(1967): 289-299.

6728. Reinhardt, Nancy. "Formal Patterns in The Iceman Cometh." MD 16(1973): 119-128.

6729. Robinson, James A. "O'Neill's Grotesque Dancers." MD 19(1976): 341-350.

6730. Rosen, Kenneth M. "O'Neill's Brown and Wilde's Gray." MD 13(1970): 347-355.

6731. Rothenberg, Albert, and Eugene Shapiro. "The Defense of Psychoanalysis in Literature: Long Day's Journey Into Night and A View From the Bridge." CD 7(1973): 22-50.

6732. Roy, Emil. "The Archetypal Unity of Eugene O'Neill's Drama." CD 3(1969): 263-274.

6733. ----------. "Eugene O'Neill's The Emperor Jones and The Hairy Ape as Mirror Plays." CD 2(1968): 21-31.

6734. Rust, R. Dilworth. "The Unity of O'Neill's S. S. Glencairn." AL 37(1965): 280-290.

6735. Scheick, William J. "The Ending of O'Neill's Beyond the Horizon." MD 20(1977): 293-298.

6736. Scrimgeour, James R. "From Loving to the Misbegotten: Despair in the Drama of Eugene O'Neill." MD 20(1977): 37-54.

6737. Shawcross, John T. "The Road to Ruin: The Beginning of O'Neill's Long Day's Journey." MD 3(1960): 289-296.

6738. Stafford, John. "Mourning Becomes America." TSLL 3(1962): 549-556.

6739. Stroupe, John H. "Marco Millions and O'Neill's 'two part two-play' Form." MD 13(1970): 382-392.

6740. ----------. "O'Neill's Marco Millions: A Road to Xanadu." MD 12(1970): 377-382.

6741. Törnqvist, Egil. "Miss Julie and O'Neill." MD 19(1976): 351-364.

6742. ----------. "O'Neill's Lazarus: Dionysus and Christ." AL 41(1970): 543-554.

6743. ----------. "Personal Nomenclature in the Plays of O'Neill." MD 8(1966): 362-373.

6744. Valgemae, Mardi. "O'Neill and German Expressionism." MD 10(1967): 111-123.

6745. Voelker, Paul D. "Eugene O'Neill and George Pierce Baker." AL 49(1977): 206-220.

6746. Weisman, Philip. "Mourning Becomes Electra and The Prodigal: Electra and Orestes." MD 3(1960): 257-259.

6747. Weixlmann, Joe. "Staged Segregation: Baldwin's Blues for Mister Charlie and O'Neill's All God's Children Got Wings." BALF 11(1977): 35-36.

6748. Winther, Sophus Keith. "Desire Under the Elms: A Modern Tragedy." MD 3(1960): 326-332.

6749. Wright, Robert C. "O'Neill's Universalizing Technique in The Iceman Cometh." MD 8(1965): 1-11.

See also 4402.

PATCHEN, KENNETH. See 4341.

PEEBLES, MELVIN. 6750. Bauerle, R. F. "The Theme of Absurdity in Melvin Van Peebles' A Bear for the FBI." NCL 1(September, 1971): 11-12.

6751. Jones, Norma R. "Sweetback: the Black Hero and Universal Myth." CLA 19(1976): 559-565.

PERCY, WALKER. 6752. Abádi-Nagy, Zoltán. "A Talk with Walker Percy." SLJ 6,#1(1973): 3-19.

6753. Dowie, William, S. J. "Walker Percy: Sensualist-Thinker." Novel 6(1972): 52-65.

6754. Johnson, Mark. "The Search for Place in Walker Percy's Novels." SLJ 8,#1(1975): 55-81.

6755. Kissell, Susan S. "Walker Percy's 'Conversions.'" SLJ 9,#2(1977): 124-136.

6756. Lawson, Lewis A. "Walker Percy's Indirect Communication." TSLL 11(1969): 867-900.

6757. ----------. "Walker Percy's Southern Stoic." SLJ 3,#1(1970): 5-31.

6758. LeClair, Thomas. "Walker Percy's Devil." SLJ 10,#1(1977): 3-13.

6759. Presley, Del. "Walker Percy's 'Larroes.'" NCL 3(January, 1973): 5-6.

6760. Sivley, Sherry. "Percy's Down Home Version of More's Utopia." NCL 7(September, 1977): 3-5.

6761. Thale, Mary. "The Moviegoer of the 1950's." TCL 14(1968): 84-89.

6762. Vauthier, Simone. "Title as Microtext: The Example of The Moviegoer." JNT 5(1975): 219-229.

PERKINS, MAXWELL. 6763. Skipp, Francis E. "Thomas Wolfe, Max Perkins, and Politics." MFS

13(1957): 503-511.

PETERKIN, JULIA.   6764. Durham, Frank. "The Reputed Demises of Uncle Tom; or, The Treatment of the Negro in Fiction by Southern Authors in the 1920's." *SLJ* 2,#2(1970): 26-50.

See also 4402.

PETERSON, LOUISE.   See 4369, 4371.

PETRY, ANN.   6765. Adams, George, R. "Riot as Ritual: Ann Petry's 'In Darkness and Confusion.'" *BALF* 6(1972): 55-57,60.

See also 4407.

PHARR, ROBERT D.   6766. O'Brien, John, and Raman K. Singh. "Interview with Robert Deane Pharr." *BALF* 8(1974): 244-246.

PLATH, SULVIA.   6767. Herman, Judith B. "Plath's 'Daddy' and the Myth of Tereus and Philomela." *NCL* 7(January, 1977): 9-10.

6768. Herman, Judith B. "Reflections on a Kitchen Table: A Note on Sylvia Plath's 'Black Rook in Rainy Weathers.'" *NCL* 7(December, 1977): 5.

6769. Libby, Anthony. "God's Lioness and the Priest of Sycorax: Plath and Hughes." *Con L* 15(1974): 386-405.

6770. Mollinger, Robert N. "Sylvia Plath's 'Private Ground.'" *NCL* 5(March, 1975): 14-15.

6771. Perloff, Marjorie. "*Angst* and Animism in the Poetry of Sylvia Plath." *JML* 1(1970): 57-74.

6772. ----------. "Extremist Poetry: Some Versions of the Sylvia Plath Myth." *JML* 2(1972): 581-588.

6773. ----------. "'A Ritual for Being Born Twice': Sylvia Plath's *The Bell Jar*." *Con L* 13 (1972): 507-522.

6774. Schwartz, Murray M., and Christopher Bollas. "The Absence of the Center: Sylvia Plath and Suicide." *Criticism* 18(1976): 147-172.

6775. Smith, Pamela A. "The Unitive Urge in the Poetry of Sylvia Plath." *NEQ* 45(1972): 323-339.

See also 4447.

POOLE, ERNEST.   6776. Hart, John E. "Heroism Through Social Awareness: Ernest Poole's *The Harbor*." *Crit* 9,#3(1967): 84-94.

PORTER, KATHERINE.   6777. Alexander, Jean. "Katherine Ann Porter's Ship in the Jungle." *TCL* 11(1966): 179-188.

6778. Bell, Vereen M. "'The Grave' Revisited." *SSF* 3(1965): 39-45.

6779. Bluefarb, Sam. "Loss of Innocence in 'Flowering Judas.'" *CLA* 7(1964): 256-262.

6780. Bride, Sister Mary. "Laura and the Unlit Lamp." *SSF* 1(1963): 61-62.

6781. Curley, Daniel. "Treasure in 'The Grave.'" *MFS* 9(1963): 377-384.

6782. Flanders, Jane. "Katherine Ann Porter and the Ordeal of Southern Womanhood." *SLJ* 9,#1 (1976): 47-60.

6783. Givner, Joan. "The Genesis of *Ship of Fools*." *SLJ* 10,#1(1977): 14-30.

6784. ----------. "A Re-Reading of Katherine Anne Porter's 'Theft.'" *SSF* 6(1969): 463-465.

6785. Gottfried, Leon. "Death's Other Kingdom: Dantesque and Theological Symbolism in 'Flowering Judas.'" *PMLA* 84(1969): 112-124.

6786. Hartley, Lodwick. "Stephen's Lost World: The Background of Katherine Anne Porter's 'The Downward Path to Wisdom.'" *SSF* 6(1969): 574-579.

6787. Hendrick, George. "Hart Crane Aboard the Ship of Fools: Some Speculations." *TCL* 9 (1963): 3-9.

6788. Joselyn, Sister M., O. S. B. "'The Grave' as Lyrical Short Story." *SSF* 1(1964): 216-221.

6789. Kramer, Dale. "Notes on Lyricism and Symbols in 'The Grave.'" *SSF* 2(1965): 331-336.

6790. Liberman, M. M. "The Responsibility of the Novelists: the Critical Reception of 'Ship of Fools.'" *Criticism* 8(1966): 377-388.

6791. ----------. "The Short Story as Chapter in *Ship of Fools*." *Criticism* 10(1968): 65-71.

6792. ----------. "Some Observations on the Genesis of *Ship of Fools*: A Letter from Katherine Anne Porter." *PMLA* 84(1969): 136-137.

6793. Madden, David. "The Charged Image in Katherine Ann Porter's 'Flowering Judas.'" *SSF* 7(1970): 277-289.

6794. Marsden, Malcom M. "Love as Threat in Katherine Anne Porter's Fiction." *TCL* 13(1967): 29-38.

6795. Poss, S. H. "Variations on a Theme in Four Stories of Katherine Anne Porter." *TCL* 4(1958): 21-29.

6796. Partridge, Colin. "'My Familiar Country': An Image of Mexico in the Work of Katherine Anne Porter." *SSF* 7(1970): 597-614.

6797. Prater, William. "'The Grave': Form and Symbol." *SSF* 6(1969): 336-338.

6798. Redden, Dorothy S. "'Flowering Judas': Two Voices." *SSF* 6(1969): 194-204.

6799. Ryan, Marjorie. "*Dubliners* and the Stories of Katherine Anne Porter." *AL* 31(1960): 464-473.

6800. Thomas, M. Wynn. "Strangers in a Strange Land: A Reading of 'Noon Wine.'" *AL* 47 (1975): 230-246.

6801. Wiesenfarth, Joseph. "Internal Opposition in Porter's 'Granny Weatherall.'" *Crit* 11,#2(1969): 47-55.

6802. Wolfe, Peter. "The Problems of Granny Weatherall." *CLA* 11(1967): 142-148.

6803. Yannella, Philip R. "The Problems of Dislocation in 'Pale Horse, Pale Rider.'" *SSF* 6 (1969): 637-642.

6804. Youngblood, Sarah. "Structure and Imagery in Katherine Anne Porter's *Pale Horse, Pale Rider*." *MFS* 5(1959): 344-352.

See also 610, 4341, 4397, 4404.

POTOK, CHAIM.   6805. Bluefarb, Sam. "The Head, the Heart, and the Conflict of Generations in Chaim Potok's *The Chosen*." *CLA* 14(1971): 402-409.

POUND, EZRA.   6806. Adams, Stephen J. "Pound's Quantities and 'Absolute Rhythms.'" *EL* 4 (1977): 95-109.

6807. Alvarez, A. "Ezra Pound: the Qualities and Limitations of Translation-Poetry." *EIC* 6(1956): 171-189.

6808. Atkinson, F. G. "Ezra Pound's Reply to an 'Old-World' Letter." *AL* 46(1974): 357-359.

6809. Baar, Ron. "Ezra Pound: Poet as Historian." AL 42(1971): 531-543.

6810. Banerjee, Ron D. K. "Dante through
the Looking Glass: Rossetti, Pound, and Eliot."
Comp L 24(1972): 136-149.

6811. Baumann, Walter. "Pound and Layamon's
Brut" JEGP 68(1969): 265-276.

6812. Bergman, Herbert. "Ezra Pound and
Walt Whitman." AL 27(1955): 56-61.

6813. Bevilaqua, Ralph. "Pound's 'In a Sta-
tion of the Metro': A Textual Note." ELN 8(1971):
293-296.

6814. Bornstein, George J., and Hugh H.
Witemeyer. "From Villain to Visionary: Pound
and Yeats on Villon." Comp L 19(1967): 308-320.

6815. Boyd, Ernest L. "Ezra Pound at Wa-
bash College." JML 4(1974): 43-54.

6816. Connolly, Thomas E. "Ezra Pound's
'Near Perigord': The Background of a Poem." Comp
L 8(1956): 110-121.

6817. Cowan, James C. "The Classical Figure
as Archetype in Pound's Cantos, I-XXX." TCL 6
(1960): 25-32.

6818. Davenport, Guy. "Ezra Pound's Radiant
Gists: A Reading of Cantos II and IV." Con L 3,
#2(1962): 50-64.

6819. Drew-Bear, Thomas. "Ezra Pound's
'Homage to Sextus Propertius.'" AL 37(1965): 204-
210.

6820. Duffey, Bernard I. "The Experimental
Lyric in Modern Poetry: Eliot, Pound, Williams."
JML 3(1974): 1085-1103.

6821. Foster, John L. "Pound's Revision of
Cantos I-III." MP 63(1966): 236-245.

6822. French, A. L. "Mauberly: A Rejoinder." EIC 16(1966): 356-359.

6823. ----------. "'Olympian Apathein':
Pound's Hugh Selwyn Mauberly and Modern Poetry."
EIC 15(1965): 428-445.

6824. Fussell, Edwin. "Dante and Pound's
Cantos." JML 1(1970): 75-87.

6825. Giannone, Richard J. "Eliot's 'Portrait of a Lady' and Pound's 'Portrait D'une
Femme.'" TCL 5(1959): 131-134.

6826. Goodwin, K. L. "Ezra Pound's Influence on Literary Criticism." MLQ 29(1968): 423-
438.

6827. Grieder, Josephine. "Robert Frost on
Ezra Pound, 1913: Manuscript Corrections of
'Portrait d'une Femme.'" NEQ 44(1971): 301-305.

6828. Halberg, Robert van. "Olson's Relation to Pound and Williams." Con L 15(1974):
15-48.

6829. Hoffa, William Walter. "Ezra Pound
and George Antheil: Vorticist Music and the
Cantos." AL 44(1972): 52-73.

6830. Holder, Alan. "The Lesson of the
Master: Ezra Pound and Henry James." AL 35
(1963): 71-79.

6831. Hungiville, Maurice. "Ezra Pound,
Educator: Two Uncollected Pound Letters." AL
44(1972): 462-469.

6832. Hurwitz, Harold M. "Hemingway's
Tutor, Ezra Pound." MFS 17(1971): 469-482.

6833. Jackson, Thomas H. "The Adventures
of Messire Wrong-Head." ELH 32(1965): 238-255.

6834. Jackson, Thomas H. "The Poetic Politics of Ezra Pound." JML 3(1974): 987-1011.

6835. Korg, Jacob. "The Music of Lost
Dynasties: Browning, Pound and History." ELH
39(1972): 420-440.

6836. Lipke, William C., and Bernard Rozran.
"Ezra Pound and Vorticism: A Polite Blast." Con L
7(1966): 201-209.

6837. Martin, Wallace. "The Sources of the
Imagist Aesthetic." PMLA 85(1970): 196-204.

6838. Materer, Timothy. "The English Vortex:
Modern Literature and the 'Patterns of Hope.'" JML
3(1974): 1123-1139.

6839. ----------. "Ezra Pound and Gaudier-
Brzeska: Sophie's Diary." JML 6(1977): 315-321.

6840. McNaughton, William F. "Ezra Pound's
Meters and Rhythms." PMLA 78(1963): 136-146.

6841. Miller, Vincent E. "The Serious Wit
of Pound's Homage to Sextus Propertius." Con L
16(1975): 452-462.

6842. Moramarco, Fred. "Concluding an Epic:
The Drafts and Fragments of The Cantos." AL 49
(1977): 309-326.

6843. Movius, Geoffrey H. "Caviar and Bread:
Ezra Pound and William Carlos Williams, 1902-
1914." JML 5(1976): 383-406.

6844. Murwitz, Harold M. "Ezra Pound and
Rabindranath Tagore." AL 36(1964): 53-63.

6845. Oakes, Lois Ann. "An Explication of
'Canto LXXC' by Ezra Pound." Con L 5(1964): 105-
109.

6846. Parkinson, Thomas. "Yeats and Pound:
The Illusion of Influence." Comp L 6(1954): 256-
264.

6847. Pondrom, Cyrena N. "The Book of the
Poet's Club and Pound's 'School of Images.'" JML
3(1973): 100-102.

6848. Ramsey, Warren. "Pound, Laforgue, and
Dramatic Structure." Comp L 3(1951): 47-56.

6849. Reiss, Christopher. "In Defense of
Mauberley." EIC 16(1966): 351-355.

6850. Schneidau, Herbert N. "Pound and
Yeats: The Question of Symbolism." ELH 32(1965):
220-237.

6851. ----------. "Vorticism and the Career
of Ezra Pound." MP 65(1968): 214-227.

6852. Slatin, Myles. "A History of Pound's
Cantos I-XVI, 1915-1925." AL 35(1963): 183-195.

6853. Sokol, B. J. "What Went Wrong between
Robert Frost and Ezra Pound." NEQ 49(1976): 521-
541.

6854. Spanos, William V. "The Modulating
Voice of Hugh Selwyn Mauberly." Con L 6(1965):
73-96.

6855. Spencer, Benjamin T. "Pound: The
American Strain." PMLA 81(1966): 457-466.

6856. Sullivan, J. P. "Pound's Homage to
Propertius: The Structure of a Mask." EIC 10
(1960): 239-249.

6857. Sutton, Walter. "Mauberley, The Waste
Land, and the Problem of Unified Form." Con L 9
(1968): 15-35.

6858. Tanselle, G. Thomas. "Two Early Letters of Ezra Pound." AL 34(1962): 114-119.

6859. Tatlow, Anthony. "Stalking the Dragon: Pound, Waley, and Brecht." Comp L 25(1973):
193-211.

6860. Teele, Roy E. "Translations of Noh

Plays." *Comp L* 9(1957): 345-368.

6861. Wagner, Linda Welshimer. "The Poetry of Ezra Pound." *JML* 1(1970): 293-298.

6861a. Wees, William C. "Ezra Pound as Vorticist." *Con L* 6(1965): 56-72.

6862. ----------. "Pound's Vorticism: Some New Evidence and Further Comments." *Con L* 7(1966): 211-234.

6863. West, T. Wilson. "D. G. Rosetti and Ezra Pound." *RES* 4(1953): 63-67.

6864. Wilhelm, James J. "The Dragon and the Duel: A Defense of Pound's *Canto 88*." *TCL* 20 (1974): 114-125.

6865. ----------. "Guido Cavalcanti as a Mask for Ezra Pound." *PMLA* 89(1974): 332-340.

6866. Willard, Charles B. "Ezra Pound's Debt to Walt Whitman." *SP* 54(1957): 573-581.

See also 488, 514, 15717a, 21025.

POWERS, J. F. 6867. Hagopian, John V. "The Fathers of J. F. Powers." *SSF* 5(1968): 139-153.

6868. ----------. "Irony and Involution in J. F. Powers' *Morte D'Urban*." *Con L* 9(1968): 151-171.

6869. Hynes, Joseph. "Father Urban's Renewal: J. F. Powers' Difficult Precision." *MLQ* 29(1968): 450-466.

6870. Poss, Stanley. "J. F. Powers and the Gin of Irony." *TCL* 14(1968): 65-74.

6871. Quinn, Sister M. Bernetta, O. S. F. "View from a Rock: The Fiction of Flannery O'Conner and J. F. Powers." *Crit* 2,#2(1958): 19-27.

6872. Schler, Alrene. "How to Recognize Heaven When You See It: The Theology of St. John of the Cross in J. F. Powers' 'Lions, Harts, and Leaping Does.'" *SSF* 14(1977): 159-164.

6873. Scouffas, George. "J. F. Powers: On the Vitality of Disorder." *Crit* 2,#2(1958): 41-58.

6874. Sisk, John P. "The Complex Moral Vision of J. F. Powers." *Crit* 2,#2(1958): 28-40.

6875. Stewart, D. H. "J. F. Powers' *Morte D'Urban* as Western." *WAL* 5(1970): 31-44.

6876. Wedge, George F. "Two Bibliographies: Flannery O'Conner, J. F. Powers." *Crit* 2,#2(1958): 59-70.

6877. Wymard, Eleanor B. "On The Revisions of *Morte D'Urban*." *SSF* 14(1977): 84-86.

PRICE, REYNOLDS. 6878. Shepherd, Alan. "Love (and Marriage) in A Long and Happy Life." *TCL* 17(1971): 29-35.

6879. ----------. "Reynolds Price's *A Long and Happy Life*: The Epigraph." *NCL* 2(May, 1972): 12-13.

6880. Stevenson, John W. "The Faces of Reynold Price's Short Fiction." *SSF* 3(1966): 300-306.

PURDY, JAMES. 6881. Baldanza, Frank. "James Purdy on the Corruption of Innocents." *Con L* 15(1974): 315-330.

6882. ----------. "The Paradoxes of Patronage in Purdy." *AL* 46(1974): 347-356.

6883. ----------. "Playing House for Keeps with James Purdy." *Con L* 11(1970): 488-510.

6884. Lorch, Thomas M. "Purdy's Malcolm: A Unique Vision of Radical Emptiness." *Con L* 6 (1965): 204-213.

6885. Skerrett, Joseph Taylor, Jr. "James Purdy and the Works: Love and Tragedy in Five Novels." *TCL* 15(1969): 25-34.

PUZO, MARIO. 6886. Crook, Eugene J. "A Christ-Figure in *The Godfather*." *NCL* 2(May, 1972): 5-6.

PYNCHON, THOMAS. 6887. Cowant, David. "Love and Death: Variations on a Theme in Pynchon's Early Fiction." *JNT* 7(1977): 157-169.

6888. Davidson, Cathy N. "Oedipa as Androgyne in Thomas Pynchon's *The Crying of Lot 49*." *Con L* 18(1977): 38-50.

6889. Friedman, Alan J. and Manfred Puetz. "Science as Metaphor: Thomas Pynchon and *Gravity's Rainbow*." *Con L* 15(1974): 345-359.

6890. Hausdorff, Don. "Thomas Pynchon's Multiple Absurdities." *Con L* 7(1966): 258-269.

6891. Henkle, Roger B. "Pynchon's Tapestries on the Western Wall." *MFS* 17(1971): 207-220.

6892. Herzberg, Bruce. "Selected Articles on Thomas Pynchon: An Annotated Bibliography." *TCL* 21(1975): 221-225.

6893. Kolodny, Annette, and Daniel James Peters. "Pynchon's *The Crying of Lot 49*: The Novel as Subversive Experience." *MFS* 19(1973): 79-88.

6894. Lhamon, W. T., Jr. "Pentecost, Promiscuity, and Pynchon's *V*: From the Scaffold to the Impulsive." *TCL* 21(1975): 163-176.

6895. McClintock, James I. "United States Revisited: Pynchon and Zamiatin." *Con L* 18(1977): 475-490.

6896. Morgan, Speer. *"Gravity's Rainbow*: What's the Big Idea?" *MFS* 23(1977): 199-216.

6897. O'Connor, Peter. "The Wasteland of Pynchon's *V*." *Coll L* 3(1976): 49-55.

6898. Ozier, Lance W. "The Calculus of Transformation: More Mathematical Imagery in *Gravity's Rainbow*." *TCL* 21(1975): 193-210.

6899. Poirier, Richard. "The Importance of Thomas Pynchon." *TCL* 21(1975): 151-162.

6900. Sanders, Scott. "Pynchon's Paranoid History." *TCL* 21(1975): 177-192.

6901. Simons, John. "Third Story Man: Biblical Irony in Thomas Pynchon's 'Entropy.'" *SSF* 14(1977): 88-93.

6902. Vesterman, William. "Pynchon's Poetry." *TCL* 21(1975): 211-220.

6903. Wagner, Linda W. "A Note on Oedipa the Roadrunner." *JNT* 4(1974): 155-161.

6904. Winston, Mathew. "The Quest for Pynchon." *TCL* 21(1975): 278-287.

6905. Wolfley, Lawrence. "Repression's Rainbow: The Prescence of Norman O. Brown in Pynchon's Big Novel." *PMLA* 92(1977): 873-889.

6906. Young, James Dean. "The Emigma Variations of Thomas Pynchon." *Crit* 10,#1(1967): 69-77.

RAKOSI, CARL. 6907. Dembo, L. S. "The 'Objectivist' Poet: Four Interviews." *Con L* 10 (1969): 155-219.

RANSOM, JOHN CROWE. 6908. Justus, James H. "A Note on John Crowe Ranson and Robert Penn Warren." *AL* 41(1969): 425-430.

6909. Mann, David, and Samuel H. Woods. "John Crowe Ransom's Poetic Revisions." *PMLA* 83 (1968): 15-21.

6910. Meyers, Walter E., Samuel Woods, Jr., and David Mann. "A Commentary on 'John Crowe Ransom's Poetic Revisions.'" *PMLA* 85(1970): 532-534.

6911. Parsons, Thorton H. "Ransom and the Poetics of Monastic Ecstasy." *MLQ* 26(1965): 571-585.

6912. Schwartz, Elias. "Ransom's 'Bells for John Whiteside's Daughter.'" *ELN* 1(1964): 284-285.

6913. Woodberry, W. Potter. "The Sword Between Them: Love and Death in Ransom's 'The Equilibrists.'" *SLJ* 9,#2(1977): 51-65.

See also 349, 19517.

RAPHAEL, FREDERIC. 6914. McDowell, Frederick P. W. "The Varied Universe of Frederic Raphael's Fiction." *Crit* 8,#1(1965): 21-50.

RAWLINGS, MARJORIE. 6915. York, Lamar. "Marjorie Kinnan Rawlings's Rivers." *SLJ* 9,#2 (1977): 91-107.

REED, ISHMAEL. 6916. Ambler, Madge. "Ishmael Reed: Whose Radio Broke Down?" *BALF* 6(1972): 125-131.

6917. Ford, Nick Aaron. "A Note on Ishmael Reed: Revolutionary Novelist." *SN* 3(1971): 216-218.

6918. McKenzie, James. "Introduction to Polevaulting in Top Hats: A Public Conversation with John Barth, William Gass, and Ishmael Read." *MFS* 22(1976): 131-152.

6919. Schmitz, Neil. "Neo-HooDoo: the Experimental Fiction of Ishmael Reed." *TCL* 20 (1974): 126-140.

REXROTH, KENNETH. 6920. Pondrom, Cyrena N. "An Interview with Kenneth Rexroth." *Con L* 10 (1969): 313-331.

REZNIKOFF, CHARLES. 6921. Dembo, L. S. "The 'Objectivist' Poet: Four Interviews." *Con L* 10(1969): 155-119.

RHODES, EUGENE. 6922. Fife, Jim L. "Two Views of the American West." *WAL* 1(1966): 34-43.

6923. Hutchinson, W. H. "I Pay for What I Break." *WAL* 1(1966): 91-96.

RICE, ELMER. 6924. Hogan, Robert. "Elmer Rice: A Bibliography." *MD* 8(1966): 440-443.

6925. ----------. "Rice: The Public Life of a Playwright." *MD* 8(1966): 426-439.

6926. Zeller, Loren L. "Two Expressionistic Interpretations of Dehumanization: Rice's *The Adding Machine* and Muñiz's *El Tintero*." *EL* 2 (1975): 245-255.

RICHARDSON, JACK. 6927. Debusscher, Gilbert. "Modern Masks of Orestes: *The Flies* and *The Prodigal*." *MD* 12(1969): 308-319.

6928. Weisman, Philip. "*Mourning Becomes Electra* and *The Prodigal*: Electra and Orestes." *MD* 3(1960): 257-259.

RIDGWAY, WILLIAM. 6929. Lockerbie, D. Bruce. "Sinclair Lewis and William Ridgway." *AL* 36(1964): 68-72.

ROBINSON, E. A. 6930. Anderson, Wallace L. "E. A. Robinson's 'Scattered Lives.'" *AL* 38(1967): 498-507.

6931. Baker, Carlos. "Robinson's Stoical Romanticism: 1890-1897." *NEQ* 46(1973): 3-16.

6932. Cary, Richard. "The First Publication of E. A. Robinson's Poem 'Broadway.'" *AL* 46 (1974): 83.

6933. Crowley, John W. "E. A. Robinson and Henry Cabot Lodge." *NEQ* 43(1970): 115-124.

6934. Donaldson, Scott. "The Alien Pity: A Study of Character in E. A. Robinson's Poetry." *AL* 38(1966): 219-229.

6935. Free, William J. "E. A. Robinson's Use of Emerson." *AL* 38(1966): 69-84.

6936. Fussell, Edwin S. "Robinson to Moody: Ten Unpublished Letters." *AL* 23(1951): 173-187.

6937. ----------. "An Unpublished Poem by E. A. Robinson." *AL* 22(1951): 487-488.

6938. Hepburn, James A. "E. A. Robinson's System of Opposites." *PMLA* 80(1965): 266-274.

6939. Joyner, Nancy. "Robinson's Pamela and Sandburg's Agatha." *AL* 40(1969): 548-549.

6940. Lowe, Robert Liddell. "Edwin Arlington Robinson to Harriet Monroe: Some Unpublished Letters." *MP* 60(1962): 31-40.

6941. ----------. "A Letter of Edwin Arlington Robinson to James Barstow." *NEQ* 37(1964): 390-392.

6942. ----------. "Two Letters of Edwin Arlington Robinson: A Note on His Early Critical Reception." *NEQ* 27(1954): 257-261.

6943. Perrine, Laurence. "The Sources of Robinson's *Merlin*." *AL* 44(1972): 313-321.

6944. Starr, Nathan C. "Edwin Arlington Robinson's Arthurian Heroines: Vivian, Guinevere, and the Two Isolts." *PQ* 56(1977): 253-258.

6945. Weeks, Lewis E., Jr. "E. A. Robinson's Poetics." *TCL* 11(1965): 131-145.

6946. Zietlow, Paul. "The Meaning of Tilbury Town: Robinson as a Regional Poet." *NEQ* 40 (1967): 188-211.

ROETHKE, THEODORE. 6947. Blessing, Richard A. "Theodore Roethke's Sometimes Metaphysical Motion." *TSLL* 14(1973): 731-749.

6948. Boyd, John D. "Texture and Form in Theodore Roethke's Greenhouse Poems." *MLQ* 32(1971): 409-424.

6949. Brown, Dennis E. "Theodore Roethke's 'Self-World' and the Modernist Position." *JML* 3 (1974): 1239-1254.

6950. Cruz, I. R. "Roethke's 'The Return.'" *NCL* 7(January, 1977): 8-9.

6951. Davis, William V. "The Escape Into Time: Theodore Roethke's 'The Waking.'" *NCL* 5 (March, 1975): 2-10.

6952. Heringman, Bernard. "Roethke's Poetry: The Forms of Meaning." *TSLL* 16(1974): 567-583.

6953. Heyen, William. "The Divine Abyss: Theodore Roethke's Mysticism." *TSLL* 11(1969): 1051-1068.

6954. Hollenberg, Susan Weidman. "Theodore Roethke: Bibliography." *TCL* 12(1967): 216-221.

6955. La Belle, Jenijoy. "Theodore Roethke's 'The Lost Son': From Archetypes to Literary History." *MLQ* 37(1976): 179-195.

6956. Libby, Anthony. "Roethke, Water Father." *AL* 46(1974): 267-288.

6957. Schutz, Fred C. "Antecedents of Roethke's 'The Lost Son' in an Unpublished Poem." *NCL* 5(May, 1975): 4-6.

6958. Staples, Hugh B. "The Rose in the Sea-Wind: A Reading of Theodore Roethke's 'North American Sequence.'" *AL* 36(1964): 189-203.

6959. Sullivan, Rosemary. "A Still Center: A Reading of Theodore Roethke's 'North American Sequence.'" *TSLL* 16(1975): 765-783.

See also 547.

ROTH, HENRY. 6960. Ferguson, James.

"Symbolic Patterns in *Call It Sleep*." *TCL* 14 (1969): 211-220.

6961. Knowles, A. Sidney, Jr. "The Fiction of Henry Roth." *MFS* 11(1965): 393-404.

6962. Ledbetter, Kenneth. "Henry Roth's *Call It Sleep*: The Revival of a Proletarian Novel." *TCL* 12(1966): 123-130.

6963. Lyons, Bonnie. "After *Call It Sleep*." *AL* 45(1974): 610-612.

6964. ----------. "'Broker': An Overlooked Story by Henry Roth." *SSF* 10(1973): 97-98.

6965. ----------. "The Symbolic Structure of Henry Roth's *Call It Sleep*." *Con L* 13(1972): 186-203.

6966. Ribalow, Harold U. "Henry Roth and His Novel *Call It Sleep*." *Con L* 3,#3(1962): 5-14.

6967. Samet, Tom. "Henry Roth's Bull Story: Guilt and Beytrayal in *Call It Sleep*." *SN* 7(1975): 569-583.

ROTH, PHILIP. 6968. Adair, William. "*Portnoy's Complaint*: A Camp Version of *Notes from Underground*." *NCL* 7(May, 1977): 9-10.

6969. Cohen, Eileen Z. "Alex in Wonderland, or *Portnoy's Complaint*." *TCL* 17(1971): 161-168.

6970. Cooperman, Stanley. "Philip Roth: 'Old Jacob's Eye' with a Squint." *TCL* 19(1973): 203-216.

6971. Davidson, Arnold E. "Kafka, Rilke, and Philip Roth's *The Breast*." *NCL* 5(January, 1975): 9-11.

6972. Donaldson, Scott. "Philip Roth: The Meanings of *Letting Go*." *Con L* 11(1970): 21-35.

6973. Levine, Mordecai H. "Philip Roth and American Judaism." *CLA* 14(1970): 163-170.

6974. Malin, Irving. "Looking at Roth's Kafka: or Some Hints about Comedy." *SSF* 14(1977): 273-275.

6975. Raban, Jonathan. "The New Philip Roth." *Novel* 2(1969): 153-163.

6976. Shakeen, Naseeb. "Binder Unbound, or, How Not to Convert the Jews." *SSF* 13(1976): 376-378.

6977. Siegel, Ben. "The Myths of Summer: Philip Roth's *The Great American Novel*." *Con L* 17(1976): 171-190.

6978. Sojka, Gregory S. "From Roth to Gaedel to Reiser: Fictional Analogues for Fictional Characters." *NCL* 7(May, 1977): 3-4.

6979. Willson, Robert F., Jr. "An Indisputable Source for the Spirited Account of a Baseball Contest Between the Port Ruppert Mundys and the Asylum Lunatics in *The Great American Novel* by Mr. Philip Roth." *NCL* 5(May, 1975): 12-14.

See also 4423.

ROTH, SAMUEL. 6980. Hamalian, Leo. "Nobody Knows My Names: Samuel Roth and the Underside of Modern Letters." *JML* 3(1974): 889-921.

6981. Roth, Samuel. "Adrift in London: An Extract from *Count Me Among the Missing*." *JML* 3(1974): 922-927.

ROTHENBERG, JEROME. 6982. McAllister, H. S. "'The Language of Shamars': Jerome Rothenberg's Contribution to American Indian Literature." *WAL* 10(1976): 293-309.

SABERHAGEN, FRED. 6983. Stewart, A. D. "Fred Saberhagen: Cybernetic Psychologist: A Study of the Berserker Stories." *Ext* 18(1976):

42-51.

SALINGER, J. D. 6984. Antico, John. "The Parody of J. D. Salinger: Esmé and the Fat Lady Exposed." *MFS* 12(1966): 325-340.

6985. Baskett, Sam S. "The Splendid/Squalid World of J. D. Salinger." *Con L* 4(1963): 48-61.

6986. Baumbach, Jonathan. "The Saint as a Young Man: A Reappraisal of *The Catcher in the Rye*." *MLQ* 25(1964): 461-472.

6987. Beebe, Maurice, and Jennifer Sperry. "Criticism of J. D. Salinger: A Selected Checklist." *MFS* 12(1966): 377-390.

6988. Bellman, Samuel Irving. "New Light on Seymour's Suicide: Salinger's *Hapworth 16, 1924*." *SSF* 3(1966): 348-351.

6989. Blotner, Joseph L. "Salinger Now: An Appraisal." *Con L* 4(1963): 100-108.

6990. Bryan, James. "The Psychological Structure of *The Catcher in the Rye*." *PMLA* 89 (1974): 1065-1074.

6991. ----------. "A Reading of Salinger's 'For Esmé-with Love and Squalor.'" *Criticism* 9 (1967): 275-288.

6992. ----------. "A Reading of Salinger's 'Teddy.'" *AL* 40(1968): 352-369.

6993. ----------. "Sherwood Anderson and *The Catcher in the Rye*: A Possible Influence." *NCL* 1(November, 1971): 2-5.

6994. Burke, Brother Fidelian, F. S. C. "Salinger's 'Esmé': Some Matters of Balance." *MFS* 12(1966): 341-348.

6995. Cohen, Hubert J. "'A Woeful Agony Which Forced Me to Bring Me to Begin My Tale': *The Catcher in the Rye*." *MFS* 12(1966): 355-366.

6996. Davis, Tom. "J. D. Salinger: 'The Sound of One Hand Clapping.'" *Con L* 4(1963): 41-47.

6997. Edwards, Duane. "Holden Caulfield: 'Don't Ever Tell Anybody Anything.'" *ELH* 44(1977): 554-565.

6998. Fiene, Donald M. "J. D. Salinger: A Bibliography." *Con L* 4(1963): 109-149.

6999. Fleissner, Robert F. "Salinger's Caulfield: A Refraction of Copperfield and His Caul." *NCL* 3(May, 1973): 5-7.

7000. French, Warren. "Holden's Fall." *MFS* 10(1964): 389.

7001. ----------. "The Phony World and the Nice World." *Con L* 4(1963): 21-30.

7002. Genthe, Charles V. "Six, Sex, Sick: Seymour, Some Comments." *TCL* 10(1965): 170-171.

7003. Goldstein, Bernice and Sanford. "'Seymour: An Introduction'—Writing as Discovery." *SSF* 7(1970): 248-256.

7004. ----------. "Zen and Salinger." *MFS* 12(1966): 313-324.

7005. Hagopian, John V. "'Pretty Mouth and Green My Eyes': Salinger's Paolo and Francesca in New York." *MFS* 12(1966): 349-354.

7006. Hassan, Ihab. "Almost the Voice of Silence: The Later Novelettes of J. D. Salinger." *Con L* 4(1963): 5-20.

7007. Howell, John M. "Salinger in the Waste Land." *MLS* 12(1966): 367-376.

7008. Kinney, Arthur F. "J. D. Salinger and the Search for Love." *TSLL* 5(1963): 111-126.

7009. Kranidas, Thomas. "Point of View in Salinger's 'Teddy.'" *SSF* 2(1964): 89-91.

7010. Lane, Gary. "Seymour's Suicide Again: A New Reading of J. D. Salinger's 'A Perfect Day for Bananafish.'" *SSF* 10(1973): 27-33.

7011. Levine, Paul. "J. D. Salinger: The Development of the Misfit Hero." *TCL* 4(1958): 92-99.

7012. Luedtke, Luther S. "J. D. Salinger and Robert Burns: *The Catcher in the Rye.*" *MFS* 16 (1970): 198-201.

7013. Lyons, John O. "The Romantic Style of Salinger's 'Seymour: An Introduction.'" *Con L* 4 (1963): 62-69.

7014. Metcalf, Frank. "The Suicide of Salinger's Seymour Glass." *SSF* 9(1972): 243-246.

7015. O'Hara, J. D. "No Catcher in the Rye." *MFS* 9(1963): 370-376.

7016. Perrine, Laurence. "Teddy? Booper? Or Blooper?" *SSF* 4(1967): 217-224.

7017. Roper, Pamela E. "Holden's Hat." *NCL* 7(May, 1977): 8-9.

7018. Russell, John. "Salinger, From Daumier to Smith." *Con L* 4(1963): 62-87.

7019. ----------. "Salinger's Feat." *MFS* 12(1966): 299-312.

7020. Schulz, Max F. "Epilogue to *Seymour: An Introduction*: Salinger and the Crisis of Consciousness." *SSF* 5(1968): 128-138.

7021. Schwartz, Arthur. "For Seymour—with Love and Judgment." *Con L* 4(1963): 88-99.

7022. Simms, L. Moody, Jr. "Seymour Glass: The Salingerian Hero as Vulgarian." *NCL* 5(November, 1975): 6-8.

7023. Slabey, Robert M. "*The Catcher in the Rye*: Christian Theme and Symbol." *CLA* 6(1963): 170-183.

7024. Stone, Edward. "Naming in Salinger." *NCL* 1(March, 1971): 2-3.

7025. ----------. "Salinger's Carousel." *MFS* 13(1967): 520-523.

7026. Strauch, Carl F. "Kings in the Back Row: Meaning Through Structure—A Reading of Salinger's *Catcher in the Rye*." *Con L* 2,#1(1961): 5-30.

7027. ----------. "Salinger: The Romantic Background." *Con L* 4(1963): 31-40.

See also 81.

SANCHEZ, SONIA. 7028. Palmer, R. Roderick. "The Poetry of Three Revolutionists: Don L. Lee, Sonia Sanchez, and Nikki Giovanni." *CLA* 15(1971): 25-36.

See also 4350, 4366.

SANDBURG, CARL. 7029. Alexander, William. "The Limited American, the Great Loneliness, and the Singing Fire: Carl Sandburg's 'Chicago Poems.'" *AL* 45(1973): 67-83.

7030. Joyner, Nancy. "Robinson's Pamela and Sandburg's Agatha." *AL* 40(1969): 548-549.

7031. Sutton, William F. "Personal Liberty Across Wide Horizons: Sandburg and the Negro." *BALF* 2(1968): 19-21.

SANDOZ, MARI. 7032. Greenwell, Scott L. "Fascists in Fiction: Two Early Novels of Mari Sandoz." *WAL* 12(1977): 133-143.

SANTAYANA, GEORGE. 7033. Ballowe, James. "Santayana on Autobiography." *AL* 41(1969): 219-230.

7034. Brown, Maurice F. "Santayana's Ameri-

can Roots." *NEQ* 33(1960): 147-163.

7035. ----------. "Santayana's Necessary Angel." *NEQ* 36(1963): 435-451.

7036. Conner, Frederick W. "*Lucifer* and *The Last Puritan*." *AL* 33(1961): 1-19.

7037. Larrabee, Harold A. "Santayana on His Works." *NEQ* 30(1957): 251-253.

7038. Porte, Joel. "Santayana at the 'Gas House.'" *NEQ* 35(1962): 337-346.

7039. Stolz, Gary R. "Santayana in America." *NEQ* 50(1977): 53-67.

7040. Wagner, C. Roland. "Conversation with Santayana, 1948: A Letter to a Friend." *AL* 40 (1968): 340-351.

7041. Wermuth, Paul C. "Santayana and *Huckleberry Finn*." *NEQ* 36(1963): 79-82.

7042. Wilson, Douglas L. "Santayana's *Metanoia*: The Second Sonnet Sequence." *NEQ* 39(1966): 3-25.

7043. Youman, A. Eliot. "Santayana's Attachments." *NEQ* 42(1969): 373-387.

7044. Young, David P. "Skeptical Music: Stevens and Santayana." *Criticism* 7(1965): 263-283.

See also 4376.

SAROYAN, WILLIAM. 7045. Rhoads, Kenneth W. "Joe as Christ-type in Sarayon's *The Time of Your Life*." *EL* 3(1976): 227-243.

7046. Shinn, Thelma. "William Saroyan: Romantic Existentialist." *MD* 15(1972): 185-194.

SAUNDERS, RUBY. See 4311.

SCHAEFER, JACK. 7047. Haslam, Gerald. "*Shane*: Twenty-five Years Later." *WAL* 9(1974): 215-216.

7048. Schaefer, Jack. "A New Direction." *WAL* 10(1976): 265-272.

SCHORER, MARK. 7049. Bluefarb, Sam. "What We Don't Know *Can* Hurt Us." *SSF* 5(1968): 163-170.

SCHUYLER, GEORGE. 7050. Peplow, Michael W. "George Schuyler, Satirist: Rhetorical Devices in *Black No More*." *CLA* 18(1974): 242-257.

SCHWARTZ, DELMORE. 7051. Lyons, Bonnie. "Delmore Schwartz and the Whole Truth." *SSF* 14 (1977): 259-264.

7052. Valenti, Lila Lee. "The Apprenticeship of Delmore Schwartz." *TCL* 20(1974): 201-216.

SEAGER, ALLAN. 7053. Bloom, Robert. "Allan Seager: Some Versions of Disengagement." *Crit* 5, #3(1962): 4-26.

7054. Hanna, Allan. "An Allan Seager Bibliography." *Crit* 5,#3(1962): 75-90.

7055. ----------. "The Muse of History: Allan Seager and the Criticism of Culture." *Crit* 5,#3(1962): 37-61.

7056. Kenner, Hugh. "The Insider." *Crit* 2, #3(1959): 3-15.

7057. Lid, R. W. "The Innocent Eye." *Crit* 5,#3(1962): 62-74.

7058. Webster, Harvey Curtis. "Allan Seager as Social Novelist." *Crit* 5,#3(1962): 27-36.

SEAY, JAMES. 7059. Bottoms, David. "Note on the Structure of James Seay's 'It All Comes Together Outside the Rest Room in Hogansville.'" *NCL* 7(September, 1977): 6-7.

SEGAL, ERICH. 7060. Kirby, David, and Eugene Crook. "*Love Story* and the Erotic Convention in Literature." *NCL* 1(November, 1971): 7-9.

SELBY, HUBERT.   7061. Peavy, Charles D.
"The Sin of Pride and Selby's *Last Exit to Brooklyn*" *Crit* 11,#3(1969): 35-42.

SELTZER, CHESTER.   7062. Halsam, Gerald.
"The Enigma of Amado Jesus Muro." *WAL* 10(1975):
3-9.

SEXTON, ANNE.   7063. "Theme and Tone in
Anne Sexton's 'To A Friend Whose Work Has Come to
Triumph.'" *NCL* 7(May, 1977): 2-3.
See also 4447.

SHANDS, H. A.   7064. Durham, Frank. "The
Reputed Demises of Uncle Tom; or, the Treatment of
the Negro in Fiction by Southern Authors in the
1920's." *SLJ* 2,#2(1970): 26-50.

SHAPIRO, KARL J.   7065. Shockley, Martin
Staples. "Shapiro's 'World.'" *AL* 21(1950): 485.

7066. Smith, Hammett W. "Karl Jay Shapiro:
A Poet of Human Relations." *CLA* 1(1958): 97-100.

SHEPARD, SAM.   7067. Bachman, Charles R.
"Defusion of Menace in the Plays of Sam Shepard."
MD 19(1976): 405-416.
See also 4372.

SILVERBERG, ROBERT.   7068. Kam, Rose Sall-
berg. "Silverberg and Conrad: Explorers of Inner
Darkness." *Ext* 17(1975): 18-28.

7069. Tuma, George W. "Biblical Myth and
Legend in *Tower of Glass*: Man's Search for Auth-
enticity." *Ext* 15(1974): 174-191.
See also 147.

SINCLAIR, UPTON.   7070. Quint, Howard H.
"Upton Sinclair's Quest for Artistic Independence—
1909." *AL* 29(1957): 194-203.

7071. Yoder, Jon A. "Upton Sinclair, Lanny,
and the Liberals." *MFS* 20(1974): 483-504.

SINGER, ISAAC B.   7072. Anderson, David M.
"Isaac Bashevis Singer: Conversations in California." *MFS* 16(1970): 423-439.

7073. Buchen, Irving H. "Isaac Bashevis
Singer and the External Past." *Crit* 8,#2(1966):
5-18.

7074. ----------. "Issac Bashevis Singer
and the Revival of Satan." *TSLL* 9(1967): 129-142.

7075. Lee, Grace Farrell. "Seeing and Blindness: A Conversation with Isaac Bashevis Singer."
Novel 9(1976): 151-164.

7076. Pinsker, Sanford. "The Fictive Worlds
of I. B. Singer." *Crit* 11,#1(1969): 26-39.

7077. ----------. "Isaac Bashevis Singer:
An Interview." *Crit* 11,#2(1969): 16-25.

7078. Pondrom, Cyrena N. "Isaac Bashevis
Singer: An Interview and a Biographical Sketch."
Con L 10(1969): 1-38.

7079. ----------. "Isaac Bashevis Singer:
An Interview, Part II." *Con L* 10(1969): 332-351.

7080. Rice, Julian C. "I. B. Singer's 'The
Captive': A False Messiah in the Promised Land."
SAF 5(1977): 267-275.

7081. Salamon, George. "In a Glass Darkly:
The Morality of the Mirror in E. T. A. "Hoffman
and I. B Singer." *SSF* 7(1970): 625-633.

7082. Siegel, Ben. "Sacred and Profane:
Isaac Bashevis Singer's Embattled Spirits." *Crit*
6,#1(1963): 24-47.

7083. Wolkenfeld, J. S. "Isaac Bashevis
Singer: The Faith of His Devils and Magicians."
Criticism 5(1963): 349-359.

7084. Zatlin, Linda G. "The Themes of

Isaac Bashevis Singer's Short Fiction." *Crit* 11,#2
(1969): 40-46.

SKINNER, B. F.   7085. Wolfe, Peter. "*Walden Two* Twenty-five years Later: A Retrospective
Look." *SLI* 6,#2(1973): 11-26.

SMITH, CORDWAINER.   See PAUL MYRON ANTHONY
LINEBARGER.

SMITH, LILLIAN.   7086. Blackwell, Louise,
and Frances Clay. "Lillian Smith, Novelist." *CLA*
15(1972): 452-458.

SMITH, WILLIAM GARDNER.   See 4415.

SNODGRASS, W. D.   See 4447.

SNYDER, GARY.   7087. Evers, Lawrence J.
"'Further Survivals of Coyote.'" *WAL* 10(1975):
233-236.

7088. Kern, Robert. "Clearing the Ground:
Gary Snyder and the Modernist Imperative." *Criticism* 19(1977): 158-177.

7089. ----------. "Recipes, Catalogues,
Open Form Poetics: Gary Snyder's Archetypal Voice."
Con L 18(1977): 173-197.

7090. Kirby, David K. "Snyder, Auden, and
the New Morality." *NCL* 1(January, 1971): 9-10.

7091. Lyon, Thomas J. "Gary Snyder, a
Western Poet." *WAL* 3(1968): 207-216.

7092. Parkinson, Thomas. "The Theory and
Practice of Gary Snyder." *JML* 2(1971): 448-452.

7093. Snyder, Gary. "The Incredible Survival
of Coyote." *WAL* 9(1975): 255-272.

SPENCER, ANNE.   See 622.

SPILLANE, MICKEY.   7094. Banks, R. Jeff.
"Anti-Professionalism in the Works of Mickey Spillane." *NCL* 3(March, 1973): 6-8.

STAFFORD, JEAN.   7095. Burns, Stuart L.
"Counterpoint in Jean Stafford's *The Mountain
Lion*." *Crit* 9,#2(1967): 20-32.

7096. Jenson, Sid. "The Noble Wicked West
of Jean Stafford." *WAL* 7(1973): 261-270.

7097. Mann, Jeanette. "Toward New Archetypal Forms: *Boston Adventure*." *SN* 8(1976): 291-
303.

7098. Vickery, Olga W. "The Novels of Jean
Stafford." *Crit* 5,#1(1962): 14-26.

STAFFORD, WILLIAM.   7099. Kyle, Carol.
"Point of View in 'Returned to Say' and the Wilderness of William Stafford." *WAL* 7(1972): 191-201.

7100. Roberts, J. Russell, Sr. "Listening
to the Wilderness with William Stafford." *WAL* 3
(1968): 217-226.

STEFFENS, LINCOLN.   7101. Cooley, Thomas W.
"Lincoln Steffens: American Innocent Abroad." *AL*
43(1972): 589-602.

STEGNER, WALLACE.   7102. Ahearn, Kerry.
"*The Big Rock Candy Mountain* and Angle of Repose:
Trial and Culmination." *WAL* 10(1975): 11-27.

7103. Ferguson, J. M., Jr. "Cellars of
Consciousness: Stegner's 'The Blue-Winged Teal.'"
SSF 14(1977): 180-182.

7104. Flora, Joseph M. "Vardis Fisher and
Wallace Stegner: Teacher and Student." *WAL* 5(1970):
121-128.

7105. Moseley, Richard. "First-Person Narration in Wallace Stegner's *All the Little Live
Things*." *NCL* 3(March, 1973): 12-13.

7106. Peterson, Audrey C. "Narrative Voice
in Wallace Stegner's *Angle of Repose*." *WAL* 10
(1975): 125-133.

See also 21115.

STEIN, GERTRUDE.   7107. Bridgman, Richard. "Melanctha." *AL* 33(1961): 350-359.

7108. Cooper, David D. "Gertrude Stein's 'Magnificent Asparagus': Horizontal Vision and Unmeaning in 'Tender Buttons.'" *MFS* 20(1974): 337-349.

7109. Couser, G. Thomas. "Of Time and Identity: Walt Whitman and Gertrude Stein as Autobiographers." *TSLL* 17(1976): 787-804.

7110. Farber, Lawren. "Fading: A Way. Gertrude Stein's Sources for Three Lives." *JML* 5(1976): 463-480.

7111. Fendelman, Earl. "Gertrude Stein Among the Cubists." *JML* 2(1972): 481-490.

7112. Fitz, L. T. "Gertrude Stein and Picasso: The Language of Surfaces." *AL* 45(1973): 228-237.

7113. Fleissner, Robert F. "Stein's Four Roses." *JML* 6(1977): 325-328.

7114. Hoffman, Michael J. "Gertrude Stein's 'Portraits.'" *TCL* 11(1965): 115-122.

7115. Purdy, Strother B. "Gertrude Stein at Marienbad." *PMLA* 85(1970): 1096-1105.

7116. Rose, Marilyn Gaddis. "Gertrude Stein and Cubist Narrative." *MFS* 22(1976): 543-555.

7117. Rother, James. "Gertrude Stein and the Translation of Experience." *EL* 3(1976): 106-119.

7118. Schmitz, Neil. "Gertrude Stein as Post-Modernist: The Rhetoric of *Tender Buttons.*" *JML* 3(1974): 1203-1218.

7119. Steele, Oliver L., Jr. "Gertrude Stein and Ellen Glasgow: Memoir of a Meeting." *AL* 33(1961): 76-77.

7120. Stewart, Allegra. "The Quality of Gertrude Stein's Creativity." *AL* 28(1957): 488-506.

7121. Wasserstrom, William. "The Sursymamericubealism of Gertrude Stein." *TCL* 21(1975): 90-106.

See also 4341.

STEINBECK, JOHN.   7122. Alexander, Stanley. "*Cannery Row:* Steinbeck's Pastoral Poem." *WAL* 2(1968): 281-295.

7123. ----------. "The Conflict of Form in *Tortilla Flat.*" *AL* 40(1968): 58-66.

7124. Antico, John. "A Reading of Steinbeck's "Flight." *MFS* 11(1965): 45-53.

7125. Astro, Richard. "Steinbeck and Ricketts: Escape or Commitment in *The Sea of Cortez.*" *WAL* 6(1971): 109-121.

7126. ----------. "Steinbeck's Post-War Trilogy: A Return to Nature and the Natural Man." *TCL* 16(1970): 109-122.

7127. Autrey, Max L. "Men, Mice, and Moths: Gradation in Steinbeck's 'The Leader of the People.'" *WAL* 10(1975): 195-204.

7128. Bedford, Richard C. "The Genesis and Consolation of Our Discontent." *Criticism* 14 (1972): 277-294.

7129. Beebe, Maurice, and Jackson R. Bryer. "Criticism of John Steinbeck: A Selected Checklist." *MFS* 11(1965): 90-103.

7130. Benson, Jackson J. "John Steinbeck: Novelist as Scientist." *Novel* 10(1977): 248-264.

7130. ----------. "John Steinbeck's *Cannery Row:* A Reconsideration." *WAL* 12(1977): 11-40.

7132. ----------. "'To Tom, Who Lived It': John Steinbeck and the Man from Weedpatch." *JML* 5(1976): 151-210.

7133. Burns, Stuart L. "The Turtle or the Gopher: Another Look at the Ending of *The Grapes of the Wrath.*" *WAL* 9(1974): 53-57.

7134. Chametzky, Jules. "The Ambivalent Endings of *The Grapes of Wrath.*" *MFS* 11(1965): 34-44.

7135. Davis, Robert Murray. "Steinbeck's 'The Murder.'" *SSF* 14(1977): 63-68.

7136. Ditsky, John M. "Music from a Dark Cave: Organic Form in Steinbeck's Fiction." *JNT* 1(1971): 59-67.

7137. French, Warren G. "The First Theatrical Production of Steinbeck's *Of Mice and Men.*" *AL* 36(1965): 525-527.

7138. ----------. "Steinbeck's Winter Tale." *MFS* 11(1965): 66-74.

7139. Gerstenberger, Donna. "Steinbeck's American Wasteland." *MFS* 11(1965): 59-65.

7140. Goldhurst, William. "*Of Mice and Men:* John Steinbeck's Parable of the Curse of Cain." *WAL* 6(1971): 123-135.

7141. Golemba, Henry L. "Steinbeck's Attempt to Escape the Literary Fallacy." *MFS* 15(1969): 231-239.

7142. Gordon, Walter K. "Steinbeck's 'Flight': Journey *to* or *from* Maturity." *SSF* 3(1966): 453-455.

7143. Griffin, Robert J., and William A. Freedman. "Machines and Animals: Pervasive Motifs in *The Grapes of Wrath.*" *JEGP* 62(1963): 569-580.

7144. Gullason, Thomas A. "Revelation and Evolution: A Neglected Dimension of the Short Story." *SSF* 10(1973): 347-356.

7145. Houghton, Donald E. "'Westering' in 'Leader of the People.'" *WAL* 4(1969): 117-124.

7146. Johnson, Curtis L. "Steinbeck: A Suggestion for Research." *MFS* 11(1965): 75-78.

7147. Kinney, Arthur F. "The Arthurian Cycle in *Tortilla Flats.*" *MFS* 11(1965): 11-20.

7148. Levant, Howard. "John Steinbeck's *The Red Pony:* A Study in Narrative Technique." *JNT* 1(1971): 77-85.

7149. ----------. "*Tortilla Flat:* The Shape of John Steinbeck's Career." *PMLA* 85(1970): 1087-1095.

7150. ----------. "The Unity of *In Dubious Battle:* Violence and Dehumanization." *MFS* 11 (1965): 21-33.

7151. Lieber, Todd M. "Talismanic Patterns in the Novels of John Steinbeck." *AL* 44(1972): 262-275.

7152. Lisca, Peter. "*The Grapes of Wrath* as Fiction." *PMLA* 72(1957): 296-309.

7153. ----------. "Motif and Pattern in *Of Mice and Men.*" *MFS* 2(1956): 228-234.

7154. ----------. "Steinbeck's Image of Man and His Decline as a Writer." *MFS* 11(1965): 3-10.

7155. Marcus, Mordecai. "The Lost Dream of Sex and Childbirth in 'The Chrysanthemums.'" *MFS* 11(1965): 54-58.

7156. Martin, Bruce K. "'The Leader of the People' Reexamined." *SSF* 8(1971): 423-432.

7157. May, Charles E. "Myth and Mystery in

Steinbeck's 'The Snake.'" *Criticism* 15(1973):
322-335.

7158. McMahan, Elizabeth E. "'The Chrysanthemums': A Study of a Woman's Sexuality." *MFS*
14(1968): 453-458.

7159. Metzger, Charles R. "Steinbeck's
Version of the Pastoral." *MFS* 6(1960): 115-124.

7160. Morsberger, Robert E. "In Defense
of "Westering." *WAL* 5(1970): 143-146.

7161. Nimitz, Jack. "Ecology in *The Grapes
of Wrath*." *HSL* 2(1970): 165-168.

7162. Noonan, Gerald. "A Note on 'The
Chrysanthemums.'" *MFS* 15(1969): 542.

7163. Osborne, William R. "The Texts of
Steinbeck's 'The Chrysanthemums.'" *MFS* 12(1966):
479-484.

7164. Pollack, Theodore. "On the Ending of
The Grapes of Wrath." *MFS* 4(1958): 177-178.

7165. Roane, Margaret. "John Steinbeck as
a Spokesman for the Mentally Retarded." *Con L*
5(1964): 127-132.

7166. Slade, Leonard A., Jr. "The Use of
Biblical Allusions in *The Grapes of Wrath*." *CLA*
11(1968): 241-247.

7167. Spilka, Mark. "Of George and Lennie
and Curley's Wife: Sweet Violence in Steinbeck's
Eden." *MFS* 20(1974): 169-179.

7168. Sweet, Charles A., Jr. "Ms. Elisa
Allen and Steinbeck's 'Chrysanthemums.'" *MFS* 20
(1974): 210-214.

7169. Tuttleton, James W. "Steinbeck in
Russia: The Rhetoric of Praise and Blame." *MFS*
11(1965): 79-89.

7170. West, Philip J. "Steinbeck's 'The
Leader of the People': A Crisis in Style." *WAL*
5(1970): 137-141.
    See also 4849.

STELOFF, FRANCES. 7171. Morgan, Kathleen.
"Frances Steloff and the Gotham Book Mart." *JML*
4(1975): 737-748.

STERLING, GEORGE. 7172. Duke, Maurice.
"Letters of George Sterling to James Branch
Cabell." *AL* 44(1972): 146-153.

STEVENS, WALLACE. 7173. Ackerman, R. D.
"Wallace Stevens: Myth, Belief, and Presence."
Criticism 14(1972): 266-276.

7174. Beehler, Michael T. "Meteoric Poetry:
Wallace Stevens' 'Description Without Place.'"
Criticism 19(1977): 241-259.

7175. Benamou, Michel. "Wallace Stevens
and Apollinaire." *Comp L* 20(1968): 289-300.

7176. ----------. "Wallace Stevens and the
Symbolist Imagination." *ELH* 31(1964): 35-63.

7177. ----------. "Wallace Stevens: Some
Relations between Poetry and Painting." *Comp L*
11(1959): 47-60.

7178. Bertholf, Robert J. "Parables and
Wallace Stevens' 'Esthetique du Mal.'" *ELH* 42
(1975): 669-689.

7179. Bevis, William B. "The Arrangement
of *Harmonium*." *ELH* 37(1970): 456-473.

7180. ----------. "Steven's Toneless
Poetry." *ELH* 41(1974): 257-286.

7181. Blessing, Richard. "Wallace Stevens
and the Necessary Reader: A Technique of Dyna-
mism." *TCL* 18(1972): 251-258.

7182. Borroff, Marie. "Wallace Stevens's

World of Words. Part I." *MP* 74(1976): 42-65.

7183. Borroff, Marie. "Wallace Stevens's
World of Words. Part II." *MP* 74(1976): 171-193.

7184. Bradley, Ardyth. "Wallace Stevens'
Decorations." *TCL* 7(1961): 114-117.

7185. Brown, Merle E. "Concordia Discors
in the Poetry of Wallace Stephens." *AL* 34(1962):
246-269.

7186. Bruns, Gerald L. "Poetry as Reality:
The Orpheus Myth and Its Modern Counterparts."
ELH 37(1970): 263-286.

7187. Bryer, Jackson R., and Joseph N. Riddel. "A Checklist of Stevens Criticism." *TCL* 8
(1962): 124-142.

7188. Butscher, Edward. "Wallace Stevens'
Neglected Fugue: 'Variations on a Summer Day.'"
TCL 19(1973): 153-164.

7189. Buttel, Robert. "Wallace Stevens and
the Grand Poem." *JML* 2(1971): 431-441.

7190. ----------. "Wallace Stevens at
Harvard: Some Origins of His Theme and Style."
ELH 29(1962): 90-119.

7191. Caldwell, Price. "Metaphoric Structures in Wallace Stevens' 'Thirteen Ways of Looking at a Blackbird.'" *JEGP* 71(1972): 321-335.

7192. Cameron, Sharon. "'The Sense Against
Calamity': Ideas of a Self in Three Poems by
Wallace Stevens." *ELH* 43(1976): 584-603.

7193. Carrier, Warren. "Commonplace Cos-
tumes and Essential Gaudiness: Wallace Stevens'
'Emperor of Ice-Cream.'" *Coll L* 1(1974): 230-235.

7194. Cecil, C. D. "An Audience for Wallace
Stevens." *EIC* 15(1965): 193-206.

7195. Collie, M. J. "The Rhetoric of Accurate Speech: A Note on the Poetry of Wallace
Stevens." *EIC* 12(1962): 54-66.

7196. Cook, Eleanor. "Wallace Stevens:
The Comedian as the Letter C." *AL* 49(1977):
192-205.

7197. Coyle, Beverly. "An Anchorage of
Thought: Defining the Role of Aphorism in Wallace Stevens' Poetry." *PMLA* 91(1976): 206-222.

7198. Culbert, Taylor, and John M. Violette.
"Wallace Stevens' Emperor." *Criticism* 2(1960):
38-47.

7199. D'Avanzo, Mario L. "Emerson and
Shakespeare in Stevens' 'Bantams in Pine-Woods.'"
AL 49(1977): 103-107.

7200. Doggett, Frank. "Abstraction and Wallace Stevens." *Criticism* 2(1960): 23-37.

7201. ----------. "Stevens on the Genesis
of a Poem." *Con L* 16(1975): 463-477.

7202. ----------. "This Invented World:
Stevens' 'Notes Toward a Supreme Fiction.'" *ELH*
28(1961): 284-299.

7203. ----------. "The Transition from
Harmonium: Factors in the Development of Stevens'
Later Poetry." *PMLA* 88(1973): 122-131.

7204. ----------. "Wallace Steven's Later
Poetry." *ELH* 25(1958): 137-154.

7205. ----------. "Wallace Stevens' Secrecy
of Words: A Note on Import in Poetry." *NEQ* 31
(1958): 375-391.

7206. Dougherty, Adelyn. "Structures of
Sound in Wallace Stevens' 'Farewell to Florida.'"
TSLL 16(1975): 755-764.

7207. Eddins, Dwight. "Wallace Stevens:

America the Primordial." *MLQ* 32(1971): 73-88.

7208. Eder, Doris L. "A Review of Stevens Criticism to Date." *TCL* 15(1969): 3-18.

7209. Enck, John J. "Stevens' Crispin as the Clown." *TSLL* 3(1961): 389-398.

7210. Feshbach, Sidney. "Wallace Stevens and Erik Satie: A Source for 'The Comedian as is the Letter C.'" *TSLL* 11(1969): 811-818.

7211. Flake, Carol. "Wallace Stevens' 'Peter Quince at the Clavier': Sources and Structure." *ELN* 12(1974): 116-120.

7212. Foster, Steven. "The *Gestalt* Configurations of Wallace Stevens." *MLQ* 28(1967): 60-76.

7213. Furia, Philip. "Nuances of a Theme by Milton: Wallace Stevens's 'Sunday Morning.'" *AL* 46(1974): 83-87.

7214. Goulet, Robert G., and Jean Rosenbaum. "The Perception of Immortal Beauty: 'Peter Quince at the Clavier.'" *Coll L* 2(1975): 66-72.

7215. Gustafson, Richard. "The Practick of the Maker in Wallace Stevens." *TCL* 9(1963): 83-88.

7216. Hartsock, Mildred E. "Image and Idea in the Poetry of Stevens." *TCL* 7(1961): 9-20.

7217. Heyen, William. "The Text of *Harmonium*." *TCL* 12(1966): 147-148.

7218. Hudson, Deatt. "Wallace Stevens." *TCL* 1(1955): 135-138.

7219. Huston, J. Dennis. "*Credences of Summer:* An Analysis." *MP* 67(1970): 263-272.

7220. King, Montgomery W. "The Two Worlds of Wallace Stevens." *CLA* 8(1964): 141-148.

7221. Lentricchia, Frank. "Wallace Stevens: The Critic's Redemption." *MLQ* 36(1975): 75-80.

7222. Lieber, Todd M. "Robert Frost and Wallace Stevens: 'What to Make of a Diminished Thing.'" *AL* 47(1975): 68-83.

7223. MacCaffrey, Isabel G. "The Other Side of Silence: 'Credences of Summer' as an Example." *MLQ* 30(1969): 417-438.

7224. ----------. "A Point of Central Arrival: Stevens' *The Rock.*" *ELH* 40(1973): 606-633.

7225. McBrearty, Paul. "Wallace Stevens's 'Like Decorations in a Nigger Cemetery.'" *TSLL* 15(1973): 341-356.

7226. McCann, Janet. "Wallace Stevens' 'The Good Man Has No Shape.'" *NCL* 6(March, 1976): 9-10.

7227. McDaniel, Judith. "Wallace Stevens and the Scientific Imagination." *Con L* 15(1974): 221-237.

7228. McFadden, George. "Poet, Nature, and Society in Wallace Stevens." *MLQ* 23(1962): 263-271.

7229. ----------. "Probings for an Integration: Color Symbolism in Wallace Stevens." *MP* 58(1961): 186-193.

7230. Miller, J. Hillis. "Wallace Stevens' Poetry of Being." *ELH* 31(1964): 86-105.

7231. Mollinger, Robert N. "An Analysis of Wallace Stevens' 'What We See Is What We Think.'" *NCL* 4(November, 1974): 4-7.

7232. Morse, Samuel French. "Wallace Stevens, Bergson, and Pater." *ELH* 31(1964): 1-34.

7233. Murphy, Francis. "'The Comedian as the Letter C.'" *Con L* 3,#2(1962): 79-99.

7234. Pearce, Roy Harvey. "Wallace Stevens: The Last Lesson of the Master." *ELH* 31(1964): 64-

85.

7235. ----------. "Wallace Stevens: The Life of the Imagination." *PMLA* 66(1951): 561-582.

7236. Perloff, Marjorie. "Irony in Wallace Stevens's *The Rock.*" *AL* 36(1964): 327-342.

7237. Pinkerton, Jan. "Political Realities and Poetic Release: Prose Statements by Wallace Stevens." *NEQ* 44(1971): 575-601.

7238. Rawson, C. J. "'Tis only Infinite Below: Speculations on Swift, Wallace Stevens, R. D. Laing and Others.'" *EIC* 22(1972): 161-181.

7239. Riddel, Joseph N. "The Contours of Stevens' Criticism." *ELH* 31(1964): 106-138.

7240. ----------. "'Poets' Politics'—Wallace Stevens' *Owl's Clover.*" *MP* 56(1958): 118-132.

7241. ----------. "The Thematic Changes of Stevens' 'Esthetique du Mal.'" *TCL* 7(1961): 65-81.

7242. ----------. "Wallace Stevens' *Ideas of Order:* The Rhetoric of Politics and the Rhetoric of Poetry." *NEQ* 34(1961): 328-351.

7243. ----------. "Wallace Stevens' 'Notes Toward a Supreme Fiction.'" *Con L* 2,#2(1961): 20-42.

7244. ----------. "Wallace Stevens' 'Visibility of Thought.'" *PMLA* 77(1962): 482-498.

7245. Rother, James. "Modernism and the Nonsense Style." *Con L* 15(1974): 187-202.

7246. Semel, Jay M. "Pennsylvania Dutch Country: Stevens' World as Meditation." *Con L* 14(1973): 310-319.

7247. Tompkins, Daniel P. "'To Abstract Reality': Abstract Language and the Intrusion of Consciousness in Wallace Stevens." *AL* 45(1973): 84-99.

7248. Turner, Myron. "The Imagery of Wallace Stevens and Henry Green." *Con L* 8(1967): 60-77.

7249. Vanderbilt, Kermit. "More Stevens and Shakespeare." *Coll L* 2(1975): 143-145.

7250. Wentersdorf, Karl P. "Wallace Stevens, Dante Alighieri, and the Emperor." *TCL* 13(1968): 197-204.

7251. Weston, Susan Brown. "The Artist as Guitarist: Stevens and Picasso." *Criticism* 17 (1975): 111-120.

7252. Whitbread, Thomas. "Wallace Stevens' 'Highest Candle.'" *TSLL* 4(1963): 465-480.

7253. Woodman, Leonora. "'A Giant on the Horizon': Wallace Stevens and the Idea of Man." *TSLL* 15(1974): 759-786.

7254. Young, David P. "Skeptical Music: Stevens and Santayana." *Criticism* 7(1965): 263-283.

7255. Zimmerman, Michael. "Wallace Stevens's Emperor." *ELN* 4(1966): 119-123.

7256. Zukofsky, Louis. "For Wallace Stevens." *JML* 4(1974): 91-104.

See also 464.

STOKES, HERBERT.   See 4366.

STONE, ROBERT.   7257. Moore, L. Hugh. "The Undersea World of Robert Stone." *Crit* 11,#3(1969): 43-56.

STRIBLING, T. S.   7258. Durham, Frank. "The Reputed Demises of Uncle Tom; or, The Treatment of the Negro in Fiction by Southern Authors in the 1920's." *SLJ* 2,#2(1970): 26-50.

See also 4402.

STUCKEY, ELNA.   7259. Roediger, David. "An Interview with Elma Stuckey." *BALF* 11(1977):

151-153.

STYRON, WILLIAM. 7260. Core, George. "*The Confessions of Nat Turner* and the Burden of the Past." *SLJ* 2,#2(1970): 117-134.

7261. Davis, Robert Gorham. "Styron and the Students." *Crit* 3,#3(1960): 37-46.

7262. Eggenschwiler, David. "Tragedy and Melodrama in *The Confessions of Nat Turner*." *TCL* 20(1974): 19-33.

7263. Foster, Richard. "An Orgy of Commerce: William Styron's *Set This House on Fire*." *Crit* 3,#3(1960): 59-70.

7264. Galloway, David D. "The Absurd Man as Tragic Hero: The Novels of William Styron." *TSLL* 6(1965): 512-534.

7265. Hays, Peter L. "The Nature of Rebellion in *The Long March*." *Crit* 8,#2(1965): 70-74.

7266. Lawson, Lewis. "Cass Kinsolving: Kierkegaardian Man of Despair." *Con L* 3,#3(1962): 54-66.

7267. Leon, Philip W. "*The Lost Boy* and a Lost Girl." *SLJ* 9,#1(1976): 61-69.

7268. Markos, Donald W. "Margaret Whitehead in *The Confessions of Nat Turner*." *SN* 4 (1972): 52-59.

7269. Mellen, Joan. "William Styron: The Absence of Social Definition." *Novel* 4(1971): 159-170.

7270. Moore, L. Hugh. "Robert Penn Warren, William Styron, and the Use of Greek Myth." *Crit* 8,#2(1965): 75-87.

7271. Nigro, August. "*The Long March*: The Expansive Hero in a Closed World." *Crit* 9,#3(1967): 103-112.

7272. O'Connell, Shaun. "Expense of Spirit: The Vision of William Styron." *Crit* 8,#2(1965): 20-33.

7273. Perry, J. Douglas, Jr. "Gothic as Vortex: The Form of Horror in Capote, Faulkner, and Styron." *MFS* 19(1973): 153-168.

7274. Pickens, Donald K. "Uncel Tom Becomes Nat Turner: A Commentary on Two American Heroes." *BALF* 3(1969): 45-48.

7275. Robb, Kenneth A. "William Styron's Don Juan." *Crit* 8,#2(1965): 34-46.

7276. Schneider, Harold W. "Two Bibliographies: Saul Bellow, William Styron." *Crit* 3,#3(1960): 71-91.

7277. Shapiro, Herbert. "*The Confession of Nat Turner*: William Styron and His Critics." *BALF* 9(1975): 99-104.

7278. Stevenson, David L. "Styron and the Fiction of the Fifties." *Crit* 3,#3(1960): 47-58.

7279. Tischler, Nancy M. "Negro Literature and Classic Form." *Con L* 10(1969): 352-365.

7280. Urang, Gunnar. "The Broader Vision: William Styron's *Set This House on Fire*." *Crit* 8,#2(1965): 47-69.

See also 4383, 4387.

SWADOS, HARVEY. 7281. Feinstein, Herbert. "Contemporary American Fiction: Harvey Swados and Leslie Fiedler (Interview)." *Con L* 2,#1(1961): 79-98.

TARKINGTON, BOOTH. 7282. Sorkin, Adam J. "'She Doesn't Last, Apparently': A Reconsideration of Booth Tarkington's *Alice Adams*." *AL* 46(1974): 182-199.

7283. Woodress, James L. "Booth Tarkington's Political Career." *AL* 26(1954): 209-222.

TATE, ALLEN. 7284. Carpenter, Lynette. "The Battle Within: The Beleaguered Consciousness in Allen Tate's *The Fathers*." *SLJ* 8,#2(1976): 3-23.

7285. Kane, Patricia. "An Irrepressible Conflict: Allen Tate's *The Fathers*." *Crit* 10,#2(1968): 9-16.

7286. Korges, James. "Allen Tate: A Checklist Continued." *Crit* 10,#2(1968): 35-52.

7287. Meniers, R. K. "The Center: Unity and Dissociation." *TCL* 9(1963): 54-79.

7288. O'Dea, Richard J. "*The Fathers*: A Revaluation." *TCL* 12(1966): 87-95.

7289. Thorp, Willard. "Allen Tate: A Checklist." *Crit* 10,#2(1968): 17-34.

TAYLOR, JEANNE A. 7290. Taylor, Jeanne A. "One Being Black and Writing for Television." *BALF* 4(1970): 79-82.

TAYLOR, PETER. 7291. Overmyer, Janet. "Sex and the Fancy Woman." *NCL* 4(September, 1974): 8-10.

7292. Pinkerton, Jan. "A Critical Distortion of Peter Taylor's 'At the Drugstore'." *NCL* 1(September, 1971): 6-7.

7293. Schuler, Barbara. "The House of Peter Taylor." *Crit* 9,#3(1967): 6-18.

7294. Smith, James Penney. "Narration and Theme in Taylor's *A Woman of Means*." *Crit* 9,#3 (1967): 19-30.

7295. ----------. "A Peter Taylor Checklist." *Crit* 9,#3(1967): 31-36.

TAYLOR, ROBERT LEWIS. See 4410.

THURBER, JAMES. 7296. Bernard, F. V. "A Thurber Letter." *ELN* 8(1971): 300-301.

7297. Black, Stephen A. "The Claw of the Sea-Puss: James Thurber's Sense of Experience." *Con L* 5(1964): 222-236.

7298. Bowden, Edwin T. "*The Thurber Carnival*: Bibliography and Printing History." *TSLL* 9(1968): 555-566.

7299. Triesch, Manfred. "Men and Animals: James Thurber and the Conversion of a Literary Genre." *SSF* 3(1966): 307.

THURMAN, WALLACE. 7300. Haslam, Gerald. "Wallace Thurman: A Western Renaissance Man." *WAL* 6(1971): 53-59.

TOLBERT, FRANK X. See 4410.

TOLSON, MELVIN. 7301. Cansler, Ronald Lee "'The White and Non-White Dichotomy' of Melvin Tolson's Poetry." *BALF* 7(1973): 115-118.

TOOMER, JEAN. 7302. Bell, Bernard. "A Key to the Poems in *Cane*." *CLA* 14(1971): 251-258.

7303. Blackwell, Louise. "Jean Toomer's *Cane* and Biblical Myth." *CLA* 17(1974): 535-542.

7304. Blake, Susan L. "The Spectatorial Artist and the Structure of *Cane*." *CLA* 17(1974): 516-534.

7305. Cancel, Rafael A. "Male and Female Interrelationship in Toomer's *Cane*." *BALF* 5(1971): 25-31.

7306. Chase, Patricia. "The Women in *Cane*." *CLA* 14(1971): 259-273.

7307. Christ, Jack M. "Jean Toomer's 'Bona and Paul': The Innocence and Artifice of Words."

BALF 9(1975): 44-46.

7308. Davis, Charles T. "Jean Toomer and the South: Region and Race as Elements within a Literary Imagination." *SLI* 7,#2(1974): 23-37.

7309. Dickerson, Mary Jane. "Sherwood Anderson and Jean Toomer: A Literary Relationship." *SAF* 1(1973): 163-175.

7310. Dillard, Mabel M. "Jean Toomer—the Veil Replaced." *CLA* 17(1974): 468-473.

7311. Duncan, Bowie. "Jean Toomer's *Cane:* A Modern Black Oracle." *CLA* 15(1972): 323-333.

7312. Farrison, W. Edward. "Jean Toomer's *Cane* Again." *CLA* 15(1972): 295-302.

7313. Fisher, Alice Poindexter. "The Influence of Ouspensky's *Tertium Organum* upon Jean Toomer's *Cane.*" *CLA* 17(1974): 504-515.

7314. Fischer, William C. "The Aggregate Man in Jean Toomer's *Cane.*" *SN* 3(1971): 190-215.

7315. Grant, Sister Mary Kathryn. "Images of Celebration in *Cane.*" *BALF* 5(1971): 32-34.

7316. Helbling, Mark. "Sherwood Anderson and Jean Toomer." *BALF* 9(1975): 35-39.

7317. Innes, Catherine L. "The Unity of Jean Toomer's *Cane.*" *CLA* 15(1972): 306-322.

7318. Jung, Udo O. H. "'Nora' Is 'Calling Jesus': A Nineteenth-Century European Dilemma in an Afro-American Garb." *CLA* 21(1977): 251-255.

7319. ----------. "'Spirit-Torsos of Exquisite Strength.'" *CLA* 19(1975): 261-267.

7320. Kopf, George. "The Tensions in Jean Toomer's 'Theatre.'" *CLA* 17(1974): 498-503.

7321. Kramer, Victor A. "The 'Mid-kingdom' of Crane's 'Black Tamborine' and Toomer's *Cane.*" *CLA* 17(1974): 486-497.

7322. Krasny, Michael. "The Aesthetic Structure of Jean Toomer's Cane." *BALF* 9(1975): 42-43.

7323. ----------. "Design in Jean Toomer's *Balo.*" *BALF* 7(1973): 103-104.

7324. ----------. "Jean Toomer's Life Prior to *Cane:* A Brief Sketch of the Emergence of a Black Writer." *BALF* 9(1975): 40-41.

7325. Leiber, Todd. "Design and Movement in *Cane.*" *CLA* 13(1969): 35-50.

7326. Matthews, George C. "Toomer's *Cane:* the Artist and His World." *CLA* 17(1974): 543-559.

7327. McCarthy, Daniel P. "'Just Americans': A Note on Jean Toomer's Marriage to Margery Latimer." *CLA* 17(1974): 474-479.

7328. McKeever, Benjamin F. "*Cane* as Blues." *BALF* 4(1970): 61-63.

7329. Quirk, Tom, and Robert E. Fleming. "Jean Toomer's Contributions to *The New Mexico Sentinel.*" *CLA* 19(1976): 524-532.

7330. Reilly, John M. "The Search for Black Redemption: Jean Toomer's Cane." *SN* 2(1970): 312-324.

7331. Riley, Roberta. "Search for Identity and Artistry." *CLA* 17(1974): 480-485.

7332. Scruggs, Charles. "Jean Toomer: Fugitive." *AL* 47(1975): 84-96.

7333. ----------. "The Mark of Cain and the Redemption of Art: A Study in Theme and Structure of Jean Toomer's *Cane.*" *AL* 44(1972): 276-291.

7334. Turner, Darwin T. "And Another Passing." *BALF* 1,#1(1967): [3-4].

7335. ----------. "The Failure of a Playwright." *CLA* 10(1967): 308-318.

7336. ----------. "An Intersection of Paths: Correspondence between Jean Toomer and Sherwood Anderson." *CLA* 17(1974): 455-467.

7337. Van Mol, Kay R. "Primitivism and Intellect in Toomer's *Cane* and McKay's *Banana Bottom:* The Need for an Integrated Consciousness." *BALF* 10(1976): 48-52.

7338. Waldron, Edward E. "The Search for Identity in Jean Toomer's 'Esther.'" *CLA* 14(1971): 277-280.

7339. Watkins, Patricia. "Is There a Unifying Theme in *Cane?*" *CLA* 15(1972): 303-305.

7340. Westerfield, Hargis. "Jean Toomer's 'Fern': A Mythical Dimension." *CLA* 14(1971): 274-276.

7341. Withrow, Dolly. "Cutting through Shade." *CLA* 21(1977): 98-99.

See also 4396, 4425.

TORRENCE, RIDGELY. 7342. Fleissner, Robert F. "Frost and Racism: The Evidence." *BALF* 9 (1975): 118-119.

7343. Monteiro, George. "Zona Gale and Ridgely Torrence." *ALR* 3(1970): 77-79.

See also 4371.

TRAVEN, B. 7344. Warner, John M. "Tragic Vision in B. Traver's 'The Night Visitor.'" *SSF* 7(1970): 377-384.

TRILLING LIONEL. 7345. Chace, William M. *"The Middel of the Journey:* Death and Politics." *Novel* 10(1977): 137-144.

7346. George, Diana L. "Thematic Structure in Lionel Trilling's 'Of This Time, of That Place.'" *SSF* 13(1976): 1-8.

7347. Green, Martin. "Lionel Trilling and the Two Cultures." *EIC* 13(1963): 375-385.

See also 4376.

TSUNEISHI, SHEISEI. 7348. Haslam, Gerald W. "Three Exotics: Yone Noguchi, Sheisei Tsuneishi, and Sadakichi Hartmann." *CLA* 19(1976): 362-373.

TURPIN, WATERS. 7349. Fleming, Robert E. "Overshadowed by Richard Wright: Three Black Chicago Novelists." *BALF* 7(1973): 75-79.

7350. Ford, Nick Aaron. "Waters Turpin: I Knew Him Well." *CLA* 21(1977) 1-18.

UPDIKE, JOHN. 7351. Bachscheider, Paula and Nick. "Updike's Couples: Squeak in the Night." *MFS* 20(1974): 45-52.

7352. Banks, R. Jeff. "The Uses of Weather in 'Tomorrow and Tomorrow and So Forth.'" *NCL* 3 (November, 1973): 8-9.

7353. Brenner, Gerry. "*Rabbit, Run:* John Updike's Criticism of 'Return to Nature.'" *TCL* 12 (1966): 3-14.

7354. Burhans, Clinton S., Jr. "Things Falling Apart: Structure and Theme in *Rabbit, Run.*" *SN* 5(1973): 336-351.

7355. Detweiler, Robert. "Updike's *Couples:* Eros Demythologized." *TCL* 17(1971): 235-246.

7356. Edwards, A. S. G. "Updike's 'A Sense of Shelter.'" *SSF* 8(1971): 467-468.

7357. Ellis, James. "Karl Barth and Socrates as Mouseketeers in *Rabbit, Run.*" *NCL* 7(December, 1977): 3.

7358. Falke, Wayne. "*Rabbit, Redux:* Time/Order/God." *MFS* 20(1974): 59-75.

7359. Galloway, David O. "The Absurd Man as Saint: The Novels of John Updike." *MFS* 10(1964): 111-127.

7360. Gingher, Robert S. "Has Updike Anything to Say?" *MFS* 20(1974): 97-105.

7361. Griffith, Albert J. "Updike's Artist's Dilemma: 'Should Wizard Hit Mommy?'" *MFS* 20(1974): 111-115.

7362. McCoy, Robert. "John Updike's Literary Apprenticeship on *The Harvard Lampoon*." *MFS* 20 (1974): 3-12.

7363. McKenzie, Alan T. "'A Craftsman's Intimate Satisfactions': The Parlor Games in *Couples*." *MFS* 20(1974): 53-58.

7364. Meyer, Arlin G., with Michael Olivas. "Criticism of John Updike: A Selected Checklist." *MFS* 20(1974): 121-133.

7365. Meyers, David. "The Questing Fear: Christian Allegory in John Updike's *The Centaur*." *TCL* 17(1971): 73-82.

7366. Oates, Joyce Carol. "Updike's American Comedies." *MFS* 21(1975): 459-472.

7367. Overmyer, Janet. "Courtly Love in the A & P." *NCL* 2(May, 1972): 4-5.

7368. Regan, Robert Alton. "Updike's Symbol of the Center." *MFS* 20(1974): 77-96.

7369. Updike's 'A Sense of Shelter.'" *SSF* 7(1970): 651-652.

7370. Rosa, Alfred F. "The Psycholinguistics of Updike's 'Museums and Women.'" *MFS* 20 (1974): 107-111.

7371. Rotundo, Barbara. *"Rabbit, Run* and *A Tale of Peter Rabbit*." *NCL* 1(May, 1971): 2-3.

7372. Russell, Mariann. "White Man's Black Man: Three Views." *CLA* 17(1973): 93-100.

7373. Shurr, William H. "The Lutheran Experience in John Updike's 'Pigeon Feathers.'" *SSF* 14(1977): 329-335.

7374. Stafford, William T. "'The Curious Greased Grace' of John Updike, Some of His Critics, and the American Tradition." *JML* 2(1972): 569-575.

7375. ----------. "Updike FourFiveSix, 'Just Like That': An Essay Review." *MFS* 20(1974): 115-120.

7376. Stubbs, John C. "The Search for Perfection in *Rabbit, Run*." *Crit* 10,#2(1968): 94-101.

7377. Sykes, Robert H. "A Commentary on Updike's Astronomer." *SSF* 8(1971): 575-579.

7378. Uphaus, Suzanne. "*The Centaur*: Updike's Mock Epic." *JNT* 7(1977): 24-36.

7379. Vanderwerken, David L. "Rabbit 'Redocks': Updike's Inner Space Odyssey." *Coll L* 2 (1975): 73-78.

7380. Vargo, Edward P. "The Necessity of Myth in Updike's *The Centaur*." *PMLA* 88(1973): 452-460.

7381. Vickery, John B. "*The Centaur*: Myth, History, and Narrative." *MFS* 20(1974): 29-43.

7382. Waldmeir, Joseph. "It's the Going That's Important, Not the Getting There: Rabbit's Questing Nonquest." *MFS* 20(1974): 13-27.

7383. Ward, J. A. "John Updike's Fiction." *Crit* 5,#1(1962): 27-40.

7384. Wyatt, Bryant N. "John Updike: The Psychological Novel in Search of Structure." *TCL* 13(1967): 89-96.

See also 483.

UNTERMEYER, LOUIS. 7385. Davison, Richard Allan. "Hart Crane, Louis Untermeyer, and T. S. Eliot: A New Crane Letter." *AL* 44(1972): 143-146.

VAN VECHTEN, CARL. 7386. Coleman, Leon. "Carl Van Vechtan Presents the New Negro." *SLI* 7,#2(1974): 85-104.

7387. Helbling, Mark. "Carl Van Vechten and the Harlem Renaissance." *BALF* 10(1976): 39-47.

7388. Larson, Charles R. "Three Harlem Novels of the Jazz Age." *Crit* 11,#3(1969): 66-78. See also 4402.

VELBEN, THORSTEIN. 7389. McIlvaine, Robert M. "Dos Passos's Reading of Thorstein Veblen." *AL* 44(1972): 471-474.

VIDAL, GORE. 7390. Boyette, Purvis E. *Myra Breckinridge* and Imitative Form." *MFS* 17 (1971): 229-238.

VONNEGUT, KURT. 7391. Adelstein, Arnold. "*Slaughterhouse-Five*: Time Out of Joint." *Coll L* 1(1974): 128-139.

7392. Buck, Lynn. "Vonnegut's World of Comic Futility." *SAF* 3(1975): 181-198.

7393. Burhans, Clinton S., Jr. "Hemingway and Vonnegut: Diminishing Vision in a Dying Age." *MFS* 21(1975): 173-191.

7394. Engel, Wilson F., III. "Pilgrim as Prisoner: Cummings and Vonnegut." *NCL* 7(January, 1977): 13-14.

7395. Godshalk, William Leigh. "The Recurring Characters of Kurt Vonnegut, Jr." *NCL* 3 (January, 1973): 2-3.

7396. Klinkowitz, Jerome. "The Literary Career of Kurt Vonnegut, Jr." *MFS* 19(1973): 57-67.

7397. May, John R. "Vonnegut's Humor and the Limits of Hope." *TCL* 18(1972): 25-36.

7398. McGinnis, Wayne D. "Names in Vonnegut's Fiction." *NCL* 3(September, 1973): 7-9.

7399. ----------. "Vonnegut's *Breakfast of Champions*: A Reductive Success." *NCL* 5(May, 1975): 6-9.

7400. Morrow, Patrick D. "The Womb Image in Vonnegut's *Cat's Cradle*." *NCL* 6(November, 1974): 11-13.

7401. O'Sullivan, Maurice J., Jr. "*Slaughterhouse-Five*: Kurt Vonnegut's Anti-Memoirs." *EL* 3 (1976): 244-250.

7402. Pauly, Rebecca M. "The Moral Stance of Kurt Vonnegut." *Ext* 15(1973): 66-71.

7403. Schriber, Mary Sue. "You've Come a Long Way Babbit! From Zenith to Ilium." *TCL* 17 (1971): 101-106.

7404. Uphaus, Robert W. "Expected Meaning in Vonnegut's Dead-End Fiction: *Breakfast of Champions,* and others." *Novel* 8(1975): 164-174.

See also 159, 203, 210.

VORSE, MARY HEATON. See 4381.

WAGONER, DAVID. 7405. Schafer, William J. "David Wagoner's Fiction: In the Mills of Satan." *Crit* 9,#1(1966): 71-89.

WAKEFIELD, PHILLIP 7406. Sheperd, Allen. "Going Down with Wakefield: Non-Father's Balloon Strategy in Starting Over." *NCL* 5(September, 1975): 8-9.

WAKOSKI, DIANE. 7407. Healey, Claire. "An Interview with Diane Wakoski." *Con L* 18(1977): 1-19.

WALKER, ALICE. 7408. Harris, Trudier. "Folklore in the Fiction of Alice Walker: A Perpetuation of Historical and Literary Traditions."

BALF 11(1977): 3-8.

7409. ----------. "Violence in *The Third Life of Grange Copeland.*" *CLA* 19(1975): 238-247.

See also 4407.

WALKER, JOSEPH. 7410. Lee, Dorothy. "Three Black Plays: Alienation and Paths to Recovery." *MD* 19(1976): 397-404.

WALKER, MARGARET. 7411. Klotman, Phyllis Rauch. "'Oh Freedom'—Women and History in Margaret Walker's *Jubilee.*" *BALF* 11(1977): 139-145.

7412. Powell, Bertie J. "The Black Experience in Margaret Walker's *Jubilee* and Lorraine Hansberry's *The Drinking Gourd.*" *CLA* 21(1977): 304-312.

See also 622.

WALLANT, EDWARD L. 7413. Gurko, Leo. "Edward Lewis Wallant as Urban Novelist." *TCL* 20 (1974): 252-261.

7414. Schulz, M. F. "Wallant and Friedman: The Glory and the Agony of Love." *Crit* 10,#3 (1968): 31-47.

WARHOL, ANDY. See 19019.

WARREN, ROBERT PENN. 7415. Burt, David J. "Robert Penn Warren's Debt to Homer in *Flood.*" *NCL* 3(January, 1973): 12-14.

7416. Beebe, Maurice, and Erin Marcus. "Criticism of Robert Penn Warren: A Selected Checklist." *MFS* 6(1960): 83-88.

7417. Berner, Robert. "The Required Past: 'World Enough and Time.'" *MFS* 6(1960): 55-64.

7418. Carter, Everett. "The 'Little Myth' of Robert Penn Warren." *MFS* 6(1960): 3-12.

7419. Casper, Leonard. "Journey to the Interior: The Cave." *MFS* 6(1960): 65-72.

7420. ----------. "Trial by Wilderness: Warren's Exemplum." *Con L* 3,#3(1962): 45-53.

7421. ----------. "Warren and the Unsuspecting Ancestor." *Con L* 2,#2(1961): 43-49.

7422. Clements, A. L. "Theme and Reality in *At Heaven's Gate* and *All the King's Men.*" *Criticism* 5(1963): 27-44.

7423. Davis, Joe. "Robert Penn Warren and the Journey to the West." *MFS* 6(1960): 73-82.

7424. Davison, Richard Allan. "Robert Penn Warren's 'Dialectical Configuration' and *The Cave.*" *CLA* 10(1967): 349-357.

7425. Ford, Newell F. "Kenneth Burke and Robert Penn Warren: Criticism by Obsessive Metaphor." *JEGP* 53(1954): 172-177.

7426. Gross, Seymour L. "Conrad and *All the King's Men.*" *TCL* 3(1957): 27-32.

7427. Hannaford, Richard. "Sugar-Boy and Violence in *All the King's Men.*" *NCL* 6(May, 1976): 10-13.

7428. Hiers, John T. "Buried Graveyards: Warren's *Flood* and Jones' *A Buried Land.*" *EL* 2 (1975): 97-104.

7429. Ilacqua, Alma A. "Amanda Starr: Victim of Her Own False Assumptions." *HSL* 8 (1976): 178-189.

7430. Justus, James H. "The Mariner and Robert Penn Warren." *TSLL* 8(1966): 117-128.

7431. ----------. "A Note on John Crowe Ransom and Robert Penn Warren." *AL* 41(1969): 425-430.

7432. ----------. "The Uses of Gesture in Warren's *The Cave.*" *MLQ* 26(1965): 448-461.

7433. ----------. "Warren's *World Enough and Time* and Beauchamp's *Confession.*" *AL* 33(1962): 500-511.

7434. Katope, Christopher G. "Robert Penn Warren's *All the King's Men*: A Novel of 'Pure Imagination.'" *TSLL* 12(1970): 493-510.

7435. Kerr, Elizabeth M. "Polarity of Themes in *All the King's Men.*" *MFS* 6(1960): 24-46.

7436. Law, Richard. "Warren's Night Rider and the Issue of Naturalism: The 'Nightmare' of Our Age." *SLJ* 8,#2(1976): 41-61.

7437. Longely, John Lewis, Jr. "*At Heaven's Gate*: The Major Themes." *MFS* 6(1960): 13-24.

7438. McCarron, William E. "Warren's *All the King's Men* and Arnold's 'To Marguerite—Continued.'" *AL* 47(1975): 115-116.

7439. McDowell, Frederick P. W. "Psychology and Theme in *Brother to Dragons.*" *PMLA* 70(1955): 565-586.

7440. ----------. "The Romantic Tragedy of Self in *World Enough and Time.*" *Crit* 1,#2(1957): 34-48.

7441. Meckier, Jerome. "Burden's Complaint: The Disintegrated Personality as Theme and Style in Warren's *All the King's Men.*" *SN* 2(1970): 7-21.

7442. Moore, L. Hugh. "Robert Penn Warren, William Styron, and the Use of Greek Myth." *Crit* 8,#2(1965): 75-87.

7443. O'Brien, Joseph M. "Cultural History in *All the King's Men.*" *NCL* 2(May, 1972): 14-15.

7444. Quinn, Sister Bernetta, O. S. F. "Warren and Jarrell: The Remembered Child." *SLJ* 8,#2(1976): 24-40.

7445. Rathbun, John W. "Philosophy, *World Enough and Time,* and the Art of the Novel." *MFS* 6(1960): 47-54.

7446. Ray, Robert J. and Ann. "Time in *All the King's Men*: A Stylistic Analysis." *TSLL* 5 (1963): 425-457.

7447. Ruoff, James. "Humpty Dumpty and All the King's Men: A Note on Robert Penn Warren's Teleology." *TCL* 3(1957): 128-134.

7448. Ryan, Alvan S. "Robert Penn Warren's *Night Rider*: The Nihilism of the Isolated Temperament." *MFS* 7(1961): 338-346.

7449. Sale, Richard B. "An Interview in New Haven with Robert Penn Warren." *SN* 2(1970): 325-354.

7450. Samuels, Charles Thomas. "In the Wilderness." *Crit* 5,#2(1962): 46-57.

7451. Shepherd, Allen. "Character and Theme in R. P. Warren's *Flood.*" *Crit* 9,#3(1967): 95-102.

7452. ----------. "The Poles of Fiction: Warren's *At Heaven's Gate.*" *TSLL* 12(1971): 709-718.

7453. ----------. "Robert Penn Warren's *Audubon: A Vision*: The Epigraph." *NCL* 3(January, 1973): 8-11.

7454. ----------. "Robert Penn Warren's 'Prime Leaf' as Prototype of *Night Rider.*" *SSF* 7 (1970): 469-471.

7455. ----------. "Sugar-Boy as A Foil in *All the King's Men.*" *NCL* 1(March, 1971): 15.

7456. ----------. "Toward an Analysis of the Prose Style of Robert Penn Warren." *SAF* 1 (1973): 188-202.

7457. Simmons, James C. "Adam's Lobectomy Operation and the Meaning of *All the King's Men.*"

PMLA 86(1971): 84-89.

7458. Stewart, John L. "Robert Penn Warren and the Knot of History." *ELH* 26(1959): 102-136.

7459. Strandberg, Victor H. "Theme and Metaphor in *Brother to Dragons*." *PMLA* 79(1964): 498-508.

7460. ----------. "Warren's Osmosis." *Criticism* 10(1968): 23-40.

7461. Sullivan, Walter. "The Historical Novel and the Existential Peril: Robert Penn Warren's *Band of Angels*." *SLJ* 2,#2(1969): 104-116.

7462. Tjenos, William. "The Poetry of Robert Penn Warren: The Art to Transfigure." *SLJ* 9,#1(1976): 3-12.

7463. Vautheir, Simone. "The Case of the Vanishing Narratee: An Inquiry into *All the King's Men*." *SLJ* 6,#2(1974): 42-69.

7464. Weathers, Winston. "'Blackberry Winter' and the Use of Archetypes." *SSF* 1(1963): 45-51.

7465. Welch, Dennis M. "Image Making: Politics and Character Development in *All the King's Men*." *HSL* 8(1976): 155-177.

See also 349, 610, 4334, 4387.

WATERS, FRANK. 7466. Davis, Jack L., and June Davis. "Frank Waters and the Native American Consciousness." *WAL* 9(1974): 33-44.

7467. Lyon, Thomas J. "An Ignored Meaning of the Old West." *WAL* 3(1968): 51-59.

7468. Pilkington, William T. "Character and Landscape: Frank Water's Colorado Trilogy." *WAL* 2(1967): 183-203.

See also 239, 4403, 4420.

WATSON, JAMES D. 7469. Cadbury, William. "On Being Literary: The Strange Case of Dr. Watson." *MLQ* 31(1970): 474-491.

WEBB, FRANK. See 4391.

WELCH, JAMES. See 621.

WELLES, ORSON. 7470. Carringer, Robert L. "Rosebud, Dead or Alive: Narrative and Symbolic Structure in *Citizen Kane*." *PMLA* 91(1976): 185-193.

7471. Goldstein, Malcom. "Welles, Welles, Welles." *JML* 3(1974): 1050-1055.

WELTY, EUDORA. 7472. Appel, Alfred, Jr. "Powerhouse's Blues." *SSF* 2(1965): 221-234.

7473. Bartel, Roland. "Life and Death in Eudora Welty's 'A Worn Path.'" *SSF* 14(1977): 288-290.

7474. Bradham, Joe Allen. "'A Visit of Charity': Menippean Satire." *SSF* 1(1964): 258-263.

7475. Carson, Franklin D. "The Passage of Time in Eudora Welty's 'Sir Rabbit.'" *SSF* 12(1975): 284-286.

7476. ----------. "Recurring Metaphors: An Aspect of Unity in *The Golden Apples*." *NCL* 5(September, 1975): 4-7.

7477. Curley, Daniel. "Eudora Welty and the Quondam Obstruction." *SSF* 5(1968): 209-224.

7478. Daly, Saralyn R. "'A Worn Path' Retrod." *SSF* 1(1964): 133-139.

7479. Davis, Charles E. "The South in Eudora Welty's Fiction: A Changing World." *SAF* 3(1975): 197-209.

7480. Dusenberry, Winifred L. "*Baby Doll* and *The Ponder Heart*." *MD* 3(1961): 393-395.

7481. Fleischauer, John F. "The Focus of Mystery: Eudora Welty's Prose Style." *SLJ* 5,#2 (1973): 64-79.

7482. Goudie, Andrea. "Eudora Welty's 'Circle': A Goddess Who Strove with Men." *SSF* 13 (1976): 481-489.

7483. Graves, Nora Calhoun. "Shirley-Tim: Eudora Welty's 'Why I Live at the P. O.'" *NCL* 7 (March, 1977): 6-7.

7484. Griffith, Albert. "The Numinous Vision: Eudora Welty's 'Clytie.'" *SSF* 4(1966): 80-82.

7485. Harrell, Don. "Death in Eudora Welty's 'The Bride of the Innisfallen.'" *NCL* 3(September, 1973): 2-7.

7485a. Harris, Wendell V. "The Thematic Unity of Welty's *The Golden Apples*." *TSLL* 6(1964): 92-95.

7486. Hartley, Lodwick. "Prosperina and the Old Ladies." *MFS* 3(1957): 350-354.

7487. Herrscher, Walter. "Is Sister Really Insane? Another Look at 'Why I Live at the P. O.'" *NCL* 5(January, 1975): 5-7.

7488. Hodgins, Audrey. "The Narrator as Ironic Device in a Story of Eudora Welty." *TCL* 1 (1956): 215-219.

7489. Holland, Robert B. "Dialogue as Reflection of Place in *The Ponder Heart*." *AL* 35 (1963): 352-358.

7490. Jones, William M. "The Plot as Search." *SSF* 5(1967): 37-43.

7491. Lief, Ruth Ann. "A Progression of Answers." *SSF* 2(1965): 343-350.

7492. Masserand, Anne. "Eudora Welty's Travellers." *SLJ* 3,#2(1971): 39-48.

7493. May, Charles E. "The Difficulty of Loving in 'A Visit of Charity.'" *SSF* 6(1969): 338-341.

7494. ----------. "Le Roi Mehaigné in Welty's 'Keela, The Outcast Indian Maiden.'" *MFS* 18(1972): 559-566.

7495. McDonald, W. U., Jr. "Eudora Welty's Revisions of 'A Piece of News.'" *SSF* 7(1970): 232-247.

7496. ----------. "Welty's 'Keela': Irony, Ambiguity, and the Ancient Mariner." *SSF* 1(1963): 59-60.

7497. ----------. "Welty's 'Social Consciousness': Revisions of 'The Whistle.'" *MFS* 16(1970): 193-198.

7498. Messerli, Douglas. "The Problem of Time in Welty's *Delta Wedding*." *SAF* 5(1977): 227-240.

7499. Moss, Grant, Jr. "'A Worn Path' Retrod." *CLA* 15(1971): 144-152.

7500. Opitz, Kurt. "Eudora Welty: The Order of a Captive Soul." *Crit* 7,#2(1964): 79-91.

7501. Semel, Jay M. "Eudora Welty's Freak Show: A Pattern in 'Why I Live at the P. O.'" NCL 3(May, 1973): 2-3.

7502. Shepherd, Allen. "Delayed Exposition in Eudora Welty's The Optimist's Daughter." NCL 4(September, 1974): 10-14.

7503. Smith, Julian. "'Livvie'—Eudora Welty's Song of Solomon." SSF 5(1967): 73-74.

7504. Stone, William B. "Eudora Welty's Hydrodynamic 'Powerhouse.'" SSF 11(1974): 93-96.

7505. Thompson, Victor H. "The Natchez Trace in Eudora Welty's 'A Still Moment.'" SLJ 6,#1(1973): 59-69.

7506. Travis, Mildred K. "A Note on 'Wakefield' and 'Old Mr. Marblehall.'" NCL 4(May, 1974): 9-10.

See 4397, 18927.

WESCOTT, GLENWAY. 7507. Gallos, Steven. "An Analysis of Wescott's The Pilgrim Hawk." Crit 8,#2(1965): 13-19.

7508. Kane, Patricia. "Glenway Wescott's Odyssey." Crit 8,#2(1965): 5-12.

WEST, DOROTHY. 7509. Daniel, Walter C. "Challenge Magazine: An Experiment that Failed." CLA 19(1976): 494-502.

WEST, EVELYN. See 4309.

WEST, NATHANAEL. 7510. Andreach, Robert J. "Nathanael West's Miss Lonelyhearts: Between the Dead Pan and the Unborn Christ." MFS 12(1966): 251-260.

7511. Brown, Daniel R. "The War Within Nathanael West: Naturalism and Existentialism." MFS 20(1974): 181-202.

7512. Frank, Mike. "The Passion of Miss Lonelyhearts According to Nathanael West." SSF 10(1973): 67-73.

7513. Galloway, David D. "Nathanael West's Dream Dump." Crit 6,#3(1963): 46-64.

7514. ----------. "A Picaresque Apprenticeship: Nathanael West's The Dream Life of Balso Snell and A Cool Million." Con L 5(1964): 110-126.

7515. Geha, Richard. "Miss Lonelyhearts: A Dual Mission of Mercy." HSL 3(1961): 116-131.

7516. Light, James. "Nathanael West, Balso Snell, and the Mundane Millstone." MFS 4(1968): 319-328.

7517. Lorch, Thomas M. "The Inverted Structure of Balso Snell." SSF 4(1966): 33.

7518. Orvell, Miles D. "The Messianic Sexuality of Miss Lonelyhearts." SSF 10(1973): 159-167.

7519. Ratner, Marc L. "'Anywhere Out of This World': Baudelaire and Nathanael West." AL 31(1960): 456-463.

7520. Smith, Marcus. "Religious Experience in Miss Lonelyhearts." Con L 9(1968): 172-188.

7521. Tibbetts, A. M. "Nathanael West's The Dream Life of Balso Snell." SSF 2(1965): 105-112.

7522. Zlotnick, Joan. "Nathanael West and Pictorial Imagination." WAL 9(1974): 177-185.

See also 6761.

WHARTON, EDITH. 7523. Ammons, Elizabeth. "The Business of Marriage in Edith Wharton's 'The Custom of the Country.'" Criticism 16(1974): 326-338.

7524. ----------. "Fairy-Tale Love and The Reef." AL 47(1976): 615-628.

7525. Bell, Millicent. "Edith Wharton and Henry James: The Literary Relation." PMLA 74 (1959): 619-637.

7526. Brennan, Joseph X. "Ethan Frome: Structure and Metaphor." MFS 7(1961): 347-356.

7527. Buchan, Alexander M. "Edith Wharton and 'The Elusive Bright-Winged Thing.'" NEQ 37 (1964): 343-362.

7528. Clough, David. "Edith Wharton's War Novels: A Reappraisal." TCL 19(1973): 1-14.

7529. Cohn, Jan. "The Houses of Fiction: Domestic Architecture in Howells and Edith Wharton." TSLL 15(1973): 537-549.

7530. Dahl, Curtis. "Edith Wharton's The House of Mirth: Sermon on a Text." MFS 21 (1975): 572-576.

7531. Dooley, R. B. "A Footnote to Edith Wharton." AL 26(1954): 78-85.

7532. Eggenschwiler, David. "The Ordered Disorder of Ethan Frome." SN 9(1977): 237-246.

7533. Evans, Elizabeth. "Musical Allusions in The Age of Innocence." NCL 4(May, 1974): 4-7.

7534. Fetterley, Judith. "'The Temptation to Be a Beautiful Object': Double Standard and Double Bind in The House of Mirth." SAF 5(1977): 199-211.

7535. Gargano, James W. "Edith Wharton's The Reef: The Genteel Woman's Quest for Knowledge." Novel 10(1976): 40-48.

7536. ----------. "The House of Mirth: Social Futility and Faith." AL 44(1972): 137-143.

7537. Hamblen, Abigail Ann. "Edith Wharton in New England." NEQ 38(1965): 239-244.

7538. Hopkins, Viola. "The Ordering Style of The Age of Innocence." AL 30(1958): 345-357.

7539. Lamar, Lillie B. "Edith Wharton's Foreknowledge in The Age of Innocence." TSLL 8 (1966): 385-389.

7540. Lawson, Richard H. "Thematic Similarities in Edith Wharton and Thomas Mann." TCL 23 (1977): 289-290.

7541. Leach, Nancy R. "Edith Wharton's Unpublished Novel." AL 25(1953): 334-353.

7542. ----------. "New England in the Stories of Edith Wharton." NEQ 30(1957): 90-98.

7543. Loney, G. M. "Edith Wharton and The House of Mirth: The Novelist Writes for the Theater." MD 4(1961): 152-163.

7544. McDowell, Margaret B. "Edith Wharton's 'After Holbein': A Paradigm of the Human Condition." JNT 1(1971): 49-58.

7545. ----------. "Edith Wharton's Ghost Stories." Criticism 12(1970): 133-152.

7546. ----------. "Viewing the Custom of Her Country: Edith Wharton's Feminism." Con L 15 (1974): 521-538.

7547. Nevius, Blake. "'Ethan Frome' and the Themes of Edith Wharton's Fiction." NEQ 24 (1951): 197-207.

7548. ----------. "'Pussie' Jones's Verses: A Bibliographical Note on Edith Wharton." AL 23 (1952): 494-497.

7549. Puknat, E. M. and S. B. "Edith Wharton and Gottfried Keller." Comp L 21(1969): 245-254.

7550. Rose, Alan Henry. "'Such Depths of Sad Initiation': Edith Wharton and New England." *NEQ* 50(1977): 423-439.

7551. Rubin, Larry. "Aspects of Naturalism in Four Novels by Edith Wharton." *TCL* 2(1957): 182-192.

7552. Saunders, Judith P. "Ironic Reversal in Edith Wharton's *Bunner Sisters*." *SSF* 14(1977): 241-245.

7553. Thmas, J. D. "Marginalia on *Ethan Frome*." *AL* 27(1955): 405-409.

7554. Tintner, Adeline R. "'The Hermit and the Wild Woman': Edith Wharton's 'Fictioning' of James." *JML* 4(1974): 32-42.

7555. Tuttleton, James W. "Edith Wharton: Form and the Epistomology of Artistic Creation." *Criticism* 10(1968): 334-351.

7556. Winner, Viola Hopkins. "Convention and Prediction in Edith Wharton's *Fast and Loose*." *AL* 42(1970): 50-69.

7557. Wolff, Cynthia Griffin. "Lily Bart and the Beautiful Death." *AL* 46(1974): 16-40.
See also 3151, 3153, 4404.

WHEELWRIGHT, JOHN. 7558. Rosenfeld, Alvin H. "The New England Notebooks of John Wheelwright." *NEQ* 45(1972): 417-421.

WHITE, EDGAR. See 4351.

WHITE, JOSEPH. See 4311.

WHITE, STEWART EDWARD. See 4380.

WHITE, WALTER. 7559. Waldron, Edward E. "Walter White and the Harlem Renaissance: Letters from 1924-1927." *CLA* 16(1973): 438-457.

WHITE, WILLIAM A. 7560. Dubbert, Joe L. "William Allen White's American Adam." *WAL* 7 (1973): 271-278.

WHITLOCK, BRAND. 7561. Thorburn, Neil. "Brand Whitlock (1869-1934)" [bibliography] *ALR* 1,#3(1968): 30-35.

WILBUR, RICHARD. 7562. Farrell, John P. "The Beautiful Changes in Richard Wilbur's Poetry." *Con L* 12(1971): 74-87.

7563. Herzman, Ronald B. "A Yeatsian Parallel in Richard Wilbur's 'Merlin Enthralled.'" *NCL* 2(November, 1972): 10-11.

7564. Kolin, Philip C. "The Subtle Drama of Richard Wilbur's 'Exeunt.'" *NCL* 5(January, 1975): 11-13.

7565. Perrine, Laurence. "Dream, Desire, or Dizziness?—Digging in 'Digging for China.'" *NCL* 1(May, 1971): 13-14.

7566. Weatherhead, A. K. "Richard Wilbur: Poetry of Things." *ELH* 35(1968): 606-617.

WILDER, THORNTON. 7567. Frenz, Horst. "The Reception of Thornton Wilder's Plays in Germany." *MD* 3(1960): 123-137.

7568. Kosok, Heinz. "Thornton Wilder: A Bibliography of Criticism." *TCL* 9(1963): 93-100.

7569. Stephens, George D. "*Our Town*—Great American Tragedy?" *MD* 1(1975): 258-264.

7570. Wixson, Douglas Charles, Jr. "The Dramatic Techniques of Thornton Wilder and Bertolt Brecht: A Study in Comparison." *MD* 15(1972): 112-124.
See also 4341.

WILLIAMS, JOHN. 7571. Brenner, Jack. "Butcher's Crossing: The Husks and Shells of Exploitation." *WAL* 7(1973): 245-259.

7572. Fleming, Robert E. "The Nightmare Level of *The Man Who Cried I Am*." *Con L* 14(1973): 186-196.

7573. Klotman, Phyllis R. "An Examination of the Black Confidence Man in Two Black Novels: *The Man Who Cried I Am* and *dem*." *AL* 44(1973): 596-611.

7574. Walcott, Ronald. "The Early Fiction of John A. Williams." *CLA* 16(1972): 198-213.

WILLIAMS, TENNESSEE. 7575. Barksdale, Richard K. "Social Backgrounds in the Plays of Miller and Williams." *CLA* 6(1963): 161-169.

7576. Beaurline, Lester A. "*The Glass Menagerie*: From Story to Play." *MD* 8(1965): 142-149.

7577. Berkman, Leonard. "The Tragic Downfall of Blanche DuBois." *MD* 10(1967): 249-257.

7578. Brooking, Jack. "Directing *Summer and Smoke*: An Existential Approach." *MD* 2(1960): 377-385.

7579. Carpenter, Charles A., and Elizabeth Cook. "Addenda to 'Tennessee Williams: A Selected Bibliography.'" *MD* 2(1959): 220-223.

7580. Costello, Donald P. "Tennessee Williams' Fugitive Kind." *MD* 15(1972): 26-43.

7581. Corrigan, Mary Ann. "Realism and Theatricalism in *A Streetcar Named Desire*." *MD* 19 (1976): 385-396.

7582. Dony, Nadine. "Tennessee Williams: A Selected Bibliography." *MD* 1(1958): 181-191.

7583. Dusenbury, Winifred L. "*Baby Doll* and *The Ponder Heart*." *MD* 3(1961): 393-395.

7584. Falk Signi. "The Profitable World of Tennessee Williams." *MD* 1(1958): 172-180.

7585. Fritscher, John J. "Some Attitudes and a Posture: Religious Metaphor and Ritual in Tennessee Williams' Query of the American God." *MD* 13(1970): 201-215.

7586. Hays, Peter L. "Arthur Miller and Tennessee Williams." *EL* 4(1977): 239-249.

7587. Hirsch, Foster. "Sexual Imagery in Tennessee Williams' *Kingdom of Earth*." *NCL* 1(March, 1971): 10-13.

7588. Hurley, Paul J. "*Suddenly Last Summer* as 'Morality Play.'" *MD* 8(1966): 392-402.

7589. ----------. "'Williams' 'Desire and the Black Masseur': An Analysis." *SSF* 2(1964): 51-55.

7590. Hurt, James R. "*Suddenly Last Summer*: Williams and Melville." *MD* 3(1961): 396-400.

7591. Jackson, Esther M. "The Problem of Form in the Drama of Tennessee Williams." *CLA* 4 (1960): 8-21.

7592. Jones, Robert Emmet. "Tennessee Williams' Early Heroines." *MD* 2(1959): 211-219.

7593. Kalson, Albert E. "Tennessee Williams Enters *Dragon Country*." *MD* 16(1973): 61-68.

7594. Kernan, Alvin B. "Truth and Dramatic Mode in the Modern Theater: Chekhov, Pirandello, and Williams." *MD* 1(1958): 101-114.

7595. Leon, Ferdinand. "Time, Fantasy, and Reality in *Night of the Iguana*." *MD* 11(1968): 87-96.

7596. Peden, William. "Mad Pilgrimage: The Short Stories of Tennessee Williams." *SSF* 1(1964): 243-250.

7597. Quirino, Leonard. "Tennessee Williams' Persistent *Battle of Angels*." *MD* 11(1968): 27-39.

7598. Riddel, Joseph N. "*A Streetcar Named Desire:* Nietzsche Descending." *MD* 5(1963): 421-430.

7599. Starnes, Leland. "The Grotesque Children of *The Rose Tatoo.*" *MD* 12(1970): 357-369.

7600. Traubitz, Nancy Baker. "Myth as a Basis of Dramatic Structure in *Orpheus Descending.*" *MD* 19(1976): 57-66.

7601. Vowles, Richard B. "Tennessee Williams and Strindberg." *MD* 1(1958): 166-171.

7602. Watson, Charles S. "The Revision of *The Glass Menagerie:* The Passing of Good Manners." *SLJ* 8,#2(1976): 74-78.

7603. Weales, Gerald. "Tennessee Williams's 'Lost' Play." *AL* 37(1965): 321-323.

See also 6715.

WILLIAMS, WILLIAM CARLOS. 7604. Baldwin, Neil E. "Discovering Common Ground: A Note on William Carlos Williams and Valery Larbaud." *AL* 45(1973): 292-297.

7605. Bollard, Margaret Lloyd. "The Interlace Element in *Paterson.*" *TCL* 21(1975): 288-304.

7606. ----------. "The 'Newspaper Landscape' of Williams' *Paterson.*" *Con L* 16(1975): 317-327.

7607. Breslin, James E. "Whitman and the Early Development William Carlos Williams." *PMLA* 82(1967): 613-621.

7608. ----------. "William Carlos Williams and Charles Demuth: Cross-Fertilization in the Arts." *JML* 6(1977): 248-263.

7609. Conarroe, Joel Osborne. "A Local Pride: The Poetry of *Paterson.*" *PMLA* 84(1969): 547-558.

7610. ----------. "The Measured Dance: Williams' 'Pictures from Brueghel.'" *JML* 1(1971): 565-577.

7611. ----------. "The 'Preface' to *Paterson.*" *Con L* 10(1969): 39-53.

7612. Cowan, James C. "The Image of Water in *Paterson.*" *JML* 1(1971): 503-511.

7613. Dietrich, R. F. "Connotations of Rape in 'The Use of Force.'" *SSF* 3(1966): 446-450.

7614. Duffey, Bernard I. "The Experimental Lyric in Modern Poetry: Eliot, Pound, Williams." *JML* 3(1974): 1085-1103.

7615. Eulbert, Donald. "Robert Lowell and W. C. Williams: Sterility in 'Central Park.'" *ELN* 5(1967): 129-135.

7616. Fiero, F. Douglas. "Williams Creates the First Book of *Paterson.*" *JML* 3(1974): 965-986.

7617. Fleissner, Robert F. "Homage to the Pentad: Williams': 'The Great Figure.'" *NCL* 1 (September, 1971): 2-6.

7618. Graham, D. B. "A Note on Howells, Williams, and the Matter of Sam Patch." *NCL* 4 (March, 1974): 10-13.

7619. Green, Jessie D. "Williams' *Kora in Hell:* The Opening of the Poem as 'Field of Action.'" *Con L* 13(1972): 295-314.

7620. Guimond, James K. "William Carlos Willimas and the Past: Some Clarifications." *JML* 1(1971): 493-502.

7621. Halberg, Robert Van. "Olson's Relation to Pound and Williams." *Con L* 15(1974): 15-48.

7622. Hardie, Jack. "'A Celebration of the Light': Selected Checklist of Writings about William Carlos Williams." *JML* 1(1971): 593-642.

7623. Heinzelman, Kurt. "Staging the Poem: William Carlos Williams' *A Dream of Love.*" *Con L* 18(1977): 491-508.

7624. Hofstadter, Marc. "A Different Speech: William Carlos Williams' Later Poetry." *TCL* 23 (1977): 451-466.

7625. Joswick, Thomas P. "Beginning with Loss: The Poetics of William Carlos Williams's *Kora in Hell: Improvisations.*" *TSLL* 19(1977): 98-118.

7626. LeClair, Thomas. "The Poet as Dog in *Paterson.*" *TCL* 16(1970): 97-108.

7627. Libby, Anthony. "'Claritas': William Carlos Williams' Epiphanies." *Criticism* 14(1972): 22-31.

7628. Leowinsohn, Ron. "'Fools Have Big Wombs': William Carlos Williams' *Kora in Hell.*" *EL* 4(1977): 221-238.

7629. Mariani, Paul. "The Eight Day of Creation: William Carlos Williams' Late Poems." *TCL* 21(1975): 305-318.

7630. ----------. "The Satyr's Defense: Williams' 'Asphodel.'" *Con L* 14(1973): 1-18.

7631. Martz, Louis L. "*Paterson:* A Plan of Action." *JML* 1(1971): 512-522.

7632. Movius, Geoffrey H. "Caviar and Bread: Ezra Pound and William Carlos Williams, 1902-1914." *JML* 5(1976): 383-406.

7633. Myers, Neil. "Decreation in Williams' 'The Descent.'" *Criticism* 14(1972): 315-327.

7634. ----------. "Sentimentalism in the Early Poetry of William Carlos Williams." *AL* 37 (1966): 458-470.

7635. ----------. "William Carlos Williams' *Spring and All.*" *MLQ* 26(1965): 285-301.

7636. ----------. "Williams' Imitation of Nature in 'The Desert Music.'" *Criticism* 12 (1970): 38-50.

7637. ----------. "Williams' 'Two Pendants: for the Ears.'" *JML* 1(1971): 477-492.

7638. Nelson, Cary. "Suffused-Encircling Shapes of Mind: Inhabited Space in Williams." *JML* 1(1971): 549-564.

7639. Quinn, Sister Bernetta. "Paterson: Landscape and Dream." *JML* 1(1971): 523-548.

7640. ----------. "William Carlos Williams: A Testament of Perpetual Change." *PMLA* 70(1955): 292-322.

7641. Ramsey, Paul. "William Carlos Williams as Metrist: Theory and Practice." *JML* 1(1971): 578-592.

7642. Schevill, James. "Notes on the Grotesque: Anderson, Brecht, and Williams." *TCL* 23 (1977): 229-238.

7643. Seamon, Roger. "The Bottle in the Fire: Resistance as Creation in William Carlos Williams' *Paterson.*" *TCL* 11(1965): 16-24.

7644. Slate, Joseph Evans. "Kora in Opacity: Williams' *Improvisations.*" *JML* 1(1971): 463-476.

7645. ----------. "William Carlos Williams, Hart Crane, and 'The Virtue of History.'" *TSLL* 6(1965): 486-511.

7646. Sutton, Walter. "Dr. Williams' *Paterson* and the Quest for Form." *Criticism* 2(1960): 242-259.

7647. Wagner, Linda Welshimer. "A Decade of Discovery, 1953-1963: Checklist of Criticism, William Carlos Williams' Poetry." *TCL* 10(1965): 166-169.

7648. ----------. "The Last Poems of William Carlos Williams." *Criticism* 6(1964): 361-378.

7649. ----------. "William Carlos Williams' *The Great American Novel*." *Novel* 3(1969): 48-61.

7650. ----------. "Williams' Search: 'To Have a Country.'" *Criticism* 12(1970): 226-238.

7651. ----------. "Williams' 'The Use of Force': An Expansion." *SSF* 4(1967): 351-353.

7652. Weatherhead, A. K. "Two Books on William Carlos Williams." *MLQ* 33(1972): 172-180.

7653. ----------. "William Carlos Williams: Poetic Invention and the World Beyond." *ELH* 32 (1965): 126-138.

7654. ----------. "William Carlos Williams: Prose, Form, and Measure." *ELH* 33(1966): 118-131.

7655. Willard, N. M. "A Poetry of Things: Williams, Rilke, Ponge." *Comp L* 17(1965): 311-324.

See also 488, 541, 2296, 4341.
WILLINGHAM, CALDER. 7656. Parr, J. L. "Calder Willingham: The Forgotten Novelist." *Crit* 11,#3(1969): 57-65.

WILSON, EDMUND. See 62, 4376.
WILSON, ETHEL. 7657. New, W. H. "The Irony of Order: Ethel Wilson's *The Innocent Traveller*." *Crit* 10,#3(1968): 22-30.

WINTERS, YVOR. 7658. Lohf, Kenneth A., and Eugene P. Sheehy. "Yvor Winters: A Bibliography." *TCL* 5(1959): 27-51.

7659. Stephens, Alan. "The *Collected Poems* of Yvor Winters." *TCL* 9(1963): 127-139.

7660. Winters, Yvor. "By Way of Clarification." *TCL* 10(1964): 130-**135**.

WINTHER, SOPHUS K. 7661. Meldrum, Barbara. "Structure and Meaning in S. K. Winther's *Beyond the Garden Gate*." *WAL* 6(1971): 191-202.

WISTER, OWEN. 7662. Bode, Carl. "Henry James and Owen Wister." *AL* 26(1954): 250-252.

7663. Kaye, Frances W. "Cooper, Sarmiento, Wister, and Hernández: The Search for a New World Hero." *CLA* 19(1976): 404-411.

7664. Lambert, Neal. "Owen Wister's 'Hank's Woman': The Writer and His Comment." *WAL* 4 (1969): 39-50.

7665. ----------. "Owen Wister's Lin McLean: The Failure of the Vernacular Hero." *WAL* 5(1970): 219-232.

7666. ----------. "Owen Wister's Virginian: The Genesis of a Cultural Hero." *WAL* 6(1971): 99-107.

7667. Marovitz, Sanford. "Owen Wister: An Annotated Bibliography of Secondary Materials." *ALR* 7(1974): 1-110.

7668. ----------. "Testament of a Patriot: The Virginian, the Tenderfoot, and Owen Wister." *TSLL* 15(1973): 511-575.

7669. Morsberger, Robert E. "Son of a Gun: Profanity and Prudery in the Movie of *The Virginian*." *ELN* 10(1973): 216-217.

7670. Solensten, John. "Richard Harding Davis, Owen Wister, and *The Virginian*: Unpublished Letters and a Commentary." *ALR* 5(1972): 123-133.

7671. Vorpahl, Ben M. "Very Much Like a Fire-cracker: Owen Wister on Mark Twain." *WAL* 6 (1971): 83-98.

See also 601, 1167.
WOLFE, BERNARD. 7672. Galloway, David. "An Erratic Geography: The Novels of Bernard Wolfe." *Crit* 7,#1(1964): 75-86.

7673. Samuelson, David N. "*Limbo*: The Great American Dystopia." *Ext* 19(1977): 76-87.

WOLFE, THOMAS. 7674. Albrecht, W. P. "The Titles of *Look Homeward Angel*: A Story of the Buried Life." *MLQ* 11(1950): 50-57.

7675. Beebe, Maurice, and Leslie A. Field. "Criticism of Thomas Wolfe: A Selected Checklist." *MFS* 11(1965): 315-328.

7676. Beja, Morris. "Why You Can't Go Home Again: Thomas Wolfe and 'The Escapes of Time and Memory.'" *MFS* 11(1965): 297-314.

7677. Boyle, Thomas E. "Frederick Jackson Turner and Thomas Wolfe: The Frontier as History and as Literature." *WAL* 4(1970): 273-285.

7678. ----------. "Thomas Wolfe: Theme Through Imagery." *MFS* 11(1965): 259-268.

7679. Bredahl, A. Carl, Jr. "*Look Homeward, Angel*: Individuation and Articulation." *SLJ* 6,#1 (1973): 47-58.

7680. Budd, Louis J. "The Grotesques of Anderson and Wolfe." *MFS* 5(1959): 304-310.

7681. Carlile, Robert Emerson. "Musical Analogues in Thomas Wolfe's *Look Homeward, Angel*." *MFS* 14(1968): 215-223.

7682. Clements, Clyde C., Jr. "Symbolic Patterns in *You Can't Go Home Again*." *MFS* 11(1965): 286-296.

7683. Cracroft, Richard. "A Pebble in the Pool: Organic Theme and Structure in Thomas Wolfe's *You Can't Go Home Again*." *MFS* 17(1971): 533-553.

7684. Delakas, Daniel L. "Thomas Wolfe and Anatole France: A Study of Some Unpublished Experiments." *Comp L* 9(1957): 33-50.

7685. Dessner, Lawrence. "Thomas Wolfe's Mr. Katamoto." *MFS* 17(1971): 561-565.

7686. Evans, Elizabeth. "Music in *Look Homeward, Angel*." *SLJ* 8,#2(1976): 62-73.

7687. Forssberg, William. "Part Two of 'The Lost Boy': Theme and Intention." *SSF* 4 (1967): 167-169.

7688. Foster, Ruel E. "Thomas Wolfe's Mountain Gloom and Glory." *AL* 44(1973): 638-647.

7689. Hawthorne, Mark D. "Thomas Wolfe's Use of the Poetic Fragment." *MFS* 11(1965): 234-244.

7690. Hill, John S. "Eugene Gant and the Ghost of Ben." *MFS* 11(1965): 245-249.

7691. Holman, C. Hugh. "Thomas Wolfe: A Bibliographical Study." *TSLL* 1(1959): 427-445.

7692. ----------. "Thomas Wolfe and America." *SLJ* 10,#1(1977): 56-74.

7693. Idol, John. "Thomas Wolfe's 'A Note in Experts.'" *SSF* 11(1974): 395-398.

7694. Kennedy, Richard S. "Thomas Wolfe and the American Experience." *MFS* 11(1965): 219-233.

7695. Leon, Philip W. "*The Lost Boy* and a
Lost Girl." *SLJ* 9,#1(1976): 61-69.

7696. McElderry, B. R. "Thomas Wolfe: Dramatist." *MD* 6(1963): 1-11.

7697. ----------. "Wolfe and Emerson on
'Flow.'" *MFS* 2(1956): 77-78.

7698. McIlvaine, Robert. "Thomas Wolfe's
GarGANTuan Family." *NCL* 6(January, 1976): 2-5.

7699. Reeves, Paschal. "Thomas Wolfe: Notes
on Three Characters." *MFS* 11(1965): 275-285.

7700. Rubin, Larry. "Thomas Wolfe and the
Lost Paradise." *MFS* 11(1965): 250-258.

7701. Scherting, Jack. "Echoes of *Look
Homeward Angel* in Dylan Thomas's 'A Child's
Christmans in Wales.'" *SSF* 9(1972): 404-406.

7702. Skipp, Francis E. "Thomas Wolfe,
Max Perkins, and Politics." *MFS* 13(1967): 503-511.

7703. Walser, Richard. "An Early Wolfe
Essay—and the Downfall of a Hero." *MFS* 11(1965):
269-274.

7704. Watkins, Floyd C. "Thomas Wolfe and
Asheville: Again and Again and Again." *SLJ* 10,
#1(1977): 31-55.

7705. ----------. "Thomas Wolfe's High Sin-
fulness of Poetry." *MFS* 2(1956): 197-206.

7706. Wilhelm, Albert E. "Borrowings from
MacBeth in Wolfe's 'The Child by Tiger.'" *SSF* 14
(1977): 179-180.

WOLFE, TOM.   7707. Hagopian, John V.
"Mau-Mauing The Literary Establishment." *SN* 3
(1971): 145-147.

WOOBY, PHILIP.   See 4309.

WOOD, CLEMENT.   See 4402.

WRIGHT, CHARLES.   7708. Foster, Frances S.
"Charles Wright: Black Black Humorist." *CLA* 15
(1971): 44-53.

WRIGHT, HAROLD BELL.   7709. Randall, Dale
B. J. "The 'Seer' and 'Seen' Themes in *Gatsby*
and Some of Their Parallels in Eliot and Wright."
TCL 10(1964): 51-63.

WRIGHT, RICHARD.   7710. Amis, Lola James.
"Richard Wright's *Native Son*: Notes." *BALF* 8
(1974): 240-243.

7711. Bayliss, John F. "*Native Son*: Protest or Psychological Study." *BALF* 1,#1(1967): [5-6].

7712. Britt, David. "*Native Son*: Watershed
of Negro Protest Poetry." *BALF* 1,#1(1967): [4-5].

7713. Brivic, Sheldon. "Conflict of Values:
Richard Wright's *Native Son*." *Novel* 7(1974): 231-
245.

7713a. Bryer, Jackson. "Richard Wright:
A Selected Checklist of Criticism." *Con L* 1,#3
(1960): 22-33.

7714. Cauley, Anne O. "A Definition of Freedom in the Fiction of Richard Wright." *CLA* 19
(1976): 327-346.

7715. Delmar, P. Jay. "Tragic Patterns in
Richard Wright's *Uncle Tom's Children*." *BALF*
10(1976): 3-12.

7716. Demarest, David P., Jr. "Richard
Wright: The Meaning Violence." *BALF* 8(1974):
236-239.

7717. Everette, Mildred W. "The Death of
Richard Wright's American Dream: 'The Man Who
Lived Underground.'" *CLA* 17(1974): 318-326.

7718. Fabre, Michael. "Richard Wright's
First Hundred Books." *CLA* 16(1973): 458-474.

7719. ----------. "Richard Wright: The Man
Who Lived Underground." *SN* 3(1971): 165-179.

7720. Felgar, Robert. "'The Kingdom of the
Beast': The Landscape of *Native Son*." *CLA* 17
(1974): 333-337.

7721. ----------. "*Soul on Ice* and *Native
Son*." *BALF* 8(1974): 235.

7722. Gaskill, Gayle. "The Effect of Black/
White Imagery in Richard Wright's *Black Boy*." *BALF*
7(1973): 46-48.

7723. Gibson, Donald B. "Richard Wright:
A Bibliographical Essay." *CLA* 12(1969): 360-365.

7724. ----------. "Richard Wright and the
Tyranny of Convention." *CLA* 12(1969): 344-357.

7725. Goede, William. "On Lower Frequencies:
The Buried Men in Wright and Ellison." *MFS* 15
(1969): 483-501.

7726. Gounard, Jean François. "Richard
Wright as a Black American Writer in Exile." *CLA*
17(1974): 307-317.

7727. Graham, Don B. "*Lawd Today* and the
Exampel of *The Waste Land*." *CLA* 17(1974): 327-332.

7728. Grenander, M. E. "Criminal Responsibility in *Native Son* and *Knock on Any Door*." *AL*
49(1977): 221-233.

7729. Hamalian, Linda Bearman. "Richard
Wright's Use of Epigraphs in *The Long Dream*."
BALF 10(1976): 120-123.

7730. Jackson, Blyden. "Richard Wright:
Black Boy from America's Black Belt and Urban
Ghettos." *CLA* 12(1969): 287-309.

7731. ----------. "Richard Wright in a
Moment of Truth." *SLJ* 3,#2(1971): 3-17.

7732. Keady, Sylvia H. "Richard Wright's
Women Characters and Inequality." *BALF* 10(1976):
124-128.

7733. Kearns, Edward. "The 'Fate' Section
of *Native Son*." *Con L* 12(1971): 146-155.

7734. Kent, George E. "On the Future Study
of Richard Wright." *CLA* 12(1969): 366-370.

7735. ----------. "Richard Wright: Blackness and the Adventure of Western Culture." *CLA*
12(1969): 322-343.

7736. Kim, Kichung. "Wright, the Protest
Novel, and Baldwin's Faith." *CLA* 17(1974): 387-
396.

7737. Kinnamon, Kenneth. "Richard Wright's
Use of *Othello* in *Native Son*." *CLA* 12(1969): 358-
359.

7738. Klotman, Phyllis R. "Moral Distancing
as a Rhetorical Technique in *Native Son*: A Note
on 'Fate.'" *CLA* 18(1974): 284-291.

7739. Klotman, Phyllis R., and Melville Yan-
cey. "Gift of Double Vision: Possible Political
Implication of Richard Wright's 'Self-Consciousness' Thesis." *CLA* 16(1972): 106-116.

7740. Larsen, R. B. V. "The Four Voices of
Richard Wright's *Native Son*." *BALF* 6(1972): 105-
109.

7741. Lawson, Lewis A. "Cross Damon:
Kirkegaardian Man of Dread." *CLA* 14(1971):
298-316.

7742. Leary, Lewis. "*Lawd Today*: Notes
on Richard Wright's First/Last Novel." *CLA* 15
(1972): 411-420.

7743. LeClair, Thomas. "The Blind Leading
the Blind: Wright's *Native Son* and a Brief Re-

ferences to Ellison's *Invisible Man*." *CLA* 13 (1970): 125-320.

7744. McCarthy, Harold T. "Richard Wright: The Expatriate as Native Son." *AL* 44(1972): 97-117.

7745. Meyer, Shirley. "The Identity of *The Man Who Lived Underground*." *BALF* 4(1970): 52-55.

7746. Miller, Eugene E. "Voodoo Parallels in *Native Son*." *CLA* 16(1972): 81-95.

7747. Moore, Gerian Steve. "Richard Wright's *American Hunger*." *CLA* 21(1977): 79-89.

7748. Oleson, Carole W. "The Symbolic Richness of Richard Wright's 'Bright and Morning Star.'" *BALF* 6(1972): 110-112.

7749. Pyros, John. "Richard Wright: A Black Novelist's Experience in Film." *BALF* 9 (1975): 53-54.

7750. Redden, Dorothy S. "Richard Wright and *Native Son:* Not Guilty." *BALF* 10(1976): 111-116.

7751. Reilly, John M. "Richard Wright's Curious Thriller, Savage Holiday." *CLA* 21(1977): 218-223.

7752. Savory, Jerold J. "Bigger Thomas and the Book of Job: The Epigraph to *Native Son*." *BALF* 9(1975): 55-56.

7753. Siegel, Paul N. "The Conclusion of Richard Wright's *Native Son*." *PMLA* 89(1974): 517-523.

7754. Singh, Raman K. "Christian Heroes and Anti-Heroes in Richard Wright's Fiction." *BALF* 6(1972): 99-104.

7755. ----------. "Some Basic Ideas and Ideals in Richard Wright's Fiction." *CLA* 13 (1969): 78-84.

7756. Smith, Sidonie Ann. "Richard Wright's *Black Boy:* The Creative Impulse as Rebellion." *SLJ* 5,#1(1972): 123-136.

7757. Starr, Alvin. "Richard Wright and the Communist Party—the James T. Farrell Factor." *CLA* 21(1977): 41-50.

7758. Tate, Claudia C. "*Black Boy:* Richard Wright's 'Tragic Sense of Life.'" *BALF* 10(1976): 117-119.

7759. Timmerman, John. "Symbolism as a Syndetic Device in Richard Wright's 'Long Black Sing.'" *CLA* 14(1971): 291-297.

7760. Turner, Darwin T. "*The Outsider:* Revision of an Idea." *CLA* 12(1969): 310-321.

7761. Wasserman, Jerry. "Embracing the Negative: *Native Son* and *Invisible Man*." *SAF* 4(1976): 93-104.

7762. Widmer, Kengsley. "The Existential Darkness: Richard Wright's *The Outsider*." *Con L* 1,#3(1960): 13-21.

See also 4335, 4396, 4400, 4407.

WYLIE, ELINOR. 7763. Wright, Celeste Turner. "Elinor Wylie: The Glass Chimera and the Minotaur." *TCL* 12(1966): 15-26.

YERBY, FRANK. 7764. Lupack, Alan C. "Frank Yerby's 'Wisdom.'" *NCL* 7(September, 1977): 8.

YOUNG, AL. 7765. Bolling, Douglass. "Artistry and Theme in Al Young's *Snakes*." *BALF* 8(1974): 223-225.

YOUNG, STARK. 7766. McAlexander, Hubert, Jr. "William Faulkner—The Young Poet in Stark Young's *The Torches Flare*." *AL* 43(1972): 647-649.

7767. Sommers, John J. "The Critic as Playwright: A Study of Stark Young's *The Saint*." *MD* 7(1965): 446-453.

ZELAZNY, ROGER. 7768. Yoke, Carl B. "Zelazny's *Damnation Alley:* Hell Noh." *Ext* 15(1973): 6-16.

ZUKOFSKY, LOUIS. 7769. Carruth, Hayden. "The Only Way to Get There from Here." *JML* 4(1974): 88-90.

7770. Dembo, L. S. "Louis Zukofsky: Objective Poetics and the Quest for Form." *AL* 44(1972): 74-98.

7771. ----------. "The 'Objectivist' Poet: Four Interviews." *Con L* 10(1969): 155-119.

7772. Yannella, Philip R. "On Louis Zukofsky." *JML* 4(1974): 74-87.

BALLAD.   7773. Bronson, B. H. "The Dialogue Song; or, Proteus Observed." *PQ* 54(1975): 117-136.

7774. Mahoney, John L. "Child's *The English and Scottish Popular Ballads* and Ballad Scholarship." *CLA* 4(1960): 126-121.

7775. Moore, Arthur K. "The Literary Status of the English Popular Ballad." *Comp L* 10(1958): 1-20.

7776. Niles, John D. "*Tam Lin*: Form and Meaning in a Traditional Ballad." *MLQ* 38(1977): 336-347.

7777. Rodger, Gillian. "Hero and Leander in Scottish Balladry." *Comp L* 9(1957): 1-16.

DRAMA.   7778. Goldsmith, Robert Hillis. "The Wild Man on the English Stage." *MLR* 53(1958): 481-491.

7779. Preston, Michael J. "The Robin Hood Folk Plays of South-Central England." *CD* 10(1976): 91-100.

FICTION.   7780. Davis, Robert Gorham. "The Sense of the Real in English Fiction." *Comp L* 3 (1951): 200-217.

7781. Gindin, James. "Review Essay: Tripartite Themes." *SN* 7(1975): 584-593.

7782. Sargent, Lyman Tower. "Ambiguous Legacy: The Role and Position of Women in English Eutopia." *Ext* 19(1977): 39-49.

POETRY.   7783. Kroeber, Alfred L. "Parts of Speech in Periods of Poetry." *PMLA* 73(1958): 309-314.

7784. Miles, Josephine. "Eras in English Poetry." *PMLA* 70(1955): 853-875.

7785. Smith, Hallett. "Love and Nature in Poetry." *MLQ* 27(1966): 80-85.

MISCELLANEOUS.   7786. Harris, Victor. "The Arts of Discourse in England, 1500-1700." *PQ* 37 (1958): 484-494.

7787. Morris, Harry. "Some Uses of Angel Iconography in English Literature." *Comp L* 10 (1958): 36-44.

7788. Rowan, D. F. "Shore's Wife." *SEL* 6 (1966): 447-464.

7789. Ward, William S. "American Authors and British Reviewers 1798-1826." *AL* 49(1977): 1-21.

OLD ENGLISH

GENERAL AND MISCELLANEOUS.   7790. Bethurum, Dorothy. "Six Anonymous Old English Codes." *JEGP* 49(1950): 449-463.

7791. Bolton, W. F. "Pre-Conquest Anglo-Latin: Perspectives and Prospects." *Comp L* 23 (1971): 151-166.

7792. Campbell, Jackson J. "Knowledge of Rhetorical Figures in Anglo-Saxon England." *JEGP* 66(1967): 1-20.

7793. Cross, J. E. "Aspects of Micrcosm and Macrocosm in Old English Literature." *Comp L* 14 (1962): 1-22.

7794. Colgrave, Bertram, and Ann Hyde. "Two Recently Discovered Leaves from Old English Manuscripts." *Speculum* 37(1962): 60-78.

7795. Davis, Norman. "'Hippopotamus' in Old English." *RES* 4(1953): 141-142.

7796. Downing, Janay Y. "An Unpublished Weather Prognostic in Cambridge University MS Ff.

5.48." *ELN* 8(1970): 87-89.

7797. Duncan, Edgar Hill. "Short Fiction in Medieval English: A Survey." *SSF* 9(1972): 1-28.

7798. Earl, James W. "Typology and Iconographic Style in Early Medieval Hagiography." *SLI* 8,#1(1975): 15-46.

7799. Greenfield, Stanley B. "The Canons of Old English Criticism." *ELH* 34(1977): 141-155.

7800. ----------. "Old English Words and Patristic Exegesis—hwyrftum scripað: A Caveat." *MP* 75(1977): 44-48.

7801. Hetherington, M.S. "Sir Simonds D'Eives and Method in Old English Lexicography." *TSLL* 17(1975): 75-92.

7802. Hill, Betty. "Notes on Five Difficult Glosses to the Lindisfarne Gospels." *MLR* 50 (1955): 487-488.

7803. Kuhn, Sherman M. "Cursus in Old English: Rhetorical Ornament or Linguistic Phenomenon." *Speculum* 47(1972): 188-206.

7804. ----------. "Some Early Mercian Manuscripts." *RES* 8(1957): 355-374.

7805. Lehmann, W. P. "Metrical Evidence for Old English Suprasegmentals." *TSLL* 1(1959): 68-72.

7806. Lerner, L. D. "Colour Words in Anglo Saxon." *MLR* 46(1951): 246-249.

7807. Magoun, Francis P., Jr. "King Aethelwulf's Biblical Ancestors." *MLR* 46(1951): 249-250.

7808. Miletich, John S. "The Quest for the Formula: A Comparative Reappraisal." *MP* 74(1976): 111-123.

7809. Rice, Robert C. "*Hreowcearig* 'Penitent, Contrite'." *ELN* 12(1975): 243-250.

7810. Robinson, Fred C. "Syntactical Glosses in Latin Manuscripts of Anglo-Saxon Provenance." *Speculum* 48(1973): 443-475.

7811. Sisam, Kenneth. "Canterbury, Lichfield, and the Vespasian Psalter." *RES* 7(1956): 1-10, 113-131.

7812. ----------. "A Gloss to Gregory's *Dialogues*." *RES* 2(1951): 48.

7813. Szarmach, Paul E. "Ms. Junius 85 f. 2r and Napier 49." *ELN* 14(1977): 241-246.

7814. Ure, James M. "The *Benedictine Office* and the Metrical Paraphrase of the Lord's Prayer in MS. C.C.C.C. 201." *RES* 4(1953): 354-356.

7815. West, Fred. "Some Notes on Word Order in Old and Middle English." *MP* 71(1973): 48-53.

7816. Wrenn, C. L. "Two Anglo-Saxon Harps." *Comp L* 14(1962): 118-128.

POETRY.   7817. Barnes, Richard. "Horse Colors in Anglo-Saxon Poetry." *PQ* 39(1960): 510-512.

7818. Benson, Larry D. "The Literary Character of Anglo-Saxon Formulaic Poetry." *PMLA* 81 (1966): 334-341.

7819. Berkout, Carl T. "Some Notes on the Old English 'Almsgiving'." *ELN* 10(1972): 81-85.

7820. Bliss, Alan, and Allen J. Frantzen. "The Integrity of *Resignation*." *RES* 27(1976): 385-402.

7821. Bloomfield, Morton W. "Patristics and Old English Literature: Notes on Some Poems." *Comp L* 14(1962): 36-43.

7822. Bonner, Joshua H. "Toward a Unified Critical Approach to Old English Poetic Composition." *MP* 73(1976): 219-228.

7823. Cable, Thomas. "Constraints on Anacrusis in Old English Meter." *MP* 69(1971): 97-104.

7824. ----------. "Metrical Simplicity and Sievers' Five Types." *SP* 69(1972): 280-288.

7825. Campbell, Jackson J. "Learned Rhetoric in Old English Poetry." *MP* 63(1965): 189-201.

7826. ----------. "Structural Patterns in Old English Advent Lyrics." *ELH* 23(1956): 239-255.

7827. Creed, Robert P. "The Andswarode-System in Old English Poetry." *Speculum* 32(1957): 523-528.

7828. Dawson, R. McGregor. "The Structure of the Old English Gnomic Poems." *JEGP* 61(1962): 14-22.

7829. Diamond, Robert E. "Theme as Ornament in Anglo-Saxon Poetry." *PMLA* 76(1961): 461-468.

7830. Eliason, Norman E. "Two Old English Scop Poems." *PMLA* 81(1966): 185-192.

7831. Elliott, Ralph W. V. "Form and Image in Old English Lyrics." *EIC* 11(1961): 1-9.

7832. Fakundiny, Lydia. "The Art of Old English Verse Composition." *RES* 21(1970): 129-142, 257-266.

7833. Frank, Roberta. "Some Uses of Paronomasia in Old English Scriptural Verse." *Speculum* 47(1972): 207-226.

7834. Frey, Leonard H. "Exile and Elegy in Anglo-Saxon Christian Epic Poetry." *JEGP* 62(1963): 293-302.

7835. Gardner, Thomas. "The Old English Kenning: A Characteristic Feature of Germanic Poetical Diction?" *MP* 67(1969): 109-117.

7836. Grant, R. J. S. "A Note on 'The Seasons for Fasting'." *RES* 23(1972): 302-304.

7837. Greenfield, Stanley B. "The Formulaic Expression of the Theme of 'Exile' in Anglo-Saxon Poetry." *Speculum* 30(1955): 200-212.

7838. Hermann, John P. "*Solomon and Saturn* (II), 339a: *Niehtes Wunde*." *ELN* 14(1977): 161-164.

7839. Hieatt, Constance B. "Alliterative Patterns in the Hypermetric Lines of Old English Verse." *MP* 71(1974): 237-242.

7840. ----------. "A New Theory of Triple Rhythm in the Hypermetric Lines of Old English Verse." *MP* 67(1969): 1-8.

7841. Hoover, David L. "Old English Meter Again." *JEGP* 76(1977): 491-505.

7842. Irving, Edward B., Jr. "Latin Prose Sources for Old English Verse." *JEGP* 56(1957): 588-595.

7843. Kliger, Samuel. "The Neo-Classical View of Old English Poetry." *JEGP* 49(1950): 516-522.

7844. Kyte, E. Clemens. "On the Composition of Hypermetric Verses in Old English." *MP* 71(1973): 160-165.

7845. LePage, R. B. "Alliterative Patterns as a Test of Style in Old English Poetry." *JEGP* 58(1959): 434-441.

7846. Lee, Alvin A. "Old English Poetry, Medieval Exegesis and Modern Criticism." *SLI* 8,#1 (1975): 47-73.

7847. Leslie, R. F. "Textual Notes on *The Seasons for Fasting*." *JEGP* 52(1953): 555-558.

7848. Lewis, Richard A. "Plurilinear Alliteration in Old English Poetry." *TSLL* 16(1975): 589-602.

7849. Magoun, Francis P., Jr. "Oral-Formulaic Character of Anglo-Saxon Narrative Poetry." *Speculum* 28(1953): 448-467.

7850. Martin, B. K. "Aspects of Winter in Latin and Old English Poetry." *JEGP* 68(1969): 375-390.

7851. Mitchell, Bruce. "Pronouns in Old English Poetry. Some Syntactical Notes." *RES* 15 (1964): 129-141.

7852. Nicholson, Lewis E. "Oral Techniques in the Composition of Expanded Anglo-Saxon Verses." *PMLA* 78(1963): 287-292.

7853. Offler, H. S. "The Date of Durham (*Carmen de situ Dunelmi*)." *JEGP* 61(1962): 591-594.

7854. Pheifer, J. D. "*Waldere* I. 29-31." *RES* 11(1960): 183-186.

7855. Rendall, Thomas. "Bondage and Freeing from Bondage in Old English Religious History." *JEGP* 73(1974): 497-512.

7856. Scargill, M. H. "'Gold Beyond Measure': A Plea for Old English Poetry." *JEGP* 52 (1953): 289-293.

7857. Short, Douglas D. "The Old English *Gifts of Men*, Line 13." *MP* 71(1974): 388-389.

7858. Starr, David. "Metrical Changes: From Old to Middle English." *MP* 68(1970): 1-9.

7859. Stevick, Robert D. "The Oral-Formulaic Analyses of Old English Verse." *Speculum* 37(1962): 382-389.

7860. Timmer, B. J. "Sectional Divisions of Poems in Old English Manuscripts." *MLR* 47(1952): 319-322.

7861. Whitbread, L. "Notes on Two Minor Old English Poems." *ELN* 4(1967): 241-243.

7862. Whitman, F. "A Major Compositional Technique in Old English Verse." *ELN* 11(1973): 81-86.

7863. Woolf, R. E. "The Devil in Old English Poetry." *RES* 4(1953): 1-12.

PROSE. 7864. Butturff, Douglas R. "Style as a Clue to Meaning: A Note on the Old English Translation of the *Epistola Alexandri ad Aristotelem*." *ELN* 8(1970): 81-86.

7865. Cross, J. E. "The dry bones speak— A Theme in Some Old English Homilies." *JEGP* 56 (1957): 434-439.

7866. Dalbey, Marcia A. "A Textual Crux in the Third Blickling Homily." *ELN* 5(1968): 241-243.

7867. Dolan, T. P. "On Claims for Syntactical Modernity in Early English Prose." *MP* 74(1977): 305-310.

7868. Sisam, Celia. "An Early Fragment of the Old English *Martyrology*." *RES* 4(1953): 209-220.

ÆLFRIC. 7869. Besserman, L. L. "A Note on the Source of Aelfric's Homily on the Book of Job." *ELN* 10(1973): 248-252.

7870. Colledge, Eric. "An Allusion to Augustine in Ælfric's *Colloquy*." *RES* 12(1961): 180-181.

7871. Gatch, Milton McC. "MS Boulogne-sur-Mer 63 and Ælfric's First Series of Catholic Homilies." *JEGP* 65(1966): 482-490.

7872. Harlow, C. G. "Punctuation in Some Manuscripts of Ælfric." *RES* 10(1959): 1-19.

7873. Kuhn, Sherman M. "Was Ælfric a Poet?" *PQ* 52(1973): 643-663.

7874. Ladd, C. A. "The 'Rubens' Manuscript and *Archbishop Ælfric's Vocabulary*." *RES* 11(1960): 353-364.

7875. Lipp, Frances Randall. "Ælfric's Old English Prose Style." *SP* 66(1969): 689-718.

7876. Minkoff, Harvey. "Some Stylistic Consequences of Ælfric's Theory of Translation." *SP* 73(1976): 29-41.

7877. Needham, Geoffrey. "Additions and Alterations in Cotton MS. Julius E VII." *RES* 9 (1958): 160-164.

7878. Nichols, Ann Eljenholm. "Ælfric and the Brief Style." *JEGP* 70(1971): 1-12.

7879. ----------. "*Awendan*: A Note on Ælfric's Vocabulary." *JEGP* 63(1964): 7-13.

7880. Raith, Josef. "Ælfric's Share in the Old English Pentateuch." *RES* 3(1952): 305-314.

7881. Temple, Winifred M. "OE. Hlædfæt— Welsh Lletwad." *RES* 6(1955): 63-65.

7882. Williams, Edna R. "Ælfric's Grammatical Terminology." *PMLA* 73(1958): 453-462.
See also 7803.

ALCUIN.   7883. Scott, Peter Dale. "Alcuin's *Versus de Cuculo*: The Vision of Pastoral Friendship." *SP* 62(1965): 510-530.

7884. Wallach, Luitpold. "Charlemagne's *De Litteris Colendis* and Alcuin: A Diplomatic—Historical Study." *Speculum* 26(1951): 288-305.

7885. ----------. "The Epitaph of Alcuin: A Model of Carolingian Epigraphy." *Speculum* 30 (1955): 367-373.
See also 7791.

ALFRED.   7786. Brown, William H., Jr. "Method and Style in the Old English *Pastoral Care*." *JEGP* 68(1969): 666-684.

7887. Cross, J. E. "The Name and Not the Deeds." *MLR* 54(1959): 66.

7888. Linderski, Jerzy. "Alfred the Great and the Tradition of Ancient Geography." *Speculum* 39(1964): 434-439.

ANDREAS.   7889. Peters, Leonard. "The Relationship of the Old English *Andreas* to *Beowulf*." *PMLA* 66(1951): 844-863.

7890. Szittya, Penn R. "The Living Stone and the Patriarchs: Typological Imagery in *Andreas*, Lines 706-810." *JEGP* 72(1973): 167-174.

7891. Willard, Rudolph. "*Andreas* and the Fates of the Apostles." *MP* 62(1964): 45-51.

ANGLO-SAXON CHRONICLE.   7892. Battaglia, Francis Joseph. "*Anglo-Saxon Chronicle* for 755: The Missing Evidence for a Traditional Reading." *PMLA* 81(1966): 173-178.

7893. Lehiste, Ilse. "Names of Scandinavians in *The Anglo-Saxon Chronicle*." *PMLA* 73(1958): 6-22.

7894. Magoun, F. P., Jr. "Orwell Havan in the 'Anglo-Saxon Chronicle'." *MLR* 50(1955): 44-45.

BEDE. 7895. Anderson, Earl R. "Passing the Harp in Bede's Story of Caldmon: A Twelfth Century Analogue." *ELN* 15(1977): 1-4.

7896. Campbell, Jackson J. "The Dialect Vocabulary of the OE Bede." *JEGP* 50(1951): 349-372.

7897. Chickering, Howell D. "Some Contexts for Bede's *Death-Song*." *PMLA* 91(1976): 91-100.

7898. Magoun, Francis P., Jr. "Bede's Story of Cædman : The Case History of an Anglo-Saxon Oral Singer." *Speculum* 30(1955): 49-63.

7899. Palmer, Robert B. "Bede as Textbook Writer: A Study of His *De Arte Metrica*." *Speculum* 34(1959): 573-584.

7900. Whitbread, L. "Bede's Verses on Doomsday: A Supplementary Note." *PQ* 51(1972): 485-486.

7901. ----------. "An Old English Gloss." *ELN* 2(1965): 245-246.
See also 7791.

BEOWULF.   7902. Anderson, Earl R. "*Beowulf* 2216b-2217: A Restoration." *ELN* 12(1974): 1-5.

7903. Baird, Joseph L. "The Happy Hurt: *Beowulf* 2,697-99." *MP* 66(1969): 328-329.

7904. ----------. "The 'Nor'—Clause of *Beowulf* 1084-85a." *MP* 69(1971): 133-135.

7905. Barnes, Daniel B. "Folktale Morphology and the structure of *Beowulf*." *Speculum* 45(1970): 416-434.

7906. Baum, Paull F. "The *Beowulf* Poet." *PQ* 39(1960): 389-399.

7907. Bevis, Richard W. "*Beowulf*: A Restoration." *ELN* 2(1965): 165-168.

7908. Blake, N. F. "The Heremod Digressions in *Beowulf*." *JEGP* 61(1962): 278-287.

7909. Bloomfield, Morton W. "Beowulf, Byrhtnoth, and the Judgement of God: Trial by Combat in Anglo-Saxon England." *Speculum* 44(1969): 545-559.

7910. Bonjour, Adrien. "Beowulf and the Beasts of Battle." *PMLA* 72(1957): 563-573.

7911. ----------. "Monsters Crouching and Critics Rampant: or the *Beowulf*." *PMLA* 68(1953): 304-312.

7912. ----------. "On Sea Images in *Beowulf*." *JEGP* 54(1955): 111-115.

7913. ----------. "The Technique of Parallel Descriptions in *Beowulf*." *RES* 2(1951): 1-10.

7914. Brodeur, Arthur G. "Design for Terror in the Purging of Heorot." *JEGP* 53(1954): 503-513.

7915. ----------. "The Structure and the Unity of *Beowulf*." *PMLA* 68(1953): 1183-1195.

7916. Brown, George Hardin. "Beowulf 1278b: 'sunu þeod wrecan'." *MP* 72(1974): 172-174.

7917. Burchfield, R. W. "'Beowulf' 219: 'ymb an tid'." *MLR* 50(1955): 485-487.

7918. Byers, John R., Jr. "The Last of the Wægmundings and a Possible Emendation of *Beowulf*." *MP* 66(1968): 45-47.

7919. ----------. "On the Decorating of Heorot." *PMLA* 80(1965): 299-300.

7920. ----------. "A Possible Emendation of *Beowulf* 461b." *PQ* 46(1967): 125-128.

7921. Cabaniss, Allen. "Beowulf and the Liturgy." *JEGP* 54(1955): 195-201.

7922. Cable, Thomas. "Parallels to the Melodic Formulas of *Beowulf*." *MP* 73(1975): 1-14.

7923. ----------. "Rules for Syntax and Metrics in *Beowulf*." *JEGP* 69(1970): 81-88.

7924. Calder, Daniel G. "Setting and Ethos: The Pattern of Measure and Limit in Beowulf." *SP* 69 (1972): 21-37.

7925. Candelaria, Frederick "'Garsecg' in *Beowulf*." *ELN* 1(1964): 243-244.

7926. Carnicelli, Thomas A. "The Function of the Messenger in *Beowulf*." *SP* 72(1975): 246-257.

7927. Chaney, William A. "Grendel and the *Gifstol*: A Legal View of Monsters." *PMLA* 77(1962): 513-520.

7928. Cherniss, Michael D. "The Progress of the Hoard in *Beowulf*."   47(1968): 473-486.

7929. Clark, George. "Beowulf and Bears' Son in the *Vishu Purana*." *PQ* 43(1964): 125-130.

7930. ----------. "Beowulf's Armor." *ELH* 32(1965): 409-441.

7931. Condren, Edward I. "*Unnyt* Gold in *Beowulf* 3168." *PQ* 52(1973): 296-299.

7932. Cosmos, Spencer. "Kuhn's Law and the Unstressed Verbs in *Beowulf*." *TSLL* 18(1976): 306-328.

7933. Creed, Robert P. "*Beowulf* 2231a: *Sinc←Faet* (sohte)" *PQ* 35(1956): 206-208.

7934. ----------. "The Making of an Anglo-Saxon Poem." *ELH* 26(1959): 445-454.

7935. ----------. "A New Approach to the Rhythm of *Beowulf*." *PMLA* 81(1966): 23-33.

7936. ----------. "On the Possibility of Criticizing Old English Poetry." *TSLL* 3(1961): 97-106.

7937. ----------. "The Singer Looks at His Sources." *Comp L* 14(1962): 44-52.

7938. Culbert, Taylor. "The Narrative Functions of Beowulf's Swords." *JEGP* 59(1960): 13-20.

7939. DuBois, Arthur E. "The Dragon in Beowulf." *PMLA* 72(1957): 819-822.

7940. ---------- and D. D. Griffith. "*Stod on Stapole*." *MLQ* 16(1955): 291-299.

7941. Eliason, Norman E. "The 'Improvised Lay' in *Beowulf*." *PQ* 31(1952): 171-179.

7942. ----------. "The þyle and Scop in *Beowulf*." *Speculum* 38(1963): 267-284.

7943. Engelhardt, George J. "*Beowulf*: A Study in Dilatation." *PMLA* 70(1955): 825-852.

7944. Fisher, Peter F. "The Trials of the Epic Hero in Beowulf." *PMLA* 73(1958): 171-183.

7945. Fry, Donald K. "The Location of Finnsburh: *Beowulf* 1125-29a." *ELN* 8(1970): 1-3.

7946. ----------. "Variation and Economy in Beowulf." *MP* 65(1068): 353-356.

7947. ----------. "Wið earm gesæt" and Beowulf's Hammerlock." *MP* 67(1970): 364-366.

7948. Gang, T.M. "Approaches to *Beowulf*." *RES* 3(1952): 1-12.

7949. Gardner, Thomas. "How Free was the *Beowulf* Poet?" *MP* 71(1973): 111-127.

7950. Green, Martin. "Man, Time, and Apocalypse in *The Wanderer, The Seafarer,* and Beowulf." *JEGP* 74(1975): 502-518.

7951. Greenfield, Stanley. "Beowulf and Epic Tragedy." *Comp L* 14(1962): 91-105.

7952. Goldsmith, Margaret E. "The Christian Perspective in Beowulf." *Comp L* 14(1962): 71-90.

7953. Halverson, John. "Ganelon's Trial." *Speculum* 42(1967): 661-669.

7954. ----------. "The World of *Beowulf*." *ELH* 36(1969): 593-608.

7955. Hanning, Robert W. "Sharing, Dividing, Depriving—The Verbal Ironies of Grendel's Last Visit to Heorot." *TSLL* 15(1973): 203-213.

7956. Helterman, Jeffrey. "*Beowulf*: The Archetype Enters History." *ELH* 35(1968): 1-20.

7957. Hoffman, Richard L. "*Guðrinc astah*: *Beowulf* 1118b." *JEGP* 64(1965): 660-667.

7958. Hollowell, Ida Masters. "Unferð the þyle in *Beowulf*." *SP* 73(1976): 239-265.

7959. Hulbert, J. R. "The Genesis of *Beowulf*: A Caveat." *PMLA* 66(1951): 1168-1176.

7960. ----------. "Surmises Concerning the *Beowulf* Poet's Source." *JEGP* 50(1951): 11-18.

7961. Hume, Kathryn. "The function of the *Hrefn Blaca*: *Beowulf* 1801." *MP* 67(1969): 60-63.

7962. ----------. "The Theme and Structure of *Beowulf*." *SP* 72(1975): 1-27.

7963. Hust, James R. "Grendel's Point of View: *Beowulf* and William Golding." *MFS* 13(1967): 264-265.

7964. Isaacs, Neil D. "Six *Beowulf* Cruces." *JEGP* 62(1963): 119-128.

7965. Johnson, William C., Jr. "Pushing and Shoving in *Beowulf*: A Semantic Inquiry." *ELN* 14 (1976): 81-87.

7966. Kahrl, Stanley J. "Feuds in *Beowulf*: A Tragic Necessity?" *MP* 69(1972): 189-198.

7967. Kaske, R.E. "*Beowulf* and the Book of Enoch." *Speculum* 46(1971): 421-431.

7968. ----------. "*Sapientia et Fortitudo* as the Controlling Theme of *Beowulf*." *SP* 55(1958): 423-456.

7969. ----------. "The Sigemund-Heremod and Hama-Hygelac Passages in *Beowulf*." *PMLA* 74(1959): 489-494.

7970. Kiessling, Nicolas K. "Grendel: A New Aspect." *MP* 65(1968): 191-201.

7971. Kinloch, A. Murray. "A Note on 'Beowulf' 1. 1828b." *MLR* 51(1956): 71.

7972. Kuhn, Sherman M. "Further Thoughts on *brand Healfdenes*." *JEGP* 76(1977): 231-237.

7973. Leake, Jane Acomb. "Middle English Glosses in the Beowulf-Codex." *MLQ* 23(1962): 229-232.

7974. Lewis, Richard A. "*Beowulf* 992A: Ironic Use of the Formulaic." *PQ* 54(1975): 663-664.

7975. Lumiansky, R.M. "The Dramatic Audience in *Beowulf*." *JEGP* 51(1952): 545-550.

7976. Malone, Kemp. "Coming Back from the Mere." *PMLA* 69(1954): 1292-1299.

7977. ----------. "A Note on 'Beowulf' 489-490." *MLR* 56(1961): 212.

7978. ----------. "A Note on *Beowulf* 2466." *JEGP* 50(1951): 19-21.

7979. McGalliard, John C. "The Complex Art of *Beowulf*." *MP* 59(1962): 276-282.

7980. McNamee, M.B. "*Beowulf*-An Allegory of Salvation." *JEGP* 59(1960): 190-207.

7981. Mezger, Fritz. "OE Hāmweorðung *Beowulf* 2998." *JEGP* 50(1951): 243-245.

7982. Moore, Bruce. "*Eacen* in *Beowulf* and Other Old English Poetry." *ELN* 13(1976): 161-165.

7983. ----------. "The Relevance of the Finnsburh Episode." *JEGP* 75(1976): 317-329.

7984. Moorman, Charles. "The Essential Paganism of Beowulf." *MLQ* 28(1967): 3-18.

7985. Ogilvy, J. D. A. "Unferth: Foil to Beowulf?" *PMLA* 79(1964): 370-375.

7986. Piper, William Bowman. "The Case for *Weard Schildinga* (*Beowulf*, 305b-306a)." *PQ* 35(1956): 202-206.

7987. Puhvel, Martin. "The Blithe-hearted Morning Raven in *Beowulf*." *ELN* 10(1973): 243-247.

7988. ----------. "*Lices Feorm*, 1. 451, *Beowulf*." *ELN* 1(1964): 159-163.

7989. Richards, Mary P. "A Reexamination of *Beowulf* 11 3180-3182." *ELN* 10(1973): 163-167.

7990. Ringler, Richard N. "*Him Seo Wen Geleah*: The Design for Irony in Grendel's Last Visit to Hearot." *Speculum* 41(1966): 49-67.

7991. Robinson, Fred C. "Beowulf's Retreat from Frisia: Some Textual Problems in 11. 2361-2362." *SP* 62(1965): 1-16.

7992. Rogers, H. L. "Beowulf's Three Great Fights." *RES* 6(1955): 339-355.

7993. Roper, Alan H. "Boethius and the Three Fates of *Beowulf*." *PQ* 41(1962): 386-400.

7994. Rosier, James L. "Design for Treachery: The Unferth Intrique." *PMLA* 77(1962): 1-7.

7995. ----------. "*icge gold* and *incge lafe* in *Beowulf*." *PMLA* 81(1966): 342-346.

7996. ----------. "The *Unhlitm* of Finn and Hengest." *RES* 17(1966): 171-174.

7997. ----------. "The Uses of Association: Hands and Feasts in *Beowulf*." *PMLA* 78(1963): 8-14.

7998. Sanborn, John Newell. "A Possible Anglo-Saxon Poetic Framework: An Alternative to an Emendation." *MP* 70(1972): 46-48.

7999. Schrader, Richard J. "Beowulf's Obsequies and the Roman Epic." *Comp L* 24(1972): 237-259.

8000. Shuman, R. Baird, and H. Charles Hutchings II. "The *un*-Prefix: A Means of Germanic Irony in *Beowulf*." *MP* 57(1960): 217-222.

8001. Sisam, Kenneth. "Beowulf's Fight with the Dragon." *RES* 9(1958): 129-140.

8002. Stevick, Robert D. "Christian Elements and the Genesis of *Beowulf*." *MP* 61(1963): 79-89.

8003. ----------. "Emendation of Old English Poetic Texts: *Beowulf* 2523." *MLQ* 20(1959): 339-343.

8004. Sutherland, Raymond Carter. "The Meaning of *Eorlscipe* in *Beowulf*." *PMLA* 70(1955): 1133-1142.

8005. Taglicht, Josef. "*Beowulf* and Old English Verse Rhythm." *RES* 12(1961): 341-351.

8006. Taylor, Paul Beekman. "*Heofon Riece Swealg*: A Sign of Beowulf's State of Grace." *PQ* 42(1963): 257-259.

8007. Tietjen, Mary C. Wilson. "God, Fate, and the Hero of *Beowulf*." *JEGP* 74(1975): 159-171.

8008. Tremaine, Hadley P. "Beowulf's *Ecg Brun* and Other Rusty Relics." *PQ* 48(1969): 145-150.

8009. Tripp, Raymond P., Jr. "The Exemplary Role of Hrothgar and Heorot." *PQ* 56(1977): 123-129.

8010. Tuso, Joseph F. "*Beowulf* 461b and Thorpe's *wara*." *MLQ* 29(1968): 259-262.

8011. Wentersdorf, Karl P. "Beowulf's Adventure with Breca." *SP* 72(1975): 140-166.

8012. ----------. "Beowulf's Withdrawal from Frisia: A Reconsideration." *SP* 68(1971): 395-415.

8013. Whallon, William. "The Christianity of *Beowulf*." *MP* 60(1962): 81-94.

8014. ----------. "The Diction of *Beowulf*." *PMLA* 76(1961): 309-318.

8015. ----------. "Formulas for Heroes in the *Iliad* and in *Beowulf*." *MP* 63(1965): 95-104.

8016. ----------. "The Idea of God in *Beowulf*." *PMLA* 80(1965): 19-23.

8017. Willard, Rudolph, and Elinar D. Clemons. "Bliss's Light Verses in the *Beowulf*." *JEGP* 66 (1967): 230-244.

8018. Wood, Cecil. "*Nis þæt seldguma: Beowulf* 249." *PMLA* 75(1960): 481-484.

8019. Wright, Herbert G. "Good and Evil; Light and Darkness; Joy and Sorrow in *Beowulf*." *RES* 8(1957): 1-11.

8020. Wright, Thomas L. "Hrothgar's Tears." *MP* 65(1967): 39-44.

8021. Vickrey, John F. "*Egesan Ne Gymeð* and the Crime of Heremod." *MP* 71(1974): 295-300.

See also 511, 514, 7821, 7827, 7849, 7889, 8202.

BRUNABURH. 8022. Berkhout, Carl T. "*Feld Dennade*—Again." *ELN* 11(1974): 161-162.

8023. Bolton, W. F. "'Variation' in *The Battle of Brunanburh*." *RES* 19(1968): 363-372.

8024. Johnson, Ann S. "The Rhetoric of *Brunanburh*." *PQ* 47(1968): 487-493.

8025. Lipp, Francis Randall. "Contrast and Point of View in *The Battle of Brunanburh*." *PQ* 48 (1969): 166-177.

CÆDMON. 8026. "Clubb, Merrel D. "Grimm's Transcript of Cædmon." *PQ* 44(1965): 152-172.

8027. Shepherd, G. "The Prophetic Cædmon." *RES* 5(1954): 113-122.

See also 7821, 7898.

CHRIST I, II, and *III.* See Cynewulf.

CHRIST AND SATAN. 8028. Finnegan, Robert Emmett. "Three Notes on the Junius XI *Christ and Satan*: Lines 78-79; Lines 236-42; Lines 435-38." *MP* 72(1974): 175-181.

8029. ----------. "Two Notes on MS. Junius *Christ and Satan*: Lines 19-2D; Lines 319 and 384." *PQ* 49(1970): 558-561.

8030. Hill, Thomas D. "Apocryphal Cosmography and the 'Stream Uton Sae': A Note on *Christ and Satan*, Lines 4-12." *PQ* 48(1969): 550-554.

8031. ----------. "'Byrht Word' and 'Hælendes Heafod': Cristological Allusion in the Old English *Christ and Satan*." *ELN* 8(1970: 6-9.

8032. ----------. "The Fall of Satan in the Old English *Christ and Satan*." *JEGP* 76(1977): 315-325.

CYNEWULF. 8033. Adams, R. W. "Christ II: Cynewulfian *Heilsgeschichte*." *ELN* 12(1973): 73-79.

8034. Anderson, Earl R. "Cynewulf's *Elene*: Manuscript Divisions and Structural Symmetry." *MP* 72(1974): 111-122.

8035. ----------. "Mary's Role as *Eiron* in *Christ I*." *JEGP* 70(1971): 230-240.

8036. Brown, George Hardin. "The Descent-Ascent Motif in *Christ II* of Cynewulf." *JEGP* 73 (1974): 1-12.

8037. Calder, Daniel G. "The Art of Cynewulf's *Juliana*." *MLQ* 34(1973): 355-371.

8038. Diamond, Robert E. "The Diction of the Signed Poems of Cynewulf." *PQ* 38(1959): 228-241.

8039. Fry, Donald K. "Themes and Type-Scenes in *Elene* 1-113." *Speculum* 44(1969): 35-50.

8040. Greenfield, Stanley P. "The Theme of Spiritual Exile in *Christ I*." *PQ* 32(1953): 321-328.

8041. Hill, Joyce. "A Sequence of Association of *Christ* 275-347." *RES* 27(1976): 296-299.

8042. Hill, Thomas D. "Vision and Judgement in the Old English *Christ III*." *SP* 70(1973): 233-242.

8043. Muinzer, L. A. "Maier's Transcript and the Conclusion of Cynewulf's *Fates of the Apostles*." *JEGP* 56(1957): 570-587.

8044. Towers, Tom H. "Thematic Unity in the Story of Cynewulf and Cyneheard." *JEGP* 62(1963): 310-316.

8045. Whatley, E. Gordon. "Old English Onomastics and Narrative Art: *Elene* 1062." *MP* 73(1975): 109-120.

DANIEL. 8046. Farrell, R. T. "The Unity of Old English *Daniel*." *RES* 18(1967): 117-135.

DEOR. 8047. Bloomfield, Morton W. "The Form of *Deor*." *PMLA* 79(1964): 534-541.

8048. Bolton, W. F. "Boethius, Alfred, and *Deor* Again." *MP* 69(1972): 222-227.

8049. Eliason, Norma E. "The Story of Geat and Mæðhild in *Deor*." *SP* 62(1965): 495-509.

8050. Markland, Murray F. "Boethius, Alfred, and Deor." *MP* 66(1968): 1-4.

8051. Tuggle, Thomas T. "The Structure of *Deor*." *SP* 74(1977): 229-242.

DREAM OF THE ROOD.   8052. Bolton, W. F. Connectives in *The Seafarer* and *The Dream of the Rood.*" MP 57(1960): 260-262.

8053. Burlin, Robert B. "The Ruthwell Cross, *The Dream of the Rood,* and the *Vita Comtemplativa.*" SP 65(1968): 23-43.

8054. Canuteson, John. "The Crucifixion and the Second Coming in *The Dream of the Rood*." MP 66(1969): 293-297.

8055. Helder, Willem. "The *Engel Dryhtnes* in *The Dream of the Rood*." MP 73(1975): 148-150.

8056. Payne, Richard C. "Convention and Originality in the Vision Framework of *The Dream of the Rood*." MP 73(1976): 329-341.

8057. Tripp, Raymond P., Jr. "*The Dream of the Rood*: 9b and Its Context." MP 69(1971): 136-137.

EXETER BOOK-RIDDLES.   8058. Blakeley, L. "Riddles 22 and 58 of the Exeter Book." RES 9 (1958): 241-252.

8059. Eliason, Norman E. "Four Old English Cryptographic Riddles." SP 49(1952): 553-565.

8060. Hacikyan, Agop. "The Exeter Manuscript: Riddle 19." ELN 3(1965): 86-88.

8061. Kennedy, Christopher B. "Old English Riddle No. 39." ELN 13(1975): 81-85.

8062. Kiernan, K. S. "*Cwene*: The Old Profession of Exeter Riddle 95." MP 72(1975): 384-389.

8063. ----------. "The Mysteries of the Seaeagle in Exeter Riddle 74." PQ 54(1975): 518-522.

8064. Kuhn, Sherman M. "A Damaged Passage in the *Exeter Book*." JEGP 50(1951): 491-493.

8065. Leslie, Roy F. "The Integrity of Riddle 60." JEGP 67(1968): 451-457.

8066. Meyvaert, Paul. "The Solution to Old English Riddle 39." *Speculum* 51(1976): 195-201.

8067. Nelson, Marie. "The Rhetoric of the Exeter Book Riddles." *Speculum* 49(1974): 421-440.

8068. ----------. "Time in the Exeter Book Riddles." PQ 54(1975): 511-518.

8069. Pope, John C. "An Unsuspected Lacuna in the Exeter Book: Divorce Proceedings for an Ill-Matched Couple in the Old English Riddles." *Speculum* 49(1974): 615-622.

8070. Russom, Geoffrey. "Exeter Riddle 47: A Moth Laid Waste to Fame." PQ 56(1977): 129-136.

8071. Whitman, F. H. "OE Riddle 74." ELN 6(1968): 1-5.

8072. ----------. "Riddle 60 and Its Source." PQ 50(1971): 108-115.

8073. Williams, Edith Whitehurst. "The Relation Between Pagan Survivals and Diction in Two Old English Riddles." PQ.54(1975): 664-670.

EXODUS.   8074. Farrell, Robert T. "A Reading of OE. *Exodus*." RES 20(1969): 401-417.

8075. Hall, J. R. "Pauline Influence on *Exodus*, 523-548." ELN 15(1977): 84-88.

8076. Hermann, John P. "The Green Rod of Moses in the Old English *Exodus*." ELN 12(1975): 241-243.

8077. ----------. "The Selection of Warriors in the Old English *Exodus*, Lines 233-240A." ELN 14(1976): 1-5.

8078. Wall, Sister Carolyn. "Stylistic Variation in the Old English *Exodus*." ELN 6(1968): 79-84.

FINNSBURH.   Fry, Donald. "Finnsburh 34a: hwearflicra hwær." ELN 6(1969): 241-242.

GENESIS.   8080. Brockman, Bennett A.

"'Heroic' and 'Christian' in *Genesis A*: The Evidence of the Cain and Abel Episode." MLQ 35(1974): 115-128.

8081. Cherniss, Michael D. "Heroic Ideals and the Moral Climate of *Genesis B*." MLQ 30(1969): 479-497.

8082. Clausen, Christopher. "A Suggested Emendation in *Genesis B*." ELN 11(1974): 249-250.

8083. Doane, A. N. "*Genesis B* 317a: *sum heard gewrinc*." PQ 56(1977): 404-407.

8084. Evans, J. M. "*Genesis B* and Its Background." RES 14(1963): 1-16, 113-123.

8085. Finnegan, Robert Emmett. "Eve and 'Vincible Ignorance' in *Genesis B*." TSLL 18(1976): 329-339.

8086. Murdoch, Brian. "The Fall of Man: A Middle High German Analogue of *Genesis B*." RES 19 (1968): 288-289.

8087. Sisam, Kenneth. "*Genesis B*, lines 273-4." RES 2(1951): 371-372.

8088. Stanley, E. G. "A Note on *Genesis B*, 328." RES 5(1954): 55-58.

8089. Vickrey, John F. "The *Micel Wundor* of *Genesis B*." SP 68(1971): 245-254.

8090. ----------. "The Vision of Eve in *Genesis B*." *Speculum* 44(1969): 86-102.

8091. Yerkes, David. "*Genesis B* 318-320 Again." ELN 12(1976): 241-242.

GUTHLAC.   8092. Bolton, W. F. "The Background and Meaning of *Guthlac*." JEGP 61(1962): 595-603.

8093. Shook, Laurence K. "The Burial Mound in *Guthlac A*." MP 58(1960): 1-10.

8094. Stracke, J. Richard. "*Eþelboda*: *Guthlac B*, 1003." MP 74(1976): 194-195.

HARROWING OF HELL.   8095. Hill, Thomas D. "Cosmic Stasis and the Birth of Christ: The Old English *Descent into Hell*, Lines 99-106." JEGP 71(1972): 382-389.

HUSBAND'S MESSAGE.   8096. Elliott, Ralph W. V. "The Runes in *The Husband's Message*." JEGP 54(1955): 1-8.

JUDGMENT DAY II.   8097. Hoffman, Richard L. "The Theme of *Judgment Day II*." ELN 6(1969): 161-164.

8098. Whitbread, L. "Old English and Old High German: A Note of *Judgment Day II*, 292-293." SP 60(1963): 514-524.

8099. ----------. "The Old English Poem *Judgment Day II* and Its Latin Source." PQ 45(1966): 635-656.

JUDITH.   8100. Campbell, Jackson J. "Schematic Technique in *Judith*." ELH 38(1971): 155-172.

8101. Fry, Donald K. "Imagery and Point of View in *Judith* 200b-231." ELN 5(1968): 157-159.

8102. Hermann, John P. "The Theme of Spiritual Warfare in the Old English *Judith*." PQ 55(1976): 1-9.

8103. Woolf, R. E. "The Last Opening to the 'Judith.'" MLR 50(1955): 168-172.

MALDON.   8104. Battaglia, F. J. "Notes on 'Maldon': Toward a Definitive *Ofermod*." ELN 2 (1965): 247-249.

8105. Bessinger, J. B. "*Maldon* and the Óláfsdrápa: An Historical Caveat." Comp L 14(1962): 23-36.

8106. Blake, N. F. "The Flyting in *The Battle of Maldon*." ELN 13(1976): 242-245.

8107. Bolton, W. F. "Byrhtnoð in the Wilderness." *MLR* 64(1969): 481-490.

8108. Clark, George. "The Battle of Maldon: A Heroic Poem." *Speculum* 43(1968): 52-71.

8109. Elliott, Ralph W. V. "Byrhtnoth and Hildebrand: A Study in Heroic Technique." *Comp L* 14(1962): 53-70.

8110. Gneuss, Helmut. *"The Battle of Maldon* 89: Byrhtnoð's *ofermod* Once Again." *SP* 73 (1976): 117-137.

8111. Harris, Joseph. "Stemnettan: *Battle of Maldon*, Line 122a." *PQ* 55(1976): 113-117.

8112. Irving, Edward B., Jr. "The Heroic Style in *The Battle of Maldon*." *SP* 58(1961): 457-467.

8113. Petty, George R., Jr., and Susan. "Geology and *The Battle of Maldon*." *Speculum* 51 (1976): 435-446.

8114. Robinson, Fred C. "Some Aspects of the *Maldon* Poet's Artistry." *JEGP* 75(1976): 25-40.

8115. Sklar, Elizabeth S. *"The Battle of Maldon* and the Popular Tradition: Some Rhymed Formulas." *PQ* 54(1975): 409-418.

8116. Swanton, Michael J. *"The Battle of Maldon*: A Literary Caveat." *JEGP* 67(1968): 441-450.

See also 7821, 7909.

ORMULUM. 8117. Stevick, Robert D. "Plus Juncture and the Spelling of the *Ormulum*." *JEGP* 64(1965): 84-89.

PHOENIX. 8118. Kantrowitz, Joanne Spencer. "The Anglo-Saxon *Phoenix* and Tradition." *PQ* 43 (1964): 1-13.

RIMING POEM. 8119. Lehmann, Ruth P. M. "A Lacuna in the Riming Poem of the Exeter Book." *ELN* 3(1965): 85-86.

8120. ----------. "The Old English *Riming Poem*: Interpretation, Text, and Translation." *JEGP* 69(1970): 437-449.

RUIN. 8121. Doubleday, James F. *"The Ruin*: Structure and Theme." *JEGP* 71(1972): 369-381.

8122. Dunleavy, Gareth W. "A "De Excidio" Tradition in the Old English *RUIN*?" *PQ* 38(1959): 112-188.

SEAFARER. 8123. Bolton, W. F. "Connectives in *The Seafarer* and *The Dream of the Rood*." *MP* 57(1960): 260-262.

8124. Campbell, Jackson J. "Oral Poetry in *The Seafarer*." *Speculum* 35(1960): 87-96.

8125. Cherniss, Michael D. "The Meaning of *The Seafarer*, Lines 97-102." *MP* 66(1968): 146-149.

8126. Goldsmith, Margaret E. *"The Seafarer* and the Birds." *RES* 5(1954): 225-235.

8127. Gordon, I. L. "Traditional Themes in *The Wanderer* and *The Seafarer*." *RES* 5(1954): 1-13.

8128. Greenfield, Stanley B. "Attitudes and Values in *The Seafarer*." *SP* 51(1954): 15-20.

8129. ----------. "Mīn, *Sylf*, and 'Dramatic Voices' in *The Wanderer* and *The Seafarer*." *JEGP* 68(1969): 212-220.

8130. Hill, Joyce M. "'Þis Deade Lif': A Note on *The Seafarer*, Lines 64-66." *ELN* 15(1977): 95-97.

8131. O'Neil, Wayne A. "Another Look at Oral Poetry in *The Seafarer*." *Speculum* 35(1960): 596-600.

8132. Pheifer, J. D. *"The Seafarer* 53-55." *RES* 16(1965): 282-284.

8133. Salmon, Vivian. "'The Wanderer' and 'The Seafarer', and the Old English Conception of the Soul." *MLR* 55(1960): 1-10.

8134. Stevick, Robert D. "The Text and the Composition of *The Seafarer*." *PMLA* 80(1965): 332-336.

See also 7950.

SOUL'S ADDRESS TO THE BODY. 8135. Ferguson, Mary Heyward. "The Structure of the *Soul's Address to the Body* in Old English." *JEGP* 69(197): 72-80.

VERCELLI BOOK. 8136. Halsall, Maureen. "Benjamin Thorpe and the Vercelli Book." *ELN* 6 (1969): 164-169.

8137. ----------. "More About C. Maier's Transcript of the Vercelli Book." *ELN* 8(1970): 3-6.

8138. ----------. "Vercelli and the Vercelli Book." *PMLA* 84(1969): 1545-1550.

8139. Peterson, Paul W. "Dialect Grouping in the Unpublished Vercelli Homilies." *SP* 50 (1953): 559-565.

WANDERER. 8140. Dean, Christopher. *"Weal Wundrum Heah, Wyrmlicum Fah* and the Narrative Background of *The Wanderer*." *MP* 63(1965): 141-143.

8141. Greenfield, Stanley B. *"The Wanderer*: A Reconsideration of Theme and Structure." *JEGP* 50(1951): 451-465.

8142. Midgley, Graham. *"The Wanderer*, lines 49-55." *RES* 10(1959): 53-54.

8143. Millns, Tony. *"The Wanderer* 98: 'weal wundrum heah wyrmlicum fah'." *RES* 28(1977): 431-438.

8144. Rosier, James L. "The Literal-Figurative Identity of *The Wanderer*." *PMLA* 79(1964): 366-370.

8145. Rumble, Thomas C. "From *Eardstapa* to *Snottor on Mode*: The Structural Principle of 'The Wanderer'." *MLQ* 19(1958): 225-230.

8146. Salmon, Vivian. "'The Wanderer' and 'The Seafarer', and the Old English Conception of the Soul." *MLR* 55(1960): 1-10.

8147. Tucker, Susie I. "Return to *The Wanderer*." *EIC* 8(1958): 229-237.

See also 7950, 8127, 8129.

WIDSITH. 8148. Malone, Kemp. "An Anglo-Latin Version of the *Hyaþningar*." *Speculum* 39 (1964): 35-44.

WIFE'S LAMENT. 8149. Bambas, Rudolph C. "Another View of the Old English 'Wife's Lament'." *JEGP* 62(1963): 303-309.

8150. Dunleavy, Gareth W. "Possible Irish Analogues for *The Wife's Lament*." *PQ* 35(1956): 208-212.

8151. Fitzgerald, Robert P. *"The Wife's Lament* and 'The Search for the Lost Husband.'" *JEGP* 62(1963): 769-777.

8152. Greenfield, Stanley B. *"The Wife's Lament* Reconsidered." *PMLA* 68(1953): 907-912.

8153. Stevick, Robert D. "Formal Aspects of *The Wife's Lament*." *JEGP* 59(1960): 21-25.

8154. Ward, J. A. *"The Wife's Lament*: An Interpretation." *JEGP* 59(1960): 26-33.

See also 8157.

WULF AND EADWACER. 8155. Kavros, Harry E. "A Note on *Wulf and Eadwacer*." *ELN* 15(1977): 83-84.

8156. Lehman, Ruth P. M. "The Metrics and Structure of 'Wulf and Eadwacer'." *PQ* 48(1969): 151-165.

8157. Malone, Kemp. "Two English *Frauen-lieder*." *Comp L* 14(1962): 106–117.

WULFSTAN. 8158. Fowler, Roger. "Some Stylistic Features of the *Sermo Lupi*." *JEGP* 65(1966): 1–18.

8159. Levin, Samuel R. "On the Authenticity of Five 'Wulfstan' Homilies." *JEGP* 60(1961): 451–459.

8160. Whitbread, L. "MS. C.C.C.C. 201: A Note on Its Character and Provenance." *PQ* 38 (1959): 106–112.

MIDDLE ENGLISH

GENERAL AND MISCELLANEOUS. 8161. Alford, John A. "Literature and Law in Medieval England." *PMLA* 92(1977): 941–951.

8162. Aston, S. C. "The Saint in Medieval Literature." *MLR* 65(1970): xxv.

8163. Baker, Donald C. "Gold Coins in Medieval English Literature." *Speculum* 36(1961): 282–289.

8164. Beichner, Paul E., C.S.C. "The Allegorical Interpretation of Medieval Literature." *PMLA* 82(1967): 33–38.

8165. Bennett, J. A. W. "Why Men Cry 'Seynt Barbara.'" *RES* 13(1962): 283.

8166. Bennett, Josephine Waters. "The Medieval Loveday." *Speculum* 33(1958): 351–370.

8167. Bivar, A. D. H. "Lyonnesse: The Evolution of a Fable." *MP* 50(1953): 162–170.

8168. Blake, N. F. *Rhythmical Alliteration.*" *MP* 67(1969): 118–124.

8169. Bliss, A. J. "Notes on the Auchinleck Manuscript." *Speculum* 26(1951): 652–658.

8196a. Bloomfield, Morton W. "Symbolism in Medieval Literature." *MP* 56(1958): 73–81.

8170. Bossy, Michel-André. "Medieval Debates of Body and Soul." *Comp L* 28(1976): 144–163.

8171. Bowers, R. H. "A Middle English Treatise on Hermenentics: Harley MS. 2276, 32^V–35^V." *PMLA* 65(1950): 590–600.

8172. Brook, Stella. "'The Charter of the Abbey of the Holy Ghost.'" *MLR* 54(1959): 481–488.

8173. Brewer, D. S. "The Ideal of Feminine Beauty in Medieval Literature, especially 'Harley Lyrics,' Chaucer, and some Elizabethans." *MLR* 50 (1955): 257–269.

8174. Bromwich, Rachel. "The Celtic Inheritance of Medieval Literature." *MLQ* 26(1965): 203–227.

8175. Bühler, Curt F. "The Middle English Texts of Morgan MS. 861." *PMLA* 69(1954): 686–692.

8176. ----------. "Owner's Jingles in Early Printed Books." *SP* 62(1965): 647–653.

8177. ----------. "Prayers and Charms in Certain Middle English Scrolls." *Speculum* 39(1964): 270–278.

8178. Cooling, June. "An Unpublished Middle English Prologue." *RES* 10(1959): 172–173.

8179. Corner, Rachel. "More Fifteenth-Century 'Terms of Association.'" *RES* 12(1962): 229–244.

8180. Duncan, Edgar Hill. "Short Fiction in Medieval English: II. The Middle English Period." *SSF* 11(1974): 227–241.

8181. Elliott, Ralph W. V. "Runes, Yews, and Magic." *Speculum* 32(1957): 250–261.

8182. Francis, W. Nelson. "Graphemic Analysis of Late Middle English Manuscripts." *Speculum* 37(1962): 32–47.

8183. Frank, Robert Worth, Jr. "The Art of Reading Medieval Personification-Allegory." *ELH* 20 (1953): 237–250.

8184. Gransden, Antonia. "Realistic Observation in Twelfth-Century England." *Speculum* 47 (1972): 29–51.

8185. Green, Richard Firth. "Three Fifteenth-Century Notes." *ELN* 14(1976): 14–17.

8186. Hanham, Alison. "The Musical Studies of a Fifteenth-Century Wool Merchant." *RES* 8(1957): 270–274.

8187. Hargreaves, Henry. "The Vocabulary of the *Surtees Psalter*." *MLQ* 17(1956): 326–339.

8188. Harrier, Richard C. "A Printed Source for 'The Devonshire Manuscript.'" *RES* 11(1960): 54.

8189. Hudson, Anne. "Tradition and Innovation in Some Middle English Manuscripts." *RES* 17(1966): 359–372.

8190. Kahrl, Stanley J. "Allegory in Practice: A Study of Narrative Styles in Medieval Exampla." *MP* 63(1965): 105–110.

8191. Keenan, Hugh T. "A Check-List on Typology and English Medieval Literature through 1972." *SLI* 8,#1(1975): 159–166.

8192. Klinefelter, Ralph A. "The Four Daughters of God: A New Version." *JEGP* 52(1953): 90–95.

8193. ----------. "A Newly-Discovered Fifteenth-Century English Manuscript." *MLQ* 14 (1953): 3–6.

8194. Kuhn, Sherman M. "The Preface to a Fifteenth-Century Concordance." *Speculum* 43(1968): 258–272.

8195. Loomis, Laura Hibbard. "The Athestan Gift Story: Its Influence on English Chronicles and Carolingian Romances." *PMLA* 67(1952): 521–537.

8196. Matonis, A. T. E. "An Investigation of Celtic Influences on MS Harley 2253." *MP* 70 (1972): 91–108.

8197. McAlindon, T. "Comedy and Terror in Middle English Literature: The Diabolical Game." *MLR* 60(1965): 323–332.

8198. Meier-Ewert, Charity. "A Middle English Version of the *Fifteen Oes*." *MP* 68(1971): 355–361.

8199. Moore, Arthur K. "Medieval English Literature and the Question of Unity." *MP* 65(1968): 285–300.

8200. Nørgaard, Holger. "Translations of the Classics into English before 1600." *RES* 9 (1958): 164–172.

8201. Robbins, Rossell H. "Medical Manuscripts in Middle English." *Speculum* 45(1970): 393–415.

8202. Robertson, D. W., Jr. "The Doctrine of Charity in Medieval Literary Gardens: A Topical Approach through Symbolism and Allegory." *Speculum* 26(1951): 24–49.

8203. Russell, J. C. "Arthur and the Romano-Celtic Frontier." *MP* 48(1951): 145–153.

8204. Sisam, Celia. "Notes on Middle English Texts." *RES* 13(1962): 385–390.

8205. ----------. "The Scribal Tradition of the Lambeth Homilies." *RES* 2(1951): 105–113.

8206. Spencer, Helen. "A Fifteenth-Century Translation of a Late Twelfth-Century Sermon Collection." *RES* 28(1977): 257-267.

8207. Szittya, Penn R. "The Antifraternal Tradition in Middle English Literature." *Speculum* 52(1977): 287-313.

8208. Woolf, Rosemary. "The Theme of Christ the Lover-Knight in Medieval English Literature." *RES* 13(1962): 1-16.

8209. Wright, C. E. "Late Middle English Parerga in a School Collection." *RES* 2(1951): 114-120.

DRAMA. 8210. Baker, D. C., and J. L. Murphy. "The Bodleian MS. *E. Mus.* 160 *Burial* and *Resurrection* and the Digby Plays." *RES* 19(1968): 290-293.

8211. Bland, D. S. "Interludes in Fifteenth-Century Revels at Furnivall's Inn." *RES* 3(1952): 263-268.

8212. Brawer, Robert A. "Dramatic Technique in the Corpus Christi Creation and Fall. *MLQ* 32(1971): 347-364.

8213. ---------- . "The Middle English Resurrection Play and Its Dramatic Antecedents." *CD* 8(1974): 77-100.

8214. Collins, Patrick J. "Narrative Bible Cycles in Medieval Art and Drama." *CD* 9(1975): 125-146.

8215. ----------. "Typology, Criticism, and Medieval Drama: Some Observations on Method." *CD* 10(1976): 298-311.

8216. Davidson, Clifford. "Medieval Drama: Diversity and Theatricality." *CD* 8(1974): 5-12.

8217. Dutka, JoAnna. "Music and the English Mystery Plays." *CD* 7(1973): 135-149.

8218. ----------. "Mysteries, Minstrels, and Music." *CD* 8(1974): 112-124.

8219. Edwards, Robert. "Techniques of Transcendence in Medieval Drama." *CD* 8(1974): 157-171.

8220. Elliott, John R. "The Sacrifice of Issac as Comedy and Tragedy." *SP* 66(1969): 36-59.

8221. Fifield, Merle. "The Community of Morality Plays." *CD* 9(1975): 332-349.

8222. Flanigan, C. Clifford. "The Liturgical Context of the *Quem Queritis* Trope." *CD* 8(1974): 45-62.

8223. Hanning, R. W. "'You Have Begun a Parlous Play': The Nature and Limits of Dramatic Mimesis as a Theme in Four Middle English 'Fall of Lucifer' Cycle Plays." *CD* 7(1973): 22-50.

8224. Harvey, Nancy Lenz, and Julie C. Dietrich. "Recent Studies in the Corpus Christi Mystery Plays." *ELR* 5(1975): 396-415.

8225. Kahrl, Stanley. "The Civic Religious Drama of Medieval England: A Review of Recent Scholarship." *RD* n.s.6(1973): 237-248.

8226. Lancashire, Ian. "The Sources of *Hyckescorner*." *RES* 22(1971): 257-273.

8227. Leigh, David J., S. J. "The Doomsday Mystery Play: An Eschatological Morality." *MP* 67(1970): 211-223.

8228. McNeir, Waldo F. "The Corpus Christi Passion Plays as Dramatic Art." *SP* 48(1951): 601-628.

8229. Maltman, Sister Nicholas, O. P. "Meaning and Art in the Croxton *Play of the Sacrament*." *ELH* 41(1974): 149-164.

8230. Meyer, Robert T. "The Middle-Cornish Play *Beunans Meriasek*." *CD* 3(1969): 54-64.

8231. Meyers, Walter E. "Typology and the Audience of the English Cycle Plays." *SLI* 8,#1 (1975): 145-158.

8232. Morgan, Margery M. "'High Fraud': Paradox and Double-Plot in the English Shepherd's Plays." *Speculum* 39(1964): 676-689.

8233. Morse, J. Mitchell. "The Unity of the Revesby Sword Play." *PQ* 33(1954): 81-86.

8234. Muir, Lynette R. "The Trinity in Medieval Drama." *CD* 10(1976): 116-129.

8235. Munson, William F. "Audience and Meaning in Two Medieval Dramatic Realisms." *CD* 9(1975): 44-66.

8236. Nelson, Alan H. "On Recovering the Lost Norwich Corpus Christi Cycle." *CD* 4(1970): 241-252.

8237. Ogden, Dunbar H. "The Use of Architectural Space in Medieval Music-Drama." *CD* 8 (1974): 63-76.

8238. Parker, John W. "Touches of Comedy and Realism in Early Religious Plays." *CLA* 2 (1958): 51-54.

8239. Robinson, J. W. "The Late Medieval Cult of Jesus and the Mystery Plays." *PMLA* 80(1965): 508-514.

8240. Sinanoglou, Leah. "The Christ Child as Sacrefice: A Medieval Tradition and the Corpus Christi Plays." *Speculum* 48(1973): 491-509.

8241. Smoldon, William L. "The Melodies of the Medieval Church-Dramas and Their Significance." *CD* 2(1968): 185-209.

8242. Staines, David. "To Out-Herod Herod: The Development of a Dramatic Character." *CD* 10 (1976): 29-53.

8243. Stemmler, Theo. "Typological Transfer in Liturgical Offices and Religious Plays of the Middle Ages." *SLI* 8,#1(1975): 123-143.

8244. Stevens, Martin, and Margaret Dorell. "The *Ordo Paginarium* Gathering of the York A/Y *Memorandum Book*." *MP* 72(1974): 45-59.

8245. Wee, David L. "The Temptation of Christ and the Motif of Divine Duplicity in the Corpus Christi Cycle Drama." *MP* 72(1974): 1-16.

8246. Wenzel, Siegfried. "An Early Reference to a Corpus Christi Play." *MP* 74(1977): 390-393.

8247. Williams, Arnold. "Typology and the Cycle Plays: Some Criteria." *Speculum* 43(1968): 677-684.

8248. Woolf, Rosemary. "The Effect of Typology on the English Mediaeval Plays of Abraham and Issac." *Speculum* 32(1957): 805-825.

POETRY. 8249. Abel, Patricia. "The Cleric, the Kitchie Boy and the Returned Sailor." *PQ* 44 (1965): 552-555.

8250. Adams, John F. "The Anglo-Saxon Riddle as Lyric Mode." *Criticism* 7(1965): 335-348.

8251. Bateson, F. W. "A Question of Spelling." *EIC* 6(1956): 363.

8252. Baugh, Albert C. "The Middle English Romance: Some Questions of Creation, Presentation, and Preservation." *Speculum* 42(1967): 1-31.

8253. Berry, Francis. "A Medieval Poem and Its Secularized Derivative." *EIC* 5(1955): 299-314.

8254. Bowers, R. H. "*Advice Resented*: A Middle-English Court of Love Poem (Corpus Christi College MS 61, Fol., 66v-67r)[with text]" *PQ* 31 (1952): 211-214.

8255. ---------- . "A Middle-English Anti-

Mendicant Squib." *ELN* 1(1964): 163-164.

8256. ----------. "A Middle English Poem on Lovedays." *MLR* 47(1952): 374-375.

8257. ----------. "The Middle-English *The Fox and the Goose*." *JEGP* 51(1952): 393-394.

8258. ----------. "Middle English Verses on the Founding of the Carthusian Order." *Speculum* 42(1967): 710-713.

8259. ----------. "Three Middle English Poems on the Apostles' Creed." *PMLA* 70(1955): 210-222.

8260. Bühler, Curt F. "Middle English Apophthegms in a Caxton Volumn." *ELN* 1(1963): 81-84.

8261. ----------. "A Middle-English Stanza on 'The Commonwealth and the Need for Wisdom'." *ELN* 2(1964): 4-5.

8262. ----------. "Middle English Verses against Thieves." *Speculum* 33(1958): 371-372.

8263. Cawley, A. C. "A York Fragment of Middle English Sacred Lyric." *Speculum* 26(1951): 142-144.

8264. Chickering, Howell D., Jr. "'Foweles in e frith': A Religious Art-Song." *PQ* 50(1971): 115-120.

8265. Clark, George. "The Traveler Recognizes His Goal: A Theme in Anglo-Saxon Poetry." *JEGP* 64(1965): 645-659.

8266. Curry, Jane L. "Waking the Well." *ELN* 2(1964): 1-4.

8267. Curschmann, Michael. "Oral Poetry in Mediaeval English, French, and German Literature." *Speculum* 42(1967): 36-52.

8268. Degginger, Stuart H. L. "'A Wayle Whyt ase Whelles Bon'—Reconstructed." *JEGP* 53 (1954): 84-90.

8269. Doyle, A. I. "An Unrecognized Piece of *Piers the Ploughman's Creed* and Other Work by Its Scribe." *Speculum* 34(1959): 428-436.

8270. Duggan, Hoyt N. "Strophic Patterns in Middle English Alliterative Poetry." *MP* 74 (1977): 223-247.

8271. Edwards, A. S. G. "A Late Medieval Refrain Poem." *ELN* 11(1973): 91-92.

8272. ----------. "A Middle English Prayer to the Cross." *PQ* 52(1973): 299-301.

8273. Fifield, Merle. "Thirteenth-Century Lyrics and the Alliterative Tradition." *JEGP* 62 (1963): 111-118.

8274. Friend, Albert C. "Fourteenth-Century Couplets of English Verse." *PMLA* 69(1954): 984.

8275. Greene, Richard. "'The Maid of the Moor' in the *Red Book of Ossory*." *Speculum* 27 (1952): 504-506.

8276. Greene, Richard Leighton. "Troubling the Well-Waters." *ELN* 4(1966): 4-6.

8277. Hatto, A. T. "The Lime-Tree and early German, Goliard and English Lyric Poetry." *MLR* 49(1954): 193-209.

8278. Hill, John M. "Middle English Poets and the Word: Notes Toward an Appraisal of Linguistic Consciousness." *Criticism* 16(1974): 153-169.

8279. Hulbert, J. R. "Quatrains in Middle English Alliterative Poems." *MP* 48(1950): 73-81.

8280. Ingham, Patricia. "The World of the Ballad." *RES* 8(1957): 22-31.

8281. Jacobs, Nicolas. "Alliterative Storms: A Topos in Middle English." *Speculum* 47(1972):

695-719.

8282. Jeremy, Sister Mary. "*Mon* in 'Fowles in the Firth'." *ELN* 5(1967): 80-81.

8283. Kinghorn, A. M. "The Medieval Makars." *TSLL* 1(1959): 73-88.

8284. Kratins, Ojars. "Treason in Middle English Metrical Romances." *PQ* 45(1966): 668-687.

8285. Lightbrown, J. "A Shorter Metrical Version of 'The Gast of Gy.'" *MLR* 47(1962): 323-329.

8286. Malone, Kemp. "Further Notes on Middle English Lyrics." *ELH* 23(1956): 1-13.

8287. Manning, Stephen. "Game and Earnest on the Middle English and Provencal Love Lyrics." *Comp L* 18(1966): 225-241.

8288. ----------. "'I Syng of a **Myden**.'" *PMLA* 75(1960): 8-12.

8289. Manning, Warren F. "The Middle English Verse *Life of Saint Dominic*: Date and Source." *Speculum* 31(1956): 82-91.

8290. Mason, H. A. "'I am as I am.'" *RES* 23(1972): 304-308.

8291. McIntosh, Angus. "Some Notes on the Text of the Middle English Poem *De Tribus Regibus Mortuis*." *RES* 28(1977): 385-392.

8292. Montgomerie, William. "'The Twa Corbies.'" *RES* 6(1955): 227-232.

8293. Ogilvie-Thomson, S. "Some Unpublished Verses in Lambeth Palace MS. 599." *RES* 25(1974): 385-395.

8294. Osberg, Richard H. "The Alliterative Lyrics and Thirteenth-Century Devotional Prose." *JEGP* 76(1977): 40-54.

8295. Parker, David. "Popular Protest in 'A Gest of Robyn Hood.'" *MLQ* 32(1971): 3-20.

8296. Peck, Russell A. "Public Dreams and Private Myths: Perspective in Middle English Literature." *PMLA* 90(1975): 461-468.

8297. Pittock, Malcolm. "A Question of Spelling." *EIC* 6(1956): 361-363.

8298. Plummer, John F., III. "The Poetic Function of Conventional Language in Middle English Lyric." *SP* 72(1975): 367-385.

8299. Raw, Barbara C. "'As Dew in Aprille.'" *MLR* 55(1960): 411-414.

8300. Raymo, Robert R. "Quod the Devill to the Frier." *ELN* 4(1967): 180.

8301. Rigg, A. G. "The Letter 'C' and the Date of Easter." *ELN* 5(1967): 1-5.

8302. Robbins, Rossell Hope. "The Bradshaw Carols." *PMLA* 81(1966): 308-310.

8308. ----------. "The Five Dogs of London." *PMLA* 71(1956): 264-268.

8304. ----------. "Isabel: A Riddling Mistress." *ELN* 1(1963): 1-4.

8305. ----------. "Middle English Carols as Processional Hymns." *SP* 56(1959): 559-582.

8306. ----------. "A Warning Against Lechery." *PQ* 35(1956): 90-95.

8307. Ross, Thomas W. "Five Fifteenth-Century 'Emblem' Verses from Brit. Mus. Addit. MS. 37049." *Speculum* 32(1957): 274-282.

8308. Salter, Elizabeth. "The Alliterative Revival I." *MP* 64(1966): 146-150.

8309. ----------. "The Alliterative Revival II." *MP* 64(1967): 233-237.

8310. Schueler, Donald G. "The Middle English *Judas*: An Interpretation." *PMLA* 91(1976): 840-845.

8311. Shannon, Ann. "The Meaning of *grein* in 'Wynter wakeneþ al my care'." *PQ* 53(1974): 425-427.

8312. Smith, Sarah Stanbury. "'Adam Lay I-Bowndyn' and the *Vinculum Amoris*." *ELN* 15(1977): 98-101.

8313. Stevick, Robert D. "The Criticism of Middle English Lyrics." *MP* 64(1966): 103-117.

8314. Strohm, Paul. "*Storie*, *Spelle*, *Geste*, *Romaunce*, *Tragedie*: Generic Distinctions in the Middle English Troy Narratives." *Speculum* 46 (1971): 348-359.

8315. Townsend, Brenda. "The Word 'Pyn' in the Harley Lyric 'Ichot A Burde in a Bour Ase Beryl So Brght'." *ELN* 11(1973): 89-91.

8316. Turville-Petre, Thorlac. "'Summer Sunday', 'De Tribus Regibus Mortius' and 'The Awntyrs Off Arthure': Three Poems in the Thirteen-Line Stanza." *RES* 25(1974): 1-14.

8317. Vann, J. Daniel, III. "Middle English Verses against Thieves: A Postscript." *Speculum* 34(1959): 636-638.

8318. Waldron, Ronald A. "Oral-Formulaic Technique and Middle English Alliterative Poetry." *Speculum* 32(1957): 792-804.

8319. Wells, Celia Townsend. "Line 21 of 'Middelerd for mon was mad'." *ELN* 10(1973): 167-169.

8320. Wenzel, Sigfried. "The Moor Maiden—A Contemporary View." *Speculum* 48(1973): 69-74.

8321. Wordsworth, Jonathan. "An Early Rudimentary Carol." *MLR* 54(1959): 221-223.

PROSE. 8322. Clark, Cecily. "Early Middle English Prose: Three Essays in Stylistics." *EIC* 18(1968): 361-382.

8323. Garmonsway, G. N., and R. R. Raymo. "A Middle-English Prose Life of St. Ursula." *RES* (1958): 353-361.

8324. Morgan, Margery M. "*A Talking of the Love of God* and the Continuity of Stylistic Tradition in Middle English Prose Meditations." *RES* 3(1952): 97-116.

8325. Zeeman, Elizabeth. "Continuity in Middle English Prose Devotional." *JEGP* 55(1956): 417-422.

ROMANCE. 8326. Duggan, Hoyt. N. "The Source of the Middle English *The Wars of Alexander*." *Speculum* 51(1976): 624-636.

8327. Hanna, Ralph, III. "*The Awntyrs off Arthure*: An Interpretation." *MLQ* 31(1970): 275-297.

8328. Harrington, Norman T. "The Problem of the Lacunae in *Ywain and Gawain*." *JEGP* 69(1970): 659-665.

8329. Holland, William E. "Formulaic Diction and the Descent of a Middle English Romance." *Speculum* 48(1973): 89-109.

8330. Hornstein, Lillian Herlands. "*King Robert of Sicily*: A New Manuscript." *PMLA* 78 (1963): 453-458.

8331. ----------. "*King Robert of Sicily*: Analogues and Origins." *PMLA* 79(1964): 13-21.

8332. Hume, Kathryn. "*Amis and Amiloun* and the Aesthetics of Middle English Romance." *SP* 70(1973): 19-39.

8333. ----------. "The Formal Nature of Middle English Romance." *PQ* 53(1974): 158-180.

8334. Hynes-Berry, Mary. "Cohesion in *King Horn* and *Sir Orfeo*." *Speculum* 50(1975): 652-670.

8335. Kiernan, Kevin S. "*Athelston* and the Rhyme of the English Romances." *MLQ* 36(1975): 339-353.

8336. ----------. "*Undo Your Door* and the Order of Chivalry." *SP* 70(1973): 345-366.

8337. Kratins, Ojars. "The Middle English *Amis and Amiloun*: Chivalric Romance or Secular Hagiography." *PMLA* 81(1966): 347-354.

8338. Koziski, Henry. "Critical Methods in the Literary Evaluation of Sir Degaré." *MLQ* 29 (1968): 3-14.

8339. Lumiansky, R. M. "The Story of Troilus and Briseida in the *Laud Troy-Book*." *MLQ* 18(1957): 238-246.

8340. Shannon, Edgar F. Jr. "Mediaeval Law in *The Tale of Gamelyn*." *Speculum* 26(1951): 458-464.

8341. Sklar, Elizabeth S. "The Dialect of *Arthour and Merlin*." *ELN* 15(1977): 88-94.

8342. Stokoe, William C., Jr. "The Double Problem of *Sir Degaré*." *PMLA* 70(1955): 518-534.

ANCRENE WISSE. 8343. Bennett, J. A. W. "'Lefunge o swefne o nore.'" *RES* 9(1958): 280-281.

8344. Rygiel, Dennis. "The Allegory of Christ the Lover-Knight in *Ancrene Wisse*: An Experiment in Stylistic Analysis." *SP* 73(1976): 343-364.

8345. Russell-Smith, Joy. "Ridiculosae Sternutationes (*o nore* in *Ancrene Wisse*)." *RES* 8 (1957): 266-269.

8346. Shepherd, Geoffrey. "'All the Wealth of Croeseus . . .': A Topic in the 'Ancren Riwle.'" *MLR* 51(1956): 161-167.

8347. Trethewey, W. H. "The Seven Deadly Sins and the Devil's Court in the Trinity College Cambridge French Text of the *Ancrene Riwle*." *PMLA* 65(1950): 1233-1246.

8348. Wilson, Edward. "The Four Loves in *Ancrene Wisse*." *RES* 19(1968): 41-47.

ASHBY, GEORGE. 8349. Bühler, Curt F. "The *Liber de dictis philosophorum antiquorum* and Common Proverbs in George Ashby's Poems." *PMLA* 65 (1950): 282-289.

ASSEMBLY OF LADIES. 8350. Pearsall, Derek. "*The Assembly of Ladies* and *Generydes*." *RES* 12 (1961): 229-237.

8351. Stephens, John. "The Questioning of Love in the *Assembly of Ladies*." *RES* 24(1973): 129-140.

BACON, ROGER. 8352. Lindberg, David C. "Lines of Influence in Thirteenth-Century Optics." *Speculum* 46(1971): 66-83.

BARGAIN OF JUDAS. 8353. Crowther, J. D. W. "'The Bargain of Judas.'" *ELN* 13(1976): 245-249.

BATTLE OF THE PSALMS. 8354. Edwards, A. S. G. "The Battle of the Psalms." *ELN* 8(1970): 89-92.

BOKE OF ST. ALBANS. 8355. Hands, Rachel. "Juliana Berners and *The Boke of St. Albans*." *RES* 18(1967): 373-386.

BROMYARD, JOHN. 8356. Boyle, Leonard E. "The Date of the *Summa Praedicantium* of John Bromyard." *Speculum* 48(1973): 533-537.

8357. Olson, Paul A. "A Note on John Bromyard and Augustine's *Christian Doctrine*." *ELN* 3 (1966): 165-168.

CASTLE OF PERSEVERANCE. 8358. Fifield, Merle. "The Arena Theatres in Vienna Codices 2535 and 2536." *CD* 2(1968): 259-282.

8359. Kelley, Michael R. "Fifteenth-Century Flamboyant Style and *The Castle of Perseverance*." *CD* 6(1972): 14-27.

8360. Nelson, Alan H. "'Of the seven ages': An Unknown Analogue of *The Castle of Perseverance*." *CD* 8(1974): 125-138.

8361. Willis, James. "Stage Directions in 'The Castell of Perseverence.'" *MLR* 51(1956): 404-405.

See also 9367, 9425.

CAXTON, WILLIAM. 8362. Bennett, J. A. W. "Caxton and Gower." *MLR* 45(1950): 215-216.

8363. Blake, N. F. "The *Vocabulary in French and English* Printed by William Caxton." *ELN* 3(1965): 7-15.

8364. ----------. "Word Borrowing in Caxton's Original Writings." *ELN* 6(1968): 87-90.

8365. Donner, Morton. "The Infrequency of Word Borrowings in Caxton's Original Writings." *ELN* 4(1966): 86-89.

8366. Finlayson, J. "The Source of Caxton's *Paris and Vienne*." *PQ* 46(1967): 130-135.

8367. Fox, Denton. "Henryson and Caxton." *JEGP* 67(1968): 586-593.

8368. Gallagher, Joseph E. "The Sources of Caxton's *Ryal Book* and *Doctrinal of Sapience*." *SP* 62(1965): 40-62.

8369. Kekewich, Margaret. "Edward IV, William Caxton, and Literary Patronage in Yorkist England." *MLR* 66(1971): 481-487.

8370. Knowles, Christine. "Caxton and his Two French Sources." *MLR* 49(1954): 417-423.

8371. Lanaghan, R. T. "Bytwene Playne Rude and Curyous: A Note on Caxton's Use of Park." *PQ* 42(1963): 95-97.

8372. McCarthy, Terence. "Caxton and the Text of Malory's Book 2." *MP* 71(1973): 144-152.

8373. Wilson, Robert H. "The Poggiana in Caxton's *Esope*." *PQ* 30(1951): 348-352.

See also 8207, 9974.

CHAUCER, GEOFFREY

GENERAL AND MISCELLANEOUS. 8374. Adams, Percy G. "Chaucer's Assonance." *JEGP* 71(1972): 527-539.

8375. Alderson, William L. "A Checklist of Supplements to Spurgeon's Chaucer Allusions." *PQ* 32(1953): 418-427.

8376. Bateson, F. W. "Could Chaucer Spell?" *EIC* 25(1975): 2-24, 392-393.

8377. Baugh, Albert C. "Fifty Years of Chaucer Scholarship." *Speculum* 26(1951): 659-672.

8378. Baum, Paull F. "Chaucer's Puns." *PMLA* 71(1956): 225-246.

8379. ----------. "Chaucer's Puns: A Supplementary List." *PMLA* 73(1958): 167-170.

8380. Bawcutt, Priscilla. "Gavin Douglas and Chaucer." *RES* 21(1970): 401-423.

8381. Bethurum, Dorothy. "Chaucer's Point of View as Narrator in the Love Poems." *PMLA* 74(1959): 511-520.

8382. Bloomfield, Morton W. "Chaucer's Sense of History." *JEGP* 51(1952): 301-313.

8383. Bonner, Francis W. "The Genesis of the Chaucer Apocrypha." *SP* 48(1951): 461-481.

8384. Braddy, Haldean. "Chaucer, Alice Perrers, and Cecily Chaumpaigne." *Speculum* 52(1977): 906-911.

8385. Brewer, D. S. "Class Distinction in Chaucer." *Speculum* 43(1968): 290-305.

8386. ----------. "The Ideal of Feminine Beauty in Medieval Literature, especially "Harley Lyrics,' Chaucer, and some Elizabethans." *MLR* 50(1955): 257-269.

8387. ----------. "Love and Marriage in Chaucer's Poetry." *MLR* 49(1954): 461-464.

8388. Camden, Carroll. "Chaucer and Two Elizabethan Pseudo-Sciences." *PQ* 38(1959): 124-126.

8389. Cline, Ruth H. "St. Anne." *ELN* 2(1964): 87-89.

8390. Clogan, Paul M. "Chaucer and the *Thebaid Scholia*." *SP* 61(1964): 599-615.

8391. Davis, Norman. "Chaucer's *Gentilesse*: A Forgotten Manuscript, with some Proverbs." *RES* 20(1969): 43-50.

8392. Delasanta, Rodney. "Chaucer and the Exegetes." *SLI* 4,#2(1971): 1-10.

8383. ----------. "James Smith and Chaucer." *EIC* 22(1972): 221-225.

8394. Dobbins, Austin C. "Chaucer Allusions: 1619-1732." *MLQ* 18(1957): 309-312.

8395. Donovan, Mortimer J. "Three Notes on Chaucerian Marine Life." *PQ* 31(1952): 439-441.

8396. Doyle, A. I., and George B. Pace. "A New Chaucer Manuscript." *PMLA* 83(1968): 22-34.

8397. Ellingwood, Leonard. "A Further Note on 'Pilates Voys'." *Speculum* 26(1951): 482.

8398. Farrell, William. "Chaucer's Use of the Catalogue." *TSLL* 5(1963): 64-78.

8399. Ferris, Sumner. "The Date of Chaucer's Annuity and of the 'Complaint to His Empty Purse.'" *MP* 65(1967): 45-52.

8400. Fisher, John H. "Chaucer's Use of *Swete* and *Swote*." *JEGP* 50(1951): 326-331.

8401. Friedman, William F. and Elizabeth S. "Acrostics, Anagrams, and Chaucer." *PQ* 38(1959): 1-20.

8402. Galway, Margaret. "Phillipa Pan, Phillipa Chaucer." *MLR* 55(1960): 481-487.

8403. Garbáty, Thomas Jay. "Chaucer in Spain, 1366: Soldier of Fortune or Agent of the Crown?" *ELN* 5(1967): 81-87.

8404. Gibaldi, Joseph. "Towards a Definition of the Novella." *SSF* 12(1975): 91-97.

8405. Hazelton, Richard. "Chaucer and Cato." *Speculum* 35(1960): 357-380.

8406. Homan, Elizabeth R. "Chaucer's Use of 'Gan.'" *JEGP* 53(1954): 389-398.

8407. Howard, Donald R. "Chaucer the Man." *PMLA* 80(1965): 337-343.

8408. Huntsman, Jeffrey F. "Caveat Editor: Chaucer and Medieval Dictionaries." *MP* 73(1976): 276-279.

8409. Huxley, Aldous. "Exhumations I. Huxley's 'Chaucer.'" *EIC* 15(1965): 6-21.

8410. Jordan, Robert M. "The Limits of Illusion: Faulkner, Fielding, and Chaucer." *Criticism* 2(1960): 278-305.

8411. Kaske, R. E. "Chaucer and Medieval Allegory." *ELH* 30(1963): 173-192.

8412. Kelly, H. A. "*Occupatio* as Negative Narration: A Mistake for *Occultatio/Praeteritio*." *MP* 74(1977): 311-315.

8413. Kennedy, E. S. "A Horoscope of

Messehalla in the Chaucer Equatorium Manuscript."
Speculum 34(1959): 629-630.

8414. Kökeritz, Helge. "Rhetorical Word-
Play in Chaucer." *PMLA* 69(1954): 937-952.

8415. Kreisler, Nocolai Von. "A Recurrent
Expression of Devotion in Chaucer's *Book of the
Duchess*, *Parliament of Fowls*, and *Knight's Tale*."
MP 68(1970): 62-64.

8416. Lunz, Elisabeth. "Chaucer's Prudence
as the Ideal of the Virtuous Woman." *EL* 4(1977):
3-10.

8417. Manzalaoui, Mahmoud. "Ars Longa,
Vita Brevis." *EIC* 12(1962): 221-224.

8418. McCall, John P. "Chaucer and John
of Legnano." *Speculum* 40(1965): 484-489.

8419. ----------. "Chaucer and the Pseudo
Origen *De Maria Magdalena*." *Speculum* 46(1971):
491-509.

8420. McPeek, James A. S. "Chaucer and
the Goliards." *Speculum* 26(1951): 332-336.

8421. Miller, Milton. "Definition by Comparison: Chaucer, Lawrence and Joyce." *EIC* 3
(1953): 369-381.

8422. Millns, Tony. "Chaucer's Suspended
Judgements." *EIC* 27(1977): 1-19.

8423. Mitchell, Jerome. "Hoccleve's
Supposed Friendship with Chaucer." *ELN* 4(1966):
9-12.

8424. Moore, Arthur K. "Chaucer's Use of
Lyric as an Ornament of Style." *Comp L* 3(1951):
32-46.

8425. Moseley, C. W. R. D. "Chaucer, Sir
John Mandeville, and the Alliterative Revival:
A Hypothesis Concerning Relationships." *MP* 72
(1974): 182-184.

8426. Mudrick, Marvin. "Chaucer as
Librettist." *PQ* 38(1959): 21-29.

8427. Murphy, James J. "A New Look at
Chaucer and the Rhetoricians." *RES* 15(1964):
1-20.

8428. Muscatine, Charles. "Chaucer in an
Age of Criticism." *MLQ* 25(1964): 473-478.

8429. North, J. D. "Kalenderes Enlumyned
Ben They. [Parts I-III]: Some Astronomical
Themes in Chaucer." *RES* 20(1969): 129-154, 257-
284, 418-444.

8430. Olson, Glending. "Deschamp's *Art de
Dictier* Chaucer's Literary Environment."
Speculum 48(1973): 714-723.

8431. Owen, Charles A., Jr. "The Problem
of Free Will in Chaucer's Narratives." *PQ* 46(1967):
433-456.

8432. Pace, George B. "Otho A. XVIII."
Speculum 26(1951): 306-316.

8433. Parker, Roscoe E. "'Pilates Voys.'"
[see also: Ellingwood, *Speculum* 26(51): 482]."
Speculum 25(1950): 237-244.

8434. Pittock, Malcolm. "Chaucer: The
Complaint Unto Pity." *Criticism* 1(1959): 160-168.

8435. Preston, Raymond. "Chaucer and the
Ballades Notées of Guillaume de Machant."
Speculum 26(1951): 615-623.

8436. Randall, Dale B. J. "A 1613 Chaucer
Allusion." *PQ* 39(1960): 131-132.

8437. Robbins, Rossell Hope. "A Love
Epistle by 'Chaucer.'" *MLR* 49(1954): 289-292.

8438. Sackton, Alexander. "A Note on Keats
and Chaucer." *MLQ* 13(1952): 37-40.

8439. Scott, Florence R. "A New Look at
'The Complaint of Chaucer to His Empty Purse'."
ELN 2(1964): 81-87.

8440. Schlauch, Margaret. "Chaucer's
Colloquial English: Its Structural Traits."
PMLA 67(1952): 1103-1116.

8441. ----------. "Chaucer's Prose
Rhythms." *PMLA* 65(1950): 568-589.

8442. Schmidt, A. V. C. "Chaucer and the
Golden Age." *EIC* 26(1976): 99-115.

8443. ----------. "Could Chaucer Spell?"
EIC 25(1975): 391-392.

8444. Shugrue, Michael. "The Urry *Chaucer*
(1721) and the London Uprising of 1384: A Phase
in Chaucerian Biography." *JEGP* 65(1966): 229-237.

8445. Smith, James. "Chaucer, Boethius,
and Recent Trends in Criticism." *EIC* 22(1972):
4-32.

8446. Smyser, H. M. "Chaucer's Use of *Gin*
and *Do*." *Speculum* 42(1967): 68-83.

8447. ----------. "A View of Chaucer's
Astronomy." *Speculum* 45(1970): 359-373.

8448. Stroud, Theodore A. "Genres and
Themes: A Reaction to Two Views of Chaucer."
MP 72(1974): 60-70.

8449. Thomson, Patricia. "The 'Canticus
Troili': Chaucer and Petrarch." *Comp L* 11(1959):
313-328.

8450. Wentersdorf, Karl P. "Chaucer and
the Lost Tale of Wade." *JEGP* 65(1966): 274-286.

8451. Wenzel, Siegfried. "Chaucer and the
Language of Contemporary Preaching." *SP* 73(1976):
138-161.

8452. Wilkins, Ernest H. "Descriptions of
Pagan Divinities from Petrarch to Chaucer."
Speculum 32(1957): 511-522.

8453. Williams, Arnold. "The 'Limitour' of
Chaucer's Time and His 'Limitacioun'." *SP* 57
(1960): 463-478.

See also 111, 8962, 8971, 9299, 12463, 14699.
BOOK OF THE DUCHESS. 8454. Baker, Donald
C. "The Dreamer Again in *The Book of the
Duchess*." *PMLA* 70(1955): 279-282.

8455. Boardman, Phillip C. "Courtly Language and the Strategy of Consolation in the *Book
of the Duchess*." *ELH* 44(1977): 567-579.

8456. Bronson, Bertrand H. "*The Book of
the Duchess* Re-opened." *PMLA* 67(1952): 863-881.

8457. Cherniss, Michael D. "The Boethian
Dialogue in Chaucer's *Book of the Duchess*." *JEGP*
68(1969): 655-665.

8458. Crampton, Georgia Ronan. "Transitions
and Meaning in *The Book of the Duchess*." *JEGP*
62(1963): 486-500.

8459. Delasanta, Rodney. "Christian
Affirmation in *The Book of the Duchess*." *PMLA* 84
(1969): 245-252.

8460. Finlayson, John. "The Book of the
Duchess: Sources for Lines 174, 203-205, 249-
253." *ELN* 10(1973): 170-172.

8461. French, W. H. "The Man in Black's
Lyric." *JEGP* 56(1957): 231-241.

8462. Fyler, John M. "Irony and the Age of
Gold in the *Book of the Duchess*." *Speculum* 52
(1977): 314-328.

8463. Grennen, Joseph E. "*Hert-huntyng* in
the *Book of the Duchess*." *MLQ* 25(1964): 131-139.

8464. Kreuzer, James R. "The Dreamer in the
Book of the Duchess." *PMLA* 66(1951): 543-547.

8465. Lawlor, John. "The Pattern of Consolation in *The Book of the Duchess*." *Speculum* 31
(1956): 626-648.

8466. Manning, Stephen. "Chaucer's Good Fair White: Woman and Symbol." *Comp L* 10(1958): 97-105.

8467. ----------. "That Dreamer Once More." *PMLA* 71(1956): 540-541.

8468. Severs, J. Burke. "Chaucer's Self-Portrait in the *Book of the Duchess*." *PQ* 43(1964): 27-39.

8469. Wilson, G. R., Jr. "The Anatomy of Comparison: Chaucer's *Book of the Duchess*." *TSLL* 14(1972): 381-388.

8470. Wimsatt, James I. "The Apotheosis of Blanche in *The Book of the Duchess*." *JEGP* 66 (1967): 26-44.

CANTERBURY TALES.   8471. Adams, George R. and Bernard S. Levy. "Good and Bad Fridays and May 3 in Chaucer." *ELN* 3(1966): 245-248.

8472. Adams, John F. "The Structure of Irony in *The Summoner's Tale*." *EIC* 12(1962): 126-132.

8473. Aiken, Pauline. "Vincent of Beauvais and the 'Houres' of Chaucer's Physician." *SP* 53 (1956): 22-24.

8474. Allen, Judson Boyce. "The Ironic Fruyt: Chauntecleer and Figura." *SP* 66(1969): 25-35.

8475. Archer, Jerome W. "In Chaucer's Source for 'Averagus' in the *Franklin's Tale*." *PMLA* 65(1950): 318-322.

8476. Bachman, W. Bryant, Jr. "Mercury, Virgil, and Arcite: *Canterbury Tales*, A 1384-1397." *ELN* 13(1976): 168-173.

8477. Baker, Donald C. "Chaucer's Clerk and the Wife of Bath on the Subject of *Gentilesse*." *SP* 59(1962): 631-640.

8478. ----------. "A Crux in Chaucer's *Franklin's Tale*: Dorigen's Complaint." *JEGP* 60(1961): 56-64.

8479. Baldwin, R. G. "The Yeoman's Canons: A Conjecture." *JEGP* 61(1962): 232-243.

8480. Barney, Stephen A. "Troilus Bound." *Speculum* 47(1972): 445-458.

8481. Beall, Chandler B. "And Gladly Teche." *ELN* 13(1975): 85-86.

8482. Beichner, Rev. Paul E., C. S. C. "Baiting the Summoner." *MLQ* 22(1961): 367-376.

8483. ----------. "Daun Piers, Monk and Business Administrator." *Speculum* 34(1959): 611-619.

8484. ----------. "The Grain of Paradise." *Speculum* 36(1961): 302-307.

8485. Beidler, Peter G. "Conrad's 'Amy Foster' and Chaucer's Prioress." *NCF* 30(1975): 111-115.

8486. Benjamin, Edwin B. "The Concept of Order in the *Franklin's Tale*." *PQ* 38(1959): 119-124.

8487. Berndt, David E. "Monastic *Acedia* and Chaucer's Characterization of Daun Piers." *SP* 68(1971): 435-450.

8488. Bettridge, William Edwin, and Francis Lee Utley. "New Light on the Origin of the Griselda Story." *TSLL* 13(1971): 153-208.

8489. Biggins, Dennis. "Chaucer: *CT* X(I) 42-46." *PQ* 42(1963): 558-562.

8490. ----------. "Erroneous Punctuation in Chaucer, *CT* I(A) 4394-96." *PQ* 44(1965): 117-119.

8491. ----------. "Sym(e)kyn/*simia*: The Ape in Chaucer's Millers." *SP* 65(1968): 44-50.

8492. Blake, Kathleen A. "Order and the Noble Life in Chaucer's *Knight's Tale*." *MLQ* 34 (1973): 3-19.

8493. Blenner-Hassett, Roland. "Autobiographical Aspects of Chaucer's Franklin." *Speculum* 28(1953): 791-800.

8494. Block, Edward A. "' . . . and It is Half-Wey Pryme'." *Speculum* 32(1957): 826-833.

8495. ----------. "Chaucer's Millers and Their Bagpipes." *Speculum* 29(1954): 239-243.

8496. ----------. "Originality, Controlling Purpose, and Craftsmanship in Chaucer's *Man of Law's Tale*." *PMLA* 68(1953): 572-616.

8497. Blodgett, E. D. "Chaucerian *Pryvetee* and the Opposition to Time." *Speculum* 51(1976): 477-493.

8498. Bloomfield, Morton W. "The Man of Law's Tale: A Tragedy of Victimization and a Christian Comedy." *PMLA* 87(1972): 384-390.

8499. Bonjour, Adrien. "Aspects of Chaucer's Irony in *The Friar's Tale*." *EIC* 11(1961): 121-127.

8500. Boyd, Beverly. "Chaucer's Prioress: Her Green Gauds." *MLQ* 11(1950): 404-416.

8501. Braddy, Haldeen. "Chaucer's Don Pedro and the Purpose of the *Monk's Tale*." *MLQ* 13(1952): 3-5.

8502. Badley, Sister Ritamary, C. H. M. "The *Wife of Bath's Tale* and the Mirror Tradition." *JEGP* 55(1956): 624-630.

8503. Brennan, John P. "Reflections on a Gloss to the *Prioress's Tale* from Jerome's *Adversus Jovinianum*." *SP* 70(1973): 243-251.

8504. Broes, Arthur T. "Chaucer's Disgruntled Cleric: *The Nun's Priest's Tale*." *PMLA* 78(1963): 156-162.

8505. Bronson, Bertrand H. "Afterthoughts on the Merchant's Tale." *SP* 58(1961): 583-596.

8506. Brosnahan, Leger. "Does the Nun's Priest's Epilogue Contain a Link?" *SP* 58(1961): 468-482.

8507. Brown, Joella Owens. "Chaucer's Daun Piers: One Monk or Two?" *Criticism* 6(1964): 44-52.

8508. Burrow, J. A. "'Sir Thopas': An Agony in Three Fits." *RES* 22(1971): 54-58.

8509. Byers, John R., Jr. "Harry Bailey's St. Madrian." *ELN* 4(1966): 6-9.

8510. Cadbury, William. "Manipulation of Sources and the Meaning of the *Manciple's Tale*." *PQ* 43(1964): 538-548.

8511. Cameron, Allen Barry. "The Heroine in *The Knight's Tale*." *SSF* 5(1968): 119-127.

8512. Carruthers, Mary. "Letter and Gloss in the Friar's and Summoner's Tales." *JNT* 2(1972): 208-214.

8513. Cespedes, Frank V. "Chaucer's Pardoner and Preaching." *ELH* 44(1977): 1-18.

8514. Chamberlain, David S. "The Nun's Priest's Tale and Boethius's *De Musica*." *MP* 68 (1970): 188-191.

8515. Clark, George. "Chauntecleer and Deduit." *ELN* 2(1965): 168-171.

8516. Clark, Roy Peter. "Christmas Games in Chaucer's 'The Miller's Tale'." *SSF* 13(1976): 277-287.

8517. Colmer, Dorothy. "Character and Class in *The Wife of Bath's Tale*." *JEGP* 72(1973): 329-339.

8518. ----------. "The Franklin's Tale: a Palimpsest Reading." EIC 20(1970): 375-380.

8519. Conley, John. "'The Peculiar Name Thopas'." SP 73(1976): 42-60.

8520. Correale, Robert M. "St. Jerome and the Conclusion of the Friar's Tale." ELN 2(1965): 171-173.

8521. Cotter, James Finn. "The Wife of Bath and the Conjugal Debt." ELN 6(1969): 169-172.

8522. Cowgill, Bruce Kent. "The Knight's Tale and the Hundred Years' War." PQ 54(1975): 670-679.

8523. Crane, John Kenny. "An Honest Debtor?: A Note on Chaucer's Merchant, Line A276." ELN 4 (1966): 81-85.

8524. Cross, James E. "On the Meaning of 'A-blakeberyed' (Canterbury Tales, C. 406)." RES 2(1951): 372-374.

8525. Cunningham, J. V. "The Literary Form of the Prologue to the Canterbury Tales." MP 49 (1952): 172-181.

8526. Dahlberg, Charles. "Chaucer's Cock and Fox." JEGP 53(1954): 277-290.

8527. David, Alfred. "The Man of Law vs. Chaucer: A Case in Poetics." PMLA 82(1967): 217-225.

8528. Dean, James. "Time Past and Time Present in Chaucer's Clerk's Tale and Gower's Confessio Amantis." ELH 44(1977): 401-418.

8529. Delany, Paul. "Constantinus Africanus and Chaucer's Merchant's Tale." PQ 46(1967): 560-566.

8530. Delasanta, Rodney. "The Theme of Judgment in The Canterbury Tales." MLQ 31(1970): 298-307.

8531. Dempster, Germaine. "The Clerk's Endlink in the d Manuscripts." PMLA 67(1952): 1177-1181.

8532. ----------. "A Period in the Development of the Canterbury Tales Marriage Group and of Blocks B^2 and C." PMLA 68(1953): 1142-1159.

8533. DeNeef, A. Leigh. "Chaucer's Pardoner's Tale and the Irony of Misinterpretation." JNT 3(1973): 85-96.

8534. Donaldson, E. T. "Chaucer, Canterbury Tales, D117: A Critical Edition." Speculum 40(1965): 626-633.

8535. Donaldson, E. Talbot. "Chaucer the Pilgrim." PMLA 69(1954): 928-936.

8536. Donovan, Mortimer J. "The Anticlaudian and Three Passages in the Franklin's Tale." JEGP 56(1957): 52-59.

8537. ----------. "Chaucer's Shipman and the Integrity of his Cargo." MLR 50(1955): 489-490.

8538. ----------. "The Image of Pluto and Proserpine in the Merchant's Tale." PQ 36(1957): 49-60.

8539. ----------. "The Moralite of the Nun's Priest's Sermon." JEGP 52(1953): 498-508.

8540. Duncan, Edgar H. "Chaucer's 'Wife of Bath's Prologue,' Lines 193-828, and Geoffrey of Vinsauf's Documentum." MP 66(1969): 199-211.

8541. ----------. "The Literature of Alchemy and Chaucer's Canon's Yeoman's Tale: Framework, Theme, and Characters." Speculum 43 (1968): 633-656.

8542. Economou, George D. "Chaucer's Use of the Bird in the Cage Image in the Canterbury Tales." PQ 54(1975): 679-684.

8543. ----------. "Januarie's Sin against Nature: The Merchant's Tale and the Roman de la Rose." Comp L 17(1965): 251-157.

8544. Eddy, Elizabeth Roth. "Sir Thopas and Sir Thomas Norny: Romance Parody in Chaucer and Dunbar." RES 22(1971): 401-409.

8545. Eliason, Mary. "The Peasant and the Lawyer." SP 48(1951): 506-526.

8546. Ethel, Garland. "Chaucer's Worste Shrewe: The Pardoner." MLQ 20(1959): 211-227.

8547. Fehrenbach, Robert J. "The Chivalric Tradition and the Red and White Gown of Chaucer's Squire." ELN 15(1977): 4-7.

8548. Fish, Stanley E. "'The Nun's Priest's Tale' and Its Analogues." CLA 5(1962): 223-228.

8549. Fisher, John H. "Chaucer's Last Revision of the 'Canterbury Tales.'" MLR 67(1972): 241-251.

8550. Fleming, John V. "The Antifraternalism of the Summoner's Tale." JEGP 65(1966): 688-700.

8551. ----------. "Chaucer's Clerk and John of Salisbury." ELN 2(1964): 5-6.

8552. Forehand, Brooks. "Old Age and Chaucer's Reeve." PMLA 69(1954): 984-989.

8553. Francis, W. Nelson. "Chaucer Shortens a Tale." PMLA 68(1953): 1126-1141.

8554. Friend, Albert C. "Analogues in Cheriton to the Pardoner and His Sermon." JEGP 53 (1954): 383-388.

8555. ----------. "The Dangerous Theme of the Pardoner." MLQ 18(1957): 305-308.

8556. Fry, Donald K. "The Ending of the Monk's Tale." JEGP 71(1972): 355-368.

8557. Gallacher, Patrick. "Food, Laxatives, and Catharsis in Chaucer's Nun's Priest's Tale." Speculum 51(1976): 49-68.

8558. Gallick, Susan. "A Look at Chaucer and His Preachers." Speculum 50(1975): 456-476.

8559. Garbáty, Thomas Jay. "Chaucer's Guildsmen and Their Fraternity." JEGP 59(1960): 691-709.

8560. ----------. "The Degradation of Chaucer's 'Geffrey.'" PMLA 89(1974): 97-104.

8561. ----------. "The Monk and the Merchant's Tale: An Aspect of Chaucer's Building Process in the Canterbury Tales." MP 67(1969): 18-24.

8562. ----------. "The Pamphilus Tradition in Ruiz and Chaucer." PQ 46(1967): 457-470.

8563. Gardner, John. "The Canon's Yeoman's Prologue and Tale: An Interpretation." PQ 46 (1967): 1-17.

8564. Gaylord, Alan T. "The Promises in The Franklin's Tale." ELH 31(1964): 331-365.

8565. ----------. "Sentence and Solaas in Fragment VII of the Canterbury Tales: Harry Bailly as Horseback Editor." PMLA 82(1967): 226-235.

8566. Gellrich, Jesse M. "Nicholas' 'Kynges Noote' and 'Melodye.'" ELN 8(1971): 249-252.

8567. ----------. "The Parody of Medieval Music in the Miller's Tale." JEGP 73(1974): 176-188.

8568. Gibbons, Robert F. "Does the Nun's Priests' Epilogue Contain a Link." SP 51(1954): 21-33.

8569. Gray, Paul Edward. "Synthesis and the Double Standard in the Franklin's Tale." TSLL 7

(1965): 213-224.

8570. Green, A. Wigfall. "Chaucer's Clerks
and the Medieval Scholarly Tradition as Repre-
sented by Richard De Burg's 'Philobiblon.'" *ELH*
18(1951): 1-6.

8571. Greenfield, S. B. "Sittingbourne and
the Order of 'The Canterbury Tales.'" *MLR* 48
(1953): 51-52.

8572. Grenner, Joseph E. "The Canon's Yeoman and the Cosmic Furnace: Language and Meaning
in the 'Canon's Yeoman's Tale.'" *Criticism* 4
(1962): 225-240.

8573. ----------. "The Canon's Yeoman's
Alchemical 'Mass.'" *SP* 62(1965): 546-560.

8574. ----------. "Chaucer's 'secree of
secrees': An Alchemical 'Topic.'" *PQ* 42(1963):
562-566.

8575. ----------. "St. Cecilia's 'Chemical
Wedding': The Unity of the *Canterbury Tales*,
Fragment VIII." *JEGP* 65(1966): 466-481.

8576. Haller, Robert S. "Chaucer's
Squire's Tale and the Uses of Rhetoric." *MP* 62
(1965): 285-295.

8577. Halverson, John. "Aspects of Order
in the *Knight's Tale*." *SP* 57(1960): 606-621.

8578. Harder, Kelsie B. "Chaucer's Use of
the Mystery Plays in the *Miller's Tale*." *MLQ* 17
(1956): 193-198.

8579. Harrington, Norman T. "Chaucer's
Merchant's Tale: Another Swing of the Pendulum."
PMLA 86(1971): 25-31.

8580. Hart, James A. "'The Droghte of
March': A Comma Misunderstanding." *TSLL* 4(1963):
525-529.

8581. Hartung, Albert E. "The Clerk's
Endlink in the d Manuscripts." *PMLA* 67(1952):
1173-1177.

8582. ----------. "Inappropriate Pointing
in the Canon Yeoman's Tale, G-1236-1239." *PMLA* 77
(1962): 508-509.

8583. ----------. "Two Notes on the
Summoner's Tale: Hosts and Swans." *ELN* 4
(1967): 175-180.

8584. Harwood, Britton J. "The Wife of
Bath and the Dream of Innocence." *MLQ* 33(1972):
257-273.

8585. Haskell, Ann Sullivan. "The Host's
precious corpus Madrian." *JEGP* 67(1968): 430-440.

8586. Hatton, Tom. "Chaucer's Friar's 'Old
Rebekke'." *JEGP* 67(1968): 266-271.

8587. Hawkins, Sherman. "Chaucer's Prioress and the Sacrifice of Praise." *JEGP* 63(1964):
599-624.

8588. Hazelton, Richard. "The *Manciple's
Tale*: Parody and Critique." *JEGP* 62(1963): 1-31.

8589. Helterman, Jeffrey. "The Dehuman-
izing Metamorphoses of the Knight's Tale." *ELH* 38
(1971): 493-511.

8590. Hench, Atcheson L. "Chaucer's
Miller's Tale, 1. 3226." *ELN* 3(1965): 88-92.

8591. Heninger, S. K., Jr. "The Concept of
Order in Chaucer's *Clerk's Tale*." *JEGP* 56(1957):
382-395.

8592. Henning, Standish. "Chauntecleer and
Taurus." *ELN* 3(1965): 1-4.

8593. Herz, Judith Scherer. *"The Canon's
Yeoman's Prologue and Tale."* *MP* 58(1961): 231-
237.

8594. ----------. "Chaucer's Elegiac

Knight." *Criticism* 6(1964): 212-224.

8595. Higdon, David Leon. "Diverse Melodies
in Chaucer's 'General Prologue.'" *Criticism* 14
(1972): 97-108.

8596. Hirsh, John C. "Why Does the Miller's
Tale Take Place on Monday?" *ELN* 13(1975): 86-90.

8597. Hoffman, Arthur W. "Chaucer's
Prologue to Pilgrimage: Two Voices." *ELH* 21
(1954): 1-16.

8598. Hoffman, Richard L. "Ovid and
Chaucer's Myth of Theseus and Pirithoüs." *ELN* 2
(1965): 252-256.

8599. ----------. "Ovid's Priapus in the
Merchant's Tale." *ELN* 3(1966): 169-172.

8600. ----------. "Two Notes on Chaucer's
Arcite." *ELN* 4(1967): 172-175.

8601. ----------. "The Wife of Bath's
Uncharitable Offerings." *ELN* 11(1974): 165-167.

8602. Holman, C. Hugh. "Courtly Love in
the Merchant's and the Franklin's Tales." *ELH* 18
(1951): 241-252.

8603. Howard, Donald R. *"The Canterbury
Tales*: Memory and Form." *ELH* 38(1971): 319-328.

8604. ----------. "The Conclusion of the
Marriage Group: Chaucer and the Human Condition."
MP 57(1959): 223-232.

8605. Hume, Kathryn. "Why Chaucer Calls
the *Franklin's Tale* a Breton Lai." *PQ* 51(1972):
365-379.

8606. Jambeck, Thomas J. "Characterization
and Syntax in the *Miller's Tale*." *JNT* 5(1975):
73-85.

8607. Jeffrey, David Lyle. "The Friar's
Rent." *JEGP* 70(1971): 600-606.

8608. Johnson, Dudley R. "The Biblical
Characters of Chaucer's Monk." *PMLA* 66(1951): 827-
843.

8609. Jones, George Fenwick. "Chaucer and
the Medieval Miller." *MLQ* 16(1955): 3-15.

8610. Johnson, Oscar E. "Was Chaucer's
Merchant in Debt? A Study in Chaucerian Syntax
and Rhetoric." *JEGP* 52(1953): 50-57.

8611. Jordan, Robert M. "Chaucer's Sense
of Illusion: Roadside Drama Reconsidered." *ELH*
29(1962): 19-33.

8612. ----------. "The Non-Dramatic Disunity of the *Merchant's Tale*." *PMLA* 78(1963):
293-299.

8613. Jungman, Robert E. "The Pardoner's
Quarrel with the Host." *PQ* 55(1976): 279-281.

8614. Kaske, R. E. "An Aube in the
Reeve's Tale." *ELH* 26(1959): 295-310.

8615. ----------. "The *Canticum
Canticorum* in the Miller's Tale." *SP* 59(1962):
479-500.

8616. ----------. "The Knight's Interruption of the *Monk's Tale*." *ELH* 24(1957): 249-
268.

8617. Kearney, Anthony. "The *Franklin's
Tale*." *EIC* 21(1971): 109-111.

8618. Kearney, A. M. "Truth and Illusion
in the *Franklin's Tale*." *EIC* 19(1969): 245-253.

8619. Kernan, Anne. "The Archwife and the
Eunuch." *ELH* 41(1974): 1-25.

8620. Kellogg, Alfred L. "An Augustian
Interpretation of Chaucer's Pardoner." *Speculum*
26(1951): 465-481.

8621. ----------. "Susannah and the
Merchant's Tale." *Speculum* 35(1960): 275-279.

8622. ----------, and Louis A. Haselmayer. "Chaucer's Satire of the Pardoner." *PMLA* 66 (1951): 251-277.

8623. Kimpel, Ben. "The Narrator of the *Canterbury Tales*." *ELH* 20(1953): 77-86.

8624. Knapp, Daniel. "The Relyk of a Saint: A Gloss on Chaucer's Pilgrimage." *ELH* 39(1972): 1-26.

8625. Labriola, Albert C. "The Doctrine of Charity and the Use of Homiletic 'Figures' in the *Man of Law's Tale*." *TSLL* 12(1970): 5-14.

8626. Langmuir, Gavin I. "The Knight's Tale of Young Hugh of Lincoln." *Speculum* 47(1972): 459-482.

8627. Lawrence, William W. "Chaucer's *Shipman's Tale*." *Speculum* 33(1958): 56-68.

8628. Lenaghan, R. T. "The Nun's Priest's Fable." *PMLA* 78(1963): 300-307.

8629. Levy, Bernard S. "The Quaint World of 'The Shipman's Tale.'" *SSF* 4(1967): 112-118.

8630. Lewis, Robert Enzer. "Chaucer's Artistic Use of Pope Innocent III's *De Miseria Humane Conditionis* in the Man of Law's Prologue and Tale." *PMLA* 81(1966): 485-492.

8631. ----------. "Glosses to the *Man of Law's Tale* from Pope Innocent III's *De Miseria Humane Conditionis*." *SP* 64(1967): 1-16.

8632. Lock, F. P. "Chaucer's Monk's Use of Lucan, Suetonius, and 'Valerie.'" *ELN* 12(1975): 251-255.

8633. Longsworth, Robert. "The Doctor's Dilemma: A Comic View of the 'Physician's Tale.'" *Criticism* 13(1971): 223-233.

8634. Loomis, Laura Hibbard. "Secular Dramatics in the Royal Palace, Paris, 1378, 1389, and Chaucer's 'Tregetoures.'" *Speculum* 33(1958): 242-255.

8635. Lumiansky, R. M. "Benoit's Portraits and Chaucer's General Prologue." *JEGP* 55(1956): 431-438.

8636. ----------. "The Nun's Priest in *The Canterbury Tales*." *PMLA* 68(1953): 896-906.

8637. Lynons, John O. "James Joyce and Chaucer's Prioress." *ELN* 2(1964): 127-132.

8638. MacDonald, Donald. "Proverbs, *Sententiae*, and *Exempla* in Chaucer's Comic Tales: The Function of Comic Misapplication." *Speculum* 41(1966): 453-465.

8639. Mahoney, John. "Alice of Bath: Her 'secte' and 'gentil text.'" *Criticism* 6(1964): 144-155.

8640. Malone, Kemp. "The Wife of Bath's Tale." *MLR* 57(1962): 481-491.

8641. Mandel, Jerome. "Other Voices in the 'Canterbury Tales.'" *Criticism* 19(1977): 338-349.

8642. Mann, Lindsay A. "'Gentilesse' and the Franklin's Tale." *SP* 63(1966): 10-29.

8643. Manning, Stephen. "The Nun's Priest's Morality and the Medieval Attitude Toward Fables." *JEGP* 59(1960): 403-416.

8644. Major, John M. "The Personality of Chaucer the Pilgrim." *PMLA* 75(1960): 160-162.

8645. Matthews, William. "Eustache Deschamps and Chaucer's 'Merchant's Tale.'" *MLR* 51(1956): 217-220.

8646. Maveety, Stanley R. "An Approach to *The Nun's Priest's Tale*." *CLA* 4(1960): 132-137.

8647. McCall, John P. "The *Clerk's Tale* and the Theme of Obedience." *MLQ* 27(1966): 260-269.

8648. McCracken, Samuel. "Confessional Prologue and the Topography of the Canon's Yeoman." *MP* 68(1971): 289-291.

8649. McCutchan, J. Wilson. "'A Solempne and a Greet Fraternitee.'" *PMLA* 74(1959): 313-317.

8650. McGalliard, John C. "Characterization in Chaucer's *Shipman's Tale*." *PQ* 54(1975): 1-18.

8651. Melton, John L. "Sir Thopas' 'Charbocle'." *PQ* 35(1956): 215-217.

8652. Merrill, Thomas F. "Wrath and Rhetric in 'The Summoner's Tale'." *TSLL* 4(1962): 341-350.

8653. Mitchell, Charles. "The Worthiness of Chaucer's Knight." *MLQ* 25(1964): 66-75.

8654. Miller, Milton. "The Heir in the *Merchant's Tale*." *PQ* 29(1950): 437-440.

8655. Miller, Robert P. "Chaucer's Pardoner, the Scriptural Eunuch, and the Pardoner's Tale." *Speculum* 30(1955): 180-199.

8656. ----------. "*The Wife of Bath's Tale* and Mediaeval Exempla." *ELH* 32(1965): 442-456.

8657. Moore, Arthur K. "*Sir Thopas* as Criticism of Fourteenth-Century Minstrelsy." *JEGP* 53(1954): 532-545.

8658. Morgan, Gerald. "The Self-revealing Tendencies of Chaucer's Pardoner." *MLR* 71(1976): 241-255.

8659. Morse, J. Mitchell. "The Philosophy of the Clerk of Oxenford." *MLQ* 19(1958): 3-20.

8660. Murtaugh, Daniel M. "Women and Geoffrey Chaucer." *ELH* 38(1971): 473-492.

8661. Muscatine, Charles. "Form, Texture, and Meaning in Chaucer's *Knight's Tale*." *PMLA* 65 (1950): 911-929.

8662. Nathan, Norman. "Pronouns of Address in the 'Friar's Tale.'" *MLQ* 17(1956): 39-42.

8663. Neuss, Paula. "*Double-Entendre* in *The Miller's Tale*." *EIC* 24(1974): 325-340.

8664. Neville, Marie. "The Function of the *Squire's Tale* in the Canterbury Scheme." *JEGP* 50 (1951): 167-179.

8665. Nevo, Ruth. "Chaucer: Motive and Mask in the 'General Prologue.'" *MLR* 58(1963): 1-9.

8666. Nichols, Robert E., Jr. "The Pardoner's Ale and Cake." *PMLA* 82(1967): 498-504.

8667. O'Connor, John J. "The Astrological Background of the *Miller's Tale*." *Speculum* 31 (1956): 120-125.

8668. Olson, Glending. "The Medieval Theory of Literature for Refreshment and Its Use in the Fablian Tradition." *SP* 71(1974): 291-313.

8669. ----------. "'The Reeves Tale' and 'Gombert'." *MLR* 64(1969): 721-725.

8670. ----------. "The *Reeve's Tale* as a Fabliau." *MLQ* 35(1974): 219-230.

8671. Olson, Paul A. "Chaucer's Merchant and January's 'Hevene in Erthe Heere.'" *ELH* 28 (1961): 203-214.

8672. ----------. "The Merchant's Lombard Knight." *TSLL* 3(1961): 259-263.

8673. ----------. "Poetic Justice in the *Miller's Tale*." *MLQ* 24(1963): 227-236.

8674. ----------. "The *Reeve's Tale*: Chaucer's *Measure for Measure*." *SP* 59(1962): 1-17.

8675. Oruch, Jack B. "Chaucer's Worldly Monk." *Criticism* 8(1966): 280-288.

8676. Owen, Charles A. "*The Canterbury Tales*: Early Manuscripts and Relative Popularity." *JEGP* 54(1955): 104-110.

8677. ----------. "The Crucial Passages in Five of the *Canterbury Tales*." *JEGP* 52(1953): 294-311.

8678. ----------. "The Development of the *Canterbury Tales*." *JEGP* 57(1958): 449-476.

8679. ----------. "The Plan of the Canterbury Pilgrimage." *PMLA* 66(1951): 820-826.

8680. ----------. "'Thy Drasty Rymyng . . ..'" *SP* 63(1966): 533-564.

8681. Owen, Nancy H. "The Pardoner's Introduction, Prologue, and Tale: Sermon and *Fabliau*." *JEGP* 66(1967): 541-549.

8682. Owen, W. J. B. "The Old Man in 'The Pardoner's Tale'." *RES* 2(1951): 49-55.

8683. Pace, George B. "Adam's Hell." *PMLA* 78(1963): 25-35.

8684. ----------. "The Scorpion of Chaucer's *Merchant's Tale*." *MLQ* 26(1965): 369-374.

8685. Palomo, Dolores. "What Chaucer Really Did to *Le Livre de Mellibee*." *PQ* 53(1974): 304-320.

8686. Park, B. A. "The Character of Chaucer's Merchant." *ELN* 1(1964): 167-175.

8687. Pearcy, Roy J. "Does the Manciple's Prologue Contain a Reference to Hell's Mouth?" *ELN* 11(1973): 167-175.

8688. Pittock, Malcolm. "'The Merchant's Tale.'" *EIC* 17(1967): 26-40.

8689. ----------. "*The Pardoner's Tale* and the Quest for Death." *EIC* 24(1974): 107-123.

8690. Pratt, Robert A. "Chaucer and the Hand that Fed Him." *Speculum* 41(1966): 619-642.

8691. ----------. "Chaucer's Title: 'The Tales of Caunterbury.'" *PQ* 54(1975): 19-25.

8692. ----------. "'Joye after Wo' in the *Knight's Tale*." *JEGP* 57(1958): 416-423.

8693. ----------. "The Order of the *Canterbury Tales*." *PMLA* 66(1951): 1141-1167.

8694. ----------. "Saint Jerome in Jankyn's Book of Wikked Wyves." *Criticism* 5(1963): 316-322.

8695. ----------. "Some Latin Sources of the Nonnes Preest on Dreams." *Speculum* 52(1977): 538-570.

8696. ----------. "Symkyn koude 'turne coppes': The *Reeve's Tale* 3928." *JEGP* 59(1960): 208-211.

8697. ----------. "Three Old French Sources of the Nonnes Preestes Tale." *Speculum* 47(1972): 422-444, 646-668.

8698. Przemysław, Mroczkowski. "Art and Aesthetics in *The Canterbury Tales*." *Speculum* 33 (1958): 204-221.

8699. Quinn, Betty Nye. "Venus, Chaucer, and Peter Bersuire." *Speculum* 38(1963): 479-480.

8700. Ramsey, Roger. "Clothing Makes a Queen in *The Clerk's Tale*." *JNT* 7(1977): 104-115.

8701. Rea, John A. "An Old French Analogue to General Prologue 1-18." *PQ* 46(1967): 128-130.

8702. Reed, Mary Brookbank. "Chaucer's Sely Carpenter." *PQ* 41(1962): 768-769.

8703. Reidy, John. "Chaucer's Canon and the Unity of *The Canon's Yeoman's* Tale." *PMLA* 80 (1965): 31-37.

8704. Reisner, Thomas Andrew. "The Wife of Bath's Dower: A Legal Interpretation." *MP* 71 (1974): 301-302.

8705. Reiss, Edmund. "Chaucer's Friar and the Man in the Moon." *JEGP* 62(1963): 481-485.

8706. ----------. "The Pilgrimage Narrative and the Canterbury Tales." *SP* 67(1970): 295-305.

8707. Richardson, Cynthia C. "The Function of the Host in *The Canterbury Tales*." *TSLL* 12 (1970): 325-344.

8708. Richardson, Janette. "The Facade of Bawdry: Image Patterns in Chaucer's *Shipman's Tale*." *ELH* 32(1965): 303-313.

8709. Rieman, Donald H. "The Real *Clerk's Tale*; or, Patient Griselda Exposed." *TSLL* 5(1963): 356-373.

8710. Roache, Joel. "Treasure Trove in the *Pardoner's Tale*." *JEGP* 64(1965): 1-6.

8711. Robbins, Rossell Hope. "Chaucer's 'To Rosemounde.'" *SLI* 4#2(1971): 73-81.

8712. Robertson, D. W., Jr. "Some Disputed Chaucerian Terminology." *Speculum* 52(1977): 571-581.

8713. Rogers, Franklin R. "*The Tale of Gamelyn* and the Editing of the *Canterbury Tales*." *JEGP* 58(1959): 49-59.

8714. Ross, Thomas W. "Notes on Chaucer's Miller's Tale, A3216 and 3320." *ELN* 13(1976): 256-258.

8715. Rowland, Beryl. "Chaucer's 'Bukke and Hare' (*Thop*, VII, 756)." *ELN* 2(1964): 6-8.

8716. ----------. "The Physician's 'Historical Thyng Notable.'" *ELH* 40(1973): 165-178.

8717. ----------. "A Sheep That Highte Malle (NPT, VII, 2831)." *ELN* 6(1968): 84-87.

8718. Rumble, T. C. "Chaucer's *Knight's Tale*, 2680-83." *PQ* 43(1964): 130-133.

8719. Scattergood, V. J. "The Manciple's Manner of Speaking." *EIC* 24(1974): 124-146.

8720. Scheps, Walter. "Chaucer's Man of Law and the Tale of Constance." *PMLA* 89(1974): 285-295.

8721. Schlauch, Margaret. "Historical Precursors of Chaucer's Constance." *PQ* 29(1950): 402-412.

8722. Schmidt, A. V. C. "The Tragedy of Arcite: A Reconsideration of the *Knight's Tale*." *EIC* 19(1969): 107-117.

8723. Schroeder, Mary C. "Fantasy in the 'Merchant's Tale.'" *Criticism* 12(1970): 167-179.

8724. Schweitzer, Edward C., Jr. "Chaucer's Pardoner and the Hare." *ELN* 4(1967): 247-250.

8725. Scott, Kathleen. "Sow-and-Bagpipe Imagery in the Miller's Portrait." *RES* 18(1967): 287-290.

8726. Severs, J. Burke. "Is the *Manciple's Tale* a Success?" *JEGP* 51(1952): 1-16.

8727. Shallers, A. Paul. "The 'Nun's Priest's Tale': An Ironic Exemplum." *ELH* 42(1975): 319-337.

8728. Shumaker, Wayne. "Alisoun in Wanda-Land: A Study in Chaucer's Mind and Literary Method." *ELH* 18(1951): 77-89.

8729. Silverman, Albert H. "Sex and Money in Chaucer's *Shipman's Tale*." *PQ* 32(1953): 329-336.

8730. Silverstein, Theodore. "Wife of Bath and the Rhetoric of Enchantment; Or, How to Make a Hero See in the Dark." *MP* 58(1961): 153-173.

8731. Silvia, Daniel S., Jr. "Chaucer's Friars: Swans or Swains? *Summoner's Tale*, D 1930."

ENL 1(1964): 248–250.

8732. ----------. "Glosses to the
Canterbury Tales from St. Jerome's *Epistola
Adversus Jovinianum*." *SP* 62(1965): 28–39.

8733. Simons, Rita Dandridge. "The Prioress's Disobedience of Benedictine Rule." *CLA* 12
(1968): 77–83.

8734. Slade, Tony. "Irony in 'The Wife of
Bath's Tale'." *MLR* 64(1969): 241–247.

8735. Sledd, James. "*The Clerk's Tale*: The
Monsters and the Critics." *MP* 51(1953): 73–82.

8736. Socola, Edward M. "Chaucer's Development of Fortune in the 'Monk's Tale.'" *JEGP* 49
(1950): 159–171.

8737. Statler, Margaret H. "The Analogues
of Chaucer's *Prioress' Tale*: the Relation of
Group C to Group A." *PMLA* 65(1950): 896–910.

8738. Steadman, John M. "The Book-Burning
Episode in the Wife of Bath's Prologue: Some
Additional Analogues." *PMLA* 74(1959): 521–525.

8739. ----------. "Chaucer's Pardoner and
the *Thesaurus Meritorium*." *ELN* 3(1965): 4–7.

8740. ----------. "The Prioress' Dogs and
Benedictine Discipline." *MP* 54(1956): 1–6.

8741. ----------. "Venus' *Citole* in Chaucer's *Knight's Tale* and Berchorius." *Speculum* 34
(1959): 620–624.

8742. Stillwell, Gardiner. "Chaucer's
Merchant: No Debts?" *JEGP* 57(1958): 192–196.

8743. ----------. "The Language of Love in
Chaucer's Miller's and Reeve's Tales and in the
Old French Fabliaux." *JEGP* 54(1955): 693–699.

8744. Storm, Melvin. "The Tercelet as
Tiger: Bestiary Hypocrisy in the Squire's Tale."
ELN 14(1977): 172–174.

8745. Strohm, Paul. "Some Generic Distinctions in the *Canterbury Tales*." *MP* 68(1971): 321–
328.

8746. Sutherland, Raymond Carter. "A Note
on Lines D 1645-1662 of Chaucer's *Friar's Tale*."
PQ 31(1952): 436–439.

8747. Szittya, Penn R. "The Friar as False
Apostle: Antifraternal Exegesis and the *Summon-
ers Tale*." *SP* 71(1974): 19–46.

8748. ----------. "The Green Yeoman as
Loathly Lady: The Friar's Parody of the Wife of
Bath's Tale." *PMLA* 90(1975): 386–394.

8749. Taylor, Estelle W. "Chaucer's 'Monk's
Tale': An Apology." *CLA* 13(1969): 172–182.

8750. Taylor, Willene P. "Chaucer's Technique in Handling Anti-Feminist Material in 'The
Merchant's Tale': An Ironic Portrayal of the
Senex-Amans and Jealous Husband." *CLA* 13(1969):
153–162.

8751. Townsend, Francis G. "Chaucer's Nameless Knight." *MLR* 49(1954): 1–4.

8752. Trask, Richard M. "The Manciple's
Problem." *SSF* 14(1977): 109–116.

8753. Tucker, S. I. "Sir Thopas and the
Wild Beasts." *RES* 10(1959): 54–56.

8754. Turner, W. Arthur. "Biblical Women
in *The Merchant's Tale* and *The Tale of Melibee*."
ELN 3(1965): 92–95

8755. Underwood, Dale. "The First of *The
Canterbury Tales*." *ELH* 26(1959): 455–469.

8756. Van, Thomas A. "Theseus and the
'Right Way' of the *Knight's Tale*." *SLI* 4,#2
(1971): 83–100.

8757. Waller, Martha S. "The Physician's Tale:

Geoffrey Chaucer and Fray Juan Garcia' de
Castrojeriz." *Speculum* 51(1976): 292–306.

8758. Watkins, Charles A. "Chaucer's
Sweete Preest." *ELH* 36(1969): 455–469.

8759. Watson, Charles S. "The Relationship
of the 'Monk's Tale' and the 'Nun's Priest's
Tale.'" *SSF* 1(1964): 277–288.

8760. Wawn, Andrew N. "Chaucer, Wyclif,
and the Court of Apollo." *ELN* 10(1972): 15–20.

8761. Wentersdorf, Karl P. "Chaucer's
Merchant's Tale and Its Irish Analogues." *SP* 63
(1966): 603–629.

8762. ----------. "Chaucer's Worthless
Butterfly." *ELN* 14(1977): 167–172.

8763. ----------. "A Spanish Analogue of
the Pear-Tree Episode in the *Merchant's Tale*."
MP 64(1967): 320–321.

8764. ----------. "Theme and Structure in
The Merchant's Tale: The Function of the Pluto
Episode." *PMLA* 80(1965): 522–527.

8765. Westlund, Joseph. "The *Knight's Tale*
as an Impetus for Pilgrimage." *PQ* 43(1964): 526–
537.

8766. White, Gertrude M. "The Franklin's
Tale: Chaucer or the Critics." *PMLA* 89(1974):
454–462.

8767. ----------. "'Hoolynesse or Dotage':
The Merchant's January." *PQ* 44(1965): 397–404.

8768. White, Robert B., Jr. "Chaucer's
Daun Piers and the Rule of St. Benedict: The
Failure of an Ideal." *JEGP* 70(1971): 13–30.

8769. Williams, Arnold. "Chaucer and the
Friars." *Speculum* 28(1953): 499–513.

8770. ----------. "Two Notes on
Chaucer's Friars." *MP* 54(1956): 117–120.

8771. Williams, Franklin B., Jr. "Alsop's
Fair Custance: Chaucer in Tudor Dress." *ELR* 6
(1976): 351–368.

8772. Wood, Chauncey. "The April Date as
a Structural Device in *The Canterbury Tales*."
MLQ 25(1964): 259–271.

8773. ----------. "Chaucer and 'Sir Thopas':
Irony or Concupiscence." *TSLL* 14(1972): 389–403.

8774. ----------. "Chaucer's Clerk and
Chalcidius." *ELN* 4(1967): 166–172.

8775. ----------. "Of Time and Tide in the
Franklin's Tale." *PQ* 45(1966): 688–711.

8776. Wright, Constance S. "On the Franklin's
Prologue, 716-721, Persius, and the Continuity of
Manuscript Style." *PQ* 52(1973): 739–746.

8777. Yunck, John A. "Religious Elements
in Chaucer's 'Man of Law's Tale.'" *ELH* 27(1960):
249–261.

See also 7787, 8202, 8207, 8314.

COMPLAINT OF MARS. 8778. Dean, Nancy.
"Chaucer's *Complaint*: A Genre Descended from the
Heroides." *Comp L* 19(1967): 1–27.

8779. Laird, Edgar S. "Chaucer's *Complaint
of Mars*, Line 145: Venus valaunse." *PQ* 51(1972):
486–489.

8780. Stillwell, Gardiner. "Convention and
Individuality in Chaucer's *Complaint of Mars*." *PQ*
35(1956): 69–89.

8781. Williams, George. "What is the Meaning of Chaucer's *Complaint of Mars*?" *JEGP* 57(1958):
167–176.

HOUSE OF FAME. 8782. Allen, Robert J.
"A Recurring Motif in Chaucer's *House of Fame*."
JEGP 55(1956): 393–405.

8783. Bevington, David M. "The Obtuse Narrator in Chaucer's *House of Fame*." *Speculum* 36 (1961): 288-298.

8784. David, Alfred. "Literary Satire in the *House of Fame*." *PMLA* 75(1960): 333-339.

8785. Delany, Sheila. "'Ars Simia Naturae' and Chaucer's *House of Fame*." *ELN* 11(1973): 1-5.

8786. ----------. "Chaucer's *House of Fame* and the *Ovide moralisé*." *Comp L* 20(1968): 254-264.

8787. Dickerson, A. Inskip. "Chaucer's *House of Fame*: A Skeptical Epistemology of Love." *TSLL* 18(1976): 171-183.

8788. Friend, Albert C. "Chaucer's Version of the Aenid." *Speculum* 28(1953): 317-323.

8789. Kelley, Michael. "Chaucer's *House of Fame*: England's Earliest Science Fiction." *Ext* 16(1974): 7-16.

8790. Magoun, Francis P., Jr., and Tauno F. Mustanoja. "Chaucer's Chimera: His Proto-Surrealist Portrait of Fame." *Speculum* 50(1975): 48-54.

8791. Neville, Marie. "Chaucer and St. Clare." *JEGP* 55(1956): 423-430.

8792. Newman, Francis X. "*House of Fame*, 7-12." *ELN* 6(1968): 5-12.

8793. Overbeck, Pat Trefzger. "The 'Man of Gret Auctorite' in Chaucer's *House of Fame*." *MP* 73(1975): 157-161.

8794. Ruggiers, Paul G. "The Unity of Chaucer's *House of Fame*." *SP* 50(1953): 16-29.

8795. Simmons, J. L. "The Place of the Poet in Chaucer's *House of Fame*." *MLQ* 27(1966): 125-135.

8796. Steadman, John M. "Chaucer's Eagle: A Contemplative Symbol." *PMLA* 75(1960): 153-159.

8797. Tisdale, Charles P. R. "*The House of Fame*: Virgilian Reason and Boethia Wisdom." *Comp L* 25(1973): 247-261.

8798. Wilson, William S. "Exegetical Grammar in the *House of Fame*." *ELN* 1(1964): 244-248.

LEGEND OF GOOD WOMEN. 8799. Bradley, D. R. "Fals Eneas and Sely Dido." *PQ* 39(1960): 122-125.

8800. Clogan, Paul M. "Chaucer's Cybele and the *Liber imaginum deorum*." *PQ* 43(1964): 272-274.

8801. Gardner, John. "The Two Prologues to the *Legend of Good Women*." *JEGP* 67(1968): 594-611.

8802. LaHood, Marvin J. "Chaucer's 'The Legend of Lucrece.'" *PQ* 43(1964): 274-276.

8803. McLaughlin, John C. "'The Honor and the Humble Obeysaunce,' *Prologue to the Legend of Good Women*, 1. 135 G-Text." *PQ* 38(1959): 515-516.

8804. Ruggiers, Paul G. "Tyrants of Lombardy in Dante and Chaucer." *PQ* 29(1959): 445-448.

8805. Weiher, Carol. "Chaucer's and Gower's Stories of Lucretia and Virginia." *ELN* 14(1976): 7-9.

PARLEMENT OF FOULES. 8806. Brewer, D. S. "The Genre of the 'Parlement of Foules.'" *MLR* 53(1958): 321-326.

8807. ----------. "Natural Love in 'The Parlement of Foules.'" *EIC* 5(1955): 407-413.

8808. ----------. "The Parlement of Foules." *EIC* 6(1956): 248.

8809. Brown, Emerson, Jr. "Pirapus and the *Parlement of Foulys*." *SP* 72(1975): 258-274.

8810. Clark, Cecily. "The Parlement of Foules.'" *EIC* 5(1955): 405-407.

8811. Cowgill, Bruce Kent. "The *Parlement of Foules* and the Body Politic." *JEGP* 74(1975): 315-335.

8812. Emslie, Macdonald. "Codes of Love and Class Distinction." *EIC* 5(1955): 1-17.

8813. ----------. "Nature Love in 'The Parlement of Foules.'" *EIC* 5(1955): 413-418.

8814. Frank, Robert W., Jr. "Structure and Meaning in the *Parlement of Foules*." *PMLA* 71 (1956): 530-539.

8815. Malone, Kemp. "Chaucer's Daughter of Cupid." *MLR* 45(1950): 63.

8816. Marshall, Linda E. "Osbern Mentions a Book." *PQ* 56(1977): 407-413.

8817. McDonald, Charles O. "An Interpretation of Chaucer's *Parlement of Foules*." *Speculum* 30(1955): 444-457.

8818. Silverstein, Theodore. "Chaucer's Modest and Homely Poem: The *Parlement*." *MP* 56 (1959): 270-276.

8819. Stillwell, Gardiner. "Chaucer's Eagles and Their Choice on February 14." *JEGP* 53(1954): 546-561.

8820. ----------. "Unity and Comedy in Chaucer's *Parlement of Foules*." *JEGP* 49(1950): 470-495.

8821. Uphaus, Robert W. "Chaucer's *Parlement* of *Foules*: Aesthetic Order and Individual Experience." *TSLL* 10(1968): 349-358.

8822. von Kreisler, Nicolai. "The *Locus Amoenus* and Eschalological Love in the *Parliament of Fouls* 204-10." *PQ* 50(1971): 16-22.

TROILUS AND CRISEYDE. 8823. Adams, John F. "Irony in Troilus' Apostrophe to the Vacant House of Criseyde." *MLQ* 24(1963): 61-65.

8824. apRoberts, Robert P. "The Boethian God and the Audience of the *Troilus*." *JEGP* 69 (1970): 425-436.

8825. ----------. "The Central Episode in Chaucer's Troilus." *PMLA* 77(1962): 373-385.

8826. ----------. "Criseyde's Infidelity and the Moral of the *Trolius*." *Speculum* 44(1969): 383-402.

8827. Beckman, Sabine. "Color Symbolism in *Troilus and Criseyde*." *CLA* 20(1976): 68-74.

8828. Bie, Wendy A. "Dramatic Chronology in *Troilus and Criseyde*." *ELN* 14(1976): 9-13.

8829. Bloomfield, Morton W. "Distance and Predestination in *Troilus and Criseyde*." *PMLA* 72 (1957): 14-26.

8830. ----------. "The Eighth Sphere: a Note on Chaucer's 'Troilus and Criseyde', v. 1809." *MLR* 53(1958): 408-410.

8831. Borthwick, Sister Mary Charlotte, F.C. S.P. "Antigone's Song as "Mirour" in Chaucer's *Troilus and Criseyde*." *MLQ* 22(1961): 227-235.

8832. Campbell, Jackson J. "A New *Troilus* Fragment." *PMLA* 73(1958): 305-308.

8833. Cassidy, Frederic G. "'Don Thyn Hood' in Chaucer's *Troilus*." *JEGP* 57(1958): 739-742.

8834. Clark, John W. "Dante and the Epilogue of Troilus." *JEGP* 50(1951): 1-10.

8835. Cook, Robert G. "Chaucer's Pandarus and the Medieval Ideal of Friendship." *JEGP* 69 (1970): 407-424.

8836. David, Alfred. "The Hero of the *Troilus*." *Speculum* 37(1962): 566-581.

8837. Davis, Norman. "The *Litera Troili*

and English Letters." *RES* 16(1965): 233-244.

8838. Devereux, James A, S. J. "A Note on *Troilus and Criseyde*, Book III, Line 1309." *PQ* 44(1965): 550-552.

8839. D'Evelyn, Charlotte. "Pandarus a Devil?" *PMLA* 71(1956): 275-279.

8840. di Pasquale, Pasquale, Jr. "'Sikernesse' and Fortune in *Troilus and Criseyde*." *PQ* 49(1970): 152-163.

8841. Friedman, John B. "Pandarus' Cushion and the '*pluma Sardanapalli*'." *JEGP* 75(1976): 41-55.

8842. Fry, Donald K. "Chaucer's *Zanzis* and a Possible Source for *Troilus and Criseyde*." *ELN* 9(1971): 81-85.

8843. Gallagher, Joseph E. "Criseyde's Dream of the Eagle: Love and War in *Troilus and Criseyde*." *MLQ* 36(1975): 115-132.

8844. Ganim, John M. "Tone and Time in Chaucer's *Troilus*." *ELH* 43(1976): 141-153.

8845. Gaylord, Alan T. "*Gentilesse* in Chaucer's *Troilus*." *SP* 61(1964): 19-34.

8846. Ham, Edward B. "Knight's Tale 38." *ELH* 17(1950): 252-261.

8847. Hatcher, Elizabeth R. "Chaucer and The Psychology of Fear: Troilus in Book V." *ELH* 40(1973): 307-324.

8848. Helterman, Jeffrey. "The Mark of Love in *Troilus and Criseyde*." *Comp L* 26(1974): 14-31.

8849. Hussey, S. S. "The Difficult Fifth Book of 'Triolus and Criseyde.'" *MLR* 67(1972): 721-729.

8850. Isaacs, Neil D. "Further Testimony in the Matter of Troilus." *SLI* 4,#2(1971): 11-27.

8851. Jordan, Robert N. "The Narrator in Chaucer's *Troilus*." *ELH* 25(1958): 237-257.

8852. Knapp, Peggy Ann. "Boccaccio and Chaucer on Cassandra." *PQ* 56(1977): 413-417.

8853. Longo, Joseph A. "The Double Time Scheme in Book II of Chaucer's *Troilus and Criseyde*." *MLQ* 22(1961): 37-40.

8854. Macey, Samuel L. "Dramatic Elements in Chaucer's *Troilus*." *TSLL* 12(1970): 307-323.

8855. Malarkey, Stoddard. "The 'Corones Tweyne': An Interpretation." *Speculum* 38(1963): 473-478.

8856. Markland, Murray F. "*Troilus and Criseyde*: The Inviolability of the Ending." *MLQ* 31(1970): 147-159.

8857. Matthews, Lloyd J. "Chaucer's Personification of Prudence in *Troilus* (v. 743-749): Sources in the Visual Arts and Manuscript Scholia." *ELN* 13(1976): 249-255.

8858. McCall, John P. "Five-Book Structure in Chaucer's *Troilus*." *MLQ* 23(1962): 297-308.

8859. ----------. "The Trojan Scene in Chaucer's *Troilus*." *ELH* 29(1962): 263-275.

8860. ---------- and George Rudisill, Jr. "The Parliament of 1386 and Chaucer's Trojan Parliament." *JEGP* 58(1959): 276-288.

8861. Moorman, Charles. "'Once More Unto the Breach': The Meaning of *Trolius and Criseyde*." *SLI* 4,#2(1971): 61-71.

8862. Nagarajan, S. "The Conclusion to Chaucer's *Troilus and Criseyde*." *EIC* 13(1963): 1-8.

8863. O'Connor, John J. "The Astronomical Dating of Chaucer's. *Troilus*." *JEGP* 55(1956): 556-562.

8864. Owen, Charles A., Jr. "Mimetic Form in the Central Love Scene of *Troilus and Criseyde*." *MP* 67(1969): 125-132.

8865. ----------. "The Significance of Chaucer's Revisions of *Troilus and Creseyde*." *MP* 55(1957): 1-5.

8866. Pratt, Robert A. "Chaucer and *Le Roman de Troyle et de Criseida*." *SP* 53(1956): 509-539.

8867. ----------. "Chaucer's 'Natal Jove' and 'Seint Jerome Agayn Jovian.'" *JEGP* 61(1962): 244-248.

8868. Reiss, Edmund. "Troilus and the Failure of Understanding." *MLQ* 29(1968): 131-144.

8869. Robertson, D. W., Jr. "Chaucerian Tragedy." *ELH* 19(1952): 1-37.

8870. Saintonge, Constance. "In Defense of Criseyde." *MLQ* 15(1954): 312-320.

8871. Scott, Forrest S. "The Seventh Sphere: a Note on "Troilus and Creseyde.'" *MLR* 51(1956): 2-5.

8872. Sharrock, Roger. "Second Thoughts: C. S. Lewis on Chaucer's *Troilus*." *EIC* 8(1958): 123-137.

8873. Schibanoff, Susan. "Argus and Argyve: Etymology and Characterization in Chaucer's Troilus." *Speculum* 51(1976): 647-658.

8874. ----------. "Criseyde's 'Impossible' Aubes." *JEGP* 76(1977): 326-333.

8875. ----------. "Prudence and Artificial Memory in Chaucer's *Troilus*." *ELH* 42(1975): 507-517.

8876. Smyser, H. M. "The Domestic Background of *Troilus and Criseyde*." *Speculum* 31 (1956): 297-315.

8877. Stroud, Theodore A. "Boethius' Influence on Chaucer's *Troilus*." *MP* 49(1951): 1-9.

8878. Sundwall, McKay. "Deiphobus and Helen: A Tantalizing Hint." *MP* 73(1975): 151-156.

8879. ----------. "The *Destruction of Troy*, Chaucer's *Troilus and Criseyde*, and Lydgate's *Troy Book*." *RES* 26(1975): 313-316.

8880. Taylor, Davis. "The Terms of Love: A Study of Troilus's Style." *Speculum* 51(1976): 69-90.

8881. Wenzel, Siegfried. "Chaucer's Troilus of Book IV." *PMLA* 79(1964): 542-547.

8882. Williams, George. "The 'Troilus and Criseyde' Frontspiece Again." *MLR* 57(1962): 173-178.

8883. Wimsatt, James I. "Medieval and Modern in Chaucer's *Troilus and Criseyde*." *PMLA* 92(1977): 203-216.

8884. Witlieb, Bernard L. "Chaucer and a French Story of Thebes." *ELN* 11(1973): 5-9.

8885. Wood, Chauncey. "On Translating Chaucer's *Troilus and Criseyde*, Book III, Lines 12-13." *ELN* 11(1973): 9-14.

See also 8182.

CHESTER CYCLE. 8886. Bryant, Joseph Allen, Jr. "Chester's Sermon for Catechumens." *JEGP* 53(1954): 399-402.

8887. Martin, Leslie Howard. "Comic Eschatology in the Chester Coming of Antichrist." *CD* 5(1971): 163-176.

8888. Travis, Peter W. "The Credal Design

of the Chester Cycle." *MP* 73(1976): 229-243.

8889. ----------. "The Dramatic Strategies of Chester's Passion Pagina." *CD* 8(1974): 275-289.

See also 8228, 8235.

THE CLOUD OF UNKNOWING. 8890. Burrow, J. A. "Fantasy and Language in *The Cloud of Unknowing*." *EIC* 27(1977): 283-298.

8891. Hodgson, Phyllis. "Walter Hilton and 'The Cloud of Unknowing': A Problem of Authority Reconsidered." *MLR* 50(1955): 395-406.

CRONICA. 8892. Robbins, Rossell Hope. "Victory at Whitby, A. D. 1451 [with text]." *SP* 67(1970): 495-504.

CROPHILL, JOHN. 8893. Robbins, Rossell Hope. "John Crophill's Ale-Pots." *RES* 20(1969): 182-189.

CURSOR MUNDI. 8894. Buehler, Philip. "The *Cursor Mundi* and Herman's *Bible*—Some additional Parallels." *SP* 61(1964): 485-499.

DE BURY, RICHARD. 8895. Cheney, Christopher R. "Richard de Bury, Borrower of Books." *Speculum* 48(1973): 325-328.

DISPUTISOUN. 8896. Ackoman, Robert W. "*The Debate of the Body and the Soul* and Parochial Christianity." *Speculum* 37(1962): 541-565.

DOUGLAS, GAVIN. 8897. Bawcutt, Priscilla. "Gavin Douglas and Chaucer." *RES* 21(1970): 401-422.

8898. Blyth, Charles R. "Gavin Douglas' Prologues of Natural Description." *PQ* 49(1970): 164-177.

8899. Dearing, Bruce. "Gavin Douglas' *Eneados*: A Reinterpretation." *PMLA* 67(1952): 845-862.

8900. Ridley, Florence H. "Did Gawin Douglas Write *King Hart*?" *Speculum* 34(1959): 402-412.

See also 8283, 11276.

DUNBAR, WILLIAM. 8901. Eddy, Elizabeth Roth. "Sir Thopas and Sir Thomas Norny: Romance Parody in Chaucer and Dunbar." *RES* 22(1971): 401-409.

8902. Fox, Denton. "The Chronology of William Dunbar." *PQ* 39(1960): 413-425.

8903. ----------. "Dunbar's *The Golden Targe*." *ELH* 26(1959): 311-334.

8904. Hyde, Isabel. "Primary Sources and Associations of Dunbar's Aureate Imagery." *MLR* 51 (1956): 481-492.

8905. Kinghorn, A. M. "Dunbar and Villon— A Comparison and a Contrast." *MLR* 62(1967): 195-208.

8906. Morgan, Edwin. "Dunbar and the Language of Poetry." *EIC* 2(1952): 138-158.

8907. Rigg, H. G. "William Dunbar: The 'Fenyeit Freir.'" *RES* 14(1963): 269-273.

8908. Shuffelton, Frank. "An Imperial Flower: Dunbar's *The Goldyn Targe* and the Court Life of James IV of Scotland." *SP* 72(1975): 193-207.

8909. Smith, A. J. "Incumbent Poets." *MLQ* 29(1968): 341-350.

8910. Wordsworth, Jonathan, and Isabel Hyde. "Dunbar's 'Quod Cinis Es': A Note and a Reply." *MLR* 54(1959): 223.

See also 8180, 8207.

ERGHOME, JOHN. 8911. Meyvaert, Paul. "John Erghome and the *Vaticinium Roberti Bridlington*." *Speculum* 41(1966): 656-664.

EVERYMAN. 8912. Adolf, Helen. "From *Everyman* and *Elckerlijc* to Hofmannsthal and Kafke." *Comp L* 9(1957): 204-214.

8913. Conley, John. "The Doctrine of Friendship in *Everyman*." *Speculum* 44(1969): 374-382.

8914. Ryan, Lawrence V. "Doctrine and Dramatic Structure in *Everyman*." *Speculum* 32 (1957): 722-735.

8915. Schreiber, Earl G. "*Everyman* in America." *CD* 9(1975): 99-115.

8916. Van Laan, Thomas F. "*Everyman*: A Structural Analysis." *PMLA* 78(1963): 465-475.

8917. Velz, John W. "Episodic Structure in Four Tudor Plays: A Virtue of Necessity." *CD* 6(1972): 87-102.

See Also 8278.

FITZRALPH, RICHARD. See 8207.

FORTESCUE, JOHN. 8918. Gill, Paul E. "Politics and Propaganda in Fifteenth-Century England: The Polemical Writings of Sr. John Fortescue." *Speculum* 46(1971): 333-347.

THE FOX AND THE WOLF. 8919. Bercovitch, Sacvan. "Clerical Satire in Þe Vox and Þe Wolf." *JEGP* 65(1966): 287-294.

8920. von Kreisler, Nicolai. "Satire in *The Vox and the Wolf*." *JEGP* 69(1970): 650-658.

FRATERNITY OF DRINKERS. 8921. Robbins, Rossell Hope. "'The Fraternity of Drinkers' [text]." *SP* 47(1950): 35-41.

GEOFFREY OF MONMOUTH. 8922. Caldwell, Robert A. "The 'History of the Kings of Britain' in College of Arms MS. Arundel XXII." *PMLA* 69 (1954): 643-654.

8923. ----------. "Wace's *Roman de Brut* and the *Variant Version* of Geoffrey of Monmouth's *Historia Regum Britanniae*." *Speculum* 31(1956): 675-682.

8924. Ditmas, E. M. R. "A Reappraisal of Geoffrey of Monmouth's Allusions to Cornwall." *Speculum* 48(1973): 510-532.

8925. Keller, Hans E. "Two Toponymical Problems in Geoffrey of Monmouth and Wace: *Estrusia* and *Siesia*." *Speculum* 49(1974): 687-698.

8926. Matthews, William. "Where Was Siesia-Sessoyne?" *Speculum* 49(1974): 680-686.

8927. Schlauch, Margaret. "Geoffrey of Monmouth and Early Polish Historiography: A Supplement." *Speculum* 44(1969): 258-263.

8928. Williams, Schafer. "Geoffrey of Monmouth and the Canon Law." *Speculum* 27(1952): 184-190.

GOWER, JOHN. 8929. Baker, Denise N. "The Priesthood of Genius: A Study of the Medieval Tradition." *Speculum* 51(1976): 277-291.

8930. Bennett, J. A. W. "Caxton and Gower." *MLR* 45(1950): 215-216.

8931. Coffman, George R. "John Gower, Mentor for Royalty: Richard II." *PMLA* 69(1954): 953-964.

8932. Dean, James. "Time Past and Time Present in Chaucer's Clerk's Tale and Gower's *Confessio Amantis*." *ELH* 44(1977): 401-418.

8933. Dwyer, J. B., S.J. "Gower's *Mirour* and Its French Sources: A Reexamination of Evidence." *SP* 48(1951): 482-505.

8934. Fisher, John H. "A Calendar of Documents Relating to the Life of John Gower the

Poet." *JEGP* 58(1959): 1-23.

8935. Fison, Peter. "The Poet in John Gower." *EIC* 8(1958): 16-26.

8936. Goolden, P. "Antiochus's Riddle in Gower and Shakespeare." *RES* 6(1955): 245-251.

8937. Murphy, James J. "John Gower's *Confessio Amantis* and the First Discussion of Rhetoric in the English Language." *PQ* 41(1962): 401-411.

8938. Pearsall, Derek. "Gower's Narrative Art." *PMLA* 81(1966): 475-484.

8939. Schueler, Donald G. "Gower's Characterization of Genius in the *Confessio Amantis*." *MLQ* 33(1972): 240-256.

8940. Weiher, Carol. "Chaucer's and Gower's Stories of Lucretia and Virginia." *ELN* 14(1976): 7-9.

See also 8180, 8207.

GROSSETESTE, ROBERT. 8941. Dales, Richard C. "Adam Marsh, Robert Gosseteste, and the Treatise on the Tides." *Speculum* 52(1977): 900-901.

8942. ----------. "The Authorship of the *Questio de fluxer et refluxer moris*." *Speculum* 52(1977): 582-588.

8943. ----------, and Servus Gieben, O.F.M. "The Prooemium to Robert Grosseteste's *Hexaemeron*." *Speculum* 43(1968): 451-461.

HAVELOCK THE DANE. 8944. Hanning, Robert W. "*Havelok the Dane*: Structure, Symbols, Meaning." *SP* 64(1967): 586-605.

8945. Reiss, Edmund. "*Havelok the Dane* and Norse Mythology." *MLQ* 27(1966): 115-124.

8946. Staines, David. "*Havelok the Dane*: A Thirteenth-Century Handbook for Princes." *Speculum* 51(1976): 602-623.

8947. Weiss, Judith. "Structure and Characterization in *Havelok the Dane*." *Speculum* 44(1969): 247-257.

HENRYSON, ROBERT. 8948. Aswell, E. Duncan. "The Role of Fortune in *The Testament of Cresseid*." *PQ* 46(1967): 471-487.

8949. Burrow, J. A. "Henryson: *The Preaching of the Swallow*." *EIC* 25(1975): 25-37.

8950. Clark, George. "Henryson and Aesop: The Fable Transformed." *ELH* 43(1976): 1-18.

8951. Crowne, David K. "A Date for the Composition of Henryson's Fables." *JEGP* 61(1962): 583-590.

8952. Duncan, Douglas. "Henryson's *Testament of Cresseid*." *EIC* 11(1961): 128-135.

8953. Elliott, Charles. "Two Notes on Henryson's *Testament of Cressid*." *JEGP* 54(1955): 241-254.

8954. Fox, Denton. "Henryson and Caxton." *JEGP* 67(1968): 586-593.

8955. ----------. "Henryson's *Fables*." *ELH* 29(1962): 337-356.

8956. ----------. "Henryson's 'Sum Practysis of Medecyne.'" *SP* 69(1972): 453-460.

8957. Friedman, John Block. "Henryson, The Friars, and the *Confessio Reynardi*." *JEGP* 66(1967): 550-561.

8958. Harth, Sydney. "Henryson Reinterpreted." *EIC* 11(1961): 471-480.

8959. Hume, Kathryn. "Leprosy or Syphilis in Henryson's *Testament of Cresseid*?" *ELN* 6 (1969): 242-245.

8960. Kreisler, Nicolai. "Henryson's

Visionary Fable: Tradition and Craftsmanship in *The Lyoun and the Mous*." *TSLL* 15(1973): 391-403.

8961. Louis, Kenneth R. R. Gros. "Robert Henryson's *Orpheus and Eurydice* and the Orpheus Traditions of the Middle Ages." *Speculum* 41(1966): 643-655.

8962. MacDonald, Donald. "Henryson and Chaucer: Cock and Fox." *TSLL* 8(1967): 451-461.

8963. Murtaugh, Daniel M. "Henryson's Animals." *TSLL* 14(1972): 405-421.

8964. Patterson, Lee W. "Christian and Pagan in *The Testament of Cresseid*." *PQ* 52(1973): 696-714.

8965. Rowland, Beryl. "The 'Seiknes Incurabill' in Henryson's *Testament of Cressid*." *ELN* 1(1964): 175-177.

8966. Sklute, Larry M. "Phoebus Descending: Rhetoric and Moral Vision in Henryson's Testament of Cresseid." *ELH* 44(1977): 189-204.

8967. Spearing, A. C. "*The Testament of Cresseid* and the 'High Concise Style'." *Speculum* 37(1962): 208-225.

See also 8207, 8283.

HILTON, WALTER. See 8891, 9003.

HOCCLEVE, THOMAS. 8968. Mitchell, Jerome. "The Autobiographical Element in Hoccleve." *MLQ* 28(1967): 269-284.

8969. ----------. "Hoccleve's Supposed Friendship with Chaucer." *ELN* 4(1966): 9-12.

8970. Rigg, A. G. "Hoccleve's *Complaint* and Isidore of Seville." *Speculum* 45(1970): 564-574.

See also 9188.

JAMES I OF SCOTLAND. 8971. Ebin, Lois A. "Boethius, Chaucer, and *The Kingis Quair*." *PQ* 53 (1974): 321-341.

8972. MacQueen, John. "Tradition and the Interpretation of the *Kingis Quair*." *RES* 12 (1961): 117-131.

8973. Preston, John. "Fortunys Exiltree. A Study of *The Kingis Quair*." *RES* 7(1956): 339-347.

8974. Rohrberger, Mary. "*The Kingis Quair*." *TSLL* 2(1960): 292-302.

See also 8283.

JOHN OF GAUNT. 8975. Friedman, Donald M. "John of Gaunt and the Rhetoric of Frustration." *ELH* 43(1976): 279-299.

JULIAN OF NORWICH. 8976. Lawlor, John. "A Note on the *Revelations* of Julian of Norwich." *RES* 2(1951): 255-258.

8977. Windeatt, B. A. "Julian of Norwich and Her Audience." *RES* 28(1977): 1-17.

LANGLAND, WILLIAM. 8978. Adams, John F. "*Piers Plowman* and the Three Ages of Man." *JEGP* 61(1962): 23-41.

8979. Adams, Robert. "Langland and the Liturgy Revisited." *SP* 73(1976): 266-284.

8980. Alford, John Alexander. "A Note on *Piers Plowman* B. xviii. 390: 'Til *Parce* It Hote.'" *MP* 69(1972): 323-325.

8981. ----------. "The Role of the Quotations in *Piers Plowman*." *Speculum* 52(1977): 80-99.

8982. ----------. "Some Unidentified Quotations in *Piers Plowman*." *MP* 72(1975): 390-399.

8983. Bloomfield, Morton W. "The Pardons of Pamplona and the Pardoner of Rounceval:

Piers Plowman B XVII 252." *PQ* 35(1956): 60-68.

8984. Burrow, John. "The Action of Langland's Second Vision." *EIC* 15(1965): 247-268.

8985. Clutterbuck, Charlotte. "Hope and Good Works: *Leaute* in the C-Text of *Piers Plowman*." *RES* 28(1977): 129-140.

8986. Davlin, Sister Mary Clemente, O.P. "Kynde Knowyng as a Major Theme in *Piers Plowman*." *RES* 22(1971): 1-19.

8987. Donaldson, E. T. "The Texts of *Piers Plowman*: Scribes and Poets." *MP* 50(1953): 269-273.

8988. Dunning, T. P., C. M. "The Structure of the B-Text of *Piers Plowman*." *RES* 7(1956): 225-237.

8989. Eliason, Mary. "The Peasant and the Lawyer." *SP* 48(1951): 506-526.

8990. Fowler, D. C. "Contamination in Manuscripts of the A-Text of *Piers the Plowman*." *PMLA* 66(1951): 495-504.

8891. ----------. "The Relationship of the Three Texts of *Piers the Plowman*." *MP* 50(1952): 5-22.

8992. Fowler, David C. "A New Interpretation of the A and B Texts of *Piers Plowman*." *MP* 71(1974): 393-404.

8993. Frank, Robert W., Jr. "The Conclusion of *Piers Plowman*." *JEGP* 49(1950): 309-316.

8994. ----------. "The Pardon Scene in *Piers Plowman*." *Speculum* 26(1951): 317-331.

8995. Gupta, Josodhara Sen. "*Piers Plowman*." *EIC* 13(1963): 201-202.

8996. Hamilton, A. C. "Spenser and Langland." *SP* 55(1958): 533-548.

8997. Harwood, Britton J. "'Clergye' and the Action of the Third Vision in *Piers Plowman*." *MP* 70(1973): 279-290.

8998. ----------. "Langland's *Kynde Wit*." *JEGP* 75(1976): 330-336.

8999. ----------. "*Liberum-Arbitrium* in the C-Text of *Piers Plowman*." *PQ* 52(1973): 680-695.

9000. Hill, Thomas D. "The Light that Blew the Saints to Heaven: *Piers Plowman* B, V. 495-503." *RES* 24(1973): 444-449.

9001. Hoffman, Richard L. "The Burning of 'Boke' in *Piers Plowman*." *MLQ* 25(1964): 57-65.

9002. Huppé, Bernard F. "*Petrus Id Est Christus*: Word Play in *Piers Plowman*, The B-Text." *ELH* 17(1950): 163-190.

9003. Hussey, S. S. "Langland, Hilton, and the Three Lives." *RES* 7(1956): 132-150.

9004. ----------. "Langland's Reading of Alliterative Poetry." *MLR* 60(1965): 163-170.

9005. Jeremy, Sister Mary. "'Leggis A-Leary,' *Piers Plowman*, A VIII, 114." *ELN* 1(1964): 250-251.

9006. Kaske, R. E. "'*Ex vi transicionis*' and Its Passage in *Piers Plowman*." *JEGP* 62(1963): 32-60.

9007. ----------. "*Gigas* the Giant in *Piers Plowman*." *JEGP* 56(1957): 177-185.

9008. ----------. "Langland's Walnut-Simile." *JEGP* 58(1959): 650-654.

9009. ----------. "A Note on *Bras* in *Piers Plowman*, A, III, 189; B, III, 195." *PQ* 31(1952): 427-430.

9010. ----------. "The Use of Simple Figures of Speech in *Piers Plowman* B: A Study in the Figurative Expression of Ideas and Opinions." *SP* 48(1951): 571-600.

9011. Kean, P. M. "Langland on the Incarnation." *RES* 16(1965): 349-363.

9012. ----------. "Love, Law, and *Lewte* in *Piers Plowman*." *RES* 15(1964): 241-260.

9013. King, John N. "Robert Crowley's Editions of *Piers Plowman*: A Tudor Apocalypse." *MP* 73(1976): 342-352.

9014. Kratins, Ojars. "*Piers Plowman* and Arthurian Romance." *EIC* 13(1963): 304.

9015. Lawlor, John. "The Imaginative Unity of *Piers Plowman*." *RES* 8(1957): 113-126.

9016. ----------. "'Piers Plowman': the Pardon Reconsidered." *MLR* 45(1950): 449-458.

9017. Martin, Jay. "Wil as Fool and Wanderer in *Piers Plowman*." *TSLL* 3(1962): 535-548.

9018. McLeod, Susan H. "The Tearing of the Pardon in *Piers Plowman*." *PQ* 56(1977): 14-26.

9019. Meroney, Howard. "The Life and Death of Long Wille." *ELH* 17(1950): 1-35.

9020. Middleton, Anne. "Two Infinities: Grammatical Metaphor in *Piers Plowman*." *ELH* 39 (1972): 169-188.

9021. Mitchell, A. G., and G. H. Russell. "The Three Texts of 'Piers the Plowman'." *JEGP* 52(1953): 445-456.

9022. Orrick, Allan H. "*Declynede*, Passus IV, 1. 133, *Piers the Plowman*, A-Text." *PQ* 35 (1956): 213-215.

9023. Paull, Michael R. "Mahomet and the Conversion of the Heathen in *Piers Plowman*." *ELN* 10(1972): 1-8.

9024. Quirk, Randolph. "Langland's Use of *Kind Wit* and *Inwit*." *JEGP* 52(1953): 182-188.

9025. ----------. "Vis Imaginativa." *JEGP* 53(1954): 81-83.

9026. Riach, Mary. "Langland's Dreamer and the Transformation of the Third Vision." *EIC* 19 (1969): 6-18.

9027. Risse, Robert G. "The Augustinian Paraphrase of Isaiah 14. 12-14 in *Piers Plowman* and the Commentary on the *Fables* of Avianus." *PQ* 45(1966): 712-717.

9028. Schroeder, Mary C. "The Character of Conscience in *Piers Plowman*." *SP* 67(1970): 13-30.

9029. ----------. "*Piers Plowman*: The Tearing of the Pardon." *PQ* 49(1970): 8-18.

9030. Schweitzer, Edward C. "'Half a Laumpe Lyne in Latyne' and Patience's Riddle in *Piers Plowman*." *JEGP* 73(1974): 313-327.

9031. Spearing, A. C. "The Development of a Theme in *Piers Plowman*." *RES* 11(1960): 241-253.

9032. ----------. "Verbal Repetition in *Piers Plowman* B and C." *JEGP* 62(1963): 722-737.

9033. Suddaby, Elizabeth. "The Poem *Piers Plowman*." *JEGP* 54(1955): 91-103.

9034. Vasta, Edward. "Truth, the Best Treasure, in *Piers Plowman*." *PQ* 44(1965): 17-29.

9035. Wesling, Donald. "Eschatology and the Language of Satire in *Piers Plowman*." *Criticism* 10(1968): 277-289.

9036. Woolf, Rosemary. "Some Non-Medieval Qualities of *Piers Plowman*." *EIC* 12(1962): 111-125.

See also 8207, 8278.

LATIMER, HUGH. 9037. Kelly, Robert L.

"Hugh Latimer as Piers Plowman." *SEL* 17(1977): 13-26.

LAY OF SORROW. 9038. Wilson, Kenneth G. "*The Lay of Sorrow* and *The Lufaris Complaynt*: An Edition [with text]." *Speculum* 29(1954): 708-726.

LAYAMON. 9039. Baumann, Walter. "Pound and Layamon's *Brut*." *JEGP* 68(1969): 265-276.

9040. Davies, H. S. "Layamon's Similes." *RES* 11(1960): 129-142.

9041. Stroud, Theodore A. "Scribal Editing in Lawman's *Brut*." *JEGP* 51(1952): 42-48.

LIFE OF ADAM AND EVE. 9042. Bliss, A. J. "The Auchinleck *Life of Adam and Eve*." *RES* 7(1956): 406-409.

LOVE, NICHOLAS. 9043. Zeeman, Elizabeth. "Nicholas Love—A Fifteenth-Century Translator." *RES* 6(1955): 113-127.

9044. ----------. "Punctuation in an Early Manuscript of Love's *Mirror*." *RES* 7 (1956): 11-18.

LOVELICH, HERRY. 9045. Ackerman, Robert W. "Herry Lovelich's *Merlin*." *PMLA* 67(1952): 473-484.

LUDUS COVENTRIAE. 9046. Bryant, Joseph Allen, Jr. "The Function of *Ludus Coventriae* 14." *JEGP* 52(1953): 340-345.

9047. Carr, Sherwyn T. "The Middle English Nativity Cherry Tree: The Dissemination of a Popular Motif." *MLQ* 36(1975): 133-147.

9048. Coletti, Theresa. "Devotional Iconography in the N-Town Marian Plays." *CD* 11(1977): 22-44.

9049. Fry, Timothy, O. S. B. "The Unity of the *Ludus Coventriae*." *SP* 48(1951): 527-570.

9050. Mills, David. "Concerning a Stage Direction in the *Ludus Coventriæ*." *ELN* 11(1974): 162-164.

9051. Poteet, Daniel P., II. "Time, Eternity, and Dramatic Form in *Ludus Coventriae* 'Passion Play I.'" *CD* 8(1974): 369-385.

9052. Reid, S. W. "Two Emendations in 'Passion Play II' of the *Ludus Coventriæ*." *ELN* 11(1973): 86-87.

See also 8228.

LUFARIS COMPLAYNT. See 9038.

LYDGATE, JOHN. 9053. Ayers, Robert W. "Medieval History, Moral Purpose, and the Structure of Lydgate's *Siege of Thebes*." *PMLA* 73(1958): 463-474.

9054. Bühler, Curt F. "The *Assembly of Gods* and Christine de Pisan." *ELN* 4(1967): 251-254.

9055. Combellack, C. R. B. "The Composite Catalogue of *The Sege of Troye*." *Speculum* 26 (1951): 624-634.

9056. Edwards, A. S. G., and A. W. Jenkins. "Lydgate's *Life of Our Lady*: An Unedited Manuscript." *ELN* 9(1971): 1-3.

9057. Klinefelter, Ralph A. "A Newly Discovered Fifteenth-Century English Manuscript." *MLQ* 14(1953): 3-6.

9058. ----------. "'The Siege of Calais': A New Text." *PMLA* 67(1952): 888-895.

9059. Parr, Johnstone. "The Astronomical Date of Lydgate's *Life of our Lady*." *PQ* 50(1971): 120-125.

9060. ----------. "Astronomical Dating for Some of Lydgate's Poems." *PMLA* 67(1952): 251-258.

9061. Robbins, Rossell Hope. "A New Lydgate Fragment." *ELN* 5(1968): 243-247.

9062. Trapp, J. B. "Verses by Lydgate at Long Melford." *RES* 6(1955): 1-11.

See also 8314, 9299.

MALORY, THOMAS. 9063. Davies, R. T. "Malory's Launcelot and the Noble Way of the World." *RES* 6(1955): 356-364.

9064. ----------. "Malory's 'Vertuouse Love.'" *SP* 53(1956): 459-469.

9065. Dichmann, Mary E. "Characterization in Malory's *Tale of Arthur and Lucius*." *PMLA* 65 (1950): 877-895.

9066. Donaldson, E. Talbot. "Malory and the Stanzaic *Le Morte Arthur*." *SP* 47(1950): 460-472.

9067. Field, P. J. C. "Description and Narration in Malory." *Speculum* 43(1968): 476-486.

9068. Hartung, Albert E. "Narrative Technique, Characterization, and the Sources in Malory's 'Tale of Sir Lancelot.'" *SP* 70(1973): 252-268.

9069. Hynes-Berry, Mary. "Malory's Translation of Meaning: *The Tale of Sankgreal*." *SP* 74(1977): 243-257.

9070. Kennedy, Edward D. "The Arthur-Guenevere Relationship in Malory's *Morte Darthur*." *SLI* 4,#2(1971): 29-40.

9071. ----------. "Malory and the 'Marriage of Edward IV.'" *TSLL* 12(1970): 155-162.

9072. Lappert, Stephen F. "Malory's Treatment of the Legend of Arthur's Survival." *MLQ* 36 (1975): 354-368.

9073. McCarthy, Terence. "Caxton and the Text of Malory's Book 2." *MP* 71(1973): 144-152.

9074. Moorman, Charles. "Courtly Love in Malory." *ELH* 27(1960): 163-176.

9075. ----------. "Internal Chronology in Malory's *Morte Darthur*." *JEGP* 60(1961): 240-249.

9076. ----------. "Malory's Treatment of the Sankgreall." *PMLA* 71(1956): 496-509.

9077. Olefsky, Ellyn. "Chronology, Factual Consistency, and the Problem of Unity in Malory." *JEGP* 68(1969): 57-73.

9078. Rumble, Thomas C. "Malory's *Balin* and the Question of Unity in the *Morte Darthur*." *Speculum* 41(1966): 68-85.

9079. ----------. "Malory's *Works* and Vinaver's Comments: Some Inconsistencies Resolved." *JEGP* 59(1960): 59-69.

9080. Schueler, Donald G. "The Tristram Section of Malory's *Morte Darthur*." *SP* 65(1968): 51-66.

9081. Snyder, Robert Lance. "Malory and 'Historical' Adaptation." *EL* 1(1974): 135-148.

9082. Tucker, P. E. "The Place of the 'Quest of the Holy Grail' in the 'Morte Darthur.'" *MLR* 48(1953): 391-397.

9083. ----------. "A Source for 'The Healing of Sir Urry' in the 'Morte Darthur.'" *MLR* 50(1955): 490-492.

9084. Whitteridge, Gweneth. "The Identity of Sr. Thomas Malory, Knight-Prisoner." *RES* 24 (1973): 257-265.

9085. Wilson, Robert H. "Addenda on Malory's Minor Characters." *JEGP* 55(1956): 563-587.

9086. ----------. "Malory's 'French Book' Again." *Comp L* 2(1950): 172-181.

9087. York, Ernest C. "The Duel of Chivalry in Malory's Book XIX." *PQ* 48(1969): 186-191.

9088. ----------. "Legal Punishment in Malory's *Le Mort Darthur*." *ELN* 11(1973): 14-21.
See also 8926.

MANKIND. 9089. Baker, Donald C. "The Date of *Mankind*." *PQ* 42(1963): 90-91.

9090. Clopper, Lawrence M. "*Mankind* and Its Audience." *CD* 8(1974): 347-355.

9091. Jones, Robert C. "Dangerous Sport: The Audience's Engagement with Vice in the Moral Interludes." *RD* n.s. 6(1973): 45-64.

9092. Stock, Lorraine Kochanske. "The Thematic and Structural Unity of *Mankind*." *SP* 72 (1975): 386-407.

MARY MAGDALENE. 9093. Velz, John W. "Sovereignty in the Digby *Mary Magdalene*." *CD* 2 (1968): 32-43.

MORTE ARTHURE. 9094. Boren, James L. "Narrative Design in the Alliterative *Morte Arthure*." *PQ* 56(1977): 310-319.

9095. Clark, Roy Peter. "*Alfin*: Invective in the Alliterative *Morte Arthure*." *ELN* 13(1976): 165-168.

9096. Finlayson, John. "*Morte Arthure*: The Date and a Source for the Contemporary References." *Speculum* 42(1967): 624-638.

9097. ----------. "Rhetorical 'Description' of Place in the Alliterative *Morte Arthure*." *MP* 61(1963): 1-11.

9098. Keiser, George R. "Edward III and the Alliterative *Morte Arthure*." *Speculum* 48 (1973): 37-51.

9099. Wertime, Richard A. "The Theme and Structure of the Stanzaic *Morte Arthur*." *PMLA* 87 (1972): 1075-1082.
See also 8926.

MUM AND THE SOTHSEGGER. 9100. Wenzel, Siegfried. "*Mum and the Sothsegger*." *SLN* 14(1976): 87-90.

NEWTON, HUMFREY. 9101. Cutler, John L. "The Versification of the 'Gawain Epigone' in Humfrey Newton's Poems." *JEGP* 51(1952): 562-570.

THE OWL AND THE NIGHTINGALE. 9102. Baldwin, Anne W. "Henry II and *The Owl and the Nightingale*." *JEGP* 66(1967): 207-229.

9103. Carson, M. Angela, O. S. U. "Rhetorical Structure in *The Owl and the Nightingale*." *Speculum* 42(1967): 92-103.

9104. Cawley, A. C. "Astrology in 'The Owl and the Nightingale.'" *MLR* 46(1951): 161-174.

9105. Colgrave, Bertram. "*The Owl* and the *Nightingale* and the 'Good Man from Rome'." *ELN* 4 (1966): 1-4.

9106. d'Ardenne, S. R. T. O. "*Smithes* in *The Owl and the Nightingale*." *RES* 9(1958): 41-43.

9107. Gottschalk, Jane. "*The Owl and the Nightingale*: Lay Preachers to a Lay Audience." *PQ* 45(1966): 657-667.

9108. Kinneavy, Gerald B. "Fortune, Providence, and the Owl." *SP* 64(1967): 655-664.

9109. Lumiansky, R. M. "Concerning *The Owl and the Nightingale*." *PQ* 32(1953): 411-417.

9110. Peterson, Douglas L. "*The Owl and the Nightingale* and Christian Dialectic." *JEGP* 55(1956): 13-26.

9111. Russell, J. C. "The Patrons of *The Owl and the Nightingale* ." *PQ* 48(1969): 178-185.

9112. Schleusener, Jay. "*The Owl and the Nightingale*: A Matter of Judgment." *MP* 70(1973): 185-189.

9113. Shippey, Thomas Alan. "Listening to the Nightingale." *Comp L* 22(1970): 46-60.

9114. Sisam, Celia. "The Broken Leaf in MS. Jesus College, Oxford, 29." *RES* 5(1954): 337-343.

PARLEMENT OF THE THRE AGES. 9115. Peck, Russell A. "The Careful Hunter in *The Parlement of Thre Ages*." *ELH* 39(1972): 333-341.

PASTON LETTERS. 9116. Davis, Norman. "A Paston Hand." *RES* 3(1952): 209-221.

9117. Jones, Kirkland C. "Biblical Sayings, Paraphrases, and Allusions in *The Paston Letters*." *CLA* 20(1976): 155-163.

PATIENCE: See *PEARL-POET*

PEARL-POET. 9118. Ackerman, Robert W. "'Pared out of Paper': *Gawain* 802 and *Purity* 1408." *JEGP* 56(1957): 410-417.

9119. Anderson, J. J. "The Prologue of *Patience*." *MP* 63(1966): 283-287.

9120. Andrew, Malcolm. "Jonah and Christ in *Patience*." *MP* 70(1973): 230-233.

9121. ----------. "*Patience*: The 'Munster Dor'." *ELN* 14(1977): 164-167.

9122. Baughan, Denver Ewing. "The Role of Morgan Le Fay in *Sir Gawain and the Green Knight*." *ELH* 17(1950): 241-251.

9123. Bazire, Joyce. "ME. $\bar{e}$ and $\bar{\varrho}$ in the Rhymes of *Sir Gawain and the Green Knight*." *JEGP* 51(1952): 234-235.

9124. Benson, Larry D. "The Source of the Beheading Episode in *Sir Gawain and the Green Knight*." *MP* 59(1961): 1-12.

9125. Bercovitch, Sacvan. "Romance and Anti-Romance in *Sir Gawain and the Green Knight*." *PQ* 44(1965): 30-37.

9126. Bishop, Ian. "The Significance of the 'Garlande Gay' in the Allegory of *Pearl*." *RES* 8(1957): 12-21.

9127. Blenker, Louis, O. S. B. "The Pattern of Traditional Images in Pearl." *SP* 68 (1971): 26-49.

9128. ----------. "Sin, Psychology, and the Structure of *Sir Gawain and the Green Knight*." *SP* 74(1977): 354-387.

9129. Bloomfield, Morton W. "*Sir Gawain and the Green Knight*: An Appraisal." *PMLA* 76 (1961): 7-19.

9130. Brewer, D. S. "The *Gawain*-Poet: A General Appreciation of the Four Poems." *EIC* 17 (1967): 130-142.

9131. Bowers, R. H. "*Gawain and the Green Knight* as Entertainment." *MLQ* 24(1963): 333-341.

9132. Burrow, John. "The Two Confession Scenes in *Sir Gawain and the Green Knight*." *MP* 57(1959): 73-79.

9133. Carson, Mother Angela, O. S. U. "Aspects of Elegy in the Middle English *Pearl*." *SP* 62(1965): 17-28.

9134. ----------. "The Green Chapel: Its Function and Its Meaning." *SP* 60(1963): 598-605.

9135. ----------. "The Green Knight's Name." *ELN* 1(1963): 84-90.

9136. ----------. "Morgain la Fée as the Principle of Unity in *Gawain and the Green Knight*." *MLQ* 23(1962): 3-16.

9137. Champion, Larry S. "Grace versus Merit in *Sir Gawain and the Green Knight*." *MLQ* 28

(1967): 413-425.

9138. Clark, Cecily. "The Green Knight
Shoeless: a Reconsideration." *RES* 6(1955): 174-
177.

9139. ----------. "*Sir Gawain and the
Green Knight*: Characterization by Syntax." *EIC*
16(1966): 361-374.

9140. Clark, John W. "'The *Gawain*-poet'
and the Substantival Adjective." *JEGP* 49(1950):
60-66.

9141. ----------. "On Certain 'Alliterative' and 'Poetic' Words in the Poems Attributed
to 'The *Gawain*-Poet.'" *MLQ* 12(1951): 387-398.

9142. Conley, John. "*Pearl* and a Lost
Tradition." *JEGP* 54(1955): 332-347.

9143. Curley, Michael J. "A Note on
Bertilak's Beard." *MP* 73(1975): 69-73.

9144. d'Ardenne, S. R. T. O. "'The Green
Count' and *Sir Gawain and the Green Knight*." *RES*
10(1959): 113-126.

9145. Davenport, W. A. "Sir Gawain's
Courteous 'Whoa!'" *ELN* 11(1973): 88-89.

9146. Davis, Norman. "A Note on *Pearl*."
RES 17(1966): 403-405.

9147. Diamond, Arlyn. "*Sir Gawain and the
Green Knight*: An Alliterative Romance." *PQ* 55
(1976): 10-29.

9148. Earl, James W. "Saint Margaret and
the Pearl Maiden." *MP* 70(1972): 1-8.

9149. Ebbs, John Dale. "Stylistic Manner-
isms of the *Gawain*-Poet." *JEGP* 57(1958): 522-525.

9150. Englehardt, George J. "The Predicament of Gawian." *MLQ* 16(1955): 218-225.

9151. Evans, W. O. "The Case for Sir
Gawain Re-opened." *MLR* 68(1973): 721-733.

9152. Field, P. J. C. "A Rereading of *Sir
Gawain and the Green Knight*." *SP* 68(1971): 255-
269.

9153. Finlayson, John. "*Pearl*: Landscape
and Vision." *SP* 71(1974): 314-343.

9154. Fowler, David C. "Cruxes in
Cleanness." *MP* 70(1973): 331-336.

9155. ----------. "On the Meaning of
Pearl, 139-40." *MLQ* 21(1960): 27-29.

9156. Friedman, Albert B. "Morgan le Fay
in *Sir Gawain and the Green Knight*." *Speculum* 35
(1960): 260-274.

9157. Ganim, John M. "Disorientation,
Style, and Consciousness in *Sir Gawain and the
Green Knight*." *PMLA* 91(1976): 376-384.

9158. Gatta, John, Jr. "Transformation
Symbolism and the Liturgy of the Mass in *Pearl*."
MP 71(1974): 243-256.

9159. Green, Richard Hamilton. "Gawain's
Shield and the Quest for Perfection." *ELH* 29
(1962): 121-139.

9160. Halverson, John. "Template Criticism: *Sir Gawain and the Green Knight*." *MP* 67
(1969): 133-139.

9161. Hamilton, Marie Padgett. "The Meaning of the Middle English *Pearl*." *PMLA* 70(1955):
805-824.

9162. ----------. "Notes on *Pearl*." *JEGP*
57(1958): 177-191.

9163. Heiserman, Arthur. "Gawain's Clean
Courtesy, or, The Task of Telling of True Love."
MLQ 27(1966): 449-457.

9164. ----------. "The Plot of *Pearl*."
PMLA 80(1965): 164-171.

9165. Hill, Ordelle G. "The Audience of
Patience." *MP* 66(1968): 103-109.

9166. ----------. "The Late-Latin *De Jona*
as a Source for *Patience*." *JEGP* 66(1967): 21-25.

9167. Hills, David Farley. "Gawain's
Fault in *Sir Gawain and the Green Knight*." *RES*
14(1963): 124-131.

9168. Hoffman, Stanton de Voren. "The
Pearl: Notes for an Interpretation." *MP* 58(1960):
73-80.

9169. Howard, Donald R. "Structure and
Symmetry in *Sir Gawain*." *Speculum* 39(1964): 425-
433.

9170. Johnson, Lynn Staley. "*Patience* and
the Poet's Use of Psalm 93." *MP* 74(1976): 67-71.

9171. Johnson, Wendell Stacy. "The Imagery
and Diction of 'The Pearl': Toward an Interpretation." *ELH* 20(1953): 161-180.

9172. Kelly, Ellen M. "Parallels between
the Middle English *Patience* and *Hymnus
Ieiunantium* of Prudentius." *ELN* 4(1967): 244-247.

9173. Kiteley, John F. "'The Endless Knot':
Magical Aspects of the Pentangle in *Sir Gawain
and the Green Knight*." *SLI* 4,#2(1971): 41-50.

9174. Lucas, Peter J. "*Pearl*'s Free-Flow-
ing Hair." *ELN* 15(1977): 94-95.

9175. Malarkey, Stoddard, and J. Barre
Toelken. "Gawain and the Green Girdle." *JEGP* 63
(1964): 14-20.

9176. Manning, Stephen. "A Psychological
Interpretation of *Sir Gawain and the Green
Knight*." *Criticism* 6(1964): 165-177.

9177. Markman, Alan M. "The Meaning of
Sir Gawain and the Green Knight." *PMLA* 72(1957):
574-586.

9178. Matouis, Ann. "*Gawain and the
Green Knight*: Flux and the Fayntyse of the
Flesche." *JNT* 1(1971): 43-48.

9179. McAlindon, T. "Magic, Fate, and
Providence in Medieval Narrative and *Sir Gawain
and the Green Knight*." *RES* 16(1965): 121-139.

9180. Mills, David. "An Analysis of the
Temptation Scenes in *Sir Gawain and the Green
Knight*." *JEGP* 67(1968): 612-630.

9181. Mills, M. "Christian Significance
and Romance Tradition in 'Sir Gawain and the
Green Knight.'" *MLR* 60(1965): 483-493.

9182. Moorman, Charles. "The Role of the
Narrator in *Patience*." *MP* 61(1963): 90-95.

9183. ----------. "The Role of the
Narrator in *Pearl*." *MP* 53(1955): 73-81.

9184. Neaman, Judith S. "Sir Gawain's
Covenant: Troth and *Timor Mortis*." *PQ* 55
(1976): 30-42.

9185. Nolan, Barbara, and David Farley-
Hills. "The Authorship of *Pearl*: Two Notes."
RES 22(1971): 295-302.

9186. Pace, George B. "Physiognomy and
Sir Gawain and the Green Knight." *ELN* 4(1967):
161-165.

9187. Pearsall, Derek A. "Rhetorical
'Descriptio' in 'Sir Gawain and the Green Knight.'"
MLR 50(1955): 129-134.

9188. Peterson, Clifford, and Edward Wilson.
"Hoccleve, the Old Hall Manuscript, Cotton Nero
A.X., and the *Pearl*-Poet." *RES* 28(1977): 49-55.

9189. Peterson, C. J. "*Pearl* and *St.
Erkenwald*: Some Evidence for Authorship." *RES*
25(1974): 49-53.

9190. ----------. "The *Pearl*-Poet and John Massey of Cotton, Cheshire." *RES* 25(1974): 257-266.

9191. Randall, Dale B. J. "Was the Green Knight a Friend?" *SP* 57(1960): 479-491.

9192. Reisner, Thomas Andrew. "The 'Cortaysye' Sequence in *Pearl*: A Legal Interpretation." *MP* 72(1975): 400-403.

9193. Revard, Carter. "A Note on Þe Fyrst fyne (*Pearl* 635)." *ELN* 1(1964): 164-166.

9194. Rigby, Marjory. "The Green Knight Shoeless Again," *RES* 7(1956): 173-174.

9195. Samson, Anne. "*Sir Gawain.*" *EIC* 18 (1968): 343-347.

9196. Savage, Henry L. "The Feast of Fools in *Sir Gawain and the Green Knight.*" *JEGP* 51 (1952: 537-544.

9197. Schleusener, Jay. "History and Action in *Patience.*" *PMLA* 86(1971): 959-965.

9198. ----------. *Patience*, Lines 35-40." *MP* 67(1969): 64-66.

9199. Shedd, Gordon M. "Knight in Tarnished Armour: The Meaning of 'Sir Gawain and the Green Knight.'" *MLR* 62(1967): 3-13.

9200. Shippey, T. A. "The Uses of Chivalry: 'Erec' and 'Gawain.'" *MLR* 66(1971): 241-250.

9201. Silverstein, Theodore. "*Sir Gawain*, Dear Brutus, and Britain's Fortunate Founding: A Study in Comedy and Convention." *MP* 62(1965): 189-206.

9202. ----------. "Sir Gawain in a Dilemma, or Keeping Faith with Marcus Tullius Cicero." *MP* 75(1977): 1-17.

9203. Sklute, Larry M. "Expectation and Fulfillment in *Pearl.*" *PQ* 52(1973): 663-608.

9204. Spearing, A. C. "Symbolic and Dramatic Development in *Pearl.*" *MP* 60(1962): 1-12.

9205. Stedman, Jane W. "The Genesis of *Patience.*" *MP* 66(1968): 48-58.

9206. Stern, Milton R. "An Approach to *The Pearl.*" *JEGP* 54(1955): 684-692.

9207. Stevens, Martin. "Laughter and Game in *Sir Gawain and the Green Knight.*" *Speculum* 47 (1972): 65-78.

9208. Tamplin, Ronald. "The Saints in *Sir Gawain and the Green Knight.*" *Speculum* 44 (1969): 403-420.

9209. Taylor, P. B. "Commerece and Comedy in *Sir Gawain.*" *PQ* 50(1971): 1-15.

9210. Turville-Petre, Thorlac, and Edward Wilson. "Hoccleve, 'Maister Massy' and the *Pearl*-Poet: Two Notes." *RES* 26(1975: 129-143.

9211. Tuttleton, James W. "The Manuscript Divisions of *Sir Gawain and the Green Knight.*" *Speculum* 41(1966): 304-310.

9212. Vasta, Edward. "*Pearl*: Immortal Flowers and the Pearl's Decay." *JEGP* 66(1967): 519-531.

9213. White, Robert B., Jr. "A Note on the Green Knight's Red Eyes (*GGK*, 304)." *ELN* 2(1965): 250-252.

9214. Williams, David. "The Point of *Patience.*" *MP* 68(1970): 127-136.

9215. Wright, Thomas L. "Sir Gawain in vayres." *PQ* 53(1974): 427-428.

9216. Wood, Ann Douglas. "The Pearl-Dreamer and the 'Hyne' in the Vineyard Parable." *PQ* 52(1973): 9-19.

See also 8197-8278.

PECHAM, JOHN. See 8325.
PIERS PLOWMAN. See WILLIAM LANGLAND.
PURITY. See *PEARL*-POET.

ROLLE, RICHARD. 9217. Alford, John A. "Biblical *Imitatio* in the Writings of Richard Rolle." *ELH* 40(1973): 1-23.

9218. Wilson, Sarah. "The Longleat Version of 'Love is Life.'" *RES* 10(1959): 337-346.

SAINT ERKENWALD. 9219. Benson, Larry D. "The Authorship of *St. Erkenwald.*" *JEGP* 64(1965): 393-405.

9220. McAlindon, T. "Hagiography into Art: A Study of *St. Erkenwald.*" *SP* 67(1970): 472-494.

9221. Petronella, Vincent F. "*St. Erkenwald*: Style as the Vehicle for Meaning." *JEGP* 66(1967): 532-540.

See also 9189.
SALISBURY, JOHN of. See 8551.
SAWLES WARDE. Johnston, G. K. W. "Two Passages in 'Sawles Warde.'" *MLR* 52(1957): 384-386.

SAYINGS OF ST. BERNARD. 9223. Cross, J. E. "*The Sayings of St. Bernard* and *Ubi Sount Qui ante Nos Fuerount.*" *RES* 9(1958): 1-7.

SIR CLEGES. 9224. Carry, Sherwyn T. "The Middle English Nativity Cherry Tree: The Dissemination of a Popular Motif." *MLQ* 36(1975: 133-147.

SIR GAWAIN AND THE GREEN KNIGHT. See *PEARL*-POET.

SIR ORFEO. 9225. Davies, Constance. "Classical Threads in 'Orfeo.'" *MLR* 56(1961): 161-166.

9226. Edwards, A. S. G. "'Sir Orfeo' 458-471 *SSF* 9(1972): 197-198.

9227. Friedman, John Block. "Eurydice, Heurodis, and the Noon-Day Demon." *Speculum* 41 (1966): 22-29.

9228. Hynes-Berry, Mary. "Cohesion in *King Horn* and *Sir Orfeo.*" *Speculum* 50(1975): 652-670.

9229. Knapp, James F. "The Meaning of *Sir Orfeo.*" *MLQ* 29(1968): 263-273.

9230. Louis, Kenneth R. R. Gros. "The Significance of Sir Orfeo's Self-Exile." *RES* 18 (1967): 245-252.

SIR TRISTREM. 9231. Rumble, Thomas C. "The Middle English *Sir Tristrem*: Toward a Reappraisal." *Comp L* 11(1959): 221-228.

9232. York, Ernest C. "Isolt's Ordeal: English Legal Customs in the Medieval Tristan Legend." *SP* 68(1971): 1-9.

SOUTH ENGLAND LEGENDARY. 9233. Boyd, Beverly. "A New Approach to the *South England Legendary.*" *PQ* 47(1968): 494-498.

THRE PRESTIS OF PEBLIS. 9234. Jack, R. D. S. "*The Thre Prestis of Peblis* and the Growth of Humanism in Scotland." *RES* 26(1975): 257-270.

TITUS AND VESPASIAN. 9235. Buler, Curt F. "The New Morgan Manuscript of *Titus and Vespasian.*" *PMLA* 76(1961): 20-24.

TOWNELEY CYCLE. 9236. Baird, Joseph L., and Amy Cassidy. "Humility and the Towneley Annunciation." *PQ* 52(1973): 301-306.

9237. Bernbrock, John E. "Notes on the Towneley Cycle *Slaying of Abel.*" *JEGP* 62(1963): 317-322.

9238. Brawer, Robert A. "The Dramatic Function of the Ministry Group in the Towneley Cycle."

CD 4(1970): 166-175.

9239. Earl, James W. "The Shape of Old Testament History in the Towneley Play." *SP* 69 (1972): 434-452.

9240. Maltman, Sister Nicholas, O. R. "Pilate—os malleatoris." *Speculum* 36(1961): 308-311.

9241. Manly, William M. "Shepherds and Prophets: Religious Unity in the Towneley *Secunda Pastorum*." *PMLA* 78(1963): 151-155.

9242. Paull, Michael. "The Figure of Mahomet in the Towneley Cycle." *CD* 6(1972): 187-204.

9243. Stevens, Martin. "The Composition of the Towneley *Talents* Play: A Linguistic Examination." *JEGP* 58(1959): 423-433.

9244. ----------. "The Missing Parts of the Towneley Cycle." *Speculum* 45(1970): 254-265.

9245. Tyson, Cynthia Haldenby. "Noah's Flood, the River Jordon, the Red Sea: Staging in the Towneley Cycle." *CD* 8(1974): 101-111.

9246. West, George A. "An Analysis of the Towneley Play of *Lazarus*." *PQ* 56(1977): 320-328.

See also 8433.

TREVET, NICHOLAS. 9247. Dean, Ruth J. "The Dedication of Nicholas Trevet's Commentary on Boethius." *SP* 63(1966): 593-603.

TREVISA, JOHN. 9248. Edwards, A. S. G. "A Sixteenth Century Version of Trevisa's *Polychronicon*." *ELN* 11(1973): 34-38.

9249. Fowler, David C. "John Trevisa and the English Bible." *MP* 58(1960): 81-98.

9250. ----------. "More About John Trevisa." *MLQ* 32(1971): 243-254.

USK, THOMAS. 9251. Heninger, S. K., Jr. "The Margarite-Pearl Allegory in Thomas Usk's *Testament of Love*." *Speculum* 32(1957): 92-98.

WAKEFIELD CYCLE. 9252. Brockman, Bennett A. "The Law of Man and the Peace of God: Judicial Process as Satiric Theme in the Wakefield *Mactacio Abel*." *Speculum* 49(1974): 699-707.

9253. Carpenter, Nan Cooke. "Music in the *Secunda Pastorum*." *Speculum* 26(1951): 698-700.

9254. Cawley, A. C. "The 'Grotesque Feast in the *Prima Pastorum*." *Speculum* 30(1955): 213-217.

9255. Cutts, John P. "The Shepherds' Gifts in *The Second Shepherds' Play* and Bosch's 'Adoration of the Magi.'" *CD* 4(1970): 120-124.

9256. Garder, John. "Theme and Irony in the Wakefield *Mactacio Abel*." *PMLA* 80(1965): 515-521.

9257. Helterman, Jeffrey. "Satan as Everyshepherd: Comic Metamorphosis in The Second Shepherds' Play." *TSLL* 12(1971): 515-530.

9258. Marshall, Linda E. "'Sacral Parody' in the *Secunda Pastorum*." *Speculum* 47(1972): 720-736.

9259. Ross, Lawrence J. "Symbol and Structure in *Secunda Pastorum*." *CD* 1(1967): 122-143.

9260. Sanders, Barry. "Who's Afraid of Jesus Christ? Games in the *Coliphizacio*." *CD* 2 (1968): 94-99.

9261. Schell, Edgar. "Seeing Through a Glass Darkly: The Action Imitated by the *Secunda Pastorum*." *MLQ* 37(1976): 3-14.

9262. Stevens, Martin. "The Dramatic Setting of the Wakefield *Annunciation*." *PMLA* 81(1966): 193-198.

9263. ----------. "Language as Theme in the Wakefield Plays." *Speculum* 52(1977): 100-117.

See also 8228, 8235.

WILSON, ROBERT. 9264. Pineas, Rainer. "Polemical Technique in *The Pedlars Prophecie*." *ELN* 6(1968): 90-94.

WISDOM. 9265. Gatch, Milton McC. "Mysticism and Satire in the Morality of *Wisdom*." *PQ* 53 (1974): 342-367.

9266. Hill, Eugene D. "The Trinitarian Allegory of the Moral Play of *Wisdom*." *MP* 73(1975): 121-135.

WOODFORD, WILLIAM. 9267. Doyle, Eric, O. F. M. "William, Woodford, O. F. M., and John Wyclif's *De Religione*." *Speculum* 50(1977): 329-340.

WYCLIF, JOHN. 9268. Dahmus, Joseph H. "John Wyclif and the English Government." *Speculum* 35(1960): 51-68.

9269. Hargreaves, Henry. "The Middle English Primers and the Wycliffite Bible." *MLR* 51(1956): 215-217.

9270. Knapp, Peggy Ann. "John Wyclif as Bible Translator, The Texts for the English Sermons." *Speculum* 46(1971): 713-720.

9271. Wawn, Andrew N. "Chaucer, Wyclif, and the Court of Apollo." *ELN* 10(1972): 15-20.

See also 8207, 9267.

WYNNERE AND WASTOURE. 9272. James, Jerry D. "The Undercutting of Conventions in *Wynnere and Wastoure*." *MLQ* 25(1964): 243-258.

WYNTOUN, ANDREW OF. 9273. Coldwell, David F. C. "Wyntoun's Anonymous Contributor." *JEGP* 58(1959): 39-48.

YORK CYCLE. 9274. Brawer, Robert A. "The Characterization of Pilate in the York Cycle Play." *SP* 69(1972): 289-303.

9275. Davidson, Clifford. "The Realism of the York Realist and the York Passion." *Speculum* 50(1975): 270-283.

9276. Dorrell, Margaret. "The Butchers', Saddlers', and Carpenters' Pageants: Misreadings of the York *Ordo*." *ELN* 13(1975): 1-4.

9277. Hanks, Dorrel T., Jr. "New Sources for York Play XLV, 'The Death of Mary': *Legenda Aurea* and Vincent's *Speculum Historiale*." *ELN* 14 (1976): 5-7.

9278. Hoy, James F. "On the Relationship of the Corpus Christi Plays to the Corpus Christi Procession at York." *MP* 71(1973): 166-168.

9279. Johnston, Alexandra F. "The Plays of the Religious Guilds of York: The Creed Play and the Peter Noster Play." *Speculum* 50(1975): 55-90.

9280. Mill, Anna J. "The York Plays of the Dying, Assumption, and Coronation of Our Lady." *PMLA* 65(1950): 866-876.

9281. Nelson, Alan H. "Principles of Processional Staging: York Cycle." *MP* 67(1970): 303-320.

9282. Reese, Jesse Byers. "Alliterative Verse in the York Cycle." *SP* 48(1951): 639-668.

9283. Robinson, J. W. "The Art of the York Realist." *MP* 60(1963): 241-251.

9284. ----------. "A Commentary on the York Play of the Birth of Jesus." *JEGP* 70(1971): 241-254.

9285. Wall, Carolyn. "York Pageant XLVI and Its Music." *Speculum* 46(1971): 689-712.

See also 8228, 8433.

SIXTEENTH CENTURY

GENERAL AND MISCELLANEOUS. 9286. Allen, Michael J. B. "The Chase: The Development of a Renaissance Theme." *Comp L* 20(1968): 301-312.

9287. Ayres, Philip J. "Degrees of Heresy: Justified Revenge and Elizabethan Narratives." *SP* 69(1972): 461-474.

9288. Baroway, Israel. "The Accentual Theory of Hebrew Prosody: A Further Study in Renaissance Interpretation of Biblical Form." *ELH* 17(1950): 115-135.

9289. Bateson, F. W. "Renaissance as Inflation." *EIC* 13(1963): 437.

9290. ----------. "Work in Progress II: Renaissance Literature." *EIC* 13(1963): 117-131.

9291. Bennett, Josephine Waters. "Britain among the Fortunate Isles." *SP* 53(1956): 114-140.

9292. Bercovitch, Sacvan. "Empedocles in the English Renaissance." *SP* 65(1968): 67-80.

9294. Caldwell, Mark L. "Allegory: The Renaissance Mode." *ELH* 44(1977): 580-600.

9295. Clements, Robert J. "Emblem Books on Literature's Role in the Revival of Learning." *SP* 54(1957): 85-100.

9296. ----------. "Princes and Literature: A Theme of Renaissance Emblem Books." *MLQ* 16 (1955): 114-123.

9297. Coldewey, John C. "Myles Blomefylde's Library: Another Book." *ELN* 14(1977): 249-250.

9298. Cochrane, Kirsty. "Orpheus Applied: Some Instances of his Importance in the Humanist View of Language." *RES* 19(1968): 1-13.

9299. Coogan, Robert, C. F. C. "Petrarch's Latin Prose and the English Renaissance." *SP* 68 (1971): 270-291.

9300. Cooper, J. P. "Renaissance as Inflation." *EIC* 13(1963): 435-437.

9301. Cutts, John P. "'Elizabeth Davenant 1624': Christ Church MS. Mus. 87." *RES* 10(1959): 26-37.

9302. Dieckmann, Liselotte. "Renaissance Hieroglyphics." *Comp L* 9(1957): 308-321.

9303. Dunlap, Rhodes. "The Allegorical Interpretation of Renaissance Literature." *PMLA* 82(1967): 39-44.

9304. Edgerton, William L. "The Calendar Year in Sixteenth-Century Printing." *JEGP* 59(1960): 439-449.

9305. Evans, Maurice. "Metaphor and Symbol in the Sixteenth Century." *EIC* 3(1953): 267-284.

9306. Frantz, David. "'Leud Priapians' and Renaissance Pornography." *SEL* 12(1972): 157-172.

9307. Giovanni, G. "Historical Realism and the Tragic Emotions in Renaissance Criticism." *PQ* 32(1953): 304-320.

9308. Hamilton, A. C. "The Modern Study of Renaissance English Literature: A Critical Survey." *MLQ* 26(1965): 150-183.

9309. Hazard, Mary E. "An Essay to Amplify 'Ornament': Some Renaissance Theory and Practice." *SEL* 16(1976): 15-32.

9310. Jayne, Sears. "Ficino and the Platonism of the English Renaissance." *Comp L* 4(1952): 214-238.

9311. Jensen, Ejner J. "The Wit of Renais-sance Satire." *PQ* 51(1972): 394-411.

9312. Jorgensen, Paul A. "Alien Military Doctrine in Renaissance England." *MLQ* 17(1956): 43-49.

9313. ----------. "Elizabethan Literature Today." *TSLL* 1(1960): 562-572.

9314. Kinney, Arthur F. "Rhetoric as Poetic: Humanist Fiction in the Renaissance." *ELH* 43(1976): 413-443.

9315. Levine, Mortimer. "Richard III—Usurper or Lawful King." *Speculum* 34(1959): 391-401.

9316. MacKinnon, M. H. M. "School Books Used at Eton College about 1600." *JEGP* 56(1957): 429-433.

9317. Matchett. William H. "The Integrity of 'Sir Patrick Spence.'" *MP* 68(1970): 25-31.

9318. May, Steven W. "'The French Primers': A Study in Renaissance Textual Transmission and Taste." *ELN* 9(1971): 102-108.

9319. Murrin, Michael. "Two Essays in Renaissance Literary History." *MLQ* 36(1975): 418-425.

9320. Nelson, William. "The Teaching of English in Tudor Grammar Schools." *SP* 49(1952): 119-143.

9321. Ong, Walter J., S. J. "Latin Language Study as a Renaissance Puberty Rite." *SP* 56(1959): 103-124.

9322. Pratt, S. M. "Antwerp and the Elizabethan Mind." *MLQ* 24(1963): 53-60.

9323. Pratt, Samuel M. "Jane Shore and the Elizabethans: Some Facts and Speculations." *TSLL* 11(1970): 1293-1306.

9324. Röstvig, Maren-Sofie. "Renaissance Numerology: Acrostics or Criticism?" *EIC* 16(1966): 6-21.

9325. Simpson, Percy, and I. A. Shapiro. "'The Mermaid Club': An answer and a rejoinder." *MLR* 46(1951): 58-63.

9326. Sisson, Charles J., and Arthur Broen. "'The Great Danseker': Literary Significance of a Chancery Suit." *MLR* 46(1951): 339-348.

9327. Sledd, James. "A Note on the Use of Renaissance Dictionaries." *MP* 49(1951): 10-15.

9328. Smith, A. J. "An Examination of Some Claims of Ramism." *RES* 7(1956): 348-359.

9329. Spencer, T. J. B. "Longinus in English Criticism: Influences before Milton." *RES* 8(1957): 137-143.

9330. Spencer, Terence. "Turks and Trojans in the Renaissance." *MLR* 47(1952): 330-333.

9331. Stein, Arnold. "On Elizabethan Wit." *SEL* 1,#1(1961): 75-91.

9332. Thomson, Patricia. "The Literature of Patronage, 1580-1630." *EIC* 2(1952): 267-284.

9333. Trousdale, Marion. "A Possible Renaissance View of Form." *ELH* 40(1973): 179-204.

9334. Vos, Alvin. "Humanistic Standards of Diction in the Inkhorn Controversy." *SP* 73(1976): 376-396.

9335. Williams, Franklin B. "Renaissance Names in Masquerade." *PMLA* 69(1954): 314-323.

9336. Wood, James O. "'*Maluolios* a Peg-a-Ramsie.'" *ELN* 5(1967): 11-15.

DRAMA. 9337. Anglo, Sydney. "The Evolution of the Early Tudor Disguising, Pageant, and Mask." *RD* n.s.1(1968): 3-44.

9338. Armstrong, William A. "The Audience of the Elizabethan Private Theatres." *RES* 10(1959): 234-249.

9339. Barish, Jonas A. "The Uniqueness of Elizabethan Drama." *CD* 11(1977): 103-112.

9340. Bawcutt, N. W. "'Policy," Machiavellianism, and the Early Tudor Drama." *ELR* 1(1971): 195-209.

9341. Beck, Ervin. "Terence Improved: The Paradigm of the Prodigal Son in English Renaissance Comedy." *RD* n.s. 6(1973): 107-122.

9342. Belsey, Catherine. "Senecan Vacillation and Elizabethan Deliberation: Influence or Confluence?" *RD* n.s. 6(1973): 65-88.

9343. Bergeron, David M. "The Elizabethan Lord Mayor's Show." *SEL* 10(1970): 269-285.

9344. Berry, Herbert. "The Stage and Boxes at Blackfriars." *SP* 63(1966): 163-186.

9345. Bevington, David M. "Drama and Polemics under Queen Mary." *RD* 9(1966): 105-124.

9346. Blissett, William. "Lucan's Caesar and the Elizabethan Villain." *SP* 53(1956): 553-575.

9347. Boyle, Harry H. "Elizabeth's Entertainment at Elvetham: War Policy in Pagentry." *SP* 68(1971): 146-166.

9348. Bradbrook, M. C. *The Comedy of Timon*: A Reveling Play of the Inner Temple." *RD* 9(1966): 83-103.

9349. ----------. "Silk? Satin? Kersey? Rags?—The Choristers' Theater under Elizabeth and James." *SEL* 1,#2(1961): 53-64.

9350. Brody, Alan. "Three Mumming Plays (with text)." *ELR* 3(1973): 105-130.

9351. Broude, Ronald. *Vindicta Filia Temporis*: Three English Forerunners of the Elizabethan Revenge Play." *JEGP* 72(1973): 489-502.

9352. Brown, Arthur. "Sebastian Westcott at York." *MLR* 47(1952): 49-50.

9353. Chang, Joseph S. M. J. "'Of Mighty Opposites': Stoicism and Machiavellianism." *RD* 9(1966): 37-57.

9354. Charney, Maurice. "The Persuaviveness of Violence in Elizabethan Plays." *RD* n.s. 2(1969): 59-70.

9355. Coldewey, Joseph E. "The Last Rise and Final Demise of Essex Town Drama." *MLQ* 36(1975): 239-260.

9356. Cole, Douglas. "The Comic Accomplice in Elizabethan Revenge Tragedy." *RD* 9(1966): 125-139.

9357. Cope, Jackson I. "The Rediscovery of Anti-Form in Renaissance Drama." *CD* 1(1967): 155-171.

9358. Dent, Robert W. "'Quality of Insight' in Elizabethan and Jacobean Tragedy." *MP* 63(1966): 252-256.

9359. Dessen, Alan C. "The 'Estates' Morality Play." *SP* 62(1965): 121-136.

9360. ----------. "The Morall as an Elizabethan Dramatic Kind: An Exploratory Essay." *CD* 5(1971): 138-159.

9361. Dollerup, Cay. "Danish Costume on the Elizabethan Stage." *RES* 25(1974): 53-58.

9362. Edmond, Mary. "Pembroke's Men." *RES* 25(1974): 129-136.

9363. Ettin, Andrew V. "Magic into Art: The Magician's Renunciation of Magic in English Renaissance Drama." *TSLL* 19(1977): 268-293.

9364. Ewbank, Inga-Stina. "'The Eloquence of Masques': A Retrospective View of Masque Criticism." *RD* n.s. 1(1968): 307-327.

9365. ----------. "The House of David in Renaissance Drama: A Comparative Study." *RD* 8 (1965): 3-40.

9366. Freeman, Arthur. "The Argument of *Meleager* (with text)." *ELR* 1(1971): 122-131.

9367. Friedenrich, Kenneth. "'You Talks Brave and Bold': The Origins of an Elizabethan Stage Device." *CD* 8(1974): 239-253.

9368. Gurr, Andrew. "Elizabethan Action." *SP* 63(1966): 144-156.

9369. Habicht, Werner. "Tree Properties and Tree Scenes in Elizabethan Theater." *RD* n.s. 4 (1971): 69-92.

9370. ----------. "The *Wit*-Interludes and the Form of Pre-Shakespearean 'Romantic Comedy'." *RD* 8(1965): 73-88.

9371. Hardison, O. B. "Three Types of Renaissance Catharsis." *RD* n.s. 2(1969): 3-22.

9372. Herrick, Marvin T. "The New Drama of the Sixteenth Century." *JEGP* 54(1955): 555-577.

9373. Homan, Sidney R. "The Uses of Silence: The Elizabethan Dumb Show and the Silent Cinema." *CD* 2(1968): 213-228.

9374. Hunter, G. K. "Italian Tragicomedy on the English Stage." *RD* n.s. 6(1973): 123-148.

9375. Ingram, William. "The Closing of the Theaters in 1597: A Dissenting View." *MP* 69(1971): 105-115.

9376. ----------. "'Neere the Playe Howse': The Swan Theatre and Community Blight." *RD* n.s. 4 (1971): 53-68.

9377. Jensen, Ejner J. "The Changing Faces of Love in English Renaissance Comedy." *CD* 6(1972): 294-309.

9378. Jones, Robert C. "Dangerous Sport: The Audiences' Engagement with Vice in the Moral Interludes." *RD* n.s. 6(1973): 45-64.

9379. ----------. "Italian Settings and the 'World' of Elizabethan Tragedy." *SEL* 10(1970): 251-268.

9380. Jorgensen, Paul A. "The Metamorphosis of Honesty in the Renaissance." *ELR* 3(1973): 369-379.

9381. Kantrowitz, Joanne Spencer. "Dramatic Allegory, or, Exploring the Moral Play." *CD* 7(1973): 68-82.

9382. Kaplan, Joel H. "The Medieval Origins of Elizabethan Comedy." *RD* n.s. 5(1972): 225-236.

9383. Kipling, Gordon. "Triumphal Drama: Form in English Civic Pageantry." *RD* n.s. 8(1977): 37-56.

9384. Klein, David. "Elizabethan Acting." *PMLA* 71(1956): 280-282.

9385. Knight, W. Nicholas. "Equity and Mercy in English Law and Drama (1405-1641)." *CD* 6(1972): 51-67.

9386. Lancashire, Anne B. "*Look About You* as a History Play." *SEL* 9(1969): 321-334.

9387. Levin, Harry. "The End of Elizabethan Drama." *CD* 3(1969): 275-281.

9388. Levin, Richard. "Elizabethan 'Clown' Subplots." *EIC* 16(1966): 84-91.

9389. ----------. "The Elizabethan 'Three-Level' Play." *RD* n.s. 2(1969): 23-57.

9390. ----------. "Some Second Thoughts on Central Themes." *MLR* 67(1972): 1-10.

9391. ----------. "Thematic Unity and the Homogenization of Character." *MLQ* 33(1972): 23-29.

9392. ----------. "The Unity of Elizabethan Multiple-Plot Drama." *ELH* 34(1967): 425-446.

9393. Levinson, Judith C. "The Sources of *Captain Thomas Stukeley*." *ELN* 9(1971): 85-90.

9394. Main, William W. "Dramaturgical Norms in Elizabethan Repetory." *SP* 54(1957): 128-148.

9395. Manheim, Michael. "The Weak King History Play of the Early 1590's." *RD* n.s. 2 (1969): 71-80.

9396. McCullen, Joseph T., Jr. "The Use of Parlor and Tavern Games in Elizabethan and Early Stuart Drama." *MLQ* 14(1953): 7-14.

9397. McDonald, Charles O. "*Decorum*, *Ethos*, and *Pathos* in the Heroes of Elizabethan Tragedy, with Particular Reference to *Hamlet*." *JEGP* 61(1962): 330-348.

9398. McMillin, Scott. "Jewel and the Queen's Men." *RES* 27(1976): 174-177.

9399. Meagher, John C. "The First Progress of Henry VII." *RD* n.s. 1(1968): 45-73.

9400. ----------. "The London Lord Mayor's Show of 1590." *ELR* 3(1973): 94-104.

9401. Mehl, Dieter. "Emblems in English Renaissance Drama." *RD* n.s. 2(1969): 39-57.

9402. ----------. "Forms and Functions of the Play within a Play." *RD* 8(1965): 41-61.

9403. Neuss, Paula. "Memorial Reconstruction of a Cornish Miracle Play." *CD* 5(1971): 129-137.

9404. Peterson, Joyce E. "The Paradox of Disintegrating Form in *Mundus et Infans*." *ELR* 7 (1977): 3-16.

9405. Pineas, Ranier. "The English Morality Play as a Weapon of Religious Controversy." *SEL* 2(1962): 157-180.

9406. Presson, Robert K. "Two Types of Dreams in the Elizabethan Drama, and their Heritage: Somnium Animale and the Prick-of-Conscience." *SEL* 7(1967): 239-256.

9407. Rabkin, Norman. "The Double Plot: Notes on the History of a Convention." *RD* 7 (1964): 55-69.

9408. Reibetang, John. "Hieronimo in Decimosexto: A Private-Theater Burlesque." *RD* n.s. 5(1972): 89-121.

9409. Ribner, Irving. "The Tudor History Play: An Essay in Definition." *PMLA* 69(1954): 591-609.

9410. Riggs, David. "'Plot' and 'Episode' in Early Neo-Classical Criticism." *RD* n.s. 6 (1973): 149-175.

9411. Rosenberg, Marvin. "Elizabethan Actors: Men or Marionettes?" *PMLA* 69(1959): 915-927.

9412. Salomon, Brownell. "Visual and Aural Signs in the Performed English Renaissance Play." *RD* n.s. 5(1972): 143-169.

9413. Schell, E. T. "*Youth* and *Hyckescorner*: Which Came First?." *PQ* 45(1966): 468-474.

9414. Scragg, Leah Lindsay. "'Love Feigned and Unfeigned': A Note on the Use of Allegory on the Tudor Stage." *ELN* 3(1966): 248-252.

9415. Shapiro, Michael. "Children's Troupes: Dramatic Illusion and Acting Style." *CD* 3(1969): 42-53.

9416. Smith, Bruce R. "Landscape with Figures: The Three Realms of Queen Elizabeth's Country-House Revels." *RD* n.s. 8(1977): 57-115.

9417. ----------. "Sir Amorous Knight and the Indecorous Romans; or, Plautus and Terence

Play Court in the Renaissance." *RD* n.s. 6(1973): 3-27.

9418. Soellner, Rolf. "The Madness of Hercules and the Elizabethans." *Comp L* 10(1958): 309-324.

9419. Stroup, Thomas B. "'All Comes Clear at Last,' but 'the Readiness is All'." *CD* 10 (1976): 61-77.

9420. ----------. "The Testing Pattern in Elizabethan Tragedy." *SEL* 3(1963): 175-190.

9421. Styan, J. L. "Elizabethan Open Staging: William Poel to Tyrone Guthrie." *MLQ* 37 (1976): 211-220.

9422. Thomas, Helen. "*Jacob and Esau*— 'rigidly Calvinistic'?" *SEL* 9(1969): 199-213.

9423. Turner, Robert K., Jr. "Act-End Notations in Some Elizabethan Plays." *MP* 72(1975): 238-247.

9424. Turner, Robert Y. "The Causal Induction in Some Elizabethan Plays." *SP* 60(1963): 183-190.

9425. Wierum, Ann. "'Actors' and 'Play Acting' in the Morality Tradition." *RD* n.s. 3(1970): 189-197.

9426. Woolf, Rosemary. "The Influence of the Mystery Plays upon the Popular Tragedies of the 1560's." *RD* n.s. 6(1973): 89-105.

9427. Young, Steven C. "A Check List of Tudor and Stuart Induction Plays." *PQ* 48(1969): 131-134.

See also 20684.

POETRY. 9428. Allen, Walter, Jr. "The Non-Existant Classical Epyllion." *SP* 55(1958): 515-518.

9429. Bateson, F. W. "Sixteenth-Century Poetry and the Common Reader." *EIC* 4(1954): 428-430.

9430. Bennett, A. L. "The Principal Rhetorical Conventions in the Renaissance Personal Elegy." *SP* 51(1954): 107-126.

9431. Biggins, Dennis. "'Solur' in *Madame d'amours*." *ELN* 3(1965): 96.

9432. Black, L. G. "Some Renaissance Children's Verse." *RES* 24(1973): 1-16.

9433. Brewer, D. S. "Metaphor and Symbol in the Sixteenth Century." *EIC* 4(1954): 108-111.

9434. Broadbent, J. B. "Sixteenth-Century Poetry and the Common Reader." *EIC* 4(1954): 421-426.

9435. Bühler, Curt F. "A Tudor 'Cross Rowe.'" *JEGP* 58(1959): 248-250.

9436. Clements, Robert J. "Iconography on the Nature and Inspiration of Poetry in Renaissance Emblem Literature." *PMLA* 70(1955): 781-804.

9437. Colie, R. L. "The Rhetoric of Transcendence." *PQ* 43(1964): 145-170.

9438. Coogan, Robert, C. F. C. "Petrarch's *Trionfi* and the English Renaissance." *SP* 67(1970): 306-327.

9439. Daley, A. Stuart. "The Uncertain Author of Poem 225, Tottle's *Miscellany*." *SP* 47 (1950): 485-493.

9440. Davie, Donald. "Sixteenth-Century Poetry and the Common Reader." *EIC* 4(1954): 426-428.

9441. Deming, Robert H. "Love and Knowledge in the Renaissance Lyric." *TSLL* 16(1974): 389-410.

9442. Fox, Denton. "Some Scribal Alterations of Dates in the Bannatyne MS." *PQ* 42(1963): 259-263.

9443. Frey, Charles. "Interpreting 'Western Wind.'" *ELH* 43(1976): 259-278.

9444. Gardner, Stanley. "Love in the Sixteenth Century." *EIC* 23(1973): 435-440.

9445. Halio, Jay L. "*Perfection* and Elizabethan Ideas of Conception." *ELN* 1(1964): 179-182.

9446. Hamer, Douglas. "Towards Restoring *The Hunting of The Cheviot*." *RES* 20(1969): 1-21.

9447. Harris, William O. "Early Elizabethan Sonnets in Sequence." *SP* 68(1971): 451-469.

9448. Hulse, S. Clark. "Elizabethan Minor Epic: Toward a Definition of Genre." *SP* 73(1976): 302-319.

9449. Hunter, G. K. "The English Hexameter and the Elizabethan Madrigal." *PQ* 32(1953): 340-342.

9450. Jack, Ronald D. S. "Imitation in the Scottish Sonnet." *Comp L* 20(1968): 313-328.

9451. Jack, R. D. S. "Petrarch in English and Scottish Renaissance Literature." *MLR* 71(1976): 801-811.

9452. Jantz, Harold. "Goethe and an Elizabethan Poem." *MLQ* 12(1951): 451-461.

9453. Kellogg, George A. "Bridge's *Milton's Prosody* and Renaissance Metrical Theory." *PMLA* 68(1953): 268-285.

9454. Kennedy, William J. "Petrarchism in Short Narrative Poetry of the Renaissance." *Comp L* 26(1974): 318-333.

9455. LaBranche, Anthony. "Imitation: Getting in Touch." *MLQ* 31(1970): 308-329.

9456. ----------. "Poetry, History, and Oratory: The Renaissance Historical Poem." *SEL* 9 (1969): 1-19.

9457. Levarie, Janet. "Renaissance Anacreontics." *Comp L* 25(1973): 221-239.

9458. Long, John H. "The Ballad Medley and the Fool." *SP* 67(1970): 505-516.

9459. Maynard, Winifred. "The *Paradyse of Daynty Deuises* Revisited." *RES* 24(1973): 295-300.

9460. Miller, Paul W. "The Elizabethan Minor Epic." *SP* 55(1958): 31-38.

9461. Piper, William Bowman. "The Inception of the Closed Heroic Couplet." *MP* 66(1969): 306-321.

9462. Rees, Christine. "The Metamorphosis of Daphne in Sixteenth- and Seventeenth- century English Poetry." *MLR* 66(1971): 251-263.

9463. Richmond, H. M. "Polyphemus in England: A Study in Comparative Literature." *Comp L* 12(1960): 229-242.

9464. ----------. "'Rural Lyricism': A Renaissance Mutation of the Pastoral." *Comp L* 16(1964): 193-210.

9465. Ringler, William A., Jr. "The Nut-brown Maid (a reconstructed text)." *ELR* 1(1971): 27-51.

9466. Ross, Ian. "Sonneteering in Sixteenth-Century Scotland." *TSLL* 6(1964): 255-268.

9467. ----------. "Verse Translation at the Court of King James VI of Scotland." *TSLL* 4(1962): 252-267.

9468. Saunders, J. W. "The Facade of Morality." *ELH* 19(1952): 81-114.

9469. ----------. "The Stigma of Print: A Note on the Social Bases of Tudor Poetry." *EIC* 1 (1951): 139-164.

9470. Sanderson, James L. "Three Unpublished Elizabethan Wedding Poems." *MLR* 58(1963): 217-219.

9471. Scammell, G. V., and H. L. Rogers. "An Elegy on Henry VII." *RES* 8(1957): 167-170.

9472. Schuman, Sharon. "Sixteenth-Century English Quantitative Verse: Its Ends, Means, and Products." *MP* 74(1977): 335-350.

9473. Seaton, Ethel. "'The Devonshire Manuscript' and its Medieval Fragments." *RES* 7 (1956): 55-56.

9474. Southall, Raymond. "The Devonshire Manuscript Collection of Early Tudor Poetry, 1532-41." *RES* 15(1964): 142-150.

9475. ----------. "Love in the Sixteenth Century." *EIC* 24(1974): 216-218.

9476. ----------. "Love Poetry in the Sixteenth Century." *EIC* 22(1972): 362-380.

9477. Wilkins, Ernest H. "A General Survey of Renaissance Petrarchism." *Comp L* 2(1950): 327-342.

PROSE. 9478. Chickera, Ernst de. "Palaces of Pleasure: The Theme of Revenge in Elizabethan Translations of Novelle." *RES* 11(1960): 1-7.

9479. Grund, Gary R. "From Formulary to Fiction: The Epistle and the English Anti-Ciceronian Movement." *TSLL* 17(1975): 379-395.

9480. Hall, Anne Drury. "Tudor Prose Style: English Humanists and the Problems of a Standard." *ELR* 7(1977): 267-298.

9481. Morgan, Margery. "A Treatise in Cadence." *MLR* 47(1952): 156-164.

9482. Nelson, William. "The Boundaries of Fiction in the Renaissance: A Treaty Between Truth and Falsehood." *ELH* 36(1969): 30-58.

9483. Ong, Walter J., S. J. "Oral Residue in Tudor Prose Style." *PMLA* 80(1965): 145-154.

9484. O'Brien, Avril S. "*Dobsons Drie Bobbes*: A Significant Contribution to the Development of Prose Fiction." *SEL* 12(1972): 55-70.

9485. Opie, B. J. "The Devil, Science, and Subjectivity." *ELR* 6(1976): 430-452.

9486. Schlauch, Margaret. "English Short Fiction in the 15th and 16th Centuries." *SSF* 3 (1966): 393-434.

9487. Starnes, D. T. "*The Institucion of a Gentleman* (1555) and Carion's Chronicles." *PQ* 36(1957): 244-252.

9488. Staton, Walter F., Jr. "The Characters of Style in Elizabethan Prose." *JEGP* 57 (1958): 197-207.

9489. Vox, Alvin. "Models and Methodologies in Renaissance Prose Stylistics." *SLI* 10,#2(1977): 1-15.

ALEXANDER, WILLIAM. See 9346.

ALSOP, THOMAS. 9490. Williams, Franklin B. Jr. "Alsop's *Fair Custance*: Chaucer in Tudor Dress." *ELR* 6(1976): 351-368.

ARDEN OF FEVERSHAM. 9491. Youngblood, Sarah. "Theme and Imagery in *Arden of Feversham*." *SEL* 3(1963): 207-218.

ARTE OF ANGLING, 1577. See 11290.

ASCHAM, ANTHONY. 9492. Perlette, John M. "Anthony Ascham's 'Of Marriage' (with text)." *ELR* 3(1973): 284-305.

9493. Robinson, Fred C. "'The Complaynt Off Sanct Cipriane, The Grett Nigromancer': A Poem by Anthony Ascham." *RES* 27(1976): 257-265.

ASCHAM, ROGER. 9494. Greene, Thomas M.

"Roger Ascham: The Perfect End of Shooting."
ELH 36(1969): 609-625.

9495. Salamon, Linda Bradley. "*The Courtier* and *The Scholemaster*." *Comp L* 25(1973): 17-36.

9496. ----------. "The Imagery of Roger Ascham." *TSLL* 15(1973): 5-23.

9497. Smith, John Hazel. "Roger Ascham's Troubled Years." *JEGP* 65(1966): 36-46.

9498. Staton, Walter F., Jr. "Roger Ascham's Theory of History Writing." *SP* 56(1959): 125-137.

9499. Strozier, Robert. "Roger Ascham and Cleanth Brooks: Renaissance and Modern Thought." *EIC* 22(1972): 396-407.

9500. Trousdale, Marion. "Recurrence and Renaissance: Rhetorical Imitation in Ascham and Sturm." *ELR* 6(1976): 156-179.

9501. Vaughan, M. F. "An Unnoted Translation of Erasmus in Ascham's *Schoolmaster*." *MP* 75(1977): 184-186.

9502. Vos, Alvin. "Form and Function in Roger Ascham's Prose." *PQ* 55(1976): 305-322.

9503. ----------. "The Formation of Roger Ascham's Prose Style." *SP* 71(1974): 344-370.

9504. ----------. "The Humanism of *Toxophilus*: A New Source." *ELR* 6(1976): 187-203.

See also 9320, 9321, 9334, 9519.

BALE, JOHN. 9505. Adams, Barry B. "Doubling in Bale's *King Johan*." *SP* 62(1965): 111-120.

9506. Miller, E. S. "The Antiphons in Bale's Cycle of Christ. *SP* 48(1951): 629-638.

9507. Pafford, J. H. P. "Two Notes on Bale's 'King John.'" *MLR* 56(1961): 553-555.

See also 9340, 9425.

BARCLAY, ALEXANDER. 9508. Lyall, R. J. "Alexander Barclay and the Edwardian Reformation 1548-52." *RES* 20(1969): 455-461.

9509. ----------. "Tradition and Innovation in Alexander Barclay's 'Towre of Vertue and Honoure.'" *RES* 23(1972): 1-19.

BARCLAY, JOHN. 9510. Fleming, David A. "Barclay's *Satyricon*: The First Satrical Roman A Clef." *MP* 65(1967): 95-102.

BARNFIELD, RICHARD. 9511. Morris, Harry. "Richard Barnfield, 'Amyntas,' and the Sidney Circle." *PMLA* 74(1959): 318-324.

BODENHAM, JOHN. 9512. Starnes, D. T. "Some Sources of *Wits Theater of the Little World* (1599) and Bodenham's *Belvedere*(1600)." *PQ* 30 (1951): 411-418.

BOOK OF SIR THOMAS MORE: 9513. Blayney, Peter W. M. "The Booke of Sir Thomas Moore Re-Examined." *SP* 69(1972): 167-191.

9514. McMillin, Scott. "*The Book of Sir Thomas More*: A Theatrical View." *MP* 68(1970): 10-24.

9515. Wentersdorf, Karl P. "Linkages of Thought and Imagery in Shakespeare and *More*." *MLQ* 34(1973): 384-405.

See also 9402.

BRETON, NICHOLAS. 9516. Ringler, William A., Jr. "Bishop Percy's Quarto Manuscript (British Museum MS Additional 34064) and Nicholas Breton." *PQ* 54(1975): 26-39.

9517. Shakeshaft, Mary. "Nicholas Breton's *The Passion of a Discontented Mind*: Some New Problems." *SEL* 5(1965): 165-174.

See also 9347, 9479.

BOYD, MARK ALEXANDER. See 9466.

BROKE, ARTHUR. See 9447.

BRYAN, FRANCIS. See 9439.

BUC, GEORGE. See 9347.

CAMDEN, WILLIAM. 9518. Johnston, George Burke, ed. "Poems by William Camden with Notes and Translations from the Latin." *SP* 72,#5(1975): 1-143.

9519. ----------. "William Camden's Elegy on Roger Ascham." [with text] *SP* 70(1973): 160-171.

9520. Oruch, Jack B. "Spenser, Camden, and the Poetic Marriage of Rivers." *SP* 64(1967): 606-624.

CAVENDISH, GEORGE. 9521. Edwards, A. S. G. "The Date of George Cavendish's Metrical Visions." *PQ* 53(1974): 128-132.

9522. Sylvester, Richard S. "Cavendish's *Life of Wolsey*: The Artistry of a Tudor Biographer." *SP* 57(1960): 44-71.

CHEKE, JOHN. See 9320, 9334.

CHETTLE, HENRY. See 9356, 11728.

CHURCHYARD, THOMAS. 9523. Goldwyn, Merrill Harvey. "Notes on the Biography of Thomas Churchyard." *RES* 17(1966): 1-15.

9524. ----------. "Some Unpublished Manuscripts by Thomas Churchyard." *SP* 64(1967): 147-158.

9525. Shirley, Charles G., Jr. "Thomas Churchyard's Forgotten Bed-Grave Poem." *ELN* 14 (1977): 182-187.

9526. Williams, Franklin B., Jr. "Thomas Churchyard's Thunder on the Right (text)." *ELR* 3 (1973): 380-399.

See also 9323, 11088.

COLET, JOHN. 9527. Surtz, Edward L. S. J. "'Oxford Reformers' and Scholasticism." *SP* 47 (1950): 547-556.

See also 9310.

COMPLAYNT OF SCOTLANDE. 9528. Blayney, Margaret S. and Glenn H. "Alain Chartier and *The Complaynt of Scotlande*." *RES* 9(1958): 8-17.

CONSTABLE, JOHN. 9529. Sylvester, Richard S. "John Constable's Poems to Thomas More." *PQ* 42(1963): 525-531.

COPLAND, ROBERT. 9530. Meagher, John C. "Robert Copland's *The Seven Sorrows*." *ELR* 7(1977): 17-50.

CORNISH, WILLIAM. 9531. Anglo, Sidney. "William Cornish in a Play, Pageants, Prison, and Politics." *RES* 10(1959): 347-360.

COX, LEONARD. See 9320, 9430.

CRAMNER, THOMAS. 9532. Devereux, James A., S.J. "The Collects of the First *Book of Common Prayer* as Words of Translation." *SP* 66(1969): 719-738.

9533. Wellington, James E. "The Litany in Cramner and Donne." *SP* 68(1971): 177-199.

CREEDE, THOMAS. 9534. Pincess, G. M. "Thomas Creede and the Repertory of the Queen's Men, 1583-1592." *MP* 67(1970): 321-330.

CROWLEY, ROBERT. 9535. King, John N. "Robert Crowley's Editions of *Piers Plowman*: A Tudo Apocalypse." *MP* 73(1976): 342-352.

DANIEL, SAMUEL. 9536. Gill, R. B. "Moral History and Daniel's *The Civil Wars*." *JEGP* 76 (1977): 334-345.

9537. Godshalk, William Leigh. "Daniel's *History*." *JEGP* 63(1964): 45-57.

9538. Goldman, Lloyd. "Samuel Daniel's *Delia* and the Emblem Tradition." *JEGP* 67(1968): 49-63.

9539. Gottfried, Rudolf B. "The Authorship of *A Breviary of the History of England*." *SP* 53 (1956): 172-190.

9540. Himelick, Raymond. "*A Fig for Momus* and Daniel's *Musophilus*." *MLQ* 18(1957): 247-250.

9541. ----------. "Montaigne and Daniel's 'To Sir Thomas Egerton.'" *PQ* 36(1957): 500-504.

9542. ----------. "Thoreau and Samuel Daniel." *AL* 24(1952): 177-185.

9543. Johnston, George Burke. "Camden, Daniel, and Shakespeare." *PMLA* 77(1962): 510-512.

9544. Logan, George M. "Daniel's *Civil Wars* and Lucan's *Pharsalia*." *SEL* 11(1971): 53-68.

9545. Maurer, Margaret. "Samuel Daniel's Poetic Epistles, Especially Those to Sir Thomas Egerton and Lucy, Countess of Bedford." *SP* 74 (1977): 418-444.

9546. Michel, Laurence, and Cecil C. Seronsy. "Shakespeare's History Plays and Daniel: An Assessment." *SP* 52(1955): 549-577.

9547. Miller, Edwin H. "Samuel Daniel's Revisions in *Delia*." *JEGP* 53(1954): 58-68.

9548. Nørgaard, Holger. "The Bleeding Captain Scene in *Macbeth* and Daniel's *Cleopatra*." *RES* 6(1955): 395-396.

9549. Norman, Arthur M. Z. "'The Tragedie of Cleopatra' and the Date of 'Antony and Cleopatra.'" *MLR* 54(1959): 1-9.

9550. Primeau, Ronald. "Daniel and the *Mirror* Tradition: Dramatic Irony in *Complaint of Rosamond*." *SEL* 15(1975): 21-36.

9551. Rees, Joan. "Samuel Daniel's 'Cleopatra' and Two French Plays." *MLR* 47(1952): 1-10.

9552. Rice, Julian C. "The Allegorical Dolabella." *CLA* 13(1970): 402-407.

9553. Saunders, J. W. "Donne and Daniel." *EIC* 3(1953): 109-114.

9554. Schanzer, Ernest. "Daniel's Revision of His *Cleopatra*." *RES* 8(1957): 375-381.

9555. Seronsy, Cecil C. "Daniel and Wordsworth." *SP* 56(1959): 187-213.

9556. ----------. "Daniel's Manuscript *Civil Wars* with Some Previously Unpublished Stanzas." *JEGP* 52(1953): 153-160.

9557. ----------. "Daniel's *Panegyricke* and the Earl of Hertford." *PQ* 32(1953): 342-344.

9558. ----------. "The Doctrine of Cyclical Recurrence and Some Related Ideas in the Works of Samuel Daniel." *SP* 54(1957): 387-407.

9559. ----------. "Well-Languaged Daniel: A Reconsideration." *SP* 52(1957): 481-497.

9560. ----------, and Robert Krueger. "A Manuscript of Daniel's *Civil Wars*, Book III." *SP* 63(1966): 157-162.

9561. Thomson, Patricia. "Sonnet 15 of Samuel Daniel's *Delia*: A Petrarchan Imitation." *Comp L* 17(1965): 151-157.

9562. Ure, Peter. "A Note on 'Opinion' in Daniel, Greville and Chapman." *MLR* 46(1951): 331-338.

9563. Wilkes, G. A. "Daniel's *Philotas* and the Essex Case: A Reconsideration." *MLQ* 23(1962): 233-242.

9564. Williamson, C. F. "The Design of Daniel's *Delia*." *RES* 19(1968): 251-260.

See also 9346, 11425.

DAVIES, SIR JOHN.   9565. Bishop, Carolyn. "Raleigh Satirized by Harington and Davies." *RES* 23(1972): 52-56.

9566. Bowers, R. H. "An Elizabethan Manuscript 'Continuation' of Sir John Davies' *Nosce teipsum*." *MP* 58(1960): 11-19.

9567. Brink, J. R. "The Masque of the Nine Muses: Sir John Davies's Unpublished 'Epithalamion' and the 'Belphoebe-Ruby' Episode in *The Faerie Queene*." *RES* 23(1972): 445-448.

9568. Huntington, John. "Philosophical Seduction in Chapman, Davies, and Donne." *ELH* 44 (1977): 40-59.

9569. Kennedy, R. F. "Another Davies Manuscript." *RES* 15(1964): 180.

9570. Krueger, Robert. "Sir John Davies: *Orchestra* Complete, *Epigrams*, Unpublished Poems." *RES* 13(1962): 17-29, 113-124.

9571. Nemser, Ruby. "*Nosce Teipsum* and the *Essais* of Montaigne." *SEL* 16(1976): 95-103.

9572. Nosworthy, J. M. "Marlowe's *Ovid* and Davies's *Epigrams*—A Postscript." *RES* 15(1964): 397-398.

9573. ----------. "The Publication of Marlowe's *Elegies* and Davies's *Epigrams*." *RES* 4 (1953): 260-261.

9574. Sanderson, James L. "Recent Studies in Sir John Davies." *ELR* 4(1974): 411-417.

9575. ----------. "Unpublished Eipgrams of Sir John Davies." *RES* 12(1961): 281-282.

9576. Schoeck, R. J. "'Nosce Teipsum' and the two John Davies." *MLR* 50(1955): 307-310.

9577. Simpson, Percy. "Unprinted Epigrams of Sir John Davies." *RES* 3(1952): 49-50.

9578. Taylor, A. B. "Sir John Davies and George Chapman: A Note on the Current Approach to *Ovids Banquet of Sence*." *ELN* 12(1975): 261-265.

See also 12549.

DELONEY, THOMAS.   9579. Dorinsville, Max. "Design in Deloney's *Jack of Newbury*." *PMLA* 88 (1973): 233-239.

9580. Hassell, J. Woodrow, Jr. "An Elizabethan Translation of the Tales of Des Périers: *The Mirrour of Mirth*, 1583 and 1592." *SP* 52(1955): 172-185.

9581. McAleer, John J. "Ballads on the Spanish Armada." *TSLL* 4(1963): 602-612.

9582. Parker, David. "*Jack of Newberry*: A New Source." *ELN* 10(1973): 172-180.

See also 9323.

DEVEREUX, ROBERT.   9583. Freeman, Arthur. "Essex to Stella: Two Letters from the Earl of Essex to Penelope Rich." *ELR* 3(1973): 248-249.

DIGGES, THOMAS.   9584. Johnson, Francis R. "Two Treatises by Thomas Digges." *RES* 9(1958): 141-145.

DOWLAND, JOHN.   9585. Reed, Victor. "Doleful Dowland." *ELN* 6(1968): 17-19.

DRANT, THOMAS.   9586. Peter, John. "'This Word Satyre.'" *RES* 6(1955): 288-290.

DRAYTON, MICHAEL.   9587. Ackerman, Catherine A. "Drayton's Revision of *The Shepheards Garland*." *CLA* 3(1959): 106-113.

9588. Bristol, Michael D. "Structural Patterns in Two Elizabethan Pastorals." *SEL* 10 (1970): 33-48.

9589. Bullitt, John M. "The Use of Rhyme Link in the Sonnets of Sidney, Drayton, and Spenser." *JEGP* 49(1950): 14-32.

9590. Davis, Walter R. "'Fantastickly I Sing': Drayton's *Idea* of 1619." *SP* 66(1969): 204-216.

9591. Grundy, Joan. "'Brave Translunary Things." *MLR* 59(1964): 501-510.

9592. Hiller, Geoffrey G. "Drayton's *Muses Elizium*: 'A New Way Over Parnassus.'" *RES* 21(1970): 1-13.

9593. Hobbs, Mary. "Drayton's 'Most Dearly-Loved Friend Henry Reynolds Esq.'" *RES* 24(1973): 414-428.

9594. LaBranche, Anthony. "Drayton's *The Barons Warres* and the Rhetoric of Historical Poetry." *JEGP* 62(1963): 82-95.

9595. ----------. "Poetry, History, and Oratory: The Renaissance Historical Poem." *SEL* 9(1969): 1-19.

9596. ----------. "The 'Twofold Vitality' of Drayton's *Odes*." *Comp L* 15(1963): 116-129.

9597. Moore, William H. "Sources of Drayton's Conception of *Poly-Olbion*." *SP* 65 (1968): 783-803.

9598. Revard, Stella P. "The Design of Nature in Drayton's *Poly-Olbion*." *SEL* 17(1977): 105-117.

9599. Robertson, Jean. "Drayton and the Countess of Pembroke." *RES* 16(1965): 49.

9600. Taylor, Dick, Jr. "Drayton and the Countess of Bedford." *SP* 49(1952): 214-228.

See also 9291.

DYER, EDWARD. 9601. May, Steven W. "The Authorship of 'My Mind to Me a Kingdom Is.'" *RES* 26(1975): 385-390.

See also 11159.

EDGEWORTH, ROGER. 9602. Blench, J. W. "John Langland and Roger Edgeworth, Two Forgotten Preachers of the Early Sixteenth Century." *RES* 5(1954): 123-143.

EDWARDS, RICHARD. 9603. Cope, Jackson I. "'The Best for Comedy': Richard Edwardes' Canon." *TSLL* 2(1961): 501-519.

9604. Holaday, Allan. "Shakespeare, Richard Edwards, and the Virtues Reconciled." *JEGP* 66(1967): 200-206.

9605. Jackson, James L. "Three Notes on Richard Edwards' *Damon and Pithias*." *PQ* 29 (1950): 209-213.

9606. Kramer, J. E. "*Damon and Pithias*: An Apology for Art." *ELH* 35(1968): 475-490.

ELYOT, SIR THOMAS. 9607. Bland, D. S. "Rhetoric and the Law Student in Sixteenth-Century England." *SP* 54(1957): 498-508.

9608. Dees, Jerome S. "Recent Studies in Elyot." *ELR* 6(1976): 336-344.

9609. Donner, H. W. "The Emperor and Sir Thomas Elyot." *RES* 2(1951): 55-59.

9610. Hogrefe, Pearl. "Sir Thomas Elyot's Intention in the Opening Chapters of the *Governour*." *SP* 60(1963): 133-144.

9611. Holmes, Elisabeth. "The Significance of Elyot's Revision of the *Gouernour*." *RES* 12(1961): 352-362.

9612. Lascelles, Mary. "Sir Thomas Elyot and the Legend of Alexander Severus." *RES* 2 (1951): 305-318.

9613. Sargent, Ralph M. "Sir Thomas Elyot and the Integrity of *The Two Gentlemen of Verona*." *PMLA* 65(1950): 1166-1180.

9614. Schoeck, R. J. "Rhetoric and the Law in Sixteenth-Century England." *SP* 50(1953): 110-127.

9615. Wilson, K. J., ed. "The Letters of Sir Thomas Elyot." *SP* 73,#5(1976): ix-xxx, 1-78.

9616. Warren, Leslie. "Patrizi's *De regno et regis institutione* and the Plan of Elyot's *The Boke Named the Governour*." *JEGP* 49(1950): 67-77.

See also 9299.

FAIRFAX, EDWARD. 9617. Bell, Charles G. "Fairfax's Tasso." *Comp L* 6(1954): 26-52.

9618. Grundy, Joan. "Tasso, Fairfax, and William Browne." *RES* 3(1952): 268-271.

FARRANT, THOMAS. 9619. Ribner, Irving. "*Tamburlaine* and *The Wars of Cyrus*." *JEGP* 53 (1954): 569-573.

FENTON, GEOFFREY. 9620. Fellheimer, Jeannette. "The Episode of 'The Villian of the Danube' in Fenton's *Golden Epistles*." *MLQ* 14(1953): 331-334.

9621. Starnes, D. T. "Geoffrey Fenton, Seneca and Shakespeare's *Lucrece*." *PQ* 43(1964): 280-283.

FERNE, JOHN. See 9614.

FISH, SIMON. 9622. Pineas, Rainer. "Thomas More's Controversy with Simon Fish." *SEL* 7(1967): 15-28.

FISHER, JOHN. 9623. Surtz, Edward, S. J. "John Fisher and the Scholastics." *SP* 55(1958): 136-153.

See also 9299.

FLEMING, ABRAHAM. 9624. Miller, William E. "Abraham Fleming: Editor of Shakespeare's Holinshed." *TSLL* 1(1959): 89-100.

FLETCHER, GILES, THE ELDER. 9625. Berry, Lloyd E. "Giles Fletcher, the Elder, and Milton's *A Brief History of Moscovia*" *RES* 11(1960): 150-156.

FLORIO, JOHN. 9626. Rees, D. G. "John Florio and Anton Francesco Doni." *Comp L* 15(1963): 33-38.

9627. Starnes, Dewitt T. "John Florio Reconsidered." *TSLL* 6(1965): 407-422.

FOWLER, WILLIAM. 9628. Jack, R. D. S. "William Fowler and Italian Literature." *MLR* 65 (1970): 481-492.

See also 9466, 9467.

FORDE, EMANUEL. 9629. Gaunt, J. L. "*The Most Excellent History of Antonius and Aurelia*: An Unusual Restoration Abridgement." *SSF* 14(1977): 399-401.

FRITH, JOHN. 9630. Pineas, Rainer. "John Frith's Polemical Use of Rhetoric and Logic." *SEL* 4(1964): 85-100.

FOXE, JOHN. 9631. Smith, John Hazel. "John Foxe on Astrology (with text)." *ELR* 1(1971): 210-225.

9632. ----------. "Sempronia, John Lyly, and John Foxe's Comedy of *Titus and Gesippus*." *PQ* 48(1969): 554-561.

GAMMER GURTON'S NEEDLE. 9633. Ingram, R. W. "*Gammer Gurton's Needle*: Comedy Not Quite of the Lowest Order?" *SEL* 7(1967): 257-268.

9634. Toole, William B. "The Aesthetics of Scatology in *Gammer Gurton's Needle*." *ELN* 10 (1973): 252-258.

GARTER, THOMAS. 9635. Sexton, Joyce Hengerer. "The Theme of Slander in *Much Ado About Nothing* and Garter's *Susanna*." *PQ* 54(1975): 419-433.

GASCOIGNE, GEORGE. 9636. Adams, Robert P. "Gascoigne's 'Master F. J.' as Original Fiction." *PMLA* 73(1958): 315-326.

9637. Bradner, Leiscester. "Point of View in George Gascoigne's Fiction." *SSF* 3(1965): 16-22.

9638. Brooks, E. L. "The Burial Place of George Gascoigne." *RES* 5(1954): 59.

9639. Fieler, Frank B. "Gascoigne's Use of Courtly Love Conventions in 'The Adventures Passed by Master F. J.'" *SSF* 1(1963): 26-33.

9640. Lanham, Richard A. "Narrative Structure in Gascoigne's *F. J.*" *SSF* 4(1966): 42-50.

9641. Maveety, Stanley R. "Versification in *The Steele Glas*." *SP* 60(1963): 166-173.

9642. McGrath, Lynette F. "George Gascoigne's Moral Satire: The Didactic Use of Convention in *The Adventures passed by Master F. J.*" *JEGP* 70(1971): 432-450.

9643. Mills, Jerry Leath. "Recent Studies in Gascoigne." *ELR* 3(1973): 322-327.

9644. Parrish, Paul A. "The Multiple Perspectives of Gascoigne's 'The Adventures of Master F. J.'" *SSF* 10(1973): 75-84.

9645. Rohr, M. R. "Gascoigne and 'my master Chaucer.'" *JEGP* 67(1968): 20-31.

9646. ----------. "Gascoigne's Fable of the Artist *as* a Young Man." *JEGP* 73(1974): 13-31.

9647. Salamon, Linda Bradley. "A Face in the Glasse: Gascoigne's Glasse of *Governement* Re-Examined." *SP* 71(1974): 47-71.

9648. Stroup, Thomas, and H. Ward Jackson. "Gascoigne's *Steele Glas* and 'The Bidding of the Beddes'." *SP* 58(1961): 52-60.

9649. Waters, Gregory. "G. T.'s 'Worthles Enterprise': A Study of the Narrator in Gascoigne's 'The Adventures of Master F. J.'" *JNT* 7(1977): 116-127.

See also 9299, 9447, 11084.

GAULTIER, THOMAS. See 9974.

GEORGE A GREEN. 9650. Nelson, Malcom A. "The Sources of *George A Green, The Pinner of Wakefield*." *PQ* 42(1962): 159-165.

9651. Pennel, Charles A. "The Authenticity of the *George a Greene* Title-Page Inscriptions." *JEGP* 64(1965): 668-676.

GOLDING, ARTHUR. 9652. Hale, David G. "The Source and Date of Golding's 'Fabletalke.'" *MP* 69(1972): 326-327.

9653. Steiner, Grundy. "Golding's Use of the Regius-Micyllus Commentary upon Ovid." *JEGP* 49(1950): 317-323.

GOODYEAR, SIR HENRY. See 9447.

GOOGE, BARNABY. 9654. Parnell, Paul E. "Barnabe Googe in Arcadia." *JEGP* 60(1961): 273-281.

9655. Sheidley, William E. "A Timely Anachronism: Tradition and Theme in Barnabe Googe's *Cupido Conquered*." *SP* 69(1972): 150-166.

GOSSON, STEPHEN. 9656. Kinney, Arthur F. "Stephen Gossen's Art of Argumentation in *The School of Abuse*." *SEL* 7(1967): 41-54.

GREENE, ROBERT. 9657. Babula, William. "Fortune or Fate: Ambiguity in Robert Greene's 'Orlando Furioso.'" *MLR* 67(1972): 481-485.

9658. Braunmuller, A. R. "The Serious Comedy of Greene's *James IV*." *ELR* 3(1973): 335-350.

9659. Drew, Philip. "Was Greene's 'Young Juvenal' Nashe or Lodge?" *SEL* 7(1967): 55-66.

9660. Esler, Anthony. "Robert Green and the Spanish Armada." *ELH* 32(1965): 314-332.

9661. Gelber, Norman. "Robert Greene's Orlando Furioso': A Study in Thematic Ambiguity." *MLR* 64(1969): 264-266.

9662. Larson, Charles H. "Robert Greene's *Ciceronis Amor*: Fictional Biography in the Romance Genre." *SN* 6(1974): 256-267.

9663. Lawlor, John. "*Pandosto* and the Nature of Dramatic Romance." *PQ* 41(1962): 96-113.

9664. Lindheim, Nancy R. "Lyly's Golden Legacy: *Rosalynde* and *Pandosto*." *SEL* 15(1975): 3-20.

9665. MacLaine, Allan H. "Greene's Borrowings from His Own Prose Fiction in *Bacon and Bungay* and *James the Fourth*." *PQ* 30(1951): 22-29.

9666. McMillin, Scott. "The Ownership of *The Jew of Malta, Friar Bacon*, and *The Ranger's Comedy*." *ELN* 9(1972): 249-252.

9667. McNeir, Waldo F. "Reconstructing the Conclusion of *John of Bordeaux*." *PMLA* 66(1951): 540-543.

9668. Miller, Edwin Haviland. "The Relationship of Robert Greene and Thomas Nashe (1588-1592)." *PQ* 33(1954): 353-367.

9669. Mortenson, Peter. "*Friar Bacon* and *Friar Bungay*: Festive Comedy and 'Three-Form'd Luna'." *ELR* 2(1972): 194-200.

9670. Parr, Johnstone. "Robert Greene and his Classmates at Cambridge." *PMLA* 77(1962): 536-543.

9671. Pennel, Charles A. "Robert Greene and 'King or Kaiser.'" *ELN* 3(1965): 24-26.

9672. Ribner, Irving. "Greene's Attack on Marlowe: Some Light on *Alphonsus* and *Selimus*." *SP* 52(1955): 162-171.

9673. Wertheim, Albert. "The Presentation of Sin in 'Friar Bacon and Friar Bungay.'" *Criticism* 16(1974): 273-286.

See also 9363, 9377, 9402, 9418, 9457.

GREVILLE, FULKE. 9674. Bennett, Paula. "Recent Studies in Greville." *ELR* 2(1972): 376-382.

9675. Caldwell, Mark L. "Sources and Analogues of the *Life of Sidney*." *SP* 74(1977): 279-300.

9676. Ewing, S. Blaine. "A New Manuscript of Greville's 'Life of Sidney.'" *MLR* 49(1954): 424-427.

9677. Farmer, Norman, Jr. "Fulke Greville and the Poetic of the Plain Style." *TSLL* 11(1969): 657-670.

9678. ----------. "Holograph Revisions in Two Poems by Fulke Greville." *ELR* 4(1974): 98-110.

9679. Levy, F. J. "Fulke Greville: The Courtier as Philosophic Poet." *MLQ* 33(1972): 433-448.

9680. Litt, Gary L. "'Images of Life': A Study of Narrative and Structure in Fulke Greville's *Caelica*." *SP* 69(1972): 217-230.

9681. Maclean, Hugh. "Fulke Greville and 'E.K.'" *ELN* 1(1963): 90-100.

9682. ----------. "Greville's 'Poetic.'" *SP* 61(1964): 170-191.

9683. Mahoney, John L. "Donne and Greville: Two Christian Attitudes toward the Renaissance Idea of Mutability and Decay." *CLA* 5(1962): 203-212.

9684. Newman, Franklin B. "Sir Fulke Greville and Giordano Bruno: A Possible Echo." *PQ* 29

(1950): 367-374.

9685. Rees, Joan. "Fulke Greville and the Revisions of *Arcadia*." *RES* 17(1966): 54-57.

9686. ----------. "Fulke Greville's Epitaph on Sidney." *RES* 19(1968): 47-51.

9687. Roberts, David A. "Fulke Greville's Aesthetic Reconsidered." *SP* 74(1977): 388-405.

9688. Ure, Peter. "Fulke Greville's Dramatic Characters." *RES* 1(1950): 308-323.

9689. ----------. "A Note on 'Opinion' in Daniel, Greville and Chapman." *MLR* 46(1951): 331-338.

9690. Wilkes, G. A. "The Sequence of the Writings of Fulke Greville, Lord Brooke." *SP* 56 (1959): 489-503.
See also 11361, 17230.

GRIMALD, NICHOLAS. 9691. Blackburn, Ruth H. "Nicholas Grimald's *Christus Redivivus*: A Protestant Resurrection Play." *ELN* 5(1968): 247-250.

9692. Turville-Petre, Thorlac. "Nicholas Grimald and *Alexander A*." *ELR* 6(1976): 180-186.
See also 9320.

HAKLUYT, RICHARD. 9693. Marsh, T. N. "An Unpublished Hakluyt Manuscript?" *NEQ* 35(1962): 247-252.

HARINGTON, JOHN. 9694. Bishop, Carolyn J. "Raleigh Satirized by Harington and Davies." *RES* 23(1972): 52-56.

9695. Goldman, Marcus Selden. "Sidney and Harington as Opponents of Superstition." *JEGP* 54(1955): 526-548.

9696. Nelson, T. G. A. "Sir John Harington as a Critic of Sir Philip Sidney." *SP* 67(1970): 41-56.

HARIOT, THOMAS. 9697. Galinsky, Hans. "Exploring the Exploration Report." *EAL* 12(1977): 5-24.

HARVEY, GABRIEL. 9698. Duhamel, P. Albert. "The Ciceronianism of Gabriel Harvey." *SP* 49 (1952): 155-170.

9699. Godshalk, W. L. "Gabriel Harvey and Sidney's 'Arcadia.'" *MLR* 59(1964): 497-500.

9700. Maxwell, J. C. "Gabriel Harvey: A Reply to Mr. G. M. Young." *EIC* 1(1951): 185-188.

9701. McPherson, David C. "Aretino and the Harvey-Nashe Quarrel." *PMLA* 84(1969): 1551-1558.

9702. Perkins, David. "Issues and Motivations in the Nashe-Harvey Quarrel." *PQ* 39(1960): 224-233.

9703. Relle, Eleanor. "Some New Marginalia and Poems of Gabriel Harvey." *RES* 23(1972): 401-416.

9704. Ribner, Irving. "Gabriel Harvey in Chancery—1608." *RES* 2(1951): 142-147.

HEYWOOD, JOHN. 9705. Bevington, David M. "Is John Heywood's *Play of the Weather* Really about the Weather." *RD* 7(1964): 11-19.

9706. Craik, T. W. "Experiment and Variety in John Heywood's Plays." *RD* 7(1964): 6-11.

9707. Sultan, Stanley. "The Audience-Participation Episode in *Johan Johan*." *JEGP* 52 (1953): 491-497.

9708. ----------. "*Johan, Johan* and Its Debt to French Farce." *JEGP* 53(1954): 23-37.

HOLINSHED, RAPHAEL. 9709. Benbow, R. Mark. "The Providential Theory of Historical Causation in Holinshed's Cronicles." *TSLL* 1(1959): 264-276.

9710. Fish, Charles. "Henry IV: Shakespeare and Holinshed." *SP* 61(1964): 205-218.

9711. Law, Robert Adger. "Holinshed's Leir Story and Shakespeare's." *SP* 47(1950): 42-50.
See also 9624.

HOLLYBAND, CLAUDIUS. 9712. Simonini, R. C., Jr. "The Italian Pedagogy of Claudius Hollyband [Claude de Sainlieus]." *SP* 49(1952): 144-154.

HOOKER, RICHARD. 9713. Chiasson, Elias J. "Swift's Clothes Philosophy in the *Tale* and Hooker's Concept of Law." *SP* 59(1962): 64-82.

9714. Cohen, Eileen Z. "The Visible Solemnity: Ceremony and Order in Shakespeare and Hooker." *TSLL* 12(1970): 181-195.

9715. Hill, W. Speed. "The Authority of Hooker's Style." *SP* 67(1970): 328-338.

9717. ----------. "Doctrine and Polity in Hooker's *Laws*." *ELR* 2(1972): 173-193.

9717. Stueber, Sister M. Stephanie, C. S. J. "The Balanced Diction of Hooker's Polity." *PMLA* 71 (1956): 808-826.

9718. Mahon, Vincent. "The 'Christian Letter': Some Puritan Pbjections to Hooker's Work; and Hooker's 'Undressed' Comments." *RES* 25(1974): 305-311.

HOWES, EDMOND. 9719. Bryant, Joseph Allen, Jr. "John Stow's Continuator and the Defence of Brute." *MLR* 45(1950): 352-354.

HUDSON, THOMAS. See 9467.

HUGHES, THOMAS. 9720. Armstrong, William A. "Elizabethan Themes in *The Misfortunes of Arthur*." *RES* 7(1956): 238-249.

9721. Logan, George M. "Hughes's Use of Lucan in *The Misfortunes of Arthur*." *RES* 20(1969): 22-32.

HULOET, RICHARD. 9722. Starnes, D. T. "Richard Huloet's *Abcedarium*: A Study in English-Latin Lexicography." *SP* 48(1951): 717-737.

JOHNSON, LAURENCE. 9723. Bevington, David M. "*Misogonus* and Laurentius BariΩna." *ELN* 2 (1964): 9-10.

JOYE, GEORGE. 9724. Pineas, Rainer. "George Joye's Use of Rhetoric and Logic as Weapons of Religious Controversy." *EL* 2(1975): 10-23.

KYD. THOMAS. 9725. Adams, Barry B. "The Audiences of *The Spanish Tragedy*." *JEGP* 68(1969): 221-236.

9726. Bercovitch, Sacvan. "Love and Strife in Kyd's *Spanish Tragedy*." *SEL* 9(1969): 215-229.

9727. Broude, Ronald. "Time, Truth, and Right in *The Spanish Tragedy*." *SP* 68(1971): 130-145.

9728. Cannon, Charles K. "The Relation of the Additions of the *Spanish Tragedy* to the Original Play." *SEL* (1962): 229-239.

9729. Chickera, Ernest de. "Divine Justice and Private Revenge in 'The Spanish Tragedy.'" *MLR* 57(1962): 228-232.

9730. Coursen, Herbert R., Jr. "The Unity of *The Spanish Tragedy*." *SP* 65(1968): 768-782.

9731. Faber, M. D., and Colin Skinner. "*The Spanish Tragedy*: Act IV." *PQ* 49(1970): 444-459.

9732. Freeman, Arthur. "Marlowe, Kyd, and the Dutch Church Liberal." *ELR* 3(1973): 44-52.

9733. Goodstein, Peter. "Hieronimo's Destruction of Babylon." *ELN* 3(1966): 172-173.

9734. Hamilton, Donna B. "*The Spanish Tragedy*: A Speaking Picture. *ELR* 4(1974): 203-217.

9735. Hunter, G. K. "Ironies of Justice in

The Spanish Tragedy." *RD* 8(1965): 89-104.

9736. Jensen, Ejner J. "Kyd's *Spanish Tragedy*: The Play Explains Itself." *JEGP* 64 (1965): 7-16.

9737. Kay, Carol McGinnis. "Deception through Words: A Reading of *The Spanish Tragedy*." *SP* 74(1977): 20-38.

9738. Laird, David. "Hieronimo's Dilemma." *SP* 62(1965): 137-146.

9739. Levin, Michael Henry. "'Vindicta mihi!': Meaning, Morality, and Motivation in *The Spanish Tragedy*." *SEL* 4(1964): 307-324.

9740. Maxwell, J. C. "Kyd's *Spanish Tragedy*, III, xiv, 168-9." *PQ* 30(1951): 86.

9741. McMillin, Scott. "The Book of Seneca in *The Spanish Tragedy*." *SEL* 14(1974): 201-208.

9742. ----------. "The Figure of Silence in *The Spanish Tragedy*." *ELH* 39(1972): 27-48.

9743. Ratliff, John D. "Hieronimo Explains Himself." *SP* 54(1957): 112-118.

9744. Tweedie, Eleanor M. "'Action is Eloquence': The Staging of Thomas Kyd's *Spanish Tragedy*." *SEL* 16(1976): 223-239.

See also 9346, 9354, 9356, 9402, 9408, 10127, 11395.

LELAND, JOHN.   9745. Bradner, Leicester. "Some Unpublished Poems by John Leland." *PMLA* 71 (1956): 827-836.

9746. Hutton, James. "John Leland's *Laudatio Pacis*." *SP* 58(1961): 616-626.

LINDSAY, SIR DAVID.   9747. Clewett, Richard M., Jr. "Rhetorical Strategy and Structure in Three of Sir David Lindsay's Poems." *SEL* 16 (1976): 3-14.

9748. MacLaine, Allan H. "*Christus Kirk on the Grene* and Sir David Lindsay's *Satyre of the Thrie Estaits*." *JEGP* 56(1957): 596-601.

See also 9425.

LODGE, THOMAS.   9749. Davis, Walter R. "Masking in Arden: The Histrionics of Lodge's *Rosalynde*." *SEL* 5(1965): 151-163.

9750. Himelick, Raymond. "*A Fig for Momus* and Daniel's *Musophilus*." *MLQ* 18(1957): 247-250.

9751. Larson, Charles. "Lodge's *Rosalind*: Decorum in Arden." *SSF* 14(1977): 117-127.

9753. Lindheim, Nancy R. "Lyly's Golden Legacy: *Rosalynde* and *Pandosto*." *SEL* 15(1975): 3-20.

9753. McAleer, John J. "Thomas Lodge's Verse Interludes." *CLA* 6(1962): 83-89.

9754. Pierce, Robert B. "The Moral Languages of *Rosalynde* and *As You Like It*." *SP* 68 (1971): 167-176.

9755. Pollack, Claudette. "Romance and Realism in Lodge's 'Robin and the Devil'." *SSF* 13(1976): 491-497.

See also 9659, 10465, 11425.

LONGLAND, JOHN.   9756. Blench, J. W. "John Longland and Roger Edgeworth, Two Forgotten Preachers of the Early Sixteenth Century." *RES* 5(1954): 123-143.

LUPTON, THOMAS.   See 9359.

LYLY, JOHN.   9757. Barish, Jonas A. "The Prose Style of John Lyly." *ELH* 23(1956): 14-35.

9758. Best, Michael R. "Lyly's Static Drama." *RD* n.s. 1(1968): 75-86.

9759. ----------. "Nashe, Lyly, and *Summer's Last Will* and Testament." *PQ* 48(1969): 1-11.

9760. ----------. "A Theory of the Literary Genesis of Lyly's *Midas*." *RES* 17(1966): 133-140.

9761. Bond, Sallie. "John Lyly's *Endimion*." *SEL* 14(1974): 189-199.

9762. Braendal, Doris Brenan. "Lyly's *Endymion*, Bronzino's *Allegory of Venus and Cupid*, Webster's *White Devil* and Botticelli's Primarera." *HSL* 4(1972): 197-215.

9763. Brown, J. R., and Margaret Cottire. "A Note on the Date of Lyly's 'Galathea.'" *MLR* 51 (1956): 220-221.

9764. Gannon, Catherine C. "Lyly's Endimion: From Myth to Allegory." *ELR* 6(1976): 220-243.

9765. Gohlke, Madelon. "Reading 'Euphues.'" *Criticism* 19(1977): 103-117.

9766. Hilliard, Stephen S. "Lyly's *Midas* as an Allegory of Tyranny." *SEL* 12(1972): 243-258.

9767. King, Walter N. "John Lyly and Elizabethan Rhetoric." *SP* 52(1955): 149-161.

9768. Knapp, Robert S. "The Monarchy of Love in Lyly's *Endimion*." *MP* 73(1976): 353-367.

9769. Lancashire, Anne C. "Lyly and Shakespeare on the Ropes." *JEGP* 68(1969): 237-244.

9770. Lenz, Carolyn Ruth Swift. "The Allegory of Wisdom in Lyly's *Endimion*." *CD* 10(1976): 235-257.

9771. Lindheim, Nancy R. "Lyly's Golden Legacy: *Rosalynde* and *Pandosto*." *SEL* 15(1975): 3-20.

9772. Parnell, Paul E. "Moral Allegory in Lyly's *Loves Metamorphosis*." *SP* 52(1955): 1-16.

9773. Sandbank, Shimon. "Euphistic Symmetry and the Image." *SEL* 11(1971): 1-13.

9774. Smith, John Hazel. "Sempronia, John Lyly, and John Foxe's Comedy of *Titus and Gesippus*." *PQ* 48(1969): 554-561.

9775. Steinberg, Theodore L. "The Anatomy of *Euphues*." *SEL* 17(1977): 27-38.

9776. Turner, Robert Y. "Some Dialogues of Love in Lyly's Comedies." *ELH* 29(1962): 276-288.

9777. Weltner, Peter. "The Antinomic Vision of Lyly's *Endymion*." *ELR* 3(1973): 5-29.

9778. Westlund, Joseph. "The Theme of Tact in *Campaspe*." *SEL* 16(1976): 213-221.

See also 111, 9286, 9363, 9377, 10372.

MARLOWE, CHRISTOPHER.   9779. Babb, Howard B. "*Policy* in Marlowe's *Jew of Malta*." *ELH* 24(1957): 85-94.

9780. Baldwin, T. W. "Marlowe's Musaeus." *JEGP* 54(1955): 478-485.

9781. Banerjee, Chinmoy. "*Hero and Leander* as Erotic Comedy." *JNT* 3(1973): 40-52.

9782. Battenhouse, Roy W. "Marlowe Reconsidered: Some Reflections on Levin's *Overreacher*." *JEGP* 52(1953): 531-542.

9783. ----------. "Protestant Apologetics and the Subplot of 2 Tamburlaine." *ELR* 3(1973): 30-43.

9784. Bawcutt, N. W. "Machiavelli and Marlowe's *The Jew of Malta*." *RD* n.s. 3(1970): 3-49.

9785. Bowers, Fredson. "The Test of Marlowe's *Faustus*." *MP* 49(1952): 195-204.

9786. Brodwin, Leonora Leet. "*Edward II*: Marlowe's Culminating Treatment of Love." *ELH* 31 (1964): 139-155.

9787. Brooks, Charles. "*Tamburlaine* and Attitudes Toward Women." *ELH* 24(1957): 1-11.

9788. Campbell, Lily B. "*Doctor Faustus*:

A Case of Conscience." *PMLA* 67(1952): 219–239.

9789. Cope, Jackson I. "Marlowe's *Dido* and the Titillating Children." *ELR* 4(1974): 315–325.

9790. Craik, T. W. "Faustus' Damnation Reconsidered." *RD* n.s. 2(1969): 189–196.

9791. Cutts, John. "Tamburlaine 'as fierce Achilles was.'" *CD* 1(1967): 105–109.

9792. Davidson, Clifford. "Doctor Faustus at Rome." *SEL* 9(1969): 231–239.

9793. ——————. "Doctor Faustus of Wittenberg." *SP* 59(1962): 514–523.

9794. Deats, Sara Munson. "*Doctor Faustus*: From Chapbook to Tragedy." *EL* 3(1976): 3–16.

9795. Dessen, Alan C. "The Elizabethan Stage Jew and Christian Example: Gerontus, Barabus, and Shylock." *MLQ* 35(1974): 231–245.

9796. Fraser, Russell A. "The Art of *Hero and Leander*." *JEGP* 57(1958): 743–754.

9797. Freeman, Arthur. "Marlowe, Kyd, and the Dutch Church Liberal." *ELR* 3(1973): 44–52.

9798. French, A. L. "The Philosophy of *Dr. Faustus*." *EIC* 20(1970): 123–142.

9799. Frey, Leonard H. "Antithetical Balance in the Opening and Close of *Doctor Faustus*." *MLQ* 24(1963): 350–353.

9800. Friedman, Alan W. "The Shackling of Accidents in Marlowe's *Jew of Malta*." *TSLL* 8 (1966): 155–167.

9801. Gill, Roma. "Marlowe, Lucan, and Sulpitius." *RES* 24(1973): 401–413.

9802. ——————. "Marlowe's Virgil: *Dido Queene of Carthage*." *RES* 28(1977): 141–155.

9803. Godshalk, William Leigh. "Marlowe's *Dido, Queen of Carthage*." *ELH* 38(1971): 1–18.

9804. Goldfarb, Russell and Clare. "The Seven Deadly Sins in *Doctor Faustus*." *CLA* 13 (1970): 350–363.

9805. Hattaway, Michael. "The Theology of Marlowe's *Doctor Faustus*." *RD* n.s. 3(1970): 51–78.

9806. Hawkins, Sherman. "The Education of Faustus." *SEL* 6(1966): 193–209.

9807. Homan, Sidney R. "Chapman and Marlowe: The Paradoxical Hero and the Divided Response." *JEGP* 68(1969): 391–406.

9808. ——————. "*Doctor Faustus*, Dekker's *Old Fortunatus*, and the Morality Plays." *MLQ* 26 (1965): 497–505.

9809. Honderich, Pauline. "John Calvin and Doctor Faustus." *MLR* 68(1973): 1–13.

9810. Hoy, Cyrus. "'Ignorance in Knowledge': Marlowe's Faustus and Ford's Giovanni." *MP* 57 (1960): 145–154.

9811. Jantz, Harold. "An Elizabethan Statement on the Origin of the German Faust Book." *JEGP* 51(1952): 137–152.

9812. Jensen, James. "Heroic Convention and *Dr. Faustus*." *EIC* 21(1971): 101–106.

9813. Keach, William. "Marlowe's Hero as 'Venus' Nun.'" *ELR* 2(1972): 307–320.

9814. Kiessling, Nicolas. "Doctor Faustus and the Sin of Demonality." *SEL* 15(1975): 205–211.

9815. Kimbrough, Robert. "*1 Tamburlaine*: A Speaking Picture in a Tragic Glass." *RD* 7(1964): 20–34.

9816. Kuriyama, Constance Brown. "Dr. Greg and *Doctor Faustus*: The Supposed Originality of the 1616 Text." *ELR* 5(1975): 171–197.

9817. Leech, Clifford. "Venus and Her Nun: Portraits of Women in Love by Shakespeare and Marlowe." *SEL* 5(1965): 247–268.

9818. Leslie, Nancy T. "*Tamburlaine* in the Theater: Tartar, Grand Guignol, or Janus?" *RD* n.s. 4(1971): 105–120.

9819. Lever, Katherine. "The Image of Man in *Tamburlaine*, Part I. *PQ* 35(1956): 421–427.

9820. Manley, Frank. "The Nature of Faustus." *MP* 66(1969): 218–231.

9821. Matalene, H. M., III. "Marlowe's *Faustus* and the Comforts of Academicism." *ELH* 39 (1972): 495–519.

9822. Maxwell, J. C. "How Bad is the Text of 'The Jew of Malta'?" *MLR* 48(1953): 435–440.

9823. McAlindon, T. "Classical Mythology and Christian Tradition in Marlowe's Doctor Faustus." *PMLA* 81(1966): 214–223.

9824. McCullen, Joseph T. "Dr. Faustus and Renaissance Learning." *MLR* 51(1956): 6–16.

9825. McMillin, Scott. "The Ownership of *The Jew of Malta, Friar Bacon*, and *The Ranger's Comedy*." *ELN* 9(1972): 249–252.

9826. Miller, Paul W. "A Function of Myth in Marlowe's 'Hero and Leander.'" *SP* 50(1953): 158–167.

9827. Mills, John. "The Courtship Ritual of Hero and Leander." *ELR* 2(1972): 298–306.

9828. Nagarajan, S. "The Philosophy of *Dr. Faustus*." *EIC* 20(1970): 485–487.

9829. Neuse, Richard. "Atheism and Some Functions of Myth in Marlowe's *Hero and Leander*." *MLQ* 31(1970): 424–439.

9830. Nosworthy, J. M. "Marlowe's *Ovid* and Davies's *Epigrams*—A Postscript." *RES* 15(1964): 397–398.

9831. ——————. "The Publication of Marlowe's *Elegies* and Davies's *Epigrams*." *RES* 4 (1953): 260–261.

9832. O'Brien, Margaret Ann. "Christian Belief in *Doctor Faustus*." *ELH* 37(1970): 1–11.

9833. Okerlund, A. N. "The Intellectual Folly of Dr. Faustus." *SP* 74(1977): 258–278.

9834. Ornstein, Robert. "The Comic Synthesis in *Doctor Faustus*." *ELH* 22(1955): 165–172.

9835. ——————. "Marlowe and God: The Tagic Theology of *Dr. Faustus*." *PMLA* 83(1968): 1378–1385.

9836. Pearce, T. M. "Marlower and Castiglione." *MLQ* 12(1951): 3–12.

9837. ——————. "Tamburlaine's 'Discipline to His Three Sonnes': An Interpretation of *Tamburlaine, Part II*." *MLQ* 15(1954): 147–167.

9838. Peet, Donald. "The Rhetoric of *Tamburlaine*." *ELH* 26(1959): 137–155.

9839. Post, Jonathan F. S. "Recent Studies in Marlowe." *ELR* 7(1977): 382–399.

9840. Quinn, Michael. "The Freedom of Tamburlaine." *MLQ* 21(1960): 315–320.

9841. Ribner, Irving. "Greene's Attack on Marlowe: Some New Light on *Alphonsus* and *Selimus*." *SP* 52(1955): 162–171.

9842. ——————. "The Idea of History in Marlowe's *Tambourlaine*." *ELH* 20(1953): 251–266.

9843. ——————. "Marlowe and Machiavelli." *Comp L* 6(1954): 348–356.

9844. ——————. "Marlowe's *Edward II* and the Tudor History Play." *ELH* 22(1955): 243–253.

9845. ——————. "*Tamburlaine* and *The Wars of Cyrus*." *JEGP* 53(1954): 569–573.

9846. Richards, Susan. "Marlowe's
Tamburlaine II: A Drama of Death." *MLQ* 26(1965):
375–387.

9847. Rothstein, Eric. "Structure as
Meaning in *The Jew of Malta*." *JEGP* 65(1966):
260–273.

9848. Sachs, Arieh. "The Religious Despair of Doctor Faustus." *JEGP* 63(1964): 625–647.

9849. Schuman, Samuel. "'Occasion's Bald
Behind': A Note on the Sources of an Emblematic
Image in *The Jew of Malta*." *MP* 70(1973): 234–
235.

9850. Segal, Erich. "Hero and Leander:
Góngora and Marlowe." *Comp L* 15(1963): 338–356.

9851. Simmons, J. L. "Elizabethan Stage
Practice and Marlowe's *The Jew of Malta*." *RD* n.s.
4(1971): 93–104.

9852. Smith, Mary E. "Staging Marlowe's
Dido Queene of Carthage" *SEL* 17(1977): 177–190.

9853. Smith, Warren D. "The Nature of Evil
in 'Doctor Faustus.'" *MLR* 60(1965): 171–175.

9854. ----------. "The Substance of Meaning in *Tamburlaine Part I*." *SP* 67(1970): 156–166.

9855. Snyder, Susan. "Marlowe's *Doctor
Faustus* as an Inverted Saint's Life." *SP* 63
(1966): 565–577.

9856. Sternfeld, Frederick W., and Mary
Joiner Chan. "'Come live with me and be my
love.'" *Comp L* 22(1970): 173–187.

9857. Stroup, Thomas B. "*Doctor Faustus*
and *Hamlet*: Contrasting Kinds of Christian
Tragedy." *CD* 5(1971): 243–253.

9858. ----------. "Ritual in Marlowe's
Plays." *CD* 7(1973): 198–221.

9859. Summers, Claude J. "Isabella's Plea
for Gaveston in Marlowe's *Edward II*." *PQ* 52
(1973): 308–310.

9860. ----------. "Tambourlaine's Opponents and Machiavelli's *Prince*." *ELN* 11(1974):
256–259.

9861. ----------, and Ted-Larry Pebworth.
"Marlowe's Faustus and the Earl of Bedford's
Motto." *ELN* 9(1972): 165–167.

9862. Thomson, J. Oliver. "Marlowe's
'River Araris'." *MLR* 48(1953): 323–324.

9863. Turner, Myron. "Pastoral and Hermap-
rodite: A Study in the Naturalism of Marlowe's
Hero and Leander." *TSLL* 17(1975): 397–414.

9864. Velz, John W. "Episodic Structure
in Four Tudor Plays: A Virtue of Necessity." *CD*
6(1972): 87–102.

9865. Waith, Eugene M. "Marlowe and the
Jades of Asia." *SEL* 5(1965): 229–245.

9866. Walsh, William P. "Sexual Discovery
and Renaissance Morality in Marlowe's *Hero and
Leander*." *SEL* 12(1972): 33–54.

9867. West, Robert H. "The Impatient Magic
of Dr. Faustus." *ELR* 4(1974): 218–240.

9868. Westlund, Joseph. "The Orthodox
Christian Framework of Marlowe's *Faustus*." *SEL*
3(1963): 191–205.

9869. Williams, Martin T. "The Temptations
in Marlowe's *Hero and Leander*." *MLQ* 16(1955): 226–
231.

9870. Zimansky, Curt A. "Marlowe's *Faustus*:
The Date Again." *PQ* 41(1962): 181–187.

See also 5094, 9346, 9354, 9356, 9363, 9367,
9395, 9445, 9460, 9463, 10377, 11619, 13368.

MARPRELATE TRACTS. 9871. Anselment, Raymond A. "Rhetoric and the Dramatic Satire of
Martin Marprelate." *SEL* 10(1970): 103–119.

9872. Coolidge, John S. "Martin Marprelate,
Marvell, and Decorum Personae on a Satirical
Theme." *PMLA* 74(1959): 526–532.

See also 11928.

MARRIAGE OF WIT AND SCIENCE. 9873. Varma,
R. S. "Philosophical and Moral Ideas in *The
Marriage of Wit and Science*." *PQ* 44(1965): 120–122.

MEDWALL, HENRY. 9874. Jones, Robert C.
"The Stage World and the 'Real' World in Medwall's
Fulgens and Lucres." *MLQ* 32(1971): 131–142.

9875. Waith, Eugene M. "*Controversia* in the
English Drama: Medwall and Massinger." *PMLA* 68
(1953): 286–303.

See also 9340, 9425.

MERBURY, FRANCIS. 9876. Lenmam, T. N. S.
"Francis Merbury, 1555-1611." *SP* 65(1968): 207–222.

MIRROR FOR MAGISTRATES. 9877. Kiefer, Frederick. "Fortune and Providence in the *Mirror for
Magistrates*." *SP* 74(1977): 146–164.

9878. Thaler, Alwin. "Literary Criticism in
A Mirror for Magistrates." *JEGP* 49(1950): 1–13.

See also 9323.

MONTGOMERIE, ALEXANDER. 9879. Jack, Ronald
D. S. "The Lyrics of Alexander Montgomerie." *RES*
20(1969): 168–181.

See also 9450, 9466.

MORE, SIR THOMAS. 9880. Abrash, Merritt.
"Missing the Point in More's Utopia." *Ext* 19(1977):
27–38.

9881. Allen, Ward. "Speculation on St. Thomas
More's Use of Hesychius." *PQ* 46(1967): 156–166.

9882. Bevington, David M. "The Dialogue in
Utopia: Two Sides to the Question." *SP* 58(1961):
498–509.

9883. Crossett, John. "More and Seneca." *PQ*
40(1961): 577–580.

9884. Duhamel, P. Albert. "Medievalism of
More's *Utopia*." *SP* 52(1955): 99–126.

9885. Elliott, Robert C. "The Shape of
Utopia." *ELH* 30(1963): 317–334.

9886. Heiserman, A. R. "Satire in the
Utopia." *PMLA* 78(1963): 163–174.

9887. Jones, Royston O. "Some Notes on More's
'Utopia' in Spain." *MLR* 45(1950): 478–482.

9888. Kincaid, Arthur Noel. "The Dramatic
Structure of Sir Thomas More's *History of King
Richard III*." *SEL* 12(1972): 223–242.

9889. McCutcheon, Elizabeth. "Thomas More,
Raphael Hythlodaeus and the Angel Raphael." *SEL* 9
(1969): 21–38.

9890. Miles, Leland. "Boethius and Thomas
More's *Dialogue of Comfort*." *ELN* 3(1965): 97–101.

9891. ----------. "The 'Dialogue of Comfort'
and More's Execution: Some Comments on Literary
Purpose." *MLR* 61(1966): 556–560.

9892. ----------. "The Literary Artistry of
Thomas More: *The Dialogue of Comfort*." *SEL* 6(1966):
7–33.

9893. ----------. "More's *Dialogue of
Comfort* as a First Draft." *SP* 63(1966): 126–134.

9894. ----------. "With a Coal? The Composition of Thomas More's *Dialogue of Comfort*." *PQ*
45(1966): 437–442.

9895. Pineas, Rainer. "More versus Tyndale:
A Study of Controversial Technique." *MLQ* 24(1963):

144-150.

9896. ----------. "Sir Thomas More's Controversy with Christopher Saint-German." *SEL* 1,#1(1961): 49-62.

9897. ----------. "Thomas More's Controversy with Simon Fish." *SEL* 7(1967): 15-28.

9898. ----------. "Thomas More's Use of Humor as a Weapon of Religious Controversy." *SP* 58(1961): 97-114.

9899. Plank, Robert. "The Geography of Utopia: Psychological Factors Shaping the Ideal Location." *Ext* 6(1965): 39-49.

9900. Rebhorn, Wayne A. "Thomas More's Enclosed Garden: *Utopia* and Renaissance Humanism." *ELR* 6(1976): 140-155.

9901. Schoek, R. J. "More, Plutarch, and King Agis: Spartan History and the Meaning of *Utopia*." *PQ* 35(1956): 366-375.

9902. ----------. "Sir Thomas More and the Lincoln's Inn Revels." *PQ* 29(1950): 426-430.

9903. Schuster, Sister Mary Faith, O.S.B. "Philosophy of Life and Prose Style in Thomas More's *Richard III* and Francis Bacon's *Henry VII*." *PMLA* 70(1955): 474-487.

9904. Surtz, Edward L. "Logic in *Utopia*." *PQ* 29(1950): 389-401.

9905. ----------. "More's *Apologia Pro Utopia Sua*." *MLQ* 19(1958): 319-324.

9906. ----------. "Richard Pace's Sketch of Thomas More." *JEGP* 57(1958): 36-50.

9907. ----------. "The Setting for More's Plea for Greek in *Utopia*." *PQ* 35(1956): 353-365.

9908. ----------. "Thomas More and the Great Books." *PQ* 32(1953): 43-57.

9909. Teunissen, John J., and Evelyn Hinz. "Roger Williams, Thomas More and the Narragansett Utopia." *EAL* 11(1977): 281-295.

See also 202, 9299, 9310, 9321, 9323, 9438, 9529, 11285, 11832.

MORLEY, HENRY PARKER. See 9438.

MULCASTER, RICHARD. 9910. DeMolen, Richard L. "Richard Mulcaster and Elizabethan Pageantry." *SEL* 14(1954): 209-221.

See also 9320.

MUNDAY, ANTHONY. 9911. Hosley, Richard. "Anthony Munday, John Heardson, and the Authorship of 'Fedele and Fortunio'." *MLR* 55(1960): 564-565.

9912. ----------. "The Date of 'Fedele and Fortunio'." *MLR* 57(1962): 385-386.

9913. Margeson, J. M. R. "Dramatic Form: the Huntington Plays." *SEL* 14(1974): 223-238.

9914. Wright, Celeste Turner. "Anthony Mundy and the Bodenham Miscellanies." *PQ* 40(1961): 449-461.

9915. ----------. "Anthony Mundy, 'Edward' Spenser, and E. K." *PMLA* 76(1961): 34-39.

9916. ----------. "'Lazarus Pyott' and Other Inventions of Anthony Mundy." *PQ* 42(1963): 532-541.

9917. ----------. "Young Anthony Mundy Again." *SP* 56(1959): 150-168.

See also 11297, 12404.

NASHE, THOMAS. 9918. Best, Michael R. "Nashe, Lyly, and *Summer's Last Will and Testament*." *PQ* 48(1969): 1-11.

9919. Drew, Philip. "Edward Daunce and *The Unfortunate Traveller*." *RES* 11(1960): 410-412.

9920. Duncan-Jones, Katherine. "Nashe and Sidney: The Tournament in 'The Unfortunate Traveller.'" *MLR* 63(1968): 3-6.

9921. Friendenreich, Kenneth. "Nash's *Strange Newes* and the Case for Professional Writers." *SP* 71(1974): 451-472.

9922. Gibbons, Sister Mariana, O.P. "Polemic, Rhetorical Tradition and *The Unfortunate Traveller*." *JEGP* 63(1964): 408-421.

9923. Gohlke, Madelon S. "Wits Wantonness: *The Unfortunate Traveller* as Picaresque." *SP* 73 (1976): 397-413.

9924. Harlow, C. G. "Nashe's Visit to the Isle of Wight and his Publications of 1592-4." *RES* 14(1963): 225-242.

9925. ----------. "A Source for Nashe's *Terrors of the Night* and the Authorship of *1 Henry VI*." *SEL* 5(1965): 31-46, 269-281.

9926. ----------. "Thomas Nashe, Robert Cotten the Antiquary, and *The Terrors of the Night*." *RES* 12(1961): 7-23.

9927. Kaula, David. "The Low Style in Nashe's *The Unfortunate Traveller*." *SEL* 6(1966): 43-57.

9928. Lanham, Richard A. "Tom Nashe and Jack Wilton: Personality as Structure in *The Unfortunate Traveller*." *SSF* 4(1967): 201-216.

9929. Leggatt, Alexander. "Artistic Coherence in *The Unfortunate Traveller*." *SEL* 14(1974): 31-46.

9930. McGinn, Donald J. "Thomas Nashe and the Marprelate Controversy: A Correction." *SP* 48 (1951): 798-799.

9931. McPherson, David C. "Aretino and the Harvey-Nashe Quarrel." *PMLA* 84(1969): 1551-1558.

9932. Miller, Edwin Haviland. "The Relationship of Robert Greene and Thomas Nashe (1588-1592)." *PQ* 33(1954): 353-367.

9933. Perkins, David. "Issues and Motivations in the Nashe-Harvey Quarrel." *PQ* 39(1960): 224-233.

9934. Sanderson, James L. "An Unnoted Text of Nashe's 'The Choice of Valentines.'" *ELN* 1 (1964): 252-253.

9935. Scoufos, Alice Lyle. "Nashe, Jonson, and the Oldcastle Problem." *MP* 65(1968): 307-324.

9936. Summersgill, Travis L. "The Influence of the Marprelate Controversy upon the Style of Thomas Nashe." *SP* 48(1951): 145-160.

9937. Trimpi, Wesley. "The Practice of Historical Interpretation and Nashe's 'Brightnesse falls from the ayre.'" *JEGP* 66(1967): 501-518.

See also 111, 504, 9287, 9306, 9659, 9944.

NEWTON, HUMFREY. 9938. Robbins, Rossell Hope. "The Poems of Humfrey Newton, Esquire, 1466-1536." *PMLA* 65(1950): 249-281.

NORTH, GEORGE. 9939. Javitch, Daniel. "*The Philosopher of the Court*: A French Satire Misunderstood." *Comp L* 23(1971): 97-124.

NOWELL, LAURENCE. 9940. Sledd, James. "Nowell's *Vocabularium Saxonicum* and the Elyot-Cooper Tradition." *SP* 51(1954): 143-148.

9941. Warnicke, Retha M. "Note on a Court of Requests Case of 1571." *ELN* 11(1974): 250-256.

PARNASSUS PLAYS. 9942. Reyburn, Marjorie L. "New Facts and Theories about the Parnassus Plays." *PMLA* 74(1959): 325-335.

9943. ----------. "A Note on Owen Gwyn and *The Returne from Parnassus*, Part II." *PMLA* 76 (1961): 298-300.

9944. Summersgill, Travis L. "Harvey, Nashe,

and the Three Parnassus Plays." *PQ* 31(1952): 94-95.

9945. Thomas, Sidney. "A Note on Owen Gwyn and *The Returne from Parnassus*, Part II." *PMLA* 76(1961): 298-300.

PALGRAVE, JOHN.   See 9320.

PATTEN, WILLIAM.   9946. Scott, David. "William Patten and the Authorship of 'Robert Lancham's Letter' (1575)." *ELR* 7(1977): 297-306.

PEELE, GEORGE.   9947. Ewbank, Inga-Stina. "The House of David in Renaissance Drama: A Comparative Study." *RD* 8(1965): 3-40.

9948. Lesnik, Henry G. "The Structural Significance of Myth and Flattery in Peele's *Arraignment of Paris*." *SP* 65(1968): 163-170.

9949. Maxwell, J. C. "Peele and Shakespeare: A Stylometric Test." *JEGP* 49(1950): 557-561.

9950. Reeves, John D. "Perseus and the Flying Horse in Peele and Heywood." *RES* 6(1955): 397-399.

9951. von Hendy, Andrew. "The Triumph of Chasitity: Form and Meaning in *The Arraignment of Paris*." *RD* n.s. 1(1968): 87-101.

See also 9291, 9343.

PERKINS, WILLIAM.   9952. Sisson, Rosemary A. "William Perkins, Apologist for the Elizabethan Church of English." *MLR* 47(1952): 495-502.

PICKERING, JOHN.   9953. Knapp, Robert S. "*Horestes*: The Uses of Revenge." *ELH* 40(1973): 205-220.

9954. Merritt, Karen Maxwell. "The Source of John Pikeryng's *Horestes*." *RES* 23(1972): 255-266.

See also 9426, 9956.

PRESTON, THOMAS.   9955. Fishman, Burton J. "Pride and Ire: Threatrical Iconography in Preston's *Cambises*." *SEL* 16(1976): 201-211.

9956. Happé, P. "Tragic Themes in Three Tudor Moralities." *SEL* 5(1965): 207-227.

9957. Myers, James Phares, Jr. "The Heart of King Cambises." *SP* 70(1973): 367-376.

See also 9354, 9426.

PUTTENHAM, GEORGE.   9958. Korn, A. L. "Puttenham and the Original Pattern-Poem." *Comp L* 6(1954): 289-303.

RALEGH, SIR WALTER.   9959. Bishop, Carolyn. "Ralegh Satirized by Harington and Davies." *RES* 23(1972): 52-56.

9960. Bowers, R. H. "Raleigh's Last Speech: The 'Elms' Document." *RES* 2(1951): 209-216.

9961. Duncan-Jones, Katherine. "The Date of Raleigh's '21th: And Last Booke of the Dream to Scinthia.'" *RES* 21(1970): 143-158.

9962. Edwards, Philip. "Who Wrote *The Passionate Man's Pilgrimage*." *ELR* 4(1974): 83-97.

9963. Horner, Joyce. "The Large Landscape: A Study of Certain Images in Ralegh." *EIC* 5 (1955): 197-213.

9964. Jacquot, Jean. "Ralegh's 'Hellish Verses' and the 'Tragicall Raigne of Selimus.'" *MLR* 48(1953): 1-9.

9965. Johnson, Michael L. "Some Problems of Unity in Sir Walter Ralegh's *The Ocean's Love to Cynthia*." *SEL* 14(1974): 17-30.

9966. Latham, A. M.C. "Sir Walter Ralegh's Will." *RES* 22(1971): 129-136.

9967. Popkin, Richard H. "A Manuscript of Ralegh's 'The Scepticke.'" *PQ* 36(1957): 253-259.

9968. Sackton, Alexander. "The Rhetoric of Literary Praise in the Poetry of Raleigh and Chapman." *TSLL* 18(1976): 409-421.

9969. Sprott, S. E. "Raleigh's 'Sceptic' and the Elizabethan Translation of Sextus Empiricus." *PQ* 42(1963): 166-175.

9970. West, Michael. "Raleigh's Disputed Authorship of 'A description of Loue.'" *ELN* 10 (1972): 92-99.

9971. Williams, Edith Whitehurst. "The Anglo-Saxon Theme of Exile in Renaissance Lyrics: A Perspective on Two Sonnets of Sir Walter Ralegh." *ELH* 42(1975): 171-188.

See also 9310, 9463.

RARE TRIUMPHS OF LOVE AND FORTUNE.   See 9363, 9402, 9418.

RASTELL, JOHN.   See 9378.

REDFORD, JOHN.   9972. Schell, Edgar T. "*Scio Ergo Sum*: The Structure of *Wit and Science*." *SEL* 16(1976): 179-199.

9973. Velz, John W., and Carl P. Daw, Jr. "Tradition and Originality in *Wit and Science*." *SP* 65(1968): 631-646.

See also 9370.

RESPUBLICA.   See 9345, 9425.

REYNARD THE FOX.   9974. Blake, N. F. "English Versions of Reynard the Fox in the Fifteenth and Sixteenth Centuries." *SP* 62(1965): 63-77.

REYNOLDS, JOHN.   See 9287.

RICH, BARNABY.   9975. Lievsay, John Leon. "A Word about Barnaby Rich." *JEGP* 55(1956): 381-392.

ROBINSON, RICHARD.   9976. Greg, W. W. "Richard Robinson and the Stationers' Register." *MLR* 50(1955): 407-413.

RUDD, ANTHONY.   9977. Barber, Lester E. "Anthony Rudd and the Authorship of *Misogonus*." *ELN* 12(1975): 255-260.

SABIE, FRANCIS.   9978. Maveety, Stanley R. "High Style, Strange Words, and the Answer to an Old Problem." *ELN* 5(1968): 159-163.

SACKVILLE, THOMAS.   9979. Bradford, Alan T. "Mirrors of Mutability: Winter Landscapes in Tudor Poetry." *ELR* 4(1974): 3-39.

9980. Davie, Donald. "Sixteenth-Century Poetry and the Common Reader: The Case of Thomas Sackville." *EIC* 4(1954): 117-127.

SHAKESPEARE, WILLIAM

GENERAL AND MISCELLANEOUS.   9981. Arthos, John. "The Undiscovered Country." *CD* 10(1976): 16-28.

9982. Babcock, R. W. "Historical Criticism of Shakespeare." *MLQ* 13(1952): 6-20.

9983. Babula, William. "The Play-Life Metaphor in Shakespeare and Stoppard." *MD* 15 (1972): 279-282.

9984. Barnet, Sylvan. "Some Limitations of a Christian Approach to Shakespeare." *ELH* 22(1955): 81-92.

9985. Barroll, J. Leeds. "Shakespeare and Roman History." *MLR* 53(1958): 327-343.

9986. Bateson, F. W. "Elementary, My Dear Hotson! A Caveat for Liteary Detectives." *EIC* 1 (1951): 81-88.

9987. Berger, Harry, Jr. "Theatre, Drama, and the Second World: A Prologue to Shakespeare."

CD 2(1968): 3-20.

9988. Berry, Ralph. "Shakespearean Comedy and Northrup Frye." *EIC* 22(1972): 33-40.

9989. Bethell, S. L. "Shakespeare's Actors." *RES* 1(1950): 193-205.

9990. Bland, D. S. "The Heroine and the Sea: An Aspect of Shakespeare's Last Plays." *EIC* 3(1953): 39-44.

9991. Boris, Edna Z. "The Tudor Constitution and Shakespeare's Two Tetralogies." *Coll L* 4(1977): 197-209.

9992. Bowers, Fredson. "The Yale Folio Facsimile and Scholarship." *MP* 53(1956): 50-57.

9993. Bradbrook, M. C. "Shakespeare and the Use of Disguise in Elizabethan Drama." *EIC* 2(1952): 159-168.

9994. Bradford, Alan T. "Mirrors of Mutability: Winter Landscapes in Tudor Poetry." *ELR* 4(1974): 3-39.

9995. Brown, Huntington. "Enter the Shakespearean Tragic Hero." *EIC* 3(1953): 285-302.

9996. Burckhardt, Sigurd. "The Poet as Fool and Priest." *ELH* 23(1956): 279-298.

9997. Carlisle, Carol Jones. "The Nineteenth-Century Actors *Versus* the Closet Critics of Shakespeare." *SP* 51(1954): 599-615.

9998. Carpenter, Nan Cooke. "Shakespeare and Music: Unexplored Areas." *RD* n.s. 7(1976): 243-255.

9999. Charney, Maurice. "Shakespeare's Unpoetic Poetry." *SEL* 13(1973): 199-207.

10000. Chapman, Raymond. "The Wheel of Fortune in Shakespeare's Historical Plays." *RES* 1(1950): 1-7.

10001. Cohen, Eileen Z. "The Visible Solemnity: Ceremony and Order in Shakespeare and Hooker." *TSLL* 12(1970): 181-195.

10002. Coke, Douglas. "Shakespearean Pastoral." *RD* n.s. 5(1972): 213-224.

10003. Craig, Hardin. "Ideational Approach to Shakespeare's Plays." *PQ* 41(1962): 147-157.

10004. ----------. "Shakespeare and the Here and Now." *PMLA* 67,#1(1952): 87-94.

10005. Cranfill, Thomas M. "Flesh's Thousand Shocks in Shakespeare." *TSLL* 17(1975): 27-60.

10006. ----------. "Shakespeare's Old Heroes." *TSLL* 15(1973): 215-230.

10007. Craven, Alan E. "Justification of Prose and Jaggard Compositor B." *ELN* 3(1965): 15-17.

10008. Cunningham, J. V. "*Tragedy* in Shakespeare." *ELH* 17(1950): 36-46.

10009. D'Avanzo, Mario L. "Emerson and Shakespeare in Stevens' 'Bantams in Pine-Woods.'" *AL* 49(1977): 103-107.

10010. Dessen, Alan C. "Two Falls and a Trap: Shakespeare and the Spectacles of Realism." *ELR* 5(1975): 291-307.

10011. Doran, Madeleine. "'Discrepant Awareness' in Shakespeare's Comedies." *MP* 60 (1962): 51-55.

10012. Draper, John W. "Shakespeare and Abbas the Great." *PQ* 30(1951): 419-425.

10013. ----------. "Shakespeare and the Turk." *JEGP* 55(1956): 523-532.

10014. Dunn, Hough-Lewis. "The Circle of Love in Hoffman and Shakespeare." *SR* 11(1972): 113-137.

10015. Eastman, Arthur M. "The Texts from Which Johnson Printed His Shakespeare." *JEGP* 49 (1950): 182-191.

10016. Evans, G. Blackemore. "The Douai Manuscript—Six Shakespearean Transcripts (1694-95)." *PQ* 41(1962): 158-172.

10017. Felheim, Marvin. "Criticism and the Films of Shakespeare's Plays." *CD* 9(1975): 147-155.

10018. Felperin, Howard. "Keats and Shakespeare: Two New Sources." *ELN* 2(1964): 105-108.

10019. Flatter, Richard. "The Veil of Beauty. Some Aspects of Verse and Prose in Shakespeare and Goethe." *JEGP* 50(1951): 437-450.

10020. Flint, M. K., and E. J. Dobson. "Weak Masters." *RES* 10(1959): 58-60.

10021. Fly, Richard D. "'So Workmanly the Blood and Tears are Drawn': Tragic Vision and Formal Beauty in Shakespearean Drama." *EL* 2(1975): 131-148.

10022. Foakes, R. A. "Atavism and Anticipation in Shakespeare's Style." *EIC* 7(1957): 455-457.

10023. Fraser, Russell. "Elizabethan Drama and the Art of Abstraction." *CD* 2(1968): 73-82.

10024. Frazier, Harriet C. "Theobald's *Double Falsehood*: A Revision of Shakespeare's *Cardenio*?." *CD* 1(1967): 219-233.

10025. Freehafer, John. "*Cardenio*, by Shakespeare and Fletcher." *PMLA* 84(1969): 501-513.

10026. Frenz, Horst, and Martin Mueller. "More Shakespeare and Less Aeschylus in Eugene O'Neill's *Mourning Becomes Electra*." *AL* 38(1966): 85-100.

10027. Frey, Charles. "Teaching Shakespeare's Romances." *Coll L* 4(1977): 252-256.

10028. Frye, Dean. "The Question of Sheakespearean 'Parody.'" *EIC* 15(1965): 22-26.

10029. Gove, Philip B. "Shakespeare's Language in Today's Dictionary." *TSLL* 7(1965): 127-136.

10030. Gray, H. David, and Percy Simpson. "Shakespeare or Heminge? A Rejoinder and a Surrejoinder." *MLR* 45(1950): 148-152.

10031. Hainsworth, J. D. "Shakespeare, Son of Beckett?" *MLQ* 25(1964): 346-354.

10032. Hamer, Douglas. "Was William Shakespeare William Shakeshafte?" *RES* 21(1970): 41-48.

10033. Hankins, John E. "The Pains of the Afterworld: Fire, Wind and Ice in Milton and Shakespeare." *PMLA* 71(1956): 482-495.

10034. Hansen, Abby J. D. "Shakespeare and the Love of Precious Stones." *Coll L* 4(1977): 210-219.

10035. Hapgood, Robert. "Shakespeare's Delayed Reactions." *EIC* 13(1963): 9-16.

10036. Harrison, G. B. "A Scholar Mislaid." *ELN* 1(1964): 183-187.

10037. Holland, Norman N. "Freud on Shakespeare." *PMLA* 75(1960): 163-173.

10038. Honigmann, E. A. J. "Shakespeare's 'Lost Source—Plays.'" *MLR* 49(1954): 293-307.

10039. Hubbs, V. C. "Treck's Romantic Fairy Tales and Shakespeare." *SR* 8(1969): 229-234.

10040. Hulme, Hilda. "Shakespeare and the *Oxford English Dictionary*: Some Supplementary Glosses." *RES* 6(1955): 128-140.

10041. ----------. "Shakespeare of Stratford." *RES* 10(1959): 20-25.

10042. Hunter, G. K. "Atavism and Anticipation in Shakespeare's Style." *EIC* 7(1957): 450-453.

10043. Jackson, J. R. de J. "Coleridge on Dramatic Illusion and Spectacle in the Performance of Shakespeare's Plays." *MP* 62(1964): 13-21.

10044. Jackson, Margaret Y. "'High Comedy' in Shakespeare." *CLA* 10(1966): 11-22.

10045. Johnston, George Burke. "Camden, Daniel, and Shakespeare." *PMLA* 77(1962): 510-512.

10046. Jorgensen, Paul A. "Divided Command in Shakespeare." *PMLA* 70(1955): 750-761.

10047. ----------. "A Formative Shakespeare Legacy: Elizabethan Views of God, Fortune, and War." *PMLA* 90(1975): 222-233.

10048. Kastan, David Scott. "The Shape of Time: Form and Value in the Shakesperean History Play." *CD* 7(1973): 259-277.

10049. Kaufmann, R. J. "The Seneca Perspective and the Shakespearean Poetic." *CD* 1(1967): 182-198.

10050. Kermode, Frank. "Opinion, Truth and Value." *EIC* 5(1955): 181-187.

10051. King, T. J. "Review Article: The Stage in the Time of Shakespeare: A Survey of Major Scholarship." *RD* n.s. 4(1971): 199-235.

10052. Kirkpatrick, R. "On the Treatment of Tragic Themes in Dante and Shakespeare." *MLR* 72(1977): 575-584.

10053. Klein, David. "Did Shakespeare Produce His Own Plays?" *MLR* 57(1962): 556-560.

10054. Knight, G. Wilson. "Shakespeare and Theology: A Private Protest." *EIC* 15(1965): 95-104.

10055. Knight, W. Nicholas. "Patrimony and Shakespeare's Daughters." *HSL* 9(1977): 175-186.

10056. Knowland, A. S. "Shakespeare in the Theatre." *EIC* 7(1957): 325-330.

10057. Lancashire, Anne C. "Lyly and Shakespeare on the Ropes." *JEGP* 68(1969): 237-244.

10058. Law, Robert Adger. "Links between Shakespeare's History Plays." *SP* 50(1953): 168-187.

10059. ----------. "Shakespeare's Historical Cycle: Rejoinder." *SP* 51(1954): 40-41.

10060. Leech, Clifford. "Shakespeare the Intellectual." *Coll L* 4(1977): 181-189.

10061. Lever, J. W. "Three Notes on Shakespeare's Plants." *RES* 3(1952): 117-129.

10062. Levin, Harry. "The Shakespearean Overplot." *RD* 8(1965): 63-71.

10063. Levin, Richard. "On Fluellen's Figures, Christ Figures, and James Figures." *PMLA* 89(1974): 302-311.

10064. ----------. "Refuting Shakespeare's Endings." *MP* 72(1975): 337-349.

10065. ----------. "Refuting Shakespeare's Endings, Part II." *MP* 75(1977): 132-158.

10066. ----------. "Third Thoughts on Thematics." *MLR* 70(1975): 481-496.

MLR 10067. Lewis, Anthony J. "The Dog, Lion, and Wolf in Shakespeare's Descriptions of Night." *MLR* 66(1971): 1-10.

10068. Marcus, Phillip L. "T. S. Eliot and Shakespeare." *Criticism* 9(1967): 22-41.

10069. Markels, Julian. "Melville's Markings in Shakespeare's Plays." *AL* 49(1977): 34-48.

10070. Matchett, William H. "Shylock, Iago, and *Sir Thomas More*: With Some Further Discussion of Shakespeare's Imagination." *PMLA* 92(1977): 217-230.

10071. Maxwell, J. C. "'At once' in Shakespeare." *MLR* 49(1954): 464-466.

10072. ----------. "Peele and Shakespeare: A Stylometric Test." *JEGP* 49(1950): 557-561.

10073. McManaway, James G. "Additional Prompt-Books of Shakespeare from the Smock Alley Theatre." *MLR* 45(1950): 64-65.

10074. ----------. "Shakespeare in the United States." *PMLA* 79(1964): 513-518.

10075. McKenzie, D. F. "Shakespearian Punctuation—A New Beginning." *RES* 10(1959): 361-370.

10076. Meyers, Jeffrey. "Shakespeare in Mann's *Doctor Faustus*." *MFS* 19(1973): 541-545.

10077. Michel, Lawrence, and Cecil Seronsy. "Shakespeare's History Plays and Daniel: An Assessment." *SP* 52(1955): 549-577.

10078. Milward, Peter. "Shakespeare and Theology." *EIC* 16(1966): 118-122.

10079. Muir, Kenneth. "In Defence of the Tribunes." *EIC* 4(1954): 331-333.

10080. ----------. "Shakespeare Among the Commonplaces." *RES* 10(1959): 283-289.

10081. ----------. "Shakespeare and Lewkenor." *RES* 7(1956): 182-183.

10082. ----------. "Shakespeare: Prose and Verse." *MLQ* 29(1968): 467-475.

10083. ----------. "Shakespeare's Use of Pliny Reconsidered." *MLR* 54(1959): 224-225.

10084. ----------. "Stratford 1956." *EIC* 7(1957): 113-118.

10085. Nock, Francis J. "E. T. A. Hoffman and Shakespeare." *JEGP* 53(1954): 369-382.

10086. Nosworthy, J. M. "Shakespeare and *Sir Thomas More*." *RES* 6(1955): 12-25.

10087. ----------. "The Shakespearian Heroic Vaunt." *RES* 2(1951): 259-262.

10088. Novy, Marianne L. "'And You Smile Not, He's Gagged': Mutuality in Shakespearean Comedy." *PQ* 55(1976): 178-194.

10089. Orisini, N. "Shakespeare in Italy." *Comp L* 3(1951): 178-180.

19980. Pafford, J. H. P. "Simon Forman's 'Bocke of Plaies.'" *RES* 10(1959): 289-291.

10091. Paolucci, Anne Bradley and Hegel on Shakespeare." *Comp L* 16(1964): 211-226.

10092. ----------. "Shakespeare and the Genius of the Absurd." *CD* 7(1973): 231-246.

10093. Pearlman, E. "Shakespeare, Freud, and the Two Usuries, or Money's a Meddler." *ELR* 2(1972): 217-236.

10094. Presson, Robert K. "Some Traditional Instances of Setting in Shakespeare's Plays." *MLR* 61(1966): 12-22.

10095. Price, Hereward T. "Shakespeare and His Young Contemporaries." *PQ* 41(1962): 37-57.

10096. Prior, Moody E. "The Elizabethan Audience and the Plays of Shakespeare." *MP* 49(1951): 101-123.

10097. Rabkin, Norman. "Shakespeare's Golden Worlds." *MLQ* 35(1974): 187-198.

10098. Rees, Joan. "Shakespeare's Use of Daniel." *MLR* 55(1960): 79-82.

10099. Replogle, Carol. "Shakespeare's Salutations: A Study in Stylistic Etiquette." *SP* 70(1973): 172-186.

10100. Ringler, William A., Jr., and Steven W. May. "An Epilogue Possibly by Shakespeare." *MP* 70(1972): 138-139.

10101. Roth, Robert. "Another World of Shakespeare." *MP* 49(1951): 42-61.

10102. Ruoff, James E. "Kierkegaard and Shakespeare." *Comp L* 20(1968): 343-354.

10103. Salingar, L. G. "Time and Art in Shakespeare's Romances." *RD* 9(1966): 3-35.

10104. Salmon, Eric. "Shakespeare on the Modern Stage: The Need for New Approaches." *MD* 15(1972): 305-320.

10105. Schanzer, Ernest. "Atavism and Anticipation in Shakespeare's Style." *EIC* 7(1957): 242-256.

10106. ----------. "Hercules and his Load." *RES* 19(1968): 51-53.

10107. ----------. "Heywood's Ages and Shakespeare." *RES* 11(1960): 18-28.

10108. Schneider, Duane B. "Dr. Garth and Shakespeare: A Borrowing." *ELN* 1(1964): 200-202.

10109. Schwartz, Kessel. "Benevente on Shakespearian Characters." *MD* 4(1961): 60-62.

10110. Sewall, Richard B. "Ahab's Quenchless Feud: The Tragic Vision in Shakespeare and Melville." *CD* 1(1967): 207-218.

10111. Shapiro, J. A. "The 'Mermaid Club.'" *MLR* 45(1950): 6-17.

10112. Sherbo, Arthur. "Warburton and the 1745 *Shakespeare*." *JEGP* 51(1952): 71-82.

10113. Sirluck, Ernest. "Shakespeare and Jonson among the Pamphleteers of the First Civil War: Some Unreported Seventeenth-Century Allusions." *MP* 53(1955): 88-99.

10114. Smith, Gordon Ross. "The Critic's Progress through Brake and Briar." with bibliography *Coll L* 4(1971): 241-251.

10116. ----------. "New Light on Stage Directions in Shakespeare." *SP* 47(1950): 173-181.

10115. Smith, Warren. "Evidence of Scaffolding on Shakespeare's Stage." *RES* 2(1951): 22-29.

10117. Smith, Warren D. "Shakespeare's Exit Cues." *JEGP* 61(1962): 884-896.

10118. ----------. "Stage Settings in Shakespeare's Dialogue." *MP* 50(1952): 32-35.

10119. Soeller, Rolf. "The Four Primary Passions: A Renaissance Theory Reflected in the Works of Shakespeare." *SP* 55(1958): 549-567.

10120. ----------. "'Hang Up Philosophy!': Shakespeare and the Limits of Knowledge." *MLQ* 23 (1962): 135-149.

10121. ----------. "The Troubled Fountain: Erasmus Formulates a Shakespearian Simile." *JEGP* 55(1956): 70-74.

10122. Spencer, Terence. "Three Shakespearian Notes." *MLR* 49(1954): 46-51.

10123. Stafford, John. "Henry Norman Hudson and the Whig Use of Shakespeare." *PMLA* 66(1951): 649-661.

10124. Stelle, Eugene. "Shakespeare, Goldoni, and the Clowns." *CD* 11(1977): 209-226.

10125. Steene, Birgitta. "Shakespearean Elements in Historical Plays of Strindberg." *Comp L* 11(1959): 209-220.

10126. Sternfeld, Frederick W., and Mary Joiner Chan. "'Come live with me and be my love.'" *Comp L* 22(1970): 173-187.

10127. Stevenson, Warren. "Shakespeare's Hand in *The Spanish Tragedy* 1602." *SEL* 8(1968): 307-321.

10128. Stoll, Elmer Edgar. "A Freudian Detective's Shakespeare." *MP* 48(1950): 122-132.

10129. ----------. "'Multi-Consciousness' in the Theatre." *PQ* 29(1950): 1-14.

10130. Stovall, Floyd. "Whitman, Shakespeare, and Democracy." *JEGP* 51(1952): 457-472.

10131. ----------. "Whitman's Knowledge of Shakespeare." *SP* 49)1952): 643-669.

10132. Sugnet, Charles J. "Exaltation at the Close: A Model for Shakespearean Tragedy." *MLQ* 38(1977): 323-335.

10133. Taylor, E. M. M. "Shelley and Shakespeare." *EIC* 3(1953): 367-368.

10134. Taylor, Estelle W. "Shakespeare's Use of *Eth* and *Es* Engings of Verbs in the First Folio." *CLA* 19(1976): 437-457.

10135. ----------. "Shakespeare's Use of *S* Endings of the Verbs *To Do* and *To Have* in the First Folio." *CLA* 16(1972): 214-231.

10136. Taylor, Michael. "A. C. Bradley and Shakespearian Tragedy." *MLR* 68(1973): 734-740.

10137. Thompson, Karl F. "Shakespeare's Romantic Comedies." *PMLA* 67(1952): 1079-1093.

10138. Tillyard, E. M. W. "Atavism and Anticipation in Shakespeare's Style." *ECI* 7(1957): 454.

10139. ----------. "Shakespeare's Historical Cycle: Organism or Compilation." *SP* 51(1954): 34-39.

10140. Tison, John L., Jr. "Shakespeare's *Consolatio* for Exile." *MLQ* 21(1960): 142-157.

10141. Toliver, Harold E. "Shakespeare and the Abyss of Time." *JEGP* 64(1965): 234-254.

10142. Trainer, James. "Some Unpublished Shakespeare Notes of Ludwig Tieck." *MLR* 54(1959): 368-377.

10143. Traversi, Derek A. "Some New Books on Shakespeare." *MLQ* 34(1973): 312-324.

10144. Trousdale, Marion. "The Question of Harley Granville-Barker and Shakespeare on Stage." *RD* n.s. 4(1971: 3-36.

10145. Turner, Robert K., Jr. "Analytical Bibliography and Shakespeare's Text." *MP* 62(1964): 51-58.

10146. Turner, Robert Y. "Characterization in Shakespeare's Early History Plays. *ELH* 31(1964): 241-258.

10147. ----------. "Shakespeare and the Public Confrontation Scene in Early History Plays." *MP* 62(1964): 1-12.

10148. Vanderbilt, Kermit. "More Stevens and Shakespeare." *Coll L* 2(1975): 143-145.

10149. Warren, Michael J. "Repunctuation as Interpretation in Editions of Shakespeare." *ELR* 7 (1977): 155-169.

10150. Watkins, Ronald. "The Only Shake-Scene." *PQ* 54(1975): 47-67.

10151. Webber, Joan. "The Renewal of the King's Symbolic Role: from *Richard II* to *Henry V*." *TSLL* 4(1963): 530-538.

10152. Weidhorn, Manfred. "The Relation of Title and Name to Identity in Shakespeare's Tragedy." *SEL* 9(1969): 303-319.

10153. Wellek, Rene. "A. C. Bradley, Shakespeare, and the Infinite." *PQ* 54(1975): 85-103.

10154. Wentersdorf, Karl P. "A Crux in the Putative Shakespearian Addition to *Sir Thomas More*." *ELN* 10(1972): 8-10.

10155. ----------. "Linkages of Thought and Imagery in Shakespeare and *More*." *MLQ* 34 (1973): 384-405.

10156. Whitakerk Virgil K. "In Search of Shakespeare's Journal." *SEL* 5(1965): 303-315.

10157. Wood, James O. "Shakespeare and the Belching Whale." *ELN* 11(1973): 40-44.

10158. Wright, Herbert G. "How Did Shakespeare come to know the 'Decameron?'" *MLR* 50 (1955): 45-48.

10159. Utterback, Raymond V. "Dramatic Perspectives on Shakespeare's History Plays: A Review Article." *SLI* 5,#1(1972): 141-162.

See also 43, 345, 474, 1587, 2688, 2929, 3114, 4265, 9354, 9377, 9395, 9402, 9406, 9419, 9445, 11369, 11711, 11868, 11980, 12164, 12871, 13368, 13579, 14167, 14203, 14329, 14392, 14511, 14627, 16215, 16296, 16305, 17374, 17376, 17490, 18010, 18257, 18486, 18662, 18837, 19034, 19172, 20387, 20621.

THE PLAYS

ALL'S WELL THAT ENDS WELL. 10160. Arthos, John. "The Comedy of Generation." *EIC* 5(1955): 97-117.

10161. Bergeron, David M. "The Mythical Structure of *All's Well that Ends Well*." *TSLL* 14 (1973): 560-568.

10162. Bradbrook, M. C. "Virtue is the True Nobility: A Study of the Structure of *All's Well That Ends Well*.: *RES* 1(1950): 289-301.

10163. Calderwood, James L. "The Mingled Yarn of *All's Well*." *JEGP* 62(1963): 61-76.

10164. ----------. "Styles of Knowing in *All's Well*." *MLQ* 25(1964): 272-294.

10165. Dennis, Carl. "*All's Well that Ends Well* and the Meaning of Agape." *PQ* 50(1971): 75-84.

10166. Donaldson, Ian. "*All's Well that Ends Well*, Shakespeare's Play of Ending." *EIC* 27 (1977): 34-55.

10167. Hapgood, Robert. "The Life of Shame: Parolles and *All's Well*." *EIC* 15(1965): 269-278.

10168. ----------, and Robert Y. Turner. "Dramatic Conventions in *All's Well that Ends Well*." *PMLA* 79(1964): 177-182.

10169. Hill, W. Speed. "Marriage as Destiny: An Essay on *All's Well That Ends Well*." *ELR* 5 (1975): 344-359.

10170. Jones, H. W. "'*All's Well*," IV, ii, 38 Again." *MLR* 55(1960): 241-242.

10171. King, Waler N. "Shakespeare's 'Mingled Yarn.'" *MLQ* 21(1960): 33-44.

10172. Leech, Clifford. "The Theme of Ambition in *All's Well That Ends Well*." *ELH* 21 (1954): 17-29.

10173. Leggatt, Alexander. "*All's Well That Ends Well*: The Testing of Romance." *MLQ* 32 (1971): 21-41.

10174. Love, John M. "'Though many of the rich are damn'd: Dark Comedy and Social Class in *All's Well that Ends Well*." *TSLL* 18(1977):517-527.

10175. Maxwell, J. C. "Helen's Pilgrimage." *RES* 20(1969): 189-192

10176. Nagarajan, S. "The Structure of *All's Well That Ends Well*." *EIC* 10(1960): 24-31.

10177. Shapiro, Michael. "'The Web of Our Life': Human Frailty and Mutual Redemption in *All's Well That Ends Well*." *JEGP* 71(1972): 514-526.

10178. Turner, Robert Y. "Dramatic Conventions in *All's Well That Ends Well*." *PMLA* 75(1960): 497-502.

10179. Wheeler, Richard P. "The King and the Physician's Daughter: *All's Well that Ends Well* and the Late Romances." *CD* 8(1974): 311-327.

ANTONY AND CLEOPATRA. 10180. Barroll, J. Leeds. "Antony and Pleasure." *JEGP* 57(1958): 708-720.

10181. Bowling, Lawrence Edward. "Antony's Internal Disunity." *SEL* 4(1964): 239-246.

10182. Cairncross, Andrew S. "A Source for Antony." *ELN* 13(1975): 4-6.

10183. Charney, Maurice. "Shakespeare's Antony: A Study of Image Themes." *SP* 54(1957): 149-161.

10184. Couchman, Gordon W. "*Antony and Cleopatra* and Subjective Convention." *PMLA* 76 (1961): 420-425.

10185. Hallett, Charles A. "Change, Fortune, and Time: Aspects of the Sublunar World in *Antony and Cleopatra*." *JEGP* 75(1976): 75-89.

10186. Harris, Duncan S. "'Again for Cydnus'" The Dramaturgical Resolution of *Antony and Cleopatra*." *SEL* 17(1977): 219-231.

10187. Heffner, Ray L. "The Messengers in Shakespeare's *Antony and Cleopatra*." *ELH* 43(1976): 154-162.

10188. Homan, Sidney R. "Divided Response and the Imagination in *Antony and Cleopatra*." *PQ* 49(1970): 460-468.

10189. Jorgensen, Paul A. "Enobabus' Broken Heart and *The Estate of English Fugitives*." *PQ* 30 (1951): 357-392.

10190. Kuriyama, Constance Brown. "The Mother of the World: A Psychoanalytic Interpretation of Shakespeare's *Antony and Cleopatra*." *ELR* 7 (1977): 324-351.

10191. Lloyd, Michel. "Antony and the Game of Chance." *JEGP* 61(1962): 548-554.

10192. Mahood, M. M. "The Fatal Cleopatra: Shakespeare and the Pun." *EIC* 1(1951): 193-207.

10193. Muir, Kenneth. "Elizabeth 1, Jodelle, and Cleopatra." *RD* n.s. 2(1969): 197-206.

10194. Norman, Arthur M. Z. "'The Tragedie of Cleopatra' and the Date of 'Antony and Cleopatra.'" *MLR* 54(1959): 1-9.

10195. Rackin, Phyllis. "Shakespeare's Boy Cleopatra, the Decorum of Nature, and the Golden World of Poetry." *PMLA* 87(1972): 201-212.

10196. Ray, Robert H. "The 'Ribaudred Nagge' of *Antony and Cleopatra*, III. x. 10: A Suggested Emendation." *ELN* 14(1976): 21-25.

10197. Rice Julian C. "The Allegorical Dolabella." *CLA* 13(1970): 402-407.

10198. Rothschild, Herbert B., Jr. "The Oblique Encounter: Shakespeare's Confrontation of Plutarch with Special Reference to *Antony and Cleopatra*." *ELR* 6(1976); 404-429.

10199. Shapiro, Stephen A. "The Varying Shore of the World: Ambivalence in *Antony and Cleopatra*." *MLQ* 27(1966): 18-32.

10200. Simmons, J. L. "The Comic Pattern and Vision in *Antony and Cleopatra*." *ELH* 36(1969):493-510.

10201. Smith, Gordon Ross. "The Melting of Authority in *Antony and Cleopatra.* *Coll L* 1 (1974): 1–18.

10202. Williamson, Marilyn L. "Fortune in *Antony and Cleopatra.*" *JEGP* 67(1968): 423–429.
See also 10410, 10545, 12097.

AS YOU LIKE IT. 10203. Berry, Ralph. "No Exit from Arden." *MLR* 66(1971): 11–20.

10204. Cirillo, Albert R. "*As You Like It:* Pastoralism Gone Awry." *ELH* 38(1971): 19–39.

10205. Cole, Howard C. "The Moral Vision of *As You Like It.*" *Coll L* 3(1976): 17–33.

10206. Fortin, René E. "'Tongues in Trees': Symbolic Patterns in *As You Like It.*" *TSLL* 14 (1973): 569–582.

10207. Goldsmith, Robert Hillis. "Touchstone: Critic in Motley." *PMLA* 68(1953): 884–895.

10208. Grennan, Eamon. "Telling the Trees from the Wood: Some Details of *As You Like It* Re-examined." *ELR* 7(1977): 197–242.

10209. Halio, Jay L. "'No Clock in the Forest': Time in *As You Like It.*" *SEL* 2(1962): 197–207.

10210. Hennessy, Michael. "'Had I Kingdoms to Give': Place in *As You Like It.*" *EL* 4(1977): 143–151.

10211. Knowles, Richard. "Myth and Type in *As You Like It.*" *ELH* 33(1966): 1–22.

10212. Kronenfield, Judy Z. "Shakespeare's Jacques and the Pastoral Cult of Solitude." *TSLL* 18(1976): 451–473.

10213. Palmer, D. J. "Art and Nature in *As You Like It.*" *PQ* 49(1970): 30–40.

10214. Pierce, Robert B. "The Moral Languages of *Rosalynde* and *As You Like It.*" *SP* 68 (1971): 167–176.

10215. Richmond, Hugh M. "'To His Mistress' Eyebrow'." *PQ* 40(1961): 157–158.

10216. Schleiner, Winifried. "' 'Tis Like the Howling of Irish Wolves Against the Moone': A Note on *As You Like It,* v. ii. 109." *ELN* 12 (1974): 5–8.

10217. Uhlig, Claus. "'The Sobbing Deer': *As You Like It,* II. i. 21–66 and the Historical Context." *RD* n.s. 3(1970): 79–109.

10218. van der Berg, Kent Talbot. "Theatrical Fiction and the Reality of Love in *As You Like It.*" *PMLA* 90(1975): 885–893.

10219. Williamson, Marilyn. "The Masque of Hymen in *As You Like It.*" *CD* 2(1968): 248–258.
See also 526, 14309.

COMEDY OF ERRORS. 10220. Arthos, John. "Shakespeare's Transformation of Plautus." *CD* 1 (1967): 239–253.

10221. Clubb, Louise George. "Italian Comedy and *The Comedy of Errors.*" *Comp L* 19 (1967): 240–251.

10222. Petronella, Vincent F. "Structure and Theme through Separation and Union in Shakespeare's 'The Comedy of Errors.'" *MLR* 69(1974): 481–488.

10223. Sanderson, James L. "Patience in *The Comedy of Errors.*" *TSLL* 16(1975): 603–618.

CORIOLANUS. Bell, Arthur H. "Coriolanus III. ii. 72–80: 'Cryptic' and 'Corrupt'?" *ELN* 9 (1971): 18–20.

10225. Berry, Ralph. "Sexual Imagery in *Coriolanus.*" *SEL* 13(1973): 301–316.

10226. Bolton, W. F. "Menenius's 'Scale't':

A New Defense." *ELN* 10(1972): 110–111.

10227. Brittin, Norman A. "Coriolanus, Alceste, and Dramatic Genres." *PMLA* 71(1956): 799–807.

10228. Browning, I. R. "Coriolanus: Boy of Tears." *EIC* 5(1955): 18–31.

10229. Calderwood, James L. "*Coriolanus:* Wordless Meanings and Meaningless Words." *SEL* 6 (1966): 211–224.

10230. Charney, Maurice. "The Dramatic Use of Imagery in Shakespeare's *Coriolanus.*" *ELH* 23 (1956): 183–193.

10231. Colman, E. A. M. "The End of Coriolanus." *ELH* 34(1967): 1–20.

10232. Danson, Lawrence N. "Metonymy and *Coriolanus.*" *PQ* 52(1973): 30–42.

10233. Enright, D. J. "Coriolanus: Tragedy or Debate?" *EIC* 4(1954): 1–19.

10234. Honig, Edwin. "*Sejanus* and *Coriolanus:* A Study in Alienation." *MLQ* 12(1951): 407–421.

10235. Lees, F. N. "*Coriolanus,* Aristotle, and Bacon." *RES* 1(1950): 114–125.

10236. Löb, Ladislaus and Lawrence Lerner. "Views of Roman History: *Corialanus* and *Coriolan.*" *Comp L* 29(1977): 35–53.

10237. McCanles, Michael. "The Dialectic of Transcendence in Shakespeare's *Coriolanus.*" *PMLA* 82 (1967): 44–53.

10238. Meszaros, Patricia K. "'There is a world elsewhere': Tragedy and History in *Coriolanus.*" *SEL* 16(1976): 273–285.

10239. Sicherman, Carol M. "Coriolanus: The Failure of Words." *ELH* 39(1972): 189–207.

10240. Stockholder, Katherine. "The Other Corialanus." *PMLA* 85(1970): 228–236.

10241. Tennenhouse, Leonard. "*Coriolanus:* History and the Crisis of Semantic Order." *CD* 10 (1976): 328–346.

10242. Zeeveld, W. Gordon. "'Coriolanus' and Jacobean Politics." *MLR* 57(1962): 321–334.

CYMBELINE. 10243. Hoeniger, F. D. "Irony and Romance in *Cymbeline.*" *SEL* 2(1962): 219–228.

10244. Jones, Emrys. "Stuart Cymbeline: Review Article." *EIC* 11(1961): 84–99.

10245. Kott, Jan. "Lucian in 'Cymbeline.'" *MLR* 67(1972): 742–744.

10246. Kirsch, Arthur C. "*Cymbeline* and Coterie Dramaturgy." *ELH* 34(1967): 285–306.

10247. Richmond, Hugh M. "Shakespeare's Roman Trilogy: The Climax in *Cymbeline.*" *SLI* 5,#1(1972): 129–139.

10248. Rogers, H. L. "The Prophetic Label in *Cymbeline.*" *RES* 11(1960): 296–299.

10249. Schork, R. J. "Allusion, Theme, and Characterization in *Cymbeline.*" *SP* 69(1972): 210–216.

10250. Smith, Warren. D. "Cloten with Carius Lucius." *SP* 49(1952): 185–194.

10251. Stone, George Winchester, Jr. "A Century of *Cymbeline;* or Garrick's Magic Touch." *PQ* 54 (1975): 310–322.

10252. Swander, Homer. "*Cymbeline* and the 'Blameless Hero.'" *ELH* 31(1964): 259–270.

HAMLET. 10253. Adler, Jacob H. "Two *Hamlet* Plays: *The Wild Duck* and *The Sea Gull.*" *JML* 1(1970): 226–248.

10254. Battenhouse, Roy W. "The Ghost in *Hamlet:* A Catholic 'Linchpin'?" *SP* 48(1951): 161–192.

10255. ----------. "Hamlet's Apostrophe on

Man: Clue to the Tragedy." *PMLA* 66(1951): 1073-1113.

10256. Brashear, William R. "Nietzche and Spengler on Hamlet: An Elaboration and Synthesis." *CD* 5(1971): 106-116.

10257. Bowers, Fredson. "Hamlet as Minister and Scourge." *PMLA* 70(1955): 740-749.

10258. Cannon, Charles K. "'As in a Theatre': *Hamlet* in the Light of Calvin's Doctrine of Predestination." *SEL* 11(1971): 203-222.

10259. Charney, Maurice. "*Hamlet* Without Words." *ELH* 32(1965): 457-477.

10260. Clarke, C. C. "A Note on 'To be or not to be.'" *EIC* 10(1960): 18-23.

10261. Cohen, Brent M. "'What is it you would see?': *Hamlet* and the Conscience of the Theatre." *ELH* 44(1977): 222-247.

10262. Collier, L. Arlen. "All the Inverted World's a Mousetrap in *Hamlet*, II. ii." *CLA* 12 (1968): 142-149.

10263. Coursen, H. R. "Hamlet and the Pirates Reconsidered." *ELN* 14(1976): 20.

10264. Crawford, Jane. "Hamlet, III. ii. 146." *RES* 18(1967): 40-45.

10265. Crocker, Lester. "*Hamlet, Don Quijote, La vida es sueño*: The Quest for Values." *PMLA* 69(1954): 278-313.

10266. Eckert, Charles W. "The Festival Structure of the Orestes-Hamlet Tradition." *Comp L* 15(1963): 321-337.

10267. Farrison, W. Edward. "Ophelia's Reply Concerning Her Father." *CLA* 1(1958): 53-57.

10268. Feynman, Alberta E. "*The Infernal Machine, Hamlet*, and Ernest Jones." *MD* 6(1963): 72-83.

10269. Friedman, Alan Warren. "Hamlet the Unready." *MLQ* 37(1976): 15-34.

10270. Gerschenkron, Erica and Alexander. "The Illogical Hamlet: A Note on Translatability." *TSLL* 8(1966): 301-336.

10271. Gelbert, Bridget. "The Iconography of Melancholy in the Graveyard Scene of *Hamlet*." *SP* 67(1970): 57-66.

10272. Green, Andrew J. "Exit Horatio." *PQ* 30(1951): 220-221.

10273. Grover, P. R. "The Ghost of Dr. Johnson: L. C. Knights and D. A. Traversi on *Hamlet*." *EIC* 17(1967): 143-157.

10274. Halio, Jay L. "Essential *Hamlet*." *Coll L* 1(1974): 83-99.

10275. ----------. "Hamlet's Alternatives." *TSLL* 8(1966): 169-188.

10276. Hallett, Charles A. "Andrea, Andrugio, and King Hamlet: The Ghost as Spirit of Revenge." *PQ* 56(1977): 43-64.

10277. Hamil, Paul. "Death's Lively Image: The Emblematic Significance of the Closet Scene in *Hamlet*." *TSLL* 16(1974): 249-262.

10278. Hardison, O. B., Jr. "The Dramatic Triad in *Hamlet*." *SP* 57(1960): 144-164.

10279. Hartwig, Joan. "Parodic Polonius." *TSLL* 13(1971): 215-225.

10280. Havely, Cicely. "The Play-Scene in *Hamlet*." *EIC* 23(1973): 217-235.

10281. Haviland, J. Barnard. "The *Hamlet* Coda." *Coll L* 2(1975): 112-119.

10281. Hawkes, Terence. "Hamlet's 'Apprehension.'" *MLR* 55(1960): 238-241.

10283. Hockey, Dorothy C. "Wormwood, Wormwood!'" *ELN* 2(1965): 174-176.

10284. Hodgdon, Barbara. "'The Mirror up to Nature': Notes on Kozintev's *Hamlet*." *CD* 9(1975): 305-317.

10285. Holstein, Michael E. "'actions that a man might play': Dirty Tricks at Elsinore and the Politics of Play." *PQ* 55(1976): 323-339.

10286. Horwich, Richard. "*Hamlet* and *Eastward Ho*." *SEL* 11(1971): 223-233.

10287. Huttar, Charles A. "'Hamlet the Dane' and the Critic's Risk." *EIC* 16(1966): 130-131.

10288. Jenkins, Harold. "How Many Gravediggers has 'Hamlet.'" *MLR* 51(1956): 562-565.

10289. ----------. "Two Readings in 'Hamlet.'" *MLR* 54(1959): 391-395.

10290. Joseph, Sister Miriam, C. S. C. "Discerning the Ghost in Hamlet." *PMLA* 76(1961): 493-502.

10291. ----------. "*Hamlet*, a Christian Tragedy." *SP* 59(1962): 119-140.

10292. Kellenberger, Hunter. "'Consummation': or 'Consumation' in Shakespeare?" *MP* 65(1968): 228-230.

10293. Kirschbaum, Leo. "Hamlet and Ophelia." *PQ* 35(1956): 376-393.

10294. Klein, Joan Larson. "The Bait of Falsehood: *Hamlet*." *Coll L* 4(1977): 220-224.

10295. Kott, Jan. "Hamlet and Orestes." *PMLA* 82(1967): 303-313.

10296. Lawlor, J. J. "The Tragic Conflict in *Hamlet*." *RES* 1(1950): 97-113.

10297. LeComte, Edward S. "Ophelia's 'Bonny Sweet Robin.'" *PMLA* 75(1960): 480.

10298. ----------. "The Ending of *Hamlet* as a Farewell to Essex." *ELH* 17(1950): 87-114.

10299. Lyons, Bridget Gellert. "The Iconography of Ophelia." *ELH* 44(1977): 60-74.

10300. Major, John M. "The 'Letters Seal'd' in *Hamlet* and the Character of Claudius." *JEGP* 57 (1958): 512-521.

10301. Manley, Frank. "The Cock Crowing in *Hamlet*." *PQ* 45(1966): 442-447.

10302. Maxwell, J. C. "'Hamlet' v. ii. 356." *MLR* 54(1959): 395-396.

10303. Mendel, Sydney. "The Revolt against the Father: *Hamlet* and *The Wild Duck*." *EIC* 14 (1964): 171-178.

10304. Moore, John Robert. "A Spanish Hamlet." *MLR* 45(1950): 512.

10305. Morris, Harry. "*Hamlet* as a *memento mori* Poem." *PMLA* 85(1970): 1035-1040.

10306. Morris, Harry C. "Ophelia's 'Bonny Sweet Robin.'" *PMLA* 73(1958): 601-603.

10307. Newell, Alex. "The Dramatic Context and Meaning of Hamlet's 'To be or not to be' Soliloquy." *PMLA* 80(1965): 38-50.

10308. Nowottny, Winifred M. T. "The Application of Textual Theory to Hamlet's Dying Words." *MLR* 52(1957): 161-167.

10309. Noland, Richard W. "Psychoanalysis and *Hamlet*." *HSL* 6(1974): 268-281.

10310. Petronella, Vincent F. "Hamlet's 'To be or not to be': Once More into the Breach." *SP* 71(1974): 72-88.

10311. Phialas, Peter G. "Hamlet and the Grave-Maker." *JEGP* 63(1964): 226-234.

10312. Olson, Elder. "*Hamlet* and the Hermeneutics of Drama." *MP* 61(1964): 225-237.

10313. Replogle, Carol. "Not Parody, Not

Burlesque: The Play within the Play in *Hamlet*."
MP 67(1969): 150-159.

10314. Rice, Julian C. "Hamlet and the
Dream of Something After Death." *HSL* 6(1974): 109-
116.

10315. Rose, Mark. "*Hamlet* and the Shape of
Revenge." *ELR* 1(1971): 132-143.

10316. Rowe, Eleanor. "Pushkin, Lermontov,
and *Hamlet*." *TSLL* 17(1975): 337-347.

10317. Russ, Jon R. "'Old Mole' in *Hamlet*,
I. v. 162." *ELN* 12(1975): 163-168.

10318. Schrickx, W. "The Background and
Context of Hamlet's Second Soliloquy." *MLR* 68
(1973): 241-255.

10319. Siegel, Paul N. "Discerning the
Ghost in *Hamlet*." *PMLA* 78(1963): 148-149.

10320. Skulsky, Harold. "'I Know My Course':
Hamlet's Confidence." *PMLA* 89(1974): 477-486.

10321. ----------. "Revenge, Honor, and
Conscience in *Hamlet*." *PMLA* 85(1970): 78-87.

10322. Stabler, A. P. "Elective Monarchy in
the Sources of *Hamlet*." *SP* 62(1965): 654-661.

10323. ----------. "King Hamlet's Ghost in
Belleforest?" *PMLA* 77(1962): 18-19.

10324. ----------. "Melancholy, Ambition,
and Revenge in Belleforest's *Hamlet*." *PMLA* 81
(1966): 207-213.

10325. Stirling, Brents. "Theme and Character in *Hamlet*." *MLQ* 13(1952): 323-332.

10326. Stroup, Thomas B. "*Doctor Faustus*
and *Hamlet*: Contrasting Kinds of Christian
Tragedy." *CD* 5(1971): 243-253.

10327. Taupin, René. "The Myth of Hamlet in
France in Mallarmé's Generation." *MLQ* 14(1953):
432-447.

10328. Taylor, Myron. "Tragic Justice and
the House of Polonius." *SEL* 8(1968): 273-281.

10329. Van Laan, Thomas F. "Ironic Reversal
in *Hamlet*." *SEL* 6(1966): 247-262.

10330. Walker, Alice. "The Textual Problem
of *Hamlet*: A Reconsideration." *RES* 2(1951): 328-
338.

10331. Warhaft, Sidney. "Hamlet's Solid
Flesh Resolved." *ELH* 28(1961): 21-30.

10332. ----------. "The Mystery of *Hamlet*."
ELH 30(1963): 193-208.

10333. West, Robert H. "King Hamlet's
Ambiguous Ghost." *PMLA* 70(1955): 1107-1117.

10334. Williams, Gwyn. "'The Pale Cast of
Thought.'" *MLR* 45(1950): 216-218.

10335. Wimsatt, James I. "The Player King
on Friendship." *MLR* 65(1970): 1-6.

See also 9371, 9397, 9419, 12192, 17921.

HENRY IV. 10336. Battenhouse, Roy. "Falstaff as Parodist and Perhaps Holy-Fool." *PMLA* 90
(1975): 32-52.

10337. Beauchamp, Gorman. "Falstaff and
Civilization's Discontents." *Coll L* 3(1976): 94-
101.

10338. Berry, Edward I. "The Rejection
Scene in *2 Henry IV*." *SEL* 17(1977): 201-218.

10339. Blanpied, John W. "'Unfathered heirs
and loathly births of nature': Bringing History
to Crisis in 2 Henry IV." *ELR* 5(1975): 212-231.

10340. Bryant, Joseph Allen, Jr. "Shakespeare's Falstaff and the Mantle of Dick Tarlton."
SP 51(1954): 149-162.

10341. Calderwood, James L. "*I Henry IV*:
Art's Gilded Lie." *ELR* 3(1973): 131-144.

10342. Craig, Hardin. "The Dering Version
of Shakespeare's *Henry IV*." *PQ* 35(1956): 218-219.

10343. Dean, Leonard F. "Three Notes on
Comic Morality: Celia, Bobadill, and Falstaff."
SEL 16(1976): 263-271.

10344. Evans, G. Blakemore. "The 'Dering
MS' of Shakespeare's *Henry IV* and Sir Edward
Dering." *JEGP* 54(1955): 498-503.

10345. Fiehler, Rudolph. "How Oldcastle
became Falstaff." *MLQ* 16(1955): 16-28.

10346. Fish, Charles. "Henry IV: Shakespeare and Holinshed." *SP* 61(1964): 205-218.

10347. Gottschalk, Paul A. "Hal and the
'Play Extempore' in *I Henry IV*." *TSLL* 15(1974):
605-614.

10348. Gross, Alan Gerald. "The Justification of Prince Hal." *TSLL* 10(1968): 27-35.

10349. Hawkins, Sherman H. "Virtue and
Kingship in Shakespeare's Henry IV." *ELR* 5(1975):
313-343.

10350. Hoyle, James. "Some Emblems in
Shakespeare's Henry IV Plays." *ELH* 38(1971): 512-
527.

10351. Humphreys, A. R. "Two Notes in '2
Henry IV'." *MLR* 59(1964): 171-172.

10352. Hunter, G. K. "*Henry IV* and the
Elizabethan Two-Part Play." *RES* 5(1954): 236-248.

10353. Jorgensen, Paul A. "The 'Dastardly
treachery' of Prince John of Lancaster." *PMLA* 76
(1961): 488-492.

10354. Kirschbaum, Leo. "The Demotion of
Falstaff." *PQ* 41(1962): 58-60.

10355. Krumpelmann, John P. "Shakespeare's
Falstaff Dramas and Kleist's 'Zerbrochener Krug'."
MLQ 12(1951): 462-472.

10356. Law, Robert Adger. "The Composition
of Shakespeare's Lancastrian Trilogy." *TSLL* 3
(1961): 321-327.

10357. Levinson, Judith C. "''Tis a Woman's
Fault.'" *ELN* 11(1973): 38-40.

10358. Manley, Frank. "The Unity of
Betrayal in *II Henry IV*." *SLI* 5#1(1972): 91-110.

10359. Musgrove, S. "The Birth of Pistol."
RES 10(1959): 56-58.

10360. Ogilvy, J. D. A. "Arcadianism in I
Henry IV." *ELN* 10(1973): 185-188.

10361. Ribner, Irving. "The Political Problem in Shakespeare's Lancastrian Tetralogy." *SP*
49(1952): 171-184.

10362. Robbins, Martin. "The Musical Meaning
of 'Mode' in *2 Henry IV*." *ELN* 8(1971): 252-257.

10363. Rothschild, Herbert B., Jr. "Falstaff
and the Picaresque Tradition." *MLR* 68(1973): 14-21.

10364. Rubinstein, E. "*I Henry IV*: The
Metaphor of Liability." *SEL* 10(1970): 287-295.

10365. Sanderson, James L. "'Buff Jerkin':
A Note to *I Henry IV*." *ELN* 4(1966): 92-95.

10366. Scoufos, Alice Lyle. "Harvey: A
Name-Change in *Henry IV*." *ELH* 36(1969): 297-318.

10367. ----------. "Nashe, Jonson, and the
Oldcastle Problem." *MP* 65(1968): 307-324.

10368. Shaaber, M. A. "Pistol Quotes St.
Augustine." *ELN* 14(1976): 90-92.

10369. Stoll, Elmer Edgar. "A Falstaff for
the 'Bright.'" *MP* 51(1954): 145-159.

10370. Tave, Stuart M. "Falstaff, Humor,
and Comic Theory in the Eighteenth Century." *MP*
50(1952): 102-115.

10371. Thomas, Mary Olive. "The Elevation

of Hal in *I Henry IV*." *SLI* 5,#1(1972): 73-89.

10372. Waggoner, G. R. "An Elizabethan Attitude toward Peace and War." *PQ* 33(1954): 20-33.

10373. Walker, Alice. "Quarto 'Copy' and the 1623 Folio: *2 Henry IV*." *RES* 2(1951): 217-225.

HENRY V. 10374. Bateson, F. W. "A Table of Green Fields." *EIC* 7(1957): 225-226.

10375. Braddy, Haldeen. "Shakespeare's *Henry V* and the French Nobility." *TSLL* 3(1961): 189-196.

10376. Cook, Dorothy. "*Henry V*: Maturing of Man and Majesty." *SLI* 5,#1(1972): 111-128.

10377. Egan, Robert. "A Muse of Fire: *Henry V* in the Light of *Tamburlaine*." *MLQ* 29 (1968): 15-28.

10378. Huffman, Clifford Chalmers. "Bergundy's Speech and France: A Note on Shakespeare's Sources." *ELN* 9(1971): 12-18.

10379. Hulme, Hilda M. "A Table of Green Fields." *EIC* 7(1957): 222-223.

10380. ----------. "The Table of Green Fields." *EIC* 6(1956): 117-119.

10381. Johnston, George Burke. "Camden, Shakespeare, and Young Henry Percy." *PMLA* 76 (1961): 298.

10382. Jorgensen, Paul A. "The Courtship Scene in *Henry V*." *MLQ* 11(1950): 180-188.

10383. Merrix, Robert P. "The Alexandrian Allusion in Shakespeare's *Henry V*." *ELR* 2(1972): 321-333.

10384. Phialas, Peter G. "Shakespeare's Henry V and the Second Tetralogy." *SP* 62(1965): 155-175.

10385. Schanzer, Ernest. "The Table of Green Fields." *EIC* 6(1956): 119-121.

10386. Smith, Warren D. "The *Henry V* Choruses in the First Folio." *JEGP* 53(1954): 38-57.

10387. Tuckey, John S. "'Table of Green Fields' Explained." *EIC* 6(1956): 486-491.

10388. Ure, Peter. "A Table of Green Fields." *EIC* 7(1957): 223-224.

10389. Wilkinson, Allan. "A Note on *Henry V*, Act IV." *RES* 1(1950): 345-346.

10390. Williamson, Marilyn L. "The Courtship of Katherine and the Second Tetralogy." *Criticism* 17(1975): 326-334.

10391. ----------. "The Episode with Williams in *Henry V*." *SEL* 9(1969): 275-282.

HENRY VI. 10392. Blanpied, John W. "'Art and Baleful Sorcery': The Counterconsciousness of *Henry VI, Part I*." *SEL* 15(1975): 213-227.

10393. Billings, Wayne L. "Ironic Lapses: Plotting in *Henry VI*." *SLI* 5,#1(1972): 27-49.

10394. Burckhardt, Sigurd. "'I Am But Shadow of Myself': Ceremony and Design in *I Henry VI*." *MLQ* 28(1967): 139-158.

10395. Cairncross, Andrew S. "An 'Inconsistency' in '3 Henry VI.'" *MLR* 50(1955): 492-494.

10396. Champion, Larry S. "'Prologue to Their Play': Shakespeare's Structural Progress in *2 Henry VI*." *TSLL* 19(1977): 294-312.

10397. Kay, Carol McGinnis. "Traps, Slaughter, and Chaos: A Study of Shakespeare's *Henry VI* Plays." *SLI* 5,#1(1972): 1-26.

10398. Kernan, Alvin. "A Comparison of the Imagery in *3 Henry VI* and *The True Tragedie of Richard Duke of York*." *SP* 51(1954): 431-442.

10399. Kirschbaum, Leo. "The Authorship of *I Henry VI*." *PMLA* 67(1952): 809-822.

10400. Williams, George Walton. "Fastolf or Falstaff." *ELR* 5(1975): 308-312.

See also 9925.

HENRY VIII. 10401. Bliss, Lee. "The Wheel of Fortune and the Maiden Phoenix of Shakespeare's *King Henry the Eighth*" *ELH* 42(1975): 1-25.

10402. Felperin, Howard. "Shakespeare's *Henry VIII*: History as Myth." *SEL* 6(1966): 225-246.

10403. Law, Robert Adger. "The Double Authorship of *Henry VIII*." *SP* 56(1959): 471-488.

10404. McBride, Tom. "*Henry VIII* as Machiavellian Romance." *JEGP* 76(1977): 26-39.

10405. Oras, Ants. "'Extra Monosyllables' in *Henry VIII* and the Problem of Authorship." *JEGP* 52(1953): 198-213.

JULIUS CAESAR. 10406. Anderson, Peter S. "Shakespeare's *Caesar*: The Language of Sacrifice." *CD* 3(1969): 3-26.

10407. Brewer, D. S. "Brutus' Crime: A Footnote to *Julius Caesar*." *RES* 3(1952): 51-54.

10408. Carson, David L. "The Dramatic Importance of Prodigies in *Julius Caesar*, Act II, Scene i." *ELN* 2(1965): 177-180.

10409. Chang, Joseph, S. M. J. "*Julius Caesar* in the Light of Renaissance Historiography." *JEGP* 69(1970): 63-71.

10410. Charney, Maurice. "Shakespeare's Style in *Julius Caesar* and *Antony and Cleopatra*." *ELH* 26(1959): 355-367.

10411. Cowsen, Herbert R., Jr. "The Fall and Decline of Julius Caesar." *TSLL* 4(1962): 241-251.

10412. Dachslager, E. L. "'The Most Unkindest Cut': A Note on *Julius Caesar* III. ii. 187." *ELN* 11(1974): 258-264.

10413. Fleissner, Robert F. "'*Non Sanz Droict*': Law and 'Heraldry' in *Julius Caesar*." *HSL* 9(1977): 196-212.

10414. Hartsock, Mildred E. "The Complexity of *Julius Caesar*." *PMLA* 81(1966): 56-62.

10415. Kaufmann, R. J., and Clifford J. Roman. "Shakespeare's *Julius Caesar*: An Apollonian and Comparative Reading." *CD* 4(1970): 18-51.

10416. Levitsky, Ruth M. "'The Elements Were So Mix&d....'" *PMLA* 88(1973): 240-245.

10417. Nathan, Norman. "'Julius Caesar' and 'The Shoemakers' Holiday.'" *MLR* 48(1953): 178-179.

10418. Ornstein, Robert. "Seneca and the Political Drama of *Julius Caesar*." *JEGP* 57(1958): 51-56.

10419. Prior, Moody E. "The Search for a Hero in *Julius Caesar*." *RD* n.s. 2(1969): 81-101.

10420. Rabkin, Norman. "Structure, Convention, and Meaning in *Julius Caesar*." *JEGP* 63(1964): 240-254.

10421. Rees, Joan. "'Julius Caesar'—an Earlier Play, and an Interpretation." *MLR* 50 (1955): 135-141.

10422. Ribner, Irving. "Political Issues in *Julius Caesar*." *JEGP* 56(1957): 10-22.

10423. Rice, Julian C. "*Julius Caesar* and the Judgment of the Senses." *SEL* 13(1973): 238-255.

10424. Schanzer, Ernest. "The Tragedy of Shakespeare's Brutus." *ELH* 22(1955): 1-15.

10425. Southwell, Michael G. "Dawn in

Brutus' Orchard." *ELN* 5(1967): 91–98.

10426. Stirling, Brents. "'Or Else This Were a Savage Spectacle.'" *PMLA* 66(1951): 765–774.

10427. Vawter, Marvin L. "*Julius Caesar*: Rupture in the Bond." *JEGP* 72(1973): 311–328.

10428. Velz, John W. "Cassius as a 'Great Observer.'" *MLR* 68(1973): 256–259.

10429. ----------. "Undular Structure in 'Julius Caesar.'" *MLR* 66(1971): 21–30.

10430. Yu, Anthony C. "O Hateful Error: Tragic *Hamartia* in Shakespeare's Brutus." *CLA* 16 (1973): 345–356.

See also 48, 9346, 10672.

KING JOHN. 10431. Bonjour, Adrien. "The Road to Swinstead Abbey: A Study of the Sense and Structure of *King John*." *ELH* 18(1951): 253–274.

10432. Burckhardt, Sigurd. "*King John*: The Ordering of this Present Time." *ELH* 33(1966): 133–153.

10433. Burgoyne, Sidney C. "Cardinal Pandulph and the 'Curse of Rome.'" *Coll L* 4(1977): 232–240.

10434. Eliott, John R., Jr. "Polydore Vergil and the Reputation of King John in the Sixteenth Century." *ELN* 2(1964): 90–92.

10435. Freeman, A. "Shakespeare and Solyman and Perseda." *MLR* 58(1963): 481–487.

10436. Law, Robert Adger. "*King John* and *King Leir*." *TSLL* 1(1960): 473–476.

10437. ----------. "On the Date of *King John*." *SP* 54(1957): 119–127.

10438. Matchett, William H. "Richard's Divided Heritage in *King John*." *EIC* 12(1962): 231–253.

10439. Ortego, Philip D. "Shakespeare and the Doctrine of Monarchy in *King John*." *CLA* 13(1970): 392–401.

10440. Pettet, E. C. "Hot Irons and Fever: A Note of Some of the Imagery of 'King John.'" *EIC* 4(1954): 128–144.

10441. Sibly, John. "The Anomalous Case of *King John*." *ELH* 33(1966): 415–421.

10442. Stroud, Ronald. "The Bastard to the Time in *King John*." *CD* 6(1972): 154–165.

KING LEAR. 10443. Adams, Robert P. "King Lear's Revenges." *MLQ* 21(1960): 223–227.

10444. Allgair, Johannes. "Is *King Lear* an Antiauthoritarian Play." *PMLA* 88(1973): 1033–1039.

10445. Anderson, Peter S. "The Fragile World of *Lear*." *CD* 5(1971): 269–282.

10446. Arnold, Judd. "How Do We Judge King Lear?" *Criticism* 14(1972): 207–226.

10447. Bache, William B. "Lear as Old Man— Father—King." *CLA* 19(1975): 1–9.

10448. Bauer, Robert J. "Despite of Mine Own Nature: Edmund and the Orders, Cosmic and Moral." *TSLL* 10(1968): 359–366.

10449. Brown, Huntington. "Lear's Fool: A Boy, Not a Man." *EIC* 13(1963): 164–171.

10450. Cairncross, Andrew S. "The Quartos and the Folio Text of *King Lear*." *RES* 6(1955): 252–258.

10451. Cutts, John P. "The Fool's Prophecy— Another Version." *ELN* 9(1972): 262–265.

10452. Delany, Paul. "*King Lear* and the Decline of Feudalism." *PMLA* 92(1977): 429–440.

10453. Donawerth, Jane. "Diogenes the Cynic and Lear's Definition of Man, *King Lear* III. iv.

101–109." *ELN* 15(1977): 10–14.

10454. Elliott, G. R. "The Initial Contrast in *Lear*." *JEGP* 58(1959): 251–263.

10455. Ellis, John. "The Gulling of Gloucester: Credibility in the Subplot of *King Lear*." *SEL* 12(1972): 275–289.

10456. Elton, William. "Lear's 'Good Years.'" *MLR* 59(1964): 177–179.

10457. Empson, William. "Basstards and Barstards." *EIC* 18(1968): 236–237.

10458. ----------. "Bastards and Barstards." *EIC* 17(1967): 407–410.

10459. Fleissner, Robert F. "Lear's 'Poor Fool' and Dickens." *EIC* 14(1964): 425.

10460. ----------. "Lear's 'Poor Fool' as the Poor Fool." *EIC* 13(1963): 425–427.

10461. Fly, Richard D. "Beyond Extremity: A Reading of *King Lear*." *TSLL* 16(1974): 45–63.

10462. Frye, Dean. "The Context of Lear's Unbuttoning." *ELH* 32(1965): 17–31.

10463. Gard, Roger. "The 'Poor Fool.'" *EIC* 14(1964): 209.

10464. Gomme, Andor. "King Lear and His Comforters." *EIC* 17(1967): 113–115.

10465. Hamilton, Donna B. "Some Romance Sources for *King Lear*: Robert of Sicily and Robert the Devil." *SP* 71(1974): 173–191.

10466. Hawkes, Terry. "'Love' in *King Lear*." *RES* 10(1959): 178–181.

10467. Hennedy, Hugh L. "*King Lear*: Recognizing the Ending." *SP* 71(1974): 371–384.

10468. Hobsbaum, Philip. "'King Lear' in the Eighteenth Century." *MLR* 68(1973): 494–506.

10469. Hogan, J. J. "Cutting His Text According to HIs Measure: A Note on the Folio *Lear*." *PQ* 41(1962): 72–81.

10470. Hole, Sandra. "The Background of Divine Action in *King Lear*." *SEL* 8(1968): 217–233.

10471. Iwasaki, Soji. "*Veritas Filia Temporis* and Shakespeare." *ELR* 3(1973): 249–263.

10472. Jones, James H. "Leir and Lear: Matthew 5:33–37, The Turning Point, and The Rescue Theme." *CD* 4(1970): 125–131.

10473. Kernan, Alvin B. "Formalism and Realism in Elizabethan Drama: The Miracles in *King Lear*." *RD* 9(1966): 59–66.

10474. Knight, G. Wilson. "Gloucester's Leap." *EIC* 22(1972): 279–282.

10475. Law, Robert Adger. "Holinshed's Leir Story and Shakespeare's." *SP* 47(1950): 42–50.

10476. Marks, Carol L. "'Speak What We Feel': The End of *King Lear*." *ELN* 5(1968): 163–171.

10477. Maxwell, J. C. "Bastards and Barstards." *EIC* 17(1967): 257–258.

10478. ----------. "Bastard or Barstard?" *EIC* 18(1968): 112.

10479. ----------. "The Technique of Invocation in 'King Lear.'" *MLR* 45(1950): 142–147.

10480. McEwan, Neil. "The Lost Childhood of Lear's Fool." *EIC* 26(1976): 209–217.

10481. McIntosh, Angus, and Colin Williamson. "*King Lear*, Act I, Scene I. A Stylistic Note." *RES* 14(1963): 54–58.

10482. McNeir, Waldo F. "Cordelia's Return in *King Lear*." *ELN* 6(1969): 172–176.

10483. ----------. "The Last Lines of *King Lear*: V. iii. 320–327." *ELN* 4(1967): 183–188.

10484. ----------. "The Role of Edmund in

King Lear." SEL 8(1968): 187-216.

10485. Meagher, John C. "The Fool's Brach." *ELN* 6(1969): 251-252.

10486. Muir, Kenneth. "Samuel Harsnett and *King Lear." RES* 2(1951): 11-21.

10487. Musgrove, S. "*King Lear* I. i. 170." *RES* 8(1957): 170-171.

10488. ----------. "The Nomenclature of *King Lear." RES* 7(1956): 294-298.

10489. Peat, Derek. "G. Wilson Knight and 'Gloucester's Leap.'" *EIC* 23(1973): 198-200.

10490. Peck, Russell A. "Edgar's Pilgrimage: High Comedy in *King Lear." SEL* 7(1967): 219-237.

10491. Presson, Robert K. "Boethius, King Lear, and 'Maystresse Philosophie.'" *JEGP* 64 (1965): 406-424.

10492. Reynolds, George F. "Two Conventions of the Open Stage (as Illustrated in *King Lear?)." PQ* 41(1962): 82-95.

10493. Rosenberg, John D. "King Lear and his Comforters." *EIC* 16(1966): 135-146.

10494. Rosier, James L. "The Lex Asterna and *King Lear." JEGP* 53(1954): 574-580.

10495. Rosinger, Lawrence. "Gloucester and Lear: Men Who Act Like Gods." *ELH* 35(1968): 491-504.

10496. Shaw, John. "*King Lear*: the Final Lines." *EIC* 16(1966): 261-267.

10497. Sinfield, Alan. "Lear and Laing." *EIC* 26(1976): 1-16.

10498. Soens, A. L. "*King Lear* III. iv. 62-65: A Fencing Pun and Staging." *ELN* 6(1968): 19-24.

10499. Stevenson, Robert. "Shakespeare's Interest in Harsnet's Declaration." *PMLA* 67(1952): 898-902.

10500. Stevenson, Warren. "Albany as Archetype in *King Lear." MLQ* 26(1965): 257-263.

10501. Summers, Claude J. "'Stand Up for Bastards!': Shakespeare's Edmund and Love's Failure." *Coll L* 4(1977): 225-231.

10502. Turner, Darwin T. "*King Lear* Re-examined." *CLA* 3(1959): 27-39.

10503. Vickers, Brian. "'King Lear' and Renaissance Paradoxes." *MLR* 63(1968): 305-314.

10504. Walker, Alice. "'King Lear'—the 1608 Quarto." *MLR* 47(1952): 376-378.

10505. Weitz, Morris. "The Coinage of Man: 'King Lear' and Camus's 'L'Etranger.'" *MLR* 66 (1971): 31-39.

10506. Young, Alan R. "The Written and Oral Sources of *King Lear* and the Problem of Justice in the Play." *SEL* 15(1975): 309-319.

See also 28, 10519, 10526, 10533, 10544, 11395, 15224, 15225.

LOVE'S LABOUR'S LOST. 10507. Calderwood, James L. "*Love's Labour's Lost*: A Wantoning with Words." *SEL* 5(1965): 317-332.

10508. Harbage, Alfred. "*Love's Labor's Lost* and the Early Shakespeare." *PQ* 41(1962): 18-36.

10509. Greenfield, Stanley B. "Moth's *L'Envoy* and the Courtiers in *Love's Labour's Lost." RES* 5(1954): 167-168.

10510. Lewis, Anthony J. "Shakespeare's Via Media in *Love's Labour's Lost." TSLL* 16 (1974): 242-248.

10511. Memmo, Paul E., Jr. "The Poetry of the *Stilnovisti* and *Love's Labour's Lost." Comp L* 18(1966): 1-15.

10512. Montrose, Louis Adrian. "'Folly, in wisdom hatch'd': The Exemplary Comedy of *Love's Labour's Lost." CD* 11(1967): 147-170.

10513. ----------. "'Sport by sport o'erthrown': *Love's Labour's Lost." TSLL* 18 (1977): 528-552.

10514. Wilders, John. "The Unresolved Conflicts of *Love's Labour's Lost." EIC* 27 (1977): 20-33.

See also 1630.

MACBETH.   10515. Allen, Michael J. B. "Macbeth's Genial Porter." *ELR* 4(1974): 326-336.

10516. Amnéus, Daniel A. "The Cawdor Episode in *Macbeth." JEGP* 63(1964): 185-190.

10517. ----------. "A Missing Scene in *Macbeth." JEGP* 60(1961): 435-440.

10518. Anderson, Ruth L. "The Pattern of Behavior Culminating in *Macbeth." SEL* 3(1963): 151-173.

10519. Bateson, F. W. "Banquo and Edgar—Character or Function?" *EIC* 7(1957): 324-325.

10520. Belsey, Catharine. "Shakespeare's 'Vaulting Ambition.'" *ELN* 10(1973): 198-201.

10521. Biggins, Dennis. "'Appal' in *Macbeth* III. iv. 60." *ELN* 4(1967): 259-261.

10522. Boyle, Robert R., S. J. "The Imagery of *Macbeth*, I, vii, 21-28." *MLQ* 16(1955): 130-136.

10523. Breuer, Horst. "Disintegration of Time in Macbeth's Soliloquy 'Tomorrow, and Tomorrow, and Tomorrow.'" *MLR* 71(1976): 256-271.

10524. Davies, Cecil W. "Action and Soliloquy in *Macbeth." EIC* 8(1958): 451-453.

10525. Flatter, Richard. "The Latest Edition of *Macbeth." MP* 49(1951): 124-132.

10526. Gillie, Christopher. "Banquo and Edgar—Character or Function." *EIC* 7(1957): 322-324.

10527. Grenander, M. E. "*Macbeth* IV. i. 44-45 and Convulsive Ergotism." *ELN* 15(1977): 102-103.

10528. Hunter, William B., Jr. "A Decorous *Macbeth." ELN* 8(1971): 169-173.

10529. Huntley, Frank L. "*Macbeth* and the Background of Jesuitical Equivocation." *PMLA* 79 (1964): 390-400.

10530. ----------, and A. E. Malloch. "Some Notes on Equivocation." *PMLA* 81(1966): 145-146.

10531. Ide, Richard S. "The Theatre of the Mind: An Essay on *Macbeth." ELH* 42(1975): 338-361.

10532. Jack, Jane H. "Macbeth, King James, and the Bible." *ELH* 22(1955): 173-193.

10533. Kirschbaum, Leo. "Banquo and Edgar: Character or Function." *EIC* 7(1957): 1-21.

10534. Maxwell, J. C. "'Macbeth,' IV, iii, 107." *MLR* 51(1956): 73.

10535. ----------. "The Punctuation of *Macbeth* I. i. 1-2." *RES* 4(1953): 356-358.

10536. Moorthy, P. Rama. "Fear in *Macbeth." EIC* 23(1973): 154-166.

10537. Norgaard, Holger. "The Bleeding Captain Scene in *Macbeth* and Daniel's *Cleopatra." RES* 6(1955): 395-396.

10538. Ramsey, Jarold. "The Perversion of Manliness in *Macbeth." SEL* 13(1973): 285-300.

10539. Rauber, D. F. "Macbeth, Macbeth, Macbeth." *Criticism* 11(1969): 59-67.

10540. Rogers, H. L. "An English Tailor and Father Garnet's Straw." *RES* 16(1965): 44–49.

10541. Sadler, Lynn Veach. "The Three Guises of Lady Macbeth." *CLA* 19(1975): 10–19.

10542. Schanzer, Ernest. "Four Notes on 'Macbeth.'" *MLR* 52(1957): 223–227.

10543. Tomlinson, T. B. "Action and Soliloquy in *Macbeth*." *EIC* 8(1958): 147–155.

10544. Ure, Peter. "Banquo and Edgar." *EIC* 7(1957): 457–459.

10545. Waith, Eugene M. "Manhood and Valor in Two Shakespearean Tragedies." *ELH* 17(1950): 262–273.

10546. Wilhelm, Albert E. "Borrowings from *Macbeth* in Wolfe's 'The Child by Tiger.'" *SSF* 14 (1977): 179–180.

10547. Zender, Karl F. "The Death of Young Siward: Providential Order and Tragic Loss in *Macbeth*." *TSLL* 17(1975): 415–425.

See also 14497.

MEASURE FOR MEASURE. 10548. Alexander, Peter. "*Measure for Measure*: A Case for the Scottish Solomon." *MLQ* 28(1967): 478–488.

10549. Caputi, Anthony. "Scenic Design in *Measure for Measure*." *JEGP* 60(1961): 423–434.

10550. Coghill, Nevill. "Two Small Points in *Measure for Measure*." *RES* 16(1965): 393–395.

10551. Cole, Howard C. "The 'Christian' Context of *Measure for Measure*." *JEGP* 64(1965): 425–451.

10552. Duncan-Jones, Katherine. "Stoicism in *Measure for Measure*: a new source." *RES* 28 (1977): 441–446.

10553. Gent, C. L. "'Measure for Measure' and the Fourth Book of Castiglione's 'Il Cortegiano.'" *MLR* 67(1972): 252–256.

10554. Gibian, George. "*Measure for Measure* and Pushkin's *Angelo*." *PMLA* 66(1951): 426–431.

10555. Harding, Davis P. "Elizabethan Betrothals and 'Measure for Measure'." *JEGP* 49 (1950): 139–158.

10556. Haskin, Dayton, S. J. "Mercy and the Creative Process in *Measure for Measure*." *TSLL* 19(1977): 348–362.

10557. Holland, Norman N. "*Measure for Measure*: The Duke and the Prince." *Comp L* 11 (1959): 16–20.

10558. Hyman, Lawrence W. "The Unity of *Measure for Measure*." *MLQ* 36(1975): 3–20.

10559. Kaufmen, Helen A. "*Trappolin Supposed a Prince* and *Measure for Measure*." *MLQ* 18(1957): 113–124.

10560. Krieger, Murray. "*Measure for Measure* and Elizabethan Comedy." *PMLA* 66(1951): 775–784.

10561. Lascelles, Mary. "'Glassie Essence,' *Measure for Measure*, II, ii. 120." *RES* 2(1951): 140–142.

10562. Mansell, Darrel, Jr. "'Seemers' in *Measure for Measure*." *MLQ* 27(1966): 270–284.

10563. Maxwell, J. C. "*Measure for Measure*: 'Vain Pity' and 'Compelled sins.'" *EIC* 16(1966): 253–255.

10564. McBride, Tom. "*Measure for Measure* and the Unreconciled Virtues." *CD* 8(1974): 264–274.

10565. Scouten, Arthur H. "An Historical Approach to *Measure for Measure*." *PQ* 54(1975): 68–84.

10566. Siegel, Paul N. "Angelo's Precise Guards." *PQ* 29(1950): 442–443.

10567. Smith, John Hazel. "Charles the Bold and the German Background of the 'Monstrous Ransom' Story." *PQ* 51(1972): 380–393.

10568. Smith, Warren D. "More Light on *Measure for Measure*." *MLQ* 23(1962): 309–322.

10569. Southall, Raymond. "*Measure for Measure* and the Protestant Ethic." *EIC* 11(1961): 10–33.

10570. Spencer, Christopher. "Lucio and the Friar's Hood." *ELN* 3(1965): 17–24.

10571. Stevenson, David L. "Design and Structure on *Measure for Measure*: A New Appraisal." *ELH* 23(1956): 256–278.

10572. ----------. "The Role of James I in Shakespeare's *Measure for Measure*." *ELH* 26 (1959): 188–208.

10573. Thaler, Alwin. "'The Devil's Crest' in *Measure for Measure*." *SP* 50(1953): 188–194.

10574. Trombetta, James T. "Versions of Dying in *Measure for Measure*." *ELR* 6(1976): 60–76.

10575. Wasson, John. "*Measure for Measure*: A Play of Incontinence." *ELH* 27(1960): 262–275.

10576. Weiser, David K. "The Ironic Hierarchy in *Measure for Measure*." *TSLL* 19(1977): 323–347.

See also 9385, 10779, 11385.

MERCHANT OF VENICE. 10577. Barnet, Sylvan. "Prodigality and Time in *The Merchant of Venice*." *PMLA* 87(1972): 26–30.

10578. Burckardt, Sigurd. "'The Merchant of Venice': The Gentle Bond." *ELH* 29(1962): 239–262.

10579. Carson, Neil. "Hazarding and Cozening in *The Merchant of Venice*." *ELN* 9(1972): 168–177.

10580. Deshpande, M. G. "Loneliness in *The Merchant of Venice*." *EIC* 11(1961): 368–369.

10581. Dessen, Alan C. "The Elizabethan Stage Jew and Christian Example: Gerontus, Barabas, and Shylock." *MLQ* 35(1974): 231–245.

10582. Fortin, Rene E. "Launcelot and the Uses of Allegory in *The Merchant of Venice*." *SEL* 14 (1974): 259–270.

10585. Fujimura, Thomas H. "Mode and Structure in *The Merchant of Venice*." *PMLA* 81(1966): 499–511.

10584. Hapgood, Robert. "Portia and *The Merchant of Venice*: The Gentle Bond." *MLQ* 28 (1967): 19–32.

10585. Hennedy, John F. "Launcelot Gobbo and Shylock's Forced Conversion." *TSLL* 15(1973): 405–410.

10586. Henze, Richard. "'Which is the Merchant Here? And Which the Jew?'" *Criticism* 16 (1974): 287–300.

10587. Holaday, Allan. "Shakespeare, Richard Edwards, and the Virtues Reconciled." *JEGP* 66 (1967): 200–206.

10588. Horwich, Richard. "Riddle and Dilemma in *The Merchant of Venice*." *SEL* 17(1977): 191–200.

10589. Hurrell, J. D. "Love and Friendship in *The Merchant of Venice*." *TSLL* 3(1961): 328–341.

10590. Hyman, Lawrence W., and Thomas H. Fujimura. "Antonio in *The Merchant of Venice*." *PMLA* 82(1967): 649–650.

10591. Kenyon, John S. "Shakespeare's Pronunciation of *Stephano*: The Merchant of Venice V. i. 28, 51." *PQ* 37(1958): 504-506.

10592. Midgley, Graham. "*The Merchant of Venice*: A Reconsideration." *EIC* 10(1960): 121-133.

10593. Mitchell, Charles. "The Conscience of Venice: Shakespeare's Merchant." *JEGP* 63(1964): 214-225.

10594. Rockas, Leo. "'A Dish of Doves': *The Merchant of Venice*." *ELH* 40(1973): 339-351.

10595. Siemon, James E. "*The Merchant of Venice*: Act V as Ritual Reiteration." *SP* 67 (1970): 201-209.

10596. Sklar, Elizabeth S. "Bassanio's Golden Fleece." *TSLL* 18(1976): 500-509.

10597. Smith, John Hazel. "Shylock: 'Devil incarnation' or 'Poor man . . . wronged'?" *JEGP* 60(1961): 1-21.

10598. Tillyard, E. M. W. "Loneliness in *The Merchant of Venice*." *EIC* 11(1961): 487-488.

10599. Velz, John W. "'Nothing Undervalued to Cato's Daughter': Plutarch's Porcia in the Shakespeare Canon." *CD* 11(1977): 303-315.

10600. Waddington, Raymond B. "Blind Gods: Fortune, Justice, and Cupid in *The Merchant of Venice*." *ELH* 44(1977): 458-477.

10601. ----------. "*The Merchant of Venice* III. i. 108-113." *ELN* 14(1976): 92-98.

See also 9385.

MERRY WIVES OF WINDSOR. 10602. Brennecke, Ernest. "Shakespeare's 'Singing Man of Windsor.'" *PMLA* 66(1951): 1188-1192.

10603. Bryant, J. A., Jr. "Falstaff and the Renewal of Windsor." *PMLA* 89(1974): 296-301.

10604. Carroll, William. "'A Received Belief': Imagination in *The Merry Wives of Windsor*." *SP* 74(1977): 186-215.

10605. Walker, Alice. "*Merry Wives of Windsor*, III. iii. 176 ('uncape')." *RES* 9(1958): 173.

MIDSUMMER NIGHT'S DREAM. 10606. Calderwood, James L. "*A Midsummer Night's Dream*: The Illusion of Drama." *MLQ* 26(1965): 506-522.

10607. Greenfield, Thomas. "*A Midsummer Night's Dream* and *The Praise of Folly*." *Comp L* 20 (1968): 236-244.

10608. Guilhamet, Leon. "*A Midsummer Night's Dream* as the Imitation of an Action." *SEL* 15(1975): 257-271.

10609. Harrison, Thomas P. "*Romeo and Juliet, A Midsummer Night's Dream*: Companion Plays." *TSLL* 13(1971): 209-213.

10610. Huston, J. Dennis. "Bottom Waking: Shakespeare's 'Most Pure Vision.'" *SEL* 13(1973): 208-222.

10611. Nitze, Wm. A. "'A Midsummer Night's Dream' V, i, 4-17." *MLR* 50(1955): 495-497.

10612. Olson, Paul A. "*A Midsummer Night's Dream* and the Meaning of Court Marriage." *ELH* 24 (1957): 95-119.

10613. Pearson, D'Orsay W. "'Vnkinde' Theseus: A Study in Renaissance Mythography." *ELR* 4(1974): 276-298.

10614. Robinson, J. W. "Palpable Hot Ice: Dramatic Burlesque in *A Midsummer-Night's Dream*." *SP* 61(1964): 192-204.

10615. Robinson, James E. "The Ritual and Rhetoric of *A Midsummer Night's Dream*." *PMLA* 83 (1968): 380-391.

10616. Taylor, Michael. "The Darker Purpose of *A Midsummer Night's Dream*." *SEL* 9(1969): 259-273.

10617. Weiner, Andrew D. "'Multiformitie Uniforme': *A Midsummer Night's Dream*." *ELH* 38 (1971): 329-349.

See also 2212, 10779.

MUCH ADO ABOUT NOTHING. 10618. Crichton, Andrew B. "Hercules Shaven: A Centering Mythic Metaphor in *Much Ado About Nothing*." *TSLL* 16 (1975): 619-626.

10619. Dennis, Carl. "Wit and Wisdom in *Much Ado About Nothing*." *SEL* 13(1973): 223-237.

10620. Draffan, Robert A. "About *Much Ado*." *EIC* 20(1970): 488-492.

10621. Gilbert, Allan. "Two Margarets: The Composition of *Much Ado About Nothing*." *PQ* 41 (1962): 61-71.

10622. Henze, Richard. "Deception in *Much Ado About Nothing*." *SEL* 11(1971): 187-201.

10623. Lewalski, Barbara K. "Love, Appearance and Reality: Much Ado About Something." *SEL* 8(1968): 235-251.

10624. Rose, Steven. "Love and Self-Love in *Much Ado About Nothing*." *EIC* 20(1970): 143-150.

10625. Sexton, Joyce Hengerer. "The Theme of Slander in *Much Ado About Nothing* and Garter's *Susanna*." *PQ* 54(1975): 419-433.

10626. Smith, Denzell S. "The Command 'Kill Claudio' in *Much Ado About Nothing*." *ELN* 4(1967): 181-183.

10627. Soens, A. L., Jr. "Benedick as 'Signor Mountanto.'" *ELN* 1(1964): 177-179.

10628. Taylor, Michael. "'Much Ado About Nothing': the Individual in Society." *EIC* 23 (1973): 146-153.

OTHELLO. 10629. Adams, Maurianne S. "'Ocular Proof' in *Othello* and its Source." *PMLA* 79(1964): 234-241.

10630. Andrews, Michael C. "Honest Othello: The Handkerchief Once More." *SEL* 13(1973): 273-284.

10631. Bache, William B. "Tension and Related Strategies in *Othello*." *Coll L* 4(1977): 257-261.

10632. Berkeley, David S. "A Vulgarization of Desdemona." *SEL* 3(1963): 233-239.

10633. Boose, Lynda E. "Othello's Handkerchief: 'The Recognizance and Pledge of Love.'" *ELR* 5(1975): 360-374.

10634. Bowman, Thomas D. "Desdemona's Last Moments." *PQ* 39(1960): 114-118.

10635. Doebler, Bettie Ann. "Othello's Angels: The *Ars Moriendi*." *ELH* 34(1967): 156-172.

10636. Doran, Madeleine. "Good Name in Othello." *SEL* 7(1967): 195-217.

10637. Faggett, Harry L. "The State of Venice Versus Shakespeare's Iago." *CLA* 1(1958): 106-108.

10638. Hawkes, Terence. "Iago's Use of Reason." *SP* 58(1961): 160-169.

10639. Hartley, Lodwick. "Dropping the Handkerchief: Pronoun Reference and Stage Direction in *Othello* III, iii." *ELN* 8(1971): 173-176.

10640. Heilman, Robert B. "The Economics of Iago and Others." *PMLA* 68(1953): 555-571.

10641. ----------. "More Fair than Black: Light and Dark in *Othello*." *EIC* 1(1951): 315-335.

10642. Hodgson, John A. "Desdemona's Handkerchief as an Emblem of Her Reputation." *TSLL* 19(1977): 313-322.

10643. Jones, Eldred D. "The Machiavel and the Moor." *EIC* 10(1960): 234-238.

10644. Jorgensen, Paul A. *"Honesty* in *Othello*." *SP* 47(1950): 557-567.

10645. Kliger, Samuel. "Othello: The Man of Judgment." *MP* 48(1951): 221-224.

10646. Lerner, Lawrence. "The Machievel and the Moor." *EIC* 9(1959): 339-360.

10647. McCullen, Joseph T., Jr. "Iago's Use of Proverbs for Persuasion." *SEL* 4(1964): 247-262.

10648. Moore, John Robert. "Othello, Iago, and Cassio as Soldiers." *PQ* 31(1952): 189-194.

10649. Poisson, Rodney. "'Othello' V. ii. 347: 'The Base Indian' Yet Again." *MLR* 62(1967): 209-211.

10650. Pryse, Majorie. "Lust for Audience: An Interpretation of *Othello*." *ELH* 43(1976): 461-478.

10651. Ricks, Christopher. "The Machiavel and the Moor." *EIC* 10(1960): 117.

10652. Rosenberg, Marvin. "The 'Refinement' of *Othello* in the Eighteenth-Century British Theatre." *SP* 51(1954): 75-94.

10653. ----------. "A Sceptical Look at Sceptical Criticism." *PQ* 33(1954): 66-77.

10654. Ross, Lawrence. "'A Fellow Almost Damn'd in a Fair Wife.'" *ELN* 5(1968): 256-264.

10655. ----------. "'Marble,' 'Crocodile,' and 'Turban'd Turk' in *Othello*." *PQ* 40(1961): 476-484.

10656. Schwartz, Elias. "Stylistic 'Impurity' and the Meaning of *Othello*." *SEL* 10(1970): 297-313.

10657. Siegel, Paul N. "The Damnation of *Othello*." *PMLA* 68(1953): 1068-1078.

10658. ----------. "The Damnation of Othello: An Addendum." *PMLA* 71(1956): 279-280.

10659. ----------. "A New Source for *Othello*?" *PMLA* 75(1960): 480.

10660. Sipahigil, T. *"Othello*, IV 2. 29-36: A Note." *ELN* 9(1971): 99-100.

10661. Snyder, Susan. *"Othello* and the Conventions of Romantic Comedy." *RD* n.s. 5(1972): 123-141.

10662. Stempel, Daniel. "The Silence of Iago." *PMLA* 84(1969): 252-263.

10663. Stockholder, Katherine. "Egregiously an Ass: Chance and Accident in *Othello*." *SEL* 13 (1973): 257-272.

10664. Stoll, Elmer Edgar. "Iago Not a 'Malcontent.'" *JEGP* 51(1952): 163-167.

10665. Sullivan, J. P. "The Machiavel and the Moor." *EIC* 10(1960): 231-234.

10666. Taylor, Estelle W. "The Ironic Equation in Shakespeare's *Othello*: Appearances Equal Reality." *CLA* 21(1977): 202-211.

10667. Taylor, Michael. "A Note on *Othello* I. iii. 1-47." *ELN* 8(1970): 99-102.

10668. Walton, J. K. "'Strength's Abundance': A View of *Othello*." *RES* 11(1960): 8-17.

10669. Watson, Thomas L. "The Detractor-Backbiter: Iago and the Tradition." *TSLL* 5(1964): 546-554.

10670. Webb, Henry J. "The Military Background in *Othello*." *PQ* 30(1951): 40-52.

10671. Weedin, E. K., Jr. "Love's Reason in *Othello*." *SEL* 15(1975): 293-308.

10672. Weidhorn, Manfred. "The Rose and Its Name: On Denomination in *Othello*, *Romeo and Juliet*, *Julius Caesar*." *TSLL* 11(1969): 671-686.

See also 7737, 14204.

PERICLES. 10673. Eggers, Walter F., Jr. "Shakespeare's Gower and the Role of the Authorial Presenter." *PQ* 54(1975): 434-443.

10674. Goolden, P. "Antiochus's Riddle in Gower and Shakespeare." *RES* 6(1955): 245-251.

10675. Knapp, Peggy Ann. "The Orphic Vision of *Pericles*." *TSLL* 15(1974): 615-626.

10676. McIntosh, William A. "Musical Design in *Pericles*." *ELN* 11(1973): 100-106.

10677. Semon, Kenneth J. *"Pericles*: An Order beyond Reason." *EL* 1(1974): 17-27.

10678. Tompkins, J. M. S. "Why Pericles?" *RES* 3(1952): 315-324.

10679. Waith, Eugene M. "Pericles and Seneca the Elder." *JEGP* 50(1951): 180-182.

10680. Wood, James O. "The Shakespearian Language of *Pericles*." *ELN* 13(1975): 98-103.

RICHARD II. 10681. Dean, Leonard F. *"Richard II*: The State and the Image of the Theater." *PMLA* 67(1952): 211-218.

10682. Elliott, John R., Jr. "History and Tragedy in *Richard II*." *SEL* 8(1968): 253-271.

10683. Fleissner, Robert F. "'Prufrock,' Pater, and Richard II: Retracing a Denial of Princeship." *AL* 38(1966): 120-123.

10684. French, A. L. *"Richard II*. a Rejoinder." *EIC* 18(1968): 229-233.

10685. ----------. "Who Deposed Richard the Second?" *EIC* 17(1967): 411-433.

10686. Gilman, Ernest B. *"Richard II* and the Perspectives of History." *RD* n.s. 7(1976): 85-115.

10687. Homan, Sidney. *"Richard II*: The Aesthetics of Judgment." *SLI* 5,#1(1972): 65-71.

10688. Leon, Harry J. "Classical Sources for the Garden Scene in *Richard II*." *PQ* 29 (1950): 65-70.

10689. Louis, Dolores Gros. "Tragedy in Christopher Fry and in Shakespeare: A Comparison of *Curtmantle* and *Richard II*." *CLA* 9(1965): 151-158.

10690. Maveety, Stanley R. "A Second Fall of Cursed Man: The Bold Metaphor in *Richard II*." *JEGP* 72(1973): 175-193.

10691. McAvoy, William C. "Form in *Richard II*, II. i. 40-66." *JEGP* 54(1955): 355-361.

10692. Phialas, Peter G. *"Richard II* and Shakespeare's Tragic Mode." *TSLL* 5(1963): 344-355.

10693. Quinn, Michael. "'The King Is Not Himself': The Personal Tragedy of Richard II." *SP* 56(1959): 169-186.

10694. Ranald, Margaret Loftus. "The Degradation of Richard II: An Inquiry into the Ritual Backgrounds." *ELR* 7(1977): 170-196.

10695. Rieman, Donald H. "Appearance, Reality, and Moral Order in *Richard II*." *MLQ* 25 (1964): 34-45.

10696. Ure, Peter. "The Looking-Glass of *Richard II*." *PQ* 34(1955): 219-224.

10697. ----------. *"Richard II*, or 'to Find Out Right with Wrong.'" *EIC* 18(1968): 225-229.

10698. Zitner, Sheldon P. "Aumerle's Conspiracy." *SEL* 14(1974): 239-257.

RICHARD III. 10699. Bogard, Travis. "Shakespeare's Second Richard." *PMLA* 70(1955): 192-209.

10700. Cairncross, Andrew S. "The Quartos and the Folio Text of *Richard III*" *RES* 8(1957): 225-233.

10701. Gurr, Andrew. "Richard III and the Democratic Process." *EIC* 24(1974): 39-47.

10702. Jones, Emrys. "Bosworth Eve." *EIC* 25(1975): 38-54.

10703. Krieger, Murray. "The Dark Generations of Richard III." *Criticism* 1(1959): 32-48.

10704. McNeir, Waldo F. "The Masks of Richard the Third." *SEL* 11(1971): 167-186.

10705. Narkin, Anthony P. "Day-Residue and Christian Reference in Clarence's Dream." *TSLL* 9(1967): 147-150.

10706. Parker, Brian. "*Richard III* and the Modernizing of Shakespeare." *MD* 15(1972): 321-330.

10707. Sheriff, William E. "The Grotesque Comedy of *Richard III*." *SLI* 5,#1(1972): 51-64.

10708. Thompson, Marjorie. "The Clarence Scenes in 'Richard III.'" *MLR* 51(1956): 221-223.

10709. Velz, John W. "Episodic Structure in Four Tudor Plays: A Virtue of Necessity." *CD* 6(1972): 87-102.

10710. Walton, J. K. "The Quarto Copy for the Folio *Richard III*." *RES* 10(1959): 127-140.

10711. Wentersdorf, Karl P. "*Richard III* (QI) and the Pembroke 'Bad' Quartos." *ELN* 14(1977): 257-264.

10712. Wheeler, Richard P. "History, Character and Conscience in *Richard III*." *CD* 5(1971): 301-321.

10713. Wilson, J. Dover. "The Composition of the Clarence Scenes in 'Richard III.'" *MLR* 53 (1958): 211-214.

10714. ----------. "A Note on 'Richard III': The Bishop of Ely's Strawberries." *MLR* 52(1957): 563-564.

See also 9323, 13906.

ROMEO AND JULIET. 10715. Adams, Barry B. "The Prudence of Prince Escalus." *ELH* 35(1968): 32-50.

10716. Bergeron, David M. "Sickness in *Romeo and Juliet*." *CLA* 20(1977): 356-364.

10717. Black, James. "The Visual Artistry of *Romeo and Juliet*." *SEL* 15(1975): 245-526.

10718. Bonnard, Georges A. "*Romeo and Juliet*: A Possible Significance?" *RES* 2(1951): 319-327.

10719. Burkhart, Robert E. "The Evidence for a Provincial Performance of Q1 *Romeo and Juliet*." *ELN* 8(1970): 9-13.

10720. Evans, Bertrand. "The Brevity of Friar Laurence." *PMLA* 65(1950): 841-865.

10721. Laird, David. "The Generation of Style in *Romeo and Juliet*." *JEGP* 63(1964): 204-213.

10722. Levin, Richard. "A Good Reading from the Bad Quarto of *Romeo and Juliet*." *RES* 23(1972): 56-58.

10723. Maxwell, J. C. "Juliet's Days, Hours, and Minutes." *RES* 2(1951): 262-267.

10724. Nevo, Ruth. "Tragic Form in *Romeo and Juliet*." *SEL* 9(1969): 241-258.

10725. Olive, W. J. "'Twenty Good Nights'—The Knight of the Burning Pestle, The Family of Love and Romeo and Juliet." *SP* 47(1950): 182-189.

10726. Smith, Warren D. "Romeo's Final Dream." *MLR* 62(1967): 579-583.

10727. Snyder, Susan. "*Romeo and Juliet*, Comedy into Tragedy." *EIC* 20(1970): 391-402.

10728. Spencer, Christopher. "'Count Paris's Wife': *Romeo and Juliet* on the Early Restoration Stage." *TSLL* 7(1966): 309-316.

10729. Thomas, Sidney. "Henry Chettle and the First Quarto of *Romeo and Juliet*." *RES* 1 (1950): 8-16.

10730. Williams, George W. "A Correction to the Text of 'Romeo and Juliet' I, v, 144." *MLR* 55 (1960): 79.

See also 10609, 10672, 12717.

TAMING OF THE SHREW. 10731. Greenfield, Thelma Nelson. "The Transformation of Christopher Sly." *PQ* 33(1954): 34-42.

10732. Heilman, Robert B. "The *Taming* Untamed, or, 'The Return of the Shrew.'" *MLQ* 27(1966): 147-161.

10733. Hosley, Richard. "Was There a 'Dramatic Epilogue' to The Taming of the Shrew." *SEL* 1,#2(1961): 17-34.

10734. Parker, John W. "Some Comments on the A Shrew-The Shrew." *CLA* 2(1959): 178-184.

10735. Ranald, Margaret Loftus. "The Manning of the Haggard; or The Taming of the Shrew." *EL* 1 (1974): 149-165.

10736. Shroeder, John W. "*The Taming of a Shrew* and *The Taming of the Shrew*: A Case Re-Opened." *JEGP* 57(1958): 424-443.

TEMPEST. 10737. Back, Guy. "Dramatic Convention in the First Scene of *The Tempest*." *EIC* 21(1971): 74-85.

10738. Baum, Bernard. "*Tempest* and *Hairy Ape*: The Literary Incarnation of Mythos." *MLQ* 14 (1953): 258-273.

10739. Bradbrook, M. C. "Romance, Farewell! *The Tempest*." *ELR* 1(1971): 239-249.

10740. Camden, Carroll. "*Songs and Chorusses in The Tempest*." *PQ* 41(1962): 114-122.

10741. Craig, Hardin. "Magic in *The Tempest*." *PQ* 47(1968): 8-15.

10742. Davidson, Frank. "*The Tempest*: An Interpretation." *JEGP* 62(1963): 501-517.

10743. Flyer, Anson, Jr. "Archetypes in *The Tempest*." *HSL* 3(1971): 45-50.

10744. Freehafer, John. "Shakespeare's *Tempest* and *The Seven Champions*." *SP* 66(1969): 87-103.

10745. Grant, Patrick. "The Magic of Charity: A Background to Prospero." *RES* 27(1976): 1-16.

10746. Kuhl, E. P. "Shakespeare and the Founders of America: *The Tempest*." *PQ* 41(1962): 123-146.

10747. McLaughlan, Juliet. "Dramatic Convention in the First Scene of *The Tempest*." *EIC* 21(1971): 424-426.

10748. Payne, Michael. "Socrates, Christ, and Prospero: Models for the Second Oldest Profession." *Coll L* 2(1975): 61-65.

10749. Robinson, James E. "Time and *The Tempest*." *JEGP* 63(1964): 255-267.

10750. Seiden, Melvin. "Utopianism in *The Tempest*." *MLQ* 31(1970): 3-21.

10751. Semon, Kenneth A. "Shakespeare's *Tempest*: Beyond a Common Joy." *ELH* 40(1973): 24-

43.

10752. Tamplin, Ronald. "*The Tempest* and *The Waste Land*." *AL* 39(1967): 352-372.

See also 9363, 19353.

TIMON OF ATHENS. 10753. Bergeron, David M. "Alchemy and *Timon of Athens*." *CLA* 13(1970): 364-373.

10754. ----------. "*Timon of Athens* and Morality Drama." *CLA* 10(1967): 181-188.

10755. Fly, Richard D. "The Ending of 'Timon of Athens': A Reconsideration." *Criticism* 15(1973): 242-252.

10756. Gomme, Andor. "*Timon of Athens*." *EIC* 9(1959): 107-125.

10757. Muir, Kenneth. "In Defence of Timon's Poet." *EIC* 3(1953): 120-121.

10758. Slights, William W. E. "*Genera mixta* and *Timon of Athens*." *SP* 74(1977): 39-62.

10759. Swigg, R. "'Timon of Athens' and the Growth of Discrimination." *MLR* 62(1967): 387-394.

10760. Walker, Lewis. "Fortune and Friendship in *Timon of Athens*." *TSLL* 18(1977): 577-600.

See also 9348, 13331.

TITUS ANDRONICUS. 10761. Cutts, John P. "Shadow and Substance: Structural Unity in *Titus Andronicus*." *CD* 2(1968): 161-172.

10762. Danson, Lawrence N. "The Device of Wonder: *Titus Andronicus* and Revenge Tragedies." *TSLL* 16(1974): 27-43.

10763. Ettin, Andrew V. "Shakespeare's First Roman Tragedy." *ELH* 37(1970): 325-341.

10764. Greg, W. W. "Alteration in Act I of 'Titus Andronicus.'" *MLR* 48(1953): 439-440.

10765. Huffman, Clifford Chalmers. "Bassanius and the British History in *Titus Andronicus*." *ELN* 11(1973): 175-181.

10766. ----------. "'Titus Andronicus': Metamorphosis and Renewal." *MLR* 67(1972): 730-741.

10767. McManaway, James G. "Writing in Sand in *Titus Andronicus*." *RES* 9(1958): 172-173.

10768. Sommers, Allan. "Structure and Symbolism in *Titus Andronicus*." *EIC* 10(1960): 275-289.

TROLIUS AND CRESSIDA. 10769. Aerol, Arnold. "The Hector-Andromache Scene in Shakespeare's *Troilus and Cressida*." *MLQ* 14(1953): 335-340.

10770. Asp, Carolyn. "In Defense of Cressida." *SP* 74(1977): 406-417.

10771. Bayley, John. "Time and the Trojans." *EIC* 25(1975): 55-73.

10772. Berger, Harry, Jr. "*Trolius and Cressida*: The Observer as Basilisk." *CD* 2(1968): 122-136.

10773. Bonheim, H. "Shakespeare's 'Goose of Winchester.'" *PQ* 51(1972): 940-941.

10774. Cox, John D. "The Error of Our Eye in *Troilus and Cressida*." *CD* 10(1976): 147-171.

10775. Enck, John J. "The Peace of the Poetomachia." *PMLA* 77(1962): 386-396.

10776. Fly, Richard D. "'I Cannot Come to Cressid but by Pandar': Mediation in the Theme and Structure of *Troilus and Cressida*." *ELR* 3 (1973): 145-165.

10777. ----------. "'Suited in like conditions as our Argument': Imitative Form in Shakespeare's *Troilus and Cressida*." *SEL* 15 (1975): 273-292.

10778. Houser, David J. "Armor and Motive in *Troilus and Cressida*." *RD* n.s. 4(1971): 121-134.

10779. Hulme, Hilda. "Three Notes: *Troilus and Cressida*, V, vii. 11; *Midsummer Night's Dream*, II. i. 54; *Measure for Measure*, II. i. 39." *JEGP* 57(1958): 721-725.

10780. Kaufmann, R. J. "'Ceremonies for Chaos:' The Status of *Troilus and Cressida*." *ELH* 32(1965): 139-159.

10781. Kaula, David. "'Mad Idolatry' in Shakespeare's *Troilus and Cressida*." *TSLL* 15 (1973): 25-38.

10782. Kimbrough, Robert A. "The Origins of *Troilus and Cressida*: Stage, Quarto, and Folio." *PMLA* 77(1962): 194-199.

10783. ----------. "The Problem of Thersites." *MLR* 59(1964): 173-177.

10784. Levenson, Jill L. "Shakespeare's *Troilus and Cressida* and the Monumental Tradition in Tapestries and Literature." *RD* n.s. 7(1976): 43-84.

10785. Main, William W. "Character Amalgams in Shakespeare's *Troilus and Cressida*." *SP* 58 (1961): 170-178.

10786. McAlindon, T. "Language, Style, and Meaning in *Troilus and Cressida*." *PMLA* 84(1969): 29-43.

10787. Nowottny, Winifred M.T. "'Opinion' and 'Value' in 'Troilus and Cressida.'" *EIC* 4 (1954): 282-296.

10788. Presson, Robert K. "The Structural Use of a Traditional Theme in *Troilus and Cressida*." *PQ* 31(1952): 180-188.

10789. Roy, Emil. "War and Manlinen in Shakespeare's *Troilus and Cressida*." *CD* 7(1973): 107-120.

10790. Sacharoff, Mark. "The Orations of Agamemnon and Nestor in Shakespeare's *Troilus and Cressida*." *TSLL* 14(1972): 223-234.

10791. ----------. "Tragic vs. Satiric: Hector's Conduct in II, ii of Shakespeare's *Troilus and Cressida*." *SP* 67(1970): 517-531.

10792. ----------, and T. McAlindon. "Critical Comment in Response to T. McAlindon's 'Language, Style, and Meaning in *Troilus and Cressida*.'" *PMLA* 87(1972): 90-99.

10793. Schwartz, Elias. "Tonal Equivocation and the Meaning of *Troilus and Cressida*." *SP* 69 (1972): 304-319.

10794. Shalvi, Alice. "'Honor' in *Troilus and Cressida*." *SEL* 5(1965): 283-302.

10795. Smith, J. Oates. "Essence and Existence in Shakespeare's *Troilus and Cressida*." *PQ* 46(1967): 167-185.

10796. Stein, Arnold. "*Troilus and Cressida*: The Disjunctive Imagination." *ELH* 36 (1969): 145-167.

10797. Ure, Peter. "*Troilus and Cressida* II. ii. 162-93." *RES* 17(1966): 405-409.

10798. Walker, Alice. "The Textual Problem of 'Troilus and Cressida.'" *MLR* 45(1950): 459-464.

10799. Wood, Robert E. "*Troilus and Cressida*: The Tragedy of a City." *PQ* 56(1977): 65-81.

TWELFTH NIGHT. 10800. Forrest, James F. "Malvolio and Puritan 'Singularity.'" *ELN* 11(1974): 259-264.

10801. Hartwig, Joan. "Feste's 'Whirligig'

and the Comic Providence of *Twelfth Night*." *ELH* 40 (1973): 501-513.

10802. Huston, J. Dennis. "'When I Came to Man's Estate': *Twelfth Night* and Problems of Identity." *MLQ* 33(1972): 274-288.

10803. King, Walter M. "Shakespeare and Parmenides: The Metaphysics of *Twelfth Night*." *SEL* 8(1968): 283-306.

10804. Melzi, Robert C. "From Lelia to Viola." *RD* 9(1966): 67-81.

10805. Taylor, Anthony Brian. "Shakespeare and Golding: Viola's Interview with Olivia and Echo and Narcissus." *ELN* 15(1977): 103-106.

10806. Williams, Porter, Jr. "Mistakes in *Twelfth Night* and their Resolution: A Study in Some Relationships of Plot and Theme." *PMLA* 76 (1961): 193-199.

See also 17492.

TWO GENTLEMEN OF VERONA. 10807. Godshalk, William Leigh. "The Structural Unity of *Two Gentlemen of Verona*." *SP* 66(1969): 168-181.

10808. Lindenbaum, Peter. "Education in *The Two Gentlemen from Verona*." *SEL* 15(1975): 229-244.

10809. Sargent, Ralph M. "Sir Thomas Elyot and the Integrity of *The Two Gentleman of Verona*." *PMLA* 65(1950): 1166-1180.

WINTER'S TALE. 10810. Blissett, William. "This Wide Gap of Time: *The Winter's Tale*." *ELR* 1 (1971): 52-70.

10811. Cox, Lee Sheridan. "The Role of Autolycus in *The Winter's Tale*." *SEL* 9(1969): 283-301.

10812. Gourlay, Patricia Southland. "'O my most sacred lady': Female Metaphor in *The Winter's Tale*." *ELR* 5(1975): 375-395.

10813. Hartwig, Joan. "The Tragicomic Perspective of *The Winter's Tale*." *ELH* 37(1970): 12-36.

10814. Honigmann, E. A. J. "Secondary Sources of *The Winter's Tale*." *PQ* 34(1955): 27-38.

10815. Hutchinson, Peter. "Franz Fühmann's 'Böhmen am Meer': A Socialist Version of 'The Winter's Tale.'" *MLR* 67(1972): 579-589.

10816. Kaula, David. "Autolycus' Trumpery." *SEL* 16(1976): 287-303.

10817. Lindenbaum, Peter. "Time, Sexual Love, and the Uses of Pastoral in *The Winter's Tale*." *MLQ* 33(1972): 3-22.

10818. Livingston, Mary L. "The Natural Art of *The Winter's Tale*." *MLQ* 30(1969): 340-355.

10819. Mueller, Martin. "Hermione's Wrinkles, or, Ovid Transformed: An Essay on *The Winter's Tale*." *CD* 5(1971): 226-239.

10820. Neely, Carol Thomas. "*The Winter's Tale*: The Triumph of Speech." *SEL* 15(1975): 321-338.

10821. Siegel, Paul N. "Leontes: A Jealous Tyrant." *RES* 1(1950): 302-307.

10822. Siemon, James Edward. "'But It Appears She Lives': Iteration in *The Winter's Tale*." *PMLA* 89(1974): 10-16.

10823. Spencer, Terence. "Shakespeare's Isle of Delphos." *MLR* 47(1952): 199-202.

10824. Taylor, John. "The Patience of *The Winter's Tale*" *EIC* 23(1973): 333-356.

THE POETRY

10825. Alter, Jean V. "Apollinaire and Two Shakespearean Sonnets." *Comp L* 14(1962): 377-385.

10826. Andrew, Malcolm. "Christian Ideas About Sin and the First Stanza of *Lucrece*." *RES* 24(1973): 179-182.

10827. Asals, Heather. "*Venus and Adonis*: The Education of a Goddess." *SEL* 13(1973): 31-51.

10828. Berry, Francis. "Pronouns in Poetry." *EIC* 9(1959): 196-197.

10829. ----------. "'Thou' and 'You' in Shakespeare's *Sonnets*." *EIC* 8(1958): 138-146.

10830. Bateson, F. W. "'Bare Ruined Choirs.'" *EIC* 3(1953): 358-362.

10831. ----------. "'Bare Ruined Choirs.'" *EIC* 4(1954): 226.

10832. Brophy, James. "Shakespeare's 'Saucy Jacks.'" *ELN* 1(1963): 11-13.

10833. Copland, Murray. "The Dead Phoenix." *EIC* 15(1965): 279-287.

10834. Cunningham, J. V. "'Essence' and *The Phoenix and the Turtle*." *ELH* 19(1952): 265-276.

10835. Davis, Jack M., and J. E. Grant. "A Critical Dialogue on Shakespeare's Sonnet 71." *TSLL* 1(1959): 214-232.

10836. Empson, William. "'Bare Ruined Choirs.'" *EIC* 3(1953): 357-358, 362-363.

10837. ----------. "*The Phoenix and the Turtle*." *EIC* 16(1966): 147-153.

10838. Evans, E. C. "Shakespeare's Sonnet 97." *RES* 14(1963): 379-380.

10839. Finkenstaedt, Thomas. "Prounouns in Poetry." *EIC* 8(1958): 456-457.

10840. Fleissner, Robert F. "Herbert's Aethiopesa and the Dark Lady: a Mannerist Parellel." *CLA* 19(1976): 458-467.

10841. ----------. "That 'Cheek of Night': Toward the Dark Lady." *CLA* 16(1973): 312-323.

10842. Gent, Lucy. "'Venus and Adonis': The Triumph of Rhetoric." *MLR* 69(1974): 721-729.

10843. Goldsmith, Ulrich K. "Words Out of a Hat? Alliteration and Assonance in Shakespeare's Sonnets." *JEGP* 49(1950): 33-48.

10844. Griffin, Robert. "'These Contraries Such Unity do Hold': Patterned Imagery in Shakespeare's Narrative Poems." *SEL* 4(1964): 43-55.

10845. Gurr, Andrew. "Shakespeare's First Poem, Sonnet 145." *EIC* 21(1971): 221-226.

10846. Hamilton, A. C. "Venus and Adonis." *SEL* 1,#1(1961): 1-15.

10847. Hulme, Hilda. "Sonnet 145: 'I Hate, from Hathaway She Threw.'" *EIC* 21(1971): 427-429.

10848. Hunter, G. K. "The Dramatic Technique of Shakespeare's Sonnets." *EIC* 3(1953): 152-164.

10849. Kaula, David. "'In War With Time': Temporal Perspectives in Shakespeare's Sonnets." *SEL* 3(1963): 45-57.

10850. Leech, Clifford. "Venus and Her Nun: Portraits of Women in Love by Shakespeare and Marlowe." *SEL* 5(1965): 247-268.

10851. Levin, Richard. "A Second English Enueg." *PQ* 53(1974): 428-430.

10852. Majors, G. "Shakespeare's First Brutus: His Role in *Lucrece*." *MLQ* 35(1974): 339-351.

10853. Matchett, William H. "The Dead Phoenix." *EIC* 16(1966): 132-133.

10854. McCanles, Michael. "'Increasing Store with Loss': Some Themes in Shakespeare's Sonnets." *TSLL* 13(1971): 391-406.

10855. Miller, Henry P. "Venus, Adonis, and the Horses." *ELH* 19(1952): 249-264.

10856. Miller, Robert P. "The Myth of Mars' Hot Minion in *Venus and Adonis*." *ELH* 26 (1959): 470-481.

10857. Muir, Kenneth. "The Order of Shakespeare's Sonnets." *Coll L* 4(1977): 190-196.

10858. Neely, Carol Thomas. "Detachment and Engagement in Shakespeare's Sonnets: 94, 116, and 129." *PMLA* 92(1977): 83-95.

10859. Nosworthy, J. M. "All too Short a Date: Internal Evidence in Shakespeare's Sonnet." *EIC* 2(1952): 311-324.

10860. Nowottny, Winifred M. T. "Formal Elements in Shakespeare's Sonnets: Sonnets I-VI." *EIC* 2(1952): 76-84.

10861. Parker, David. "Verbal Moods in Shakespeare's Sonnets." *MLQ* 30(1969): 331-339.

10862. Piper, William Bowman. "A Poem Turned in Process." *ELH* 43(1976): 444-460.

10863. Purdum, Richard. "Shakespeare's Sonnet 128." *JEGP* 63(1964): 235-239.

10864. Sheidley, William E. "'Unless it be a boar': Love and Wisdom in Shakespeare's *Venus and Adonis*." *MLQ* 35(1974): 3-15.

10865. Smith, Gordon Ross. "*Venus and Adonis*." *HSL* 3(1971): 1-11.

10866. Starnes, D. T. "Geoffrey Fenton, Seneca and Shakespeare's *Lucrece*." *PQ* 43(1964): 280-283.

10867. Stirling, Brents. "A Shakespeare Sonnet Group." *PMLA* 75(1960): 340-349.

10868. Stone, Walter B. "Shakespeare and the Sad Augers." *JEGP* 52(1953): 457-479.

10869. Taylor, Dick. Jr. "The Earl of Pembroke and the Youth of Shakespeare's Sonnets: An Essay in Rehabilitation." *SP* 56(1959): 26-54.

10870. Walley, Harold R. "*The Rape of Lucrece* and Shakespearean Tragedy." *PMLA* 76 (1961): 480-487.

10871. Weiser, David K. "'I' and 'Thou' in Shakespeare's *Sonnets*." *JEGP* 76(1977): 506-524.

10872. Wheeler, Charles B. "'Bare Ruined Choirs.'" *EIC* 4(1954): 224-226.

10873. White, Robert L. "Sonnet 73 Again—A Rebuttal and New Reading." *CLA* 6(1962): 125-132.

10874. Williamson, C. F. "Themes and Patterns in Shakespeare's Sonnets." *EIC* 26(1976): 191-208.

See also 9454, 17049.

SHEPHERD, LUKE. 10875. Wheat, Cathleen Hayhurst. "Luke Shepherd's *Antipi Amicus*." *PQ* 30 (1951): 58-68.

SIDNEY, MARY. See 9438.

SIDNEY, SIR PHILIP. 10876. Anderson, D. M. "The Trial of the Princes in the *Arcadia*, Book V." *RES* 8(1957): 409-412.

10877. Barnes, Catherine. "The Hidden Persuader: The Complex Speaking Voice of Sidney's *Defence of Poetry*." *PMLA* 86(1971): 422-427.

10878. Baughan, Denver Ewing. "Sidney's *Defence of the Earl of Leicester* and the Revised *Arcadia*." *JEGP* 51(1952): 35-41.

10879. Beach, D. M. "The Poetry of Idea: Sir Philip Sidney and the Theory of Allegory." *TSLL* 13(1971): 365-389.

10880. Bergbusch, Martin. "Rebellion in the *New Arcadia*." *PQ* 53(1974): 29-41.

10881. Brodwin, Leonora Leet. "The Structure of Sidney's *Astrophel and Stella*." *MP* 67(1969): 25-40.

10882. Bullitt, John M. "The Use of Rhyme Link in the Sonnets of Sidney, Drayton, and Spenser." *JEGP* 49(1950): 14-32.

10883. Buxton, John. "A New Letter from Sir Philip Sidney." *ELR* 2(1972): 28.

10884. ----------. "Sidney and Theophrastus." *ELR* 2(1972): 79-82.

10885. Chalifour, Clark L. "Sir Philip Sidney's *Old Arcadia* as Terentian Comedy." *SEL* 16 (1976): 51-63.

10886. Challis, Lorna. "The Use of Oratory in Sidney's Arcadia." *SP* 62(1965): 561-576.

10887. Cotter, James Finn. "The 'Baiser' Group in Sidney's *Astrophil and Stella*." *TSLL* 12 (1970): 381-403.

10888. --------. "The Songs in *Astrophil and Stella*." *SP* 67(1970): 178-200.

10889. Cutts, John P. "More Manuscript Versions of Poems by Sidney." *ELN* 9(1971): 3-12.

10890. Dana, Margaret E. "Heroic and Pastoral: Sidney's *Arcadia* as Masquerade." *Comp L* 25(1977): 308-320.

10891. ----------. "The Providential Plot of the *Old Arcadia*." *SEL* 17(1977): 39-57.

10892. Davis, Walter R. "Actaeon in Arcadia." *SEL* 2(1962): 95-110.

10893. ----------. "Thematic Unity in the *New Arcadia*." *SP* 57(1960): 123-143.

10894. Dipple, Elizabeth. "The Captivity Episode and the *New Arcadia*." *JEGP* 70(1971): 418-431.

10895. ----------. "Harmony and Pastoral in the *Old Arcadia*." *ELH* 35(1968): 309-328.

10896. ----------. "Metamorphosis in Sidney's *Arcadias*." *PQ* 50(1970): 47-62.

10897. ----------. "'Unjust Justice' in the *Old Arcadia*." *SEL* 10(1970): 83-101.

10898. Donno, Elizabeth Story. "Old Mouse-eaten Records: History in Sidney's *Apology*." *SP* 72(1975): 275-298.

10899. Dorsten, Jan A. Van. "Gruterus and Sidney's *Arcadia*." *RES* 16(1965): 174-177.

10900. Duncan-Jones, Katherine. "Nashe and Sidney: The Tournament in 'The Unfortunate Traveller.'" *MLR* 63(1968): 3-6.

10901. ----------. "Sidney's Urania." *RES* 17(1966): 123-132.

10902. ----------. "Sidney in Samothea: A Forgotten National Myth." *RES* 25(1974): 174-177.

10903. Fabry, Frank J. "Sidney's Poetry and Italian Song-Form." *ELR* 3(1973): 232-248.

10904. Ford, P. Jeffrey. "Philosophy, History, and Sidney's *Old Arcadia*." *Comp L* 26(1974): 32-50.

10905. Godshalk, W. L. "Gabriel Harvey and Sidney's 'Arcadia.'" *MLR* 59(1964): 497-500.

10906. ----------. "Recent Studies in Sidney." *ELR* 2(1972): 148-164.

10907. ----------. "Sidney's Revision of the *Arcadia*, Books III–V." *PQ* 43(1964): 171–184.

10908. Goldman, Marcus Selden. "Sidney and Harington as Opponents of Superstition." *JEGP* 54 (1955): 526–548.

10909. Grennblatt, Stephen J. "Sidney's *Arcadia* and the Mixed Mode." *SP* 70(1973): 269–278.

10910. Hamilton, A. C. "Et in Arcadia ego." *MLQ* 27(1966): 332–350.

10911. ----------. "Sidney and Agrippa." *RES* 7(1956): 151–157.

10912. ----------. "Sidney's *Arcadia* as Prose Fiction: Its Relation to its Sources." *ELR* 2(1972): 29–60.

10913. ----------. "Sidney's *Astrophel and Stella* as a Sonnet Sequence." *ELH* 36(1969): 59–87.

10914. ----------. "Sidney's Idea of the 'Right Poet.'" *Comp L* 9(1957): 51–59.

10915. Hardison, O. B., Jr. "The Two Voices of Sidney's *Apology for Poetry*." *ELR* 2(1972): 83–99.

10916. Heltzel, Virgil B. "The Arcadian Hero." *PQ* 41(1962): 173–180.

10917. Howe, Ann Romayne. "*Astrophel and Stella*: 'Why and how.'" *SP* 61(1964): 150–169.

10918. Hyman, Virginia Riley. "Sidney's Definition of Poetry." *SEL* 10(1970): 49–62.

10919. Isler, Alan D. "The Allegory of the Hero and Sidney's Two *Arcadias*." *SP* 65(1968): 171–191.

10920. ----------. "Heroic Poetry and Sidney's Two *Arcadias*." *PMLA* 83(1968): 368–379.

10921. John, Lisle Cecil. "Sir Stephen Le Sieur and Sir Philip Sidney." *MLQ* 17(1956): 340–351.

10922. Jones, Dorothy. "Sidney's Erotic Pen: An Interpretation of One of the *Arcadia* Poems." *JEGP* 73(1974): 32–47.

10923. Kalstone, David. "Sir Philip Sidney and 'Poore *Petrarchs* Long Deceased Woes.'" *JEGP* 63 (1964): 21–32.

10924. ----------. "The Transformation of Arcadia: Sannazaro and Sir Philip Sidney." *Comp L* 15(1963): 234–249.

10925. Kimbrough, Robert, and Philip Murphy. "The Helmingham Hall Manuscript of Sidney's *The Lady of May*: A Commentary and Transcription." *RD* n.s. 1(1968): 103–119.

10926. Kinney, Arthur F. "Parody and Its Implications in Sidney's *Defense of Poesie*." *SEL* 12 (1972): 1–19.

10927. Krouse, F. Michael. "Plato and Sidney's *Defence of Poesie*." *Comp L* 6(1954): 138–147.

10928. Lanlam, Richard A. "*Astrophil and Stella*: Pure and Impure Persuasion." *ELR* 2(1972): 100–115.

10929. Levy, Charles S. "The Sidney–Hanau Correspondence (with texts)." *ELR* 2(1972): 19–28.

10930. ----------. "A Supplementary Inventory of Sir Philip Sidney's Correspondence." *MP* 67 (1969): 177–181.

10931. Levy, F. J. "Philip Sidney Reconsidered." *ELR* 2(1972): 5–18.

10932. Lindheim, Nancy Rothwax. "Sidney's *Arcadia*, Book II: Retrospective Narrative." *SP* 64(1967): 159–186.

10933. ----------. "Vision, Revision, and the 1593 Text of the *Arcadia*." *ELR* 2(1972): 139–147.

10934. Mahl, Mary R. "Sir Philip Sidney's Scribe: The New *Arcadia* and the *Apology for Poetry*." *ELN* 10(1972): 90–91.

10935. Mallock, A. E. "'Architectonic' Knowledge and Sidney's 'Apologie.'" *ELH* 20(1953): 181–185

10936. Marenco, Franco. "Double Plot in Sidney's Old 'Arcadia.'" *MLR* 64(1969): 248–263.

10937. Martin, L. C. "Marvell, Massinger, and Sidney." *RES* 2(1951): 374–375.

10938. McIntyre, John P., S. J. "Sidney's 'Golden World.'" *Comp L* 14(1962): 356–365.

10939. Montrose, Louis Adrian. "Celebration and Insinuation: Sir Philip Sidney and the Motives of Elizabethan Courtship." *RD* n.s. 8(1977): 3–35.

10940. Murphy, Karl M. "The 109th and 110th Sonnets of *Astrophel and Stella*." *PQ* 34(1955): 349–352.

10941. Nelson, T. G. A. "Sir John Harrington as a Critic of Sir Philip Sidney." *SP* 67(1970): 41–56.

10942. Parker, Robert W. "Tertian Structure and Sidney's Original *Arcadia*." *ELR* 2(1972): 61–78.

10943. Payne, Michael. "Taking Poets Seriously." *Coll L* 3(1976): 83–93.

10944. Pickett, Penney. "Sidney's Use of *Phaedrus* in *The Lady of May*." *SEL* 16(1976): 33–50.

10945. Rees, Joan. "Fulke Greville and the Revisions of *Arcadia*." *RES* 17(1966): 54–57.

10946. Regan, Mariann S. "Astrophel: Full of Desire, Emptie of Wit." *ELN* 14(1977): 251–256.

10947. Ribner, Irving. "Machiavelli and Sidney: The *Arcadia* of 1590." *SP* 47(1950): 152–172.

10948. Ringler, William. "Master Drant's Rules." *PQ* 29(1950): 70–74.

10949. ----------. "Poems Attributed to Sir Philip Sidney." *SP* 47(1950): 126–151.

10950. Roberts, Mark. "The Pill and the Cherries: Sidney and the Neo-Classical Tradition." *EIC* 16(1966): 22–31.

10951. Robertson, Jean. "Sir Philip Sidney and Lady Penelope Rich." *RES* 15(1964): 296–297.

10952. Rose, Mark. "Sidney's Womanish Man." *RES* 15(1964): 353–363.

10953. Ryken, Leland. "The Drama of Choice in Sidney's *Astrophel and Stella*" *JEGP* 68(1969): 648–654.

10954. Scanlon, James J. "Sidney's *Astrophil and Stella*: 'See what it is to Love' Sensually." *SEL* 16(1976): 65–74.

10955. Schleiner, Winfried. "Differences of Theme and Structure of the Erona Episode in the *Old* and *New Arcadia*." *SP* 70(1973): 377–391.

10956. Sinfield, Alan. "Sexual Puns in *Astrophel and Stella*." *EIC* 24(1974): 341–355.

10957. ----------. "Sidney and Du Bartas." *Comp L* 27(1975): 8–20.

10958. Skretkowicz, Victor, Jr. "Sidney and Amyot: Heliodorus in the Structure and Ethos of the *New Arcadia*." *RES* 27(1976): 170–174.

10959. Stanford, Ann. "Anne Bradstreet's Portrait of Sir Philip Sidney." *EAL* 1,#3(1967): 11–13.

10960. Stillinger, Jack. "The Biographical Problem of *Astrophel and Stella*." *JEGP* 59(1960): 617–639.

10961. Stroup, Thomas B. "The 'Speaking Picture' Realized: Sidney's 45th Sonnet." *PQ* 29 (1950): 440-442.

10962. Thorne, J. P. "A Ramistical Commentary on Sidney's *An Apologie for Poetrie*." *MP* 54 (1957): 158-164.

10963. Turner, Myron. "The Disfigured Face of Metaphor in the Revised *Arcadia*." *ELR* 2(1972): 116-135.

10964. ----------. "The Heroic Ideal in Sidney's Revised *Arcadia*." *SEL* 10(1970): 63-82.

10965. ----------. "'When Rooted Moisture Failes': Sidney's Pastoral Elegy (OA 75) and the Radical Humour." *ELN* 15(1977): 7-10.

10966. Waller, G. F. "The Text and Manuscript Variants of the Countess of Pembroke's Psalms." *RES* 26(1975): 1-18.

10967. Weiner, Andrew D. "'In a grove most rich of shade': A Figurative Reading of the Eighth Song of *Astrophil and Stella*." *TSLL* 18 (1976): 341-361.

10968. ----------. "Structure and 'Fore Conceit' in 'Astorphil and Stella.'" *TSLL* 16 (1974): 1-25.

See also 9287, 9371, 9441, 9457, 9583, 9675, 9686, 11419.

SKELTON, JOHN.   10969. Atchity, Kenneth John. "Skelton's *Colyn Clout*: Visions of Perfectibility." *PQ* 52(1973): 715-727.

10970. Brownlow, F. W. "The Boke Compiled by Maister Skelton, Poet Laureate, called *Speake Parrot*." *ELR* 1(1971): 3-26.

10971. ----------. "*Speke, Parrot*: Skelton's Allegorical Denunciation of Cardinal Wolsey." *SP* 65(1968): 124-139.

10972. Carpenter, Nan Cooke. "Skelton and Music." *RES* 6(1955): 279-284.

10973. ----------. "Skelton and Music: A Gloss on *Hippates*." *ELN* 8(1970): 93-97.

10974. ----------. "Skelton's Hand in William Cornish's Musical Parable." *Comp L* 22 (1970): 157-172.

10975. Fishman, Burton. "Recent Studies in Skelton." *ELR* 1(1971): 89-96.

10976. Harris, William O. "The Thematic Importance of Skelton's Allusion to Horace in *Magnyfycence*." *SEL* 3(1963): 9-18.

10977. ----------. "Wolsey and Skelton's *Magnyfycence*: A Re-evaluation." *SP* 57(1960): 99-122.

10978. Kinsman, Robert S. "The 'Buck' and the 'Fox' in Skelton's *Why Come Ye Not to Courte?*" *PQ* 29(1950): 61-64.

10979. ----------. "*Phyllip Sparowe*: Titulus." *SP* 47(1950): 473-484.

10980. ----------. "Skelton's *Magnyfycence*: The Strategy of the 'Olde Sayde Sawe.'" *SP* 63 (1966): 99-125.

10981. ----------. "Skelton's 'Uppon a Deedmans Hed': New Light on the Origin of the Skeltonic." *SP* 50(1953): 101-109.

10982. Larson, Judith Sweitzer. "What Is *The Bowge of Courte*?" *JEGP* 61(1962): 288-295.

10983. McLane, Paul E. "Skelton's *Colyn Cloute* and Spenser's *Shepheardes Calender*." *SP* 70 (1973): 141-159.

10984. ----------. "Wolsey's Forced Loans and the Dating of Skelton's *Colyn Clout*." *ELN* 10 (1972): 85-89.

10985. Norton-Smith, John. "The Origins of 'Skeltonics.'" *EIC* 23(1973): 57-62.

10986. Phillips, Norma. "Observations on the Stylistic Features of Skelton's Realism." *JEGP* 65(1966): 19-35.

10987. Smith, A. J. "Incumbent Poets." *MLQ* 29(1968): 341-350.

10988. Spina, Elaine. "Skeltonic Meter in *Elynour Rummyng*." *SP* 64(1967): 665-684.

10989. Swallow, Alan. "The Pentameter Lines in Skelton and Wyatt." *MP* 48(1950): 1-11.

10990. ----------. "John Skelton: The Structure of the Poem." *PQ* 32(1953): 29-42.

10991. Tucker, Melvin J. "Skelton and Sheriff Hutton." *ELN* 4(1967): 254-259.

10992. West, Michael. "Skelton and the Renaissance Theme of Folly." *PQ* 50(1971): 23-35.

10993. Winser, Leigh. "*The Bowge of Courte*: Drama Doubling as Dream." *ELR* 6(1976): 3-39.

10994. ----------. "'The Garlande of Laurel': Masque Spectacular." *Criticism* 19(1977): 51-69.

See also 9425.

SMITH, WILLIAM.   10995. Sasek, Lawrence A. "William Smith and *The Shepheardes Calender*." *PQ* 39(1960): 251-253.

10996. van den Berg, Kent T. "An Elizabethan Allegory of Time by William Smith." *ELR* 6(1976): 40-59.

SOUTHWELL, ROBERT.   10997. Brown, Nancy Pollard. "The Structure of Southwell's 'Saint Peter's Complaint.'" *MLR* 61(1966): 3-11.

10998. Maurer, Warren. "Spee, Southwell, and the Poetry of Meditation." *Comp L* 15(1963): 15-22.

10999. Roberts, John R. "The Influence of *The Spiritual Exercises* of St. Ignatius on the Nativity Poems of Robert Southwell." *JEGP* 59(1960): 450-456.

11000. White, Helen. "Southwell: Metaphysical and Baroque." *MP* 61(1964): 159-168.

See also 11429.

SPENSER, EDMUND.   11001. Allen, Don Cameron. "On Spenser's *Muiopotmos*." *SP* 53(1956): 141-158.

11002. ----------. "Three Poems on Eros." *Comp L* 8(1956): 177-193.

11003. Alpers, Paul J. "Narrative and Rhetoric in the *Faerie Queene*." *SEL* 2(1962): 27-46.

11004. ----------. "Narration in *The Faerie Queene*." *ELH* 44(1977): 19-39.

11005. ----------. "Review Article: How to read *The Faerie Queene*." *EIC* 18(1968): 429-443.

11006. Anderson, Judith H. "'Come, let's away to prison': Fortune and Freedom in *The Faerie Queene*, Book VI." *JNT* 2(1972): 133-137.

11007. ----------. "The July Eclogue and the House of Holiness: Perspective in Spenser." *SEL* 10(1970): 17-32.

11008. ----------. "The Knight and the Palmer in *The Faerie Queene*, Book II." *MLQ* 31 (1970): 160-178.

11009. ----------. "'Nor Man It Is': Knight of Justice in Book V of Spenser's *Faerie Queene*." *PMLA* 85(1970): 65-77.

11010. ----------. "Redcrosse and the Descent into Hell." *ELH* 36(1969): 470-492.

11011. ----------. "Whatever Happened to Amoret? The Poet's Role in Book IV of 'The Faerie Queene.'" *Criticism* 13(1971): 180-200.

11012. Atchity, Kenneth John. "Spenser's *Mother Hubberds Tale*: Three Themes of Order."

PQ 52(1973): 161-172.

11013. Bean, John C. "Cosmic Order in *The
Faerie Queene:* From Temperance to Chastity."
SEL 17(1977): 67-79.

11014. Berger, Harry, Jr. "At Home and
Abroad with Spenser." *MLQ* 25(1964): 102-109.

11015. ----------. "Busirane and the War
Between the Sexes: An Interpretation of *The Faerie
Queene* III. xi-xii." *ELR* 1(1971): 99-121.

11016. ----------. "The Discarding of Mal-
becco: Conspicuous Allusion and Cultural Exhaustion in *The Faerie Queene* III. ixx." *SP* 66
(1969): 135-154.

11017. ----------. "*Faerie Queene* Book III:
A General Description."*Criticism* 11(1969): 234-261.

11018. ----------. "Mode and Diction in
The Shepheardes Calender." *MP* 67(1969): 140-149.

11019. ----------. "The Prospect of
Imagination: Spenser and the Limits of Poetry."
SEL 1,#1(1961): 93-120.

11020. ----------. "The Spenserian
Dynamics." *SEL* 8(1969): 1-18.

11021. ----------. "Spenser's
Prothalamion: An Interpretation." *EIC* 15(1965):
363-380.

11022. ----------. "The Structure of
Merlin's Chronicle in *The Faerie Queene* III(iii)."
SEL 9(1969): 39-51.

11023. ----------. "Two Spenserian Retro-
spects: The Antique Temple of Venus and the Primitive Marriage of Rivers." *TSLL* 10(1968): 5-25.

11024. Berleth, Richard J. "Heavens
Favorable and Free: Belphoebe's Nativity in
The Faerie Queene." *ELH* 40(1973: 479-500.

11025. Berry, Jerbert, and E. K. Timings.
"Spenser's Pension." *RES* 11(1960): 254-259.

11026. Blayney, M. S. and G. H. *"The
Faerie Queen* and an English Version of Chartier's
Traité de l'Esperance." *SP* 55(1958): 154-163.

11027. Blissett, William. "Florimell and
Marinell." *SEL* 5(1965): 87-104.

11028. Blitch, Alice Fox. Proserpina
Preserved: Book VI of *The Faerie Queene,*" *SEL* 13
(1973): 15-30.

11029. Blythe, John Heiges. "Spenser and the
Seven Deadly Sins: Book I, Cantos IV and V." *ELH*
39(1972): 343-352.

11030. Braden, Gordon. "Riverrun: An Epic
Catalogue in *The Faerie Queene.*" *ELR* 5(1975): 25-
48.

11031. Bradford, Alan T. "Mirrors of
Mutability: Winter Landscapes in Tudor Poetry."
ELR 4(1974): 3-39.

11032. Brill, Lesley W. "Battles that Need
Not Be Fought: *The Faerie Queene*, III." *ELR* 5
(1979): 198-211.

11033. ----------. "Chastity as Ideal
Sexuality in the Third Book of *The Faerie Queene.*"
SEL 11(1971): 15-26.

11034. Brink, J. R. "The Masque of the
Nine Muses: Sir John Davier's Unpublished 'Epith-
alamion' and the 'Belphoebe-Ruby' Episode in
The Faerie Queene." *RES* 23(1972): 445-448.

11035. Bristol, Michael D. "Structural
Patterns in Two Elizabethan Pastorals." *SEL* 10
(1970): 33-48.

11036. Browning, I. R. "Spenser and Iconography." *EIC* 11(1961): 480-481.

11037. Bryan, Robert A. "Apostasy and the
Fourth Bead-Man in the *Faerie Queene.*" *ELN* 5
(1967): 87-91.

11038. Bullitt, John M. "The Use of Rhyme
Link in the Sonnets of Sidney, Drayton, and
Spenser." *JEGP* 49(1950): 14-32.

11039. Burchmore, David W. "The Image Centre
in *Colin Clouts Come Home Againe.*" *RES* 28(1977):
393-406.

11040. Cain, Thomas. "The Strategy of
Praise in Spenser's 'Aprill.'" *SEL* 8(1968):
45-58.

11041. Carpenter, Nan. "Spenser and Timotheus:
A Musical Gloss on E. K.'s Gloss." *PMLA* 71(1956:
1141-1151.

11042. Cheney, Donald. "Spenser's Hermaphrodite and the 1590 *Faerie Queene.*" *PMLA* 87(1972):
192-200.

11043. Cirillo, A. R. "The Fair Hermaphrodite: Love-Union in the Poetry of Donne and
Spenser.: *SEL* 9(1969): 81-95.

11044. ----------. "Spenser's *Epithalamion:*
The Harmonius Universe of Love." *SEL* 8(1968):
19-34.

11045. ----------. "Spenser's 'Faire
Hermaphrodite.'" *PQ* 47(1968): 136-137.

11046. Comito, Terry. "A Dialectic of Images
in Spenser's *Fowre Hymnes.*" *SP* 74(1977): 301-321.

11047. Cosman, Madeleine Pelner. "Spenser's
Ark of Animals: Animal Imagery in the *Faery
Queene.*" *SEL* 3(1963): 85-107.

11048. Cowt, Franklin E. "The Theme and
Structure of Spenser's *Muiopotmos.*" *SEL* 10(1970):
1-15.

11049. Craig, Joanne. "The Image of Mortality:
Myth and History in *The Faerie Queene.*" *ELH* 39(1972):
520-544.

11050. Crampton, Georgia Ronan. "Spenser's
Lyric Theodicy: The Complaints of *The Faerie
Queene* III. iv." *ELH* 44(1977): 205-221.

11051. Cullen Patrick. "Guyon *Micro-
christus:* The Cave of Mammon Reexamined." *ELH* 37
(1970): 153-174.

11052. ----------. "Imitation and Metamorphosis: The Golden-Age Eclogue in Spenser, Milton,
and Marvell." *PMLA* 84(1969): 1559-1570.

11053. Culp, Dorothy Woodward. "Courtesy
and Fortune's Change in Book 6 of *The Faerie
Queene.*" *MP* 68(1971): 254-259.

11054. ----------. "Courtesy and Moral
Virtue." *SEL* 11(1971): 37-51.

11055. Cummings, L. "Spenser's *Amoretti* VIII:
New Manuscript Versions."*SEL* 4(1964): 125-135.

11056. Cummings, Peter M. "Spenser's
Amoretti as an Allegory of Love."*TSLL* 12(1970):
163-179.

11057. Cutts, John P. "Spenser's Mermaids."
ELN 5(1968): 250-256.

11058. Dallett, Joseph B. "Ideas of Sight
in *The Faerie Queene.*" *ELH* 27(1960): 87-121.

11059. Davidson, Clifford. "The Idol of Isis
Church." *SP* 66(1969): 70-86.

11060. Davis, Walter R. "Arthur, Partial
Exegesis, and the Reader." *TSLL* 18(1977): 553-576.

11061. Dees, Jerome S. "The Narrator of
Christ's Victorie and Triumph: What Giles Fletcher
Learned from Spenser." *ELR* 6(1976): 453-465.

11062. ----------. "The Narrator of *The*

Faerie Queene: Patterns of Response." *TSLL* 12 (1971): 537-568.

11063. ----------. "The Ship Conceit in *The Faerie Queene*: 'Conspicuous Allusion' and Poetic Structure." *SP* 72(1975): 208-225.

11064. Dixon, Michael F. "Rhetorical Patterns and Methods of Advocacy in Spenser's *Shepheardes Calender*." *ELR* 7(1977): 131-154.

11065. Doyle, Charles Clay. "Christian Vision in *The Faerie Queene*." *Coll L* 3(1976): 33-41.

11066. Dundas, Judith. *"The Faerie Queene*: The Incomplete Poem and the Whole Meaning." *MP* 71(1974): 257-265.

11067. _____. "The Rhetorical Basis of Spenser's Imagery." *SEL* 8(1968): 59-75.

11068. Durling, Robert M. "The Bower of Bliss and Armida's Palace." *Comp L* 6(1954): 335-347.

11069. Durr, Robert Allen. "Spenser's Calendar of Christian Time." *ELH* 24(1957): 269-295.

11070. Eade, J. C. "The Pattern in the Astronomy of Spenser's *Epithalamion*." *RES* 23 (1972): 173-178.

11071. Edwards, Calvin R. "The Narcissus Myth in Spenser's Poetry." *SP* 74(1977): 63-88.

11072. English, H. M., Jr. "Spenser's Accommodation of Allegory to History in the Story of Timias and Belphoebe." *JEGP* 59(1960): 417-429.

11073. Entzminger, Robert L. "Courtesy: The Cultural Imperative." *PQ* 53(1974): 389-400.

11074. Evans, Maurice. "The Fall of Guyon." *ELH* 28(1961): 215-224.

11075. ----------. "Guyon and the Bower of Sloth." *SP* 61(1964): 140-149.

11076. ----------. "Platonic Allegory in *The Faerie Queene*." *RES* 12(1961): 132-143.

11077. Falls, Mother Mary Robert, O. S. U. "Spenser's Kirkrapine and the Elizabethans." *SP* 50(1953): 457-475.

11078. Fish, Stanley E. "Nature as Concept and Character in the *Mutabilitie Cantos*." *CLA* 6 (1963): 210-215.

11079. Fowler, A. D. S. "Emblems of Temperance in *The Faerie Queene*, Book II." *RES* 11 (1960): 143-149.

11080. Fowler, Alastair. "The Owl and the Turtle-Dove." *EIC* 12(1962): 227-229.

11081. ----------. "Six Knights at Castle Joyous." *SP* 56(1959): 583-599.

11082. ----------. "Spenser and Renaissance Iconography." *EIC* 11(1961): 235-238.

11083. Fox, Robert C. "Temperance and the Seven Deadly Sins in *The Faerie Queene*, Book II." *RES* 12(1961): 1-6.

11084. Friedland, Louis S. "A Source of Spenser's 'The Oak and the Briar.'" *PQ* 33(1954): 222-224.

11085. ----------. "Spenser's Sabaoth's Rest." *MLQ* 17(1956): 199-203.

11086. Friedmann, Anthony E. "The Diana-Acteon Episode in Ovid's *Metamorphoses* and *The Faerie Queene*." *Comp L* 18(1966): 289-299.

11087. Gang, Theodore. "Nature and Grace in *The Faerie Queene*: The Problem Reviewed." *ELH* 26(1959): 1-22.

11088. Geimer, Roger A. "Spenser's Rhyme or Churchyard's Reason: Evidence of Churchyard's First Pension." *RES* 20(1969): 306-309.

11089. Geller, Lila. "The Acidalian Vision: Spenser's Graces in Book VI of *The Faerie Queene*." *RES* 23(1972): 267-278.

11090. ----------. "Spenser's Theory of Nobility in Book VI of *The Faerie Queene*." *ELR* 5 (1975): 49-57.

11091. ----------. "Venus and the Three Graces: A Neoplatonic Paradigm for Book III of *The Faerie Queene*." *JEGP* 75(1976): 56-74.

11092. Gilde, Helen Cheney. "Spenser's Hellenore and Some Ovidian Associations." *Comp L* 23(1971): 233-239.

11093. ----------. "'The Sweet Lodge of Love and Deare Delight': The Problem of Amoret." *PQ* 50(1971): 63-74.

11094. Glazier, Lyle. "The Nature of Spencer's Imagery." *MLQ* 16(1955): 300-310.

11095. Goldberg, Jonathan. "The Mothers in Book III of *The Faerie Queene*." *TSLL* 17(1975): 5-26.

11096. Goldstein, Lawrence. "Immortal Longings and 'The Ruines of Time.'" *JEGP* 75(1976): 337-351.

11097. Gottfried, Rudolf B. "Our New Poet: Archetypal Criticism and *The Faerie Queene*." *PMLA* 83(1968): 1362-1378.

11098. ----------. "The Pictorial Element in in Spenser's Poetry." *ELH* 19(1952): 203-213.

11099. Gransden, K. W. "Allegory and Personality in Spencer's Heroes." *EIC* 20(1970): 298-310.

11100. Gray, J. C. "Bondage and Deliverance in the 'Faerie Queene': Varieties of a Moral Imperative." *MLR* 70(1975): 1-12.

11101. Graziani, René. "Elizabeth at Isis Church." *PMLA* 79(1964): 376-389.

11102. Grellner, Sister Mary Adelaide, S. C. L. "Britomart's Quest for Maturity." *SEL* 8 (1968): 35-43.

11103. Greene, Thomas. "Spenser and the Epithalamic Convention." *Comp L* 9(1957): 215-228.

11104. Guth, Hans P. "Allegorical Implications of Artifice in Spenser's *Faerie Queene*." *PMLA* 76(1961): 474-479.

11105. Hamilton, A. C. "The Argument of Spenser's *Shepheardes Calender*." *ELH* 23(1956): 171-182.

11106. ----------. "'Like race to runne': The Parallel Structure of *The Faerie Queene*, Books I and II." *PMLA* 73(1958): 327-334.

11107. ----------. "Review Article: Spencer's Pastoral." *ELH* 33(1966): 518-531.

11108. ----------. "Spenser and Langland." *SP* 55(1958): 533-548.

11109. ----------. "Spenser and the Common Reader." *ELH* 35(1968): 618-633.

11110. ----------. "Spenser and Tourneur's *Transformed Metamorphosis*." *RES* 8(1957): 127-136.

11111. ----------. "Spencer's Treatment of Myth." *ELH* 26(1959): 335-354.

11112. ----------. "A Theological Reading of *The Faerie Queene*, Book II." *ELH* 25(1958): 155-162.

11113. Hardin, Richard F. "The Resolved Debate of Spenser's 'October.'" *MP* 73(1976): 257-263.

11114. Hardison, O. B., Jr. *"Amoretti* and the *Dolce Stil Novo*." *ELR* 2(1972): 208-216.

11115. Harrison, Thomas P., Jr. "Turner and Spenser's *Mother Hubberds Tale*." *JEGP* 49

(1950): 464-469.

11116. Heffner, Ray, Dorothy E. Mason, and Frederick M. Padelford. "Spenser Allusions in the Sixteenth and Seventeenth Centuries, Part I: 1580-1625." *SP* 68,#5(1971): 3-172.

11117. ----------. "Spenser Allusions in the Sixteenth and Seventeenth Centuries, Part II: 1626-1700." *SP* 69,#5(1972): 175-351.

11118. Heninger, S. K., Jr. "The Orgoglio Episode in *The Faerie Queene*." *ELH* 26(1959): 171-187.

11119. Hieatt, A. Kent. "Scudamour's Practice of *Maistrye* upon Amoret." *PMLA* 77(1962): 509-510.

11120. Hill, Iris Tillman. "Britomart and *Be Bold, Be Not Too Bold*." *ELH* 38(1971): 173-187.

11121. Hill, John M. "Braggadocchio and Spenser's Golden World Concept: The Function of Unregenerative Comedy." *ELH* 37(1970): 315-324.

11122. Hill, R. F. "Colin Clout's Courtesy." *MLR* 57(1962): 492-503.

11123. ----------. "Spenser's Allegorical 'Houses.'" *MLR* 65(1970): 721-733.

11124. Hinton, Stan. "The Poet and His Narrator: Spenser's Epic Voice." *ELH* 41(1974): 165-181.

11125. Holahan, Michael. " *Iamque opus exegi*: Ovid's Changes and Spenser's Brief Epic of Mutability." *ELR* 6(1976): 244-270.

11126. Holland, Joanne Field. "The Cantor of Mutabilities and the Form of *The Faerie Queene*." *ELH* 35(1968): 21-31.

11127. Hollander, John. "Spenser and the Mingled Measure." *ELR* 1(1971): 226-238.

11128. Holloway, J. "The Seven Deadly Sins in *The Faerie Queene*, Book II." *RES* 3(1952): 13-18.

11129. Hoopes, Robert. "'God Guide Thee, Guyon': Nature and Grace Reconciled in *The Faerie Queene*, Book II." *RES* 5(1954): 14-24.

11130. Hough, Graham. "Spenser and Renaissance Iconography." *EIC* 11(1961): 233-235.

11131. Hume, Anthea. "Spenser, Puritanism, and the 'Maye' Eclogue." *RES* 20(1969): 155-167.

11132. Huston, J. Dennis. "The Function of the Mock Heroic in Spenser's *Faerie Queen*." *MP* 66(1969): 212-217.

11133. Ingham, Patricia. "Spenser's Use of Dialect." *ELN* 8(1971): 164-168.

11134. Iredale, Roger O. "Giants and Tyrants in Book Five of *The Faerie Queene*." *RES* 17(1966): 373-381.

11135. Jenkins, Raymond. "Spenser and Ireland." *ELH* 19(1952): 131-142.

11136. Johnson, William C. "Spenser's *Amoretti* and the Art of Liturgy." *SEL* 14(1974): 47-61.

1137. Jordan, Richard Douglas. "Una among the Satyrs: *The Faerie Queene*, 1.6." *MLQ* 38 (1977): 123-131.

11138. Kaske, Carol V. "The Dragon's Spark and Sting and the Structure of Red Cross's Dragonfight: *The Faerie Queene*, I. xi-xii." *SP* 66(1960): 609-638.

11139. Kellogg, Robert L., and Oliver L. Steele. "On the Punctuation of Two Lines in *The Faerie Queene*." *PMLA* 78(1963): 147-148.

11140. Kennedy, William J. "Rhetoric, Allegory, and Dramatic Modality in Spenser's

Fradubio Episode." *ELR* 3(1973): 351-368.

11141. Knight, W. Nicholas. "The Narrative Unity of Book V of *The Faerie Queene*: 'That Part of Justice Which is Equity.'" *RES* 21(1970): 267-294.

11142. Koller, Katherine. "Art, Rhetoric, and Holy Dying in the *Faerie Queene* with Special Reference to the Despair Canto." *SP* 61(1964): 128-139.

11143. Landrum, Grace Warren. "St. George Redivivius." *PQ* 29(1950): 381-388.

11144. Lanham, Richard A. "The Literal Britomart." *MLQ* 28(1967): 426-445.

11145. MacCaffrey, Isabel G. "Allegory and Pastoral in *The Shepheardes Calender*." *ELH* 36 (1969): 88-109.

11146. MacIntyre, Jean. "Artegall's Sword and *The Mutabilitie Cantos*." *ELH* 33(1966): 405-414.

11147. Maclean, Hugh. "Fulke Greville and 'E.K.'" *ELN* 1(1963): 90-100.

11148. MacLure, Millar. "Nature and Art in *The Faerie Queene*." *ELH* 28(1961): 1-20.

11149. Magill, A. J. "Spenser's Guyon and the Mediocrity of the Elizabethan Settlement." *SP* 67(1970): 167-177.

11150. Mallette, Richard. "Poet and Hero in Book VI of 'The Faerie Queene.'" *MLR* 72(1977): 257-267.

11151. Marotti, Arthur F. "Animal Symbolism in *The Faerie Queene*: Tradition and the Poetic Context." *SEL* 5(1965): 69-86.

11152. Maxwell, J. C. "Guyon, Phaedria, and the Palmer." *RES* 5(1954): 388-390.

11153. ----------. "The Truancy of Calidore." *ELH* 19(1952): 143-149.

11154. May, Steven W. "Spenser's 'Amyntas': Three Poems by Fernandino Stanley, Lord Strange, Fifth Earl of Darby." *MP* 70(1972): 49-52.

11155. Maynard, John. "Perspectives on Change: Narrative Technique in Spenser's Cantos of Mutabilitie." *JNT* 5(1975): 100-118.

11156. McKim, William M. Jr. "The Divine and Infernal Comedy of Spenser's Mammon." *EL* 1 (1974): 3-16.

11157. McLane, Paul E. "Skelton's *Colyn Cloute* and Spenser's *Shepheardes Calender*." *SP* 70 (1973): 141-159.

11158. ----------. "Spenser and the Primitive Church." *ELN* 1(1963): 6-11.

11159. ----------. "Spenser's Cuddie: Edward Dyer." *JEGP* 54(1955): 230-240.

11160. ----------. "Spenser's Political and Religious Position in the *Shepheardes Calender*." *JEGP* 49(1950): 324-332.

11161. ----------. "Spenser's Oak and Briar." *SP* 52(1955): 463-477.

11162. Meyer, Sam. "the Figures of Rhetoric in Spenser's *Colin Clout*." *PMLA* 79(1964): 206-218.

11163. Miller, Lewis H., Jr. "Phaedria, Mammon, and Sir Guyon's Education by Error." *JEGP* 63(1964): 33-44.

11164. ----------. "A Secular Reading of the *Faerie Queene*, Book II." *ELH* 33(1966): 154-169.

11165. Miller, Milton. "Nature in the *Faerie Queene*." *ELH* 18(1951): 191-200.

11166. Milne, Fred L. "The Doctrine of Act and Potency: A Metaphysical Ground for Interpretation of Spenser's Garden of Adonis Passages."

SP 70(1973): 279-287.

11167. Mills, Jerry Leath. "A Source for Spenser's Anamnestes." *PQ* 47(1968): 137-139.

11168. ----------. "Spenser and the Numbers of History: A Note on the British and Elfin Chronicles in *The Faerie Queene*." *PQ* 55(1976): 281-287.

11169. ----------. "Spenser, Lodowick Bryskett, and the Mortalist Controversy: *The Faerie Queene*, II. ix. 22." *PQ* 52(1973): 173-186.

11170. ----------. "Spenser's Letter to Raleigh and the Averroistic *Poetics*." *ELN* 14 (1977): 246-249.

11171. ----------. "Symbolic Tapestry in *The Faerie Queene*, II. ix. 33." *PQ* 49(1970): 568-569.

11172. Moloney, Michael F. "St. Thomas and Spenser's Virtue of Magnificence." *JEGP* 52(1953): 58-62.

11173. Moore, Geoffrey. "The Cave of Mammon: Ethics and Metaphysics in Secular and Christian Perspective." *ELH* 42(1975): 157-170.

11174. Moore, John W., Jr. "Colin Breaks His Pipe: A Reading of the 'January' Eclogue." *ELR* 5(1975): 3-24.

11175. Mounts, Charles E. "Spenser and the Countess of Leicester." *ELH* 19(1952): 191-202.

11176. Mueller, William R. "Edmund Spenser and Recent Scholarship." *TSLL* 3(1961): 409-420.

11177. Murrin, Michael. "The Varieties of Criticism." *MP* 70(1973): 342-356.

11178. Murtaugh, Daniel M. "The Garden and the Sea: The Topography of *The Faerie Queene*, III." *ELH* 40(1973): 325-338.

11179. Neill, Kerby. "The Degradation of the Red Cross Knight." *ELH* 19(1952): 173-190.

11180. Nellish, B. "The Allegory of Guyon's Voyage: An Interpretation." *ELH* 30 (1963): 89-106.

11181. Nestrick, William V. "The Virtuous and Gentle Discipline of Gentlemen and Poets." *ELH* 29(1962): 357-371.

11182. Neuse, Richard. "Book VI as Conclusion to *The Faerie Queene*." *ELH* 35(1968): 329-353.

11183. ----------. "The Triumph over Hasty Accidents: A Note on the Symbolic Mode of the 'Epithalamion.'" *MLR* 61(1966): 163-174.

11184. O'Connell, Michael. "Spenser's *Astrophel Elegy*." *SEL* 11(1971): 27-35.

11185. ----------. "History and the Poet's Golden World: The Epic Catalogues in *The Faerie Queene*." *ELR* 4(1974): 241-267.

11186. Okerlund, Arlene N. "Spenser's Wanton Maidens: Reader Psychology and the Bower of Bliss." *PMLA* 88(1973): 62-68.

11187. Orange, Linwood E. "Sensual Beauty in Book I of *The Faerie Queene*." *JEGP* 61(1962): 555-561.

11188. Oras, Ants. "Intensified Rhyme Links in *The Faerie Queene*: An Aspect of Elizabethan Rhymecraft." *JEGP* 54(1955): 39-60.

11189. Oruch, Jack B. "Spenser, Camden, and the Poetic Marriage of Rivers." *SP* 64(1967): 606-624.

11190. Owen, W. J. B. "'In these XII Books Severally Handled and Discoursed.'" *ELH* 19(1952): 165-172.

11191. ----------. "Narrative Logic and Imitation in *The Faerie Queene*." *Comp L* 7(1955): 324-337.

11192. ----------. "Spenser's Letter to Ralegh." *MLR* 45(1950): 511-512.

11193. ----------. "The Structure of *The Faerie Queene*." *PMLA* 68(1953): 1079-1100.

11194. Parker, Patricia. "The Progress of Phaedria's Bower: Spenser to Coleridge." *ELH* 40 (1973): 372-397.

11195. Payne, Michael. "Taking Poets Seriously." *Coll L* 3(1976): 83-93.

11196. Pecheux, Mother N. Christopher, O. S. U. "Spenser's Red Cross and Milton's Adam." *ELN* 6(1969): 246-251.

11197. Phillips, James E. "Spenser's Synretistic Religious Imagery." *ELH* 36(1969): 110-130.

11198. Pichaske, David R. "*The Faerie Queene* IV. ii and iii: Spenser on the Genesis of Friendship." *SEL* 17(1977): 81-93.

11199. Reamer, Owen J. "Spenser's Debt to Marot—Re-examined." *TSLL* 10(1969): 504-527.

11200. Ricks, Beatrice. "Catholic Sacramentals and Symbolism in Spenser's *Faerie Queene*." *JEGP* 52(1953): 322-331.

11201. Ringler, Richard N. "The Faunus Episode." *MP* 63(1965): 12-19.

11202. ----------. "Spenser and the Achilleid." *SP* 60(1963): 174-182.

11203. Roche, Thomas P. Jr. "The Challenge to Chastity: Britomart at the House of Busyrane." *PMLA* 76(1961): 340-344.

11204. Rollinson, Philip B. "A Generic View of Spenser's Four Hymns." *SP* 68(1971): 292-304.

11205. Rosinger, Lawrence. "Spenser's Una and Queen Elizabeth." *ELN* 6(1968): 12-17.

11206. Rusche, Harry. "Pride, Humility, and Grace in Book I of *The Faerie Queene*." *SEL* 7(1967): 29-39.

11207. Satterthwaite, Alfred W. "Moral Vision in Spenser, du Ballay and Ronsard." *Comp L* 9(1957): 136-149.

11208. ----------. "A Re-examination of Spenser's Translations of the 'Sonets' from *A Theatre for Worldlings*." *PQ* 38(1959): 509-515.

11209. Saunders, J. W. "The Facade of Morality." *ELH* 19(1952): 81-114.

11210. Shore, David R. "Colin and Rosalind: Love and Poetry in the *Shepheardes Calender*." *SP* 73(1976): 176-188.

11211. Shroeder, John W. "Spenser's Erotic Drama: The Orgoglio Episode." *ELH* 29(1962): 140-159.

11212. Sims Dwight J. "The Syncretic Myth of Venus in Spenser's Legend of Chastity." *SP* 71 (1974): 427-450.

11213. Sirluck, Ernest. "The *Faerie Queene*, Book II, and the *Nicomachean Ethics*." *MP* 49(1951): 73-100.

11214. ----------. "Milton Revises *The Faerie Queene*." *MP* 48(1950): 90-96.

11215. Smith, J. Norton. "Spenser's *Protholamion*: a New Genre." *RES* 10(1959): 173-178.

11216. Smith, Roland M. "Origines Arthurianae: The Two Crosses of Spenser's Red Cross Knight." *JEGP* 54(1955): 670-683.

11217. Sonn, Carl Robinson. "Sir Guyon in the Cave of Mammon." *SEL* 1,#1(1961): 17-30.

11218. ----------. "Spenser's Imagery."

ELH 26(1959): 156-170.

11219. South, Malcolm H. "A Note on Spenser and Sir Thomas Browne." MLR 62(1967): 14-16.

11220. Spitzer, Leo. "Spenser, Shepherdes Calender, March 11. 61-114, and the Variorum Edition." SP 47(1950): 494-505.

11221. Stambler, Peter D. "The Development of Guyon's Christian Temperance." ELR 7(1977): 51-89.

11222. Staton, Walter F., Jr. "Italian Pastorals and the Conclusion of the Serena Story." SEL 6(1966): 35-42.

11223. ----------. "Ralegh and the Amyos—Aemylia Episode (F. Q. IV, viii-ix)." SEL 5(1965): 105-114.

11224. ----------. "Spenser's 'April' Lay as a Dramatic Chorus." SP 59(1962): 111-118.

11225. Steadman, John M. "The 'Inharmonious Blacksmith': Spenser and the Pythagoras Legend." PMLA 79(1964): 664-665.

11226. ----------. "Sin, Echidna, and the Viper's Blood." MLR 56(1961): 62-66.

11227. ----------. "Spenser and Martianus Capella." MLR 53(1958): 545-546.

11228. Stewart, James T. "Renaissance Psychology and the Ladder of Love in Castiglione and Spenser." JEGP 56(1957): 225-230.

11229. Swearingen, Roger G. "Guyon's Faint." SP 74(1977): 165-185.

11230. Thompson, Claud A. "Spenser's 'Many Faire Pourtraicts, and Many a Faire Feate.'" SEL 12(1972): 21-32.

11231. Tonkin, Humphrey. "Some Notes on Myth and Allegory in the Faerie Queene." MP 70 (1973): 291-301.

11232. ----------. "Spenser's Garden of Adonis and Britomart's Quest." PMLA 88(1973): 408-417.

11233. ----------. "Theme and Emblem in Spenser's Fairie Queene." ELH 40(1973): 221-230.

11234. Tonkin, James E. "Discussing Spenser's Cave of Mammon." SEL 13(1973): 1-13.

11235. Torczon, Vern. "Spenser's Orgoglio and Despair." TSLL 3(1961): 123-128.

11236. Tosello, Matthew, I. M. C. "Spenser's Silence about Dante." SEL 17(1977): 59-66.

11237. Tourney, Leonard D. "Spenser's Astrophel: Myth and the Critique of Values." EL 3(1976): 145-151.

11238. Travis, Mildred K. "Of Hawthorne's 'The Artist of the Beautiful' and Spenser's 'Muiopotmos.'" PQ 54(1975): 537.

11239. Wagner, Geoffrey. "Talus." ELH 17 (1950): 79-86.

11240. Waters, D. Douglas. "Errour's Den and Archimago's Hermitage: Symbolic Lust and Symbolic Witchcraft." ELH 33(1966): 279-298.

11241. ----------. "Prince Arthur as Christian Magnanimity in Book One of The Faerie Queene." SEL 9(1969): 53-62.

11242. ----------. "Spenser and Symbolic Witchcraft in The Shepheardes Calender." SEL 14 (1974): 3-15.

11243. ----------. "Spenser's 'Well of Life' and 'Tree of Life' Once More." MP 67(1969): 67-68.

11244. Webster, John. "Oral Form and Written Craft in Spenser's Faerie Queene." SEL 16(1976): 75-93.

11245. Weld, J. S. "The Complaint of

Britomart: Word-Play and Symbolism." PMLA 66 (1951): 548-551.

11246. West, Michael. "Prothalamia in Propertius and Spenser." Comp L 26(1974): 346-353.

11247. West, Michael. "Spenser and the Renaissance Ideal of Christian Heroism." PMLA 88 (1973): 1013-1032.

10248. Whitaker, Virgil K. "The Theological Structure of The Faerie Queene, Book I." ELH 19(1952): 151-164.

11249. Wickert, Max A. "Structure and Ceremony in Spenser's Epithalamion." ELH 35(1968): 135-157.

11250. Williams, Kathleen. "Courtesy and Pastoral in The Faerie Queene, Book VI." RES 13 (1962): 337-346.

11251. ----------. "'Eterne in Mutabilitie': The Unified World of The Faerie Queene." ELH 19 (1952): 115-130.

11252. ----------. "The Present State of Spenser Studies." TSLL 7(1965): 225-238.

11253. ----------. "Venus and Diana: Some Uses of Myth in The Faerie Queene." ELH 28(1961): 101-120.

11254. ----------. "Vision and Rhetoric: The Poet's Voice in The Faerie Queene." ELH 36 (1969): 131-144.

11255. Wilson, Rawdon. "Images and 'Allegoremes' of Time in the Poetry of Spenser." ELR 4(1974): 56-82.

11256. Wine, M. L. "Spenser's 'Sweete Themmes': Of Time and the River." SEL 2(1962): 111-117.

11257. Wright, Celeste Turner. "Anthony Munday, 'Edward' Spenser, and E. K." PMLA 76 (1961): 34-39.

11258. Wright, Lloyd A. "Guyon's Heroism in the Bower of Bliss." TSLL 15(1974): 597-603.

11259. Woodhouse, A. S. P. "Nature and Grace in Spenser: a Rejoinder." RES 6(1955): 284-288.

11260. ----------. Spenser, Nature and Grace: Mr. Gang's Mode of Argument Reviewed." ELH 27(1960): 1-15.

11261. Woods, Susanne. "Closure in The Faerie Queene." JEGP 76(1977): 195-216.

11262. Woodward, Daniel H. "Some Themes in Spenser's Prothalamion." ELH 29(1962): 34-46.

11263. Young, Frank B. "Medusa and the Epithalamion: A Problem in Spenserian Imagery." ELN 11(1973): 21-29.

11264. Zitner, S. P. "Spenser's Diction and Classical Precedent." PQ 45(1966): 360-371.

11265. Zivley, Sherry. "Hawthorne's 'The Artist of the Beautiful' and Spenser's 'Muiopotmos.'" PQ 48(1969): 134-137.

See also 515, 2236, 2300, 2319, 2440, 3538, 3715, 9286, 9287, 9291, 9310, 9324, 10995, 11431, 13127, 14519, 14649, 16339.

STANLEY, FERNANDINO. 11266. May, Steven W. "Spenser's 'Amyntas': Three Poems by Fernandino Stanley, Lord Strange, Fifth Earl of Derby." MP 70(1972): 49-52.

STEWART, JOHN. See 9450, 9466, 9467.

STOW, JOHN. 11267. Bryant, Joseph Allen, Jr. "John Stow's Continuator and the Defence of Brut." MLR 45(1950): 352-354.

STUBBES, PHILLIP. 11268. Pearson, Terry P. "The Composition and Development of Phillip

Stubbes's 'Anatomie of Abuses.'" *MLR* 56(1961): 321-332.

SURREY, HENRY HOWARD.   11269. Davis, Walter R. "Contexts in Surrey's Poetry." *ELR* 4(1974): 40-55.

11270. Fishman, Burton. "Recent Studies in Wyatt and Surrey." *ELR* 1(1971): 178-191.

11271. Harris, William O. "'Love that doth raine': Surrey's Creative Imitation." *MP* 66 (1969): 298-305.

11272. Jentoft, C. W. "Surrey's Five Elegies: Rhetoric, Structure, and the Poetry of Praise." *PMLA* 91(1976): 23-32.

11273. Nathan, Leonard. "The Course of the Particular: Surrey's Epitaph on Thomas Clere and the Fifteenth-Century Lyric Tradition." *SEL* 17(1977): 3-12.

11274. Oras, Ants. "Surrey's Technique of Phonetic Echoes: A Method and Its Background." *JEGP* 50(1951): 289-299.

11275. Richardson, David A. "Humanistic Intent in Surrey's *Aeneid*." *ELR* 6(1976): 204-219.

11276. Ridley, Florence H. "Surrey's Debt to Gawain Douglas." *PMLA* 76(1961): 25-33.

See also 9438.

TALLIS, THOMAS.   11277. Lenz, Carolyn R. S. "An Earlier Version of a Religious Lyric by Thomas Tallis." *RES* 24(1973): 301-304.

TILNEY, EDMUND.   11278. Moncada, Ernest J. "The Spanish Source of Edmund Tilney's 'Flower of Friendshippe.'" *MLR* 65(1970): 241-247.

TOFTE, ROBERT.   11279. Williams, F. B., Jr. "Robert Tofte an Oxford Man." *RES* 6(1955): 177-179.

TURBERVILE, GEORGE.   11280. Sheidley, William E. "George Turbervile and the Problem of Passion." *JEGP* 69(1970): 631-649.

11281. ----------. "George Turbervile's Epigrams from the Greek Anthology: A Case-Study of 'Englishing.'" *SEL* 12(1972): 71-84.

11282. ----------. "'Lycidas': An Early Elizabethan Analogue by George Turbervile." *MP* 69(1972): 228-230.

See also 9287.

TURNER, WILLIAM.   11283. Harrison, Thomas P. "Turner and Spenser's *Mother Hubberd's Tale*." *JEGP* 49(1950): 464-469.

TYNDALE, WILLIAM.   11284. Maveety, Stanley R. "Doctrine in Tyndale's New Testament: Translation as Tendentious Art." *SEL* 6(1966): 151-158.

11285. Pineas, Rainer. "William Tyndale: Controversialist." *SP* 60(1963): 117-132.

See also 9895.

UDALL, NICHOLAS.   11286. Edgerton, William L. "The Date of *Roister Doister*." *PQ* 44(1965): 555-560.

11287. ----------. "Nicholas Udall in the Indexes of Prohibited Books." *JEGP* 55(1956): 247-252.

11288. Plumstead, A. W. "Satirical Parody in *Roister Doister*: A Reinterpretation." *SP* 60 (1963): 141-154.

See also 9320, 9345, 9367.

WAGER, WILLIAM.   11289. Kutrieh, Ahmad Ramez. "The Doubling of Parts in *Enough Is As Good As A Feast*." *ELN* 12(1974): 79-84.

See also 9425.

WAPULL, GEORGE.   See 9359.

WARDE, WILLIAM.   11290. Coon, Arthur M. "Dr. William Warde (1534-1609) Author of *The Arte of Angling, 1577*." *JEGP* 61(1962): 578-582.

WATSON, THOMAS.   11291. Morris, Harry. "Thomas Watson and Abraham Fraunce." *PMLA* 76 (1961): 152-153.

11292. Murphy, William M. "Thomas Watson's *Hecatompathia* [1582] and the Elizabethan Sonnet Sequence." *JEGP* 56(1957): 418-428.

11293. Stanton, Walter F., Jr. "Thomas Watson and Abraham Fraunce." *PMLA* 76(1961): 150-152.

See also 9347.

WEALTH AND HEALTH.   11294. Craik, T. W. "The Political Interpretation of Two Tudor Interludes: *Temperance and Humility* and *Wealth and Health*." *RES* 4(1953): 98-108.

11295. Pineas, Rainer. "The Revision of *Wealth and Health*." *PQ* 44(1965): 560-562.

WESTCOTT, SEBASTIAN.   11296. Brown, Arthur. "A Note on Sebastian Westcott and the Plays Presented by the Children of Paul's." *MLQ* 12(1951): 134-136.

WEVER, R.   See 9425.

WHITNEY, GEOFFREY.   11297. Bergeron, David M. "The Emblematic Nature of English Civic Pageantry." *RD* n.s. 1(1968): 167-198.

11298. Hunter, Kathryn. "Geoffrey Whitney's 'To Richard Cotton, Esq.': an Early English Country-House Poem." *RES* 28(1977): 438-441.

WHITTINGTON, ROBERT.   See 9320.

WILSON, ROBERT.   11299. Dessen, Alan C. "The Elizabethan Stage Jew and Christian Example: Gerontus, Barabas, and Shylock." *MLQ* 35(1974): 231-245.

See also 9359.

WILSON, SIR THOMAS.   11300. Anderson, D. M. "Sir Thomas Wilson's Translation of Montemayor's *Diana*." *RES* 7(1956): 176-181.

See also 9334, 9430, 9614.

WYATT, THOMAS.   11301. Bath, Michael. "Wyatt and 'Liberty.'" *EIC* 23(1973): 322-328.

11302. Boyd, John Douglas "Literary Interpretation and the *Subjective* Correlative: an Illustration from Wyatt." *EIC* 21(1971): 327-346.

11303. Candelaria, Frederick H. "The Necklace of Wyatt's 'Diere.'" *ELN* 1(1963): 4-5.

11304. Daalder, Joost. "Wyatt and 'Liberty.'" *EIC* 23(1973): 63-67.

11305. ----------. "Wyatt's 'There Was Never Nothing More Me Payned': A Reply to John Douglas Boyd." *EIC* 21(1971): 418-424.

11306. Evans, Robert O. "Some Aspects of Wyatt's Metrical Technique." *JEGP* 53(1954): 197-213.

11307. Fishman, Burton. "Recent Studies in Wyatt and Surrey." *ELR* 1(1971): 178-191.

11308. Friedman, Donald M. "The Mind in the Poem: Wyatt's 'They Fle From Me.'" *SEL* 7(1967): 1-13.

11309. ----------. "The 'Thing' in Wyatt's Mind." *EIC* 16(1966): 375-381.

11310. ----------. "Wyatt and the Ambiguities of Fancy." *JEGP* 67(1968): 32-48.

11311. ----------. "Wyatt's *Amoris Personae*." *MLQ* 27(1966): 136-146.

11312. Fuller, J. O. "Wyatt and Petrarch." *EIC* 14(1964): 324-326.

11313. Gerard, Albert S. "Wyatt's 'They Fle

from Me.'" *EIC* 11(1961): 359-366.

11314. Graziani, René. "Sir Thomas Wyatt at a Cockfight, 1539." *RES* 27(1976): 299-303.

11315. Greene, Richard Leighton. "A Carol of Anne Boleyn by Wyatt." *RES* 25(1974): 437-439.

11316. ----------. "Wyatt's 'I am as I am' in Carol-form." *RES* 15(1964): 175-180.

11317. Hainsworth, J. D. "Sir Thomas Wyatt's Use of the Love Convention." *EIC* 7(1957): 90-95.

11318. ----------. "Wyatt's 'They Fle from Me.'" *EIC* 11(1961): 366-368.

11319. Harrier, Richard C. "Notes on Wyatt and Ann Boleyn." *JEGP* 53(1954): 581-584.

11320. Low, Anthony. "Wyatt's 'What Word is That.'" *ELN* 10(1972): 89-90.

11321. Luria, Maxwell S. "Wyatt's 'The Lover Compareth His State' and the Petrarchan Commentators." *TSLL* 12(1971): 531-535.

11322. Maxwell, J. C. "Wyatt and 'Liberty.'" *EIC* 24(1974): 104.

11323. Maynard, Winifred. "The Lyrics of Wyatt: Poems or Songs." *RES* 16(1965): 1-13, 245-257.

11324. ----------. "'To Smithe of Camden.'" *RES* 18(1967): 162-163.

11325. McCanles, Michael. "Love and Power in the Poetry of Sir Thomas Wyatt." *MLQ* 29(1968): 145-160.

11326. Morris, Harry. "Birds, Does, and Manliness in 'They Fle From Me.'" *EIC* 10(1960): 484-492.

11327. Muir, Kenneth. "An Unpublished Wyatt Poem." *EIC* 10(1960): 229-230.

11328. Nathan, Leonard E. "Tradition and New-fangledness in Wyatt's *They Fle from Me*" *ELH* 32(1965): 1-16.

11329. Nelson, C. E. "A Note on Wyatt and Ovid." *MLR* 58(1963): 60-63.

11330. Ogle, Robert B. "Wyatt and Petrarch: A Puzzle in Prosody." *JEGP* 73(1974): 189-208.

11331. Rees, D. G. "Sir Thomas Wyatt's Translations from Petrarch." *Comp L* 7(1955): 15-24.

11332. ----------. "Wyatt and Petrarch." *MLR* 52(1957): 389-391.

11333. Schwartz, Elias. "The Meter of Some Poems of Wyatt." *SP* 60(1963): 155-165.

11334. Southall, Raymond. "The Personality of Sir Thomas Wyatt." *EIC* 14(1964): 43-64.

11335. ----------. "Wyatt and Petrarch." *EIC* 14(1964): 326-327.

11336. ----------. "Wyatt's 'Ye Old Mule.'" *ELN* 5(1967): 5-11.

11337. Swallow, Alan. "The Pentameter Lines in Skelton and Wyatt." *MP* 48(1950): 1-11.

11338. Thomson, Patricia. "Wyatt and the Petrarchan Commentators." *RES* 10(1959): 225-233.

11339. ----------. "Wyatt and the School of Serafino." *Comp L* 13(1961): 289-315.

11340. ----------. "Wyatt's Boethian Ballade." *RES* 15(1964): 262-267.

11341. Twombley, Robert G. "Beauty and the (Subverted) Beast; Wyatt's 'They fle me.'" *TSLL* 10(1969): 489-503.

11342. ----------. "Thomas Wyatt's Paraphrase of the Penitential Psalms of David." *TSLL* 12(1970): 345-380.

11343. Whiting, George W. "Fortune in Wyatt's 'They Fle from Me.'" *EIC* 10(1960): 220-222.

11344. Wiatt, William H. "On the Date of Sir Thomas Wyatt's Knighthood." *JEGP* 60(1961): 268-272.

11345. ----------. "Sir Thomas Wyatt and Anne Boleyn." *ELN* 6(1968): 94-102.

11346. ----------. "Sir Thomas Wyatt's Astrologer." *ELN* 4(1966): 89-92.

11347. Winser, Leigh. "The Question of Love Tradition in Wyatt's 'They Flee from Me.'" *EL* 2(1975): 3-9.

   See also 9439, 9447, 11425.
YATES, JAMES. See 9447.
YORKSHIRE TRAGEDY. See 9354.

SEVENTEENTH CENTURY

GENERAL AND MISCELLANEOUS. 11348. Brevold, Louis I. "The Rise of English Classicism: Study in Methodology." *Comp L* 2(1950): 253-268.

11349. Cope, Jackson I. "Seventeenth-Century Quaker Style." *PMLA* 71(1956): 725-754.

11350. Cruttwell, Patrick. "The War's and Fortune's Son." *EIC* 2(1952): 24-37.

11351. Davies, Paul C. "Restoration Liberalism." *EIC* 22(1972): 226-238.

11352. ----------. "Who were the Restoration Liberals?" *EIC* 24(1974): 213-216.

11353. Hardin, Richard F. "Ovid in Seventeenth-Century England." *Comp L* 24(1972): 44-62.

11354. Hughes, Richard E. "'Wit': The Genealogy of a Theory." *CLA* 5(1961): 142-144.

11355. Jarrett, Hobart. "Some Exceptional Allusions to the Negro in Non-Dramatic Literature of Seventeenth-Century England." *CLA* 6(1962): 19-22.

11356. Jensen, James H. "A Note on Restoration Aesthetics." *SEL* 14(1974): 317-326.

11357. Joseph. "A Seventeenth-Century Guide to Character Writing." *RES* 1(1950): 144.

11358. Miller, Henry Knight. "The Paradoxical Encomium with Special Reference to Its Vogue in England, 1600-1800." *MP* 53(1956): 145-178.

11359. Mish, Charles C. "Black Letter as a Social Discriminant in the Seventeenth Century." *PMLA* 68(1953): 627-630.

11360. Parsons, Leila. "Prince Henry (1594-1612) as a Patron of Literature." *MLR* 47(1952): 503-507.

11361. Perella, Nicolas J. "Amarilli's Dilemma: The *Pastor Fido* and Some English Authors." *Comp L* 12(1960): 348-359.

11362. Praz, Mario. "Baroque in England." *MP* 61(1964): 169-179.

11363. Salmon, Vivian. "Early Seventeenth-Century Punctuation as a Guide to Sentence Structure." *RES* 13(1962): 347-360.

11364. Seidel, Michael A. "The Restoration Mob: Drones and Dregs." *SEL* 12(1972): 429-443.

11365. Sprott, S. E. "The Damned Crew." *PMLA* 84(1969): 492-500.

11366. Summers, Joseph H. "Notes on Recent Studies in English Literature of the Earlier Seventeenth Century." *MLQ* 26(1965): 135-149.

11367. Weitzman, Arthur J. "Who Were the Restoration Liberals?" *EIC* 23(1973): 200-205, and 24(1974): 323-324.

11368. Ziff, Lazar. "The Literary Consequences of Puritanism." *ELH* 30(1963): 293-305.

DRAMA. 11369. Adams, Robert P. "Transformations in the Late Elizabethan Tragic Sense of Life: New Criticial Approaches." *MLQ* 35 (1974): 352-363.

11370. Anderson, Donald K. "The Banquet of Love in English Drama (1595-1642)." *JEGP* 63 (1964): 422-432.

11371. Andrews, Michael C. "The Sources of *Andromana*." *RES* 19(1968): 295-300.

11372. Avery, Emmett L. "The Resotration Audience." *PQ* 45(1966): 54-61.

11373. Bateson, F. W. "Second Throught. II L. C. Knights and Resotration Comedy." *EIC* 7 (1957): 56-57.

11374. Barranger, Milly S. "The Cankered Rose: A Consideration of the Jacobean Tragic Heroine." *CLA* 14(1970): 178-186.

11375. Bergeron, David M. "The Christmas Family: Artificers in English Civic Pageantry." *ELH* 35(1968): 354-364.

11376. Berkeley, David S. "The Art of 'Whining' Love." *SP* 52(1955): 478-496.

11377. ----------. "The Penitent Rake in Restoration Comedy." *MP* 49(1952): 223-233.

11378. Blayney, Glenn H. "Enforcement of Marriage in English Drama (1600-1650)." *PQ* 38 (1959): 459-472.

11379. Cecil, C. D. "Delicate and Indelicate Puns in Restoration Comedy." *MLR* 61(1966): 572-578.

11380. ----------. "Libertine and *Précieux* Elements in Restoration Comedy." *EIC* 9(1959): 239-253.

11381. Empson, William. "Restoration Comedy Again." *EIC* 7(1957): 318.

11382. Eversole, Richard. "A Source for the Plot of *The Fair Maide of Bristow*." *RES* 24 (1973): 305-310.

11383. Gossett, Suzanne. "Drama in the English College, Rome, 1591-1660." *ELR* 3(1973): 60-93.

11384. Holland, Norman H. "Restoration Comedy Again." *EIC* 7(1957): 319-322.

11385. Horwich, Richard. "Wives, Courtesans, and the Economics of Love in Jacobean City Comedy." *CD* 7(1973): 291-309.

11386. Hosley, Richard. "Three Renaissance English Indoor Playhouses." *ELR* 3(1973): 166-182.

11387. Hoy, Cyrus. "Renaissance and Restoration Dramatic Plotting." *RD* 9(1966): 247-264.

11388. Hume, Robert D. "The Myth of the Rake in 'Restoration Comedy.'" *SLI* 10,#1(1977): 25-55.

11389. ----------. "Theory of Comedy in the Resotration." *MP* 70(1973): 302-318.

11390. Jensen, Ejner J. "The Style of the Boy Actors." *CD* 2(1968): 100-114.

11391. Kirsch, Arthur C. "A Caroline Commentary on the Drama." *MP* 66(1969): 256-261.

11392. Lancashire, Anne. "*The Second Maiden's Tragedy*: A Jacobean Saint's Life." *RES* 25(1974): 267-279.

11393. Levin, Richard. "The Proof of Parody." *EIC* 24(1974): 312-317.

11394. Maxwell, Baldwin. "The Attitude Toward the Duello in Later Jacobean Drama—a Postscript." *PQ* 54(1975): 104-116.

11395. McCullen, Joseph T., Jr. "Madness

and the Isolation of Characters in Elizabethan and Early Stuart Drama." *SP* 48(1951): 206-218.

11396. McDonald, Charles O. "Restoration Comedy as Drama of Satire: An Investigation into Seventeenth-Century Aesthetics." *SP* 61(1964): 522-544.

11397. McManaway, James G. "Notes on Two Pre-Restoration Stage Curtains." *PQ* 41(1962): 270-274.

11398. McKenzie, D. F. "A Cambridge Playhouse of 1638." *RD* n.s. 3(1970): 263-272.

11399. Novak, Maximillian E. "Margery Pinchwife's 'London Disease': Restoration Comedy and the Libertine Offensive of the 1670's." *SLI* 10,#1(1977): 1-23.

11400. Ross, Robert H., Jr. "Samuel Sandford: Villain from Necessity." *PMLA* 76(1961): 367-372.

11401. Rothstein, Eric. "English Tragic Theory in the Late Seventeenth Century." *ELH* 29 (1962): 306-323.

11402. Rowan, D. F. "The English Playhouse: 1595-1630." *RD* n.s. 4(1971): 37-51.

11403. Rubin, Barbara L. "'Anti-Husbandry' and Self-Creation: A Comparison of Restoration Rake and Beaudelaire's Dandy." *TSLL* 14(1973): 583-592.

11404. Scouten, A. H. "Notes toward a History of Restoration Comedy." *PQ* 45(1966): 62-70.

11405. Spikes, Judith Doolin. "The Jacobean History Play and the Myth of the Elect Nation." *RD* n.s. 8(1977): 117-149.

11406. Stephenson, William E. "Religious Drama in the Restoration." *PQ* 50(1971): 599-609.

11407. Traugott, John. "The Rake's Progress from Court to Comedy: A Study in Comic Form." *SEL* 6(1966): 381-407.

11408. Vernon, P. F. "Marriage of Convenience and the Moral Code of Restoration Comedy." *EIC* 12(1962): 370-387.

11409. Wain, John. "Restoration Comedy and its Modern Critics." *EIC* 6(1956): 367-385.

11410. Waith, Eugene M. "Aristophanes, Plautus, Terence, and the Refinement of English Comedy." *SLI* 10,#1(1977): 91-108.

11411. Williams, Aubrey. "Of 'One Faith': Authors and Auditors in the Restoration Theatre." *SLI* 10,#1(1977): 57-76.

11412. Williams, Gwyn. "The Cuckoo, the Welsh Ambassador." *MLR* 51(1956): 223-225.

11413. Wilson, John Harold. "Rant, Cant, and Tone on the Restoration Stage." *SP* 52(1955): 592-598.

POETRY. 11414. Budick, Sanford. "The Demythological Mode in Augustan Verse." *ELH* 37 (1970): 389-414.

11415. Buxton, J. "The Poets' Hall called Apollo." *MLR* 48(1953): 52-54.

11416. Chernaik, Warren L. "The Heroic Occasional Poem: Panegyric and Satire in the Restoration." *MLQ* 26(1965): 523-535.

11417. Duncan, Joseph E. "The Revival of Metaphysical Poetry, 1872-1912." *PMLA* 68(1953): 658-671.

11418. Ellrodt, Robert. "Scientific Curiosity and Metaphysical Poetry in the Seventeenth Century." *MP* 61(1964): 180-189.

11419. Fisher, William N. "*Occupatio* in

Sixteenth- and Seveenteenth-Century Verse." *TSLL* 14(1972): 203-222.

11420. Gros Louis, Kenneth R. R. "The Triumph and Death of Orpheus in the English Renaissance." *SEL* 9(1969): 63-80.

11421. Hart, E. F. "The Answer-Poem of the Early Seventeenth Century." *RES* 7(1956): 19-29.

11422. Hawkins, Annabel L. "A Strain of Trivia in Minor Metaphysical Poetry." *CLA* 12 (1969): 257-262.

11423. Hughes, Richard E. "Metaphysical Poetry as Event." *HSL* 3(1971): 191-196.

11424. Judkins, David C. "Recent Studies in the Cavalier Poets: Thomas Carew, Richard Lovelace, John Suckling, and Edmund Waller." *ELR* 7(1977): 243-258.

11425. Levine, Jay Arnold. "The Status of the Verse Epistle before Pope." *SP* 59(1962): 658-684.

11426. MacCaffrey, Isabel G. "The Meditative Paradigm." *ELH* 32(1965): 388-407.

11427. Maresca, Thomas E. "Language and Body in Augustan Poetic." *ELH* 37(1970): 374-388.

11428. Mazzeo, Joseph Anthony. "A Critique of Some Modern Theories of Metaphysical Poetry." *MP* 50(1952): 88-96.

11429. McCann, Eleanor. "Oxymora in Spanish Mystics and English Metaphysical Writers." *Comp L* 13(1961): 16-25.

11430. McGuire, Philip C. "Private Prayer and English Poetry in the Early Seventeenth Century." *SEL* 14(1974): 63-77.

11431. Miller, Paul W. "The Decline of the English Epithalamion." *TSLL* 12(1970): 405-416.

11432. Murrin, Michael. "Poetry as Literary Criticism." *MP* 65(1968): 202-207.

11433. Osmond, Rosalie. "Body and Soul Dialogues in the Seventeenth Century." *ELR* 4 (1974): 364-403.

11435. Quaintance, Richard E. "French Sources of the Restoration 'Imperfect Enjoyment' Poem." *PQ* 42(1963): 190-199.

11436. Richmond, H. M. "The Intangible Mistress." *MP* 56(1959): 217-223.

11437. Röstrig, Maren-Sofie. "Casimire Sarbiewski and the English Ode." *SP* 51(1954): 443-460.

11438. Sanderson, James L. "Poems on an Affair of State—The Marriage of Somerset and Lady Essex." *RES* 17(1966): 57-61.

11439. Selden, R. "Juvenal and Restoration Modes of Translation." *MLR* 68(1973): 481-493.

11440. Stein, Arnold. "The Paradise Within and the Paradise Without." *MLQ* 26(1965): 586-600.

11441. Tokson, Elliot H. "The Image of the Negro in Four Seventeenth-Century Love Poems." *MLQ* 30(1969): 508-522.

11442. Watson, George. "Ramus, Miss Tuve, and the New Petromachia." *MP* 55(1958): 259-262.

11443. Weinbrot, Howard. "Translation and Parody: Towards the Genealogy of the Augustan Imitation." *ELH* 33(1966): 434-447.

11444. Youngren, William H. "Generality, Science and Poetic Language in the Restoration." *ELH* 35(1968): 158-187.

PROSE. 11445. Cope, Jackson I. "Modes of Modernity in Seventeenth-Century Prose." *MLQ* 31 (1970): 92-111.

11446. Fisch, Harold. "The Puritans and the Reform of Prosectyle." *ELH* 19(1952): 229-248.

11447. McIntosh, Carey. "A Matter of Style: Stative and Dynamic Predicates." *PMLA* 92(1977): 110-121.

11448. Miner, Earl. "Patterns of Stoicism in Thought and Prose Styles, 1530-1700." *PMLA* 85 (1970): 1023-1034.

11449. Mish, Charles C. "English Short Fiction in the Seventeenth Century." *SSF* 6(1969): 233-330.

11450. Novak, Maximillian E. "Some Notes Toward a History of Fictional Forms: From Aphra Behn to Daniel Defoe." *Novel* 6(1973): 120-133.

11451. Pebworth, Ted-Larry. "Not Being, but Passing: Defining the Early English Essay." *SLI* 10,#2(1977): 17-27.

11451a. Peterson, Spiro. "William Morrell and Late Seventeenth-Century Fiction." *PQ* 42 (1963): 200-206.

ALEXANDER, SIR WILLIAM. See 9450.

ANDREWES, LANCELOT. 11452. McCutcheon, Elizabeth. "Lancelot Andrewes' *Preces Privatae*: A Journey through Time." *SP* 65(1968): 223-241.

11453. Webber, Joan. "Celebration of Word and World in Lancelot Andrewes' Style." *JEGP* 64 (1965): 255-269.

AYRES, PHILIP. See 18124.

AYTON, ROBERT. 11454. Gullans, Charles B. "New Poems by Sir Robert Ayton." *MLR* 55(1960): 160-168.

11455. Roberts, William. "Saint-Amant, Aytoun, and the Tobacco Sonnet." *MLR* 54(1959): 499-506.

BACON, FRANCIS. 11456. Bierman, Judah. "New Atlantis Revisited." *SLI* 4,#1(1971): 121-141.

11457. ----------. "Science and Society in the *New Atlantis* and Other Renaissance Utopias." *PMLA* 78(1963): 492-500.

11458. Callahan, Patrick. "*Frankenstein*, Bacon, and the 'Two Truths.'" *Ext* 14(1972): 39-48.

11459. Cochrane, Rexmond C. "Francis Bacon in Early Eighteenth-Century English Literature." *PQ* 37(1958): 58-79.

11460. Davis, Walter R. "The Imagery of Bacon's Late Work." *MLQ* 27(1966): 162-173.

11461. Farrington, Benjamin. "Frances Bacon after His Fall." *SLI* 4,#1(1971): 143-158.

11462. Fisch, H., and H. W. Jones. "Bacon's Influence on Sprat's *History of the Royal Society*." *MLQ* 12(1951): 399-406.

11463. Guibbory, Achsah. "Francis Bacon's View of History: The Cycles of Error and the Progress of Truth." *JEGP* 74(1975): 336-350.

11464. Hopkins, Vivian C. "Emerson and Bacon." *AL* 29(1958): 408-430.

11465. Lees, F. N. "*Coriolanus*, Aristotle, and Bacon." *RES* 1(1950): 114-125.

11466. McCutcheon, Elizabeth. "Bacon and the Cherubim: An Iconographical Reading of the *New Atlantis*." *ELR* 2(1972): 334-355.

11467. McNamee, Maurice P., S. J. "Bacon's Inductive Method and Humanistic Grammar." *SLI* 4,#1 (1971): 81-106.

11468. Nisbet, H. B. "Herder and Francis Bacon." *MLR* 62(1967): 267-283.

11469. Patrick, J. Max. "Hawk versus Dove: Frances Bacon's Advocacy of a Holy War by James I against the Turks." *SLI* 4,#1(1971): 159-171.

11470. Rickert, Corinne. "An Addition to the Canon of Bacon's Writings." *MLR* 51(1956): 71-72.

11471. Schultz, H. Stefan. "Hofmannsthal and Bacon: The Sources of the Chandos Letter." *Comp L* 13(1961): 1-15.

11472. Schuster, Sister Mary Faith, O. S. B. "Philosophy of Life and Prose Style in Thomas More's *Richard III* and Francis Bacon's *Henry VII*." *PMLA* 70(1955): 474-487.

11473. Steadman, John M. "Beyond Hercules: Bacon and the Scientist as Hero." *SLI* 4,#1 (1971): 3-47.

11474. Stephens, James. "Bacon's Fable-making: A Strategy of Style." *SEL* 14(1974): 111-127.

11475. Vickers, Brian. "Bacon's Use of Theatrical Imagery." *SLI* 4,#1(1971): 189-226.

11476. Wallace, Karl R. "Chief Guides for the Study of Bacon's Speeches." *SLI* 4,#1(1971): 173-188.

11477. Warhaft, Sidney. "The Providential Order in Bacon's New Philosophy." *SLI* 4,#1(1971): 49-64.

11478. Wheeler, Thomas. "The Purpose of Bacon's *History of Henry the Seventh*" *SP* 54(1957): 1-13.

11479. Whitaker, Virgil K. "Francesco Patrizi and Francis Bacon." *SLI* 4,#1(1971): 107-120.

11480. Wiley, Margaret L. "Frances Bacon: Induction and/or Rhetoric." *SLI* 4,#1(1971): 65-79.

See also 1927, 11451, 18048.

BEAUMONT AND FLETCHER. 11481. Davison, Peter. "The Serious Concerns of *Philaster*." *ELH* 30(1963): 1-15.

11482. Eddy, D. Mathis. "Melville's Response to Beaumont and Fletcher: A New Source for *The Encantadas*." *AL* 40(1968): 374-380.

11483. Finkelpearl, Philip J. "Beaumont, Fletcher, and 'Beaumont and Fletcher': Some Distinctions." *ELR* 1(1971): 144-164.

11484. Gossett, Suzanne. "Masque Influence on the Dramaturgy of Beaumont and Fletcher." *MP* 69(1972): 199-208.

11485. ----------. "The Term 'Masque' in Shakespeare and Fletcher, and *The Coxcomb*." *SEL* 14(1974): 285-295.

11486. Huebert, Ronald. "'An Artificial Way to Grieve': The Forsaken Woman in Beaumont and Fletcher, Massinger and Ford." *ELH* 44(1977): 601-621.

11487. Neill, Michael. "'The Simetry, Which Gives a Poem Grace': Masque, Imagery, and the Fancy of *The Maid's Tragedy*." *RD* n.s. 3(1970): 111-135.

See also 9402, 11374, 11395.

BEAUMONT, FRANCIS. 11488. Finkelpearl, Philip J. "'Wit' in Francis Beaumont's Poems." *MLQ* 28(1967): 33-44.

11489. Doebler, John. "Beaumont's *The Knight of the Burning Pestle* and the Prodigal Son Plays." *SEL* 5(1965): 333-344.

11490. Olive, W. J. "'Twenty Good Nights'— *The Knight of the Burning Pestle*, *The Family of Love*, and *Romeo and Juliet*." *SP* 47(1950): 182-189.

11491. Simpson, Percy. "Francis Beaumont's Verse-Letter to Ben Jonson: 'The Sun, Which Doth the Greatest Comfort Bring. . . .'" *MLR* 46(1951): 435-436.

BEAUMONT, JOHN. 11492. Wallerstein, Ruth. "Sir John Beaumont's *Crowne of Thornes*: a Report." *JEGP* 53(1954): 410-434.

BEAUMONT, JOSEPH. 11493. Stanwood, Paul Grant. "St. Teresa and Joseph Beaumont's *Psyche*." *JEGP* 62(1963): 533-550.

See also 11429.

BEHN, APHRA. 11494. Brownley, Martine Watson. "The Narrator in *Oroonoko*." *EL* 4(1977): 174-181.

11495. Seeber, Edward D. "Oroonoko and Crusoe's Man Friday." *MLQ* 12(1951): 286-291.

11496. Sheffey, Ruthe T. "Some Evidence for a New Source of Aphra Behn's *Oroonoko*." *SP* 59 (1962): 52-53.

See also 7780, 13601.

BENLOWES, EDWARD. 11497. Duncan-Jones, Elsie. "Benlowes's Borrowings from George Herbert." *RES* 6(1955): 179-180.

11498. Hill, Christopher. "Benlowes and his Times." *EIC* 3(1953): 143-151.

11499. Roditi, Edouard. "The Wisdom and Folly of Edward Benlowes." *Comp L* 2(1950): 343-353.

See also 11437.

BIRKENHEAD, JOHN. 11500. Doyle, Charles Clay. "An Unhonored English Anacreon: John Birkenhead." *SP* 71(1974): 192-205.

BOLTON, EDMUND. 11501. Blackburn, Thomas H. "The Date and Evolution of Edmund Bolton's *Hypercritics*." *SP* 63(1966): 196-202.

BRATHWAIT, RICHARD. 11502. Boyce, Benjamin. "History and Fiction in *Panthalia: or the Royal Romance*." *JEGP* 57(1958): 477-491.

BREWER, ANTH. 11503. Dent, Robert W. "The Love-Sick King: Turk Turned Dane." *MLR* 56 (1961): 555-557.

BROME, ALEXANDER. See 12098.

BROME, RICHARD. 11504. Cutts, John. "The Anonymous Masque-like Entertainment in Egerton MS. 1994, and Richard Brome." *CD* 1(1967): 277-287.

11505. Freehafer, John. "Brome, Suckling and Davenant's Theater Project of 1639." *TSLL* 10 (1968): 367-383.

11506. Haaker, Ann. "The Plague, the Theater, and the Poet." *RD* n.s. 1(1968): 283-306.

11507. Ingram, R. W. "The Musical Art of Richard Brome's Comedies." *RD* n.s. 7(1976): 219-242.

11508. Kaufmann, R. J. "Suckling and Davenant Satirized by Brome." *MLR* 55(1960): 332-344.

11509. Panek, LeRoy L. "Asparagus and Brome's *The Sparagus Garden*" *MP* 68(1971): 362-363.

BROWNE, THOMAS. 11510. Ardolino, Frank. "The Saving of God: The Significance of the Emblematic Frontspiece of the *Religio Medici*." *ELN* 15 (1977): 19-23.

11511. Breiner, Laurence A. "The Generation of Metaphor in Thomas Browne." *MLQ* 38(1977): 261-275.

11512. Childs, Herbert E. "Emily Dickinson and Sir Thomas Browne." *AL* 22(1951): 455-465.

11513. Davis, Walter R. "*Urne Buriall*: A Descent into the Underworld." *SLI* 10,#2(1977): 73-87.

11514. Donovan, Dennis G. "Recent Studies in Browne." *ELR* 2(1972): 271-279.

11515. Guibbory, Achsah. "Sir Thomas Browne's

Allusions to Janus." *ELN* 12(1975): 269-273.

11516. ----------. "Sir Thomas Browne's *Pseudodoxia Epidemica* and the Circle of Knowledge." *TSLL* 18(1976): 486-499.

11517. Huntley, Frank Livingston. "The Occasion and Date of Sir Thomas Browne's *A Letter to a Friend*." *MP* 48(1951): 157-171.

11518. ----------. "Sir Thomas Browne: The Relationship of *Urn Burial* and *The Garden of Cyrus*." *SP* 53(1956): 204-219.

11519. Moloney, Michael F. "Metre and *Cursus* in Sir Thomas Browne's Prose." *JEGP* 58 (1959): 60-66.

11520. Parr, Johnstone. "Sir Thomas Browne's Birthday." *ELN* 11(1973): 44-46.

11521. Pritchard, Allan. "Wither's *Motto* and Browne's *Religio Medici*." *PQ* 40(1961): 302-307.

11522. Shabber, M. A. "A Crux in *Religio Medici*." *ELN* 3(1966): 263-265.

11523. Sloane, Cecile A. "Imagery of Conflict in *Religio Medici*." *ELN* 8(1971): 260-262.

11524. South, Malcolm H. "A Note on Spenser and Sir Thomas Browne." *MLR* 62(1967): 14-16.

11525. Whallon, William. "Hebraic Synonymy in Sir Thomas Browne." *ELH* 28(1961): 335-352.

11526. Williamson, George. "The Purple of *Urn Burial*." *MP* 62(1964): 110-117.

See also 9302, 12916.

BROWNE, WILLIAM. 11527. Grundy, Joan. "Keats and William Browne." *RES* 6(1955): 44-52.

11528. ----------. "Tasso, Fairfax, and William Browne." *RES* 3(1952): 268-271.

11529. ----------. "William Browne and the Italian Pastoral." *RES* 4(1953): 305-316.

BUNYAN, JOHN. 11530. Alpaugh, David J. "Emblem and Interpretation in *The Pilgrim's Progress*." *ELH* 33(1966): 299-314.

11531. Fish, Stanley Eugene. "Progress in *The Pilgrim's Progress*." *ELR* 1(1971): 261-293.

11532. Forrest, James F. "Bunyan's Ignorance and the Flatterer: A Study in the Literary Art of Damnation." *SP* 60(1963): 12-22.

11533. ----------. "Mercy With Her Mirror." *PQ* 42(1963): 121-126.

11534. Frye, Roland Mushat. "Bunyan, Dürer, and the Byway to Hell." *ELR* 1(1971): 288-289.

11535. Hardin, Richard F. "Bunyan, Mr. Ignorance, and the Quakers." *SP* 69(1972): 496-508.

11536. Johnson, W. Stacy. "Hawthorne and *The Pilgrim's Progress*." *JEGP* 50(1951): 156-166.

11537. Knott, John R., Jr. "Bunyan's Gospel Day: A Reading of *The Pilgrim's Progress*." *ELR* 3(1973): 443-461.

11538. Mandel, Barrett John. "Bunyan and the Autobiographer's Artistic Purpose." *Criticism* 10(1968): 225-243.

11539. Newey, Vincent. "Wordsworth, Bunyan, and the Puritan Mind." *ELH* 41(1954): 212-232.

11540. O'Donnell, Norbert F. "Shaw, Bunyan, and Puritanism." *PMLA* 72(1957): 520-533.

11541. Pascal, Roy. "The Present Tense in 'The Pilgrim's Progress.'" *MLR* 60(1965): 13-16.

11542. Price, Lawrence Marsden. "The Pilgrim Journeys of Bunyan and Henrich Jung-Stilling." *Comp L* 12(1960): 14-18.

11543. Scheer-Schäzler, Brigitte. "Heracles and Bunyan's Pilgrim." *Comp L* 23(1971): 240-254.

11544. Sharrock, Roger. "The Origin of *A Relation of the Imprisonment of Mr. John Bunyan*." *RES* 10(1959): 250-256.

See also 4917, 1662, 7780.

BURTON, HENRY. See 12200.

BURTON, ROBERT. 11545. Browne, Robert M. "Robert Burton and the New Cosmology." *MLQ* 13(1952): 131-148.

11546. Dewey, Nicholas. "Burton's *Melancholy*: A Paradox Disinterred." *MP* 68(1971): 292-293.

11547. Donovan, Dennis G. "Recent Studies in Burton and Walton." *ELR* 1(1971): 294-303.

11548. Friederich, Reinhard H. "Training His Melancholy Spaniel: Persona and Structure in Robert Burton's 'Democritus Junior to the Reader.'" *PQ* 55(1976): 194-210.

11549. Grace, William J. "Notes on Robert Burton and John Milton." *SP* 52(1955): 578-591.

11550. Höltgen, Karl Josef. "Robert Burton and the Rectory of Seagrave." *RES* 27(1976): 129-136.

11551. Jackson, H. J. "Sterne, Burton, and Ferriar: Allusions to the *Anatomy of Melancholy* in Volumes Five to Nine of *Tristram Shandy*." *PQ* 54 (1975): 457-470.

11552. Mueller, William R. "Robert Burton's 'Satyricall Preface.'" *MLQ* 15(1954): 28-35.

11553. Nochimson, Richard L. "Robert Burton's Authorship of *Alba*: A Lost Letter Recovered." *RES* 21(1970): 325-331.

11554. Renaker, David. "Robert Burton's Tricks of Memory." *PMLA* 87(1972): 391-396.

11555. Tillman, James S. "The Satirist Satirized: Burton's Democritus Jr." *SLI* 10,#2 (1977): 89-96.

See also 17449.

BUTLER, SAMUEL. 11556. Quintana, Ricardo. "Samuel Butler: A Restoration Figure in a Modern Light." *ELH* 18(1951): 7-31.

11557. Totten, Charles F. "Hypocrisy and Corruption in Four Characters of Samuel Butler." *EL* 2(1975): 164-170.

11558. Wasserman, George R. "*Hudibras* and Male Chauvinism." *SEL* 16(1976): 351-361.

11559. ----------. "Samuel Butler and the Problem of Unnatural Man." *MLQ* 31(1970): 179-194.

11560. ----------. "'A Strange *Chimaera* of Beasts and Men': The Argument and Imagery of *Hudibras*, Part I." *SEL* 13(1973): 405-421.

11561. Wilding, R. M. "The Date of Samuel Butler's Baptism." *RES* 17(1966): 174-177.

CAMPION, THOMAS. 11562. Bryan, Margaret B. "Recent Studies in Campion." *ELR* 4(1974): 404-411.

11563. Cunningham, J. V. "Campion and Propertius." *PQ* 31(1952): 96.

11564. Davis, Walter R. "Melodic and Poetic Structure: The Examples of Campion and Dowland." *Criticism* 4(1962): 89-107.

11565. ----------. "A Note on Accent and Quantity in *A Book of Ayres*." *MLQ* 22(1961): 32-36.

11566. DeNeef, A. Leigh. "Structure and Theme in Campion's *Lords Maske*." *SEL* 17(1977): 95-103.

11567. Irwin, John T. "Thomas Campion and the Musical Emblem." *SEL* 10(1970): 121-141.

11568. Orrell, John. "The Agent of Savoy at *The Somerset Masque*." *RES* 28(1977): 301-304.

11569. Peltz, Catharine W. "Thomas Campion, An Elizabethan Neo-Classicist." *MLQ* 11(1950): 3-6.

CAREW, THOMAS. 11570. Blanshard, Rufus A. "Carew and Jonson." *SP* 52(1955): 195-211.

11571. Duncan-Jones, E. E. "Carew and Guez de Balzac." *MLR* 46(1951): 439-440.

11572. Johnson, Paula. "Carew's 'A Rapture': The Dynamics of Fantasy." *SEL* 16(1976): 145-155.

11573. Rauber, D. F. "Carey Redivivus." *TSLL* 13(1971): 17-28.

See also 11424.

CAREY, ELIZABETH. 11574. Pearse, Nancy Cotton. "Elizabeth Cary, Renaissance Playwright." *TSLL* 18(1977): 601-608.

CAVENDISH, MARGARET. 11575. Gagen, Jean. "Honor and Fame in the Works of the Duchess of Newcastle." *SP* 56(1959): 519-538.

11576. Mintz, Samuel I. "The Duchess of Newcastle's Visit to the Royal Society." *JEGP* 51 (1952): 168-176.

CHAMBERLAYNE, WILLIAM. 11577. Parsons, A. E. "A Forgotten Poet: William Chamberlayne and 'Pharonnida.'" *MLR* 45(1950): 296-311.

CHAPMAN, GEORGE. 11578. Adams, Robert P. "Critical Myths and Chapman's Original *Bussy D'Ambois*." *RD* 9(1966): 141-161.

11579. Bement, Peter. "The Imagery of Darkness and of Light in Chapman's *Bussy D'Ambois*." *SP* 64(1967): 187-198.

11580. ----------. "The Stoicism of Chapman's *Clermont D'Ambois*." *SEL* 12(1972): 345-357.

11581. Bergson, Allen. "The Ironic Tragedies of Marston and Chapman: Notes on Jacobean Tragic Form." *JEGP* 69(1970): 613-630.

11582. ----------. "Stoicism Achieved: Cato in Chapman's *Tragedy of Caesar and Pompey*." *SEL* 17(1977): 295-302.

11583. ----------. "The Worldly Stoicism of George Chapman's *The Revenge of Bussy D'Ambois* and *The Tragedy of Chabot, Admiral of France*." *PQ* 55 (1976): 43-64.

11584. Braunmuller, A. R. "Chapman's Use of Plutarch's *De Fortuna Romanorum* in *The Tragedy of Charles, Duke of Byron*." *RES* 23(1972): 178-179.

11585. ----------. "'A Greater Wound': Corruption and Human Frailty in Chapman's 'Chabot, Admiral of France.'" *MLR* 70(1975): 241-259.

11586. ----------. "The 'hot Low Countries' in Chapman's *Hero and Leander*." *ELN* 8(1970): 97-99.

11587. Brodwin, Leonora Leet. "Authorship of *The Second Maiden's Tragedy*: A Reconsideration of the Manuscript Attribution to Chapman." *SP* 63 (1966): 51-77.

11588. Broude, Ronald. "George Chapman's Stoic-Christian Revenger." *SP* 70(1973): 51-61.

11589. Brown, John Russell. "Chapman's 'Caesar and Pompey': An Unperformed Play?" *MLR* 49(1954): 466-469.

11590. Burton, K. M. "The Political Tragedies of Chapman and Ben Jonson." *EIC* 2(1952): 397-412.

11591. Cannon, Charles Kendrick. "Chapman on the Unity of Style and Meaning." *JEGP* 68(1969): 245-264.

11592. Crawley, Derek. "Decision and Character in Chapman's *The Tragedy of Caesar and Pompey*." *SEL* 7(1967): 277-297.

11593. ----------. "The Effect of Shirley's Hand on Chapman's *The Tragedy of Chabot Admiral of France*." *SP* 63(1966): 677-696.

11594. Freije, George F. "Chapman's *Byron* and Bartholomaeus Anglicus." *ELN* 12(1975): 168-171.

11595. Fay, H. C. "Chapman's Materials for His Translation of Homer." *RES* 2(1951): 121-128.

11596. ----------. "Poetry, Pedantry, and Life in Chapman's *Iliads*." *RES* 4(1953): 13-25.

11597. Gabel, John Butler. "The Date of Chapman's *Conspiracy and Tragedy of Byron*." *MP* 66 (1969): 330-332.

11598. ----------. "The Original Version of Chapman's *Tragedy of Byron*." *JEGP* 63(1964): 433-440.

11599. Haddakin, Lilian. "A Note on Chapman and Two Medieval English Jurists." *MLR* 47(1952): 550-553.

11600. Herring, Thelma. "Chapman and an Aspect of Modern Criticism." *RD* 8(1965): 153-179.

11601. Hogan, A. P. "Thematic Unity in Chapman's *Monsieur D'Olive*." *SEL* 11(1971): 295-306.

11602. Homan, Sidney R. "Chapman and Marlowe: The Paradoxical Hero and the Divided Response." *JEGP* 68(1969): 391-406.

11603. Huntington, John. "Condemnation and Pity in Chapman's *Hero and Leander*." *ELR* 7(1977): 307-323.

11604. ----------. "Philosophical Seduction in Chapman, Davies, and Donne." *ELH* 44(1977): 40-59.

11605. Ingledew, J. E. "Chapman's Use of Lucan in *Caesar and Pompey*." *RES* 13(1962): 283-288.

11606. ----------. "The Date of Composition of Chapman's *Caesar and Pompey*." *RES* 12(1961): 144-159.

11607. Kaufman, Helen Andrews. "*The Blind Beggar of Alexandria*: A Reappraisal." *PQ* 38(1959): 101-106.

11608. Kennedy, Edward D. "James I and Chapman's Byron Plays." *JEGP* 64(1965): 677-690.

11609. Krisak, Len. "Chapman's Missing Couplet." *ELN* 11(1973): 30-33.

11610. Lancashire, Anne. "*The Second Maiden's Tragedy*: Chapman Reconsidered and Rejected." *ELN* 14(1977): 174-182.

11611. Lordi, R. J. "Proofreading in *The Revenge of Bussy D'Ambois*." *ELN* 10(1973): 188-197.

11612. MacLure, Millar. "The Minor Translations of George Chapman." *MP* 60(1963): 172-182.

11613. Myers, James Phares, Jr. "'This Curious Frame': Chapman's *Ovid's Banquet of Sense*." *SP* 65(1968): 192-206.

11614. Nicoll, Allardyce. "The Dramatic Portrait of George Chapman." *PQ* 41(1962): 215-228.

11615. Orbison, Tucker. "The Case for the Attribution of a Chapman Letter." *SP* 72(1975): 72-84.

11616. O'Callaghan, James F. "Chapman's Caesar." *SEL* 16(1976): 319-331.

11617. Ornstein, Robert. "The Dates of Chapman's Tragedies, Once More." *MP* 59(1961): 61-64.

11618. Presson, Robert K. "Wrestling with This World: A View of George Chapman." *PMLA* 84 (1969): 44-50.

11619. Rees, Ennis. "Chapman's *Blind Beggar* and the Marlovian Hero." *JEGP* 57(1958): 60-63.

11620. Reese, Jack E. "Unity in Chapman's *Masque of the Middle Temple and Lincoln's Inn*." *SEL* 4(1964): 291-305.

11621. Ribner, Irving. "Character and Theme

in Chapman's *Bussy D'Ambois*." *ELH* 26(1959): 482-496.

11622. ----------. "The Meaning of Chapman's 'Tragedy of Chabot.'" *MLR* 55(1960): 321-331.

11623. Sackton, Alexander. "The Rhetoric of Literary Praise in the Poetry of Raleigh and Chapman." *TSLL* 18(1976): 409-421.

11624. Schwartz, Elias. "Chapman's Renaissance Man: Byron Reconsidered." *JEGP* 58(1959): 613-626.

11625. ----------. "The Date of Bussy d'Ambois." *MP* 59(1961): 126-127.

11626. ----------. "The Date of Chapman's Byron Plays." *MP* 58(1961): 201-202.

11627. ----------. "The Dates and Order of Chapman's Tragedies." *MP* 57(1959): 80-82.

11628. ----------. "A Neglected Play by Chapman." *SP* 58(1961): 140-159.

11629. ----------. "Seneca, Homer, and Chapman's *Bussy D'Ambois*." *JEGP* 56(1957): 163-176.

11630. Sisson, Charles J., and Robert Butman. "George Chapman, 1612-1622: Some New Facts." *MLR* 46(1951): 185-190.

11631. Smith, John Hazel. "The Genesis of the Strozza Subplot in George Chapman's *The Gentleman Usher*." *PMLA* 83(1968): 1448-1452.

11632. Taylor, A. B. "Sir John Davies and George Chapman: A Note on the Current Approach to *Ovids Banquet of Sence*." *ELN* 12(1975): 261-265.

11633. Tricomi, Albert H. "The Focus of Satire and the Date of *Monsieur D'Olive*." *SEL* 17 (1977): 281-294.

11634. ----------. "The Revised *Bussy D'Ambois* and *The Revenge of Bussy D'Ambois*: Joint Performance in Thematic Counterpoint." *ELN* 9 (1972): 253-262.

11635. ----------. "The Revised Version of Chapman's *Bussy D'Ambois*: A Shift in Point of View." *SP* 70(1973): 288-305.

11636. ----------. "The Social Order of Chapman's *The Widow's Tears*." *JEGP* 72(1973): 350-359.

11637. Ure, Peter. "Chapman's 'Tragedy of Bussy d'Ambois': Problems of the Revised Quarto." *MLR* 48(1953): 257-269.

11638. ----------. "Chapman's 'Tragedy of Byron.'" *MLR* 54(1959): 557-558.

11639. ----------. "Chapman's Use of North's Plutarch in *Caesar and Pompey*." *RES* 9 (1958): 281-284.

11640. ----------. "The Main Outline of Chapman's Byron." *SP* 47(1950): 568-588.

11641. ----------. "A Note on 'Opinion' in Daniel, Greville, and Chapman." *MLR* 46(1951): 331-338.

11642. Waddington, Raymond B. "Chapman and Persius: The Epigraph to *Ovids Banquet of Sence*." *RES* 19(1968): 158-162.

11643. ----------. "Chapman's *Andromeda Liberata*: Mythology and Meaning." *PMLA* 81(1966): 34-44.

11644. ----------. "Prometheus and Hercules: The Dialectic of *Bussy D'Ambois*." *ELH* 34(1967): 21-48.

11645. Weidner, Henry M. "The Dramatic Uses of Homeric Idealism: The Significance of Theme and Design in George Chapman's *The Gentleman Usher*." *ELH* 28(1961): 121-136.

11646. ----------. "Homer and the Fallen World: Focus of Satire in George Chapman's *The Widow's Tears*." *JEGP* 62(1963): 518-532.

11647. Wilkes, G. A. "Chapman's 'Lost' Play, *The Fount of New Fashions*." *JEGP* 62(1963): 77-81.

See also 24, 9310, 9346, 9389, 9407, 10372, 11369, 11425, 12403, 12472, 13372.

CHUDLEIGH, MARY. See 11437.

CLARENDON, EDWARD HYDE. 11648. Watson, George. "The Reader in Clarendon's *History of the Rebellion*." *RES* 25(1974): 396-409.

11649. Wilson, Gayle Edward. "Clarendon's Hamlet: The 'Character' of Lucius Cary, Viscount Falkland." *CLA* 14(1970): 171-177.

CLEVELAND, JOHN. 11650. Kimmey, John L. "John Cleveland and the Satiric Couplet in the Restoration." *PQ* 37(1958): 410-423.

11651. Stanford, Donald E. "Edward Taylor and the 'Hermophrodite' Poems of John Cleveland." *EAL* 8,#1(1973): 59-61.

11652. Woolf, Henry Bosley. "John Cleveland's 'West Saxon poet.'" *PQ* 30(1951): 443-447.

See also 504, 11441.

CODRINGTON, CHRISTOPHER. 11653. Chapple, J. A. V. "Christopher Codrington's Verses to Elizabeth Cromwell." *JEGP* 60(1961): 75-78.

COKAIN, SIR ASTON. 11654. Kaufman, Helen A. "*Trappolin Supposed a Prince* and *Measure for Measure*." *MLQ* 18(1957): 113-124.

COLLIER, JEREMY. 11655. Williams, Aubrey. "No Cloistered Virtue: Or, Playwright versus Priest in 1698." *PMLA* 90(1975): 234-246.

CONGREVE, WILLIAM. 11656. Corman, Brian. "'The Mixed Way of Comedy': Congreve's *The Double-Dealer*." *MP* 71(1974): 356-365.

11657. Gagen, Jean. "Congreve's Mirabell and the Ideal of the Gentleman." *PMLA* 79(1964): 422-427.

11658. Gosse, Anthony. "The Omitted Scene in Congreve's *Love for Love*." *MP* 61(1963): 40-42.

11659. ----------. "Plot and Character in Congreve's *Double-Dealer*." *MLQ* 29(1968): 274-288.

11660. Hinnant, Charles H. "Wit, Propriety, and Style in *The Way of the World*." *SEL* 17(1977): 373-386.

11661. Jarvis, F. P. "The Philosophical Assumptions of Congreve's *Love for Love*." *TSLL* 14 (1972): 423-434.

11662. Kaufman, Anthony. "Language and Character in Congreve's *The Way of the World*." *TSLL* 15(1973): 411-427.

11663. Kenny, Shirley Strum. "Perennial Favorites: Congreve, Vanbrugh, Cibber, Farquhar, and Steele." *MP* 73(1976): S4-S11.

11664. Leech, Clifford. "Congreve and the Century's End." *PQ* 41(1962): 275-293.

11665. Lynch, Kathleen M. "References to William Congreve in the Evelyn MSS." *PQ* 32(1953): 337-340.

11666. Lyons, Charles R. "Congreve's Miracle of Love." *Criticism* 6(1964): 331-348.

11667. McComb, John King. "Congreve's *The Old Bachelour*: A Satiric Anatomy." *SEL* 17(1977): 361-372.

11668. Novak, Maximillian E. "Congreve's *Incognita* and the Art of the Novella." *Criticism*

11(1969): 329-342.

11669. ----------. "Congreve's *The Old Bachelor*: from Formula to Art." *EIC* 20(1970): 182-199.

11670. Noyes, Robert Gale. "Congreve and His Comedies in the Eighteenth-Century Novel." *PQ* 39(1960): 464-480.

11671. Rogers, J. P. W. "Congreve's First Biographer: The Identity of 'Charles Wilson.'" *MLQ* 31(1970): 330-344.

11672. Roper, Alan. "Language and Action in *The Way of the World*, *Love's Last Shift*, and *The Relapse*." *ELH* 40(1973): 44-69.

11673. Rosowski, Susan J. "Thematic Development in the Comedies of Congreve: The Individual in Society." *SEL* 16(1976): 387-406.

11674. Stephenson, Peter S. "Congreve's 'Incognita': The Popular Spanish Novela Form Burlesqued." *SSF* 9(1972): 333-342.

11675. Turner, Darwin T. "The Servant in the Comedies of William Congreve." *CLA* 1(1958): 68-74.

11676. Williams, Aubrey. "No Cloistered Virtue: Or, Playwright versus Priest in 1698." *PMLA* 90(1975): 234-246.

11677. ----------. "Political Justice, the Contrivances of Providence, and The Works of William Congreve." *ELH* 35(1968): 540-565.

See also 11396, 11425, 11447.

COWLEY, ABRAHAM. 11678. Donovan, Dennis G. "Recent Studies in Cowley." *ELR* 6(1976): 466-475.

11679. Goldstein, Harvey D. "*Anglorum Pindarus*: Model and Milieu." *Comp L* 17(1965): 299-310.

11680. Hinman, Robert B. "'Truth in Truest Poetry.'" *ELH* 23(1956): 194-203.

11681. Keough, James R. "Cowley's Brutus Ode: Historical Precepts and the Politics of Defeat." *TSLL* 19(1977): 382-391.

11682. Korshin, Paul J. "The Theoretical Bases of Cowley's Later Poetry." *SP* 66(1969): 756-776.

11683. McGaw, William D. "The Civil War in Cowley's *Destinie*." *ELN* 14(1977): 268-270.

11684. Miller, Clarence H. "The Order of Stanzas in Cowley and Crashaw's 'On Hope.'" *SP* 61(1964): 64-73.

11685. Pritchard, Allan. "Six Letters by Cowley." *RES* 18(1967): 253-263.

11686. Rawlinson, David. "Cowley." *EIC* 14 (1964): 426.

11687. ----------. "Cowley and the Current Status of Metaphysical Poetry." *EIC* 13(1963): 323-340.

11688. Walton, Geoffrey. "Cowley." *EIC* 14 (1964): 216-219.

See also 525, 9457, 11437, 12098.

CRASHAW, RICHARD. 11689. Barbato, Louis R. "Marino, Crashaw, and *Sospetto d'Herode*." *PQ* 54 (1975): 522-527.

11690. Bertonasco, Marc. "A New Look at Crawshaw and 'The Weeper.'" *TSLL* 10(1968): 177-188.

11691. Cirillo, A. R. "Crashaw's 'Epiphany Hymn': The Dawn of Christian Time." *SP* 67(1970): 67-88.

11692. Collmer, Robert G. "Crashaw's 'death more misticall and high.'" *JEGP* 55(1956): 373-380.

11693. Larsen, Kenneth J. "Some Light on Richard Crashaw's Final Years in Rome." *MLR* 66 (1971): 492-496.

11694. Manning, Stephen. "The Meaning of 'The Weeper.'" *ELH* 22(1955): 34-57.

11695. Maxwell, J. C. "*Steps to the Temple*: 1646 and 1648." *PQ* 29(1950): 216-220.

11696. Miller, Clarence H. "The Order of Stanzas in Cowley and Crashaw's 'On Hope.'" *SP* 61 (1964): 64-73.

11697. Pettoello, Laura. "A Current Misconception concerning the Influence of Marino's Poetry on Crashaw's." *MLR* 52(1957): 321-328.

11698. Schwenger, Peter. 'Crashaw's Perspectivist Metaphor." *Comp L* 28(1976): 65-74.

11699. Strier, Richard. "Crashaw's Other Voice." *SEL* 9(1969): 135-151.

11700. Yoklavich, John. "A Manuscript of Crashaw's Poems from Loseley." *ELN* 2(1964): 92-97.

11701. ----------. "Not by Crashaw, but Cornwallis." *MLR* 59(1964): 517-518.

See also 11429, 11431.

CROWNE, JOHN. 11702. McMullin, B. J. "The Songs from John Crowne's *Justice Buisy, or the Gentleman-Quack*." *RES* 28(1977): 168-175.

11703. Seward, Patricia M. "An Additional Spanish Source for John Crowne's 'Sir Courtly Nice.'" *MLR* 67(1972): 486-489.

CUDWORTH, RALPH. 11704. Wood, D. N. C. "Ralph Cudworth the Elder and Henri Estienne's *World of Wonders*." *ELN* 11(1973): 93-100.

DABORNE, ROBERT. 11705. Maxwell, Baldwin. "Notes on Robert Daborne's Extant Plays." *PQ* 50 (1971): 85-98.

11706. McManaway, James G. "Additional Notes on 'The Great Danseker.'" *MLR* 47(1952): 202-203.

DAVENANT, WILLIAM. 11707. Berry, Herbert. "Three New Poems by Davenant." [with text]. *PQ* 31 (1952): 70-74.

11708. Dust, Alvin I. "*The Seventh and Last Canto of Gondibert* and Two Dedicatory Poems." *JEGP* 60(1961): 282-285.

11709. Feil, J. P. "Davenant Exonerated." *MLR* 58(1963): 335-342.

11710. Gibbs, A. M. "A Davenant Imitation of Donne?" *RES* 18(1967): 45-48.

See also 11419, 11505, 11508, 12314.

DAVENPORT, ROBERT. 11711. Olive, W. J. "Davenport's Debt to Shakespeare in *City-Night-Cap*." *JEGP* 49(1950): 333-344.

DAVYS, MARY. 11712. McBurney, William H. "Mrs. Mary Davys: Forerunner of Fielding." *PMLA* 74(1959): 348-355.

DAY, JOHN. 11713. Peery, William. "*The Noble Soldier* and *The Parliament of Bee*." *SP* 48 (1951): 219-233.

DEAN, JOHN. 11714. Levy, Robert H. "The Date of *The Badger in the Fox-Trap*." *ELN* 1(1964): 253-256.

DEKKER, THOMAS. 11715. Ashton, J. W. "Dekker's Use of Folklore in *Old Fortunatus*, *If This Be Not a Good Play*, and *The Witch of Edmonton*." *PQ* 41(1962): 240-248.

11716. Berlin, Normand. "Thomas Dekker: A Partial Reappraisal." *SEL* 6(1966): 263-277.

11717. Bowers, Fredson. "Essex's Rebellion and Dekker's *Old Fortunatus*." *RES* 3(1952): 365-366.

11718. Brodwin, Leonora Leet. "The Domestic Tragedy of Frank Thorney in *The Witch of Edmonton*." *SEL* 7(1967): 311-328.

11719. Champion, Larry S. "From Melodrama to Comedy: A Study of the Dramatic Perspective in Dekker's *The Honest Whore*, Parts I and II." *SP* 69(1972): 192-209.

11720. Clubb, Louise George. "*The Virgin Martyr* and the *Tragedia Sacra*." *RD* 7(1964): 103-126.

11721. Freeman, Arthur. "The Authorship of *The Tell-Tale*." *JEGP* 62(1963): 288-292.

11722. ----------. "The Date of Dekker's *If This Be Not a Good Play, The Devil Is In It*." *PQ* 44(1965): 122-124.

11723. Homan, Sidney R., Jr. "Dekker as Collaborator in Ford's *Perkin Warbeck*." *ELN* 3 (1965): 104-106.

11724. ----------. "*Doctor Faustus*, Dekker's *Old Fortunatus*, and the Morality Plays." *MLQ* 26(1965): 497-505.

11725. Johnson, Paula. "Jacobean Ephemera and the Immortal World." *RD* n.s. 8(1977): 151-171.

11726. Kaplan, Joel H. "Virtue's Holiday: Thomas Dekker and Simon Eyre." *RD* n.s. 2(1969): 103-122.

11727. Keyishian, Harry. "Dekker's *Whore* and Marston's *Courtesan*." *ELN* 4(1967): 261-266.

11728. ----------. "Griselda on the Elizabethan Stage: The Patient Grissil of Chettle, Dekker, and Haughton." *SEL* 16(1976): 253-261.

11729. Manheim, Michael. "The Construction of *The Shoemaker's Holiday*." *SEL* 10(1970): 315-323.

11730. ----------. "The Thematic Structure of Dekker's *2 Honest Whore*." *SEL* 5(1965): 363-381.

11731. Martin, Mary Forster. "Stow's 'Annals' and 'The Famous Historie of Sir Thomas Wyat.'" *MLR* 53(1958): 75-77.

11732. Mortenson, Peter. "The Economics of Joy in *The Shoemaker's Holiday*." *SEL* 16(1976): 241-252.

11733. Nathan, Norman. "'Julius Caesar' and 'The Shoemakers' Holiday.'" *MLR* 48(1953): 178-179.

11734. Novarr, David. "Dekker's Gentle Craft and the Lord Mayor of London." *MP* 57(1960): 233-239.

11736. Pendry, E. D. "Thomas Dekker in the Magistrates' Court." *ELR* 3(1973): 53-59.

11735. Peery, William. "*The Noble Soldier* and *The Parliament of Bees*." *SP* 48(1951): 219-233.

11737. Pineas, Rainer. "Dekker's *The Whore of Babylon* and Milton's *Paradise Lost*." *ELN* 2 (1965): 257-260.

11738. Shaw, Phillip. "*Sir Thomas Wyat* and the Scenario of *Lady Jane*." *MLQ* 13(1952): 227-238.

11739. Thomson, Patricia. "The Old Way and the New Way in Dekker and Massinger." *MLR* 51 (1956): 168-178.

See also 9942, 11297, 11385, 11395, 12144, 12164, 12527.

DENHAM, JOHN. 11740. Berry, Herbert. "Sir John Denham at Law." *MP* 71(1974): 266-276.

11741. O Hehir, Brendan. "Denham's *Coopers Hill* and Poole's *English Parnassus*." *MP* 61(1964): 253-260.

11742. ----------. "'Lost,' 'Authorized,' and 'Pirated' Editions of John Denham's *Cooper's Hill*." *PMLA* 79(1964): 242-253.

11743. ----------. "Vergil's First *Georgic* and Denham's *Coopers Hill*." *PQ* 42(1963): 542-547.

11744. Wallace, John M. "*Cooper's Hill*: The Manifesto of Parliamentary Royalism, 1641." *ELH* 41(1974): 494-540.

DIGBY, KENELM. 11745. Ackerman, Catherine A. "Fashionable Platonism and Sir Kenelm Digby's *Private Memoirs*." *CLA* 5(1961): 136-141.

D'URFEY, THOMAS. 11746. Ellis, William D., Jr. "Thomas D'Urfey, the Pope-Phillips Quarrel and *The Shepherd's Week*." *PMLA* 74(1959): 203-212.

11747. Vaughn, Jack A. "A D'Urfey Play Dated." *MP* 64(1967): 322-323.

DONNE, JOHN. 11748. Allen, D. C. "Donne's 'Sapho to Philaenis.'" *ELN* 1(1964): 188-191.

11749. Andreasen, N. J. C. "Donne's *Devotions* and the Psychology of Assent." *MP* 62 (1964): 207-216.

11750. ----------. "Theme and Structure in Donne's *Satyres*." *SEL* 3(1963): 59-75.

11751. Anselnent, Raymond A. "'Ascensio Mendax, Descensio Crudelis: The Image of Babel in the *Anniversaries*." *ELH* 38(1971): 188-205.

11752. Applebaum, Wilbur. "Donne's Meeting with Kepler: A Previously Unknown Episode." *PQ* 50(1971): 132-134.

11753. Archer, Stanley. "Meditation and the Structure of Donne's 'Holy Sonnets.'" *ELH* 28 (1961): 137-147.

11754. Armitage, C. M. "Donne's Poems in Huntington Manuscript 198: New Light on 'The Funerall.'" *SP* 63(1966): 678-707.

11755. Armstrong, Alan. "The Apprenticeship of John Donne: Ovid and the *Elegies*." *ELH* 44 (1977): 419-442.

11756. Ayres, Philip J. "Donne's 'The Dampe,' Engraved Hearts, and the 'Passion' of St. Clare of Montefalco." *ELN* 13(1976): 173-175.

11757. Bald, R. C. "A Latin Version of Donne's Problems." *MP* 61(1964): 198-203.

11758. Baker-Smith, Dominic. "Donne's 'Litanie.'" *RES* 26(1975): 171-173.

11759. Bateson, F. W. "As We Read the Living? An Argument." *EIC* 23(1973): 175-178.

11760. Beck, Rosalie. "A Precedent for Donne's Imagery in 'Goodfriday, 1613. Riding Westward.'" *RES* 19(1968): 166-169.

11761. Bellette, Anthony F. "Art and Imitation in Donne's *Anniversaries*." *SEL* 15(1975): 83-96.

11762. ----------. "'Little Worlds Made Cunningly': Significant Forms in Donne's *Holy Sonnets* and 'Good Friday, 1613.'" *SP* 72(1975): 322-347.

11763. Bennett, J. A. W. "A Note on Donne's *Crosse*." *RES* 5(1954): 168-169.

11764. Benson, Donald R. "Platonism and Neoclassic Metaphor: Dryden's Elenora and Donne's Anniversaries." *SP* 68(1971): 340-356.

11765. Bozanich, Robert. "Donne and Ecclesiastes." *PMLA* 90(1975): 270-276.

11766. Brown, Nancy P. "A Note on the Imagery of Donne's 'Love's Growth.'" *MLR* 48(1953): 324-327.

11767. Bryan, Robert A. "John Donne's Use of the Anathema." *JEGP* 61(1962): 305-312.

11768. Cameron, Barry A. "Donne's Deliberative Verse Epistles." *ELR* 6(1976): 369-403.

11769. Carey, John. "Notes on Two of Donne's *Songs and Sonnets*." *RES* 16(1965): 50-53.

11770. Chambers, A. B. "The Fly in Donne's 'Canonization.'" *JEGP* 65(1966): 252-259.

11771. ----------. "Goodfriday, 1613. Riding Westward: The Poem and Its Tradition." *ELH* 28(1961): 31-53.

11772. ----------. "The Meaning of 'Temple' in Donne's *La Corona*." *JEGP* 59(1960): 212-217.

11773. Cirillo, A. R. "The Fair Hermaphrodite: Love-Union in the Poetry of Donne and Spenser." *SEL* 9(1969): 81-95.

11774. Clair, John A. "Donne's 'The Canonization.'" *PMLA* 80(1965): 300-302.

11775. Colie, R. L. "The Rhetoric of Transcendence." *PQ* 43(1964): 145-170.

11776. Dawson, S. W. "As we Read the Living?" *EIC* 24(1974): 94-97.

11777. Donald, Roslyn L. "Another Source for Three of John Donne's Elegies." *ELN* 14 (1977): 264-268.

11778. Duncan, Joseph E. "The Intellectual Kinship of John Donne and Robert Browning." *SP* 50 (1953): 81-100.

11779. Duncan-Jones, E. E. "Donne's Praise of Autumnal Beauty: Greek Sources." *MLR* 56 (1961): 213-215.

11780. Durand, Laura G. "Sponde and Donne: Lens and Prism." *Comp L* 21(1969): 319-336.

11781. Durr, R. A. "Donne's 'The Primrose.'" *JEGP* 59(1960): 218-222.

11782. Eldredge, Frances. "Further Allusions and Debts to John Donne." *ELH* 19(1952): 214-228.

11783. Elliott, Emory. "The Narrative and Allusive Unity of Donne's *Satyres*." *JEGP* 75(1976): 105-116.

11784. Elliott, Roger. "As we Read the Living?" *EIC* 24(1974): 100-104.

11785. Evans, G. Blakemore. "Two Notes on Donne: 'The Undertaking'; 'A Valediction: of my Name, in the Window." *MLR* 57(1962): 60-62.

11786. Finkelpearl, P. J. "Donne and Everard Gilpin: Additions, Corrections, and Conjectures." *RES* 14(1963): 164-167.

11787. Freccero, John. "Donne's 'Valediction: Forbidding Mourning.'" *ELH* 30(1963): 335-376.

11788. French, A. L. "Dr. Gardner's Dating of the *Songs and Sonets*." *EIC* 17(1967): 115-120.

11789. Friedman, Donald M. "Memory and the Art of Salvation in Donne's Good Friday Poem." *ELR* 3(1973): 418-442.

11790. Fox, Ruth A. "Donne's *Anniversaries* and the Art of Living." *ELH* 38(1971): 528-541.

11791. Gallant, Gerald, and A. L. Clements. "Harmonized Voices in Donne's 'Songs and Sonets': 'The Dampe.'" *SEL* 15(1975): 71-82.

11792. Gardner, Helen. "Another Note on Donne: 'Since she whome I lov'd.'" *MLR* 52(1957): 564-565.

11793. Geraldine, Sister M. "John Donne and the Mindes Indeavors." *SEL* 5(1965): 115-131.

11794. Gifford, William. "Time and Place in Donne's Sermons." *PMLA* 82(1967): 388-398.

11795. Gill, Roma. "As We Read the Living? An Argument." *EIC* 23(1973): 167-175.

11796. Gleason, John B. "Dr. Donne in the Court of Kings: A Glimpse from Marginalia." *JEGP* 69(1970): 599-612.

11797. Goldberg, Jonathan. "Donne's Journey East: Aspects of a Seventeenth-Century Trope." *SP* 68(1971): 470-483.

11798. ----------. "Hesper-Vesper: Aspects of Venus in a Seventeenth-Century Trope." *SEL* 15(1975): 37-55.

11799. Grant, Patrick. "Augustinian Spirituality and the *Holy Sonnets* of John Donne." *ELH* 38 (1971): 542-561.

11800. Graziani, Rene. "John Donne's 'The Extasie' and Ecstasy." *RES* 19(1968): 121-136.

11801. Guss, Donald L. "Donne's Conceit and the Petrarchan Wit." *PMLA* 78(1963): 308-314.

11802. ----------. "Donne's Petrarchism." *JEGP* 64(1965): 17-28.

11803. Harris, Victor. "John Donne and the Theatre." *PQ* 41(1962): 257-269.

11804. Hassel, R. Chris, Jr. "Donne's *Ignatius His Conclave* and The New Astronomy." *MP* 68(1971): 329-337.

11805. Heatherington, Madelon E. "'Decency' and 'Zeal' in the Sermons of John Donne." *TSLL* 9 (1967): 307-316.

11806. Henrickson, Bruce. "Donne's Orthodoxy." *TSLL* 14(1972): 5-16.

11807. Hester, M. Thomas. "John Donne's 'Hill of Truth.'" *ELN* 14(1976): 100-105.

11808. Höltgen, Karl Josef. "Unpublished Early Verses 'On Dr. Donnes Anatomy.'" *RES* 22 (1971): 302-306.

11809. Hughes, Merrit Y. "Some of Donne's 'Ecstasies.'" *PMLA* 75(1960): 509-518.

11810. Hughes, Richard E. "The Woman in Donne's *Anniversaries*." *ELH* 34(1967): 307-326.

11811. Huntington, John. "Philosophical Seduction in Chapman, Davies, and Donne." *ELH* 44 (1977): 40-59.

11812. Hynes, Sam L. "A Note on Donne and Aquinus." *MLR* 48(1953): 179-181.

11813. Kerrigan, William. "The Fearful Accomodations of John Donne." *ELR* 4(1974): 337-363.

11814. Korkowski, Eugene. "Donne's *Ignatius* and Menippean Satire." *SP* 72(1975): 419-438.

11815. Krueger, Robert. "The Publication of John Donne's Sermons." *RES* 15(1964): 151-160.

11816. LaBranche, A. "'Blanda Elegeia': The Background to Donne's 'Elegies.'" *MLR* 61(1966): 357-369.

11817. Lander, Clara. "A Dangerous Sickness Which Turned to a Spotted Fever." *SEL* 11(1971): 89-108.

11818. Lauritsen, John R. "Donne's *Satyres*: The Drama of Self-Discovery." *SEL* 16(1976): 117-130.

11819. Lebans, W. M. "Donne's *Anniversaries* and the Tradition of Funeral Elegy." *ELH* 39 (1972): 545-559.

11820. ----------. "The Influence of the Classics in Donne's *Epicedes and Obsequies*." *RES* 23(1972): 127-137.

11821. Lein, Clayton D. "Donne's 'The Storme': The Poem and the Tradition." *ELR* 4(1974): 137-163.

11822. Levine, Jay Arnold. "'The Dissolution': Donne's Twofold Elegy." *ELH* 28(1961): 301-315.

11823. Lewalski, Barbara K. "A Donnean Perspective on 'The Extasie.'" *ELN* 10(1973): 258-262.

11824. Louthan, Doniphan. "The *Tome-Tomb* Pun in Renaissance England." *PQ* 29(1950): 375-380.

11825. Love, Harold. "The Argument of Donne's *First Anniversary*." *MP* 64(1966): 125-131.

11826. Low, Donald A. "An Eighteenth Century Imitation of Donne's First Satire." *RES* 16 (1965): 291-298.

11827. MacColl, Alan. "A New Manuscript of Donne's Poems." *RES* 19(1968): 293-295.

11828. ----------. "The New Edition of Donne's Love Poems." *EIC* 17(1967): 258-263.

11829. Mahoney, John L. "Donne and Greville: Two Christian Attitudes toward the Renaissance Idea of Mutability and Decay." *CLA* 5(1962): 203-212.

11830. Mahony, Patrick. "*The Anniversaries*: Donne's Rhetorical Approach to Evil." *JEGP* 68 (1969): 407-413.

11831. Malloch. A. E. "John Donne and the Casuists." *SEL* 2(1962): 57-76.

11832. ----------. "The Techniques and Function of the Renaissance Paradox." *SP* 53(1956): 191-203.

11833. Mann, Lindsay A. "The Marriage Analogue of Letter and Spirit in Donne's Devotional Prose." *JEGP* 70(1971): 607-616.

11834. Marotti, Arthur F. "Donne's 'Love Progress,' 11. 37-38, and Renaissance Bawdry." *ELN* 6(1968): 24-25.

11835. Matchett, William H. "Donne's 'Peece of Chronicle.'" *RES* 18(1967): 290-292.

11836. Maurer, Margaret. "John Donne's Verse Letters." *MLQ* 37(1976): 234-259.

11837. McCanles, Michael. "Distinguish in Order to Unite: Donne's 'The Extasie.'" *SEL* 6 (1966): 59-75.

11838. Miller, Clarence H. "Donne's 'A Nocturnall upon S. Lucies Day' and the Nocturne of Matins." *SEL* 6(1966): 77-86.

11839. Mitchell, Charles. "Donne's 'The Extasie': Love's Sublime Knot." *SEL* 8(1968): 91-101.

11840. Mizejewski, Linda. "Darkness and Disproportion: A Study of Donne's 'Storme' and 'Calme.'" *JEGP* 76(1977): 217-230.

11841. Moloney, Michael F. "Donne's Metrical Practice." *PMLA* 65(1950): 232-239.

11842. Moore, Arthur K. "Donne's *Loves Deitie* and De planctu Naturae." *PQ* 42(1963): 102-105.

11843. Moore, Thomas V. "Donne's Use of Uncertainty as a Vital Force in *Satyre III*." *MP* 67(1969): 41-49.

11844. Morillo, Marvin. "Donne's Compasses: Circles and Right Lines." *ELN* 3(1966): 173-176.

11845. Mueller, Janel M. "Death and the Maiden: The Metaphysics of Christian Symbolism in Donne's *Anniversaries*." *MP* 72(1975): 280-286.

11846. ----------. "Donne's Epic Venture in the *Metampsychosis*." *MP* 70(1972): 109-137.

11847. ----------. "The Exegesis of Experience: Dean Donne's *Devotions upon Emergent Occasions*." *JEGP* 67(1968): 1-19.

11848. ----------. "Exhuming Donne's Enigma." *MP* 69(1972): 231-249.

11849. Murray, W. A. "What was the Soul of that Apple?" *RES* 10(1959): 141-155.

11850. Nellist, B. F. "Donne's 'Storm' and 'Calm' and the Descriptive Tradition." *MLR* 59 (1964): 511-516.

11851. Newton, Richard C. "Donne the Satirist." *TSLL* 16(1974): 427-445.

11852. Novarr, David. "The Dating of Donne's *La Corona*." *PQ* 36(1957): 259-265.

11853. ----------. "Donne's 'Epithalamion Made at Lincoln's Inn': Context and Date." *RES* 7 (1956): 250-263.

11854. ----------. "The Two Hands of John Donne." *MP* 62(1964): 142-154.

11855. Ong, Walter J., S. J. "Gospel, Existence, and Print." *MLQ* 35(1974): 66-77.

11856. Ornstein, Robert. "Donne, Montaigne, and Natural Law." *JEGP* 55(1956): 213-229.

11857. Otten, Charlotte F. "Donne's Manna in 'The Primrose.'" *ELN* 13(1976): 260-262.

11858. Ousby, Heather Dubrow. "Donne's 'Epithalamion made at Lincolnes Inn': An Alternative Interpretation." *SEL* 16(1976): 131-143.

11859. Parfitt, George A. E. "Donne, Herbert and the Matter of Schools." *EIC* 22(1972): 381-395.

11860. Peterson, Donald L. "John Donne's *Holy Sonnets* and the Anglican Doctrine of Contrition." *SP* 56(1959): 504-518.

11861. Pritchard, Allan. "Donne's Mr. Tilman." *RES* 24(1953): 38-42.

11862. Powers, Doris C. "Donne's Compass." *RES* 9(1958): 173-175.

11863. Quinn, Dennis. "Donne and the Wane of Wonder." *ELH* 36(1969): 626-647.

11864. ----------. "Donne's *Anniversaries* as Celebration." *SEL* 9(1969): 97-105.

11865. ----------. "Donne's Christian Eloquence." *ELH* 27(1960): 276-297.

11866. ----------. "John Donne's Principles of Biblical Exegesis." *JEGP* 61(1962): 313-329.

11867. Raspa, Anthony. "Theology and Poetry in Donne's *Conclave*." *ELH* 32(1965): 478-489.

11868. Richmond, H. M. "Donne's Master: The Young Shakespeare." *Criticism* 15(1973): 126-145.

11869. ----------. "The Intangible Mistress." *MP* 56(1959): 217-223.

11870. Ricks, Don M. "The Westmoreland Manuscript and the Order of Donne's 'Holy Sonnets.'" *SP* 63(1966): 187-195.

11871. Ringler, Richard N. "Donne's Specular Stone." *MLR* 60(1965): 333-339.

11872. Roberts, John R. "Donne's *Satyre III* Reconsidered." *CLA* 12(1968): 105-115.

11873. Roberts, Mark. "The New Edition of Donne's Love Poems." *EIC* 17(1967): 263-278.

11874. ----------. "Review Article: If It Were Donne When 'Tis Done. . .." *EIC* 16(1966): 309-329.

11875. Rockett, William. "John Donne: The Ethical Argument of *Elegy III*." *SEL* 15(1975): 57-69.

11876. Rooney, William J. "'The Canonization'—The Language of Paradox Reconsidered." *ELH* 23(1956): 36-47.

11877. ----------. "John Donne's 'Second Prebend Sermon'—A Stylistic Analysis." *TSLL* 4 (1962): 24-34.

11878. Sackton, Alexander. "Donne and the Privacy of Verse." *SEL* 7(1967): 67-82.

11879. Saunders, J. W. "Donne and Daniel." *EIC* 3(1953): 109-114.

11880. Selden, R. "Donne's 'The Dampe,' Lines 22-24." *MLR* 64(1969): 726-727.

11881. Shapiro, I. A. "Walton and the Occasion of Donne's *Devotions*." *RES* 9(1958): 18-22.

11882. Shawcross, John T. "Donne's 'A Lecture Upon the Shadow.'" *ELN* 1(1964): 187-188.

11883. Sherwood, Terry G. "Reason, Faith, and Just Augustinian Lamentation in Donne's Elegy on Prince Henry." *SEL* 13(1973): 53-67.

11884. ----------. "Reason in Donne's Sermons." *ELH* 39(1972): 353-374.

11885. Sicherman, Carol Marks. "Donne's Discovery." *SEL* 11(1971): 69-88.

11886. Simpson, Evelyn M. "The Biographical Value of Donne's Sermons." *RES* 2(1951): 339-357.

11887. ----------. "Two Notes on Donne." *RES* 16(1965): 140-151.

11888. Slights, Camille. "'To Stand Inquiring Right': The Casuistry of Donne's 'Satyre III.'" *SEL* 12(1972): 85-101.

11889. Sloan, Thomas O. "The Rhetoric in the Poetry of John Donne." *SEL* 3(1963): 31-44.

11890. Smith, A. J. "The Metaphysic of Love." *RES* 9(1958): 362-375.

11891. ----------. "Two Notes on Donne." *MLR* 51(1956): 405-407.

11892. Smith, M. van Wyk. "John Donne's *Metampsychosis*. Parts I-II." *RES* 24(1973): 17-26, 141-152.

11893. Snyder, Susan. "Doone and DuBartas: *The Progresse of the Soul* as Parody." *SP* 70(1973): 392-407.

11894. Spenko, James L. "Circular Form in Two Donne Lyrics." *ELN* 13(1975): 103-107.

11895. Stanwood, P. G. "'Essentiall Joye' in Donne's *Anniversaries*." *TSLL* 13(1971): 227-238.

11896. Stapleton, Laurence. "The Theme of Virtue in Donne's Verse Epistles." *SP* 55(1958): 187-200.

11897. Steig, Michael. "Donne's Divine Rapist: Unconscious Fantasy in Holy Sonnet XIV." *HSL* 1(1969): 52-58.

11898. Stein, Arnold. "Donne and the 1920's: A Problem in Historical Consciousness." *ELH* 27 (1960): 16-29.

11899. Storhoff, Gary P. "Social Mode and Poetic Strategies: Donne's Verse Letters to His Friends." *EL* 4(1977): 11-18.

11900. Tepper, Michael. "John Donne's Fragment Epic: 'The Progresse of the Soule.'" *ELN* 13 (1976): 262-266.

11901. Tourney, Leonard D. "Convention and Wit in Donne's *Elegie* on Prince Henry." *SP* 71 (1974): 473-483.

11902. van Laan, Thomas F. "John Donne's *Devotions* and the Jesuit Spiritual Exercises." *SP* 60(1963): 191-202.

11903. Wall, John N., Jr. "Donne's Wit of Redemption: The Drama of Prayer in the *Holy Sonnets*." *SP* 73(1976): 189-203.

11904. Waller, G. F. "John Donne's Changing Attitudes to Time." *SEL* 14(1974): 79-89.

11905. Warren, Austin. "Donne's 'Extasie.'" *SP* 55(1958): 472-480.

11906. Wellington, James E. "The Litany in Cramner and Donne." *SP* 68(1971): 177-199.

11907. Whitlock, Baird W. "Ye Curioust Schooler in Cristendom." *RES* 6(1955): 365-371."

11908. Williamson, George. "The Design of

Donne's *Anniversaries*." *MP* 60(1963): 183-191.

11909. ----------. "Donne's Satircial *Progresse of the Soule*." *ELH* 36(1969): 250-264.

11910. Wilson, G. R., Jr. "The Interplay of Perception and Reflection: Mirror Image in Donne's Poetry." *SEL* 9(1969): 107-121.

11911. Wyke, Clement H. "Edmund Gosse as Biographer and Critic of Donne: His Fallible Role in the Poet's Rediscovery." *TSLL* 17(1976): 805-819.

11912. Yoklavich, John. "Donne and the Countess of Huntingdon." *PQ* 43(1964): 283-288.

11913. Zivley, Sherry. "Imagery in John Donne's *Satyres*." *SEL* 6(1966): 87-95.

See also 474, 9291, 9463, 9441, 11361, 11425, 11429, 11430, 11431, 11710, 12498, 14432, 14660.

DRUMMOND OF HAWTHORDEN, WILLIAM. 11914. Barker, J. R. "A Pendant to Drummond of Hawthorden's *Conversations*." *RES* 16(1965): 284-288.

11915. Ellrodt, Robert. "William Drummond's Revision of 'A Cypresse Grove.'" *MLR* 47(1952): 50-52.

11916. MacDonald, R. H. "Drummond of Hawthornden, Miss Euphemia Kyninghame, and the 'Poems.'" *MLR* 60(1965): 494-499.

11917. ----------. "Drummond of Hawthornden: The Season at Bourges, 1607." *CD* 4(1970): 89-109.

DRYDEN, JOHN. 11918. Adams, Percy G. "'Harmony of Numbers': Dryden's Alliteration, Consonance, Assonance." *TSLL* 9(1967): 333-343.

11919. Aden, John M. "Dryden and Boileau: The Question of Critical Influence." *SP* 50(1953): 491-509.

11920. ----------. "Dryden and the Imagination: The First Phase." *PMLA* 74(1959): 28-40.

11921. ----------. "Dryden, Corneille, and the *Essay of Dramatic Poesy*." *RES* 6(1955): 147-156.

11922. Allen, Ned B. "The Sources of Dryden's *The Mock Astrologer*." *PQ* 36(1957): 453-464.

11923. Alssid, Michael W. "The Design of Dryden's *Aureng-Zebe*." *JEGP* 64(1965): 452-469.

11924. ----------. "The Impossible Form of Art: Dryden, Purcell, and *King Arthur*." *SLI* 10,#1 (1977): 125-144.

11925. ----------. "The Perfect Conquest: A Study of Theme, Structure and Characters in Dryden's *The Indian Emperor*." *SP* 59(1962): 539-559.

11926. ----------. "Shadwell's *MacFlecknoe*." *SEL* 7(1967): 387-402.

11927. Anderberg, Gary T. "*Cleomenes* and Affective Tragedy." *EL* 3(1976): 41-51.

11928. Anselment, Raymond A. "Martin Marprelate: A New Source for Dryden's Fable of the Martin and the Swallows." *RES* 17(1966): 256-267.

11929. Archer, Stanley. "Benaiah in *Absalom and Achitophel II*." *ELN* 3(1966): 183-185.

11930. Armistead, J. M. "The Mythic Dimension of Dryden's *The Hind and the Panther*." *SEL* 16(1976): 377-386.

11931. ----------. "The Narrator as Rhetorician in Dryden's *The Hind and the Panther*." *JNT* 3(1973): 208-218.

11932. Atkins, G. Douglas. "The Function and Significance of the Priest in Dryden's *Troilus and Cressida*." *TSLL* 13(1971): 29-37.

11933. Bache, William. "Dryden and Oldham: Hail and Farewell." *CLA* 12(1969): 237-243.

11934. Bachorik, Lawrence L. "*The Duke of Guise* and Dryden's *Vindication*: A New Consideration." *ELN* 10(1973): 208-212.

11935. Ball, Albert. "Charles II: Dryden's Christian Hero." *MP* 59(1961): 25-35.

11936. Barnard, John. "The Dates of Six Dryden Letters." *PQ* 42(1963): 396-403.

11937. Bateley, Janet M. "Dryden's Revisions in the *Essay of Dramatic Poesy*: The Preposition at the End of the Sentence and the Expression of the Relative." *RES* 15(1964): 268-282.

11938. Baumgartner, A. M. "Dryden's Caleb and Agag." *RES* 13(1962): 394-397.

11939. Bell, Robert H. "Dryden's 'Aeneid' as English Augustan Epic." *Criticism* 19(1977): 34-50.

11940. Benson, Donald R. "The Artistic Image and Dryden's Conception of Reason." *SEL* 11 (1971): 427-435.

11941. ----------. "Platonism and Neoclassic Metaphor: Dryden's *Elenora* and Donne's *Anniversaries*." *SP* 68(1971): 340-356.

11942. ----------. "Theology and Politics in Dryden's Conversion." *SEL* 4(1964): 393-412.

11943. ----------. "Who 'Bred' *Religio Laici*?" *JEGP* 65(1966): 238-251.

11944. Beer, E. S. de. "Historical Allusions in *Absalom and Achitophel*." *RES* 7(1956) 410-415.

11945. Blair, Joel. "Dryden on the Writings of Fanciful Poetry." *Criticism* 12(1970): 89-104.

11946. ----------. "Dryden's Ceremonial Hero." *SEL* 9(1969): 379-393.

11947. Boddy, Margaret P. "The Dryden-Lauderdale Relationships, Some Bibliographical Notes and a Suggestion." *PQ* 42(1963): 267-272.

11948. ----------. "The 1692 *Fourth Book of Virgil*" *RES* 15(1964): 364-380.

11949. Bowers, Fredson. "Current Theories of Copy-Text, with an Illustration from Dryden." *MP* 48(1950): 12-20.

11950. ----------. "The 1665 Manuscript of Dryden's *Indian Emperour*." *SP* 48(1951): 738-760.

11951. Brodwin, Leonora Leet. "Miltonic Allusion in *Absalom and Achitophel*: Its Function in Political Satire." *JEGP* 68(1969): 24-44.

11952. Brooks, Harold F. "Dryden's Juvenal and the Harveys." *PQ* 48(1969): 12-19.

11953. Brower, Reuben A. "An Allusion to Europe: Dryden and Tradition." *ELH* 19(1952): 38-48.

11954. Brown, David D. "Dryden's 'Religio Laici' and the 'Judicious and Learned Friend.'" *MLR* 56(1961): 66-69.

11955. ----------. "John Tillotson's Revisions and Dryden's 'Talent for English Prose.'" *RES* 12(1961): 24-39.

11956. Buck, John Dawson Carl. "The Ascetic's Banquet: The Morality of *Alexander's Feast*." *TSLL* 17(1975): 573-589.

11957. Canfield, J. Douglas. "The Jewel of Great Price: Mutability and Constancy in Dryden's *All for Love*." *ELH* 42(1975): 38-61.

11958. Castrop, Helmut. "Dryden and Flecknoe." *RES* 23(1972): 455-458.

11959. Cope, Jackson I. "Dryden vs. Hobbes: An Adaptation from the Platonists." *JEGP* 57 (1958): 444-448.

11960. Corder, Jim W. "Rhetoric and Meaning in *Religio Laici*." *PMLA* 82(1967): 245-249.

11961. Daly, Robert. "Dryden's Ode to Anne Killegrew and the Communal Work of Poets." *TSLL* 18(1976): 184-197.

11962. Davis, Ira B. "Religious Controversy: John Dryden's 'The Hind and the Panther.'" *CLA* 4(1961): 207-214.

11963. Dobbins, Austin C. "Dryden's 'Character of a Good Parson': Background and Interpretation." *SP* 53(1956): 51-59.

11964. Donnelly, Jerome. "Movement and Meaning in Dryden's *MacFlecknoe*." *TSLL* 12(1971): 569-582.

11965. Doyle, Anne. "Dryden's Authorship of *Notes and Observations on the Empress of Morocco* (1674)." *SEL* 6(1966): 421-445.

11966. Duggan, Margaret. "Mythic Components in Dryden's *Hind and Panther*." *Comp L* 26(1974): 110-123.

11967. Eleanor, Mother Mary, S. H. C. J. "*Anne Killigrew* and *Mac Flecknoe*." *PQ* 43(1964): 47-54.

11968. Empson, William. "A Deist Tract by Dryden." *EIC* 25(1975): 74-100.

11969. ----------. "Dryden's Apparent Scepticism." *EIC* 20(1970): 172-181.

11970. ----------. "Dryden's Apparent Scepticism." *EIC* 21(1971): 111-115.

11971. Emslie, McD. "Dryden's Complete." *EIC* 11(1961): 264-273.

11972. Faulkner, Thomas C. "Dryden and *Great and Weighty Considerations*: An Incorrect Attribution." *SEL* 11(1971): 417-425.

11973. Feder, Lillian. "John Dryden's Use of Classical Rhetoric." *PMLA* 69(1954): 1258-1278.

11974. Fisher, Alan S. "Daring to be Absurd: The Paradoxes of *The Conquest of Granada*." *SP* 73(1976): 414-439.

11975. ----------. "Necessity and the Winter: The Tragedy of *All for Love*." *PQ* 56(1977): 183-203.

11976. Fowler, Alastair, and Douglas Brooks. "The Structure of Dryden's *Song for St. Cecilia's Day*, *1687*." *EIC* 17(1967): 434-447.

11977. Freedman, Morris. "Dryden's Miniature Epic." *JEGP* 57(1958): 211-219.

11978. ----------. "Satan and Shaftesbury." *PMLA* 74(1959): 544-547.

11979. French, A. L. "Dryden, Marvell, and Political Poetry." *SEL* 8(1968): 397-413.

11980. Frost, William. "*Aureng-Zebe* in Context: Dryden, Shakespeare, Milton, and Racine." *JEGP* 74(1975): 26-49.

11981. ----------. "Dryden and 'Satire.'" *SEL* 11(1971): 401-416.

11982. ----------. "Dryden's Versions of Ovid." *Comp L* 26(1974): 193-202.

11983. Fujimura, Thomas H. "The Appeal of Dryden's Heroic Plays." *PMLA* 75(1960): 37-45.

11984. ----------. "Dryden's Poetics" The Expressive Values in Poetry." *JEGP* 74(1975): 195-208.

11985. ----------. "Dryden's *Religio Laici*: An Anglican Poem." *PMLA* 76(1961): 205-217.

11986. ----------. "The Personal Drama of Dryden's *The Hind and the Panther*." *PMLA* 87 (1972): 406-416.

11987. ----------. "The Personal Element in Dryden's Poetry." *PMLA* 89(1974): 1007-1023.

11988. ----------. "The Temper of John

Dryden." *SP* 72(1975): 348-366.

11989. Gardener, William Bradford. "John Dryden's Interest in Judicial Astrology." *SP* 47 (1950): 506-521.

11990. Garrison, James D. "A Quotation from Waller in Dryden's *Love Triumphant*." *ELN* 15 (1977): 27-29.

11991. Gagen, Jean. "Love and Honor in Dryden's Heroic Plays." *PMLA* 77(1962): 208-220.

11992. Gransden, K. W. "Milton, Dryden, and the Comedy of the Fall." *EIC* 26(1976): 116-133.

11993. ----------. "What Kind of Poem is *Religio Laici*." *SEL* 17(1977): 397-406.

11994. Griffin, Dustin. "Dryden's 'Oldham' and the Perils of Writing." *MLQ* 37(1976): 133-150.

11995. Guibbory, Achsah. "Dryden's Views of History." *PQ* 52(1973): 187-204.

11996. Guilhamet, Leon M. "Dryden's Debasement of Scripture in *Absalom and Achitophel*." *SEL* 9(1969): 395-413.

11997. Hamm, Victor M. "Dryden's *Religio Laici* and Roman Catholic Apologetics." *PMLA* 80 (1965): 190-198.

11998. ----------. "Dryden's *The Hind and the Panther* and Roman Catholic Apologetics." *PMLA* 83(1968): 400-415.

11999. Hammond, H. "'One Immortal Song.'" *RES* 5(1954): 60-62.

12000. Hardin, Richard F. "Convention and Design in Drayton's *Heroicall Epistles*." *PMLA* 83 (1968): 35-41.

12001. Harth, Phillip. "Empson's Interpretation of *Religio Laici*." *EIC* 20(1970): 446-450.

12002. ----------. "Religion and Politics in Dryden's Poetry and Plays." *MP* 70(1973): 236-242.

12003. Hemphill, George. "Dryden's Heroic Line." *PMLA* 72(1957): 863-879.

12004. Hinnant, Charles H. "The Background of the Early Version of Dryden's *The Duke of Guise*." *ELN* 6(1968): 102-106.

12005. ----------. "Dryden's Gallic Rooster." *SP* 65(1968): 647-656.

12006. Hopkins, D. W. "Dryden's 'Baucis and Philemon.'" *Comp L* 28(1976): 135-143.

12007. Hooker, Edward N. "Dryden and the Atoms of Epicurus." *ELH* 24(1957): 177-190.

12008. Horsman, E. A. "Dryden's French Borrowings." *RES* 1(1950): 346-351.

12009. Hughes, Derek W. "The Significance of *All for Love*." *ELH* 37(1970): 540-563.

12010. Hughes, R. E. "John Dryden's Greatest Compromise." *TSLL* 2(1961): 458-463.

12011. Hume, Robert D. "Dryden on Creation: 'Imagination' in the Later Criticism." *RES* 21 (1970): 295-314.

12012. ----------. "Dryden's Apparent Scepticism." *EIC* 20(1970): 492-495.

12013. ----------. "Dryden's 'Heads of an Answer to Rymer': Notes Toward a Hypothetical Revolution." *RES* 19(1968): 373-386.

12014. Illo, JOhn. "Dryden, Sylvester, and the Correspondence of Melancholy Winter and Cold Age." *ELN* 1(1963): 101-104.

12015. Jackson, Wallace. "Dryden's Emperor

and Lillo's Merchant: The Relevant Bases of Action." *MLQ* 26(1965): 536-544.

12016. Jefferson, D. W. "Aspects of Dryden's Imagery." *EIC* 4(1954): 20-41.

12017. Johnson, Maurice. "Dryden's 'Cousin Swift.'" *PMLA* 68(1953): 1234-1237.

12018. ----------. "A Literary Chestnut: Dryden's 'Cousin Swift.'" *PMLA* 67(1952): 1024-1034.

12019. Kearful, Frank J. "'Tis past recovery': Tragic Consciousness in *All for Love*." *MLQ* 34(1973): 227-246.

12020. Keast, W. R. "Dryden Studies, 1895-1948." *MP* 48(1951): 205-210.

12021. King, Bruce. "Anti-Whig Satire in *The Duke of Guise*." *ELN* 2(1965): 190-193.

12022. ----------. "Dryden, Tillotson, and *Tyrannic Love*." *RES* 16(1965): 364-377.

12023. ----------. "Dryden's Ark: The Influence of Filmer." *SEL* 7(1967): 403-414.

12024. ----------. "The Significance of Dryden's *State of Innocence*." *SEL* 4(1964): 371-391.

12025. Kinsley, James. "Dryden and the *Encomium Musicae*." *RES* 4(1953): 263-267.

12025a. ----------. "Dryden's Bestiary." *RES* 4(1953): 331-336.

12026. ----------. "Dryden's 'Character of a Good Parson' and Bishop Ken." *RES* 3(1952): 155-158.

12027. ----------. "Historical Allusions in *Absalom and Achitophel*." *RES* 6(1955): 291-297.

12028. ----------. "The 'Three Glorious Victories' in *Annus Mirabilis*." *RES* 7(1956): 30-37.

12029. Kirsch, Arthur C. "Dryden, Corneille, and the Heroic Play." *MP* 59(1962): 248-264.

12030. ----------. "The Significance of Dryden's *Aureng-Zebe*." *ELH* 29(1962): 160-174.

12031. LeClercq, R. V. "Corneille and *An Essay of Dramatic Poesy*." *Comp L* 22(1970): 319-327.

12032. Levine, Jay Arnold. "Dryden's *Song for St. Cecilia's Day, 1687*." *PQ* 44(1965): 38-50.

12033. ----------. "John Dryden's Epistle to John Driden." *JEGP* 63(1964): 450-474.

12034. Lewalski, Barbara Kiefer. "The Scope and Function of Biblical Allusion in *Absalom and Achitophel*." *ELN* 3(1965): 29-35.

12035. Loftis, John. "'El Principe Constante' and 'The Indian Emperour': A Reconsideration." *MLR* 65(1970): 761-767.

12036. ----------. "Exploration and Enlightenment: Dryden's *The Indian Emperour* and Its Background." *PQ* 45(1966): 71-84.

12037. Love, Harold. "Dryden, Durfey, and the Standard of Comedy." *SEL* 13(1973): 422-436.

12038. Lowens, Irving. "St. Evremond, Dryden, and the Theory of Opera." *Criticism* 1(1959): 226-248.

12039. Maresca, Thomas E. "The Context of Dryden's *Absalom and Achitophel*." *ELH* 41(1974): 340-358.

12040. Martin, Leslie Howard. "*All for Love* and the Millenarian Tradition." *Comp L* 27(1975): 289-306.

12041. ----------. "The Consistency of Dryden's *Aureng-Zebe*." *SP* 70(1973): 306-328.

12042. ----------. "Dryden and the Art of Transversion." *CD* 6(1972): 3-13.

12043. ----------. "The Source and Originality of Dryden's Melantha." *PQ* 52(1973): 746-753.

12044. Martin, R. H. "A Note on Dryden's *Aeneid.*" *PQ* 30(1951): 89-91.

12045. Maurer, Wallace. "Who Prompted Dryden to Write *Absalom and Achitophel.*" *PQ* 40 (1961): 130-138.

12046. ----------. "Dryden's Ballam Well Hung?" *RES* 10(1959): 398-401.

12047. McFadden, George. "Elkanah Settle and the Genesis of *Mac Flecknoe.*" *PQ* 43(1964): 55-72.

12048. Miller, Clarence H. "The Styles of *The Hind and the Panther.*" *JEGP* 61(1962): 511-527.

12049. Miner, Earl. "Dryden and the Issue of Human Progress." *PQ* 40(1961): 120-129.

12050. ----------. "Dryden as Prose Controversialist: His Role in *A Defence of the Royal Papers.*" *PQ* 43(1964): 412-419.

12051. ----------. "Dryden's Apparent Scepticism." *EIC* 21(1971): 410-411.

12052. ----------. "Dryden's Messianic Eclogue." *RES* 11(1960): 299-302.

12053. ----------. "Mr. Dryden and Mr. Rymer." *PQ* 54(1975): 137-151.

12054. ----------. "Some Characteristics of Dryden's Use of Metaphor." *SEL* 2(1962): 309-320.

12055. Moore, Frank Harper. "Dr. Pelling, Dr. Pell, and Dryden's Lord Nonsuch." *MLR* 49 (1954): 349-351.

12056. ----------. "Heroic Comedy: A New Interpretation of Dryden's Assignation." *SP* 51 (1954): 585-598.

12057. Moore, John Robert. "*Alexander's Feast*: A Possible Chronology of Development." *PQ* 37(1958): 495-498.

12058. ----------. "Dryden and Rupert Brooke." *MLR* 54(1959): 226.

12059. ----------. "Dryden's 'Cousin Swift.'" *PMLA* 68(1953): 1232-1234, 1237-1240.

12060. ----------. "Political Allusions in Dryden's Later Plays." *PMLA* 73(1958): 36-42.

12061. Myers, William. "Politics in *The Hind and the Panther.*" *EIC* 19(1969): 19-34.

12062. Newman, Robert S. "Irony and the Problem of Tone in Dryden's *Aureng-Zebe.*" *SEL* 10(1970): 439-458.

12063. Novak, Maximillian E. "The Demonology of Dryden's *Tyrannick Love* and 'Anti-Scott.'" *ELN* 4(1966): 95-98.

12064. Osborn, Scott C. "Heroical Love in Dryden's Heroic Drama." *PMLA* 73(1958): 480-490.

12065. Parkin, Rebecca P. "Heroic and Anti-Heroic Elements in *The Hind and the Panther.*" *SEL* 12(1972): 459-466.

12066. Perkins, Merle L. "Dryden's *The Indian Emperour* and Voltaire's *Algire.*" *Comp L* 9 (1957): 229-237.

12067. Peterson, R. G. "Larger Manners and Events: Sallust and Virgil in *Absalom and Achitophel.*" *PMLA* 82(1967): 236-244.

12068. ----------. "The Unavailing Gift: Dryden's Roman Farewell to Mr. Oldham." *MP* 66 (1969): 232-236.

12069. Proffitt, Bessie. "Political Satire in Dryden's *Alexander's Feast.*" *TSLL* 11(1970): 1307-1316.

12070. Purpos, Eugene R. "Some Notes on a Deistical Essay Attributed to Dryden." *PQ* 29

(1950): 347-349.

12071. Ricks, Christopher. "Dryden's Absalom." *EIC* 11(1961): 273-289.

12072. Ringler, Richard N. "Two Dryden Notes." *ELN* 1(1964): 256-261.

12073. ----------. "Two Sources for Dryden's *The Indian Emperour.*" *PQ* 42(1963): 423-429.

12074. Roberts, William. "Saint-Amant, Orinda, and Dryden's Miscellany." *ELN* 1(1964): 191-196.

12075. Roper, Alan. "Characteristics of Dryden's Prose." *ELH* 41(1974): 668-692.

12076. ----------. "Dryden's *Medal* and the Divine Analogy." *ELH* 29(1962): 396-417.

12077. ----------. "Dryden's 'Secular Masque.'" *MLQ* 23(1962): 29-40.

12078. Rosenberg, Bruce A. "*Annus Mirabilis* Distilled." *PMLA* 79(1964): 254-258.

12079. Salter, C. H. "Dryden and Addison." *MLR* 69(1974): 29-39.

12080. Saslow, Edward L. "Dryden in 1684." *MP* 72(1975): 248-255.

12081. ----------. "Dryden's Authorship of the Defence of the Royal Papers." *SEL* 17(1977): 387-395.

12082. Schless, Howard H. "Dryden's *Absalom and Achitophel* and *A Dialogue between Nathan and Absalome.*" *PQ* 40(1961): 139-143.

12083. Selden, R. "Roughness in Satire from Horace to Dryden." *MLR* 66(1971): 264-272.

12084. Shawcross, John T. "Some Literary Uses of Numerology." *HSL* 1(1969): 50-61.

12085. ----------. "An Unnoticed Reaction to Dryden's 'The Hind and the Panther.'" *ELN* 11 (1973): 110-112.

12086. Sherbo, Arthur. "Virgil, Dryden, Gay, and Matters Trivial." *PMLA* 85(1970): 1063-1071.

12087. Shergold, N. D., and Peter Ure. "Dryden and Calderón: A New Spanish Source for 'The Indian Emperour.'" *MLR* 61(1966): 369-383.

12088. Sherwood, John C. "Dryden and the Critical Theories of Tasso." *Comp L* 18(1965): 351-359.

12089. ----------. "Dryden and the Rules: The Preface to the *Fables.*" *JEGP* 52(1953): 13-26.

12090. ----------. "Dryden and the Rules: The Preface to *Troilus and Cressida.*" *Comp L* 2 (1950): 73-83.

12091. ----------. "Precept and Practice in Dryden's Criticism." *JEGP* 68(1969): 432-440.

12092. Simon, Irene. "Dryden's Revision of the *Essay of Dramatic Poesy.*" *RES* 14(1963): 132-141.

12093. Sloman, Judith. "Dryden's Originality in *Sigismonda and Guiscardo.*" *SEL* 12(1972): 445-457.

12094. Smith, John Harrington. "Dryden and Flecknoe: A Conjecture." *PQ* 33(1954): 338-341.

12095. ----------. "The Dryden-Howard Collaboration." *SP* 51(1954): 54-74.

12096. ----------. "Dryden's Prologue to Epilogue to *Mithridates*, Revived." *PMLA* 68(1953): 251-267.

12097. Starnes, D. T. "Imitation of Shakespeare in Dryden's *All For Love.*" *TSLL* 6(1964): 39-47.

12098. Swedenberg, H. T., Jr. "England's Joy: *Astraea Redux* in Its Setting." *SP* 50(1953):

30-44.

12099. Sweney, John R. "Dryden's 'Lines to Mrs. Creed.'" *PQ* 51(1972): 489-490.

12100. Tarbet, David W. "Reason Dazzled: Perspective and Language in Dryden's 'Aureng-Zebe.'" *Criticism* 18(1976): 256-272.

12101. Thale, Mary. "Dryden's Dramatic Criticism." *Comp L* 18(1966): 36-54.

12102. Thomas, W. K. "The Matrix of *Absalom and Achitophel*." *PQ* 49(1970): 92-99.

102103. Towers, Tom H. "The Lineage of Shadwell: An Approach to *MacFlecknoe*." *SEL* 3 (1963): 323-334.

12104. Tritt, Carleton S. "The Title of *All for Love*." *ELN* 10(1973): 273-275.

12105. Vieth, David M. "Irony in Dryden's Ode to Anne Killigrew." *SP* 62(1965): 91-100.

12106. ----------. "Irony in Dryden's Verses to Sir Robert Howard." *EIC* 22(1972): 239-243.

12107. Waith, Eugene M. "The Voice of Mr. Bayes." *SEL* 3(1963): 335-343.

12108. Wallace, John M. "Dryden and History: A Problem in Allegorical Reading." *ELH* 36(1969): 265-290.

12109. Wasserman, Earl R. "Dryden's Epistle to Charleton." *JEGP* 55(1956): 201-212.

12110. Wasserman, George R. "The Domestic Metaphor in *Astraea Redux*." *ELN* 3(1965): 106-111.

12111. Watson, George. "Dryden's First Answer to Rymer." *RES* 14(1963): 17-23.

12112. Weinbrot, Howard D. "Alexas in *All for Love*: His Genealogy and Function." *SP* 64 (1967): 625-639.

12113. Welcher, Jeanne K. "The Opening of *Religio Laici* and Its Virgilian Associations." *SEL* 8(1968): 391-396.

12114. Wendorf, Richard. "Dryden, Charles II, and the Interpretation of Historical Character." *PQ* 56(1977): 82-103.

12115. West, Michael. "Some Neglected Continental Analogues for Dryden's *MacFlecknoe*." *SEL* 13(1973): 437-449.

12116. Wilding, Michael. "Allusion and Innuendo in *MacFlecknoe*." *EIC* 19(1969): 355-370.

12117. Wimsatt, W. K., Jr. "Samuel Johnson and Dryden's *Du Fresnoy*." *SP* 48(1951): 26-39.

12118. Winterbottom, John. "The Development of the Hero in Dryden's Tragedies." *JEGP* 52 (1953): 161-173.

12119. ----------. "The Place of Hobbesian Ideas in Dryden's Tragedies." *JEGP* 57(1958): 665-683.

12120. ----------. "Stoicism in Dryden's Tragedies." *JEGP* 61(1962): 868-883.

12121. Zwicker, Steven N. "The King and Christ: Figural Imagery in Dryden's Restoration Panegyrics." *PQ* 50(1971): 582-598.

See also 11348, 11353, 11388, 11399, 11410, 11416, 11425, 11650, 12195, 12313, 12615, 13040, 13579, 13612, 13617, 13627.

DUGDALE, WILLIAM. 12122. Yerkes, David. "Dugdale's Dictionary and Somner's *Dictionarium*." *ELN* 14(1976): 110-112.

ETHEREGE, GEORGE. 12123. Berman, Ronald. "The Comic Passions of *The Man of Mode*." *SEL* 10 (1970): 459-468.

12124. Brown, Harold Clifford, Jr. "Etherege and Comic Shallowness." *TSLL* 16(1975):

675-690.

12125. Boyette, Purvis E. "Songs of George Etherege." *SEL* 6(1966): 409-419.

12126. Cox, R. S., Jr. "Richard Flecknoe and *The Man of Mode*." *MLQ* 29(1968): 183-189.

12127. Fujimura, Thomas H. "Etherege at Constantinople." *PMLA* 71(1956): 465-481.

12128. Hayman, John G. "Dorimant and the Comedy of a Man of Mode." *MLQ* 30(1969): 183-197.

12129. Hume, Robert D. "Reading and Misreading 'The Man of Mode.'" *Criticism* 14(1972): 1-11.

12130. Martin, Leslie H. "Past and Parody in *The Man of Mode*." *SEL* 16(1976): 363-376.

12131. Rosenfeld, Sybil. "The Second Letterbook of Sir George Etherege." *RES* 3(1952): 19-27. See also 11399, 11409.

FARQUHAR, GEORGE. 12132. Berman, Ronald. "The Comedy of Reason." *TSLL* 7(1965): 162-168.

12133. Cope, Jackson I. "*The Constant Couple*: Farquhar's Four-Plays-In-One." *ELH* 41(1974): 477-493.

12134. Kenny, Shirley Strum. "Perennial Favorites: Congreve, Vanbrugh, Cibber, Farquhar, and Steele." *MP* 73(1976): S4-S11.

12135. James, Eugene Nelson. "The Burlesque of Restoration Comedy in *Love and a Bottle*." *SEL* 5(1965): 469-490.

12136. Rothstein, Eric. "Farquhar's *Twin-Rivals* and the Reform of Comedy." *PMLA* 79(1964): 33-41.

12137. Wertheim, Albert. "Bertolt Brecht and George Farquhar's *The Recruiting Officer*." *CD* 7(1973): 179-190.

FELTHAM, OWEN. 12138. Hazlett, McCrea. "'New Frame and Various Composition': Development in the Form of Owen Feltham's *Resolves*." *MP* 51 (1953): 93-101.

FLECKNOE, RICHARD. See 12126.

FLETCHER, GILES (the younger). 12139. Dees, Jerome S. "The Narrator of *Christs Victorie and Triumph*: What Giles Fletcher Learned from Spenser." *ELR* 6(1976): 453-465.

12140. Holaday, Allan. "Giles Fletcher and the Puritans." *JEGP* 54(1955): 578-586.

See also 12153.

FLETCHER, JOHN. 12142. Cutts, John P. "A Newly Discovered Musical Setting from Fletcher's *Beggars' Bush*." *CD* 5(1971): 101-105.

12143. Freehafer, John. "*Cardenio*, by Shakespeare and Fletcher." *PMLA* 84(1969): 501-513.

12144. Forker, Charles R. "*Wit Without Money*: A Fletcherian Antecedent to *Keep the Widow Waking*." *CD* 8(1974): 172-183.

12145. Howarth, W. D. "Cervantes and Fletcher: A Theme with Variations." *MLR* 56(1961): 563-566.

12146. Hughes, Leo, and A. H. Scouten. "The Penzance Promptbook of *The Pilgrim*." *MP* 73(1975): 33-53.

12147. Law, Robert Adger. "The Double Authorship of *Henry VIII*." *SP* 56(1959): 471-488.

12148. Mincoff, Marco. "The Faithful Shepherdess: A Fletcherian Experiment." *RD* 9(1966): 163-177.

12149. ----------. "Fletcher's Early Tragedies." *RD* 7(1964): 70-94.

12150. Waith, Eugene M. "John Fletcher and the Art of Declamation." *PMLA* 66(1951): 226-234.

See also 9407.

FLETCHER, PHINEAS.   12151. Baldwin, R. G.
"Phineas Fletcher: His Modern Readers and His
Renaissance Ideas." *PQ* 40(1961): 462-475.

12152. Berry, Lloyd E. "Phineas Fletcher's
Account of His Father." *JEGP* 60(1961): 258-267.

12153. Sheldon, David C. "A Note on a
Latin Poem by either Giles Fletcher the Younger
or his brother Phineas." *MLR* 46(1951): 437-438.

See also 11431, 13275.

FORD, JOHN.   12154. Anderson, Donald K.,
Jr. "The Heart and the Banquet: Imagery in
Ford's *'Tis Pity* and *The Broken Heart*." *SEL* 2
(1962): 209-217.

12155. ----------. "Kingship in Ford's
Perkin Warbeck." *ELH* 27(1960): 177-193.

12156. Barish, Jonas A. "*Perkin Warbeck*
as Anti-History." *EIC* 20(1970): 151-171.

12157. Blayney, Glenn H. "Convention, Plot,
and Structure in *The Broken Heart*." *MP* 56(1958):
1-9.

12158. Brissenden, Alan. "Impediments to
Love: A Theme in John Ford." *RD* 7(1964): 95-102.

12159. Burbridge, Roger T. "The Moral
Vision of Ford's *The Broken Heart*." *SEL* 10(1970):
397-407.

12160. Carsangia, Giovanni M. "'The Truth'
in John Ford's *The Broken Heart*." *Comp L* 10
(1958): 344-348.

12161. Champion, Larry S. "Ford's *'Tis
Pity She's a Whore* and the Jacobean Tragic Perspective." *PMLA* 90(1975): 78-87.

12162. Greenfield, Thelma. "The Language
of Process in Ford's *The Broken Heart*." *PMLA* 87
(1972): 397-405.

12163. Hogan, A. P. "*'Tis Pity She's a
Whore*: The Overall Design." *SEL* 17(1977): 303-
316.

12164. Homan, Sidney R., Jr. "Shakespeare
and Dekker as Keys to Ford's *'Tis Pity She's a
Whore*." *SEL* 7(1967): 269-276.

12165. Hoy, Cyrus. "'Ignorance in Knowledge': Marlowe's Faustus and Ford's Giovanni."
MP 57(1960): 145-154.

12166. Huebert, Ronald. "'An Artificial
Way to Grieve': The Forsaken Woman in Beaumont
and Fletcher, Massinger and Ford." *ELH* 44(1977):
601-621.

12167. Kaufman, R. J. "Ford's Tragic
Perspective." *TSLL* 1(1960): 522-537.

12168. ----------. "Ford's 'Waste Land':
The Broken Heart." *RD* n.s. 3(1970): 167-187.

12169. Kistner, Arthur L. and M. K. "The
Dramatic Functions of Love in the Tragedies of
John Ford." *SP* 70(1973): 62-76.

12170. Leech, Clifford. "A Projected
Restoration Performance of Ford's 'The Lover's
Melancholy'?" *MLR* 56(1961): 378-381.

12171. Levin, Richard. "'The Ass in
Compound': A Lost Pun in Middleton, Ford, and
Jonson." *ELN* 4(1966): 12-15.

12172. McDonald, Charles O. "The Design
of John Ford's *The Broken Heart*: A Study in the
Development of Caroline Sensibility." *SP* 59
(1962): 141-161.

12173. McMaster, Juliet. "Love, Lust, and
Sham: Structural Pattern in the Plays of John
Ford." *RD* n.s. 2(1969): 157-166.

12174. Monsarrat, G. D. "John Ford's
Authorship of *Christes Bloodie Sweat*." *ELN* 9
(1971): 20-25.

12175. Neill, Michael. "'Anticke
Pageantrie': The Mannerist Art of *Perkin
Warbeck*." *RD* n.s. 7(1976): 117-150.

12176. Novarr, David. "'Gray Dissimulation': Ford and Milton." *PQ* 41(1962): 500-
504.

12177. Reinecke, George F. "John Ford's
'Missing' Ralegh Passage." *ELN* 6(1969): 252-254.

12178. Rosen, Carol C. "The Language of
Cruelty in Ford's *'Tis Pity She's a Whore*." *CD*
8(1974): 356-368.

12179. Sensabaugh, George F. "John Ford
Revisited." *SEL* 4(1964): 195-216.

12180. Sutton, Juliet. "Platonic Love
in Ford's *The Fancies, Chaste and Noble*." *SEL* 7
(1967): 299-309.

12181. Ure, Peter. "Cult and Initiates
in Ford's *Love's Sacrifice*." *MLQ* 11(1950): 298-
306.

12182. Weathers, Winston. "*Perkin Warbeck*:
A Seventeenth-Century Psychological Play." *SEL* 4
(1964): 217-226.

See also 11374, 11718, 12144.

FREKE, JOHN.   12183. Ellis, Frank H.
"John Freke and *The History of Insipids*." *PQ* 44
(1965): 472-483.

See also 13313.

FULLER, THOMAS.   12184. Resnick, Robert B.
"An Ounce of Mirth: The Function of Thomas
Fuller's Wit." *CLA* 11(1967): 124-134.

12185. Sandler, Florence. "The Temple of
Zerubbabel: A Pattern for Reformation in Thomas
Fuller's *Pisgah-Sight* and *Church-History of
Britain*." *SLI* 10,#2(1977): 29-42.

See also 12098.

GAYTON, EDMUND.   12186. Wilson, Edward M.
"Edmund Gayton on Don Quixote, Andres, and Juan
Halududo." *Comp L* 2(1950): 64-72.

GILDON, CHARLES.   12187. Maxwell, J. C.
"Charles Gildon and the Quarrel of the Ancients
and Moderns." *RES* 1(1950): 55-57.

GILL, ALEXANDER.   12188. Little, Marguerite.
"Milton's *Ad Patrem* and the Younger Gill's *In
Natalem mei Parentis*." *JEGP* 49(1950): 345-351.

GLANVILLE, JOSEPH.   12189. Cope, Jackson I.
"Joseph Glanvill, Anglican Apologist: Old Ideas
and New Style in the Restoration." *PMLA* 69(1954):
223-250.

GODWIN, FRANCIS.   12190. Copeland, Thomas A.
"Francis Godwin's *The Man in the Moone*: A
Picaresque Satire." *Ext* 16(1975): 156-163.

12191. Knowlson, James R. "A Note on Bishop
Godwin's *Man in the Moone*: The East Indies Trade
Route and a 'Language' of Musical Notes." *MP* 65
(1968): 357-361.

GOFFE, THOMAS.   12192. O'Donnell, Norbert F.
"Shakespeare, Marston, and the University: The
Sources of Thomas Goffe's *Orestes*." *SP* 50(1953):
476-490.

GOTT, SAMUEL.   12193. Patrick, J. Max.
"*Nova Solyma*: Samuel Gott's Puritan Utopia." *SLI*
10,#2(1977): 43-55.

GOUGH, JOHN.   12194. O'Donnell, Norbert F.
"The Authorship of *The Careless Shepherdess*." *PQ*
33(1954): 43-47.

GOULD, ROBERT.   12195. Weinbrot, Howard D.
"Robert Gould: Some Borrowings from Dryden." *ELN*
3(1965): 36-40.

HABINGTON, WILLIAM.   See 11437.

HALL, JOHN.   12196. Turnbull, G. H. "John

Hall's Letters to Samuel Hartilib." *RES* 4(1953): 221-223.

HALL, JOSEPH. 12197. Chew, Audrey. "Joseph Hall and John Milton." *ELH* 17(1950): 274-295.

12198. ----------. "Joseph Hall and Neo-Stoicism." *PMLA* 65(1950): 1130-1145.

12199. Huntley, Frank Livingstone. "Bishop Joseph Hall and the Protestant Meditation." *SLI* 10,#2(1977): 57-71.

12200. Kirk, Rudolf. "A Seventeenth-Century Controversy: Extremism vs. Moderation." *TSLL* 9 (1967): 5-35.

12201. MacKinnon, M. H. M. "Sir John Harington and Bishop Hall" *PQ* 37(1958): 80-86.

12202. Müller-Schwefe, Gerhard. "Joseph Hall's *Characters of Vertues and Vices*: Notes Toward a Revaluation." *TSLL* 14(1972): 235-251.

12203. Stout, Gardner D., Jr. "Sterne's Borrowings from Bishop Joseph Hall's *Quo Vadis*?" *ELN* 2(1965): 196-200.

See also 9291, 9479, 12538.

HARE, NICHOLAS. 12204. Carey, John. "The Poems of Nicholas Hare." *RES* 11(1960): 365-383.

HARSNETT, SAMUEL. 12205. Berry, Herbert. "Italian Definitions of Tragedy and Comedy Arrive in England." *SEL* 14(1974): 179-187.

HARVEY, CHRISTOPHER. 12206. Howell, A. C. "Christopher Harvey's *The Synagogue* (1640)." *SP* 49(1952): 229-247.

HAWKINS, HENRY. 12207. Lottes, Wolfgang. "Henry Hawkins and *Parthenia Sacra*." *RES* 26(1975): 144-153, 271-286.

HERBERT, EDWARD. See 12254.

HERBERT, GEORGE. 12208. Asals, Heather. "The Voice of George Herbert's 'The Church.'" *ELH* 36(1969): 511-528.

12209. Bell, Ilona. "'Setting Foot into Divinity': George Herbert and the English Reformation." *MLQ* 38(1977): 219-241.

12210. Bowers, Fredson. "Herbert's Sequential Imagery: 'The Temper.'" *MP* 59(1962): 202-213.

12211. Carnes, Valerie. "The Unity of George Herbert's *The Temple*: A Reconsideration." *ELH* 35(1968): 505-526.

12212. Carpenter, Margaret. "From Herbert to Marvell: Poetics in 'A Wreath' and 'The Coronet.'" *JEGP* 69(1970): 50-62.

12213. Charles, Amy M. "George Herbert, Deacon." *MP* 72(1975): 272-276.

12214. ----------. "Mrs. Herbert's Kitchin Booke (with texts)." *ELR* 4(1974): 164-173.

12215. "'Lord, in Thee the *Beauty* Lies in the Discovery': 'Love Unknown' and Reading Herbert." *ELH* 39(1972): 560-584.

12216. Clements, A. L. "Theme, Tone, and Tradition in Herbert's Poetry." *ELR* 3(1973): 264-283.

12217. Daniels, Edgar F. "Herbert's *The Quip*, Line 23: 'Say, I am Thing.'" *ELN* 2(1964): 10-12.

12218. Duncan-Jones, Elsie. "Benlowes's Borrowings from George Herbert." *RES* 6(1955): 179-180.

12219. Dust, Phillip. "The Sorrow of a Black Woman in a Seventeenth-Century Neo-Latin Poem." *CLA* 18(1975): 516-520.

12220. El-Gabalawy, Saad. "The Pilgrimage: George Herbert's Favourite Allegorical Technique." *CLA* 13(1970): 408-419.

12221. Fish, Stanley E. "Letting Go: The Reader in Herbert's Poetry." *ELH* 37(1970): 475-494.

12222. Fleissner, Robert F. "Herbert's Aethiopesa and the Dark Lady: A Mannerist Parallel." *CLA* 19(1976): 458-467.

12223. Forsyth, R. A. "Herbert, Clough, and Their Church-Windows." *VP* 7(1969): 17-30.

12224. Freeman, Rosemary. "Parody as a Literary Form: George Herbert and Wilfred Owen." *EIC* 13(1963): 307-322.

12225. Gallagher, Michael P., S. J. "Rhetoric, Style, and George Herbert." *ELH* 37 (1970): 495-516.

12226. Gallagher, Philip J. "George Herbert's 'The Forerunners.'" *ELN* 15(1977): 14-18.

12227. Greenwood, E. B. "George Herbert's Sonnet 'Prayer': A Stylistic Study." *EIC* 15 (1965): 27-45.

12228. ----------. "Putting the 'Romance' Back into Stylistics." *EIC* 17(1967): 256-257.

12229. Hanley, Sister Sara William, C. S. J. "George Herbert's Ana$<^{Mary}_{Army}>$Gram." *ELN* 4(1966): 16-19.

12230. ----------. "Temples in *The Temple*: Herbert's Study of the Church." *SEL* 8(1968): 121-135.

12231. Harman, Barbara Leah. "George Herbert's 'Affliction (I)': The Limits of Representation." *ELH* 44(1977): 267-285.

12232. Harnack, H. Andrew. "George Herbert's 'Aaron': The Aesthetics of Shaped Typology." *ELN* 14(1976): 25-32.

12233. Higbie, Robert. "Images of Enclosure in George Herbert's *The Temple*." *TSLL* 15 (1974): 627-638.

12234. Hughes, R. E. "George Herbert's Rhetorical World." *Criticism* 3(1961): 86-94.

12235. Huntley, Frank L. "A Crux in George Herbert's *The Temple*." *ELN* 8(1970): 13-17.

12236. Johnson, Lee Ann. "The Relationship of 'The Church Militant' to *The Temple*." *SP* 68 (1971): 200-206.

12237. Jordan, Richard Douglas. "Herbert's First Sermon." *RES* 27(1976): 178-179.

12238. Knieger, Bernard. "The Purchase-Sale: Patterns of Business Imagery in the Poetry of George Herbert." *SEL* 6(1966): 111-124.

12239. ----------. "The Religious Verse of George Herbert." *CLA* 4(1960): 138-147.

12240. ----------. "Teaching George Herbert in Israel—and in America?" *CLA* 10(1966): 143-148.

12241. Levang, Dwight. "George Herbert's 'The Church Militant' and the Chances of History." *PQ* 36(1957): 265-268.

12242. Levitt, Paul M., and Kenneth G. Johnston. "Herbert's 'The Collar': A Nautical Metaphor." *SP* 66(1969): 217-224.

12243. Low, Anthony. "Herbert's 'Jordan (I)' and the Court Masque." *Criticism* 14(1972): 109-118.

12244. McLaughlin, Elizabeth, and Gail Thomas. "Communion in *The Temple*." *SEL* 15(1975): 111-124.

12245. Mills, Jerry Leath. "Recent Studies in Herbert." *ELR* 6(1976): 105-118.

12246. Mollenkott, Virginia R. "George Herbert's 'Redemption.'" *ELN* 10(1973): 262-267.

12247. ----------. "The Many and the One in George Herbert's 'Providence.'" *CLA* 10(1966): 34-41.

12248. Montgomery, Robert L., Jr. "The Province of Allegory in George Herbert's Verse." *TSLL* 1(1960): 457-472.

12249. Morillo, Marvin. "Herbert's Chairs: Notes to *The Temple*." *ELN* 11(1974): 271-275.

12250. Ostriker, Alicia. "Song and Speech in the Metrics of George Herbert." *PMLA* 80(1965): 62-68.

12251. Parfitt, George A. E. "Donne, Herbert and the Matter of Schools." *EIC* 22(1972): 381-395.

12252. Primeau, Ronald. Reading George Herbert: Process vs. Rescue." *Coll L* 2(1975): 50-60.

12253. Rickey, Mary Ellen. "Herbert's Technical Development." *JEGP* 62(1963): 745-760.

12254. ----------. "Rhymecraft in Edward and George Herbert." *JEGP* 57(1958): 502-511.

12255. Sheick, William J. "Typology and Allegory: A Comparative Study of George Herbert and Edward Taylor." *EL* 2(1975): 76-86.

12256. Smithson, Bill. "Herbert's 'Affliction' Poems." *SEL* 15(1975): 125-140.

12257. Stanford, Donald E. "The Imagination of Death in the Poetry of Philip Pain, Edward Taylor, and George Herbert." *SLI* 9,#2 (1976): 53-67.

12258. Stewart, Stanley. "Time and *The Temple*." *SEL* 6(1966): 97-110.

12259. Story, G. M. "George Herbert's *Inventa Bellica*: A New Manuscript." *MP* 59(1962): 270-272.

12260. Strier, Richard. "'Humanizing' Herbert." *MP* 74(1976): 78-88.

12261. Stroup, Thomas B. "'A Reasonable, Holy, and Living Sacrifice': Herbert's 'The Altar.'" *EL* 2(1975): 149-163.

12262. Summers, Joseph H. "Herbert's Form." *PMLA* 66(1951): 1055-1072.

12263. von Ende, Frederick. "George Herbert's 'The Sonne': In Defense of the English Language." *SEL* 12(1972): 173-182.

12264. Walker, John David. "The Architectonics of George Herbert's *The Temple*." *ELH* 29 (1962): 289-305.

12265. West, Michael. "Ecclestical Controversy in George Herbert's 'Peace.'" *RES* 22 (1971): 445-451.

12266. Williams, R. Darby. "Two Baroque Game Poems on Grace Herbert's 'Paradise' and Milton's 'On Time.'" *Criticism* 12(1970): 180-194.

12267. Williamson, Karina. "Herbert's Reputation in the Eighteenth Century." *PQ* 41 (1962): 769-775.

12268. Wolfe, Jane E. "George Herbert's 'Assurance.'" *CLA* 5(1962): 213-222.

See also 11419, 11441.

HERRICK, ROBERT.   12269. Asals, Heather. "King Solomon in the Land of the *Hesperides*." *TSLL* 18(1976): 362-380.

12270. Bache, William B. "Experiment with a Poem." *Coll L* 1(1974): 65-67.

12271. Cain, T. G. S. "The Bell/White MS."

ELR 2(1972): 260-270.

12272. Chambers, A. B. "Herrick and the Trans-shifting of Time." *SP* 72(1975): 85-114.

12273. ----------. "Herrick, Corinna, Canticles, and Catallus." *SP* 74(1977): 216-227.

12274. Crum, Margaret. "An Unpublished Fragment of Verse by Herrick." *RES* 11(1960): 186-189.

12275. Deming, Robert H. "Herrick's Funeral Poems." *SEL* 9(1969): 153-167.

12276. ----------. "Robert Herrick's Classical Ceremony." *ELH* 34(1967): 327-348.

12277. Glaser, Joseph A. "Recent Herrick Criticism: Sighting in on One of the Most Elusive of Poets." *CLA* 20(1976): 292-302.

12278. Godshalk, William Leigh. "Art and Nature: Herrick and History." *EIC* 17(1967): 121-124.

12279. Hageman, Elizabeth H. "Recent Studies in Herrick." *ELR* 3(1973): 462-471.

12280. Heinemann, Alison. "*Balme* in Herrick's 'A Meditation for His Mistresse.'" *ELN* 8(1971): 176-180.

12281. Höltgen, Karl Josef. "Herrick, the Wheeler Family, and Quarles." *RES* 16(1965): 399-405.

12282. Jenkins, Paul R. "Rethinking What Moderation Means to Robert Herrick." *ELH* 39(1972): 49-65.

12283. Kimmey, John. "Order and Form in Herrick's *Hesperides*." *JEGP* 70(1971): 255-268.

12284. ----------. "Robert Herrick's Persona." *SP* 67(1970): 221-236.

12285. Marcus, Leah Sinanoglou. "Herrick's *Noble Numbers* and the Politics of Playfulness." *ELR* 7(1977): 108-126.

12286. Reed, Mark L. "Herrick Among the Maypoles: Dean Prior and the Hesperides." *SEL* 5 (1965): 133-150.

12287. Ross, Richard J. "Herrick's Julia in Silks." *EIC* 15(1965): 171-180.

12288. Schleiner, R. Louise. "Herrick's Songs and the Character of *Hesperides*." *ELR* 6 (1976): 77-91.

12289. Whitaker, Thomas R. "Herrick and the Fruits of the Garden." *ELH* 22(1955): 16-33.

12290. Woodward, Daniel H. "Herrick's Oberon Poems." *JEGP* 64(1965): 270-284.

See also 9291, 9457, 9463, 11431.

HEYWOOD, THOMAS.   12291. Belton, Ellen R. "'A Plaine and Direct Course': The Unity of Thomas Heywood's *Ages*." *PQ* 56(1977): 169-182.

12292. Berry, Lloyd E. "A Note on Heywood's 'A Woman Killed with Kindness.'" *MLR* 58(1963): 64-65.

12293. Brown, Arthur. "Two Notes on Thomas Heywood." *MLR* 50(1955): 497-498.

12294. Canuteson, John. "The Theme of Forgiveness in the Plot and Subplot of *A Woman Killed with Kindness*." *RD* n.s. 2(1969): 123-141.

12295. Coursen, Herbert R., Jr. "The Subplot of *A Woman Killed with Kindness*." *ELN* 2(1965): 180-185.

12296. Holaday, Allan. "Thomas Heywood and the Puritans." *JEGP* 49(1950): 192-203.

12297. Hooper, Gifford. "Heywood's *A Woman Killed with Kindness* Scene XIV: Sir Charles's Plan." *ELN* 11(1974): 181-188.

12298. Janzen, Henry D. "A Note on the

Authorship of *The Escapes of Jupiter*." *ELN* 10 (1973): 270-273.

12299. Patrides, C. A. "Thomas Heywood and Literary Piracy." *PQ* 39(1960): 118-122.

12300. Prager, Carolyn. "Heywood's **Adaptation of Plautus'** *Rudens*: The Problem of Slavery in *The Captives*." *CD* 9(1975): 116-124.

12301. Rabkin, Norman. "Dramatic Deception in Heywood's *The English Traveller*." *SEL* 1,#2 (1961): 3-16.

12302. Reeves, John D. "Perseus and the Flying Horse in Peele and Heywood." *RES* 6(1955): 397-399.

12303. Schanzer, Ernest. "Heywood's *Ages* and Shakespeare." *RES* 11(1960): 18-28.

12304. Spacks, Patricia Meyers. "Honor and Perception in *A Woman Killed with Kindness*." *MLQ* 20(1959): 321-332.

See aslo 7787, 9371, 9389, 9407, 9418, 11297, 11374.

HICKES, WILLIAM. 12305. Smith, Courtney Craig. "William Hickes, Compiler of Drolleries." *MLQ* 12(1951): 259-266.

HOBBES, THOMAS. 12306. Alexander, Richard W. "The Myth of Power: Hobbes *Leviathan*." *JEGP* 70(1971): 31-50.

12307. Cope, Jackson I. "Dryden vs. Hobbes: An Adaptation from the Platonists." *JEGP* 57(1958): 444-448.

12308. Dodd, Mary C. "The Rhetorics in Molesworth's Edition of Hobbes." *MP* 50(1952): 36-42.

12309. Henry, Nathaniel H. "Milton and Hobbes: Mortalism and the Intermediate State." *SP* 48(1951): 234-249.

12310. Hinnant, Charles H. "Hobbes on Fancy and Judgment." *Criticism* 18(1976): 15-26.

12311, Pinto, V. de S. "Was Hobbes an Ogre?" *EIC* 7(1957): 22-27.

12312. Wikelund, Philip R. "'Thus I Passe my Time in This Place': An Unpublished Letter of Thomas Hobbes." *ELN* 6(1969): 263-268.

See also 12119, 15189.

HOWARD, JAMES. 12313. Hume, Robert D. "Dryden, James Howard, and the Date of *All Mistaken*." *PQ* 51(1972): 422-429.

12314. Spencer, Christopher. "'Count Paris's Wife': *Romeo and Juliet* on the Early Restoration Stage." *TSLL* 7(1965): 309-316.

See also 11388.

HOWARD, ROBERT. 12315. Roscioni, Gian Carlo. "Sir Robert Howard's 'Sceptical Curiosity.'" *MP* 65 (1967): 53-59.

12316. Smith, John Harrington. "The Dryden-Howard Collaboration." *SP* 51(1954): 54-74.

HOWELL, JAMES. 12317. Hirst, Verona M. "The Authenticity of James Howell's Familiar Letters." *MLR* 54(1959): 558-561.

See also 9479.

JAMES I. 12318. Dunlap, Rhodes. "King James and Some Witches: The Date and Text of the *Daemonologie*." *PQ* 54(1975): 40-46.

12319. ----------. "King James's Own Masque." *PQ* 41(1962): 249-256.

See also 9450.

JONES, INIGO. 12320. Orgel, Stephen. "To Make Boards to Speak: Inigo Jones's Stage and the Jonsonian Masque." *RD* n.s. 1(1968): 121-152.

JONSON, BEN.   12321. Anderson, Mark A. "The Successful Unity of *Epicoene*: A Defense of Ben Jonson." *SEL* 10(1970): 349-366.

12322. Arnold, Judd. "Lovewit's Triumph and Jonsonian Morality: A Reading of *The Alchemist*." *Criticism* 11(1969): 151-166.

12323. Babb, Howard S. "The 'Epitaph on Elizabeth, L. H.' and Ben Jonson's Style." *JEGP* 62(1963): 738-744.

12324. Barish, Jonas A. "Baroque Prose in the Theater: Ben Jonson." *PMLA* 73(1958): 184-195.

12325. ----------. "*Bartholomew Fair* and Its Puppets." *MLQ* 20(1959): 3-17.

12326. ----------. "The Double Plot in *Volpone*." *MP* 51(1953): 83-92.

12327. ----------. "Feasting and Judging in Jonsonian Comedy." *RD* n.s. 5(1972): 3-35.

12328. ----------. "Ovid, Juvenal, and *The Silent Woman*." *PMLA* 71(1956): 213-224.

12329. Beaurline, L. A. "Ben Jonson and the Illusion of Completeness." *PMLA* 84(1969): 51-59.

12330. ----------. "The Selective Principle in Jonson's Shorter Poems." *Criticism* 8 (1966): 64-74.

12331. ----------. "Volpone and the Power of Gorgeous Speech." *SLI* 6,#1(1973): 61-75.

12332. Blanshard, Rufus A. "Carew and Jonson." *SP* 52(1955): 195-211.

12333. Blissett, William. "The Venter Tripartite in *The Alchemist*." *SEL* 8(1968): 323-334.

12334. Borroff, Marie. "The Triumph of Charis: Through *Swards*, not *Swords*." *ELN* 8(1971): 257-259.

12335. Boughner, Daniel C. "Sejanus and Machiavelli." *SEL* 1,#2(1961): 81-100.

12336. Bradbrook, M. C. "Social Change and the Evolution of Ben Jonson's Court Masques." *SLI* 6,#1(1973): 101-138.

12337. Bryant, Joseph Allen, Jr. "*Catiline* and the Nature of Jonson's Tragic Fable." *PMLA* 69 (1954): 265-277.

12338. ----------. "Jonson's Revision of *Every Man in His Humor*." *SP* 59(1962): 641-650.

12339. ----------. "The Significance of Ben Jonson's First Requirement for Tragedy: 'Truth of Argument.'" *SP* 49(1952): 195-213.

12340. Burton, K. M. "The Political Tragedies of Chapman and Ben Jonson." *EIC* 2(1952): 397-412.

12341. Carlson, Peter. "Judging Spectators." *ELH* 44(1977): 443-457.

12342. Clary, Frank N., Jr. "The Vol and the Pone: A Reconsideration of Jonson's Volpone." *ELN* 10(1972): 102-107.

12343. Clubb, Roger L. "The Paradox of Ben Jonson's 'A Fit of Rime against Rime.'" *CLA* 5(1961): 145-147.

12344. Colley, John Scott. "*Bartholomew Fair*: Ben Jonson's 'A Midsummer Night's Dream.'" *CD* 11(1977): 63-71.

12345. Cope, Jackson I. "*Bartholomew Fair* as Blasphemy." *RD* 8(1965): 127-152.

12346. Creaser, John. "The Popularity of Jonson's Tortoise." *RES* 27(1976): 38-46.

12347. ----------. "*Volpone*: The Mortifying of the Fox." *EIC* 25(1975): 329-356.

12348. ----------. "Volpone's Mortification." *EIC* 26(1976): 277-278.

12349. Cubeta, Paul M. "'A Celebration of Charis': An Evaluation of Jonsonian Poetic Strategy." *ELH* 25(1958): 163-180.

12350. ----------. "A Jonsonian Ideal: 'To Penshurst.'" *PQ* 42(1963): 14-24.

12351. ----------. "Ben Jonson's Religious Lyrics." *JEGP* 62(1963): 96-110.

12352. Cunningham, Delora. "The Jonsonian Masque as a Literary Form." *ELH* 22(1955): 108-124.

12353. Cutts, John P. "Seventeenth-Century Illustrations of Three Masques by Jonson." *CD* 6 (1972): 125-134.

12354. ----------. "'When were the *senses* in such order plac'd?'" *CD* 4(1970): 52-62.

12355. Davis, Tom. "Ben Jonson's Ode to Himself: An Early Version." *PQ* 51(1972): 410-421.

12356. Davison, P. H. "*Volpone* and the Old Comedy." *MLQ* 24(1963): 151-157.

12357. Dean, Leonard F. "Three Notes on Comic Morality: Celia, Bobadill, and Falstaff." *SEL* 16(1976): 263-271.

12358. Dessen, Alan C. "*The Alchemist*: Jonson's 'Estates' Play." *RD* 7(1964): 33-54.

12359. ----------. "Jonson's 'Knaue of Clubs' and 'The Play of the Cards.'" *MLR* 62(1967): 584-585.

12360. ----------. "*Volpone* and the Late Morality Tradition." *MLQ* 25(1964): 383-399.

12361. Donaldson, Ian. "Jonson's Ode to Sir Lucius Cary and Sir H. Morison." *SLI* 6,#1 (1973): 139-152.

12362. ----------. "Jonson's Tortoise." *RES* 19(1968): 162-166.

12363. ----------. "'A Martyrs Resolution': Jonson's *Epicoene*." *RES* 18(1967): 1-15.

12364. ----------. "Volpone." *EIC* 22(1972): 216-218.

12365. "*Volpone*—Quick and Dead." *EIC* 21 (1971): 121-134.

12366. Dorenkamp, Angela G. "Jonson's *Catiline*: History as the Trying Faculty." *SP* 67 (1970): 210-220.

12367. Duncan, Douglas. "A Guide to *The New Inn*." *EIC* 20(1970): 311-326.

12368. Dutton, A. Richard. "The Significance of Jonson's Revision of 'Every Man in his Humour.'" *MLR* 69(1974): 241-249.

12369. Earley, Robert. "Sir Luckless Woo-All's 'Wast Wife' and the *OED* (Jonson's *Epigramme* XLVI)." *ELN* 12(1975): 265-268.

12370. Echeruo, Michael J. C. "The Conscience of Politics and Jonson's *Catiline*." *SEL* 6(1966): 341-356.

12371. Enck, John Jacob. "*The Case Is Altered*: Initial Comedy of Humors." *SP* 50(1953): 195-214.

12372. ----------. "The Peace of the Poetomachia." *PMLA* 77(1962): 386-396.

12373. Evans, K. W. "*Sejanus* and the Ideal Prince Tradition." *SEL* 11(1971): 249-264.

12374. Ferns, John. "Ovid, Juvenal, and 'The Silent Woman': A Reconsideration." *MLR* 65 (1970): 248-253.

12375. Fetrow, Fred M. "Disclaimers Reclaimed: A Consideration of Jonson's Praise of Shakespeare." *EL* 2(1975): 24-31.

12376. Fischer, Jeffrey. "*Love Restored*: A Defense of Masquing." *RD* n.s. 8(1977): 231-244.

12377. Fitton Brown, A. D. "Drink to me, Celia." *MLR* 54(1959): 554-557.

12378. Flachmann, Michael. "Ben Jonson and the Alchemy of Satire." *SEL* 17(1977): 259-280.

12379. Fowler, Alastair. "The 'Better Marks' of Jonson's *To Penshurst*." *RES* 24(1973): 266-282.

12380. Fraser, Russell. "Elizabethan Drama and the Art of Abstraction." *CD* 2(1968): 73-82.

12381. Freidberg, Harris. "Ben Jonson's Poetry: Pastoral, Georgie, Epigram." *ELR* 4 (1974): 111-136.

12382. French, John Thatcher. "Ben Jonson: His Aesthetic of Relief." *TSLL* 10(1968): 161-175.

12383. Furniss, W. Todd. "The Annotation of Ben Jonson's *Masque of Queens*." *RES* 5(1954): 344-360.

12384. Gardiner, Judith K., and Susanna S. Epp. "Ben Jonson's Social Attitudes: A Statistical Analysis." *CD* 9(1975): 68-86.

12385. Gertmenian, Donald. "Comic Experience in *Volpone* and *The Alchemist*." *SEL* 17 (1977): 247-258.

12386. ----------. "Volpone's Mortification." *EIC* 26(1976): 274-277.

12387. Gianakaras, C. J. "Jonson's Use of 'Avocatori' in *Volpone*." *ELN* 12(1974): 8-15.

12388. ----------. "The Humanism of Ben Jonson." *CLA* 14(1970): 115-126.

12389. Goldberg, S. L. "Folly into Crime: The Catastrophe of *Volpone*." *MLQ* 20(1959): 233-242.

12390. Graziani, R. I. C. "Ben Jonson's *Chlorida*: Fame and Her Attendants." *RES* 7(1956): 56-58.

12391. Greenblatt, Stephen J. "The False Ending in *Volpone*." *JEGP* 75(1976): 90-104.

12392. Greene, Thomas M. "Ben Jonson and the Centered Self." *SEL* 10(1970): 325-348.

12393. Hallett, Charles A. "Jonson's Celia: A Reinterpretation of *Volpone*." *SP* 68(1971): 50-69.

12394. ----------. "The Satanic Nature of Volpone." *PQ* 49(1970): 41-55.

12395. Hamilton, Gary D. "Irony and Fortune in Sejanus." *SEL* 11(1971): 265-281.

12396. Hawkins, Harriett B. "Folly, Incurable Disease, and *Volpone*." *SEL* 8(1968): 335-348.

12397. ----------. "Jonson's Use of Traditional Dream Theory in *The Vision of Delight*." *MP* 64(1967): 285-292.

12398. ----------. "The Idea of a Theater in Jonson's *The New Inn*." *RD* 9(1966): 205-226.

12399. Hedrick, Don K. "Cooking for the Anthropophagi: Jonson and His Audience." *SEL* 17 (1977): 233-245.

12400. Hill, W. Speed. "Biography, Autobiography, and *Volpone*." *SEL* 12(1972): 309-328.

12401. Honig, Edwin. "*Sejanus* and *Coriolanus*: A Study in Alienation." *MLQ* 12(1951): 407-421.

12402. Holleran, James V. "Character Transmutation in *The Alchemist*." *CLA* 11(1968): 221-227.

12403. Horwich, Richard. "*Hamlet* and *Eastward Ho*." *SEL* 11(1971): 223-233.

12404. Huntley, Frank L. "Ben Jonson and Anthony Munday, or, *The Case is Altered* Again." *PQ* 41(1962): 205-215.

12405. Hutchinson, Barbara. "Ben Jonson's 'Let Me Be What I Am': an Apology in Disguise." *ELN* 2(1965): 185-190.

12406. John, Lisle Cecil. "Ben Jonson's 'To Sir William Sidney, on his Birthday.'" *MLR* 52 (1957): 168-176.

12407. Johnson, Paula. "Jacobean Ephemera and the Immortal World." *RD* n.s. 8(1977): 151-171.

12408. Johnston, George Burke. "Jonson's 'Perseus upon Pegasus.'" *RES* 6(1955): 65-67.

12409. Jones, Robert C. "The Satirist's Retirement in Jonson's 'Apologetical Dialogue.'" *ELH* 34(1967): 447-467.

12410. Kaplan, Joel H. "Dramatic and Moral Energy in Ben Jonson's *Bartholomew Fair*." *RD* n.s. 3(1970): 137-156.

12411. Kay, W. David. "*Bartholomew Fair*: Ben Jonson in Praise of Folly." *ELR* 6(1976): 299-316.

12412. ----------. "The Christian Wisdom of Ben Jonson's 'On My First Sonne.'" *SEL* 11 (1971): 125-136.

12413. ----------. "The Shaping of Ben Jonson's Career: A Reexamination of Facts and Problems." *MP* 67(1970): 224-237.

12414. Kelley, Ann Cline. "The Challenge of the Impossible: Ben Jonson's *Masque of Blackness*." *CLA* 20(1977): 341-355.

12415. Kernan, Alvin B. "Alchemy and Acting: The Major Plays of Ben Jonson." *SLI* 6,#1 (1973): 1-22.

12416. Kerrigan, William. "Ben Jonson Full of Shame and Scorn." *SLI* 6,#1(1973): 199-217.

12417. Kiefer, Frederick. "Pretense in Ben Jonson's *Sejanus*." *EL* 4(1977): 19-26.

12418. Kifer, Devra Rowland. "*The Staple of News*: Jonson's Festive Comedy." *SEL* 12(1972): 329-344.

12419. ----------. "Too Many Cookes: An Addition to the Printed Text of Jonson's *Staple of News*." *ELN* 11(1974): 264-271.

12420. LeClercq, R. V. "The Reciprocal Harmony of Jonson's 'A Celebration of Charis.'" *TSLL* 16(1975): 627-650.

12421. Lemly, John. "Masks and Self-Portraits in Jonson's Late Poetry." *ELH* 44(1977): 248-266.

12422. Levin, Lawrence L. "Clement Justice in *Every Man in His Humor*." *SEL* 12(1972): 291-307.

12423. ----------. "Replication as Dramatic Strategy in the Comedies of Ben Jonson." *RD* n.s. 5(1972): 37-74.

12424. Levin, Richard. "'The Ass in Compound': A Lost Pun in Middleton, Ford, and Jonson." *ELN* 4(1966): 12-15.

12425. ----------. "'No Laughing Matter': Some New Readings of *The Alchemist*." *SLI* 6,#1 (1973): 85-99.

12426. ----------. "The New *New Inn* and the Proliferation of Good Bad Drama." *EIC* 22(1972): 41-47.

12427. ----------. "*The Staple of News*, The Society of Jeerers, and Canters' College." *PQ* 44(1965): 445-453.

12428. ----------. "The Structure of *Bartholomew Fair*." *PMLA* 80(1965): 172-179.

12429. Livingston, Mary L. "Ben Jonson: The Poet to the Painter." *TSLL* 18(1976): 381-392.

12430. Major, John M. "A Reading of Jonson's 'Epitaph on Elizabeth, L. H.'" *SP* 73 (1976): 62-86.

12431. Marotti, Arthur F. "All About Jonson's Poetry." *ELH* 39(1972): 208-237.

12432. ----------. "The Self-Reflexive Art of Ben Jonson's *Sejanus*." *TSLL* 12(1970): 197-220.

12433. McCanles, Michael. "Festival in Jonsonian Comedy." *RD* n.s. 8(1977): 203-219.

12434. McFarland, Ronald E. "Jonson's *Magnetic Lady* and the Reception of Gilbert's *De Magnete*." *SEL* 11(1971): 283-293.

12435. McMillin, Scott. "Jonson's Early Entertainments: New Information from Hatfield House." *RD* n.s. 1(1968): 153-166.

12436. McPherson, David. "Ben Jonson Meets Daniel Heinsius, 1613." *ELN* 14(1976): 105-109.

12437. ----------. "*Ben Jonson's Library and Marginalia*." *SP* 71,#5(1971): 3-106.

12438. ----------. "The Origins of Overdo: A Study in Jonsonian Invention." *MLQ* 37(1976): 221-233.

12439. ----------. "Rough Beast into Tame Fox: The Adaptations of Volpone." *SLI* 6,#1 (1973): 77-84.

12440. ----------. "Some Renaissance Sources for Jonson's Early Comic Theory." *ELN* 8 (1971): 180-182.

12441. Medine, Peter E. "Object and Intent in Jonson's 'Famous Voyage.'" *SEL* 15(1975): 97-110.

12442. Miskimin, Alice S. "Ben Jonson and Captain Cox: Elizabethan Gothic Reconsidered." *RD* n.s. 8(1977): 173-202.

12443. Mortimer, Anthony. "The Feigned Commonwealth in the Poetry of Ben Jonson." *SEL* 13(1973): 69-79.

12444. Nash, Ralph. "Ben Jonson's Tragic Poems." *SP* 55(1958): 164-186.

12445. ----------. "The Parting Scene in Jonson's *Poetaster*(IV, ix)." *PQ* 31(1952): 54-62.

12446. Newton, Richard C. "'Goe, quit'hem all': Ben Jonson and Formal Verse Satire." *SEL* 16(1976): 105-116.

12447. Nosworthy, J. M. "*The Case is Altered*." *JEGP* 51(1952): 61-70.

12448. Olive, W. F. "A Chance Allusion in Jonsons' *Bartholomew Fair*." *MLQ* 13(1952): 21-22.

12449. Orgel, Stephen. "To Make Boards to Speak: Inigo Jones's Stage and the Jonsonian Masque." *RD* n.s. 1(1968): 121-152.

12450. Parfitt, George A. E. "Compromise Classicism: Language and Rhythm in Ben Jonson's Poetry." *SEL* 11(1971): 109-123.

12451. ----------. "Ethical Thought and Ben Jonson's Poetry." *SEL* 9(1969): 123-134.

12452. ----------. "The Nature of Translation in Ben Jonson's Poetry." *SEL* 13(1973): 344-359.

12453. ----------. "The Poetry of Ben Jonson." *EIC* 18(1968): 18-31.

12454. ----------. "Virtue and Pessimism in Three Plays by Ben Jonson." *SLI* 6,#1(1973):

23-40.

12455. ----------. "Volpone." *EIC* 21(1971): 411-412.

12456. Parker, R. B. "*Volpone* and *Reynard the Fox*." *RD* n.s. 7(1976): 3-42.

12457. Partridge, Edward B. "The Allusiveness of *Epicoene*." *ELH* 22(1955): 93-107.

12458. ----------. "Jonson's *Epigrammes*: The Named and the Nameless." *SLI* 6,#1(1973): 153-198.

12459. ----------. "The Symbolism of Clothes in Jonson's Last Plays." *JEGP* 56(1957): 396-409.

12460. Paster, Gail Kern. "Ben Jonson's Comedy of Limitation." *SP* 72(1975): 51-71.

12461. Peterson, Richard S. "Virtue Reconciled to Pleasure: Jonson's 'A Celebration of Charis.'" *SLI* 6,#1(1973): 219-268.

12462. Potter, John M. "Old Comedy in *Bartholomew Fair*." *Criticism* 10(1968): 290-299.

12463. Putney, Rufus. "Jonson's Poetic Comedy." *PQ* 41(1962): 188-204.

12465. Rackin, Phyllis. "Poetry Without Paradox: Jonson's 'Hymne' to Cynthia." *Criticism* 4(1962): 197-209.

12466. Rathwell, J. C. A. "Jonson, Lord Lisle, and Penshurst." *ELR* 1(1971): 250-260.

12467. Redwine, James D., Jr. "Beyond Psychology: The Moral Basis of Jonson's Theory of Humour Characterization." *ELH* 28(1961): 316-334.

12468. Ribeiro, Alvaro. "Sir John Roe: Ben Jonson's Friend." *RES* 24(1973): 153-164.

12469. Robinson, James E. "*Bartholomew Fair*: Comedy of Vapors." *SEL* 1,#2(1961): 65-80.

12470. Scheve, D. A. "Jonson's *Volpone* and Traditional Fox Lore." *RES* 1(1950): 242-244.

12471. Seronsy, Cecil C. "Sir Politic Would-Be in Laputa." *ELN* 1(1963): 17-24.

12472. Shapiro, Michael. "Audience vs. Dramatist in Jonson's *Epicoene* and Other Plays of the Children's Troupes." *ELR* 3(1973): 400-417.

12473. Simmons, J. L. "Volpone as Antinous: Jonson and 'Th' Overthrow of Stage-Plays.'" *MLR* 70(1975): 13-19.

12474. Simpson, Percy. "Francis Beaumont's Verse-Letter to Ben Jonson: 'The Sun, Which Doth the Greatest Comfort Bring. . . .'" *MLR* 46(1951): 435-436.

12475. Sirluck, Ernest. "Shakespeare and Jonson Among the Pamphleteers of the First Civil War: Some Unreported Seventeenth-Century Allusions." *MP* 53(1955): 88-99.

12476. Slights, William W. E. "*Epicoene* and the Prose Paradox." *PQ* 49(1970): 178-187.

12477. Smith, Bruce R. "Ben Jonson's *Epigrammes*: Portrait-Gallery, Theater, Commonwealth." *SEL* 14(1974): 91-109.

12478. Spanos, William V. "The Real Toad in Jonsonian Garden: Resonance in the Nondramatic Poetry." *JEGP* 68(1969): 1-23.

12479. Soufos, Alice Lyle. "Nashe, Jonson, and the Oldcastle Problem." *MP* 65(1968): 307-324.

12480. South, Malcolm H. "The 'Vncleane Birds, in Seuenty-Seuen': *The Alchemist*." *SEL* 13(1973): 331-343.

12481. Stein, Arnold. "Plain Style, Plain Criticism, Plain Dealing, and Ben Jonson." *ELH* 30(1963): 306-316.

12482. Thayer, C. G. "Theme and Structure in *The Alchemist*." *ELH* 26(1959): 23-35.

12483. Thron, E. M. "Jonson's *Cynthia's Revels*: Multiplicity and Unity." *SEL* 11(1971): 235-247.

12484. Trimpi, Wesley. "Jonson and the Neo-Latin Authorities for the Plain Style." *PMLA* 77(1962): 21-26.

12485. Vawter, Marvin L. "The Seeds of Virtue: Political Imperatives in Jonson's *Sejanus*." *SLI* 6,#1(1973): 41-60.

12486. Van Der Berg, Sara. "The Play of Wit and Love: Demetrius' *On Style* and Jonson's 'A Celebration of Charis.'" *ELH* 41(1974): 26-36.

12487. Van Deusen, Marshall. "Criticism and Ben Jonson's 'To Celia.'" *EIC* 7(1957): 95-103.

12488. Waith, Eugene M. "The Poet's Morals in Jonson's *Poetaster*." *MLQ* 12(1951): 13-19.

12489. ----------. "Spectacles of State." *SEL* 13(1973): 317-330.

12490. ----------. "The Staging of *Bartholomew Fair*." *SEL* 2(1962): 181-195.

12491. Warren, Michael J. "The Location of Jonson's *Catiline* III. 490-754." *PQ* 48(1969): 561-565.

12492. Weld, John S. "Christian Comedy: *Volpone*." *SP* 51(1954): 172-193.

12493. Williams, Mary C. "Ben Jonson's 'Apology' for *Bartholomew Fair*." *ELN* 10(1973): 180-185.

12494. ----------. "*Merlin and the Prince*: The Speeches at Prince Henry's Barriers." *RD* n.s. 8(1977): 221-230.

12495. Wilson, Gayle Edward. "Jonson's Use of the Bible and the Great Chain of Being in 'To Penshurst.'" *SEL* 8(1968): 77-89.

12496. Young, R. V., Jr. "Style and Structure in Jonson's Epigrams." *Criticism* 17(1975): 210-222.

See also 24, 935, 5105, 9291, 9302, 9346, 9363, 9385, 9389, 9402, 9463, 9942, 11348, 11361, 11369, 11385, 11410, 11419, 11425, 11430, 11431, 11447, 11491.

KILLIGREW, WILLIAM. 12497. Johnston, Joseph S., Jr. "Sir William Killigrew's Revised Copy of His *Four New Plays*: Confirmation of His Claim to *The Imperial Tragedy*." *MP* 74(1976): 72-74.

12498. Keast, William R. "Killigrew's Use of Donne in 'The Parson's Wedding.'" *MLR* 45(1950): 512-515.

KING, HENRY. 12499. Clark, Roger G. "Henry King and the Rise of Modern Prose Style." *JEGP* 74(1975): 172-182.

12500. Low, Anthony. "A Metrical Device in 'The Exequy.'" *MLR* 63(1968): 7-12.

See also 11441.

LEANERD, JOHN. See 13573.

LEE, HENRY. 12501. Clayton, Thomas. "'Sir Henry Lee's Farewell to the Court': The Texts and Authorship of 'His Golden Locks Time Hath to Silver Turned.'" *ELR* 4(1974): 268-275.

LEE, NATHANIEL. 12502. Armistead, J. M. "Lee, Renaissance Conventions, and the Psychology of Providence: The Design of *Caesar Borgia*." *EL* 4(1977): 159-173.

12503. Bachorik, Lawrence L. "*The Duke of Guise* and Dryden's *Vindication*: A New Consideration." *ELN* 10(1973): 208-212.

12504. Cooke, A. L., and Thomas B. Stroup. "The Political Implications in Lee's *Constantine the Great*." *JEGP* 49(1950): 506-515.

12505. Hume, Robert D. "The Satiric Design of Nat. Lee's *The Princess of Cleve*." *JEGP* 75(1976): 117-138.

LLEWELLYN, MARTIN. 12506. Cutts, John P. "The Dramatic Writing of Martin Llewellyn." *PQ* 47(1968): 16-29.

LOCKE, JOHN. 12507. Brown, F. Andrew. "German Interest in John Locke's *Essay*, 1688-1800." *JEGP* 50(1951): 466-482.

12508. Colie, Rosalie L. "John Locke and the Publication of the Private." *PQ* 45(1966): 24-47.

12509. Maskell, Duke. "Locke and Sterne; or Can Philosophy Influence Literature." *EIC* 23 (1973): 22-39.

12510. Tuveson, Ernest. "Locke and the 'Dissolution of the Ego.'" *MP* 52(1955): 159-174.

LOVEDAY, ROBERT. 12511. Huntley, Frank Livingstone. "Robert Loveday: Commonwealth Man of Letters." *RES* 2(1951): 262-267.

LOVELACE, RICHARD. 12512. Allen, Don Cameron. "An Explication of Lovelace's 'The Grasse-hopper.'" *MLQ* 18(1957): 35-43.

12513. Anselment, Raymond A. "'Griefe Triumphant' and 'Victorious Sorrow': A Reading of Richard Lovelace's 'The Falcon.'" *JEGP* 70 (1971): 404-417.

12514. Duncan-Jones, E. E. "Two Allusions in Lovelace's Poems." *MLR* 51(1956): 407-409.

12515. Jones, George Fenwick. "Lov'd I Not Honour More: The Durability of a Literary Motif." *Comp L* 11(1959): 131-143.

12516. Palmer, Pauline. "Lovelace's Treatment of Some Marinesque Motifs." *Comp L* 29 (1977): 300-312.

12517. Wadsworth, Randolph L., Jr. "On 'The Snayl' by Richard Lovelace." *MLR* 65(1970): 750-760.

12518. Williamson, C. F. "Two Notes on the Poems of Richard Lovelace." *MLR* 52(1957): 227-229.

See also 11424.

LUKE, JOHN. 12519. Kaufman, Paul. "Spanish Players at Tangier: A New Chapter in Stage History." *Comp L* 12(1960): 125-132.

MARSTON, JOHN. 12520. Berland, Ellen. "The Function of Irony in Marston's *Antonio and Mellida*." *SP* 66(1969): 739-755.

12521. Ayres, Philip J. "Marston's *Antonio's Revenge*: The Morality of the Revenging Hero." *SEL* 12(1972): 359-374.

12522. Bergson, Allen. "Dramatic Style as Parody in Marston's *Antonio and Mellida*." *SEL* 11(1971): 307-325.

12523. ----------. "The Ironic Tragedies of Marston and Chapman: Notes on Jacobean Tragic Form." *JEGP* 69(1970): 613-630.

12524. Brettle, R. E. "Everard Guilpin and John Marston (1576-1634)." *RES* 16(1965): 396-399.

12525. ----------. "Notes on John Marston." *RES* 13(1962): 390-393.

12526. Colley, John Scott. "'Opinion' and the Reader in John Marston's *The Metamorphosis of Pigmalions Image*." *ELR* 3(1973): 221-231.

12527. Cross, K. Gustav. "The Authorship of 'Lust's Dominion.'" *SP* 55(1958): 39-61.

12528. ----------. "The Date of *The Malcontent* Once More." *PQ* 39(1960): 104-113.

12529. ----------. "Marston, Montaigne, and Morality: *The Dutch Courtesan*." *ELH* 27 (1960): 30-43.

12530. ----------. "An Unrecognized Poem by John Marston?" *MLQ* 19(1958): 325-330.

12531. Davis, Gilbert R. "The Characterization of Mamon in *Jack Drum's Entertainment*." *ELN* 3(1965): 22-24.

12532. Finkelpearl, Philip J. "From Petrarch to Ovid: Metamorphoses in John Marston's *Metamorphosis of Pygmalions Image*." *ELH* 32 (1965): 333-348.

12533. ----------. "The Use of the Middle Temple's Christmas Revels in Marston's *The Fawne*." *SP* 64(1967): 199-209.

12534. Foakes, R. A. "John Marston's Fantastical Plays: *Antonio and Mellida* and *Antonio's Revenge*." *PQ* 41(1962): 229-239.

12535. Geckle, George L. "*Antonio's Revenge*: 'Never more woe in lesser plot was found.'" *CD* 6(1972): 323-335.

12536. ----------. "Fortune in Marston's *The Malcontent*." *PMLA* 86(1971): 202-209.

12537. ----------. "John Marston's *Histriomastix* and the Golden Age." *CD* 6(1972): 205-222.

12538. Gill, R. B. "A Purchase of Glory: The Persona of Late Elizabethan Satire." *SP* 72 (1975): 408-438.

12539. Gunby, D. C. "Marston, Mecho, and Supererogation." *ELN* 14(1976): 98-99.

12540. Hamilton, Donna B. "Language as Theme in *The Dutch Courtesan*." *RD* n.s. 5(1972): 75-87.

12541. Houser, David J. "Purging the Commonwealth: Marston's Disguised Dukes and *A Knack to Know a Knave*." *PMLA* 89(1974): 993-1006.

12542. Jackson, James L. "Sources of the Subplot of Marston's *The Dutch Courtezan*." *PQ* 31 (1952): 223-224.

12543. Jensen, Ejner J. "Theme and Imagery in *The Malcontent*." *SEL* 10(1970): 367-384.

12544. Kaplan, Joel. "John Marston's *Fawn*: A Saturnalian Satire." *SEL* 9(1969): 335-350.

12545. Kernan, Alvin. "John Marston's Play *Histriomastix*." *MLQ* 19(1958): 134-140.

12546. Keyishian, Harry. "Dekker's *Whore* and Marston's *Courtesan*." *ELN* 4(1967): 261-266.

12547. Kiefer, Christian. "Music and Marston's *The Malcontent*." *SP* 51(1954): 163-171.

12548. McGrath, Lynette. "John Marston's Mismanaged Irony: The Poetic Satires." *TSLL* 18 (1976): 393-408.

12549. McNeir, Waldo F. "Marston versus Davies and Terpsichore." *PQ* 29(1950): 430-434.

12550. O'Connor, John J. "The Chief Source of Marston's *Dutch Courtezan*." *SP* 54(1957): 509-515.

12551. O'Neill, David G. "The Commencement of Marston's Career as a Dramatist." *RES* 22 (1971): 442-445.

12552. Presson, Robert K. "Marston's *Dutch Courtezan*: The Study of an Attitude in Adaptation." *JEGP* 55(1956): 406-413.

12553. Salomon, Brownell. "The Theological Basis of Imagery and Structure in *The Malcontent*." *SEL* 14(1974): 271-284.

12554. Schoenbaum, Samuel. "The Precarious Balance of John Marston." *PMLA* 67(1952): 1069-1078.

12555. Slights, William W. E. "'Elder in a Deform'd Church': The Function of Marston's *Malcontent*." *SEL* 13(1973): 360-373.

12556. ----------. "Political Morality and the Ending of *The Malcontent*." *MP* 69(1971): 138-139.

12557. Weiss, Adrian. "Rhetoric and Satire: New Light on John Marston's *Pigmalion* and the Satires." *JEGP* 71(1972): 22-35.

12558. Wharton, T. F. *"The Malcontent* and 'Dreams, Visions, Fantasies.'" *EIC* 24(1974): 261-274.

12559. ----------. "Old Marston or New Marston: The *Antonio* Plays." *EIC* 25(1975): 357-369.

12560. Yearling, Elizabeth M. "Lost for Words (Marston's Antonio Plays)." *EIC* 26(1976): 371-373.

12561. Zall, Paul M. "John Marston, Moralist." *ELH* 20(1953): 181-193.

See also 9306, 9356, 9377, 9389, 9415, 9402, 9407, 9418, 11369, 11385, 11390, 12192, 12403, 12472.

MARVELL, ANDREW.   12562. Allen, D. C. "Marvell's 'Nymph.'" *ELH* 23(1956): 93-111.

12563. Anselment, Raymond A. "'Betwixt Jest and Earnest': Ironic Reversal in Marvell's 'The Rehearsal Transpos'd.'" *MLR* 66(1971): 282-293.

12565. ----------. "Satiric Strategy in Marvell's *The Rehearsal Transpros'd*." *MP* 68 (1970): 137-150.

12565. Bain, Carl E. "The Latin Poetry of Andrew Marvell." *PQ* 38(1959): 436-449.

12566. Baruch, Elaine Hoffman. "Theme and Counterthemes in 'Damon the Mower.'" *Comp L* 26 (1974): 242-259.

12567. Berek, Peter. "The Voices of Marvell's Lyrics." *MLQ* 32(1971): 143-157.

12568. Berger, Harry, Jr. "Marvell's 'Garden': Still Another Interpretation." *MLQ* 28 (1967): 285-304.

12569. Berthoff, Ann Evans. "The Allegorical Metaphor: Marvell's 'The Definition of Love.'" *RES* 17(1966): 16-29.

12570. ----------. "The Voice of Allegory: Marvell's 'The Unfortunate Lover.'" *MLQ* 27(1966): 41-50.

12571. Burroughs, Franklin G., Jr. "Marvell's Cromwell and May's Caesar: 'An Horatian Ode' and the *Continuation of the Pharsalia*." *ELN* 13(1975): 115-122.

12572. Carpenter, Margaret. "From Herbert to Marvell: Poetics in 'A Wreath' and 'The Coronet.'" *JEGP* 69(1970): 50-62.

12573. ----------. "Marvell's 'Garden.'" *SEL* 10(1970): 155-169.

12574. Clayton, Thomas. "'Morning Glew' and Other Sweal Leaves in the Folio Text of Andrew Marvell's Major Pre-Restoration Poems." *ELR* 2 (1972): 356-375.

12575. Coolidge, John S. "Martin Marprelate, Marvell, and *Decorum Personae* as a Satirical

Theme." *PMLA* 74(1959): 526-532.

12576. ----------. "Marvell and Horace." *MP* 63(1965): 111-120.

12577. Creaser, John. "Marvell's Effortless Superiority." *EIC* 20(1970): 403-423.

12578. Cullen, Patrick. "Imitation and Metamorphosis: The Golden-Age Eclogue in Spenser, Milton, and Marvell." *PMLA* 84(1969): 1559-1570.

12579. Cummings, R. M. "The Difficulty of Marvell's 'Bermudas.'" *MP* 67(1970): 331-340.

12580. Datta, Kitty. "Marvell and Wotton: A Reconsideration." *RES* 19(1968): 403-405.

12581. ----------. "Marvell's Prose and Poetry: More Notes." *MP* 63(1966): 319-321.

12582. Davison, Dennis. "Marvell's 'The Definition of Love.'" *RES* 6(1955): 141-146.

12583. Day, Robert A. "Marvell's 'Glew.'" *PQ* 32(1953): 344-346.

12584. Delany, Paul. "Marvell's 'Mourning.'" *MLQ* 33(1972): 30-36.

12585. Dorenkamp, Angela G. "Marvell's Geometry of Love." *ELN* 9(1971): 111-115.

12586. Evett, David. "'Paradice's Only Map': The *Topos* of the *Locus Amoenus* and the Structure of Marvell's *Upon Appleton House*." *PMLA* 85(1970): 504-513.

12587. Fisher, Alan S. "The Augustan Marvell: *The Last Instructions to a Painter*." *ELH* 38(1971): 223-238.

12588. Fizdale, Tay. "Irony in Marvell's 'Bermudas.'" *ELH* 42(1975): 203-213.

12589. French, A. L. "Dryden, Marvell, and Political Poetry." *SEL* 8(1968): 397-413.

12590. Gearin-Tosh, Michael. "The Structure of Marvell's 'Last Instructions to a Painter.'" *EIC* 22(1972): 48-57.

12591. Godshalk, William Leigh. "Marvell's 'Garden' and the Theologians." *SP* 66(1969): 639-653.

12592. Goldberg, Jonathan. "The Typology of 'Musicks Empire.'" *TSLL* 13(1971): 421-430.

12593. Greenwood, E. B. "Marvell's Impossible Love." *EIC* 27(1977): 100-111.

12594. Guild, Nicholas. "Marvell's 'The Nymph Complaining for the Death of Her Fawn.'" *MLQ* 29(1968): 385-394.

12595. Hardman, C. B. "Marvell's Rowers." *EIC* 27(1977): 93-99.

12596. Hartman, Geoffrey. "Marvell, St. Paul, and the Body of Hope." *ELH* 31(1964): 175-194.

12597. ----------. *"The Nymph Complaining for the Death of her Fawn*." *EIC* 18(1968): 113-135.

12598. Herron, Dale. "Marvell's 'Garden' and the Landscape of Poetry." *JEGP* 73(1974): 328-337.

12599. Hetherington, Edith W., and Norriss S. "Andrew Marvell, 'Upon Appleton House' and Fleas in Multiplying Glasses." *ELN* 13(1975): 122-124.

12600. Hodge, R. I. V. "Marvell's Fairfax Poems: Some Considerations concerning Dates." *MP* 71(1974): 347-355.

12601. Hogan, Patrick G., Jr. "Marvell's 'Vegetable Love.'" *SP* 60(1963): 1-11.

12602. Hyman, Lawrence W. "Marvell's 'Coy Mistress' as Fact or Poem." *MLQ* 26(1965): 462-466.

12603. ----------. "Marvell's *Garden*." *ELH*

25(1958): 13-22.

12604. ----------. "Politics and Poetry in Andrew Marvell." *PMLA* 73(1958): 475-479.

12605. Kalstone, David. "Marvell and the Fictions of Pastoral." *ELR* 4(1974): 174-188.

12606. Kawasaki, Toshihiko. "Marvell's 'Bermudas'—A Little World, or a New World?" *ELH* 43(1976): 53-73.

12607. Kelliher, W. Hilton. "Marvell's 'A Letter to Doctor Ingelo.'" *RES* 20(1969): 50-57.

12608. Kermode, Frank. "The Argument of Marvell's 'Garden.'" *EIC* 2(1952): 225-241.

12609. ----------. "Definitions of Love." *RES* 7(1956): 183-185.

12610. King, Bruce. "A Reading of Marvell's 'The Coronet.'" *MLR* 68(1973): 741-749.

12611. LeComte, Edward S. "Marvell's 'The Nymph Complaining for the Death of her Fawn.'" *MP* 50(1952): 97-101.

12612. Legouis, Pierre. "Marvell and the New Critics." *RES* 8(1957): 382-389.

12613. ----------. "Marvell and 'the two learned brothers of St. Marthe.'" *PQ* 38(1959): 450-458.

12614. ----------. "Marvell's 'Nymph Complaining for the Death of Her Fawn': A *Mise au point*." *MLQ* 21(1960): 30-32.

12615. Lippincott, Henry F., Jr. "Marvell's 'On *Paradise Lost*.'" *ELN* 9(1972): 265-272.

12616. Lord, George. "From Contemplation to Action: Marvell's Poetical Career." *PQ* 46(1967): 207-224.

12617. Love, Harold. "Marvell's Impossible Love." *EIC* 27(1977): 374-375.

12618. Low, Anthony, and Paul J. Pival. "Rhetorical Pattern in Marvell's 'To His Coy Mistress.'" *JEGP* 68(1969): 414-421.

12619. Maccaffrey, Isabel G. "Some Notes on Marvell's Poetry, Suggested by a Reading of His Prose." *MP* 61(1964): 261-269.

12620. Martin, L. C. "Marvell, Massinger, and Sidney." *RES* 2(1951): 374-375.

12621. McGaw, William D. "Marvell's 'Salmon-Fishers'—A Contemporary Joke." *ELN* 13(1976): 177-180.

12622. McQueen, William A. "The Missing Stanzas in Marvell's *Hortus*." *PQ* 44(1965): 173-179.

12623. Miller, Clarence H. "Sophistry and Truth in 'To His Coy Mistress.'" *Coll L* 2(1975): 97-104.

12624. Miner, Earl. "The Death of Innocence in Marvell's *Nymph Complaining for the Death of Her Fawn*." *MP* 65(1967): 9-16.

12625. ----------. "The 'Poetic Picture, Painted Poetry' of *Last Instructions to a Painter*." *MP* 63(1966): 288-294.

12626. Moldenhauer, Joseph J. "The Voices of Seduction in 'To His Coy Mistress': A Rhetorical Analysis." *TSLL* 10(1968): 189-206.

12627. Molesworth, Charles. "Marvell's 'Upon Appleton House': The Persona as Historian, Philosopher, and Priest." *SEL* 13(1973): 149-162.

12628. Nevo, Ruth. "Marvell's 'Songs of Innocence and Experience.'" *SEL* 5(1965): 1-21.

12629. Norford, Don Parry. "Marvell and the Arts of Contemplation and Action." *ELH* 41(1974): 50-73.

12630. ----------. "Marvell's 'Holy Mathematicks.'" *MLQ* 38(1977): 242-260.

12631. Patterson, Annabel. "Against Polarization: Literature and Politics in Marvell's Cromwell Poems." *ELR* 5(1975): 251-272.

12632. ----------. "*Bermudas* and *The Coronet*: Marvell's Protestant Poetics." *ELH* 44(1977): 478-499.

12633. Pitman, M. R. "Andrew Marvell and Sir Henry Wotten." *RES* 13(1962): 157-158.

12634. Potter, John M. "Another Porker in the Garden of Epicurus: Marvell's 'Hortus' and 'The Garden.'" *SEL* 11(1971): 137-151.

12635. Quivey, James. "Marvell's Couplet Art: 'Last Instructions to a Painter.'" *EL* 1(1974): 28-36.

12636. Rees, Christine. "'Tom May's Death' and Ben Jonson's Ghost: A Study of Marvell's Satiric Method." *MLR* 71(1976): 481-488.

12637. Roth, Frederic H., Jr. "Marvell's 'Upon Appleton House': A Study in Perspective." *TSLL* 14(1972): 269-281.

12638. Salerno, Nicholas A. "Andrew Marvell and the *Furor Hortensis*." *SEL* 8(1968): 103-120.

12639. Schmitter, Dean Morgan, and Pierre Legouis. "The Cartography of 'The Definition of Love.'" *RES* 12(1961): 49-54.

12640. Schwenger, Peter T. "Marvell's 'Unfortunate Lover' as Device." *MLQ* 35(1974): 364-375.

12641. Spitzer, Leo. "Marvell's 'Nymph Complaining for the Death of Her Faun': Sources versus Meaning." *MLQ* 19(1958): 231-243.

12642. Summers, Joseph H. "Marvell's 'Nature.'" *ELH* 20(1953): 121-135.

12643. Sutherland, James R. "A Note on the Satirical Poetry of Andrew Marvell." *PQ* 45(1966): 46-53.

12644. Swan, Jim. "At Play in the Garden of Ambivalence: Andrew Marvell and the Green World." *Criticism* 17(1975): 295-307.

12645. ----------. "'Betwixt Two Labyrinths': Andrew Marvell's Rational Amphibian." *TSLL* 17(1975): 551-572.

12646. Syfret, R. H. "Marvell's 'Horatian Ode.'" *RES* 12(1961): 160-172.

12647. Szanto, Gillian. "Recent Studies in Marvell." *ELR* 5(1975): 273-286.

12648. Toliver, Harold E. "Pastoral Form and Idea in Some Poems of Marvell." *TSLL* 5(1963): 83-97.

12649. ----------. "The Strategy of Marvell's Resolve against Created Pleasure." *SEL* 4(1964): 57-69.

12650. Turner, James. "Marvell's Impossible Love." *EIC* 27(1977): 375-377.

12651. Wallace, John M. "Andrew Marvell and Cromwell's Kingship: The First Anniversary." *ELH* 30(1963): 209-235.

12652. ----------. "Marvell's Horatian Ode." *PMLA* 77(1962): 33-45.

12653. Warnke, Frank J. "Play and Metamorphosis in Marvell's Poetry." *SEL* 5(1965): 23-30.

12654. Wilding, Michael. "'Apples' in Marvell's 'Bermudas.'" *ELN* 6(1969): 254-257.

12655. Williamson, Karina. "Marvell's

'The Nymph Complaining for the Death of Her Faun': A Reply." *MP* 51(1954): 268-271.

12656. Wilson, A. J. N. "Andrew Marvell's 'The First Anniversary of the Government Under Cromwell': The Poem and Its Frame of Reference." *MLR* 69(1974): 254-273.

12657. Withington, Eleanor. "Marvell and Montague: Another Source for 'The Definition of Love.'" *RES* 4(1953): 261-263.

12658. Zwicker, Steven N. "Models of Governance in Marvell's 'The First Anniversary.'" *Criticism* 16(1974): 1-12.

See also 474, 504, 526, 2171, 5178, 9286, 9291, 9463, 11361, 11419, 11798, 13313.

MASON, JOHN. 12659. Wadsworth, Frank W. "The Relation of *Lusts' Dominion* and John Mason's *The Turk*." *ELH* 20(1953): 194-199.

MASSINGER, PHILIP. 12660. Bliss, Michael D. "Massinger's *City Madam* and the Lost *City Honest Man*." *ELR* 7(1977): 368-381.

12661. Bowers, R. H. "A Note on Massinger's 'New Way.'" *MLR* 53(1958): 214-215.

12662. Burelbach, Frederich M., Jr. "*A New Way to Pay Old Debts*: Jacobean Morality." *CLA* 12(1969): 205-213.

12663. Clubb, Louise, George. "*The Virgin Martyr* and the *Tragedia Sacra*." *RD* 7 (1964): 103-126.

12664. Edwards, Philip. "The Sources of Massinger's *The Bondman*." *RES* 15(1964): 21-26.

12665. Gibson, C. A. "Massinger's London Merchant and the Date of 'The City Madam.'" *MLR* 65(1970): 737-749.

12666. Gill, Roma. "Collaboration and Revision in Massinger's *A Very Woman*." *RES* 18 (1967): 136-148.

12667. Gray, J. E. "The Source of *The Emperour of the East*." *RES* 1(1950): 126-135.

12668. Gross, Allen. "Contemporary Politics in Massinger." *SEL* 6(1966): 279-290.

12669. ----------. "Social Change and Philip Massinger." *SEL* 7(1967): 329-342.

12670. Hogan, A. P. "Imagery of Acting in 'The Roman Actor.'" *MLR* 66(1971): 273-281.

12671. ----------. "Massinger as Tragedian: *Believe as You Lust*." *TSLL* 13 (1971): 407-419.

12672. Hoy, Cyrus. "Verbal Formulae in the Plays of Philip Massinger." *SP* 56(1959): 600-618.

12673. Huebert, Ronald. "'An Artificial Way to Grieve': The Forsaken Woman in Beaumont and Fletcher, Massinger and Ford." *ELH* 44(1977): 601-621.

12674. Martin, L. C. "Marvell, Massinger, and Sidney." *RES* 2(1951): 374-375.

12675. Mullany, Peter F. "Religion in Massinger's *The Maid of Honour*." *RD* n.s. 2 (1969): 143-156.

12676. Phialas, Peter G. "The Sources of Massinger's *Emperour of the East*." *PMLA* 65 (1950): 473-482.

12677. Thomson, Patricia. "The Old Way and the New Way in Dekker and Massinger." *MLR* 51 (1956): 168-178.

12678. Waith, Eugene M. "*Controversia* in the English Drama: Medwall and Massinger." *PMLA* 68(1953): 286-303.

See also 9402, 11395, 13500, 14835.

MIDDLETON, THOMAS. 12679. Berger, Thomas L. "Further Notes on the Text of *Blurt Master-Constable*." *ELN* 13(1975): 90-98.

12680. Bullough, Geoffrey. "'The Game at Chesse': How It Struck a Contemporary." *MLR* 49 (1954): 156-163.

12681. Chatterji, Ruby. "Theme, Imagery, and Unity in *A Chaste Maid in Cheapside*." *RD* 8 (1965): 105-126.

12682. ----------. "Unity and Disparity in *Michaelmas Term*." *SEL* 8(1968): 349-363.

12683. Dessen, Alan C. "Middleton's *The Phoenix* and the Allegorical Tradition." *SEL* 6 (1966): 291-308.

12684. Doob, Penelope B. R. "A Reading of *The Changeling*." *ELR* 3(1973): 183-206.

12685. Duffy, Joseph M. "Madhouse Optics: *The Changeling*." *CD* 8(1974): 184-198.

12686. Eccles, Mark. "'Thomas Middleton a Poett.'" *SP* 54(1957): 516-536.

12687. Engelberg, Edward. "Tragic Blindness in *The Changeling* and *Women Beware Women*." *MLQ* 23(1962): 20-28.

12688. Foakes, R. A. "On the Authorship of 'The Revenger's Tragedy.'" *MLR* 48(1953): 129-138.

12689. Farr, Dorothy M. "'The Changeling.'" *MLR* 62(1967): 586-597.

12690. George, David. "Thomas Middleton at Oxford." *MLR* 65(1970): 734-736.

12691. Gross, Alan Gerald. "Middleton's *Your Five Gallants*: The Fifth Act." *PQ* 44(1965): 124-129.

12692. Hallett, Charles A. "Middleton's Allwit: The Urban Cynic." *MLQ* 30(1969): 498-507.

12693. ----------. "Penitent Brothel, the Succubus and Parsons' *Resolution*: A Reappraisal of Penitent's Position in Middleton's Canon." *SP* 69(1972): 72-86.

12694. ----------. "The Psychological Drama of *Women Beware Women*." *SEL* 12(1972): 375-389.

12695. Hébert, Catherine A. "A Note on the Significance of the Title of Middleton's *The Changeling*." *CLA* 12(1968): 66-69.

12696. Heineman, Margot. "Middleton's *A Game of Chess*: Parliamentary Puritans and Opposition Drama." *ELR* 5(1975): 232-250.

12697. Holdsworth, R. V. "The Medical Jargon in *A Fair Quarrel*." *RES* 23(1972): 448-454.

12698. Holmes, David M. "Thomas Middleton's 'Blurt Master-Constable or, The Spaniard's Night-Walk.'" *MLR* 64(1969): 1-10.

12699. Jacobs, Henry E. "The Constancy of Change: Character and Perspective in *The Changeling*." *TSLL* 16(1975): 651-674.

12700. Janzen, Henry D. "Two Cruxes in Dyce's Edition of Middleton's *Blurt Master-Constable*." *ELN* 10(1972): 100-101.

12701. Johnson, Paula. "Dissimulation Anatomized: *The Changeling*." *PQ* 56(1977): 329-338.

12702. Jordan, Robert. "Myth and Psychology in *The Changeling*." *RD* n.s. 3(1970): 157-165.

12703. Kaplan, Joel H. "Middleton's Tamburlaine." *ELN* 13(1976): 258-260.

12704. Kehler, Dorothea. "Rings and Jewels in *The Changeling*." *ELN* 5(1967): 15-17.

12705. Kistner, A. L. and M. K. "Will, Fate, and Social Order in *Women Beware Women*." *EL* 3(1976): 17-31.

12706. Lieblein, Leanore. "Thomas Middleton's Prodigal Play." *CD* 10(1976): 54-60.

12707. Levin, Richard. "'The Ass in Compound': A Lost Pun in Middleton, Ford, and Jonson." *ELN* 4(1966): 12-15.

12708. ----------. "The Dampit Scenes in *A Trick to Catch The Old One*." *MLQ* 25(1964): 140-152.

12709. ----------. "The Family of Lust and *The Family of Love*." *SEL* 6(1966): 309-322.

12710. ----------. "The Four Plots of *A Chaste Maid in Cheapside*." *RES* 16(1965): 14-24.

12711. ----------. "The Three Quarrels of *A Fair Quarrel*." *SP* 61(1964): 219-231.

12712. Marotti, Arthur F. "Fertility and Comic Form in *A Chaste Maid in Cheapside*." *CD* 3 (1969): 65-74.

12713. Maxwell, Baldwin. "Thomas Middleton's *Your Five Gallants*." *PQ* 30(1951): 30-39.

12714. McElroy, John F. "Middleton, Entertainer or Moralist? An Interpretation of *The Family of Love* and *Your Five Gallants*." *MLQ* 37(1976): 35-46.

12715. Mulholland, P. A. "The Date of *The Roaring Girl*." *RES* 28(1977): 18-31.

12716. Mulryne, J. R. "The French Source for the Sub-Plot of Middleton's *Women Beware Women*." *RES* 25(1974): 439-445.

12717. Olive, W. J. "Imitation of Shakespeare in Middleton's *The Family of Love*." *PQ* 29 (1950): 75-78.

12718. ----------. "'Twenty Good Nights'—*The Knight of the Burning Pestle*, *The Family of Love*, and *Romeo and Juliet*." *SP* 47(1950): 182-189.

12719. Paster, Gail Kern. "The City in Plautus and Middleton." *RD* n.s. 6(1973): 29-44.

12720. Pentzell, Raymond J. "*The Changeling*: Notes on Mannerism in Dramatic Form." *CD* 9(1975): 3-29.

12721. Phialas, P. G. "Middleton's Early Contact with the Law." *SP* 52(1955): 186-194.

12722. Ricks, Christopher. "Word-Play in *Women Beware Women*." *RES* 12(1961): 238-250.

12723. Rowe, George E., Jr. "The *Old Law* and Middleton's Comic Vision." *ELH* 42(1975): 189-202.

12724. ----------. "Prodigal Sons, New Comedy, and Middleton's *Michaelmas Term*." *ELR* 7 (1977): 90-107.

12725. Schoenbaum, Samuel. "*Hengist, King of Kent* and the Sexual Preoccupation in Jacobean Drama." *PQ* 29(1950): 182-198.

12726. ----------. "Middleton's Tragicomedies." *MP* 54(1956): 7-19.

12727. ----------. "A New Middleton Record." *MLR* 55(1960): 82-84.

12728. Ricks, Christopher. "The Moral of Poetic Structure of *The Changeling*." *EIC* 10 (1960): 290-306.

12729. Sargent, Roussel. "Theme and Structure in Middleton's 'A Game at Chess.'" *MLR* 66(1971): 721-730.

12730. Slights, William W. E. "The Trickster Hero and Middleton's *A Mad World, My Masters*." *CD* 3(1969): 87-98.

12731. Tomlinson, T. B. "Poetic Naturalism—*The Changeling*." *JEGP* 63(1964): 648-659.

12732. Williams, Robert I. "Machiavelli's *Mandragola*, Touchwood Senior, and the Comedy of Middleton's *A Chaste Maid in Cheapside*." *SEL* 10 (1970): 385-396.

12733. Wigler, Stephen. "If Looks Could Kill: Fathers and Sons in *The Revenger's Tragedy*." *CD* 9(1975): 206-225.

See also 9389, 9402, 11297, 11385, 13368, 13500.

MILTON, JOHN.   12734. Adams, Robert Martin. "Reading *Comus*." *MP* 51(1953): 18-32.

12735. ----------. "The Text of *Paradise Lost*; Emphatic and Unemphatic Spellings." *MP* 52 (1954): 84-91.

12736. Adamson, J. H. "Milton and the Creation." *JEGP* 61(1962): 756-778.

12737. ----------. "The War in Heaven: Milton's Version of the *Merkabah*." *JEGP* 57(1958): 690-703.

12738. Allen, D. C. "Milton and the Descent to Light." *JEGP* 60(1961): 614-630.

12739. Archer, Stanley. "Satan and the Colures: Paradise Lost IX, 62-66." *ELN* 10(1972): 115-116.

12740. Arthos, John. "Milton and the Passions: A Study of *Samson Agonistes*." *MP* 69 (1972): 209-221.

12741. Aryanpur, Manoocher. "*Paradise Lost* and *The Odyssey*." *TSLL* 9(1967): 151-166.

12742. Asals, Heather R. "In Defense of Dalila: *Samson Agonistes* and the Reformation Theology of the Word." *JEGP* 74(1975): 183-194.

12743. Atkins, Samuel D., and Maurice Kelley. "Milton's Annotations of Aratus." *PMLA* 70(1955): 1090-1106.

12744. Atkinson, Michael. "The Structure of the Temptations in Milton's *Samson Agonistes*." *MP* 69(1972): 285-291.

12745. Auksi, Peter. "Milton's 'Sanctifi'd Bitternesse': Polemical Technique in the Early Prose." *TSLL* 19(1977): 363-381.

12746. Ayers, Robert W. "The Date of the John Phillips-John Milton *Joannis Philippi Angli Responsio*." *PQ* 38(1959): 95-101.

12747. ----------. "The Editions of Milton's *Readie & Easie Way to Establish a Free Commonwealth*." *RES* 25(1974): 280-292.

12748. Baker, Stewart A. "Sannazaro and Milton's Brief Epic." *Comp L* 20(1968): 116-132.

12749. Baruch, Franklin R. "Milton's Blindness: The Conscious and Unconscious Patterns of Autobiography." *ELH* 42(1975): 26-37.

12750. ----------. "Time, Body, and Spirit at the Close of *Samson Agonistes*." *ELH* 36(1969): 319-339.

12751. Baumgartner, Paul R. "Milton and Patience." *SP* 60(1963): 203-213.

12752. Bedford, R. D. "Milton's Logic." *EIC* 27(1977): 84-86.

12753. ----------. "Similies of Unlikeness in *Paradise Lost*." *EIC* 25(1975): 179-196.

12754. Beer, Gillian. "Richardson, Milton, and the Status of Evil." *RES* 19(1968): 261-270.

12755. Bell, Millicent. "The Fallacy of the Fall in *Paradise Lost*." *PMLA* 68(1953): 863-883.

12756. ----------. "The Fallacy of the Fall

in *Paradise Lost*." *PMLA* 70(1955): 1187-1197, 1203.

12757. Benham, Allen R. "'Things Unattempted Yet in Prose or Rime.'" *MLQ* 14(1953): 341-347.

12758. Bennett, Joan S. "God, Satan, and King Charles: Milton's Royal Portraits." *PMLA* 92(1977): 441-457.

12759. Berek, Peter. "'Plain' and 'Ornate' Styles and the Structure of *Paradise Lost*." *PMLA* 85(1970): 237-246.

12760. Berry, Boyd M. "Puritan Soldiers in *Paradise Lost*." *MLQ* 35(1974): 376-402.

12761. Berry, Lloyd E. "Giles Fletcher, the Edler, and Milton's *A Brief History of Moscovia*." *RES* 11(1960): 150-156.

12762. Berthold, Dennis. "The Concept of Merit in *Paradise Lost*." *SEL* 15(1975): 153-167.

12763. Beum, Robert. "The Rhyme in *Samson Agonistes*." *TSLL* 4(1962): 177-182.

12764. Boddy, Margaret. "Milton's Translation of Psalms 80-88." *MP* 64(1966): 1-9.

12765. Bolton, W. F. "A Further Echo of the Old English *Genesis* in Milton's *Paradise Lost*." *RES* 25(1974): 58-61.

12766. Boswell, Jackson C. "Milton and Prevenient Grace." *SEL* 7(1967): 83-94.

12767. Bottkol, Joseph McG. "The Holograph of Milton's Letter to Holstenius." *PMLA* 68 (1953): 617-627.

12768. Bowers, A. Robin. "Milton and Salmasius: The Rhetorical Imperatives." *PQ* 52 (1973): 55-68.

12769. Bowers, Fredson. "Adam, Eve, and the Fall in *Paradise Lost*." *PMLA* 84(1969): 264-273.

12770. Bradley, S. A. J. "Ambiorix Ariovistus, Detractor of Milton's *Defensio*, Identified." *MP* 73(1976): 382-388.

12771. Brantlinger, Patrick. "To See New Worlds: Curiosity in *Paradise Lost*." *MLQ* 33 (1972): 355-369.

12772. Brisman, Leslie. "'All Before Them Where To Choose': 'L'Allegro' and 'Il Penseroso.'" *JEGP* 71(1972): 226-240.

12773. Broadbent, J. B. "Milton and Arnold." *EIC* 6(1956): 404-417.

12774. ----------. "Milton's Hell." *ELH* 21(1954): 161-192.

12775. ----------. "Milton's Paradise." *MP* 51(1953): 160-176.

12776. ----------. "Milton's Rhetoric." *MP* 56(1959): 224-242.

12777. Brooks, Cleanth. "Milton and Critical Re-estimates." *PMLA* 66(1951): 1045-1054.

12778. Brown, Cedric C. "Milton's *Arcades*: Context, Form, and Function." *RD* n.s. 8(1977): 245-274.

12779. Bryan, Robert A. "Adam's Tragic Vision in *Paradise Lost*." *SP* 62(1965): 197-214.

12780. Bryant, Joseph Allen, Jr. "Milton and the Art of History: A Study of Two Influences on *A Brief History of Moscovia*." *PQ* 29(1950): 15-30.

12781. ----------. "A Note on Milton's Use of Machiavelli's *Discorsi*." *MP* 47(1950): 217-221.

12782. ----------. "A Reply to 'Milton's Moscovia Not History.'" *PQ* 31(1952): 221-223.

12783. Bush, Douglas. "Calculus Racked Him." *SEL* 6(1966): 1-6.

12784. ----------. "The Date of Milton's *Ad Patrem*." *MP* 61(1964): 204-208.

12785. ----------. "Ironic and Ambiguous Allusion in *Paradise Lost*." *JEGP* 60(1961): 631-640.

12786. ----------. "Three More Views of *Paradise Lost*." *MLQ* 34(1973): 78-84.

12787. Buxton, John. "A Note on *Paradise Lost*, X. 71-79." *RES* 15(1964): 52-53.

12788. Campbell, Gordon. "The Satire on Aristotelian Logic in Milton's 'Vacation Exercise.'" *ELN* 15(1977): 106-110.

12789. Canfield, J. Douglas. "The Birthday of the Son in *Paradise Lost*." *ELN* 13(1975): 113-115.

12790. Carey, John. "The Date of Milton's Italian Poems." *RES* 14(1963): 383-386.

12791. ----------. "Milton's *Ad Patrem*, 35-37." *RES* 15(1964): 180-184.

12792. ----------. "Sea, Snake, Flower, and Flame in 'Samson Agonistes.'" *MLR* 62(1967): 395-399.

12793. Carlisle, A. J. "Milton and Ludwig Lavater." *RES* 5(1954): 249-255.

12794. Carnes, Valerie. "Time and Language in Milton's *Paradise Lost*." *ELH* 37(1970): 517-539.

12795. Carpenter, Nan Cooke. "Milton and Music: Henry Lawes, Dante, and Casella." *ELR* 2 (1972): 237-242.

12796. Carrithers, Gale H., Jr. "Milton's Ludlow *Mask*: From Chaos to Community." *ELH* 33 (1966): 23-42.

12797. Carson, Barbara Harrell. "Milton's Samson as *Parvus Sol*." *ELN* 5(1968): 171-176.

12798. Cavanagh, Michael. "A Meeting of Epic and History: Books XI and XII of Paradise Lost." *ELH* 38(1971): 206-222.

12799. Chambers, A. B. "Milton's Proteus and Satan's Visit to the Sun." *JEGP* 62(1963): 280-287.

12800. ----------. "Milton's 'Upon the Circumcision': Background and Meanings." *TSLL* 17 (1975): 687-697.

12801. ----------. "More Sources for Milton." *MP* 63(1965): 61-66.

12802. ----------. "Three Notes on Eve's Dream in Paradise Lost." *PQ* 46(1967): 186-193.

12803. ----------. "Wisdom and Fortitude in *Samson Agonistes*." *PMLA* 78(1963): 315-320.

12804. ----------. "Wisdom at One Entrance Quite Shut Out: *Paradise Lost*, III, 1-55." *PQ* 42(1963): 114-120.

12805. Chang, Y. Z. "Why Did Milton Err on Two Chinas." *MLR* 65(1970): 493-498.

12806. Chatman, Seymour. "Milton's Participial Style." *PMLA* 83(1968): 1386-1399.

12807. Cheek, Macon. "Milton's 'In Quintum Novembris': An Epic Foreshadowing." *SP* 54(1957): 172-184.

12808. Chester, Allan G. "Milton, Latimer, and the Lord Admiral." *MLQ* 14(1953): 15-20.

12809. Chew, Audrey. "Joseph Hall and John Milton." *ELH* 17(1950): 274-295.

12810. Christopher, Georgia. "Homeopathic Physic and Natural Renovation in *Samson Agonistes*." *ELH* 37(1970): 361-373.

12811. ----------. "The Verbal Gate to

Paradise: Adam's 'Literary Experience' in Book X of *Paradise Lost*." *PMLA* 90(1975): 69-77.

12812. ----------. "The Virginity of Faith: *Comus* as a Reformation Conceit." *ELH* 43(1976): 479-499.

12813. Cirillo, Albert R. "'Hail Holy Light' and Divine Time in *Paradise Lost*." *JEGP* 68 (1969): 45-56.

12814. ----------. "Moon-Midnight and the Temporal Structure of *Paradise Lost*." *ELH* 29 (1962): 372-395.

12815. Clark, David R. "Asmodeus and the Fishy Fume: *Paradise Lost*, IV, 153-171." *SEL* 12 (1972): 121-128.

12816. Clark, Evert Mordecai. "Milton and Whither." *SP* 56(1959): 626-646.

12817. ----------. "Milton's English Poetical Vocabulary." *SP* 53(1956): 220-238.

12818. Clark, Ira. "Milton and the Image of God." *JEGP* 68(1969): 422-431.

12819. ----------. "*Paradise Regained* and the Gospel according to John." *MP* 71(1973): 1-15.

12820. Clavering, Rose, and John T. Shawcross. "Anne Milton and the Milton Residences." *JEGP* 59(1960): 680-690.

12821. ----------. "Milton's European Itinerary and His Return Home." *SEL* 5(1965): 49-59.

12822. Cleveland, Edward. "On the Identity Motive of *Paradise Regained*." *MLQ* 16(1955): 232-236.

12823. Cobb, Carl W. "Milton and Blank Verse in Spain." *PQ* 42(1963): 264-267.

12824. Coffin, Charles Monroe. "Creation and the Self in *Paradise Lost*." *ELH* 29(1962): 1-18.

12825. Cohen, Kitty. "A Note on Milton's Azazel." *PQ* 49(1970): 248-249.

12826. Collette, Carolyn P. "Milton's Psalm Translations: Petition and Praise." *ELR* 2 (1972): 243-259.

12827. Collett, Jonathan H. "Milton's Use of Classical Mythology in *Paradise Lost*." *PMLA* 85 (1970): 88-96.

12828. Condee, Ralph Waterbury. "Formalized Openings of Milton's Epic Poems." *JEGP* 50 (1951): 502-508.

12829. ----------. "Ovid's Exile and Milton's Rustication." *PQ* 37(1958): 498-502.

12830. ----------. "The Structure of Milton's 'Epitaphium Damonis.'" *SP* 62(1965): 577-594.

12831. Coolidge, John S. "Boethius and 'That Last Infirmity of Noble Mind.'" *PQ* 42 (1963): 176-182.

12832. Collidge, Lowell W. "'That Two-Handed Engine.'" *PQ* 29(1950): 444-445.

12833. Cope, Jackson I. "Fortunate Falls as Form in Milton's 'Fair Infant.'" *JEGP* 63(1964): 660-674.

12834. ----------. "Milton's Muse in *Paradise Lost*." *MP* 55(1957): 6-10.

12835. ----------. "Time and Space as Miltonic Symbol." *ELH* 26(1959): 497-513.

12836. Cox, John D. "Poetry and History in Milton's Country Masque." *ELH* 44(1977): 622-640.

12837. Cox, Lee Sheridan. "Food-Word Imagery in *Paradise Regained*." *ELH* 28(1961): 225-243.

12838. ----------. "Milton's 'I did but prompt,' 11. 13-14." *ELN* 3(1965): 102-104.

12839. ----------. "Natural Science and Figurative Design in *Samson Agonistes*." *ELH* 35 (1968): 51-74.

12840. Cullen, Patrick. "Imitation and Metamorphosis: The Golden-Age Eclogue in Spenser, Milton, and Marvell." *PMLA* 84(1969): 1559-1570.

12841. Curry, Walter Clyde. "Milton's Dual Concept of God as Related to Creation." *SP* 47 (1950): 190-210.

12842. ----------. "Some Travels of Milton's Satan and the Road to Hell." *PQ* 29 (1950): 225-235.

12843. Day, Douglas. "Adam and Eve in *Paradise Lost*, IV." *TSLL* 3(1961): 369-381.

12844. Demaray, John G. "Love's Epic Revel in *Paradise Lost*: A Theatrical Vision of Marraige." *MLQ* 38(1977): 3-20.

12845. Doyle, Charles Clay. "Nature's Fair Defect: Milton and William Cartwright on the Paradox of Woman." *ELN* 11(1973): 107-110.

12846. Duhamel, P. Albert. "Milton's Alleged Ramism." *PMLA* 67(1952): 1035-1053.

12847. Duncan, Edgar Hill. "Satan-Lucifer: Lightning and Thunderbolt." *PQ* 30(1951): 441-443.

12848. Duvall, Robert F. "Time, Place, Persons: The Background for Milton's *Of Reformation*." *SEL* 7(1967): 107-118.

12849. Dyson, A. E. "The Meaning of Paradise Regained." *TSLL* 3(1961): 197-211.

12850. Ebbs, John Dale. "Milton's Treatment of Poetic Justice in *Samson Agonistes*." *MLQ* 22(1961): 377-389.

12851. Egan, James. "Public Truth and Personal Witness in Milton's Last Tracts." *ELH* 40(1973): 231-248.

12852. ----------. "The Satiric Wit of Milton's Prose Controversies." *SLI* 10,#2(1977): 97-104.

12853. Ethel, Garland. "Hell's Marching Music." *MLQ* 18(1957): 295-302.

12854. Evans, G. Blakemore. "Addison's Early Knowledge of Milton." *JEGP* 49(1950): 204-207.

12855. ----------. "The State of Milton's Text: The Prose, 1643-48." *JEGP* 59 (1960): 497-505.

12856. Evans, John X. "Imagery as Argument in Milton's Areopagitica." *TSLL* 8(1966): 189-205.

12857. Feinstein, Blossom. "On the Hymns of John Milton and Gian Francesco Pico." *Comp L* 20(1968): 245-253.

12858. Fenderson, Lewis H. "The Onomato-Musical Element in *Paradise Lost*." *CLA* 9(1966): 255-264.

12859. Fields, Albert W. "Milton and Self-Knowledge." *PMLA* 83(1968): 392-399.

12860. Fiske, Dixon. "Milton in the Middle of Life: Sonnet XIX." *ELH* 41(1974): 37-49.

12861. Fixler, Michael. "The Orphic Technique of 'L'Allegro' and 'Il Penseroso.'" *ELR* 1(1971): 165-177.

12862. ----------. "Plato's Four Furors and the Real Structure of *Paradise Lost*." *PMLA* 92 (1977): 952-962.

12863. Fletcher, Harris. "Milton's *Apologus* and Its Mantuan Model." *JEGP* 55(1956):

230-233.

12864. ----------. "Milton's *E nostro suburbano*." *JEGP* 51(1952): 154-159.

12865. ----------. "Milton's Demogorgon—*Prolusion I* and *Paradise Lost*, II, 960-65." *JEGP* 57(1958): 684-689.

12866. ----------. "Milton's 'Old Damoetas.'" *JEGP* 60(1961): 250-257.

12867. ----------. "A Possible Origin of Milton's 'Counterpoint' or Double Rhythm." *JEGP* 54(1955): 521-525.

12868. ----------. "The Seventeenth-Century Separate Printing of Milton's *Epitaphium Damonis*." *JEGP* 61(1962): 788-796.

12869. Flower, Annette C. "The Critical Context of the Preface to *Samson Agonistes*." *SEL* 10(1970): 409-423.

12870. Foley, Jack. "'Sin, not Time': Satan's First Speech in *Paradise Lost*." *ELH* 37(1970): 37-56.

12871. Forker, Charles R. "Milton and Shakespeare: The First Sonnet on Blindness in Relation to a Speech From *Troilus and Cressida*." *ELN* 11(1974): 188-192.

12872. Fox, Robert C. "The Allegory of Sin and Death in *Paradise Lost*." *MLQ* 24(1963): 354-364.

12873. ----------. "The Character of Mammon in *Paradise Lost*." *RES* 13(1962): 30-39.

12874. ----------. "Milton's 'Sin': Addenda." *PQ* 42(1963): 120-121.

12875. ----------. "Satan's Triad of Vices." *TSLL* 2(1960): 261-280.

12876. Freeman, James A. "'The Roof Was Fretted Gold.'" *Comp L* 27(1975): 254-266.

12877. French, J. Milton. "Milton and the Barbarous Dissonance." *TSLL* 4(1962): 376-389.

12878. ----------. "The Reliability of Anthony Wood and Milton's Oxford, M. A." *PMLA* 75(1960): 22-30.

12879. ----------. "A Royalist Gibe at Milton's Antagonist Salmasius." *PQ* 42(1963): 109-114.

12880. ----------. "Some Notes on Milton's *Accedence Commenc't Grammar*." *JEGP* 60(1961): 641-650.

12881. ----------. "An Unpublished Reply (1659): to Milton's *Defensio*." *MP* 55(1957): 164-169.

12882. French, Roberts W. "Voice and Structure in *Lycidas*." *TSLL* 12(1970): 15-25.

12883. Friendman, Donald. "Harmony and the Poet's Voice in Some of Milton's Early Poems." *MLQ* 30(1969): 523-544.

12884. Frye, Northrup. "The Typology of *Paradise Regained*." *MP* 53(1956): 227-238.

12885. Gallagher, Philip J. "'Real or Allegoric': The Ontology of Sin and Death in *Paradise Lost*." *ELR* 6(1976): 317-335.

12886. Garber, Marjorie B. "Fallen Landscape: The Art of Milton and Poussin." *ELR* 5(1975): 96-124.

12887. Geckle, George L. "Milton's Idealism: *L'Allegro* and *Il Penseroso*." *TSLL* 9(1968): 455-473.

12888. Gleason, John B. "The Nature of Milton's *Moscovia*." *SP* 61(1964): 640-649.

12889. Gilbert, Allan. "Form and Matter in *Paradise Lost*, Book III." *JEGP* 60(1961): 651-663.

12890. Gilliam, J. F. "Scylla and Sin." *PQ* 29(1950): 345-347.

12891. Goldman, Jack. "Milton's Intrusion of Abraham and Isaac upon Psalm 114." *PQ* 55(1976): 117-126.

12892. ----------. "The Name and Function of Harapha in Milton's *Samson Agonistes*." *ELN* 12(1974): 84-91.

12893. ----------. "Insight into Milton's Abdiel." *PQ* 49(1970): 249-254.

12894. Gossman, Ann. "Milton's Samson as the Tragic Hero Purified by Trial." *JEGP* 61(1962): 528-541.

12895. ----------. "The Ring Pattern: Image, Structure, and Theme in *Paradise Lost*." *SP* 68(1971): 326-339.

12896. ----------. "The Use of The Tree of Life in *Paradise Lost*." *JEGP* 65(1966): 680-687.

12897. ----------, and George W. Whiting. "*Comus*, Once More, 1761." *RES* 11(1960): 56-60.

12898. ----------, with a reply by Fitzroy Pyle. "Milton's First Sonnet on his Blindness." *RES* 12(1961): 364-390.

12899. Grace, William J. "Notes on Robert Burton and John Milton." *SP* 52(1955): 578-591.

12900. Gransden, K. W. "Milton, Dryden, and the Comedy of the Fall." *EIC* 26(1976): 116-133.

12901. ----------. "*Paradise Lost* and the *Aeneid*." *EIC* 17(1967): 281-303.

12902. Grose, Christopher. "Lucky Words: Process of Speech in *Lycidas*." *JEGP* 70(1971): 383-403.

12903. Gross, Barry Edward. "Free Love and Free Will in *Paradise Lost*." *SEL* 7(1967): 95-106.

12904. Guss, Donald L. "A Brief Epic: Paradise Regained." *SP* 68(1971): 223-243.

12905. Hamilton, Gary D. "Creating the Garden Anew: The Dynamics of *Paradise Regained*." *PQ* 50(1971): 567-581.

12906. ----------. "Milton's Defensive God: A Reappraisal." *SP* 69(1972): 87-100.

12907. Hankins, John E. "The Pains of the Afterworld: Fire, Wind and Ice in Milton and Shakespeare." *PMLA* 71(1956): 482-495.

12908. Harada, Jun. "The Mechanism of Human Reconciliation in *Paradise Lost*." *PQ* 50(1971): 543-552.

12909. Harding, Davis P. "Milton's Bee-Simile." *JEGP* 60(1961): 664-669.

12910. Hardison, O. B., Jr. "Milton's 'On Time' and Its Scholastic Background." *TSLL* 3(1961): 107-122.

12911. Harris, William O. "Despair and 'Patience as the Truest Fortitude' in *Samson Agonistes*." *ELH* 30(1963): 107-120.

12912. Hartman, Geoffrey. "Adam on the Grass with Balsamum." *ELH* 36(1969): 168-192.

12913. ----------. "False Themes and Gentle Minds." *PQ* 47(1968): 55-68.

12914. ----------. "Milton's Counterplot." *ELH* 25(1958): 1-12.

12915. Haskin, Dayton, S. J. "Divorce as a Path to Union with God in *Samson Agonistes*." *ELH* 38(1971): 358-376.

12916. Henry, Nathaniel H. "Milton and Hobbes: Mortalism and the Intermediate State."

SP 48(1951): 234-249.

12917. Hill, Archibald A. "Imagery and Meaning: A Passage from Milton, and from Blake." *TSLL* 11(1969): 1093-1105.

12918. Holloway, John. "Milton and Arnold." *EIC* 7(1957): 226-228.

12919. Hone, Ralph E. "'The Pilot of the *Galilean* Lake.'" *SP* 56(1959): 55-61.

12920. Hoyle, James. "'If Sion Hill Delight Thee More': The Muse's Choice in *Paradise Lost*." *ELN* 12(1974): 20-26.

12921. Hughes, Merritt Y. "'Earth Felt the Wound.'" *ELH* 36(1969): 193-214.

12922. ----------. "Milton and the Symbol of Light." *SEL* 4(1964): 1-33.

12923. ----------. "The Miltonic Future." *MLR* 66(1971): xxi.

12924. ----------. "'Myself Am Hell.'" *MP* 54(1956): 80-94.

12925. ----------. "New Evidence on the Charge that Milton Forged the Pamela Prayer in the *Eikon Basilike*." *RES* 3(1952): 130-140.

12926. ----------. "Some Illustrators of Milton: The Expulsion from Paradise." *JEGP* 60 (1961): 670-679.

12927. Hulme, Hilda M. "Milton's Use of Colloquial Language in 'Paradise Lost' (with a new interpretation of 'drugd as oft' (x, 568)." *MLR* 64(1969): 491-499.

12928. Hunt, Winifred. "On Even Ground: A Note on the Extramundane Location of Hell in *Paradise Lost*." *MLQ* 23(1962): 17-19.

12929. Hunter, William B., Jr. "The Date and Occasion of *Arcades*." *ELN* 11(1973): 46-47.

12930. ----------. "The Date of Milton's Sonnet 7." *ELN* 13(1975): 10-14.

12931. ----------. "The Liturgical Context of *Comus*." *ELN* 10(1972): 11-15.

12932. ----------. "Milton and Richard Cromwell." *ELN* 3(1966): 252-259.

12933. ----------. "Milton and the Waldensians." *SEL* 11(1971): 153-164.

12934. ----------. "Milton on the Exultation of the Son: The War in Heaven in *Paradise Lost*." *ELH* 36(1969): 215-231.

12935. ----------. "Milton Translates the Psalms." *PQ* 40(1961): 485-494.

12936. ----------. "Milton's Urania." *SEL* 4(1964): 35-42.

12937. ----------. "Satan as Comet: *Paradise Lost* II. 708-711." *ELN* 5(1967): 17-21.

12938. Huntley, Frank L. "A Justification of Milton's 'Paradise of Fools' (*P.L.* III, 431-499)." *ELH* 21(1954): 107-113.

12939. ----------. "Milton Studies in Japan." *Comp L* 13(1961): 97-113.

12940. Huntley, John F. "Aristotle's Physics as a Gloss on *PL* VIII. 152." *PQ* 44(1965): 129-132.

12941. ----------. "Milton's 23rd Sonnet." *ELH* 34(1967): 468-481.

12942. ----------. "*Proaresis, Synteresis*, and the Ethical Orientation of Milton's *Of Education*." *PQ* 43(1964): 40-46.

12943. ----------. "The Poet-Critic and His Poem-Culture in 'L'Allegro' and 'Il Penseroso.'" *TSLL* 13(1972): 541-553.

12944. ----------. "A Revaluation of the Chorus' Role in Milton's *Samson Agonistes*." *MP* 64

(1966): 132-145.

12945. Hurley, C. Harold. "The Cheerful Man's 'Sorrow': A Key to the Meaning of 'L'Allegro,' 45-46." *ELN* 11(1974): 275-278.

12946. Hyman, Lawrence W. "Milton's 'On the Late Massacre in Piedmont.'" *ELN* 3(1965): 26-29.

12947. ----------. "The Reader's Attitude in *Paradise Regained*." *PMLA* 85(1970): 496-503.

12948. Jackson, Elizabeth. "Milton's Sonnet XX." *PMLA* 65(1950): 328-329.

12949. Jacobs, Laurence H. "'Unexpressive Notes': The Decorum of Milton's Nativity Ode." *EL* 1(1974): 166-177.

12950. Jarrett-Kerr, Martin, C. R. "Milton, Poet and Paraphrast." *EIC* 10(1960): 373-389.

12951. Jayne, Sears. "The Subject of Milton's Ludlow Mask." *PMLA* 74(1959): 533-543.

12952. Jochums, Milford C. "'As Ancient as *Constantine*.'" *SEL* 4(1964): 101-107.

12953. Johnson, Clarence D. "A Note on Milton's Use of *Gamut* in *Areopagitica*." *ELN* 14 (1977): 187-189.

12954. Jones, Frederick L. "Shelley and Milton." *SP* 49(1952): 488-519.

12955. Kastor, Frank S. "'By Force or Guile Eternal War': *Paradise Lost*, IV, 776-1015." *JEGP* 70(1971): 269-278.

12956. ----------. "'In His Own Shape': The Stature of Satan in *Paradise Lost*." *ELN* 5 (1968): 264-269.

12957. Kates, Judith A. "The Revaluation of the Classical Heroic in Tasso and Milton." *Comp L* 26(1974): 299-317.

12958. Kell, Richard. "Thesis and Action in Milton's *Comus*." *EIC* 24(1974): 48-54.

12959. Kelley, Maurice, and Samuel Atkins. "Milton's Annotations of Euripedes." *JEGP* 60 (1961): 680-687.

12960. ----------. "Milton's Later Sonnets and the Cambridge Manuscript." *MP* 54(1956): 20-25.

12961. Kellogg, George A. "Bridge's *Milton's Prosody* and Renaissance Metrical Theory." *PMLA* 68(1953): 268-285.

12962. Kenrick, Edward F. "*Paradise Lost* and the *Index* of Prohibited Books." *SP* 53(1956): 485-500.

12963. Kermode, Frank. "Milton's Hero." *RES* 4(1953): 317-330.

12964. Kerrigan, William. "The Heretical Milton: From Assumption to Mortalism." *ELR* 5 (1975): 125-166.

12965. Kliger, Samuel. "Milton in Italy and the Lost Malatesti Manuscript." *SP* 51(1954): 208-213.

12966. Knoepflmacher, U. C. "The Post-Romantic Imagination: *Adam Bede*, Wordsworth and Milton." *ELH* 34(1967): 518-540.

12967. Knott, John R. "Milton's Heaven." *PMLA* 85(1970): 487-495.

12968. ----------. "The Pastoral Day in *Paradise Lost*." *MLQ* 29(1968): 168-182.

12969. ----------. "The Visit of Raphael: *Paradise Lost*, Book V." *PQ* 47(1968): 36-42.

12970. Koehler, G. Stanley. "Milton on 'Numbers,' 'Quantity,' and 'Rime.'" *SP* 55(1958): 201-217.

12971. Kranidas, Thomas. "Adam and Eve in the Garden: A Study of *Paradise Lost*, Book V." *SEL* 4(1964): 71-83.

12972. ----------. "Dalila's Role in *Samson Agonistes*." *SEL* 6(1966): 125-137.

12973. ----------. "'Decorum' and the Style of Milton's Antiprelatical Tracts." *SP* 62(1965): 176-187.

12974. ----------. "Manoa's Role in *Samson Agonistes*." *SEL* 13(1973): 95-109.

12975. ----------. "Milton and the Rhetoric of Zeal." *TSLL* 6(1965): 423-432.

12976. ----------. "Satan's First Disguise." *ELN* 2(1964): 13-15.

12977. Kuby, Lolette. "The World is Half the Devil's: Cold-Warmth Imagery in *Paradise Lost*." *ELH* 41(1974): 182-191.

12978. Labriola, Albert C. "Divine Urgency as a Motive for Conduct in *Samson Agonistes*." *PQ* 50(1971): 99-107.

12979. Landy, Marcia. "Character Portrayal in *Samson Agonistes*." *TSLL* 7(1965): 239-253.

12980. Langford, Thomas. "The Temtations in *Paradise Regained*." *TSLL* 9(1967): 37-46.

12981. Lawrey, Jon S. "'Eager Thought': Dialect in Lycidas." *PMLA* 77(1962): 27-32.

12982. ----------. "'The Faithful Herdman's Art' in *Lycidas*." *SEL* 13(1973): 111-125.

12983. Leahy, William. "Pollution and *Comus*." *EIC* 11(1961): 111.

12984. LeComte, Edward S. "Milton Remembers *The Praise of Folly*." *PMLA* 71(1956): 840.

12985. ----------. "Milton's Infernal Council and Mantuan." *PMLA* 69(1954): 979-983.

12986. ----------. "'That Two-Handed Engine' and Savonarola." *SP* 47(1950): 589-606.

12987. ----------. "'That Two-Handed Engine' and Savonarola: Supplement." *SP* 49 (1952): 548-550.

12988. Lerner, Laurence. "Farewell, Rewards and Fairies: An Essay on *Comus*." *JEGP* 70(1971): 617-631.

12989. ----------. "The Miltonic Simile." *EIC* 4(1954): 297-308.

12990. Lewalski, Barbara K. "Milton: Political Beliefs and Polemical Methods, 1659-60." *PMLA* 74(1959): 191-202.

12991. ----------. "*Paradise Lost* 'Introduced' and 'Structured in Space.'" *MP* 61 (1963): 122-126.

12992. ----------. "*Samson Agonistes* and the 'Tragedy' of the Apocalypse." *PMLA* 85 (1970): 1050-1062.

12993. ----------. "Structure and Symbolism of Vision in Michael's Prophecy, *Paradise Lost*, Books XI-XII." *PQ* 42(1963): 25-35.

12994. ----------. "Theme and Structure in *Paradise Regained*." *SP* 57(1960): 186-220.

12995. Lieb, Michael. "'Holy Place': A Reading of *Paradise Lost*." *SEL* 17(1977): 129-147.

12996. ----------. "'Holy Rest': A Reading of *Paradise Lost*." *ELH* 39(1972): 238-253.

12997. ----------. "Milton and the Kenotic Christology: Its Literary Bearing." *ELH* 37(1970): 342-360.

12998. ----------. "Milton and the Metaphysics of Form." *SP* 71(1974): 206-224.

12999. ----------. "Three Monographs on Milton: An Assessment." *MP* 74(1977): 204-212.

13000. Little, Marguerite. "Milton's *Ad Patrem* and the Younger Gill's *In Natalem mei Parentis*." *JEGP* 49(1950): 345-351.

13001. Lloyd, Michael. "The Two Worlds of *Lycidas*." *EIC* 11(1961): 390-402.

13002. Low, Anthony. "Action and Suffering: *Samson Agonistes* and the Irony of Alternatives." *PMLA* 84(1969): 514-519.

13003. ----------. "The Astronomy of *Paradise Lost*." *ELN* 8(1971): 263-267.

13004. ----------. "The Image of the Tower in *Paradise Lost*." *SEL* 10(1970): 171-214.

13005. ----------. "The Parting in the Garden in *Paradise Lost*." *PQ* 47(1968): 30-35.

13006. ----------. "Some Notes on *Lycidas* and the *Aeneid*." *ELN* 13(1976): 175-177.

13007. ----------. "Tragic Pattern in *Samson Agonistes*." *TSLL* 11(1969): 915-930.

13008. MacLean, Hugh N. "Milton's *Fair Infant*." *ELH* 24(1957): 296-305.

13009. Madsen, William G. "Earth the Shadow of Heaven: Typological Symbolism in *Paradise Lost*." *PMLA* 75(1960): 519-526.

13010. ----------. "The Voice of Michael in *Lycidas*." *SEL* 3(1963): 1-7.

13011. Major, John M. "Milton's View of Rhetoric." *SP* 64(1967): 685-711.

13012. Marilla, Esmond L. "That 'Two-handed Engine' Finally." *PMLA* 67(1952): 1181-1184.

13013. Martz, Louis L. "*Paradise Lost*: Princes of Exile." *ELH* 36(1969): 232-249.

13014. ----------. "*Paradise Lost*: The Realms of Light." *ELR* 1(1971): 71-88.

13015. ----------. "*Paradise Regained*: The Meditative Combat." *ELH* 27(1960): 223-248.

13016. Maxwell, J. C. "Milton's Knowledge of Aeschylus: The Argument from Parallel Passages." *RES* 3(1952): 366-371.

13017. ----------. "Milton's Samson and Sophocles' Heracles." *PQ* 33(1954): 90-91.

13018. ----------. "'The Sensible of Pain': *Paradise Lost*, II. 278." *RES* 5(1954): 268.

13019. ----------. "'*Paradise Lost*,' xi, 829-38." *MLR* 45(1950): 515-516.

13020. McAlister, Flloyd L. "Milton and the Anti-Academics." *JEGP* 61(1962): 779-787.

13021. McCarthy, William. "The Continuity of Milton's Sonnets." *PMLA* 92(1977): 96-111.

13022. McColley, Diane Kelsey. "Free Will and Obedience in the Separation Scene of *Paradise Lost*." *SEL* 12(1972): 103-120.

13023. ----------. "The Voice of the Destroyer in Adam's Diatribes." *MP* 75(1977): 18-28.

13024. McDavid, Raven I., Jr. "*Samson Agonistes* 1096: A Rexamination." *PQ* 33(1954): 86-89.

13025. McGuire, Mary Ann. "'A Most Just

Vituperation': Milton's Christian Orator in *Pro Se Defensio*." *SLI* 10,#2(1977): 105-128.

13026. McHaney, Thomas L. "*The Confidence-Man* and Satan's Disguises in *Paradise Lost*." *NCF* 30(1975): 200-205.

13027. McQueen, William. "*Paradise Lost*, V, VI: The War in Heaven." *SP* 71(1974): 89-104.

13028. Meier, T. K. "Milton's 'Nativity Ode': Sectarian Discord." *MLR* 65(1970): 7-10.

13029. Meyers, Robert R. "Was There a Toad in the Bower?" *MLQ* 33(1972): 37-43.

13030. Miller, David M. "From Delusion to Illumination: A Larger Structure for L'Allegro-Il Penseroso." *PMLA* 86(1971): 32-39.

13031. Miller, Dorothy Durkee. "Eve." *JEGP* 61(1962): 542-547.

13032. Miller, Martin E. "*Pathos* and *Katharsis* in *Samson Agonistes*." *ELH* 31(1964): 156-174.

13033. Miller, Sonia. "The Text of the Second Edition of Milton's *Eikonoklastes*." *JEGP* 52(1953): 214-220.

13034. ----------. "Two References in Milton's *Tenure of Kings*." *JEGP* 50(1951): 320-325.

13035. Miner, Earl. "*Felix Culpa* in the Redemptive Order of *Paradise Lost*." *PQ* 47(1968): 43-54.

13036. Mollenkott, Virginia R. "The Cycle of Sins in *Paradise Lost*, Book XI." *MLQ* 27(1966): 33-40.

13037. ----------. Relativism in *Samson Agonistes*." *SP* 67(1970): 89-102.

13038. Moloney, Michael F. "Plato and Plotinus in Milton's Cosmogony." *PQ* 40(1961): 34-43.

13039. Moore, Frank Harper. "Astraea, the Scorpion, and the Heavenly Scales." *ELH* 38(1971): 350-357.

13040. Moore, John Robert. "Milton among the Augustans: The Infernal Council." *SP* 48(1951): 15-25.

13041. Morkan, Joel. "Wrath and Laughter: Milton's Ideas on Satire." *SP* 69(1972): 475-495.

13042. Morris, David B. "Drama and Stasis in Milton's 'Ode on the Morning of Christ's Nativity.'" *SP* 68(1971): 207-222.

13043. Morse, J. Mitchell. "*Le Pucelle* and *Paradise Lost*." *Comp L* 9(1957): 238-242.

13044. Moss, Leonard. "The Rhetorical Style of *Samson Agonistes*." *MP* 62(1965): 296-301.

13045. Mueller, Martin. "Sixteenth-Century Italian Criticism and Milton's Theory of Catharsis." *SEL* 6(1966): 139-150.

13046. Muldrow, George M. "The Beginning of Adam's Repentance." *PQ* 46(1967): 194-206.

13047. Mundhenk, Rosemary Karmelich. "Dark Scandal and The Sun-Clad Power of Chastity: The Historical Milieu of Milton's *Comus*." *SEL* 15(1975): 141-152.

13048. Murrin, Michael. "The Language of Milton's Heaven." *MP* 74(1977): 350-365.

13049. Nelson, Lowry, Jr. "Góngra and Milton: Toward a Definition of the Baroque." *Comp L* 6(1954): 53-63.

13050. Neuse, Richard. "Metamorphosis and Symbolic Action in *Comus*." *ELH* 34(1967): 49-64.

13051. Nicholas, Constance. "The Edition of the Early Church Historians Used by Milton." *JEGP* 51(1952): 160-162.

13052. Nitchie, George W. "Milton and His Muses." *ELH* 44(1977): 75-84.

13053. Norford, Don Parry. "'My other half': The Coincidence of Opposites in *Paradise Lost*." *MLQ* 36(1975): 21-53.

13054. Novarr, David. "'Gray Dissimulation': Ford and Milton." *PQ* 41(1962): 500-504.

13055. Ogden, H. V. S. "The Crisis of *Paradise Lost* Reconsidered." *PQ* 35(1956): 1-19.

13056. Onuska, John T., Jr. "The Equation of Action and Passion in *Samson Agonistes*." *PQ* 52(1973): 69-84.

13057. Oras, Ants. "'Goddess Humane' ('Paradise Lost' IX, 732)." *MLR* 49(1954): 51-53.

13058. ----------. "Milton's Early Rhyme Schemes and the Structure of *Lycidas*." *MP* 52(1954): 12-22.

13059. Oruch, Jack B. "Milton as Adjutant-General?" *SEL* 5(1965): 61-67.

13060. Otten, Charlotte F. "Milton's Daffadillies." *ELN* 11(1973): 48-49.

13061. ----------. "Milton's Haemony." *ELR* 5(1975): 81-95.

13062. ----------. "Milton's Myrtle's." *EIC* 24(1974): 105.

13063. Parish, John E. "Milton and an Anthropomorphic God." *SP* 56(1959): 619-625.

13064. ----------. "Milton and God's Curse on the Serpent." *JEGP* 58(1959): 241-247.

13065. Parker, William R. "The Dates of Milton's Sonnets on Blindness." *PMLA* 73(1958): 196-200.

13066. ----------. "Notes on the Text of *Samson Agonistes*." *JEGP* 60(1961): 688-698.

13067. ----------, and Fitzroy Pile. "Milton's Last Sonnet Again." *RES* 2(1951): 147-154.

13068. Parks, George B. "Milton's *Muscovia* Not History." *PQ* 31(1952): 218-221.

13069. Patrides, C. A. "The Godhead in *Paradise Lost*: Dogma or Drama." *JEGP* 64(1965): 29-34.

13070. ----------. "Milton and the Protestant Theory of the Atonement." *PMLA* 74(1959): 7-13.

13071. ----------. "*Paradise Lost* and the Theory of Accomodation." *TSLL* 5(1963): 58-63.

13072. ----------. "The 'Protevangelium' in Renaissance Theology and *Paradise Lost*." *SEL* 3(1963): 19-30.

13073. Pecheux, Mother Mary Christopher, O. S. U. "Abraham, Adam, and the Theme of Exile in *Paradise Lost*." *PMLA* 80(1965): 365-371.

13074. ----------. "The Concept of the Second Eve in *Paradise Lost*." *PMLA* 75(1960): 359-366.

13075. ----------. "The Conclusion of Book VI of *Paradise Lost*." *SEL* 3(1963): 109-117.

13076. ----------. "'O Foul Descent!': Satan and the Serpent Form." *SP* 62(1965): 188-196.

13077. ----------. "The Second Adam and The Church in *Paradise Lost*." *ELH* 34(1967): 173-

187.

13078. ----------. "Spenser's Red Cross and Milton's Adam." *ELN* 6(1969): 246-251.

13079. Pequigney, Joseph. "Milton's Sonnet XIX Reconsidered." *TSLL* 8(1967): 485-498.

13080. Phillips, Norma. "Milton's Limbo of Vanity and Dante's Vestibule." *ELN* 3(1966): 177-182.

13081. Pineas, Rainer. "Dekker's *The Whore of Babylon* and Milton's *Paradise Lost*." *ELN* 2(1965): 257-260.

13082. Pittion, J-P. "Milton, La Place, and Socianism." *RES* 23(1972): 138-146.

13083. Price, Alan F. "Incidental Imagery in *Areopagitica*." *MP* 49(1952): 217-222.

13084. Pyle, Fitzroy. "Milton's First Sonnet on His Blindness." *RES* 9(1958): 376-387.

13085. Raben, Joseph. "Milton's Influence on Shelley's Translation of Dante's 'Matilda Gathering Flowers.'" *RES* 14(1963): 142-156.

13086. Radzinowicz, M. A. N. "*Samson Agonistes* and Milton the Politican in Defeat." *PQ* 44(1965): 454-471.

13087. Rajan, B. "*Lycidas*: The Shattering of the Leaves." *SP* 64(1967): 51-64.

13088. ----------. "In Order Serviceable: Milton's 'On the Morning of Christ's Nativity.'" *MLR* 63(1968): 13-22.

13089. Rans, Geoffrey. "Mr. Wilkinson on *Comus*." *EIC* 10(1960): 364-369.

13090. Rauber, D. F. "Milton's Sonnet XI—'I did but prompt.'" *PQ* 49(1970): 561-564.

13091. Rebhorn, Wayne A. "The Humanist Tradition and Milton's Satan: The Conservative as Revolutionary." *SEL* 13(1973): 81-93.

13092. Redman, Harry, Jr. "Villemain on Milton: A Document in Romantic Criticism." *Comp L* 10(1958): 241-245.

13093. Revard, Stella Purce. "The Dramatic Function of the Son in *Paradise Lost*: A Commentary on Milton's 'Trinitarianism.'" *JEGP* 66(1967): 45-58.

13094. ----------. "Eve and the Doctrine of Responsibility in *Paradise Lost*." *PMLA* 88 (1973): 69-78.

13095. ----------. "Milton's Critique of Heroic Warfare in *Paradise Lost* V and VI." *SEL* 7 (1967): 119-139.

13096. ----------. "Satan's Envy of the Kingship of the Son of God: A Reconsideration of *Paradise Lost*, Book 5, and Its Theological Background." *MP* 70(1973): 190-198.

13097. ----------. "The Warring Saints and the Dragon: A Commentary upon Revelation 12: 7-9 and Milton's War in Heaven." *PQ* 53(1974): 181-194.

13098. Richardson, Janette. "Virgil and Milton Once Again." *Comp L* 14(1962): 321-331.

13099. Riffe, Nancy Lee. "'A Fragment of Milton, from the Italian.'" *PQ* 45(1966): 447-450.

13100. Robins, Harry F. "The Crystalline Sphere and the 'Waters Above' in *Paradise Lost*." *PMLA* 69(1954): 903-914.

13101. ----------. "The Key to a Problem in Milton's *Comus*." *MLQ* 12(1951): 422-428.

13102. ----------. "Milton's First Sonnet on His Blindness." *RES* 7(1956): 360-366.

13103. ----------. "Milton's 'Two-Handed Engine at the Door' and St. Matthew's Gospel." *RES* 5(1954): 25-36.

13104. ----------. "Satan's Journey: Direction in *Paradise Lost*." *JEGP* 60(1961): 699-711.

13105. Rollinson, Phillip B. "The Central Debate in *Comus*." *PQ* 49(1970): 481-488.

13106. ----------. "The Traditional Contexts of Milton's 'Two-Handed Engine.'" *ELN* 9 (1971): 28-35.

13107. Roscelli, William John. "The Metaphysical Milton (1625-1631)." *TSLL* 8(1967): 463-484.

13108. Rose, Marilyn Gaddis. "Milton, Chateaubriand, and Villiers de L'Isle Adam: *Paradise Lost* and *Axël*." *SR* 9(1970): 37-43.

13109. Rosenberg, D. M. "Milton's Masque: A Social Occasion for Philosophical Laughter." *SP* 67(1970): 245-253.

13110. ----------. "Style and Meaning in Milton's Anti-Episcopal Tracts." *Criticism* 15 (1973): 43-57.

13111. Rosenblatt, Jason P. "Adam's Pisgah Vision: *Paradise Lost*, Books XI and XII." *ELH* 39(1972): 66-86.

13112. ----------. "'Audacious Neighborhood': Idolatry in *Paradise Lost*, Book I." *PQ* 54(1975): 553-568.

13113. ----------. "Milton's Bee-lines." *TSLL* 18(1977): 609-623.

13114. ----------. "Structural Unity and Temporal Concordance: The War in Heaven in *Paradise Lost*." *PMLA* 87(1972): 31-41.

13115. Rudrum, Alan. "Polygamy in *Paradise Lost*." *EIC* 20(1970): 18-23.

13116. Sadler, Lynn Veach. "Regeneration and Typology: *Samson Agonistes* and Its Relation to *De Doctrina Christiana*, *Paradise Lost* and *Paradise Regained*." *SEL* 12(1972): 141-156.

13117. ----------. "Typological Imagery in *Samson Agonistes*: Noon and the Dragon." *ELH* 37(1970): 195-210.

13118. Samuel, Irene. "The Development of Milton's Poetics." *PMLA* 92(1977): 231-240.

13119. ----------. "The Dialogue in Heaven: A Reconsideration of *Paradise Lost* III. 1-417." *PMLA* 72(1957): 601-611.

13120. ----------. "*Purgatorio* and the Dream of Eve." *JEGP* 63(1964): 441-449.

13121. ----------. "Satan and the 'Diminisht' Stars." *MP* 59(1962): 239-247.

13122. ----------. "The Vally of Serpents: *Inferno* xxiv-xxv and *Paradise Lost* x. 504-577." *PMLA* 78(1963): 449-451.

13123. Sankey, Benjamin T., Jr. "Coleridge on Milton's Satan." *PQ* 41(1962): 504-508.

13124. Saunders, J. W. "Milton, Diomede, and Amaryllis." *ELH* 22(1955): 254-286.

13125. Savage, J. B. "*Comus* and Its Tradition." *ELR* 5(1975): 58-80.

13126. ----------. "Freedom and Necessity in *Paradise Lost*." *ELH* 44(1977): 286-311.

13127. Schoen, Raymond G. "Milton and Spenser's Cave of Mammon Episode." *PQ* 54(1975): 684-689.

13128. Schultz, Howard. "Christ and Antichrist in *Paradise Regained*." *PMLA* 67(1952): 790-808.

13129. ----------. "A fairer Paradise? Some Recent Studies of *Paradise Regained*." *ELH* 32(1965): 275-302.

13130. Scott, William O. "Ramism and Milton's Concept of Poetic Fancy." *PQ* 42(1963): 183-189.

13131. Seaman, John E. "Homeric Parody at the Gates of Milton's Hell." *MLR* 62(1967): 212-213.

13132. Seigel, Catherine F. "The Reconciliation in Book X of 'Paradise Lost.'" *MLR* 68 (1973): 260-263.

13133. Sellin, Paul R. "Milton's Epithet *Agonistes*." *SEL* 4(1964): 137-162.

13134. ----------. "Sources of Milton's Catharsis: A Reconsideration." *JEGP* 60(1961): 712-730.

13135. Sendry, Joseph. "*In Memoriam* and *Lycidas*." *PMLA* 82(1967): 437-443.

13136. Sensabaugh, George F. "Milton Bejesuited." *SP* 47(1950): 224-242.

13137. Shaheen, Naseeb. "'Of *Oreb*, or of *Sinai*.'" *ELN* 9(1971): 25-28.

13138. Shaklee, Margaret E. "Grammatical Agency and the Argument for Responsibility in *Paradise Lost*." *ELH* 42(1975): 518-530.

13139. Shattuck, Charles H. "Macready's *Comus*: A Prompt-Book Study." *JEGP* 60(1961): 731-748.

13140. Shaw, William P. "Milton's Choice of the Epic for *Paradise Lost*." *ELN* 12(1974): 15-20.

13141. Shawcross, John T. "The Balanced Structure of Paradise Lost." *SP* 62(1965): 696-718.

13142. ----------. "The Chronology of Milton's Major Poems." *PMLA* 76(1961): 345-358.

13143. ----------. "The Dating of Certain Poems, Letters, and Prolusions Written by Milton." *ELN* 2(1965): 261-266.

13144. ----------. "Milton's Decision to Become a Poet." *MLQ* 24(1963): 21-30.

13145. ----------. "A Note on Milton's Hobson Poems." *RES* 18(1967): 433-437.

13146. ----------. "Notes on Milton's Amanuenses." *JEGP* 58(1959): 29-38.

13147. ----------. "Of Chronology and the Dates of Milton's Translation from Horace and the *New Forcers of Conscience*." *SEL* 3 (1963): 77-84.

13148. ----------. "One Aspect of Milton's Spelling: Idle Final 'E.'" *PMLA* 78 (1963): 501-510.

13149. ----------. "*Paradise Lost* and 'Novelistic' Technique." *JNT* 5(1975): 1-15.

13150. ----------. "Some Literary Uses of Numerology." *HSL* 1(1969): 50-61.

13151. ----------. "The Son in His Ascendance: A Reading of *Paradise Lost*." *MLQ* 27 (1966): 388-401.

13152. Sheidley, William E. "'Lycidas': An Early Elizabethan Analogue by George Turberville." *MP* 69(1972): 228-230.

13153. Sherbo, Arthur. "'Magic Error': 'Paradise Lost' IV, 239." *MLR* 67(1972): 745-751.

13154. Shumaker, Wayne. "The Fallacy of the Fall in *Paradise Lost*." *PMLA* 70(1955): 1185-1187, 1197-1202.

13155. ----------. "Flowerets and Sounding Seas: A Study in the Affective Structure of *Lycidas*." *PMLA* 66(1951): 485-494.

13156. Sigmon, Dennis H. "The Negatives of *Paradise Lost*: An Introduction." *SP* 73(1976): 320-341.

13157. Sirluck, Ernest. "*Areopagitica* and a Forgotten Licensing Controversy." *RES* 11(1960): 260-274.

13158. ----------. "Certain Editorial Tendencies Exemplified: A New Edition of Milton's *An Apology*." *MP* 50(1953): 201-205.

13159. ----------. "Milton Revises *The Faerie Queene*." *MP* 48(1950): 90-96.

13160. ----------. "Milton's Critical Use of Historical Sources: An Illustration." *MP* 50 (1953): 226-231.

13161. ----------. "Milton's Idle Right Hand." *JEGP* 60(1961): 749-785.

13162. ----------. "Milton's Political Thought: The First Cycle." *MP* 61(1964): 209-224.

13163. Slakey, Roger L. "Milton's Sonnet 'On His Blindness.'" *ELH* 27(1960): 122-130.

13164. Slights, Camille W. "A Hero of Conscience: *Samson Agonistes* and Casuitry." *PMLA* 90(1975): 395-413.

13165. Smith, George William, Jr. "Iterative Rhetoric in *Paradise Lost*." *MP* 74(1976): 1-19.

13166. Smith, Russell E., Jr. "Adam's Fall." *ELH* 35(1968): 527-539.

13167. Spencer, Terence. "Milton, the First English Philhellene." *MLR* 47(1952): 553-554.

13168. Stackhouse, Janifer Gerl. "Early Critical Response to Milton in Germany: The *Dialogi* of Martin Zeiller." *JEGP* 73(1974): 487-496.

13169. Stapleton, Laurance. "Perspectives of Time in *Paradise Lost*." *PQ* 45(1966): 734-748.

13170. Starkman, M. K. "The Militant Miltonist; or The Retreat from Humanism." *ELH* 26(1959): 209-228.

13171. Steadman, John M. "Adam and the Prophesied Redeemer (*Paradise Lost*, XII, 359-623)." *SP* 56(1959): 214-225.

13172. ----------. "Allegory and Verisimilitude in *Paradise Lost*: The Problem of the 'Impossible Credible.'" *PMLA* 78(1963): 36-39.

13173. ----------. "Archangel to Devil: The Background of Satan's Metamorphosis." *MLQ* 21(1960): 321-335.

13174. ----------. "'Bitter Ashes': Protestant Exegesis and the Serpent's Doom." *SP* 59(1962): 201-210.

13175. ----------. "Dalila, the Ulysses Myth, and Renaissance Allegorical Tradition." *MLR* 57(1962): 560-565.

13176. ----------. "Image and Idol: Satan and the Element of Illusion in *Paradise Lost*." *JEGP* 59(1960): 640-654.

13177. ----------. "'Like Turbulencies': The Tempest of *Paradise Regain'd* as Adversity Symbol." *MP* 59(1961): 81-88.

13178. ----------. "'Magnific Titles': Satan's Rhetoric and the Argument of Nobility." *MLR* 61(1966): 561-571.

13179. ----------. "'Man of Renown':

Heroic Virtue and the Giants of Genesis 6:4 (*Paradise Lost*, XI, 638-99)." *PQ* 40(1961): 580-586.

13180. ----------. "Milton, Valvasone, and the Schoolmen." *PQ* 37(1958): 502-504.

13181. ----------. "Milton's *Haemony*: Etymology and Allegory." *PMLA* 77(1962): 200-207.

13182. ----------. "Milton's Harapha and Goliath." *JEGP* 60(1961): 786-795.

13183. ----------. "Milton's 'Summa Epitasis': The End of the Middle of 'Samson Agonistes.'" *MLR* 69(1974): 730-744.

13184. ----------. "Satan in Orbit and Medieval Demonology (*Paradise Lost*, IX, 64-66)." *ELN* 12(1975): 161-163.

13185. ----------. "Satan's Metamorphoses and the Heroic Convention of the Ignoble Disguise." *MLR* 52(1957): 81-85.

13186. ----------. "'Sin' and the Serpent of Genesis 3: *Paradise Lost*, II, 650-53." *MP* 54(1957): 217-220.

13187. ----------. "Tantalus and the Dead Sea Apples (*Paradise Lost*, X, 547-73)." *JEGP* 64(1965): 35-40.

13188. ----------. "Tradition and Innovation in Milton's 'Sin': The Problem of Literary Indebtedness." *PQ* 39(1960): 93-103.

13189. ----------. "The 'Tree of Life' Symbolism in *Paradise Regain'd*." *RES* 11(1960): 384-391.

13190. Stein, Arnold. "The Kingdoms of the World: Paradise Regained." *ELH* 23(1956): 112-126.

13191. ----------. "Milton's War in Heaven—An Extended Metaphor." *ELH* 18(1951): 201-220.

13192. ----------. "Satan: the Dramatic Role of Evil." *PMLA* 65(1950): 221-230.

13193. Stempel, Daniel. "John Knox and Milton's 'Two-Handed Engine.'" *ELN* 3(1966): 259-263.

13194. St. George, Priscilla P. "Psychomachia in Books V and VI of *Paradise Lost*." *MLQ* 27(1966): 185-196.

13195. Stollman, Samuel S. "Milton's Dichotomy of 'Judaism' and 'Hebraism.'" *PMLA* 89(1974): 105-112.

13196. ----------. "Milton's Understanding of 'Hebraic' in *Samson Agonistes*." *SP* 69(1972): 334-347.

13197. Stringer, Gary. "The Unity of 'L'Allegro' and 'Il Penseroso.'" *TSLL* 12(1970): 221-229.

13198. Stroup, Thomas B. "Aeneas' Vision of Creüsa and Milton's Twenty-third Sonnet." *PQ* 39(1960): 125-126.

13199. ----------. "*The Cestus*: Manuscript of an Anonymous Eighteenth-Century Imitation of *Comus*." *SEL* 2(1962): 47-55.

13200. ----------. "'When I Consider': Milton's Sonnet XIX." *SP* 69(1972): 242-258.

13201. Summers, Joseph H. "'Grateful Vicissitude' in *Paradise Lost*." *PMLA* 69(1954): 251-264.

13202. ----------. "The Two Great Sexes in *Paradise Lost*." *SEL* 2(1962): 1-26.

13203. ----------. "The Voice of the Redeemer in *Paradise Lost*." *PMLA* 70(1955): 1082-1089.

13204. Sullivan, Edward E., Jr. "'Sweet Societies That Sing': The Voice of the Saints in *Lycidas*." *EL* 23(1976): 32-40.

13205. Svendsen, Kester. "John Milton and the Expulsion Scene of *Paradise Lost*." *SEL* 1,#1 (1961): 63-73.

13206. ----------. "Milton and Alexander More: New Documents." *JEGP* 60(1961): 796-807.

13207. ----------. "Milton's *Pro Se Defensio* and Alexander More." *TSLL* 1(1959): 11-29.

13208. ----------. "Science and Structure in Milton's *Doctrine of Divorce*." *PMLA* 67(1952): 435-445.

13209. Swaim, Kathleen M. "The Art of the Maze in Book IX of *Paradise Lost*." *SEL* 12(1972): 129-140.

13210. ----------. "Cycle and Circle: Time and Structure in 'L'Allegro' and 'Il Penseroso.'" *TSLL* 18(1976): 422-432.

13211. ----------. "Lycidas and the Dolphins of Apollo." *JEGP* 72(1973): 340-349.

13212. ----------. "'Mighty Pan': Tradition and an Image in Milton's Nativity *Hymn*." *SP* 68(1971): 484-495.

13213. Taaffe, James G. "Michaelmas, The 'Lawless Hour,' and the Occasion of Milton's *Comus*." *ELN* 6(1969): 257-262.

13214. Tayler, E. W. "Milton's *Samson*: The Form of Christian Tragedy." *ELR* 3(1973): 306-321.

13215. Thompson, Claud Adelburt. "'That Two-Handed Engine' Will Smite: Time Will Have a Stop." *SP* 59(1962): 184-200.

13216. Tillyard, E. M. W. "On Annotating *Paradise Lost*, Books IX and X." *JEGP* 60(1961): 808-816.

13217. Tobin, J. J. M. "*Samson* and Sea-Imagery Again." *ELN* 15(1977): 23-27.

13218. ----------. "The Trojan Harapha." *ELN* 12(1975): 273-279.

13219. Toliver, Harold E. "Complicity of Voice in *Paradise Lost*." *MLQ* 25(1964): 153-170.

13220. ----------. "Symbol-Making and the Labors of Milton's Eden." *TSLL* 18(1976): 433-450.

13221. Tung, Mason. "The Abdiel Episode: A Contextual Reading." *SP* 62(1965): 595-609.

13222. ----------. "Samson Impatiens: A Reinterpretation of Milton's *Samson Agonistes*." *TSLL* 9(1968): 475-492.

13223. Turner, W. Arthur. "Milton's Two-Handed Engine." *JEGP* 49(1950): 562-565.

13224. Tuve, Rosemond. "Baroque and Mannerist Milton?" *JEGP* 60(1961): 817-833.

13225. Ulreich, John C., Jr. "'A Bright Golden Flow'r': Haemony as a Symbol of Transformation." *SEL* 17(1977): 119-128.

13226. Varandyan, Emmanuel P. "Milton's *Paradise Lost* and Zoroaster's *Zenda Vesta*." *Comp L* 13(1961): 208-220.

13227. Viswanathan, S. "Milton and the 'Seasons' Difference.'" *SEL* 13(1973): 127-133.

13228. Waddington, Raymond B. "Appearance and Reality in Satan's Disguises." *TSLL* 4(1962): 390-398.

13229. ----------. "The Death of Adam: Vision and Voice in Books XI and XII of *Paradise Lost*." *MP* 70(1972): 9-21.

13230. Waggoner, George R. "The Challenge

to Single Combat in *Samson Agonistes*." *PQ* 39 (1960): 82-92.

13231. Wallace, John Malcom. "Milton's *Arcades*." *JEGP* 58(1959): 627-636.

13232. Watson, J. R. "Divine Providence and the Structure of *Paradise Lost*." *EIC* 14 (1964): 148-155.

13233. Webber, Joan. "Milton's God." *ELH* 40(1973): 514-531.

13234. ----------. "The Son of God and Power of Life in Three Poems by Milton." *ELH* 37(1970): 175-194.

13235. Weber, Burton J. "The Schematic Structure of *Paradise Regained*: A Hypothesis." *PQ* 50(1971): 553-566.

13236. Weidhorn, Manfred. "The Anxiety Dream in Literature from Homer to Milton." *SP* 64(1967): 65-82.

13237. Weinbrot, Howard D. "John Clarke's *Essay on Study* and Samuel Johnson on *Paradise Lost*." *MP* 72(1975): 404-407.

13238. Weinkauf, Mary S. "Dalila: The Worst of All Possible Wives." *SEL* 13(1973): 135-147.

13239. West, Robert H. "The Names of Milton's Angels." *SP* 47(1950): 211-223.

13240. Wheeler, Thomas. "Milton's Blank Verse Couplets." *JEGP* 66(1967): 359-368.

13241. ----------. "Milton's Twenty-Third Sonnet." *SP* 58(1961): 510-515.

13242. White, Robert B., Jr. "Milton's Allegory of Sin and Death: A Comment on Background." *MP* 70(1973): 337-341.

13243. Whiteley, M. "Verse and Its Feet." *RES* 9(1958): 268-279.

13244. Whiting, George W. "Abdiel and the Prophet Abdias." *SP* 60(1963): 214-226.

13245. ----------. "'And without Thorn the Rose.'" *RES* 10(1959): 60-63.

13246. ----------. "Pareus, the Stuarts, Laud, and Milton." *SP* 50(1953): 215-229.

13247. ----------, and Ann Gossman. "Siloas's Brook, The Pool of Siloam, and Milton's Muse." *SP* 58(1961): 193-205.

13248. Widmer, Kingsley. "The Iconography of Renunciation: The Miltonic Simile." *ELH* 25(1958): 258-269.

13249. Wilkenfeld, Roger B. "Act and Emblem: The Conclusion of *Samson Agonistes*." *ELH* 32(1965): 160-168.

13250. ----------. "The Seat at the Center: An Interpretation of *Comus*." *ELH* 33 (1966): 170-197.

13251. ----------. "Theoretics or Polemics? Milton Criticism and the 'Dramatic Axiom.'" *PMLA* 82(1967): 505-515.

13252. Wilkinson, David. "The Escape from Pollution: A Comment on *Comus*." *EIC* 10 (1960): 32-43.

13253. Williams, R. Darby. "Two Baroque Game Poems on Grace: Herbert's 'Paradise' and Milton's 'On Time.'" *Criticism* 12(1970): 180-194.

13254. Williamson, George. "The Education of Adam." *MP* 61(1963): 96-109.

13255. ----------. "Milton the Anti-Romantic." *MP* 60(1962): 13-21.

13256. Williamson, Marilyn L. "The Myth of Orpheus in 'L'Allegro' and 'Il Penseroso.'"

MLQ 32(1971): 377-386.

13257. Wittreich, Joseph Anthony, Jr. "Milton's 'Destin'd Urn': The Art of *Lycidas*." *PMLA* 84(1969): 60-70.

13258. ----------. "Pico and Milton: A Gloss on *Aeropagitica*." *ELN* 9(1971): 108-110.

13259. Wright, B. A. "'Mainly': *Paradise Lost*, XI. 519." *RES* 4(1953): 143.

13260. ----------. "A Note on Milton's Punctuation." *RES* 5(1954): 170.

13261. ----------. "*Paradise Lost*, IX, 1079-80." *RES* 10(1959): 62-67.

13262. Woodhouse, A. S. P. "The Historical Criticism of Milton." *PMLA* 66(1951): 1033-1044.

13263. Wolfe, Don M. "Limits of Miltonic Toleration." *JEGP* 60(1961): 834-846.

13264. Woolrych, Austin. "Milton and Richard Heath." *PQ* 53(1974): 132-135.

13265. Zwicky, Laurie. "Kairos in *Paradise Regained*: the Divine Plan." *ELH* 31 (1964): 271-277.

See also 474, 894, 903, 935, 1173, 1275, 2212, 2336, 3144, 3869, 4653, 9324, 9419, 9463, 11420, 11440, 11798, 11951, 11978, 11980, 12200, 12615, 13292, 13697, 13800, 14606, 15265, 16303, 16335, 17373, 17389, 17426, 17524, 18029.

MINSHEU, JOHN. 13266. Rosier, James L. "The Sources and Methods of Minsheu's *Guide into the Tongues*." *PQ* 40(1961): 68-76.

MORE, HENRY. 13267. Brown, C. C. "Henry More's 'Deep Retirement': New Material on the Early Years of the Cambridge Platonist." *RES* 20(1969): 445-454.

13268. ----------. "The Mere Numbers of Henry More's Cabbala." *SEL* 10(1970): 143-153.

NABBES, THOMAS. 13269. Vince, R. W. "Thomas Nabbes's *Hannibal* and *Scipio*." *SEL* 11 (1971): 327-343.

NEALE, THOMAS. See 13500.

NEVILLE, HENRY. 13270. Aldridge, A. Owen. "Polygamy in Early Fiction: Henry Neville and Denis Veiras." *PMLA* 65(1950): 464-472.

NEWTON, ISAAC. 13271. Bevilacqua, Vincent M. "Two Newtonian Arguments concerning Taste." *PQ* 47(1968): 585-590.

13272. Elliott, Ralph W. V. "Isaac Newton's 'Of an Universall Language.'" *MLR* 52 (1957): 1-18.

NORTH, ROGER. 13273. Millard, P. T. "The Chronology of Roger North's Main Works." *RES* 24(1973): 283-294.

OLDHAM, JOHN. 13274. Brooks, Harold F. "John Oldham: Some Problems of Biography and Annotation." *PQ* 54(1975): 569-578.

13275. ----------. "Oldham and Phineas Fletcher: An Unrecognized Source for *Satyrs Upon the Jesuits*." *RES* 22(1971): 410-422, *RES* 23(1972): 19-34.

13276. Mackin, Cooper R. "The Satiric Technique of John Oldham's *Satyrs upon the Jesuits*." *SP* 62(1965): 78-90.

13277. Vieth, David M. "John Oldham, the Wits, and *A Satyr Against Vertue*." *PQ* 32 (1953): 90-93.

See also 11348, 11650, 11933.

OTWAY, THOMAS. 13278. Berman, Ronald. "Nature in *Venice Preserv'd*." *ELH* 36(1969): 529-543.

13279. Durant, Jack D. "'Honor's Toughest

Task': Family and State in *Venice Preserved*." *SP* 71(1974): 484-503.

13280. Hauser, David R. "Otway Preserved: Theme and Form in *Venice Preserv'd*." *SP* 55 (1958): 481-493.

13281. Hughes, Derek W. "A New Look at *Venice Preserv'd*." *SEL* 11(1971): 437-457.

13282. Hume, Robert D. "Otway and the Comic Muse." *SP* 73(1976): 87-116.

13283. Klieneberger, H. R. "Otway's 'Venice Preserved' and Hofmannsthal's 'Das Gerettete Venedig.'" *MLR* 62(1967): 292-297.

13284. Marshall, Geoffrey. "The Coherence of *The Orphan*." *TSLL* 11(1969): 931-943.

13285. McBurney, William H. "Otway's Tragic Muse Debauched: Sensuality in *Venice Preserv'd*." *JEGP* 58(1959): 380-399.

13286. Ross, J. C. "An Attack on Thomas Shadwell in Otway's *The Atheist*." *PQ* 52(1973): 753-760.

See also 11388, 13628.

PAYNE, HENRY NEVILLE. See 11399.

PECKE, THOMAS. See 12098.

PENKETHMAN, JOHN. 13287. Butler, Francella. "John Penkethman's Pseudonymous Plague Works, 1625-1636." *SP* 57(1960): 622-633.

PEPYS, SAMUEL. 13288. Rousseau, G. S. "Two New Pepys Letters." *RES* 19(1968): 169-172.

13289. Taylor, Ivan E. "Mr. Pepys's Use of Colloquial English." *CLA* 7(1963): 22-36.

PHILIPS, KATHERINE. 13290. Elmen, Paul. "Some Manuscript Poems by the Matchless Orinda." *PQ* 30(1951): 53-57.

13291. Roberts, William. "Saint-Amant, Orinda, and Dryden's Miscellany." *ELN* 1(1964): 191-196.

PHILLIPS, EDWARD. 13292. Fletcher, Harris. "Milton's [Index Poeticus] —The *Theatrum Poetarum* by Edward Phillips." *JEGP* 55(1956): 35-40.

13293. Golding, Sanford. "The Sources of the *Theatrum Poetarum*." *PMLA* 76(1961): 48-53.

13294. Howarth, R. G. "Edward Phillips's 'Compendiosa Enumeratio Poetarum.'" *MLR* 54(1959): 321-328.

POETA de TRISTIBUS. 13295. Love, Harold. "The Satirised Characters in *Poeta de Tristibus*." *PQ* 47(1968): 547-562.

POOLE, JOSHUA. 13296. O Hehir, Brendan. "Denham's *Cooper's Hill* and Poole's *English Parnassus*." *MP* 61(1964): 253-260.

QUARLES, FRANCIS. 13297. Davies, H. Neville. "Quarles's Hybrid Strain." *ELN* 4(1967): 266-268.

13298. Meserole, Harrison T. "'Come dry-Brained Marble eyed Porticks': James Allen and Francis Quarles." *EAL* 1,#3(1967): 6-7.

See also 12281, 15245.

RATSEY PAMPHLETS. 13299. O'Connor, John J. "On the Authorship of the Ratsey Pamphlets." *PQ* 30(1951): 381-386.

RANDOLPH, THOMAS. 13300. Kelliher, W. Hilton. "Two Notes on Thomas Randolph." *PQ* 51 (1972): 941-945.

REYNOLDS, HENRY. 13301. Cinquemani, A. M. "Henry Reynolds' *Mythomystes* and the Continuity of Ancient Modes of Allegoresis in Seventeenth-Century England." *PMLA* 85(1970): 1041-1049.

ROCHESTER, JOHN WILMOT. 13302. Brooks, Elmer L. "An Unpublished Restoration Satire on the Court Ladies." *ELN* 10(1973): 201-208.

13303. Davies, Paul C. "Rochester and Boileau: A Reconsideration." *Comp L* 21(1969): 348-355.

13304. Fabricant, Carole. "Rochester's World of Imperfect Enjoyment." *JEGP* 73(1974): 338-350.

13305. ----------. "The Writer as Hero and Whore: Rochester's *Letter from Artemisia to Chloe*." *EL* 2(1976): 152-166.

13306. Fujimura, Thomas H. "Rochester's 'Satyr against Mankind': An Analysis." *SP* 55 (1958): 576-590.

13307. Johnson, Ronald W. "Rhetoric and Drama in Rochester's 'Satyr Against Reason and Mankind.'" *SEL* 15(1975): 365-373.

13308. Jordan, Robert. "The First Printing of Rochester's 'Tunbridge Wells.'" *ELN* 10 (1973): 267-270.

13309. Knight, Charles A. "The Paradox of Reason: Argument in Rochester's 'Satyr against Mankind.'" *MLR* 65(1970): 254-260.

13310. McVeagh, John. "Rochester and Defoe: A Study in Influence." *SEL* 14(1974): 327-341.

13311. Paulson, Kristoffer F. "Pun Intended: Rochester's *Upon Nothing*." *ELN* 9(1971): 118-121.

13312. ----------. "The Reverend Edward Stillingfleet and the 'Epilogue' to Rochester's *A Satyr against Reason and Mankind*." *PQ* 50 (1971): 657-663.

13313. Pinto, Vivian De S. "'The History of Insipids': Rochester, Freke, and Marvell." *MLR* 65(1970): 11-15.

13314. Treglown, Jeremy. "Rochester: Three Forgotten Letters." *MLR* 71(1976): 19-25.

13315. ----------. "The Satirical Inversion of Some English Sources in Rochester's Poetry." *RES* 24(1973): 42-48.

13316. Vieth, David M. "Poems by 'My Lord R.': Rochester Versus Radclyffe." *PMLA* 72(1957): 612-619.

13317. ----------. "Rochester's 'Scepter' Lampoon on Charles II." *PQ* 37(1958): 424-432.

13318. Weinbrot, Howard D. "The Swelling Volume: The Apocalyptic Satire of Rochester's *Letter from Artemisia in the Town to Chloe in the Country*." *SLI* 5,#2(1972): 19-37.

13319. ----------. "The 'Allusion to Horace': Rochester's Imitative Mode." *SP* 69 (1972): 348-368.

13320. Wilcoxon, Reba. "Pornography, Obscenity, and Rochester's 'The Imperfect Enjoyment.'" *SEL* 15(1975): 375-390.

ROSS, ALEXANDER.

ROWLEY, SAMUEL. 13321. Somerset, J. A. "New Facts Concerning Samuel Rowley." *RES* 17 (1966): 293-297.

ROWLEY, WILLIAM. 13322. Robb, Dewar M. "The Canon of William Rowley's Plays." *MLR* 45 (1950): 129-141.

13323. Shapiro, I. A. "*Tityre-Tu* and the Date of William Rowley's *Woman Never Vext*." *RES* 11(1960): 55-56.

See entries for *The Changeling* and *A Fair*

Quarrel under **Thomas Middleton**.

    See also 9389, 12144, 12685, 12699, 12702.

    RUDYERD, BENJAMIN. Sanderson, James L. "*Epigrames p[er] B[enjamin] R[udyerd]* and Some More 'Stolen Feathers' of Henry Parrot." *RES* 17 (1966): 241-255.

    RYMER, THOMAS. 13325. Miner, Earl. "Mr. Dryden and Mr. Rymer." *PQ* 54(1975): 137-151.

    13326. Osborn, James M. "Thomas Rymer as Rhymer." *PQ* 54(1975): 152-177.

    13327. Zimansky, Curt A. "A Manuscript Poem to Thomas Rymer." [with text of anonymous poem]." *PQ* 30(1951): 217-220.

    SANDYS, GEORGE. See 11353.

    SECOND MAIDEN'S TRAGEDY. 11328. Levin, Richard. "The Double Plot of *The Second Maiden's Tragedy.*" *SEL* 3(1963): 219-231.

    SEDLEY, CHARLES. 13329. Boddy, Margaret P. "The 1692 *Fourth Book of Virgil.*" *RES* 15 (1964): 364-380.

    SHADWELL, THOMAS. 13330. Berman, Ronald. "The Values of Shadwell's *Squire of Alsatia.*" *ELH* 39(1972): 375-386.

    13331. Edmunds, John. "'Timon of Athens' blended with 'Le Misanthrope': Shadwell's Recipe for Satirical Tragedy." *MLR* 64(1969): 500-507.

    13332. Fisher, Alan S. "The Significance of Thomas Shadwell." *SP* 71(1974): 225-246.

    13333. Gilde, Joseph M. "Shadwell and the Royal Society: Satire in *The Virtuoso.*" *SEL* 10(1970): 469-490.

    13334. Hume, Robert D. "Formal Intention in *The Brothers* and *The Squire of Alsatia.*" *ELN* 6(1969): 176-184.

    See also 11388, 11399.

    SHIPMAN, THOMAS. 13335. Zimansky, Curt A., and Robert D. Hume. "Thomas Shipman's *Henry the Third of France*: Some Questions of Date, Performance, and Publication." *PQ* 55(1976): 436-444.

    SHIRLEY, JAMES. 13336. Bas, Georges. "Two Misrepresented Biographical Documents Concerning James Shirley." *RES* 27(1976): 303-310.

    13337. Bland, D. S. "A Word in Shirley's *The Cardinal.*" *RES* 4(1953): 358-359.

    13338. Cogan, Nathan. "James Shirley's *The Example* (1634): Some Reconsiderations." *SEL* 17(1977): 317-331.

    13339. Crawley, Derek. "The Effect of Shirley's Hand on Chapman's *The Tragedy of Chabot Admiral of France.*" *SP* 63(1966): 677-696.

    13340. Feil, J. P. "James Shirley's Years of Service." *RES* 8(1957): 413-416.

    13341. Levin, Richard. "The Triple Plot of 'Hyde Park.'" *MLR* 62(1967): 17-27.

    13342. McGrath, Juliet. "James Shirley's Uses of *Language.*" *SEL* 6(1966): 323-339.

    13343. Morillo, Marvin. "Shirley's 'Preferment' and the Court of Charles I." *SEL* 1,#2(1961): 101-117.

    13344. Morton, Richard. "Deception and Social Dislocation: An Aspect of James Shirley's Drama." *RD* 9(1966): 227-245.

    13345. Riemer, A. P. "Shirley's Revisions and the Date of *The Constant Maid.*" *RES* 17(1966): 141-148.

    13346. ----------. "A Source for Shirley's

The Traitor." *RES* 14(1963): 380-383.

    See also 9389.

    SOUTHERNE, THOMAS. 13347. Kaufman, Anthony. "'This hard condition of a woman's fate': Southerne's *The Wives' Excuse.*" *MLQ* 34 (1973): 36-47.

    STRODE, WILLIAM. 13348. Main, C. F. "Notes on Some Poems Attributed to William Strode." *PQ* 34(1955): 444-448.

    SUCKLING, JOHN. 13349. Anselment, Raymond A. "'Men Most of All Enjoy, When Least They Do': The Love Poetry of John Suckling." *TSLL* 14(1972): 17-32.

    13350. Beaurline. L. A. "The Canon of Sir John Suckling's Poems." *SP* 57(1960): 492-518.

    13351. ----------. "New Poems by Sir John Suckling." *SP* 59(1962): 651-657.

    13352. ----------. "'Why So Pale and Wan': An Essay in Critical Method." *TSLL* 4(1963): 553-563.

    13353. Freehafer, John. "*The Italian Night Piece* and Suckling's *Aglaura.*" *JEGP* 67(1968): 249-265.

    13354. Markel, Michael H. "John Suckling's Semi-serious Love Poetry." *EL* 4(1977): 152-158.

    See also 11424, 11505, 11508.

    SYLVESTER, JOSHUA. 13355. Illo, John. "Dryden, Sylvester, and the Correspondence of Melancholy Winter and Cold Age." *ELN* 1(1963): 101-104.

    13356. Williams, Franklin B., Jr. "The Bear Facts About Joshua Sylvester, The Woodman." *ELN* 9(1971): 90-98.

    TAYLOR, JEREMY. 13357. Elmen, Paul. "Jeremy Taylor and the Fall of Man." *MLQ* 14(1953): 139-148.

    TEMPLE, WILLIAM. 13358. French, David P. "Swift, Temple, and 'A Digression on Madness.'" *TSLL* 5(1963): 42-57.

    13359. Halewood, William H. "Young William Temple and Young Jonathan Swift." *CLA* 10(1966): 105-113.

    See also 11361, 15096, 15150.

    TILLOTSON, JOHN. 13360. Brown, David D. "John Tillotson's Revisions and Dryden's 'Talent for English Prose.'" *RES* 12(1961): 24-39.

    TOURNEUR, CYRIL. 13361. Ayres, Philip J. "Parallel Action and Reductive Technique in *The Revenger's Tragedy.*" *ELN* 8(1970): 103-107.

    13362. Champion, Larry S. "Tourner's *The Revenger's Tragedy* and the Jacobean Tragic Perspective." *SP* 72(1975): 299-321.

    13363. Craik, T. W. "The Revenger's Tragedy." *EIC* 6(1956): 482-485.

    13364. Ekeblad, Inga-Stina. "An Approach to Tourneur's Imagery." *MLR* 54(1959): 489-498.

    13365. Foakes, R. A. "On the Authorship of 'The Revenger's Tragedy.'" *MLR* 48(1953): 129-138.

    13366. Hamilton, A. C. "Spenser and Tourneur's *Transformed Metamorphosis.*" *RES* 8 (1957): 127-136.

    13367. Hunter, G. K. "A Source for *The Revenger's Tragedy.*" *RES* 10(1959): 181-182.

    13368. Jacobson, Daniel J. "'There It Goes'—Or Does It? Thunder in *The Revenger's Tragedy* and a Catch-Phrase in Shakespeare, Marlowe, and Middleton." *ELN* 13(1975): 6-10.

    13369. Kaufmann, R. J. "Theodicy, Tragedy

and the Psalmist: Tourner's *Atheist's Tragedy*." *CD* 3(1969): 241-262.

13370. Kistner, Arthur L., and M. K. Kistner. "Morality and Inevitability in *The Revenger's Tragedy*." *JEGP* 71(1972): 36-46.

13371. Layman, B. J. "Tourner's Artificial Noon: The Design of *The Revenger's Tragedy*." *MLQ* 34(1973): 20-35.

13372. Leech, Clifford. "*The Atheist's Tragedy* as a Dramatic Comment on Chapman's *Bussy* Plays." *JEGP* 52(1953): 525-530.

13373. Lisca, Peter. "*The Revenger's Tragedy*: A Study in Irony." *PQ* 38(1959): 242-251.

13374. Ornstein, Robert. "*The Atheist's Tragedy* and Renaissance Naturalism." *SP* 51 (1954): 194-207.

13375. ----------. "The Ethical Design of *The Revenger's Tragedy*." *ELH* 21(1954): 81-93.

13376. Pearce, Howard. "*Virtu* and *Poesis* in *The Revenger's Tragedy*." *ELH* 43(1976): 19-52.

13377. Peter, John. "The Revenger's Tragedy." *EIC* 6(1956): 485-486.

13378. ----------. "*The Revenger's Tragedy* Reconsidered." *EIC* 6(1956): 131-143.

13379. Salingar, L. G. "'The Revenger's Tragedy': Some Possible Sources." *MLR* 60(1965): 3-12.

13380. Schoenbaum, Samuel. "*The Revenger's Tragedy*: Jacobean Dance of Death." *MLQ* 15(1954): 201-207.

13381. Simmons, J. L. "The Tongue and Its Office in *The Revenger's Tragedy*." *PMLA* 92 (1977): 56-68.

13382. Tomlinson, T. W. "The Morality of Revenge: Tourneur's Critics." *EIC* 10(1960): 134-147.

13383. Wadsworth, Frank W. "'The Revenger's Tragedy.'" *MLR* 50(1955): 307.

13384. Wigler, Stephen. "'Tis Well He Died; He Was a Witch'; A Note on *The Revenger's Tragedy*, V. iii. 117." *ELN* 14(1976): 17-20.

13385. Wilds, Nancy G. "'Of Rare Fire Compact': Image and Rhetoric in *The Revenger's Tragedy*." *TSLL* 17(1975): 61-74.

See also 9354, 9389, 12733.

TRAHERNE, THOMAS. 13386. Clements, A. L. "On the Mode and Meaning of Traherne's Mystical Poetry: 'The Preparative.'" *SP* 61(1964): 500-521.

13387. Cox, Gerard H., Jr. "Traherne's *Centuries*: A Platonic Devotion of 'Divine Philosophy.'" *MP* 69(1971): 10-24.

13388. Day, Malcom M. "'Naked Truth' and the Language of Thomas Traherne." *SP* 68(1971): 305-325.

13389, ----------. "Traherne and the Doctrine of Pre-existence." *SP* 65(1968): 81-97.

13390. Dees, Jerome S. "Recent Studies in Traherne." *ELR* 4(1974): 189-196.

13391. Drake, Ben. "Thomas Traherne's Songs of Innocence." *MLQ* 31(1970): 492-503.

13392. Grant, Patrick. "Original Sin and the Fall of Man in Thomas Traherne." *ELH* 38 (1971): 40-61.

13392. Marks, Carol L. "Thomas Traherne and Cambridge Platonism." *PMLA* 81(1966): 521-534.

13394. Owen, Catharine A. "The Authorship of the 'Meditations on the Six Days of Creation'

and the 'Meditations and Devotions on the Life of Christ.'" *MLR* 56(1961): 1-12.

13395. Ridler, Anne. "Traherne: Some Wrong Attributions." *RES* 18(1967): 48-49.

13396. Ridlon, Harold C. "The Function of the 'Infant-Ey' in Traherne's Poetry." *SP* 61 (1964): 627-639.

13397. Russell, Angela. "The Life of Thomas Traherne." *RES* 6(1955): 34-43.

13398. Sauls, Lynn. "Traherne's Debt to Puente's *Meditations*." *PQ* 50(1971): 161-174.

13399. Selkin, Carl M. "The Language of Vision: Traherne's Cataloguing Style." *ELR* 6 (1976): 92-104.

13400. Trimpey, John E. "An Analysis of Traherne's 'Thoughts I.'" *SP* 68(1971): 88-104.

13401. Wallace, John Malcolm. "Thomas Traherne and the Structure of Meditation." *ELH* 25(1958): 79-89.

See also 11440.

TURKISH MAHOMET. 13402. O'Connor, John J. "A Jacobean Allusion to *The Turkish Mahomet* and *Hiren the Fair Greek*." *PQ* 35(1956): 427-429.

VANBRUGH, JOHN. 13403. Faller, Lincoln B. "Between Jest and Earnest: The Comedy of Sir John Vanbrugh." *MP* 72(1974): 17-29.

13404. Kenny, Shirley Strum. "Perrenial Favorites: Congreve, Vanbrugh, Cibber, Farquhar, and Steele." *MP* 73(1976): S4-S11.

13405. Kropf, C. R. "*The Relapse* and the Sentimental Mask." *JNT* 1(1971): 193-199.

13406. Harley, Graham D. "*Squire Trelooby* and *The Cornish Squire*: A Reconsideration." *PQ* 49(1970): 520-529.

13407. Hughes, Leo, and A. H. Scouten. "The Penzance Promptbook of *The Pilgrim*." *MP* 73 (1975): 33-53.

13407a. Huseboe, Arthur R. "Vanbrugh: Additions to the Correspondence." *PQ* 53(1974): 135-140.

13408. Patterson, Frank M. "The Revised Scenes of *The Provok'd Wife*." *ELN* 4(1966): 19-23.

13409. Peterson, William M. "Cibber's *She Wou'd and She Wou'd Not* and Vanbrugh's *Aesop*." *PQ* 35(1956): 429-435.

13410. Roper, Alan. "Language and Action in *The Way of the World*, *Love's Last Shift*, and *The Relapse*." *ELH* 40(1973): 44-69.

13411. Rosenberg, Albert. "New Light on Vanbrugh." *PQ* 45(1966): 603-613.

13412. Shipley, John B. "The Authorship of *The Cornish Squire*." *PQ* 47(1968): 145-156.

VAUGHAN, HENRY. 13413. Allen, Don Cameron. "Vaughan's 'Cock-Crowing' and the Tradition." *ELH* 21(1954): 94-106.

13414. Bourdette, Robert E., Jr. "Recent Studies in Henry Vaughan." *ELR* 4(1974): 299-310.

13415. Bowers, Fredson. "Henry Vaughan's Multiple Time Scheme." *MLQ* 23(1962): 291-296.

13416. Chambers, Leland H. "Henry Vaughan's Allusive Technique: Biblical Allusions in 'The Night.'" *MLQ* 27(1966): 371-387.

13417. ----------. "Vaughan's 'The World': The Limits of Extrinsic Criticism." *SEL* 8(1968): 137-150.

13418. Christopher, Georgia B. "In Arcadia, Calvin. . .: A Study of Nature in Henry Vaughan." *SP* 70(1973): 408-426.

13419. Durr, R. A. "Vaughan's Pilgrim and the Birds of Night: 'The Proffer.'" *MLQ* 21 (1960): 45-48.

13420. ----------. "Vaughan's 'The Night.'" *JEGP* 59(1960): 34-40.

13421. ----------. "Vaughan's Theme and Its Pattern: 'Regeneration.'" *SP* 54(1957): 14-28.

13422. Farnham, Fern. "The Imagery of Henry Vaughan's 'The Night.'" *PQ* 38(1959): 425-435.

13423. Gesner, Carol. "A Note on Henry Vaughan." *MLR* 50(1955): 172-173.

13424. Grant, P. "Hermetic Philosophy and the Nature of Man in Vaughan's *Silex Scintillans*." *JEGP* 67(1968): 406-422.

13425. Kermode, Frank. "The Private Imagery of Henry Vaughan." *RES* 1(1950): 206-225.

13426. Malpezzi, Frances M. "An Approach to Vaughan's 'Isaacs Marriage.'" *ELN* 14(1976): 112-117.

13427. Marcus, Leah Sinanoglon. "Vaughan, Wordsworth, Coleridge, and the *Encomium Asini*." *ELH* 42(1975): 224-241.

13428. Marilla, E. L. "The Mysticism of Henry Vaughan." *RES* 18(1967): 164-166.

13429. Martz, Louis L. "Henry Vaughan: The Man Within." *PMLA* 78(1963): 40-49.

13430. Oliver, H. J. "The Mysticism of Henry Vaughan: A Reply." *JEGP* 53(1954): 352-360.

13431. Olson, Paul A. "Vaughan's *The World*: The Pattern of Meaning and Tradition." *Comp L* 13(1961): 26-32.

13432. Rickey, Mary Ellen. "Vaughan, *The Temple*, and Poetic Form." *SP* 59(1962): 162-170.

13433. Rudrum, Alan. "An Aspect of Vaughan's Hermeticism: The Doctrine of Cosmic Sympathy." *SEL* 14(1974): 129-138.

13434. ----------. "The Influence of Alchemy in the Poems of Henry Vaughan." *PQ* 49 (1970): 469-480.

13435. ----------. "Vaughan's 'The Night': Some Hermetic Notes." *MLR* 64(1969): 11-18.

13436. ----------. "Vaughan's 'Welshness': The Verb 'Trample.'" *ELN* 9(1971): 115-118.

13437. Sandbank, S. "Henry Vaughan's Apology for Darkness." *SEL* 7(1967): 141-152.

13438. Sandler, Florence. "The Ascents of the Spirit: Henry Vaughan on the Atonement." *JEGP* 73(1974): 209-226.

13439. Simmonds, James D. "Henry Vaughan's Amoret and Etesia." *PQ* 42(1963): 137-142.

13440. ----------. "The Identity of Henry Vaughan's Suppressed Poems." *MLQ* 22(1961): 390-398.

13441. ----------. "Vaughan's Masterpiece and its Critics: 'The World' Revaluated." *SEL* 2(1962): 77-93.

13442. Stewart, Bain Tate. "Hermetic Symbolism in Henry Vaughan's 'The Night.'" *PQ* 29(1950): 417-422.

13443. Summers, Claude J., and Ted-Larry Pepworth. "Vaughan's Temple in Nature and the Context of 'Regeneration.'" *JEGP* 74(1975): 351-360.

13444. Underwood, Horace H. "Time and Space in the Poetry of Vaughan." *SP* 69(1972): 231-241.

13445. Wanamaker, Melissa Cynthia. "*Discordia Concors*: The Metaphysical Wit of Henry Vaughan's *Silex Scintillans*." *TSLL* 16 (1974): 463-477.

13446. Wyly, Thomas J. "Vaughan's 'Regeneration' Reconsidered." *PQ* 55(1976): 340-353.

See also 11429, 11437, 11440.

WALLER, EDMUND. 13447. Atterbury, Francis. "Exhumations III: Atterbury's Preface to Waller." *EIC* 15(1965): 288-293.

13448. Berman, Ronald. "The Comic Passions of *The Man of Mode*." *SEL* 10(1970): 459-468.

13449. Cherniak, Warren L. "Waller's *Panegyric to My Lord Protector* and the Poetry of Praise." *SEL* 4(1964): 109-124.

13450. Höltgen, Karl Josef. "Why Was Man Created in the Evening? On Waller's 'An Apologie for Having Loved Before.'" *MLR* 69(1974): 23-28.

13451. Wikelund, Philip R. "Edmund Waller's Fitt of Versifying: Deducations from a Holograph Fragment, Folger MS. X. d. 309." *PQ* 49(1970): 68-91.

See also 11416, 11424.

WALSH, WILLIAM. 13452. Sambrook, A. J. "William Walsh and *The Golden Age from the Fourth Eclogue of Virgil* (1703)." *MP* 64(1967): 324-325.

WALTON, IZAAK. 13453. Donovan, Dennis G. "Recent Studies in Burton and Walton." *ELR* 1 (1971): 294-303.

13454. Greenslade, B. D. "*The Compleat Angler* and the Sequestered Clergy." *RES* 5(1954): 361-366.

13455. Manley, Francis. "The Age of Walton's Ancient Pike of Haylprunn." *PQ* 40(1961): 587-589.

13456. Novarr, David. "Izaak Walton Bishop Morley, and *Love and Truth*." *RES* 2(1951): 30-39.

13457. Shapiro, I. A. "Walton and the Occasion of Donne's *Devotions*." *RES* 9(1958): 18-22.

WEBSTER, JOHN. 13458. Allison, Alexander W. "Ethical Themes in *The Duchess of Malfi*." *SEL* 4(1964): 263-273.

13459. Belton, Ellen R. "The Function of Antonio in *The Duchess of Malfi*." *TSLL* 18(1976): 474-485.

13460. Bennett, Robert B. "John Webster's Strange Dedication: An Inquiry into Literary Patronage and Jacobean Court Intrigue." *ELR* 7 (1977): 352-367.

13461. Bliss, Lee. "Destructive Will and Social Chaos in 'The Devil's Law-Case.'" *MLR* 72 (1977): 513-525.

13462. Brennan, Elizabeth M. "The Relationship between Brother and Sister in the Plays of John Webster." *MLR* 58(1963): 488-494.

13463. Brown, John Russell. "On the Dating of Webster's *The White Devil* and *The Duchess of Malfi*." *PQ* 31(1952): 353-362.

13464. Calderwood, James L. "*The Duchess of Malfi*: Styles of Ceremony." *EIC* 12(1962): 133-147.

13465. Champion, Larry S. "Webster's *The White Devil* and the Jacobean Tragic Perspective." *TSLL* 16(1974): 447-462.

13466. Dent, Robert W. "John Webster and Nicholas de Montreux." *PQ* 35(1956): 418-421.

13467. ----------. "The White Devil, or Vittoria Corombona." *RD* 9(1966): 179-203.

13468. Emslie, McD. "Motives in *Malfi*: Review Article." *EIC* 9(1959): 391-405.

13469. Ekeblad, Inga-Stina. "The 'Impure Act' of John Webster." *RES* 9(1958): 253-267.

13470. ----------. "Webster's Constructional Rhythm." *ELH* 24(1957): 165-176.

13471. Fieler, Frank B. "The Eight Madmen in *The Duchess of Malfi*." *SEL* 7(1967): 343-350.

13472. Forker, Charles R. "Two Notes on John Webster and Anthony Munday: Unpublsihed Entries in The Records of the Merchant Taylors." *ELN* 6(1968): 26-34.

13473. ----------. "'Wit's descant on any plain song': The Prose Characters of John Webster." *MLQ* 30(1969): 33-52.

13474. Franklin, H. Bruce. "The Trial Scene of Webster's *The White Devil* Examined in Terms of Renaissance Rhetoric." *SEL* 1,#2(1961): 35-51.

13475. Giannetti, Louis D. "A Contemporary View of *The Duchess of Malfi*." *CD* 3(1969): 297-307.

13476. Gunby, D. C. "'The Devil's Law-Case': An Interpretation." *MLR* 63(1968): 545-558.

13477. ----------. "'In Her Effected': A Websterian Crux Resolved?" *ELN* 10(1972): 107-110.

13478. Holland, George. "the Function of the Minor Characters in *The White Devil*." *PQ* 52 (1973): 43-54.

13479. Howarth, R. G. "Two Notes on John Webster." *MLR* 63(1968): 785-798.

13480. ----------. "Webster's *Appius and Virginia*." *PQ* 46(1967): 135-137.

13481. Hurt, James R. "Inverted Rituals in Webster's *The White Devil*." *JEGP* 61(1962): 42-47.

13482. Kroll, Norma. "The Democritean Universe in Webster's *The White Devil*." *CD* 7 (1973): 3-21.

13483. Layman, B. J. "The Equilibrium of Opposites in *The White Devil*: A Reinterpretation." *PMLA* 74(1959): 336-347.

13484. Leech, Clifford. "An Addendum on Webster's Duchess." *PQ* 37(1958): 253-256.

13485. Lord, Joan M. "*The Duchess of Malfi*: 'the Spirit of Greatness' and 'of Woman.'" *SEL* 16(1976): 305-317.

13486. Luecke, Jane Marie, O. S. B., "*The Duchess of Malfi*: Comic and Satiric Confusion in a Tragedy." *SEL* 4(1964): 275-290.

13487. Martin, Mary Forster. "Stow's 'Annals' and 'The Famous History of Sir Thomas Wyat.'" *MLR* 53(1958): 75-77.

13488. Price, Hereward T. "The Function of Imagery in Webster." *PMLA* 70(1955): 717-739.

13489. Rawcutt, N. W. "'Don Quixote,' Part I, and 'The Duchess of Malfi.'" *MLR* 66 (1971): 488-491.

13490. Schuman, Samuel. "The Ring and the Jewel in Webster's Tragedies." *TSLL* 14(1972): 253-268.

13491. Seiden, Melvin. "Two Notes on Webster's *Appius and Virginia*" *PQ* 35(1956): 408-417.

13492. Sensebaugh, George F. "Tragic Effect in Webster's *The White Devil*." *SEL* 5 (1965): 345-361.

13493. Shaw, Phillip. "*Sir Thomas Wyat* and the Scenario of *Lady Jane*." *MLQ* 13(1952): 227-238.

13494. Thayer, C. G. "The Ambiguity of Bosola." *SP* 54(1957): 162-171.

13495. Topp, F. M. "Webster and Cervantes." *MLR* 51(1956): 321-323.

13496. Wadsworth, Frank W. "Webster's *Duchess of Malfi* in the Light of Some Contemporary Ideas on Marriage and Remarraige." *PQ* 35 (1956): 394-407.

13497. Whitman, Robert F. "The Moral Paradox of Webster's Tragedy." *PMLA* 90(1975): 894-903.

See also 9354, 9402, 9762, 11374, 11395, 12144.

WHITLOCK, RICHARD. 13498. Bentley, Christopher. "The Life of Richard Whitlock." *ELN* 10(1972): 111-115.

WILL SUMMERS. 13499. Mish, Charles C. "*Will Summers*: An Unrecorded Jest Book." *PQ* 31 (1952): 215-218.

WILKINS, GEORGE. 13500. Blayney, Glenn H. "Wardship in English Drama (1600-1650." *SP* 53(1956): 470-484.

13501. ----------. "Wilkins's Revisions in *The Miseries of Inforst Mariage*." *JEGP* 56 (1957): 23-41.

WILKINS, JOHN. 13502. DeMott, Benjamin. "The Sources and Development of John Wilkins' Philosophical Language." *JEGP* 57(1958): 1-13.

WITHER, GEORGE. 13503. Calhoun, Thomas O. "George Wither: Origins and Consequences of a Loose Poetics." *TSLL* 16(1974): 263-279.

13504. Clark, Evert Mordecai. "Milton and Whither." *SP* 56(1959): 626-646.

13505. Kendall, Lyle H., Jr. "Notes on Some Works Attributed to George Wither." *RES* 5(1954): 390-394.

13506. Pritchard, Allan. "*Abuses Stript and Whipt* and Wither's Imprisonment." *RES* 14 (1963): 337-345.

13507. ----------. "George Wither: The Poet as Prophet." *SP* 59(1962): 211-230.

13508. ----------. "An Unpublished Poem by George Wither." *MP* 61(1963): 120-121.

13509. ----------. "Wither's *Motto* and Browne's *Religio Medici*." *PQ* 40(1961): 302-307.

See also 12098.

WIT'S TRIUMVIRATE. 13510. Schoenbaum, S. "*Wit's Triumvirate*: A Caroline Comedy Recovered." *SEL* 4(1964): 227-237.

WOOD, ANTHONY. 13511. Pritchard, Allan. "According to Wood: Sources of Anthony Wood's Lives of Poets and Dramatists." *RES* 28(1977): 268-290, 407-420.

WRIGHT, ABRAHAM. 13512. Kirsch, Arthur C. "A Caroline Commentary on the Drama." *MP* 66 (1969): 256-261.

WYCHERLEY, WILLIAM. 13513. Beauchamp, Gorman. "The Amorous Machiavellism of

Gorman. "The Amorous Machiavellism of *The Country Wife*." *CD* 11(1977): 316-330.

13514. Berman, Ronald. "The Ethics of *The Country Wife*." *TSLL* 9(1967): 47-55.

13515. Candido, Joseph. "Theatricality and Satire in *The Country Wife*." *EL* 4(1977): 27-36.

13516. Dearing, Vinton A. "Pope, Theobald, and Wycherley's *Posthumous Works*." *PMLA* 68(1953): 223-236.

13517. Donaldson, Ian. "'Tables Turned': *The Plain Dealer*." *EIC* 17(1967): 304-321.

13518. Friedman, Arthur. "Two Notes on William Wycherley." *MP* 75(1977): 186-190.

13519. Friedson, A. M. "Wycherley and Moliere: Satirical Point of View in *The Plain Dealer*." *MP* 64(1967): 189-197.

13520. Morrissey, L. J. "Wycherley's *Country Dance*." *SEL* 8(1968): 415-429.

13521. O Regan, M. J. "Furetière and Wycherley." *MLR* 53(1958): 77-81.

13522. Rogers, K. N. "Fatal Inconsistency: Wycherly and *The Plain-Dealer*." *ELH* 28(1961): 148-162.

13523. Roper, Alan. "Sir Harbottle Grimstone and the Country Wife." *SLI* 10,#1 (1977): 109-123.

13524. Vernon, P. F. "Wycherley's First Comedy and Its Spanish Source." *Comp L* 18 (1966): 132-144.

13525. Zimbardo, Rose A. "The Satiric Design in *The Plain Dealer*." *SEL* 1,#3(1961): 1-18.

See also 11399.

Eighteenth Century

GENERAL AND MISCELLANEOUS. 13526. Bloom, Edward A. "Neoclassic 'Paper wars' for a Free Press." *MLR* 56 (1961): 481-496.

13527. ----------. "'Labors of the Learned': Neoclassic Book Reviewing Aims and Techniques." *SP* 54 (1957): 537-563.

13528. Brenner, C.D. "The Eighteenth-Century Vogue of 'Malbrough' and Marlborough." *MLR* 45 (1950): 177-180.

13530. Cruttwell, Patrick. "'These Are Not Whigs' (Eighteenth-Century Attitudes to the Scottish Highlanders)." *EIC* 15(1965): 394-413.

13529. Clifford, James L. "The Eighteenth Century." *MLQ* 26(1965): 111-134.

13530. Cruttwell, Patrick. "'These Are Not Whigs' (Eighteenth-Century Attitudes to the Scottish Highlanders)." *EIC* 15(1965): 394-413.

13531. Davies, Paul C. "Augustan Smells." *EIC* 25(1975): 395-406.

13532. Elliot, Robert C. "The Early Scots Magazine." *MLQ* 11(1950): 189-196.

13533. Freimarck, Vincent. "The Bible and Neo-Classical Views of Style." *JEGP* 51(1952): 507-526.

13534. Frye, Northrup. "Towards Defining an Age of Sensibility." *ELH* 23(1956): 144-152.

13535. Greene, Donald. "Latitudinarianism and Sensibility: The Geneology of th 'Man of Feeling' Reconsidered." *MP* 75(1977): 159-183.

13536. Havens, Raymond D. "Solitude and the Neoclassicists." *ELH* 21(1954): 251-273.

13537. Hume, Robert D. "Marital Discord in English Comedy from Dryden to Fielding." *MP* 74 (1977): 248-272.

13538. Irwin, W. R. "Prince Frederick's Mask of Patriotism." *PQ* 37(1958): 368-384.

13539. Jones, George Hilton. "The Jacobites, Charles Molloy, and Common Sense." *RES* 4(1953): 144-147.

13540. Jones, W. Powell. "The Captive Linnet: A Footnote on Eighteenth-Century Sentiment." *PQ* 33(1954): 330-337.

13541. ----------. "Science in Biblical Paraphrases in Eighteenth-Century England." *PMLA* 74(1959): 41-51.

13542. Korshin, Paul J. "The Development of Intellectual Biography in the Eighteenth Century." *JEGP* 73(1974): 513-523.

13543. Kuhn, Albert J. "English Deism and the Development of Romantic Mythological Syncretism." *PMLA* 71(1956): 1094-1116.

13544. ----------. "Nature Spiritualized: Aspects of Anti-Newtonianism." *ELH* 41(1974): 400-412.

13545. Landa, Louis A. "London Observed: The Progress of a Simile." *PQ* 54(1975): 275-288.

13545. Landa, Louis A. "London Observed: The Progress of a Simile." *PQ* 54(1975): 275-288.

13546. Langhans, Edward A. "Three Early Eighteenth-Century Manuscript Promptbooks." *MP* 65(1967): 114-129.

13547. Lockwood, Thomas. "The Augustan Author-Audience Relationship: Satiric vs. Comic Forms." *ELH* 36(1969): 648-658.

13548. Loftis, John. "The Social Milieu of Early-Eighteenth-Century Comedy." *MP* 53(1955): 100-112.

13549. Maclean, Norman. "Personification but not Poetry." *ELH* 23(1956): 163-170.

13550. Miller, Henry Knight. "The Paradoxical Encomium with Special Reference to its Vogue in England, 1600-1800." *MP* 53(1956): 145-178.

13551. Page, Alex. "Faculty Psychology and Metaphor in Eighteenth-Century Criticism." *MP* 66 (1969): 237-247.

13552. Parks, George B. "The Turn to the Romantic in the Travel Literature of the Eighteenth Century." *MLQ* 25(1964): 22-33.

13553. Piper, William Bowman. "Common Sense as a Basis of Literary Style." *TSLL* 18 (1977): 609-641.

13554. Purpose, Eugene R. "The 'Plain, Easy, and Familiar Way': The Dialogue in English Literature, 1660-1725." *ELH* 17(1950): 47-58.

13555. Rawson, C.J. "Order and Misrule: Eighteenth-Century Literature in the 1970's." *ELH* 42(1975): 471-505.

13556. Stanlis, Peter J. "British Views of the American Revolution: A Conflict Over Rights of Sovereignty." *EAL* 11(1976): 191-201.

13557. Staves, Susan. "Don Quixote in Eighteenth-Century England." *COMP L* 24(1972): 193-215.

13558. Stewart, Keith. "History, Poetry, and the Terms of Fiction in the Eighteenth Century." *MP* 66(1968): 110-120.

13559. Thacker, Christopher. "'Wish'd, Wint'ry, Horrors': The Storm in the Eighteenth Century." *COMP L* 19(1967): 36-57.

13560. Thornton, Robert D. "The University of Edinburgh and the Scottish Enlightenment." *TSLL* 10(1968): 415-422.

13561. Trowbridge, Hoyt. "Some Varieties of Intellectual History." *MP* 73(1976): 399-406.

13562. Tuveson, Ernest. "Space, Deity, and the 'Natural Sublime.'" *MLQ* 12(1951): 20-38.

13561. Trowbridge, Hoyt. "Some Varieties of Intellectual History." *MP* 73(1976): 399-406.

13562. Tuveson, Ernest. "Space, Diety, and the 'Natural Sublime.'" *MLQ* 12(1951): 20-38.

13563. Ward, Addison. "The Tory View of Roman History." *SEL* 4(1964): 413-456.

13564. Wasserman, Earl R. "The Inherent Values of Eighteenth-Century Personification." *PMLA* 65(1950): 435-463.

13565. ----------. "Nature Moralized: The Divine Analogy in the Eighteenth Century." *ELH* 20 (1953): 39-76.

13566. Woodruff, James F. "The *Tatler Revived*, 1750: a Competitor of the *Rambler*." *RES* 26(1975): 174-181.

13567. Wright, Herbert G. "Boccaccio and English Highwaymen." *RES* 1(1950): 17-22.

13568. Zwerdling, Alex. "The Mythographers and the Romantic Revival of Greek Myth." *PMLA* 79 (1964): 447-456.

DRAMA. 13569. Avery, Emmett L. "Some New Prologues and Epilogues, 1704-1708." *SEL* 5 (1965): 455-467.

13570. Hnatko, Eugene. "The Failure of Eighteenth-Century Tragedy." *SEL* 11(1971): 459-468.

13571. Kenny, Shirley Strum. "Humane Comedy." *MP* 75(1977): 29-43.

13572. Jones, Claude E. "Dramatic Criticism in the *Critical Review,* 1756-1785." *MLQ* 20(1959): 18-26, 133-144.

13573. Loftis, John. "Spanish Drama in Neoclassical England." *Comp L* 11(1959): 29-34.

13574. MacMillan, Dougald. "The Rise of Social Comedy in the Eighteenth Century. *PQ* 41 (1962): 330-338.

13575. Matlaw, Myron. "Modern Versions of *Die Spanier in Peru*." *MLQ* 16(1955): 63-67.

13576. Parnell. Paul E. "The Sentimental Mask." *PMLA* 78(1963): 529-535.

13577. Pedicord, Harry William. "White Gloves at Five: Fraternal Patronage of London Theatres in the Eighteenth Century." *PQ* 45(1966): 270-288.

13578. Vincent, Howard P. "John Rich and the First Covent Garden Theatre." *ELH* 17(1950): 296-306.

13579. Winton, Calhoun. "The Roman Play in the Eighteenth Century." *SLI* 10,#1(1977): 77-90.

FICTION. 13580. Adams, Percy G. "The Anti-Hero in Eighteenth-Century Fiction." *SLI* 9,#1 (1976): 29-51.

13581. Beasley, Jerry C. "English Fiction in the 1740's: Some Glances at the Major and Minor Novels." *SN* 5(1973): 155-175.

13582. Boyce, Benjamin. "English Short Fiction in the Eighteenth Century." *SSF* 5(1968): 95-112.

13583. Braudy, Leo. "The Form of the Sentimental Novel." *Novel* 7(1973): 5-13.

13584. Cooke, Arthur L. "Some Lights on the Theory of the Gothic Romance." *MLQ* 12(1951): 429-436.

13585. Duncan, Jeffrey L. "The Rural Ideal in Eighteenth-Century Fiction." *SEL* 8(1968): 517-535.

13586. Foster, James R. "A Forgotten Noble Savage, Tsonnonthouan." *MLQ* 14(1953): 348-359.

13587. Jones, Claude E. "The English Novel: A *Critical* View, 1756-1785." *MLQ* 19(1958): 147-159, 213-224.

13588. Mayo, Robert D. "Gothic Romance in the Magazines." *PMLA* 65(1950): 762-789.

13589. New, Melvyn. "'The Grease of God': The Form of Eighteenth-Century English Fiction." *PMLA* 91(1976): 235-244.

13590. Noyes, Robert Gale. "Congreve and His Comedies in the Eighteenth-Century Novel." *PQ* 39(1960): 464-480.

13591. Park, William. "Change in the Criticism of the Novel After 1760." *PQ* 46(1967): 34-41.

13592. ----------. "What Was New About the 'New Species of Writing.'" *SN* 2(1970): 112-130.

13593. Pickering, Samuel F., Jr. "The Evolution of a Genre: Fictional Biographies for Children in the Eighteenth-Century." *JNT* 7(1977): 1-23.

13594. Pierce, Robert B. "Moral Education in the Novel of the 1750's." *PQ* 44(1965): 73-87.

13595. Pitcher, E.W. "Changes in Short Fiction in Britain 1785-1810: Philosophic Tales, Gothic Tales, and Fragments and Visions." *SSF* 13 (1976): 331-354.

13596. ----------. "On the Conventions of Eighteenth-Century British Short Fiction: Part I: 1700-1760." *SSF* 12(1975): 199-212.

13597. ----------. "On the Conventions of Eighteenth-Century British Short Fiction: 1760-1785." *SSF* 12(1975): 327-341.

13598. ----------. "The Short Story in Anthology and Miscellany 1750-1800: A Response to Robert Mayo." *SSF* 14(1977): 1-11.

13599. Roddier, Henri. "The Pre-Romantic Novel in England." *MP* 48(1951): 263-270.

13600. Rothstein, Eric. "The Muse of Satire: A Harlot's Progress." *MLQ* 29(1968): 222-229.

13601. Schulz, Dieter. "'Novel,' 'Romance,' and Popular Fiction in the First Half of the Eighteenth Century." *SP* 70(1973): 77-91.

13602. Sherbo, Arthur. "A Postscript to

Studies in the Eighteenth-Century Novel." JNT 4 (1974): 226-232.

13603. Spacks, Patricia Meyer. "Early Fiction and the Frightened Male." *Novel* 8 (1974): 5-15.

LITERARY CRITICISM. 13604. Cohen, Ralph. "Association of Ideas and Poetic Unity." *PQ* 36 (1957): 465-474.

13605. Danziger, Marlies K. "Heroic Villains in Eighteenth-Century Criticism." *Comp L* 11(1959): 35-46.

13606. Foerster, Donald M. "Scottish Primitivism and the Historical Approach." *PQ* 29 (1950): 307-323.

13607. Hamm, Victor M. "Antonio Conti and English Aesthetics." *Comp L* 8(1956): 12-27.

13608. Hayman, John G. "On Reading an Eighteenth-Century Page." *EIC* 12(1962): 388-401.

13609. Ong, Walter J. "Psyche and the Geometers: Aspects of Associationist Critical Theory." *MP* 49(1951): 16-27.

13610. Page, Alex. "Origin of Language and Eighteenth-Century English Criticism." *JEGP* 71 (1972): 12-21.

13611. Preston, Thomas R. "Historiography as Art in Eighteenth-Century England. *TSLL* 11 (1969): 1209-1221.

13612. Sherbo, Arthur. "'Characters of Manners': Notes Toward the History of a Critical Term." *Criticism* 11(1969): 343-357.

POETRY. 13613. Bronson, Bertrand H. "The Pre-Romantic or Post-Augustan Mode." *ELH* 20(1953): 15-28.

13614. Eland, Rosamund G. "Problems of the Middle Style: La Fontaine in Eighteenth-Century England." *MLR* 66(1971): 731-737.

13615. Foster, John Wilson. "A Re definition of Topographical Poetry." *JEGP* 69(1970): 394-406.

13616. Gaston, James C. "Richard Prescott and Mud Island: Epitomes of the American Revolution as Seen by London's Poets." *EAL* 11(1976): 147-155.

13617. Greene, D.J. "'Logical Structure' in Eighteenth-Century Poetry." *PQ* 31(1952): 315-336.

13618. Jones, William Powell. "Newton Further Demands the Muse." *SEL* 3(1963): 287-306.

13619. Lockwood, Thomas. "On the Relationship of Satire and Poetry After Pope." *SEL* 14 (1974): 387-402.

13620. Mace, Dean Tolle. "The Doctrine of Sound and Sense in Augustan Poetic Theory." *RES* 2(1951): 129-139.

13621. Marks, Emerson R. "In Search of the Godly Language." *PQ* 54(1975): 289-309.

13622. Miner, Earl. "From Narrative to 'Description' and 'Sense' in Eighteenth-Century Poetry." *SEL* 9(1969): 471-487.

13623. Sitter, John E. "Mother, Memory, Muse and Poetry after Pope." *ELH* 44(1977): 312-336.

13624. Spacks, Patricia Meyer. "Horror-'ersonification in Late Eighteenth-Century Poetry."

SP 59(1962): 560-578.

13625. Stevenson, John W. "Arcadia Re-Settled: Pastoral Poetry and Romantic Theory." *SEL* 7(1967): 629-638.

13626. Stewart, Keith. "The Ballad and the *Genres* of the Eighteenth Century." *ELH* 24(1957): 120-137.

13627. Thorpe, Peter. "'No Metaphor Swell'd High': The Relative Unimportance of Imagery or Figurative Language in Augustan Poetry." *TSLL* 13 (1972): 593-612.

13628. ----------. "Some Fallacies in the Study of Augustan Poetry." *Criticism* 9(1967): 326-336.

13629. Weinbrot, Howard D. "The Pattern of Formal Verse Satire in the Restoration and the Eighteenth Century."*PMLA* 80(1965): 394-401.

13630. Wimsatt, W.K., Jr. "The Augustan Mode in English Poetry." *ELH* 20(1953): 1-14.

13631. Woolley, James. "English Verse, 1701-1750." *MP* 75(1977): 59-73.

13632. Yohannan, John D. "The Persian Poetry Fad in England, 1770-1825." *Comp L* 4(1952): 137-160.

SATIRE. 13633. Bloom, Edward A. "*Sacramentum Militiae*: The Dynamics of Religious Satire." *SLI* 5,#2(1972)· 119-142.

13634. Carnochan, W.B. "Augustan Satire and the Gates of Dreams: A Utopian Essay." *SLI* 5,#2 (1972): 1-18.

13635. ----------. "Satire, Sublimity, and Sentiment: Theory and Practice in Post-Augustan Satire." *PMLA* 85(1970): 260-267.

13636. Donaldson, Ian. "The Satirists' London." *EIC* 25(1975): 101-122.

13637. Goldgar, Bertrand A. "Satires on Man and 'The Dignity of Human Nature.'" *PMLA* 80 (1965): 535-541.

13638. Wilkinson, Andrew M. "The Decline of English Verse Satire in the Middle Years of the Eighteenth Century." *RES* 3(1952): 222-233.

ADDISON, JOSEPH. 13629. Battersby, James L. "Johnson and Shiels: Biographers of Addison." *SEL* 9(1969): 521-537.

13640. Bloom, Edward A., and Lillian Bloom. "Addison's 'Enquiry After Truth': The Moral Assumptions of His Proof for Divine Existence." *PMLA* 65(1950): 198-220.

13641. Bond, Donald F. "Addison in Perspective." *MP* 54(1956): 124-128.

13642. ----------. "The First Printing of the *Spectator*." *MP* 47(1950): 164-177.

13643. Brown, F. Andrew. "Addison's 'Imagination' and the Gesellschaft der Mahlern.'" *MLQ* 15(1954): 57-66.

13644. Campbell, Hilbert H. "Addison's 'Cartesian' Passage and Nicholas Malebranche." *PQ* 46(1967): 408-411.

13645. ----------. "The Sale Catalogue of Addison's Library." *ELN* 4(1967): 269-273.

13646. Chambers, Robert D. "Addison at Work on the *Spectator*." *MP* 56(1959): 145-153.

13647. Cooke, Arthur L. "Addison's Aristocratic Wife." *PMLA* 72(1957): 373-389.

13648. ----------. "Addison vs. Steele, 1708." *PMLA* 68(1953): 313-320.

13649. Dust, Alvin I. "An Aspect of the Addison-Steele Literary Relationship." *ELN* 1(1964): 196-200.

13650. Evans, G. Blakemore. "Addison's Early Knowledge of Milton." *JEGP* 49(1950): 204-207.

13651. Friedman, Albert B. "Addison's Ballad Papers and the Reaction to Metaphysical Wit." *Comp L* 12(1960): 1-13.

14652. Furtwangler, Albert. "The Making of Mr. Spectator." *MLQ* 38(1977): 21-39.

13653. Halsband, Robert. "Addison's *Cato* and Lady Mary Wortley Montagu."' *PMLA* 65(1950): 1122-1129.

13654. Hodgart, M.J.C. "The Eighth Volume of the *Spectator*." *RES* 5(1954): 367-387.

13655. Hopkins, Robert H. "'The Good Old Cause' in Pope, Addison, and Steele." *RES* 17(1966): 62-68.

13656. Jackson, Wallace. "Addison: Empiricist of the Moral Consciousness." *PQ* 45 (1966): 455-459.

13657. Kelsall, M.M. "The Meaning of Addison's *Cato*." *RES* 17(1966): 149-162.

13658. Kinsley, William. "Meaning and Format: Mr. Spectator and His Folio Half-Sheets." *ELH* 34(1967): 482-494.

13659. Marsh, Robert. "Akenside and Addison: The Problem of Ideational Debt." *MP* 59(1961): 36-48.

13660. Osborn, James M. "Addison's Tavern Companion and Pope's 'Umbra.'" *PQ* 42(1963): 217-225.

13661. Rogers, Pat. "Addison's Official Correspondence: A Supplement to Graham." *MP* 69 (1972): 328-329.

13662. Salter, C.H. "Dryden and Addison." *MLR* 69(1974): 29-39.

13663. Turner, Margaret. "The Influence of La Brurjère on the 'Tatler' and the 'Spectator.'" *MLR* 48(1953): 10-16.

13664. Wheatley, Katherine E. "Addison's Portrait of the Neo-Classical Critic (The *Tatler*, No. 165)." *RES* 1(1950): 245-247.

See also 11353, 11425, 13596, 13607, 13879, 14050, 14237, 14568.

AIKEN, ANN L. See 13597.

AKENSIDE, MARK. 13665. Hart, Jeffrey. "Akenside's Revision of *The Pleasures of Imagination*." *PMLA* 74(1959): 67-74.

13666. Marsh, Robert. "Akenside and Addison: The Problem of Ideational Debt." *MP* 59 (1961): 36-48.

See also 17408.

ARBUTHNOT, JOHN. 13667. Erickson, Robert A. "Situations of Identity in the *Memoirs of Martin Scriblerus*."." *MLQ* 26(1965): 388-400.

13668. Köster, P.J. "Arbuthnot's Use of Quotation and Parody in His Account of the Sacheverell Affair." *PQ* 48(1969): 201-211.

See also 15193.

ATTERBURY, FRANCES. 13669. Atterbury, Francis. "Exhumations III: Atterbury's Preface to Waller." *EIC* 15(1965): 288-293.

BAGE, ROBERT. 13670. Sutherland, John H. "Robert Bage: Novelist of Ideas." *PQ* 36(1957): 211-220.

BAILEY, NATHANIEL. 13671. McCracken, David. "The Drudgery of Defining: Johnson's Debt to Bailey's *Dictionarium Britannicum*." *MP* 66(1969): 338-341.

BAKER, HENRY. 13672. Havens, Raymond D. "Unusual Opinions in 1725 and 1716." *PQ* 30(1951): 447-448.

BAKER, THOMAS. 13673. Smith, John Harrington. "Thomas Baker and *The Female Tatler*." *MP* 49(1952): 182-188.

BAKER, JANE. 13674. McBarney, William H. "Edmund Curll, Mrs. Jane Barker, and the English Novel." *PQ* 37(1959): 385-399.

BEATTIE, JAMES. 13675. Eberwein, Robert. "James Beattie and David Hume on the Imagination and Truth." *TSLL* 12(1971): 595-603.

13676. Hudson, Randolph. "Henry Mackenzie, James Beattie, *et al*, and the Edinburgh *Mirror*." *ELN* 1(1963): 104-108.

13677. Land, Stephen K. "James Beattie on Language." *PQ* 51(1972): 887-904.

BECKFORD, WILLIAM. 13678. Gemmett, Robert J. "The Composition of William Beckford's *Biographical Memoirs of Extraordinary Painters*." *PQ* 47(1968): 139-141.

13679. Thompson, Karl F. "Henley's Share in Beckford's *Vathek*." *PQ* 31(1952): 75-80.

BENTHAM, JEREMY. 13679a. Allentuck, Marcia. "Jeremy Bentham: An Unpublished Letter." *ELN* 6(1969): 185-186.

13680. Korshin, Paul J. "Dr. Johnson and Jeremy Bentham: an Unnoticed Relationship." *MP* 70(1972): 38-45.

BERKELEY, GEORGE. See 15294.

BICKERSTAFF, ISSAC. 13681. Tasch, Peter A. "Garrick's Revisions of Bickerstaff's *The Sultan*." *PQ* 50(1971): 141-149.

BIRCH, THOMAS. 13692. Ruhe, E.L. "Pope's Hand in Thomas Birch's Account of Gay." *RES* 5 (1954): 171-174.

BLACKMORE, RICHARD. 13683. Moore, John Robert. "Gay's Burlesque of Sir Richard Blackmore's Poetry." *JEGP* 50(1951): 83-89.

BLAIR, HUGH. 13684. Dettlaff, Shirley M. "The Concept of Beauty in 'The Artist of the Beautiful': and Hugh Blair's *Rhetoric*." *SSF* 13 (1976): 512-515.

13685. Warfel, Harry R. "Structural Concepts of Language in the Eighteenth Century and Now." *CLA* 5(1962): 179-183.

See also 13611.

BLAKE, WILLIAM. 13686. Adams, Hazard. "Reading Blake's Lyrics." *TSLL* 2(1960): 18-37.

13687. Adlard, John. "Blake's Crystal Cabinet." *MLR* 62(1967): 28-30.

13688. Aers, D. "William Blake and the Dialectics of Sex." *ELH* 44(1977): 500-514.

13689. Ault, Donald. "Incommensurability and Interconnection in Blake's Anti-Newtonian Text." *SR* 16(1977): 277-304.

13690. Baine, Mary, and Rodney M. Baine. "Blake's Other Tigers, and 'The Tyger.'" *SEL* 15(1975): 563-578.

13691. ----------. "'Then Mars Thou Wast Our Center.'" *ELN* 13(1975): 14-18.

13692. Blaine, Rodney M. "Blake's 'Tyger': The Nature of the Beast." *PQ* 46(1967): 488-498.

13693. ----------. "Thel's Northern Gate." *PQ* 51(1972): 957-961.

13694. Baird, Julian. "Swinburne, Sade, and Blake: The Pleasure-Pain Paradox." *VP* 9(1971): 49-75.

13695. Balakian, Anna. "The Literary Fortune of William Blake in France." *MLQ* 17(1956): 261-272.

13697. Bateson, F. W. "'Intention' and Blake's *Jerusalem*." *EIC* 2(1952): 106-110, 113-114.

13697. Behrendt, Stephen C. "Blake's Illustrations to Milton's *Nativity Ode*." *PQ* 55 (1976): 65-95.

13698. Bentley, G.E., Jr. "Blake and Cromek: The Wheat and the Tares." *MP* 71(1974): 366-379.

13699. ----------. "Blake, Hayley, and Lady Hesketh." *RES* 7(1956): 264-286.

13700. ----------. "Byron, Shelley, Wordsworth, Blake, and *The Seaman's Recorder*." *SR* 9(1970): 21-36.

13701. ----------. "The Printing of Blake's *America*." *SR* 6(1966): 46-57.

13702. ----------. "Thomas Butts, White Collar Maecenas." *PMLA* 71(1956): 1052-1066.

13703. ----------. "William Blake and 'Johnny of Norfolk.'" *SP* 53(1956): 60-74.

13704. Bidney, Martin. "Urizen and the Comedy of Automatism in Blake's *The Four Zoas*." *PQ* 56(1977): 204-220.

13705. Bloom, Harold. "Dialectic in *The Marriage of Heaven and Hell*." *PMLA* 73(1958): 501-504.

13706. Bogen, Nancy. "An Early Listing of William Blake's *Poetical Sketches*." *ELN* 3 (1966): 194-196.

13707. Brogan, Howard O. "Blake and the Occult." *WC* 8(1977): 147-160.

13708. Chayes, Irene H. "Blake and the Seasons of the Poet." *SR* 11(1972): 225-240.

13709. ----------. "Plato's *Stateman* Myth in Shelley and Blake." *Comp L* 13(1961): 358-369.

13710. Connolly, Thomas E., and George R. Levine. "Pictorial and Poetic Design in Two Songs of Innocence." *PMLA* 82(1967): 257-264.

13711. Curtis, F.B. "Blake and the 'Moment of Time': an Eighteenth-Century Controversy in Mathematics." *PQ* 51(1972): 460-470.

13712. Deck, Raymond H., Jr. "New Light on C.A. Tulk, Blake's Nineteenth-Century Patron." *SR* 16(1977): 217-236.

13713. DeLuca, Vincent A. "Ariston's Immortal Palace: Icon and Allegory in Blake's Prophecies." *Criticism* 11(1969): 1-19.

13714. Dike, Donald A. "The Difficult Innocence: Blake's Songs and Pastoral." *ELH* 28 (1961): 353-375.

13715. DiSalvo, Jackie. "William Blake on the Unholy Alliance." *WC* 3(1972): 212-222.

13716. Doherty, Francis. "Blake's 'The Tyger' and Henry Needler." *PQ* 46(1967): 566-567.

13717. Doyno, V. "Blake's Revision of 'London.'" *EIC* 22(1972): 58-63.

13718. Eaves, Morris. "Blake and the Artistic Machine: An Essay in Decorum and Technology." *PMLA* 92(1977): 903-927.

13719. Erdman, David V. "Blake's Early Swedenborgiannism: a Twentieth-Century Legend." *Comp L* 5(1953): 247-261.

13720. ----------. "The Dating of William Blake's Engravings." *PQ* 31(1952): 337-343.

13721. ----------. "Lambeth and Bethlehem in Blake's *Jerusalem*." *MP* 48(1951): 184-192.

13722. ----------. "The Symmetries of *The Song of Los*." *SR* 16(1977): 179-188.

13723. ----------. "William Blake's Debt to Joel Barlow." *AL* 26(1954): 94-98.

13724. Evans, James C. "The Apocalypse as Contrary Vision: Prolegomena to an Analogical Reading of *The Four Zoas*." *TSLL* 14(1972): 313-328.

13725. Fisher, Peter. "Blake and the Druids." *JEGP* 58(1959): 589-612.

13726. ----------. "Blake's Attacks on the Classical Tradition." *PQ* 40(1961): 1-18.

13727. Gallagher, Philip J. "The Word Made Flesh: Blake's 'A Poison Tree' and the Book of Genesis." *SR* 16(1977): 237-250.

13728. Gleckner, Robert F. "Blake and Satire." *WC* 8(1977): 311-326.

13729. ----------. "Blake and the Four Daughters of God." *ELN* 15(1977): 110-115.

13730. ----------. "Blake and the Senses." *SR* 5(1965): 1-15.

13731. ----------. "Blake, Gray, and the Illustrations." *Criticism* 19(1977): 118-140.

13732. ----------. "Blake's Seasons." *SEL* 5(1962): 533-551.

13733. ----------. "Blake's *Tirel* and the State of Experience." *PQ* 36(1957): 195-210.

13734. ----------. "Most Holy Forms of Thought: Some Observations on Blake and Language." *ELH* 41(1974): 555-577.

13735. ----------. "William Blake and the Human Abstract." *PMLA* 76(1961): 373-379.

13736. Goslee, Nancy M. "'In Englands Green and Pleasant Land': The Building of Vision in Blake's Stanzas From *Milton*." *SR* 13(1974): 105-126.

13737. Grant, John E. "Apocalypse in Blake's 'Auguries of Innocence.'" *TSLL* 5(1964): 489-508.

13738. ----------. "The Art and Arugment of 'The Tyger.'" *TSLL* 2(1960): 38-60.

13739. ----------. "Blake: Original and New." *MLQ* 25(1964): 356-364.

13740. ----------. "Misreadings of *The Fly*." *EIC* 11(1961): 481-487.

13741. ----------. "Redemptive Action in Blake's *Arlington Court Picture*." *SR* 10(1971): 21-26.

13742. ----------. "Review Article: Blake's *Songs of Innocence and of Experience*." *PQ* 47(1968): 571-580.

13743. ----------, and Fred C. Robinson. "Tense and the Sense of Blake's 'The Tyger.'" *PMLA* 81(1966): 596-603.

13744. Green, Richard G. "Blake and Dante on Paradise." *Comp L* 26(1974): 51-61.

13745. Hagstrum, Jean H. "Kathleen Raine's Blake." *MP* 68(1970): 76-82.

13746. Halliburton, David G. "Blake's *French Revolution*: The *Figura* and Yesterday's News." *SR* 5(1966): 158-168.

13747. Harper, George Mills. "Blake's Lost Letter to Hayley, 4 December, 1804." [with text] SP 61(1964): 573-585.

13748. ----------. "Blake's Nebuchadnezzer in 'The City of Dreadful Night.'" SP 50(1953): 68-80.

13749. ----------. "Blake's Neo-Platonic Interpretation of Plato's Atlantis Myth." JEGP 54 (1955): 72-79.

13750. ----------. "The Neo-Platonic Concept of Time in Blake's Prophetic Books." PLMA 69(1954): 142-155.

13751. ----------. "The Source of Blake's 'Ah! Sun-Flower.'" MLR 48(1953): 139-142.

13752. ----------. "Thomas Taylor and Blake's Drama of Persephone." PQ 34(1955): 378-394.

13753. Heinzelman, Kurt. "Blake's Golden Word." ELN 15(1977): 33-38.

13754. Helms, Randel. "Ezekiel and Blake's Jerusalem." SR 13(1974): 127-140.

13755. Helmstadter, Thomas H. "Blake and Religion: Iconographical Themes in the Night Thoughts." SR 10(1971): 199-212.

13756. ----------. "Blake's Night Thoughts: Interpretations of Edward Young." TSLL 12(1970): 27-54.

13757. Hill, Archibald A. "Imagery and Meaning: A Passage From Milton, and From Blake." TSLL 11(1969): 1093-1105.

13758. Hirsch, E.D., Jr. "The Two Blakes." RES 12(1961): 373-390.

13759. Jackson, Mary V. "Prolific and Devourer: From Nonmythic to Mythic Statement in The Marriage of Heaven and Hell and A Song to Liberty." JEGP 70(1971): 207-219.

13760. Jackson, Wallace. "William Blake in 1789: Unorganized Innonence." MLQ 33(1972): 396-404.

13761. James, G. Ingli. "Blake Illuminated." EIC 26(1976): 91-92.

13762. Johnson, Mary Lynn. "Beulah, 'Mne Seraphim,' and Blake's Thel." JEGP 69(1970): 258-277.

13763. Jones, William Powell. "The Ideas of the Limitations of Science from Prior to Blake." SEL 1,#3(1961): 97-114.

13764. Kaplan, Fred. "'The Tyger' and Its Maker: Blake's Vision of Art and the Artist." SEL 7(1967): 617-627.

13765. Keogh, J.G., Thomas E. Connolly, and George R. Levine. "Two Songs of Innocence." PMLA 84(1969): 137-141.

13766. King, James. "The Meredith Family, Thomas Taylor, and William Blake." SR 11(1972): 153-157.

13767. Kiralis, Karl. "A Guide to the Intellectual Symbolism of William Blake's Late Prophetic Writings." Criticism 1(1959): 190-210.

13768. ----------. "Joyce and Blake: A Basic Source for Finnegans Wake." MFS 4(1958): 329-334.

13769. ----------. "The Theme and Structure of Blake's Jerusalem." ELH 23(1956): 127-143.

13770. Kirschbaum, Leo. "Blake's The Fly." (with a postscript by F.W. Bateson) EIC 11(1961): 154-163.

13771. Kreiter, Carmen S. "Evolution and William Blake." SR 4(1965): 110-120.

13772. Lefcowitz, Barbara F. "Blake and the Natural World." PMLA 89(1974): 121-131.

13773. Manlove, C.N. "Engineered Innocence: Blake's 'The Little Black Boy' and 'The Fly.'" EIC 27(1977): 112-121.

13774. Margoliouth, H.M. "Blake's Drawings for Young's Night Thoughts." RES 5(1954): 47-54.

13775. Marks, Mollyanne. "Structure and Irony in Blake's 'The Book of Urizen.'" SEL 15 (1975): 579-590.

13776. McClelland, Jane, and George Mills Harper. "Blake's Demonic Triad." WC 8(1977): 172-182.

13777. Mellor, Anne Kostelanetz. "Blake's Design for The Book of Thel: An Affirmation of Innocence." PQ 50(1971): 193-207.

13778. ----------. "The Human Form Divine and the Structure of Blake's Jerusalem." SEL 11 (1971): 595-620.

13779. Miner, Paul. "The Polyp as a Symbol in Blake." TSLL 2(1960): 198-205.

13780. ----------. "'The Tyger': Genesis and Evolution in the Poetry of William Blake." Criticism 4(1962): 59-73.

13781. ----------. "William Blake's 'Divine Analogy.'" Criticism 3(1961): 46-61.

13782. Mitchell, W.J.T. "Style as Epistemology: Blake and the Movement Toward Abstraction in Romantic Art. SR 16(1977): 145-164.

13783. Murray, Roger. "Blake and the Ideal of Simplicity." SR 13(1974): 89-104.

13784. Myers, Victoria. "The Dialogues as Interpretative Focus in Blake's The Four Zoas." PQ 56(1977): 221-239.

13785. Nathan, Norman. "Blake and Nontheism." PMLA 75(1960): 147.

13786. Nurmi, Martin K. "Blake's Revision of The Tyger." PMLA 71(1956): 669-685.

13787. ----------. "Joy, Love, and Innocence in Blake's 'The Mental Traveller.'" SR 3(1964): 109-117.

13788. Paley, Morton D. "The Female Babe and 'The Mental Traveller.'" SR 1(1962): 97-104.

13789. ----------. "The Truchsessian Gallery Revisited. SR 16(1977): 165-178.

13790. ----------. "Tyger of Wrath." PMLA 81(1966): 540-551.

13791. Parsons, Coleman O. "Tygers Before Blake." SEL 8(1968): 573-592.

13792. Pederson, Glenn. "Blake's Urizen as Hawthorne's Ethan Brand." NCF 12(1958): 304-314.

13793. Peterson, Jane E. "The Visions of the Daughters of Albion: A Problem in Perception." PQ 52(1973): 252-264.

13794. Phillips, Michael. "The Reputation of Blake's Poetical Sketches, 1783-1863." RES 26 (1975): 19-33.

13795. Punter, David. "Blake: Creative and Uncreative Labour." SR 16(1977): 535-562.

13796. Robinson, Fred C. "Verb Tense in Blake's 'The Tyger.'" PMLA 79(1964): 666-669.

13797. Robson, W.W. "'Intention' and Blake's Jerusalem." EIC 2(1952): 111-113.

13798. Rose, Edward. "Blake's Hand: Symbol and Design in Jerusalem." TSLL 6(1964): 47-58.

13799. ----------. "Blake's Human Insect: Symbol, Theory, and Design." TSLL 10(1968): 215-232.

13800. ----------. "Blake's Illustrations for Paradise Lost, L'Allegro and Il Penseroso." HSL 2(1970): 40-67.

13801. ----------. "Circumcision Symbolism in Blake's *Jerusalem*." *SR* 8(1968): 16-25.

13802. ----------. "The Spirit of the Bounding Line: Blake's Los." *Criticism* 13(1971): 54-76.

13803. ----------. "The Symbolism of the Opened Center and Poetic Theory in Blake's *Jerusalem*." *SEL* 5(1965): 587-606.

13804. ----------. "Visionary Forms Dramatic: Grammatical and Iconographical Movement in Blake's Verse and Design." *Criticism* 8(1966): 111-125.

13805. ----------. "Wheels Within Wheels in Blake's *Jerusalem*." *SR* 11(1972): 36-47.

13806. Rose, William J. "Blake's Fourfold Art." *PQ* 49(1970): 400-423.

13807. Ryskamp, Charles. "Blake's Cowperian Sketches." *RES* 9(1958): 48-49.

13808. Simmens, Robert, and Janet Warner. "Blake's *Arlington Court Picture*: The Moment of Truth." *SR* 10(1971): 3-20.

13809. Stevenson, W.H. "Blake's 'Jerusalem.'" *EIC* 9(1959): 254-264.

13810. ----------. "On the Nature of Blake's Symbolism." *TSLL* 15(1973): 445-460.

13811. ----------. "The Shaping of Blake's 'America.'" *MLR* 55(1960): 497-503.

13812. Stevenson, Warren. "Artful Irony in Blake's 'The Fly.'" *TSLL* 10(1968): 77-82.

13813. Sugnet, Charles J. "The Role of Christ in Blake's *The Four Zoas*." *EL* 3(1976): 167-180.

13814. Sutherland, John. "Blake: A Crisis of Love and Jealousy." *PMLA* 87(1972): 424-431.

13815. ----------. "Blake's 'Mental Traveller.'" *ELH* 22(1955): 136-147.

13816. Tannenbaum, Leslie. "Blake's News from Hell: *The Marriage of Heaven and Hell* and the Lucianic Tradition." *ELH* 43(1976): 74-99.

13817. ----------. "Lord Byron in the Wilderness: Biblical Tradition in Byron's *Cain* and Blake's *The Ghost of Abel*." *MP* 72(1975): 350-364.

13818. Taylor, Gary J. "The Structure of *The Marriage*: A Revolutionary Primer." *SR* 13 (1974): 141-146.

13819. Trawick, Leonard. "Blake's Empirical Occult." *WC* 8(1977): 161-171.

13820. Twitchell, James B. "'The Mental Traveller,' Infinity, and the 'Arlington Court Picture.'" *Criticism* 17(1975): 1-14.

13821. Wain, John. "'Intention' and Blake's *Jerusalem*." *EIC* 2(1952): 105-106, 110-111.

13822. Wardle, Judith.. "Blake's Leutha." *ELN* 5(1967): 105-106.

13823. ----------. "'Satan not having the Science of Wrath, but only of Pity.'" *SR* 13(1974): 147-154.

13824. White, Wayne. "William Blake: Mystic or Visionary?" *CLA* 9(1966): 284-288.

13825. Wilkinson, A.M. "Illuminated—or Not? A Note on Blake's 'Songs of Innocence and Experience.'" *MLR* 57(1962): 387-391.

13826. Williams, Porter, Jr. "'Duty' in Blake's 'The Chimney Sweeper' of *Songs of Innocence*." *ELN* 12(1974): 92-96.

13827. Witke, Joanne. "*Jerusalem*: A Synoptic Poem." *Comp L* 22(1970): 265-278.

13828. Wittreich, Joseph Anthony, Jr.

"Blake's Philosophy of Contraries: A New Source." *ELN* 4(1966): 105-110.

13829. ----------. "Dome of Mental Pleasure: Blake's Epics and Hayley's Epic Theory." *SP* 69 (1972): 101-129.

13830. ----------. "The 'Satanism' of Blake and Shelley Reconsidered." *SP* 65(1968): 816-833.

13831. Worrell, David. "Blake's *Jerusalem* and the Visionary History of Britain." *SR* 16(1977): 189-216.

See also 15275, 15293, 17958, 19174, 19878, 20733.

BOLINGBROKE, HENRY ST. JOHN. 13832. Aldridge, Alfred Owen. "Shaftesbury and Bolingbroke." *PQ* 31(1952): 1-16.

13833. Riely, John C. "Chesterfield, Mallet, and the Publication of Bolingbroke's *Works*." *RES* 25(1974): 61-65.

See also 14599.

BOSWELL, JAMES. 13834. Baldwin, Louis. "The Conversation in Boswell's *Life of Johnson*." *JEGP* 51(1952): 492-506.

13835. Bell, Robert H. "Boswell's Notes Toward a Supreme Fiction: From *London Journal* to *Life of Johnson*." *MLQ* 38(1977): 132-148.

13836. Brady, Frank. "Boswell's Self-presentation and his Critics." *SEL* 12(1972): 545-555.

13837. Brooks, A. Russell. "Pleasure and Spiritual Turmoil in Boswell." *CLA* 3(1959): 12-19.

13838. Cole, R.C. "James Boswell's Agreeable Mr. Eccles." *PQ* 54(1975): 533-537.

13839. Fifer, C.N. "Boswell and the Decorous Bishop." *JEGP* 61(1962): 48-56.

13840. Fussell, Paul, Jr. "The Force of Literary Memory in Boswell's *London Journal*." *SEL* 2(1962): 351-357.

13841. Hart, Edward. "The Contributions of John Nichols to Boswell's *Life of Johnson*." *PMLA* 67(1952): 391-410.

13842. Hart, Francis R. "Boswell and the Romantics: A Chapter in the History of Biographical Theory." *ELH* 27(1960): 44-65.

13843. Leigh, R.A. "Boswell and Rousseau." *MLR* 47(1952): 289-318.

13844. Lustig, Irma S. "Boswell and the Descendants of Venerable Abraham." *SEL* 14(1974): 435-448.

13845. ----------. "Boswell's Literary Criticism in *The Life of Johnson*." *SEL* 6(1966): 529-541.

13846. ----------. "Boswell at Work: The 'Animadversions' on Mrs. Piozzi." *MLR* 67(1972): 11-30.

13847. ----------. "Boswell on Politics in *The Life of Johnson*." *PMLA* 80(1965): 387-393.

13848. Molin, Sven Eric. "Boswell's Account of the Johnson-Wilkes Meeting. *SEL* 3(1963): 307-322.

13849. Nussbaum, Felicity A. "Boswell's Treatment of Johnson's Temper: 'A Warm West-Indian Climate.'" *SEL* 14(1974): 421-433.

13850. Riely, John C. "Lady Knight's Role in the Boswell-Piozzi Rivalry." *PQ* 51(1972): 961-965.

13851. Schwalm, David. "The *Life of Johnson*: Boswell's Rhetoric and Reputation." *TSLL* 18(1976): 240-289.

13852. Sheldon, Ester K. "Boswell's English in *The London Journal*." *PMLA* 71(1956): 1067-1093.

13853. Siebenschuh, William R. "The Relationship Between Factual Accuracy and Literary Art in the *Life of Johnson*." *MP* 74(1977): 273-288.

13854. Stewart, Mary Margaret. "Boswell and the Infidels." *SEL* 4(1964) 475-483.

13855. ----------. "Boswell's Denominational Dilemma." *PMLA* 76(1961): 503-511.

13856. Woolley, James D. "Johnson as Despot: Anna Seward's Rejected Contribution to Boswell's *LIFE*." *MP* 70(1972): 140-145.

BOYSE, SAMUEL. 13857. Hart, Edward. "Portrait of a Grub: Samuel Boyse." *SEL* 7(1967): 415-425.

BROWN, JOHN. 13858. Eddy, Donald D. "John Brown: 'The Columbus of Keswick.'" *MP* 73(1976): S74-S84.

See also 13624.

BURKE, EDMUND. 13859. Allentuck, Marcia Epstein. "Edmund Burke to John Barrow: A New Discovery." *PQ* 50(1971): 675-677.

13860. Cannon, Garland H. "Sir William Jones and Edmund Burke." *MP* 54(1957): 165-186.

13861. May, Gita. "Diderot and Burke: A Study in Aesthetic Affinity." *PMLA* 75(1960): 527-539.

13862. Sarason, Bertram D. "Edmund Burke and the Two *Annual Registers*." *PMLA* 68(1953): 496-508.

13863. Stewart, Larry L. "Ossian, Burke, and the 'Joy of Grief.'" *ELN* 15(1977): 29-32.

13864. Vincitorio, Gaetano L. "Edmund Burke and Charles Lucas." *PMLA* 68(1953): 1047-1055.

13865. Weston, John C., Jr. "Edmund Burke's Irish History: A Hypothesis." *PMLA* 77(1962): 397-403.

See also 13559.

BURNEY, CHARLES. 13866. Benkovitz, Mariam. "Dr. Burney's Memoirs." *RES* 10(1959): 257-268.

13867. Lonsdale, Roger. "Dr. Burney and the *Monthly Review*." *RES* 14(1963): 346-358.

13868. ----------. "Dr. Burney and the *Monthly Review*, Part II." *RES* 15(1964): 27-37.

BURNEY, FANNY. 13869. Copeland, Edward W. "Money in the Novel of Fanny Burney." *SN* 8(1976): 24-37.

13870. Cutting, Rose Marie. "Defiant Women: The Growth of Feminism in Fanny Burney's Novels." *SEL* 17(1977): 519-530.

13871. ----------. "A Wreath for Fanny Burney's Last Novel: *The Wanderer*'s Contribution to Women's Studies." *CLA* 20(1976): 57-68.

13872. Erickson, James P. "*Evelina* and *Betsy Thoughtless*." *TSLL* 6(1964): 96-103.

13873. Glock, Waldo S. "Appearance and Reality: The Education of Evelina." *EL* 2(1975): 32-41.

13874. Hemlow, Joyce. "Fanny Burney and the Courtesy Books." *PMLA* 65(1950): 732-761.

13875. Moler, Kenneth L. "Fanny Burney's *Cecelia* and Jane Austen's 'Jack and Alice.'" *ELN* 3(1965): 40-42.

13876. Sambrook, A.J. "Fanny Burney's First Letter to Dr. Johnson." *RES* 14(1963): 273-275.

13877. Staves, Susan. "*Evelina*, or Female Difficulties. *MP* 73(1976): 368-381.

13878. Vopat, James B. "*Evelina*: Life as Art—Notes Toward Becoming a Performer on the Stage of Life." *EL* 2(1975): 42-52.

See also 15333.

BURNS, ROBERT. 13879. Beaty, Frederick. "'AE Spark O'Natures Five.'" *ELN* 1(1964): 203-207.

13880. ----------. "Burns's Comedy of Romantic Love." *PMLA* 83(1968): 429-438.

13881. Bentman, Raymond. "Robert Burns's Declining Fame." *SR* 11(1972): 207-224.

13882. ----------. "The Romantic Poets and Critics on Robert Burns." *TSLL* 6(1964): 104-118.

13883. Buchan, A.M. "Word and Word—Tune in Burns." *SP* 48(1951): 40-48.

13884. Gillies, A. "Emilie von Berlepsch and Burns." *MLR* 55(1960): 584-587.

13885. Lewis, Mary Ellen Brown. "The Progress of 'Lady Mary Ann.'" *PQ* 52(1973): 97-107.

13886. MacLaine, Allan H. "Burns' Use of Parody in 'Tam O'Shanter.'" *Criticism* 1(1959): 308-316.

13887. Morton, Richard. "Narrative Irony in Robert Burns's *Tam O'Shanter*." *MLQ* 22(1961): 12-20.

13888. Werkmeister, Lucyle. "Robert Burns and the London Daily Press." *MP* 63(1966): 322-335.

13889. Weston, John C., Jr. "An Example of Robert Burns' Contribution to the Scottish Vernacular Tradition." *SP* 57(1960): 634-647.

13890. ----------. "The Narrator of *Tam O'Shanter*." *SEL* 8(1968): 537-550.

13891. ----------. "Robert Burns' Use of the Scots Verse-Epistle Form." *PQ* 49(1970): 188-210.

See also 7012, 13559, 17212.

CHATTERTON, THOMAS. 13892. Bronson, Bertrand H. "Chattertoniana." *MLQ* 11(1950): 417-424.

13893. Krosse, Irvin B. "Chatterton's *Aella* and Chatterton." *SEL* 12(1972): 557-566.

13894. Taylor, Donald S. "Chatterton: The Problem of Rowley Chronology and its Implications." *PQ* 46(1967): 268-276.

13895. ----------. "Chatterton's Suicide." *PQ* 31(1952): 63-69.

13896. White, Eric Walter. "Chatterton and the English Burletta." *RES* 9(1958): 43-48.

CHESTERFIELD, PHILIP DORMER STANHOPE. 13897. Pullen, Charles. "Lord Chesterfield and Eighteenth-Century Appearance and Reality." *SEL* 8 (1968): 501-515.

13898. Nelick, Frank C. "Lord Chesterfield's Adoption of Philip Stanhope." *PQ* 38(1959): 370-378.

13899. Shipley, John B. "A Note on the Authorship of *The Whale*." *RES* 18(1967): 166-169.

CHETWOOD, WILLIAM RUFUS. 13900. Dorris, George. "*The Projector, The Mock Mason*, and Miss Littlewood." *MD* 16(1973): 265-268.

CHURCHILL, CHARLES. 13901. Fisher, Alan S. "The Stretching of Augustan Satire: Charles Churchill's 'Dedication' to Warburton." *JEGP* 72 (1973): 360-377.

13902. Golden, Morris. "Churchill's Literary Influence on Cowper." *JEGP* 58(1959): 655-665.

13903.   Golden, Morris. "Sterility and Em-
minence in the Poetry of Charles Churchill." *JEGP*
66(1967): 333-346.
   See also 13635.
   CIBBER, COLLEY.   13904. Fuller, John.
"Cibber, *The Rehearsal at Goatham*, and the Sup-
pression of *Polly*." *RES* 13(1962): 125-134.
   13905. Hayley, R. L. "The Scriblerians
and the South Sea Bubble: a hit by Cibber." *RES*
24(1973): 452-458.
   13906. Kalson, Albert E. "The Chronicles
in Cibber's *Richard III*." *SEL* 3(1963): 253-267.
   13907. Kenny, Shirley Strum. "Perennial
Favorites: Congreve, Vanbrugh, Cibber, Farquhar,
and Steele." *MP* 73(1976): S4-S11.
   13908. Parnell, Paul E. "Equivocation in
Cibber's *Love's Last Shift*." *SP* 57(1960): 519-
534.
   13909. Peterson, William M. "Cibber's *She
Wou'd and She Wou'd Not* and Vanbrugh's *Aesop*."
PQ 35(1956): 429-435.
   13910. Roper, Alan. Language and Action in
The Way of the World, Love's Last Shift, and *The
Relapse*." *ELH* 40(1973): 44-69.
   See also 13573, 14192.
   CLARKE, JOHN.   13911. Weinbrot, Howard D.
"John Clarke's *Essay on Study* and Samuel Johnson
on *Paradise Lost*." *MP* 72(1975): 404-407.
   CLELAND, JOHN.   13912. Copland, Edward W.
"*Clarissa* and *Fanny Hill*: Sisters in Distress."
SN 4(1972): 343-352.
   13913. Morrissey, L. J., and B. Slepian.
"What is *Fanny Hill*?" *EIC* 14(1964): 65-75.
   CLEMENTS, SAMUEL.   13914. Snyder, Henry L.
"The Authorship of *Faults on Both Sides* (1701)."
PQ 56(1977): 266-272.
   COLLINS, WILLIAM.   13915. Baine, Rodney M.
"Warton, Collins, and Skelton's *Necromancer*." *PQ*
49(1970): 245-248.
   13916. Brown, Merle E. "On William Collins'
Ode to Evening." *EIC* 11(1961): 136-153.
   13917. Collins, Martha. "The Self-Conscious
Poet: The Case of William Collins." *ELH* 42(1975):
362-377.
   13918. Crider, John R. "Structure and Effect
in Collins' Progress Poems." *SP* 60(1963): 57-72.
   13919. Kallich, Martin. "'Plain in Thy Neat-
ness': Horace's Pyrrha and Collins' Evening."
ELN 3(1966): 265-271.
   13920. Lamont, Claire. "William Collins's
'Ode on the Popular Superstitions.'" *RES* 19(1968):
137-147.
   13921. Pettit, Henry. "Collins's 'Ode to
Evening' and the Critics." *SEL* 4(1964): 361-369.
   13922. Spacks, Patricia Meyer. "Collins'
Imagery." *SP* 62(1965): 719-736.
   13923. Stewart, Mary Margaret. "Further
Notes on William Collins." *SEL* 10(1970): 569-578.
   13924. ----------. "William Collins and
Cackham Manor." *RES* 20(1969): 310-314.
   13925. ----------. "William Collins and
Thomas Barrow." *PQ* 48(1969): 212-219.
   13926. Wasserman, Earl R. "Collins' 'Ode on
the Poetical Character.'" *ELH* 34(1967): 92-115.
   COVENTRY, FRANCIS. See 13593.
   COWPER, WILLIAM.   13927. Golden, Morris.
"Churchill's Literary Influence on Cowper." *JEGP*
58(1959): 655-665.
   13928. Gregory, Hoover K. "Cowper's Love of

Subhuman Nature: A Psychoanalytic Approach." *PQ*
46(1967): 42-57.
   13929. Hartley, Lodwick. "Cowper and the
Evangelicals: Notes on Early Biographical Interpretations." *PMLA* 65(1950): 719-731.
   13930. ----------. "Cowper and the Polyga-
mous Parson." *MLQ* 16(1955): 137-141.
   13931. ----------. "An Uncollected Cowper
Letter." *RES* 17(1966): 299-301.
   13932. Jones, Myrddin. "Wordsworth and Cowper: the Eye made Quiet." *EIC* 21(1971): 236-247.
   13933. Kroiter, Harry P. "The Influence of
Popular Science on William Cowper." *MP* 61(1964):
281-287.
   13934. Link, Frederick. "Two Cowper Letters."
MP 62(1964): 137-138.
   13935. Mandel, Barrett John. "Artistry and
Pyschology in William Cowper's *Memoir*." *TSLL* 12
(1970): 431-442.
   13936. Martin, Bernard. "Fresh Light on
William Cowper." *MLQ* 13(1952): 253-255.
   13937. Newey, Vincent. "Cowper and the Des--
cription of Nature." *EIC* 23(1973): 102-108.
   13938. Quinlan, Maurice J. "William Cowper
and the French Revolution." *JEGP* 50(1951): 483-490.
   13939. Ringler, Richard N. "The Genesis of
Cowper's 'Yardley Oak.'" *ELN* 5(1967): 27-32.
   13940. Spacks, Meyer. "The Soul's Imaginings:
PMLA 91(1976): 420-435.
   CRABBE, GEORGE.   13941. Broman, Walter E.
"Factors in Crabbe's Eminence in the Early Nineteenth Century." *MP* 51(1953): 42-49.
   13942. Chamberlin, Robert L. "George Crabbe
and Darwin's Amorous Plants." *JEGP* 61(1962): 833-
852.
   13943. Duncan-Jones, E. E. "Jane Austen and
Crabbe." *RES* 5(1954): 174.
   13944. Edwards, Gavin. "The Grimeses." *EIC*
27(1977): 122-140.
   13945. Faulkner, Thomas C. "Letters of
George Crabbe and Francis Fulford." *RES* 26(1975):
56-63.
   13946. Link, Frederick M. "Three Crabbe Letters." *ELN* 2(1965): 200-206.
   13947. Pollard, Arthur. "Two New Letters of
Crabbe." *RES* 2(1951): 375-377.
   13948. Hatch, Ronald B. "George Crabbe and
the Work-houses of the Suffolk Incorporations." *PQ*
54(1975): 689-698.
   13949. ----------. "George Crabbe, the Duke
of Rutland, and the Tories." *RES* 24(1973): 429-443.
   13950. Swingle, L. J. "Late Crabbe in Relation to the Augustans and Romantics: The Temporal Labyrinth of his *Tales in Verse*, 1812." *ELH*
42(1975): 580-594.
   13951. Thale, Rose Marie. Crabbe's *Village*
and Topographical Poetry." *JEGP* 55(1956): 618-623.
   13952. Thomas, W. K. "George Crabbe: Not
Quite the Sternest." *SR* 7(1968): 166-175.
   CROFT, HERBERT.   13953. Pettet, Henry.
"The Making of Croft's Life of Young for Johnson's
Lives of the Poets." *PQ* 54(1975): 333-341.
   CROWE, WILLIAM.   13954. Martin, C. G.
"Coleridge and William Crowes's 'Lewesdon Hill.'"
MLR 62(1967): 400-406.
   CROWNE, JOHN. See 13579.
   CUMBERLAND, RICHARD. See 13579.
   CURLL, EDMUND. See 13674.
   DALRYMPLE, DAVID.   13955. Campbell, Jackson J.

"Sir David Dalrymple's Ballad Work." *PQ* 29(1950): 324-332.

DARWIN, ERASMUS.   13956. Dean, Dennis R. "Erasmus Darwin's Botanic Terms." *ELN* 10(1972): 27-29.

13957. Ritterbush, Philip C. "Erasmus Darwin's Second Published Poem." *RES* 13(1962): 158-160.

See also 13624.

DEFOE, DANIEL.   13958. Alkon, Paul K. "Defoe's Argument in *The Shortest Way with the Dissenters*." *MP* 73(1976): S12-S23.

13959. Ayers, Robert W. *Robinson Crusoe*: 'Allusive Allegorick History.'" *PMLA* 82(1967): 399-407.

13960. Baine, Rodney M. "The Apparition of Mrs. Veal: A Neglected Account." *PMLA* 69(1954): 523-541.

13961. ----------. "Chalmers' First Bibliography of Daniel Defoe." [with text] *TSLL* 10 (1969): 547-568.

13962. ----------. "Daniel Defoe and Captain Carleton's *Memoirs of an English Officer*." *TSLL* 13(1972): 613-627.

13963. ----------. "Daniel Defoe and Robert Drury's *Journal*." *TSLL* 16(1974): 479-491.

13964. ----------. "Defoe and Mrs. Bargrave's Story." *PQ* 33(1954): 388-395.

13965. ----------. "Defoe and the Angels." *TSLL* 9(1967): 345-369.

13966. ----------. "Dainel Defoe's Imaginary Voyages to the Moon." *PMLA* 81(1966): 377-380.

13967. ----------. "Roxana's Georgian Setting." *SEL* 15(1975): 459-471.

13968. Bastian, F. "Defoe's *Journal of the Plague Year*." *RES* 16(1965): 151-173.

13969. Benjamin, Edwin. B. "Symbolic Elements in *Robinson Crusoe*." *PQ* 30(1951): 206-211.

13970. Blewett, David. "'Roxana' and the Masquerades." *MLR* 65(1970): 499-501.

13971. Brink, Andrew W. "*Robinson Crusoe* and *The Life of the Reverend Mr. George Trosse*." *PQ* 48 (1969): 433-451.

13972. Brooks, Douglas. "*Moll Flanders* Again." *EIC* 20(1970): 115-181.

13973. ----------. "*Moll Flanders*: an Interpretation." *EIC* 19(1969): 46-59.

13974. Brown, Homer O. "The Displaced Self in the Novels of Daniel Defoe." *ELH* 38(1971): 562-590.

13975. Bond, Clinton S. "*Street Robberies, Consider'd* and the Canon of Daniel Defoe." *TSLL* 13 (1971): 431-445.

13976. Boyce, Benjamin. "The Question of Emotion in Defoe." *SP* 50(1953): 45-58.

13977. Clark, Paul Odell. "A *Gulliver* Dictionary." *SP* 50(1953): 592-624.

13978. Cohan, Steven. "Other Bodies: Roxana's Confession of Guilt." *SN* 8(1976): 406-418.

13979. Columbus, Robert R. "Conscious Artistry in *Moll Flanders*." *SEL* 3(1963): 415-432.

13980. Damrosch, Leopold, Jr. "Defoe as Ambiguous Impersonator." *MP* 71(1973): 153-159.

13981. Davies, Godfrey. "Daniel Defoe's *A Tour thro' the Whole Island of Great Britain*." *MP* 48(1950): 21-36.

13982. Downie, J. A. "'Mistakes on all Sides': a New Defoe Manuscript." *RES* 27(1976): 431-437.

13983. Egan, James. "Crusoe's Monarchy and the Puritan Concept of Self." *SEL* 13(1973): 451-460.

13984. Ganzel, Dewey. "Chronology in *Robinson Crusoe*." *PQ* 40(1961): 495-512.

13985. Girdler, Lew. "Defoe's Education at Newington Green Academy." *SP* 50(1953): 573-591.

13986. Greif, Martin J. "The Conversion of Robinsoe Crusoe." *SEL* 6(1966): 551-574.

13987. Hahn, H. G. "The Approach to Character Development in Defoe's Narrative Prose." *PQ* 51(1972): 845-858.

13988. Halewood, William H. "Religion and Invention in *Robinson Crusoe*." *EIC* 14(1964): 339-351.

13989. Horsley, L. S. "Contemporary Reactions to Defoe's *Shortest Way with the Dissenters*." *SEL* 16(1976): 407-420.

13990. ----------. "Rogues or Honest Gentlemen: The Public Characters of Queen Anne Journalists." *TSLL* 18(1976): 198-228.

13991. Howard, William J. "Truth Preserves Her Shape: An Unexplored Influence on Defoe's Prose Style." *PQ* 47(1968): 193-205.

13992. Hunter, J. Paul. "Friday as a Convert: Defoe and the Accounts of Indian Missionaries." *RES* 14(1963): 243-248.

13993. Jackson, Wallace. "*Roxana* and the Development of Defoe's Fiction." *SN* 7(1975): 181-194.

13994. Jenkins, Ralph E. "The Structure of *Roxana*." *SN* 2(1970): 145-158.

13995. Johnson, Abby Arthur. "Old Bones Uncovered: A Reconsideration of *Robinson Crusoe*." *CLA* 17(1973): 271-278.

13996. Karl, Frederick R. "Moll's Many-Colored Coat: Veil and Disguise in the Fiction of Defoe." *SN* 5(1973): 86-97.

13997. ----------. "Review-Essay: Defoe and the Novel: Two Recent Studies." *SN* 8(1976): 468-473.

13998. Koonce, Howard L. "Moll's Muddle: Defoe's Use of Irony in *Moll Flanders*." *ELH* 30 (1963): 377-394.

13999. Krier, William J. "A Courtesy Which Grants Integrity: A Literal Reading of *Moll Flanders*." *ELH* 38(1971): 397-410.

14000. Kropf, C. R. "Theme and Structure in Defoe's *Roxana*." *SEL* 12(1972): 467-480.

14001. MacLaine, Allan H. "Robinson Crusoe and the Cyclops." *SP* 52(1955): 599-604.

14002. Martin, Terence. "The Unity of *Moll Flanders*." *MLQ* 22(1961): 115-124.

14003. McBurney, William H. "*Colonel Jacque*: Defoe's Definition of the Complete English Gentleman." *SEL* 2(1962): 321-336.

14004. McMaster, Juliet. "The Equation of Love and Money in *Moll Flanders*." *SN* 2(1970): 131-144.

14005. McVeagh, John. "Rochester and Defoe: A Study in Influence." *SEL* 14(1974): 327-341.

14006. Moore, John Robert. "Defoe's Persona as Author: The Quaker's Sermon." *SEL* 11(1971): 507-516.

14007. Novak, Maximillian E. "Crime and Punishment in Defoe's *Roxana*." *JEGP* 65(1966): 445-465.

14008. ----------. "Crusoe the King and the Political Evolution of His Island." *SEL* 2(1962):

337-350.

14009. ----------. "Defoe and the Disordered City." *PMLA* 92(1977): 241-252.

14010. ----------. "Defoe, Thomas Burnet and the 'Deistical' Passages of Robert Drury's Journal." *PQ* 42(1963): 207-216.

14011. ----------. "Defoe's *Shortest Way With the Dissenters*: Hoax, Parody, Paradox, Fiction, Irony, and Satire." *MLQ* 27(1966): 402-417.

14012. ----------. "Defoe's Theory of Fiction." *SP* 61(1964): 650-668.

14013. ----------. "The Problem of Necessity in Defoe's Fiction." *PQ* 40(1961): 513-524.

14014. ----------. "Robinson Crusoe's Fear and the Search for Natural Man." *MP* 58(1961): 238-245.

14015. ----------. "Robinson Crusoe's 'Original Sin.'" *SEL* 1,#6(1961): 19-29.

14016. ----------. "'Simon Forecastle's Weekly Journal': Some Notes on Defoe's Conscious Artistry." *TSLL* 6(1965): 433-440.

14017. Olshin, Toby A. "'Thoughtful of the Main Chance': Defoe and the Cycle of Anxiety." *HSL* 6(1974): 117-128.

13018. Payne, William L. "Defoe in the Pamphlets." *PQ* 52(1973): 85-96.

14019. Peck, Daniel H. "*Robinson Crusoe*: The Moral Geography of Limitation." *JNT* 3(1973): 20-31.

14020. Peterson, Spiro. "The Matrimonial Theme of Defoe's *Roxana*." *PMLA* 70(1955): 166-191.

14021. Piper, William Bowman. "*Moll Flanders* as a Structure of Topics." *SEL* 9(1969): 489-502.

14022. Robins, Harry F. "How Smart Was Robinson Crusoe?" *PMLA* 67(1952): 782-789.

14023. Rodway, A.E. "*Moll Flanders* and *Manon Lescaut*." *EIC* 3(1953): 303-320.

14024. Rogal, Samuel J. "The Profit and Loss of Moll Flanders." *SN* 5(1973): 98-103.

14025. Rogers, Pat. "Crusoe's Home." *EIC* 24(1974): 375-390.

14026. ----------. "Defoe as Plagiarist: Camden's *Britannia* and *A Tour Thro' The Whole Island of Great Britain*." *PQ* 52(1973): 771-774.

14027. ----------. "Defoe in the Fleet Prison." *RES* 22(1971): 451-455.

14028. Rosenberg, Albert. "Defoe's *Pacificator* Reconsidered." *PQ* 3(1958): 433-439.

14029. Schonhorn, Manuel. "Defoe's *Four Years Voyages of Capt. George Roberts* and *Ashton's Memorial*." *TSLL* 17(1975): 93-102.

14030. ----------. "Defoe's *Journal of the Plague Year*: Topography and Intention." *RES* 19 (1968): 387-402.

14031. ----------. "Defoe's Pirates: A New Source." *RES* 14(1963): 386-389.

14032. Scouten, Arthur. "An Early Printed Report on the Apparition of Mrs. Veal." *RES* 6 (1955): 259-263.

14033. Secord, A.W. "The Correspondence of Daniel Defoe." *MP* 54(1956): 45-52.

14034. ----------. "Defoe in Stoke Newington." *PMLA* 66(1951): 211-225.

14035. ----------. " A September Day in Canterbury: The Veal-Bargrave Story." *JEGP* 54 (1955): 639-650.

14036. Seeber, Edward D. "Oroonoko and Crusoe's Man Friday." *MLQ* 12(1951): 286-291.

14037. Sherbo, Arthur. "Defoe's Limited Genius." *EIC* 19(1969): 351-354.

14038. Snow, Malinda. "Diabolic Intervention in Defoe's *Roxana*." *EL* 3(1976): 52-60.

14039. ----------. "The Origins of Defoe's First-Person Narrative Technique: An Overlooked Aspect of the Rise of the Novel." *JNT* 6(1976): 175-187.

14040. Spacks, Meyer. "The Soul's Imaginings: Daniel Defoe, William Cowper." *PMLA* 91 (1976): 420-435.

14041. Starr, G.A. "Defoe's Prose Style: The Language of Interpretation." *MP* 71(1974): 277-294.

14042. ----------. "'Sauces to whet our gorg'd Appetites': Defoe at Seventy in the Anchovy Trade." *PQ* 54(1975): 531-533.

14043. Taylor, S. Oritz. "Episodic Structure and the Picaresque Novel." *JNT* 7(1977): 218-225.

14044. Watt, Ian. "Defoe and Richardson on Homer: A Study of the Relation of Novel and Epic in the Early Eighteenth Century." *RES* 3 (1952): 325-340.

14045. ----------. "Robinson Crusoe as a Myth." *EIC* 1(1951): 95-119.

14046. Wilkinson, Andrew M. "The 'Meditations' of Daniel Defoe." *MLR* 46(1951): 349-354.

14047. Zimmerman, Everett. "Defoe and Crusoe." *ELH* 38(1971): 377-396.

14048. ----------. "H.F.'s Meditations: *A Journal of the Plague Year*." *PMLA* 87(1972): 417-423.

14049. ----------. "Language and Character in Defoe's *Roxanna*." *EIC* 21(1971): 227-235.

See also 135, 7780, 13040, 13589, 13596, 14323, 14579, 15043, 19687.

DENNIS, JOHN. 14050. Tyre, Richard H. "Versions of Poetic Justice in the Early Eighteenth Century." *SP* 54(1954): 29-44.

See also 11396, 13579, 13612, 15264.

DODSLEY, ROBERT. 14051. Tierney, James E. "*The Museum*, the 'Super-Excellent Magazine.'" *SEL* 13(1973): 503-515.

DRURY, ROBERT. See 13963.

DUNBAR, JAMES. 14052. Berry, Christopher J. "'Climate' in the Eighteenth Century: James Dunbar and the Scottish Case." *TSLL* 16(1974): 281-292.

FALCONER, WILLIAM. 14053. Joseph, M.K. "William Falconer." *SP* 47(1950): 72-101.

See also 13559.

FIELDING, HENRY. 14054. Allott, Miriam. "A Note on Fielding's Mr. Square." *MLR* 56(1961): 69-72.

14055. Alter, Robert. "Fielding and the Uses of Style." *Novel* 1(1967): 53-63.

14056. Amory, Hugh. "Henry Fielding and the Criminal Legislation of 1751-2." *PQ* 50 (1971): 175-192.

14057. ----------. "Henry Fielding's *Epistle to Walpole*: A Reexamination." *PQ* 46 (1967): 236-247.

14058. ----------. "Magistrate or Censor? The Problem of Authority in Fielding's Later Writings." *SEL* 12(1972): 503-518.

14059. ----------. "*Shamela* as Aesopic Satire." *ELH* 38(1971): 239-253.

14060. Anderson, Howard. "Answers to the Author of *Clarissa*: Theme and Narrative Technique in *Tom Jones* and *Tristram Shandy*." *PQ* 51(1972): 859-873.

14061. Baker, John Ross. "From Imitation to Rhetoric: The Chicago Critics, Wayne Booth, and *Tom Jones*." *Novel* 6(1973): 197-217.

14062. Baker, Sheridan. "Fielding's *Amelia* and the Materials of Romance." *PQ* 41(1962): 437-449.

14063. ----------. "Henry Fielding and the Cliché." *Criticism* 1(1959): 354-361.

14064. ----------. "Henry Fielding's *The Female Husband*." *PMLA* 74(1959): 213-224.

14065. ----------. "Political Allusion in Fielding's *Author's Farce, Mock Doctor,* and *Tumble-Down Dick*." *PMLA* 77(1962): 221-231.

14066. Battestin, Martin C. "Fielding and 'Master Punch' in Panton Street." *PQ* 45(1966): 191-208.

14067. ----------. "Fielding and Ralph Allen: Benevolism and Its Limits as an Eighteenth-Century Ideal." *MLQ* 28(1967): 368-377.

14068. ----------. "Fielding's Changing Politics and *Joseph Andrews*." *PQ* 39(1960): 39-55.

14069. ----------. "Fielding's Definition of Wisdom: Some Functions of Ambiguity and Emblem in *Tom Jones*." *ELH* 35(1968): 188-217.

14070. ----------. "Lord Hervey's Role in *Joseph Andrews*." *PQ* 42(1963): 226-241.

14071. ----------. "Pope's 'Magus' in Fielding's *Vernoniad*: The Satire of Walpole." *PQ* 46(1967): 137-141.

14072. ----------. "The Problem of *Amelia*: Hume, Barrow, and the Conversion of Captain Booth." *ELH* 41(1974): 613-648.

14073. ----------. "*Tom Jones* and 'His Egyptian Majesty': Fielding's Parable of Government." *PMLA* 82(1967): 68-77.

14074. Beasley, Jerry C. "Romance and the 'New' Novels of Richardson, Fielding, and Smollett." *SEL* 16(1976): 437-450.

14075. Bell, Michael. "A Note on Drama and the Novel: Fielding's Contribution." *Novel* 3 (1970): 119-128.

14076. Bliss, Michael. "Fielding's Bill of Fare in *Tom Jones*." *ELH* 30(1963): 236-243.

14077. Bloch, Tuvia. "*Amelia* and Booth's Doctrine of the Passions." *SEL* 13(1973): 461-473.

14078. ----------. "The Prosecution of the Maidservant in *Amelia*." *ELN* 6(1969): 269-271.

14079. Brooks, Douglas. "Abraham Adams and Parson Trulliber: The Meaning of 'Joseph Andrews,' Book II, Chapter 14." *MLR* 63(1968): 794-801.

14080. ----------. "The Interpolated Tales in *Joseph Andrews* Again." *MP* 65(1968): 208-213.

14081. ----------. "*Joseph Andrews* and *Pamela*." *EIC* 19(1969): 348-351.

14082. ----------. "*Pamela* and *Joseph Andrews*." *EIC* 18(1968): 348-349.

14083. ----------. "Richardson's *Pamela* and Fielding's *Joseph Andrews*." *EIC* 17(1967): 158-168.

14084. Brown, Jack Richard. "Henry Fielding's *Grub-Street Opera*." *MLQ* 16(1955): 32-41.

14085. Butler, Marilyn. "Fielding, Whose Contemporary?" *EIC* 25(1975): 478-479.

14086. Cleary, Thomas. "Jacobitism in *Tom Jones*: The Basis for an Hypothesis." *PQ* 52 (1973): 239-251.

14087. Coley, William B. "The Authorship of *An Address to the Electors of Great Britain* (1740)." *PQ* 36(1957): 488-495.

14088. ----------. "The Background of Fielding's Laughter." *ELH* 26(1959): 229-254.

14089. ----------. "Fielding and the Two 'Covent-Garden Journals.'" *MLR* 57(1962): 386-387.

14090. ----------. "Fielding, Hogarth, and Three Italian Masters." *MLQ* 24(1963): 386-391.

14091. ----------. "Fielding's Two Appointments to the Magistracy." *MP* 63(1965): 144-149.

14092. ----------. "Gide and Fielding." *Comp L* 11(1959): 1-15.

14093. ----------. "Henry Fielding and the Two Walpoles." *PQ* 45(1966): 157-178.

14094. ----------. "The 'Remarkable Queries' in the *Champion*." *PQ* 41(1962): 426-436.

14095. Colmer, Dorothy. "Fielding's Debt to John Lacy in *The Mock Doctor*." *ELN* 9(1971): 35-39.

14096. Coolidge, John S. "Fielding and 'Conservation of Character.'" *MP* 57(1960): 245-259.

14097. Dircks, Richard J. "The Perils of Heartfree: A Sociological Preview of Fielding's Adaptatation of Dramatic Convention." *TSLL* 8 (1966): 5-13.

14098. Dyson, A.E. "Satiric and Comic Theory in Relation to Fielding." *MLQ* 18(1957): 225-237.

14099. Eaves, T. C. Duncan, and Ben D. Kimpel. "Two Names in *Joseph Andrews*." *MP* 72(1975): 408-409.

14100. Edwards, P.D. "Education and Nature in 'Tom Jones' and 'The Ordeal of Richard Feverel.'" *MLR* 63(1968): 23-32.

14101. Evans, James E. "Fielding's Lady Booby and Fénolon's Calypso." *SN* 8(1976): 210-213.

14102. Farrell, William J. "Fielding's Familiar Style." *ELH* 34(1967): 65-77.

14103. ----------. "The Mock-Heroic Form of *Jonathan Wild*." *MP* 63(1966): 216-226.

14104. Feil, J.P. "Fielding's Character of Mrs. Whitefield." *PQ* 39(1960): 508-510.

14105. Ferguson, Oliver W. "Partridge's Vile Encomium: Fielding and Honest Billy Mills." *PQ* 43(1964): 73-78.

14106. Folkenflik, Robert. "Critical Exchange: Purpose and Narration in Fielding's *Amelia*." *Novel* 7(1974): 168-174.

14107. Goggin, L.P. "Development of Techniques in Fielding's Comedies." *PMLA* 67(1952): 769-781.

14108. ----------. "Fielding and the *Select Comedies of Mr. de Moliere*." *PQ* 31(1952): 344-350.

14109. ----------. "Fielding's *The Masquerade*." *PQ* 36(1957): 475-487.

14110. Goldberg, Homer. "Comic Prose Epic or Comic Romance: The Argument of the Preface to *Joseph Andrews*." *PQ* 43(1964): 193-215.

14111. ----------. "The Interpolated Stories in *Joseph Andrews* or 'The History of the World in General' Satirically Revised." *MP* 63 (1966): 295-310.

14112. Goldgar, Bertrand A. "The Politics of Fielding's *Coffee-House Politician*." *PQ* 49 (1970): 424-429.

14113. Goldknopf, David. "The Failure of Plot in *Tom Jones*." *Criticism* 11(1969): 262-274.

14114. Greason, A. LeRoy, Jr. "Fielding's *An Address to the Electors of Great Britain*." *PQ* 33(1954): 347-352.

14115. ----------. "Fielding's *The History of the Present Rebellion in Scotland*." *PQ* 37 (1958): 119-123.

14116. Grundy, Isobel M. "New Verse by Henry Fielding." *PMLA* 87(1972): 213-245.

14117. Hartwig, Robert J. "*Pharsamon* and *Joseph Andrews*." *TSLL* 14(1972): 45-52.

14118. Hassall, Anthony J. "Fielding's *Amelia*: Dramatic and Authorial Narration." *Novel* 5(1972): 225-233.

14119. ----------. "Fielding's Puppet Image." *PQ* 53(1974): 71-83.

14120. Hatfield, Glenn W. "Puffs and Pollitricks: *Jonathan Wild* and the Political Corruption of Language." *PQ* 46(1967): 248-267.

14121. ----------. "Quacks, Pettyfoggers, and Parsons: Fielding's Case Against the Learned Professions." *TSLL* 9(1967): 69-83.

14122. ----------. "The Serpent and the Dove: Fielding's Irony and the Prudence Theme of *Tom Jones*." *MP* 65(1967): 17-32.

14123. Hopkins, Robert H. "Language and Comic Play in Fielding's *Jonathan Wild*." *Criticism* 8(1966): 213-228.

14124. Hunter, J. Paul. "Fielding's Reflexive Plays and the Rhetoric of Discovery." *SLI* 5,#2(1972): 65-100.

14125. Hutchens, Eleanor N. "'Prudence' in *Tom Jones*: A Study of Connotative Irony." *PQ* 39(1960): 496-507.

14126. ----------. "Verbal Irony in *Tom Jones*." *PMLA* 77(1962): 46-50.

14127. Jenkins, Owen. "Richardson's *Pamela* and Fielding's 'Vile Forgeries.'" *PQ* 44(1965): 200-210.

14128. Jobe, Alice. "Fielding's Novels: Selected Criticism (1940-1969)." *SN* 2(1970): 246-259.

14129. Johnson, E.D.H. "*Vanity Fair* and *Amelia*: Thackeray in the Perspective of the Eighteenth Century." *MP* 59(1961): 100-113.

14130. Jones, Claude E. "Fielding's 'True Patriot' and the Henderson Murder." *MLR* 52 (1957): 498-503.

14131. Jordan, Robert M. "The Limits of Illusion: Faulkner, Fielding, and Chaucer. *Criticism* 2(1960): 278-305.

14132. Kaplan, Fred. "Fielding's Novel about Novels: The 'Prefaces' and the 'Plot' of *Tom Jones*." *SEL* 13(1973): 535-549.

14133. Kearney, A.M. "*Pamela* and *Joseph Andrews*." *EIC* 18(1968): 105-107, 479-480.

14134. Kern, Jean B. "Fielding's Dramatic Satire." *PQ* 54(1975): 239-257.

14135. Kishler, Thomas C. "Fielding's Experiments with Fiction in the *Champion*." *JNT* 1 (1971): 95-107.

14136. Knight, Charles A. "Multiple Structures and the Unity of 'Tom Jones.'" *Criticism* 14 (1972): 227-242.

14137. Kropf, C.R. "Educational Theory and Human Nature in Fielding's Works." *PMLA* 89(1974): 113-120.

14138. LePage, Peter V. "The Prison and the Dark Beauty of 'Amelia.'" *Criticism* 9(1967): 337-354.

14139. Levine, George R. "Henry Feilding's 'Defense' of the Stage Licensing Act." *ELN* 2 (1965): 193-196.

14140. Longmire, Samuel E. "Allworthy and Barrow: The Standards of Good Judgement." *TSLL* 13 (1972): 629-639.

14141. ----------. "Partridge's Ghost Story." *SSF* 11(1974): 423-426.

14141a: Macey, Samuel L. "Fielding's *Tom Thumb* as the Heir to Buckingham's *The Rehearsal*." *TSLL* 10(1968): 405-414.

14142. McCullen, J.T., Jr. "Fielding's Beau Didapper." *ELN* 2(1964): 98-100.

14143. Miller, Henry K. "Benjamin Stillingfleet's *Essay on Conversation*, 1737, and Henry Fielding." *PQ* 33(1954): 427-428.

14144. ----------. "'Digressive' Tales in Fielding's *Tom Jones* and the Perspective of Romance." *PQ* 54(1975): 258-274.

14145. ----------. "Henry Fielding's Satire on the Royal Society." *SP* 57(1960): 72-86.

14146. ----------. "Some Functions of Rhetoric in *Tom Jones*." *PQ* 45(1966): 209-235.

14147. Oakman, Robert L. "The Character of the Hero: A Key to Fielding's Amelia. *SEL* 16 (1976): 473-489.

14148. Palmer, E. Taiwo. "Irony in 'Tom Jones.'" *MLR* 66(1971): 497-510.

14149. Palmer, Eustace. "*Amelia*—the Decline of Fielding's Art." *EIC* 21(1971): 135-151.

14150. Park, William. Fielding *and* Richardson." *PMLA* 81(1966): 381-388.

14151. ----------. "Tom and Oedipus." *HSL* 7(1975): 207-215.

14152. Poovey, Mary. "Journeys from this World to the Next: The Providential Promise in *Clarissa* and *Tom Jones*." *ELH* 43(1976): 316-341.

14153. Preston, John. "The Ironic Mode: a Comparison of *Jonathan Wild* and *The Beggar's Opera*." *EIC* 16(1966): 268-280.

14154. ----------. "Plot as Irony: The Reader's Role in *Tom Jones*." *ELH* 35(1968): 365-380.

14155. ----------. "*Tom Jones* and the 'Pursuit of True Judgment.'" *ELH* 33(1966): 315-326.

14156. Rawson, C.J. "Fielding, Whose Contemporary?" *EIC* 25(1975): 272-276.

14157. ----------. "Fielding, Whose Contemporary?" *EIC* 26(1976): 283.

14158. ----------. "Fielding's 'Good' Merchant: The Problem of Heartfree in *Jonathan Wild* (with Comments on Other 'Good' Characters in Fielding)." *MP* 69(1972): 292-313.

14159. Ribble, Frederick G. "The Constitution of the Mind and the Concept of Emotion in Fielding's *Amelia*." *PQ* 56(1977): 104-123.

14160. Rinehart, Hollis. "*Jonathan Wild* and the Cant Dictionary." *PQ* 48(1969): 220-225.

14161. Roberts, Edgar V. "Mr. Seedo's London Career and His Work with Henry Fielding." *PQ* 45(1966): 179-190.

14162. Rogers, Katharine M. "Sensitive Feminism vs. Conventional Sympathy: Richardson and Fielding on Women." *Novel* 9(1976): 256-270.

14163. Rogers, Pat. "Fielding's Parody of Oldmixon." *PQ* 49(1970): 262-266.

14164. Roscoe, Adrian A. "Fielding and the Problem of Allworthy." *TSLL* 7(1965): 167-172.

14165. Rothstein, Eric. "The Framework of *Shamela*." *ELH* 35(1968): 381-402.

14166. Schonhorn, Manuel. "Fielding's Digressive-Parodic Artistry: *Tom Jones* and The Man of the Hill." *TSLL* 10(1968): 207-214.

14167. ----------. "Heroic Allusion in *Tom Jones*: Hamlet and the Temptations of Jesus." *SN* 6(1974): 218-227.

14168. Shea, Bernard. "Machiavelli and Fielding's *Jonathan Wild*." *PMLA* 72(1957): 55-73.

14169. Sherburn, George. "Fielding's Social Outlook." *PQ* 35(1956): 1-23.

14170. Shepperson, Archibald Bolling. "Additions and Corrections to Facts about Fielding." *MP* 51(1954): 217-224.

14171. Shesgreen, Sean. "The Moral Function of Thwackum, Square, and Allworthy." *SN* 2(1970): 159-167.

14172. Shipley, John B. "A New Fielding Essay from the *Champion*." *PQ* 42(1963): 417-422.

14173. Smith, LeRoy W. "Fielding and Mandeville: The 'War Against Virtue.'" *Criticism* 3 (1961): 7-15.

14174. ----------. "Fielding and 'Mr. Bayle's' *Dictionary*." *TSLL* 4(1962): 16-20.

14175. Spilka, Mark. "Fielding and the Epic Impulse." *Criticism* 11(1969): 68-77.

14176. Stern, Guy. "A German Imitation of Fielding: Musäus' *Grandison der Zweite*." *Comp L* 10(1985): 335-343.

14177. Stevick. "Fielding and the Meaning of History." *PMLA* 79(1964): 561-568.

14178. ----------. "On Fielding Talking." *Coll L* 1(1974): 19-34.

14179. Stewart, Mary Margaret. "Henry Fielding's Letter to the Duke of Richmond." *PQ* 50(1971): 135-140.

14180. Tannenbaum, Earl. "A Note on Tom Jones and the Man of the Hill." *TSLL* 4(1961): 215-217.

14181. Thomas, D. S. "Fortune and the Passions in Fielding's 'Amelia.'" *MLR* 60(1965): 176-187.

14182. Towers, A. R. "*Amelia* and the State of Matrimony." *RES* 5(1954): 144-157.

14183. Vopat, James B. "Narrative Technique in *Tom Jones*: the Balance of Art and Nature." *JNT* 4(1974): 144-154.

14184. Warner, John N. "The Interpolated Narratives in the Fiction of Fielding and Smollett: An Epistemological View." *SN* 5(1973): 271-283.

14185. Weinbrot, Howard D. "Chastity and Interpolation: Two Aspects of *Joseph Andrews*." *JEGP* 69(1970): 14-31.

14186. Wendt, Allan. "The Moral Allegory of *Jonathan Wild*." *ELH* 24(1957): 306-320.

14187. ----------. "The Naked Virtue of Amelia." *ELH* 27(1960): 131-148.

14188. Wess, Robert V. "The Probable and the Marvelous in *Tom Jones*." *MP* 68(1970): 32-45.

14189. Wisenfarth, Joseph. "'High' People and 'Low' in *Joseph Andrews*: A Study of Structure and Style." *CLA* 16(1973): 357-365.

14190. Wolff, Cynthia Griffin. "Fielding's *Amelia*: Private Virtue and Public Good." *TSLL* 10(1968): 37-55.

14191. Wood, Carl. "*Shamela*'s Subtle Satire: Fielding's Characterization of Mrs. Jewkes and Mrs. Jervis." *ELN* 13(1976): 266-270.

14192. Woods, Charles B. "Cibber in Fielding's Author's Farce: Three Notes." *PQ* 44(1965): 145-151.

14193. ----------. "The 'Miss Lucy' Plays of Fielding and Garrick." *PQ* 41(1961): 294-310.

14194. ----------. "Theobald and Fielding's Don Tragedio." *ELN* 2(1965): 266-271.

14195. Wright, Andrew. "Work in Progress III: *Joseph Andrews* and Mask and Feast." *EIC* 13(1963): 209-221.

14196. Zirker, Malvin R. "Fielding and Reform in the 1750's." *SEL* 7(1967): 453-465.

See also 59, 7780, 13557, 13581, 13585, 13589, 13596, 14472, 14881, 14965, 16347, 18421, 18427.

FORSTER, GEORG. 14197. Robson-Scott, W. D. "Georg Forster and the Gothic Revival." *MLR* 51 (1956): 42-48.

GARRICK, DAVID. 14198. Bergman, Frederick L. "David Garrick and *The Clandestine Marriage*." *PMLA* 67(1952): 148-162.

14198a. ----------. "Garrick's *Zara*: *PMLA* 74 (1959): 225-232.

14198b. Hainsworth, J. D. "The Date of David Garrick's Lines to George Lyttelton." *RES* 24 (1973): 458-460.

14199. ----------. "David Garrick's Address to the Audience on Behalf of the Drury Lane Theatrical Fund." *RES* 26(1975): 50-55.

14200. Knapp, Mary E. "Garrick's Verses to the Marquis of Rockingham." *PQ* 29(1950): 78-81.

14201. Price, Cecil. "David Garrick and Evan Lloyd." *RES* 3(1952): 28-38.

14202. Stone, George Winchester, Jr. "A Century of Cymbeline; or Garrick's Magic Touch." *PQ* 54(1975): 310-322.

14203. ----------. "David Garrick's Significance in the History of Shaksperean Criticism." *PMLA* 65(1950): 183-197.

14204. ----------. "Garrick and *Othello*." *PQ* 45(1966): 304-320.

See also 13681, 14192.

GARTH, SAMUEL. 14205. Cook, Richard I. "Garth's *Dispensary* and Pope's *Rape of the Lock*." *CLA* 6(1962): 107-116.

14206. Schneider, Duane B. "Dr. Garth and Shakespeare: A Borrowing." *ELN* 1(1964): 200-202.

14207. Sena, John F. "Samuel Garth's *The Dispensary*." *TSLL* 15(1974): 639-648.

GAY, JOHN. 14208. Aden, John M. "The 1720 Version of *Rural Sports* and the Georgic Tradition." *MLQ* 20(1959): 228-231.

14209. Battestin, Martin C. "Menalca's Song: The Meaning of Art and Artifice in Gay's Poetry." *JEGP* 65(1966): 662-679.

14210. Bronson, Bertrand H. "The True Proportions of Gay's *Acis and Galatea*." *PMLA* 80(1965): 325-331.

14211. Burgess, C. F. "John Gay and *Polly* and a Letter to the King." *PQ* 47(1968): 596-598.

14212. Burgess, C. F. "John Gay to the Countess of Burligton: An Unpublished Letter." *PQ* 43 (1964): 420-422.

14213. Conolly, L. W. "Anna Margaretta Larpent, Duchess of Queensbury and Gay's *Polly* in 1777." *PQ* 51(1972): 955-957.

14214. Lewis, Peter. "Another Look at John Gay's 'The Mohocks.'" *MLR* 63(1968): 790-793.

14215. Moore, John Robert. "Gay's Burlesque of Sir Richard Blackmore's Poetry." *JEGP* 50(1951): 83-89.

14216. Preston, John. "The Ironic Mode: a Comparison of *Jonathan Wild* and *The Beggar's Opera*." *EIC* 16(1966): 268-280.

14217. Rawson, C. J. "Gay's Horses." *EIC* 14(1964): 426-427.

14218. ----------. "Some Unpublished Letters of Pope and Gay; and some Manuscript Sources of Goldsmith's *Life of Thomas Parnell*." *RES* 10(1959): 371-387.

14219. Rees, Christine. "Gay, Swift, and the Nymphs of Drury-Lane." *EIC* 23(1973): 1-21.

14220. Rosenberg, Albert. "The Date of John Gay's 'An Epistle to Burlington.'" *PQ* 30(1951): 94-96.

14221. Ruhe, E. L. "Pope's Hand in Thomas Birch's Account of Gay." *RES* 5(1954): 171-174.

14222. Sherbo, Arthur. "Virgil, Dryden, Gay, and Matters Trivial." *PMLA* 85(1970): 1063-1071.

14223. Spacks, Patricia Meyer. "John Gay: a Satirist's Progress." *EIC* 14(1964): 156-170.

See also 11361, 15193.

GAYLARD, DOCTOR. 14224. Limouze. A. Sanford. "Doctor Gaylard's *Loyal Observer Reviv'd*." *MP* 48 (1950): 97-103.

GIBBON, EDWARD. 14227. Dilworth, Ernest. "A Letter of Gibbon to Adam Smith." *RES* 10(1959): 410-402.

14228. Frost, William. "The Irony of Swift and Gibbon: a Reply to F. R. Leavis." *EIC* 17 (1967): 41-47.

14229. Hayes, Curtis W. "A Study in Prose Styles: Edward Gibbon and Ernest Hemingway." *TSLL* 7(1966): 371-386.

14230. Keast, William R. "The Elements in Art in Gibbon's *History*." *ELH* 23(1956): 153-162.

14231. King, R. W. "A Note on Shelley, Gibbon, Voltaire, and Southey." *MLR* 51(1956): 255-227.

14232. Mandel, Barrett John. "The Problems of Narration in Edward Gibbon's *Autobiography*." *SP* 67(1970): 550-564.

14233. Oliver, Dennis. "The Character of an Historian: Edward Gibbon." *ELH* 38(1971): 254-273.

14234. ----------. "Gibbon's Use of Architecture as Symbol." *TSLL* 14(1972): 77-92.

14235. Price, Martin. "The Inquisitition of Truth: Memory and Freedom in Gibbon's Memoirs." *PQ* 54(1975): 391-408.

14236. Voth, Grant L. "Gibbon and the Christian Soldier: Tonal Manipulation as Moral Judgment." *SEL* 14(1974): 449-457.

See also 13634.

GILDON, CHARLES. 14237. Anderson, G. L. "Lord Halifax in Gildon's *New Rehearsal*." *PQ* 33 (1954): 423-426.

14238. Moore, John Robert. "Gildon's Attack on Steele and Defoe in *The Battle of the Authors*."

PMLA 66(1951): 534-538.

GILPIN, WILLIAM. 14239. Boudreau, Gordon V. "H. D. Thoreau, William Gilpin, and the Metaphysical Ground of the Picturesque." *AL* 45(1973): 357-369.

GODWIN, WILLIAM. 14240. Albrecht, W. P. "Godwin and Malthus." *PMLA* 70(1950): 552-555.

14241. Barker, Gerard A. "Justice to Caleb Williams." *SN* 6(1974): 377-388.

14242. Colmer, John. "Godwin's *Mandeville* and Peacock's *Nightmare Abbey*." *RES* 21(1970): 331-336.

14243. Denman, Peter. "Caleb Williams and the Real." *EIC* 27(1977): 280-282.

14244. Duerksen, Roland A. "*Caleb Williams*, *Political Justice*, and *Billy Budd*." *AL* 38(1966): 372-376.

14245. Dumas, D. Gilbert. "Things as They Were: The Original Ending of *Caleb Williams*." *SEL* 6(1966): 575-597.

14246. Flanders, Wallace Austin. "Godwin and Gothicism: *St. Leon*." *TSLL* 8(1967): 533-545.

14247. Furbank, P. N. "Godwin's Novels." *EIC* 5(1955): 214-228.

14248. Gold, Alex, Jr. "It's Only Love: The Politics of Passion in Godwin's *Caleb Williams*." *TSLL* 19(1977): 135-160.

14249. Griffith, Ben. "An Experiment on the American Bookseller: Two Letters from Irving to Godwin." *NCF* 12(1957): 237-239.

14250. Grob, Alan. "Wordsworth and Godwin: A Reassessment." *SR* 6(1967): 98-119.

14251. Gross, Harvey. "The Puruser and the Pursued: A Study of *Caleb Williams*." *TSLL* 1(1959): 401-411.

14252. Harvey, A. D. "The Nightmare of *Caleb Williams*." *EIC* 26(1976): 236-249.

14253. Kelly, Gary. "History and Fiction: Bethlem Gabor in Godwin's *St. Leon*." *ELN* 14(1976): 117-120.

14254. Kropf, C. R. "*Caleb Williams* and the Attack on Romance." *SN* 8(1976): 81-87.

14255. Marken, Jack W. "William Godwin's History of the United Provinces." *PQ* 45(1966): 379-386.

14256. McCracken, David. "Godwin's Literary Theory: The Alliance between Fiction and Political Philosophy." *PQ* 49(1970): 113-133.

14257. Myers, Mitzi. "Godwin's Changing Conception of *Caleb Williams*." *SEL* 12(1972): 591-628.

14258. Pollin, Burton R. "Poe and Godwin." *NCF* 20(1965): 237-253.

14259. ----------. "William Godwin's 'Fragment of a Romance.'" *Comp L* 16(1964): 40-54.

14260. Pulos, C. E. "Godwin and Malthus." *PMLA* 70(1955): 555-556.

14261. Roemer, Donald. "The Achievement of Godwin's 'Caleb Williams': The Proto-Byronic Squire Falkland." *Criticism* 18(1976): 43-56.

14262. Rosen, Frederick. "Godwin and Holcroft." *ELN* 5(1968): 183-186.

14263. Sherburn, George. "Godwin's Later Novels." *SR* 1(1962): 65-82.

14264. Stallbaumer, Virgil. "Holcroft's Influence on *Political Justice*." *MLQ* 14(1953): 21-30.

14265. Storch, Rudolph F. "Metaphors of Private Guilt and Social Rebellion in Godwin's *Caleb Williams*." *ELH* 34(1967): 188-207.

14266. Uphaus, Robert. "*Caleb Williams*: Godwin's Epoch of Mind." *SN* 9(1977): 279-296.

14267. Werkmeister, Lucyle. "Coleridge and Godwin on the Communication of Truth." *MP* 55 (1958): 170-177.

See also 3252.

GOLDSMITH, OLIVER.   14268. Andrews, William. "Goldsmith and Freneau in 'The American Village.'" *EAL* 5,#2(1970): 14-23.

14269. Bäckman, Sven. "The Real Origin of One of the 'Manufactured Anecdotes' in Goldsmith's *Life of Nash*." *MP* 72(1975): 277-279.

14270. Booth, Wayne C. "'The Self-Portraiture of Genius': *The Citizen of the World* and Critical Method." *MP* 73(1976): S85-S96.

14271. Cole, Richard C. "Oliver Goldsmith's Reputation in Ireland, 1762-74." *MP* 68(1970): 65-70.

14272. Dahl, Curtis. Patterns of Disguise in *The Vicar of Wakefield*." *ELH* 25(1958): 90-104.

14273. Dircks, Richard J. "The Genesis of Goldsmith's *Retaliation*." *MP* 75(1977): 48-52.

14274. Durant, David. "*The Vicar of Wakefield* and the Sentimental Novel." *SEL* 17(1977): 477-491.

14275. Eversole, Richard. "The Oratorical Design of *The Deserted Village*." *ELN* 4(1966): 99-104.

14276. Ferguson, Oliver W. "Dr. Primrose and Goldsmith's Clerical Ideal." *PQ* 54(1975): 323-332.

14277. ----------. "The Materials of History: Goldsmith's *Life of Nash*." *PMLA* 80(1965): 372-386.

14278. Friedman, Arthur. "Goldsmith and the Jest-books." *MP* 53(1955): 47-49.

14279. ----------. "Goldsmith's 'Essay on Friendship': Its First Publication and the Problem of Authorship." *PQ* 35(1956): 346-349.

14280. Gassman, Byron. "French Sources of Goldsmith's *The Good Natur'd Man*." *PQ* 39(1960): 56-65.

14281. Golden Morris. "The Family-Wanderer Theme in Goldsmith." *ELH* 25(1958): 181-193.

14282. ---------. "Goldsmith, *The Vicar of Wakefield*, and the Periodicals." *JEGP* 76(1977): 525-536.

14283. Goldstein, Laurence. "The Auburn Syndrome: Change and Loss in 'The Deserted Village' and Wordsworth's Grasmere." *ELH* 40(1973): 352-371.

14284. Helgerson, Richard. "The Two Worlds of Oliver Goldsmith." *SEL* 13(1973): 516-534.

14285. Hennig, John. "The Auerbachs Keller Scene and *She Stoops to Conquer*." *Comp L* 7(1955): 193-202

14286. Hopkins, Robert H. "Matrimony in *The Vicar of Wakefield* and the Marriage Act of 1753. *SP* 74(1977): 322-339.

14287. Hunting, Robert. "The Poems in 'The Vicar of Wakefield.'" *Criticism* 15(1973): 234-241.

14288. Jaarsma, Richard. J. "Biography as Tragedy: Fictive Style in Oliver Goldsmith's *The Life of Richard Nash, Esq.*'" *JNT* 1(1971): 15-29.

14289. ----------. "Ethics in the Wasteland: Image and Structure in Goldsmith's *The Deserted Village*." *TSLL* 13(1971): 447-459.

14290. ----------. "Satiric Intent in *The Vicar of Wakefield*." *SSF* 5(1968): 331-341.

14291. McDonald, Daniel. "*The Vicar of Wakefield*: A Paradox." *CLA* 10(1966): 23-33.

14292. Quintana, Ricardo. "Oliver Goldsmith as a Critic of the Drama." *SEL* 5(1965): 435-454.

14293. ----------. "*The Vicar of Wakefield*: The Problem of Critical Approach." *MP* 71(1973): 59-65.

14294. Rawson, C. J. "Some Unpublished Letters of Pope and Gay; and some Manuscript Sources of Goldsmith's *Life of Thomas Parnell*." *RES* 10 (1959): 371-387.

14295. Storm, Leo. "Conventional Ethics in Goldsmith's *The Traveller*." *SEL* 17(1977): 463-476.

14296. Weinbrot, Howard D., and Eric Rothstein. "The Vicar of Wakefield, Mr. Wilmot, and the 'Whistonean Controversy.'" *PQ* 55(1976): 225-240.

14297. Yearling, Elizabeth M. "The Good-Natured Heroes of Cumberland, Goldsmith, and Sheridan." *MLR* 67(1972): 490-500.

14298. Suits, C. B. "Who Wrote *The History of Francis Wills*?" *PQ* 43(1964): 216-223.

See also 13585, 13596.

GRAVES, RICHARD. See 13557.

GRAY, THOMAS.   14299. Berry, Francis. "The Sound of Personification in Gray's *Elegy*." *EIC* 12 (1962): 442-445.

14300. Carper, Thomas R. "Gray's Personal Elegy." *SEL* 17(1977): 451-462.

14301. Doherty, F. "The Two Voices of Gray." *EIC* 13(1963): 222-230.

14302. Dyson, A. E. "The Ambivalence of Gray's Elegy." *EIC* 7(1957): 257-261.

14303. Eaves, T. C. Duncan. "Further Pursuit of Selima." *PQ* 30(1951): 91-94.

14304. Ellis, Frank H. "Gray's *Elegy*: The Biographical Problem in Literary Criticism." *PMLA* 66(1951): 971-1008.

14305. Foladare, Joseph. "Gray's 'Frail Memorial' to West." *PMLA* 75(1960): 61-65.

14306. Johnston, Arthur. "Gray's 'The Triumph of Owen.'" *RES* 11(1960): 275-285.

14307. ----------. "Gray's Use of the Gorchest y Beirdd in 'The Bard.'" *MLR* 59(1964): 335-338.

14308. ----------. "'The Purple Year' in Pope and Gray." *RES* 14(1963): 389-393.

14309. Jones, Myrddin. "Gray, Jagues, and the the Man of Feeling." *RES* 25(1974): 39-48.

14310. Jones, W. Powell. "Johnson and Gray: A Study in Literary Anatgonism." *MP* 56(1959): 243-253.

14311. Macdonald, Alastair. "The Poet Gray in Scotland." *RES* 13(1962): 245-256.

14312. Saslow, Edward L. "Richard West: A Correction." *PQ* 47(1968): 592-596.

14313. Spacks, Patricia Meyer. "'Artful Strife': Conflict in Gray's Poetry." *PMLA* 81 (1966): 63-69.

14314. ----------. "Statement and Artifice in Thomas Gray. *SEL* 5(1965): 519-532.

14315. Sparrow, John. Gray's 'Spring of Tears.'" *RES* 14(1963): 58-61.

14316. Sutherland, John. "The Stonecutter in Gray's 'Elegy.'" *MP* 55(1957): 11-13.

14317. Swearingen, James E. "Wordsworth on Gray." *SEL* 14(1974): 489-509.

14318. Vernon, P.F. "The Structure of Gray's Early Poems." *EIC* 15(1965): 381-393.

14319. Wright, George T. "Eliot Written in a Country Churchyard." *ELH* 43(1976): 227-243.

14320. ----------. "Stillness and the Argument of Gray's *Elegy*." *MP* 74(1977): 381-389.

See also 13731.

GRIFFIN, BENJAMIN. See 13579.

HALL-STEVENSON, JOHN. 14321. Hartley, Lodwick. "Sterne's Eugenius as Indiscreet Author: The Literary Career of John Hall-Stevenson." *PMLA* 86(1971): 428-445.

See also 3866.

HAMMOND, ANTHONY. 14322. Watt, Ian. *"Considerations Upon Corrupt Elections of Members to Serve in Parliament, 1701:* by Anthony Hammond, Not Defoe." *PQ* 31(1952): 45-53.

HARRIS, JAMES. 14323. Malek, James. "Art as Mind Shaped by Medium: The Significance of James Harris' 'A Disourse on Music, Painting, and Poetry' in Eighteenth-Century Aesthetics." *TSLL* 12(1970): 231-239.

HAWKESWORTH, JOHN. 14324. Eddy, Donald D. "John Hawkesworth: Book Reviewer in the *Gentleman's Magazine*." *PQ* 43(1964): 223-238.

14325. Fairer, David. "Authorship Problems in *The Adventurer*." *RES* 25(1974): 137-151.

See also 13596.

HAYLEY, WILLIAM. 14326. Wittreich, Joseph Anthony, Jr. "Dome of Mental Pleasure: Blake's Epics and Hayley's Epic Theory." *SP* 69(1972): 101-129.

See also 13611, 13624, 13747, 18124.

HAYWOOD, ELIZA. 14327. Erickson, James P. *"Evelina* and *Betsy Thoughtless*." *TSLL* 6(1964): 96-103.

See also 13601.

HERON, ROBERT. 14328. Mendilow, A. A. "Robert Heron and Wordsworth's Critical Essays." *MLR* 52(1957): 329-338.

HILL, AARON. 14329. Sutherland, W. O. S. "Polonius, Hamlet, and Lear in Aaron Hill's *Prompter*." *SP* 49(1952): 605-618.

See also 14198.

HILL, JOHN. See 13611.

HOGARTH, WILLIAM. 14330. Jackson, Wallace. "Hogarth's *Analysis:* The Fate of a Late Rococo Document." *SEL* 6(1966): 543-550.

See also 14090.

HOLCROFT, THOMAS. See 13597.

HOME, JOHN. 14331. Malek, James S. "The Ossianic Source of John Home's *The Fatal Discovery*." *ELN* 9(1971): 39-42.

See also 13579.

HUGHES, JOHN. See 11437.

HUME, DAVID. 14332. Bell, Robert H. "David Hume's Fables of Identity." *PQ* 54(1975): 471-483.

14333. Cohen, Ralph. "David Hume's Experimental Method and the Theory of Taste." *ELH* 25 (1958): 270-289.

14334. ----------. "The Transformation of Passion: A Study of Hume's Theories of Tragedy." *PQ* 41(1962): 450-464.

14335. Eberwein, Robert. "James Beattie and David Hume on the Imagination and Truth." *TSLL* 12(1971): 595-603.

14336. Hunter, Geoffrey. "David Hume: Some Unpublished Letters." [with text] *TSLL* 2 (1960): 127-150.

14337. Meyer, Paul H. "The Manuscript of Hume's Account of His Dispute with Rousseau." *Comp L* 4(1952): 341-350.

14338. ----------. "Voltaire and Hume as Historians: A Comparative Study of the *Essai sur les moers* and the *History of England*. *PMLA* 73 (1958): 51-68.

14339. Morrisroe, Michael, Jr. "Did Hume Read Berkeley? A Conclusive Answer." *PQ* 52(1973): 310-315.

14340. ----------. "Hume's Rhetorical Strategy: A Solution to the Riddle of the Dialogues Concerning Natural Religion." *TSLL* 11 (1969): 963-974.

14341. Mossner, Ernest Campbell. "Hume's *Four Dissertations:* An Essay in Biography and Bibliography. *MP* 48(1950): 37-57.

14342. ----------. "New Hume Letters to Lord Elibank, 1748-1776." [with text] *TSLL* 4 (1962): 431-460.

14343. Popkin, Richard H. "Hume and Isaac de Pinto." *TSLL* 12(1970): 417-430.

14344. Price, John Valdimir. "Concepts of Englightenment in Eighteenth-Century Scottish Literature." *TSLL* 9(1967): 371-389.

14345. ----------. "Empirical Theists in Cicero and Hume." *TSLL* 5(1963): 255-264.

14346. Ross, Ian. "Le Bon David Again: Three New Hume Letters." [with text] *TSLL* 10 (1969): 537-545.

14347. White, Thomas I. "Some Remarks on Hume's Conversion Theory in 'Of Tragedy.'" *PQ* 55 (1976): 287-291.

HURD, RICHARD. 14348. Curry, Stephe, J. "Richard Hurd's Genre Criticism." *TSLL* 8(1966): 207-217.

14349. Nankivell, James. "Extracts from the Destroyed Letters of Richard Hurd to William Mason." *MLR* 45(1950): 153-163.

HUTCHESON, FRANCIS. See 13607.

JOHNSON, SAMUEL. 14350. Abbott, John Lawrence. "Dr. Johnson and the Amazons." *PQ* 44 (1965): 484-495.

14351. ----------. "Dr. Johnson, Fontenelle, Le Clerc, and Six 'French' Lives." *MP* 63(1965): 121-127.

14352. Aden, John M. *"Rasselas* and *The Vanity of Human Wishes*." *Criticism* 3(1961): 295-303.

14353. Adler, Joseph H. "Notes on the Prosody of *The Vanity of Human Wishes*." *SLI* 5, #2(1972): 101-117.

14354. Alkon, Paul K. "The Intention and Reception of Johnson's *Life of Savage*." *MP* 72 (1974): 139-150.

14355. ----------. "Johnson's Conception of Admiration." *PQ* 48(1969): 59-81.

14356. ----------. "Robert South, William Low, and Samuel Johnson." *SEL* 6(1966): 499-528.

14357. Allison, James. "Joseph Warton's Reply to Dr. Johnson's *Lives*." *JEGP* 51(1952): 186-191.

14358. Amis, George T. "The Style of *The Vanity of Human Wishes*." *MLQ* 35(1974): 16-29.

14359. Atkinson, A.D. "Dr. Johnson and Newton's *Opticks*." *RES* 2(1951): 226-237.

14360. Baker, Sheridan. "*Rasselas:* Psychological Irony and Romance." *PQ* 45(1966): 249-261.

14361. Balderston, Katharine. "Dr. Johnson and William Law." *PMLA* 75(1960): 382-394.

14362. ----------. "Dr. Johnson's Use of William Law in the Dictionary." *PQ* 39(1960): 379-388.

14363. Batten, Charles L. "Samuel Johnson's Sources for 'The Life of Roscommon.'" *MP* 74(1974): 185-189.

14364. Battersby, James L. "Johnson and Shiels: Biographers of Addison." *SEL* 9(1969): 521-537.

14365. Bernard, F. V. "The Hermit of Paris and the Astronomer in Rasselas." *JEGP* 67(1968): 272-278.

14366. ----------. "Johnson and the Authorship of Four Debates." *PMLA* 82(1967): 408-419.

14367. ----------. "New Evidence on the Pamphilus Letters." *MP* 62(1964): 42-44.

14368. ----------. "A New Preface by Samuel Johnson." *PQ* 55(1976): 445-449.

14369. ----------. "A Possible Source for Johnson's Life of the King of Prussia." *PQ* 47 (1968): 206-215.

14370. Bloom, Edward A. "Symbolic Names in Johnson's Periodical Essays." *MLQ* 13(1952): 333-352.

14371. ----------. "*The Vanity of Human Wishes:* Reason's Images." *EIC* 15(1965): 181-192.

14372. Booth, Mark W. "Johnson's Critical Judgments in the *Lives of the Poets.*" *SEL* 16 (1976): 505-515.

14373. Bowers, Fredson. "The Text of Johnson." *MP* 61(1964): 298-309.

14374. Boyce, Benjamin. "Johnson and Chesterfield Once More." *PQ* 32(1953): 93-96.

14375. ----------. "Johnson's *Life of Savage* and Its Literary Background." *SP* 53(1956): 576-598.

14376. ----------. "Samuel Johnson's Criticism of Pope in the *Life of Pope.*" *RES* 5 (1954): 37-46.

14377. Boyd, D. V. "Vanity and Vacuity: A Reading of Johnson's Verse Satires." *ELH* 39 (1972): 387-403.

14378. Braudy, Leo. "Lexicography and Biography in the *Preface* to Johnson's *Dictionary,*" *SEL* 10(1970): 551-556.

14379. Bronson, Bertrand H. "The Double Tradition of Dr. Johnson." *ELH* 18(1951): 90-106.

14380. Campbell, Hilbert. "Shiels and Johnson: Biographers of Thomson." *SEL* 12(1972): 535-544.

14381. Cannon, Garland. "Sir William Jones and Dr. Johnson's Literary Club." *MP* 63(1965): 20-37.

14382. Carnochan, W. B. "Johnsonian Metaphor and the 'Adamant of Shakespeare.'" *SEL* 10(1970): 541-549.

14383. Chapin, Chester F. "Johnson and the 'Proofs' of Revelation." *PQ* 40(1961): 297-302.

14384. ----------. "Johnson, Rousseau, and Religion." *TSLL* 2(1960): 95-102.

14385. ----------. "Samuel Johnson's Religious Development." *SEL* 4(1964): 457-474.

14386. Clifford, James L. "Johnson and Lauder." *PQ* 54(1975): 342-356.

14387. Cornu, Donald. "Dr. Johnson at Fort Augustus: Captain Lewis Ourry." *MLQ* 11 (1950): 27-49.

14388. ----------. "The Historical Authenticity of Dr. Johnson's 'Speaking Cat.'" *RES* 2 (1951): 358-370.

14389. Damrosch, Leopold, Jr. "Johnson's Manner of Proceeding in the *Rambler.*" *ELH* 40 (1973): 70-89.

14390. Donaldson, Ian. "Johnson's 'Falling Houses.'" *EIC* 26(1976): 378.

14391. Dussinger, John A. "Style and Intention in Johnson's *Life of Savage.*" *ELH* 37 (1970): 564-580.

14392. Eastman, Arthur M. "Johnson's Shakespeare and the Laity: A Textual Study." *PMLA* 65(1950): 1112-1121.

14393. ----------. "The Texts From Which Johnson Printed His Shakespeare." *JEGP* 49(1950): 182-191.

14394. Eaves, T.C. Duncan. "Dr. Johnson's Letters to Richardson." *PMLA* 75(1960): 377-381.

14395. Edinger, William. "Johnson on Conceit: The Limits of Particularity." *ELH* 39(1972): 597-619.

14396. Elder, A. T. "Thematic Patterning and Development in Johnson's Essays." *SP* 62(1965): 610-632.

14397. Emden, Cecil S. "Dr. Johnson and Imagery." *RES* 1(1950): 23-38.

14398. Fifer, Charles N. "Dr. Johnson and Bennet Langton." *JEGP* 54(1955): 504-506.

14399. Fleeman, J.D. "Some Notes on Johnson's Prayers and Meditations." *RES* 19(1968): 172-179.

14400. Fox, Robert C. "The Imaginary Submarines of Dr. Johnson and Richard Owen Cambridge." *PQ* 40(1961): 112-119.

14401. Fussel, Paul. "A Note on Samuel Johnson and the Rise of Accentual Prosodic Theory." *PQ* 33(1954): 431-433.

14402. Gifford, Henry. "*The Vanity of Human Wishes.*" *RES* 6(1955): 157-173.

14403. Gilbert, Vedder M. "The Altercations of Thomas Edwards with Samuel Johnson." *JEGP* 51 (1952): 326-335.

14404. Gold, Joel J. "Johnson's Translation of Lobo." *PMLA* 80(1965): 51-61.

14405. Greene, D. J. "Johnson." *EIC* 14 (1964): 427-428.

14406. ----------. "The Johnsonian Canon: A Neglected Attribution." *PMLA* 65(1950): 427-434.

14407. ----------. "Johnsonian Critics." *EIC* 10(1960): 476-480.

14408. ----------. "Johnson's Contributions to the *Literary Magazine.*" *RES* 7(1956): 367-392.

14409. ----------. "Some Notes on Johnson and the *Gentleman's Magazine.*" *PMLA* 74(1959): 75-84.

14410. ----------. "Was Johnson Theatrical Critic of the *Gentleman's Magazine?*" *RES* 3 (1952): 158-161.

14411. Griffin, Dustin. "Johnson's Funeral Writings." *ELH* 41(1974): 192-211.

14412. Hagstrum, J.H. "The Nature of Dr. Johnson's Rationalism." *ELH* 17(1950): 191-205.

14413. Hanchock, Paul. "The Structure of Johnson's *Lives:* A Possible Source." *MP* 74(1976): 75-77.

14414. Hart, Edward. "Some New Sources of Johnson's *Lives*." *PMLA* 65(1950): 1088-1111.

14415. Hart, Francis R. "Johnson as Philosophic Traveler: The Perfecting of an Idea." *ELH* 36(1969): 679-695.

14416. Hardy, John. "Hope and Fear in Johnson." *EIC* 26(1976): 285-299.

14417. ----------. "Johnson and *Don Bellianis*." *RES* 17(1966): 297-299.

14418. Hart, Jeffrey. "Johnson's *A Journey to the Western Islands:* History as Art." *EIC* 10 (1960): 44-59.

14419. Hilles, Frederick W. "Dr. Johnson on Swift's Last Years: Some Misconceptions and Distortions." *PQ* 54(1975): 370-379.

14420. ----------. "Johnson's Correspondence with Nichols: Some Facts and a Query." *PQ* 48(1969): 226-233.

14421. Horne, Colin J. "The Biter Bit: Johnson's Strictures on Pope." *RES* 27(1976): 310-313.

14422. ----------. "The Roles of Swift and Marlborough in *The Vanity of Human Wishes*." *MP* 73(1976): 280-283.

14423. Hovey, Richard P. "Dr. Samuel Johnson, Psychiatrist." *MLQ* 15(1954): 321-325.

14424. Ingham, Patricia. "Dr. Johnson's 'Elegance.'" *RES* 19(1968): 271-278.

14425. Jack, Ian. "The Choice of Life' in Johnson and Matthew Prior." *JEGP* 49(1950): 523-530.

14426. Jemielity, Thomas. "Dr. Johnson and the Uses of Travel." *PQ* 51(1972): 448-459.

14427. ----------. "Samuel Johnson, the Second Sight, and His Sources." *SEL* 14(1974): 403-420.

14428. Jenkins, Ralph E. "'And I Travelled After Him': Johnson and Pennant in Scotland." *TSLL* 14(1972): 445-462.

14429. Jones, Emrys. "The Artistic Form of *Rasselas*." *RES* 18(1967): 387-401.

14430. Jones, W. Powell. "Johnson and Gray: A Study in Literary Antagonism." *MP* 56 (1959): 243-253.

14431. Kaul, R. K. "*A Journey to the Western Isles Reconsidered*." *EIC* 13(1963): 341-350.

14432. Keast, William R. "Johnson's Criticism of the Metaphysical Poets." *ELH* 17(1950): 59-70.

14433. ----------. "Johnson's Plan of a Dictionary: A Textual Crux." *PQ* 33(1954): 341-347.

14434. ----------. "Some Emendations in Johnson's Preface to the *Dictionary*." *RES* 4 (1953): 52-57.

14435. ----------. "The Two *Clarissas* in Johnson's *Dictionary*." *SP* 54(1957): 429-439.

14436. Kelly, Richard. "Johnson Among the Sheep." *SEL* 8(1968): 475-485.

14437. Kenney, William. "*Rasselas* and the Theme of Diversification." *PQ* 38(1959): 84-89.

14438. Kolb, Gwin J. "The Intellectual Background of the Discourse on the Soul in *Rasselas*." *PQ* 54(1975): 357-369.

14439. ----------. "More Attributions to Dr. Johnson." *SEL* 1,#3(1961): 77-95.

14440. ----------. "Notes on Four Letters by Dr. Johnson: Addenda to Chapman's Edition." *PQ* 38(1959): 379-383.

14441. ----------. "The 'Paradise' in Abyssinia and the 'Happy Valley' in Rasselas." *MP* 56(1958): 10-16.

14442. ----------. "Rousseau and the Background of the 'Life Led According to Nature' in Chapter 22 of *Rasselas*." *MP* 73(1976): S66-S73.

14443. ----------. "The Structure of *Rasselas*." *PMLA* 66(1951): 698-717.

14444. ----------, and James H. Sledd. "Johnson's *Dictionary* and Lexicographical Tradition." *MP* 50(1953): 171-194.

14445. Korshin, Paul J. "Dr. Johnson and Jeremy Bentham: An Unnoticed Relationship." *MP* 70(1972): 38-45.

14446. ----------. "Johnson and Swift: A Study in the Genesis of Literary Opinion." *PQ* 48 (1969): 464-478.

14447. ----------. "The Johnson—Chesterfield Relationship: A New Hypothesis." *PMLA* 85(1970): 247-259.

14448. Knapp, Lewis M. "Smollett and Johnson, Never Cater-Cousins?" *MP* 66(1968): 152-154.

14449. Kupesmith, William. "'More Like an Orator than a Philosopher': Rhetorical Structure in *The Vanity of Human Wishes*." *SP* 72(1975): 454-472.

14450. Lascelles, Mary. "Johnson's Last Allusion to Mary Queen of Scotts." *RES* 8(1957): 32-37.

14451. ----------. "*Rasselas:* A Rejoinder." *RES* 21(1970): 49-56.

14452. Leed, Jacob. "Two New Pieces by Johnson in the *Gentleman's Magazine*." *MP* 54(1957): 221-229.

14453. Leyburn, Ellen Douglass. "'No Romantick Absurdities or Incredible Fictions': The Relation of Johnson's *Rasselas* to Lobo's *Voyage to Abyssinia*." *PMLA* 70(1955): 1059-1067.

14454. Lipking, Lawrence. "Learning to Read Johnson: *The Vision of Theodore* and *The Vanity of Human Wishes*." *ELH* 43(1976): 517-537.

14455. Lockhart, Donald M. "'The Fourth Son of the Mighty Emperor': The Ethiopian Background of Johnson's *Rasselas*." *PMLA* 78(1963): 516-528.

14456. McAdam, E.L., Jr. "Dr. Johnson and Saunders Welch's *Proposals*." *RES* 4(1953): 337-345.

14457. ----------. "Johnson, Percy and Warton." *PMLA* 70(1955): 1203-1204.

14458. McCarthy, William. "The Moral Art of Johnson's *Lives*." *SEL* 17(1977): 503-517.

14459. McClure, Ruth K. "Johnson's Criticism of the Foundling Hospital and Its Consequences." *RES* 27(1976): 17-26.

14460. McCracken, David. "The Drudgery of Defining: Johnson's Debt to Bailey's *Dictionarium Britannicum*." *MP* 66(1969): 338-341.

14461. McGlynn, Paul D. "Rhetoric as Metaphor in *The Vanity of Human Wishes*." *SEL* 15(1975): 473-482.

14462. McIntosh, Carey. "Johnson's Debate with Stoicism." *ELH* 33(1966): 327-336.

14463. McKenzie, Alan T. "Two Letters from Giuseppe Baretti to Samuel Johnson." *PMLA* 86(1971): 218-224.

14464. Meier, T. K. "Johnson on Scotland." *EIC* 18(1968): 349-352.

14465. Middendorf, John H. "Dr. Johnson and Adam Smith." *PQ* 40(1961): 281-296.

14466. Mild, Warren. "Johnson and Lauder: A Reexamination." *MLQ* 14(1953): 149-153.

14467. Misenheimer, James B., Jr. "Dr. Johnson's Concept of Literary Fiction." *MLR* 62 (1967): 598-605.

14468. Monaghan, T. J. "Johnson's Additions to his *Shakespeare* for the Edition of 1773." *RES* 4(1953): 234-248.

14469. Moody, A. D. "The Creative Critic: Johnson's Revisions of *London* and *The Vanity of Human Wishes*." *RES* 22(1971): 137-150.

14470. Moore, John Robert. "Conan Doyle, Tennyson, and *Rasselas*." *NCF* 7(1952): 221-223.

14471. ----------. "*Rasselas* and the Early Travelers to Abyssinia." *MLQ* 15(1954): 36-41.

14472. Moore, Robert Etheridge. "Dr. Johnson on Fielding and Richardson." *PMLA* 66 (1951): 162-181.

14473. Noyes, Gertrude E. "The Critical Reception of Johnson's *Dictionary* in the Latter Eighteenth Century." *MP* 52(1955): 175-191.

14474. O'Flaherty, Patrick. "Dr. Johnson as Equivocator: The Meaning of *Rasselas*." *MLQ* 31(1970): 195-208.

1447a. ----------. "Johnson as Satirist: A New Look at *The Vanity of Human Wishes*." *ELH* 34(1967): 78-91.

14475. ----------. "Johnson's *Idler*: The Equipment of a Satirist." *ELH* 37(1970): 211-225.

11476. Ong, Walter J., S. J. "Gospel, Existence, and Print." *MLQ* 35(1974): 66-77.

14477. O'Sullivan, Maurice J., Jr. "Ex Alieno Igenio Poeta: Johnson's Translation of Pope's *Messiah*." *PQ* 54(1975): 579-591.

14478. Perkins, David. "Johnson on Wit and Metaphysical Poetry." *ELH* 20(1953): 200-217.

14479. Pettit, Henry. "The Making of Craft's Life of Young for Johnson's *Lives of the Poets*." *PQ* 54(1975): 333-341.

14480. Preston, Thomas R. "The Biblical Context of Johnson's *Rasselas*." *PMLA* 84(1969): 274-281.

14481. Quinlan, Maurice J. "The Reaction to Dr. Johnson's *Prayers and Meditations*." *JEGP* 52(1953): 125-139.

14482. Reichard, Hugo M. "The Pessimist's Helpers in *Rasselas*." *TSLL* 10(1968): 57-64.

14483. Rhodes, Rodman D. "*Idler* No. 24, and Johnsons' Epistemology." *MP* 64(1966): 10-21.

14484. Ricks, Christopher. "Johnson's 'Battle of the Pygmies and Cranes.'" *EIC* 16 (1966): 281-289.

14485. ----------. "Notes on Swift and Johnson." *RES* 11(1960): 412-413.

14486. Ruhe, Edward L. "Birch, Johnson, and Elizabeth Carter: An Episode of 1738-39." *PMLA* 73(1958): 491-500.

14487. Sachs, Arieh. "Generality and Particularity in Johnson's Thought." *SEL* 5(1965): 491-511.

14488. ----------. "Reason and Unreason in Johnson's Religion." *MLR* 59(1964): 519-526.

14489. ----------. "Samuel Johnson on 'The Art of Forgetfulness.'" *SP* 63(1966): 578-588.

14490. ----------. "Samuel Johnson on 'The Vacuity of Life.'" *SEL* 3(1963): 345-363.

14491. Sambrook, A. J. "Fanny Burney's First Letter to Dr. Johnson." *RES* 14(1963): 273-275.

14492. Savage, George H. "'Roving Among the Hebrides': The Odyssey of Samuel Johnson." *SEL* 17(1977): 493-501.

14493. Scholes, Robert. "Dr. Johnson and Jane Austen." *PQ* 54(1975): 380-390.

14494. Schwartz, Richard B. "Johnson's *Journey*." *JEGP* 69(1970): 292-303.

14495. ----------. "Johnson's Philosopher of Nature: *Rasselas*, Chapter 22." *MP* 74 (1976): 196-200.

14496. Selden, R. "Dr. Johnson and Juvenal: A Problem in Critical Method." *Comp L* 22(1970): 289-302.

14497. Sherbo, Arthur. "Dr. Johnson on *Macbeth*: 1745 and 1765." *RES* 2(1951): 40-47.

14498. ----------. "Dr. Johnson's *Dictionary*: A Preliminary Puff." *PQ* 31(1952): 91-93.

14499. ----------. "Dr. Johnson's *Dictionary* and Warburton's Shakespeare." *PQ* 33 (1954): 94-96.

14500. ----------. "Dr. Johnson's Revision of HIs *Dictionary*." *PQ* 31(1952): 372-382.

14501. ----------. "Johnson's 'Falling Houses.'" *EIC* 26(1976): 376-378.

14502. ----------. "Johnson's Intent in the *Journey to the Western Islands of Scotland*." *EIC* 16(1966): 382-397.

14503. ----------. "The Making of *Ramblers* 186 and 187." *PMLA* 67(1952): 575-580.

14504. ----------. "A Possible Addition to the Johnson Canon." *RES* 6(1955): 70-71.

14505. ----------. "Samuel Johnson and Certain Poems in the May 1747 *Gentleman's Magazine*." *RES* 17(1966): 382-390.

14506. ----------. "Samuel Johnson and Giuseppe Baretti: A Question of Translation." *RES* 19(1968): 405-411.

14507. ----------. "Two Additions to the Johnson Canon." *JEGP* 52(1953): 543-548.

14508. ----------. "Two Notes on Johnson's Revisions." *MLR* 50(1955): 311-315.

14509. Sherburn, George. "*Rasselas* Returns—To What?" *PQ* 38(1959): 383-384.

14510. Siebenschuh, William R. "The Relationship between Factual Accuracy and Literary Art in the *Life of Johnson*." *MP* 74(1977): 273-288.

14511. Siebert, Donald T., Jr. "The Scholar as Satirist: Johnson's Edition of Shakespeare." *SEL* 15(1975): 483-503.

14512. Sitter, John E. "To *The Vanity of Human Wishes* through the 1740's." *SP* 74(1977): 445-464.

14513. Sledd, James, and Gwin Kolb. "Johnson's Definitions of *Whig* and *Tory*." *PMLA* 67(1952): 882-887.

14514. Sutherland, Raymond Carter. "Dr. Johnson and the Collect." *MLQ* 17(1956): 111-112.

14515. Swearingen, James E. "Johnson's *Life of Gray*." *TSLL* 14(1972): 283-302.

14516. Tillotson, Kathleen. "Arnold and Johnson." *RES* 1(1950): 145-147.

14517. Todd, William B. "Leigh Hunt's Annotations in Johnson's *Dictionary*." *MP* 73

(1976): S110–112.

14518. Tucker, Susie I., and Henry Gifford. "Johnson's Poetic Imagination." *RES* 8(1957): 241–248.

14519. Turnage, Maxine. "Samuel Johnson's Criticism of the Works of Edmund Spenser." *SEL* 10(1970): 557–567.

14520. Vesterman, William. "Johnson and *The Life of Savage*." *ELH* 36(1969): 659–678.

14521. Walker, Ian C. "Dr. Johnson and *The Weekly Magazine*." *RES* 19(1968): 14–24.

14522. Ward, John C. "Johnson's Conversation." *SEL* 12(1972): 519–533.

14523. Wasserman, Earl R. "Johnson's *Rasselas*: Implicit Contexts." *JEGP* 74(1975): 1–25.

14524. Weinbrot, Howard D. "John Clarke's *Essay on Study* and Samuel Johnson on *Paradise Lost*." *MP* 72(1975): 404–407.

14525. ----------. "Johnson's *Dictionary* and *The World*: The Papers of Lord Chesterfield and Richard Owen Cambridge." *PQ* 50(1971): 663–669.

14526. ----------. "Johnson's *London* and Juvenal's Third Satire: The Country as 'Ironic' Norm." *MP* 73(1976): S56–S65.

14527. Weitzman, Arthur J. "More Light on *Rasselas*: The Background of the Egyptian Episodes." *PQ* 48(1969): 42–58.

14528. Whitley, Alvin. "The Comedy of *Rasselas*." *ELH* 23(1956): 48–70.

14529. Wimsatt, W. K. "Images of Samuel Johnson." *ELH* 41(1974): 359–374.

14530. ----------. "Philosophic Words." *PQ* 29(1950): 84–88.

14531. ----------. "Samuel Johnson and Dryden's *Du Fresnoy*." *SP* 48(1951): 26–39.

14532. Woolley, James D. "Johnson as Despot: Anna Seward's Rejected Contribution to Boswell's *Life*." *MP* 70(1972): 140–145.

14533. Wright, John W. "Samuel Johnson and Traditional Methodology." *PMLA* 86(1971): 40–50.

See also 272, 2196, 7780, 13596, 13611, 13612, 13617, 13627, 13848, 13849, 14325, 15160, 15616.

JONES, WILLIAM. 14534. Cannon, Garland. "Five New Letters by Sir William Jones." *PQ* 51 (1972): 951–955.

14535. ----------. "Sir William Jones and Edmund Burke." *MP* 54(1957): 165–186.

See also 13632.

KAMES, HENRY HOME, LORD. 14536. Horn, Andras. "Kames and the Anthropological Approach to Criticism." *PQ* 44(1965): 211–233.

14537. McGuinness, Arthur E. "Lord Kames on the Ossian Poems: Anthropology and Criticism." *TSLL* 10(1968): 65–75.

14538. Ross, Ian. "Quaffing the 'Mixture of Wormwood and Aloes': A Consideration of Lord Kames's *Historical Law-Tracts*." *TSLL* 8(1967): 499–518.

14539. ----------. "Scots Law and Scots Criticism: The Case of Lord Kames." *PQ* 45 (1966): 614–623.

KEATE, GEORGE. See 13597.

KELLY, HUGH. 14540. Rawson, C. J. "Some Remarks on Eighteenth-Century 'Delicacy,' with a Note on Hugh Kelly's *False Delicacy* (1768)." *JEGP* 61(1962): 1–13.

KENDRICK, WILLIAM. 14541. Fussell, Paul Jr. "William Kendrick's 'Courtesy' Book." *PMLA* 66(1951): 538–540.

14542. Irwin, W. R. "William Kendrick: Volunteer Moralist." *PMLA* 67(1952): 288–291.

KENNETT, BASIL. 14543. Hopkins, W. D., and I. D. MacKillop. "'Immortal Vida' and Basil Kennett." *RES* 27(1976): 137–146.

LETTERS FROM AN ARMENIAN. 14544. Crisafulli, Alessandro S. "A Neglected English Imitation of Montesquieu's *Lettres Persanes*." *MLQ* 14(1953): 209–216.

LILLO, GEORGE. 14545. Burgess, C. F. "Further Notes for a Biography of George Lillo." *PQ* 46(1967): 424–428.

14546. ----------. "Lillo Sans Barnwell, or the Playwright Revisited." *MP* 66(1968): 5–29.

14547. Jackson, Wallace. "Dryden's Emperor and Lillo's Merchant: The Relevant Bases of Action." *MLQ* 26(1965): 536–544.

14548. Pedicord, Harry W. "George Lillo and 'Speculative Masonry.'" *PQ* 53(1974): 401–412.

14549. Price, Lawrence Marsden. "George Barnwell Abroad." *Comp L* 2(1950): 126–156.

LYTTLETON, GEORGE. See 3428, 13596.

MACKENZIE, HENRY. 14550. Hudson, Randolph. "Henry Mackenzie, James Beattie, *et al.*, and the Edinburgh *Mirror*." *ELN* 1(1963): 104–108.

14551. Kramer, Dale. "The Structural Unity of *The Man of Feeling*." *SSF* 1(1964): 191–199.

14552. Platzner, Robert L. "Mackenzie's Martyr: The Man of Feeling as Saintly Fool." *Novel* 10(1976): 59–64.

14553. Quaintance, Richard E., Jr. "Charles Churchill as Man of Feeling: A Forgotten Poem by Mackenzie." *MLR* 56(1961): 73–77.

See also 13597.

MACKLIN, CHARLES. 14554. Findlay, Robert R. "Macklin's Acting Version of *Love à la Mode*." *PQ* 45(1966): 749–760.

MACPHERSON, JAMES. 14555. Fitzgerald, Robert P. "The Style of Ossian." *SR* 6(1966): 22–33.

14556. Stewart, Larry L. "Ossian, Burke, and the 'Joy of Grief.'" *ELN* 15(1977): 29–32.

14557. Thomas, R. George. "Lord Bute, John Home, and Ossian: Two Letters." *MLR* 51 (1956): 73–75.

See also 14537.

MANDEVILLE, BERNARD. 14558. Chiasson, Elias J. "Bernard Mandeville: A Reappraisal." *PQ* 49(1970): 489–519.

14559. Edwards, Thomas H., Jr. "Mandeville's Moral Prose." *ELH* 31(1964): 195–212.

14560. Jones, Harry L. "Holberg on Mandeville's *Fable of the Bees*." *CLA* 4(1960): 116–125.

14561. Skarsten, A. Keith. "Nature in Mandeville." *JEGP* 53(1954): 562–568.

14562. Smith, LeRoy W. "Fielding and Mandeville: The 'War Against Virtue.'" *Criticism* 3(1961): 7–15.

14563. Vichert, Gordon S. "Some Recent Mandeville Attributions." *PQ* 45(1966): 459–463.

See also 13627.

MANLEY, MARIA. 14564. Snyder, Henry L. "New Light on Mrs. Manley?" *PQ* 52(1973): 767–770.

See also 13601.

MASON, WILLIAM.   14565. Day, Martin S. "The influence of Mason's *Heroic Epistle*." *MLQ* 14 (1953): 235-252.

See also 14349, 18758.

MAVOR, WILLIAM F.   See 13597.

MAYNWARING, ARTHUR.   14566. Snyder, Henry L. "The Prologues and Epilogues of Arthur Maynwaring." *PQ* 50(1971): 610-629.

MCNALLY, LEONARD.   See 13597.

MICKLE, WILLIAM JULIUS.   14567. Letzring, Monica. "Mickle, Boswell, Liberty, and the 'Prospects of Liberty and of Slavery.'" *MLR* 69 (1974): 489-501.

MIST, NATHANIEL.   14568. Limouze, A. Sanford. "Burlesque Criticism of the Ballad in *Mist's Weekly Journal*." *SP* 47(1950): 607-618.

MONTAGU, LADY MARY WORTLEY.   14569. Grundy, Isobel. "Ovid and Eighteenth-Century Divorce: An Unpublished Poem by Lady Mary Wortley Montagu." *RES* 23(1972): 417-428.

14570. Halsband, Robert. "Am Imitation of Perrault in England: Lady Mary Wortley Montagu's 'Carabosse.'" *Comp L* 3(1951): 174-178.

14571. ----------. "Lady Mary Wortley Montagu and Eighteenth-Century Fiction." *PQ* 45 (1966): 145-156.

14572. ----------. "Lady Mary Wortley Montagu as Letter Writer." *PMLA* 80(1965): 155-163.

14573. ----------. "A 'New' Lady Mary Letter." *PQ* 44(1965): 180-184.

MOOR, JAMES.   See 13611.

MORE, HANNAH.   14574. Bennett, Charles H. "The Text of Horace Walpole's Correspondence with Hannah More." *RES* 3(1952): 341-345.

14575. Pickering, Sam. "*The Cheap Repository Tracts* and the Short Story." *SSF* 12 (1975): 15-21.

MORGANN, MAURICE.   14576. Tave, Stuart Malcolm. "Notes on the Influence of Morgann's Essay on Falstaff." *RES* 3(1952): 371-375.

MORRIS, CORBYN.   14577. Tave, Stuart M. "Corbyn Morris: Falstaff, Humor, and Comic Theory in the Eighteenth Century." *MP* 50(1952): 102-115.

NEEDLER, HENRY.   14578. Doherty, F. M. J. "Blake's 'The Tyger' and Henry Needler." *PQ* 46 (1967): 566-567.

NICHOLS, JOHN.   See 13841.

OGILVE, JOHN.   See 13624.

OLDMIXON, JOHN.   14579. Rogers, Pat. "The Dunce Answers Back: John Oldmixon on Swift and Defoe." *TSLL* 14(1972): 33-43.

OLDYS, WILLIAM.   14580. Lipking, Lawrence. "The Curiosity of William Oldys: An Approach to the Development of English Literary History." *PQ* 46(1967): 385-407.

PARNELL, THOMAS.   14581. Rawson, C. J. "Swift's Certificate to Parnell's 'Posthumous Works.'" *MLR* 57(1962): 179-182.

PENNANT, THOMAS.   14582. Jenkins, Ralph E. "'And I travelled after him': Johnson and Pennant in Scotland." *TSLL* 14(1972): 445-462.

PERCY, THOMAS.   14583. Friedman, Albert B. "The First Draft of Percy's *Reliques*." *PMLA* 69 (1954): 1233-1249.

14584. ----------. "Percy's Folio Manuscript Revalued." *JEGP* 53(1954): 524-531.

14585. Mayhew, George P. "The Early Life of John Partridge." *SEL* 1,#3(1961): 31-42.

See also 14457.

POMFRET, JOHN.   See 13628.

PHILIPS, AMBROSE.   14586. Joost, Nicholas. "The *Fables* of Fénelon and Philips' *Free-Thinker*." *SP* 47(1950): 51-61.

14587. Parnell, Paul E. "*The Distrest Mother*, Ambrose Philips' Morality Play." *Comp L* 11(1959): 111-123.

14588. Winton, Calhoun. "Some Manuscripts By and Concerning Ambrose Philips." *ELN* 5 (1967): 99-101.

POPE, ALEXANDER.   14589. Adams, Percy G. "Pope's Concern with Assonance." *TSLL* 9(1968): 493-502.

14590. Aden, John M. "Another Analogue to Pope's Vice Triumphant." *MP* 66(1968): 150-151.

14591. ----------. "Bethel's Sermon, Pope's *Exemplum*: Towards a Critique." *SEL* 9 (1969): 463-470.

14592. ----------. "'The Change of Scepters, and impending Woe': Political Allusion in Pope's Statius." *PQ* 52(1973): 728-738.

14593. ----------. "'*First* follow Nature': Strategy and Stratification in *An Essay on Criticism*." *JEGP* 55(1956): 604-617.

14594. ----------. "Pope and the Satiric Adversary." *SEL* 2(1962): 267-286.

14595. Adler, Jacob H. "Pope and the Rules of Prosody." *PMLA* 76(1961): 218-226.

14596. Alpers, Paul J. "Pope's *To Bathurst* and the Mandevillian State." *ELH* 25 (1958): 23-42.

14597. Altenbernd, A. Lynn. "On Pope's 'Horticultural Romanticism.'" *JEGP* 54(1955): 470-477.

14598. Arlidge, Elizabeth. "A New Pope Letter." *RES* 12(1961): 398-402.

14599. Askstens, Thomas. "Pope and Bolingbroke on 'Examples': An Echo of the *Letters on History* in Pope's Correspondence." *PQ* 52(1973): 232-238.

14600. Auden, W. H. "Alexander Pope." *EIC* 1(1951): 208-224.

14601. Barrett, John Mandel. "Pope's 'Eloisa to Abelard.'" *TSLL* 9(1967): 57-68.

14602. Bateson, F. W. "Prose and Poetry and Mack." *EIC* 10(1960): 115-116.

14603. ----------. "Pun and Metaphor and Pope." *EIC* 9(1959): 437-439.

14604. Battestin, Martin C. "Pope's 'Magus' in Fielding's *Vernoniad*: The Satire of Valpole." *PQ* 46(1967): 137-141.

14605. Beaumont, Charles. "Pope and the Palladians." *TSLL* 17(1975): 461-479.

14606. Beyette, Kent. "Milton and Pope's *The Rape of the Lock*." *SEL* 16(1976): 421-436.

14607. Bluestone, Max. "Pun and Metaphor and Pope." *EIC* 9(1959): 440-443.

14608. ----------. "The Suppressed Metaphor in Pope." *EIC* 8(1958): 347-354.

14609. Bond, Donald F. "The Importance of Pope's Letters." *MP* 56(1958): 55-59.

14610. Boyce, Benjamin. "Baroque into Satire: Pope's Frontispiece for the 'Essay on Man.'" *Criticism* 4(1962): 14-27.

14611. ----------. "The Poet and the Postmaster: The Friendship of Alexander Pope and Ralph Allen." *PQ* 45(1966): 114-122.

14612. ----------. "Samuel Johnson's Criticism of Pope in the *Life of Pope*." *RES* 5

(1954): 37-46.

14613. Brady, Frank. "The History and Structure of Pope's *To A Lady*." *SEL* 9(1969): 439-462.

14614. Brückman, Patricia. "Pope's Shock and the Count of Gabalis." *ELN* 1(1964): 261-262.

14615. Callan, Norman. "Pope's *Iliad*: A New Document." *RES* 4(1953): 109-121.

14616. Chambers, Jessie Rhodes. "The Episode of Annius and Mummius: *Dunciad* IV 347-96." *PQ* 43(1964): 185-192.

14617. Chapman, R. W. "Crousaz on Pope." *RES* 1(1950): 57.

14618. Clark, Donald B. "The Italian Fame of Alexander Pope." *MLQ* 22(1961): 357-366.

14619. Clarke, Howard W. "Pope's Homeric Notes." *Coll L* 3(1976): 203-218.

14620. Clements, Frances M. "Lansdowne, Pope, and the Unity of *Windsor Forest*." *MLQ* 33 (1972): 44-53.

14621. Clever, Glenn. "The Narrative Effectiveness of Pope's *The Rape of the Lock* and *The Dunciad*." *JNT* 1(1971): 122-134.

14622. Cohen, Murray. "Versions of the Lock: Readers of 'The Rape of the Lock.'" *ELH* 43(1976): 53-73.

14623. Cook, Richard I. "Garth's *Dispensary* and Pope's *Rape of the Lock*." *CLA* 6 (1962): 107-116.

14624. Crossley, Robert. "Pope's *Iliad*: The Commentary and the Translation." *PQ* 56 (1977): 339-357.

14625. Dearing, Vinton A. "Pope, Theobald, and Wycherley's *Posthumous Works*." *PMLA* 68(1953): 223-236.

14626. DeLisle, Harold F. "Structure in Part I of Pope;s *Essay on Criticism*." *ELN* 1 (1963): 14-17.

14627. Dixon, P. "Pope's Shakespeare." *JEGP* 63(1964): 191-203.

14628. Dorris, George E. "Scipione Maffei amid the Dunces." *RES* 16(1965): 288-290.

14629. Douglass, Richard. "More on the Rhetoric and Imagery of Pope's *Arbuthnot*." *SEL* 13 (1973): 488-502.

14630. Durant, David S. "Man and Nature in Alexander Pope's *Pastorals*." *SEL* 11(1971): 469-485.

14631. Edwards, Thomas R. "Reconciled Extremes: Pope's *Epistle to Bathurst*." *EIC* 11 (1961): 290-308.

14632. Effross, Susi Hillburn. "The Influence of Alexander Pope in Eighteenth-Century Spain." *SP* 63(1966): 78-92.

14633. Erskine-Hill, Howard. "Alexander Pope at Fifteen: A New Manuscript." *RES* 17 (1966): 268-277.

14634. Ewards, Thomas R., Jr. "Light and Nature: A Reading of the *Dunciad*." *PQ* 39 (1960): 447-463.

14635. Farnham, Fern. "Achilles' Shield: Some Observations on Pope's *Iliad*." *PMLA* 84 (1969): 1571-1581.

14636. Fenner, Arthur, Jr. "The Unity of Pope's *Essay on Criticism*." *PQ* 39(1960): 435-446.

14637. Fineman, Daniel A. "The Case of the Lady 'Killed' by Alexander Pope." *MLQ* 12 (1951): 137-149.

14638. Fisher, Alan S. "Cheerful Noonday, 'Gloomy' Twilight: Pope's *Essay on Criticism*."

PQ 51(1972): 832-844.

14639. Fuller, John. "A New Epilogue by Pope?" *RES* 17(1966): 409-413.

14640. Gibson, William A. "Three Principles of Renaissance Architectural Theory in Pope's *Epistle to Burlington*." *SEL* 11(1971): 487-505.

14641. Goldgar, Bertrand A. "Pope and the *Grub-street Journal*." *MP* 74(1977): 366-380.

14642. ----------. "Pope's Theory of the Passions: The Background of Epistle II of the *Essay on Man*." *PQ* 47(1962): 730-743.

14643. Griffin, Dustin. "Revisions in Pope's 'Ode on Solitude.'" *MLQ* 36(1975): 369-375.

14644. Grundy, Isobel. "Pope, Peterborough, and the Characters of Women." *RES* 20 (1969): 461-468.

14645. Haber, Grace Stevenson. "A. Pope—'imployed in Grottofying.'" *TSLL* 10(1968): 385-403.

14646. Halsband, Robert. "Pope, Lady Mary, and the *Court Poems* (1716)." *PMLA* 68 (1953): 237-250.

14647. ----------. "Two New Letters from Lady Mary Wortley Montagu to Alexander Pope." *PQ* 29(1950): 349-352.

14648. Hauser, David R. "Pope's Lodona and the Uses of Mythology." *SEL* 6(1966): 465-482.

14649. Hoffman, Arthur W. "Spenser and *The Rape of the Lock*." *PQ* 49(1970): 530-546.

14650. Hoilman, Dennis R. "Pope's *An Essay on Man*, IVm 195-196." *PQ* 50(1971): 308-309.

14651. Hoover, Evelyn. "Racine and Pope's Eloisa." *EIC* 24(1974): 368-374.

14652. Hopkins, Robert H. "'The Good Old Cause' in Pope, Addison, and Steele." *RES* 17(1966): 62-68.

14653. Hotch, Ripley. "The Dilemma of an Obedient Son: Pope's *Epistle to Dr. Arbuthnot*." *EL* 1(1974): 37-45.

14654. ----------. "Pope Surveys His Kingdom: *An Essay on Criticism*." *SEL* 13 (1973): 474-487.

14655. Howard, Leon. "The American Revolt against Pope." *SP* 49(1952): 48-65.

14656. Howard, William J. "The Mystery of the Cibberian *Dunciad*." *SEL* 8(1968): 463-474.

14657. Hunter, G. K. "The 'Romanticism' of Pope's Horace." *EIC* 10(1960): 390-404.

14658. Hunter, J. Paul. "Satiric Apology as Satiric Instance: Pope's *Arbuthnot*." *JEGP* 68(1969): 625-647.

14659. Hunting, Robert S. "The 'Cura Cuiusdam Anonymi' of Pope's *Anthologia*." *PQ* 31(1952): 430-432.

14660. Jack, Ian. "Pope and 'the weighty Bullion of Dr. Donne's Satires.'" *PMLA* 66(1951): 1009-1022.

14661. Jackson, James L. "Pope's *The Rape of the Lock* Considered as a Five-Act Epic." *PMLA* 65(1950): 1283-1287.

14662. James, G. Ingli. "Prose and Poetry and Mask." *EIC* 10(1960): 114-115.

14663. Johnston, Arthur. "'The Purple Year' in Pope and Gray." *RES* 14(1963): 389-393.

14664. Kelmey, Robert P. "Pope's *Eloisa*

to *Abelard* and 'Those Celebrated Letters.'"
PQ 47(1968): 164-178.

14665. Kenner, Hugh. "Pope's Reasonable
Rhymes." *ELH* 41(1974): 74-88.

14666. Kerman, Alvin B. *The Dunciad*
and the Plot Satire." *SEL* 2(1962): 255-266.

14667. Kinsley, William. "Physico-demon-
ology in Pope's 'Dunciad' IV, 71-90." *MLR* 70
(1975): 20-31.

14668. Knight, Douglas. "The Development
of Pope's *Iliad* Preface: A Study of the Manuscript." *MLQ* 16(1955): 237-246.

14669. ----------. "Pope as a Student of
Homer." *Comp L* 4(1952): 75-82.

14670. Knoepflmacher, U. C. "Impersonations
of Alexander Pope: Current Views Within a
Nineteenth-Century Perspective." *MLQ* 34(1973):
448-461.

14671. ----------. "The Poet as Physician:
Pope's *Epistle to Dr. Arbuthnot*." *MLQ* 31(1970):
440-449.

14672. Kropf, C. R. "Education and the
Neoplatonic Idea of Wisdom in Pope's *Dunciad*."
TSLL 14(1973): 593-604.

14673. Lauren, Barbara. "Pope's *Epistle
to Bolingbroke*: Satire from the Vantage of
Retirement." *SEL* 15(1975): 419-430.

14674. Lawlor, Nancy K. "Pope's *Essay on
Man*: Oblique Light for a False Mirror." *MLQ* 28
(1967): 305-316.

14675. Lawler, Traugott. "'Wafting Vapours
from the Land of Dreams': Virgil's Fourth and
Sixth Eclogues and the *Dunciad*." *SEL* 14(1974):
373-386.

14676. Levine, Jay Arnold. "Pope's
Epistle to Augustus, Lines 1-30." *SEL* 7(1967):
427-451.

14677. Link, Frederick M. "A New Pope
Letter." *RES* 15(1964): 398-399.

14678. Litz, Francis E. "Pope and
Twickenhem's Famous Preacher." *MLQ* 17(1956): 204-
212.

14679. ----------. "Pope's Use of Derham."
JEGP 60(1961): 65-74.

14680. Loomis, Emerson Robert. "The Turning Point in Pope's Reputation: A Dispute Which
Preceded the Bowles-Byron Controversy." *PQ* 42
(1963): 249-248.

14681. Lunn, A. Coyle. "A New Pope Letter
in the Trumbull Correspondence." *RES* 24(1973):
310-315.

14682. Mack, Maynard. "Some Annotations
in the Second Earl of Oxford's Copies of Pope's
Epistle to Dr. Arbuthnot and *Sober Advice from
Horace*." *RES* 8(1957): 416-420.

14683. Mahaffey, Kathleen. "Pope's
'Artimesia' and 'Phryne' as Personal Satire."
RES 21(1970): 466-471.

14684. ----------. "Timon's Villa:
Walpole's Houghton." *TSLL* 9(1967): 193-222.

14685. Maresca, Thomas E. "Pope's Defense
of Satire: The First Satire of the Second Book
of Horace Imitated." *ELH* 31(1964): 366-394.

14686. Marks, Emerson R. "Pope on Poetry
and the Poet." *Criticism* 12(1970): 271-280.

14687. Maud, Ralph N. "Some Lines from
Pope." *RES* 9(1958): 146-151.

14688. Maxwell, J. C. "*Dunciad* IV. 121-
2." *RES* 3(1952): 55.

14689. Mell, Donald C., Jr. "Pope's Idea
of the Imagination and the Design of 'Elegy to
the Memory of an Unfortunate Lady.'" *MLQ* 29
(1968): 395-406.

14690. Mengel, Elias F., Jr. "Patterns
of Imagery in Pope's *Arbuthnot*." *PMLA* 69(1954):
189-197.

14691. Miller, John H. "Pope and the
Principles of Reconciliation." *TSLL* 9(1967):
185-192.

14692. Morris, David B. "The Kinship of
Madness in Pope's *Dunciad*." *PQ* 51(1972): 813-831.

14693. ----------. "Virgilian Attitudes
in Pope's *Windsor-Forest*." *TSLL* 15(1973): 231-
250.

14694. ----------. "'The visionary maid':
Tragic Passion and Redemptive Sympathy in Pope's
'Eloisa to Abelard.'" *MLQ* 34(1973): 247-271.

14695. Moskovit, Leonard A. "Pope and the
Tradition of the Neoclassical Imitation." *SEL*
8(1968): 445-462.

14696. ----------. "Pope's Purpose in
Sober Advice." *PQ* 44(1965): 195-199.

14697. Newey, Vincent. "Pope, Reymond
Williams, and the Man of Ross." *EIC* 27(1977):
368-373.

14698. Nokes, David. "Pope and Heidegger:
A Forgotten Fragment." *RES* 23(1972): 308-313.

14699. ----------. "Pope's Chaucer." *RES*
27(1976): 180-182.

14700. Nussbaum, Felicity A. "Pope's 'To
a Lady' and the Eighteenth-Century Woman." *PQ*
54(1975): 444-456.

14701. Odell, Daneil W. "Young's *Nights
Thoughts* as an Answer to Pope's *Essay on Man*."
SEL 12(1972): 481-501.

14702. Osborn, James M. "Addison's Tavern
Companion and Pope's 'Umbra.'" *PQ* 42(1963): 217-
225.

14703. ----------. "Pope, the Byzantine
Empress, and Walpole's Whore." *RES* 6(1955): 372-
382.

14704. ----------. "Spence, Natural
Genius and Pope." *PQ* 45(1966): 123-144.

14705. Park, Douglas B. "'At Once the
Source, and *End*': Nature's Defining Pattern in
An Essay on Criticism." *PMLA* 90(1975): 861-873.

14706. Parkin, Rebecca P. "Mythopoeic
Activity in the *Rape of the Lock*." *ELH* 21(1954):
30-38.

14707. ----------. "The Role of Time in
Alexander Pope's *Epistle to a Lady*." *ELH* 32
(1965): 490-501.

14708. Perella, Nocolas J. "Pope's Judgment of the *Pastor Fido* and a Case of Plagiarism."
PQ 40(1961): 444-448.

14709. Peterson, R. G. "Renaissance
Classicism in Pope's *Dunciad*." *SEL* 15(1975): 431-
445.

14710. Piper, William Bowman. "The Con-
versational Poetry of Pope." *SEL* 10(1970): 505-
524.

14711. Rawson, C. J. "Some Unpublished
Letters of Pope and Gay; and Some Manuscript
Sources of Goldsmith's *Life of Thomas Parnell*."
RES 10(1959): 371-387.

14712. Reichard, Hugo M. "The Independence
of Pope as a Political Satirist." *JEGP* 54(1955):
309-317.

14713. ----------. "The Love Affair in Pope's *Rape of the Lock*." *PMLA* 69(1954): 887-902.

14714. ----------. "Pope's Social Satire: Belles-Lettres and Business." *PMLA* 67(1952): 420-434.

14715. Rogers, Pat. "The Conduct of the Earl of Nottingham: Curll, Oldmixon and the Finch Family." *RES* 21(1970): 175-181.

14716. ----------. "Faery Lore and *The Rape of the Lock*." *RES* 25(1974): 25-38.

14717. ----------. "Pope to Fortescue: A New Text for Eighteen Letters." *MP* 73(1975): 74-76.

14718. ----------. "Pope, Sattle, and the Fall of Troy." *SEL* 15(1975): 447-458.

14719. ----------. "An Uncollected Pope Letter." *PQ* 50(1971): 306-308.

14720. ----------. "Wit and Grammar in *The Rape of the Lock*." *JEGP* 72(1973): 17-31.

14721. Rogers, Robert W. "Alexander Pope's *Universal Prayer*." *JEGP* 54(1955): 612-624.

14722. Rothman, Irving N. "The Quincunx in Pope's Moral Áesthetics." *PQ* 55(1976): 374-388.

14723. Rousseau, G. S. "A New Pope Letter." *PQ* 45(1966): 409-418.

14724. Ruhe, E. L. "Pope's Hand in Thomas Birch's Account of Gay." *RES* 5(1954): 171-174.

14725. Ryley, Robert M. "A Note on the Authenticity of Some Lines from Pope." *PQ* 46 (1967): 417-420.

14726. Schmitz, R. M. "Peterborough and Pope's Nymphs: Pope at Work." *PQ* 48(1969): 192-200.

14727. ----------. "Two New Holographs of Pope's Birthday Lines to Martha Blount." *RES* 8 (1957): 234-248.

14728. Schonhorn, Manuel. "The Audacious Contemporaneity of Pope's *Epistle to Augustus*." *SEL* 8(1968): 431-443.

14729. Sherbo, Arthur. "No Single Scholiast: Pope's 'The Dunciad.'" *MLR* 65(1970): 503-516.

14730. Sherburn, George. "Letters from Alexander Pope, Chiefly to Sir William Trumbull." *RES* 9(1958): 388-406.

14731. Sitter, John E. "The Argument of Pope's *Epistle to Cobham*." *SEL* 17(1977): 435-449.

14732. Spacks, Patricia Meyer. "Imagery and Method in *An Essay on Criticism*." *PMLA* 85 (1970): 97-106.

14733. ----------. "Pope's Satiric Use of Nature." *SLI* 5,#2(1972): 39-52.

14734. Sparrow, John. "Pope's *Anthologies* Again." *PQ* 33(1954): 428-431.

14735. Stumpf, Thomas A. "Pope's *To Cobham*, *To A Lady*, and the Traditions of Inconstancy." *SP* 67(1970): 339-358.

14736. Sutherland, John. "Wit, Reason, Vision, and *An Essay on Man*." *MLQ* 30(1969): 356-369.

14737. Torchiana, Donald T. "Brutus: Pope's Last Hero." *JEGP* 61(1962): 853-867.

14738. Trimble, John. "Clarissa's Role in *The Rape of the Lock*." *TSLL* 15(1974): 673-691.

14739. Tuveson, Ernest. "*An Essay on Man* and 'The Way of Ideas.'" *ELH* 26(1959): 368-386.

147040. ----------. "*An Essay on Man* and 'The Way of Ideas': Some Further Remarks." *PQ* 40 (1961): 262-269.

14741. Wasserman, Earl R. "The Limits of Allusion in *The Rape of the Lock*." *JEGP* 65(1966): 425-44.

14742. ----------. "Pope's *Ode for Musick*." *ELH* 28(1961): 163-186.

14743. Weinbrot, Howard D. "Pope's 'Elegy to the Memory of an Unfortunate Lady.'" *MLQ* 32 (1971): 255-267.

14744. Wellington, James E. "Pope and Charity." *PQ* 46(1967): 225-235.

14745. Williams, Aubrey. "The 'Angel, Goddess, Montague' of Pope's *Sober Advice from Horace*." *MP* 71(1973): 56-58.

14746. ----------. "The 'Fall' of China and *The Rape of the Lock*." *PQ* 41(1962): 412-425.

14747. ----------. "Literary Backgrounds to Book Four of the *Dunciad*." *PMLA* 68(1953): 806-813.

14748. ----------. "Pope's 'Duchesses and Lady Mary's.'" *RES* 4(1953): 359-361.

14749. ----------. "Submerged Metaphor in Pope." *EIC* 9(1959): 197-201.

14750. Williams, Kathleen. "The Moralized Song: Some Renaissance Themes in Pope." *ELH* 41 (1974): 578-612.

14751. Wimsatt, W. K., Jr. "The Augustan Mode in English Poetry." *ELH* 20(1953): 1-14.

14752. ----------. "The Game of Ombre in *The Rape of the Lock*." *RES* 1(1950): 136-143.

See also 494, 11361, 11425, 13617, 13627, 13634, 13667, 14237, 14421, 14477, 14543, 15024, 15101, 15160, 15186, 15193, 15261, 16087.

POPPLE, WILLIAM. See 14329.

PORRETT, ROBERT. 14753. Wilson, Stuart. "The First Dramatic Version of *Clarissa*." *ELN* 2 (1964): 21-25.

PRATT, SAMUEL JACKSON. See 13597.

PRIOR, MATTHEW. 14754. Griffith, R. H. "Not by Prior." *RES* 6(1955): 67-69.

14755. Jack, Ian. "The 'Choice of Life' in Johnson and Matthew Prior." *JEGP* 49(1950): 523-530.

14756. Jones, William Powell. "The Idea of the Limitations of Science from Prior to Blake." *SEL* 1,#3(1961): 97-114.

14757. Kline, Richard B. "Matthew Prior and 'Dear Will Nuttley': An Addition to the Canon." *PQ* 47(1968): 157-163.

14758. ----------. "Tory Prior and Whig Steele" A Measure of Respect." *SEL* 9(1969): 427-437.

14759. Rosenberg, Albert. "Prior's Feud with the Duchess of Marlborough." *JEGP* 52(1953): 27-31.

14760. Wright, H. Bunker. "Ideal Copy and Authoritative Text: The Problem of Prior's *Poems on Several Occasions*." *MP* 49(1952): 234-241.

See also 11425.

RADCLIFFE, ANN. 14761. Beaty, Frederick L. "Mrs. Radcliffe's Fading Gleam." *PQ* 42(1963): 126-129.

14762. Epstein, Lynne. "Anne Radcliffe's Reliance on Claude Lorrain, Salvatore Rosa and Nicholas Poussin." *HSL* 1(1969): 107-120.

14763. Frank, Frederick S. "A Bibliography of Writings about Ann Radcliff." *Ext* 17(1975): 54-62.

14764. Smith, Nelson C. "Sense, Sensibility and Ann Radcliffe." *SEL* 13(1973): 577-590.

See also 59, 13597.

REEVE, CLARA.   See 13597.

REID, THOMAS.   14765. Ross, Ian. "Unpublished Letters of Thomas Reid to Lord Kames, 1762-1782." [with text] *TSLL* 7(1965): 17-66.

14766. Todd, D. D. "Reid Redivivus?" *TSLL* 14(1970): 303-312.

RELLY, JAMES.   14767. Barbow, J. Murray. "The Texts of Billings' Church Music." *Criticism* 1(1959): 49-61.

REYNOLDS, JOSHUA.   14768. Gerber, Helmut E. "Reynolds' Pendulum Figure and the Watchmaker." *PQ* 38(1959): 66-83.

14769. Macklem, Michael. "Reynolds and the Ambiguities of Neo-Classical Criticism." *PQ* 31(1952): 383-398.

RICHARDSON, SAMUEL.   14770. Allentuck, Marcia Epstein. "Narration and Illustration: The Problem of Richardson's *Pamela*." *PQ* 51 (1972): 874-886.

14771. Babb, Howard S. "Richardson's Narrative Mode in *Clarissa*." *SEL* 16(1976): 451-460.

14772. Ball, Donald L. "*Pamela II*: A Primary Link in Richardson's Development as a Novelist." *MP* 65(1968): 334-342.

14773. Barker, Gerard A. "Clarissa's 'Command of Her Passions': Self-Censorship in the Third Edition." *SEL* 10(1970): 525-539.

14774. ----------. "The Complacent Paragon: Exemplary Characterization in Richardson." *SEL* 9(1969): 503-519.

14775. Beasley, Jerry C. "Romance and the 'New' Novels of Richardson, Fielding, and Smollett." *SEL* 16(1976): 437-450.

14776. Beer, Gillian. "Richardson, Milton, and the Status of Evil." *RES* 19(1968): 261-270.

14777. Bell, Michael Devitt. "Pamela's Wedding and the Marriage of the Lamb." *PQ* 49 (1970): 100-112.

14778. Bonnard, G. A. "Samuel Richardson and Guillaume-Antoine de Luc." *MLR* 46(1951): 440-441.

14779. Brooks, Douglas. "*Joseph Andrews* and *Pamela*." *EIC* 19(1969): 348-351.

14780. ----------. "*Pamela* and *Joseph Andrews*." *EIC* 18(1968): 348-349.

14781. ----------. "Richardson's *Pamela* and Fielding's *Joseph Andrews*." *EIC* 17(1967): 158-168.

14782. Cohan, Stevan M. "*Clarissa* and the Individuation of Character." *ELH* 43(1976): 163-183.

14783. Cohen, Richard. "The Social-Christian and Christian-Social Doctrines of Samuel Richardson." *HSL* 4(1972): 135-146.

14784. Copeland, Edward. "Allegory and Analogy in *Clarissa*: The 'Plan' and the 'No-Plan.'" *ELH* 39(1972): 254-265.

14785. ----------. "*Clarissa* and *Fanny Hill*: Sisters in Distress." *SN* 4(1972): 343-352.

14786. ----------. "Samuel Richardson and Naive Allegory: Some Beauties of the Mixed Metaphor." *Novel* 4(1971): 231-239.

14787. Costa, Richard Hauer. "The Epistolary Monitor in *Pamela*." *MLQ* 31(1970): 38-47.

14788. Donovan, Robert A. "The Problem of Pamela, or, Virtue Unrewarded." *SEL* 3 (1963): 377-395.

14789. Dussinger, John A. "Conscience and the Pattern of Christian Perfection in *Clarissa*." *PMLA* 81(1966): 236-245.

14790. ----------. "Richardson's Tragic Muse." *PQ* 46(1967): 18-33.

14791. ----------. "What Pamela Knew: An Interpretation." *JEGP* 69(1970): 377-393.

14792. Eaves, T. C. Duncan, and Ben D. Kimpel. "The Composition of *Clarissa* and Its Revision Before Publication." *PMLA* 83(1968): 416-428.

14793. Erickson, Robert A. "Mother Jewkes, Pamela, and the Midwives." *ELH* 43 (1976): 500-516.

14794. Farrell, William J. "The Style and the Action in *Clarissa*." *SEL* 3(1963): 365-375.

14795. Folkenflik, Robert. "A Room of Pamela's Own." *ELH* 39(1972): 585-596.

14796. Golden, Morris. "Richardson's Repetitions." *PMLA* 82(1967): 64-67.

14797. Hill, Christopher. "Clarissa Harlowe and her Times." *EIC* 5(1955): 315-340.

14798. Hilles, Frederick W. "The Plan of *Clarissa*." *PQ* 45(1966): 236-248.

14799. Kaplan, Fred. "'Our Short Story': The Narrative Devices of *Clarissa*." *SEL* 11 (1971): 549-562.

14800. Kearney, A. M. "*Pamela* and *Joseph Andrews*." *EIC* 18(1968): 105-107, 479-480.

14801. ----------. "*Clarissa* and the Epistolary Form." *EIC* 16(1966): 44-56.

14802. Kinkead-Weekes, M. "*Clarissa* Restored?" *RES* 10(1959): 156-171.

14803. Klotman, Phyllis R. "Sin and Sublimation in the Novels of Samuel Richardson." *CLA* 20(1977): 365-373.

14804. Knight, Charles A. "The Function of Wills in Richardson's *Clarissa*." *TSLL* 11 (1969): 1183-1190.

14805. Konigsberg, Ira. "The Dramatic Background of Richardson's Plots and Characters." *PMLA* 83(1968): 42-53.

14806. ----------. "The Tragedy of Clarissa." *MLQ* 27(1966): 285-298.

14807. Jenkins, Owen. "Richardson's *Pamela* and Fielding's 'Vile Forgeries.'" *PQ* 44 (1965): 200-210.

14808. Lyles, Albert M. "Pamela's Trials." *CLA* 8(1965): 290-292.

14809. McIntosh, Carey. "Pamela's Clothes." *ELH* 35(1968): 75-83.

14810. McKillop, Alan D. "Richardson's Early Writings—Another Pamphlet." *JEGP* 53 (1954): 72-75.

14811. Miles, Kathleen. "Richardson's Response to Fielding's Felon." *SN* 1(1969): 373-374.

14812. Morton, Donald E. "Theme and Structure in *Pamela*." *SN* 3(1971): 242-257.

14813. Muecke, D. C. "Beauty and Mr. B." *SEL* 7(1967): 467-474.

14814. Napier, Elizabeth R. "'Tremble and Reform': The Inversion of Power in Richardson's *Clarissa*." *ELH* 42(1975): 214-223.

14815. Newcomb, Robert. "Franklin and

Richardson." *JEGP* 57(1958): 27-35.

14816. Palmer, William J. "Two Dramatists: Lovelace and Richardson in *Clarissa*." *SN* 5(1973): 7-21.

14817. Park, William. "*Clarissa* as Tragedy." *SEL* 16(1976): 461-471.

14818. ----------. "Fielding *and* Richardson." *PMLA* 81(1966): 381-388.

14819. Parker, Dorothy. "The Time Scheme in *Pamela* and the Character B." *TSLL* 11(1969): 695-704.

14820. Paulson, Ronald. "Review-Essay: All about Richardson." *SN* 5(1973): 110-116.

14821. Poovey, Mary. "Journeys from this World to the Next: The Providential Promise in *Clarissa* and *Tom Jones*." *ELH* 43(1976): 300-315.

14822. Rabkin, Norman. "*Clarissa*: A Study in the Nature of Convention." *ELH* 23(1956): 204-217.

14823. Rogers, Katharine M. "Sensitive Feminism vs. Conventional Sympathy: Richardson and Fielding on Women." *Novel* 9(1976): 256-270.

14824. Roussel, Roy. "Reflections on the Letter: The Reconciliation of Distance and Presence in *Pamela*." *ELH* 41(1974): 375-399.

14825. Sacks, Sheldon. "Novelists as Storytellers." *MP* 73(1976): S97-S109.

14826. Sherburn, George. "Samuel Richardson's Novels and the Theatre: A Theory Sketched." *PQ* 41(1962): 325-329.

14827. Watt, Ian. "Defoe and Richardson on Homer: A Study of the Relation of Novel and Epic in the Early Eighteenth Century." *RES* 3 (1952): 325-340.

14828. Wendt, Allan. "Clarissa's Coffin." *PQ* 39(1960): 481-495.

14829. Wilson, Stuart. "The First Dramatic Version of *Clarissa*." *ELN* 2(1964): 21-25.

14830. ----------. "Richardson's *Pamela*: An Interpretation." *PMLA* 88(1973): 79-91.

14831. Wilt, Judith. "He Could Go No Farther: A Modest Proposal about Lovelace and Clarissa." *PMLA* 92(1977): 19-32.

14832. Winner, Anthony. "Richardson's Lovelace: Character and Prediction." *TSLL* 14 (1972): 53-75.

See also 7780, 13581, 13589, 14060, 14191, 14394, 14435, 14472, 15282.

ROWE, ELIZABETH. 14833. Chapman, Clayton Harding. "Benjamin Colman and Philomela." *NEQ* 42(1969): 214-231.

14834. Richetti, John J. "Mrs. Elizabeth Rowe: The Novel as Polemic." *PMLA* 82(1967): 522-529.

ROWE, NICHOLAS. 14835. Clark, Donald B. "An Eighteenth-Century Adaptation of Massinger." *MLQ* 13(1952): 239-252.

14836. Schwarz, Alfred. "An Example of Eighteenth-Century Pathetic Tragedy: Rowe's *Jane Shore*." *MLQ* 22(1961): 236-247.

14837. Wyman, Lindley A. "The Tradition of the Formal Meditation in Rowe's *The Fair Penitent*." *PQ* 42(1963): 412-416.

SAYERS, FRANK. See 15319.

SEWARD, ANNA. 14838. Woolley, James D. "Johnson as Despot: Anna Seward's Rejected Contribution to Boswell's *Life*." *MP* 70(1972): 140-145.

SHAFTESBURY, ANTHONY ASHLEY COOPER. 14839.

Aldridge, Alfred Owen. "Shaftesbury and Bolingbroke." *PQ* 31(1952): 1-16.

14840. Hayman, John G. "The Evolution of 'The Moralists.'" *MLR* 64(1969): 728-733.

14841. ----------. "Shaftesbury and the Search for a Persona." *SEL* 10(1970): 491-504.

14842. Marsh, Robert. "Shaftesbury's Theory of Poetry: The Importance of the 'Inward Colloquy.'" *ELH* 28(1961): 54-69.

14843. Shepard, John B. "The Significance of the Cartouche in Shaftesbury's *Characteristicks*." *ELN* 13(1976): 180-184.

14844. Tuveson, Ernest. "Shaftesbury on the Not So Simple Plan of Human Nature." *SEL* 5 (1965): 403-434.

14845. ----------. "The Importance of Shaftesbury." *ELH* 20(1953): 267-299.

14846. Voitle, Robert B. "Shaftesbury's Moral Sense." *SP* 52(1955): 17-38.

SHENSTONE, WILLIAM. 14847. Burns, F. D. A. "The First Published Version of Shenstone's 'Pastoral Ballad.'" *RES* 24(1973): 182-185.

14848. Gregg, Richard A. "Pushkin and Shenstone: The Case Re-opened." *Comp L* 17 (1965): 109-116.

14849. Sambrook, A. J. "Another Early Version of Shenstone's *Pastoral Ballad*." *RES* 18 (1967): 169-173.

SHERIDAN, RICHARD BRINSLEY. 14850. Auburn, Mark S. "The Pleasures of Sheridan's *The Rivals*: A Critical Study in the Light of Stage History." *MP* 72(1975): 256-271.

14851. Bloch, Tuvia. "The Antecedents of Sheridan's Faulkland." *PQ* 49(1970): 266-268.

14852. Deelman, Christian. "The Original Cast of *The School for Scandal*." *RES* 13(1962): 257-266.

14853. Nettleton, George H. "Sheridan's Introduction to the American Stage." *PMLA* 65 (1950): 163-182.

14854. Price, Cecil. "The First Prologue to *The Rivals*." *RES* 20(1969): 192-195.

14855. Schiller, Andrew. "*The School for Scandal*: The Restoration Unrestored." *PMLA* 71 (1956): 694-704.

14856. Sen, Sailendra Kumar. "Sheridan's Literary Debt: *The Rivals* and *Humphry Clinker*." *MLQ* 21(1960): 291-300.

14857. Williams, George Woods. "A New Source of Evidence for Sheridan's Authorship of *The Camp* and *The Wonders of Derbyshire*." *SP* 47 (1950): 619-628.

14858. Yearling, Elizabeth M. "The Good-Natured Heroes of Cumberland, Goldsmith, and Sheridan." *MLR* 67(1972): 490-500.

SHIELS, ROBERT. 14859. Battersby, James L. "Johnson and Shiels: Biographers of Addison." *SEL* 9(1969): 521-537.

14860. Campbell, Hilbert. "Shiels and Johnson: Biographers of Thomson." *SEL* 12(1972): 535-544.

SMART, CHRISTOPHER. 14861. Adams, Francis. "Wordplay in the D Fragment of *Jubilate Agno*." *PQ* 48(1969): 82-91.

14862. Dearnley, Moira. "Christopher Smart: 'Some Young Cymro in Cambridge.'" *RES* 19(1968): 53-58.

14863. Fitzgerald, Robert P. "The Form of Christopher Smart's *Jubilate Agno*." *SEL* 8(1968):

487-499.

14864. Friedman, John Block. "The Cosmology of Praise: Smart's *Jubilate Agno*." *PMLA* 82(1967): 250-256.

14865. Hartman, Geoffrey H. "Christopher Smart's *Magnificat*: Toward a Theory of Representation." *ELH* 41(1974): 429-454.

14866. Kuhn, Albert J. "Christopher Smart: The Poet and Patriot of the Lord." *ELH* 30(1963): 121-136.

14867. Lonsdale, Roger. "Christopher Smart's First Publication in English." *RES* 12(1961): 402-404.

14868. Parkin, Rebecca Price. "Christopher Smart's Sacramental Cat." *TSLL* 11(1969): 1191-1196.

14869. Parish, Charles. "Christopher Smart's Knowledge of Hebrew." *SP* 58(1961): 516-532.

14870. ----------. "Christopher Smart's 'Pillars of the Lord.'" *MLQ* 24(1963): 158-163.

14871. Price, Cecil. "Six Letters by Christopher Smart." *RES* 8(1957): 144-148.

14872. Rogers, K. M. "The Pillars of the Lord: Some Sources of 'A Song to David.'" *PQ* 40 (1961): 525-534.

14873. Rizzo, Betty. "A New Secular Hymn by Christopher Smart." *RES* 26(1975): 317-319.

14874. Sherbo, Arthur. "Christopher Smart, Free and Accepted Mason." *JEGP* 54(1955): 664-669.

14875. ----------. "Christopher Smart's Three Translations of Horace." *JEGP* 66(1967): 347-358.

14876. ----------. "The Probably Time of Composition of Christopher Smart's *Song to David*, *Psalms*, and *Hymns and Spiritual Songs*." *JEGP* 55(1956): 41-57.

14877. ----------. "Two Pieces Newly Ascribed to Christopher Smart." *MLR* 62(1967): 214-220.

14878. Williamson, Karina. "Christopher Smart in the Songbooks." *RES* 25(1974): 410-421.

14879. ----------. "Christopher Smart's Hymns and Spiritual Songs." *PQ* 38(1959): 413-424.

SMITH, ADAM. 14880. Bevilacqua, Vincent M. "Adam Smith and some Philosophical Origins of Eighteenth-century Rhetorical Theory." *MLR* 63 (1968): 559-568.

14881. Brissender, R. F. "Authority, Guilt, and Anxiety in *The Theory of Moral Sentiments*." *TSLL* 11(1969): 945-962.

14882. Dankert, Clyde E. "Adam Smith—Man of Letters." *TSLL* 3(1961): 212-223.

SMITH, CHARLOTTE. 14883. Bushnell, Nelson S. "Artistic Economy in *Jane Eyre*: A Contrast with *The Old Manor House*." *ELN* 5(1968): 197-202.

14884. Ehrenpreis, Anne Henry. "*Northanger Abbey*: Jane Austen and Charlotte Smith." *NCF* 25(1970): 343-348.

See also 15646.

SMOLLETT, TOBIAS. 14885. Beasley, Jerry C. "Romance and the 'New' Novels of Richardson, Fielding, and Smollett." *SEL* 16(1976): 437-450.

14886. Bevis, Richard W. "Smollett and *The Israelites*." *PQ* 45(1966): 387-394.

14887. Bloch, Tuvia. "Smollett's Quest for Form." *MP* 65(1967): 103-113.

14888. Boucé, Paul-Gabriel. "The 'Chinese Pilot' and 'Sa-rouf' in Smollett's *Atom*." *ELN* 4 (1967): 273-275.

14889. ----------. "A Note on Smollett's *Continuation of the Complete History of England*." *RES* 20(1969): 57-61.

14890. ----------. "Smollett and the Expidition against Rochefort." *MP* 65(1967): 33-38.

14891. Brack, O M, Jr. "Toward a Critical Edition of Smollett's *Peregrine Pickle*." *SN* 7 (1975): 361-374.

14892. Copeland, Edward. "*Humphry Clinker*: A Comic Pastoral Poem in Prose?" *TSLL* 16(1974): 493-501.

14893. Cordasco, Francesco. "Smollett and the Translation of *Don Quixote*." *MLQ* 13 (1952): 23-36.

14894. de la Torre, Lillian. "The Melting Scot: A Postscript to *Peregrine Pickle* (1751-1772)." *ELN* 10(1972): 20-27.

14895. ----------. "New Light on Smollett and the Annesley Cause." *RES* 22(1971): 274-281.

14896. Dillingham, William B. "Melville's Long Ghost and Smollett's Count Fathom." *AL* 42 (1970): 232-235.

14897. Driskell, Leon V. "Looking for Dustwich." *TSLL* 9(1967): 85-90.

14898. Dunn, Richard J. "*Humphry Clinker's* Humane Humor." *TSLL* 18(1976): 229-239.

14899. Evans, David L. "*Humphry Clinker*: Smollett's Tempered Augustanism." *Criticism* 9 (1967): 257-274.

14900. ----------. "Peregrine Pickle: The Complete Satirist." *SN* 3(1971): 258-274.

14901. Folkenflik, Robert. "Self and Society: Comic Union in *Humphry Clinker*." *PQ* 53(1974): 195-204.

14902. Foster, James R. "Smollett and the *Atom*." *PMLA* 68(1953): 1032-1046.

14903. Gassman, Byron. "The *Briton* and *Humphry Clinker*." *SEL* 3(1963): 397-414.

14904. ----------. "'Humphry Clinker' and the Two Kingdoms of George III." *Criticism* 16 (1974): 95-108.

14905. Hunter, Richard A., and Ida Macalpine. "Smollett's Reading in Psychistry." *MLR* 51 (1956): 409-411.

14906. Jeffrey, David K. "Smollett's Irony in *Peregrine Pickle*." *JNT* 6(1976): 137-146.

14907. Kent, John P. "Smollett's Translation of the *Gil Blas*: A Question of Text." *ELN* 5(1967): 21-26.

14908. Knapp, Lewis M. "Early Scottish Attitudes toward Tobias Smollett." *PQ* 45(1966): 262-269.

14909. ----------. "The Keys to Smollett's *Atom*." *ELN* 2(1964): 100-102.

14910. ----------. "The 'Prophecy' attributed to Smollett." *RES* 16(1965): 177-182.

14911. ----------. "Smollett and Johnson, Never Cater-Cousins?" *MP* 66(1968): 152-154.

14912. ----------. "Smollett's Transaction of Fénelon's *Télémaque*." *PQ* 44(1965): 405-407.

14913. Knapp, Lewis M., and Lillian de la Torre. "Smollett, MacKercher, and the Annesley Claimant." *ELN* 1(1963): 28-33.

14914. Knowles, Edwin B. "A Note on Smollett's *Don Quixote*." *MLQ* 16(1955): 29-31.

14915. Orr, John. "Did Smollett Know Spanish?" *MLR* 45(1950): 218.

14916. Paulson, Ronald. "Satire in the Early Novels of Smollett." *JEGP* 59(1960): 381-402.

14917. ----------. "Smollett and Hogarth: The Identity of Pallet." *SEL* 4(1964): 351-359.

14918. Piper, William Bowman. "The Large Diffused Picture of Life in Smollett's Early Novels." *SP* 60(1963): 45-56.

14919. Preston, Thomas R. "Smollett and the Benevolent Misanthrope Type." *PMLA* 79(1964): 51-57.

14920. ----------. "The 'Stage Passions' and Smollett's Characterizations." *SP* 71(1974): 105-125.

14921. Rice, Scott. "Smollett's Seventh Travel Letter and the Design of Formed Verse Satire." *SEL* 16(1976): 491-503.

14922. Roper, Derek. "Smollett's 'Four Gentlemen': The First Contributors to the *Critical Review*." *RES* 10(1959): 38-44.

14923. Rosenblum, Michael. "Smollett and the Old Conventions." *PQ* 55(1976): 389-402.

14924. ----------. "Smollett as Conservative Satirist." *ELH* 42(1975): 556-579.

14925. Rousseau, G. S., and Roger Hambridge. "Smollett and Politics: Originals for the Election Scene in *Sir Launcelot Greaves*." *ELN* 14(1976): 32-37.

14926. Scott, William. "Smollett's *The Tears of Scotland*. A Hitherto Unnoticed Printing and some comments on the Text." *RES* 8(1957): 38-42.

14927. Sena, John F. "Smollett's Portrait of Narcissa's Aunt: The Genesis of an 'Original.'" *ELN* 14(1977): 270-275.

14928. Siebert, Donald T., Jr. "The Role of the Senses in *Humphry Clinker*." *SN* 6(1974): 17-26.

14929. Speer, Diane Parkin. "Heinlein's *The Door into Summer* and *Roderick Random*." *Ext* 12(1970): 30-34.

14930. Stevick, Philip. "Stylistic Energy in the Early Smollett." *SP* 64(1967): 712-719.

14931. Taylor, S. Oritz. "Episodic Structure and the Picaresque Novel." *JNT* 7(1977): 218-225.

14932. Underwood, Gary N. "Linquistic Realism in *Roderick Random*." *JEGP* 69(1970): 32-40.

14933. Warner, John M. "The Interpolated Narratives in the Fiction of Fielding and Smollett: An Epistemological View." *SN* 5(1973): 271-283.

14934. ----------. "Smollett's Development as a Novelist." *Novel* 5(1972): 148-161.

14935. West, William A. "Matt Bramble's Journey to Health." *TSLL* 11(1969): 1197-1208.

See also 7780, 13557, 13559, 13581, 13585, 13589, 14856.

SPENCE, JOSEPH. 14936. Osborn, James M. "Spence, Natural Genius and Pope." *PQ* 45(1966): 123-144.

STANLEY, THOMAS. 14937. O'Regan, M. J. "The French Sources of Thomas Stanley's Paraphrases of Psalms 139 and 148." *MLR* 59(1964): 179-181.

STEELE, RICHARD. 14938. Averill, James H. "The Death of Stephen Clay and Richard Steele's *Spectators* of August 1711." *RES* 28 (1977): 305-310.

14939. Blanchard, Rae. "Richard Steele and William Lord Cowper: New Letters." *PMLA* 80 (1965): 303-306.

14940. Bond, Richmond P. "A Letter to Steele on the *Spectator*." *MLQ* 18(1957): 303-304.

14941. Cole, Douglas. "Albee's *Virginia Woolf* and Steele's *Tatler*." *AL* 40(1968): 81-82.

14942. Dust, Alvin I. "An Aspect of the Addison-Steele Literary Relationship." *ELN* 1 (1964): 196-200.

14943. Furtwangler, Albert. "The Making of Mr. Spectator." *MLQ* 38(1977): 21-39.

14944. Hodgart, M. J. C. "The Eighth Volume of the *Spectator*." *RES* 5(1954): 367-387.

14945. Hopkins, Robert H. "'The Good Old Cause' in Pope, Addison, and Steele." *RES* 17 (1966): 62-68,

14946. ----------. "The Issue of Anonymity and the Beginning of the Steele-Swift Controversy of 1713-14." *ELN* 2(1964): 15-21.

14947. Kenny, Shirley Strum. "Perennial Favorites: Congreve, Vanbrugh, Cibber, Farquhar, and Steele." *MP* 73(1976): S4-S11.

14948. ----------. "Richard Steele and the 'Pattern of Genteel Comedy.'" *MP* 70(1972): 22-37.

14949. Kline, Richard B. "Tory Prior and Whig Steele." *SEL* 9(1969): 427-437.

14950. Köster, Patricia. "'Monoculus' and Party Satire." *PQ* 49(1970): 259-262.

14951. Loftis, John. "The Blenheim Papers and Steele's Journalism, 1715-18." *PMLA* 66 (1951): 197-210.

14952. Snyder, Henry L. "The Identity of Monoculus in *The Tatler*." *PQ* 48(1969): 20-26.

14953. Stephens, John C., Jr. "Steele and the Bishop of St. Asaph's Preface." *PMLA* 67 (1952): 1011-1023.

14954. Turner, Margaret. "The Influence of La Bruyère on the 'Tatler' and the 'Spectator.'" *MLR* 48(1953): 10-16.

14955. Winton, Calhoun. "New Documents Concerning Richard Steele's Father." *JEGP* 58 (1959): 264-269.

14956. ----------. "Steele and the Fall of Harley in 1714." *PQ* 37(1958): 440-447.

14957. ----------. "Steele, Mrs. Manley, and John Lacy." *PQ* 42(1963): 272-275.

14958. White, Robert B., Jr. "Character of the Tatler." *PQ* 45(1966): 450-454.

See also 13557, 13597, 13647.

STERNE, LAURENCE. 14959. Anderson, Howard. "Answers to the Author of *Clarissa*: Theme and Narrative Technique in *Tom Jones* and *Tristram Shandy*." *PQ* 51(1972): 859-873.

14960. ----------. "Associationism and Wit in *Tristram Shandy*." *PQ* 48(1969): 27-41.

14961. ----------. "*Tristram Shandy* and the Reader's Imagination." *PMLA* 86(1971): 966-973.

14962. ----------. "A Version of Pastoral: Class and Society in *Tristram Shandy*." *SEL* 7 (1967): 509-529.

14963. Banerjee, Chinmoy. "*Tristram Shandy* and the Association of Ideas." *TSLL* 15 (1974): 693-706.

14964. Booth, Wayne. "Did Sterne Complete *Tristam Shandy*?" *MP* 48(1951): 172-183.

14965. ----------. "The Self-Conscious Narrator in Comic Fiction before *Tristram Shandy*." *PMLA* 67(1952): 163-185.

14966. Burckhardt, Sigurd. "*Tristam Shandy*'s Law of Gravity." *ELH* 28(1961): 70-88.

14967. Cash, Arthur. "The Lockean

Psychology of *Tristram Shandy*." *ELH* 22(1955): 125-135.

14968. ----------. "The Sermon in *Tristram Shandy*" *ELH* 31(1964): 395-417.

14969. Cook, Albert. "Reflexive Attitude: Sterne, Gogol, Gide." *Criticism* 2(1960): 164-174.

14970. Donaldson, Ian. "The Clockwork Novel: Three Notes on an Eighteenth-Century Analogy." *RES* 21(1970): 14-22.

14971. Fabricant, Carole. "*Tristram Shandy* and *Moby-Dick*: A Cock and Bull Story and a Tale of a Tub." *JNT* 7(1977): 57-69.

14972. Fardon, Michael. "A Rabelaisian Source for the 'Key' to Sterne's *A Political Romance*." *RES* 26(1975): 47-50.

14973. Farrell, William J. "Nature Versus Art as a Comic Pattern in *Tristram Shandy*." *ELH* 30(1963): 16-35.

14974. Faurot, Ruth Marie. "Mrs. Shandy Observed." *SEL* 10(1970): 579-589.

14975. Freedman, William. "*Tristram Shandy*: The Art of Literary Counterpoint." *MLQ* 32(1971): 268-280.

14976. Evans, James E. "Tristram as Critic: Momus's Glass vs. Hobby-Horse." *PQ* 50(1971): 669-671.

14977. Gold, Joel J. "Tristram Shandy at the Ambassador's Chapel." *PQ* 48(1969): 421-424.

14978. Hafter, Ronald. "Garrick and *Tristram Shandy*." *SEL* 7(1967): 475-489.

14979. Hall, Joan Joffe. "The Hobby-horsical World of *Tristram Shandy*." *MLQ* 24 (1963): 131-143.

14980. Hamilton, Harlan W. "William Combe and the *Original Letters of the Late Reverend Mr. Laurence Sterne* (1788)." *PMLA* 82(1967): 420-429.

14981. Harper, Kenneth E. "A Russian Critic and *Tristram Shandy*." *MP* 52(1954): 92-99.

14982. Hartley, Lodwick. "The Eustace-Sterne Correspondence: A Note on Sterne's Reputation in America." *ELN* 5(1968): 176-183.

14983. ----------. "The North American Review on Laurence Sterne: A Document in a Literary Reputation." *AL* 44(1972): 299-306.

14984. ----------. "Yorick Redivivus: A Bicentenary Review of Studies on Laurence Sterne." *SN* 1(1969): 81-89.

14985. Hnatko, Eugene. "*Tristram Shandy*'s Wit." *JEGP* 65(1966): 47-64.

14986. Hunter, J. Paul. "Response as Reformation: *Tristram Shandy* and the Art of Interruption." *Novel* 4(1971): 132-146.

14987. Jackson, H. J. "Sterne, Burton, and Ferriar: Allusion to the *Anatomy of Melancholy* in Volumes Five to Nine of *Tristram Shandy*." *PQ* 54(1975): 457-470.

14988. Jefferson, D. W. "*Tristram Shandy* and the Tradition of Learned Wit." *EIC* 1(1951): 225-248.

14989. Klotman, Phyllis R. "'Reconciliation of Contrasts' in *Tristram Shandy*." *CLA* 20 (1976): 48-56.

14990. Koppel, Gene. "Fulfillment through Frustration: Some Aspects of Sterne's Art of the Incomplete in *A Sentimental Journey*." *SN* 2 (1970): 168-172.

14991. Korkowski, Eugene. "The *Second Tale of a Tub*: A Link from Swift to Sterne."

SN 6(1974): 470-475.

14992. Kuist, James M. "New Light on Sterne: An Old Man's Recollections of the Young Vicar." *PMLA* 80(1965): 549-553.

14993. Kyle, Carol A. "A Note on Laurence Sterne and the Cannon-Bullet of John Locke." *PQ* 50(1971): 672-674.

14994. Lounsberry, Barbara. "Sermons and Satire: Anti-Catholicism in Sterne." *PQ* 55 (1976): 403-417.

14995. Maskell, Duke. "Locke and Sterne; or Can Philosophy Influence Literature." *EIC* 23(1973): 22-39.

14996. McMaster, Juliet. "Experience to Expression: Thematic Character Contrasts in *Tristram Shandy*." *MLQ* 32(1971): 42-57.

14997. New, Melvyn. "Laurence Sterne and Henry Baker's *The Microscope Made Easy*." *SEL* 10(1970): 591-604.

14998. ----------. "Sterne and Swift: Sermons and Satire." *MLQ* 30(1969): 198-211.

14999. ----------. "Sterne's Rabelaisian Fragment: A Text from the Holograph Manuscript." *PMLA* 87(1972): 1083-1093.

15000. Parish, Charles. "The Shandy Bull Vindicated." *MLQ* 31(1970): 48-52.

15001. Park, William. "*Tristram Shandy* and the New 'Novel of Sensibility.'" *SN* 6 (1974): 268-279.

15002. Pellan, Françoise. "Laurence Sterne's Indebtedness to Charron." *MLR* 67 (1972): 752-755.

15003. Petrakis, Byron. "The Jester in the Pulpit: Sterne and Pulpit Eloquence." *PQ* 51(1972): 430-447.

15004. Petrie, Graham. "Rhetoric as Fictional Technique in *Tristram Shandy*." *PQ* 48(1969): 479-494.

15005. ----------. "A Rhetorical Topic in 'Tristram Shandy.'" *MLR* 65(1970): 261-266.

15006. Piper, William Bowman. "Tristram Shandy's Digressive Artistry." *SEL* 1,#3(1961): 65-76.

15007. ----------. "Tristram Shandy's Tragicomical Testimony." *Criticism* 3(1961): 171-185.

15008. Rosenblum, Michael. "Shandean Geometry and the Challange of Contingency." *Novel* 10(1977): 237-247.

15009. Sallé, Jean-Claude. "A Source of Sterne's Conception of Time." *RES* 6(1955): 180-182.

1510. Schaefer, Josephine O'Brien. "Sterne's *Sentimental Journey* and Woolf's *Jacob's Room*." *MFS* 23(1977): 189-197.

15011. Scher, Steven Paul. "Hoffman and Sterne: Unmediated Parallels in Narrative Method." *Comp L* 28(1976): 309-325.

15012. Smitten, Jeffrey R. "Spatial Form as Narrative Technique in *A Sentimental Journey*." *JNT* 5(1975): 208-218.

15013. Stedmond, J. M. "Genre and *Tristram Shandy*." *PQ* 38(1959): 37-51.

15014. ----------. "Satire and *Tristram Shandy*." *SEL* 1,#3(1961): 53-63.

15015. ----------. "Style and *Tristram Shandy*." *MLQ* 20(1959): 243-251.

15016. Stewart, Jack F. "Some Critical Metaphors for Shandean Style." *CLA* 13(1969):

183-187.

15017. Stout, Gardner D., Jr. "Some Borrowings in Sterne from Rabelais and Cervantes." *ELN* 3(1965): 111-118.

15018. ----------. "Sterne's Borrowings from Bishop Joseph Hall's *Quo Vadis?*" *ELN* 2 (1965): 196-200.

15019. ----------. "Yorick's 'Sentimental Journey': A Comic 'Pilgrim's Progress' for the Man of Feeling." *ELH* 30(1963): 395-412.

15020. Traugott, John. "Auxiliary Verbs: A Review of Two Books on Sterne." *MLQ* 30(1969): 112-120.

15021. Towers, A. R. "Sterne's Cock and Bull Story." *ELH* 24(1957): 12-29.

15022. Wagoner, Mary S. "Satire of the Reader in *Tristram Shandy*." *TSLL* 8(1966): 337-344.

15023. Wright, Andrew. "The Artifice of Failure in *Tristram Shandy*." *Novel* 2(1969): 212-220.

See also 7780, 13557, 13585, 13597, 19919.

STOCKDALE, PERCIVAL. 15024. Hardy, John. "Stockdale's Defense of Pope." *RES* 18(1967): 49-54.

SWIFT, JONATHAN. 15025. Adams, Robert Martin. "Jonathan Swift, Thomas Swift, and the Authorship of *A Tale of a Tub*." *MP* 64(1967): 198-232.

15026. Aden, John M. "Corinna and the Sterner Muse of Swift." *ELN* 4(1966): 23-31.

15027. Allen, Robert J. "Swift's *Contests and Dissensions* in Boston." *NEQ* 29(1956): 73-82.

15028. Andreasen, M. J. C. "Swift's Satire on the Occult in *A Tale of a Tub*." *TSLL* 5(1963): 410-421.

15029. Barroll, J. Leeds. "Gulliver and the Struldbruggs." *PMLA* 73(1958): 43-50.

15030. ----------. "Gulliver in Luggnagg." *PQ* 36(1957): 504-508.

15031. Bentman, Raymond. "Satiric Structure and Tone in the Conclusion of *Gulliver's Travels*." *SEL* 11(1971): 535-548.

15032. Brown, James. "Swift as Moralist." *PQ* 33(1954): 368-387.

15033. Brown, William J. "Gulliver's Passage on the Dutch *Amboyna*." *ELN* 1(1964): 262-264.

15034. Byers, John R., Jr. "Another Source for *Gulliver's Travels*." *JEGP* 57(1958): 14-20.

15035. Calderwood, James L. "Sturctural Parody in Swift's *Fragment*." *MLQ* 23(1962): 243-253.

15036. Carnochan, W. B. "The Complexity of Swift: Gulliver's Fourth Voyage." *SP* 60(1963): 23-44.

15037. ----------. "*Gulliver's Travels*: An Essay on the Human Understanding?" *MLQ* 25 (1964): 5-21.

15038. ----------. "Some Roles of Lemuel Gulliver." *TSLL* 5(1964): 520-529.

15039. Champion, Larry S. "Gulliver's Voyages: The Framing Events as a Guide to Interpretation." *TSLL* 10(1969): 529-536.

15040. Chiasson, Elias J. "Swift's Clothes Philosophy in the *Tale* and Hooker's Concept of Law." *SP* 59(1962): 64-82.

15041. Clark, John R. "Further Iliads in Swift's Nut-Shell." *PQ* 51(1972): 945-950.

15042. ----------. "Swift's Knaves and Fools in the Tradition: Rhetoric Versus Poetic in *A Tale of a Tub*, Section IX." *SP* 66(1969): 777-796.

15043. Clark, Paul Odell. "Lapponia, Lapland, and Laputa." *MLQ* 19(1958): 343-351.

15044. Cohan, Steven M. "Gulliver's Fiction." *SN* 6(1974): 7-16.

15045. Cook, Richard I. "The Audience of Swift's Tory Tracts, 1710-14." *MLQ* 24(1963): 31-41.

15046. ----------. "Swift as Tory Rhetorician." *TSLL* 4(1962): 72-86.

15047. ----------. "The Uses of *Saeva Indignatio*." *SEL* 2(1962): 267-307.

15048. Coulling, Sidney M. B. "Carlyle and Swift." *SEL* 10(1970): 741-758.

15049. Danchin, Pierre. "The Text of *Gulliver's Travels*." *TSLL* 2(1960): 233-250.

15050. Dircks, Richard J. "Gulliver's Tragic Rationalism." *Criticism* 2(1960): 134-149.

15051. Drew, Philip. "Further Thoughts on *A Tale of A Tub*." *EIC* 21(1971): 412-418.

15052. Ehrenpreis, Irvin. "The Date of Swift's 'Sentiments.'" *RES* 3(1952): 272-274.

15053. ----------. "The Origins of *Gulliver's Travels*." *PMLA* 72(1957): 880-899.

15054. ----------. "The Pattern of Swift's Women." *PMLA* 70(1955): 706-716.

15055. ----------. "Swift's First Poem." *MLR* 49(1954): 210-211.

15056. ----------. "Swift's History of England." *JEGP* 51(1952): 177-185.

15057. Elliott, Robert C. "Gulliver as Literary Artist." *ELH* 19(1952): 49-63.

15058. ----------. "Swift and Dr. Eachard." *PMLA* 69(1954): 1250-1257.

15059. ----------. "Swift's *Tale of a Tub*: An Essay in Problems of Structure." *PMLA* 66(1951): 441-455.

15060. ----------. "Swift's Satire: Rules of the Game." *ELH* 41(1974): 413-428.

15061. England, A. B. "Private and Public Rhetoric in the *Journal to Stella*." *EIC* 22(1972): 131-141.

15062. ----------. "The Subversion of Logic in Some Poems by Swift." *SEL* 15(1975): 409-418.

15063. ----------. "World Without Order: Some Thoughts on the Poetry of Swift." *EIC* 16 (1966): 32-43.

15064. Fabricant, Carole. "The Garden as City: Swift's Landscape of Alienation." *ELH* 42 (1975): 531-555.

15065. Ferguson, Oliver W. "The Authorship of 'Apollo's Edict.'" *PMLA* 70(1955): 433-441.

15066. ----------. "Swift's *Saeva Indignatio* and *A Modest Proposal*." *PQ* 38(1959): 473-479.

15067. Fisher, Alan S. "Swift's Verse Portraits: A Study in His Originality as an Augustan Satirist." *SEL* 14(1974): 343-356.

15068. Fischer, John Irwin. "How to Die: *Verses on the Death of Dr. Swift*." *RES* 21(1970): 422-442.

15069. Fitzgerald, Robert P. "The Allegory of Luggnagg and the Struldbruggs in Gulliver's Travels." *SP* 65(1968): 657-676.

15070. ----------. "The Structure of

Gulliver's Travels." *SP* 71(1974): 247-263.

15071. French, David P. "Swift, Temple, and 'A Digression on Madness.'" *TSLL* 5(1963): 42-57.

15072. Frese, Jerry. "Swift's Houyhnhms and Utopian Law." *HSL* 9(1977): 187-195.

15073. Frost, William. "The Irony of Swift and Gibbon: A Reply to F. R. Leavis." *EIC* 17(1967): 41-47.

15074. Fussell, Paul, Jr. "Speaker and Style in *A Letter of Advice to a Young Poet* (1721) and the Problem of Attribution." *RES* 10 (1959): 63-67.

15075. Gill, James E. "Beast over Man: Theriophilic Paradox in Gulliver's 'Voyage to the Country of the Houyhnhnms.'" *SP* 67(1970): 532-549.

15076. Gilmore, Thomas B., Jr. "The Comedy of Swift's Scatological Poems." *PMLA* 91 (1976): 33-43.

15077. ----------. "Swift's 'Modest Proposal': A Possible Source." *PQ* 47(1968): 590-592.

15078. Graham, Edward. "Smedley and Swift—'Further Reasons for Their Enmity.'" *PQ* 48(1969): 416-420.

15079. Greenberg, Robert A. "'A Modest Proposal' and the Bible." *MLR* 55(1960): 568-569.

15080. Guskin, Phyllis J. "'A very remarkable Book': Abel Boyer's View of Gulliver's Travels." *SP* 72(1975): 439-453.

15081. Halewood, William H. "*Gulliver's Travels I, vi*." *ELH* 33(1966): 422-433.

15082. ----------. "Plutarch in Houyhnhnmland: A Neglected Source for Gulliver's Fourth Voyage." *PQ* 44(1965): 185-194.

15085. ----------. "Young William Temple and Young Jonathan Swift." *CLA* 10(1966): 105-113.

15084. Harris, Kathryn Montgomery. "'Occasions so few': Satire as a Strategy of Praise in Swift's Early Odes." *MLQ* 31(1970): 22-37.

15085. Hart, Jeffrey. "The Ideologue as Artist: Some Notes on *Gulliver's Travels*." *Criticism* 2(1960): 125-133.

15086. Harth, Phillip. "Ehrenpreis's *Swift*: The Biographer as Critic." *MP* 67(1970): 273-278.

15087. ----------. "The Problem of Political Allegory in *Gulliver's Travels*." *MP* 73 (1976): S40-S47.

15088. ----------, and Leland D. Peterson. "Swift's *Project*: Tract or Travesty." *PMLA* 84 (1969): 336-343.

15089. Holzknecht, R. K. "Swift and Mr. Rawson." *EIC* 20(1970): 496-497.

15090. Hopkins, Robert H. "The Issue of Anonymity and the Beginning of the Steete-Swift Controversy of 1713-14." *ELN* 2(1964): 15-21.

15091. ----------. "The Personation of Hobbism in Swift's *Tale of a Tub* and *Mechanical Operation of the Spirit*." *PQ* 45(1966): 372-378.

15092. Horne, Colin J. "Hazlitt on Swift." *EIC* 25(1975): 276-277.

15093. ----------. "The Roles of Swift and Marlborough in *The Vanity of Human Wishes*." *MP* 73(1976): 280-283.

15094. ----------, and Hugh Powell. "A German Analogue for 'A Tale of a Tub.'" *MLR* 55 (1960): 488-496.

15095. Horsley, L. S. "Rogues or Honest Gentlemen: The Public Characters of Queen Anne Journalists." *TSLL* 18(1976): 198-228.

15096. Irwin, Archibald B. "Swift as Translator of the French of Sir William Temple and His Correspondents." *SEL* 6(1966): 483-498.

15097. Irwin, W. R. "Swift and the Novelists." *PQ* 45(1966): 102-113.

15098. ----------. "Swift the Verse Man." *PQ* 54(1975): 222-238.

15099. Jarrell, Mackie L. "The Handwriting of the Lilliputians." *PQ* 37(1958): 116-119.

15100. ----------. "A New Swift Attribution: The Prefaces to Sheridan's Sermon on St. Cecilia's Day." *PMLA* 78(1963): 511-515.

15101. ----------. "'Ode to the King': Some Contests, Dissensions, and Exchanges among Jonathan Swift, John Dutton, and Henry James." *TSLL* 7(1965): 145-159.

15102. Johnson, Maurice. "Swift and 'The Greatest Epitaph in History.'" *PMLA* 68(1953): 814-827.

15103. ----------. "Text and Possible Occasion for Swift's 'Day of Judgement.'" *PMLA* 86 (1971): 210-217.

15104. Jones, Gareth. "Swift's *Cadenus* and *Vanetta*: a Question of Positives." *EIC* 20 (1970): 424-440.

15105. Jones, Myrddin. "*Further Thoughts on Religion*: Swift's Relationship to Filmer and Locke." *RES* 9(1958): 284-286.

15106. ----------. "Swift, Harrington and Corruption in England." *PQ* 53(1974): 59-70.

15107. Juan, E. San, Jr. "The Anti-Poetry of Jonathan Swift." *PQ* 44(1965): 387-396.

15108. Kallich, Martin. "Three Ways of Looking at a Horse: Jonathan Swift's 'Voyage to the Houyhnhnms' Again." *Criticism* 2(1960): 107-124.

15109. Kelley, Ann Cline. "Swift's Explorations of Slavery in Houyhnhnmland and Ireland." *PMLA* 91(1976): 846-855.

15110. ----------. "Swift's *Polite Conservation*: An Eschatological Vision." *SP* 73 (1976): 204-224.

15111. Kelling, Harold D. "Reason in Madness: *A Tale of a Tub*." *PMLA* 69(1954): 198-222.

15112. ----------. "Some Significant Names in *Gulliver's Travels*." *SP* 48(1951): 761-778.

15113. Kelsall, M. M. "*Iterum* Houyhnhnm: Swift's Sextumvirate and the Horses." *EIC* 19 (1969): 35-45.

15114. Kesterson, David B. "Swift and Music." *TSLL* 11(1969): 687-694.

15115. Kinahan, Frank. "The Melancholy of Anatomy: Voice and Theme in *A Tale of a Tub*." *JEGP* 69(1970): 278-291.

15116. Klima, S. "A Possible Source for Swift's Struldbrugs?" *PQ* 42(1963): 566-569.

15117. Korkowski, Eugene. "The *Second Tale of a Tub*: A Link from Swift to Sterne." *SN* 6(1974): 470-474.

15118. ----------. "With an Eye to the Bunghole: Figures of Containment in *A Tale of a Tub*." *SEL* 15(1975): 391-408.

15119. Korshin, Paul J. "The Intellectual

Context of Swift's Flying Island." *PQ* 50(1971): 630-646.

15120. ----------. "Johnson and Swift: A Study in the Genesis of Literary Opinion." *PQ* 48 (1969): 464-478.

15121. Kulishek, Clarence L. "Swift's Octosyllabics and the Hudibrastic Tradition." *JEGP* 53(1954): 361-368.

15122. Lacase, Steward. "The Fall of Gulliver's Master." *EIC* 20(1970): 327-333.

15123. Lawlis, Merritt. "Swift's Use of Narrative: The Third Chapter of the Voyage to Lilliput." *JEGP* 72(1973): 1-16.

15124. Lawry, Jon S. "Dr. Lemuel Gulliver and 'the Thing which was not.'" *JEGP* 67(1968): 212-234.

15125. Lein, Clayton D. "Rhetoric and Allegory in Swift's *Examiner 14*." *SEL* 17(1977): 407-417.

15126. Levine, Jay Arnold. "The Design of 'A Tale of a Tub' (with a Digression on a Mad Modern Critic)." *ELH* 33(1966): 198-227.

15127. Leyburn, Ellen Douglass. "Swift's View of the Dutch." *PMLA* 66(1951): 734-745.

15128. Manley, Francis. "Swift Marginalia in Howell's *Medulla Historiae Anglicane*." *PMLA* 73 (1958): 335-338.

15129. Mayhew, George. "Swift and the Tripos Tradition." *PQ* 45(1966): 85-101.

15130. ----------. "Swift's Bickerstaff Hoax as an April Fools' Joke." *MP* 61(1964): 270-280.

15131. ----------. "Swift's 'On the Day of Judgement' and Theophilus Swift." *PQ* 54(1975): 213-221.

15132. ----------. "Some Dramatizations of Swift's *Polite Conversation* (1738)." *PQ* 44(1965): 51-72.

15133. McAleer, John J. "Swift's Letcombe Admonition to Bolingbroke." *CLA* 4(1961): 188-195.

15134. McKenzie, Alan T. "'The Lamentation of Glumdalclitch for the Loss of Grildrig. A Pastoral': What We Have Been Missing." [with text] *TSLL* 12(1971): 583-594.

15135. Mezciems, Jenny. "The Unity of Swift's 'Voyage to Laputa': Structure as Meaning in Utopian Fiction." *MLR* 72(1977): 1-21.

15136. Moore, John Robert. "Swift as Historian." *SP* 49(1952): 583-604.

15137. Nandy, Dipak. "Jonathan Swift, Thomas Swift, and the Authorship of *A Tale of a Tub*." *MP* 66(1969): 333-337.

15138. New, Melvyn. "Sterne and Swift: Sermons and Satire." *MLQ* 30(1969): 198-211.

15129. Nokes, David. "Swift and the Beggars." *EIC* 26(1976): 218-235.

15140. O Hehir, Brendan. "Meaning in Swift's 'Description of a City Shower.'" *ELH* 27 (1960): 194-207.

15141. Ohlin, Peter. "'Cadenus and Vanessa: Reason and Passion." *SEL* 4(1964): 485-496.

15142. Ong, Walter J., S. J. "Swift on the Mind: The Myth of Asepis." *MLQ* 15(1954): 208-221.

15143. Olson, R. C. "Swift's Use of the *Philosophical Transactions* in Section V of *A Tale of a Tub*." *SP* 49(1952): 459-467.

15144. Paulson, Ronald. "Swift, Stella, and Permanence." *ELH* 27(1960): 298-314.

15145. Peake, Charles. "Swift and the Passions." *MLR* 55(1960): 169-180.

15146. Peterson, Leland D. "On the Keen Appetitite for Perpetuity of Life." *ELN* 1(1964): 265-267.

15147. ----------. "Swift's *Project*: A Religious and Political Satire." *PMLA* 82(1967): 54-63.

15148. Philmus, Robert M. "The Language of Utopia." *SLI* 6,#2(1973): 61-78.

15149. ----------. "Swift, Gulliver, and 'The Thing Which Was Not.'" *ELH* 38(1971): 62-79.

15150. Pierre, Gerald J. "Gulliver's Voyage to China and Moor Park: The Influence of Sir William Temple upon *Gulliver's Travels*." *TSLL* 17(1975): 428-437.

15151. Pinkus, Philip. "*A Tale of a Tub* and the Rosy Cross." *JEGP* 59(1960): 669-679.

15152. Quinlan, Maurice J. "Lemuel Gulliver's Ships." *PQ* 46(1967): 412-417.

15153. ----------. "The Prosecution of Swift's *Public Spirit of the Whigs*." *TSLL* 9 (1967): 167-184.

15154. ----------. "Swift's *Project for the Advancement of Religion and the Reformation of Manners*." *PMLA* 71(1956): 201-212.

15155. ----------. "Swift's Use of Literalization as a Rhetorical Device." *PMLA* 82(1967): 516-521.

15156. ----------. "Treason in Lilliput and in England." *TSLL* 11(1970): 1317-1332.

15157. Quintana, Ricardo. "Two Paragraphs in *A Tale of a Tub*, Section IX." *MP* 73(1975): 15-32.

15158. Radner, John B. "The Struldbruggs, The Houyhnhnms, and the Good Life." *SEL* 17(1977): 419-433.

15159. Rawson, C. J. "Mr. Holzknecht on Rawson on Swift." *EIC* 21(1971): 115-116.

15160. ----------. "Order and Cruelty: a Reading of Swift (with some Comments on Pope and Johnson)." *EIC* 20(1970): 24-56.

15161. ----------. "Swift's Certificate to Parnell's 'Posthumous Words.'" *MLR* 57(1962): 179-182.

15162. ----------. "'Tis only Infinite Below: Speculations on Swift, Wallace Stevens, R. D. Laing and Others." *EIC* 22(1972): 161-181.

15163. Real, Hermann J. "'That Malignant Deity': An Interpretation of *Criticism* in Swift's Battle of the Books." *PQ* 52(1973): 760-766.

15164. Rees, Christine. "Gay, Swift, and the Nymphs of Drury-Lane." *EIC* 23(1973): 1-21.

15165. Reichert, John F. "Plato, Swift, and the Houyhnhnms." *PQ* 47(1968): 179-192.

15166. Reiss, Edmund. "The Importance of Swift's Glubbdubdrib Episode." *JEGP* 59(1960): 223-228.

15167. Ricks, Christopher. "Notes on Swift and Johnson." *RES* 11(1960): 412-413.

15168. Roberts, Philip. "Swift, Queene Anne, and *The Windsor* Prophecy." *PQ* 49(1970): 254-258.

15169. Robertson, Mary F. "Swift's *Argument*: The Fact and the Fiction of Fighting with Beasts." *MP* 74(1976): 124-141.

15170. Rogers, Katharine. "'My Female Friends': The Mysogyny of Jonathan Swift."

TSLL 1(1959): 366-379.

15171. Rogers, Pat. "Form in *A Tale of a Tub*." *EIC* 22(1972): 142-160.

15172. ----------. "Gulliver and the Engineers." *MLR* 70(1975): 260-270.

15173. Roscelli, William John. "*A Tale of a Tub* and the 'Cavils of the Sour.'" *JEGP* 64(1965): 41-56.

15174. Rosenheim, Edward, Jr. "The Fifth Voyage of Lemuel Gulliver: A Footnote." *MP* 60 (1962): 103-119.

15175. ----------. "A 'Source' for the Rope-Dancing in *Gulliver's Travels*." *PQ* 31(1952): 208-211.

15176. ----------. "Swift and the Martyred Monarch." *PQ* 54(1975): 178-194.

15177. ----------. "Swift's *Ode to Sancroft*: Another Look." *MP* 73(1976): S24-S39.

15178. ----------. "The Text and Context of Swift's *Contests and Dissentions*." *MP* 66 (1968): 59-74.

15179. Ryley, Robert M. "Gulliver, Flimnap's Wife, and the Critics." *SLI* 5,#2(1972): 53-63.

15180. Sams, Henry W. "An End to Writing about Swift." *EIC* 24(1974): 275-285.

15181. ----------. "Swift's Satire of the Second Person." *ELH* 26(1959): 36-44.

15182. Samuel, Irene. "Swift's Reading of Plato." *SP* 73(1976): 440-462.

15183. Schakel, Peter J. "The Politics of Opposition in 'Verses on the Death of Dr. Swift.'" *MLQ* 35(1974): 246-256.

15184. ----------. "Swift's 'dapper clerk' and the Matrix of Allusion in 'Cadenus and Vanessa.'" *Criticism* 17(1975): 246-261.

15185. ----------. "Virgil and the Dean: Christian and Classical Allusion in *The Legion Club*." *SP* 70(1973): 427-438.

15186. Scouten, Arthur H., and Robert D. Hume. "Pope and Swift: Text and Interpretation of Swift's Verses on His Death." *PQ* 52(1973): 205-231.

15187. Scruggs, Charles. "Swift's Use of Lucretius in *A Tale of a Tub*." *TSLL* 15(1973): 39-49.

15188. ----------. "Swift's Views on Language: The Basis of His Attack on Poetic Diction." *TSLL* 13(1972): 581-592.

15189. Seelye, John D. "Hobbes' *Leviathan* and the Giantism Complex in the First Book of *Gulliver's Travels*." *JEGP* 60(1961): 228-239.

15190. Sena, John F. "Swift as Moral Physician: Scatology and the Tradition of Love Melancholy." *JEGP* 76(1977): 346-362.

15191. Seronsy, Cecil. "Sir Politic Would-Be in Laputa." *ELN* 1(1963): 17-24.

15192. Shaw, Sheila. "The Rape of Gulliver: Case Study of a Source." *PMLA* 90(1975): 62-68.

15193. Sherburn, George. "The 'Copies of Verse' about Gulliver." *TSLL* 3(1961): 3-7.

15194. ----------. "Errors concerning the Houyhnhnms." *MP* 56(1958): 92-97.

15195. Slepian, Barry. "The Ironic Intention of Swift's Verses on his Own Death." *RES* 14 (1963): 249-256.

15196. Smith, Frederick N. "The Epistemology of Fictional Failure: Swift's *Tale of a Tub* and Beckett's *Watt*." *TSLL* 15(1974): 649-672.

15197. ----------. "Swift's Correspondence: The 'Dramatic' Style and the Assumption of Roles." *SEL* 14(1974): 357-371.

15198. Smith, Roland M. "Swift's Little Language and Nonsense Names." *JEGP* 53(1954): 178-196.

15199. Spiller, Michael R. G. "The Idol of the Stove: The Background to Swift's Criticism of Descartes." *RES* 25(1974): 15-25.

15200. Thorpe, Annette P. "Jonathan Swift's Prescriptions Concerning the English Language." *CLA* 3(1960): 173-180.

15201. Timpe, Eugene F. "Swift as Railleur." *JEGP* 69(1970): 41-49.

15202. Torchiana, Donald T. "Jonathan Swift, the Irish, and the Yahoos: The Case Reconsidered." *PQ* 54(1975): 195-212.

15203. ----------. "W. B. Yeats, Jonathan Swift, and Liberty." *MP* 61(1963): 26-39.

15204. Traugott, John. "The Refractory Swift." *MLQ* 25(1964): 205-211.

15205. Treadwell, J. M. "Jonathan Swift: The Satirist as Projector." *TSLL* 17(1975): 439-460.

15206. Tyne, James L., S. J. "Gulliver's Maker and Gullibility." *Criticism* 7(1965): 151-167.

15207. ----------. "Vanessa and the Houyhnhnms: A Reading of 'Cademus and Vanessa.'" *SEL* 11(1971): 517-534.

15208. Uphaus, Robert W. "Swift's 'Whole character': The Delany Poems and 'Verses on the Death of Dr. Swift.'" *MLQ* 34(1973): 406-416.

15209. ----------. "From Panegyric to Satire: Swift's Early Odes and *A Tale of a Tub*." *TSLL* 13(1971): 55-70.

15210. Van Meter, Jan R., and Leland D. Peterson. "On Peterson on Swift." *PMLA* 86 (1971): 1017-1025.

15211. Waingrow, Marshall. "*Verses on the Death of Dr. Swift*." *SEL* 5(1965): 513-518.

15212. Wasiolek, Edward. "Relativity in *Gulliver's Travels*." *PQ* 37(1958): 110-116.

15213. White, Douglas H. "Swift and the Definition of Man." *MP* 73(1976): S48-S55.

15214. White, John H. "Swift's Trojan Horses: 'Reasoning But to Err.'" *ELN* 3(1966): 185-194.

15215. Williams, Kathleen M. "'Animal Rationis Capax.' A Study of Certain Aspects of Swift's Imagery." *ELH* 21(1954): 193-207.

15216. ----------. "Gulliver's Voyage to the Houyhnhnms." *ELH* 18(1951): 275-286.

15217. ----------. "Restoration Themes in the Major Satires of Swift." *RES* 16(1965): 258-271.

15218. Wood, James O. "Gulliver and the Monkey of Tralee." *SEL* 9(1969): 415-426.

15219. Woodring, Carl R. "The Aims, Audience, and Structure of the Drapier's Fourth Letter." *MLQ* 17(1956): 50-59.

15220. Zimmerman, Everett. "Gulliver the Preacher." *PMLA* 89(1974): 1024-1032.

See also 272, 7780, 11425, 13634, 14419, 14579, 14585, 19874, 19933, 20157.

SWIFT, THOMAS. 15221. Adams, Robert Martin. "Jonathan Swift, Thomas Swift, and the Authorship of *A Tale of a Tub*." *MP* 64

(1967): 198-232.

15222. Nandy, Dipak. "Jonathan Swift, Thomas Swift, and the Authorship of *A Tale of a Tub*." *MP* 66(1969): 333-337.

TATE, NAHUM. 15223. Black, James. "The Influence of Hobbes on Nahum Tate's *King Lear*." *SEL* 7(1967): 377-385.

15224. Green, Lawrence D. "'Where's My Fool?'—Some Consequences of the Omission of the Fool in Tate's *Lear*." *SEL* 12(1972): 259-274.

15225. Spencer, Christopher. "A Word for Tate's *King Lear*." *SEL* 3(1963): 241-251.

THEOBALD, LEWIS. 15226. Dearing, Vinton A. "Pope, Theobald, and Wycherley's *Posthumous Works*." *PMLA* 68(1953): 223-236.

15227. Frazier, Harriet C. "Theobald's *The Double Falsehood*: A Revision of Shakespeare's *Cardenis*?" *CD* 1(1967): 219-233.

15228. Woods, Charles B. "Theobald and Fielding's Don Tragedio." *ELN* 2(1965): 266-271.

THOMSON, JAMES. 15229. Campbell, Hilbert H. "Thomson and the Countess of Hertford Yet Again." *MP* 67(1970): 367-369.

15230. ----------. "Thomson's *Seasons*, the Countess of Hertford, and Elizabeth Young: A Footnote to *The Unfolding of the Seasons*." *TSLL* 14(1972): 435-444.

15231. Cohen, Ralph. "*Spring*: The Love Song of James Thomson." *TSLL* 11(1969): 1107-1182.

15232. Cooke, Arthur L. "James Thomson and William Hinchliffe." *JEGP* 57(1958): 755-761.

15233. Kern, Jean B. "James Thomson's Revisions of *Agamemnon*." *PQ* 45(1966): 289-303.

15234. Marsh, Robert. "The Seasons of Discrimmation." *MP* 64(1967): 238-252.

15235. McKillop, Alan D. "The Early History of *Alfred*." *PQ* 41(1962): 311-324.

15236. ----------. "The Early History of Thomson's *Liberty*." *MLQ* 11(1950): 307-316.

15237. ----------. "Thomson and the Jail Committee." *SP* 47(1950): 62-71.

15238. ----------. "Thomson and the Licensers of the Stage." *PQ* 37(1958): 448-453.

15239. ----------. "Two More Thomson Letters." *MP* 60(1962): 128-130.

15240. Sherbo, Arthur. "Solomon Mendes, A Friend of the Poets." [with text of a letter by Thomson] *PQ* 36(1957): 508-511.

15241. Spacks, Patricia M. "Vision and Meaning in James Thomson." *SR* 4(1965): 206-219.

15242. Werkmeister, Lucyle. "Thomson and the London Daily Press, 1789-97." *MP* 62(1965): 237-240.

See also 13538, 13559, 13627, 14380.

THORNTON, BONNELL. 15243. Brown, Wallace Cable. "A Belated Augustan: Bonnell Thornton, Esq." *PQ* 34(1955): 335-348.

15244. Lams, Victor J., Jr. "The 'A' Papers in the *Adventurer*: Bonnell Thornton, not Dr. Bathurst, Their Author." *SP* 64(1967): 83-96.

TOPLADY, AUGUSTUS MONTAGUE. 15245. Howell, Almonte C. "Augustus Toplady and Quarles' Emblems." *SP* 57(1960): 178-185.

TRAPP, JOSEPH. 15246. Freimarck, Vincent. "Joseph Trapp's Advanced Conception of Metaphor." *PQ* 29(1950): 413-417.

TUTCHIN, JOHN. 15247. Horsley, L. S. "Rogues or Honest Gentlemen: The Public Characters of Queen Anne Journalists." *TSLL* 18(1976): 198-228.

TWINING, THOMAS. 15248. Malek, James. "Thomas Twining's Analysis of Poetry and Music as Imitative Arts." *MP* 68(1971): 260-268.

TYRWHITT, THOMAS. 15249. Starnes, Dewitt T. "Thomas Tyrwhitt's Copy of Polydore Vergil's *De Inventoribus Rerum*." *TSLL* 7(1965): 255-263.

WALKER, GEORGE. 15250. Harvey, A. D. "George Walker and the Anti-Revolutionary Novel." *RES* 28(1977): 290-300.

WALLACE, ROBERT. 15251. Smith, Norah. "Robert Wallace's 'Of Venery.'" *TSLL* 15(1973): 429-444.

WALPOLE, HORACE. 15252. Bennett, Charles H. "The Text of Horace Walpole's Correspondence with Hannah More." *RES* 3(1952): 341-345.

15253. Conolly, L. W. "Horace Walpole, Unofficial Play Censor." *ELN* 9(1971): 42-46.

15254. Walpole, Horace. "Exhumations II: Horace Walpole's 'Thoughts on Comedy.'" *EIC* 15 (1965): 162-170.

WALSH, WILLIAM. 15255. Freeman, Phyllis. "Two Fragments of Walsh Manuscripts." *RES* 8 (1957): 390-401.

WARBURTON, WILLIAM. 15256. Cherpack, Clifton. "Warburton and Some Aspects of the Search for the Primitive in Eighteenth-Century France." *PQ* 36(1957): 221-233.

15257. ----------. "Warburton and the *Encyclopédie*." *Comp L* 7(1955): 226-239.

See also 13634.

WARTON, JOSEPH. 15258. Fenner, Arthur, Jr. "The **Wartons 'Romanticize" Their Verse**." *SP* 53(1956): 501-508.

5259. Hysham, Julia. "Joseph Warton's Reputation as a Poet." *SR* 1(1962): 220-229.

15260. Morris, David B. "Joseph Warton's Figure of Virtue: Poetic Indirection in 'The Enthusiast.'" *PQ* 50(1971): 678-683.

15261. Pittock, Joan. "Joseph Warton and His Second Volume of the *Essay on Pope*." *RES* 18 (1967): 264-273.

WARTON, THOMAS. 15262. Sambrook, A. J. "Thomas Warton's *German Eclogues*." *RES* 20 (1969): 61-62.

See also 15258, 16269.

WARTON, THOMAS (the elder). 15263. Fairer, David. "The Poems of Thomas Warton the Elder?" *RES* 26(1975): 287-300, 395-406.

WATTS, ISAAC. 15264. Steese, Peter B. "Dennis's Influence on Watts's Preface to *Horae Lyricae*." *PQ* 42(1963): 275-277.

See also 1847, 11437.

WEBB, DANIEL. See 13624.

WESLEY, JOHN. 15265. Sherwin, Oscar. "Milton for the Masses: John Wesley's Edition of *Paradise Lost*." *MLQ* 12(1951): 267-285.

WOLLSTONECRAFT, MARY. 15266. Hickey, Damon D. "Mary Wollstonecraft and *The Female Reader*." *ELN* 13(1975): 128-129.

15267. Sulloway, Alison G. "Emma Woodhouse and *A Vindication of the Rights of Women*." *WC* 7(1976): 320-332.

YOUNG, EDWARD. 15286. Forster, H. B. "The Ordination of Edward Young" *ELN* 1(1963): 24-28.

15296. Hall, Mary S. "On Light in Young's *Night Thoughts*." *PQ* 48(1969): 452-463.

15270. Odell, D. W. "Locke, Cudworth, and Young's *Night Thoughts*." *ELN* 4(1967): 188-193.

15271. ----------. Young's *Night Thoughts* as an Answer to Pope's *Essay on Man*." *SEL* 12(1972):

481-501.

15272. Stevens, Irma Ned. "Beckett's 'Texts for Nothing': An Inversion of Young's 'Night-Thoughts.'" *SSF* 11(1974): 131-139.

See also 13755.

NINETEENTH CENTURY

GENERAL. 15273. Badger, Kingsbury. "Christianity and Victorian Religious Confessions." *MLQ* 15(1964): 86-101.

15274. Ball, Patricia. "Sincerity: The Rise and Fall of a Critical Term." *MLR* 58(1963): 1-12.

15275. Banta, Martha. "Adonais and the Angle: Light, Color, and the Occult Sublime." *WC* 8(1977): 113-120.

15276. Bloom, Harold. "First and Last Romantics." *SR* 9(1970): 225-233.

15277. Boas, George. "The Romantic Self: An Historical Sketch." *SR* 4(1964): 1-16.

15278. Bosse, Heinrich. "The Marvellous and Romantic Semiotics." *SR* 14(1975): 211-236.

15279. Chaffee, Alan J. "The Rendezvous of Mind." *WC* 3(1972): 196-203.

15280. Chapman, R. W. "The Reading Public in 1803." *RES* 1(1950): 144-145.

15281. Curnow, Wystan. "Romanticism and Modern American Criticism." *SR* 12(1973): 777-799.

15282. Dijkstra, Bram. "The Androgyne in Nineteenth-Century Art and Literature." *Comp L* 26(1974): 62-73.

15283. Foerster, Donald M. "The Critical Attack upon the Epic in the English Romantic Movement." *PMLA* 69(1954): 432-447.

15284. Fredeman, William E. "Impediments and Motives: Biography as Unfair Sport." *MP* 70 (1972): 149-154.

15285. Furst, Lillian. "The Romantic Hero, or Is He an Anti-Hero." *SLI* 9,#1(1976): 53-67.

15286. Garber, Frederick. "Nature and the Romantic Mind: Egotism, Empathy, Irony." *Comp L* 29(1977): 193-212.

15287. Gray, Donald J. "Humor as Poetry in Nineteenth-Century English Criticism." *JEGP* 61(1962): 249-257.

15288. Griest, G. "A Victorian Leviathan: Mudie's Select Library." *NCF* 20(1965): 103-126.

15289. Harper, Kenneth E, and B. A. Booth. "Russian Translations of Nineteenth-Century English Fiction." *NCF* 8(1953): 188-197.

15290. Harris, R. J. "Emilia Francis Strong: Portraits of a Lady." *NCF* 8(1953): 81-98.

15291. Hartman, Geoffrey. "Theories on the Theory of Romanticism." *WC* 2(1971): 51-56.

15292. Harvey, W. J. "Some Notes on the Study of Nineteenth-Century Literature." *MLQ* 26 (1965): 93-110.

15293. Havens, Raymond D. "Discontinuity in Literary Development: The Case of English Romanticism." *SP* 47(1950): 102-111.

15294. Holloway, John. "Thought, Style and the Idea of Co-Variance in Some Mid-Nineteenth-Century Prose." *SLI* 8,#2(1975): 1-14.

15295. Jackson, Wallace. "Sincerity: A Postscript on Antecedents and Correlatives." *MLR* 61(1966): 355-356.

15296. Keith, Sara. "Mudie's Circulating Library." *NCF* 11(1956): 156-157.

15297. Maniquis, Robert M. "The Puzzling *Mimosa*: Sensitivity and Plant Symbols in Roman-

ticism." *SR* 8(1969): 129-155.

15298. McGann, Jerome J. "The Beauty of the Medusa: A Study in Romantic Literary Iconography." *SR* 11(1972): 3-25.

15299. ----------. "Romanticism and the Embarrassements of Critical Tradition." *MP* 70 (1973): 243-257.

15300. Merriman, James. "The Other Arthurians in Victorian England." *PQ* 56(1977): 249-253.

15301. Monsman, Gerald C. "Old Morality at Oxford." *SP* 67(1970): 359-389.

15302. Nadelhaft, Janice. "*Punch* and the Syncretics: An Early Victorian Prologue to the Aesthetic Movement." *SEL* 15(1975): 627-640.

15303. Peckman, Morse. "On Romanticism." *SR* 9(1970): 217-224.

15304. ----------. "Towards a Theory of Romanticism: II. Reconsiderations." *SR* 1(1961): 1-8.

15305. Reed, John R. "Emblems in Victorian Literature." *HSL* 2(1970): 19-39.

15306. ----------. "The Public Schools in Victorian Literature." *NCF* 29(1974): 58-76.

15307. Rinehart, Keith. "The Victorian Approach to Autobiography." *MP* 51(1954): 177-186.

15308. Robinson, James K. "A Neglected Phase of the Aesthetic Movement: English Parnassianism." *PMLA* 68(1953): 733-754.

15309. Rockwell, Frederick S. "More About Wife-Selling." *NCF* 5(1951): 329.

15310. Rulfs, Donald J. "The Romantic Writers and Edmund Kean." *MLQ* 11(1950): 425-437.

15311. San Juan, E., Jr. "Toward a Definition of Victorian Activism." *SEL* 4(1964): 583-600.

15312. Shea, F. X., S.J. "Religion and the Romantic Movement." *SR* 9(1970): 285-296.

15313. Taylor, Anya. "The Occult and Romanticism." *WC* 8(1977): 97-102.

15314. Thorslev, Peter. "Romantic Writers and the Now Generation." *WC* 2(1971): 42-45.

15315. Wasserman, Earl. "The English Romantics: The Grounds of Knowledge." *SR* 4(1964): 17-34.

15316. Wellek, René. "German and English Romanticism: A Confrontation." *SR* 4(1964): 35-56.

15317. Woodring, Carl. "Nature and Art in the Nineteenth Century." *PMLA* 92(1977): 193-202.

15318. Zall, Paul M. "Lord Eldon's Censorship." *PMLA* 68(1953): 436-443.

DRAMA. 15319. Culler, A. Dwight. "Monodrama and the Dramatic Monologue." *PMLA* 90(1975): 366-385.

15320. Ganzel, Dewey. "Patent Wrongs and Patent Theatres: Drama and the Law in the Early Nineteenth Century." *PMLA* 76(1961): 384-396.

15321. Herring, Paul D. "Nineteenth-Century Drama." *MP* 68(1970): 83-90.

15322. Stratman, Carl J. "English Tragedy: 1819-1823." [checklist] *PQ* 41(1962): 465-474.

FICTION. 15323. Brantlinger, Patrick. "Bluebook, the Social Organism, and the Victorian Novel." *Criticism* 14(1972): 328-344.

15324. Brightfield, Myron F. "America and the Americans, 1840-1860, as Depicted in English Novels of the Period." *AL* 31(1959): 309-324.

15325. Bostrom, Irene. "The Novel and Catholic Emancipation." *SR* 2(1963): 155-176.

15326. Colburn, William E. "Victorian Translations of Zola." *SLI* 1,#2(1968): 23-32.

15327. Elsbree, Langdon. "The Purest and Most Perfect Form of Play: Some Novelists and the Dance." *Criticism* 14(1972): 361-372.

15328. Folsom, James K. "English Westerns." *WAL* 2(1967): 3-13.

15329. Garrett, Peter K. "Double Plots and Dialogical Form in Victorian Fiction." *NCF* 32 (1977): 1-17.

15330. Graham, John. "Character Description and Meaning in the Romantic Novel." *SR* 5(1966): 208-218.

15331. Harris, Wendell V. "English Short Fiction in the Nineteenth-Century." *SSF* 6(1968): 1-93.

15332. ----------. "John Lane's Keynotes Series and the Fiction of the 1890's." *PMLA* 83 (1968): 1407-1413.

15333. Haworth, H. E. "Romantic Female Writers and the Critics." *TSLL* 17(1976): 725-736.

15334. Hume, Robert D. "Gothic versus Romantic: A Revaluation of the Gothic Novel." *PMLA* 84(1969): 282-290.

15335. Keech, James M. "The Survival of the Gothic Response." *SN* 6(1974): 130-144.

15336. Killham, John. "The Idea of Community in the English Novel." *NCF* 31(1977): 379-396.

15337. Knoepflmacher, U. C. "Review-Essay: Reprinting Religious Novels: Losses or Gain?" *SN* 9(1977): 217-222.

15338. Laski, Audrey L. "Myths of Character: As Aspects of the Novel." *NCF* 14(1960): 333-343.

15339. Millhauser, Milton. "Dr. Newton and Mr. Hyde: Scientists in Fiction from Swift to Stevenson." *NCF* 28(1973): 287-304.

15340. Mitchell, Sally. "Implications of Realism: Four Stories From *The London Journal*." *SSF* 12(1975): 145-154.

15341. Moynahan, Julian. "Pastoralism as Culture and Counter-Culture in English Fiction, 1800-1928: From a View to a Death." *Novel* 6(1972): 20-35.

15342. Orel, Harold. "The First Russian Novels in Victorian England." *NCF* 9(1954): 228-231.

15343. Platzner, Robert L, and Robert D. Hume. "'Gothic versus Romantic': A Rejoinder." *PMLA* 86(1971): 266-274.

15344. Polsgrove, Carol. "They Made It Pay: British Short Fiction Writers, 1820-1840." *SSF* 11(1974): 417-421.

15345. Rosengarten, Herbert. "'From the Social Side': Two Studies of Nineteenth-Century Fiction." *MLQ* 38(1977): 381-389.

15346. Smith, Sheila M. "Blue Books and Victorian Novelists." *RES* 21(1970): 23-40.

15347. Stevenson, Lionel. "Darwin and the Novel." *NCF* 15(1960): 29-38.

15348. ----------. "The Modern Values of Victorian Fiction." *CLA* 4(1960): 1-7.

15349. ----------. "The Rationale of Victorian Fiction." *NCF* 27(1973): 391-404.

15350. Weintraub, Stanley. "Ibsen's Doll's House Metaphor Foreshadowed in Victorian Fiction." *NCF* 13(1958): 67-69.

PERIODICALS. 15351. Buckler, William E. "*Once a Week* under Samuel Lucas, 1859-65." *PMLA* 67(1952): 924-941.

15352. Carnall, Geoffrey. "The *Monthly Magazine*." *RES* 5(1954): 158-164.

15353. Colby, Robert A. "'How it Strikes a Contemporary': *The Spectator* as Critic." *NCF* 11 (1956): 182-206.

15354. Fenner, Theodore. "Edward Quin and the *Traveller*." *SR* 14(1975): 133-164.

15355. Jump, J. D. "Weekly Reviewing in the Eighteen-Sixties." *RES* 3(1952): 244-262.

15356. Maurer, Oscar. "*Punch* and the Opera War, 1847-1867." *TSLL* 1(1959): 139-170.

15357. Milhauser, Milton. "The Literary Impact of *Vestiges of Creation*." *MLQ* 17(1956): 213-226.

15358. Osbourn, R. V. "*The British Quarterly Review*." *RES* 1(1950): 147-152.

15359. Vivian, Charles H. "Radical Journalism in the 1830's: The *True Sun* and *Weekly True Sun*." *MLQ* 15(1954): 222-232.

POETRY. 15360. Amis, Kingley. "Communication and the Victorian Poet." *EIC* 4(1954): 386-399.

15361. Bauer, N. Stephen. "Romantic Poetry and the Unstamped Political Press, 1830-1836." *SR* 14(1975): 411-424.

15362. Bose, A. "The Verse of the English 'Annuals.'" *RES* 4(1953): 38-51.

15363. Chayes, Irene H. "Rhetoric as Drama: An Approach to the Romantic Ode." *PMLA* 79(1964): 67-79.

15364. Doggett, Frank. "Romanticism's Singing Bird." *SEL* 14(1974): 547-561.

15365. Dudley, Fred A. "Dating the Term 'Lake School.'" *ELN* 1(1964): 267-270.

15366. Duffy, Edward. "The Cunning Spontaneities of Romanticism." *WC* 3(1972): 232-240.

15367. Eskin, Stanley G. "Revolution and Poetry: Some Political Patterns in the Romantic Tradition and After." *CLA* 11(1968): 189-205.

15368. Ewbank, David R. "Kidding the Victorian Poets: A Collection of Parodies." *VP* 15 (1977): 66-74.

15369. Foerster, Donald M. "Critical Approval of Epic Poetry in the Age of Wordsworth." *PMLA* 70(1955): 682-705.

15370. Forsyth, R. A. "The Myth of Nature and Victorian Compromise of the Imagination." *ELH* 31(1964): 213-240.

15371. Harvey, A. D. "The English Epic in the Romantic Period." *PQ* 55(1976): 241-259.

15372. Langbaum, Robert. "Review Article: Victorians Reconsidered." *EIC* 20(1970): 451-465.

15373. Lindenberger, Herbert. "On Commentary, Romanticism, and Critical Method." *MLQ* 27 (1966): 212-220.

15374. Merivale, Patricia. "The Pan Figure in Victorian Poetry: Landor to Meredith." *PQ* 44 (1965): 258-277.

15375. Miles, Josephine. "The Romantic Mode in Poetry." *ELH* 20(1953): 29-38.

15376. Omans, Glen. "The Villon Cult in England." *Comp L* 18(1966): 16-35.

15377. Peters, Robert L. "Whistler and the English Poets of the 1890's." *MLQ* 18(1957): 251-261.

15378. Prince, Jeffrey R. "The Iconic Poem and the Aesthetic Tradition." *ELH* 43(1976): 567-583.

15379. Selkirk, J. B. "Exhumations IV: Extracts from J. B. Selkirk's *Ethics and Aesthetics of Modern Poetry*." *EIC* 16(1966): 73-85.

15380. Starzyk, Lawrence J. "'The Fiery Consciousness of His Own Activity': The Poet as Outcast in Early Victorian Poetic Theory." *TSLL* 16(1974): 109-134.

15381. Swingle, L. J. "On Reading Romantic Poetry." *PMLA* 86(1971): 974-981.

15382. ----------. "Romantic Unity and English Romantic Poetry." *JEGP* 74(1975): 361-374.

15383. Taylor, Dennis. "Natural Supernaturalism's New Clothes." *WC* 5(1974): 33-40.

15384. Throslev, Peter L., Jr. "The Romantic Mind." *Comp L* 15(1963): 250-268.

15385. Warburg, Jeremy. "Poetry and Industrialism: Some Refractory Material in Nineteenth-Century and Later English Verse." *MLR* 53(1958): 161-170.

15386. Winchester, Otis. "The Victorian Autumnal-Evening Pastoral." *VP* 6(1968): 184.

ADAMS, FRANCIS W. L.   15387. Arinshtein, Leonid M. "A Francis William Lauderdale Adams Unknown Poem." *VP* 7(1969): 55-56.

AINSWORTH, WILLIAM.   15388. Ligocki, Llewellyn. "Ainsworth's Tudor Novels: History as Theme." *SN* 4(1972): 364-377.

ARNOLD, EDWIN.   15389. Clausen, Christopher. "Sir Edwin Arnold's Lost Last Poem." *ELN* 14(1977): 197-201.

ARNOLD, MATTHEW.   15390. Alaya, Flavia M. "'Two Worlds' Revisited: Arnold, Renan, The Monastic Life, and the 'Stanzas from the Grande Chartreuse.'" *VP* 5(1967): 237-254.

15391. Alexander, Edward. "Arnold, Ruskin, and the Hanwell Insane Asylum." *ELN* 9(1971): 53-55.

15392. ----------; Addendum by Kenneth Allott. "A Note on the Date and Meaning of 'The New Sirens.'" *VP* 8(1970): 347-349.

15393. Allott, Kenneth. "An Allusion to Pope in an Early Unpublished Arnold Letter." *VP* 7(1969): 70-71.

15394. ----------. "Matthew Arnold's 'Stagirius' and Saint-Marc Girardin." *RES* 9 (1958): 286-292.

15395. ----------. "Matthew Arnold's 'The Neckan': The Real Issues." *VP* 2(1964): 60-63.

15396. ----------. "Matthew Arnold's 'The New Sirens' and George Sand." *VP* 1(1963): 156-158.

15397. ----------. "Pater and Arnold." *EIC* 2(1952): 219-221.

15398. ----------. "The 'Scythian' in 'The Strayed Reveller." *VP* 11(1973): 163-166.

15399. Armytage, W. H. G. "Matthew Arnold and a Reviewer." *RES* 6(1955): 297.

15400. ----------. "Matthew Arnold and T. H. Huxley: Some New Letters 1870-80." *RES* 4 (1953): 346-353.

15401. Balliet, Conrad A. "'Growing Old' along with 'Rabbi Ben Ezra.'" *VP* 1(1963): 300-301.

15402. Barksdale, Richard K. "Arnold and Tennyson on Etna." *CLA* 2(1958): 87-103.

15403. Bateson, F. W. "The Fuction of Criticism at the Present Time." *EIC* 3(1953): 1-27.

150404. Becht, Ronald E. "Matthew Arnold's 'Switzerland': The Drama of Choice." *VP* 13(1975): 35-46.

15405. Bevington, Merle M. "Matthew Arnold and John Bright: A Typographical Error and Some Ironic Consequences." *PMLA* 70(1955): 543-548.

15406. Blount, Paul G. "Matthew Arnold on Wordsworth." *SLI* 1,#1(1968): 3-11.

15407. Broadbent, J. B. "Milton and Arnold." *EIC* 6(1956): 404-417.

15408. Broderick, James H. "Two Notes on Arnold's 'Grand Chartreuse.'" *MP* 66(1968): 157-162.

15409. Brooks, Roger L. "'A Deptford Poet': An Addition and a Correction to the Matthew Arnold Bibliography." *PQ* 41(1962): 515-517.

15410. ----------. "The Genesis of Matthew Arnold's 'Thyrsis.'" *RES* 14(1963): 172-174.

15411. ----------. "Letters of Matthew Arnold: A Supplementary Checklist." *SP* 63(1966): 93-98.

15412. ----------. "Matthew Arnold and His Contemporaries: A Check List of Unpublished and Published Letters." *SP* 56(1959): 647-653.

15413. ----------. "Matthew Arnold and the *London Review*." *PMLA* 76(1961): 622-623.

15414. ----------. "Matthew Arnold and the *Pall Mall Gazette*." *MP* 58(1961): 202-203.

15415. ----------. "Matthew Arnold and Ticknor & Fields." *AL* 35(1964): 514-519.

15416. ----------. "A Matthew Arnold Letter to James Russell Lowell: The Reason for the American Lecture Tour." *AL* 31(1959): 336-338.

15417. ----------. "Matthew Arnold's 'A Few Words about the Education Act': A Signed, Unrecorded, and Uncollected Article." *MP* 66(1969): 262-264.

15418. ----------. "Matthew Arnold's Correspondence." *MP* 59(1962): 273-275.

15419. ----------. "Matthew Arnold's Revision of *Tristram and Iseult*: Some Instances of Clough's Influence." *VP* 2(1964): 57-60.

15420. ----------. "Matthew Arnold's 'Sohrab and Rustum': An Oriental Detail." *ELN* 4 (1967): 198-199.

15421. ----------. "A New Source for Matthew Arnold's 'Sohrab and Rustum." *PQ* 42(1963): 129-131.

15422. ----------. "'A Septuagenarian Poet': An Addition to the Matthew Arnold Bibliography." *MP* 57(1960): 262-263.

15423. Bruns, Gerald L. "The Formal Nature of Victorian Thinking." *PMLA* 90(1975): 904-918.

15424. Buckler, William E. "An American Edition of Matthew Arnold's Poems." *PMLA* 69(1954): 678-680.

15425. ----------. "Matthew Arnold in America: The 'Reason.'" *AL* 29(1958): 464-470.

15426. ----------. "Studies in Three Arnold Problems." *PMLA* 73(1958): 260-269.

15427. Burwick, Fred L. "Hölderlin and Arnold: *Empelocles on Etna*." *Comp L* 17(1965): 24-42.

15428. Cadbury, William. "Coming to Terms with 'Dover Beach.'" *Criticism* 8(1966): 126-138.

15429. Carnall, Geoffrey. "Matthew Arnold's 'Great Critical Effort.'" *EIC* 8(1958): 256-268.

15430. Carrithers, Gale H., Jr. "Missing Persons on Dover Beach?" *MLQ* 26(1965): 264-266.

15431. Carroll, David R. "Arnold's Tyrian Trader and Grecian Coaster." *MLR* 64(1969): 27-33.

15432. Christensen, Merton A. "Thomas Arnold's Debt to German Theologians: A Prelude to Matthew Arnold's *Literature and Dogma*." *MP* 55

(1958): 14-20.

15433. Corner, Martin. "Arnold, Lessing, and the Preface of 1853." *JEGP* 72(1973): 223-235.

15434. Coursen, Herbert R., Jr. "'The Moon Lies Fair': The Poetry of Matthew Arnold." *SEL* 4 (1964): 569-581.

15435. Coulling, Sidney M. P. "The Evolution of *Culture and Anarchy*." *SP* 60(1963): 637-668.

15436. ----------. "The Background of 'The Function of Criticism at the Present Time.'" *PQ* 42(1963): 36-54.

15437. ----------. "Matthew Arnold and the *Daily Telegraph*." *RES* 12(1961): 173-179.

15438. ----------. "Swinburne and Arnold." *PQ* 49(1970): 211-233.

15439. Davis, Mary Byrd. "George Sand and the Poetry of Matthew Arnold." *TSLL* 19(1977): 204-226.

15440. ----------. "A Source for Arnold's Tale of Merlin and Vivian." *ELN* 14(1976): 120-123.

15441. DeLaura, David J. "Arnold and Carlyle." *PMLA* 79(1964): 104-129.

15442. ----------. "Arnold and Hazlitt." *ELN* 9(1972): 277-283.

15443. ----------. "Arnold, Clough, Dr. Arnold, and 'Thyrsis.'" *VP* 7(1969): 191-202.

15444. ----------. "Four Arnold Letters." [with text] *TSLL* 4(1962): 276-284.

15445. ----------. "Matthew Arnold and John Henry Newman: The 'Oxford Sentiment' and the Religion of the Future.'" *TSLL* 6(1965): 573-702.

15446. ----------. "What, Then, Does Matthew Arnold Mean?" *MP* 66(1969): 345-355.

15447. ----------. "The 'Wordsworth' of Pater and Arnold: 'The Supreme, Artistic View of Life.'" *SEL* 6(1966): 651-667.

15448. Dietrich, Manfred. "Arnold's *Empedocles on Etna* and the 1853 Preface." *VP* 14 (1976): 311-324.

15449. Donovan, Robert A. "The Method of Arnold's *Essays in Criticism*." *PMLA* 71(1956): 922-931.

15450. Douglas, Dennis. "Matthew Arnold's Historic Sense: The Conflict of Greek and Tyrian in 'The Scholar-Gipsy.'" *RES* 25(1974): 422-436.

15451. Dyson, A. E. "The Last Enchantments." *RES* 8(1957): 257-265.

15452. Ebel, Henry. "Matthew Arnold and Marcus Aurelius." *SEL* 3(1963): 555-566.

15453. Eggenschwiler, David L. "Arnold's Passive Questers." *VP* 5(1967): 1-11.

15454. Engelberg, Edward. "James and Arnold: Conscience and Consciousness in a Victorian 'Kunstlerroman.'" *Criticism* 10(1968): 93-115.

15455. Farmer, Andrew. "Arnold's Gipsy Reconsidered." *EIC* 22(1972): 64-73.

15456. Farrell, John P. "Matthew Arnold's Tragic Vision." *PMLA* 85(1970): 107-117.

15457. Feshbach, Sidney. "Empedocles at Dover Beach." *VP* 4(1966): 271-275.

15458. Forbes, George. "Arnold's 'Oracles.'" *EIC* 23(1973): 41-56.

15459. ----------. "Arnold's 'The World and the Quietist' and the *Bagavad Gita*." *Comp L* 25(1973): 153-160.

15460. ----------. "The Reluctant Lover and the World: Structure and Meaning in Arnold's 'Resignation' and 'Stanzas in Memory of the Author of *Obermann*.'" *SEL* 16(1976): 661-676.

15461. Forsyth, R. A. '"The Buried Life'— The Contrasting Views of Arnold and Clough in the Context of Dr. Arnold's Historiography." *ELH* 35 (1968): 218-253.

15462. Friedman, Norman. "The Young Matthew Arnold 1847-1849: Self, Art, and the World." *VP* 9 (1971): 405-428.

15463. Frierson, J. W. "The Strayed Reveller of Fox How." *VP* 5(1967): 137-140.

15464. Fulweiler, Howard W. "Matthew Arnold: The Metamorphosis of a Merman." *VP* 1(1963): 208-222.

15465. ----------. "The Real Issues in Arnold's 'The Neckan.'" *VP* 2(1964): 205-208.

15466. Giannone, Richard. "The Quest Motif in 'Thyrsis.'" *VP* 3(1965): 71-80.

15467. Giordano, Frank, Jr. "Rhythm and Rhyme in 'Self-Dependence.'" *ELN* 13(1975): 29-35.

15468. Godshalk, William L. "Autograph Fragments of Two Arnold Poems." *PMLA* 85(1970): 118-119.

15469. Gordon, Jan B. "Disenchantment with Intimations: A Reading of Arnold's 'In Utrumque Paratus.'" *VP* 3(1965): 192-196.

15470. Gottfried, Leon A. "Matthew Arnold's 'The Strayed Reveller.'" *RES* 11(1960): 403-409.

15471. Greenberg, Robert A. "Matthew Arnold's Mournful Rhymes: A Study of 'The World and the Quietist.'" *VP* 1(1963): 284-290.

15472. ----------. "Patterns of Imagery: Arnold's 'Shakespeare.'" *SEL* 5(1965): 723-733.

15473. Harris, Wendell V. "Arnold, Pater, Wilde, and the Object as Themselves They See It." *SEL* 11(1971): 733-747.

15474. ----------. "Eighteenth-Century Straws in Arnoldian Amber and a Conjecture 'How the Devil They Got There.'" *VP* 13(1975): 70-74.

15475. Holloway, John. "Matthew Arnold and the Modern Tradition." *EIC* 1(1951): 1-16.

15476. ----------. "Milton and Arnold." *EIC* 7(1957): 226-228.

15477. Honan, Park. "Matthew Arnold and Cacaphony." *VP* 1(1963): 115-122.

15478. Hornstein, Lillian Herlands. "'Rugby Chapel' and Exodus." *MLR* 47(1952): 208-209.

15479. Hubenthal, John. "'Growing Old,' 'Rabbi Ben Ezra,' and 'Tears, Idle Tears.'" *VP* 3(1965): 61-63.

15480. Johnson, W. Stacy. "Matthew Arnold's Sea of Life." *PQ* 31(1952): 195-207.

15481. Kau, Joseph. "'In Utrumque Paratus': Impresa of the Stoic." *VP* 10(1972): 181-184.

15482. Kendall, J. L. "The Unity of Arnold's *Tristram and Iseult*." *VP* 1(1963): 140-145.

15483. Kerpneck, Harvey. "'Kings of Modern Thought.'" *MLQ* 24(1963): 392-395.

15484. Knight, G. Wilson. "*The Scholar Gypsy*: An Interpretation." *RES* 6(1955): 53-62.

15485. Knoepflmacher, U. C. "Dover Revisited: The Wordsworthian Matrix in the Poetry of Matthew Arnold." *VP* 1(1963): 17-26.

15486. Lee, Robert A. "James Baldwin and Matthew Arnold: Thoughts on 'Relevance.'" *CLA*

14(1971): 324-330.

15487. Lowe, Robert Liddell. "A Further Note on Arnold in America." *AL* 30(1959): 530-533.

15488. ----------. "A Note on Arnold in America." *AL* 23(1951): 250-252.

15489. ----------. "Two Arnold Letters." *MP* 52(1955): 262-264.

15490. Lubell, Albert J. "Matthew Arnold: Between Two Worlds." *MLQ* 22(1961): 248-263.

15491. Maider, Francine B. "Matthew Arnold and the Circle of Recurrence." *VP* 14(1976): 293-310.

15492. Mainwaring, Marion. "Arnold and Tolstoi." *NCF* 6(1952): 269-274.

15493. ----------. "Notes Toward a Matthew Arnold Bibliography." *MP* 49(1952): 189-194.

15494. Maxwell, J. C. "'One Who Most Has Suffered': Arnold and Leopardi." *RES* 6(1955): 182-188.

15495. Mazzaro, Jerome L. "Corydon in Matthew Arnold's 'Thyrsis.'" *VP* 1(1963): 304-306.

15496. McCarrow, William E. "Warren's *All the King's Men* and Arnold's 'To Marguerite—Continued.'" *AL* 47(1975): 115-116.

15497. McCarthy, Patrick J. "Mrs. Matthew Arnold." *TSLL* 12(1971): 647-662.

15498. Mermin, Dorothy M. "The Two Worlds in Arnold's 'The Strayed Reveller.'" *SEL* 12 (1972): 735-743.

15499. Middlebrook, Jonathan. "'Resignation,' 'Rugby Chapel,' and Thomas Arnold." *VP* 8(1970): 291-298.

15500. Moyer, Charles R. "The Idea of History in Thomas and Matthew Arnold." *MP* 67(1969): 160-167.

15501. Nagarajan, S. "Arnold and the *Bhagavad Gita*: A Reinterpretation of *Empedocles on Etna*." *Comp L* 12(1960): 335-347.

15502. Neiman, Fraser. "Some Newly Attributed Contributions of Matthew Arnold to the *Pall Mall Gazette*." *MP* 55(1957): 84-92.

15503. ----------. "The Zeitgeist of Matthew Arnold." *PMLA* 72(1957): 977-996.

15504. Pitman, Ruth. "On Dover Beach." *EIC* 23(1973): 109-136.

15505. Plotinsky, Melvin L. "Help for Pain: The Narrative Verse of Matthew Arnold." *VP* 2(1964): 165-177.

15506. Perkins, David. "Arnold and the Function of Literature." *ELH* 18(1951): 287-309.

15507. Peterson, William S. "'Rugby Chapel' and *Tom Brown's School-Days*." *ELN* 3(1966): 204-206.

15508. Racin, John. "'Dover Beach' and the Structure of Meditation." *VP* 8(1970): 49-55.

15509. Raisor, Philip. "Matthew Arnold's 'Balder Dead': An Exercise in Objectivity." *SEL* 13(1973): 653-669.

15510. Ranta, Jerrald. "The Metrics of 'Rugby Chapel.'" *VP* 10(1972): 333-350.

15511. Ray, Linda Lee. "Callicles on Etna: The Other Mask." *VP* 7(1969): 309-320.

15512. Reed, John R. "Matthew Arnold and the Soul's Horizons." *VP* 8(1970): 15-24.

15513. Robertson, David Allen, Jr. "'Dover Beach' and 'Say Not the Struggle Nought Availeth.'" *PMLA* 66(1951): 919-926.

15514. Roll-Hansen, Diderik. "Matthew Arnold and the *Academy*: A Note on English Criticism in the Eighteenth-Seventies." *PMLA* 68 (1953): 384-396.

15515. Roos, David A. "Matthew Arnold and Thomas Henry Huxley: Two Speeches at the Royal Academy, 1881 and 1883." *MP* 74(1977): 316-324.

15516. Roper, Alan H. "The Moral Landscape of Arnold's Poetry." *PMLA* 77(1962): 289-296.

15517. Russ, Jon R. "A Possible Source for the Death Scene in Arnold's *Tristram and Iseult*." *VP* 9(1971): 336-338.

15518. Ryals, Clyde de L. "Arnold's *Balder Dead*." *VP* 4(1966): 67-81.

15519. Savory, Jerold J. "Matthew Arnold and 'The Author of *Supernatural Religion*': The Background to *God and the Bible*." *SEL* 16(1976): 677-691.

15520. Schneider, Mary W. "Orpheus in Three Poems by Matthew Arnold." *VP* 10(1972): 29-44.

15521. Shumaker, Wayne. "Matthew Arnold's Humanism: Literature as a Criticism of Life." *SEL* 2(1962): 385-402.

15522. Seturaman, V. S. "*The Scholar Gypsy* and Oriental Wisdom." *RES* 9(1958): 411-413.

15523. Siegchrist, Mark. "The Role of Vivian in Arnold's 'Tristram and Iseult.'" *Criticism* 16(1974): 136-152.

15524. Smidt, Kristian. "The Beaches of Calais and Dover: Arnold's Counterstatement to Wordsworth's Confession of Faith." *VP* 14(1976): 256-257.

15525. Starzyk, Lawrence J. "Arnold and Carlyle." *Criticism* 12(1970): 281-300.

15526. Stitelman, Alice N. "Lyrical Process in Three Poems by Matthew Arnold." *VP* 15 (1977): 133-146.

15527. Sundell, M. G. "The Intellectual Background and Structure of Arnold's *Tristram and Iseult*." *VP* 1(1963): 272-283.

15528. ----------. "Life, Imagination, and Art in Arnold's Oxford Elegies." *Criticism* 15(1973): 309-321.

15529. ----------. "Story and Context in 'The Strayed Reveller.'" *VP* 3(1965): 161-170.

15530. ----------. "'Tintern Abbey' and 'Resignation.'" *VP* 5(1967): 255-264.

15531. Super, R. H. "American Piracies of Matthew Arnold." *AL* 38(1966): 123-125.

15532. ----------. "Arnold's Notebooks and Arnold Bibliography." *MP* 56(1959): 268-269.

15533. ----------. "Documents in the Matthew Arnold-Sainte-Beuve Relationship." *MP* 60(1963): 206-210.

15534. ----------. "Emerson and Arnold's Poetry." *PQ* 33(1954): 396-403.

15535. ----------. "Seeing How the World Is Going." *MLQ* 27(1966): 458-471.

15536. ----------. "Vicacity and the Philistines." *SEL* 6(1966): 629-637.

15537. Tener, Robert H. "Hutton's Earliest Review of Arnold: An Attribution." *ELN* 12(1974): 102-109.

15538. Tillotson, Kathleen. "Arnold and Johnson." *RES* 1(1950): 145-147.

15539. ----------. "Rugby 1850: Arnold, Clough, Walrond, and *In Memorium*." *RES* 4(1953): 122-140.

15540. ----------. "'Yes: In the Sea of

Life.'" *RES* 3(1952): 346-364.

15541. Timko, Michael. "Arnold, Tennyson, and the English Idyll: Ancient Criticism and Modern Poetry." *TSLL* 16(1974): 135-146.

15542. Tobias, Richard Clark. "On Dating Matthew Arnold's 'General Note-books.'" *PQ* 39 (1960): 426-434.

15543. Townsend, Francis G. "Matthew Arnold's Letters to George Smith." *PQ* 35(1956): 195-198.

15544. ----------. "A Neglected Edition of Arnold's *St. Paul and Protestantism*." *RES* 5(1954): 66-69.

15545. ----------. "The Third Installment of Arnold's *Literature and Dogma*." *MP* 50(1953): 195-200.

15546. Trawick, Buckner B. "The Sea of Faith and the Battle by Night in *Dover Beach*." *PMLA* 65(1950): 1282-1283.

15547. Trotter, David. "Hidden Ground Within: Matthew Arnold's Lyric and Elegiac Poetry." *ELH* 44(1977): 526-553.

15548. Vogeler, Martha Salmon. "Matthew Arnold and Frederic Harrison: The Prophet of Culture and the Prophet of Positivism." *SEL* 2(1962): 441-462.

15549. Walker, Warren S. "Burnes's Influence on *Sohrab and Rustum*: A Closer Look." *VP* 8(1970): 151-157.

15550. Waller, John O. "Doctor Arnold's Sermons and Matthew Arnold's 'Rugby Chapel.'" *SEL* 9(1969): 633-646.

15551. Wilkenfed, Roger B. "The Argument of 'The Scholar-Gipsy.'" *VP* 7(1969): 117-128.

15552. Wilkinson, D. R. M. "Carlyle, Arnold, and Literary Justice." *PMLA* 86(1971): 225-235.

15553. Williamson, Eugene L. "Matthew Arnold and the Archbishops." *MLQ* 24(1963): 245-252.

15554. ----------. "Significant Points of Comparison between the Biblical Criticism of Thomas and Matthew Arnold." *PMLA* 76 (1961): 539-543.

15555. ----------. "Words from Westminister Abbey: Matthew Arnold and Arthur Stanley." *SEL* 11(1971): 749-761.

15556. Wright, Charles D. "Matthew Arnold on Heine as 'Continuator of Goethe.'" *SP* 65 (1968): 693-701.

15557. ----------. "How Matthew Arnold Altered 'Goethe on Poetry.'" *VP* 5(1967): 57-61. See also 3345, 15294, 18161.

ARNOLD, THOMAS. 15558. Christensen, Merton A. "Thomas Arnold's Debt to German Theologians: A Prelude to Matthew Arnold's *Literature and Dogma*." *MP* 55(1958): 14-20.

15559. Moyer, Charles R. "The Idea of History in Thomas and Matthew Arnold." *MP* 67 (1969): 160-167.

AUSTEN, JANE. 15560. Anderson, Walter E. "Plot, Character, Speech, and Place in *Pride and Prejudice*." *NCF* 30(1975): 367-382.

15561. ----------. "The Plot of *Mansfield Park*." *MP* 71(1973): 16-27.

15562. apRoberts, Ruth. "*Sense and Sensibility*: or Growing Up Dichotomous." *NCF* 30(1975): 351-366.

15563. Auerbach, Nina. "Austen and Alcott on Matriarchy: New Women or New Wives." *Novel* 10 (1976): 6-26.

15564. ----------. "O Brave New World: Evolution and Revolution in *Persuasion*." *ELH* 39 (1972): 112-128.

15565. Banfield, Ann. "The Moral Landscape of *Mansfield Park*." *NCF* 26(1971): 1-24.

15566. Bennett, James R. "'Doating on you, faults and all': Mr. George Knightley." *SN* 5 (1973): 248-250.

15567. Berger, Carole. "The Rake and the Reader in Jane Austen's Novels." *SEL* 15(1975): 531-544.

15568. Booth, Wayne C. "Point of View and the Control of Distance in *Emma*." *NCF* 16(1961): 95-116.

15569. Bradbrook, M. C. "A Note on Fanny Price." *EIC* 5(1955): 289-292.

15570. Bradbury, Malcolm. "*Persuasion* Again." *EIC* 18(1968): 383-396.

15571. Branton, Clarence L. "The Ordinations in Jane Austen's Novels." *NCF* 10(1955): 156-159.

15572. Brenner, Gerry. "*Mansfield Park*: Reading for 'Improvement.'" *SN* 7(1975): 24-32.

15573. Brogan, Howard D. "Science and Narrative Structure in Austen, Hardy and Woolf." *NCF* 11(1957): 276-287.

15574. Brown, Jane K. "*Die Wahlverwandtschaften* and the English Novel of Manners." *Comp L* 28(1976): 97-108.

15575. Brown, Lloyd W. "The Comic Conclusion in Jane Austen's Novels." *PMLA* 84(1969): 1582-1587.

15576. ----------. "Jane Austen and the Feminist Tradition." *NCF* 28(1973): 321-338.

15577. Burchell, Samuel C. "Jane Austen: The Theme of Isolation." *NCF* 10(1955): 146-150.

15578. Burgan, Mary A. "Mr. Bennet and the Failures of Fatherhood in Jane Austen's Novels." *JEGP* 74(1975): 536-552.

15579. Carroll, David R. "*Mansfield Park, Daniel Deronda*, and Ordination." *MP* 62(1965): 217-226.

15580. Chandler, Alice. "'A Pair of Fine Eyes': Jane Austen's Treatment of Sex." *SN* 7 (1975): 88-103.

15581. Chapman, R. W. "A Reply to Mr. Duffy on *Persuasion*." *NCF* 9(1954): 154.

15582. ----------. "Jane Austen's Titles." *NCF* 9(1954): 238.

15583. Chard, Leslie F., III. "Jane Austen and the Obituaries: the Names of *Northanger Abbey*." *SN* 7(1975): 133-136.

15584. Cohen, Louise D. "Insight, the Essence of Jane Austen's Artistry." *NCF* 8(1953): 213-224.

15585. Collins, K. K. "Mrs. Smith and the Morality of *Persuasion*." *NCF* 30(1975): 383-398.

15586. Copeland, Catherine H. "*Pride and Prejudice*: A Neo-Classical Work in a Romantic Age." *CLA* 14(1970): 156-162.

15587. Crowley, J. Donald. "Review Essay: Jane Austen Studies: A Portrait of the Lady and Her Critics." *SN* 7(1975): 137-160.

15588. DeRose, Peter L. "Hardship, Recollection, and Discipline: Three Lessons in *Mansfield Park*." *SN* 9(1977): 261-278.

15589. Donohue, Joseph W., Jr. "Ordination and the Divided House at Mansfield Park." *ELH* 32 (1965): 169-178.

15590. Dooley, D. J. "Pride, Prejudice, and Vanity in Elizabeth Bennet." *NCF* 20(1965): 185-188.

15591. Duckworth, Alistair. "*Mansfield Park* and Estate Improvements: Jane Austen's Grounds of Being." *NCF* 26(1971): 25-48.

15592. Duffy, Joseph M., Jr. "*Emma*: The Awakening from Innocence." *ELH* 21(1954): 39-53.

15593. ----------. "Moral Integrity and Moral Anarchy in *Mansfield Park*." *ELH* 23(1956): 71-92.

15594. ----------. "Structure and Idea in Jane Austen's *Persuasion*." *NCF* 8(1954): 272-289.

15595. Duncan-Jones, E. E. "Jane Austen and Crabbe." *RES* 5(1954): 174.

15596. Draffan, Robert A. "*Mansfield Park*: Jane Austen's Bleak House." *EIC* 19(1969): 371-384.

15597. Drew, Philip. "A Significant Incident in *Pride and Prejudice*." *NCF* 13(1959): 356-358.

15598. Dry, Helen. "Syntax and Point of View in Jane Austen's *Emma*." *SR* 16(1977): 87-100.

15599. Edge, Charles E. "*Mansfield Park* and Ordination." *NCF* 16(1961): 269-274.

15600. Edwards, Thomas R., Jr. "The Difficult Beauty of *Mansfield Park*." *NCF* 20(1965): 51-67.

15601. Ehrenpreis, Anne Henry. "*Northanger Abbey*: Jane Austen and Charlotte Smith." *NCF* 25 (1970): 343-348.

15602. Elsbree, Langdon. "Jane Austen and the Dance of Fidelity and Complaisance." *NCF* 15 (1960): 113-136.

15603. Emden, Cecil S. "The Composition of *Northanger Abbey*." *RES* 19(1968): 279-287.

15604. Fleishman, Avrom. "*Mansfield Park* in its Time." *NCF* 22(1967): 1-18.

15605. ----------. "The Socialization of Catherine Morland." *ELH* 41(1974): 649-667.

15606. ----------. "The State of the Art: Recent Jane Austen Criticism." *MLQ* 37(1976): 281-289.

15607. Fox, Robert C. "Elizabeth Bennett: Prejudice or Vanity?" *NCF* 17(1962): 185-187.

15608. Frost, William. "*Emma*: A Defense." *NCF* 4(1950): 325-328.

15609. Gallon, D. N. "Comedy in 'Northanger Abbey.'" *MLR* 63(1968): 802-809.

15610. Gillie, Christopher. "*Sense and Sensibility*: An Assessment." *EIC* 9(1959): 1-9.

15611. Gomme, Andor. "On Not Being Persuaded." *EIC* 16(1966): 170-184.

15612. ----------. "*Persuasion*." *EIC* 16 (1966): 481.

15613. Greene, D. J. "Jane Austen and the Peerage." *PMLA* 68(1953): 1017-1031.

15614. Greene, Donald. "New Verses by Jane Austen." *NCF* 30(1975): 257-260.

15615. Griffin, Cynthia. "The Development of Realism in Jane Austen's Early Novel." *ELH* 30 (1963): 36-52.

15616. Gullans, Charles B. "Jane Austen's *Mansfield Park* and Dr. Johnson." *NCF* 27(1972): 206-208.

15617. Hagan, John. "The Closure of *Emma*." *SEL* 15(1975): 545-561.

15618. Halliday, E. M. "Narrative Perspective in *Pride and Prejudice*." *NCF* 15(1960): 65-71.

15619. Halperin, John. "The Trouble with *Mansfield Park*." *SN* 7(1975): 6-23.

15620. Hart, Francis R. "The Spaces of Privacy: Jane Austen." *NCF* 30(1975): 305-334.

15621. Harvey, W. J. "The Plot of *Emma*." *EIC* 17(1967): 48-63.

15622. Hellstrom, Ward. "Francophobia in *Emma*." *SEL* 5(1965): 607-617.

15623. Hennedy, Hugh L. "Acts of Perception in Jane Austen's Novels." *SN* 5(1973): 22-38.

15624. Hogan, Charles Beecher. "Jane Austen and her Early Public." *RES* 1(1950): 39-54.

15625. Hughes, R. E. "The Education of Emma Woodhouse." *NCF* 16(1961): 69-74.

15626. Joukovsky, Nicholas A. "Another Unnoted Contemporary Review of Jane Austen." *NCF* 29(1974): 336-338.

15627. Kauvar, Elain M. "Jane Austen and *The Female Quixote*." *SN* 2(1970): 211-221.

15628. Kearful, Frank J. "Satire and the Form of the Novel: The Problem of Aesthetic Unity in *Northanger Abbey*." *ELH* 32(1965): 511-527.

15629. Kestner, Joseph A., III. "The 'I' Persona in the Novels of Jane Austen." *SN* 4(1972): 6-16.

15630. ----------. "Jane Austen: The Tradition of the English Romantic Novel, 1800-1832." *WC* 7(1976): 297-311.

15631. King, Noel J. "Jane Austen in France." *NCF* 8(1953): 1-26.

15632. Kinkead-Weekes, Mark. "This Old Maid: Jane Austen Replies to Charlotte Brontë and D. H. Lawrence." *NCF* 30(1975): 399-420.

15633. Kissane, James. "Comparison's Blessed Felicity: Character Arrangement in Emma." *SN* 2(1970): 173-184.

15634. Knight, Charles A. "Irony and Mr. Knightley." *SN* 2(1970): 185-193.

15635. Knoepflmacher, U. C. "The Importance of Being Frank: Character and Letter-Writing in *Emma*." *SEL* 7(1967): 639-658.

15636. Kroeber, Karl. "Jane Austen, Romantic." *WC* 7(1976): 291-296.

15637. Lauber, John. "Jane Austen's Fool." *SEL* 14(1974): 511-524.

15638. ----------. "Minds Bewildered and Astray: The Crawfords in *Mansfield Park*." *SN* 2 (1970): 194-210.

15639. ----------. "*Sanditon*: The Kingdom of Folly." *SN* 4(1972): 353-363.

15640. Lawry, J. S. "'Decided and Open': Structure in *Emma*." *NCF* 24(1969): 1-15.

15641. Levine, George. "Translating The Monstrous: *Northanger Abbey*." *NCF* 30(1975): 335-350.

15642. Levine, Jay Arnold. "*Lady Susan*: Jane Austen's Character of the Merry Widow." *SEL* 1,#4(1961): 23-34.

15643. Lewis, C. S. "A Note on Jane Austen." *EIC* 4(1954): 359-371.

15644. Litz, Walton. "*The Loiterer*: A Reflection of Jane Austen's Early Environment." *RES* 12(1961): 251-261.

15645. Lodge, David. "A Question of Judgment: The Theatricals at Mansfield Park." *NCF* 17 (1962): 275-282.

15646. Magee, William H. "The Happy Marriage: The Influence of Charlotte Smith on Jane Austen." *SN* 7(1975): 120-132.

15647. Marcus, Mordecai. "A Major Thematic Pattern in *Pride and Prejudice*." *NCF* 16(1961): 274-279.

15648. Mathison, John K. "*Northanger Abbey* and Jane Austen's Conception of the Value of Fiction." *ELH* 24(1957): 138-152.

15649. McCann, Charles J. "Setting and Character in *Pride and Prejudice*." *NCF* 19(1964): 65-75.

15650. McMaster, Juliet. "The Continuity of Jane Austen's Novels." *SEL* 10(1970): 723-739.

15651. Minter, David Lee. "Aesthetic Vision and the World of *Emma*." *NCF* 21(1966): 49-59.

15652. Moler, Kenneth L. "The Bennet Girls and Adam Smith on Vanity and Pride." *PQ* 46(1967): 567-569.

15653. ----------. "Fanny Burney's *Cecelia* and Jane Austen's 'Jack and Alice.'" *ELN* 3(1965): 40-42.

15654. ----------. "*Pride and Prejudice*: Jane Austen's 'Patrician Hero.'" *SEL* 7(1967): 491-508.

15655. ----------. "*Sense and Sensibility* and its Sources." *RES* 17(1966): 413-419.

15656. Monagham, David M. "The Decline of the Gentry: A Study of Jane Austen's Attitude to Formality in *Persuasion*." *SN* 7(1975): 73-87.

15657. Moore, E. Margaret. "Emma and Miss Bates: Early Experiences of Separation and the Theme of Dependency in Jane Austen's Novels." *SEL* 9(1969): 573-585.

15658. Morgan, Susan J. "Emma Woodhouse and the Charms of Imagination." *SN* 7(1975): 33-48.

15659. ----------. "Intelligence in *Pride and Prejudice*." *MP* 73(1975): 54-68.

15660. ----------. "Polite Lies: The Veiled Heroine of *Sense and Sensibility*." *NCF* 31(1976): 188-205.

15661. Mummel, Madeline. "Emblematic Charades and the Observant Woman in *Mansfield Park*." *TSLL* 15(1973): 251-265.

15662. Myers, Sylvia H. "Womanhood in Jane Austen's Novels." *Novel* 3(1970): 225-232.

15663. Nardin, Jane. "Charity in *Emma*." *SN* 7(1975): 61-72.

15664. Nash, Ralph. "The Time Scheme for *Pride and Prejudice*." *ELN* 4(1967): 194-198.

15665. Page, Norman. "Categories of Speech in 'Persuasion.'" *MLR* 64(1969): 734-741.

15666. Parks, Edd Winfield. "A Human Failing in *Pride and Prejudice*." *NCF* 10(1955): 237-240.

15667. ----------. "Jane Austen's Lure of the Next Chapter." *NCF* 7(1952): 56-60.

15668. Patterson, Emily H. "Family and Pilgrimage Themes in Austen's *Mansfield Park* CLA 20(1976): 14-18.

15669. Pikoulis, John. "Jane Austen: The Figure in the Carpet." *NCF* 27(1972): 38-60.

15670. Price, Martin. "Manners, Morals, and Jane Austen." *NCF* 30(1975): 261-280.

15671. Roth, Barry. "Review-Essay: Celebrating the Bicentennial: Jane Austen and Her Critics." *SN* 8(1976): 474-482.

15672. Ruoff, Gene W. "Anne Elliott's Dowry: Reflections on the Ending of *Persuasion*." *WC* 7(1976): 342-351.

15673. Sabiston, Elizabeth. "The Prison of Womanhood." *Comp L* 25(1973): 336-351.

15674. Sacks, Sheldon. "Novelists as Storytellers." *MP* 73(1976): S97-S109.

15675. Schneider, Sister M. Lucy, C.S.J. "The Little White Attic and the East Room: Their Function in Mansfield Park." *MP* 63(1966): 227-235.

15676. Scholes, Robert. "Dr. Johnson and Jane Austen." *PQ* 54(1975): 380-390.

15677. Shannon, Edgar F., Jr. "*Emma*: Character and Construction." *PMLA* 71(1956): 637-650.

15678. Shaw, Valerie. "Jane Austen's Subdued Heroines." *NCF* 30(1975): 281-304.

15679. Southam, B. C. "Mrs. Leavis and Miss Austen: The 'Critical Theory' Reconsidered." *NCF* 17(1962): 21-32.

15680. Southam, Brian. "*Persuasion*." *EIC* 16(1966): 480.

15681. Steig, Michael. "Psychological Realism and Fantasy in Jane Austen: *Emma* and *Mansfield Park*." *NCF* 5(1973): 126-134.

15682. Stone, Donald D. "Sense and Semantics in Jane Austen." *NCF* 25(1970): 31-50.

15683. Suddaby, Elizabeth. "Jane Austen and the Delphic Oracle." *NCF* 9(1954): 235-238.

15684. Sulloway, Alison, G. "Emma Woodhouse and *A Vindication of the Rights of Women*." *WC* 7(1976): 320-332.

15685. Swingle, L. J. "The Perfect Happiness of the Union: Jane Austen's *Emma* and English Romanticism." *WC* 7(1976): 312-319.

15686. Walling, William A. "The Glorious Anxiety of Motion: Jane Austen's *Persuasion*." *WC* 7(1976): 333-341.

15687. Ward, William S. "Three Hitherto Unnoted Contemporary Reviews of Jane Austen." *NCF* 26(1972): 469-477.

15688. Watson, J. R. "Mr. Perry's Patients: a View of *Emma*." *EIC* 20(1970): 334-343.

15689. White, Edward M. "A Critical Theory of *Mansfield Park*." *SEL* 7(1967): 659-677.

15690. ----------. "*Emma* and the Parodic Point of View." *NCF* 18(1963): 55-63.

15691. Weinsheimer, Joel. "Chance and the Hierarchy of Marriages in *Pride and Prejudice*." *ELH* 39(1972): 404-419.

15692. ----------. "*Mansfield Park*: Three Problems." *NCF* 29(1974): 185-205.

15693. Wilhelm, Albert E. "Three Word Clusters in *Emma*." *SN* 7(1975): 49-60.

15694. Willis, Lesley H. "Object Association and Minor Characters in Jane Austen's Novels." *SN* 7(1975): 104-119.

15695. Wiesenfarth, Joseph. "*Persuasion*: History and Myth." *WC* 2(1971): 160-168.

15696. Wolfe, Thomas P. "The Achievement of *Persuasion*." *SEL* 11(1971): 687-700.

15697. Wright, Andrew. "Jane Austen Adapted." *NCF* 30(1975): 421-454.

15698. ----------. "A Reply to Mr. Burchell on Jane Austen." *NCF* 10(1956): 315-319.

15699. Zietlow, Paul N. "Luck and Fortuitous Circumstance in *Persuasion*: Two

Interpretations." *ELH* 32(1965): 179-195.

15700. Zimmerman, Everett. "Jane Austen and *Mansfield Park*: A Discrimination of Ironies." *SN* 1(1969): 347-356.

15701. ----------. "The Function of Parody in *Northanger Abbey*." *MLQ* 30(1969): 53-63.

15702. ----------. "Pride and Prejudice in *Pride and Prejudice*." *NCF* 23(1968): 64-73.

See also 59, 71, 80, 13557, 15327, 15333, 18161.

BAGEHOT, WALTER. 15703. Chapman, R. W. "The Text of Bagehot's *Constitution*." *PQ* 31 (1952): 446-447.

15704. Davis, Frances L. "Walter Bagehot: Follower of Edmund Burke." *CLA* 21(1977): 292-303.

BARING-GOULD, SABINE. 15705. Hyde, William J. "The Stature of Baring-Gould as a Novelist." *NCF* 15(1960): 1-16.

BARNES, WILLIAM. 15706. Keith, W. J. "Thomas Hardy's Edition of William Barnes." *VP* 15(1977): 121-132.

15707. Zietlow, Paul. "Thomas Hardy and William Barnes: Two Dorset Poets." *PMLA* 84 (1969): 291-303.

BARRINGTON, JONAH. 15708. Torchiana, Donald T. "The World of Sir Jonah Barrington's *Personal Sketches*." *PQ* 45(1966): 321-345.

BAYLAY, W. FREDERICK. 15709. Butler, James A. "A Summer in the Lakes, 1800: A Manuscript Journal." *WC* 7(1976): 153-160.

BEDDOES, THOMAS L. See 478, 5783.

BESANT, WALTER. 15711. Boege, Fred W. "Sir Walter Besant: Novelist." *NCF* 10(1956): 249-280.

15712. Spilka, Mark. "Henry James and Walter Besant: 'The Art of Fiction' Controversy." *Novel* 6(1973): 101-119.

BINDLOSS, HAROLD. 15713. Miller, Carrol. "'The Two Priests of Konnoto': A Satire on British Colonialism." *SSF* 11(1974): 251-255.

BLACKMORE, R. D. 15714. Buckler, William A. "Blackmore's Novels before *Lorna Doone*." *NCF* 10(1955): 169-187.

15715. Sutton, Max Keith. "The Mythic Appeal of *Lorna Doone*." *NCF* 28(1974): 435-449.

BLACKWOOD, JOHN. 15716. Anderson, Roland F. "George Eliot Provoked: John Blackwood and Chapter Seventeen of *Adam Bede*." *MP* 71(1973): 39-47.

BLUNT, WILFRID S. 15717. Going, William T. "Blunt's Sonnets and Skittles: A Further Word." *VP* 4(1966): 136-141.

15717a. ----------. "A Peacock Dinner: The Homage of Pound and Yeats to Wilfred Scawen Blunt." *JML* 1(1971): 303-310.

15718. ----------. "Wilfrid Scawan Blunt, Victorian Sonneteer." *VP* 2(1964): 67-86.

15719. Scott, Kenneth W. "Blunt's Sonnets and Another Poem to 'Skittles.'" *VP* 3 (1965): 141-143.

BOWLES, WILLIAM L. 15720. Fayen, George S. "The Pencil and the Harp of William Lisle Bowles." *MLQ* 21(1960): 301-314.

See also 18124.

BRADDON, MARY E. 15721. Heywood, C. "Flaubert, Miss Braddon, and George Moore." *Comp L* 12(1960): 151-158.

15722. ----------. "*The Return of the*

Native and Miss Braddon's *The Doctor's Wife*: A Probable Source." *NCF* 18(1963): 91-94.

BRONTË, CHARLOTTE. 15723. Blackall, Jean Frantz. "Point of View in *Villette*." *JNT* 6(1976): 14-28.

15724. ----------. "A Suggestive Book for Charlotte Brontë?" *JEGP* 76(1977): 363-383.

15725. Benvenuto, Richard. "The Child of Nature, The Child of Grace, and the Unresolved Conflict of *Jane Eyre*." *ELH* 39(1972): 620-638.

15726. Blom, M. A. "'Jane Eyre': Mind as Law Unto Itself." *Criticism* 15(1973): 350-364.

15727. Brammer, M. M. "The Manuscript of *The Professor*." *RES* 11(1960): 157-170.

15728. Burkhart, Charles. "Another Key Word for *Jane Eyre*." *NCF* 16(1961): 177-179.

15729. Bushnell, Nelson S. "Artistic Economy in *Jane Ayre*: A Contrast with *The Old Manor House*." *ELN* 5(1968): 197-202.

15730. Drew, Philip. "Charlotte Brontë as a Critic of *Wuthering Heights*." *NCF* 18(1964): 365-381.

15731. Dunbar, George S. "Proper Names in *Villette*." *NCF* 15(1960): 77-80.

15732. Gribble, Jennifer. "Jane Eyre's Imagination." *NCF* 23(1968): 279-293.

15733. Grudin, Peter. "Jane and the Other Mrs. Rochester: Excess and Restraint in *Jane Eyre*." *Novel* 10(1977): 145-157.

15734. Hagan, John. "Enemies of Freedom in 'Jane Eyre.'" *Criticism* 13(1971): 351-376.

15735. Heilman, Robert B. "Charlotte Brontë, Reason, and the Moon." *NCF* 14(1960): 283-302.

15736. Hughes, R. E. "*Jane Eyre*: The Unbaptized Dionysus." *NCF* 18(1964): 347-364.

15737. Johnson, E. D. H. "'Daring the Dread Glance': Charlotte Brontë's Treatment of the Supernatural in *Villette*." *NCF* 20(1966): 325-336.

15738. Kinkead-Weekes, Mark. "This Old Maid: Jane Austen Replies to Charlotte Brontë and D. H. Lawrence." *NCF* 30(1975): 399-420.

15739. Korg, Jacob. "The Problem of Unity in *Shirley*." *NCF* 12(1957): 125-136.

15740. Langford, Thomas A. "Prophetic Imagination and the Unity of *Jane Eyre*." *SN* 6 (1974): 228-235.

15741. Martin, Robert B. "Charlotte Brontë and Harriet Martineau." *NCF* 7(1952): 198-201.

15742. Millgate, Jane. "Narrative Distance in 'Jane Eyre': The Relevance of the Pictures." *MLR* 63(1968): 315-319.

15743. Momberger, Philip. "Self and World in the Works of Charlotte Brontë." *ELH* 32(1965): 349-369.

15744. Moser, Lawrence E., S.J. "From Portrait to Person: A Note on the Surrealistic in *Jane Eyre*." *NCF* 20(1965): 275-281.

15745. Pell, Nancy. "Resistance, Rebellion, and Marriage: The Economics of *Jane Eyre*." *NCF* 31(1977): 397-420.

15746. Rosengarten, Herbert J. "Charlotte Brontë's *Shirley* and the *Leeds* Mercury." *SEL* 16 (1976): 591-600.

15747. Shannon, Edgar F., Jr. "The Present Tense in *Jane Eyre*." *NCF* 10(1955): 141-145.

15748. Shapiro, Arnold. "In Defense of Jane Eyre." *SEL* 8(1968): 681-698.

15749. Siebenschuh, William R. "The Image

of the Child and the Plot of *Jane Eyre*." *SN* 8 (1976): 304-317.

15750. Wilson, F. A. C. "The Primrose Wreath: The Heroes of the Brontë Novels." *NCF* 29 (1974): 40-57.

15751. Yeazell, Ruth Bernard. "More True than Real: Jane Eyre's 'Mysterious Summons.'" *NCF* 29(1974): 127-143.

See also 15335.

BRONTË, EMILY. 15752. Adams, Ruth M. "*Wuthering Heights*: The Land East of Eden." *NCF* 13(1958): 58-62.

15753. Allott, Miriam. "*Wuthering Heights*: The Rejection of Heathcliff." *EIC* 8(1958): 27-47.

15754. Bell, Vereen M. "*Wuthering Heights* and the Unforgivable Sin." *NCF* 17(1962): 188-191.

15755. Brick, Allan R. "Lewes's Review of *Wuthering Heights*." *NCF* 14(1960): 355-359.

15756. Buchen, Irving H. "Emily Brontë and the Metaphysics of Childhood and Love." *NCF* 22 (1967): 63-70.

15757. Buckler, William F. "Chapter VII of *Wuthering Heights*: A Key to Interpretation." *NCF* 7(1952): 51-55.

15758. Burns, Wayne. "In Death They Were Not Divided: The Moral Magnificence of Unmoral Passion in *Wuthering Heights*." *HSL* 5(1973): 135-159.

15759. Carmody, Francis J. "Two Recent French Books on Emily Brontë." *NCF* 5(1950): 239-242.

15760. Cott, Jeremy. "Structures of Sound: The Last Sentence of *Wuthering Heights*." *TSLL* 6(1964): 280-289.

15761. Davies, Cecil W. "A Reading of *Wuthering Heights*." *EIC* 19(1969): 254-272.

15762. Fike, Francis. "Bitter Herbs and Wholesome Medicines: Love as Theological Affirmation in *Wuthering Heights*." *NCF* 23(1968): 127-149.

15763. Fine, Ronald E. "Lockwood's Dreams and the Key to *Wuthering Heights*." *NCF* 24(1969): 16-30.

15764. Fraser, John. "The Name of Action: Nelly Dean and *Wuthering Heights*." *NCF* 20(1965): 223-236.

15765. Ghent, Dorothy Van. "The Window Figure and the Two-Children Figure in *Wuthering Heights*." *NCF* 7(1952): 189-197.

15766. Gleckner, Robert F. "Time in *Wuthering Heights*." *Criticism* 1(1959): 328-338.

15767. Gose, Elliott B., Jr. "*Wuthering Heights*: The Heath and the Hearth." *NCF* 21(1966): 1-19.

15768. Grudin, Peter D. "*Wuthering Heights*: The Question of Unquiet Slumbers." *SN* 6(1974): 389-407.

15769. Hafley, James. "The Villain in *Wuthering Heights*." *NCF* 13(1958): 199-215.

15770. Hagan, John. "Control of Sympathy in *Wuthering Heights*." *NCF* 21(1967): 305-323.

15771. Hinz, Evelyn J. "Hierogamy versus Wedlock: Types of Marriage Plots and Their Relationship to Genres of Prose Fiction." *PMLA* 91 (1976): 900-913.

15772. Jordan, John E. "The Ironic Vision of Emily Brontë." *NCF* 20(1965): 1-18.

15773. Krupat, Arnold. "The Strangeness of *Wuthering Heights*." *NCF* 25(1970): 269-281.

15774. Langman, F. H. "*Wuthering Heights*." *EIC* 15(1965): 294-312.

15775. Madden, William A. "*Wuthering Heights*: The Binding of Passion." *NCF* 27(1972): 127-154.

15776. Mathison, John K. "Nelly Dean and the Power of *Wuthering Heights*." *NCF* 11(1956): 106-129.

15777. McKibben, Robert C. "The Image of the Book in *Wuthering Heights*." *NCF* 15(1960): 159-169.

15778. Moser, Thomas. "What is the Matter with Emily Jane? Conflicting Impulses in *Wuthering Heights*." *NCF* 17(1962): 1-19.

15779. Shannon, Edgar F. "Lockwood's Dreams and the Exegesis of *Wuthering Heights*." *NCF* 14 (1959): 95-109.

15780. Shapiro, Arnold. "*Wuthering Heights* as a Victorian Novel." *SN* 1(1969): 284-296.

15781. Shunami, Gideon. "The Unreliable Narrator in *Wuthering Heights*." *NCF* 27(1973): 449-468.

15782. Solomon, Eric. "The Incest Theme in *Wuthering Heights*." *NCF* 14(1959): 80-83.

15783. Sonstroem, David. "*Wuthering Heights* and the Limits of Vision." *PMLA* 86(1971): 51-62.

15784. Starzyk, Lawrence. "Emily Brontë: Poetry in a Mingled Tone." *Criticism* 14(1972): 119-136.

15785. ----------. "The Faith of Emily Bronte's Immortality Creed." *VP* 11(1973): 295-305.

15786. Thompson, Wade. "Infantcide and Sadism in *Wuthering Heights*." *PMLA* 78(1963): 69-74.

15787. Thomson, Patricia. "*Wuthering Heights* and *Mauprat*." *RES* 24(1973): 26-37.

15788. Vargish, Thomas. "Revenge and *Wuthering Heights*." *SN* 3(1971): 7-17.

15789. Wilson, F. A. C. "The Primrose Wreath: The Heroes of the Brontë Novels." *NCF* 29(1974): 40-57.

15790. Woodring, Carl R. "The Narrators of *Wuthering Heights*." *NCF* 11(1957): 298-305.

15791. Worth, George J. "Emily Brontë's Mr. Lockwood." *NCF* 12(1958): 315-320.

See also 67, 15335, 15730.

BROWNING, ELIZABETH BARRETT. 15792. Arinshtein, Leonid M. "'A Curse for a Nation': A Controversial Episode in Elizabeth Barrett Browning's Political Poetry." *RES* 20(1969): 33-42.

15793. Gladish, Robert W. "Mrs. Browning's 'A Curse for a Nation': Some Further Comments." *VP* 7(1969): 275-280.

15794. Green, David Bonnell. "Elizabeth Barrett to Hugh Stuart Boyd: An Additional Letter." *PMLA* 76(1961): 154-155.

15795. Kelley, Philip, and Ronald Hudson. "The Letters of the Brownings." *VP* 1(1963): 238-239.

15796. McAleer, Edward C. "New Letters from Mrs. Browning to Isa Blagden." *PMLA* 66(1951): 594-612.

15797. Paroissien, David. "Mrs. Browning's Influence on and Contribution to *A New Spirit of the Age*." *ELN* 8(1971): 274-281.

15798. Thale, Mary. "T. S. Eliot and Mrs. Browning on the Metaphysical Poets." *CLA* 11(1968):

255-258.

15799. Weaver, Bennett. "Twenty Unpublished Letters of Elizabeth Barrett to Hugh Stuart Boyd." *PMLA* 65(1950): 397-418.

See also 18124.

BROWNING, ROBERT. 15800. Adams, Laura. Browning's Rings and Posies." *VP* 8(1970): 346-347.

15801. Adler, Joshua. "Structure and Meaning in Browning's 'My Last Duchess.'" *VP* 15 (1977): 219-228.

15802. Adrian, Arthur A. "The Browning-Rossetti Friendship: Some Unpublished Letters." *PMLA* 73(1958): 538-544.

15803. Aiken, Susan Hardy. "On Clothes and Heroes: Carlyle and 'How It Strikes a Contemporary.'" *VP* 13(1975): 99-109.

15804. Allen, Frank. "Ariosto and Browning: A Reexamination of 'Count Gismond.'" *VP* 11 (1973): 15-26.

15805. Altick, Richard D. "Browning's 'Transcendentalism.'" *JEGP* 58(1959): 24-28.

15806. ----------. "'A Grammarian's Funeral': Browning's Praise of Folly?" *SEL* 3(1963): 449-460.

15807. ----------. "Memo to the Next Annotator of Browning." *VP* 1(1963): 61-68.

15808. ----------. "The Symbolism of Browning's 'Master Hugues of Saxe-Gotha.'" *VP* 3(1965): 1-7.

15809. Antippas, A. P. "Browning's 'The Guardian Angel': A Possible Early Reference to Ruskin." *VP* 11(1973): 342-344.

15810. Armstrong, Isobel. "A Note on the Conversion of Caponsacchi." *VP* 6(1968): 271-280.

15811. ----------. "Browning's *Mr. Sludge, 'The Medium.'*" *VP* 2(1964): 1-10.

15812. Armytage, W. H. G. "Some New Letters of Robert Browning, 1871-1889." *MLQ* 12(1951): 155-158.

15813. Baker, Joseph E. "Religious Implications in Browning's Poetry." *PQ* 36(1957): 436-452.

15814. Ball, Patricia. "Browning's Godot." *VP* 3(1965): 245-253.

15815. Balliet, Conrad A. "'Growing Old' along with 'Rabbi Ben Ezra.'" *VP* 1(1963): 300-301.

15816. Bargainnier, Earl F. "Browning, James, and 'The Private Life.'" *SSF* 14(1977): 151-158.

15817. Beckson, Karl, and John M. Munroe. "Symons, Browning, and the Development of the Modern Aesthetic." *SEL* 10(1970): 687-699.

15818. Bennett, James R. "Lazarus in Browning's 'Karshish.'" *VP* 3(1965): 189-191.

15819. Benvenuto, Richard. "Lippo and Andrea: The Pro and Contra of Browning's Realism." *SEL* 13(1973): 643-652.

15820. Beresford, Rosemary. "'Mark Rutherford' and Hero-Worship." *RES* 6(1955): 264-272.

15821. Bieman, Elizabeth. "An Eros *Manqué*: Browning's 'Andrea del Sarto.'" *SEL* 10(1970): 651-668.

15822. Bishop, Alan, and John Ferns. "Art in Obedience to Laws': Form and Meaning in Browning's 'Abt Vogler.'" *VP* 12(1974): 25-32.

15823. Boo, Sister Mary Richard. "The Ordeal of Giusseppe Caponsacchi." *VP* 3(1965): 179-188.

15824. Boulton, J. A. "Browning—A Potential Revolutionary." *EIC* 3(1953): 165-176.

15825. Bright, Michael H. "Browning's Celebrated *Pictor Ignotus*." *ELN* 13(1976): 192-194.

15826. ----------. "John the Baptist in Browning's 'Fra Lippo Lippi.'" *VP* 15(1977): 75-77.

15827. Bross, Addison C. "*Easter-Day*: Browning's Changing Concept of Faith." *VP* 14 (1976): 11-24.

15828. Brown, Bernadine. "Robert Browning's 'The Italian in England.'" *VP* 6(1968): 179-184.

15829. Bullen, J. B. "Browning's 'Pictor Ignotus' and Vasari's 'Life of Fra Bartolommeo di San Marco.'" *RES* 23(1972): 313-319.

15830. Burr, Michael A. "Browning's Note to Forster." *VP* 12(1974): 343-350.

15831. Campbell, William R. "A Note on the Flowers in *Pippa Passes*." *VP* 14(1976): 59-63.

15832. Chandler, Alice. "'The Eve of St. Agnes' and 'Porphyria's Lover.'" *VP* 3(1965): 273-274.

15833. Clarke, C. C. "Humor and Wit in 'Childe Roland.'" *MLQ* 23(1962): 323-336.

15834. Colburn, William E. "Ruskin and Browning: The Poet's Responsibility." *SLI* 1,#1 (1968): 37-46.

15835. Collins, R. G. "Browning's Practical Prelate: The Lesson of *Bishop Blougram's Apology*." *VP* 13(1975): 1-20.

15836. Collins, Thomas J. "Browning's *Essay on Shelley*: In Context." *VP* 2(1964): 119-124.

15837. ----------. "The Poetry of Robert Browning: A Proposal for Reexamination." *TSLL* 15(1973): 325-340.

15838. ----------. "Shelley and God in Browning's *Pauline*: Unresolved Problems." *VP* 3 (1965): 151-160.

15839. Columbus, Claudette Kemper. "*The Ring and the Book*: A Masque for the Making of Meaning." *PQ* 53(1974): 237-255.

15840. Columbus, Robert R. and Claudette Kemper. "Sordello and the Speaker: A Problem in Identity." *VP* 2(1964): 251-268.

15841. Corrigan, Beatrice. "New Documents on Browning's Roman Murder Case." *SP* 49(1952): 520-533.

15842. Cox, Ollie. "The 'Spot of Joy' in 'My Last Duchess.'" *CLA* 12(1968): 70-76.

15843. Coyle, William. "Molinos: 'The Subject of the Day' in *The Ring and the Book* *PMLA* 67(1952): 308-314.

15844. Cramer, Maurice B. "Maisie Ward and Browning Biography: A New Era." *MP* 68(1971): 294-300.

15845. Cundiff, Paul A. "Browning's Old Bishop." *VP* 9(1971): 452-453.

15846. D'Avanzo, Mario L. "'Childe Roland to the Dark Tower Came': The Shelleyan and Shakespearean Context." *SEL* 17(1977): 695-708.

15847. ----------. "King Francis, Lucrezia, and the Figurative Language of 'Andrea del Sarto.'" *TSLL* 9(1968): 523-536.

15848. DeBaun, Vincent C. "Browning: Art Is Life Is Thought." *CLA* 14(1971): 387-401.

15849. DeLaura, David J. "A Robert Browning Letter: The Occasion of Mrs. Browning's 'A Curse for a Nation.'" *VP* 4(1966): 210-212.

15850. Donaghy, Henry J. "*The Ring and the*

Book: Its Conception, Current Reputation, and Meaning." *SLI* 1,#1(1968): 47-66.

15851. Drew, Philip. "Another View of *Fifine at the Fair*." *EIC* 17(1967): 244-255.

15852. ----------. "Browning's *Essay on Shelley*." *VP* 1(1963): 1-6.

15853. ----------. "Henry Jones on Browning's Optimism." *VP* 2(1964): 29-41.

15854. ----------. "A Note on the Lawyers." *VP* 6(1968): 297-308.

15855. Duncan, Joseph E. "The Intellectual Kinship of John Donne and Robert Browning." *SP* 50(1953): 81-100.

15856. Eggenschwiler, David. "Psychological Complexity in 'Porphyria's Lover.'" *VP* 8 (1970): 39-48.

15857. Erdman, David V. "Browning's Industrial Nightmare." *PQ* 36(1957): 417-435.

15858. Ewbank, David R. "Bishop Blougram's Argument." *VP* 10(1972): 257-264.

15859. Fairchild, Hoxie N. *"La Saisiaz* and The Nineteenth Century." *MP* 48(1950): 104-111.

15860. Fleck, Richard. "Browning's 'Up at a Villa—Down in the City' as Satire." *VP* 7(1969): 345-349.

15861. Fleisher, David. "Browning's 'Rabbi Ben Ezra': A New Key to an Old Crux." *VP* 1(1963): 46-52.

15862. Fleissner, R. F. "Browning's Last Lost Duchess: A Purview." *VP* 5(1967): 217-219.

15863. Fontana, Ernest L. "Browning's St. Praxed's Bishop: A Naturalistic View." *VP* 10 (1972): 278-282.

15864. Friedman, Barton R. "To Tell the Sun from the Druid Fire: Imagery of Good and Evil in *The Ring and the Book*." *SEL* 6(1966): 693-708.

15865. Friend, Joseph H. "Euripides Browningized: The Meaning of *Balaustion's Adventure*." *VP* 2(1964): 179-186.

15866. Gabbard, G. N. "Browning's Metamorphoses." *VP* 4(1966): 29-31.

15867. Gainer, Patrick W. "'Hy, Zy, Hine.'" *VP* 1(1963): 158-160.

15868. Garrett, Marvin P. "Language and Design in *Pippa Passes*." *VP* 13(1975): 47-60.

15869. Garratt, Robert F. "Browning's Dramatic Monologue: The Strategy of the Double Mask." *VP* 11(1973): 115-126.

15870. Goldfarb, Russell M. "Sexual Meaning in 'The Last Ride Together.'" *VP* 3(1965): 255-261.

15871. Govil, O. P. "A Note on Mill and Browning's *Pauline*." *VP* 4(1966): 287-291.

15872. Guerin, Wilfred L. "Browning's 'Cleon': A Teilhardian View." *VP* 12(1974): 13-24.

15873. ----------. "Irony and Tension in Browning's 'Karshish.'" *VP* 1(1963): 132-139.

15874. Guralnick, Elissa Schagrin. "Archimagical Fireworks: The Function of Light-Imagery in *Sordello*." *VP* 13(1975): 111-128.

15875. Guskin, Phyllis J. "Ambiguities in the Structure and Meaning of Browning's *Christmas-Eve*." *VP* 4(1966): 21-28.

15876. Greenberg, Robert A. "Ruskin, Pugin, and the Contemporary Context of 'The Bishop Orders His Tomb.'" *PMLA* 84(1969): 1588-1594.

15877. Gridley, Roy E. "Browning's

Caponsacchi: 'How the Priest Caponsacchi said his say.'" *VP* 6(1968): 281-296.

15878. ----------. "Browning's *Pompilia*." *JEGP* 67(1968): 64-83.

15879. Griffith, George V. "'Andrea del Sarto' and the New Jerusalem.'" *VP* 15(1977): 371-372.

15880. Grillo, Virgil F. "Browning's Cuckold of St. Praxed's." *VP* 11(1973): 66-68.

15881. Gross, Dalton H. "Browning's Positivist Count in Search of a Miracle: A Grim Parody in *The Ring and the Book*." *VP* 12(1974): 178-180.

15882. Hagopian, John V. "The Mask of Browning's Countess Gismond." *PQ* 40(1961): 153-155.

15883. Harden, Edgar F. "A New Reading of Browning's 'A Toccata of Galuppi's.'" *VP* 11(1973): 330-336.

15884. Harrison, Thomas P. "Birds in the Poetry of Browning." *RES* 7(1956): 393-405.

15885. Hellstrom, Ward. "Time and Type in Browning's *Saul*." *ELH* 33(1966): 370-389.

15886. Hetzler, Leo A. "The Case of Prince Hohenstiel-Schwangau: Browning and Napoleon III." *VP* 15(1977): 335-350.

15887. Hilton, Earl. "Browning's *Sordello* as a Study of the Will." *PMLA* 69(1954): 1127-1136.

15888. Hitner, John M. "Browning's Grotesque Period." *VP* 4(1966): 1-13.

15889. Holloway, Sister Marcella M. "A Further Reading of 'Count Gismond.'" *SP* 60(1963): 549-553.

15890. Honan, Park. "Browning's Poetic Laboratory: The Uses of *Sordello*." *MP* 56(1959): 162-166.

15891. ----------. "Browning's Testimony on His Essay on Shelley in 'Shepherd v. Francis.'" *ELN* 2(1964): 27-31.

15892. ----------. "The Murder Poem for Elizabeth." *VP* 6(1968): 215-230.

15893. ----------. "The Texts of Fifteen Fugitives by Robert Browning." *VP* 5(1967): 157-169.

15894. Howard, John. "Caliban's Mind." *VP* 1(1963): 249-257.

15895. Huebenthal, John. "The Dating of Browning's 'Love Among the Ruins,' 'Women and Roses,' and 'Childe Roland.'" *VP* 4(1966): 51-54.

15896. ----------. "'Growing Old,' 'Rabbi Ben Ezra,' and 'Tears, Idle Tears.'" *VP* 3(1965): 61-63.

15897. Hyde, Virginia M. "The Fallible Parchment: Structure in Robert Browning's *A Death in the Desert*." *VP* 12(1974): 125-136.

15898. Irvine, William. "Four Monologues in Browning's *Men and Women*." *VP* 2(1964): 155-164.

15899. Jerman, B. R. "Browning's Witless Duke." *PMLA* 72(1957): 488-493.

15900. Jennings, C. Wade. "Diderot: A Suggested Source of the Jules-Phene Episode in *Pippa Passes*." *ELN* 2(1964): 32-36.

15901. Johnson, Alan P. "*Sordelo*: Apollo, Bacchus, and the Pattern of Italian History." *VP* 7(1969): 321-338.

15902. Kelley, Philip, and Ronald Hudson. "The Letters of the Brownings." *VP* 1(1963):

238-239.

15903. Kelly, Richard, and Neil D. Isaacs. "Dramatic Tension and Irony in Browning's 'The Glove.'" *VP* 8(1970): 157-160.

15904. Kelly, Robert L. "Dactyls and Curlews: Satire In 'A Grammarian's Funeral.'" *VP* 5 (1967): 105-112.

15905. Kemper, Claudette. "Irony Anew, with Occasional Reference to Byron and Browning." *SEL* 7(1967): 705-719.

15906. Kintgen, Eugene R. "Childe Roland and the Perversity of the Mind." *VP* 4(1966): 253-258.

15907. Kirk, Carey H. "Checkmating Bishop Blougram." *VP* 10(1972): 265-272.

15908. Kishler, Thomas C. "A Note on 'Soliloguy of the Spanish Cloister.'" *VP* 1(1963): 70-71.

15909. Korg, Jacob. "Browning's Art and 'By the Fire-Side.'" *VP* 15(1977): 147-158.

15910. ----------. "The Music of Lost Dynasties: Browning, Pound and History." *ELH* 39 (1972): 420-440.

15911. ----------. "A Reading of *Pippa Passes*." *VP* 6(1968): 5-20.

15912. Kramer, Dale. "Character and Theme in *Pippa Passes*." *VP* 2(1964): 241-250.

15913. Kroeber, Karl. "Touchstones for Browning's Victorian Complexity." *VP* 3(1965): 101-107.

15914. Kvapil, Charline R. "'How it Strikes a Contemporary': a Dramatic Monologue." *VP* 4 (1966): 279-283.

15915. Langbaum, Robert. "Browning and the Question of Myth." *PMLA* 81(1966): 575-584.

15916. ----------. "Is Guido Saved? The Meaning of Browning's Conclusion to *The Ring and the Book*." *VP* 10(1972): 289-306.

15917. ----------. "*The Ring and the Book*: A Relativist Poem." *PMLA* 71(1956): 131-154.

15918. Lee, Young G. "The Human Condition: Browning's 'Cleon.'" *VP* 7(1969): 56-62.

15919. Lewis, Hanna Ballin. "Hofmannsthal and Browning." *Comp L* 19(1967): 142-159.

15920. Loschky, Helen M. "Free Will Versus Determinism in *The Ring and the Book*." *VP* 6 (1968): 333-352.

15921. Loucks, James F. "'Hy, Zy, Hine' and Peter of Abano." *VP* 12(1974): 165-169.

15922. MacEachen, Dougald B. "Browning's Use of his Sources in 'Andrea del Sarto.'" *VP* 8 (1970): 61-64.

15923. Malbone, Raymond Gates. "That Blasted Rose-Aracia: A Note on Browning's 'Soliloquy of the Spanish Cloister.'" *VP* 4(1966): 218-221.

15924. Marshall, George O. "Evelyn Hope's Lover." *VP* 4(1966): 32-34.

15925. Maurer, Oscar. "Bishop Blougram's 'French Book.'" *VP* 6(1968): 177-179.

15926. Maxwell, J. C. "Browning's Concept of the Poet: A Revision in *Pauline*." *VP* 1(1963): 237-238.

15927. ----------. "A Horatian Echo in Browning's 'Saul.'" *VP* 3(1965): 144.

15928. Maynard, John. "The Dating of Browning's 'Lines to the Memory of James Dow': A Mythling and Some Small Facts." *VP* 14(1976): 67-69.

15929. McAleer, Edward C. "Browning's 'Cleon' and Auguste Comte." *Comp L* 8(1956): 142-145.

15929a. McCarthy, John F. "Browning's *Waring*: The Real Subject of the 'Fancy Portrait.'" *VP* 9(1971): 371-382.

15930. McComb, John King. "Beyond the Dark Tower: Childe Roland's Painful Memories." *ELH* 42 (1975): 460-470.

15931. McCormick, James Patton. "Robert Browning and the Experimental Drama." *PMLA* 68 (1953): 982-991.

15932. McNally, James. "Suiting Sight and Sound to Sense in 'Meeting at Night' and 'Parting at Morning.'" *VP* 5(1967): 219-224.

15933. ----------. "Two Small Verses of Browning." *VP* 9(1971): 338-341.

15934. Melchiori, Barbara. "Browning's 'Andrea del Sarto': A French Source in De Musset." *VP* 4(1966): 132-136.

15935. ----------. "Browning's Don Juan." *EIC* 16(1966): 416-440.

15936. ----------. "Robert Browning's Courtship and the Mutilation of Monsieur Léonce Miranda." *VP* 5(1967): 303-304.

15937. Meyers, Joyce S. "'Childe Roland to the Dark Tower Came': A Nightmare Confrontation with Death." *VP* 8(1970): 335-339.

15938. Millhouser, Milton. "Poet and Burgher: A Comic Variation on a Serious Theme." *VP* 7 (1969): 163-168.

15939. Mishler, Mark K. "God Versus God: The Tension in 'Karshish.'" *ELN* 13(1975): 132-137.

15940. Monteiro, George. "The Apostasy and Death of St. Praxed's Bishop." *VP* 8(1970): 209-218.

15941. ----------. "Browning's 'My Last Duchess.'" *VP* 1(1963): 234-237.

15942. ----------. "A Proposal for Settling the Grammarian's Estate." *VP* 3(1965): 266-270.

15943. Mudford, P. G. "The Artistic Consistency of Browning's *In A Balcony*." *VP* 7(1969): 31-40.

15944. Nelson, Charles Edwin. "Role-Playing in *The Ring and the Book*." *VP* 4(1966): 91-98.

15945. Neufeldt, Victor A. "Browning's 'Saul' in the Context of the Age." *JEGP* 73(1974): 48-59.

15946. Nitchie, Elizabeth. "Browning's 'Duchess.'" *EIC* 3(1953): 475-476.

15947. Omans, Glen. "Browning's 'Fra Lippo Lippi,' A Transcendentalist Monk." *VP* 7(1969): 129-145.

15948. O'Neal, Michael J. "Miltonic Allusions in *Bishop Blougram's Apology*." *VP* 15 (1977): 177-182.

15949. Ower, John. "The Abuse of the Hand: A Thematic Motif in Browning's 'Fra Lippo Lippi.'" *VP* 14(1976): 135-141.

15950. Page, David. "And so is Browning." *EIC* 13(1963): 146-154.

15951. Palmer, Rupert E., Jr. "The Uses of Character in 'Bishop Blougram's Apology.'" *MP* 58 (1960): 108-118.

15952. Parr, Johnstone. "Browning's *Fra Lippo Lippi*, Baldinucci, and the Milanesi Edition of Vasari." *ELN* 3(1966): 197-201.

15953. ----------. "Browning's *Fra Lippo Lippi*, Vasari's Masaccio, and Mrs. Jameson." *ELN*

5(1968): 277-283.

15954. Parr, Johnstone. "The Date of Composition of Browning's *Love Among the Ruins*." *PQ* 32(1953): 443-446.

15955. ----------. "The Site and Ancient City of Browning's *Love Among the Ruins*." *PMLA* 68(1953): 128-137.

15956. Pearsall, Robert B. "Browning's Texts in Galatians and Deuteronomy." *MLQ* 13 (1952): 256-258.

15957. Peckham, Morse. "Historiography and *The Ring and the Book*." *VP* 6(1968): 243-258.

15958. Perrine, Laurence. "Browning's 'Calaban Upon Setebos': A Reply." *VP* 2(1964): 124-127.

15959. ----------. "Browning's Shrewd Duke." *PMLA* 74(1959): 157-159.

15960. ----------. "Browning's 'Too Late': A Re-Interpretation." *VP* 7(1969): 339-345.

15961. ----------. "Family Relationships at Saint Praxeds." *VP* 12(1974): 175-177.

15962. Peterson, William S. "An Unpublished Memoir of Robert Browning." *VP* 7(1969): 147-151.

15963. Phipps, Charles T., S.J. "Adaptation from the Past, Creation for the Present: A Study of Browning's 'The Pope.'" *SP* 65(1968): 702-722.

15964. ----------. "The Bishop as Bishop: Clerical Motif and Meaning in 'The Bishop Orders His Tomb at St. Praxed's Church.'" *VP* 8(1970): 199-208.

15965. ----------. "Browning's Canon Giuseppe Caponsacchi: Warrior-Priest, Dantean Lover, Critic of Society." *ELH* 36(1969): 696-718.

15966. ----------. "Browning's 'Soliloquy of the Spanish Cloister': Lines 71-72." *VP* 7 (1969): 158-159.

15967. ----------. "The Monsignor in *Pippa Passes*: Browning's First Clerical Character." *VP* 7(1969): 66-70.

15968. Plotinsky, Melvin L. "The Kingdom of Infinite Space." *TSLL* 11(1969): 837-849.

15969. Poston, Lawrence, III. "Browning's Political Skepticism: *Sordello* and the Plays." *PMLA* 88(1973): 260-270.

15970. Preyer, Robert. "Robert Browning: A Reading of the Early Narratives." *ELH* 26(1959): 531-548.

15971. ----------. "Two Styles in the Verse of Robert Browning." *ELH* 32(1965): 62-84.

15972. Raisor, Philip. "'Palmyra's Ruined Palaces': The Influence of Shelley's *Queen Mab* on Browning's 'Love Among the Ruins.'" *VP* 14(1976): 142-149.

15973. Raymond, William O. "'The Jewelled Bow': A Study in Browning's Imagery and Humanism." *PMLA* 70(1955): 115-131.

15974. ----------. "The Pope in *The Ring and the Book*." *VP* 6(1968): 323-332.

15975. Reed, Joseph W., Jr. "Browning and Macready: The Final Quarrel." *PMLA* 75(1960): 597-603.

15976. Ridenour, George M. "Browning's Music Poems: Fancy and Fact." *PMLA* 78(1963): 369-377.

15977. Russo, Francine Gomberg. "Browning's 'James Lee's Wife': A Study in Neurotic Love." *VP* 12(1974): 219-234.

15978. Ryals, Clyde de L. "*Balaustion's Adventure*: Browning's Greek Parable." *PMLA* 88 (1973): 1040-1048.

15979. ----------. "Browning's Amphibian: Don Juan at Home." *EIC* 19(1969): 210-217.

15980. Ryan, William M. "The Classifications of Browning's 'Difficult' Vocabulary." *SP* 60(1963): 542-548.

15981. Sanders, Charles Richard. "Some Lost and Unpublished Carlyle-Browning Correspondence." *JEGP* 62(1963): 323-335.

15982. Sandstrom, Glenn. "'James Lee's Wife'—and Browning's." *VP* 4(1966): 259-270.

15983. Scheer, Thomas Frederick. "Mythopoeia and the Renaissance Mind: A Reading of 'A Grammarian's Funeral.'" *JNT* 5(1975): 119-128.

15984. Shapiro, Arnold. "A New (Old) Reading of *Bishop Blougram's Apology*: The Problem of the Dramatic Monologue." *VP* 10(1972): 243-256.

15985. Shaw, W. David. "The Analogical Argument of Browning's 'Saul.'" *VP* 2(1964): 277-282.

15986. ----------. "Character and Philosophy in 'Fra Lippo Lippi.'" *VP* 2(1964): 127-132.

15987. Short, Clarice. "Childe Roland, Pedestrian." *VP* 6(1968): 175-177.

15988. Shmiefsky, Marvel. "Yeats and Browning: The Shock of Recognition." *SEL* 10 (1970): 701-721.

15989. Siegchrist, Mark. "Browning's *Red Cotten Night-Cap Country*: The Process of Imagination." *VP* 12(1974): 137-152.

15990. ----------. "Pollyanna or Polyanthus: Clara de Millefleurs in Browning's *Red Cotten Night-Cap Country*." *ELN* 11(1974): 283-287.

15991. ----------. "Thematic Coherence in Browning's *Dramatic Idyls*." *VP* 15(1977): 229-239.

15992. Slakey, Roger L. "A Note on Browning's 'Rabbi Ben Ezra.'" *VP* 5(1967): 291-294.

15993. Slinn, Warwick. "Experience as Pageant: Subjectivism in *Fifine at the Fair*." *ELH* 42(1975): 651-668.

15994. Smalley, Donald. "Joseph Arnould and Robert Browning: New Letters (1842-50) and a Verse Epistle." *PMLA* 80(1965): 90-101.

15995. Sonstroem, David. "Animal and Vegetable in the Spanish Cloister." *VP* 6(1968): 70-73.

15996. ----------. "'Fine Speeches Like Gold' in Browning's 'The Glove.'" *VP* 15(1977): 85-90.

15997. ----------. "On Resisting Brother Lippo." *TSLL* 15(1974): 721-734.

15998. Spånberg, Sven-Johan. "The Don Juan Figure in Browning's *Fifine at the Fair*." *Comp L* 28(1976): 19-33.

15999. Stasny, John F. "Selected Bibliography." [*The Ring and the Book*] *VP* 6(1968): 374-375.

16000. Stempel, Daniel. "Browning's *Sordello*: The Art of the Makers-See." *PMLA* 80 (1965): 554-561.

16001. Stevens, L. Robert. "Aestheticism in Browning's Early Renaissance Monologues." *VP* 3(1965): 19-24.

16002. Stone, Wilfred H. "Browning and 'Mark Rutherford.'" *RES* 4(1953): 249-259.

16003. Sullivan, Mary Rose. "The Function of Book I in *The Ring and the Book*." *VP* 6(1968):

231-242.

16004. Sullivan, Ruth Elizabeth. "Browning's 'Childe Roland' and Dante's 'Inferno.'" VP 5(1967): 296-302.

16005. Svaglic, Martin J. "Browning's Grammarian: Apparent Failure or Real?" VP 5 (1967): 93-104.

16006. Swingle, L. J. "Truth and The Ring and the Book: A Negative View." VP 6(1968): 259-270.

16007. Talon, Henri-A. "The Ring and the Book: Truth and Fiction in Character-painting." VP 6(1968): 353-365.

16008. Thale, Jerome. "Browning's 'Popularity' and the Spasmodic Poets." JEGP 54 (1955): 348-354.

16009. Thompson, Gordon W. "Authorial Detachment and Imagery in The Ring and the Book." SEL 10(1970): 669-686.

16010. Tilton, John W, and R. Dale Tuttle. "A New Reading of 'Count Gismond.'" SP 59(1962): 83-95.

16011. Timko, Michael. "Ah, Did You Once See Browning Plain?" SEL 6(1966): 731-742.

16012. ----------. "Browning upon Butler; or, Natural Theology in the English Isle." Criticism 7(1965): 141-150.

16013. Vogel, C. S. "Browning's Salomé: An Allusion in 'Fra Lippo Lippi.'" VP 14(1976): 346-348.

16014. Viswanathan, S. "'Ay, Note that Potter's Wheel': Browning and 'That Metaphor.'" VP 7(1969): 349-352.

16015. Waddington, Patrick. "Two Unpublished Letters of Robert Browning to Pauline Viardot-Garcia." ELN 13(1975): 35-37.

16016. Waters, D. Douglas, Jr. "Does Browning's 'Great Text in Galatians' Entail 'Twenty-nine Distinct Damnations?'" MLR 55 (1960): 243-244.

16017. Watkins, Charlotte C. "The 'Abstruser Themes' of Browning's Fifine at the Fair." PMLA 74(1959): 426-437.

16018. ----------. "Browning's 'Fame within These Four Years.'" MLR 53(1958): 492-500.

16019. ----------. "Browning's Men and Women and the Spasmodic School." JEGP 57(1958): 57-59.

16020. Wear, Richard. "Further Thoughts on Browning's Spanish Cloister." VP 12(1974): 67-70.

16021. Willoughby, John W. "Browning's 'Childe Roland to the Dark Tower Came.'" VP 1 (1963): 291-299.

16022. Witt, Robert W. "Caliban Upon Plato." VP 13(1975): 136.

16023. Wyant, Jerome L. "The Legal Episodes in The Ring and the Book." VP 6(1968): 309-322.

16024. Yetman, Michael G. "'Count Guido Franceschini': The Villain as Artist in The Ring and the Book." PMLA 87(1972): 1093-1102.

16025. ----------. "Exorcising Shelley Out of Browning: Sordello and the Problem of Poetic Identity." VP 13(1975): 79-98.

See also 2948, 4693, 5123, 15319, 15374.

BUCHANAN, ROBERT. 16026. Cassidy, John A. "Robert Buchanan and the Fleshly Controversy." PMLA 67(1952): 65-93.

16027. Forsyth, R. A. "Nature and the Victorian City: The Ambivalent Attitude of Robert Buchanan." ELH 36(1969): 382-439.

16028. ----------. "Robert Buchanan and the Dilemma of the Brave New Victorian World." SEL 9(1969): 647-657.

16029. Storey, George G. "Robert Buchanan's Critical Principles." PMLA 68(1953): 1228-1232.

BULWER-LYTTON, EDWARD. 16030. Barnes, James J. "Edward Lytton Bulwer and the Publishing Firm of Harper & Brothers." AL 38(1966): 35-48.

16031. Christensen, Allan C. "Edward Bulwer, First Baron Lytton of Knebworth: 25 May 1803-18 January 1873." NCF 28(1973): 85-86.

16032. Dahl, Curtis. "Bulwer-Lytton and the School of Catastrophe." PQ 32(1953): 428-442.

16033. Eigner, Edwin M. "Bulwer-Lytton and the Changed Ending of Great Expectations." NCF 25(1970): 104-109.

16034. Eigner, Edwin M., and Joseph I. Fradin. "Bulwer-Lytton and Dickins' Jo." NCF 24 (1969): 98-103.

16035. Fradin, Joseph I. "'The Absorbing Tyranny of Everyday Life': Bulwer-Lytton's A Strange Story." NCF 16(1961): 1-16.

16036. Ganzel, Dewey. "Bulwer and His Lady." MP 58(1960): 41-52.

16037. Kelly, Richard. "The Haunted House of Bulwer-Lytton." SSF 8(1971): 581-587.

16038. Simmons, James C. "Bulwer and Vesuvius: The Topicality of The Last Days of Pompeii." NCF 24(1969): 103-105.

16039. Wagner, Geoffrey. "A Forgotten Satire: Bulwer-Lytton's The Coming Race." NCF 19 (1965): 379-385.

16040. Wildman, John Hazard. "Unsuccessful Return from Avalon." VP 12(1974): 291-296.

See also 144, 211, 20580.

BURDETT-COUTTS, ANGELA. 16041. Adams, Ruth M. "Miss Dunstable and Miss Coutts." NCF 9 (1954): 231-235.

16042. Fielding, K. J. "Miss Burdett-Coutts: Some Misconceptions." NCF 8(1954): 314-318.

BUTLER, SAMUEL. 16043. Breuer, Hans-Peter. "Samuel Butler's 'The Book of the Machines' and the Argument from Design." MP 72(1975): 365-383.

16044. Marshall, William H. "The Way of All Flesh: The Dual Function of Edward Overton." TSLL 4(1963): 583-590.

16045. Shoenberg, Robert E. "The Literal-Mindedness of Samuel Butler." SEL 4(1964): 601-616.

See also 144, 18927.

BYRON, GEORGE GORDON. 16046. Allentuck, Marcia. "Byron and Goethe: New Unpublished References by Henry Gally Knight." PQ 52(1973): 777-779.

16047. Ashton, Thomas L. "Byronic Lyrics for David's Harp: The Hebrew Melodies." SEL 12 (1972): 665-681.

16048. ----------. "Marino Faliero: Byron's 'Poetry of Politics.'" SR 13(1974): 1-14.

16049. Baender, Paul. "Mark Twain and the Byron Scandal." AL 30(1959): 467-485.

16050. Barker, Kathleen M. D. "The First English Performance of Byron's Werner." MP 66 (1969): 342-344.

16051. Beaty, Frederick L. "Byron and the Story of Francesca da Rimini." PMLA 75(1960):

395–401.

16052. Beaty, Frederick. "Byron's Imita-
tions of Juvenal and Persius." *SR* 15(1976): 333–
356.

16053. ----------. "Byron's Longbow and
Strongbow." *SEL* 12(1972): 653–663.

16054. ----------. "Harlequin Don Juan."
JEGP 67(1968): 395–405.

16055. Bentley, G. E., Jr. "Byron, Shelley,
Wordsworth, Blake, and *The Seaman's Recorder*."
SR 9(1970): 21–36.

16056. Bostetter, Edward E. "Byron and
the Politics of Paradise." *PMLA* 75(1960): 571–
576.

16057. ----------. "Masses and Souls:
Byron's View of the External World." *MLQ* 35
(1974): 257–271.

16058. Brisman, Leslie. "Byron: Troubled
Stream from a Pure Source." *ELH* 42(1975): 623–
650.

16059. Brownstein, Rachel Mayer. "Byron's
Don Juan: Some Reasons for the Rhymes." *MLQ* 28
(1967): 177–191.

16060. Bruffee, Kenneth A. "The Synthetic
Hero and the Narrative Structure of *Childe
Harold* III." *SEL* 6(1966): 669–678.

16061. Butler, Maria Hogan. "An Examination of Byron's Revision of *Manfred*, Act III."
SP 60(1963): 627–636.

16062. Cline, C. L. "Sacrilege at Lucca
and the Pisan Circle." *TSLL* 9(1968): 503–509.

16063. Clubbe, John. "Byron and Scott."
TSLL 15(1973): 67–91.

16064. Cooke, M. G. "The Restoration
Ethos of Byron's Classical Plays." *PMLA* 79
(1964): 569–578.

16065. Cooke, Michael G. "Byron's *Don
Juan*: The Obsession and Self-Discipline of
Spontaneity." *SR* 14(1975): 285–302.

16066. Deen, Leonard W. "Liberty and
License in Byron's *Don Juan*." *TSLL* 8(1966):
345–357.

16067. DePorte, Michael V. "Byron's
Strange Perversity of Thought." *MLQ* 33(1972):
405–419.

16068. Diakonova, Nina. "Byron's Prose and
Byron's Poetry." *SEL* 16(1976): 547–561.

16069. Dowden, Wilfred S. "A Jacobin
Journel's View of Byron." *SP* 48(1951): 56–66.

16070. Eggenschwiler, David. "Byron's
Cain and the Antimythological Myth." *MLQ* 37
(1976): 324–338.

16071. ----------. "The Tragic and Comic
Rhythms of *Manfred*." *SR* 13(1974): 63–78.

16072. Elledge, W. Paul. "Byron's Hungry
Sinner: The Quest Motif in *Don Juan*." *JEGP* 69
(1970): 1–13.

16073. Everett, Edwin M. "Lord Byron's
Lakist Interlude." *SP* 55(1958): 62–75.

16074. Fiess, Edward. "Byron's Dark Blue
Ocean and Melville's Rolling Sea." *ELN* 3(1966):
274–278.

16075. Fitzpatrick, William P. "Byron's
Mysteries: The Paradoxical Drive Toward Eden."
SEL 15(1975): 615–625.

16076. Gleckner, Robert F. "Ruskin and
Byron." *ELN* 3(1965): 47–51.

16077. Goldstein, Stephen L. "Byron's *Cain*
and the Painites." *SR* 14(1975): 391–410.

16078. Hoisington, Sona Stephan. "*Eugene
Onegin*: An Inverted Byronic Poem." *Comp L* 27
(1975): 136–152.

16079. Hudson, Arthur Palmer. "The 'Super-
stitious' Lord Byron." *SP* 63(1966): 708–721.

16080. Kahn, Arthur D. "Seneca and *Sarda-
napalus*: Byron, the Don Quixote of Neo-Classicism."
SP 66(1969): 654–671.

16081. Kemper, Claudette. "Irony Anew,
with Occasional Reference to Byron and Browning."
SEL 7(1967): 705–719.

16082. Kleinfield, H. L. "Infidel on
Parnassus: Lord Byron and the *North American
Review*." *NEQ* 33(1960): 164–185.

16083. Lauber, John. "*Don Juan* as Anti-
Epic." *SEL* 8(1968): 607–619.

16084. Leach, Sally. "The Byron Sesquicen-
tenary Exhibition Held in 1974 at the Humanities
Research Center of the University of Texas at
Austin." [catalog] *TSLL* 17(1975): 119–156.

16085. Lefevre, Carl. "Lord Byron's Fiery
Convert of Revenge." *SP* 49(1952): 468–487.

16086. Luke, Hugh J., Jr. "The Publishing
of Byron's *Don Juan*." *PMLA* 80(1965): 199–209.

16087. Marshall, William H. "Some Byron
Comments on Pope and Boileau." *PQ* 38(1959): 252–
253.

16088. McConnell, Frank D. "Byron's Reduc-
tions: 'Much Too Poetical.'" *ELH* 37(1970): 415–
432.

16089. McGann, Jerome J. "Byronic Drama in
Two Venetian Plays." *MP* 66(1968): 30–44.

16090. ----------. "A Reply to George M.
Ridenour." *SR* 16(1977): 571–583.

16091. Michaels, Leonard. "Byron's *Cain*."
PMLA 84(1969): 71–78.

16092. Mortenson, Robert. "Another Continuation of *Don Juan*." *SR* 2(1963): 244–247.

16093. Ogle, Robert B. "A Byron Contradiction: Some Light on his Italian Study." *SR* 12
(1973): 436–442.

16094. Pafford, Ward. "Byron and the Mind
of Man: *Childe Harold III-IV* and *Manfred*." *SR* 1
(1962): 105–128.

16095. Quinlan, Maurice J. "Byron's *Manfred*
and Zoroastrianism." *JEGP* 57(1958): 726–738.

16096. Reiman, Donald H. "*Don Juan* in Epic
Context." *SR* 16(1977): 587–594.

16097. Ridenour, George M. "*Don Juan* and
the Romantics." *SR* 16(1977): 563–570, 584–586.

16098. ----------. "The Mode of Byron's
Don Juan." *PMLA* 79(1964): 442–446.

16099. Robertson, J. Michael. "Aristocratic
Individualism in Byron's *Don Juan*." *SEL* 17(1977):
639–655.

16100. Robertson, Michael. "The Byron of
Don Juan as Whig Aristocrat." *TSLL* 17(1976):
709–724.

16101. Rutherford, Andrew. "The Influence
of Hobhouse on *Childe Harold's Pilgrimage*, Canto
IV." *RES* 12(1961): 391–397.

16102. Salomon, Roger B. "Mock-Heroes and
Mock-Heroic Narrative: Byron's *Don Juan* in the
Context of Cervantes." *SLI* 9,#1(1976): 69–86.

16103. Sanders, Charles Richard. "The
Byron Closed in *Sartor Resartus*." *SR* 3(1964):
77–108.

16104. Sarmiento, Edward. "A Parallel
between Lord Byron and Fray Luis de León." *RES*

4(1953): 267-273.

16105. Shilstone, Frederick W. "Byron's 'Mental Theatre' and the German Classical Present." *CD* 10(1976): 187-199.

16106. Slater, Joseph. "Byron's Hebrew Melodies." *SP* 49(1952): 75-94.

16107. Sperry, Stuart M. "Byron and the Meaning of 'Manfred.'" *Criticism* 16(1974): 189-202.

16108. Stavrou, C. N. "Religion in Byron's *Don Juan*." *SEL* 3(1963): 567-594.

16109. Steffan, Guy. "The Devil a Bit of Our *Beppo*." *PQ* 32(1953): 154-171.

16110. Sundell, Michael G. "The Development of *The Giaour*." *SEL* 9(1969): 587-599.

16111. Tannenbaum, Leslie. "Lord Byron in the Wilderness: Biblical Tradition in Byron's *Cain* and Blake's *The Ghost of Abel*." *MP* 72(1975): 350-364.

16112. Twitchell, James. "The Supernatural Structure of Byron's *Manfred*." *SEL* 15(1975): 601-614.

16113. Walling, William. "Tradition and Revolution: Byron's *Vision of Judgement*." *WC* 3 (1972): 223-231.

See also 446, 3410, 4018, 13632, 13882, 15285, 15286, 15367, 15384.

CAMPBELL, THOMAS.   See 4292.

• CARLYLE, THOMAS.   16114. Aiken, Susan Hardy. "On Clothes and Heroes: Carlyle and 'How It Strikes a Contemporary.'" *VP* 13(1975): 99-109.

16115. Arac, Jonathan. "Narrative Form and Social Sense in *Bleak House* and *The French Revolution*." *NCF* 32(1977): 54-72.

16116. Ashton, Rosemary D. "Carlyle's Apprenticeship: His Early German Criticism and his Relationship with Goethe." *MLR* 7(1976): 1-18.

16117. Barbour, James, and Leon Howard. "Carlyle and the Conclusion of *Moby-Dick*." *NEQ* 49(1976): 214-224.

16118. Brantlinger, Patrick. "'Romance,' 'Biography,' and the Making of *Sartor Resartus*." *PQ* 52(1973): 108-118.

• 16119. ----------. "'Teufeldsdröckh' Resartus." *ELN* 9(1972): 191-193.

• 16120. Bruns, Gerald L. "The Formal Nature of Victorian Thinking." *PMLA* 90(1975): 904-918.

16121. Calder, Grace J. "Carlyle and 'Irving's London Circle': Some Unpublished Letters by Thomas Carlyle and Mrs. Edward Strachey." *PMLA* 69(1954): 1135-1149.

16122. ----------. "Erasmus A. Darwin, Friend of Thomas and Jane Carlyle." *MLQ* 20(1959): 36-48.

16123. Campbell, Ian. "Carlyle and Sir Gideon Dunn." *ELN* 9(1972): 185-191.

16124. ----------. "Carlyle and the Negro Question Again." *Criticism* 13(1971): 279-290.

16125. Coulling, Sidney M. B. "Carlyle and Swift." *SEL* 10(1970): 741-758.

16126. Deen, Leonard W. "Irrational Form in *Sartor Resartus*." *TSLL* 5(1963): 438-451.

16127. DeLaura, David J. "Arnold and Carlyle." *PMLA* 79(1964): 104-129.

16128. ----------. "Ishmael as Prophet: *Heroes and Hero-Worship* and the Self-Expressive Basis of Carlyle's Art." *TSLL* 11(1969): 705-732.

16129. Dibble, Jerry Allen. "Carlyle's 'British Reader' and the Structure of *Sartor*

Resartus." *TSLL* 16(1974): 293-304.

16130. Gilbert, Elliot L. "'A Wondrous Contiguity': Anachronism in Carlyle's Prophecy and Art." *PMLA* 87(1972): 432-442.

16131. Gragg, Wilson B. "Trollope and Carlyle." *NCF* 13(1958): 266-270.

16132. Haber, Grace Stevenson. "Echoes from Carlyle's 'Goethe's *Helena*' in *The Mayor of Casterbridge*." *NCF* 12(1957): 89-90.

16133. Hall, N. John. "Trollope and Carlyle." *NCF* 27(1972): 197-205.

16134. Hopwood, Alison L. "Carlyle and Conrad: *Past and Present* and 'Heart of Darkness.'" *RES* 23(1972): 162-172.

16135. Johnson, Wendell Stacy. "Swinburne and Carlyle." *ELN* 1(1963): 117-121.

16136. King, Marjorie P. "'Illudo Chartis': an Initial Study in Carlyle's Mode of Composition." *MLR* 49(1954): 164-175.

16137. Landow, George P. "'Swim or Drown': Carlyle's World of Shipwrecks, Castaways, and Stranded Voyagers." *SEL* 15(1975): 641-655.

• 16138. Metzger, Lore. "*Sartor Resartus*: A Victorian *Faust*." *Comp L* 13(1961): 316-331.

16139. Moore, Carlisle. "The Persistence of Carlyle's 'Everlasting Yea.'" *MP* 54(1957): 187-196.

16140. ----------. "*Sartor Resartus* and the Problem of Carlyle's 'Conversion.'" *PMLA* 70 (1955): 662-681.

16141. Nobbe, Susanne H. "Four Unpublished Letters to Carlyle." *PMLA* 70(1955): 876-884.

• 16142. Reed, Walter L. "The Pattern of Conversion in *Sartor Resartus*." *ELH* 38(1971): 411-431.

16143. Roberts, Mark. "Carlyle and the Rhetoric of Unreason." *EIC* 18(1968): 397-419.

16144. Roellinger, Francis X., Jr. "The Early Development of Carlyle's Style." *PMLA* 72 (1957): 936-951.

16145. Sanders, Charles Richard. "The Byron Closed in *Sartor Resartus*." *SR* 3(1964): 77-108.

16146. ----------. "Carlyle and Tennyson." *PMLA* 76(1961): 82-97.

16147. ----------. "Some Lost and Unpublished Carlyle-Browning Correspondence." *JEGP* 62(1963): 323-335.

16148. Sigman, Joseph. "Adam-Kadmon, Nifl, Muspel, and the Biblical Symbolism of *Sartor Resartus*." *ELH* 41(1974): 233-256.

16149. Slater, Joseph. "George Ripley and Thomas Carlyle." *PMLA* 67(1952): 341-349.

16150. Slater, Michael. "Carlyle and Jerrold into Dickens: A Study of *The Chimes*." *NCF* 24(1970): 506-526.

16151. Smeed, J. W. "Thomas Carlyle and Jean Paul Richter." *Comp L* 16(1964): 226-253.

16152. Starzyk, Lawrence J. "Arnold and Carlyle." *Criticism* 12(1970): 281-300.

16153. Tarr, Rodger L. "Mary Aitken Carlyle: An Unpublished Letter to Her Son." *ELN* 8 (1971): 281-283.

16154. ----------. "Some Unpublished Letters of Varnhagen von Ense to Thomas Carlyle." *MLR* 68(1973): 22-27.

16155. Tennyson, G. B. "Carlyle's Poetry to 1840: A Checklist and Discussion, a New Attribution, and Six Unpublished Poems." *VP* 1

1963: 161-181.

16156. Tennyson, G. B. "Unnoted Encyclopedia Articles by Carlyle." *ELN* 1(1963): 108-112.

16157. Tobias, Richard C. "The Eighth Hero and the Eighth Day." *MP* 73(1976): 284-289.

16158. Wilkinson, D. R. M. "Carlyle, Arnold, and Literary Justice." *PMLA* 86(1971): 225-235.

16159. Worth, George J. "Three Carlyle Documents." *PMLA* 71(1956): 542-544.

See also 13882, 16178, 16482, 16740.

CARROLL, LEWIS. 16160. Johnson, Paula. "Alice among the Analysts." *HSL* 4(1972): 113-122.

16161. Kincaid, James R. "Alice's Invasion of Wonderland." *PMLA* 88(1973): 92-99.

16162. Matthews, Charles. "Satire in the Alice Books." *Criticism* 12(1970): 105-119.

16163. Miller, Edmund. "Lewis Carroll's Genealogical Oversight in 'The Tangled Tale.'" *ELN* 12(1974): 109-111.

16164. Rackin, Donald. "Alice's Journey to the End of Night." *PMLA* 81(1966): 313-326.

16165. Sewell, Elizabeth. "Bats and Tea-Trays: A Note on Nonsense." *EIC* 1(1951): 376-386.

CHOLMODELEY, MARY. 16166. Colby, Vineta. "'Devoted Amateur': Mary Cholmondeley and *Red Potage*." *EIC* 20(1970): 213-228.

CLARE, JOHN. 16167. Frosch, Thomas R. "The Descriptive Style of John Clare." *SR* 10 (1971): 137-149.

16168. Green, David Bonnell. "New Letters of John Clare to Taylor and Hessey." *SP* 64(1967): 720-734.

16169. Robinson, Eric, and Geoffrey Summerfield. "John Clare: An Interpretation of Certain Asylum Letters." *RES* 13(1962): 135-146.

16170. ----------. "John Taylor's Editing of Clare's *The Shepherd's Calendar*." *RES* 14 (1963): 359-369.

16171. Storey, Mark. "Some Previously Unpublished Letters from John Clare." *RES* 25 (1974): 177-185.

16172. Swingle, L. J. "Stalking the Essential John Clare: Clare in Relation to His Contemporaries." *SR* 14(1975): 273-284.

16173. Todd, Janet M. "'Very copys of nature': John Clare's Descriptive Poetry." *PQ* 53 (1974): 84-99.

CLOUGH, ARTHUR HUGH. 16174. Badger, Kingsbury. "Arthur Hugh Clough as Dipsychus." *MLQ* 12 (1951): 39-56.

16175. Barish, Evelyn. "A New Clough Manuscript." *RES* 15(1964): 168-174.

16176. Bertram, James. "The Ending of Clough's *Dipsychus*." *RES* 7(1956): 59-60.

16177. Bowers, Frederick. "Arthur Hugh Clough: The Modern Mind." *SEL* 6(1966): 709-716.

16178. Castan, Constanine. "Clough's 'Epi-strauss-ium' and Carlyle." *VP* 4(1966): 54-56.

16179. ----------. "The Marriage of Epithalamium and Elegy in a Poem by Clough." *VP* 10(1972): 145-160.

16180. Dalglish, Doris N. "Arthur Hugh Clough: the Shorter Poems." *EIC* 2(1952): 38-53.

16181. DeLaura, David J. "Arnold, Clough, Dr. Arnold, and 'Thyrsis.'" *VP* 7(1969): 191-202.

16182. Forsyth, R. A. "'The Buried Life'—The Contrasting Views of Arnold and Clough in the Context of Dr. Arnold's Historiography." *ELH*

35(1968): 218-253.

16183. ----------. "Herbert, Clough, and Their Church-Windows." *VP* 7(1969): 17-30.

16184. Gollin, Richard M. "The 1951 Edition of Clough's *Poems*: A Critical Re-Examination." *MP* 60(1962): 120-127.

16185. Greenberger, Evelyn Barish. "Clough's 'The Judgement of Brutus': A Newly Found Poem." *VP* 8(1970): 127-150.

16186. ----------. "'Salsette and Elephanta': An Unpublished Poem by Clough." *RES* 20 (1969): 284-305.

16187. Houghton, Walter E. "Arthur Hugh Clough: A Hundred Years of Disparagement." *SEL* 1,#4(1961): 35-61.

16188. Johari, G. P. "Arthur Hugh Clough at Oriel and at University Hall." *PMLA* 66(1951): 405-425.

16189. Leedham-Green, E.S. "Four Unpublished Translations by Arthur Hugh Clough." *RES* 23(1972): 179-187.

16190. McGhee, Richard D. "'Blank Misgivings': Arthur Hugh Clough's Search for Poetic Form." *VP* 7(1969): 105-115.

16191. McGrail, John P. "Three Image Motifs in Arthur Hugh Clough's *The Bothie of Tober-Na-Vuolich*." *VP* 13(1975): 75-78.

16192. McGrane, P. S. "Clough's 'Salsette and Elephanta' and *The Christian Year*." *RES* 25 (1974): 445-449.

16193. ----------. "Unpublished Poetic Fragments and Manuscripts of Arthur Hugh Clough." *VP* 14(1976): 359-364.

16194. Miyoshi, Masao. "Clough's Poems of Self-Irony." *SEL* 5(1965): 691-704.

16195. Norrington, A. L. P. "Clough and *In Memoriam*." *RES* 4(1953): 364.

16196. Robertson, David Allen, Jr. "'Dover Beach' and 'Say Not the Struggle Nought Availeth.'" *PMLA* 66(1951): 919-926.

16197. Rutland, R. B. "The Genesis of Clough's *Bothie*." *VP* 11(1973): 277-284.

16198. ----------. "Some Notes on the Highland Setting of Clough's *Bothie*." *VP* 14 (1976): 125-134.

16199. Ryals, Clyde De L. "An Interpretation of Clough's *Dipsychus*." *VP* 1(1963): 182-187.

16200. Savory, Jerold J. "An Epitaph Poem by Arthur Hugh Clough." *VP* 14(1976): 264.

16201. Tillotson, Kathleen. "Rugby 1850: Arnold, Clough, Walrond, and *In Memoriam*." *RES* 4(1953): 122-140.

16202. Timko, Michael. "The Satiric Poetry of Arthur Hugh Clough." *VP* 1(1963): 104-114.

16203. ----------. "The 'True Creed' of Arthur Hugh Clough." *MLQ* 21(1960): 208-222.

16204. Townsend, Francis G. "Clough's 'The Struggle': The Text, Title, and Date of Publication." *PMLA* 67(1952): 1191-1192.

See also 17545.

COBBETT, WILLIAM. 16205. Duff, Gerald A. "An Unpublished William Cobbett Letter." *ELN* 4 (1966): 110-112.

16206. ----------. "William Cobbett and the Prose of Revelation." *TSLL* 11(1970): 1349-1365.

16207. Lemrow, Lynne. "A New Letter of William Cobbett." *ELN* 10(1973): 275-278.

COLERIDGE, H. N. 16208. Holt, Palmer C.

"Poe and H. N. Coleridge's *Greek Classic Poets*: 'Pinakidia,' 'Politian,' and 'Morella' Sources." *AL* 34(1962): 8-30.

COLERIDGE, SAMUEL TAYLOR.   16209. Adlard, John. "The Quantock *Christabel*." *PQ* 50(1971): 230-238.

16210. Aldrich, Ruth I. "The Wordsworths and Coleridge: 'Three Persons' but *not* 'One Soul.'" *SR* 2(1962): 61-63.

16211. Angus, Douglas. "The Theme of Love and Guilt in Coleridge's Three Major Poems." *JEGP* 59(1960): 655-668.

16212. Appleyard, J. A. "Structuring Coleridge's Ideas." *MLQ* 32(1971): 206-213.

16213. Ashton, Rosemary D. "Coleridge and Faust." *RES* 28(1977): 156-167.

16214. Averill, James H. "Another Early Coleridge Reference to *An Evening Walk*." *ELN* 13 (1976): 270-273.

16215. Badawi, M. M. "Coleridge's Formal Criticism of Shakespeare's Plays." *EIC* 10(1960): 148-162.

16216. Bailey, Dudley. "Coleridge's Revision of *The Friend*." *MP* 59(1961): 89-99.

16217. Barnard, John. "An Echo of Keats in 'The Eolian Harp.'" *RES* 28(1977): 311-313.

16218. Barnes, Sam G. "Was *Theory of Life* Coleridge's 'Opus Maximum?'" *SP* 55(1958): 494-514.

16219. Barnet, Sylvan. "Coleridge on Puns: A Note to His Shakespeare Criticism." *JEGP* 56 (1957): 602-609.

16220. Barth, J. Robert, S.J. "Symbol as Sacrement in Coleridge's Thought." *SR* 11(1972): 320-331.

16221. Beaty, Frederick L. "Dorothy Wordsworth and the Coleridges: A New Letter." *MLR* 51 (1956): 411-413.

16222. ----------. "Two Manuscript Poems of Coleridge." *RES* 7(1956): 185-187.

16223. Beer, John. "Coleridge, the Wordsworths, and the State of Trance." *WC* 8(1977): 121-138.

16224. Bellis, George. "The Fixed Crime of the *Ancient Mariner*." *EIC* 24(1974): 243-260.

16225. Benziger, James. "Organic Unity: Leibniz to Coleridge." *PMLA* 66(1951): 24-48.

16226. Berkoben, Lawrence D. "*Christabel*: A Variety of Evil Experience." *MLQ* 25(1964): 400-411.

16227. ----------. "The Composition of Coleridge's 'Hymn Before Sunrise': Some Mitigating Circumstances." *ELN* 4(1966): 32-37.

16228. Beyer, Werner W. "Coleridge's Early Knowledge of German." *MP* 52(1955): 192-200.

16229. Bostetter, Edward E. "*Christabel*: The Vision of Fear." *PQ* 36(1957): 183-194.

16230. ----------. "The Nightmare World of *The Ancient Mariner*." *SR* 1(1962): 241-254.

16231. Boulger, James D. "Coleridge on Imagination Revisited." *WC* 4(1973): 13-24.

16232. ----------. "Coleridge: The Marginalia, Myth-Making, and the Later Poetry." *SR* 11 (1972): 304-319.

16233. ----------. "Imagination and Speculation in Coleridge's Conversation Poems." *JEGP* 64(1965): 691-711.

16234. Bouslog, Charles S. "Structure and Theme in Coleridge's 'Dejection: An Ode.'" *MLQ*

24(1963): 42-52.

16235. Brooks, E. L. "Coleridge's Second Packet for Blackwood's Magazine." *PQ* 30(1951): 426-430.

16236. Broughton, Panthea R. "The Modifying Metaphor in 'Dejection: An Ode.'" *WC* 4(1973): 241-249.

16237. Buchan, A. M. "The Sad Wisdom of the Mariner." *SP* 61(1964): 669-688.

16238. Carafiol, Peter C. "James Marsh's American *Aids to Reflection*: Influence Through Ambiguity." *NEQ* 49(1976): 27-45.

16239. Chadwick, Elizabeth. "Coleridge's Headlong Horseman: Insinuating the Supernatural." *WC* 8(1977): 47-55.

16240. Chandler, Alice. "Structure and Symbol in 'The Rime of the Ancient Mariner.'" *MLQ* 26(1965): 401-413.

16241. Chayes, Irene. "A Coleridgean Reading of *The Ancient Mariner*." *SR* 4(1965): 81-103.

16242. ----------. "Coleridge, Metampsychosis, and 'Almost All the Followers of Fenelon.'" *ELH* 25(1958): 290-315.

16243. ----------. "'Kubla Khan' and the Creative Process." *SR* 6(1966): 1-21.

16244. Christensen, Jerome C. "Coleridge's Marginal Method in the *Biographia Literaria*." *PMLA* 92(1977): 928-940.

16245. Christensen, Morton. "Udolpho, Horrid Mysteries and Coleridge's Machinery of Imagination." *WC* 2(1971): 153-159.

16246. Coburn, Kathleen. "S.T.C. in His Letters." *MP* 57(1960): 264-268.

16247. Coffin, Tristram P. "Coleridge's Use of the Ballad Stanza in 'The Rime of the Ancient Mariner.'" *MLQ* 12(1951): 437-445.

16248. Colmer, J. A. "Coleridge on Addington's Administration." *MLR* 54(1959): 69-72.

16249. Colmer, John. "Coleridge and the Life of Hope." *SR* 11(1972): 332-341.

16250. Cooke, M. G. "*Quisque Sui Faber*: Coleridge in the *Biographia Literaria*." *PQ* 50 (1971): 208-229.

16251. Crawford, Walter B., and Edward S. Lauterbach. "Coleridge in Narrative and Drama, Part I." [bibliography] *WC* 3(1972): 117-122.

16251a. ----------. "Coleridge in Narrative and Drama, Part II." *WC* 4(1973): 36-40.

16252. Creed, Howard H. "Coleridge's Metacriticism." *PMLA* 69(1954): 1160-1180.

16253. D'Avanzo, Mario. "Wordsworth's and Coleridge's 'Genial Spirits.'" *WC* 2(1971): 17-20.

16254. Delson, Abe. "The Symbolism of the Sun and Moon in *The Rime of the Ancient Mariner*." *TSLL* 15(1974): 707-720.

16255. Deen, Leonard W. "Coleridge and the Radicalism of Religious Dissent." *JEGP* 61(1962): 496-510.

16256. Dendurent, H. O. "The Coleridge Collection in Victoria University Library, Toronto." [bibliography] *WC* 5(1974): 225-286.

16257. Deneau, Daniel P. "Coleridge's 'Limbo': A 'Riddling Tale'?" *WC* 3(1972): 97-105.

16258. Dowden, Wilfred S. "Thomas Moore and the Review of *Christabel*." *MP* 60(1962): 47-50.

16259. Duffy, John J. "Problems in

Publishing Coleridge: James Marsh's First American Edition of *Aids to Reflection*." *NEQ* 43(1970): 193-208.

16260. Dunlap, Rhodes. "Verses by Coleridge." *PQ* 42(1963): 282-284.

16261. Durr, R. A. "'This Lime-Tree Bower My Prison' and a Recurrent Action in Coleridge." *ELH* 26(1959): 514-530.

16262. Dyck, Sarah. "Perspective in 'The Rime of the Ancient Mariner.'" *SEL* 13(1973): 591-604.

16263. Ebbatson, J. R. "Coleridge's Mariner and the Rights of Man." *SR* 11(1972): 171-206.

16264. Emslie, MacDonald, and Paul Edwards. "The Limitations of Langdale: a Reading *Christabel*." *EIC* 20(1970): 57-70.

16265. Erdman, David V. "Coleridge and the 'Review Business.'" *WC* 6(1975): 3-50.

16266. ----------. "Coleridge on Coleridge." *SR* 1(1961): 47-64.

16267. ---------- and Paul M. Zall. "Coleridge and Jeffrey in Controversy." *SR* 14(1975): 75-84.

16268. Evans, B. Ivor. "Coleorton Manuscripts of 'Resolution and Independence' and 'Ode to Dejection.'" *MLR* 46(1951): 355-360.

16269. Fairbanks, A. Harris. "Coleridge and Thomas Warton, the Younger." *WC* 6(1975): 313-315.

16270. ----------. "Coleridge's Opinion of 'France: an Ode.'" *RES* 26(1975): 181-182.

16271. ----------. "The Form of Coleridge's Dejection Ode." *PMLA* 90(1975): 874-884.

16272. Farrison, W. Edward. "Coleridge's *Christabel*, 'The Conclusion to Part II.'" *CLA* 5(1961): 83-94.

16273. Fleissner, Robert F. "Hwæt! Wē Gardēna: 'Kubla Khan' and Those Anglo-Saxon Words." *WC* 5(1974): 50-54.

16274. ----------. "'Kubla Khan' as an Integrationist Poem." *BALF* 8(1974): 254-256.

16275. Foakes, R. A. "Repairing the Damaged Archangel." *EIC* 24(1974): 423-427.

16276. Fogle, Richard Harter. "The Dejection of Coleridge's Ode." *ELH* 17(1950): 71-77.

16277. ----------. "Hawthorne and Coleridge on Credibility." *Criticism* 13(1971): 234-241.

16278. Fogle, Stephen F. "The Unity of Coleridge's 'Dejection.'" *SP* 48(1951): 49-55.

16279. Forstner, Lorne J. "Coleridge's 'The Ancient Mariner' and the Case for Justifiable 'Mythocide': An Argument on Psychological, Epistemological and Formal Grounds." *Criticism* 18(1976): 211-229.

16280. Fox, Arnold B. "Political and Biographical Background of Coleridge's *Osorio*." *JEGP* 61(1962): 258-267.

16281. Fulmer, O. Bryan. "The Ancient Mariner and the Wandering Jew." *SP* 66(1969): 797-815.

16282. Garber, Frederick. "The Hedging Consciousness in Coleridge's Conversation Poems." *WC* 4(1973): 124-138.

16283. Gatta, John, Jr. "Coleridge and Allegory." *MLQ* 38(1977): 62-79.

16284. Gerard, Albert. "Coleridge, Keats and the Modern Mind." *EIC* 1(1951): 249-261.

16285. ----------. "Counterfeiting

Infinity: *The Eolian Harp* and the Growth of Coleridge's Mind." *JEGP* 60(1961): 411-422.

16286. ----------. "The Systolic Rhythm: The Structure of Coleridge's Conversation Poems." *EIC* 10(1960): 307-319.

16287. Gilpin, George H. "Coleridge and the Spiral of Poetic Thought." *SEL* 12(1972): 639-652.

16288. Glickfield, Charlotte Woods. "Coleridge's Prose Contributions to the *Morning Post*." *PMLA* 69(1954): 681-685.

16289. Gose, Elliott B., Jr. "Coleridge and the Luminous Gloom: An Analysis of the 'Symbolical Language' in 'The Rhime of the Ancient Mariner.'" *PMLA* 75(1960): 238-244.

16290. Griggs, Earl Leslie. "Ludwig Tieck and Samuel Taylor Coleridge." *JEGP* 54(1955): 262-268.

16291. Haeger, J. H. "Coleridge's 'Bye Blow': The Composition and Date of *Theory of Life*." *MP* 74(1976): 20-41.

16292. ----------. "Coleridge's Speculations on Race." *SR* 13(1974): 333-358.

16293. Harding, Anthony John. "Coleridge's College Declamation, 1792." *WC* 8(1977): 361-367.

16294. Hardy, Barbara. "Coleridge's Marginalia in Fuller's 'Pisgah-Sight of Palestine.'" *MLR* 47(1952): 203-208.

16295. ----------. "Distinction without Difference: Coleridge's Fancy and Imagination." *EIC* 1(1951): 336-344.

16296. ----------. "'I Have a Smack of Hamlet': Coleridge and Shakespeare's Characters." *EIC* 8(1958): 229-255.

16297. ----------. "Imagination and Fancy." *EIC* 2(1952): 347-349.

16298. Harris, John. "Coleridge's Readings in Medicine." *WC* 3(1972): 85-95.

16299. Harris, Wendell V. "The Shape of Coleridge's 'Public' System." *MP* 68(1970): 46-61.

16300. Harvey, W. J. "Help!" *EIC* 16 (1966): 259-260.

16301. Haven, Richard. "The Ancient Mariner in the Nineteenth Century." *SR* 11(1972): 360-374.

16302. ----------. "Anna Vardill Niven's 'Christobell': An Addendum." *WC* 7(1976): 117-118.

16303. ----------. "Coleridge on Milton: A Lost Lecture." *WC* 3(1972): 21-22.

16304. Hayden, John O. "Coleridge, the Reviewers, and Wordsworth." *SP* 68(1971): 105-119.

16305. Hoheisel, Peter. "Coleridge on Shakespeare: Method Amid the Rhetoric." *SR* 13 (1974): 15-24.

16306. Holstein, Michael E. "Coleridge's *Christabel* as Psychodrama: Five Perspectives on the Intruder." *WC* 7(1976): 119-128.

16307. Hunt, Bishop C., Jr. "Coleridge and the Endeavor of Philosophy." *PMLA* 91(1976): 829-839.

16308. Hunting, Constance. "Another Look at 'The Conclusion to Part II' of *Christabel*." *ELN* 12(1975): 171-176.

16309. Jackson, H. J. "Coleridge on the King's Evil." *SR* 16(1977): 337-348.

16310. Jackson, J. R. deJ. "Coleridge on

Dramatic Illusion and Spectacle in the Performance of Shakespeare's Plays." *MP* 62(1964): 13-21.

16311. Johnson, Mary Lynn. "Gillman's Discovery of the 'Lost' *Times* Review of *Christabel*." *WC* 6(1975): 55-58.

16312. Johnson, S. F. "Coleridge's *The Watchman*: Decline and Fall." *RES* 4(1953): 147-148.

16313. Jordan, Hoover H. "Thomas Moore and the Review of *Christabel*." *MP* 54(1956): 95-105.

16314. King, E. H. "Beattie and Coleridge: New Light on the Damaged Archangel." *WC* 7 (1976): 142-152.

16315. Knieger, Bernard. "Wordsworth and Coleridge as Playwrights." *CLA* 6(1962): 57-63.

16316. Landon, Carol. "Wordsworth, Coleridge, and the *Morning Post*: An Early Version of 'The Seven Sisters.'" *RES* 11(1960): 392-402.

16317. Lange, Donald. "A New Reynolds-Milnes Letter: Were there two Meetings between Keats and Coleridge?" *MLR* 72(1977): 769-772.

16318. Levere, Trevor H. "Coleridge, Chemistry, and the Philosophy of Nature." *SR* 16 (1977): 349-380.

16319. Little, G. L. "Christabess: by S. T. Colebritche, Esq." *MLR* 56(1961): 215-220.

16320. Lyon, Judson S. "Romantic Psychology and the Inner Senses." *PMLA* 81(1961): 246-260.

16321. Magnuson, Paul A. "The Dead Calm in the Conversation Poems." *WC* 3(1972): 53-60.

16322. Mahoney, John L. "'The Reptile's Lot': Theme and Imagery in Coleridge's Later Poetry." *WC* 8(1977): 349-360.

16323. Maier, Rosemarie. "The Bitch and the Bloodhound: Generic Similarity in 'Christabel' and 'The Eve of St. Agnes.'" *JEGP* 70(1971): 62-75.

16324. Mann, Peter. "Coleridge, Gerrald and the Slave Trade." *WC* 8(1977): 38-46.

16325. ----------. "Two Autograph Letters of S. T. Coleridge." *RES* 25(1974): 312-317.

16326. Marcus, Leah Sinanoglon. "Vaughan, Wordsworth, Coleridge, and the *Encomium Asini*." *ELH* 42(1975): 224-241.

16327. Marks, Emerson. "Means and Ends in Coleridge's Critical Method." *ELH* 26(1959): 387-401.

16328. Marsh, Florence. "The Ocean Desert: *The Ancient Mariner* and *The Waste Land*." *EIC* 9 (1959): 107-133.

16329. Martin, C. G. "Coleridge and William Crowe's 'Lewesdon Hill.'" *MLR* 62(1967): 400-406.

16330. ----------. "Coleridge, Edward Rushton, and the Cancelled Note to the 'Monody on the Death of Chatterton.'" *RES* 17(1966): 391-402.

16331. Martin, Richard T. "Coleridge's Use of 'sermoni propriora.'" *WC* 3(1972): 71-75.

16332. Mayo, Robert. "The Contemporaneity of the *Lyrical Ballads*." *PMLA* 69(1954): 486-522.

16333. McDonald, Daniel. "Too Much Reality: A Discussion of 'The Rime of the Ancient Mariner.'" *SEL* 4(1964): 543-554.

16334. McFarland, Thomas. "The Symbiosis of Coleridge and Wordsworth." *SR* 11(1972): 263-303.

16335. McLaughlin, Elizabeth T. "Coleridge and Milton." *SP* 61(1964): 545-572.

16336. Metzger, Lore. "Coleridge: The Legacy of an Adventurous Conservative." *MLQ* 30 (1969): 121-131.

16337. Milne, Fred. "'Pantisocracy': A Reflection of Coleridge's Opium Use?" *ELN* 9 (1972): 177-182.

16338. Modiano, Rainmonda. "Words and 'Languageless' Meanings: Limits of Expression in *The Rime of the Ancient Mariner*." *MLQ* 38(1977): 40-61.

16339. Mounts, Charles E. "Coleridge's Self-Identification with Spenserian Characters." *SP* 47(1950): 522-533.

16340. Ober, Warren U. "Southey, Coleridge and 'Kubla Kahn.'" *JEGP* 58(1959): 414-433.

16341. Orsini, G. N. G. "Coleridge and Schlegel Reconsidered." *Comp L* 16(1964): 97-118.

16342. Pafford, Ward. "Coleridge's Wedding-Guest." *SP* 60(1963): 618-626.

16343. Park, Roy. "Coleridge's Two Voices as a Critic of Wordsworth." *ELH* 36(1969): 361-381.

16344. Parrish, Stephen M. "Dramatic Technique in the *Lyrical Ballads*." *PMLA* 74(1959): 85-97.

16345. ----------. "Wordsworth and Coleridge on Meter." *JEGP* 59(1960): 41-49.

16346. ----------. "The Wordsworth-Coleridge Controversy." *PMLA* 73(1953): 367-374.

16347. Passler, Susan Miller. "Coleridge, Fielding and Arthur Murphy." *WC* 5(1974): 55-58.

16348. Patterson, Charles I. "The Authenticity of Coleridge's Reviews of Gothic Romances." *JEGP* 50(1951): 517-521.

16349. ----------. "Coleridge's Conception of Dramatic Illusion in the Novel." *ELH* 18 (1951): 123-137.

16350. ----------. "A Unidentified Criticism by Coleridge Related to *Christabel*." *PMLA* 67(1952): 973-988.

16351. Patterson, Charles I., Jr. "The Daemonic in *Kubla Kahn*." *PMLA* 89(1974): 1033-1042.

16352. Peter, John. "Symbol and Implication: Notes Apropos of a Dictum of Coleridge's." *EIC* 4(1954): 145-167.

16353. Piper, H. W. "The Two Paradises in *Kubla Khan*." *RES* 27(1976): 148-158.

16354. Potts, L. J. "Imagination and Fancy." *EIC* 2(1952): 345-347.

16355. Powell, Grosvenor. "Coleridge's 'Imagination' and the Infinite Regress of Consciousness." *ELH* 39(1972): 266-278.

16356. Pradham, S. V. "Coleridge's 'Philocrisy' and His Theory of Fancy and Secondary Imagination." *SR* 13(1974): 235-254.

16357. ----------. "Fancy and Imagination: Coleridge versus Wordsworth." *PQ* 54(1975): 604-623.

16358. Prickett, Stephen. "The Living Educts of the Imagination: Coleridge on Religious Language." *WC* 4(1973): 99-110.

16359. Purser, J. W. R. "Interpretations of *The Ancient Mariner*." *RES* 8(1957): 249-256.

16360. Purves, Alan C. "Formal Structure in 'Kubla Khan.'" *SR* 1(1962): 187-192.

16361. Radley, Virginia L. "*Christabel*:

Directions Old and New." *SEL* 4(1964): 531-541.

16362. Rahme, Mary. "Coleridge's Concept of Symbolism." *SEL* 9(1969): 619-632.

16363. Rainsberry, Frederick B. "Coleridge and the Paradox of the Poetic Imperative." *ELH* 21 (1954): 114-145.

16364. Rauber, D. F. "The Fragment as Romantic Form." *MLQ* 30(1969): 212-221.

16365. Raysor, Thomas M. "Coleridge's Comment on the Moral of 'The Ancient Mariner.'" *PQ* 31(1952): 88-91.

16366. ----------. "Notes on Coleridge's 'Lewti.'" *PQ* 32(1953): 207-210.

16367. Reiman, Donald H. "Christabel; or, The Case of the Sequel Preemptive." *WC* 6(1975): 283-289.

16368. Ridenour, George M. "Source and Allusion in Some Poems of Coleridge." *SP* 60 (1963): 73-95.

16369. Roper, Derek. "Coleridge and the 'Critical Review.'" *MLR* 55(1960): 11-16.

16370. Robinson, Charles E. "The Shelley Circle and Coleridge's *The Friend*." *ELN* 8(1971): 269-274.

16371. Rowell, Charles H. "Coleridge's Symbolic Albatross." *CLA* 6(1962): 133-135.

16372. Sanderson, David R. "Coleridge's Political 'Sermons': Discursive Language and the Voice of God." *MP* 70(1973): 319-330.

16373. Sankey, Benjamin. "Coleridge and the Visible World." *TSLL* 6(1964): 59-67.

16374. ----------. "Coleridge on Milton's Satan." *PQ* 41(1962): 504-508.

16375. Savage, Basil. "Another 'Lost' Manuscript." *WC* 3(1972): 49.

16376. Scheuerle, William H. "A Reexamination of Coleridge's 'The Eolian Harp.'" *SEL* 15 (1975): 591-599.

16377. Schneider, Elisabeth. "Notes on *Christabel*." *PQ* 32(1953): 197-206.

16378. ----------. "Tom Moore and the *Edinburgh* Review of *Christabel*." *PMLA* 77(1962): 71-76.

16379. ----------. "The Unknown Reviewer of *Christabel*: Jeffrey, Hazlitt, Tom Moore." *PMLA* 70(1955): 417-432.

16380. Schulz, Max F. "Coleridge Agonistes." *JEGP* 61(1962): 268-277.

16381. ----------. "Coleridge, Wordsworth, and the 1800 Preface to the *Lyrical Ballads*." *SEL* 5(1965): 619-639.

16382. ----------. "The New Coleridge." *MP* 69(1971): 142-151.

16383. Schwartz, Lewis M. "A New Review of Coleridge's *Christabel*." *SR* 9(1970): 114-124.

16384. Sells, A. Lytton. "Zannella, Coleridge, and Shelley." *Comp L* 2(1950): 16-30.

16385. Seronsy, Cecil C. "Marginalia by Coleridge in Three Copies of His Published Works." *SP* 51(1954): 470-481.

16386. ----------. "More Coleridge Marginalia." *SP* 52(1955): 497-501.

16387. Sewell, Elizabeth. "Coleridge on Revolution." *SR* 11(1972): 342-359.

16388. Sgammato, Joseph. "A Note on Coleridge's 'symphony and song.'" *WC* 6(1975): 303-306.

16389. Smith, Charles J. "Wordsworth and Coleridge: The Growth of a Theme." *SP* 54(1957): 53-64.

16390. Smith, Gayle S. "A Reappraisal of the Moral Stanzas in *The Rime of the Ancient Mariner*." *SR* 3(1963): 42-52.

16391. Smyser, Jane Worthington. "Coleridge's Use of Wordsworth's Juvenilia." *PMLA* 65 (1950): 419-426.

16392. Spatz, Jonas. "The Mystery of Eros: Sexual Initiation in Coleridge's 'Christabel.'" *PMLA* 90(1975): 107-116.

16393. Stelzig, Eugene L. "The Landscape of 'Kubla Kahn' and the *Valley of Rocks*." *WC* 6 (1975): 316-318.

16394. Stempel, Daniel. "Coleridge and Organic Form: The English Tradition." *SR* 6 (1967): 89-97.

16395. Stevenson, Warren. "'Kubla Khan' as Symbol." *TSLL* 14(1973): 605-630.

16396. Stone, Edward. "Melville's Pip and Coleridge's Servant Girl." *AL* 25(1953): 358-360.

16397. Strickland, Edward. "Metamorphoses of the Muse in Romantic Poesis: *Christabel*." *ELH* 44(1977): 641-658.

16398. Sundell, Michael G. "The Theme of Self-Realization in 'Frost at Midnight.'" *SR* 7 (1967): 34-39.

16399. Taylor, Anya. "Magic in Coleridge's Poetry." *WC* 3(1972): 76-84.

16400. Teich, Nathaniel. "Coleridge's *Biographia* and the Contemporary Controversy About Style." *WC* 3(1972): 61-70.

16401. Teichman, Milton. "Wordsworth's Two Replies to Coleridge's 'Dejection: An Ode.'" *PMLA* 86(1971): 982-989.

16402. Twitchell, James B. "*The Rime of the Ancient Mariner* As Vampire Poem." *Coll L* 4 (1977): 21-39.

16403. ----------. "The World above the Ancient Mariner." *TSLL* 17(1975): 103-117.

16404. Ward, Patricia A. "Coleridge's Critical Theory of the Symbol." *TSLL* 8 (1966): 15-32.

16405. Ware, Malcolm. "Coleridge's 'Spectre Bark': A Slave Ship." *PQ* 40(1961): 589-593.

16406. ----------. "*The Rime of the Ancient Mariner*: A Discourse on Prayer?" *RES* 11(1960): 303-304.

16407. Watson, George C. "*Contributions to a Dictionary of Critical Terms*: Imagination and Fancy." *EIC* 3(1953): 201-214.

16408. Wells, G. A. "Herder's and Coleridge's Evaluation of the Historical Approach." *MLR* 48(1953): 167-175.

16409. ----------. "Man and Nature: an Elucidation of Coleridge's Rejection of Herder's Thought." *JEGP* 15(1952): 214-325.

16410. Wendling, Ronald C. "Coleridge and the Consistency of 'The Eolian Harp.'" *SR* 8 (1968): 26-42.

16411. Werkmeister, Lucyle. "Coleridge and Godwin on the Communication of Truth." *MP* (1958): 170-177.

16412. ----------. "Coleridge and 'The Work for Which Poor Palm Was Murdered.'" *JEGP* 53 (1954): 347-351.

16413. ----------. "Coleridge's 'Anthem': Another Debt to Bowles." *JEGP* 58(1959): 270-275

16414. ----------. "Coleridge's *The Plot Discovered*: Some Facts and a Speculation." *MP*

56(1959): 254-263.

16415. Werkmeister, Lucyle. "'High Jinks' at Highgate." *PQ* 40(1961): 104-111.

16416. ----------. "Some Whys and Wherefores of Coleridge's 'Lines Composed in a Concert-Room.'" *MP* 60(1963): 201-205.

16417. ---------- and P. M. Zall. "Possible Additions to Coleridge's 'Sonnets on Eminent Characters.'" *SR* 8(1969): 121-127.

16418. Whalley, George. "Coleridge and Southey in Bristol, 1795." *RES* 1(1950): 324-340.

16419. ----------. "Coleridge on Classical Prosody: An Unidentified Review of 1797." *RES* 2(1951): 238-247.

16420. Wilcox, Stewart C. "The Arguments and Motto of *The Ancient Mariner*." *MLQ* 22(1961): 264-268.

16421. Wiley, Margaret L. "Coleridge and the Wheels of Intellect." *PMLA* 67(1952): 101-112.

16422. Will, Frederic. "Cousin and Coleridge: The Aesthetic Ideal." *Comp L* 8(1956): 63-77.

16423. Wilson, Douglas Brownlow. "Two Modes of Apprehending Nature: A Gloss on the Coleridgean Symbol." *PMLA* 87(1972): 42-52.

16424. Wilson, James D. "A Note on Coleridge and *The Quarterly Review*." *WC* 6(1975): 51-33.

16425. Woodring, Carl R. "Coleridge and the Kahn." *EIC* 9(1959): 361-368.

16426. ----------. "The Mariner's Return." *SR* 11(1972): 375-380.

16427. Zall, Paul M. "The Cool World of Samuel Taylor Coleridge: Bawdy Books and Obscene Ballads." *WC* 5(1974): 59-64.

16428. ----------. "The Cool World of Samuel Taylor Coleridge: Citizen John Up Against the Wall." *WC* 3(1972): 111-116.

16429. ----------. "The Cool World of Samuel Taylor Coleridge: 1) Do Ye Ken Tom Poole." *WC* 8(1977): 56-61.

16430. ----------. "The Cool World of Samuel Taylor Coleridige: Dr. Beddoes the Bristol Brunonian." *WC* 2(1971): 67-72.

16431. ----------. "The Cool World of Samuel Taylor Coleridge: George Canning, Comical Poet/Politician." *WC* 8(1977): 306-310.

16432. ----------. "The Cool World of Samuel Taylor Coleridge: Implacable Christian." *WC* 5(1974): 169-173.

16433. ----------. "The Cool World of Samuel Taylor Coleridge: James Perry: *Vox Pop*." *WC* 6(1975): 59-64.

16434. ----------. "The Cool World of Samuel Taylor Coleridge: Joseph Johnson, on the Perils of Publishing." *WC* 3(1972): 25-30.

16435. ----------. "The Cool World of Samuel Taylor Coleridge: More for the Millions." *WC* 4(1973): 152-157.

16436. ----------. "The Cool World of Samuel Taylor Coleridge: Mrs. Barbauld's Crew and the Building of a Mass Reading Class." *WC* 2(1971): 74-79.

16437. ----------. "The Cool World of Samuel Taylor Coleridge: Richard Brothers—The Law and the Prophet." *WC* 4(1973): 25-30.

16438. ----------. "The Cool World of Samuel Taylor Coleridge: Richard Porson, Don or Devil." *WC* 6(1975): 255-260.

16439. ----------. "The Cool World of Samuel Taylor Coleridge: The American Connection: Dr. Richard Price (1723-91)." *WC* 7(1976): 95-100.

16440. ----------. "The Cool World of Samuel Taylor Coleridge: The Trials of William Friend." *WC* 2(1971): 26-31.

16441. ----------. "The Cool World of Samuel Taylor Coleridge: Up Loyal Sock Creek." *WC* 3(1972): 161-167.

16442. ----------. "Checklist: Coleridge in the Huntingdon Literary (1794-1834)." [bibliography] *WC* 2(1971): 1-16.

See also 349, 368, 478, 1988, 2212, 7430, 13604, 13882, 15293, 15294, 15363, 17189, 17531, 18076.

COLLINS, WILKIE. 16443. Ashley, Robert P., Jr. "Wilkie Collins and the American Theater." *NCF* 8(1954): 241-255.

16444. ----------. "Wilkie Collins and the Detective Story." *NCF* 6(1951): 47-60.

16445. ----------. "Wilkie Collins Reconsidered." *NCF* 4(1950): 265-273.

16446. Booth, Bradford. "Wilkie Collins and the Art of Fiction." *NCF* 6(1951): 131-143.

16447. Caracciolo, Peter. "Wilkie Collins's 'Divine Comedy': The Use of Dante in *The Woman in White*." *NCF* 25(1971): 383-404.

16448. Corrigan, Beatrice. "Antonio Fogazzaro and Wilkie Collins." *Comp L* 13(1961): 39-51.

16449. Kendrick, Walter M. "The Sensationalism of *The Woman in White*." *NCF* 32(1977): 18-35.

16450. MacEachen, Dougald. "Wilkie Collins and British Law." *NCF* 5(1950): 121-139.

CORELLI, MARIA. 16451. Kowalczyk, Richard L. "Marie Corelli and Arthur Severn's Reputation as an Artist." *MP* 66(1969): 322-327.

CORVO, BARON. See ROLFE, FREDERICK.

COUTTS, ANGELA. See BURDETT-COUTTS, ANGELA.

CRACKENTHORPE, HUBERT. 16452. Peden, William. "'A Fellside Tragedy': An Uncollected Crackenthorpe Story." *SSF* 9(1972): 401-402.

16453. ----------. "Hubert Crackenthorpe: Forgotten Pioneer." *SSF* 7(1970): 539-548.

CROKER, JOHN W. 16454. Beer, E. S. de. "Macaulay and Croker: The Review of Croker's Boswell." *RES* 10(1959): 388-397.

16455. Morgan, Peter. "Croker as Literary Critic." *WC* 8(1977): 62-68.

DARLEY, GEORGE. 16456. Brisman, Leslie. "George Darley: The Poet as Pigmy." *SR* 15(1976): 119-142.

16457. Curran, Eileen M. "George Darley and the London English Professorship." *MP* 71 (1973): 28-38.

16458. Lange, Donald. "George Darley: New Manuscript Poems and Notes on 'It is not beautie I demande.'" *RES* 27(1976): 437-445.

DAVIDSON, JOHN. 16459. Lester, John A., Jr. "Prose-Poetry Transmutation in the Poetry of John Davidson." *MP* 56(1958): 38-44.

DE QUINCEY, THOMAS. 16460. Blake, Kathleen. "The Whispering Gallery and Structural Coherence in De Quincey's Revised *Confessions of an English Opium-Eater*." *SEL* 13(1973): 632-642.

16461. Brown, Calvin S. "De Quincey and the Participles in Mallarné's *Coup de dés*."

Comp L 16(1964): 65-69.

16462. Burwick, Frederick. "The Dream-Visions of Jean Paul and Thomas De Quincey." *Comp L* 20(1968): 1-26.

16463. Byrns, Richard H. "De Quincey's Revisions in the 'Dream Fugue.'" *PMLA* 77(1962): 97-101.

16464. ----------. "Some Unpublished Works of De Quincey." *PMLA* 71(1956): 990-1003.

16465. Clarke, David F. "Incompleteness of the *Confessions of an English Opium Eater*." *WC* 8(1977): 368-376.

16466. De Luca, V. A. "De Quincey's 'Knocking at the Gate in *Macbeth*': Dream and Prose Art." *ELN* 13(1976): 273-278.

16467. ----------. "Satanic Fall and Hebraic Exodus: An Interpretation of De Quincey's 'Revolt of the Tartars.'" *SR* 8(1969): 95-108.

16468. ----------. "'The Type of a Mighty Mind': Mutual Influence in Wordsworth and De Quincey." *TSLL* 13(1971): 239-247.

16469. Hayden, John O. "De Quincey's *Confessions* and the Reviewers." *WC* 6(1975): 273-279.

16470. Hopkins, Robert. "De Quincey on War and the Pastoral Design of *The English Mail-Coach*." *SR* 6(1967): 129-151.

16471. Jack, Ian. "De Quincey Revises His *Confessions*." *PMLA* 72(1957): 122-146.

16472. Jordon, John E. "De Quincey on Wordsworth's Theory of Diction." *PMLA* 68(1953): 764-778.

16473. ----------. "De Quincey's Dramatic Criticism." *ELH* 18(1951): 32-49.

16474. Patterson, Charles I. "De Quincey's Conception of the Novel as Literature of Power." *PMLA* 70(1955): 375-389.

16475. Rockwell, Frederick S. "De Quincey and the Ending of *Moby Dick*." *NCF* 9(1954): 161-168.

16476. Vann, J. Don. "An Unpublished De Quincey Letter." *PQ* 50(1971): 683-684.

16477. Wright, Brooks. "The Cave of Trophonius: Myth and Reality in De Quincey." *NCF* 8(1954): 290-299.

DICKENS, CHARLES. 16478. Adamowski, Thomas H. "Dombey and Son and Sutpen and Son." *SN* 4(1972): 378-389.

16479. Adrian, Arthur A. "Charles Dickens as Verse Editor." *MP* 58(1960): 99-107.

16480. ----------. "*David Copperfield*: A Century of Critical and Popular Acclaim." *MLQ* 11(1950): 325-331.

16481. ----------. "Dickens and the Brick-and-Mortar Sects." *NCF* 10(1955): 188-201.

16482. ----------. "Dickens on American Slavery: A Carlylean Slant." *PMLA* 67(1952): 315-329.

16483. Alter, Robert. "The Demons of History in Dickens *Tale*." *Novel* 2(1969): 135-142.

16484. Arac, Jonathan. "Narrative Form and Social Sense in *Bleak House* and *The French Revolution*." *NCF* 32(1977): 54-72.

16485. Axton, William. "*Dombey and Son*: from Stereotype to Archetype." *ELH* 31(1964): 301-317.

16486. ----------. "Religious and Scientific Imagery in *Bleak House*." *NCF* 22(1968): 349-359.

16487. ----------. "Tonal Unity in *Dombey and Son*." *PMLA* 78(1963): 341-348.

16488. ----------. "The Trouble with Esther." *MLQ* 26(1965): 545-557.

16489. ----------. "Unity and Coherence in *The Pickwick Papers*." *SEL* 5(1965): 663-676.

16490. Baker, Richard M. "What Might Have Been: A Study for Droodians." *NCF* 4(1950): 275-297; 5(1950): 47-66.

16491. Baker, Robert S. "Imagination and Literacy in Dickens' 'Our Mutual Friend.'" *Criticism* 18(1976): 57-72.

16492. Bandelin, Carl. "David Copperfield: A Third Interesting Penitent." *SEL* 16(1976): 601-611.

16493. Barrett, Edwin B. "*Little Dorrit* and the Disease of Modern Life." *NCF* 25(1970): 199-215.

16494. Bell, Vereen M. "The Emotional Matrix of *David Copperfield*." *SEL* 8(1968): 633-649.

16495. ----------. "Mrs. General as Victorian England: Dickens's Image of His Times." *NCF* 20(1965): 177-184.

16496. Benjamin, Edwin B. "The Structure of *Martin Chuzzlewit*." *PQ* 34(1955): 39-47.

16497. Bennett, Rachel. "Punch Versus Christian in *The Old Curiosity Shop*." *RES* 22(1971): 423-435.

16498. Berman, Ronald. "The Human Scale: A Note on *Hard Times*." *NCF* 22(1967): 288-293.

16499. Bevington, David M. "Seasonal Relevance in *The Pickwick Papers*." *NCF* 16(1961): 219-230.

16500. Blount, Trevor. "The Chadbands and Dickens' View of Dissenters." *MLQ* 25(1964): 295-307.

16501. ----------. "Dickens's Ironmaster Again." *EIC* 21(1971): 429-436.

16502. ----------. "Dickens's Slum Satire in 'Bleak House.'" *MLR* 60(1965): 340-351.

16503. ----------. "The Graveyard Satire of *Bleak House*." *RES* 14(1963): 370-378.

16504. ----------. "The Ironmaster and the New Acquisitiveness: Dickens's Views on the Rising Industrial Classes as Exemplified in *Bleak House*." *EIC* 15(1965): 414-427.

16505. ----------. "Poor Jo, Education, and the Problem of Juvinile Delinquency in Dickens' *Bleak House*." *MP* 62(1965): 325-339.

16506. ----------. "Sir Leicester Dedlock and 'Deportment' Turveydrop: Some Aspects of Dickens's Use of Parallelism in *Bleak House*." *NCF* 21(1966): 149-165.

16507. Boege, Fred W. "Point of View in Dickens." *PMLA* 65(1950): 90-105.

16508. ----------. "Recent Criticism of Dickens." *NCF* 8(1953): 171-187.

16509. Bornstein, George. "Miscultivated Field and Corrupted Garden: Imagery in *Hard Times*." *NCF* 26(1971): 158-170.

16510. Brantlinger, Patrick. "Dickens and the Factories." *NCF* 26(1971): 270-285.

16511. Breslow, Julian W. "The Narrator in Sketches by Boz." *ELH* 44(1977): 127-149.

16512. Broderick, James H, and John E. Grant. "The Identity of Esther Summerson." *MP* 55(1958): 252-258.

16513. Buckler, William E. "Dickens the

Paymaster." *PMLA* 66(1951): 1177-1180.

16514. Burgan, William. "Little Dorrit in Italy." *NCF* 29(1975): 393-411.

16515. ----------. "People in the Setting of *Little Dorrit*." *TSLL* 15(1973): 111-128.

16516. ----------. "Tokens of Winter in Dickens's Pastoral Settings." *MLQ* 36(1975): 293-315.

16517. Burke, Alan R. "The Strategy and Theme of Urban Observation in *Bleak House*." *SEL* 9(1969): 659-676.

16518. Butt, John. "*Bleak House* in the Context of 1851." *NCF* 10(1955): 1-21.

16519. ----------. "*David Copperfield*: From Manuscript to Print." *RES* 1(1950): 247-251.

16520. Butwin, Joseph. "*Hard Times*: The News and the Novel." *NCF* 32(1977): 166-187.

16521. Byrd, Max. "'Reading' in *Great Expectations*." *PMLA* 91(1976): 259-265.

16522. Carlisle, Janice. "*Dombey and Son*: The Reader and the Present Tense." *JNT* 1(1971): 146-158.

16523. ----------. "*Little Dorrit*: Necessary Fictions." *SN* 7(1975): 195-214.

16524. Carlton, William J. "The Third Man at Newgate." *RES* 8(1957): 402-407.

16525. Carolan, Katherine. "Dickensian Echoes in a Thackeray Christmas Book." *SSF* 11 (1974): 196-199.

16526. Christensen, Allan C. "A Dickensian Hero Retailored: The Carlylean Apprenticeship of Martin Chuzzlewit." *SN* 3(1971): 18-25.

16527. Collins, P. A. W. "Bleak House and Dickens's *Household Narrative*." *NCF* 14(1960): 345-349.

16528. Collins, Philip. "Dickens and the *Edinburgh Review*." *RES* 14(1963): 167-172.

16529. ----------. "Dickens' Public Readings: The Performer and the Novelist." *SN* 1 (1969): 118-132.

16530. ----------. "Some Unpublished Comic Duologues of Dickens." *NCF* 31(1977): 440-449.

16531. Connolly, Thomas E. "Technique in *Great Expectations*." *PQ* 34(1955): 48-55.

16532. Costigan, Edward. "Drama and Everyday Life in *Sketches by Boz*." *RES* 27(1976): 403-421.

16533. Craig, David. "Fiction and the Rising Industrial Classes." *EIC* 17(1967): 64-74.

16534. Crompton, Louis. "Satire and Symbolism in *Bleak House*." *NCF* 12(1958): 284-303.

16535. Curran, Stuart. "The Lost Paradises of *Martin Chuzzlewit*." *NCF* 25(1970): 51-68.

16536. Deen, Leonard W. "Style and Unity in *Bleak House*." *Criticism* 3(1961): 206-218.

16537. Delespinasse, Doris Stringham. "The Significance of Dual Point of View in *Bleak House*." *NCF* 23(1968): 253-264.

16538. Dennis, Carl. "Dickens' Moral Vision." *TSLL* 11(1969): 1237-1246.

16539. Dessner, Lawrence Jay. "*Great Expectations*: 'The ghost of a man's own father.'" *PMLA* 91(1976): 436-449.

16540. Dilnot, A. F. "The Case of Mr. Jaggers." *EIC* 25(1975): 437-443.

16541. Dobie, Ann B. "Early Stream-of-Consciousness Writing: *Great Expectations*." *NCF* 25(1971): 405-416.

16542. Donoghue, Denis. "The English Dickens and *Dombey and Son*." *NCF* 24(1970): 383-403.

16543. Donovan, Robert A. "Structure and Idea in *Bleak House*." *ELH* 29(1962): 175-201.

16544. Duffy, Joseph M., Jr. "Another Version of Pastoral: *Oliver Twist*." *ELH* 35(1968): 403-421.

16545. Dunn, Richard J. "Dickens and Mayhew Once More." *NCF* 25(1970): 348-353.

16546. ----------. "Dickens and the Tragic-Comic Grotesque." *SN* 1(1969): 147-156.

16547. ----------. "Review-Essay: The Imaginative Dickens." *SN* 8(1976): 223-233.

16548. Dyson, A. E. "The Case for Dombey Senior." *Novel* 2(1969): 123-134.

16549. Edminson, Mary. "The Date of the Action in *Great Expectations*." *NCF* 13(1958): 22-35.

16550. Eigner, Edwin M. "Bulwer-Lytton and the Changed Ending of *Great Expectations*." *NCF* 25(1970): 104-109.

16551. ---------- and Joseph I. Fradin. "Bulwer-Lytton and Dickens' Jo." *NCF* 24(1969): 98-103.

16552. Engel, Monroe. "Dickens on Art." *MP* 53(1955): 25-38.

16553. ----------. "The Politics of Dickens' Novels." *PMLA* 71(1956): 945-974.

16554. Eoff, Sherman. "*Oliver Twist* and the Spanish Picaresque Novel." *SP* 54(1957): 440-447.

16555. Erickson, Donald H. "Harold Skimpole: Dickens and the Early 'Art for Art's Sake' Movement." *JEGP* 72(1973): 48-59.

16556. Fielding, E. K. and Anne Smith. "*Hard Times* and the Factory Controversy: Dickens vs. Harriet Martineau." *NCF* 24(1970): 404-427.

16557. Fielding, K. J. "'American Notes' and Some English Reviewers." *MLR* 59(1964): 527-538.

16558. ----------. "Charles Dickens and Colin Rae Brown." *NCF* 7(1952): 103-110.

16559. ----------. "Charles Dickens and the Department of Practical Art." *MLR* 48(1953): 270-277.

16560. ----------. "Charles Whitehead and Charles Dickens." *RES* 3(1952): 141-154.

16561. ----------. "Dickens and Scott: An 'Unusual Borrowing' Queried." *NCF* 7(1952): 223-224.

16562. ----------. "Dickens and the Hogarth Scandal." *NCF* 10(1955): 64-74.

16563. ----------. "Dickens and the Royal Literary Fund." *RES* 6(1955): 383-394.

16564. ----------. "Mill and Gradgrind." *NCF* 11(1956): 148-151.

16565. ----------. "Sir Francis Burdett and *Oliver Twist*." *RES* 2(1951): 154-157.

16566. Finkel, Robert J. "Another Boy Brought up 'By Hand.'" *NCF* 20(1966): 389-390.

16567. Fleishman, Avrom. "The Apocalyptic Dickens." *MLQ* 34(1973): 191-199.

16568. ----------. "Master and Servant in *Little Dorrit*." *SEL* 14(1974): 575-586.

16569. Fleissner, Robert F. "Lear's 'Poor Fool' and Dickens." *EIC* 14(1964): 425.

16570. Flibbert, Joseph T. "Dickens and the French Debate over Realism: 1838-1856." *Comp L* 23(1971): 18-31.

16571. Fogle, Stephen F. "Skimpole Once More." *NCF* 7(1952): 1-18.

16572. Folland, Harold F. "The Doer and the Deed: Theme and Pattern in *Barnaby Rudge*." *PMLA* 74(1959): 406-417.

16573. Ford, George H. "Dickens and the Voices of Time." *NCF* 24(1970): 428-448.

16574. ----------. "Dickens's Notebook and *Edwin Drood*." *NCF* 6(1952): 275-280.

16575. ----------. "Leavises, Levi's, and Some Dickinsian Priorities." *NCF* 26(1971): 95-114.

16576. Forker, Charles R. "The Language of Hands in *Great Expectations*." *TSLL* 3(1961): 280-293.

16577. Fradin, Joseph I. "Will and Society in *Bleak House*." *PMLA* 81(1966): 95-109.

16578. Fraser, Russell. "A Charles Dickens Original." *NCF* 9(1955): 301-307.

16579. French, A. L. "Beating and Cringing: *Great Expectations*." *EIC* 24(1974): 147-168.

16580. ----------. "Mr. Jaggers." *EIC* 26 (1976): 279-282.

16581. Friedman, Stanley. "The Motif of Reading in *Our Mutual Friend*." *NCF* 28(1973): 38-61.

16582. Gard, Roger. "*David Copperfield*." *EIC* 15(1965): 313-325.

16583. Gardner, Joseph H. "Dickens, Romance, and *McTeague*: A Study in Mutual Interpretation." *EL* 1(1974): 69-82.

16584. ----------. "Gaffer Hexam and Pap Finn." *MP* 66(1968): 155-156.

16585. ----------. "Howells: The 'Realist' as Dickensian." *MFS* 16(1970): 323-344.

16586. Gibson, Priscilla. "Dickens's Uses of Animism." *NCF* 7(1953): 283-291.

16587. Gilbert, Elliot L. "The Ceremony of Innocence : Charles Dickens' *A Christmas Carol*." *PMLA* 90(1975): 22-31.

16588. Gill, Stephen C. "Allusion in *Bleak House*: A Narrative Device." *NCF* 22(1967): 145-154.

16589. ----------. "'Pickwick Papers' and the 'Chroniclers by the Line': A Note on Style." *MLR* 63(1968): 33-36.

16590. Goldberg, Michael. "Dickens and Lawrence: More on Rocking Horses." *MFS* 17(1971): 574.

16591. Gottshall, James K. "Devils Abroad: The Unity and Significance of *Barnaby Rudge*." *NCF* 16(1961): 133-146.

16592. Green, Robert. "*Hard Times*: The Style of a Sermon." *TSLL* 11(1970): 1375-1396.

16593. Gregory, Marshall W. "Values and Meaning in *Great Expectations*: the Two Endings Revisited." *EIC* 19(1969): 402-409.

16594. Grenander, M. E. "The Mystery and the Moral: Point of View in Dickens's *Bleak House*." *NCF* 10(1956): 301-305.

16595. Gribble, Jennifer. "Depth and Surface in *Our Mutual Friend*." *EIC* 25(1975): 197-214.

16596. Griffith, Ben W. "Dickens the Philanthropist: An Unpublished Letter." *NCF* 12 (1957): 160-163.

16597. Grob, Shirley. "Dickens and Some Motifs of the Fairy Tale." *TSLL* 5(1964): 567-579.

16598. Grove, T. N. "The Psychological Prison of Arthur Clennam in Dickens's 'Little Dorritt.'" *MLR* 68(1973): 750-761.

16599. Grubb, Gerald G. "Dickens and the *Daily News*: Preliminaries to Publication." *NCF* 6(1951): 174-194.

16600. ----------. "Dickens and the *Daily News*: Resignation." *NCF* 7(1952): 19-38.

16601. ----------. "Dickens and the *Daily News*: The Early Issues." *NCF* 6(1952): 234-246.

16602. ----------. "Dickens' Western Tour and the Cairo Legend." *SP* 48(1951): 87-97.

16603. ----------. "The Personal and Literary Relationships of Dickens and Poe." *NCF* 5(1950): 1-22, 101-120, 209-221.

16604. Grylls, R. Glynn. "Dickens and Holman Hunt." *TSLL* 6(1964): 76-79.

16605. Hagan, John H. "The Poor Labyrinth: *Great Expectations*." *NCF* 9(1954): 169-178.

16606. ----------. "Structural Patterns in Dickens's *Great Expectations*." *ELH* 21(1954): 54-66.

16607. Haight, Gordon S. "Dickens and Lewes." *PMLA* 71(1956): 166-179.

16608. ----------. "Dickens and Lewes on Spontaneous Combustion." *NCF* 10(1955): 53-63.

16609. Hannaford, Richard. "Fairy-tale Fantasy in 'Nicholas Nickleby.'" *Criticism* 16 (1974): 247-259.

16610. Hardy, Barbara. "Dickens and the Passions." *NCF* 24(1970): 449-466.

16611. ----------. "Work in Progress IV: Food and Ceremony in *Great Expectations*." *EIC* 13(1963): 351-363.

16612. Hark, Ina Rae. "Marriage in the Symbolic Framework of *The Mystery of Edwin Drood*." *SN* 9(1977): 154-168.

16613. Harvey, William R. "Charles Dickens and the Byronic Hero." *NCF* 24(1969): 305-316.

16614. Hauck, Richard. "The Dickens Controversy in the *Spirit of the Times*." *PMLA* 85 (1970): 278-283.

16615. Herbert, Christopher. "Converging Worlds in *Pickwick Papers*." *NCF* 27(1972): 1-20.

16616. Herring, Paul D. "Dickens' Monthly Number Plans for *Little Dorrit*." *MP* 64(1966): 22-63.

16617. ----------. "The Number Plans for *Dombey and Son*: Some Further Observations." *MP* 68(1970): 151-187.

16618. Hersch, David H. "*Hard Times* and F. R. Leavis." *Criticism* 6(1964): 1-16.

16619. Hobsbaum, Philip. "The Critics and *Our Mutual Friend*." *EIC* 13(1963): 231-240.

16620. Hornback, Bert G. "Frustration and Resolution in *David Copperfield*." *SEL* 8(1968): 651-667.

16621. Houtchens, Lawrence H. "*The Spirit of the Times* and a 'New Work by Boz.'" *PMLA* 67 (1952): 94-100.

16622. Hutter, Albert D. "The High Tower of His Mind: Psychoanalysis and the Reader of 'Bleak House.'" *Criticism* 19(1977): 296-316.

16623. ----------. "Psychoanalysis and Biography: Dickens' Experiences at Warren's Blacking." *HSL* 8(1976): 23-37.

16624. Hughes, Felicity. "Narrative Complexity in *David Copperfield*." *ELH* 41(1974):

89-105.

16625. Hynes, Joseph A. "Image and Symbol in *Great Expectations*." *ELH* 30(1963): 258-292.

16626. Jefferson, D. W. "The Moral Centre of *Little Dorrit*." *EIC* 26(1976): 300-317.

16627. Johnson, Edgar. "*Bleak House*: The Anatomy of Society." *NCF* 7(1952): 73-89.

16628. ----------. "The Garrick Club Affair." *PMLA* 71(1956): 256-259.

16629. Kaplan, Fred. "Dickens' Flora Finching and Joyce's Molly Bloom." *NCF* 23(1968): 343-346.

16630. Kelley, Alice van Buren. "The Bleak Houses of *Bleak House*." *NCF* 25(1970): 252-268.

16631. Kelly, Thomas. "Character in Dickens' Late Novels." *MLQ* 30(1969): 386-401.

16632. Kennedy, G. W. "Dickens's Endings." *SN* 6(1974): 280-287.

16633. ----------. "Naming and Language in *Our Mutual Friend*." *NCF* 28(1973): 165-178.

16634. Kincaid, James R. "Dickens's Subversive Humor: *David Copperfield*." *NCF* 22(1968): 313-329.

16635. ----------. "The Education of Mr. Pickwick." *NCF* 24(1969): 127-141.

16636. ----------. "Laughter and *Oliver Twist*." *PMLA* 83(1968): 63-70.

16637. ----------. "Symbol and Subversion in *David Copperfield*." *SN* 1(1969): 196-206.

16638. Krentz, Irving W. "Sly of Manner, Sharp of Tooth: A Study of Dickens's Villains." *NCF* 22(1968): 331-348.

16639. Lane, Lauriat, Jr. "Dickens and Scott: A Reply to Mr. Fielding." *NCF* 8(1953): 78.

16640. ----------. "Dickens and Scott: An Unusual Borrowing." *NCF* 6(1951): 223-224.

16641. ----------. "Dickens' Archetypal Jew." *PMLA* 73(1958): 94-100.

16642. ----------. "Dickens Studies, 1958-1968: An Overview." *SN* 1(1969): 240-254.

16643. ----------. "Mr. Pickwick and *The Dance of Death*." *NCF* 14(1959): 171-172.

16644. ----------. "Review Essay: Satire, Society, and Symbol in Recent Dickens Criticism." *SN* 5(1973): 125-138.

16645. Lane, William G. "R. H. Barham and Dickens's Clergymen of *Oliver Twist*." *NCF* 10 (1955): 159-162.

16646. Lasson, Angus. "Dickens's Marchioness Again." *MLR* 65(1970): 517-522.

16647. Levine, George. "Communication in *Great Expectations*." *NCF* 18(1963): 175-181.

16648. Levine, Richard A. "Dickens, the Two Nations, and Individual Possibility." *SN* 1 (1969): 157-180.

16649. Librach, Ronald S. "The Burdens of Self and Society: Release and Redemption in *Little Dorrit*." *SN* 7(1975): 538-551.

16650. Linehan, Tom. "The Importance of Plot in *Little Dorrit*." *JNT* 6(1976): 116-131.

16651. Lougy, Robert E. "Pickwick and 'The Parish Clerk.'" *NCF* 25(1970): 100-104.

16652. MacAndrew, Elizabeth. "A Second Level of Symbolism in *Great Expectations*." *EL* 2(1975): 65-75.

16653. Maclean, H. N. "Mr. Pickwick and the Seven Deadly Sins." *NCF* 8(1953): 198-212.

16654. Manheim, Leonard. "The Dickens Hero as Child." *SN* 1(1969): 189-195.

16655. ----------. "Floras and Doras: The Women in Dickens' Novels." *TSLL* 7(1965): 181-200.

16656. ----------. "The Law as 'Father': An Aspect of the Dickens Pattern." *HSL* 9(1977): 100-109.

16657. Marcus, David D. "The Carlean Vision of *A Tale of Two Cities*." *SN* 8(1976): 56-69.

16658. Marlow, James E. "Memory, Romance, and the Expressive Symbol in Dickens." *NCF* 30 (1975): 20-32.

16659. Marten, Harry P. "The Visual Imaginations of Dickens and Hogarth: Structure and Scene." *SN* 6(1974): 145-164.

16660. Mauskopf, Charles. "Thackeray's Attitude Towards Dickens's Writings." *NCF* 21 (1966): 21-33.

16661. Maxwell, J. C. "Jagger's Case." *EIC* 26(1976): 98.

16662. ----------. "Mrs. Christian's Reminiscences of Dickens." *RES* 2(1951): 59-63.

16663. Maxwell, Richard C., Jr. "G. M. Reynolds, Dickens, and the Mysteries of London." *NCF* 32(1977): 188-213.

16664. McDonald, Andrew. "The Preservation of Innocence in *Dombey and Son*: Florence's Identity and the Role of Walter Gay." *TSLL* 18 (1976): 1-19.

16665. McLean, Robert Simpson. "Another Source for Quilp." *NCF* 26(1971): 337-339.

16666. McMaster, R. D. "Dickens, the Dandy, and the Savage: A Victorian View of the Romantic." *SN* 1(1969): 133-146.

16667. Meckier, Jerome. "Suspense in *The Old Curiosity Shop*: Dickens' Contrapuntal Artistry." *JNT* 2(1972): 199-207.

16668. Meisel, Martin. "The Ending of *Great Expectations*." *EIC* 15(1965): 326-331.

16669. ----------. "Miss Havisham Brought to Book." *PMLA* 81(1966): 278-285.

16670. Miller, J. Hillis. "The Sources of Dickens's Comic Art: From *American Notes* to *Martin Chuzzlewit*." *NCF* 24(1970): 467-476.

16671. Millhauser, Milton. "*David Copperfield*: Some Shifts of Plan." *NCF* 27(1972): 339-345.

16672. Milner, Ian. "The Dickens Drama: Mr. Dombey." *NCF* 24(1970): 477-487.

16673. Mitchell, Charles. "*The Mystery of Edwin Drood*: The Interior and Exterior of Self." *ELH* 33(1966): 228-246.

16674. Monod, Sylvère. "Dickens's Attitudes in *A Tale of Two Cities*." *NCF* 24(1970): 488-505.

16675. Morris, William E. "The Conversion of Scrooge: A Defense of that Good Man's Motivation." *SSF* 3(1965): 46-55.

16676. Moynahan, Julian. "Dickens Criticism." *EIC* 11(1961): 239-241.

16677. ----------. "The Hero's Guilt: the Case of *Great Expectations*." *EIC* 10(1960): 60-79.

16678. Nadel, Ira Bruce. "'Wonderful Deception': Art and the Artist in 'Little Dorrit.'" *Criticism* 19(1977): 17-33.

16679. Nadlehaft, Janice. "The English

Malady, Corrupted Humors, and Krook's Death." *SN* 1(1969): 230-239.

16680. Needham, Gwendolyn B. "The Undisciplined Heart of David Copperfield." *NCF* 9(1954): 81-107.

16681. Nelson, Harland S. "Dickens's *Our Mutual Friend* and Henry Mayhew's *London Labour and the London Poor*." *NCF* 20(1965): 207-222.

16682. Nisbet, Ada B. "New Light on the Dickens-Poe Relationship." *NCF* 5(1951): 295-302.

16683. ----------. "Poe and Dickens." *NCF* 9(1955): 313-314.

16684. Olshin, Toby A. "'The Yellow Dwarf' and *The Old Curiosity Shop*." *NCF* 25 (1970): 96-99.

16685. Ousby, Ian. "The Broken Glass: Vision and Comprehension in *Bleak House*." *NCF* 29(1975): 381-392.

16686. ----------. "Language and Gesture in 'Great Expectations.'" *MLR* 72(1977): 784-793.

16687. Palmer, William J. "The Movement of History in *Our Mutual Friend*." *PMLA* 89(1974): 487-495.

16688. Parker, Dorothy. "Allegory and the Extension of Mr. Bucket's Forefinger." *ELN* 12 (1974): 31-35.

16689. Parish, Charles. "A Boy Brought Up 'By Hand.'" *NCF* 17(1962): 286-288.

16690. Paroissien, David. "*The Life and Adventures of Nicholas Nickleby*: Alberto Cavalcanti Interprets Dickens." *HSL* 9(1977): 17-28.

16691. Patten, Robert L. "The Art of *Pickwick's* Interpolated Tales." *ELH* 34(1967): 349-366.

16692. ----------. "Boz, Phiz, and Pickwick in the Pound." *ELH* 36(1969): 575-591.

16693. ----------. "Capitalism and Compassion in *Oliver Twist*." *SN* 1(1969): 207-221.

16694. ----------. "The Fight at the Top of the Tree: *Vanity Fair* versus *Dombey and Son*." *SEL* 10(1970): 759-773.

16695. Pratt, Branwen Bailey. "Dickens and Father: Notes on the Family Romance." *HSL* 8 (1976): 4-22.

16696. ----------. "Dickins and Freedom: Young Bailey in *Martin Chuzzlewit*." *NCF* 30(1975): 185-199.

16697. ----------. "Sympathy for the Devil: A Dissenting View of Quilp." *HSL* 6(1974): 129-146.

16698. Quirk, Eugene F. "Tulkinghorn's Buried Life: A Study of Character in *Bleak House*." *JEGP* 72(1973): 526-535.

16699. Raleigh, John Henry. "Dickens and the Sense of Time." *NCF* 13(1958): 127-138.

16700. Ray, Gordon N. "Dickens versus Thackeray: The Garrick Club Affair." *PMLA* 69 (1954): 815-832.

16701. ----------. "The Garrick Club Affair." *PMLA* 71(1956): 259-263.

16702. Rice, Thomas Jackson. "The End of Dickens's Apprenticeship: Variable Focus in *Barnaby Rudge*." *NCF* 30(1975): 172-184.

16703. Ridland, J. M. "Huck, Pip, and Plot." *NCF* 20(1965): 286-290.

16704. Rogers, Philip. "The Dynamics of Time in *The Old Curiosity Shop*." *NCF* 28(1973): 127-144.

16705. ----------. "Mr. Pickwick's

Innocence." *NCF* 27(1972): 21-37.

16706. Rosenberg, Marvin. "The Dramatist in Dickens." *JEGP* 59(1960): 1-12.

16707. Rouse, H. Blair. "Charles Dickens and Henry James: Two Approaches to the Art of Fiction." *NCF* 5(1950): 151-157.

16708. Rubin, Stan S. "Spectator and Spectacle: Narrative Evasion and Narrative Voice in *Pickwick Papers*." *JNT* 6(1976): 188-203.

16709. Rust, James D. "Dickens and the Americans: An Unnoticed Letter." *NCF* 11(1956): 70-72.

16710. Saint Victor, Carol de. "*Master Humphry's Clock*: Dickens' 'Lost' Book." *TSLL* 10 (1969): 569-584.

16711. Serlen, Ellen. "The Two Worlds of *Bleak House*." *ELH* 43(1976): 551-603.

16712. Sherer, Ray J. "Laughter in *Our Mutual Friend*." *TSLL* 13(1971): 509-521.

16713. Sipe, Samuel M. "The Intentional World of Dickens's Fiction." *NCF* 30(1975): 1-20.

16714. ----------. "Memory and Confession in *Great Expectations*." *EL* 2(1975): 53-64.

16715. Slater, Michael. "Carlyle and Jerrold into Dickens: A Study of *The Chimes*." *NCF* 24(1970): 506-526.

16716. Smith, Anne G. M. "Dickens's Ironmaster Again." *EIC* 22(1972): 218-220.

16717. ----------. "The Ironmaster in *Bleak House*." *EIC* 21(1971): 159-169.

16718. Sonstroem, David. "Fettered Fancy in *Hard Times*." *PMLA* 84(1969): 520-529.

16719. Stacy, Paul H. "David Copperfield: Novel and Film." *HSL* 9(1977): 1-16.

16720. Steig, Michael. "*Barnaby Rudge* and *Vanity Fair*: A Note on a Possible Influence." *NCF* 25(1970): 353-354.

16721. ----------. "A Chapter of Noses: George Cruikshank's Psychonography of the Nose." *Criticism* 17(1975): 308-325.

16722. ----------. "Dickens' Characters and Psychoanalytic Criticism." *HSL* 8(1976): 38-45.

16723. ----------. "Dickens, Hablôt Browne, and the Tradition of English Craicature." *Criticism* 11(1969): 219-233.

16724. ----------. "The Iconography of *David Copperfield*." *HSL* 2(1970): 1-18.

16725. ----------. "*Martin Chuzzlewit*: Pinch and Pecksniff." *SN* 1(1969): 181-188.

16726. ----------. "*Re* Quilp: A Comment." *HSL* 6(1974): 282-283.

16727. ----------, and F. A. C. Wilson. "Hortense versus Bucket: The Ambiguity of Order in *Bleak House*." *MLQ* 33(1972): 289-298.

16728. Stewart, Garrett. "The 'Golden Bower' of *Our Mutual Friend*." *ELH* 40(1973): 105-130.

16729. Stone, Harry. "An Added Note on Dickens and Miss Havisham." *NCF* 10(1955): 85-86.

16730. ----------. "Charles Dickens and Harriet Beecher Stowe." *NCF* 12(1957): 188-202.

16731. ---------- "Dickens and Interior Monologue." *PQ* 38(1959): 52-65.

16732. ----------. "Dickens Rediscovered: Some Lost Writings Retrieved." *NCF* 24(1970): 527-548.

16733. ----------. "Dickens' Use of His American Experiences in *Martin Chuzzlewit*." *PMLA* 72(1957): 464-478.

16734. ----------. "Dickens's Tragic Universe: 'George Silverman's Explanation.'" *SP* 55 (1958): 86-97.

16735. ----------. "Fairy Tales and Ogres: Dickens' Imagination and David Copperfield." *Criticism* 6(1964): 324-330.

16736. Sucksmith, Harvey Peter. "Dickens and Mayhew: A Further Note." *NCF* 24(1969): 345-349.

16737. ----------. "The Dust-Heaps in *Our Mutual Friend*." *EIC* 23(1973): 206-211.

16738. ----------. "The Secret of Immediacy: Dickens' Debt to the Tale of Horror in *Blackwood's*." *NCF* 26(1971): 145-157.

16739. Tarr, Rodger L. "Dickens' Debt to Carlyle's 'Justice Metaphor' in *The Chimes*." *NCF* 27(1972): 208-215.

16740. ----------. "The 'Foreign Philanthropy' Question in *Bleak House*: A Carlylean Influence." *SN* 3(1971): 275-283.

16741. Tedlock, E. W., Jr. "Kafka's Imitation of *David Copperfield*." *Comp L* 7(1955): 52-62.

16742. Thale, Jerome. "The Imagination of Charles Dickens: Some Preliminary Discriminations." *NCF* 22(1967): 127-144.

16743. Thompson, Leslie M. "Mrs. Nickleby's Monologue: The Dichotomy of Pessimism and Optimism in *Nicholas Nickleby*." *SN* 1(1969): 222-229.

16744. Tick, Stanley. "The Memorializing of Mr. Dick." *NCF* 24(1969): 142-153.

16745. ----------. "The Unfinished Business of *Dombey and Son*." *MLQ* 36(1975): 390-402.

16746. Vande Kieft, Ruth M. "Patterns of Communication in *Great Expectations*." *NCF* 15 (1961): 325-334.

16747. Vann, J. Don. "Dickens Criticism, 1963-1967." *SN* 1(1969): 255-278.

16748. Vivian, Charles H. "Dickens, the 'True Son,' and Samuel Laman Blanchard." *NCF* 4 (1950): 328-330.

16749. Waller, John O. "Charles Dickens and the American Civil War." *SP* 57(1960): 535-548.

16750. Walton, James. "Conrad, Dickens, and the Detective Novel." *NCF* 23(1969): 446-462.

16751. Webb, Howard W., Jr. "A Further Note on the Dickens-Poe Relationship." *NCF* 15 (1960): 80-82.

16752. Welsh, Alexander. "Waverley, Pickwick, and Don Quixote." *NCF* 22(1967): 19-30.

16753. Wentersdorf, Karl P. "Mirror-Images in *Great Expectations*." *NCF* 21(1966): 203-224.

16754. Westburg, Barry. "'His Allegorical Way of Expressing It': Civil War and Psychic Conflict in *Oliver Twist* and *A Child's History*." *SN* 6(1974): 27-37.

16755. Wilde, Alan. "Mr. F's Aunt and the Analogical Structure of *Little Dorrit*." *NCF* 19 (1964): 33-44.

16756. Wilkinson, Ann Y. "*Bleak House*: From Faraday to Judgment Day." *ELH* 34(1967): 225-247.

16757. Williamson, Colin. "Two Missing Links in *Oliver Twist*." *NCF* 22(1967): 225-234.

16758. Wilt, Judith. "Confusion and Consciousness in Dickens's Esther." *NCF* 32(1977): 285-309.

16759. Wing, George. "*Edwin Drood* and *Desperate Remedies*: Prototypes of Detective Fiction in 1870." *SEL* 13(1973): 677-687.

16760. Winslow, Joan D. "Esther Summerson: The Betrayal of the Imagination." *JNT* 6(1976): 1-13.

16761. Whitlow, Roger. "Animal and Human Personalities in Dicken's Novels." *CLA* 19 (1975): 65-74.

16762. Worth, George J. "The Genesis of Jo the Crossing-Sweeper." *JEGP* 60(1961): 44-47.

16763. Zambrano, Ana Laura. "*David Copperfield*: Novel and Film." *HSL* 9(1977): 1-16.

16764. ----------. "*Great Expectations*: Dickens Style in Terms of Film." *HSL* 4(1972): 104-112.

16765. Zwerdling, Alex. "Esther Summerson Rehabilitated." *PMLA* 88(1973): 429-439.

See also 135, 472, 1435, 3995, 15323, 15335, 15351, 19868, 20132.

DISRAELI, BENJAMIN.   16766. Fido, Martin. "'From his own Observation': Sources of Working Class Passages in Disraeli's 'Sybil.'" *MLR* 72 (1977): 268-284.

16767. Greene, D. J. "Becky Sharp and Lord Steyne—Thackeray or Disraeli." *NCF* 16 (1961): 157-164.

16768. Hirsch, David H. "Another Source for Poe's 'The Duc De L'Omelette.'" *AL* 38 (1967): 532-536.

16769. Hoeltje, Hubert H. "Benjamin Disraeli's Letters to Robert Carter." *PQ* 31 (1952): 17-26.

16770. Holloway, John. "Disraeli's 'View of Life' in the Novels." *EIC* 2(1952): 413-433.

16771. Jerman, Bernard R. "Disraeli's Fan Mail: A Curiosity Item." *NCF* 9(1954): 61-71.

16772. Levine, Richard A. "Disraeli's *Tancred* and 'The Great Asian Mystery.'" *NCF* 22 (1967): 71-85.

16773. O'Kell, Robert. "The Autobiographical Nature of Disraeli's Early Fiction." *NCF* 31(1976): 253-284.

16774. Merritt, James D. "Disraeli as a Byronic Poet." *VP* 3(1965): 138-139.

16775. ----------. "The Novelist St. Barbe in Disraeli's *Endymion*: Revenge on Whom?" *NCF* 23(1968): 85-88.

16776. Schwarz, Daniel R. "Art and Argument in Disraeli's *Sybil*." *JNT* 4(1974): 19-31.

16777. Smith, Sheila M. "Willenhall and Wodgate: Disraeli's Use of Blue Book Evidence." *RES* 13(1962): 368-384.

D'ISRAELI, ISAAC.   16778. Tuerk, Richard. "Melville's 'Bartlely' and Isaac D'Israeli's *Curiosities of Literature*, Second Series." *SSF* 7(1970): 647-649.

16779. West, Muriel. "Poe's 'Ligeia' and Isaac D'Israeli." *Comp L* 16(1964): 19-28.

DOBSON, AUSTIN.   16780. Robinson, James Keith. "Austin Dobson and the Roundeliers." *MLQ* 14(1953): 31-42.

DOWSON, ERNEST.   16781. Baker, Houston A. "A Decadent's Nature: The Poetry of Ernest Dowson." *VP* 6(1968): 21-28.

16782. Cushman, Keith. "The Quintessence of Dowsonism: 'The Dying of Francis Donne.'" *SSF* 11(1974): 45-51.

16783. Goldfarb, Russell M. "The Dowson Legend Today." *SEL* 4(1964): 653-662.

16784. Harris, Wendell. "Innocent Decadence: The Poetry of the *Savoy*." *PMLA* 77(1962): 629-636.

16785. Marshall, L. Birkett. "A Note on Ernest Dowson." *RES* 3(1952): 162-164.

16786. Reed, John R. "Bedlamite and Pierrot: Ernest Dowson's Esthetic of Futility." *ELH* 35(1968): 94-113.

EDGEWORTH, MARIA. 16787. Altieri, Joanne. "Style and Purpose in Maria Edgeworth's Fiction." *NCF* 23(1968): 265-278.

16788. Brooks, Gerry H. "The Didacticism of Edgeworth *Castle Rackrent*." *SEL* 17(1977): 593-605.

16789. Butler, Marilyn. "The Uniqueness of Cynthia Kirkpatrick: Elizabeth Gaskell's *Wives and Daughters* and Maria Edgeworth's *Helen*." *RES* 23(1972): 278-290.

16790. Butler, R. F. "Maria Edgeworth and Sir Walter Scott: Unpublished Letters, 1823." *RES* 9(1958): 23-40.

16791. Kennedy, Sister Eileen, S.C. "Genesis of a Fiction: The Edgeworth-Turgenev Relationship." *ELN* 6(1969): 271-273.

16792. Newcomer, James. "*Castle Rackrent*: Its Structure and Its Irony." *Criticism* 8(1966): 170-179.

16793. ----------. "The Disingenuous Thady Quirk." *SSF* 2(1964): 44-50.

16794. Solomon, Stanley J. "Ironic Perspective in Maria Edgeworth's *Castle Rackrent*." *JNT* 2(1972): 68-73.

See also 15333.

ELIOT, GEORGE. 16795. Adam, Ian. "Character and Destiny in George Eliot's Fiction." *NCF* 20(1965): 127-143.

16796. ----------. "The Structure of Realisms in *Adam Bede*." *NCF* 30(1975): 127-149.

16797. Anderson, Roland F. "George Eliot Provoked: John Blackwood and Chapter Seventeen of *Adam Bede*." *MP* 71(1973): 39-47.

16798. Auerbach, Nina. "The Power of Hunger: Demonism and Maggie Tulliver." *NCF* 30 (1975): 150-171.

16799. Baker, William. "George Eliot's Projected Napoleonic War Novel: An Unnoted Reading List." *NCF* 29(1975): 453-460.

16800. ----------. "John Walter Cross to Herbert Spencer, December 23, 1880: An Unpublished Letter Concerning George Eliot's Death." *ELN* 13(1975): 39-40.

16801. Beaty, Jerome. "The Forgotten Past of Will Ladislaw." *NCF* 13(1958): 159-163.

16802. ----------. "'Into the Irrevocable': A New George Eliot Letter." *JEGP* 57(1958): 704-707.

16803. ----------. "Visions and Revisions: Chapter lxxxi of Middlemarch." *PMLA* 72(1957): 662-679.

16804. Benvenuto, Richard. "At a Crossroads: The Life and Thought of George Eliot." *SN* 2(1970): 355-361.

16805. Benson, James D. "'Sympathetic' Criticism: George Eliot's Response to

Contemporary Reviewing." *NCF* 29(1975): 428-440.

16806. Bissell, Claude T. "Social Analysis in the Novels of George Eliot." *ELH* 18(1951): 221-239.

16807. Blake, Kathleen. "*Middlemarch* and the Woman Question." *NCF* 31(1976): 285-312.

16808. Bullen, J. B. "George Eliot's *Romola* as a Positivist Allegory." *RES* 26(1975): 425-435.

16809. Byrd, Scott. "The Fractured Crystal in *Middlemarch* and *The Golden Bowl*." *MFS* 18 (1972): 551-554.

16810. Carroll, David R. "*Felix Holt*: Society as Protagonist." *NCF* 17(1962): 237-257.

16811. ----------. "An Image of Disenchantment in the Novels of George Eliot." *RES* 11 (1960): 29-41.

16812. Carroll, David R. "*Mansfield Park, Daniel Deronda*, and Ordination." *MP* 62(1965): 217-226.

16813. ----------. "The Unity of *Daniel Deronda*." *EIC* 9(1959): 369-380.

16814. Christ, Carol. "Aggression and Providential Death in George Eliot's Fiction." *Novel* 9(1976): 130-140.

16815. Colby, Robert A. "An American Sequel to *Daniel Deronda*." *NCF* 12(1957): 231-235.

16816. ----------. "Miss Evans, Miss Mulock, and Hetty Sorrel." *ELN* 2(1965): 206-211.

16817. Creeger, George R. "An Interpretation of *Adam Bede*." *ELH* 23(1956): 218-238.

16818. DeLaura, David J. "*Romola* and the Origin of the Paterian View of Life." *NCF* 21 (1966): 225-234.

16819. Deneau, Daniel P. "Inconsistencies and Inaccuracies in *Adam Bede*." *NCF* 14(1959): 71-75.

16820. Dunham, Robert H. "*Silas Marner* and the Wordsworthian Child." *SEL* 16(1976): 645-659.

16821. Eliot, George. "'Quarry for Middlemarch,' edited with introduction and notes by Anna Theresa Kitchel." *NCF* 4(1950): supplement.

16822. Ermarth, Elizabeth. "Maggie Tulliver's Long Suicide." *SEL* 14(1974): 587-601.

16823. ----------. "Incarnations: George Eliot's Conception of 'Undeviating Law.'" *NCF* 29(1974): 273-286.

16824. Fast, Robin Riley. "Getting to the Ends of *Daniel Deronda*." *JNT* 7(1977): 200-217.

16825. Feltes, N. N. "George Eliot and the Unified Sensibility." *PMLA* 79(1964): 130-136.

16826. ----------. "George Eliot's 'Pier-Glass': The Development of a Metaphor." *MP* 67 (1969): 69-71.

16827. ----------. "Phrenology: from Lewes to George Eliot." *SLI* 1,#1(1968): 13-22.

16828. Ferguson, Suzanne C. "Mme. Laure and Operative Irony in *Middlemarch*: A Structural Analogy." *SEL* 3(1963): 509-516.

16829. Fernando, Lloyd. "Special Pleading and Art in 'Middlemarch': The Relations between the Sexes." *MLR* 67(1972): 44-49.

16830. Fisch, Harold. "*Daniel Deronda* or *Gwendolyn Harleth*." *NCF* 19(1965): 345-356.

16831. Freeman, Janet H. "Authority in *The Mill on the Floss*." *PQ* 56(1977): 374-388.

16832. French, A. L. "A Note on *Middlemarch*." *NCF* 26(1971): 339-347.

16833. Fricke, Douglas C. "Art and Artists in *Daniel Deronda*." *SN* 5(1973): 220-228.

16834. Fulmer, Constance Marie. "Contrasting Pairs of Heroines in George Eliot's Fiction." *SN* 6(1974): 288-294.

16835. Fyfe, Albert J. "The Interpretation of *Adam Bede*." *NCF* 9(1954): 134-139.

16836. Greenberg, Robert A. "The Heritage of Will Ladislaw." *NCF* 15(1961): 355-358.

16837. ----------. "Plexuses and Ganglia: Scientific Allusion in *Middlemarch*." *NCF* 30 (1975): 33-52.

16838. Hagan, John. "*Middlemarch*: Narrative Unity in the Story of Dorothea Brooke." *NCF* 16(1961): 17-31.

16839. ----------. "A Reinterpretation of *The Mill on the Floss*." *PMLA* 87(1972): 53-63.

16840. Hardy, Barbara. "Imagery in George Eliot's Last Novels." *MLR* 50(1955): 6-14.

16841. ----------. "The Moment of Disenchantment in George Eliot's Novels." *RES* 5 (1954): 256-264.

16842. ----------. "Mr. Browning and George Eliot." *EIC* 6(1956): 121-123.

16843. Harvey, W. J. "George Eliot and the Omniscient Author Convention." *NCF* 13(1958): 81-108.

16844. ----------. "Ideas in George Eliot." *MLQ* 27(1966): 86-91.

16845. Herbert, Christopher. "Preachers and the Schemes of Nature in *Adam Bede*." *NCF* 29 (1975): 412-427.

16846. Hester, Erwin. "George Eliot's Messengers." *SEL* 7(1967): 679-690.

16847. ----------. "George Eliot's Use of Historical Events in *Daniel Deronda*." *ELN* 4 (1966): 115-118.

16848. Higdon, David Leon. "Failure of Design in *The Mill on the Floss*." *JNT* 3(1973): 183-192.

16849. ----------. "George Eliot and the Art of the Epigraph." *NCF* 25(1970): 127-151.

16850. ----------. "The Iconographic Backgrounds of *Adam Bede*, Chapter 15." *NCF* 27 (1972): 155-170.

16851. Hill, Donald L. "Pater's Debt to *Romola*." *NCF* 22(1968): 361-377.

16852. Hollahan, Eugene. "The Concept of 'Crisis' in *Middlemarch*." *NCF* 28(1974): 450-457.

16853. Horowitz, Lenore Wisney. "George Eliot's Vision of Society in *Felix Holt the Radical*." *TSLL* 17(1975): 175-191.

16854. Hulme, Hilda M. "*Middlemarch* as Science-Fiction: Notes on Language and Imagery." *Novel* 2(1968): 36-45.

16855. Hurley, Edward T. "Death and Immortality: George Eliot's Solution." *NCF* 24 (1969): 222-227.

16856. ----------. "'The Lifted Veil': George Eliot as Anti-Intellectual." *SSF* 5 (1968): 257-262.

16857. Hussey, Maurice. "Structure and Imagery in *Adam Bede*." *NCF* 10(1955): 115-129.

16858. Hyde, William J. "George Eliot and the Climate of Realism." *PMLA* 72(1957): 147-164.

16859. Isaacs, Neil D. "*Middlemarch*: Crescendo of Obligatory Drama." *NCF* 18(1963): 21-34.

16860. Jones, W. Gareth. "George Eliot's 'Adam Bede' and Tolstoy's Conception of 'Anna Karenina.'" *MLR* 61(1966): 473-481.

16861. Kaminsky, Alice R. "George Eliot, George Henry Lewes, and the Novel." *PMLA* 70 (1955): 997-1013.

16862. Kearney, John P. "Time and Beauty in *Daniel Deronda*: "Was she beautiful or not beautiful?'" *NCF* 26(1971): 286-306.

16863. Ker, I. T. "George Eliot's Rhetoric of Enthusiasm." *EIC* 26(1976): 134-155.

16864. Knoepflmacher, U. C. "*Middlemarch*: An Avuncular View." *NCF* 30(1975): 53-81.

16865. ----------. "The Post-Romantic Imagination: *Adam Bede*, Wordsworth and Milton." *ELH* 34(1967): 518-540.

16866. Kropf, Carl R. "Time and Typology in George Eliot's Early Fiction." *SN* 8(1976): 430-440.

16867. Levine, George. "Determinism and Responsibility in the Works of George Eliot." *PMLA* 77(1962): 268-279.

16868. ----------. "Intelligence as Deception: *The Mill on the Floss*." *PMLA* 80(1965): 402-409.

16869. ----------. "Isabel, Gwendolen, and Dorothea." *ELH* 30(1963): 244-257.

16870. Levenson, Shirley Frank. "The Use of Music in *Daniel Deronda*." *NCF* 24(1969): 317-334.

16871. Lothamer, Eileen. "Science and Pseudo-Science in George Eliot's *The Lifted Veil*." *Ext* 17(1976): 125-132.

16872. Lyons, Richard S. "The Method of *Middlemarch*." *NCF* 21(1966): 35-47.

16873. Luecke, Sr. Jane Marie. "Ladislaw and the *Middlemarch* Vision." *NCF* 19(1964): 55-64.

16874. Makurath, Paul A., Jr. "The Symbolism of the Flood in Eliot's *Mill on the Floss*." *SN* 7(1975): 298-300.

16875. Mansell, Darrel, Jr. "George Eliot's Conception of 'Form.'" *SEL* 5(1965): 651-662.

16876. ----------. "George Eliot's Conception of Tragedy." *NCF* 22(1967): 155-172.

16877. ----------. "Ruskin and George Eliot's 'Realism.'" *Criticism* 7(1965): 203-216.

16878. Martin, Bruce K. "Rescue and Marriage in *Adam Bede*." *SEL* 12(1972): 745-763.

16879. ----------. "Similarity Within Dissimilarity: The Dual Structure of *Silas Marner*." *TSLL* 14(1972): 479-489.

16880. Mason, Michael York. "*Middlemarch* and *History*." *NCF* 25(1971): 417-431.

16881. ----------. "*Middlemarch* and *Science*: Problems of Life and Mind." *RES* 22 (1971): 151-171.

16882. McCarthy, Patrick J. "Lydgate, 'The New, Young Surgeon' of *Middlemarch*." *SEL* 10(1970): 805-816.

16883. McCobb, E. A. "Aaron Bernstein's *Mendel Gibbor*: A Minor Source for *Daniel Deronda*?" *ELN* 14(1976): 42-44.

16884. Miller, J. Hillis. "Narrative and History." *ELH* 41(1974): 455-473.

16885. Milner, Ian. "Distortion in *Felix Holt*." *EIC* 17(1967): 406-407.

16886. ----------. "Structure and Quality in *Silas Marner*." *SEL* 6(1966): 717-729.

16887. Moldstad, David. "George Eliot's *Adam Bede* and Smiles's *Life of George Stephenson*." *ELN* 14(1977): 189-192.

16888. ----------. "*The Mill on the Floss* and *Antigone*." *PMLA* 85(1970): 527-531.

16889. Newton, K. M. "The Role of the Narrator in George Eliot's Novels." *JNT* 3(1973): 97-107.

16890. Paris, Bernard J. "George Eliot, Science Fiction, and Fantasy." *Ext* 5(1964): 26-30.

16891. ----------. "George Eliot's Religion of Humanity." *ELH* 29(1962): 418-443.

16892. ----------. "George Eliot's Unpublished Poetry." [with texts] *SP* 56(1959): 539-558.

16893. ----------. "The Otherness of George Eliot." *JML* 1(1970): 272-277.

16894. ----------. "Toward a Revaluation of George Eliot's *The Mill on the Floss*." *NCF* 11(1956): 18-31.

16895. Pinney, Thomas. "Another Note on the Forgotten Past of Will Ladislaw." *NCF* 17(1962): 69-73.

16896. ----------. "The Authority of the Past in George Eliot's Novels." *NCF* 21(1966): 131-147.

16897. Poston, Lawrence, III. "Setting and Theme in *Romola*." *NCF* 20(1966): 355-366.

16898. Putzell, Sara M. "'An Antigonism of Valid Claims': The Dynamics of *The Mill on the Floss*." *SN* 7(1975): 227-244.

16899. Quick, Jonathan R. "*Silas Marner* as Romance: The Example of Hawthorne." *NCF* 29(1974): 287-298.

16900. Roberts, Lynne Tidaback. "Perfect Pyramids: *The Mill on the Floss*." *TSLL* 13(1971): 111-124.

16901. Robinson, Carole. "The Severe Angel: a Study of *Daniel Deronda*." *ELH* 31(1964): 278-300.

16902. Rogal, Samuel J. "Hymns in George Eliot's Fiction." *NCF* 29(1974): 173-184.

16903. Rubenstein, Elliot T. "A Forgotten Tale by George Eliot." *NCF* 17(1962): 175-183.

16904. Rust, James D. "The Art of Fiction in George Eliot's Reviews." *RES* 7(1956): 164-172.

16905. Sabiston, Elizabeth. "The Prison of Womanhood." *Comp L* 25(1973): 336-351.

16906. Sealy, R. J. "Brunetière, Montégut—and George Eliot." *MLR* 66(1971): 66-75.

16907. Selig, Robert L. "The Red Haired Lady Orator: Parallel Passages in *The Bostonians* and *Adam Bede*." *NCF* 16(1961): 169-173.

16908. Smith, Grover. "A Source for Hopkins' 'Spring and Fall' in the *Mill on the Floss*." *ELN* 1(1963): 43-46.

16909. Smith, Jane S. "The Reader as Part of the Fiction: *Middlemarch*." *TSLL* 19(1977): 188-203.

16910. Spivey, Ted R. "George Eliot: Victorian Romantic and Modern Realist." *SLI* 1,#2 (1968): 5-21.

16911. Squires, Michael. "*Adam Bede* and the *Locus Amoenus*." *SEL* 13(1973): 670-676.

16912. Stang, Richard. "The Literary Criticism of George Eliot." *PMLA* 72(1957): 952-961.

16913. Steig, Michael. "Anality in *The Mill on the Floss*." *Novel* 5(1971): 42-53.

16914. Steiner, F. George. "A Preface to *Middlemarch*." *NCF* 9(1955): 262-279.

16915. Stwertka, Eve Maria. "The Web of Utterance: *Middlemarch*." *TSLL* 19(1977): 179-187.

16916. Sudrann, Jean. "*Daniel Deronda* and the Landscape of Exile." *ELH* 37(1970): 433-455.

16917. Sullivan, William J. "The Allusion to Jenny Lind in *Daniel Deronda*." *NCF* 29(1974): 211-214.

16918. ----------. "Music and Musical Allusion in 'The Mill on the Floss.'" *Criticism* 16(1974): 232-246.

16919. ----------. "Piero di Cosimo and the Higher Primitivism in *Romola*." *NCF* 26 (1972): 390-405.

16920. Svaglic, Martin J. "Religion in the Novels of George Eliot." *JEGP* 53(1954): 145-159.

16921. Swann, Brian. "George Eliot's Ecumenical Jew, or The Novel as Outdoor Temple." *Novel* 8(1974): 39-50.

16922. Swann, Brian. "Eyes in the Mirror: Imagery and Symbolism in *Daniel Deronda*." *NCF* 23(1969): 434-445.

16923. ----------. "Middlemarch and Myth." *NCF* 28(1973): 210-214.

16924. ----------. "*Middlemarch*: Realism and Symbolic Form." *ELH* 39(1972): 279-308.

16925. ----------. "'Silas Marner' and the New Mythus." *Criticism* 18(1976): 101-121.

16926. Thale, Jerome. "*Daniel Deronda*: The Darkened World." *MFS* 3(1951): 119-126.

16927. ----------. "River Imagery in *Daniel Deronda*." *NCF* 8(1954): 300-306.

16928. Thomson, Fred C. "*Felix Holt* as Classic Tragedy." *NCF* 16(1961): 47-58.

16929. ----------. "The Genesis of *Felix Holt*." *PMLA* 74(1959): 576-584.

16930. ----------. "The Legal Plot in *Felix Holt*." *SEL* 7(1967): 691-704.

16931. ----------. "The Theme of Alienation in *Silas Marner*." *NCF* 20(1965): 69-84.

16932. Thompson, Patricia. "The Three Georges." *NCF* 18(1963): 137-150.

16933. Tye, J. R. "George Eliot's Unascribed Mottoes." *NCF* 22(1967): 235-249.

16934. Waddington, Patrick. "Turgenev and George Eliot: A Literary Friendship." *MLR* 66(1971): 751-759.

16935. Watson, Charles N. "The 'Accidental' Drownings in *Daniel Deronda* and *An American Tragedy*." *ELN* 13(1976): 288-291.

16936. Watson, Kathleen. "Dinah Morris and Mrs. Evans: A Comparative Study of Methodist Diction." *RES* 22(1971): 282-294.

16937. ----------. "George Eliot and Mrs. Oliphant: a Comparison in Social Attitudes." *EIC* 19(1969): 410-419.

16938. Welsh, Alexander. "George Eliot and the Romance." *NCF* 14(1959): 255-264.

16939. Wiesenfarth, Joseph. "George Eliot's Notes for *Adam Bede*." *NCF* 32(1977):

127-165.

16940. Wiesenfarth, Joseph. "Demythologizing *Silas Marner*." *ELH* 37(1970): 226-244.

16941. ----------. "Legend in *The Mill on the Floss*." *TSLL* 18(1976): 20-41.

16942. Williams, Raymond. "The Knowable Community in George Eliot's Novel." *Novel* 2 (1969): 255-268.

16943. Witemeyer, Hugh. "English and Italian Portraiture in *Daniel Deronda*." *NCF* 30 (1976): 477-494.

16944. Yuill, W. E. "'Character is Fate': A Note on Thomas Hardy, George Eliot, and Novalis." *MLR* 57(1962): 401-402.

16945. Zimmerman, Bonnie S. "'Radiant as a Diamond': George Eliot, Jewelry and the Female Role." *Criticism* 19(1977): 212-222.

See also 59, 80, 1868, 2666, 15290, 15294, 15327.

FIELD, MICHAEL. 16946. Ireland, Kenneth R. "*Sight and Song*: A Study of the Interrelations between Painting and Poetry." *VP* 15(1977): 9-20.

FITZGERALD, EDWARD. 16947. Cadbury, William. "Fitzgerald's Rubáiyát as a Poem." *ELH* 34 (1967): 541-563.

FRAZIER, JAMES. 16948. Fitz, L. T. "'The Rocking-Horse Winner' and the Golden Bough." *SSF* 11(1974): 199-200.

FROUDE, ANTHONY. 16949. Badger, Kingsbury. "The Ordeal of Anthony Froude, Protestant Historian." *MLQ* 13(1952): 41-55.

16950. Mulhauser, Frederick L. "An Unpublished Poem of James Anthony Froude." *ELH* 12 (1974): 26-30.

GALT, JOHN. 16951. Costain, Keith M. "Theoretical History and the Novel: The Scottish Fiction of John Galt." *ELH* 43(1976): 342-365.

GASKELL, ELIZABETH. 16952. Altick, Richard D. "Dion Boucicault Stages *Mary Barton*." *NCF* 14(1959): 129-141.

16953. Auerbach, Nina. "Elizabeth Gaskell's 'Sly Javelins': Governing Women in Cranford and Haworth." *MLQ* 38(1977): 276-291.

16954. Axton, William F. "Mrs. Gaskell in Apotheosis." *MLQ* 28(1967): 240-247.

16955. Bland, D. S. "*Mary Barton* and Historical Accuracy." *RES* 1(1950): 58-60.

16956. Butler, Marilyn. "The Uniqueness of Cynthia Kirkpatrick: Elizabeth Gaskell's *Wives and Daughters* and Maria Edgeworth's *Helen*." *RES* 23(1972): 278-290.

16957. Chapple, J. A. V. "*North and South*: a Reassessment." *EIC* 17(1967): 461-472.

16958. Collins, H. P. "The Naked Sensibility: Elizabeth Gaskell." *EIC* 3(1953): 60-72.

16959. Dodsworth, Martin. "Women Without Men at Cranford." *EIC* 13(1963): 132-145.

16960. Eagleton, Terry. "*Sylvia's Lovers* and Legality." *EIC* 26(1976): 17-27.

16961. Gill, Stephen. "Price's Patent Candles: New Light on *North and South*." *RES* 27 (1976): 313-321.

16962. Hopkins, Annette B. "A Uniquely Illustrated *Cranford*." *NCF* 4(1950): 299-314.

16963. Lauterback, Edward S. "A Note on 'A Uniquely Illustrated *Cranford*.'" *NCF* 8 (1953): 232-234.

16964. McVeagh, John. "The Making of 'Sylvia's Lovers.'" *MLR* 65(1970): 272-281.

16965. ----------. "Mrs. Gaskell's Narrative Technique." *EIC* 18(1968): 461-470.

16966. Shusterman, David. "William Rathbone Gregg and Mrs. Gaskell." *PQ* 36(1957): 268-272.

16967. Sucksmith, Harvey Peter. "Mrs. Gaskell's *Mary Barton* and William Mudford's *The Iron Shroud*." *NCF* 29(1975): 460-463.

16968. Tarratt, Margaret. "*Cranford* and 'the Strict Code of Gentility.'" *EIC* 18(1968): 152-163.

16969. Wolfe, Patricia A. "Structure and Movement in *Cranford*." *NCF* 23(1968): 161-176.

See also 17253, 18204.

GIFFORD, WILLIAM. 16970. Tunnicliffe, Stephen. "A Newly Discovered Source for the Early Life of William Gifford." *RES* 16(1965): 25-34.

GILBERT, W. S. 16971. Jenkins, William D. "Swinburne, Robert Buchanan, and W. S. Gilbert: The Pain that Was All but a Pleasure." *SP* 69 (1972): 369-387.

16972. Jones, John B. "In Search of Archibald Grosvenor: A New Look at Gilbert's *Patience*." *VP* 3(1965): 45-53.

16973. ----------. "Mr. Gilbert and Dr. Bowdler: A Further Note on *Patience*." *VP* 12 (1974): 65-66.

See also 20066.

GISSING, GEORGE. 16974. Adams, Elsie B. "Gissing's Allegorical 'House of Cobwebs.'" *SSF* 7(1970): 324-326.

16975. Adams, Ruth M. "George Gissing and Clara Collet." *NCF* 11(1956): 72-77.

16976. Cope, Jackson I. "Definition as Structure in Gissing's 'Ryecroft Papers.'" *MFS* 3(1957): 127-140.

16977. Francis, C. J. "Gissing and Schopenhauer." *NCF* 15(1960): 53-63.

16978. Gettmann, Royal A. "Bentley and Gissing." *NCF* 11(1957): 306-314.

16979. Halperin, John. "The Gissing Revival, 1961-1974." *SN* 8(1976): 103-120.

16980. Harris, W. V. "An Approach to Gissing's Short Stories." *SSF* 2(1965): 137-144.

16981. Jameson, Fredric. "Authentic *Ressentiment*: The 'Experimental' Novels of Gissing." *NCF* 31(1976): 127-149.

16982. Korg, Jacob. "Division of Purpose in George Gissing." *PMLA* 20(1955): 323-336.

16983. Selig, Robert L. "A Sad Heart at the Late-Victorian Culture Market: George Gissing's *In the Year of Jubilee*." *SEL* 9(1969): 703-720.

16984. ----------. "'The Valley of the Shadow of Books': Alienation in Gissing's *New Grub Street*." *NCF* 25(1970): 188-198.

16985. Sporn, Paul. "Gissing's *Demos*: Late-Victorian Values and the Displacement of Conjugal Love." *SN* 1(1969): 334-346.

16986. Thomas, J. D. "The Public Purposes of George Gissing." *NCF* 8(1953): 118-123.

16987. Ware, Thomas C. "Jerusalem Artichokes in Gissing's Garden." *SSF* 9(1972): 86-89.

16988. Wolff, Joseph J. "Gissing's Revision of *The Unclassed*." *NCF* 8(1953): 42-52.

16989. Young, Arthur C. "George Gissing's Friendship with Eduard Bertz." *NCF* 13(1958):

227–237.

GRAND, SARAH. See 20635.

GOSSE, EDMUND. 16990. Buckhart, Charles B. "George Moore and *Father and Son*." *NCF* 15 (1960): 71–77.

16991. Gracie, William J., Jr. "Truth of Form in Edmund Gosse's *Father and Son*." *JNT* 4 (1974): 176–187.

16992. Porter, Roger J. "Edmund Gosses's *Father and Son*: Between Form and Flexibility." *JNT* 5(1975): 174–195.

16993. Traubitz, Nancy Baker. "Heavenly Mother: The Trinity as Structural Device in Edmund Gosse's *Father and Son*." *JNT* 6(1976): 147–154.

16994. Vincent, Paul. "Sir Edmund Gosse and Frederik van Eeden: Some Reflections on an Unpublished Correspondence." *MLR* 66(1971): 125–138.

16995. Wyke, Clement H. "Edmund Gosse as Biographer and Critic of Donne: His Fallible Role in the Poet's Rediscovery." *TSLL* 17(1976): 805–819.

GRAY, JOHN. 16996. Dowling, Linda C. "Nature and Decadence: John Gray's *Silverpoints*." *VP* 15(1977): 159–170.

GORDON, MARY. 16997. Wilson, F. A. C. "Checklist of Writings by Mary Gordon." *VP* 9 (1971): 257.

16998. ----------. "Swinburne in Love: Some Novels by Mary Gordon." *TSLL* 11(1970): 1415–1426.

HAGGARD, HENRY RIDER. 16999. Hinz, Evelyn. "Rider Haggard's *She*: an Archetypal 'History of Adventure.'" *SN* 4(1972): 416–431.

HALLAM, ARTHUR. 17000. Friedman, Norma. "Hallam on Tennyson: An Early Aesthetic Doctrine and Modernism." *SLI* 8,#2(1975): 37–62.

17001. Kolb, Jack. "Arthur Hallam and Emily Tennyson." *RES* 28(1977): 32–48.

17002. ----------. "'They were no kings': An Unrecorded Sonnet by Hallam." *VP* 15(1977): 373–376.

17003. Leach, Stephen J. "An Unpublished Poem by Arthur Hallam." *PQ* 54(1975): 698–703.

HANNAY, JAMES. 17004. Worth, George J. "Thackeray and James Hannay: Three New Letters." *JEGP* 55(1956): 414–416.

HARDY, THOMAS. 17005. Alexander, B. J. "Criticism of Thomas Hardy's Novels: A Selected Checklist." *SN* 4(1972): 630–654.

17006. Amy, E. F. "Laying a Ghost." *NCF* 9(1954): 150–153.

17007. Anderson, Carol Reed. "Time, Space, and Perspective in Thomas Hardy." *NCF* 9(1954): 192–208.

17008. Atkinson, F. G. "Thomas Hardy in 1916—A New Letter." *RES* 22(1971): 172–173.

17009. Babb, Howard. "Setting and Theme in *Far From the Madding Crowd*." *ELH* 30(1963): 147–161.

17010. Bailey, J. O. "Evolutionary Meliorism in the Poetry of Thomas Hardy." *SP* 60 (1963): 569–587.

17011. ----------. "Hardy's Vision of the Self." *SP* 56(1959): 74–101.

17012. Baker, Donald. "Thomas Hardy: Prophet of Total Theatre." *CD* 7(1973): 121–134.

17013. Baker, James R. "Thematic Ambiguity in *The Mayor of Casterbridge*." *TCL* 1(1955): 13–16.

17014. Bartlett, Phyllis. "'Seraph of Heaven': A Shelleyan Dream in Hardy's Fiction." *PMLA* 70(1955): 624–635.

17015. Beckman, Richard. "A Character Typology for Hardy's Novels." *ELH* 30(1963): 70–87.

17016. Beebe, Maurice, Bonnie Culotta, and Erin Marcus. "Criticism of Thomas Hardy: A Selected Checklist." *MFS* 6(1960): 258–279.

17017. Benvenuto, Richard. "Another Look at the Other Eustacia: Critical Exchange." *Novel* 4(1970): 77–79.

17018. ----------. "Modes of Perception: The Will to Live in *Jude the Obscure*." *SN* 2 (1970): 31–41.

17019. ----------. "*The Return of the Native* as a Tragedy in Six Books." *NCF* 26(1971): 83–94.

17020. Block, Haskell M. "James Joyce and Thomas Hardy." *MLQ* 19(1958): 337–342.

17021. Brick, Allan. "Paradise and Consciousness in Hardy's *Tess*." *NCF* 17(1962): 115–134.

17022. Brogan, Howard O. "Science and Narrative Structure in Austen, Hardy, and Woolf." *NCF* 11(1957): 276–287.

17023. ----------. "'Visible Essences' in *The Mayor of Casterbridge*." *ELH* 17(1950): 307–323.

17024. Burstein, Janet. "The Journey beyond Myth in *Jude the Obscure*." *TSLL* 15(1973): 499–515.

17025. Carpenter, Richard C. "Hardy's 'Gurgoyles.'" *MFS* 6(1960): 223–232.

17026. ----------. "The Mirror and the Sword: Imagery in *Far from the Madding Crowd*." *NCF* 18(1964): 331–345.

17027. Casagrande, Peter J. "The Shifted 'Centre of Altruism' in *The Woodlanders*: Thomas Hardy's Third 'Return of a Native.'" *ELH* 38 (1971): 104–125.

17028. Cassidy, John A. "The Original Source of Hardy's *Dynasts*." *PMLA* 69(1954): 1085–1100.

17029. Clifford, Emma. "The Impressionistic View of History in *The Dynasts*." *MLQ* 22 (1961): 21–31.

17030. ----------. "Thomas Hardy and the Historians." *SP* 56(1959): 654–668.

17031. ----------. "'The Trumpet Major Notebook' and *The Dynasts*." *RES* 8(1957): 149–161.

17032. ----------. "*War and Peace* and *The Dynasts*." *MP* 54(1956): 33–44.

17033. Cronin, Frank C. "The Dimension of Time in *Jude the Obscure*." *CLA* 12(1968): 123–128.

17034. Cushman, Keith. "Lawrence's Use of Hardy in 'The Shades of Spring.'" *SSF* 9 (1972): 402–404.

17035. ----------. "Review-Essay: Seven Versions of Hardy." *SN* 9(1977): 223–230.

17036. Davis, W. Eugene. "*Tess of the d'Urbervilles*: Some Ambiguities About a Pure Woman." *NCF* 22(1968): 397–401.

17037. Deen, Leonard W. "Heroism and Pathos in Hardy's *Return of the Native*." *NCF* 15

(1960): 207-219.

17038. De Laura, David J. "'The Ache of Modernism' in Hardy's Later Novels." *ELH* 34 (1967): 380-399.

17039. De Vitas, A. A. and William J. Palmer. "*A Pair of Blue Eyes* Flash at *The French Lieutenant's Woman*." *Con L* 15(1974): 90-101.

17040. Dike, D. A. "A Modern Oedipus: The Mayor of Casterbridge." *EIC* 2(1952): 169-179.

17041. Dowling, Linda C. "Pursuing Antithesis: Lionel Johnson on Hardy." *ELN* 12(1975): 287-292.

17042. Drake, Robert Y., Jr. "*A Laodicean*: A Note on a Minor Novel." *PQ* 40(1961): 602-606.

17043. ----------. "*The Mayor of Casterbridge*: A New Fiction Defined." *MFS* 6(1960): 195-213.

17044. ----------. "'*The Woodlanders*' as Traditional Pastoral." *MFS* 6(1960): 251-257.

17045. Edwards, Duane D. "*The Mayor of Casterbridge* as Aeschylean Tragedy." *SN* 4 (1972): 608-618.

17046. Eggenschwiler, David. "Eustacia Vye, Queen of the Night and Courtly Pretender." *NCF* 25(1971): 444-454.

17047. Elsbree, Langdon. "*Tess* and the Local Cerealia." *PQ* 40(1961): 606-613.

17048. Evans, Robert. "Hardy Heroine Festival—Part One: The Other Eustacia." *Novel* 1(1968): 251-259.

17049. Faber, M. D. "*Tess* and *The Rape of Lucrece*." *ELN* 5(1968): 292-293.

17050. Fairchild, Hoxie N. "The Immediate Source of *The Dynasts*." *PMLA* 67(1952): 43-64.

17051. Fayen, George S., Jr. "Hardy's *The Woodlanders*: Inwardness and Memory." *SEL* 1,#4 (1961): 81-100.

17052. Fischler, Alexander. "'Theatrical Techniques' in Thomas Hardy's Short Stories." *SSF* 3(1966): 435-445.

17053. Fleissner, Robert F. "'Ideas, Striking, Novel, or Beautiful': A Hitherto Unpublished Comment of Hardy's." *SN* 4(1972): 628-629.

17054. Friedman, Alan Warren. "'Beeny Cliff' and 'Under the Waterfall': An Approach to Hardy's Love Poetry." *VP* 5(1967): 224-228.

17055. Gerber, Helmut E. "Hardy's The Well-Beloved as a Comment on the Well-Despised." *ELN* 1(1963): 48-53.

17056. Gindin, James. "Toward Literary Biography." *MLQ* 37(1976): 82-92.

17057. Giordano, Frank R., Jr. "Characterization and Conflict in Hardy's 'The Fiddler of the Reels.'" *TSLL* 17(1975): 617-633.

17058. ----------. "*Jude the Obscure* and the *Bildungsroman*." *SN* 4(1972): 580-591.

17059. ----------. "A Source for Thomas Hardy's 'Valenciennes.'" *VP* 14(1976): 349-355.

17060. ----------. "Thomas Hardy on Lenz's *Napoleon*: A New Letter." *ELN* 10(1972): 122-123.

17061. Goldberg, M. A. "Hardy's Double-Visioned Universe." *EIC* 7(1957): 374-382.

17062. Goodheart, Eugene. "Thomas Hardy and the Lyrical Novel." *NCF* 12(1957): 215-225.

17063. Gordon, Walter K. "Father Time's Suicide Note in *Jude the Obscure*." *NCF* 22(1967):

298-300.

17064. Gordon, Jan B. "Origins, History, and the Reconstitution of Family: Tess' Journey." *ELH* 43(1976): 366-388.

17065. Gose, Elliott B., Jr. "Psychic Evolution: Darwinism and Initiation in *Tess of the d'Urbervilles*." *NCF* 18(1963): 261-272.

17066. Gregor, Ian. "Hardy's World." *ELH* 38(1971): 274-293.

17067. ----------. "What Kind of Fiction did Hardy Write?" *EIC* 16(1966): 290-308.

17068. Haber, Grace Stevenson. "Echoes from Carlyle's 'Goethe's Helena' in *The Mayor of Casterbridge*." *NCF* 12(1957): 89-90.

17069. Hagan, John. "A Note on the Significance of Diggory Venn." *NCF* 16(1961): 147-155.

17070. Harper, George G., Jr. "An Unpublished Thomas Hardy Letter." *ELN* 3(1966): 207-208.

17071. Hassett, Michael E. "Compromised Romanticism in *Jude the Obscure*." *NCF* 25(1971): 432-443.

17072. Hazen, James. "Angel's Hellenism in *Tess of the D'Urbervilles*." *Coll L* 4(1977): 129-135.

17073. ----------. "The God-Curst Sun: Love in 'Neutral Tones.'" *VP* 9(1971): 331-336.

17074. ----------. "The Tragedy of Tess Durbeyfield." *TSLL* 11(1969): 779-794.

17075. Heilman, Robert B. "Hardy's *Mayor* and the Problem of Intention." *Criticism* 5 (1963): 199-213.

17076. ----------. "Hardy's *Mayor*: Notes on Style." *NCF* 18(1964): 307-329.

17077. ----------. "Hardy's Sue Bridehead." *NCF* 20(1966): 307-323.

17078. Herbert, Lucille. "Hardy's Views in *Tess of the D'Urbervilles*." *ELH* 37(1970): 77-94.

17079. Herzog, Tobey C. "The Grand Design of Hardy's Major Novels." *SN* 6(1974): 418-438.

17080. Heywood, C. "*The Return of the Native* and Miss Braddon's *The Doctor's Wife*: A Probable Source." *NCF* 18(1963): 91-94.

17081. Holland, Norman, Jr. "*Jude the Obscure*: Hardy's Symbolic Indictment of Christianity." *NCF* 9(1954): 50-60.

17082. Hoopes, Kathleen R. "Illusion and Reality in *Jude the Obscure*." *NCF* 12(1957): 154-157.

17083. Hornback, Berg G. "Thomas Hardy: The Poet in Search of His Voice." *VP* 12(1974): 55-64.

17084. Horne, Lewis B. "'The Art of Renunciation' in Hardy's Novels." *SN* 4(1972): 556-567.

17085. ----------. "The Darkening Sun of Tess Durbyfield." *TSLL* 13(1971): 299-311.

17086. Hutchins, Patricia. "Thomas Hardy and Some Younger Writers." *JML* 3(1973): 35-44.

17087. Hyde, William J. "Hardy's Spider Webs." *VP* 8(1970): 265-268.

17088. ----------. "Theoretic and Practical Unconventionality in *Jude the Obscure*." *NCF* 20(1965): 155-164.

17089. Hyman, Virginia Riley. "The Ethical Dimension in Hardy's Novels." *EL* 1(1974):

178-192.

17090. Hynes, Samuel. "Hardy in His Times and Places." *MLQ* 34(1973): 325-330.

17091. Ingham, Patricia. "The Evolution of *Jude the Obscure*." *RES* 27(1976): 27-37; 159-169.

17092. Jacobus, Mary. "Sue the Obscure." *EIC* 25(1975): 304-328.

17093. ----------. "Tess's Purity." *EIC* 26(1976): 318-338.

17094. Jarrett, David W. "Eustacia Vye and Eula Varner, Olympians: The Worlds of Thomas Hardy and William Faulkner." *Novel* 6(1973): 163-174.

17095. ----------. "Hawthorne and Hardy as Modern Romancers." *NCF* 28(1974): 458-471.

17096. Jason, Philip K. "A Possible Allusion in Thomas Hardy's 'Going and Staying.'" *VP* 14(1976): 261-263.

17097. Jones, Lawrence O. "*Desperate Remedies* and the Victorian Sensation Novel." *NCF* 20(1965): 35-50.

17098. ----------. "Imitation and Expression in Thomas Hardy's Theory of Fiction." *SN* 7(1975): 507-525.

17099. ----------. "Thomas Hardy's 'Idiosyncratic Mode of Regard.'" *ELH* 42(1975): 433-459.

17100. Karl, Frederick R. "*The Mayor of Casterbridge*: A New Fiction Defined—1960,, 1965." *MFS* 21(1975): 405-428.

17101. Keith, W. J. "Thomas Hardy and the Literary Pilgrims." *NCF* 24(1969): 80-92.

17102. ----------. "Thomas Hardy and the Name 'Wessex.'" *ELN* 6(1968): 42-44.

17103. ----------. "Thomas Hardy's Edition of William Barnes." *VP* 15(1977): 121-132.

17104. Kiely, Robert. "Vision and Viewpoint in *The Mayor of Casterbridge*." *NCF* 23 (1968): 189-200.

17105. King, R. W. "Verse and Prose Parallels in the Works of Thomas Hardy." *RES* 13(1962): 52-61.

17106. Lentz, Vern B., and Douglas D. Short. "Hardy, Shelley, and the Statues." *VP* 12(1974): 370-372.

17107. Lodge, David. "Critical Exchange: Thomas Hardy and Cinematographic Form." *Novel* 7 (1974): 246-254.

17108. Lowe, Robert Liddell. "Three New Hardy Letters." *MLR* 54(1959): 396-397.

17109. Luedtke, Luther. "Sherwood Anderson, Thomas Hardy, and 'Tandy.'" *MFS* 20(1974): 531-540.

17110. Marshall, George O. "Hardy's *Tess* and Ellen Glasgow's *Barren Ground*." *TSLL* 1 (1960): 517-521.

17111. Martin, Bruce. "Whatever Happened to Eustacia Vye?" *SN* 4(1972): 619-627.

17112. Matchett, William. "*The Woodlanders*, or Realism in Sheep's Clothing." *NCF* 9(1955): 241-261.

17113. May, Charles E. "Hardy's 'Darkling Thrush': The 'Nightingale' Grown Old." *VP* 11 (1973): 62-65.

17114. ----------. "Thomas Hardy and the Poetry of the Absurd." *TSLL* 12(1970): 63-73.

17115. McCann, Eleanor. "Blind Will or Blind Hero: Philosophy and Myth in Hardy's *Return of the Native*." *Criticism* 3(1961): 140-157.

17116. McCullen, J. T., Jr. "Henchard's Sale of Susan in *The Mayor of Casterbridge*." *ELN* 2(1965): 217-218.

17117. McDowell, Frederick P. W. "Hardy's 'Seemings on Personal Impressions.': The Symbolic Use of Contrast in *Jude the Obscure*." *MFS* 6(1960): 233-250.

17118. ----------. "In Defense of Arabella: A Note on *Jude the Obscure*." *ELN* 1(1964): 274-280.

17119. Migdal, Seymour. "History and Archetype in *The Mayor of Casterbridge*." *SN* 3(1971): 284-292.

17120. Miller, Bruce E. "Motives of Annihilation in Hardy's Late Novels." *CLA* 19(1976): 389-403.

17121. Millgate, Jane. "Two Versions of Regional Romance: Scott's *Bride of Lammermoor* and Hardy's *Tess of the d'Urbervilles*." *SEL* 17 (1977): 729-738.

17122. Mills, Nicolaus C. "The Discovery of Nil in *Pierre* and *Jude the Obscure*." *TSLL* 12 (1970): 249-262.

17123. Mitchell, Charles. "Hardy's 'Afterwards.'" *VP* 1(1963): 68-70.

17124. Moore, John Robert. "Two Notes on Thomas Hardy." *NCF* 5(1950): 159-163.

17125. Morgan, William W. "Form, Tradition, and Consolation in Hardy's 'Poems of 1912-13.'" *PMLA* 89(1974): 496-505.

17126. ----------. "Syntax in Hardy's 'Neutral Tones,' Lines Seven and Eight." *VP* 11 (1973): 167-168.

17127. Morrell, Roy. "'The Dynasts' Reconsidered." *MLR* 58(1963): 161-171.

17128. Moynahan, Julian. "*The Mayor of Casterbridge* and the Old Testament's First Book of Samuel: A Study in Literary Relationships." *PMLA* 71(1956): 118-130.

17129. Neiman, Gilbert. "Thomas Hardy, Existentialist." *TCL* 1(1956): 207-214.

17130. ----------. "Was Hardy Anthropomorphic?" *TCL* 2(1956): 86-91.

17131. Neumeyer, Peter F. "The Transfiguring Vision." *VP* 3(1965): 263-266.

17132. Newton, William. "Chance as Employed by Hardy and the Naturalists." *PQ* 30(1951): 154-175.

17133. ----------. "Hardy and the Naturalists: Their Use of Physiology." *MP* 49(1951): 28-41.

17134. O'Grady, Walter. "On Plot in Modern Fiction: Hardy, James, and Conrad." *MFS* 11(1965): 107-115.

17135. Osborne, L. MacKenzie. "The 'Chronological Frontier' in Thomas Hardy's Novels." *SN* 4(1972): 543-555.

17136. Page, Norman. "Hardy's Short Stories: A Reconsideration." *SSF* 11(1974): 75-84.

17137. Paris, Bernard J. "'A Confusion of Many Standards': Conflicting Value Systems in *Tess of the d'Urbervilles*." *NCF* 24(1969): 57-79.

17138. Parrish, John E. "Thomas Hardy on the Evidence of Things Unseen." *VP* 2(1964): 203-205.

17139. Paterson, John. "The Genesis of *Jude the Obscure*." *SP* 57(1960): 87-98.

17140. ----------. "The 'Poetics' of *The*

Return of the Native." *MFS* 6(1960): 214-222.

17141. Paterson, John. "*The Return of the Native* as Anti-Christian Document." *NCF* 14(1959): 111-127.

17142. Perkins, David. "Hardy and the Poetry of Isolation." *ELH* 26(1959): 253-270.

17143. Perrine, Laurence. "Thomas Hardy's 'God Forgotten.'" *VP* 6(1968): 187-188.

17144. Roberts, James L. "Legend and Symbol in Hardy's 'The Three Strangers.'" *NCF* 17 (1962): 191-194.

17145. Salter, C. H. "Hardy's 'Pedantry.'" *NCF* 28(1973): 145-164.

17146. ----------. "Unusual Words Beginning with *Un, En, Out, Up,* and *On* in Thomas Hardy's Verse." *VP* 11(1973): 257-261.

17147. Sankey, Benjamin. "Hardy's Plotting." *TCL* 11(1965): 82-97.

17148. ----------. "Hardy's Prose Style." *TCL* 11(1965): 3-15.

17149. ----------. "Henchard and Faust." *ELN* 3(1965): 123-125.

17150. Saunders, Mary M. "The Significance of the Man-Trap in *The Woodlanders*." *MFS* 20(1974): 529-531.

17151. Schwartz, Barry N. "*Jude the Obscure* in the Age of Anxiety." *SEL* 10(1970): 793-804.

17152. Schwartz, Daniel R. "The Narrator as Character in Hardy's Major Fiction." *MFS* 18 (1972): 155-172.

17153. Schweik, Robert C. "Character and Fate in Hardy's *The Mayor of Casterbridge*." *NCF* 21(1966): 249-262.

17154. ----------. "The Early Development of Hardy's *Far from the Madding Crowd*." *TSLL* 9 (1967): 415-428.

17155. ----------. "Theme, Character, and Perspective in Hardy's *The Return of the Native*." *PQ* 41(1962): 757-767.

17156. Scott, James F. "Spectacle and Symbol in Thomas Hardy's Fiction." *PQ* 44(1965): 527-544.

17157. ----------. "Thomas Hardy's Use of the Gothic: An Examination of Five Representative Works." *NCF* 17(1963): 363-380.

17158. Sherman, G. W. "Thomas Hardy and the Agricultural Laborer." *NCF* 7(1952): 111-118.

17159. Short, Clarice. "In Defense of *Ethelberta*." *NCF* 13(1958): 48-57.

17160. Slack, Robert C. "The Text of Hardy's *Jude the Obscure*." *NCF* 11(1957): 261-275.

17161. Smart, Alastair. "Pictorial Imagery in the Novels of Thomas Hardy." *RES* 12 (1961): 262-280.

17162. Snell, Reginald. "A Self-Plagiarism by Thomas Hardy." *EIC* 2(1952): 114-115.

17163. Spivey, Ted R. "Thomas Hardy's Tragic Hero." *NCF* 9(1954): 179-191.

17164. Squires, Michael. "*Far From the Madding Crowd* as Modified Pastoral." *NCF* 25 (1970): 299-326.

17165. Stanford, Raney. "Thomas Hardy and Lawrence's *The White Peacock*." *MFS* 5(1959): 19-28.

17166. Starr, William T. "Romain Rolland and Thomas Hardy." *MLQ* 17(1956): 99-103.

17167. Starzyk, Lawrence J. "The Coming Universal Wish Not to Live in Hardy's 'Modern' Novels." *NCF* 26(1972): 419-435.

17168. ----------. "Hardy's *Mayor*: The Antitraditional Basis of Tragedy." *SN* 4(1972): 592-607.

17169. Steig, Michael. "Hardy Heroine Festival—Part Two: Sue Bridehead." *Novel* 1 (1968): 260-266.

17170. ----------. "Political Caricature and *The Dynasts*." *ELN* 8(1971): 287-293.

17171. ----------. "The Problem of Literary Value in Two Early Hardy Novels." *TSLL* 12(1970): 55-62.

17172. Strong, L. A. G. "Dorset Hardy." *EIC* 1(1951): 42-50.

17173. Taylor, Dennis. "The Patterns in Hardy's Poetry." *ELH* 42(1975): 258-275.

17174. ----------. "The Riddle of Hardy's Poetry." *VP* 11(1973): 263-276.

17175. ----------, and Paul Doherty. "Syntax in Hardy's 'Neutral Tones.'" *VP* 12(1974): 285-290.

17176. Thomson, George H. "The Trumpet-Major Chronicle." *NCF* 17(1962): 45-56.

17177. Tillman-Hill, Iris. "Hardy's Skylark and Shelley's." *VP* 10(1972): 79-82.

17178. Toliver, Harold E. "The Dance under the Greenwood Tree: Hardy's Bucolics." *NCF* 17(1962): 57-68.

17179. Weber, Carl J. "Hardy's Comet." *ELN* 1(1964): 215-218.

17180. ----------. "Hardy's Debt to Sir Frederick Macmillan." *ELN* 5(1967): 120-129.

17181. Wheeler, Otis B. "Four Versions of *The Return of the Native*." *NCF* 14(1959): 27-44.

17182. Winfield, Christine. "Factual Sources of Two Episodes in *The Mayor of Casterbridge*." *NCF* 25(1970): 224-231.

17183. Wing, George. "*Edwin Drood* and *Desperate Remedies*: Prototypes of Detective Fiction in 1870." *SEL* 13(1973): 677-687.

17184. ----------. "'Forbear, Hostler, Forbear': Social Satire in *The Hand of Ethelberta*." *SN* 4(1972): 468-479.

17185. Zellefrow, Ken. "*The Return of the Native*: Hardy's Map and Eustacia's Suicide." *NCF* 28(1973): 214-220.

17186. Zietlow, Paul. "The Tentative Mode of Hardy's Poems." *VP* 5(1967): 113-126.

17187. ----------. "Thomas Hardy and William Barnes: Two Dorset Poets." *PMLA* 84(1969): 291-303.

17188. Yuill, W. E. "'Character is Fate': A Note on Thomas Hardy, George Eliot, and Novalis." *MLR* 57(1962): 401-402.

See also 59, 80, 5064, 15327.

HAYDON, B. R.   17189. Jones, Stanley. "B. R. Haydon on Some Contemporaries." *RES* 26 (1975): 183-189.

See also 17204.

HAZLITT, WILLIAM.   17190. Albrecht, W. P. "Hazlitt on the Poetry of Wit." *PMLA* 75(1960): 245-249.

17191. ----------. "Hazlitt's Preference for Tragedy." *PMLA* 71(1956): 1042-1051.

17192. ----------. "More on Hazlitt's Preference for Tragedy." *PMLA* 73(1958): 444-445.

17193. ----------, and J. D. O'Hara. "More on Hazlitt and the Functions of the Imagination."

PMLA 83(1968): 151-155.

17194. Barnet, Sylvan. "More on Hazlitt's Preference for Tragedy." *PMLA* 73(1958): 443-444.

17195. Cheshire, Ardner R., Jr. "William Hazlitt, 'Slangwhanger.'" *WC* 7(1976): 107-108.

17196. DeLaura, David J. "Arnold and Hazlitt." *ELN* 9(1972): 277-283.

17197. Donohue, Joseph W., Jr. "Hazlitt's Sense of the Dramatic Actor as Tragic Character." *SEL* 5(1965): 705-721.

17198. Friedman, Martin B. "Hazlitt, Jerrold, and Horne: *Liber Amoris* Twenty Years After." *RES* 22(1971): 455-462.

17199. Hassler, Donald M. "The Discovery of the Future and Indeterminacy in William Hazlitt." *WC* 8(1977): 75-79.

17200. Hayden, John O. "Hazlitt Reviews Hazlitt?" *MLR* 64(1969): 20-26.

17201. Horne, Colin J. "Hazlitt on Swift." *EIC* 25(1975): 276-277.

17202. Houck, James Ashley. "Hazlitt on the Obligations of the Critic." *WC* 4(1973): 250-258.

17203. ----------. "Hazlitt's Divorce: The Court Records." *WC* 6(1975): 115-120.

17204. Jones, Stanley. "Haydon and Northcote on Hazlitt: A Fabrication." *RES* 24(1973): 165-178.

17205. ----------. "Hazlitt and *John Bull*: A Neglected Letter." *RES* 17(1966): 163-170.

17206. ----------. "Hazlitt's Missing Essay 'On Individuality.'" *RES* 28(1977): 421-430.

17207. Kinnaird, John. "The Faith of the Centaur: Hazlitt's Sceptical Triumph over Scepticism." *WC* 6(1975): 85-96.

17208. ----------. "Hazlitt as Poet: The Probable Authorship of Some Anonymous Verses on Wordsworth's Appointment as Stamp-Distributor." *SR* 12(1973): 426-435.

17209. ----------. "Hazlitt, Keats, and the Poetics of Intersubjectivity." *Criticism* 19(1977): 1-16.

17210. Klingopulos, G. D. "Hazlitt as Critic." *EIC* 6(1956): 386-403.

17211. Lahey, Gerald. "The Hazlitt Correspondence, Based upon a Prospective Edition." *WC* 6(1975): 121-128.

17212. Low, Donald. "Hazlitt on Burns." *WC* 2(1971): 100.

17213. Miller, Edmund. "Hazlitt and Fawcett." *WC* 8(1977): 377-382.

17214. Moyne, Ernest J. "An Unpublished Letter of William Hazlitt." *PMLA* 77(1962): 341-344.

17215. O'Hara, J. D. "Hazlitt and the Functions of the Imagination." *PMLA* 81(1966): 552-562.

17216. Park, Roy. "The Painter as Critic: Hazlitt's Theory of Abstraction." *PMLA* 85(1970): 1072-1081.

17217. Patterson, Charles I. "William Hazlitt as a Critic of Prose Fiction." *PMLA* 68 (1953): 1001-1016.

17218. Ready, Robert. "Hazlitt as an English Comic Writer." *WC* 6(1975): 109-114.

17219. ----------. "Hazlitt: In and Out of 'Gusto.'" *SEL* 14(1974): 537-546.

17220. ----------. "The Logic of Passion: Hazlitt's *Liber Amoris*." *SR* 14(1975): 41-58.

17221. Sallé, J.-C. "Hazlitt the Associationist." *RES* 15(1964): 38-51.

17222. Story, Patrick L. "A Contemporary Continuation of Hazlitt's *Spirit of the Age*." *WC* 1(1970): 59-65.

17223. ----------. "Hazlitt's Definition of the Spirit of the Age." *WC* 6(1975): 97-108.

17224. Trawick, Leonard M., III. "Hazlitt, Reynolds, and the Ideal." *SR* 4(1965): 240-247.

17225. ----------. "Sources of Hazlitt's 'Metaphysical Discovery.'" *PQ* 42(1963): 277-282.

17226. Wardle, Ralph M. "'Moore's Present to Hazlitt.'" *WC* 6(1975): 80-84.

See also 13882, 15286, 16379, 17189, 17419.

HENLEY, WILLIAM EARNEST. 17227. Cohen, Edward H. "An Early Sonnet-Portrait by W. E. Henley." *VP* 14(1976): 258-260.

17228. Schaefer, William D. "Henley and 'The Hound of Heaven.'" *VP* 5(1967): 171-181.

17229. Weintraub, Joseph. "Henley Puffing Stevenson." *MP* 74(1976): 201-203.

See also 5064, 15376.

HOGG, JAMES. 17230. Georgas, Marilyn. "A New Source for Hogg's *Justified Sinner*: Greville's *Life of Sidney*." *NCF* 29(1974): 338-345.

17231. Strout, Alan Lang. "James Hogg's 'Chaldee Manuscript.'" *PMLA* 65(1950): 695-718.

HOOD, THOMAS. 17232. Henning, John. "The Literary Relations Between Goethe and Thomas Hood." *MLQ* 12(1951): 57-66.

17233. Lauterbach, Edward S. "Tom Hood Discovers Bret Harte." *AL* 34(1962): 285-287.

17234. Stone, Edward. "Bartleby and Miss Norman." *SSF* 9(1972): 271-274.

HOPE, ANTHONY. 17235. Putt, S. Gorley. "The Prisoner of *The Prisoner of Zenda*: Anthony Hope and the Novel of Society." *EIC* 6(1956): 38-59.

HOPKINS, GERARD MANLEY. 17236. August, Eugene. "The Growth of 'The Windhover.'" *PMLA* 82(1967): 465-468.

17237. ----------. "Hopkins' Dangerous Fire." *VP* 1(1963): 72-74.

17238. Bates, Ronald. "'The Windhover.'" *VP* 2(1964): 63-64.

17239. Baum, Paull F. "Sprung Rhythm." *PMLA* 74(1959): 418-425.

17240. Baxter, Ralph C. "Shakespeare's Dauphin and Hopkins' Windhover." *VP* 7(1969): 71-75.

17241. Bernard, Miguel A. "Hopkins' *Pied Beauty*: A Note on its Ignatian Inspiration." *EIC* 12(1962): 217-220.

17242. Beyette, Kent. "Grace and Time as Latent Structures in the Poetry of Gerad Manley Hopkins." *TSLL* 16(1975): 705-721.

17243. Beyette, Thomas K. "Hopkins' Phenomonology of Art in 'The Shepherd's Brow.'" *VP* 11(1973): 207-214.

17244. Boyd, John D., S.J. "Hopkins' Blessed Understanding: A Source for a Line in *The Wreck of the Deutschland*." *ELN* 5(1968): 293-297.

17245. Boyle, Robert, S.J. "Hopkins' Use of 'Fancy.'" *VP* 10(1972): 17-28.

17246. Bump, Jerome. "Hopkins and Keats." *VP* 12(1974): 33-44.

17247. ----------. "Hopkins' Imagery and Medievalist Poetics." *VP* 15(1977): 99-120.

17248. ----------. "'The Wreck of the

Deutschland' and The Dynamic Sublime." *ELH* 41 (1974): 106-129.

17249. Carson, J. Angela. "The Metaphor of Struggle in 'Carrion Comfort.'" *PQ* 49(1970): 547-557.

17250. Chard, Leslie F., II. "Once More Into *The Windhover*." *ELN* 2(1965): 282-285.

17251. Cohen, Selma Jeanne. "'As King-fishes Catch Fire.'" *MLQ* 11(1950): 197-204.

17252. Dawson, S. W. "An Early Poem by Hopkins." *EIC* 19(1969): 100-105.

17253. DeLaura, David J. "Hopkins and Mrs. Gaskell: Margaret, Are You Grieving?" *VP* 14(1976): 341-345.

17254. Doherty, Francis. "A Note on *Spelt from Sibyl's Leaves*." *EIC* 14(1964): 428-432.

17255. Doherty, Paul C. "Hopkins' 'Spring and Fall: To A Young Child.'" *VP* 5(1967): 140-143.

17256. Downes, David A. "Hopkins and Thomism." *VP* 3(1965): 270-272.

17257. Driscoll, John P., S.J. "'The Wreck of the Deutschland': Stanza 33." *VP* 13(1975): 137-142.

17258. Eble, Joseph. "Levels of Awareness: A Reading of Hopkins' 'Felix Randall.'" *VP* 13(1975): 129-135.

17259. Eagleton, Terry. "Nature and the Fall in Hopkins: a Reading of 'God's Grandeur.'" *EIC* 23(1973): 68-75.

17260. Epstein, E. L. "Hopkins's 'Heaven-Haven': a Linguistic-Critical Description." *EIC* 23(1973): 137-145.

17261. Ferns, John. "The Wreck of the Deutschland: Voice and Structure." *VP* 9(1971): 383-393.

17262. Fike, Francis. "Gerard Manley Hopkins' Interest in Painting after 1868: Two Notes." *VP* 8(1970): 315-334.

17263. Fox, Judith H. "*The Queen of the Air*: Transformation of Myth in Ruskin and Hopkins." *VP* 12(1974): 335-342.

17264. Freije, George F. "Grace in Hopkins's 'Deutschland.'" *ELN* 13(1975): 37-38.

17265. Giffard, C. Anthony. "The Springs of Goldengrove." *VP* 15(1977): 60-65.

17266. Gomme, Andor. "A Note on Two Hopkins Sonnets." *EIC* 14(1964): 327-331.

17267. Graves, William L. "Gerard Manley Hopkins as Composer: An Interpretive Postscript." *VP* 1(1963): 146-155.

17268. Hallgarth, Susan A. "A Study of Hopkins' Use of Nature." *VP* 5(1967): 79-92.

17269. Harrison, Thomas P. "The Birds of Gerard Manley Hopkins." *SP* 54(1957): 448-463.

17270. Haskell, Ann Sullivan. "An Image of 'The Windhover.'" *VP* 6(1968): 75-77.

17271. Hentz, Ann Louise. "Language in Hopkins' 'Carrion Comfort.'" *VP* 9(1971): 343-347.

17272. Hill, Archibald A. "An Analysis of *The Windhover*: An Experiment in Structural Method." *PMLA* 70(1955): 968-978.

17273. ----------. "'The Windhover' Revisited: Linguistic Analysis of Poetry Reassessed." *TSLL* 7(1966): 349-359.

17274. Humiliata, Sister Mary. "Hopkins and the Prometheus Myth." *PMLA* 70(1955): 58-68.

17275. Johnson, Michael L. "Hopkins,

Heraclitus, Cosmic Instress and of the Comfort of the Resurrection." *VP* 10(1972): 235-242.

17276. Johnson, Wendell Stacy. "Auden, Hopkins, and the Poetry of Reticence." *TCL* 20 (1974): 165-171.

17277. Kennedy, Eileen. "Lightning, Lashed Rod, and Dove in 'The Wreck of the Deutschland." *VP* 11(1973): 247-251.

17278. Korg, Jacob. "Hopkins' Linguistic Deviations." *PMLA* 92(1977): 977-986.

17279. Kretz, Thomas, S.J. "Advents Three for Three: A Study of 'The Wreck of the Deutschland.'" *VP* 11(1973): 252-254.

17280. Litzinger, Boyd. "The Pattern of Ascent in Hopkins." *VP* 2(1964): 43-47.

17281. ----------. "Once More, 'The Windhover.'" *VP* 5(1967): 228-230.

17282. Lowenstein, Amy. "Seeing 'Pied Beauty': A Key to Theme and Structure." *VP* 14 (1976): 64-66.

17283. MacKenzie, Norman H. "Gerard Manley Hopkins: The Dragon's Treasure Horde Unlocked." *MLQ* 31(1970): 236-244.

17284. Mariani, Paul L. "The Artistic and Tonal Integrity of Hopkins' 'The Shepherd's Brow.'" *VP* 6(1968): 63-68.

17285. ----------. "Hopkins' 'Andromeda' and The New Aestheticism." *VP* 11(1973): 39-54.

17286. Matchett, William. "An Analysis of 'The Windhover.'" *PMLA* 72(1957): 310-311.

17287. Mellown, Elgin W. "Gerard Manley Hopkins and His Public, 1889-1918." *MP* 57(1959): 94-99.

17288. ----------. "The History of the Critical Reception of 'The Wreck of the Deutschland.'" *VP* 14(1976): 1-10.

17289. ----------. "Hopkins and the *Odyssey*." *VP* 8(1970): 263-265.

17290. ----------. "The Reception of Gerard Manley Hopkins' *Poems*, 1918-1930." *MP* 63(1965): 38-51.

17291. Miller, Bruce E. "On 'The Windhover.'" *VP* 2(1964): 115-119.

17292. Miller, J. Hillis. "The Creation of the Self in Gerard Manley Hopkins." *ELH* 22(1955): 293-319.

17293. Montag, George E. "Hopkins' 'God's Grandeur' and 'The Ooze of Oil Crushed.'" *VP* 1 (1963): 302-303.

17294. ----------. "'The Windhover': Crucifixion and Redemption." *VP* 3(1965): 109-118.

17295. Murphy, Michael W. "Violent Imagery in the Poetry of Gerard Manley Hopkins." *VP* 7 (1969): 1-16.

17296. O'Dea, Richard J. "'The Loss of the Eurydice': A Possible Key to the Reading of Hopkins." *VP* 4(1966): 291-293.

17297. Pace, George B. "On the Octave Rhymes of *The Windhover*." *ELN* 2(1965): 285-286.

17298. Page, Philip. "Unity and Subordination in 'Carrion Comfort.'" *VP* 14(1976): 25-32.

17299. Proffitt, Edward. "'The Wreck of the Deutschland': Stanza 25-28." *ELN* 14(1977): 201-206.

17300. Rader, Louis. "Hopkins' Dark Sonnets: Another New Expression." *VP* 5(1967): 13-20.

17301. Reiman, Donald H. "Hopkins' 'Ooze of Oil' Rises Again." *VP* 4(1966): 39-42.

17302. Rodway, Allan. "Hopkins's 'Heaven-

Haven.'" *EIC* 23(1973): 430-434.

17303. Rose, Alan M. "Hopkins' 'Carrion Comfort': The Artful Disorder of Prayer." *VP* 15 (1977): 207-218.

17304. Schneider, Elisabeth W. "Sprung Rhythm: A Chapter in the Evolution of Nineteenth-Century Verse." *PMLA* 80(1965): 237-253.

17305. ----------. *The Wreck of the Deutschland* : A New Reading." *PMLA* 81(1966): 110-122.

17306. Sharples, Sister Marian, I. H. M. "Conjecturing a Date for Hopkins' 'St. Thecla.'" *VP* 4(1966): 204-209.

17307. Shea, F. X., S.J. "Another Look at 'The Windhover.'" *VP* 2(1964): 219-240.

17308. Shurr, William H. "Sylvester Judd and G. M. Hopkins' Margaret." *VP* 11(1973): 337-339.

17309. Slakey, Roger L. "The Grandeur in Hopkins' 'God's Grandeur.'" *VP* 7(1969): 159-163.

17310. Smith, Grover. "A Source for Hopkins' 'Spring and Fall' in *The Mill on the Floss.*" *ELN* 1(1963): 43-46.

17311. Sonstroem, David. "Making Earnest of Game: G. M. Hopkins and Nonsense Poetry." *MLQ* 28(1967): 192-206.

17312. Sutherland, John. "'Tom's Garland': Hopkins' Political Poem." *VP* 10(1972): 111-122.

17313. Templeman, William Darby. "Hopkins and Whitman: Evidence of Influence and Echoes." *PQ* 33(1954): 48-65.

17314. Thesing, William B. "'Tom's Garland' and Hopkins' Inscapes of Humanity." *VP* 15 (1977): 37-48.

17315. Thomas, A. "G. M. Hopkins: An Unpublished Triolet." *MLR* 61(1966): 183-187.

17316. ----------. "G. M. Hopkins: 'The Windhover'; Sources, 'Underthought' and Significance." *MLR* 70(1975): 497-507.

17317. ----------. "G. M. Hopkins: Two Bibliographical Discoveries." *RES* 22(1971): 58-61.

17318. ----------. "Hopkinsharvest: The Meeting of the 'Wrecks.'" *VP* 12(1974): 71-73.

17319. Thornton, R. K. R. "Hopkins and the Histories." *VP* 9(1971): 341-343.

17320. Tucker, Herbert F., Jr. "Hopkins: Bloomfall and Inthought." *PQ* 55(1976): 133-140.

17321. Ward, Sister M. Eucharista. "Suffering as Passivity: Pierre Teilhard de Chardin as a Gloss on Gerard Manley Hopkins." *VP* 10 (1972): 321-332.

17322. White, Gertrude M. "Hopkins' 'God's Grandeur': A Poetic Statement of Christian Doctrine." *VP* 4(1966): 284-287.

17323. White, Norman. "A Date for G. M. Hopkins's 'What Being in Rank-Old Nature. . ..'" *RES* 20(1969): 319-320.

17324. ----------. "The Probable Identity of Hopkins' 'Two Beautiful Young People.'" *ELN* 8(1971): 206-208.

17325. ----------. "The Setting of Hopkins' 'Epithalamion.'" *VP* 10(1972): 83-86.

17326. Winter, J. L. "Notes on 'The Windhover.'" *VP* 4(1966): 212-213.

17327. Wolfe, Patricia A. "The Paradox of Self: A Study of Hopkins' 'Terrible' Sonnets." *VP* 6(1968): 85-104.

17328. Wooton, Carl. "The Terrible Fire of Gerard Manley Hopkins." *TSLL* 4(1962): 367-375.
  See also 547.

HOWITT, WILLIAM. 17329. Woodring, Carl R. "Charles Reade's Debt to William Howitt." *NCF* 5 (1950): 39-46.

HUNT, LEIGH. 17330. Davies, James Atterbury. "Leigh Hunt and John Forster." *RES* 19 (1968): 25-40.

17331. Duff, Gerald. "Leigh Hunt's Criticism of the Novel." *CLA* 13(1969): 109-118.

17332. Fogle, Stephen F. "Leight Hunt and the Laureatship." *SP* 55(1958): 603-615.

17333. Todd, William B. "Leight Hunt's Annotations in Johnson's *Dictionary.*" *MP* 73 (1976): S110-S112.

HUTTON, RICHARD. 17334. Colby, Robert A. "How it Strikes a Contemporary: The *Spectator* as Critic." *NCF* 11(1956): 182-206.

HUXLEY, THOMAS H. 17335. Roos, David A. "Matthew Arnold and Thomas Henry Huxley: Two Speeches at the Royal Academy, 1881 and 1883." *MP* 74(1977): 316-324.

INGLIS, HENRY DAVID. 17336. McDonald, W. U., Jr. "Inglis' *Rambles*: A Romantic Tribute to *Don Quixoite.*" *Comp L* 12(1960): 33-41.

JEFFREY, FRANCIS. 17337. Guyer, Byron. "The Philosophy of Francis Jeffrey." *MLQ* 11 (1950): 17-26.

17338. Hatch, Ronald B. "'This Will Never Do.'" *RES* 21(1970): 56-62.

17339. Owen, W. J. B. "Wordsworth and Jeffrey in Collaboration." *RES* 15(1964): 161-167.

JEFFRIES, RICHARD. 17340. Hyde, William J. "Richard Jeffries and the Naturalistic Peasant." *NCF* 11(1956): 207-217.

JERROLD, DOUGLAS. 17341. Slater, Michael. "Carlyle and Jerrold into Dickens: A Study of *The Chimes.*" *NCF* 24(1970): 506-526.

JEWSBURY, GERALDINE. 17342. Fahnestock, Jeanne Rosenmayer. "Geraldine Jewsbury: The Power of the Publisher's Reader." *NCF* 28(1973): 253-272.

JOHNSON, LIONEL. 17343. Dowling, Linda C. "Pursuing Antithesis: Lionel Johnson on Hardy." *ELN* 12(1975): 287-292.

JOHNSON, RICHARD. 17344. Hirsch, Richard S. M. "The Source of Richard Johnson's *Look on Me London.*" *ELN* 13(1975): 107-113.

KEATS, JOHN. 17345. Allott, Kenneth. "Keats's 'Ode to Psyche.'" *EIC* 6(1956): 278-301.

17346. Amis, Kingsley. "The Curious Elf: A Note on Rhyme in Keats." *EIC* 1(1951): 189-192.

17347. Beer, Gillian. "Aesthetic Debate in Keats's Odes." *MLR* 64(1969): 742-748.

17348. Benvenuto, Richard. "'The Ballance of Good and Evil' in Keats's Letters and 'Lamia.'" *JEGP* 71(1972): 1-11.

17349. Beyer, Werner W. "Some Notes to Keats's Letters." *JEGP* 51(1952): 336-344.

17350. Blake, Robert. "The Dating of *Endymion.*" *RES* 17(1966): 177-182.

17351. Bland, D. S. "'Logical Structure' in the *Ode to Autumn.*" *PQ* 33(1954): 219-222.

17352. ----------. "Painting and the Poetry of Keats: Some Further Identifications." *MLR* 50(1955): 502-504.

17353. Bloom, Harold. "Keats and Romanticism." *MLQ* 25(1964): 479-485.

17354. Boulger, James D. "Keats' Symbolism." ELH 28(1961): 244-259.

17355. Bump, Jerome. "Hopkins and Keats." VP 12(1974): 33-44.

17356. Bunn, James H. "Keats's Ode to Psyche and the Transformation of Mental Landscape." ELH 37(1970): 581-594.

17357. Burrow, John. "Keats and Edward Thomas." EIC 7(1957): 404-415.

17358. Chandler, Alice. "'The Eve of St. Agnes' and 'Porphyria's Lover.'" VP 3(1965): 273-274.

17359. Chayes, Irene H. "Dreamer, Poet, and Poem in the Fall of Hyperion." PQ 46(1967): 499-515.

17360. Coombes, H. "Keats and Edward Thomas." EIC 8(1958): 227-228.

17361. Davies, R. T. "Was 'Negative Capability' Enough for Keats? A Re-assessment of the Evidence in the Letters." SP 55(1958): 76-85.

17362. de Man, Paul. "Keats and Hölderlin." Comp L 8(1956): 28-45.

17363. Eggers, J. Phillip. "Memory in Mankind: Keats's Historical Imagination." PMLA 86 (1971): 990-998.

17364. Ende, Stuart A. "Keats's Music of Truth." ELH 40(1973): 90-104.

17365. Felperin, Howard. "Keats and Shakespeare: Two New Sources." ELN 2(1964): 105-108.

17366. Fogle, Richard Harter. "Keats's Ode to a Nightingale." PMLA 68(1953): 211-222.

17367. Ford, Newell F. "Keats's Saturn: Person or Statue?" MLQ 14(1953): 253-257.

17368. Garlitz, Barbara. "Egypt and Hyperion." PQ 34(1955): 189-196.

17369. Gelfant, Blanche F. "Faulkner and Keats: The Ideality of Art in 'The Bear.'" SLJ 2,#1(1969): 43-65.

17370. Gerard, Albert. "Coleridge, Keats and the Modern Mind." EIC 1(1951): 249-261.

17371. Gleckner, Robert F. "Keats's Odes: The Problem of the Limited Canon." SEL 5(1965): 577-585.

17372. Goldberg, M. A. "The 'Fears' of John Keats." MLQ 18(1957): 125-131.

17373. Goslee, Nancy M. "'Under a Cloud in Prospect': Keats, Milton, and Stationing." PQ 53(1974): 205-219.

17374. Gradman, Barry. "Measure for Measure and Keats's 'Nightingale' Ode." ELN 12 (1975): 177-182.

17375. Green, Eugene and Rosemary M. "Keats's Use of Names in Endymion and in the Odes." SR 16(1977): 15-34.

17376. Grennan, Eamon. "Keats's Contemptus Mundi: A Shakespearean Influence on the 'Ode to a Nightingale.'" MLQ 36(1975): 272-292.

17377. Grundy, Joan. "Keats and William Browne." RES 6(1955): 44-52.

17378. Hardison, O. B., Jr. "The Decorum of Lamia." MLQ 19(1958): 33-42.

17379. Harrison, Robert. "Symbolism of the Cyclical Myth in Endymion." TSLL 1(1960): 538-554.

17380. Harrold, William E. "Keats's 'Lamia' and Peacock's 'Rhododaphne.'" MLR 61(1966): 579-584.

17381. Hartman, Geoffrey H. "Spectral Symbolism and the Authorial Self: an Approach to Keats's Hyperion." EIC 24(1974): 1-19.

17382. Havens, Raymond D. "Of Beauty and Reality in Keats." ELH 17(1950): 206-213.

17383. Haworth, Helen E. "Keats and the Metaphor of Vision." JEGP 67(1968): 371-394.

17384. ----------. "The Titans, Apollo, and the Fortunate Fall in Keats's Poetry." SEL 10(1970): 637-649.

17385. Heinen, Hubert. "Interwoven Time in Keats's Poetry." TSLL 3(1961): 382-388.

17386. Itzkowitz, Martin E. "Freneau's 'Indian Burying Ground' and Keats' 'Grecian Urn.'" EAL 6,#3(1972): 258-262.

17387. Jones, Leonidas M. "Keats's Favorite Play." ELN 15(1977): 43-44.

17388. Koch, June Q. "Politics in Keats's Poetry." JEGP 71(1972): 491-501

17389. Lams, Victor J., Jr. "Ruth, Milton, and Keats's 'Ode to a Nightingale.'" MLQ 34 (1973): 417-435.

17390. Lange, Donald. "A New Reynolds-Milnes Letter: Were there two Meetings between Keats and Coleridge?" MLR 72(1977): 769-772.

17391. Lott, James. "Keats's To Autumn: The Poetic Consciousness and the Awareness of Process." SR 9(1970): 71-81.

17392. Luke, David. "The Eve of Saint Mark: Keats's 'ghostly Queen of Spades' and the Textual Superstition." SR 9(1970): 161-176.

17393. Maier, Rosemarie. "The Bitch and the Bloodhound: Generic Similarity in 'Christabel' and 'The Eve of St. Agnes.'" JEGP 70(1971): 62-75.

17394. Manierre, William Reid. "Versification and Imagery in The Fall of Hyperion." TSLL 3(1961): 264-279.

17395. Margolis, John D. "Keats's 'Men of Genius' and 'Men of Power.'" TSLL 11(1970): 1333-1347.

17396. McCall, Dan. "'The Self-Same Song that Found a Path': Keats and The Great Gatsby." AL 42(1971): 521-530.

17397. Miller, Bruce E. "On the Incompleteness of Keats' Hyperion." CLA 8(1965): 234-239.

17398. Mincoff, Marco. "Beauty is Truth—Once More." MLR 65(1970): 267-271.

17399. Mooney, Stephen. "James, Keats, and the Religion of Consciousness." MLQ 22(1961): 399-401.

17400. Muir, Kenneth. "The Meaning of Hyperion." EIC 2(1952): 54-75.

17401. Nelson, Lowry, Jr. "The Rhetoric of Ineffability: Toward a Definition of Mystical Poetry." Comp L 8(1956): 323-336.

17402. Notopoulos, James A. "'Truth-Beauty' in the 'Ode on a Grecian Urn' and the Elgin Marbles." MLR 61(1966): 180-182.

17403. Osler, Alan. "Keats and Baldwin's 'Pantheon.'" MLR 62(1967): 221-225.

17404. Parsons, Coleman O. "The Refining of Lamia." WC 8(1977): 183-192.

17405. Patterson, Charles I. "The Keats-Hazlitt-Hunt Copy of Palmerin of England in Relation to Keats's Poetry." JEGP 60(1961): 31-43.

17406. ----------. "Passion and Permanence

in Keats's *Ode on a Grecian Urn*." *ELH* 21(1954): 208-220.

17407. Pettet, E. C. "Echoes of *The Lay of the Last Minstrel* in *The Eve of St. Agnes*." *RES* 3(1952): 39-48.

17408. Pollard, Arthur. "Keats and Akenside: A Borrowing in the 'Ode to a Nightingale.'" *MLR* 51(1956): 75-77.

17409. Pratt, Willis W. "*The Eve of St. Agnes* and W. S. Rose's *Partenopex de Blois*." *TSLL* 10(1968): 83-90.

17410. Ragussis, Michael. "Narrative Structure and the Problem of the Divided Reader in *The Eve of St. Agnes*." *ELH* 42(1975): 378-394.

17411. Reiman, Donald H. "Keats and the Humanistic Paradox: Mythological History in *Lamia*." *SEL* 11(1971): 659-669.

17412. Ruthven, K. K. "Keats and *Dea Moneta*." *SR* 15(1976): 445-460.

17413. Ryan, Robert M. "Keats and the Truth of Imagination." *WC* 4(1973): 259-266.

17414. ----------. "Christ and Moneta." *ELN* 13(1976): 190-192.

17415. Sackton, Alexander H. "A Note on Keats and Chaucer." *MLQ* 13(1952): 37-40.

17416. Sallé, Jean-Claude. "The Pious Frauds of Art: A Reading of the 'Ode on a Grecian Urn.'" *SR* 11(1972): 79-93.

17417. Schulz, Max F. "Keats' Timeless Order of Things: A Modern Reading of Ode to Psyche." *Criticism* 2(1960): 55-65.

17418. Severs, J. Burke. "Keats's 'Mansion of Many Apartments,' *Sleep and Poetry*, and *Tintern Abbey*." *MLQ* 20(1959): 128-132.

17419. Sikes, Herschel M. "The Poetic Theory and Practice of Keats: The Record of a Debt to Hazlitt." *PQ* 38(1959): 401-412.

17420. Simpson, David E. "Keats's Lady, Metaphor, and the Rhetoric of Neurosis." *SR* 15(1976): 265-288.

17421. Slote, Bernice. "The Climate of Keats's 'La Belle Dame sans Merci.'" *MLQ* 21(1960): 195-207.

17422. ----------. "La Belle Dame as Naiad." *JEGP* 60(1961): 22-30.

17423. Smith, Barbara Hernstein. "'Sorrow's Mysteries': Keats's 'Ode on Melancholy.'" *SEL* 6(1966): 679-691.

17424. Smith, Louise Z. "The Material Sublime: Keats and *Isabella*." *SR* 13(1974): 299-312.

17425. Spens, Janet. "A Study of Keats's 'Ode to a Nightingale.'" *RES* 3(1952): 234-243.

17426. Sperry, Stuart M., Jr. "The Allegory of *Endymion*." *SR* 2(1962): 38-53.

17427. ----------. "Keats and the Chemistry of Poetic Creation." *PMLA* 85(1970): 268-277.

17428. ----------. "Keats, Milton, and *The Fall of Hyperion*." *PMLA* 77(1962): 77-84.

17429. ----------. "Keats's *Epistle to John Hamilton Reynolds*." *ELH* 36(1969): 562-574.

17430. ----------. "Romance as Wish-Fulfillment in Keats's *The Eve of Saint Agnes*." *SR* 10(1971): 27-43.

17431. ----------. "Some Versions of Keats." *MLQ* 38(1977): 178-185.

17432. Spitzer, Leo. "The 'Ode on a Grecian Urn,' or Content vs. Metagrammar." *Comp L* 7(1955): 203-225.

17433. Stevenson, Warren. "*Lamia*: A Stab at the Gordian Knot." *SR* 11(1972): 241-252.

17434. Stewart, Garrett. "*Lemia* and the Language of Metamorphosis." *SR* 15(1976): 3-42.

17435. Stillinger, Jack. "The Hoodwinking of Madeline: Scepticism in 'The Eve of St. Agnes.'" *SP* 58(1961): 533-555.

17436. ----------. "Keats and Romance." *SEL* 8(1968): 593-605.

17437. ----------. "Keats's Grecian Urn and the Evidence of Transcripts." *PMLA* 73(1958): 447-448.

17438. ----------. "The Meaning of 'poor cheated soul' in Keats's 'The Eve of St. Mark.'" *ELN* 5(1968): 193-196.

17439. ----------. "The Order of Poems in Keats's First Volume." *PQ* 48(1969): 92-101.

17440. Teich, Nathaniel. "Criticism and Keats's *Grecian Urn*." *PQ* 44(1965): 496-502.

17441. Thurston, Norman. "Biography and Keats's Pleasure Thermometer." *WC* 4(1973): 267-270.

17442. Utley, Francis Lee. "The Infernos of Lucretius and of Keats's *La Belle Dame Sans Merci*." *ELH* 25(1958): 105-121.

17443. Vendler, Helen. "The Experiential Beginnings of Keats's Odes." *SR* 12(1973): 591-606.

17444. Vitoux, Pierre. "Keats's Epic Design in *Hyperion*." *SR* 14(1975): 165-184.

17445. Waldoff, Leon. "From Abandonment to Scepticism in Keats." *EIC* 21(1971): 152-158.

17446. ----------. "Porphyro's Imagination and Keats's Romanticism." *JEGP* 76(1977): 177-194.

17447. ----------. "The Theme of Mutability in the 'Ode to Psyche.'" *PMLA* 92(1977): 410-419.

17448. Ward, Aileen. "The Date of Keats's 'Bright Star' Sonnet." *SP* 52(1955): 75-85.

17449. ----------. "Keats and Burton: A Reappraisal." *PQ* 40(1961): 535-552.

17450. ----------. "Keats's Sonnet, 'Nebuchadnezzar's Dream.'" *PQ* 34(1955): 177-188.

17451. Ware, Malcolm. "Keats's 'Stout Cortez': A Deliberate Error." *ELN* 4(1966): 113-115.

17452. Webster, Grant T. "Keats's 'La Belle Dame': A New Source." *ELN* 3(1965): 42-47.

17453. Wicker, Brian. "The Disputed Lines in *The Fall of Hyperion*." *EIC* 7(1957): 28-41.

17454. Wigod, Jacob D. "Keats's Ideal in the *Ode on a Grecian Urn*." *PMLA* 72(1957): 113-121.

17455. ----------. "The Meaning of *Endymion*." *PMLA* 68(1953): 779-790.

17456. ----------. "Negative Capability and Wise Passiveness." *PMLA* 67(1952): 383-390.

17457. Wills, Garry. "Classicism in Keats's Chapman Sonnet." *EIC* 17(1967): 456-460.

17458. Wright, Herbert G. "Possible Indebtedness of Keats's 'Isabella' to the *Decameron*." *RES* 2(1951): 248-254.

17459. Yost, George, Jr. "An Identification in Keats's *Ode to Psyche*." *PQ* 36(1957): 496-500.

17460. ----------. "Keats' Early Religious Phraseology." *SP* 59(1962): 579-591.

17461. ----------. "The Poetic Drive in

the Early Keats." *TSLL* 5(1964): 555-566.

17462. Yost, George, Jr. "A Source and Interpretation of Keats's Minos." *JEGP* 57(1958): 220-229.

17463. Zeff, Jacqueline. "Strategies of Time in Keats's Narratives." *SEL* 17(1977): 621-637.

See also 2254, 3152, 13882, 15286, 15293, 15363, 16217, 17689, 17781, 17958, 18022.

KINGLAKE, ALEXANDER WILLIAM. 17464. Dunlap, Benjamin. "Kinglake's *Eothen*." *SLI* 8,#2 (1975): 77-91.

17465. Johnston, William M. "William Kinglake's 'A Summer in Russia': A Neglected Memoir of Saint Petersburg in 1845." *TSLL* 9(1967): 103-115.

KINGSLEY, CHARLES. 17466. Coleman, Dorothy. "Rabelais and 'The Water-Babies.'" *MLR* 66(1971): 511-521.

17467. Waller, John O. "Charles Kingsley and the American Civil War." *SP* 60(1963): 554-568.

KINGSLEY, HENRY. 17468. Buckler, William E. "Henry Kingsley and *The Gentleman's Magazine*." *JEGP* 50(1951): 90-100.

17469. Scheuerle, William H. "'Magdalen at Michael's Gate': A Neglected Lyric." *VP* 5 (1967): 144-146.

17470. Thirkell, Angela. "Henry Kingsley 1830-1876." *NCF* 5(1950): 175-187.

17471. Thirkell, Angela. "The Works of Henry Kingsley." *NCF* 5(1951): 273-293.

See also 21105.

KIPLING, RUDYARD. 17472. Cook, Richard. "Rudyard Kipling and George Orwell." *MFS* 7(1961): 125-135.

17473. Fussell, Paul, Jr. "Irony, Freemasonry, and Humane Ethics in Kipling's 'The Man Who Would Be King.'" *ELH* 25(1958): 216-233.

17474. Gilbert, Elliot L. "Kipling's 'The Gardner': Craft into Art." *SSF* 7(1970): 308-319.

17475. ----------. "What Happens in 'Mrs. Bathurst.'" *PMLA* 77(1962): 450-458.

17476. Hagemann, E. R. "'Correspondents Three' in the Graeco-Turkish War: Some Parodies." *AL* 30(1958): 339-344.

17477. Hill, Donald L. "Kipling in Vermont." *NCF* 7(1952): 153-170.

17478. Isani, Mukhtar Ali. "The Origin of Kipling's 'Gunga Din.'" *VP* 15(1977): 83-84.

17479. Karim, M. Enamul. "Rudyard Kipling's Uncollected Poem: 'Exchange.'" *VP* 12 (1974): 181-182.

17480. ----------. "Rudyard Kipling's Uncollected Poem: *Alnaschar*." *ELN* 13(1975): 40-42.

17481. Kaufman, Esther. "Kipling and the Technique of Action." *NCF* 6(1951): 107-120.

17482. Meyers, Jeffrey. "The Idea of Moral Authority in *The Man Who Would Be King*." *SEL* 8(1968): 711-723.

17483. ----------. "The Quest for Identity in *Kim*." *TSLL* 12(1970): 101-110.

17484. Montefiore, Janet. "Day and Night in Kipling." *EIC* 27(1977): 299-314.

17485. Ridley, Hugh. "Hans Grimm and Rudyard Kipling." *MLR* 68(1973): 863-869.

17486. Shippey, T. A. "Borrowing and Independence in Kipling's 'The Story of Muhammed Din.'" *MLR* 67(1972): 264-271.

17487. ----------, and Michael Short. "Framing and Distancing in Kipling's *The Man Who Would Be King*." *JNT* 2(1972): 75-87.

17488. Tompkins, J. M. S. "Kipling's Later Tales: The Theme of Healing." *MLR* 45(1950): 18-32.

17489. Wallis, Bruce E. "The Resurrection Motif in Kipling's 'The Gardner.'" *SSF* 10(1973): 99-100.

See also 6286, 18922.

LAMB, CHARLES. 17490. Ades, John I. "Charles Lamb, Shakespeare, and Early Nineteenth-Century Theater." *PMLA* 85(1970): 514-526.

17491. ----------. "Friendly Persuasion: Lamb as Critic of Wordsworth." *WC* 8(1977): 18-24.

17492. Barnet, Sylvan. "Charles Lamb and the Tragic Malvolio." *PQ* 33(1954): 178-188.

17493. ----------. "Charles Lamb's Contribution to the Theory of Dramatic Illusion." *PMLA* 69(1954): 1150-1159.

17494. Barnett, George L. "Charles Lamb to John Britton: An Unpublished Letter." *MLQ* 13 (1952): 353-355.

17495. ----------. "Charles Lamb's Part in an Edition of Hogarth." *MLQ* 20(1959): 315-320.

17496. ----------. "The Pronunciation of *Elia*." *SR* 5(1965): 51-55.

17497. ----------. "An Unpublished Review by Charles Lamb." *MLQ* 17(1956): 352-356.

17498. Braendel, Doris. "The Lamb Collection at the Rosenbach Foundation: A Checklist." *WC* 2(1971): 80-91.

17499. Brier, Peter A. "An Unpublished Poem by Charles Lamb: 'Acrostic to E. B.'" *ELN* 10 (1972): 29-30.

17500. ----------. "Charles Lamb in the Huntington Library (1796-1833)." [bibliography] *WC* 3(1972): 123-146.

17501. Davies, James A. "Charles Lamb, John Forster, and a Victorian Shakespeare." *RES* 26(1975): 442-450.

17502. Fenderson, Lewis H. "Charles Lamb as Critic." *CLA* 7(1964): 235-239.

17503. Green, David Bonnell. "Charles Lamb, Bradbury and Evans, and the Title of *The Last Essays of Elia*." *ELN* 1(1963): 37-40.

17504. Haven, Richard. "The Romantic Art of Charles Lamb." *ELH* 30(1963): 137-146.

17505. Henderson, Arnold. "Some Constants of Charles Lamb's Criticism." *SR* 7(1968): 104-116.

17506. Kelly, Michael J. "Claggart's 'Equivocal Words' and Lamb's 'Popular Fallacies.'" *SSF* 9(1972): 183-186.

17507. Khazoum, Violet. "The Novel and Characters in the Essays of Elia." *SEL* 16 (1976): 563-577.

17508. Larrabee, Stephen A. "Some American Notices of Lamb in 1828." *PMLA* 74(1959): 157.

17509. Mulcahy, Daniel J. "Charles Lamb: The Antithetical Manner and the Two Planes." *SEL* 3(1963): 517-542.

17510. Nabholtz, John R. "Drama and Rhetoric in Lamb's Essays of the Imagination." *SEL* 12(1972): 683-703.

17511. Patterson, Charles I. "Charles Lamb's Insight into the Nature of the Novel." *PMLA* 67(1952): 375-382.

17512. Pollin, Burton R. "Charles Lamb and

Charles Lloyd as Jacobins and Anti-Jacobins."
SR 12(1973): 633-647.

17513. Randel, Fred V. "Eating and Drinking in Lamb's Elia Essays." *ELH* 37(1970): 57-76.

17514. Reiman, Donald H. "Thematic Unity in Lamb's Familiar Essays." *JEGP* 64(1965): 470-478.

17515. Scoggins, James. "Images of Eden in the Essays of Elia." *JEGP* 71(1972): 198-210.

17516. Shokoff, James. "Charles Lamb and the Elizabethan Dramatists." *WC* 4(1973): 3-11.

17517. Standley, Fred L. "Charles Lamb: An Unpublished Album Verse." *ELN* 5(1967): 33-34.

See also 3377.

LANDON, LETITIA. See 478.

LANDOR, WALTER SAVAGE. 17518. Davie, Donald A. "Landor and Poetic Diction." *EIC* 2 (1952): 218-219.

17519. ----------. "The Shorter Poems of Walter Savage Landor." *EIC* 1(1951): 345-355.

17520. Harvey, W. J. "Landor and Poetic Diction." *EIC* 2(1952): 214-218.

17521. Kestner, Joseph. "The Genre of Landor's *Gebir*: 'Eminences Excessively Bright.'" *WC* 5(1974): 41-49.

17522. Mariani, John F. "Lady Blessington's 'Ever Obliged Friend and Servant, W. S. Landor': A Study of Their Literary Relationship." *WC* 7(1976): 17-30.

17523. Perrine, Laurence. "Landor and Immortality." *VP* 2(1964): 50-57.

17524. Proudfit, Charles L. "Landor on Milton: The Commentator's Commentator." *WC* 7 (1976): 3-11.

17525. ----------. "Landor's Hobbyhorse: A Study in Romantic Orthography." *SR* 7(1968): 207-217.

17526. ----------. "Southey and Landor: A Literary Friendship." *WC* 5(1974): 105-112.

17527. Ruoff, A. LaVonne. "Landor's Conception of the Great Leader." *WC* 7(1976): 38-50.

17528. ----------. "The Publication of Landor's *Imaginary Conversations*: 1825-38." *JEGP* 72(1973): 32-47.

17529. Super, R. H. "Landor and Catullus." *WC* 7(1976): 31-37.

17530. ----------. "Landor's American Publications." *MLQ* 14(1953): 360-374.

17531. ----------. "Landor's Letters to Wordsworth and Coleridge." *MP* 55(1957): 73-83.

17532. Vitoux, Pierre. "*Gebir* as an Heroic Poem." *WC* 7(1976): 51-57.

See also 13882, 15374, 18088.

LANG, ANDREW. See 15376.

LEAR, EDWARD. See 16165.

LEVER, CHARLES. 17533. Alexander, Doris. "Eugene O'Neill and Charles Lever." *MD* 5(1963): 415-420.

LEWES, GEORGE. 17534. Brick, Allan R. "Lewes's Review of *Wuthering Heights*." *NCF* 14 (1960): 355-359.

17535. David, Kenneth W. "George Henry Lewes's Introduction to the Blackwood Circle." *ELN* 1(1963): 113-114.

17536. Haight, Gordon S. "Dickens and Lewes on Spontaneous Combustion." *NCF* 10(1955): 53-63.

See also 16827.

LEWIS, MATTHEW. 17537. Brooks, Peter. "Virtue and Terror: *The Monk*." *ELH* 40(1973): 249-263.

17538. Grudin, Peter. "*The Monk*: Matilda and the Rhetoric of Deceit." *JNT* 5(1975): 136-146.

17539. Peck, Louis F. "On the Date of *Tales of Wonder*." *ELN* 2(1964): 25-27.

17540. ----------. "*The Monk* and Musäus' 'Die Entfürung.'" *PQ* 32(1953): 346-348.

MACAULAY, THOMAS. 17541. Beer, E. S. de. "Macaulay and Croker: The Review of Croker's Boswell." *RES* 10(1959): 388-397.

17542. Jones, Frederick L. "Macaulay's Theory of Poetry in *Milton*." *MLQ* 13(1952): 356-362.

17543. Millgate, Jane. "Father and Son: Macauley's *Edinburgh* Debut." *RES* 21(1970): 159-167.

MACLEOD, FIONA. See WILLIAM SHARP.

MALLOCK, W. H. 17544. Patrick, J. Max. "The Portrait of Huxley in Mallock's *New Republic*." *NCF* 11(1956): 61-69.

17545. Scott, P. G. "Mallock and Clough: A Correction." *NCF* 26(1971): 347-348.

17546. Woodring, Carl R. "Notes on Mallock's *The New Republic*." *NCF* 6(1951): 71-74.

17547. Yarker, P. M. "W. H. Mallock's Other Novels." *NCF* 14(1959): 189-205.

MANGEN, JAMES. See 19967.

MARRYAT, FREDERICK. 17548. Doubleday, Neal F. "Jack Easy and Billy Budd." *ELN* 2 (1964): 39-42.

17549. Rosenthal, Bernard. "Melville, Marryat, and the Evil-Eyed Villain." *NCF* 25 (1970): 221-224.

17550. Zanger, Jules. "Marryat, Monsieur Violet, and Edward La Salle." *NCF* 12(1957): 226-231.

MARTINEAU, HARRIETT. 17551. Vann, J. Don. "An Unpublished Harriet Martineau Letter." *ELN* 2 (1964): 109-111.

See also 16556.

MATURIN, CHARLES. 17552. Dawson, Leven M. "*Melmouth the Wanderer*: Paradox and the Gothic Novel." *SEL* 8(1968): 621-632.

See also 15282, 15335.

MAYHEW, HENRY. 17553. Bradley, John L. "Henry Mayhew and Father William." *ELN* 1(1963): 40-42.

17554. Nelson, Harland S. "Dickens's *Our Mutual Friend* and Henry Mayhew's *London Labour and the London Poor*." *NCF* 20(1965): 207-222.

MEREDITH, GEORGE. 17555. Baker, Robert S. "*The Ordeal of Richard Feverel*: A Psychological Approach to Structure." *SN* 6(1974): 200-217.

17556. ----------. "Sir Willoughby Patterne's 'Inner Temple': Psychology and 'Sentimentalism' in *The Egoist*." *TSLL* 16(1975): 691-703.

17557. ----------. "Sanctuary and Dungeon: The Imagery of Sentimentalism in Meredith's *Diana of the Crossways*." *TSLL* 18 (1976): 63-81.

17558. ----------. "Victorian Conventions and Imagery in George Meredith's 'One of Our Conquerors.'" *Criticism* 18(1976): 317-333.

17559. Baylen, Joseph O. "George Meredith:

An Unpublished Letter, 1893." [with text] *SLI* 8,#2(1975): 103-104.

17560. Baylen, Joseph O. "George Meredith and W. T. Stead: Two Unpublished Letters." *TSLL* 4(1962): 21-23.

17561. Beer, Gillian. "George Meredith and *The Satirist*." *RES* 15(1964): 283-295.

17562. ----------. "Meredith's Contributions to 'The Pall Mall Gazette.'" *MLR* 61(1966): 395-400.

17563. ----------. "Meredith's Revisions of *The Tragic Comedians*." *RES* 14(1963): 33-53.

17564. ----------. "Meredith's Idea of Comedy: 1876-1880." *NCF* 20(1965): 165-176.

17565. Bogner, Delmar. "The Sexual Side of Meredith's Poetry." *VP* 8(1970): 107-126.

17566. Brunner, Bernard A. "Meredith's Symbolism: *Lord Ormont and His Aminta*." *NCF* 8 (1953): 124-133.

17567. Buchen, Irving H. "The Egoists in *The Egoist*: The Sensualists and the Ascetics." *NCF* 19(1964): 255-269.

17568. ----------. "'The Ordeal of Richard Feverel': Science versus Nature." *ELH* 29(1962): 47-66.

17569. Buckler, William E. "The Artistic Unity of Richard Feverel: Chapter XXXIII." *NCF* 7(1952): 119-123.

17570. Casten, C. "The Influence of F. Max Muller's *German Love* on Meredith's *Modern Love*." *ELN* 10(1973): 282-286.

17571. Cline, C. L. "The Betrothal of George Meredith to Marie Vulliamy." *NCF* 16(1961): 231-243.

17572. ----------. "On the Editing of Collected Editions of Letters." *SLI* 8,#2(1975): 93-101.

17573. ----------. "Two Early George Meredith Letters." [with text] *TSLL* 17(1975): 591-597.

17574. Collins, Arthur Nethaway. "Meredith's Ataxia: A Corrective Note." *ELN* 2(1964): 111-115.

17575. Conrow, Margaret. "The Relevance of the Feverel Crest." *ELN* 13(1976): 285-288.

17576. Crunden, Patricia. "'The Woods of Westermain.'" *VP* 5(1967): 265-282.

17577. Curtin, Frank D. "Adrian Harley: The Limits of Meredith's Comedy." *NCF* 7(1953): 272-282.

17578. Eaker, J. Gordon. "Meredith's Human Comedy." *NCF* 5(1951): 253-272.

17579. Edwards, P. D. "Education and Nature in 'Tom Jones' and 'The Ordeal of Richard Feverel.'" *MLR* 63(1968): 23-32.

17580. Fanger, Donald. "George Meredith as Novelist." *NCF* 16(1962): 317-328.

17581. ----------. "Joyce and Meredith: A Question of Influence and Tradition." *MFS* 6 (1960): 125-130.

17582. Foster, David E. "Rhetorical Strategy in *Richard Feverel*." *NCF* 26(1971): 185-195.

17583. ----------. "'The Pecuniary Pen': Meredith's Personal Dilemma." *ELN* 13(1976): 184-190.

17584. Friedman, Norman. "The Jangled Harp: Symbolic Structure in *Modern Love*." *MLQ* 18(1957): 9-26.

17585. Golden, Arline. "'The Game of Sentiment': Tradition and Innovation in Meredith's *Modern Love*." *ELH* 40(1973): 264-284.

17586. Green, David Bonnell. "George Meredith's 'Austrian Poets': A Newly Identified Review Essay with Translations." *MLR* 54(1959): 329-336.

17587. Haight, Gordon S. "George Meredith and the 'Westminister Review.'" *MLR* 53(1958): 1-16.

17588. Hardy, Barbara. "The Structure of Imagery in *Harry Richmond*." *EIC* 10(1960): 163-180.

17589. Hergenhan, L. T. "Meredith Receives Recognition: The Reception of *Beauchamp's Career* and *the Egoist*." *TSLL* 11(1969): 1247-1268.

17590. ----------. "Meredith's Attempts to Win Popularity: Contemporary Reactions." *SEL* 4 (1964): 637-651.

17591. ----------. "Meredith's Revisions of *Harry Richmond*." *RES* 14(1963): 24-32.

17592. ----------. "Meredith's Use of Revision: A Consideration of the Revisions of 'Richard Feverel' and 'Evan Harrington.'" *MLR* 59 (1964): 539-544.

17593. ----------. "The Reception of George Meredith's Early Novels." *NCF* 19(1964): 213-235.

17594. Hill, Charles J. "George Meredith's 'Plain Story.'" *NCF* 7(1952): 90-102.

17595. ----------. "The Portrait of the Author in *Beauchamp's Career*." *JEGP* 52(1953): 332-339.

17596. Holt, Carolyn D. "Sir Austin and His *Scrip*: A New Approach to *The Ordeal of Richard Feverel*." *JNT* 4(1974): 129-143.

17597. Hudson, Richard B. "Meredith's Autobiography and *The Adventures of Harry Richmond*." *NCF* 9(1954): 38-49.

17598. Karl, Frederick R. "*Beauchamp's Career*: An English Ordeal." *NCF* 16(1961): 117-131.

17599. Kerpneck, Harvey. "George Meredith, Sun-Worshipper, and Diana's Redworth." *NCF* 18 (1963): 77-82.

17600. Ketcham, Carl H. "Meredith and the Wilis." *VP* 1(1963): 241-248.

17601. ----------. "Meredith at Work: 'The Tale of Chloe.'" *NCF* 21(1966): 235-248.

17602. Korg, Jacob. "Expressive Styles in *The Ordeal of Richard Feverel*." *NCF* 27(1972): 253-267.

17603. Kruppa, Joseph E. "Meredith's Late Novels: Suggestions for a Critical Approach." *NCF* 19(1964): 271-286.

17604. Kwinn, David. "Meredith's Psychological Insight in *Modern Love* XXIII." *VP* 7 (1969): 151-153.

17605. Mermin, Dorothy M. "Poetry as Fiction: Meredith's *Modern Love*." *ELH* 43(1976): 100-119.

17606. Morris, Christopher. "Richard Feverel and the Fictional Lineage of Desire." *ELH* 42(1975): 242-257.

17607. Morris, John W. "The Germ of Meredith's 'Lucifer in Starlight.'" *VP* 1(1963): 76-80.

17608. ----------. "Inherent Principles of Order in *Richard Feverel*." *PMLA* 78(1963): 333-340.

17609. Mueller, William R. "Theological Dualism and the 'System' in *Richard Feverel*." *ELH* 18(1951): 138–154.

17610. Perkus, Gerald H. "Toward Disengagement: A Neglected Early Meredith Manuscript Poem." *VP* 8(1970): 268–272.

17611. Poston, Lawrence, III. "Dramatic Reference and Structure in *The Ordeal of Richard Feverel*." *SEL* 6(1966): 743–752.

17612. Reader, Willie D. "The Autobiographical Author as Fictional Character: Point of View in Meredith's *Modern Love*." *VP* 10(1972): 131–144.

17613. Rodenbeck, John von B. "The Classicism of Meredith's 'Love in the Valley.'" *VP* 11(1973): 27–38.

17614. Sage, Judith Ann. "George Meredith and Thomas Love Peacock: A Note on Literary Influence." *ELN* 4(1967): 279–283.

17615. Shaheen, M. Y. "Forster on Meredith." *RES* 24(1973): 185–191.

17616. Simpson, Arthur L., Jr. "Meredith's Pessimistic Humanism: A New Reading of *Modern Love*." *MP* 67(1970): 341–356.

17617. Smirlock, Daniel. "Rough Truth: Synechdoche and Interpretation in *The Egoist*." *NCF* 31(1976): 313–328.

17618. Stevenson, Lionel. "Meredith and the Interviewers." *MP* 51(1953): 50–63.

17619. Stevenson, Richard C. "Innovations of Comic Method in George Meredith's *Evan Harrington*." *TSLL* 15(1973): 311–323.

17620. ----------. "Laetitia Dale and the Comic Spirit in *The Egoist*." *NCF* 26(1972): 406–418.

17621. Sudrann, Jean. "'The Linked Eye and Mind': A Concept of Action in the Novels of George Meredith." *SEL* 4(1964): 617–635.

17622. Sundell, Michael G. "The Functions of Flitch in *The Egoist*." *NCF* 24(1969): 227–235.

17623. Thomson, Fred C. "The Design of *One of Our Conquerors*." *SEL* 2(1962): 463–480.

17624. Tompkins, J. M. S. "Meredith's *Periander*." *RES* 11(1960): 286–295.

17625. Tucker, Cynthia Grant. "Meredith's Broken Laurel: *Modern Love* and the Renaissance Sonnet Tradition." *VP* 10(1972): 351–366.

17626. Watson, Robert. "George Meredith's *Sandra Belloni*." *ELH* 24(1957): 321–335.

17627. Wilkinfield, Roger B. "Hands Around: Image and Theme in *The Egoist*." *ELH* 34(1967): 367–379.

17628. Williams, I. M. "The Organic Structure of *The Ordeal of Richard Feverel*." *RES* 18(1967): 16–29.

17629. Wilson, Phillip E. "Affective Coherence: a Principle of Abated Action, and Meredith's *Modern Love*." *MP* 72(1974): 151–171.

17630. Wilt, Judith. "Meredith's Diana: Freedom, Fiction, and the Female." *TSLL* 18(1976): 42–62.

See also 80, 15374, 17820.

MILL, JOHN STUART. 17631. August, Eugene R. "Mill's *Autobiography* as Philosophic Commedia." *VP* 11(1973): 143–162.

17632. ----------. "Mill as Sage: The Essay on Bentham." *PMLA* 89(1974): 142–153.

17633. Fielding, K. J. "Mill and Gradgind." *NCF* 11(1956): 148–151.

17634. McDonnell, James. "'A Season of Awakening': An Analysis of Chapter Five of Mill's 'Autobiography.'" *MLR* 72(1977): 773–783.

17635. Millhauser, Milton. "The Two Boyhoods." *HSL* 4(1972): 36–50.

17636. Ong, Walter, J., S.J. "J. S. Mill's Pariah Poet." *PQ* 29(1950): 333–344.

MITFORD, MARY RUSSELL. 17637. Owen, J. C. "Utopia in Little: Mary Russell Mitford and *Our Village*." *SSF* 5(1968): 245–256.

MONTGOMERY, ROBERT. 17638. Hopkins, Kenneth." Reflections on Satan Montgomery." *TSLL* 4 (1962): 351–366.

MOORE, GEORGE. 17639. Blissett, William F. "George Moore and Literary Wagnerism." *Comp L* 13(1961): 52–71.

17640. Brown, Calvin S. "Balzac as a Source of George Moore's *Sister Teresa*." *Comp L* 11(1959): 124–130.

17641. Burkhart, Charles B. "George Moore and *Father and Son*." *NCF* 15(1960): 71–77.

17642. Chaikin, Milton. "The Composition of George Moore's *A Modern Lover*." *Comp L* 7(1955): 259–264.

17643. Heywood, C. "Flaubert, Miss Braddon, and George Moore." *Comp L* 12(1960): 151–158.

17644. Jernigan, Jay. "The Forgotten Serial Version of George Moore's *Esther Waters*." *NCF* 23(1968): 99–103.

17645. Ohmann, Carol. "George Moore's *Esther Waters*." *NCF* 25(1970): 174–187.

17646. McFate, Patricia Ann. "'A Letter to Rome' and 'Clay': Similarities in Character and Conclusion." *SSF* 9(1972): 277–279.

17647. Morton, Donald E. "Lyrical Form and the World of *Esther Waters*." *SEL* 13(1973): 688–700.

17648. Schwab, Arnold T. "Irish Author and American Critic: George Moore and James Hunecker." *NCF* 8(1954): 256–271, 9(1955): 22–37.

MOORE, THOMAS. 17649. Dowden, Wilfred S. "Thomas Moore and the Review of *Christabel*." *MP* 60(1962): 47–50.

17650. Eldridge, Herbert G. "Anacreon Moore and America." *PMLA* 83(1968): 54–62.

17651. Hawthorne, Mark D. "Thomas Moore's *The Epicurean*: The Anacreontic Poet in Search of Eternity." *SR* 14(1975): 249–272.

17652. Jackson, H. J. "Thomas Moore and Robert Burton." *ELN* 13(1975): 130–132.

17653. Jordan, Hoover, H. "Thomas Moore: Artistry in the Song Lyric." *SEL* 2(1962): 403–440.

17654. ----------. "Thomas Moore and the Review of *Christabel*." *MP* 54(1956): 95–105.

See also 16379.

MORIER, JAMES. 17655. Grabar, Terry H. "Fact and Fiction; Morier's *Hajji Baba*." *TSLL* 11 (1969): 1223–1236.

MORRIS, WILLIAM. 17656. Balch, Dennis R. "Guenevere's Fidelity to Arthur in 'The Defence of Guenevere' and 'King Arthur's Tomb.'" *VP* 13, #3/4(1975): 61–70.

17657. Berry, Ralph. "A Defense of Guenevere." *VP* 9(1971): 277–286.

17658. Bono, Barbara J. "The Prose Fictions of William Morris: A Study in the Literary Aesthetic of a Victorian Social Reformer." *VP* 13,#3/4(1975): 43–60.

17659. Carson, Mother Angela, O.S.U. "Morris' Guenevere: A Further Note." *PQ* 42(1963): 131-134.

17660. Dahl, Curtis. "Morris's 'The Chapel in Lyoness': An Interpretation." *SP* 51(1954): 482-491.

17661. DeLaura, David J. "An Unpublished Poem of William Morris." *MP* 62(1965): 340-341.

17662. Dunlap, Joseph R. "Morris and the Book Arts before the Kelmscott Press." *VP* 13, #3/4(1975): 141-158.

17663. Fleissner, R. F. "*Percute Hic*: Morris' Terrestial Paradise." *VP* 3(1965): 171-177.

17664. Fredeman, William E. "Introduction: William Morris: 'What May He Not Yet Do?'" *VP* 13,#3/4(1975): xix-xxx.

17665. Galyon, Aubrey E. "William Morris: The Past as Standard." *PQ* 56(1977): 245-249.

17666. Goodwin, K. L. "An Unpublished Tale from *The Earthly Paradise*." *VP* 13,#3/4 (1975): 91-102.

17667. Harris, Richard L. "William Morris, Eiríkur Magnússon, and Iceland: A Survey of Unpublished Correspondence." *VP* 13,#3/4(1975): 119-130.

17668. Hollow, John. "William Morris and the Judgement of God." *PMLA* 86(1971): 446-451.

17669. ----------. "William Morris' 'The Haystack in the Floods.'" *VP* 7(1969): 353-355.

17670. Kirchhoff, Frederick. "*Love is Enough*: A Crisis in William Morris' Poetic Development." *VP* 15(1977): 297-306.

17671. Kocmanová, Jessie. "'Landscape and Sentiment': Morris' First Attempt in Longer Prose Fiction." *VP* 13,#3/4(1975): 103-118.

17672. Life, Allan R. "Illustration and Morris' 'Ideal Book.'" *VP* 13,#3/4(1975): 131-140.

17673. Lourie, Margaret A. "The Embodiment of Dreams: William Morris' 'Blue Closet' Group." *VP* 15(1977): 193-206.

17674. MacEachen, Dougald B. "Trial by Water in William Morris' 'The Haystack in the Floods.'" *VP* 6(1968): 73-75.

17675. Maurer, Oscar. "William Morris and *Laxoela Saga*." *TSLL* 5(1963): 422-437.

17676. McAlindon, T. "The Idea of Byzantium in William Morris and W. B. Yeats." *MP* 64 (1967): 307-319.

17677. Morris, Barbara. "William Morris and the South Kensington Museum." *VP* 13,#3/4 (1975): 159-176.

17678. Perrine, Laurence. "Morris's Guenevere: An Interpretation." *PQ* 39(1960): 234-241.

17679. Raymond, Meredith B. "The Arthurian Group in *The Defense of Guenevere and Other Poems*." *VP* 4(1966): 213-218.

17680. Sadoff, Dianne F. "Erotic Murders: Structural and Rhetorical Irony in William Morris' Froissart Poems." *VP* 13,#3/4(1975): 11-26.

17681. ----------. "Imaginative Transformation in William Morris' 'Rapunzel.'" *VP* 12 (1974): 153-164.

17682. Silver, Carole G. "'The Defence of Guenevere': A Further Interpretation." *SEL* 9 (1969): 695-702.

17683. ----------. "*The Earthly Paradise*: Lost." *VP* 13,#3/4(1975): 27-42.

17684. Spatt, Hartley S. "Morrissaga: *Sigurd the Volsung*." *ELH* 44(1977): 355-375.

17685. ----------. "William Morris and the Uses of the Past." *VP* 13,#3/4(1975): 1-10.

17686. Staines, David. "Morris' Treatment of His Medieval Sources in *The Defence of Guenevere and Other Poems*." *SP* 70(1973): 439-464.

17687. Stallman, Robert L. "The Lovers' Progress: An Investigation of William Morris' 'The Defence of Guenevere' and 'King Arthur's Tomb.'" *SEL* 15(1975): 657-670.

17688. ----------. "'Rapunzel' Unravelled." *VP* 7(1969): 221-232.

17689. Strode, Elizabeth. "The Crisis of *The Earthly Paradise*: Morris and Keats." *VP* 13,#3/4(1975): 71-82.

17690. Valentine, K. B. "Motifs from Nature in the Design Work and Prose Romances of William Morris, 1876-1896." *VP* 13,#3/4(1975): 83-90.

MOTHERWELL, WILLIAM. 17691. Montgomerie, William. "William Motherwell and Robert A. Smith." *RES* 9(1958): 152-159.

MUDFORD, WILLIAM. 17692. Sucksmith, Harvey Peter. "Mrs. Gaskell's *Mary Barton* and William Mudford's *The Iron Shroud*." *NCF* 29(1975): 460-463.

MULOCK, DINAH. 17693. Colby, Robert A. "Miss Evans, Miss Mulock, and Hetty Sorrel." *ELN* 2(1965): 206-211.

NADEN, CONSTANCE. 17694. Smith, Philip E., and Susan Harris Smith. "Constance Naden: Late Victorian Feminist Poet and Philosopher." *VP* 15 (1977): 367-370.

NEWMAN, CHARLES. 17695. Svaglic, Martin J. "Charles Newman and His Brothers." *PMLA* 71(1956): 370-385.

NEWMAN, FRANCIS WILLIAM. 17696. Winslow, Donald F. "Francis W. Newman's Assessment of John Sterling: Two Letters." *ELN* 11(1974): 278-283.

NEWMAN, JOHN HENRY. 17697. Crawford, Charlotte E. "Newman's 'Callista' and the Catholic Popular Library." *MLR* 45(1950): 219-221.

17698. Deen, Leonard W. "The Rhetoric of Newman's *Apologia*." *ELH* 29(1962): 224-238.

17699. DeLaura, David J. "Some Victorian Experiments in Closure." *SLI* 8,#2(1975): 19-35.

17700. Friedman, Norman. "Newman, Aristotle, and the New Criticism: On the Modern Element in Newman's Poetics." *PMLA* 81(1966): 261-271.

17701. Ker, I. T. "Apology for Newman." *EIC* 24(1974): 319-322.

17702. Lawler, Justus George. "Newman's *Apologia* and the Burthens of Editing." *MLQ* 32 (1971): 291-304.

17703. Levine, George. "Newman's Fiction and the Failure of Reticence." *TSLL* 8(1966): 359-373.

17704. Mendel, Sydney. "Metaphor and Rhetoric in Newman's *Apologia*." *EIC* 23(1973): 357-371.

17705. Svaglic, Martin J. "Newman and the Oriel Fellowship." *PMLA* 70(1955): 1014-1032.

17706. ----------. "The Revision of

Newman's *Apologia*." *MP* 50(1952): 43-49.

17707. ----------. "The Structure of New-man's *Apologia*." *PMLA* 66(1951): 138-148.

17708. Wildman, John Hazard. "Newman in the Pulpit: The Power of Simplicity." *SLI* 8,#2 (1975): 63-75.

See also 15445, 15483.

OLIPHANT, MARGARET. 17709. Colby, Robert and Vineta. "*A Beleagured City*: A Fable for the Victorian Age." *NCF* 16(1962): 283-301.

17710. Watson, Kathleen. "George Eliot and Mrs. Oliphant: a Comparison in Social Atti-tudes." *EIC* 19(1969): 410-419.

PATER, WALTER. 17711. Allott, Kenneth. "Pater and Arnold." *EIC* 2(1952): 219-221.

17712. Bassett, Sharon. "Wordsworth, Pater, and the 'Anima Mundi.'" *Criticism* 17(1975): 262-275.

17713. Bizot, Richard. "Pater and Yeats." *ELH* 43(1976): 389-412.

17714. ----------. "Pater in Transition." *PQ* 52(1973): 129-141.

17715. Brake, Laurel. "A Commentary on 'Arezzo': An Unpublished Manuscript by Walter Pater." *RES* 27(1976): 266-276.

17716. ----------. "Problems in Victorian Biography: The *DNB* and the *DNB* 'Walter Pater.'" *MLR* 70(1975): 731-742.

17717. Brzenk, Eugene J. "Pater and Apuleius." *Comp L* 10(1958): 55-60.

17718. ----------. "The Unique Fictional World of Walter Pater." *NCF* 13(1958): 217-226.

17719. Court, Franklin E. "Change and Suffering in Pater's Fictional Heroes." *MFS* 13 (1967): 443-453.

17720. ----------. "Virtue Sought 'As a Hunter His Sustenance': Pater's 'Amoral Aesthet-ic.'" *ELH* 40(1973): 549-563.

17721. Dahl, Curtis. "Pater's *Marius* and Historical Novels on Early Christian Times." *NCF* 28(1973): 1-25.

17722. DeLaura, David J. "Pater and Eliot: The Origin of the 'Objective Correlative.'" *MLQ* 26(1965): 426-431.

17723. ----------. "*Romola* and the Origin of the Paterian View of Life." *NCF* 21(1966): 225-234.

17724. ----------. "Some Victorian Ex-periments in Closure." *SLI* 8,#2(1975): 19-35.

17725. ----------. "The 'Wordsworth' of Pater and Arnold: 'The Supreme, Artistic View of Life.'" *SEL* 6(1966): 651-667.

17726. Duffey, Bernard. "The Religion of Pater's Marius." *TSLL* 2(1960): 103-114.

17727. Fleissner, Robert F. "'Prufrock,' Pater, and Richard II: Retracing a Denial of Princeship." *AL* 38(1966): 120-123.

17728. Gordon, Jan B. "Pater's Gioconda Smile: A Reading of 'Emerald Uthwart.'" *SSF* 6 (1969): 136-143.

17729. Hafley, James. "Walter Pater's 'Marius' and the Techniques of Modern Fiction." *MFS* 3(1957): 99-109.

17730. Harris, Wendell V. "Arnold, Pater, Wilde, and the Object as Themselves They See It." *SEL* 11(1971): 733-747.

17731. ----------. "Pater as Prophet." *Criticism* 6(1964): 349-360.

17732. Herendeen, Warren. "Three Unpublished Letters of Walter Pater." *RES* 20(1969): 63-65.

17733. Hill, Donald L. "Pater's Debt to *Romola*." *NCF* 22(1968): 361-377.

17734. Hughes, Daniel. "*Marius* and the Diaphane." *Novel* 9(1975): 55-65.

17735. Inman, Billie Andrew. "The Organic Structure of *Marius the Epicurean*." *PQ* 41(1962): 475-491.

17736. ----------. "Pater's Appeal to His Readers: A Study of Two of Pater's Prose Styles." *TSLL* 14(1973): 643-665.

17737. ----------. "'Sebastian van Storck': Pater's Exploration Into Nihilism." *NCF* 30(1976): 457-476.

17738. Johnson, R. V. "Pater and the Vic-torian Anti-Romantics." *EIC* 4(1954): 42-57.

17739. Knoepflmacher, U. C. "Historicism as Fiction: Motion and Rest in the Stories of Walter Pater." *MFS* 9(1963): 139-148.

17740. Lenaghan, R. T. "Pattern in Walter Pater's Fiction." *SP* 58(1961): 69-91.

17741. Lyons, Richard S. "The 'Complex, Many-Sided' Unity of *The Renaissance*." *SEL* 12 (1972): 765-781.

17742. Osbourn, R. V. "Marius the Epicu-rean." *EIC* 1(1951): 387-403.

17743. Roellinger, Francis X. "Intimations of Winckelmann in Pater's *Diaphaneitè*." *ELN* 2 (1965): 277-282.

17744. Rosenblatt, Louise M. "The Genesis of Pater's *Marius the Epicurean*." *Comp L* 14(1962): 242-260.

17745. Ryan, Michael. "Narcissus Auto-biographer: *Marius the Epicurean*." *ELH* 43(1976): 184-208.

17746. Shmiefsky, Marvel. "A Study in Aesthetic Relativism: Pater's Poetics." *VP* 6 (1968): 105-124.

17747. Shuter, William. "History as Palingenesis in Pater and Hegel." *PMLA* 86(1971): 411-421.

17748. Sudrann, Jean. "Victorian Compro-mise and Modern Revolution." *ELH* 26(1959): 425-444.

17749. Vogeler, Martha Salmon. "The Re-ligious Meaning of *Marius the Epicurean*." *NCF* 19(1964): 287-299.

17750. Zietlow, Paul. "Pater's Impres-sionism Reconsidered." *ELH* 44(1977): 150-170.

See also 5123, 7232, 15301.

PATMORE, COVENTRY. Cadbury, William. "The Structure of Feeling in a Poem by Patmore: Meter, Phonology, Form." *VP* 4(1966): 237-251.

17752. Cohen, J. M. "Prophet without Re-sponsibility: A Study in Coventry Patmore's Poetry." *EIC* 1(1951): 283-297.

17753. Dunn, John J. "Love and Eroticism: Coventry Patmore's Mystical Imagery." *VP* 7(1969): 203-219.

PAYNE, JOHN. See 15376.

PEACOCK, THOMAS LOVE. 17754. Brogan, Howard S. "Romantic Classicism in Peacock's Verse Satire." *SEL* 14(1974): 525-536.

17755. Colmer, John. "Godwin's *Mande-ville* and Peacock's *Nightmare Abbey*." *RES* 21 (1970): 331-336.

17756. Gallon, D. N. "T. L. Peacock's Later Years: The Evidence of Unpublished Letters."

RES 20(1969): 315-319.

17757. Green, David Bonnell. "Two Letters of Thomas Love Peacock." PQ 40(1961): 593-596.

17758. Hewitt, Douglas. "Entertaining Ideas: A Critique of Peacock's Crochet Castle." EIC 20(1970): 200-212.

17759. Hoff, Peter Sloat. "The Paradox of the Fortunate Foible: Thomas Love Peacock's Literary Vision." TSLL 17(1975): 481-488.

17760. ----------. "The Voices of Crotchet Castle." JNT 2(1972): 186-198.

17761. Joukovsky, Nicholas A. "The Composition of Peacock's Melincourt and the Date of the 'Calidore' Fragment." ELN 13(1975): 18-25.

17762. ----------. "Thomas Love Peacock on Sir Robert Peel: An Unpublished Satire." MP 73(1975): 81-84.

17763. Kennedy, William F. "Peacock's Economists: Some Mistaken Identities." NCF 21 (1966): 185-191.

17764. Sage, Judith Ann. "George Meredith and Thomas Love Peacock: A Note on Literary Influence." ELN 4(1967): 279-283.

17765. Salz, Pauline June. "Peacock's Use of Music in His Novels." JEGP 55(1955): 370-379.

See also 17380.

PINERO, ARTHUR WING.   17766. Leggatt, Alexander. "Pinero: From Farce to Social Drama." MD 17(1974): 329-344.

17767. Miner, Edmund J. "The Limited Naturalism of Arthur Pinero." MD 19(1976): 147-160.

17768. Wearing, J. P. "Two Early Absurd Plays in England." MD 16(1973): 259-264.

READE, CHARLES.   17769. Bowers, R. H. "The Canceled 'Song of Solomon' Passage in Reade's Hard Cash." NCF 6(1952): 225-233.

17770. Gettmann, Royal A. "The Serialization of Reade's A Good Fight." NCF 6(1951): 21-32.

17771. Woodring, Carl R. "Charles Reade's Debt to William Howitt." NCF 5(1950): 39-46.

REID, MAYNE.   17772. Meyer, Roy W. "The Western Fiction of Mayne Reid." WAL 3(1968): 115-132.

REYNOLDS, GEORGE W. M.   17773. Maxwell, Richard C., Jr. "G. M. Reynolds, Dickens, and the Mysteries of London." NCF 32(1977): 188-213.

ROGERS, CHARLES.   17774. Flory, Claude R. "Charles Rogers: Late Victorian Provincial Playwright." MD 4(1961): 117-130.

ROGERS, SAMUEL.   17775. Knieger, Bernard. "Samuel Rogers, Forgotten Maecenas." CLA 3(1960): 187-192.

ROLFE, FREDERICK.   17776. Jones, G. P. "Literalism and Beyond: The Characterization of Public Figures in Hadrian the Seventh." JML 3 (1974): 928-950.

See also 18922.

ROSE, W. S.   17777. Pratt, Willis W. "The Eve of St. Agnes and W. S. Rose's Partenopex de Blois." TSLL 10(1968): 83-90.

ROSSETTI, CHRISTINA.   17778. Brzenk, Eugene J. "'Up-hill' and 'Down' by Christina Rossetti." VP 10(1972): 367-372.

17779. Curran, Stuart. "The Lyric Voice of Christina Rossetti." VP 9(1971): 287-299.

17780. Dombrowski, Theo. "Dualism in the Poetry of Christina Rossetti." VP 14(1976): 70-76.

17781. Fass, Barbara. "Christina Rossetti and St. Agnes' Eve." VP 14(1976): 33-46.

17782. Festa, Conrad. "Symbol and Meaning in 'A Birthday.'" ELN 11(1973): 50-56.

17783. Garlitz, Barbara. "Christina Rossetti's Sing-Song and Nineteenth-Century Children's Poetry." PMLA 70(1955): 539-543.

17784. Grott, H. B. de. "Christina Rossetti's 'A Nightmare': A Fragment Completed." RES 24(1973): 48-52.

17785. Honninghausen, Gisela. "Emblematic Tendencies in the Works of Christina Rossetti." VP 10(1972): 1-16.

17786. Janowitz, K. E. "The Antipods of Self: Three Poems by Christina Rossetti." VP 11 (1973): 195-206.

17787. Lynde, Richard D. "A Note on the Imagery in Christina Rossetti's 'A Birthday.'" VP 3(1965): 261-263.

17788. Packer, Lona M. "Symbol and Reality in Christina Rossetti's Goblin Market." PMLA 73 (1953): 375-385.

17789. Standley, Fred L. "Christina Georgina to Dante Gabriel: An Unpublished Letter." ELN 5(1968): 283-285.

17790. Weathers, Winston. "Christina Rossetti: The Sisterhood of Self." VP 3(1965): 81-89.

ROSSETTI, DANTE GABRIEL.   17791. Adrian, Arthur A. "The Browning-Rossetti Friendship." PMLA 73(1958): 538-544.

17792. ----------. "The Genesis of Rossetti's 'Found.'" TSLL 5(1963): 79-82.

17793. Baker, Houston A., Jr. "The Poet's Progress: Rossetti's The House of Life." VP 8 (1970): 1-14.

17794. Banerjee, Ron D. K. "Dante through the Looking Glass: Rossetti, Pound, and Eliot." Comp L 24(1972): 136-149.

17795. Bentley, D. M. R. "The Belle Assemblée Versions of 'My Sister's Sleep.'" VP 12 (1974): 321-334.

17796. ----------. "Rossetti and the Hypnerotomachia Poliphili." ELN 14(1977): 279-283.

17797. ----------. "Rossetti's 'Ave' and Related Pictures." VP 15(1977): 21-36.

17798. Bequette, M. K. "Dante Gabriel Rossetti: The Synthesis of Picture and Poem." HSL 4(1972): 216-227.

17799. Brown, Thomas H. "The Quest of Dante Gabriel Rossetti in 'The Blessed Damozel.'" VP 10(1972): 273-277.

17800. Bund, Van Aiken. "Ruskin, Rossetti, and William Bell Scott: A Second Arrangement." PQ 48(1969): 102-107.

17801. Eldredge, Harrison. "On an Error in a Sonnet of Rossetti's." VP 5(1967): 302-303.

17802. Fisher, Benjamin Franklin, IV. "Rossetti and Swinburne in Tandem: 'The Laird of Waristoun.'" VP 11(1973): 229-240.

17803. Fisher, Benjamin Franklin, IV. "Rossetti's 'William and Marie': Hints of the Future." ELN 9(1971): 121-129.

17804. Franklin, Colin. "The Blessed Damozel At Penkill." EIC 14(1964): 331-335.

17805. Gitter, Elisabeth G. "Rossetti's Translations of Early Italian Lyrics." VP 12 (1974): 351-362.

17806. Gordon, Jan B. "A Portrait of Jenny." *HSL* 1(1969): 89-106.

17807. Harris, Wendell V. "A Reading of Rossetti's Lyrics." *VP* 7(1969): 299-308.

17808. Hobbs, John N. "Love and Time in Rossetti's 'The Stream's Secret.'" *VP* 9(1971): 395-404.

17809. Holberg, Stanley M. "Rossetti and the Trance." *VP* 8(1970): 299-314.

17810. Howard, Ronnalie Roper. "Rossetti's *A Last Confession*: A Dramatic Monologue." *VP* 5 (1967): 21-29.

17811. Hyder, Clyde K. "Rossetti's *Rose Mary*: A Study in the Occult." *VP* 1(1963): 197-207.

17812. Johnson, Wendell Stacy. "D. G. Rossetti as Painter and Poet." *VP* 3(1965): 9-18.

17813. Keane, Robert N. "Rossetti: The Artist and 'The Portrait.'" *ELN* 12(1974): 96-102.

17814. Leggett, Bernie. "A Picture and Its Poem by Dante Gabriel Rossetti." *VP* 11(1973): 241-246.

17815. Lindsay, Jack, and William E. Fredeman. "Dante Gabriel Rossetti's 'The Death of Topsy.'" *VP* 13 #3/4(1975): 177-179.

17816. McGann, Jerome J. "Rossetti's Significant Details." *VP* 7(1969): 41-54.

17817. Nelson, James G. "Aesthetic Experience and Rossetti's 'My Sister Sleep.'" *VP* 7 (1969): 154-158.

17818. ----------. "The Rejected Harlot: 'A Last Confession' and 'Jenny.'" *VP* 10(1972): 123-130.

17819. Packer, Lona Mosk. "Maria Francesca to Dante Gabriel Rossetti: Some Unpublished Letters." *PMLA* 79(1964): 613-619.

17820. Peterson, Carl A. "The Iliad, George Meredith's 'Cassandra,' and D. G. Rossetti's 'Cassandra' Drawing." *TSLL* 7(1966): 329-337.

17821. ----------. "Rossetti's *A Last Confession* As Dramatic Monologue." *VP* 11(1973): 127-142.

17822. Pittman, Philip McM. "The Strumpet and the Snake: Rossetti's Treatment of Sex as Original Sin." *VP* 12(1974):45-54.

17823. Prince, Jeffrey R. "D. G. Rossetti and the Pre-Raphaelite Conception of the Special Moment." *MLQ* 37(1976): 349-369.

17824. Ryals, Clyde deL. "The Narrative Unity of *The House of Life*." *JEGP* 69(1970): 241-257.

17825. Seigel, Jules Paul. "*Jenny*: The Divided Sensibility of a Young and Thoughtful Man of the World." *SEL* 9(1969): 677-693.

17826. Spector, Stephen J. "Love, Unity, and Desire in the Poetry of Dante Gabriel Rossetti." *ELH* 38(1971): 432-458.

17827. ----------. "Rossetti's Self-Destroying 'Moment's Monument': 'Silent Noon.'" *VP* 14 (1976): 54-58.

17828. Stein, Richard L. "Dante Gabriel Rossetti: Painting and the Problem of Poetic Form." *SEL* 10(1970); 775-792.

17829. Vogel, Joseph F. "'White Rose' or 'White Robe' in 'The Blessed Damozel.'" *ELN* 1 (1963): 121-123.

17830. Warner, Janet. "D. G. Rossetti: Love, Death and Art." *HSL* 4(1972): 228-240.

17831. Weatherby, Harold L. "Problems of Form and Content in the Poetry of Dante Gabriel Rossetti." *VP* 2(1964): 11-20.

17832. West, T. Wilson. "D. G. Rossetti and Ezra Pound." *RES* 4(1953): 63-67.

RUSKIN, JOHN. 17833. Alexander, Edward. "Arnold, Ruskin, and the Hanwell Insane Asylum." *ELN* 9(1971): 53-55.

17834. ----------. "*Praeterita*: Ruskin's Remembrance of Things Past." *JEGP* 73(1974): 351-362.

17835. ----------. "Ruskin and Science." *MLR* 64(1969): 508-521.

17836. Bidney, Martin. "Ruskin, Dante, and the Enigma of Nature." *TSLL* 18(1976): 290-305.

17837. Bradley, John Lewis. "Ruskin's Advice to an Amateur Artist: Some New Letters to Louisa, Marchioness of Waterford." *SEL* 1,#4(1961): 101-122.

17838. Bruns, Gerald L. "The Formal Nature of Victorian Thinking." *PMLA* 90(1975): 904-918.

17839. Burd, Van Akin. "Another Light on the Writing of *Modern Painters*." *PMLA* 68(1953): 755-763.

17840. ----------. "Background to *Modern Painters*: The Tradition and the Turner Controversy." *PMLA* 74(1959): 254-267.

17841. ----------. "Ruskin, Rossetti, and William Bell Scott: A Second Arrangement." *PQ* 48(1969): 102-107.

17842. ----------. "Ruskin's Defense of Turner: The Imitative Phase." *PQ* 37(1958): 465-483.

17843. ----------. "Ruskin's Quest for a Theory of Imagination." *MLQ* 17(1956): 60-72.

17844. ----------. "A Week at Winnington: Two New Ruskin Letters of 1864." *ELN* 12(1974): 38-43.

17845. Claiborne, Jay W. "John Ruskin and Charles Augustus Howell: Some New Letters." [with text] *TSLL* 15(1973): 471-498.

17846. Colburn, William E. "Ruskin and Browning: The Poet's Responsibility." *SLI* 1,#1 (1968): 37-46.

17847. Curtin, Frank D. "Ruskin in French Criticism: A Possible Reappraisal." *PMLA* 77(1962): 102-108.

17848. Fain, John Tyree. "Ruskin and Mill." *MLQ* 12(1951): 150-154.

17849. ----------. "Ruskin and Hobson." *PMLA* 67(1952): 297-307.

17850. Ferguson, Oliver W. "Ruskin's Continental Letters to Mrs. Severn, 1888." *JEGP* 51 (1952): 527-536.

17851. Fox, Judith H. "*The Queen of the Air*: Transformation of Myth in Ruskin and Hopkins." *VP* 12(1974): 335-342.

17852. Gleckner, Robert F. "Ruskin and Byron." *ELN* 3(1965): 1947-1951.

17853. Hayman, John. "Ruskin and his Oxford Tutor: an Unpublished Letter from Venice." *RES* 27(1976): 46-54.

17854. ----------. "Ruskin, Mallock, and the Pre-Raphaelites." *ELN* 14(1977): 283-289.

17855. Helsinger, Elizabeth K. "Ruskin and the Poets: Alterations in Autobiography." *MP* 74(1976): 142-170.

17856. ----------. "The Ruskin Renaissance." *MP* 73(1975): 166-177.

17857. Landow, George P. "'I heard of a delightful ghost': A New Ruskin Letter." *PQ* 52 (1973): 779-783.

17858. Landow, George P. "John Ruskin and W. J. Linton: A New Letter." *ELN* 10(1972): 38–41.

17859. Levin, Gerald. "The Imagery of Ruskin's 'A Walk in Chamouni.'" *VP* 5(1967): 283–290.

17860. Litzenberg, Karl. "Controversy over Ruskin: Review Article." *JEGP* 50(1951): 529–531.

17861. Miller, J. Hillis. "Myth as 'Heiroglyph' in Ruskin." *SLI* 8,#2(1975): 15–18.

17862. Millhauser, Milton. "The Two Boyhoods." *HSL* 4(1972): 36–50.

17863. Mills, John F. "Ruskin and Burckhardt in Venice." *Criticism* 1(1959): 139–151.

17864. Monteiro, George. "Ruskin and Stillman: A New Letter." *ELN* 3(1966): 202–204.

17865. Shapiro, Harold I. "Ruskin and Spiritualism: A Correction." *PQ* 55(1976): 140–141.

17866. Smallwood, Osborn T. "John Ruskin and the Oxford Movement." *CLA* 3(1959): 114–118.

17867. Thomas, J. D. "Poetic Truth and Pathetic Fallacy." *TSLL* 3(1961): 342–347.

17868. Townsend, Francis G. "The American Estimate of Ruskin, 1847–1860." *PQ* 32(1953): 69–82.

17869. Wesling, Donald. "Ruskin and the Adequacy of Landscape." *TSLL* 9(1967): 253–272.
See also 15294, 15809, 16877.

RUTHERFORD, MARK. See WILLIAM HALE WHITE.

RUXTON, GEORGE FREDERICK. 17870. Crafroft, Richard H. "'Half Froze for Mountain Doins': The Influence and Significance of George F. Ruxton's *Life in the Far West*." *WAL* 10(1975): 29–43.

SCOTT, JOHN. 17871. Jones, Leonidas M. "The Scott–Christie Duel." *TSLL* 12(1971): 605–629.

SCOTT, SIR WALTER. 17872. Adams, Ruth M. "A Letter by Sir Walter Scott." *MP* 54(1956): 121–123.

17873. Ambrose, Mary E. "'La donna del lago': The First Italian Translations of Scott." *MLR* 67(1972): 74–82.

17874. Berkeley, David S. "Sir Walter Scott and Restoration 'Préciosité.'" *NCF* 10(1955): 240–242.

17875. Butler, R. F. "Maria Edgeworth and Sir Walter Scott: Unpublished Letters, 1823." *RES* 9(1958): 23–40.

17876. Cadbury, William. "The Two Structures of *Rob Roy*." *MLQ* 29(1968): 42–60.

17877. Chandler, Alice. "Chivalry and Romance: Scott's Medieval Novels." *SR* 14(1975): 185–200.

17878. ----------. "Sir Walter Scott and the Medieval Revival." *NCF* 19(1965): 315–332.

17879. Clubbe, John. "Byron and Scott." *TSLL* 15(1973): 67–91.

17880. Cooney, Seamus. "Scott and Progress: The Tragedy of 'The Highland Widow.'" *SSF* 11(1974): 11–16.

17881. Cowley, John. "Lockhart and the Publication of *Marmion*." *PQ* 32(1953): 172–183.

17882. Craig, David. "*The Heart of Midlothian*; Its Religious Basis." *EIC* 8(1958): 217–225.

17883. Cruttwell, Patrick. "Scott Rehabilitated? Edgar Johnson, *Sir Walter Scott: The Great Unknown*." *NCF* 27(1972): 95–102.

17884. Daiches, David. "Scott's Achievement as a Novelist." *NCF* 6(1951): 80–95, 153–173.

17885. Dean, Dennis R. "Scott and Mackenzie: New Poems." *PQ* 52(1973): 265–273.

17886. Devlin, D. D. "Character and Narrative in Scott: *A Legend of Montrose* and *Rob Roy*." *EIC* 18(1968): 136–151.

17887. Duncun, Joseph. "The Anti-Romantic in *Ivanhoe*." *NCF* 9(1955): 293–300.

17888. Elbers, Joan S. Isolation and Community in *The Antiquary*." *NCF* 27(1973): 405–423.

17889. Fisher, P. F. "Providence, Fate, and the Historical Imagination in Scott's *The Heart of Midlothian*." *NCF* 10(1955): 99–114.

17890. French, Richard. "Sir Walter Scott and His Literary Contemporaries." *CLA* 11(1968): 248–254.

17891. Garside, P. D. "Scott, the Romantic Past, and the Nineteenth Century." *RES* 23(1972): 147–161.

17892. ----------. "Waverley's Pictures of the Past." *ELH* 44(1977): 659–682.

17893. Gordon, Robert C. "A Victorian Anticipation of Scott Criticism." *PQ* 36(1957): 272–275.

17894. ----------. "In Defense of *Rob Roy*." *EIC* 18(1968): 470–475.

17895. ----------. "*The Bride of Lammermoor*: A Novel of Tory Pessimism." *NCF* 12(1957): 110–124.

17896. Gordon, S. Stewart. "*Waverley* and 'Unified Design.'" *ELH* 18(1951): 107–122.

17897. Goslee, Nancy M. "Romance as Theme and Structure in *The Lady of the Lake*." *TSLL* 17(1976): 737–757.

17898. Grabar, Terry H. "The English Dialogue of *Waverley*." *JNT* 1(1971): 30–42.

17899. Green, F. C. "Scott's French Correspondence." *MLR* 52(1957): 35–49.

17900. Guest, Ann M. "Imagery of Color and Light in Scott's Narrative Poems." *SEL* 12(1972): 705–720.

17901. Hafter, Monroe Z. "The Spanish Version of Scott's 'Don Roderick.'" *SR* 13(1974): 225–234.

17902. Haggos, D. R. "Scott, Balzac, and the Historical Novel as Social and Political Analysis: 'Waverley' and 'Les Chouans.'" *MLR* 68(1973): 51–68.

17903. Hahn, H. G. "Historiographic and Literary: The Fusion of Two Eighteenth-Century Modes in Scott's *Waverley*." *HSL* 6(1974): 243–267.

17904. Heist, William W. "The Collars of Gurth and Wamba." *RES* 4(1953): 361–364.

17905. Hennelly, Mark M., Jr. "*Waverley* and Romanticism." *NCF* 28(1973): 194–209.

17906. Hennig, John. "Goethe's Translation of Scott's Criticism of Hoffman." *MLR* 51(1956): 369–377.

17907. Henry, Nathaniel H. "Wordsworth's 'Thorn' an Analogue in Scott's *Heart of Midlothian*." *ELN* 3(1965): 118–120.

17908. Hook, Andrew. D. "*The Bride of Lammermoor*: A Reexamination." *NCF* 22(1967): 111–126.

17909. Hyde, William J. "Jeanie Deans and the Queen: Appearance and Reality." *NCF* 28(1973): 86–92.

17910. Jacobson, Sibyl. "The Narratie Framing of History: A Discussion of *Old Mortality*." *JNT* 1(1971): 179–192.

17911. Johnson, Edgar. "Sceptered Kings and Laureled Conquerors: Scott in London and Paris, 1815." *NCF* 17(1963): 299–320.

17912. Jordon, Frank. "Scott and Wordsworth;

or, Reading Scott Well." *WC* 4(1973): 112-124.

17913. Kestner, Joseph. "Linguistic Transmission in Scott: *Waverley, Old Mortality, Rob Roy*, and *Redgauntlet*." *WC* 8(1977): 333-348.

17914. Krause, Sidney J. "Twain and Scott: Experience versus Adventures." *MP* 62(1965): 227-236.

17915. Lane, Lauriat, Jr. "Dickens and Scott: An Unusual Borrowing." *NCF* 6(1951): 223-224.

17916. Lauber, John. "Scott on the Art of Fiction." *SEL* 3(1963): 543-554.

17917. Lightfoot, Martin. "Scott's Self-Renewal: Manuscript and Other Evidence." *NCF* 23 (1968): 150-160.

17918. Marshall, William H. "Point of View and Structure in *The Heart of Midlothian*." *NCF* 16 (1961): 257-262.

17919. Maxwell, J. C. "An Uncollected Scott Letter." *RES* 9(1958): 410-411.

17920. Mayhead, Robin. "*The Heart of Midlothian*: Scott as Artist." *EIC* 6(1956): 266-277.

17921. McCombie, Frank. "Scott, *Hamlet*, and *The Bride of Lammermoor*." *EIC* 25(1975): 419-436.

17922. McDonald, W. U., Jr. "A Letter of Sir Walter Scott to William Scott on the Jeffrey-Swift Controversy." *RES* 12(1961): 404-408.

17923. Millgate, Jane. "Two Versions of Regional Romance: Scott's *Bride of Lammermoor* and Hardy's *Tess of the d'Urbervilles*." *SEL* 17(1977): 729-738.

17924. Montgomerie, William. "Sir Walter Scott as Ballad Editor." *RES* 7(1956): 158-163.

17925. Murdoch, J. D. W. "Scott, Pictures, and Painters." *MLR* 67(1972): 31-43.

17926. Nunnally, Clay. "The Manna of Saint Nicholas." *ELN* 5(1967): 106-108.

17927. Pikoulis, John. "Scott and 'Marmion': The Discovery of Identity." *MLR* 66(1971): 738-750.

17928. Pittock, Joan H. "*The Heart of Midlothian*: Scott as Artist?" *EIC* 7(1957): 477-479.

17929. Poston, Lawrence, III. "The Commercial Motif of the Waverley Novels." *ELH* 42(1975): 62-87.

17930. Raleigh, John Henry. "*Waverley* as History, or 'Tis One Hundred and Fifty-Six Years Since." *Novel* 4(1970): 14-29.

17931. Roberts, Paul. "Sir Walter Scott's Contributions to the English Vocabulary." *PMLA* 68 (1953): 189-210.

17932. Rubenstein, Jill. "The Defeat and Triumph of Bourgeois Pacificism: Scott's *Fair Maid of Perth* and *The Fortunes of Nigel*." *WC* 2(1971): 136-141.

17933. ----------. "The Dilemma of History: A Reading of Scott's *Bridal of Triermain*." *SEL* 12 (1972): 721-734.

17934. Russell, Norma H. "New Letters of Sir Walter Scott." *RES* 14(1963): 61-65.

17935. Sroka, Kenneth M. "Fact, Fiction, and the Introductions to the Waverley Novels." *WC* 2(1971): 142-152.

17936. "Struve, Gleb. "Russian Friends and Correspondents of Sir Walter Scott." *Comp L* 2 (1950): 307-326.

17937. Thomas, L. H. C. "'Walladmor': A Psuedo-Translation of Sir Walter Scott." *MLR* 46 (1951): 218-231.

17938. Walker, Warren S. "A 'Scottish Cooper' for an 'American Scott.'" *AL* 40(1969): 536-537.

17939. Weinstein, Mark A. "Imagination and Reality in Romantic Fiction." *WC* 2(1971): 126-135.

17940. Welsh, Alexander. "Contrast of Styles in the Waverley Novels." *Novel* 6(1973): 218-228.

See also 4019, 13557, 16561, 18479.

SHARP, WILLIAM. 17941. Halloran, William F. "William Sharp as Bard and Craftsman." *VP* 10(1972): 57-78.

17942. Havens, Raymond D. "Assumed Personality, Insanity, and Poetry." *RES* 4(1953): 26-37.

SHELLEY, MARY. 17943. Buchen, Irving H. "Frakenstein and the Alchemy of Creation and Evolution." *WC* 8(1977): 103-112.

17944. Callahan, Patrick. "*Frankenstein*, Bacon, and the 'Two Truths.'" *Ext* 14(1972): 39-48.

17945. Dunn, Richard J. "Narrative Distance in *Frankenstein*." *SN* 6(1974): 408-417.

17946. Dussinger, John A. "Kinship and Guilt in Mary Shelley's *Frankenstein*." *SN* 8(1976): 38-55.

17947. Fleck, P. D. "Mary Shelley's Notes to Shelley's Poems and *Frankenstein*." *SR* 6(1967): 226-254.

17948. Gardner, Joseph H. "Mary Shelley's Divine Tragedy." *EL* 4(1977): 182-197.

17949. Hirsch, Gordon D. "The Monster Was a Lady: On the Psychology of Mary Shelley's *Frankenstein*." *HSL* 7(1975): 116-153.

17950. Jones, Frederick L. "Mary Shelley to Maria Gisborne: New Letters, 1818-1822." *SP* 52 (1955): 39-74.

17951. Joseph, Gerhard. "Frankenstein's Dream: The Child as Father of the Monster." *HSL* 7 (1975): 97-115.

17952. Levine, George. "*Frankenstein* and the Tradition of Realism." *Novel* 7(1973): 14-30.

17953. Lewis, Paul. "Victor Frankenstein and Owen Warland: The Artist as Satan as God." *SSF* 14(1977): 279-282.

17954. Rieger, James. "Dr. Polidori and the Genesis of *Frankenstein*." *SEL* 3(1963): 461-472.

17955. Rubenstein, Marc A. "'My Accursed Origin': The Search for the Mother in *Frankenstein*." *SR* 15(1976): 165-194.

17956. Shug, Charles. "The Romantic Form of Mary Shelley's *Frankenstein*." *SEL* 17(1977): 607-619.

17597. Spatt, Hartley S. "Mary Shelley's last Men: The Truth of Dreams." *SN* 7(1975): 526-537.

17958. Swingle, L. J. "Frankenstein's Monster and Its Romantic Relatives: Problems of Knowledge in English Romanticism." *TSLL* 15(1973): 51-65.

SHELLEY, PERCY BYSSHE. 17959. Allott, Kenneth. "Bloom on *The Triumph of Life*." *EIC* 10 (1960): 222-228.

17960. Bateson, F. W. "Shelley on Wordsworth: Two Unpublished Stanzas from *Peter Bell the Third*." *EIC* 17(1967): 125-129.

17961. Baxter, B. M. "Verwey and Shelley." *MLR* 55(1960): 221-233.

17962. Bentley, G. E., Jr. "Byron, Shelley, Wordsworth, Blake, and *The Seaman's Recorder*."

SR 9(1970): 21-36.

17963. Berrian, Albert H. "Lamartine and Shelley." *CLA* 3(1959): 40-45.

17964. Bostetter, Edward E. "Shelley and the Mutinous Flesh." *TSLL* 1(1959): 203-213.

17965. Brisman, Susan Hawk. "'Unsaying His High Language': The Problem of Voice in *Prometheus Unbound*." *SR* 16(1977): 51-86.

17966. Butler, P. H. "Sun and Shape in Shelley's *The Triumph of Life*." *RES* 13(1962): 40-51.

17967. Caldwell, Richard S. "'The Sensitive Plant' as Original Fantasy." *SR* 15(1976): 221-252.

17968. Casto, Robert C. "Shelley as Translator of *Faust*: The 'Prologue.'" *RES* 26(1975): 407-424.

17969. Chayes, Irene H. "Plato's Myth in Shelley and Blake." *Comp L* 13(1961): 358-369.

17970. Chernaik, Judith S. "The Figure of the Poet in Shelley." *ELH* 35(1968): 566-590.

17971. Cronin, Richard. "Shelley's Language of Dissent." *EIC* 27(1977): 203-215.

17972. DeLasanta, Rodney. "Shelley's 'Sometimes Embarrassing Declaration': A Defense." *TSLL* 7 (1965): 173-179.

17973. Duerkson, Roland A. "Shelley and Shaw." *PMLA* 78(1963): 114-127.

17974. ----------. "Shelley's 'Deep Truth' Reconsidered." *ELN* 13(1975): 25-27.

17975. --------. "Unidentified Shelley Texts in Medwin's *Shelley Papers*." *PQ* 44(1965): 407-410.

17976. Duncan-Jones, Katherine. "Miss Mitford and *Adonais*." *RES* 22(1971): 170-172.

17977. Erdman, David. "Reading Shelley." *EIC* 4(1954): 96-99.

17978. Ehrsam, Theodore G. "Concerning Shelley Forgeries." *PQ* 32(1953): 217-219.

17979. Fitzpatrick, W. P. "Down and Down I Go: A Note on Shelley's *Prometheus Unbound* and Gardner's *Grendel*." *NCL* 7(January, 1977): 2-5.

17980. Flagg, John S. "Shelley and Aristotle: Elements of the *Poetics* in Shelley's Theory of Poetry." *SR* 9(1970): 44-67.

17981. Ford, Newell F. "Paradox and Irony in Shelley's Poetry." *SP* 57(1960): 648-662.

17982. ----------. "The Symbolism of Shelley's Nightingales." *MLR* 55(1960): 569-574.

17983. ----------. "The Symbolism of Shelley's Swans." *SR* 1(1962): 175-183.

17984. ----------. "The Wit in Shelley's Poetry." *SEL* 1,#4(1961): 1-22.

17985. Gerard, Albert. "*Alastor*, or the Spirit of Solipsism." *PQ* 33(1954): 164-177.

17986. Hall, Spencer. "Shelley's 'Mont Blanc.'" *SP* 70(1973): 199-221.

17987. Hartley, Robert A. "The Uroboros in Shelley's Poetry." *JEGP* 73(1974): 524-542.

17988. Havens, Raymond D. "Structure and Prosodic Pattern in Shelley's Lyrics." *PMLA* 65 (1950): 1076-1087.

17989. Hildebrand, W. H. "Shelley's Early Vision Poems." *SR* 8(1969): 198-215.

17990. Hill, James L. "Dramatic Structure in Shelley's *Julian and Maddalo*." *ELH* 35(1968): 84-93.

17991. Hirsch, E. D. "Further Comments on 'Music, When Soft Voices Die.'" *JEGP* 60(1961): 296-298.

17992. Hodgson, John A. "The World's Mysterious Doom: Shelley's *The Triumph of Life*." *ELH* 42(1975): 595-622.

17993. Houston, Ralph. "Reading Shelley." *EIC* 4(1954): 93-96, 99.

17994. ----------. "Shelley and the Principle of Association." *EIC* 3(1953): 45-59.

27995. Hughes, D. J. "Coherence and Collapse in Shelley, With Particular Reference to *Epipsychidion*." *ELH* 28(1961): 260-283.

17996. ----------. "Potentiality in *Prometheus Unbound*." *SR* 2(1963): 107-128.

17997. Huges, Daniel. "Shelley, Leonardo, and the Monsters of Thought." *Criticism* 12(1970): 195-212.

17998. Hunter, Parks C., Jr. "Texture Differences in Drafts of Shelley's 'Una Favola.'" *SR* 6(1966): 58-64.

17999. ----------. "Undercurrents of Anacreontics in Shelley's 'To A Skylark' and 'The Cloud.'" *SP* 65(1968): 677-692.

18000. Jones, Frederick L. "Hogg's Peep at Elizabeth Shelley." *PQ* 29(1950); 422-426.

18001. ----------. "A Seriously Misdated Shelley Letter." *PQ* 38(1959): 126.

18002. ----------. "Shelley and Milton." *SP* 49(1952): 488-519.

18003. Joukovsky, Nicholas A. "An Unnoticed Obituary of Shelley." *ELN* 15(1977): 44-47.

18004. Kessel, Marcel. "*The Cenci* as a Stage Play." *PMLA* 75(1960): 147-148.

18005. King, R. W. "A Note on Shelley, Gibbon, Voltaire, and Southey." *MLR* 51(1956): 225-227.

18006. Kroeber, Karl. "Experience as History: 'Shelley's Venice, Turner's Carthage." *ELH* 41(1974): 321-339.

18007. Maddox, David L. "Shelley's *Alastor* and the Legacy of Rousseau." *SR* 9(1970): 82-98.

18008. Mahony, Patrick J. "An Analysis of Shelley's Craftsmanship in *Adonais*." *SEL* 4(1964): 555-568.

18009. Male, Roy R., Jr., and James A. Notopoulos. "Shelley's Copy of Diogenes Laertius." *MLR* 54(1959): 10-21.

18010. Margolis, John D. "Shakespeare and Shelley's Sonnet 'England in 1819.'" *ELN* 4(1967): 276-277.

18011. Marshall, William. "The Father-Child Symbolism in *Prometheus Unbound*." *MLQ* 22(1961): 41-45.

18012. Massey, Irving. "Shelley's 'Music, When Soft Voices Die': Text and Meaning." *JEGP* 59 (1960): 430-438.

18013. ----------. "Shelley's 'Time': An Unpublished Sequel." *SR* 2(1962): 57-60.

18014. Matthews, G. M. "Shelley's Grasp upon the Actual." *EIC* 4(1954): 328-331.

18015. ----------. "Shelley and Jane Williams." *RES* 12(1961): 40-48.

18016. ----------. "'The Triumph of Life.'" *EIC* 18(1968): 352-356.

18017. ----------. "A Volcano's Voice in Shelley." *ELH* 24(1957): 191-228.

18018. Maxwell, J. C. "Shelley and Manzoni." *MLR* 46(1951): 442.

18019. McGill, Mildred S. "The Role of Earth in Shelley's *Prometheus Unbound*." *SR* 7(1968): 117-128.

18020. McNiece, Gerald. "The Poet as Ironist in 'Mont Blanc' and 'Hymn to Intellectual Beauty.'" *SR* 14(1975): 311-336.

18021. Milgate, W. "Reading Shelley." *EIC* 4(1954): 87-93.

18022. Milne, Fred L. "Shelley on Keats: A Notebook Dialogue." *ELN* 13(1976): 278-284.

18023. Mortenson, Peter. "Image and Structure in Shelley's Longer Lyrics." *SR* 4 (1965): 104-109.

18024. Murray, E. B. "'Elective Affinity' in *The Revolt of Islam*." *JEGP* 67(1968): 570-585.

18025. Norman, Sylva. "Twentieth-Century Theories on Shelley." *TSLL* 9(1967): 223-237.

18026. Notopoulos, James A. "Shelley's 'Disinterested Love' and Aristotle." *PQ* 32 (1953): 214-217.

18027. ----------. "Two Notes on Shelley." *MLR* 48(1953): 440-443.

18028. O'Malley, Glenn. "Shelley's 'Air Prism': The Synesthetic Scheme of Alastor." *MP* 55(1958): 178-187.

18029. Oras, Ants. "The Multitudinous Orb: Some Miltonic Elements in Shelley." *MLQ* 16(1955): 247-257.

18030. Palacio, Jean L. De. "Music and Musical Themes in Shelley's Poetry." *MLR* 59(1964): 345-360.

18031. Parr, Johnstone. "Shelley's 'Ozymandias' Again." *MLR* 46(1951): 441-442.

18032. Pitt, Valerie. "Reading Shelley." *EIC* 4(1954): 99-103.

18033. Pottle, Frederick A. "The Case of Shelley." *PMLA* 67(1952): 589-608.

18034. Pulos, C. E. "Shelley and Malthus." *PMLA* 67(1952): 113-124.

18035. Raben, Joseph. "Coleridge as the Prototype of the Poet in Shelley's *Alastor*." *RES* 17(1966): 278-292.

18036. ----------. "Milton's Influence on Shelley's Translation of Dante's 'Matilda Gathering Flowers.'" *RES* 14(1963): 142-156.

18037. ----------. "Shelley's Invocation to Misery': An Expanded Text." *JEPG* 65(1966): 65-74.

18038. ----------. "Shelley's 'The Boat on the Serchio.'" *PQ* 46(1967): 58-68.

18039. Rees, Joan. "'But for such Faith.' A Shelley Crux." *RES* 15(1964): 185-186.

18040. ----------. "The Preface to *The Cenci*." *RES* 8(1957): 172-173.

18041. Reiman, Donald H. "Roman Scenes in *Prometheus Unbound* III. iv." *PQ* 46(1967): 69-78.

18042. ----------. "Shelley's 'The Triumph of Life': The Biographical Problem." *PMLA* 78(1963): 536-550.

18043. ----------. "Structure, Symbol, and Theme in 'Lines Written among the Euganean Hills.'" *PMLA* 77(1962): 404-413.

18044. Rieger, James. "Shelley's Paterin Beatrice." *SR* 4(1965): 169-184.

18045. Robinson, C. E. "The Shelley Circle and Coleridge's *The Friend*." *ELN* 8(1971): 269-274. 269-274.

18046. Robertson, Lorraine. "Unpublished Verses by Shelley." *MLR* 48(1953): 181-184.

18047. Rubin, David. "A Study of Antinomies in Shelley's *The Witch of Atlas*." *SR* 8(1969): 216-228.

18048. Scott, William O. "Shelley's Admiration for Bacon." *PMLA* 73(1958): 228-236.

18049. Sells, A. Lytton. "Zannella, Coleridge, and Shelley." *Comp L* 2(1950); 16-30.

18050. Smith, Wiltrude L. "An Overlooked Source for *Prometheus Unbound*." *SP* 48(1951): 783-792.

18051. States, Bert O., Jr. "Addendum: The Stage History of Shelley's *The Cenci*." *PMLA* 72 (1957): 633-744.

18052. ----------. "*The Cenci* as a Stage Play." *PMLA* 75(1960): 148-149.

18053. Steffan, Truman Guy. "Seven Accounts of the Cenci and Shelley's Drama." *SEL* 9(1969): 610-618.

18054. St. George, Priscilla P. "Another Look at Two Famous Lyrics in *Prometheus Unbound*." *JEGP* 67(1968): 279-295.

18055. ----------. "The Styles of Good and Evil in 'The Sensitive Plant.'" *JEGP* 64(1965): 479-488.

18056. Taylor, Charles H. "The Errata Leaf to Shelley's *Posthumous Poems* and Some Surprising Relationships Between the Earliest Collected Editions." *PMLA* 70(1955): 408-416.

18057. Taylor, E. M. M. "Shelley and Shakespeare." *EIC* 3(1953): 367-368.

18058. Thurston, Norman. "Author, Narrator, and Hero in Shelley's *Alastor*." *SR* 14(1975): 119-132.

18059. ----------. "The Second Language of *Prometheus Unbound*." *PQ* 55(1976): 126-133.

18050. Tillman-Hill, Iris. "Hardy's Skylark and Shelley's." *VP* 10(1972): 79-83.

18061. Turner, Paul. "Shelley and Lucretius." *RES* 10(1959): 269-282.

18062. Vitoux, Pierre. "Jupiter's Fatal Child in 'Prometheus Unbound.'" *Criticism* 10(1968): 115-125.

18063. Wasserman, Earl R. "*Adonais*: Progressive Revelation as a Poetic Mode." *ELH* 21 (1954): 274-326.

18064. Weaver, Bennett. "Pre-Prometheus Thought in Three Longer Poems of Shelley." *PQ* 29 (1950): 353-366.

18065. ----------. "Shelley: The First Beginnings." *PQ* 32(1953): 184-196.

18066. Webb, Timothy. "Coleridge and Shelley's *Alastor*." *RES* 18(1967): 402-411.

18067. ----------. "Shelley and the Religion of Joy." *SR* 15(1976): 357-382.

18068. ----------. "Shelley's 'Hymn to Venus': A New Text." *RES* 21(1970): 315-325.

18069. White, Harry. "Shelley's Defense of Science." *SR* 16(1977): 319-330.

18070. Whitman, Robert F. "Beatrice's 'Pernicious Mistake' in *The Cenci*." *PMLA* 74(1959): 249-253.

18071. Wilcox, Stewart C. "Imagery, Ideas, and Design in Shelley's *Ode to the West Wind*." *SP* 47(1950): 634-649.

18072. Wittreich, Joseph Anthony, Jr. "The 'Satanism' of Blake and Shelley Reconsidered." *SP* 65(1968): 815-833.

18073. Woodings, R. B. "Shelley's Sources for 'Charles the First.'" *MLR* 64(1969): 267-275.

18074. ----------. "Shelley's Widow Bird." *RES* 19(1968): 411-414.

See also 15275, 15293, 15297, 15363, 15367, 15384, 15836, 15838, 15852, 15891, 15972, 16025, 16062, 17106, 17958, 18160, 18284.

SHORTER, DORA S.   18075. Hanley, Evelyn A. "Dora Sigerson Shorter: Late Victorian Romantic." *VP* 3(1965): 233-234.

SOTHEBY, WILLIAM.   18076. Cohen, Ralph. "S. T. Coleridge and Sotheby's 'Orestes.'" *MLR* 52 (1957): 19-27.

18077. Weaver, Ann C. "William Sotheby's Translation of Schiller's 'Lied von der Glocke.'" *MLR* 57(1962): 573-575.

SOUTHEY, ROBERT. . 18078. Antippas, Andy P. "Four New Southey Letters." *WC* 5(1974): 91-96.

18079. Berhardt-Kabisch, Ernest. "Southey in the Tropics: *A Tale of Paraguay* and the Problem of Romantic Faith. *WC* 5(1974): 97-104.

18080. Brown, Simon. "Ebenezer Elliott and Robert Southey: Southey's Break with the Quarterly Review." *RES* 22(1971): 307-311.

18081. Carnall, Geoffrey. "A Note on Southey's Later Religious Opinions." *PQ* 31(1952): 399-406.

18082. Curry, Kenneth. "Southey's Portraits." *WC* 5(1974): 67-71.

18083. ----------, and Robert Dedmon. "Southey's Contributions to *The Quarterly Review*." *WC* 6 (1975): 261-272.

18084. Elias, Robert H., and Michael N. Stanton. "Thomas Atwood Digges and *Adventures of Alonzo*: Evidence from Robert Southey." *AL* 44(1972): 118-122.

18085. Hoffpauir, Richard. "The Thematic Structure of Southey's Epic Poetry." *WC* 6(1975): 240-248.

18086. ----------. "The Thematic Structure of Southey's Poetry, Part II." *WC* 7(1976): 109-116.

18087. Jacobus, Mary. "Southey's Debt to *Lyrical Ballads* (1798)." *RES* 22(1971): 20-36.

18088. Joukovsky, Nicholas A. "Southey on Landor: An Unpublished Letter." *WC* 7(1976): 13-16.

18089. King, R. W. "A Note on Shelley, Gibbon, Voltaire, and Southey." *MLR* 51(1956): 225-227.

18090. Llorens, Vincente. "Blanco White and Robert Southey: Fragments of a Correspondence." *SR* 11(1972): 147-152.

18091. Morgan, Peter F. "Southey: A Critical Spectrum." *WC* 5(1974): 71-75.

18092. Ober, Warren V. "Southey, Coleridge, and 'Kubla Kahn.'" *JEGP* 58(1959): 414-422.

18093. ----------, and Kenneth H. Ober. "Zukovsky and Southey's Ballads: The Translator as Rival." *WC* 5(1974): 76-88.

18094. Pollin, Burtin R. "Southey's *Curse of Kehama* in Poe's 'City in the Sea.'" *WC* 7(1976): 101-106.

18095. Proudfit, Charles L. "Southey and Landor: A Literary Friendship." *WC* 5(1974): 105-112.

18096. Runyun, William Ronald. "Bob Southey's Diabolical Doggerel." *WC* 6(1975): 249-254.

18097. ----------. "Bob Southey's Diabolical Doggerel: Source and Authorship." *WC* 7(1976): 58-62.

18098. Stanton, Michael N. "Southey and the Art of Autobiography." *WC* 5(1974): 113-119.

18099. Volz, Robert, and James Rieger. "The Rochester Southey Collection." *WC* 5(1974): 89-91.

18100. Whalley, George. "Coleridge and Southey in Bristol, 1795." *RES* 1(1950): 324-340.

18101. Zall, Paul M. "The Gothic Voice of Father Bear." *WC* 5(1974): 124-128.

See also 15319, 17553.

SPENCER, HERBERT.   18102. Katope, Christopher. "*Sister Carrie* and Spencer's *First Principles*." *AL* 41(1969): 64-75.

STANLEY, ARTHUR.   18103. Williamson, Eugene L. "Words from Westminster Abbey: Matthew Arnold and Arthur Stanley." *SEL* 11(1971): 749-761.

STEAD, WILLIAM T.   18104. Baylen, Joseph O., and Patrick G. Hogan, Jr. "G. B. Shaw and W. T. Stead: An Unexplained Relationship." *SEL* 1,#4 (1961): 123-147.

18105. Baylen, Joseph, and Robert B. Holland. "Whitman, W. T. Stead, and the *Pall Mall Gazette*: 1886-1887." *AL* 33(1961): 68-72.

STEPHEN, LESLIE.   18106. Sheen, Edwin D. "Leslie Stephen and Modern Criticism." *CLA* 2 (1958): 1-14.

STERLING, JOHN. See 17696.

STEVENSON, ROBERT LOUIS.   18107. Daiches, David. "Which R. L. S.?" *NCF* 6(1951): 61-70.

18108. Egan, Joseph J. "Dark in the Poet's Corner: Stevenson's 'A Lodging for the Night.'" *SSF* 7(1970): 402-408.

18109. ----------. "From History to Myth: A Symbolic Reading of *The Master of Ballantrae*." *SEL* 8(1968): 699-710.

18110. ----------. "'Markheim': A Drama of Moral Psychology." *NCF* 20(1966): 377-384.

18111. Faurot, Ruth Marie. "From Records to Romance: Stevenson's *The Black Arrow* and *The Paston Letters*." *SEL* 5(1965): 677-690.

18112. Gossman, Ann. "On the Knocking at the Gate in 'Markheim.'" *NCF* 17(1962): 73-76.

18113. Hardesty, William H. III, and David Mann. "Historical Reality and Fictional Daydream in *Treasure Island*." *JNT* 7(1977): 94-103.

18114. Poston, Lawrence, III. "'Markheim' and Chesterton's 'The Hammer of God.'" *NCF* 12(1957): 235-236.

18115. Saposnik, Irving S. "The Anatomy of *Dr. Jekyll and Mr. Hyde*." *SEL* 11(1971): 715-731.

18116. ----------. "Stevenson's 'Markheim': A Fictional 'Christmas Sermon.'" *NCF* 21(1966): 277-282.

18117. Sharp, Robert L. "Stevenson and James' Childhood." *NCF* 8(1953): 236-237.

18118. Stevenson, Robert. "Robert Louis Stevenson's Musical Interests." *PMLA* 72(1957): 700-704.

18119. Ward, Hayden W. "'The Pleasure of Your Heart': *Treasure Island* and the Appeal of Boys' Adventure Fiction." *SN* 6(1974): 304-317.

18120. Warner, Fred B., Jr. "Stevenson's First Scottish Story." *NCF* 24(1969): 335-344.

18121. Weintraub, Joseph. "Henley Puffing Stevenson." *MP* 74(1976): 201-203.

See also 15376.

STRACHEY, LYTTON.   18122. Sanders, Charles Richard. "Lytton Strachey's 'Point of View.'" *PMLA* 68(1953): 75-94.

18123. ----------. "Lytton Strachey's Conception of Biography." *PMLA* 66(1951): 295-315.

STRANGFORD, PERCY SMYTH.   18124. Letzring, Monica. "Strangford's *Poems from the Portuguese of Luis de Camoens*." *Comp L* 23(1971): 289-311.

STURGIS, HOWARD.   18125. Borklund, Elmer. "Howard Sturgis, Henry James, and *Belchamber*." *MP* 58(1961): 255-269.

18126. Thompson, George H. "E. M. Forster and Howard Sturgis." *TSLL* 10(1968): 423-433.

SURTEES, R. S. 18127. Collison, Robert L. "Surtees: Satirist and Sociologist." *NCF* 7(1952): 202-207.

SWINBURNE, ALGERNON. 18128. Baird, Julian. "Swinburne, Sade, and Blake: The Pleasure-Pain Paradox." *VP* 9(1971): 49-75.

18129. Bass, Eben. "Swinburne, Greene, and 'The Triumph of Time.'" *VP* 4(1966): 56-61.

18130. Baum, Paull F. "The Fitzwilliam Manuscript of Swinburne's 'Atalanta,' Verses 1038-1204." *MLR* 54(1959): 161-178.

18131. Burnett, T. A. "Swinburne's 'The Ballad of Bulgarie.'" *MLR* 64(1969): 276-282.

18132. Connolly, Thomas E. "Swinburne on 'The Music of Poetry.'" *PMLA* 72(1957): 680-688.

18133. ----------. "Swinburne's Theory of the End of Art." *ELH* 19(1952): 277-290.

18134. Cook, David A. "The Content and Meaning of Swinburne's 'Anactoria.'" *VP* 9(1971): 77-93.

18135. Coulling, Sidney M. B. "Swinburne and Arnold." *PQ* 49(1970): 211-233.

18136. Dahl, Curtis. "Autobiographical Elements in Swinburne's Trilogy on Mary Stuart." *VP* 3(1965): 91-99.

18137. Davis, Mary Byrd. "Swinburne's Use of His Sources in *Tristram of Lyonesse*." *PQ* 55 (1976): 96-112.

18138. Ehrenpreis, Anne Henry. "Swinburne's Edition of Popular Ballads." *PMLA* 78(1963): 559-571.

18139. Fricke, Douglas C. "The Idea of Love in Swinburne's 'The Sundew.'" *ELN* 13(1976): 194-201.

18140. Findlay, Leonard. "Swinburne and Tennyson." *VP* 9(1971): 217-236.

18141. Fisher, Benjamin Franklin IV. "Rossetti and Swinburne in Tandem: 'The Laird of Waristoun.'" *VP* 11(1973): 229-240.

18142. ----------. "Swinburne's *Tristram of Lyonesse* in Process." *TSLL* 14(1972): 510-528.

18143. Greenberg, Robert A. "Gross's Swinburne, 'The Triumph of Time' and the Context of 'Les Noyades.'" *VP* 9(1971): 95-110.

18144. ----------. "Swinburne and the Redefinition of Classical Myth." *VP* 14(1976): 175-196.

18145. Grosskurth, P. M. "Swinburne and Symonds: An Uneasy Literary Relationship." *RES* 14(1963): 257-268.

18146. Hyder, Clyde K. "Swinburne and Plautus: 'A Man of Three.'" *VP* 15(1977): 377-378.

18147. Johnson, Wendell Stacy. "Swinburne and Carlyle." *ELN* 1(1963): 117-121.

18148. Jordan, John O. "The Sweet Face of Mothers: Psychological Patterns in *Atalanta in Calydon*." *VP* 11(1973): 101-114.

18149. Harrison, Anthony H. "Swinburne's *Tristram of Lyonesse*: Visionary and Courtly Epic." *MLQ* 37(1976): 370-389.

18150. Kinneavy, Gerald B. "Character and Action in Swinburne's *Chastelard*." *VP* 5(1967): 31-39.

18151. Kolaski, Bernard J. "The Swinburne Lines in *The Awakening*." *AL* 45(1974): 608-610.

18152. Landow, George P. "Swinburne to W. J. Linton and J. W. Inchbold: Two New Letters." *MLR* 68(1973): 264-267.

18153. Lang, Cecil Y. "Swinburne's Lost Love." *PMLA* 74(1959): 123-130.

18154. Lougy, Robert E. "Thematic Imagery and Meaning in *Atalanta in Calydon*." *VP* 9(1971): 17-34.

18155. Mathews, Richard. "Heart's Love and Heart's Division." *VP* 9(1971): 35-48.

18156. McGann, Jerome J. "'Ave Atque Vale': An Introduction to Swinburne." *VP* 9(1971): 145-163.

18157. McGhee, Richard D. "'Thalassius': Swinburne's Poetic Myth." *VP* 5(1967): 127-136.

18158. McSweeney, Kerry. "Swinburne's 'A Nympholet' and 'The Lake of Gaube.'" *VP* 9(1971): 201-216.

18159. ----------. "Swinburne's *Poems and Ballads* (1866)." *SEL* 11(1971): 671-685.

18160. Meyers, Terry L. "Shelley's Influence on *Atalanta in Calydon*." *VP* 14(1976): 150-154.

18161. ----------. "Swinburne's Later Opinion of Arnold." *ELN* 10(1972): 118-122.

18162. Murfin, Ross C. "Athens Unbounded: A Study of Swinburne's *Erectheus*." *VP* 12(1974): 205-218.

18163. Peters, Robert. "A. C. Swinburne's 'Hymn to Proserpine': The Work Sheets." *PMLA* 83 (1968): 1400-1406.

18164. ----------. "Swinburne and the Moral Design of Art." *VP* 2(1964): 139-154.

18165. ----------. "Swinburne's Idea of Form." *Criticism* 5(1963): 45-63.

18166. Raymond, Meredith B. "'The Lake of Gaube': Swinburne's Dive in the Dark and the 'Indeterminate Moment.'" *VP* 9(1971): 185-199.

18167. ----------. "Swinburne Among the Nightingales." *VP* 6(1968): 125-142.

18168. Reed, John R. "Swinburne's *Tristram of Lyonesse*: The Poet-Lover's Song of Love." *VP* 4 (1966): 99-120.

18169. Ridenour, George M. "Swinburne on 'The Problem to Solve in Expression.'" *VP* 9(1971): 129-144.

18170. Schuldt, Edward P. "Three Ballad Essays of A. C. Swinburne." *RES* 27(1976): 422-430.

18171. Shmiefsky, Marvel. "Swinburne's Anti-Establishment Poetics." *VP* 9(1971): 261-276.

18172. Stuart, Donald. "Swinburne: The Composition of a Self-Portrait." *VP* 9(1971): 111-128.

18173. Sypher, Francis Jacques. "Swinburne and Wagner." *VP* 9(1971): 165-183.

18174. ----------. "Swinburne's Debt to Campbell in 'A Forsaken Garden.'" *VP* 12(1974): 74-78.

18175. Wilson, F. A. C. "Fabrication and Fact in Swinburne's *The Sisters*." *VP* 9(1971): 237-248.

18176. ----------. "Swinburne and Kali: The Confessional Element in *Atalanta in Calydon*." *VP* 11(1973): 215-228.

18177. ----------. "Swinburne in Love: Some Novels by Mary Gordon." *TSLL* 11(1970): 1415-1426.

18178. ----------. "Swinburne, Racine, and the Permissive Morality." *ELN* 10(1973): 212-216.

18179. ----------. "Swinburne's Prose Heroines and Mary's *Femmes Fatales*." *VP* 9(1971): 249-256.

18180. Wymer, Thomas L. "Swinburne's Tragic Vision in *Atalanta in Calydon*." *VP* 9(1971): 1-16.

See also 15301, 15367, 15376.

SYMONDS, JOHN ADDINGTON. 18181. Going, William T. "John Addington Symonds and the Victorian Sonnet Sequence." *VP* 8(1970): 25-38.

18182. Grosskurth, Phyllis. "The Genesis of

of Symonds's Elizabethan Criticism." *MLR* 59(1964): 183-194.

18183. Grosskurth, P. M. "Swinburne and Symonds: An Uneasy Literary Relationship." *RES* 14 (1963): 257-268.

18184. Landow, G. P. "John Addington Symonds to R. H. Horne: A New Letter." *MP* 71(1974): 303.

SYMONS, ARTHUR.   18185. Beckson, Karl, and John M. Munro. "Symons, Browning, and the Development of the Modern Aesthetic." *SEL* 10(1970): 687-699.

18186. Gibbons, Tom. "The Shape of Things to Come: Arthur Symons and the Futurists." *JML* 5 (1976): 515-521.

18187. Goldfarb, Russell M. "Arthur Symons' Decadent Poetry." *VP* 1(1963): 231-234.

18188. Gordon, Jan B. "The Danse Macabre of Arthur Symons: *London Nights*." *VP* 9(1971): 429-443.

18189. Harris, Wandell. "Innocent Decadence: The Poetry of the *Savoy*." *PMLA* 77(1962): 629-636.

18190. Peters, Robert L. "The Salome of Arthur Symons and Aubrey Beardsley." *Criticism* 2 (1960): 150-163.

18191. Peterson, William S. "Arthur Symons as a Browningite." *RES* 19(1968): 148-157.

TALFOURD, THOMAS NOON.   18192. Ward, William S. "An Early Champion of Wordsworth: Thomas Noon Talfourd." *PMLA* 68(1953): 992-1000.

TENNYSON, ALFRED, LORD.   18193. Adey, Lionel. "Tennyson's Sorrow and Her Lying Lip." *VP* 8 (1970): 261-263.

18194. Adler, Joshua. "Tennyson's 'Mother of Sorrows': 'Rizpah.'" *VP* 12(1974): 363-369.

18195. Adler, Thomas P. "The Uses of Knowledge in *Merlin and Vivien*." *TSLL* 11(1970): 1397-1403.

18196. Alaya, Flavia M. "Tennyson's 'The Lady of Shalott': The Triumph of Art." *VP* 8(1970): 273-290.

18197. Antippas, Andy P. "Tennyson, Hallam, and *The Palace of Art*." *VP* 5(1967): 294-296.

18198. August, Eugene R. "Tennyson and Teilhard: The Faith of *In Memoriam*." *PMLA* 84 (1969): 217-226.

18199. Ball, Patricia. "Tennyson and the Romantics." *VP* 1(1963): 7-16.

18200. Barksdale, Richard K. "Arnold and Tennyson on Etna." *CLA* 2(1958): 87-103.

18201. Battaglia, Francis Joseph. "The Use of Contradiction in '*In Memoriam*.'" *ELN* 4(1966): 41-46.

18202. Baum, Paull F. "Crossing the Bar." *ELN* 1(1963): 115-116.

18203. Bergman, Herbert. "Whitman and Tennyson." *SP* 51(1954): 492-504.

18204. Bishoff, **Brigitte**. "Tennyson, Mrs. Gaskell, and the Weaver Poet." *VP* 14(1976): 356-358.

18205. Boyd, John D. "*In Memoriam* and the 'Logic of Feeling.'" *VP* 10(1972): 95-110.

18206. ----------. "*In Memoriam*, Section CXXI." *VP* 14(1976): 161-164.

18207. Brashear, William R. "Tennyson's Third Voice: A Note." *VP* 2(1964): 283-286.

18208. ----------. "Tennyson's Tragic Vitalism: *Idylls of the King*." *VP* 6(1968): 29-50.

18209. Buckler, William E. "Tennyson's *Lucretius* Bowdlerized?" *RES* 5(1954): 269-271.

18210. Bufkin, E. C. "Imagery in 'Locksley Hall.'" *VP* 2(1964): 21-28.

18211. Burchell, S. C. "Tennyson's 'Allegory in the Distance.'" *PMLA* 68(1953): 418-424.

18212. Cadbury, William. "Tennyson's 'The Palace of Art' and the Rhetoric of Structure." *Criticism* 7(1965): 23-44.

18213. ----------. "The Utility of the Poetic Mask in Tennyson's 'Supposed Confessions.'" *MLQ* 24(1963): 374-385.

18214. Cannon, Garland. "'The Lady of Shalott' and *The Arabian Night's Tales*." *VP* 8(1970): 344-346.

18215. Chandler, Alice. "Cousin Clara de Vere." *VP* 5(1967): 55-57.

18216. ----------. "Tennyson's Maud and the Song of Songs." *VP* 7(1969): 91-104.

18217. Collins, Joseph J. "Tennyson and Kierkegaard." *VP* 11(1973): 345-350.

18218. Collins, Winston. "Enoch Arden, Tennyson's Heroic Fisherman." *VP* 14(1976): 47-53.

18219. ----------. "*The Princess*: The Education of the Prince." *VP* 11(1973): 285-294.

18220. Crawford, John W. "A Unifying Element in Tennyson's *Maud*." *VP* 7(1969): 64-66.

18221. Danzig, Allan. "The Contraries: A Central Concept in Tennyson's Poetry." *PMLA* 77 (1962): 577-585.

18222. ----------. "Tennyson's *The Princess*: A Definition of Love." *VP* 4(1966): 83-89.

18223. Davies, James A. "Dylan Thomas' 'One Warm Saturday' and Tennyson's *Maud*." *SSF* 14(1977): 284-286.

18224. Drake, Constance. "A Topical Dating for 'Locksley Hall Sixty Years After.'" *VP* 10 (1972): 307-320.

18225. Duncan-Jones, Katherine. "A Note on Tennyson's 'Claribel.'" *VP* 9(1971): 348-350.

18226. Durham, Margery Stricker. "Tennyson's Wellington Ode and the Cosmology of Love." *VP* 14 (1976): 277-292.

18227. Edwards, P. D. "Tennyson and the Young Person." *VP* 15(1977): 78-82.

18228. Eggers, John Phillip. "The Weeding of the Garden: Tennyson's Geraint Idylls and *The Mabinogion*." *VP* 4(1966): 45-51.

18229. Eidson, John Olin. "The First Performance of Tennyson's *Harold*." *NEQ* 37(1964): 387-390.

18230. ----------. "The Reception of Tennyson's Plays in America." *PQ* 35(1956): 435-443.

18231. ----------. "Tennyson's First Play on the American Stage." *AL* 35(1964): 519-528.

18232. ----------. "Tennyson's *The Foresters* on the American Stage." *PQ* 43(1964): 549-557.

18233. Elliott, Philip L. "*In Memoriam*, II and CXXVII." *ELN* 2(1965): 275-277.

18234. ----------. "*In Memoriam*, Section XCVI." *VP* 3(1965): 191-192.

18235. ----------. "Tennyson's Sir Galahad." *VP* 9(1971): 445-452.

18236. Engelberg, Edward. "The Beast Image in Tennyson's *Idylls of the King*." *ELH* 22(1955): 287-292.

18237. Fass, I. Leonard. "Green as a Motif of Alfred Tennyson." *VP* 3(1965): 139-141.

18238. Fichter, Andrew. "Ode and Elegy: Idea and Form in Tennyson's Early Poetry." *ELH* 40(1973): 398-427.

18239. Findlay, Leonard M. "Swinburne and Tennyson." *VP* 9(1971): 217-236.

18240. Francis, Elizabeth A. "Tennyson's Political Poetry, 1852-1855." *VP* 14(1976): 113-124.

18241. Freeman, James A. "Tennyson, 'Lucretius' and the 'Breasts of Helen.'" *VP* 11(1973): 69-75.

18242. Fulweiler, Howard W. "Tennyson and the 'Summons from the Sea.'" *VP* 3(1965): 25-44.

18243. Gallant, Christine. "Tennyson's Use of the Nature Goddess in 'The Hesperides,' 'Tithonus,' and 'Demeter and Persephone.'" *VP* 14(1976): 155-160.

18244. Gillett, Peter J. "Tennyson's Mind at the Work of Creation." *VP* 15(1977): 321-334.

18245. Goslee, David F. "Character and Structure in Tennyson's *The Princess*." *SEL* 14(1974): 563-573.

18246. ----------. "Spatial and Temporal Vision in Early Tennyson." *VP* 11(1973): 323-329.

18247. ----------. "Three Stages of Tennyson's 'Tiresias.'" *JEGP* 75(1976): 154-167.

18248. Grant, Stephen Allen. "The Mystical Implications of *In Memoriam*." *SEL* 2(1962): 481-495.

18249. Gray, J. M. "The Creation of Excalibur: An Apparent Inconsistencey in *The Idylls*." *VP* 6(1968): 68-70.

18250. ----------. "The Purpose of an Epic List in 'The Coming of Arthur.'" *VP* 8(1970): 339-341.

18251. ----------. "Source and Symbol in 'Geraint and Enid': Tennyson's Doorm and Limours." *VP* 4(1966): 131-132.

18252. Green, Joyce. "Tennyson's Development During the 'Ten Years' Silence' (1832-1842)." *PMLA* 66(1951): 662-697.

18253. Grob, Alan. "Tennyson's *The Lotus-Eaters*: Two Versions of Art." *MP* 62(1964): 118-129.

18254. Gwynn, Frederick L. "Tennyson's 'Tithon,' 'Tears, Idle Tears,' and 'Tithonus.'" *PMLA* 67(1952): 572-575.

18255. Hagen, June Steffensen. "The 'Crescent Promise' of 'Locksley Hall': A Crisis in Poetic Creativity." *VP* 11(1973): 169-171.

18256. Hirsch, Gordon D. "Tennyson's *Commedia*." *VP* 8(1970): 93-106.

18257. Hoge, James O., Jr. "Tennyson on Shakespeare: His Talk about the Plays." *TSLL* 18(1976): 147-170.

18258. Hubenthal, John. "'Growing Old,' 'Rabbi Ben Ezra,' and 'Tears, Idle Tears.'" *VP* 3(1965): 61-63.

18259. Hughes, Linda K. "Tennyson's 'Columbus': 'Sense at War with Soul' Again." *VP* 15(1977): 171-176.

18260. Hunt, John Dixon. "The Symbolist Vision of *In Memoriam*." *VP* 8(1970): 187-198.

18261. Jamieson, Paul F. "Tennyson and His Audience in 1832." *PQ* 31(1952): 407-413.

18262. John, Brian. "Tennyson's 'Recollections of the Arabian Nights' and the Individuation Process." *VP* 4(1966): 275-279.

18263. Joseph, Gerhard. "The Idea of Mortality in Tennyson's Classical and Arthurian Poems: 'Honor Comes with Mystery.'" *MP* 66(1968): 136-145.

18264. ----------. "Poe and Tennyson." *PMLA* 88(1973): 418-428.

18265. ----------. "Tennyson's Concepts of Knowledge, Wisdom, and Pallas Athene." *MP* 69(1972): 314-322.

18266. ----------. "Tennyson's Optics: The Eagle's Gaze." *PMLA* 92(1977): 420-428.

18267. Kaplan, Fred. "Woven Hands: Tennyson's Merlin as Fallen Artist." *VP* 7(1969): 285-298.

18268. Kennedy, Ian H. C. "The Crisis of Language in Tennyson's *Maud*." *TSLL* 19(1977): 161-178.

18269. ----------. "*In Memoriam* and the Tradition of Pastoral Elegy." *VP* 15(1977): 351-366.

18270. Kilroy, James. "The Chiastic Structure of *In Memoriam, A. H. H.*" *PQ* 56(1977): 358-373.

18271. Kincaid, James R. "Rhetorical Irony, the Dramatic Monologue, and Tennyson's *Poems* (1842)." *PQ* 53(1974): 220-236.

18272. ----------. "Tennyson's 'Crossing the Bar': A Poem of Frustration." *VP* 3(1965): 57-61.

18273. ----------. "Tennyson's 'Gareth and Lynette.'" *TSLL* 13(1972): 663-671.

18274. ----------. "Tennyson's Ironic Camelot: Arthur Breathes His Last." *PQ* 56(1977): 241-245.

18275. Kissane, James. "Tennyson: The Passion of the Past and the Curse of Time." *ELH* 32(1965): 85-109.

18276. Kozicki, Henry. "'Meaning' in Tennyson's *In Memoriam*." *SEL* 17(1977): 673-694.

18277. ----------. "The 'Medieval Ideal' in Tennyson's 'The Princess.'" *Criticism* 17(1975): 121-130.

18278. ----------. "Philosophy of History in Tennyson's Poetry to the 1842 *Poems*." *ELH* 42(1975): 88-106.

18279. ----------. "Tennyson's *Idylls of the King* as Tragic Drama." *VP* 4(1966): 15-20.

18280. Krause, Anna. "Unamuno and Tennyson." *Comp L* 8(1956): 122-135.

18281. Laird, Robert G. "Tennyson and 'The Bar of Michael Angelo': A Possible Source for *In Memoriam* LXXXVII. 40." *VP* 14(1976): 253-255.

18282. Litzinger, Boyd. "The Structure of Tennyson's 'The Last Tournament.'" *VP* 1(1963): 53-60.

18283. Marshall, George O., Jr. "Tennyson's 'Oh! That 'Twere Possible': A Link Between *In Memoriam* and *Maud*." *PMLA* 78(1963): 225-229.

18284. ----------. "Tennyson's 'The Poet': Mis-seeing Shelley Plain." *PQ* 40(1961): 156-157.

18285. Martin, David M. "Romantic Perspectivism in Tennyson's 'The Lady of Shallot.'" *VP* 11(1973): 255-256.

18286. Mason, Michael Y. "*In Memoriam*: The Dramatization of Sorrow." *VP* 10(1972): 161-178.

18287. McLuhan, H. M. "Tennyson and Picturesque Poetry." *EIC* 1(1951): 262-282.

18288. McSweeney, Kerry. "The Pattern of Natural Consolation in *In Memoriam*." *VP* 11(1973): 87-100.

18289. ----------. "Tennyson's Quarrel with Himself: The Tristram Group of *Idylls*." *VP* 15(1977): 49-59.

18290. Mermin, Dorothy M. "Tennyson's *Maud*: A Thematic Analysis." *TSLL* 15(1973): 267-277.

18291. Metzger, Lore. "The Eternal Process:

Some Parallels Between Goethe's *Faust* and Tennyson's *In Memoriam*." *VP* 1(1963): 189-196.

18292. Millhouser, Milton. "'Magnetic Mockeries': The Background of a Phrase." *ELN* 5 (1967): 108-113.

18293. ----------. "Structure and Symbol in 'Crossing the Bar.'" *VP* 4(1966): 34-39.

18294. ----------. "Taylor and Alfred Tennyson." *HSL* 1(1969): 37-49.

18295. ----------. "Tennyson's *Princess* and *Vestiges*." *PMLA* 69(1954): 337-343.

18296. Mitchell, Charles. "The Undying Will of Tennyson's 'Ulysses.'" *VP* 2(1964): 87-96.

18297. Moews, Daniel D. "The 'Prologue' to *In Memoriam*: A Commentary on Lines 5, 17, and 32." *VP* 6(1968): 185-187.

18298. Monteiro, George. "Tennyson to Sir Frances Palgrave: A Letter." *ELN* 6(1968): 106-107.

18299. Moore, John Robert. "Conan Doyle, Tennyson, and *Rasselas*." *NCF* 7(1952): 221-223.

18300. Norrington, A. L. P. "Clough and *In Memoriam*." *RES* 4(1953): 364.

18301. Ostriker, Alicia. "The Three Modes of Tennyson's Prosody." *PMLA* 82(1967): 273-284.

18302. Perrine, Laurence. "When Does Hope Mean Doubt? The Tone of 'Crossing the Bar.'" *VP* 4(1966): 127-131.

18303. Pettigrew, John. "Tennyson's 'Ulysses': A Reconciliation of Opposites." *VP* 1(1963): 27-45.

18304. Pipes, B. N. Jr. "A Slight Meteorological Disturbance: The Last Two Stanzas of Tennyson's 'The Poet.'" *VP* 1(1963): 74-76.

18305. Poston, Lawrence, III. "The Argument of the Geraint-Enid Books in *Idylls of the King*." *VP* 2(1964): 269-275.

18306. ----------. "'Pelleas and Ettarre': Tennyson's 'Troilus.'" *VP* 4(1966): 199-204.

18307. ----------. "The Two Provinces of Tennyson's 'Idylls.'" *Criticism* 9(1967): 372-382.

18308. Pratt, Linda Ray. "The Holy Grail: Subversion and Revival of a Tradition in Tennyson and T. S. Eliot." *VP* 11(1973): 307-322.

18309. Preyer, Robert. "Tennyson as an Oracular Poet." *MP* 55(1958): 239-251.

18310. Puckett, Harry. "Subjunctive Imagination in *In Memoriam*." *VP* 12(1974): 97-124.

18311. Pugh, Anthony R. "Tennyson: 'Armageddon' into 'Timbuctoo.'" *MLR* 61(1966): 23-24.

18312. Rackin, Phyllis. "Recent Misreadings of 'Break, Break, Break' and Their Implication for Poetic Theory." *JEGP* 65(1966): 217-228.

18313. Rader, Ralph Wilson. "The Composition of Tennyson's *Maud*." *MP* 59(1962): 265-269.

18314. ----------. "Tennyson in the Year of Hallam's Death." *PMLA* 77(1962): 419-424.

18315. Ricks, Christopher. "Hallam's 'Youthful Letters' and Tennyson." *ELN* 3(1965): 120-122.

18316. ----------. "Tennyson and Persian." *ELN* 4(1966): 46-47.

18317. ----------. "Tennyson: Three Notes." *MP* 62(1964): 139-141.

18318. ----------. "Tennyson's 'Hail Briton!' and 'Tithon': Some Corrections." *RES* 15 (1964): 53-55.

18319. ----------. "Tennyson's 'Rifle

Clubs." *RES* 15(1964): 401-404.

18320. ----------. "Two Early Poems by Tennyson." *VP* 3(1965): 55-57.

18321. Robbins, Tony. "Tennyson's 'Ulysses': The Significance of the Homeric and Dantesque Backgrounds." *VP* 11(1973): 177-194.

18322. Rosenberg, John D. "Tennyson and the Landscape of Consciousness." *VP* 12(1974): 303-310.

18323. ----------. "The Two Kingdoms of *In Memoriam*." *JEGP* 58(1959): 228-240.

18324. Rutenberg, Daniel. "Crisscrossing the Bar: Tennyson and Lionel Johnson on Death." *VP* 10(1972): 179-180.

18325. Ryals, Clyde de L. "The 'Fatal Woman' Symbol in Tennyson." *PMLA* 74(1959): 438-443.

18326. ----------. "The Moral Paradox of the Hero in *Idylls of the King*." *ELH* 30(1963): 53-69.

18327. ----------. "The 'Weird Seizures' in *The Princess*." *TSLL* 4(1962): 268-275.

18328. Sanders, Charles Richard. "Carlyle and Tennyson." *PMLA* 76(1961): 82-97.

18329. Sendry, Joseph. "*In Memoriam* and *Lycidas*." *PMLA* 82(1967): 437-443.

18330. ----------. "'The Palace of Art' Revisited." *VP* 4(1966): 149-162.

18331. ----------. "Tennyson's 'Butcher's Books' as Aids to Composition." *VP* 11(1973): 55-59.

18332. Shannon, Edgar F., Jr. "The Critical Reception of Tennyson's 'Maud.'" *PMLA* 68(1953): 397-417

18333. ----------. "Tennyson's 'Balloon Stanzas.'" *PQ* 31(1952): 441-445.

18334. Shaw, Marion. "*In Memoriam* and Popular Religious Poetry." *VP* 15(1977): 1-8.

18335. Shaw, W. David. "Consolation and Cartharsis in *In Memoriam*." *MLQ* 37(1976): 47-67.

18336. ----------. "The Idealist's Dilemma in *Idylls of the King*." *VP* 5(1967): 41-53.

18337. ----------. "*Idylls of the King*: A Dialectical Reading." *VP* 7(1969): 175-190.

18338. ----------. "Imagination and Intellect in Tennyson's 'Lucretius.'" *MLQ* 33(1972): 130-139.

18339. ----------. "*In Memoriam* and the Rhetoric of Confession." *ELH* 38(1971): 80-103.

18340. ----------. "The Passion of the Past: Tennyson and Francis Grose." *ELN* 5(1968): 269-277.

18341. ----------. "Tennyson's Late Elegies." *VP* 12(1974): 1-12.

18342. ----------. "Tennyson's 'Tithonus' and the Problem of Mortality." *PQ* 52(1973): 274-285.

18343. ----------. "The Transcendentalist Problem in Tennyson's Poetry of Debate." *PQ* 46 (1967): 79-94.

18344. ----------, and Carl W. Gartlein. "The Aurora: A Spiritual Metaphor in Tennyson." *VP* 3(1965): 213-222.

18345. Shmiefsky, Marvel. "'In Memoriam': Its Seasonal Imagery Reconsidered." *SEL* 7(1967): 721-739.

18346. Short, Clarice. "Tennyson and 'The Lover's Tale.'" *PMLA* 82(1967): 78-84.

18347. Simpson, Arthur L., Jr. "Aurora as Artist: A Reinterpretation of Tennyson's *Tithonus*." *PQ* 51(1972): 905-921.

18348. Sinfield, Alan. "'That Which Is': The

Platonic Indicative in *In Memoriam* XCV." *VP* 14 (1976): 247-252.

18349. Slinn, E. Warwick. "Deception and Artifice in *Idylls of the King*." *VP* 11(1973): 1-14.

18350. Smalley, Donald. "A New Look at Tennyson—and Especially the *Idylls*." *JEGP* 61 (1962): 349-357.

18351. Solomon, Stanley J. "Tennyson's Paradoxical King." *VP* 1(1963): 258-271.

18352. Sonn, Carl Robinson. "Poetic Vision and Religious Certainty in Tennyson's Earlier Poetry." *MP* 57(1959): 83-93.

18353. Sonstroem, David. "'Crossing the Bar' as Last Word." *VP* 8(1970): 55-61.

18354. Spatz, Jonas. "Love and Death in Tennyson's *Maud*." *TSLL* 16(1974): 503-510.

18355. Staines, David M. "Tennyson's 'The Holy Grail': The Tragedy of Percivale." *MLR* 69 (1974): 745-756.

18356. Stange, G. Robert. "Tennyson's Garden of Art: A Study of *The Hesperides*." *PMLA* 67 (1952): 732-743.

18357. ----------. "Tennyson's Mythology: A Study of *Demeter and Persephone*." *ELH* 21(1954): 67-80.

18358. Stevenson, Catherine Barnes. "Tennyson's 'Mutability Canto': Time, Memory, and Art in *The Princess*." *VP* 13(1975): 21-33.

18359. Stokes, Edward. "The Metrics of *Maud*." *VP* 2(1964): 97-110.

18360. Storch, R. F. "The Fugitive from the Ancestral Hearth: Tennyson's 'Ulysses.'" *TSLL* 13 (1971): 281-297.

18361. Sutherland, Raymond Carter. "The 'St. John Sense' underlying 'The Eagle: a Fragment' by Tennyson—'To Whom the Vision Came.'" *SLI* 1,#1 (1968): 23-35.

18362. Svaglic, Martin J. "A Framework for Tennyson's *In Memoriam*." *JEGP* 61(1962): 810-825.

18363. Sypher, F. J. "Politics in the Poetry of Tennyson." *VP* 14(1976): 101-112.

18364. Taafe, James G. "Circle Imagery in Tennyson's *In Memoriam*." *VP* 1(1963): 123-131.

18365. Templeman, William Darby. "A Consideration of the Fame of 'Locksley Hall.'" *VP* 1 (1963): 81-103.

18366. Tennyson, Sir Charles. "Tennyson's "Doubt and Prayer' Sonnet." *VP* 6(1968): 1-4.

18367. Timko, Michael. "Arnold, Tennyson, and the English Idyll: Ancient Criticism and Modern Poetry." *TSLL* 16(1974): 135-146.

18368. Tryon, W. S. "Nationalism and International Copyright: Tennyson and Longfellow in America." *AL* 24(1952): 310-309.

18369. Turner, Paul. "Some Ancient Light on Tennyson's *Oenone*." *JEGP* 61(1962: 57-72.

18370. Walton, James. "Tennyson's Patrimony: From 'The Outcast' to 'Maud.'" *TSLL* 11(1969): 733-759.

18371. Ward, Arthur D. "'Ulysses' and 'Tithonus': Tunnel-Vision and the Idle Tears." *VP* 12 (1974): 311-320.

18372. Welch, James Donald. "Tennyson's Landscapes of Time and a Reading of 'The Kraken.'" *VP* 14(1976): 197-204.

18373. Whitbread, L. G. "Tennyson's 'In the Garden at Swainston.'" *VP* 13(1975): 61-69.

18374. Wilkenfeld, Roger B. "'Columbus' and

'Ulysses': Notes on the Development of a Tennysonian Theme." *VP* 12(1974): 170-174.

18375. ----------. "The Shape of Two Voices." *VP* 4(1966): 163-173.

18376. Wilson, James D. "Tennyson's Emendations to Wordsworth's 'Tintern Abbey.'" *WC* 5(1974): 7-8.

18377. Wordsworth, Jonathan. "'What is it, that has been done?': the Central Problem of *Maud*." *EIC* 24(1974): 356-362.

See also 3288, 15219, 17000.

TENNYSON, EMILY. 18378. Hoge. James O. "Emily Tennyson's Narrative for Her Sons." [with text] *TSLL* 14(1972): 93-106.

THACKERAY, WILLIAM MAKEPEACE. 18379. Baker, Joseph E. "Thackeray's Recantation." *PMLA* 77(1962): 586-594.

18380. ----------. "*Vanity Fair* and the Celestial City." *NCF* 10(1955): 89-98.

18381. Bledsoe, Robert. "Fitz-boodle Among the Harpies: A Reading of 'Dennis Hagarty's Wife.'" *SSF* 12(1975): 181-184.

18382. ----------. "*Pendennis* and the Power of Sentimentality: A Study of Motherly Love." *PMLA* 91(1976): 871-883.

18383. ----------. "*Sibi Constet*: The Goddess of Castlewood and the Goddess of Walcot." *SN* 5(1973): 211-219.

18384. Blodgett, Harriet. "Necessary Presence: The Rhetoric of the Narrator in *Vanity Fair*." *NCF* 22(1967): 211-223.

18385. Cabot, Frederick C. "The Two Voices in Thackeray's *Catherine*." *NCF* 28(1974): 404-416.

18386. Carolan, Katherine. "Dickensian Echoes in a Thackeray Christmas Book." *SSF* 11 (1974): 196-199.

18387. Colby, Robert A. "Barry Lyndon and the Irish Hero." *NCF* 21(1966): 109-130.

18388. ----------. "*Catherine*: Thackeray's Credo." *RES* 15(1964): 381-396.

18389. Dooley, D. J. "Thackeray's Use of Vanity Fair." *SEL* 11(1971): 701-713.

18390. Ferris, Ina. "The Breakdown of Thackeray's Narrator: *Lovel the Widower*." *NCF* 32(1977): 36-53.

18391. Fido, Martin. "*The History of Pendennis*: A Reconsideration." *EIC* 14(1964): 363-379.

18392. Fraser, Russell A. "Pernicious Casuistry: A Study of Character in *Vanity Fair*." *NCF* 12(1957): 137-147.

18393. ----------. "Shooting Niagara in the Novels of Thackeray and Trollope." *MLQ* 19(1958): 141-146.

18394. Greene, D. J. "Becky Sharp and Lord Steyne—Thackeray or Disraeli?" *NCF* 16(1961): 157-164.

18395. Hagan, John. "'Bankruptcy of His Heart': The Unfulfilled Life of Harry Esmond." *NCF* 27(1972): 293-316.

18396. ----------. "A Note on the Napoleonic Background of *Vanity Fair*." *NCF* 15(1961): 358-361.

18397. ----------. "*Vanity Fair*: Becky Brought to Book Again." *SN* 7(1975): 479-506.

18398. Harden, Edgar. "The Artistry of a Serial Novelist: Parts 10, 14, and 15 of *The Newcomes*." *NCF* 16(1976): 613-630.

18399. ----------. "The Challanges of Serialization: Parts 4, 5, and 6 of *The Newcomes*." *NCF* 29(1974): 3-21.

18400. Harden, Edgar F. "The Discipline and Significance of Form in *Vanity Fair*." *PMLA* 82 (1967): 530–541.

18401. ----------. "A Partial Outline for Thackeray's *The Virginians*." *JEGP* 75(1976): 168–187.

18402. Hawes, Donald. "Thackeray and the *National Standard*." *RES* 23(1972): 35–51.

18403. Hendy, Andrew Von. "Misunderstandings about Becky's Characterization in *Vanity Fair*." *NCF* 18(1963): 279–283.

18404. James, David L. "Story and Substance in *Lovel the Widower*." *JNT* 7(1977): 70–79.

18405. ----------. "Thackeray and his Narrator." *EIC* 26(1976): 189–190.

18406. Johnson, E. D. H. "*Vanity Fair* and *Amelia*: Thackeray in the Perspective of the Eighteenth Century." *MP* 59(1961): 100–113.

18407. Klein, J. T. "The Dual Center: A Study of Narrative Structure in *Vanity Fair*." *Coll L* 4(1977): 122–128.

18408. Landow, George P. "Some New Thackeray Letters." *ELN* 10(1973): 279–281.

18409. Lerner, Lawrence. "Thackeray and Marriage." *EIC* 25(1975): 279–303.

18410. Lester, John A., Jr. "Thackeray's Narrative Technique." *PMLA* 69(1954): 392–409.

18411. Lougy, Robert E. "Vision and Satire: The Warped Looking Glass in *Vanity Fair*." *PMLA* 90 (1975): 256–269.

18412. Nolan, Edward F. "The Death of Bryan Lyndon: An Analogue in *Gone With the Wind*." *NCF* 8 (1953): 225–228.

18413. Mathison, John K. "The German Sections of *Vanity Fair*." *NCF* 18(1963): 235–246.

18414. Mauskopf, Charles. "Thackeray's Attitudes Towards Dickens's Writings." *NCF* 21 (1966): 21–33.

18415. ----------. "Thackeray's Concept of the Novel: A Study of Conflict." *PQ* 50(1971): 239–252.

18416. Maxwell, J. C. "*The History of Pendennis*." *EIC* 15(1965): 245.

18417. McMaster, Juliet. "Theme and Form in *The Newcomes*." *NCF* 23(1968): 177–188.

18418. McMaster, R. D. "The Pygmalion Motif in *The Newcomes*." *NCF* 29(1974): 22–39.

18419. Moler, Kenneth L. "Evelina in Vanity Fair: Becky Sharp and Her Patrician Heroes." *NCF* 27(1972): 171–181.

18420. Patten, Robert L. "The Flight of the Top of the Tree: *Vanity Fair* Versus *Dombey and Son*." *SEL* 10(1970): 759–773.

18421. Rader, Ralph Wilson. "Thackeray's Injustice to Fielding." *JEGP* 56(1957): 203–212.

18422. Ray, Gordon N. "Dickens Versus Thackeray: The Garrick Club Affair." *PMLA* 69(1954): 815–832.

18423. ----------. "Thackeray's *Book of Snobs*." *NCF* 10(1955): 22–33.

18424. Redvine, Bruce. "The Uses of Memento Mori in *Vanity Fair*." *SEL* 17(1977): 657–672.

18425. Rogers, Katherine M. "The Pressure of Convention on Thackeray's Women." *MLR* 67(1972): 257–263.

18426. ----------. "A Defense of Thackeray's Amelia." *TSLL* 11(1970): 1367–1374.

18427. Rogers, Winslow. "Thackeray and Fielding's 'Amelia.'" *Criticism* 19(1977): 141–157.

18428. Segal, Elizabeth Towne. "Truth and Authenticity in Thackeray." *JNT* 2(1972): 46–59.

18429. Sharp, Sister M. Corona. "Sympathetic Mockery: A Study of the Narrator's Character in *Vanity Fair*." *ELH* 29(1962): 324–336.

18430. Sheets, Robin Ann. "Art and Artistry in *Vanity Fair*." *ELH* 42(1975): 420–432.

18431. Sherbo, Arthur. "A Suggestion for the Original of Thackeray's Rawdon Crawley." *NCF* 10 (1955): 211–216.

18432. Shillingsburg, Peter L. "Miss Horrocks Again." *NCF* 28(1973): 92–95.

18433. Spilka, Mark. "A Note on Thacheray's Amelia." *NCF* 10(1955): 202–210.

18434. Steig, Michael. "*Barnaby Rudge* and *Vanity Fair*: A Note on a Possible Influence." *NCF* 25(1970): 353–354.

18435. Stevens, Joan. "A Note on Thackeray's 'Manager of the Performance.'" *NCF* 22(1968): 391–397.

18436. Stokes, Geoffrey C. "Thackeray as Historian: Two Newly Identified Contributions to *Fraser's Magazine*." *NCF* 22(1967): 281–288.

18437. Summerfield, Henry, ed. "Letters from a Club Arm Chair." *NCF* 18(1963): 205–233.

18438. Sutherland, J. A. "The Expanding Narrative of *Vanity Fair*." *JNT* 3(1973): 149–169.

18439. Sutherland, John. "*Henry Esmond* and the Virtues of Carelessness." *MP* 68(1971): 345–354.

18439. ----------. "The Inhibiting Secretary in Thackeray's Fiction." *MLQ* 32(1971): 175–188.

18441. ----------. "Thackeray as Victorian Racialist." *EIC* 20(1970): 441–445.

18442. Talon, Henri-A. "Time and Memory in Thackeray's *Henry Esmond*." *RES* 13(1962): 147–156.

18443. Taube, Myron. "Contrast as a Principle of Structure in *Vanity Fair*." *NCF* 18(1963): 119–135.

18444. ----------. "The Puppet Frame of *Vanity Fair*." *ELN* 6(1968): 40–42.

18445. ----------. "Thackeray and the Reminiscential Vision." *NCF* 18(1963): 247–259.

18446. ----------. "Thackeray at Work: The Significance of Two Deletions from *Vanity Fair*." *NCF* 18(1963): 273–279.

18447. Tilford, John E., Jr. "The Love Theme of *Henry Esmond*." *PMLA* 67(1952): 684–701.

18448. ----------. "The 'Unsavoury Plot' of *Henry Esmond*." *NCF* 6(1951): 121–130.

18449. ----------. "The Untimely Death of Rachel Esmond." *NCF* 12(1957): 148–153.

18450. Tobias, Richard Clark. "American Criticism of Thackeray." *NCF* 8(1953): 53–65.

18451. White, Edward M. "Thackeray, 'Dolly Duster,' and Lady Charlotte Campbell Bury." *RES* 16 (1965): 35–43.

18452. Wilkenfeld, Roger B. "'Before the Curtain' and *Vanity Fair*." *NCF* 26(1971): 307–319.

18453. Wilkinson, Ann Y. "The Thomeavesian Way of Knowing the World: Technique and Meaning in *Vanity Fair*." *ELH* 32(1965): 370–387.

18454. Williamson, Karina. "A Note on the Function of Castlewood in *Henry Esmond*." *NCF* 18 (1963): 71–77.

18455. Wolff, Cynthia Griffin. "Who is the Narrator of *Vanity Fair* and Where Is He Standing?" *Coll L* 1(1974): 190–203.

18456. Worth, Geroge J. "More on the German Sections of *Vanity Fair*." *NCF* 19(1965): 402–405.

18457. Worth, George J. "Thackeray and James Hanning: Three New Letters." *JEGP* 55(1956): 414-416.

18458. ----------. "The Unity of *Henry Esmond*." *NCF* 15(1961): 345-353.

THOMPSON, FRANCIS. 18459. Buchen, Irving H. "Francis Thompson and the Aesthetics of the Incarnation." *VP* 3(1965): 235-244.

18460. ----------. "Source-Hunting Versus Tradition: Thompson's 'The Hound of Heaven.'" *VP* 2(1964): 111-115.

THOMSON, JAMES. 18561. Forsyth, R. A. "Evolutionisn and the Pessimism of James Thomson (B. V.)." *EIC* 12(1962): 148-166.

18462. Harper, Geroge M. "Blake's *Nebuchadnezzer* in 'The City of Dreadful Night.'" *SP* 50 (1953): 68-80.

18463. NcGann, Jerome J. "The Woven Hymns of Day and Night." *SEL* 3(1963): 493-507.

18464. Noel-Bentley, Peter C. "'Fronting the Dreadful Mysteries of Time': Dürer's *Melencholia* in Thomson's *City of Dreadful Night*." *VP* 12(1974): 193-204.

18465. Schaefer, William D. "The Two Cities of Dreadful Night." *PMLA* 77(1962): 609-616.

18466. Steele, Michael R. "James Thomson's Angel and Sphinx: A Possible Source." *VP* 12(1974): 373-376.

TONNA, CHARLOTTE ELIZABETH. 18467. Kovacević, Ivanka, and S. Barbara Kanner. "Blue Book Into Novel: The Forgotten Industrial Fiction of Charlotte Elizabeth Tonna." *NCF* 25(1970): 152-173.

TRENCH, RICHARD C. 18468. Kaufman, Paul. "To Wordsworth from Archbishop Trench: A Volume and a Letter." *ELN* 4(1966): 37-41.

TROLLOPE, ANTHONY. 18469. Adams, Robert Martin. "*Orley Farm* and Real Fiction." *NCF* 8 (1953): 27-41.

18470. ----------. "Miss Dunstable and Miss Counts." *NCF* 9(1954): 231-235.

18471. Aitken, David. "Anthony Trollope on 'the Genus Girl.'" *NCF* 28(1974): 417-434.

18472. ----------. "'A kind of Felicity': Some Notes about Trollope's Style." *NCF* 20(1966): 337-353.

18473. apRoberts, Ruth. "*Cousin Henry*: Trollope's Note from Antiquity." *NCF* 24(1969): 93-98.

18474. ----------. "Trollope's Casuistry." *Novel* 3(1969): 17-27.

18475. Arthur, Anthony. "The Death of Mrs. Proudie: 'Frivolous Slaughter' of Calculated Dispatch." *NCF* 26(1972): 477-484.

18476. Arthur, R. Anthony. "Authorial Intrusions as Art in *The Last Chronicle of Berset*." *JNT* 1(1971): 200-206.

18477. Bloomfield, Morton W. "Trollope's Use of Canadian History in *Phineas Finn* (1867-1869)." *NCF* 5(1950): 67-74.

18478. Booth, Bradford A. "Trollope and the Royal Literary Fund." *NCF* 7(1952): 208-216.

18479. ----------. "Trollope on Scott: Some Unpublished Notes." *NCF* 5(1950): 223-230.

18480. Butte, George. "Ambivalence and Affirmation in *The Duke's Children*." *SEL* 17(1977): 709-727.

18481. Cadbury, William. "Character and Mock Heroic in *Barchester Towers*." *TSLL* 5(1964): 509-519.

18482. ----------. "Shape and Theme: Determinations of Trollope's Form." *PMLA* 78(1963): 326-332.

18483. ----------. "The Uses of the Village: Form and Theme in Trollope's *The Vicar of Bullhampton*." *NCF* 18(1963): 151-163.

18484. Chamberlaine, David. "Unity and Irony in Trollope's *Can You Forgive Her?*" *SEL* 8 (1968): 669-680.

18485. Corsa, Helen Storm. "'The Cross-Grainedness of Man': The Rev. Josiah Crawley—Trollope's Study of a Paranoid Personality." *HSL* 5(1973): 160-172.

18486. Coyle, William. "An Error in Trollope's Last Novel." *NCF* 6(1951): 222.

18487. ----------. "The Friendship of Anthony Trollope and Richard Henry Dana." *NEQ* 25 (1952): 255-262.

18488. ----------. "Trollope and the Bi-columned Shakespeare." *NCF* 6(1951): 33-46.

18489. Dinwiddy, J. R. "Who's Who in Trollope's Political Novels." *NCF* 22(1967): 31-46.

18490. Donovan, Robert A. "Trollope's Prentice Work." *MP* 53(1956): 179-186.

18491. Dustin, John E. "Thematic Alteration in Trollope." *PMLA* 77(1962): 280-288.

18492. Edwards, P. D. "Trollope Changes His Mind: The Death of Melmotte in *The Way We Live Now*." *NCF* 18(1963): 89-91.

18493. Fraser, Russell A. "Anthony Trollope's Younger Characters." *NCF* 6(1951): 96-106.

18494. ----------. "Shooting Niagara in the Novels of Thackeray and Trollope." *MLQ* 19(1958): 141-146.

18495. Ganzel, Carol H. "*The Times* Correspondent and *The Warden*." *NCF* 21(1967): 325-336.

18496. Glavin, John J. "Trollope's 'Most Natural English Girl.'" *NCF* 28(1974): 477-486.

18497. Goldberg, M. A. "Trollope's *The Warden*: A Commentary on the 'Age of Equipoise.'" *NCF* 17(1963): 381-390.

18498. Gragg, Wilson B. "Trollope and Carlyle." *NCF* 13(1958): 266-270.

18499. Grossman, Richard H., and Andrew Wright. "Anthony Trollope's Librarians." *NCF* 31 (1976): 48-64.

18500. Hagan, John. "The Divided Mind of Anthony Trollope." *NCF* 14(1959): 1-26.

18501. ----------. "*The Duke's Children*: Trollope's Psychological Masterpiece." *NCF* 13(1958): 1-21.

18502. Hall, N. John. "Trollope and Carlyle." *NCF* 27(1972): 197-205.

18503. ----------. "Trollope's Commonplace Book, 1835-40." *NCF* 31(1976): 15-25.

18504. ----------. "An Unpublished Trollope Manuscript on a Proposed History of World Literature." *NCF* 29(1974): 206-210.

18505. Hamer, Mary. "*Framley Parsonage*: Trollope's First Serial." *RES* 26(1975): 154-170.

18506. Harden, Edgar F. "The Alien Voice: Trollope's Western Senator." *TSLL* 8(1966): 219-234.

18507. Harvey, Geoffrey M. "The Form of the Short Story: Trollope's *The Last Chronicle of Barset*." *TSLL* 18(1976): 82-97.

18508. ----------. "Scene and Form: Trollope as a Dramatic Novelist." *SEL* 16(1976): 631-644.

18509. Hawkins, Sherman. "Mr. Harding's Church Music." *ELH* 29(1962): 202-223.

18510. Jillson, Frederick. "The 'Professional' Clergyman in Some Novels by Anthony Trollope." *HSL* 1(1969): 185-197.

18511. Kenney, Blair G. "Trollope's Ideal Statesman: Plantagenet Palliser and Lord John Russell." *NCF* 20(1965): 281-285.

18512. Kerr, Albert S. "Two Problems in *John Caldigate*." *NCF* 5(1951): 75-76.

18513. Kincaid, James R. "*Barchester Towers* and the Nature of Conservative Comedy." *ELH* 37 (1970): 595-612.

18514. ----------. "Bring Back *The Trollopian*." *NCF* 31(1976): 1-14.

18515. King, Margaret F. "Trollope's *Orley Farm*: Chivalry versus Commercialism." *EL* 3(1976): 181-193.

18516. Kleis, John Christopher. "Passion vs. Prudence: Theme and Technique in Trollope's Palliser Novels." *TSLL* 11(1970): 1405-1414.

18517. Lee, James W. "Trollope's Theological Concerns: The Low Church Clergyman." *HSL* 1(1969): 198-208.

18518. McMaster, Juliet. "'The Naming of Words and the Nature of Things': Trollope's *Can You Forgive Her?*" *SEL* 14(1974): 603-618.

18519. ----------. "'The Unfortunate Moth': Unifying Theme in *The Small House at Allington*." *NCF* 26(1971): 127-144.

18520. Maxwell, J. C. "Cockshut on *Dr. Wortle's School*." *NCF* 13(1958): 153-159.

18521. Nelson, Raymond A. "An Inconsistency in *Barchester Towers*." *NCF* 8(1953): 234-236.

18522. Overton, W. J. "Trollope: An Interior View." *MLR* 71(1976): 489-499.

18523. Parks, Edd Winfield. "Trollope and the Defense of Exegesis." *NCF* 7(1953): 265-271.

18524. Pickering, Samuel F., Jr. "Trollope's Poetics and Authorial Intrusion in *The Warden* and *Barchester Towers*." *JNT* 3(1973): 131-140.

18525. Polhemus, Robert M. "*Cousin Henry*: Trollope's Note from Underground." *NCF* 20(1966): 385-389.

18526. Pringle, Virginia Williams. "Barsetshire Under Fire." *NCF* 4(1950): 330-333.

18527. Robbins, Frank F. "Chronology and History in Trollope's Barset and Parliamentary Novels." *NCF* 5(1951): 303-316.

18528. Robinson, Clement Franklin. "Trollope's Jury Trials." *NCF* 6(1952): 247-268.

18529. Sharp, R. L. "Trollope's Mathematics in *The Warden*." *NCF* 17(1962): 288-289.

18530. Shaw, W. David. "Moral Drama in *Barchester Towers*." *NCF* 19(1964): 45-54.

18531. Skilton, David. "*The Fixed Period*: Anthony Trollope's Novel of 1980." *SLI* 6,#2(1973): 39-50.

18532. Slakey, Roger L. "Melmotte's Death: A Prism of Meaning in *The Way We Live Now*." *ELH* 34 (1967): 248-259.

18533. ----------. "Trollope's Case for Moral Imperative." *NCF* 28(1973): 305-320.

18534. Smalley, Donald. "Henry Trollope: Poems in America." *NCF* 4(1950): 251-263.

18535. Stone, Donald D. "Trollope as a Short Story Writer." *NCF* 31(1976): 26-47.

18536. Stryker, David. "The Significance of Trollope's *American Senator*." *NCF* 5(1950): 141-149.

18537. Terry, R. C. "Three Lost Chapters of Trollope's First Novel." *NCF* 27(1972): 71-80.

18538. Thale, Jerome. "The Problem of Structure in Trollope." *NCF* 15(1960): 147-157.

18539. Tingay, Lance O. "The Reception of Trollope's First Novel." *NCF* 6(1951): 195-200.

18540. ----------. "Trollope and the Beverly Election." *NCF* 5(1950): 23-37.

18541. ----------. "Trollope's Popularity: A Statistical Approach." *NCF* 11(1956): 223-229.

18542. Wall, Stephen. "Trollope, Balzac, and the Reappearing Character." *EIC* 25(1975): 123-144.

See also 59, 144.

TURNER, CHARLES TENNYSON. 18543. Ebbatson, J. R. "The Lonely Garden: The Sonnets of Charles Tennyson Turner." *VP* 15(1977): 307-320.

VOYNICH, E. L. 18544. Kettle, Arnold. "E. L. Voynich: A Forgotten English Novelist." *EIC* 7 (1957): 163-174.

WARD, MARY ARNOLD (MRS. HUMPHREY). 18545. Lederer, Clara. "Mary Arnold Ward and the Victorian Ideal." *NCF* 6(1951): 201-208.

18546. Peterson, William S. "Gladstone's Review of *Robert Elsmere*: Some Unpublished Correspondence." *RES* 21(1970): 442-461.

18547. Smith, J. Norton. "An Introduction to Mrs. Humphrey Ward, Novelist." *EIC* 18(1968): 420-428.

WARREN, SAMUEL. 18548. Steig, Michael. "The Subversive Grotesque in Samuel Warren's *Ten Thousand a-Year*." *NCF* 24(1969): 154-168.

WEBB, BEATRICE. 18549. Nadel, Ira Bruce. "Beatrice Webb's Literary Success." *SSF* 13(1976): 441-446.

WHITE, WILLIAM HALE. 18550. Holderness, Graham. "*The Revolution in Tanner's Lane*." *EIC* 21(1971): 412-417.

18551. Merton, E. S. "The Autobiographical Novels of Mark Rutherford." *NCF* 5(1950): 189-217.

18552. ----------. "The Personality of Mark Rutherford." *NCF* 6(1951): 1-20.

18553. Rayson, R. J. "Is *The Revolt in Tanner's Lane* broken-backed?" *EIC* 20(1970): 71-80.

18554. Thomson, Patricia. "The Novels of Mark Rutherford." *EIC* 14(1964): 256-267.

WHITEHEAD, CHARLES. 18555. Fielding, K. J. "Charles Whitehead and Charles Dickens." *RES* 3 (1952): 141-154.

WHYTE-MELVILLE, GEORGE JOHN. 18556. Freeman, James C. "Whyte-Melville and Galsworthy's 'Bright Beings.'" *NCF* 5(1950): 85-100.

WILDE, OSCAR. 18557. Baker, Houston A., Jr. "A Tragedy of the Artist: *The Picture of Dorian Gray*." *NCF* 24(1969): 349-355.

18558. Beckson, Karl. "A New Oscar Wilde Letter." *ELN* 8(1971): 284-287.

18559. Brooks, Michael. "Oscar Wilde, Charles Ricketts, and the Art of the Book." *Criticism* 12(1970): 301-315.

18560. Davis, Lisa E. "Oscar Wilde in Spain." *Comp L* 25(1973): 136-152.

18561. Dieckmann, Liselotte. "The Dancing Electra." *TSLL* 2(1960): 3-17.

18562. Ganz, Arthur. "The Divided Self in the Society Comedies of Oscar Wilde." *MD* 3(1960): 16-23.

18563. ----------. "The Meaning of *The Importance of Being Earnest*." *MD* 6(1963): 42-52.

18564. Gordon, Jan B. "Parody as Initiation—

The Sad Education of 'Dorian Gray.'" *Criticism* 9 (1967): 355-371.

18565. Harris, Wendell V. "Arnold, Pater, Wilde, and the Object as Themselves They See it." *SEL* 11(1971): 733-747.

18566. Keefe, Robert. "Artist and Model in *The Picture of Dorian Gray*." *SN* 5(1973): 63-70.

18567. Lawler, Donald L., and Charles E. Knott. "The Context of Invention: Suggested Origins of *Dorian Gray*." *MP* 73(1976): 389-398.

18568. Mikhail, E. H. "The Four-Act Version of *The Importance of Being Earnest*." *MD* 11(1968): 263-266.

18569. ----------. "Oscar Wilde and His First Comedy." *MD* 10(1968): 394-396.

18570. ----------. "Self-Revelation in *An Ideal Husband*." *MD* 11(1968): 180-186.

18571. Monteiro, George. "A Contemporary View of Henry James and Oscar Wilde, 1882." *AL* 35(1964): 528-530.

18572. Nethercot, Arthur H. "Prunes and Miss Prism." *MD* 6(1963): 112-116.

18573. Nicholas, Brian. "Two Nineteenth-Century Utopias: The Influence of Renan's 'L'Avenir de la Science' on Wilde's 'The Soul of Man Under Socialism.'" *MLR* 59(1964): 361-370.

18574. Parker, David. "Oscar Wilde's Great Farce: *The Importance of Being Earnest*." *MLQ* 35(1974): 173-186.

18575. Poague, L. A. "*The Importance of Being Earnest*: The Texture of Wilde's Story." *MD* 16(1973): 251-257.

18576. Poteet, Lewis J. "*Dorian Gray* and the Gothic Novel." *MFS* 17(1971): 239-248.

18577. ----------. "Romantic Aesthetics in Oscar Wilde's 'Mr. W. H.'" *SSF* 7(1970): 458-464.

18578. Reinert, Otto. "The Courtship Dance in *The Importance of Being Earnest*." *MD* 1(1959): 256-257.

18579. Rose, Marilyn Gaddis. "The Daughters of Herodias in *Hérodiade*, *Salomé*, and *A Full Moon in March*." *CD* 1(1967): 172-181.

18580. Rosen, Kenneth M. "O'Neill's *Brown* and Wilde's *Gray*." *MD* 13(1970): 347-355.

18581. Rossi, Dominick. "Parallels in Wilde's *The Picture of Dorian Gray* and Goethe's *Faust*." *CLA* 13(1969): 188-191.

18582. Stone, Geoffrey. "Serious Bunburyism: The Logic of *The Importance of Being Earnest*." *EIC* 26(1976): 28-41.

18583. Sussman, Herbert. "Criticism as Art: Form in Oscar Wilde's Critical Writings." *SP* 70 (1973): 108-122.

18584. Toliver, Harold E. "Wilde and the Importance of 'Sincere and Studied Triviality.'" *MD* 5 (1963): 389-399.

WILSON, JOHN. 18585. Munday, Michael. "John Wilson and the Distionction between Fancy and Imagination." *SR* 13(1974): 313-322.

See also 3861.

WORDSWORTH, DOROTHY. 18586. Aldrich, Ruth I. "The Wordsworths and Coleridge: 'Three Persons' but *not* 'One Soul.'" *SR* 2(1962): 61-63.

18587. Beaty, Frederick L. "Dorothy Wordsworth and the Coleridges: A New Letter." *MLR* 51 (1956): 411-413.

18588. Brownstein, Rachel Mayer. "The Private Life: Dorothy Wordsworth's Journals." *MLQ* 34 (1973): 48-63.

18589. Nabholtz, John R. "Dorothy Wordsworth and the Picturesque." *SR* 3(1964): 118-128.

18590. Siemens, Reynold. "Checklist: Dorothy Wordsworth at University of Alberta." *WC* 2 (1971): 104-106.

See also 18602.

WORDSWORTH, WILLIAM. 18591. Ahearn, Edward J. "The Search for Community: The City in Hölderlin, Wordsworth, and Beaudelaire." *TSLL* 13 (1971): 71-89.

18592. Albrecht, W. P. "Tragedy and Wordsworth's Sublime." *WC* 8(1977): 83-94.

18593. Aldrich, Ruth I. "The Wordsworths and Coleridge: 'Three Persons' but *not* 'One Soul.'" *SR* 2(1962): 61-63.

18594. Alford, John Alexander. "Wordsworth's Use of the Present Perfect." *MLQ* 33(1972): 119-129.

18595. Altieri, Charles. "Wordsworth's 'Preface' as Literary Theory." *Criticism* 18(1976): 122-146.

18596. ----------. "Wordsworth's Wavering Balance: The Thematic Rhythm of *The Prelude*." *WC* 4 (1973): 226-240.

18597. Averill, James H. "Suffering and Calm in Wordsworth's Early Poetry." *PMLA* 91(1976): 223-234.

18598. Baird, James R. "Wordsworth's 'Inscrutable Workmanship' and the Emblems of Reality." *PMLA* 68(1953): 444-457.

18599. Baker, Jeffrey. "'Deliberate Holiday': Wordsworth's Doctrine of the Necessity of Idleness." *Criticism* 13(1971): 242-264.

18600. "Wordsworth, Pater, and the 'Anima Mundi.'" *Criticism* 17(1975): 262-275.

18601. Bauer, N. Stephen. "Early Burlesques and Parodies of Wordsworth." *JEGP* 74(1975): 553-569.

18602. Beer, John. "Coleridge, the Wordsworths, and the State of Trance." *WC* 8(1977): 121-138.

18603. Bentley, G. E., Jr. "Byron, Shelley, Wordsworth, Blake, and *The Seaman's Recorder*." *SR* 9(1970): 21-36.

18604. Benziger, James. "*Tintern Abbey* Revisited." *PMLA* 65(1950): 154-162.

18605. Bernhardt-Kabisch, Ernest. "Wordsworth: The Monumental Poet." *PQ* 44(1965): 503-519.

18606. Betz, Paul F. "An Unpublished Wordsworth Letter." *WC* 1(1970): 53-54.

18607. Birdsall, Eric R. "Revisions to *Descriptive Sketches*: The Wellesley Copy." *WC* 5 (1974): 9-14.

18608. Bishop, Jonathan. "Wordsworth and the 'Spots of Time.'" *ELH* 26(1959): 45-65.

18609. Black, M. H. "On Six Lines of Wordsworth." *MLR* 59(1964): 339-344.

18610. Blount, Paul G. "Matthew Arnold on Wordsworth." *SLI* 1,#1(1968): 3-11.

18611. Brantley, Richard E. "Spiritual Maturity and Wordsworth's 1783 Christmas Vacation." *SEL* 14(1974): 479-487.

18612. Brier, Peter A. "Reflections on Tintern Abbey." *WC* 5(1974): 4-6.

18613. Bostetter, Edward. "Wordsworth's Dim and Perilous Way." *PMLA* 71(1956): 433-450.

18614. Borck, Jim Springer. "Wordsworth's *The Prelude* and the Failure of Language." *SEL* 13

(1973): 605-616.

18615. Boyd, David. "Wordsworth as Satirist: Book VII of *The Prelude*." *SEL* 13(1973): 617-631.

18616. Boyd, Julian and Zelda. "The Perfect Experience." *SR* 16(1977): 3-14.

18617. Buchen, Irving H. "The Poet as Poetry: An Aesthetic Reading of *The Prelude*." *WC* 1(1970): 133-140.

18618. Bullough, Geoffrey. "The Wordsworth-Laing Letters." *MLR* 46(1951): 1-15.

18619. Bunting, Basil. "The Poet's Voice." *WC* 2(1971): 16.

18620. Burke, Richard C. "A Hitherto Unrecorded Wordsworth Holograph." *WC* 7(1976): 83-86.

18621. Butler, James A. "Christopher Wordsworth and the Text of *Home at Grasmere*." *WC* 3 (1972): 179-180.

18622. ----------. "The Chronology of Wordsworth's *The Ruined Cottage* After 1800." *SP* 74 (1977): 89-112.

18623. ----------. "Wordsworth, Cottle, and the *Lyrical Ballads*: Five Letters, 1797-1800." *JEGP* 75(1976): 139-153.

18624. ----------. "Wordsworth in the Philadelphia Libraries, 1787-1850." *WC* 4(1973): 41-64.

18625. ----------. "Wordsworth's Funeral: A Contemporary Report." *ELN* 13(1975): 27-29.

18626. ----------. "Wordsworth's *Tuft of Primroses*: 'An Unrelenting Doom.'" *SR* 14(1975): 237-248.

18627. Caviglia, Anne Marie. "A Very Rare Wordsworthian Pun." *WC* 4(1973): 158-159.

18628. Christensen, Francis. "Intellectual Love: The Second Theme of *The Prelude*." *PMLA* 80 (1965): 69-75.

18629. Cohen, B. Bernard. "Haydon, Hunt, and Scott, and Six Sonnets (1816) by Wordsworth." *PQ* 29(1950): 434-437.

18630. Conran, Anthony E. M. "The Dialectic of Experience: A Study of Wordsworth's *Resolution and Independence*." *PMLA* 75(1960): 66-74.

18631. Cook, Peter. "Chronology of the 'Lake School' Argument: Some Revisions." *RES* 28 (1977): 175-181.

18632. Curry, Kenneth. "A Note on Wordsworth's 'Fidelity.'" *PQ* 32(1953): 212-214.

18633. Curtis, Jared R. "Wordsworth in the Lilly Library." [bibliography] *WC* 3(1972): 173-178.

18634. D'Avanzo, Mario L. "Immortality's Winds and Fields of Sleep: A Virgilian Elysium." *WC* 3(1972): 168-171.

18635. ----------. "Wordsworth's and Coleridge's 'Genial Spirits.'" *WC* 2(1971): 17-20.

18636. Davies, Hugh Sykes. "Another New Poem by Wordsworth." *EIC* 15(1965): 135-161.

18637. DeLuca, Vincent A. "'The Type of a Mighty Mind': Mutual Influence in Wordsworth and De Quincey." *TSLL* 13(1971): 239-247.

18638. Eakin, Sybil S. "The Spots of Time in Early Versions of *The Prelude*." *SR* 12(1973): 389-405.

18639. Eggenschwiler, David. "Wordsworth's *Discordia Discors*." *SR* 8(1969): 78-94.

18640. Emslie, McD. "The Sloitary Reaper." *EIC* 15(1965): 360-361.

18641. Erdman, David V. "A Note on a Guide to Tintern Abbey." *WC* 8(1977): 95-96.

18642. Evans, B. Ifor. "Coleorton Manuscripts of 'Resolution and Independence' and 'Ode to Dejection.'" *MLR* 46(1951): 355-360.

18643. Ferguson, Frances C. "The Lucy Poems: Wordsworth's Quest for a Poetic Object." *ELH* 40(1973): 532-548.

18644. Finch, John A. "'The Ruined Cottage' Restored: Three Stages of Composition, 1795-1798." *JEGP* 66(1967): 179-199.

18645. Fink, Zera S. "'Dion' and Wordsworth's Political Thought." *SP* 50(1953): 510-514.

18646. Fox, Arnold B., and Martin Kallich. "Theme and Image in 'The World is Too Much With Us.'" *WC* 8(1977): 327-332.

18647. Fussell, Paul, Jr. "Some Observations on Wordsworth's 'A POET!—He hath put his heart to school.'" *PQ* 37(1958): 454-464.

18648. Garber, Frederick. "Wordsworth at the Universal Dance." *SR* 8(1969): 168-182.

18649. Garlitz, Barbara. "The Immortality Ode: Its Cultural Progeny." *SEL* 6(1966): 639-649.

18650. Gates, Barbara T. "Wordsworth's Lessons from the Past." *WC* 7(1976): 133-141.

18651. ----------. "Wordsworth's Symbolic White Doe: 'The Power of History in the Mind.'" *Criticism* 17(1975): 234-245.

18652. Gatti-Taylor, Marisa. "The Myth of the Children in Wordsworth and Pascoli." *EL* 4 (1977): 250-264.

18653. Gerard, Albert S. "Dark Passages: Exploring *Tintern Abbey*." *SR* 3(1963): 10-23.

18654. ----------. *Of Trees and Men*: The Unity of Wordsworth's *The Thorn*." *EIC* 14 (1964): 237-255.

18655. Gill, Stephen C. "'Adventures on Salisbury Plain' and Wordsworth's Poetry of Protest 1795-97." *SR* 11(1972): 48-66.

18656. ----------. "Wordsworth's Breeches Pocket: Attitudes to the Didactic Poet." *EIC* 19 (1969): 385-401.

18657. ----------. "Wordsworth's 'Never Failing Principle of Joy.'" *ELH* 34(1967): 208-224.

18658. Gohn, Jack Benoit. "Who Wrote *Benjamin the Waggoner*?" *WC* 8(1977): 69-74.

18659. Goldstein, Laurence. "The Auburn Syndrome: Change and Loss in 'The Deserted Village' and Wordsworth's Grasmere." *ELH* 40(1973): 352-371.

18660. Gomme, A. H. "Some Wordsworthian Transparencies." *MLR* 68(1973): 507-520.

18661. Green, David Bonnell. "William Wordsworth and Lydia Huntley Sigourney." *NEQ* 37 (1964): 527-531.

18662. ----------. "An Uncollected Wordsworth Letter on Shakespeare." *RES* 15(1964): 399-401.

18663. ----------. "Wordsworth and Edward Du Bois." *PQ* 33(1954): 435-437.

18664. ----------. "Wordsworth in the Westmorland Election of 1818: A New Letter to John Taylor." *MLR* 62(1967): 606-607.

18665. Griffin, Andrew L. "Wordsworth and the Problem of Imaginative Story: The Case of 'Simon Lee.'" *PMLA* 92(1977): 392-409.

18666. Griggs, Earl Leslie. "A Note on

Wordsworth's *A Character*." *RES* 4(1953): 57-63.

18667. Grob, Alan. "Process and Permanence in *Resolution and Independence*." *ELH* 28(1961): 89-100.

18668. ----------. "Wordsworth and Godwin: A Reassessment." *SR* 6(1967): 98-119.

18669. ----------. "Wordsworth's *Immortality Ode* and the Search for Identity." *ELH* 32 (1965): 32-61.

18670. ----------. "Wordsworth's *Nutting*." *JEGP* 61(1962): 826-832.

18671. Hall, Spencer. "Wordsworth's 'Lucy' Poems: Context and Meaning." *SR* 10(1971): 159-175.

18672. Hamilton, John Bowen. "Restoration of 'The Happy Warrior.'" *MLQ* 16(1955): 311-324.

18673. Harper, George Mills. "A Source of Wordsworth's Ages of Man." *TSLL* 1(1959): 277-280.

18674. Hartman, Geoffrey H. "A Poet's Progress: Wordsworth and the Via Naturaliter Negativa." *MP* 59(1962): 214-224.

18675. ----------. "Wordsworth's *Descriptive Sketches* and the Growth of a Poet's Mind." *PMLA* 76(1961): 519-527.

18676. ----------. "Wordsworth, *The Borderers*, and 'Intellectual Murder.'" *JEGP* 62(1963): 761-768.

18677. Hayden, John O. "Coleridge, the Reviewers, and Wordsworth." *SP* 68(1971): 105-119.

18678. Heath, William W. "Wordsworth's Experiments with Truth." *WC* 4(1973): 87-98.

18679. Heffernan, James A. W. "Wordsworth and Dennis: The Discrimination of Feelings." *PMLA* 82(1967): 430-436.

18680. ----------. "Wordsworth on Imagination: The Emblemizing Power." *PMLA* 81(1966): 389-399.

18681. ----------. "Wordsworth on the Sublime: The Quest for Interfusion." *SEL* 7(1967): 605-615.

18682. Heffernan, Thomas F. "Melville and Wordsworth." *AL* 49(1977): 338-351.

18683. Helms, Randel. "On the Genesis of Wordsworth's *Michael*." *ELN* 15(1977): 38-43.

18684. Herman, Judith B. "A Note on 'The Sailor's Mother.'" *WC* 6(1975): 302.

18685. Hertz, Neil H. "Wordsworth and the Tears of Adam." *SR* 7(1967): 15-33.

18686. Hill, Alan G. "Wordsworth, Comenius, and the Meaning of Education." *RES* 26(1975): 301-312.

18687. Hodgson, John A. "Wordsworth's Dialectical Transcentalism, 1798: 'Tintern Abbey.'" *Criticism* 18(1976): 367-380.

18688. Holkeboer, Robert, and Nadean Bishop. "Wordsworth on Words." *WC* 6(1975): 307-313.

18689. Holland, Patrick. "The Two Contrasts in Wordsworth's 'Westminster Bridge." *WC* 8(1977): 32-34.

18690. ----------. "Wordsworth and the Sublime: Some Further Considerations." *WC* 5(1974): 17-22.

18691. Holland, William H., Jr. "'The Proposed Publication': An Unpublished Letter from Wordsworth to James Dyer." *ELN* 6(1968): 34-37.

18692. Howe, Evelyn. "Lady Beaumont, Wordsworth's Friend." *SR* 4(1965): 143-157.

18693. Hunt, Bishop C., Jr. "Wordsworth and Charlotte Smith." *WC* 1(1970): 85-103.

18694. Irwin, Michael. "Wordsworth's 'Dependency Sublime.'" *EIC* 14(1964): 352-362.

18695. Jackson, Wallace. "Wordsworth and His Predecessors: Private Sensations and Public Tones." *Criticism* 17(1975): 41-58.

18696. Jacobus, Mary. "*Peter Bell* the First." *EIC* 24(1974): 219-242.

18697. James, G. Ingli. "The Solitary Reaper." *EIC* 15(1965): 361-362.

18698. ----------. "Wordsworth's *Solitary Reaper*." *EIC* 15(1965): 65-76.

18699. Jay, Eileen. "Walking with Wordsworth." *WC* 2(1971): 111-114.

18700. Johnston, Kenneth R. "'Home at Grasmere': Reclusive Song." *SR* 14(1975): 1-28.

18701. ----------. "Recollecting Forgetting: Forcing Paradox to the Limit in the 'Intimation Ode.'" *WC* 2(1971): 59-64.

18702. Jaye, Michael C. "*The Prelude*, *The Excursion*, and *The Recluse*: An Unpublished *Prelude* Variant." *PQ* 54(1975): 484-493.

18703. Jones, Myrddin. "Wordsworth and Cowper: The Eye made Quiet." *EIC* 21(1971): 236-247.

19704. Jordon, John E. "De Quincey on Wordsworth's Theory of Diction." *PMLA* 68(1953): 764-778.

18705. ----------. "The Hewing of *Peter Bell*." *SEL* 7(1967): 559-603.

18706. ----------. "Wordsworth's 'Minuteness and Fidelity.'" *PMLA* 72(1957): 433-445.

18707. ----------. "Wordsworth's Humor." *PMLA* 73(1958): 81-93.

18708. Kabisch-Bernhardt, Ernest. "Wordsworth's Expostulator: Taylor or Hazlitt?" *ELN* 2 (1964): 102-105.

18709. Kaufman, Paul. "John Peace to William Wordsworth: Four Unpublished Letters." *ELN* 11(1974): 193-199.

18710. ----------. "To Wordsworth from Archbishop Trench: A Volume and a Letter." *ELN* 4 (1966): 37-41.

18711. Knieger, Bernard. "Wordsworth and Coleridge as Playwrights." *CLA* 6(1962): 57-63.

18712. Knoepflmacher, U. C. "The Post-Romantic Imagination: *Adam Bede*, Wordsworth and Milton." *ELH* 34(1967): 518-540.

18713. Kostelanetz, Anne. "Wordsworth's *Conversations*: A Reading of *The Two April Mornings* and *The Fountain*." *ELH* 33(1966): 43-52.

18714. Kroeber, Karl. "'Home at Grasmere': Ecological Holiness." *PMLA* 89(1974): 132-141.

18715. ----------. "A New Reading of 'The World is Too Much With Us.'" *SR* 2(1963): 183-188.

18716. ----------. "The Reaper and the Sparrow: A Study in Romantic Style." *Comp L* 10 (1958): 203-214.

18717. Lainoff, Seymour. "Wordsworth's 'Answer to Mathetes': A Re-Appraisal." *ELN* 3 (1966): 271-274.

18718. ----------. "Wordsworth's Final Phase: Glimpses of Eternity." *SEL* 1,#4(1961): 63-79.

18719. Landon, Carl. "Wordsworth, Coleridge, and the *Morning Post*: An Early Version of 'The Seven Sisters.'" *RES* 11(1960): 392-402.

18720. Langbaum, Robert. "The Evolution of Soul in Wordsworth's Poetry." *PMLA* 82(1967): 265-272.

18721. ----------. "Magnifying Wordsworth." *ELH* 33(1966): 271-278.

18722. Leyburn, Ellen D. "Radiance in *The White Doe of Rlystone*." *SP* 47(1950): 629-633.

18723. Lim, Paulino M., Jr. "Zen and Wordsworth." *WC* 7(1976): 129-132.

18724. Lincoln, Kenneth R. "Wordsworth's Mortality Ode." *JEGP* 71(1972): 211-225.

18725. Little, Geoffrey. "Tintern Abbey and Llyswen Farm." *WC* 8(1977): 80-82.

18726. Lyon, Judson Stanley. "Wordsworth and Ticknor." *PMLA* 66(1951): 432-440.

18727. MacGillivray, J. R. "An Early Poem and Letter by Wordsworth." *RES* 5(1954): 62-66.

18728. MacLean, Kenneth. "Levels of Imagination in Wordsworth's *Prelude* (1805)." *PQ* 38(1959): 385-400.

18729. Maniquis, Robert. "Comparison, Intensity, and Time in *Tintern Abbey*." *Criticism* 11(1969): 358-382.

18730. Manning, Peter J. "'Michael,' Luke, and Wordsworth." *Criticism* 19(1977): 195-211.

18731. ----------. "Wordsworth, Margaret, and The Pedlar." *SR* 15(1976): 195-220.

18732. Marcus, Leah. "Vaughan, Wordsworh, and the *Encomium Asini*." *ELH* 42(1975): 224-241.

18733. Marsh, Florence G. "Wordsworth's *Ode*: Obstinate Questionings." *SR* 5(1966): 219-230.

18734. Martin, John S. "Wordsworth's Echoes." *ELN* 5(1968): 186-192.

18735. Martin, B. W. "Wordsworth, Faber, and Keble: Commentary on a Triangular Relationship." *RES* 26(1975): 436-442.

18736. Maxwell, J. C. "Wordsworth and the Subjugation of Switzerland." *MLR* 65(1970): 16-18.

18737. Mayo, Robert. "The Contemporaneity of the *Lyrical Ballads*." *PMLA* 69(1954): 486-522.

18738. McAdam, E. L., Jr. "Wordsworth's Shipwreck." *PMLA* 77(1962): 240-247.

18739. McCarthy, John F. "The Conflict in Books I-II of *The Prelude*." *MLQ* 30(1969): 370-385.

18740. McFarland, Thomas. "Creative Fantasy and Matter-of-Fact Reality in Wordsworth's Poetry." *JEGP* 75(1976): 1-24.

18741. ----------. "The Symbiosis of Coleridge and Wordsworth." *SR* 11(1972): 263-303.

18742. McGavran, James Holt, Jr. "The 'Creative Soul' of *The Prelude* and the 'Sad Incompetence of Human Speech.'" *SR* 16(1977): 35-50.

18743. McGhee, Richard D. "'And Earth and Stars Composed a Universal Heaven': A View of Wordsworth's Later Poetry." *SEL* 11(1971): 641-657.

18744. ----------. "'Conversant with Infinity': Form and Meaning in Wordsworth's 'Laodamia.'" *SP* 68(1971): 357-369.

18745. Mellown, Muriel. "The Development of Imagery in 'Home at Grasmere.'" *WC* 5(1974): 23-27.

18746. Mendilow, A. A. "Robert Heron and Wordsworth's Critical Essays." *MLR* 52(1957): 329-338.

18747. Metzger, Lore. "Wordsworth's Pastoral Covenant." *MLQ* 37(1976): 307-323.

18748. Minot, W. S., John T. Ades, and Gordon K. Thomas. "Notes on Wordsworthian Puns." *WC* 5 (1974): 28-32.

18749. Morgan, Edwin. A Prelude to *The Prelude*." *EIC* 5(1955): 341-353.

18750. Morkan, Joel. "Structure and Meanings in *The Prelude*, Book V." *PMLA* 87(1972): 244-254.

18751. Mortenson, Robert. "'The Nose-Drop': A Parody of Wordsworth." *WC* 2(1971): 91-100.

18752. Murray, Roger. "Betty Foy: An Early Mental Traveler." *JEGP* 70(1971): 51-61.

18753. Murray, Roger. "Synechdoche in Wordsworth's *Michael*." *ELH* 32(1965): 502-510.

18754. Muir, Kenneth. "Contemporary Eclogue: A Conversation about Wordsworth." *EIC* 1(1951): 17-37.

18755. ----------. "An Epilogue to 'The Prelude.'" *EIC* 6(1956): 245-247.

18756. Nabholtz, John R. "The Journeys Homeward: Drama and Rhetoric in Book IV of *The Prelude*." *SR* 10(1971): 79-93.

18757. ----------. "The Integrity of Wordsworth's 'Tintern Abbey.'" *JEGP* 73(1974): 227-238.

18758. ----------. "Wordsworth and William Mason." *RES* 15(1964): 297-302.

18759. ----------. "Wordsworth's *Guide to the Lakes* and Picturesque Tradition." *MP* 61(1964): 288-297.

18760. New, Melvyn. "Wordsworth's Shell of Poetry." *PQ* 53(1974): 275-281.

18761. Newey, Vincent. "Wordsworth, Bunyan, and the Puritan Mind." *ELH* 41(1974): 212-232.

18762. Noyes, Russell. "More on Wordsworth in Japan." *WC* 1(1970): 65-68.

18763. ----------. "Why Read *The Excursion*?" *WC* 4(1973): 139-151.

18764. ----------. "Wordsworth: An Unpublished Letter to John Kenyon." *MLR* 53(1958): 546-547.

18765. ----------. "Wordsworth and the Copyright Act of 1842: *Addendum*." *PMLA* 76(1961): 380-383.

18766. ----------, K. Kamijima, M. Okachi, and K. Senbokuya. "Wordsworth in Japan." *WC* 1(1970): 5-13.

18767. Ogden, John. "The Power of Distance in Wordsworth's *Prelude*." *PMLA* 88(1973): 246-259.

18768. ----------. "The Structure of Imaginative Experience in Wordsworth's *Prelude*." *WC* 6 (1975): 290-298.

18796. O'Hara, J. D. "Ambiguity and Assertion in Wordsworth's 'Elegiac Stanzas.'" *PQ* 47 (1968): 69-82.

18770. Owen, W. J. B. "*The Borderers* and the Aesthetics of Drama." *WC* 6(1975): 227-239.

18771. ----------. "Literary Echoes in *The Prelude*." *WC* 3(1972): 3-16.

18772. ----------. "The Major Theme of Wordsworth's 1800 Preface." *EIC* 6(1956): 144-159.

18773. ----------. "A Shock of Mild Surprise." *WC* 8(1977): 291-305.

18774. ----------. "The Sublime and the Beautiful in *The Prelude*." *WC* 4(1973). 67-86.

18775. ----------. "'The Thorn' and the Poet's Intention." *WC* 8(1977): 3-17.

18776. ----------. "Wordsworth and Jeffrey in Collaboration." *RES* 15(1964): 161-167.

18777. ----------. "Wordsworth's Aesthetics of Landscape." *WC* 7(1976): 70-81.

18778. Park, Roy. "Coleridge's Two Voices as a Critic of Wordsworth." *ELH* 36(1969): 361-381.

18779. Parker, Reeve. "'Finer Distance': The Narrative Art of Wordsworth's 'The Wanderer.'" *ELH* 39(1972): 87-111.

18780. Parrish, Stephen. "Dramatic Technique in the *Lyrical Ballads*." *PMLA* 74(1959): 85-97.

18781. ----------. "'The Thorn': Wordsworth's Dramatic Monologue." *ELH* 24(1957): 153-163.

18782. ----------. "Wordsworth and Coleridge on Meter." *JEGP* 59(1960): 41-49.

18783. ----------. "The Wordsworth-Coleridge Controversy." *PMLA* 73(1958): 367-374.

18784. Parrish, Stephen. "The Worst of Wordsworth." *WC* 7(1976): 89-91.

18785. Patterson, Charles. "The Daemonic in *Peter Bell*." *WC* 8(1977): 139-146.

18786. ----------. "The Meaning and Significance of Wordsworth's *Peele Castle*." *JEGP* 56(1957): 1-9.

18787. Pfeffer, Arthur, and James Heffernan. "Wordsworth and Imagination." *PMLA* 84(1969): 141-147.

18788. Pittock, Malcolm. "The Solitary Reaper." *EIC* 15(1965): 243-245.

18789. ----------. "'The Solitary Reaper.'" *EIC* 16(1966): 131.

18790. Pollin, Burton. "Permutations of Names in *The Borderers*, or Hints of Godwin, Charles Lloyd, and a Real Renegade." *WC* 4(1973): 31-35.

18791. ----------. "Wordsworth's 'Misserrimus' Sonnet: Several Errors Corrected." *WC* 1(1970): 22-24.

18792. ----------. "'The World is Too Much With Us': Two More Sources—Dryden and Godwin." *WC* 1(1970): 50-52.

18793. Pradhan, S. V. "Fancy and Imagination: Coleridge vs. Wordsworth." *PQ* 54(1975): 604-623.

18794. Preston, John. "The Structure of 'The Solitary Reaper.'" *EIC* 19(1969): 60-66.

18795. Price, Martin. "Imagination in *The White Doe of Rylstone*." *PQ* 33(1954): 189-199.

18796. Pritchard, John Paul. "On the Making of Wordsworth's 'Dion.'" *SP* 49(1952): 66-74.

18797. Priestman, Donald. "Superstition and Imagination: Complementary Faculties of Wordsworth's Narrator in 'The Thorn.'" *JNT* 5(1975): 196-207.

28798. Pulos, C. E. "The Unity of Wordsworth's Immortality Ode." *SR* 13(1974): 179-188.

18799. Ragussis, Michael. "Language and Metamorphosis in Wordsworth's Arab Dream." *MLQ* 36(1975): 148-165.

18800. Ramsey, Jonathan. "Seeing and Perceiving in Wordsworth's *An Evening Walk*." *MLQ* 36(1975): 376-389.

18801. ----------. "Wordsworth and the Childhood of Language." *Criticism* 18(1976): 243-255.

18802. ----------. "Wordsworth's Silent Poet." *MLQ* 37(1976): 260-280.

18803. Randel, Fred. "Wordsworth's Homecoming." *SEL* 17(1977): 575-591.

18804. Rayan, Krishna. "Statement by Omission: The Case of *The Prelude*." *EIC* 17(1967): 448-455.

18805. Raysor, Thomas. "The Establishment of Wordsworth's Reputation." *JEGP* 54(1955): 61-71.

18806. ----------. "The Themes of Immortality and Natural Piety in Wordsworth's Immortality Ode." *PMLA* 69(1954): 861-875.

18807. ----------. "Wordsworth's Early Drafts of *The Ruined Cottage* in 1797-98." *JEGP* 55(1956): 1-7.

18808. Reid, Ian. "'A Naked Guide-Post's Double Head': The Wordsworthian." *ELH* 43(1976): 538-550.

18809. Ricks, Christopher. "Wordsworth: 'A Pure Organic Pleasure from the Lines.'" *EIC* 21(1971): 1-32.

18810. Robinson, Jeffrey. "'The Prelude,' Book XIV and the Problem of Concluding." *Criticism* 16(1974): 301-310.

18811. ----------. "Unpublished Letter of W. W. to Henry Robinson of York." *WC* 5(1974): 15-16.

18812. Ross, Isabel. "Wordsworth and Colthouse near Hawkshead." *MLR* 50(1955): 499-501.

18813. Rubenstein, Jill. "Wordsworth and 'Localised Romance': The Scottish Poems of 1831." *SEL* 16(1976): 579-590.

18814. Ruoff, Gene. "Another New Poem by Wordsworth." *EIC* 16(1966): 359-360.

18815. ----------. "Religious Implications of Wordsworth's Imagination." *SR* 12(1973): 670-692.

18816. ----------. "Wordsworth on Language: Toward a Radical Poetics." *WC* 3(1972): 204-211.

18817. ----------. "Wordsworth's 'Yew-Trees' and Romantic Perception." *MLQ* 34(1973): 146-160.

18818. Sabin, Margery. "Imagination in Rousseau and Wordsworth." *Comp L* 22(1970): 328-345.

18819. Sanderson, David. "Wordsworth's World, 1809: A Stylistic Study of the Cintra Pamphlet." *WC* 1(1970): 104-113.

18820. Schell, Richard. "Wordsworth's Revisions of the Ascent of Snowden." *PQ* 54(1975): 592-603.

18821. Schier, Rudolf. "The Experience of the Noumenal in Goethe and Wordsworth." *Comp L* 25(1973): 37-59.

18822. Schleifer, Ronald. "Wordsworth's Yarrow and the Poetics of Repetition." *MLQ* 38(1977): 348-366.

18823. Schneider, Robert. "The Failure of Solitude: Wordsworth's Immortality Ode." *JEGP* 54(1955): 625-633.

18824. Schulz, Max F. "Coleridge, Wordsworth, and the 1800 Preface to the Lyrical Ballads." *SEL* 5(1965): 619-639.

18825. Sellers, W. H. "Wordsworth and Spender: Some Speculations on the Use of Rhyme." *SEL* 5(1965): 641-650.

18826. Seronsy, Cecil C. "Daniel and Wordsworth." *SP* 56(1959): 187-213.

18827. Shakir, Evelyn. "Books, Death, and Immortality: A Study of Book V of *The Prelude*." *SR* 8(1969): 156-167.

18828. Sharp, Steven. "The Unmerited Contempt of Reviewers: Wordsworth's Response to Contemporary Reviewers of *Descriptive Sketches*." *WC* 8(1977): 25-31.

18829. Sharrock, Roger. "Speech and Prose in Wordsworth's Preface." *EIC* 7(1957): 108-113.

18830. ----------. "Wordsworth's Revolt Against Literature." *EIC* 3(1953): 396-412.

18831. Shaver, C. L. "Wordsworth's Vaudracour and Wilkinson's *The Wanderer*." *RES* 12(1961): 55-57.

18832. Sheats, P. D. "Excursion and Return in *The Prelude*." *WC* 1(1970): 123-130.

18833. ----------. "Wordsworth's 'Retrogrades' and the Shaping of *The Prelude*." *JEGP* 71(1972): 473-490.

18834. Serbo, Arthur. "A Note on *The Prelude*." *WC* 4(1973): 11-12.

18835. Slakey, Roger. "At Zero: A Reading of Wordsworth's 'She Dwelt Among the Untrodden Ways.'" *SEL* 12(1972): 629-638.

18836. Smith, Charles. "The Contrarieties: Wordsworth's Dualistic Imagery." *PMLA* 69(1954): 1181-1199.

18837. ----------. "The Effect of Shakespeare's Influence on Wordsworth's 'The Borderers.'" *SP* 50(1953): 625-639.

18838. ----------. "Wordsworth and Coleridge: The Growth of a Theme." *SP* 54(1957): 53-64.

18839. Smyser, Jane. "'An eye to perceive and a heart to rejoice.'" *WC* 8(1977): 35-37.

18840. ----------. "Wordsworth's Dream of Poetry and Science: *The Prelude*, V." *PMLA* 71

(1956): 269-275.

18841. Solomon, Gerald. "Wordsworth and the 'Art of Lying.'" *EIC* 27(1977): 141-156.

18842. Sonn, Carl R. "An Approach to Wordsworth's Earlier Imagery." *ELH* 27(1960): 208-222.

18843. Spector, S. J. "Wordsworth's Minor Imagery and the Picturesque Tradition." *ELH* 44(1977): 85-107.

18844. Sperry, Stuart M., Jr. "From 'Tintern Abbey' to the 'Intimations Ode': Wordsworth and the Function of Memory." *WC* 1(1970): 40-49.

18845. Spiegelman, Willard. "Wordsworth's *Aeneid.*" *Comp L* 26(1974): 97-109.

18846. Stang, Richard. "The False Dawn: A Study of the Opening of Wordsworth's *The Prelude*." *ELH* 33(1966): 53-65.

18847. Stevens, Bonnie Klomp. "Biblical Allusions in *Peter Bell*: The Story of Balaam's Ass." *ELN* 14(1977): 275-278.

18848. Stevenson, Warren. "Cosmic Irony in Wordsworth's 'A Slumber Did My Spirit Seal.'" *WC* 7(1976): 92-94.

18849. Stobie, W. G. "A Reading of *The Prelude*, Book V." *MLQ* 24(1963): 365-373.

18850. Stoddard, F. G. "Two Autograph Letters of William Wordsworth." *MP* 69(1971): 140-141.

18851. Stone, C. F., III. "Narrative Variations in Wordsworth's Versions of 'The Discharged Soldier.'" *JNT* 4(1974): 32-44.

18852. Storch, R. F. "Another New Poem by Wordsworth." *EIC* 15(1965): 473-476.

18853. ----------. "Wordsworth and Constable." *SR* 5(1966): 121-138.

18854. ----------. "Wordsworth and the City: 'Social Reason's Inner Sense.'" *WC* 1(1970): 114-122.

18855. ----------. "Wordsworth's Experimental Ballads: The Radical Uses of Intelligence and Comedy." *SEL* 11(1971): 621-639.

18856. ----------. "Wordsworth's *The Borderers*: The Poet as Anthropologist." *ELH* 36(1969): 340-360.

18857. Swearingen, James E. "Wordsworth on Gray." *SEL* 14(1974): 489-509.

18858. Swetnam, Ford. "The Controversial Uses of Wordsworth's Comedy." *WC* 3(1972): 31-40.

18859. Swingle, L. J. "Wordsworth's Contrarieties: A Prelude to Wordsworthian Complexity." *ELH* 44(1977): 337-354.

18860. Sundell, M. G. "'Tintern Abbey' and 'Resignation.'" *VP* 5(1967): 255-264.

18861. Taaffee, J. G. "Poet and Lover in Wordsworth's 'Lucy' Poems." *MLR* 61(1966): 175-179.

18862. ----------. The 'Spots of Time' Passage in *The Prelude*." *ELN* 2(1965): 271-275.

18863. Teich, Nathaniel. "Wordsworth's Reception and Copleston's *Advice*." *WC* 6(1975): 280-282.

18864. Teichman, Milton. "Wordsworth's Two Replies to Coleridge's 'Dejection: An Ode.'" *PMLA* 86(1971): 982-989.

18865. Tetreault, Ronald. "Wordsworth on Enthusiasm: A New Letter to Thomas Clarkson on the Slavery Question." *MP* 75(1977): 53-58.

18866. Thorslev, Peter. "Wordsworth's and the Romantic Villain-Hero." *SR* 5(1966): 84-103.

18867. Todd, F. M. "Wordsworth's Monody on Lamb: Another Copy." *MLR* 50(1955): 48-50.

18868. ----------. "Wordsworth in Germany." *MLR* 47(1952): 508-511.

18869. Townsend, R. C. "John Wordsworth and His Brother's Poetic Development." *PMLA* 81(1966):

70-78.

18870. Waldoff, Leon. "Wordsworth's Healing Power: Basic Trust in 'Tintern Abbey.'" *HSL* 4 (1972): 147-166.

18871. Ward, William S. "An Early Champion of Wordsworth: Thomas Noon Talfourd." *PMLA* 68 (1953): 992-1000.

18872. Watson, J. R. "Lucy and the Earth-Mother." *EIC* 27(1977): 187-202.

18873. ----------. "Wordsworth and Constable." *RES* 13(1962): 361-367.

18874. ----------. "Wordsworth and Constable: a Correction." *RES* 14(1963): 275.

18875. ----------. "Wordsworth's Card Games." *WC* 6(1975): 299-302.

18876. Watson, Melvin. "The Redemption of Peter Bell." *SEL* 4(1964): 519-530.

18877. Weaver, Bennett. "Wordsworth: Poet of the Unconquerable Mind." *PMLA* 75(1960): 231-237.

18878. Wesling, Donald. "The Inevitable Ear: Freedom and Necessity in Lyric Form, Wordsworth and After." *ELH* 36(1969): 544-561.

18879. Whalley, George. "The Fields of Sleep." *RES* 9(1958): 49-53.

18880. Whitney, Ross. "A New Wordsworth Letter: A Testimonial for Derwent Coleridge." *WC* 7(1976): 87-88.

18881. Wiener, David. "Wordsworth, Books, and the Growth of a Poets' Mind." *JEGP* 74(1975): 209-220.

18882. Wigod, Jacob. "Negative Capability and Wise Passiveness." *PMLA* 67(1952): 383-390.

18883. Wilcox, S. C. "The Sources of Wordsworth's 'After-Thought' Sonnet." *PQ* 32(1953): 210-212.

18884. ----------. "Wordsworth's River Dudden Sonnets." *PMLA* 69(1954): 131-141.

18885. Wilhelm, Albert E. "The Dramatized Narrator in Wordsworth's *The Idiot Boy*." *JNT* 5 (1975): 16-23.

18886. Wilkie, Brian. "Wordsworth and the Tradition of the Avant-Garde." *JEGP* 72(1973): 194-222.

18887. Wilson, James. "Tennyson's Emendations fo Wordsworth's 'Tintern Abbey.'" *WC* 5(1974): 7-8.

18888. Woodring, Carl. "On Liberty in the Poetry of Wordsworth." *PMLA* 70(1955): 1033-1048.

18889. ----------. "Peter Bell and 'The Pious': A New Letter." *PQ* 30(1951): 430-434.

18890. Wooley, Mary Lynn. "Wordsworth's Symbolic Vale as it Functions in *The Prelude*." *SR* 7(1968): 176-189.

18891. Wordsworth, Jonathan. "The Five-Book *Prelude* of Early Spring 1804." *JEGP* 76 (1977): 1-25.

18892. ----------. "A New Poem by Wordsworth." *EIC* 16(1966): 122-123.

18893. ----------, and Stephen Gill. "The Two-Part *Prelude* of 1798-99." *JEGP* 72(1973): 503-525.

18894. Zall, Paul M. "Old Knight Revisited." *PMLA* 71(1956): 1173-1177.

18895. ----------. "Wordsworth and the Copyright Act of 1842." *PMLA* 70(1955): 132-144.

18896. ----------. "Wordsworth's 'Ode' and Mrs. Barbauld's *Hymns*." *WC* 1(1970): 177-179.

18897. ----------, E. W. Zall, and Doris Braendel. "Wordsworth in the Huntington Library: A Preliminary Checklist." *WC* 1(1970): 141-160.

See also 455, 464, 3871, 13882, 15293, 15367,

15447, 15524, 16214, 16391, 16820, 17189, 17418, 17491, 17531, 17907, 17912, 17960, 18087, 19217.

ZANGWILL, ISRAEL. 18898. Winehouse, Bernard. "Israel Zangwill's 'The King of Schnorrers.'" *SSF* 10(1973): 227-233.

TWENTIETH CENTURY

GENERAL AND MISCELLANEOUS. 18889. Bateson, F. W. "The Alternative to *Scrutiny*." *EIC* 14 (1964): 10-20.

18900. Dawson, S. W. "*Scrutiny* and the Idea of a University." *EIC* 14(1964): 1-9.

18901. Gibbons, Tom. "Modernism and Reactionary Politcs." *JML* 3(1974): 1-9.

18902. Hobsbaum, Philip. "The Growth of English Modernism." *Con L* 6(1965): 97-105.

18903. Jackson, G. R. "Mr. Trodd and *Scrutiny*." *EIC* 14(1964): 335-337.

18904. Jean, Denis-J. "Was There an English Surrealist Group in the Forties? Two Unpublished Letters." *TCL* 21(1975): 81-89.

18905. Knight, G. Wilson. "*Scrutiny* and Criticism." *EIC* 14(1964): 32-36.

18906. Landini, R. G. "The Tenth Anniversary of *Nine*: A Bibliographical Guide." *TCL* 5(1959): 52-55.

18907. Roberts, Mark, and Allen Rodway. "English in the University: II 'Practical Criticism' in Principle and Practice." *EIC* 10(1960): 1-17.

18908. Roberts, Warren. "Modern Literary Materials at the University of Texas: Their Scope and Usefulness." *JML* 2(1971): 329-341.

18909. Staley, Thomas F. "The Artist as Autobiographer." *JML* 2(1972): 576-581.

18910. Storm, Leo. "J. M. Robertson and T. S. Eliot." *JML* 5(1976): 315-321.

18911. Trodd, Kenneth. "*Scrutiny*: Report from the Younger Generation." *EIC* 14(1964): 21-32.

18912. Vaizey, John. "*Scrutiny* and Education." *EIC* 14(1964): 36-42.

DRAMA. 18913. Armstrong, William A. "Tradition and Innovation in the London Theater, 1960-61." *MD* 4(1961): 184-195.

18914. Browne, E. Martin. "A Last Look Round the English Theatre." *CD* 3(1969): 133-142.

18915. Feynman, A. E. "The Fetal Quality of 'Character' in Plays of the Absurd." *MD* 9(1966): 18-25.

18916. Flory, Claude R. "A Rare Theatrical Journal: *The Arthurian Theatre Magazine*." *MD* 13 (1970): 129-132.

18917. Hays, H. R. "Transcending Naturalism." *MD* 5(1962): 27-36.

18918. Jurak, Mirko. "Dramaturgic Concepts of the English Group Theatre: The Totality of Artistic Involvement." *MD* 16(1973): 81-86.

18919. Kennedy, Andrew K. "Old and New in London Now." *MD* 11(1969): 437-446.

18920. Trilling, Ossia. "The Young British Drama." *MD* 3(1960): 168-177.

18921. Williams, Raymond. "Criticism into Drama, 1880-1950." *EIC* 1(1951): 120-138.

FICTION. 18922. Armytage, W. H. G. "The Disenchanted Mechanophobes in Twentieth-Century England." *Ext* 9(1968): 33-60.

18923. Daiches, David. "Time and Sensibility." *MLQ* 25(1964): 486-492.

18924. Gindin, James. "The Fable Begins to Break Down." *Con L* 8(1967): 1-18.

18925. ----------. "Well Beyond Laughter: Directions from Fifties' Comic Fiction." *SN* 3 (1971): 357-364.

18926. Haberman, Donald. "Destiny's New Voice." *Con L* 17(1976): 191-203.

18927. Harris, Wendell V. "Molly's 'Yes': The Transvaluation of Sex in Modern Fiction." *TSLL* 10(1968): 107-118.

18928. Martin, P. A. "The Short Story in England: 1930's Fiction Magazines." *SSF* 14(1977): 322-240.

18929. McDowell, Frederick, P. W. "The Devious Involutions of Human Character and Emotions: Reflections on Some Recent British Novels." *Con L* 4(1963): 339-366.

18930. Melchiori, Giorgio. "The Moment as Time-Unit in Fiction." *EIC* 3(1953): 434-445.

18931. O'Connor, William Van. "Two Types of 'Heroes' in Post-War British Fiction." *PMLA* 77 (1962): 168-174.

POETRY. 18932. Johnson, Abby Arthur. "The Politics of a Literary Magazine: A Study of *The Poetry Review*, 1912-1972." *JML* 3(1974): 951-964.

18933. Ransom, John Crowe. "The Poetry of 1900-1950." *ELH* 18(1951): 155-162.

18934. Rosenthal, M. L. "Dynamics of Form and Motive in Some Representative Twentieth-Century Lyric Poems." *ELH* 37(1970): 136-151.

18935. Wood, M. "We All Hate Home: English Poetry Since World War II." *Con L* 18(1977): 315-318.

ALDISS, BRIAN. 18936. Aldiss, Brian. "On Being a Literary Pariah." *Ext* 17(1976): 168-171.

ALLEN, WALTER. 18937. Sale, Richard B. "An Interview in New York with Walter Allen." *SN* 3(1971): 405-429.

AMIS, KINGSLEY. 18938. Boyle, Ted E, and Terence Brown. "The Serious Side of Kingsley Amis's *Lucky Jim*." *Crit* 9,#1(1966): 100-112.

18939. Fallis, Richard. "*Lucky Jim* and Academic Wishful Thinking." *SN* 9(1977): 65-72.

18940. Hopkins, R. H. "The Satire of Kingsley Amis's *I Like It Here*." *Crit* 8,#3(1966): 62-70.

18941. Hurrell, John D. "Class and Conscience in John Braine and Kingsley Amis." *Crit* 2,#1(1958): 39-53.

18942. Parker, R. "Farce and Society: The Range of Kingsley Amis." *Con L* 2,#3(1927): 27-38.

18943. Salwak, Dale. "An Interview with Kingsley Amis." *Con L* 16(1975): 1-18.

ARDEN, JOHN. 18944. Adler, Thomas P. "Religious Ritual in John Arden's *Serjeant Musgrave's Dance*." *MD* 16(1973): 163-166.

18945. Blindheim, Joan Tindale. "John Arden's Use of the Stage." *MD* 11(1968): 306-316.

18946. Day, P. W. "Individual and Society in the Early Plays of John Arden." *MD* 18(1975): 239-250.

18947. Hampton, Nigel. "Freedom and Order in Arden's *Ironhand*." *MD* 19(1976): 129-134.

18948. Jordan, Robert. "Sarjeant Musgrave's Problem." *MD* 13(1970): 54-62.

18949. O'Connell, Mary B. "Ritual Elements in John Arden's *Sarjeant Musgrave's Dance*." *MD* 13(1970): 356-359.

18950. Page, Malcolm, and Virginia Evans. "Approaches to John Arden's *Squire Jonathan*." *MD* 13(1970): 360-365.

AUDEN, W. H. 18951. Bloom, Robert. "The Humanization of Auden's Early Style." *PMLA* 83 (1968): 443-455.

18952. ----------. "Poetry's Auden." *JML*

1(1970): 119-122.

18953. Brooke-Rose, Christine. "Notes on the Metre of Auden's *The Age of Anxiety*." *EIC* 13 (1963): 253-264.

18954. Bruehl, William J. "*Polus Naufragia*: A Key Symbol in *The Ascent of F6*." *MD* 10 (1967): 161-164.

18955. Callan, Edward. "Allegory in Auden's *The Age of Anxiety*." *TCL* 10(1965): 155-165.

18956. ----------. "An Annotated Check List of the Works of W. H. Auden." *TCL* 4(1958): 30-50.

18957. ----------. "Auden Triumphant." *JML* 3(1974): 1055-1062.

18958. ----------. "The Development of W. H. Auden's Poetic Theory Since 1940." *TCL* 4(1958): 79-91.

18959. ----------. "W. H. Auden: Annotated Checklist II (1958-1969)." *TCL* 16(1970): 27-56.

18960. ----------. "W. H. Auden's First Dramatization of Jung: The Charade of the Loving and Terrible Mothers." *CD* 11(1977): 287-302.

18961. Charney, Maurice. "Sir Lewis Namier and Auden's 'Musée des Beaux Arts.'" *PQ* 39(1960): 129-131.

18962. Cohen, Edward H. "Auden's 'A Shock.'" *NCL* 4(Sept., 1974): 7-8.

18963. Cook, F. W. "Primordial Auden." *EIC* 12(1962): 402-412.

18964. Enright, D. J. "Reluctant Admiration: A Note on Auden and Rilke." *EIC* 2(1952): 180-195.

18965. Firchow, Peter E. "Private Faces in Public Places: Auden's *The Orators*." *PMLA* 92(1977): 253-272.

18966. Gerstenberger, Donna. "Poetry and Politics: The Verse Drama of Auden and Isherwood." *MD* 5(1962): 123-132.

18967. Hazard, Forrest E. "The Father Christmas Passage in Auden's 'Paid on Both Sides.'" *MD* 12(1969): 155-164.

18968. Hyde, Virginia M. "The Pastoral Formula of W. H. Auden and Piero di Cosimo." *Con L* 14(1973): 332-346.

18969. Irwin, John T. "MacNeice, Auden, and the Art Ballad." *Con L* 11(1970): 58-79.

18970. Johnson, Wendall Stacy. "Auden, Hopkins, and the Poetry of Reticence." *TCL* 20 (1974): 165-171.

18971. Kirby, David K. "Snyder, Auden, and the New Morality." *NCL* (Jan., 1971): 9-10.

18972. Lehman, John. "Two of the Conspirators." *TCL* 22(1976): 264-275.

18973. Leithauser, Gladys Garner. "W. H. Auden's 'Meiosis.'" *ELN* 8(1970): 120-126.

18974. McDiarmid, Lucy S. "Auden and the Redeemed City: Three Allusions." *Criticism* 13 (1971): 340-350.

18975. ----------. "Poetry's Landscape in Auden's Elogy for Yeats." *MLQ* 38(1977): 167-177.

18976. ---------- and John. "Artifice and Self-Consciousness in Auden's 'The Sea and the Mirror.'" *Con L* 16(1975): 353-377.

18977. McDowell, Frederick P. W. "'Subtle, Various, Ornamental, Clever': Auden in His Recent Poetry." *Con L* 3,#3(1962): 29-44.

18978. Mendelson, Edward. "Auden." *EIC* 26 (1976): 96-97.

18979. ----------. "The Auden-Isherwood Collaboration." *TCL* 22(1976): 276-285.

18980. ----------. "The Coherence of Auden's *The Orators*." *ELH* 35(1968): 114-133.

18981. Moore, Gerald. "Luck in Auden." *EIC* 7(1957): 103-108.

18982. Parkin, Rebecca Price. "The Facsimile of Immediacy in W. H. Auden's 'In Praise of Limestone.'" *TSLL* 7(1965): 295-304.

18983. Replogle, Justin. "The Auden Group." *Con L* 5(1964): 133-150.

18984. ----------. "Auden's Intellectual Development 1950-1960." *Criticism* 7(1965): 250-262.

18985. ----------. "Auden's Marxism." *PMLA* 80(1965): 584-595.

18986. ----------. "Auden's Religious Leap." *Con L* 7(1966): 47-75.

18987. ----------. "The Gang Myth in Auden's Early Poetry." *JEGP* 61(1962): 481-495.

18988. ----------. "Social Philosophy in Auden's Early Poetry." *Criticism* 2(1960): 351-361.

18989. Roth, Robert. "The Sophistication of W. H. Auden: A Sketch in Longinian Method." *MP* 48(1951): 193-204.

18990. Sellers, W. H. "New Light on Auden's *The Orators*." *PMLA* 82(1967): 455-464.

18991. Sharp, Sr. Corona. "The Dance of Death in Modern Drama: Auden, Dürrenmatt and Ionesco." *MD* 20(1977): 107-116.

18992. Waidson, H. M. "Auden and German Literature." *MLR* 70(1975): 347-365.

18993. Weatherhead, A. Kingsley. "The Good Place in the Latest Poems of W. H. Auden." *TCL* 10(1964): 99-107.

18994. Weisstein, Ulrich. "Reflections on a Golden Style: W. H. Auden's Theory of Opera." *Comp L* 22(1970): 108-124.

See also 4341, 18922.

BALLARD, J. G. 18995. Wright, A. J. "Allegory of the Ruin: J. G. Ballard's 'The Drowned Giant.'" *NCL* 6(Sept., 1976): 14-15.

BARBELLION, W. N. P. 18996. Abbott, H. Porter. "The Journals of W. N. P. Barbellion." *JML* 3(1973): 45-62.

BARKER, GEORGE. 18997. Pondrom, Cyrena N. "An Interview with George Barker." *Con L* 12(1971): 375-401.

BARKER, GRANVILLE. 18998. Morgan, Margery M., and Frederick May. "The Early Plays of Harley Granville Barker." *MLR* 51(1956): 324-338.

18999. Norton, Roger C. "Hugo van Hofmansthal's *Der Schwierige* and Granville-Barker's *Waste*." *Comp L* 14(1962): 272-279.

19000. Ritchie, Harry M. "Harley Granville Barker's *The Madras House* and the Sexual Revolution." *MD* 15(1972): 150-158.

BARRIE, JAMES. 19001. Lamacchia, Grace A. "Textual Variations for Act IV of *The Admirable Crichton*." *MD* 12(1970): 408-418.

19002. McGraw, William R. "James M. Barrie's Concept of Dramatic Action." *MD* 5(1962): 133-141.

19003. Williams, David Park. "Hook and Ahab: Barrie's Strange Satire on Melville." *PMLA* 80(1965): 483-488.

BECKETT, SAMUEL. 19004. Abbott, H. Porter. "Farewell to Incompetence: Beckett's *How It Is* and *Imagination Dead Imagine*." *Con L* 11(1970): 36-47.

19005. Abbott, H. Porter. "A Grammar for Being Elsewhere." *JML* 6(1977): 39-46.

19006. ----------. "A Poetics of Radical Displacement: Samuel Beckett Coming up to Seventy." *TSLL* 17(1975): 219-238.

19007. Admussen, Richard L. "The Manuscripts of Beckett's *Play*." *MD* 16(1973): 23-28.

19008. Alpaugh, David. "*Embers* and the Sea: Beckettian Intimations of Mortality." *MD* 16 (1973): 317-328.

19009. ----------. "Negative Definition in Samuel Beckett's *Happy Days*." *TCL* 11(1966): 202-210.

19010. ----------. "The Symbolic Structure of Samuel Beckett's *All That Fall*." *MD* 9(1966) 324-332.

19011. Atkins, Anselm. "A Note on the Structure of Lucky's Speech." *MD* 9(1966): 309.

19012. Avigal, Shoshana. "Beckett's *Play*: The Circular Line of Existence." *MD* 18(1975): 251-258.

19013. Barge, Laura. "'Colored Images' in the 'Black Dark': Samuel Beckett's Later Fiction." *PMLA* 92(1977): 273-284.

19014. Beckett, Samuel. "Come and Go." *MD* 19(1976): 255-260.

19015. Brater, Enoch. "Beckett, Ionesco, and the Tradition of Tragicomedy." *SSF* 11(1974): 113-127.

19016. ----------. "Brecht's Alienated Actor in Beckett's Theatre." *CD* 9(1975): 195-205.

19017. ----------. "Dada, Surrealism, and the Genesis of *Not I*." *MD* 18(1975): 49-59.

19018. ----------. "The Empty Can: Samuel Beckett and Andy Warhol." *JML* 3(1974): 1255-1264.

19019. ----------. "The 'I' in Beckett's *Not I*." *TCL* 20(1974): 189-200.

19020. ----------. "Noah, *Not I*, and Beckett's 'Incomprehensibly Sublime.'" *CD* 8 (1974): 254-263.

19021. ----------. "Still/Beckett: The Essential and the Incidental." *JML* 6(1977): 3-16.

19022. ----------. "The Thinking Eye in Beckett's *Film*." *MLQ* 36(1975): 166-176.

19023. ----------, and Susan Brienza. "The Composition of Beckett's *Lessness*." *ELH* 43(1976): 244-258.

19024. Breyer, Rolf. "The Solution as Problem: Beckett's *Waiting for Godot*." *MD* 19 (1976): 225-236.

19025. Brick, Allen. "A Note on Perception and Communication in Beckett's *Endgame*." *MD* 4 (1961): 20-22.

19026. Brienza, Susan D. "The *Lost Ones*: The Reader as Searcher." *JML* 6(1977): 148-168.

19027. Brooks, Curtis M. "The Mythic Pattern in *Waiting for Godot*." *MD* 9(1966): 292-299.

19028. Bruns, Gerald L. "The Storyteller and the Problem of Language in Samuel Beckett's Fiction." *MLQ* 30(1969): 265-281.

19029. Chase, N. C. "Images of Man: *Le Malentendu* and *En Attendant Godot*." *Con L* 7 (1966): 295-310.

19030. Cleveland, Louise D. "Trials in the Sound-scape: The Radio Plays of Samuel Beckett." *MD* 11(1968): 267-282.

19031. Coetzee, J. M. "The Manuscript Revisions of Beckett's *Watt*." *JML* 2(1972): 472-480.

19032. Cohen, Robert S. "Parallels and the Possibility of Influence Between Simone Weil's *Waiting for God* and Samuel Beckett's *Waiting for Godot*." *MD* 6(1964): 425-436.

19033. Cohn, Ruby. "Acting for Beckett." *MD* 9(1966): 237.

19034. ----------. "Beckett and Shakespeare." *MD* 15(1972): 223-230.

19035. ----------. "The Beginning of *Endgame*." *MD* 9(1966): 319-323.

19036. ----------. "Outward Bound Soliloquies." *JML* 6(1977): 17-38.

19037. ----------. "Philosophical Fragments in the Works of Samuel Beckett." *Criticism* 6(1964): 33-43.

19038. ----------. "Samuel Beckett Self-Translator." *PMLA* 76(1961): 613-621.

19039. ----------. "*Treatrum Mundi* and Contemporary Theatre." *CD* 1(1967): 28-35.

19040. ----------. "Waiting is All." *MD* 3 (1960): 162-167.

19041. ----------. "*Watt* in the Light of *The Castle*." *Comp L* 13(1961): 154-166.

19042. Conely, James. "Edgar Varese's *Arcana* and Samuel Beckett's *Three Novels: Malloy, Malone Dies, The Unnamable*: A Brief Comparison of Forms." *HSL* 4(1972): 187-196.

19043. Cornwell, Ethel F. "Samuel Beckett: The Flight from Self." *PMLA* 88(1973): 41-51.

19044. Dearlove, J. E. "'Last Images': Samuel Beckett's Residual Fiction." *JML* 6(1977) 104-126.

19045. Dubois, Jacques. "Beckett and Ionesco: The Tragic Awareness of Pascal and the Ironic Awareness of Flaubert." *MD* 9(1966): 283-291.

19046. Dukore, Bernard F. "*Krapp's Last Tape* as Tragicomedy." *MD* 15(1973): 351-354.

19047. Easthope, Antony. "Hamm, Clov, and Dramatic Method in *Endgame*." *MD* 10(1968): 424-433.

19048. Eastman, Richard M. "Samuel Beckett and *Happy Days*." *MD* 6(1964): 417-424.

19049. ----------. "The Strategy of Samuel Beckett's *Endgame*." *MD* 2(1959): 36-44.

19050. Esslin, Martin. "Beckett's *Rough for Radio*." *JML* 6(1977): 95-103.

19051. Finney, Brian. "A Reading of Beckett's *Imagination Dead Imagine*." *TCL* 17 (1971): 65-71.

19052. Fletcher, John. "Action and Play in Beckett's Theater." *MD* 9(1966): 242-250.

19053. ----------. "The Arrival of Godot." *MLR* 64(1969): 34-38.

19054. ----------. "Samuel Beckett and the Philosophers." *Comp L* 17(1965): 43-56.

19055. Francis, Richard Lee. "Beckett's Meta-Physical Tragicomedy." *MD* 8(1965): 259-267.

19056. Friedman, Melvin J. "Crritic!" *MD* 9(1966): 300-308.

19057. ----------. "The Novels of Samuel Beckett: An Amalgam of Joyce and Proust." *Comp L* 12(1960): 47-58.

19058. ----------. "Review-Essay: Samuel Beckett and His Critics Enter the 1970's." *SN* 5 (1973): 383-399.

19059. ----------. "Samuel Beckett and the *Nouveau Roman*." *Con L* 1,#2(1960): 22-36.

19060. Gaddis, Marilyn Rose. "The Lyrical Structure of Beckett's *Texts for Nothing*." *Novel*

4(1971): 223-230.

19061. Gontarski, S. E. "Crapp's First Tape: Beckett's Manuscript Revisions of *Krapp's Last Tape*." *JML* 6(1977): 61-68.

19062. Greene, Naomi. "Creation and the Self: Artaud, Beckett, Michaux." *Criticism* 13 (1971): 265-278.

19063. Hampton, Charles C., Jr. "Samuel Beckett's *Film*." *MD* 11(1968): 299-305.

19064. Harvey, Lawrence E. "Art and the Existential in *En Attendant Godot*." *PMLA* 75 (1960): 137-146.

19065. Hassan, Ihab. "Joyce-Beckett: A Scenario in Eight Scenes and a Voice." *JML*: (1970): 7-18.

19066. Hasselbach, Hans-Peter. "Samuel Beckett's *Endgame*: A Structural Analysis." *MD* 19(1976): 25-34.

19067. Hesla, David H. "The Shape of Chaos: A Reading of Beckett's *Watt*." *Crit* 6,#1 (1963): 85-105.

19068. Hubert, Renée Riese. "Beckett's *Play* Between Poetry and Performance." *MD* 9 (1966): 339-346.

19069. Iser, Wolfgang. "Samuel Beckett's Dramatic Language." *MD* 9(1966): 251-259.

19070. Jones, Louisa. "Narrative Salvation in *Waiting for Godot*." *MD* 17(1974): 179-188.

19071. Kellman, Steven G. "Imagining the Novel Dead: Recent Variations on a Theme by Proust." *MLQ* 35(1974): 45-55.

19072. Kern, Edith. "Beckett and the Spirit of the Commedia dell'Arte." *MD* 9(1966): 260-267.

19073. ----------. "Beckett as *Homo Ludens*." *JML* 6(1977): 47-60.

19074. ----------. "Surrealism: The Language of the Unthought." *TCL* 21(1975): 37-47.

19075. Kroll, Jeri L. "Beckett and Grock: Kings of Clowns." *NCL* 6(Jan., 1976): 7-14.

19076. Leventhal, A. J. "The Beckett Hero." *Crit* 7,#2(1964): 18-35.

19077. London, Merrie. "'To Make a Short Beckett Piece.'" *MD* 18(1975): 60.

19078. Lyons, Charles R. "Beckett's *Endgame*: An Anti-Myth Creation." *MD* 7(1964): 204-209.

19079. ----------. "Beckett's Major Plays and the Trilogy." *CD* 5(1971): 254-268.

19080. ----------. "Some Analogies Between the Epic Brecht and the Absurdist Beckett." *CD* 1(1967-68): 297-304.

19081. Marker, Frederick J. "Beckett Criticism in *Modern Drama*: A Checklist." *MD* 19 (1976): 261-264.

19082. Mayoux, Jean Jacques. "Beckett and Expressionism." *MD* 9(1966): 238-241.

19083. Mihalyi, Gabor. "Beckett's *Godot* and the Myth of Alienation." *MD* 9(1966): 277-282.

19084. Mitchell, Breon. "Art in Microcosm: The Manuscript Stages of Beckett's *Come and Go*." *MD* 19(1976): 245-254.

19085. Mood, John J. "'The Personal System'—Samuel Beckett's *Watt*." *PMLA* 86(1971): 255-265.

19086. Murphy, Vincent J. "Being and Perception: Beckett's *Film*." *MD* 18(1975): 43-48.

19087. ----------. La Peinture de l'empêchement—Samuel Beckett's 'Watt.'" *Criticism*

18(1976): 353-366.

19088. Oberg, Arthur K. "*Krapp's Last Tape* and the Proustian Vision." *MD* 9(1966): 333-338.

19089: Park, Eric. "Fundamental Sounds: Music in Samuel Beckett's *Murphy* and *Watt*." *MFS* 21(1975): 157-171.

19090. Pearce, Richard. "Old Bottles for Now Beckett." *JML* 2(1971): 442-448.

19091. Perlmutter, Ruth. "Beckett's *Film* and Beckett and Film." *JML* 6(1977): 83-94.

19092. Pountney, Rosemary. "Samuel Beckett's Interest in Form: Structural Patterning in *Play*." *MD* 19(1976): 237-244.

19093. Rabinovitz, Rubin. "Style and Obscurity in Beckett's Early Fiction." *MFS* 20 (1974): 399-406.

19094. Rechtien, Brother John, S.M. "Time and Eternity Meet in the Present." *TSLL* 6(1964): 5-21.

19095. Rickels, Milton. "Existentialist Themes in Beckett's *Unnamable*." *Criticism* 4(1962): 134-147.

19096. Riva, Raymond T. "Beckett and Freud." *Criticism* 12(1970): 120-132.

19097. Rose, Marilyn Gaddis. "The Irish Memories of Beckett's Voice." *JML* 2(1971): 127-132.

19098. Schechner, Richard. "There's Lots of Time in *Godot*." *MD* 9(1966): 268-276.

19099. Schoell, Konrad. "The Chain and the Circle: A Structural Comparison of *Waiting for Godot* and *Endgame*." *MD* 11(1968): 48-53.

19100. Segrè, Elisabeth Bregman. "Style and Structure in Beckett's 'Ping': *That Something Itself*." *JML* 6(1977): 127-147.

19101. Senneff, Susan Field. "Song and Music in Samuel Beckett's *Watt*." *MFS* 10(1964): 137-149.

19102. Sheedy, John J. "The Comic Apocalypse of King Hamm." *MD* 9(1966): 310-318.

19103. Skerl, Jennie. "Fritz Mauthner's 'Critique of Language' in Samuel Beckett's *Watt*." *Con L* 15(1974): 474-487.

19104. Smith, Frederick N. "Beckett and the Seventeenth-Century *Port-Royal Logic*." *JML* 5(1976): 99-108.

19105. ----------. "The Epistemology of Fictional Failure: Swift's *Tale of a Tub* and Beckett's *Watt*." *TSLL* 15(1974): 649-672.

19106. Sparling, Russell. "The Anti-Transcendental Function of Pozzo and Lucky in Beckett's *Waiting for Godot*." *NCL* 7(Dec., 1977): 2.

19107. Stein, William Bysshe. "Beckett's 'Whoroscope': Turdy Ooscopy." *ELH* 42(1975): 125-155.

19108. Steinberg, S. C. "The External and Internal in *Murphy*." *TCL* 18(1972): 93-110.

19109. Stempel, Daniel. "History Electrified into Analogy: A Reading of *Waiting for Godot*." *Con L* 17(1976): 263-278.

19110. Stevens, Irma Ned. "Beckett's 'Texts for Nothing': An Inversion of Young's 'Night-Thoughts.'" *SSF* 11(1974): 131-139.

19111. Strauss, Walter A. "Dante's Belacqua and Beckett's Tramps." *Comp L* 11(1959): 250-261.

19112. Swanson, Eleanor. "Samuel Beckett's *Watt*: A Coming and A Going." *MFS* 17(1971): 264-268.

19113. Tindall, William York. "Beckett's Bums." *Crit* 2,#1(1958): 3-15.

19114. Todd, Robert E. "Proust and Redemption in *Waiting for Godot*." *MD* 10(1967): 175-181.

19115. Torrance, Robert M. "Modes of Being and Time in the World of *Godot*." *MLQ* 28(1967): 77-95.

19116. Trousdale, Marion. "Dramatic Form: The Example of *Godot*." *MD* 11(1968): 1-9.

19117. Warhaft, Sidney. "Threne and Theme in *Watt*." *Con L* 4(1963): 261-278.

19118. Webb, Eugene. "Pozzo in Bloomsberry: A Possible Allusion in Beckett's *Waiting for Godot*." *JML* 5(1976): 326-331.

19119. Wicker, Brian. "Samuel Beckett and the Death of the God-Narrator." *JNT* 4(1974): 62-74.

19120. Winston, Mathew. "*Watt*'s First Footnote." *JML* 6(1977): 69-82.

19121. Zilliacus, Clas. "Samuel Beckett's *Embers*: 'A Matter of Fundamental Sounds.'" *MD* 13 (1970): 216-225.

19122. ----------. "Three Times Godot: Beckett, Brecht, Bulatovic." *CD* 4(1970): 3-19.

19123. Zeifman, Hersh. "Being and Non-Being: Samuel Beckett's *Not I*." *MD* 19(1976): 35-46.

See also 5, 38, 83, 84.

BEERBOHM, MAX. 19124. Bross, Addison C. "Beerbohm's 'The Feast' and Conrad's Early Fiction." *NCF* 26(1971): 329-336.

19125. Langbaum, Robert. "Max and Dandyism." *VP* 4(1966): 121-126.

19126. Roselli, Daniel N. "Max Beerbohm's Unpublished Parody of Henry James." *RES* 22(1971): 61-63.

BEHAN, BRENDAN. 19127. Burca, Seamus De. "The Essential Brendan Behan." *MD* 8(1966): 374-381.

19128. Wall, Richard. "*An Giall and The Hostage* Compared." *MD* 18(1975): 165-172.

BENNETT, ARNOLD. 19129. Hepburn, James G. "The Notebook for *Riceyman Steps*." *PMLA* 78 (1963): 257-261.

19130. ----------. "Some Curious Realism in *Riceyman Steps*." *MFS* 8(1962): 116-126.

19131. Hynes, Samuel. "The Whole Contention Between Mr. Bennett and Mrs. Woolf." *Novel* 1(1967): 34-44.

19132. Kreutz, Irving. "Mr. Bennett and Mrs. Woolf." *MFS* 8(1962): 103-115.

19133. Roby, Kinley E. "Arnold Bennett's Social Consciousness." *MFS* 17(1971): 513-524.

See also 60, 18927.

BOLT, ROBERT. 19135. Atkins, Anselm. "Robert Bolt: Self, Shadow, and the Theater of Recognition." *MD* 10(1967): 182-188.

19136. McElrath, Joseph, Jr. "The Metaphoric Structure of *A Man for All Seasons*." *MD* 14(1971): 84-92.

BOND, EDWARD. 19137. Babula, William. "Scene Thirteen of Bond's *Saved*." *MD* 15(1972): 147-149.

19138. Barth, Adolf K. H. "The Aggressive 'Theatrum Mundi' of Edward Bond: *Narrow Road to the Deep North*." *MD* 18(1975): 189-214.

19139. Duncan, Joseph E. "The Child and the Old Man in the Plays of Edward Bond." *MD* 19 (1976): 1-10.

19140. Stoll, Karl-Heinz. "Interviews with Edward Bond and Arnold Wesker." *TCL* 22(1976): 411-432.

BOWEN, ELIZABETH. 19141. Davis, Robert Murray. "Contributions to *Night and Day* by Elizabeth Bowen, Graham Greene, and Anthony Powell." *SN* 3(1971): 401-404.

19142. Dorenkamp, Angela G. "'Fall or Leap': Bowens' *The Heart of the Day*." *Crit* 10,#3 (1968): 13-21.

19143. Heinemann, Alison. "The Indoor Landscape in Bowens' *The Death of the Heart*." *Crit* 10,#3(1968): 5-12.

19144. Hughes, Douglas A. "Cracks in the Psyche: Elizabeth Bowen's 'The Demon Lover'." *SSF* 10(1973): 411-413.

19145. Mitchell, Edward. "Themes in Elizabeth Bowen's Short Stories." *Crit* 8,#3(1966): 41-54.

19146. Van Duyn, Mona. "Pattern and Pilgrimage: A Reading of *The Death of the Heart*." *Crit* 4,#2(1961): 52-66.

19147. Wagner, Geoffrey. "Elizabeth Bowen and the Artificial Novel." *EIC* 13(1963): 155-163.

BRAINE, JOHN. 19148. Hurrell, John D. "Class and Conscience in John Braine and Kingsley Amis." *Crit* 2,#1(1958): 39-53.

See also 18925.

BRIDGES, ROBERT. 19149. Green, David Bonnell. "A New Letter of Robert Bridges to Coventry Patmore." *MP* 55(1958): 198-199.

19150. Peck, John. "Bridges' *Nero* and the Closet Tradition." *ELH* 38(1971): 591-615.

19151. Stanford, Donald. "Robert Bridges and the Free Verse Rebellion." *JML* 2(1971): 19-32.

19152. ----------. "Robert Bridges on His Poems and Plays: Unpublished Letters by Robert Bridges to Samuel Butler." *PQ* 50(1971): 281-291.

BRIDIE, JAMES. 19153. Luyben, Helen L. "Bridie's Last Play." *MD* 5(1963): 400-414.

19154. ----------. "James Bridie and the Prodigal Son Story." *MD* 7(1964): 35-45.

19155. Michie, James A. "Educating the Prophets." *MD* 11(1969): 429-431.

BROOKE, RUPERT. 19156. Moore, John Robert. "Dryden and Rupert Brooke." *MLR* 54 (1959): 226.

BROOKE-ROSE CHRISTINE. 19157. Hayman, David, and Keith Cohen. "An Interview with Christine Brooke-Rose." *Con L* 17(1976): 1-23.

BROPHY, BRIGID. 19158. Dock, Leslie. "An Interview with Brigid Brophy." *Con L* 17 (1976): 151-170.

BUNTING, BASIL. 19159. Suter, Anthony. "Time and the Literary Past in the Poetry of Basil Bunting." *Con L* 12(1971): 510-526.

BURGESS, ANTHONY. 19160. Aggeler, Geoffrey. "Incest and the Artist: Anthony Burgess's *MF* as Summation." *MFS* 18(1972): 529-543.

19161. Anderson, Ken. "A Note on A *Clockwork Orange*." *NCL* 2(Nov., 1972): 5-7.

19162. Brophy, Elizabeth. "'A Clockwork Orange': English and Nadsat." *NCL* 2(March, 1972): 4-6.

19163. Bunting, Charles T. "An Interview in New York with Anthony Burgess." *SN* 5(1973):

504-529.

19164. Connelly, Wayne C. "Optimism in Anthony Burgess's *A Clockwork Orange*." *Ext* 14 (1972): 25-29.

19165. Cullinan, John. "Anthony Burgess' *A Clockwork Orange*: Two Versions." *ELN* 9(1972): 287-292.

19166. ----------. "Anthony Burgess' 'The Muse: A Sort of SF Story.'" *SSF* 9(1972): 213-220.

19167. David, Beverly R. "Anthony Burgess: A Checklist (1956-1971)." *TCL* 19(1973): 181-188.

19168. Evans, Robert O. "Nadsat: The Orgot and Its Implications in Anthony Burgess' *A Clockwork Orange*." *JML* 1(1971): 406-410.

19169. ----------. "The *nouveau roman*, Russian Dystopias, and Anthony Burgess." *SLI* 6,#2(1973): 27-37.

19170. Holte, Carlton. "Additions to *Anthony Burgess: A Checklist (1956-1971)*." *TCL* 20(1974): 44-52.

19171. Plank, Robert. "The Place of Evil in Science Fiction." *Ext* 14(1973): 100-111.

19172. Stinson, John J. "*Nothing Like the Sun*: The Faces in Bella Cohen's Mirror." *JML* 5 (1976): 131-147.

CAMPBELL, ROY. 19173. Smith, Rowland. "Roy Campbell and His French Sources." *Comp L* 22(1970): 1-18.

CARY, JOYCE. 19174. Adams, Hazard. "Blake and Gully Jimson: English Symbolists." *Crit* 3,#1(1959): 3-14.

19175. ----------. "Joyce Cary: Posthumous Volumes and Criticism to Date." *TSLL* 1 (1959): 289-298.

19176. ----------. "Joyce Cary's Three Speakers." *MFS* 5(1959): 108-120.

19177. Battalia, Francis J. "Spurious Armageddon: Joyce Cary's *Not Honour More*." *MFS* 13(1967): 479-491.

19178. Beebe, Maurice, James Lee, and Sam Henderson. "Criticism of Joyce Cary: A Selected Checklist." *MFS* 9(1963): 284-288.

19179. Brawer, Judith. "The Triumph of Defeat: A Study of Joyce Cary's *First Trilogy*." *TSLL* 10(1969): 629-634.

19180. Eastman, Richard M. "Historical Grace in Cary's *A Fearful Joy*." *Novel* 1(1968): 150-157.

19181. Foster, Malcolm. "Fell of the Lion, Fleece of the Sheep." *MFS* 9(1963): 257-262.

19182. Fraser, Keath. "Potboiler to Artist: Joyce Cary and the Short Story." *SSF* 8 (1971): 617-626.

19183. French, Warren G. "Joyce Cary's American Rover Girl." *TSLL* 2(1960): 281-291.

19184. Friedman, Alan Warren. "Joyce Cary's Cubistic Morality." *Con L* 14(1973): 78-96.

19185. Fyfe, Christopher. "The Colonial Situation in *Mister Johnson*." *MFS* 9(1963): 226-230.

19186. Garrett, George. "The Major Poetry of Joyce Cary." *MFS* 9(1963): 245-256.

19187. Galligan, Edward L. "Intuition and Concept: Joyce Cary and the Critics." *TSLL* 8 (1967): 581-587.

19188. Hardy, Barbara. "Form in Joyce Cary's Novels." *EIC* 4(1954): 180-190.

19189. Hoffmann, Charles G. "The Captive and the Free: Joyce Cary's Unfinished Trilogy."

TSLL 5(1963): 17-24.

19190. ----------. "The Genesis and Development of Joyce Cary's First Trilogy." *PMLA* 78(1963): 431-439.

19191. ----------. "'They Want to Be Happy': Joyce Cary's Unfinished *Castle Corner* Series." *MFS* 9(1963): 217-225.

19192. Hopwood, Alison. "Separate Worlds: Joyce Cary's Nimmo Triology." *TSLL* 13(1971): 523-535.

19193. Karl, Frederick R. "Joyce Cary: The Moralist as Novelist." *TCL* 5(1960): 183-196.

19194. Lyons, Richard S. "Narrative Method in Cary's *To Be a Pilgrim*." *TSLL* 6(1964): 269-279.

19195. Meriwether, James B. "The Books of Joyce Cary: A Preliminary Bibliography of English and American Editions." *TSLL* 1(1959): 299-310.

19196. Mitchell, Giles. "Joyce Cary's *Prisoner of Grace*." *MFS* 9(1963): 263-275.

19197. Moody, Peter R. "Joyce Cary's Criticism of Flaubert." *CLA* 12(1968): 161-163.

19198. Nyce, Benjamin. "Joyce Cary's Political Trilogy: The Atmosphere of Power." *MLQ* 32(1971): 89-106.

19199. Pittock, Malcolm. "Joyce Cary; *A Fearful Joy*." *EIC* 13(1963): 428-432.

19200. Reed, Peter J. "'The Better the Heart': Joyce Cary's Sara Monday." *TSLL* 15(1973): 357-370.

19201. ----------. "Getting Stuck: Joyce Cary's Gulley Jimson." *TCL* 16(1970): 241-252.

19202. ----------. "Holding Back: Joyce Cary's *To Be a Pilgrim*." *Con L* 10(1969): 103-116.

19203. Rosenthal, Michael. "Joyce Cary's Comic Sense." *TSLL* 13(1971): 337-346.

19204. Ryan, Marjorie. "An Interpretation of Joyce Cary's *The Horse's Mouth*." *Crit* 2,#1 (1958): 29-38.

19205. Seltzer, Alvin J. "Speaking Out of Both Sides of *The Horse's Mouth*: Joyce Cary vs. Gulley Jimson." *Con L* 15(1974): 488-502.

19206. Shapiro, Stephen A. "Joyce Cary's *To Be a Pilgrim*: Mr. Facing-Both-Ways." *TSLL* 8 (1966): 81-91.

19207. ----------. "Leopold Bloom and Gulley Jimson: The Economics of Survival." *TCL* 10(1964) 3-11.

19208. Smith, B. R. "Moral Evaluation in *Mister Johnson*." *Crit* 11,#2(1969): 101-110.

19209. Stevenson, Lionel. "Joyce Cary and the Anglo-Irish Tradition." *MFS* 9(1963): 210-216.

19210. Stockholder, Fred. "The Triple Vision in Joyce Cary's First Trilogy." *MFS* 9 (1963): 231-244.

19211. Teeling, John, S. J. "Joyce Cary's Moral World." *MFS* 9(1963): 276-283.

19212. Weintraub, Stanley. "*Castle Corner*: Joyce Cary's *Buddenbrooks*." *Con L* 5(1964): 54-63.

19213. Wright, Andrew. "A Note on Joyce Cary's Reputation." *MFS* 9(1963): 207-209.

CHESTERTON, G. K. 19214. Poston, Lawrence, III. "'Markheim' and Chesterton's 'The Hammer of God.'" *NCF* 12(1957): 235-236.

See also 18922.

CLARKE, ARTHUR C. 19215. Beja, Mavis. "*2001*: Odyssey to Byzantium." *Ext* 10(1969): 67-68.

19216. Cary, Meredith. "Faustus Now." *HSL*

4(1972): 167-173.

19217. Plank, Robert. "1001 Interpretations of *2001*." *Ext* 11(1969): 23-24.

See also 100.

COMPTON-BURNETT, IVY. 19218. Curtis, Mary M. "The Moral Comedy of Miss Compton-Burnett." *Con L* 5(1964): 213-221.

19219. Greenfield, Stanley B. "'Pastors and Masters': The Spoils of Genius." *Criticism* 2 (1960): 66-80.

19220. McCabe, Bernard. "Ivy Compton-Burnett, An English Eccentric." *Crit* 3,#2(1960): 47-63.

CONRAD, JOSEPH. 19221. Andreach, Robert J. "The Two Narrators of 'Amy Foster.'" *SSF* 2 (1965): 262-269.

19222. Bantock, G. H. "Conrad and Politics." *ELH* 25(1958): 122-136.

19223. ----------. "The Two 'Moralities' of Joseph Conrad." *EIC* 3(1953): 125-142.

19224. Beebe, Maurice. "Criticism of Joseph Conrad: A Selected Checklist." *MFS* 10(1964): 81-106.

19225. ----------. "Criticism of Joseph Conrad: A Selected Checklist with an Index to Studies of Separate Works." *MFS* 1,#1(1955): 30-45.

19226. Beidler, Peter G. "Conrad's 'Amy Foster' and Chaucer's Prioress." *NCF* 30(1975): 111-115.

19227. Benson, Carl. "Conrad's Two Stories of Initiation." *PMLA* 69(1954): 46-56.

19228. Benson, Donald R. "'Heart of Darkness': The Grounds of Civilization in an Alien Universe." *TSLL* 7(1966): 339-347.

19229. Berman, Jeffrey. "Joseph Conrad: 'The Figure Behind the Veil.'" *JML* 6(1977): 196-208.

19230. Bojarski, Edmund A, and Harold Ray Stevens. "Joseph Conrad and the *Falconhurst*." *JML* 1(1970): 197-208.

19231. Bonney, William W. "Joseph Conrad and the Discontinuous Point of View." *JNT* 2(1972): 99-115.

19232. ----------. "Narrative Perspective in *Victory*: the Sematic Relevance." *JNT* 5(1975): 24-39.

19233. ----------. "Semantic and Structural Indeterminancy in *The Nigger of the 'Narcissus'*: An Experiment in Reading." *ELH* 40 (1973): 564-583.

19234. Boyle, Ted E. "Marlow's 'Lie' in *Heart of Darkness*." *SSF* 1(1964): 159-163.

19235. Bross, Addison C. "Beerbohm's 'The Feast' and Conrad's Early Fiction." *NCF* 26(1971): 329-336.

19236. Brown, Christopher. "Marlow and Dowell." *PQ* 56(1977): 136-140.

19237. Bruffee, Kenneth A. "The Lesser Nightmare: Marlowe's Lie in *Heart of Darkness*." *MLQ* 25(1964): 322-329.

19238. Bruss, Paul S. "Conrad's 'Youth': Problems in Interpretation." *Coll L* 1(1974): 218-229.

19239. ----------. "'The End of the Tether': Teleological Diminishing in Conrad's Early Metaphor of Navigation." *SSF* 13(1976): 311-320.

19240. ----------. "Marlow's Interview with Stein: The Implications of the Metaphor." *SN* 5(1973): 491-503.

19241. Bufkin, E. C. "Conrad, Grand Opera and *Nostromo*." *NCF* 30(1975): 206-214.

19242. Burgess, C. F. "Conrad's Pesky Russian." *NCF* 18(1963): 189-193.

19243. Burnstein, Janet. "On Ways of Knowing in *Lord Jim*." *NCF* 26(1972): 456-468.

19244. Canario, John W. "The Harlequin in *Heart of Darkness*." *SSF* 4(1967): 225-244.

19245. Carpenter, Richard C. "The Geography of Costaguana, or Where *Is* Sulaco?" *JML* 5 (1976): 321-326.

19246. Carroll, Welsey. "The Novelist as Artist." *MFS* 1,#1(1955): 2-8.

19247. Casey, Bill. "Andre Malraux's Heart of Darkness." *TCL* 5(1959): 21-26.

19248. Chaiken, Milton. "Zola and Conrad's 'The Idiots.'" *SP* 52(1955): 502-507.

19249. Cheney, Lynne. "Joseph Conrad's *The Secret Agent* and Graham Greene's *It's a Battle-field*: A Study in Structural Meaning." *MFS* 16 (1970): 117-131.

19250. Cook, Albert. "Conrad's Void." *NCF* 12(1958): 326-330.

19251. Covino, William A. "Lugubrious Drollery: Humor and Horror in Conrad's Fiction." *MFS* 23(1977): 217-225.

19252. Culbertson, Diana. "'The Informer' as Conrad's Little Joke." *SSF* 11(1974): 430-433.

19253. Curley, Daniel. "The Writer and His Use of Material: The Case of 'The Secret Sharer.'" *MFS* 13(1967): 179-194.

19254. Dahl, James C. "Kurtz, Marlow, Conrad and the Human Heart of Darkness." *SLI* 1,#2 (1968): 33-40.

19255. D'Avanzo, Mario L. "Conrad's Motley as an Organizing Metaphor in *Heart of Darkness*." *CLA* 9(1966): 289-291.

19256. Davis, Harold E. "Conrad's Revisions of *The Secret Agent*: A Study in Literary Impressionism." *MLQ* 19(1958): 244-254.

19257. ----------. "Symbolism in *The Nigger of the 'Narcissus.'*" *TCL* 2(1956): 26-29.

19258. Dike, Donald A. "The *Tempest of Axel Heyst*." *NCF* 17(1962): 95-113.

19259. Duncan-Jones, E. E. "Some Sources of *Chance*." *RES* 20(1969): 468-471.

19260. Dussinger, Gloria R. "'The Secret Sharer': Conrad's Psychological Study." *TSLL* 10 (1969): 599-608.

19261. Eddleman, Floyd Eugene, and David Leon Higdon. "The Typescript of Conrad's *Almayers' Folly*." *TSLL* 18(1976): 98-123.

19262. Emmet, Victor J. "The Aesthetics of Antiimperialism: Ironic Distributions of the Vergilian Epic Mode in Conrad's *Nostromo*." *SN* 4 (1972): 459-472.

19263. Epstein, Harry S. "*Lord Jim* as a Tragic Action." *SN* 5(1973): 229-247.

19264. Evans, Robert O. "Conrad's Underworld." *MFS* 2(1956): 55-62.

19265. ----------. "Further Comment on *The Heart of Darkness*." *MFS* 3(1957): 358-360.

19266. Feaster, John. "Conrad and Ford: Criticism at the End of the Tether." *JML* 2(1971): 417-421.

19267. Feder, Lillian. "Marlow's Descent into Hell." *NCF* 9(1955): 280-292.

19268. Fernando, Lloyd. "Conrad's Eastern Expatriates." *PMLA* 91(1976): 78-90.

19269. Fleishman, Avrom. "The Symbolic World of *The Secret Agent*." *ELH* 32(1965): 196-219.

19270. Foulke, Robert. "Postures of Belief in *The Nigger of the Narcissus*." *MFS* 17(1971): 249-292.

19271. Foye, Paul F., Bruce Harkness, and Nathan L. Marvin. "The Sailing Maneuver in 'The Secret Sharer.'" *JML* 2(1971): 119-123.

19272. Fradin, Joseph I. "Anarchist, Detective, and Saint: The Possibilities of Action in *The Secret Agent*." *PMLA* 83(1968): 1414-1422.

19273. ----------. Conrad's Everyman: *The Secret Agent*." *TSLL* 11(1969): 1023-1038.

19274. Freeman, Rosemary. "Conrad's *Nostromo*: A Source and its Use." *MFS* 7(1961): 317-326.

19275. Gatch, Katherine Haynes. "Conrad's Axel." *SP* 48(1951): 98-106.

19276. Geary, Edward A. "An Ashy Halo: Women as Symbols in *Heart of Darkness*." *SSF* 13 (1976): 499-506.

19277. Gertzman, Jay A. "Commitment and Sacrifice in 'Heart of Darkness': Marlow's Response to Kurtz." *SSF* 9(1972): 187-196.

19278. Gilliam, Harriett. "Time in Conrad's *Under Western Eyes*." *NCF* 31(1977): 421-439.

19279. ----------. "Two Russians in the West: Conrad's Razumov and Count Razumovsky." *JML* 6(1977): 311-315.

19280. ----------. "Vision in Conrad's *Under Western Eyes*." *TSLL* 19(1977): 24-41.

19281. Goens, Mary B. "The 'Mysterious and Effective Star': The Mythic World-View in Conrad's *Victory*." *MFS* 13(1967): 455-463.

19282. Goldknopf, David. "What's Wrong with Conrad: Conrad on Conrad." *Criticism* 10(1968): 54-64.

19283. Goodin, George. "The Personal and Political in *Under Western Eyes*." *NCF* 25(1970): 327-342.

19284. Gose, Elliott B., Jr. "'Cruel Devourer of the World's Light': *The Secret Agent*." *NCF* 15(1960): 39-51.

19285. ----------. "Pure Exercise of Imagination: Archetypal Symbolism in *Lord Jim*." *PMLA* 79(1964): 137-147.

19286. Gossman, Ann M, and Geo. W. Whiting. "The Essential Jim." *NCF* 61(1975): 75-80.

19287. Graver, Lawrence. "Conrad's First Story." *SSF* 2(1965): 164-169.

19288. ----------. "Critical Confusion and Conrad's 'The End of the Tether.'" *MFS* 9(1963): 390-393.

19289. Green, R. J. "Messrs. Wilcox and Kurtz, Hollow Men." *TCL* 14(1969): 231-240.

19290. Greene, Jesse D. "Diabolism, Pessimism, and Democracy: Notes on Melville and Conrad." *MFS* 8(1962): 287-305.

19291. Grieff, Louis K. and Shirley A. "Sucalo and Panama: A Geographical Source in Conrad's *Nostromo*." *JML* 3(1973): 102-104.

19292. Gross, Seymour L. "Conrad and *All the King's Men*." *TCL* 3(1957): 27-32.

19293. ----------. "The Devil in Samburan: Jones and Ricardo in *Victory*." *NCF* 16 (1961): 81-85.

19294. ----------. "A Further Note on the Function of the Frame in *The Heart of Darkness*." *MFS* 3(1957): 167-170.

19295. Gurko, Leo. "Death Journey in *The Nigger of the 'Narcissus*.'" *NCF* 15(1961): 301-311.

19296. ----------. "'The Secret Agent': Conrad's Vision of Megalopolis." *MFS* 4(1958): 307-318.

19297. Hagan, John. "Conrad's *Under Western Eyes*: The Question of Razumov's Guilt and Remorse." *SN* 1(1969): 310-322.

19298. ----------. "The Design of Conrad's *The Secret Agent*." *ELH* 22(1955): 148-164.

19299. Hagopian, John V. "The Pathos of 'Il Conde.'" *SSF* 3(1965): 31-38.

19300. Halverson, John, and Ian Watt. "The Original Nostromo: Conrad's Source." *RES* 10 (1959): 45-52.

19301. Hamer, Douglas. "Conrad: Two Biographical Episodes." *RES* 18(1967): 54-56.

19302. Harkness, Bruce. "Conrad on Galsworthy: The Time Scheme in *Fraternity*." *MFS* 1,#2(1955): 12-18.

19303. ----------. The Epigraph of Conrad's *Chance*." *NCF* 9(1954): 209-222.

19304. Harper, George Mills. "Conrad's Knitters and Homer's Cave of the Nymphs." *ELN* 1(1963): 53-57.

19305. Haugh, Robert F. "Conrad's *Chance*: Progression d'Effect." *MFS* 1,#1(1955): 9-15.

19306. Hay, Eloise Knapp. "Conrad Between Satre and Scorates." *MLQ* 34(1973): 85-97.

19307. Hay, Eloise K. "*Lord Jim*: From Sketch to Novel." *Comp L* 12(1960): 289-309.

19308. Heimer, Jackson W. "Betrayal, Confession, Attempted Redemption, and Punishment in *Nostromo*." *TSLL* 8(1967): 561-579.

19309. Helder, Jack. "Fool Convention and Conrad's Hollow Harlequin." *SSF* 12(1975): 361-368.

19310. Herndon, Richard. "The Genesis of Conrad's 'Amy Foster.'" *SP* 57(1960): 549-566.

19311. Hicks, John H. "Conrad's *Almayer's Folly*: Structure, Theme, and Critics." *NCF* 19 (1964): 17-31.

19312. Higdon, David Leon. "Chateau Borel, Pétrus Borel, and Conrad's *Under Western Eyes*." *SN* 3(1971): 99-102.

19313. ----------. "Conrad's *The Rover*: The Grammar of a Myth." *SN* 1(1969): 17-26.

19314. Hollahan, Eugene. "Beguiled into Action: Silence and Sound in *Victory*." *TSLL* 16 (1974): 349-362.

19315. Holland, Norman N. "Style as Character: *The Secret Agent*." *MFS* 12(1966): 221-231.

19316. Hoffman, Stanton de Voren. "The Hole in the Bottom of the Pail: Comedy and Theme in *Heart of Darkness*." *SSF* 2(1965): 113-123.

19317. Hopwood, Alison L. "Carlyle and Conrad: *Past and Present* and 'Heart of Darkness.'" *RES* 23(1972): 162-172.

19318. Hudspeth, Robert N. "Conrad's Use of Time in *Chance*." *NCF* 21(1966): 283-289.

19319. Izsak, Emily K. "*Under Western Eyes* and the Problems of Serial Publication." *RES* 23 (1972): 429-444.

19320. Jacobs, Robert G. "Comrade Ossipon's Favorite Saint: Lombroso and Conrad." *NCF* 23 (1968): 74-84.

19321. Johnson, Bruce. "Conrad's 'Falk': Manuscript and Meaning." *MLQ* 26(1965): 267-284.

19322. ----------. "Conrad's 'Karain' and *Lord Jim*." *MLQ* 24(1963): 13-20.

19323. ----------. "'Heart of Darkness' and the Problem of Emptiness." *SSF* 9(1972): 387-400.

19324. ----------. "Names, Naming, and the 'Inscrutable' in Conrad's *Heart of Darkness*." *TSLL* 12(1971): 675-688.

19325. Johnson, J. W. "Marlow and *Chance*: A Reappraisal." *TSLL* 10(1968): 91-105.

19326. Karn, Rose Salberg. "Silverberg and Conrad: Explorers of Inner Darkness." *Ext* 17 (1975): 18-28.

19327. Kaehele, Sharon, and Howard German. "Conrad's *Victory*: A Reassessment." *MFS* 10 (1964): 55-72.

19328. Karl, Frederick R. "Conrad and Gide: A Relationship and a Correspondence." *Comp L* 29(1977): 148-171.

19329. ----------. "Conrad and Pinker: Some Aspects of the Correspondence." *JML* 5(1976): 59-78.

19330. ----------. "Conrad, Wells, and the Two Voices." *PMLA* 88(1973): 1049-1065.

19331. ----------. "Conrad's Stein: The Destructive Element." *TCL* 3(1958): 163-169.

19332. ----------. "Introduction to the *Danse Macabre*: Conrad's *Heart of Darkness*." *MFS* 14(1968): 143-156.

19333. ----------. "Joseph Conrad, Norman Douglas, and the English Review." *JML* 2(1971): 342-356.

19334. ----------. "Joseph Conrad's Literary Theory." *Criticism* 2(1960): 317-335.

19335. ----------. "Review-Essay: Conrad Studies." *SN* 9(1977): 326-332.

19336. ----------. "The Rise and Fall of *Under Western Eyes*." *NCF* 13(1959): 313-327.

19337. ----------. "The Significance of the Revisions in the Early Versions of *Nostromo*." *MFS* 5(1959): 129-144.

19338. Kauver, Gerald B. "Marlowe as Liar." *SSF* 5(1968): 290-292.

19339. Kaye, Julian B. "Conrad's *Under Western Eyes* and Mann's *Doctor Faustus*." *Comp L* 9(1957): 60-65.

19340. Kehler, Joel R. "A Note on the Epigraph to Conrad's *The Rescue*." *ELN* 12(1975): 184-187.

19341. Ketterer, David. "'Beyond the Threshold' in Conrad's *Heart of Darkness*." *TSLL* 11(1969): 1013-1022.

19342. Kimpel, Ben, and T. C. Duncan Eaves. "The Geography and History in *Nostromo*." *MP* 56 (1958): 45-54.

19344. Kirschner, Paul. "Conrad's Strong Man." *MFS* 10(1964): 31-36.

19345. Kleiner, Elaine L. "Joseph Conrad's Forgotten Role in the Emergence of Science Fiction." *Ext* 15(1973): 25-34.

19346. Kramer, Dale. "Marlow, Myth, and Structure in *Lord Jim*." *Criticism* 8(1966): 263-279.

19347. Leiter, Louis H. "Echo Structures: Conrad's *The Secret Sharer*." *TCL* 5(1960): 159-175.

19348. Levin, Gerald H. "An Allusion to Tasso in Conrad's *Chance*." *NCF* 13(1958): 145-152.

19349. ----------. "The Scepticism of Marlow." *TCL* 3(1958): 177-183.

19350. Little, Roger. "Saint-John Perse and Joseph Conrad: Some Notes and an Uncollected Letter." *MLR* 72(1977): 811-814.

19351. Lincoln, Kenneth R. "Comic Light in *Heart of Darkness*." *MFS* 18(1972): 183-197.

19352. ----------. "Conrad's Mythic Humor." *TSLL* 17(1975): 635-651.

19353. Lodge, David. "Conrad's 'Victory' and 'The Tempest': An Amplification." *MLR* 59(1964): 195-200.

19354. Long, Robert Emmet. "*The Great Gatsby* and the Tradition of Joseph Conrad. Part I." *TSLL* 8(1966): 257-276.

19355. ----------. "*The Great Gatsby* and the Tradition of Joseph Conrad. Part II." *TSLL* 8(1966): 407-422.

19356. Lorch, Thomas M. "The Barrier Between Youth and Maturity in the Works of Joseph Conrad." *MFS* 10(1964): 73-80.

19357. Luecke, Sister Jane Marie. O.S.B. "Conrad's Secret and Its Agent." *MFS* 10(1964): 37-48.

19358. Lynskey, Winifred. "The Role of the Silver in *Nostromo*." *MFS* 1,#1(1955): 16-21.

19359. MacShawe, Frank. "Conrad on Melville." *AL* 29(1958): 463-464.

19360. Marten, Harry. "Conrad's Skeptic Reconsidered: A Study of Martin Decoud." *NCF* 27(1972): 81-94.

19361. Martin, David M. "The Function of the Intended in Conrad's 'Heart of Darkness.'" *SSF* 11(1974): 27-33.

19362. ----------. "The Paradox of Perspectivism in Conrad's 'The Lagoon.'" *SSF* 11 (1974): 306-307.

19363. Martin, Joseph H. "Edward Garnett and Conrad's Plunge into the 'Destructive Element.'" *TSLL* 15(1973): 517-536.

19364. Malbone, Raymond Gates. "'How to Be': Marlow's Quest in *Lord Jim*." *TCL* 10(1965): 172-180.

19365. Mathews, James W. "Ironic Symbolism in Conrad's 'Youth.'" *SSF* 11(1974): 117-123.

19366. Maxwell, J. C. "Mr. Stephens on *Heart of Darkness*." *EIC* 19(1969): 461-462.

19367. ----------. "Mr. Stephens on *Heart of Darkness*." *EIC* 20(1970): 118-119.

19368. McClure, John A. "The Rhetoric of Restraint in *Heart of Darkness*." *NCF* 32(1977): 310-326.

19369. McDowell, Frederick P. W. "Joseph Conrad's: Current Criticism and the 'Achievement and Decline' Question." *JML* 1(1970): 261-272.

19370. ----------. "Review Article: Recent Books on Joseph Conrad as Artist and Philosopher." *PQ* 51(1972): 922-939.

19371. ----------. "Review Article: Two Books on Conrad." *PQ* 46(1967): 109-124.

19372. McIntyre, Allan O. "Conrad on the Functions of the Mind." *MLQ* 25(1964): 187-197.

19373. McLauchlan, Juliet. "The Politics of *Nostromo*." *EIC* 17(1967): 398-406.

19374. ----------. "The Politics of *Nostromo*." *EIC* 18(1968): 475-477.

19375. Messenger, Ann P, and William E. Messenger. "'One of Us': A Biblical Allusion in

Conrad's *Lord Jim*." *ELN* 9(1971): 129-132.

19376. Miller, James E., Jr. "*The Nigger of the 'Narcissus*': A Re-examination." *PMLA* 66 (1951): 911-918.

19377. Moore, Carlisle. "Conrad and the Novel as Ordeal." *PQ* 42(1963): 55-74.

19378. Moynihan, William T. "Conrad's 'The End of the Tether': A New Reading." *MFS* 4(1958): 173-177.

19379. Mudrick, Marvin. "The Artist's Conscience and *The Nigger of the Narcissus*." *NCF* 11(1957): 288-297.

19380. Nash, Christopher. "More Light on *The Secret Agent*." *RES* 20(1969): 322-327.

19381. Nettels, Elsa. "The Grotesque in Conrad's Fiction." *NCF* 29(1974): 144-163.

19382. ----------. "James and Conrad on the Art of Fiction." *TSLL* 14(1972): 529-543.

19383. Newell, Kenneth B. "The Destructive Element and Related 'Dream' Passages in the *Lord Jim* Manuscript." *JML* 1(1970): 30-44.

19384. ----------. "The Yellow-Dog Incident in Conrad's *Lord Jim*." *SN* 3(1971): 26-33.

19385. Oates, Joyce Carol. "'The Immense Indifference of Things': The Tragedy of Conrad's *Nostromo*." *Novel* 9(1975): 5-22.

19386. O'Grady, Walter. "On Plot in Modern Fiction: Hardy, James, and Conrad." *MFS* 11(1965): 107-115.

19387. Owen, Guy, Jr. "A Note on *Heart of Darkness*." *NCF* 12(1957): 168-169.

19388. Park, Douglas B. "Conrad's *Victory*: The Anatomy of a Pose." *NCF* 31(1976): 150-169.

19389. Perry, John Oliver. "Action, Vision, or Voice: The Moral Dilemmas in Conrad's Tale-Telling." *MFS* 10(1964): 3-14.

19390. Philips, Steven R. "The Monomyth and Literary Criticism." *Coll L* 2(1975): 1-16.

19391. Raskin, Jonah. "*Heart of Darkness*: The Manuscript Revisions." *RES* 18(1967): 30-39.

19392. ----------. "*Nostromo*: the Argument from Revision." *EIC* 18(1968): 183-192.

19393. Reid, Stephen. "The 'Unspeakable Rites' in *Heart of Darkness*." *MFS* 9(1963): 347-356.

19394. Ridley, Florence H. "The Ultimate Meaning of 'Heart of Darkness.'" *NCF* 18(1963): 43-53.

19395. Rogers, William N., II. "The Game of Dominoes in *Heart of Darkness*." *ELN* 13(1975): 42-45.

19396. Rose, Alan M. "Conrad and the Sirens of Decadence." *TSLL* 11(1969): 795-810.

19397. Rosenfield, Claire. "An Archetypal Analysis of Conrad's *Nostromo*." *TSLL* 3(1962): 510-534.

19398: Ryf, Robert S. "Conrad's Stage *Victory*." *MD* 7(1964): 148-160.

19399. ----------. "*The Secret Agent* on Stage." *MD* 15(1972): 54-67.

19400. Said, Edward W. "Conrad: The Presentation of Narrative." *Novel* 7(1974): 116-132.

19401. Saveson, John E. "Conrad's View of Primitive Peoples in *Lord Jim* and *Heart of Darkness*." *MFS* 16(1970): 163-183.

19402. ----------. "Contemporary Psychology in 'The Nigger of the *Narcissus*.'" *SSF* 7 (1970): 219-231.

19403. ----------. "Marlow's Psychological Vocabulary in *Lord Jim*." *TSLL* 12(1970): 457-470.

19404. ----------. "The Moral Discovery of 'Under Western Eyes.'" *Criticism* 14(1972): 32-48.

19405. ----------. "*Nostromo* and the London *Times*." *RES* 24(1973): 52-58.

19406. Schenck, Mary-Low. "Seamanship in Conrad's 'The Secret Sharer.'" *Criticism* 15(1973): 1-15.

19407. Schneider, Daniel J. "Symbolism in Conrad's *Lord Jim*: The Total Pattern." *MFS* 12 (1966): 427-438.

19408. Schwab, Arnold T. "Conrad's American Speeches and His Reading from *Victory*." *MP* 62(1965): 342-347.

19409. ----------. "Joseph Conrad and Warrington Dawson." *MP* 68(1971): 364-374.

19410. ----------. "Joseph Conrad's American Friend: Correspondence with James Huneker." *MP* 52(1955): 222-232.

19411. Schwartz, Daniel R. "The Journey to Patusan: The Education of Jim and Marlow in Conrad's *Lord Jim*." *SN* 4(1972): 442-458.

19412. ----------. "The Lepidopterist's Revenge: Theme and Structure in Conrad's 'An Anarchist.'" *SSF* 8(1971): 330-334.

19413. ----------. "The Self-Deceiving Narrator of Conrad's 'Il Conde.'" *SSF* 6(1969): 187-193.

19414. ----------. "The Significance of the Language Teacher in Conrad's *Under Western Eyes*." *JNT* 6(1976): 101-115.

19415. Sherry, Norman. "Conrad and the Bangkok *Times*." *NCF* 20(1965): 255-266.

19416. ----------. "Conrad and the S. S. *Vidar*." *RES* 14(1963): 157-163.

19417. ----------. "Conrad's Source for Lord Jim." *MLR* 59(1964): 545-558.

19418. ----------. "Conrad's Ticket-of-Leave Apostle." *MLR* 64(1969): 749-758.

19419. ----------. "'Exact Biography' and *The Shadow-Line*." *PMLA* 79(1964): 620-625.

19420. ----------. "The Greenwich Bomb Outrage and *The Secret Agent*." *RES* 18(1967): 412-428.

19421. ----------. "*Lord Jim* and 'The Secret Sharer.'" *RES* 16(1965): 378-392.

19422. ----------. "The Pilgrim Ship in *Lord Jim*: Conrad's Two Sources." *PQ* 44(1965): 88-99.

19423. ----------. "Sir Ethelred in *The Secret Agent*." *PQ* 48(1969): 108-115.

19424. ----------. "'Rajah Laut'—A Quest for Conrad's Source." *MP* 62(1964): 22-41.

19425. Simmons, J. L. "The Dual Morality in Conrad's 'Secret Sharer.'" *SSF* 2(1965): 209-220.

19426. Smith, David R. "Nostromo and the Three Sisters." *SEL* 2(1962): 497-508.

19427. ----------. "'One More Word' about *The Nigger of the 'Narcissus*.'" *NCF* 23(1968): 201-216.

19428. Smoller, Sanford J. "A Note on Joseph Conrad's Fall and Abyss." *MFS* 155(1969): 261-264.

19429. Spector, Robert D. "Irony as Theme: Conrad's *Secret Agent*." *NCF* 13(1958): 69-71.

19430. Stark, Bruce R. "Kurtz's Intended: The Heart of *Heart of Darkness*." *TSLL* 16(1974): 535-555.

19431. Stallman, Robert Wooster. "Conrad and *The Great Gatsby*." *TCL* 1(1955): 5-12.

19432. ----------. "Time and *The Secret Agent*." *TSLL* 1(1959): 101-122.

19433. Stegmaier, E. "The 'Would-scene' in Joseph Conrad's 'Lord Jim' and 'Nostromo.'" *MLR* 67(1972): 517-523.

19434. Stein, William Bysshe. "Conrad's East: Time, History, Action, and *Maya*." *TSLL* 7 (1965): 265-283.

19435. ----------. "The Lotus Posture and *The Heart of Darkness*." *MFS* 2(1956): 235-237.

19436. Stephens, R. C. "*Heart of Darkness*." *EIC* 19(1969): 463-466.

19437. ----------. "*Heart of Darkness*: Marlow's 'Spectral Moonshine.'" *EIC* 19(1969): 273-284.

19438. Tanner, J. E. "The Chronology and the Enigmatic End of *Lord Jim*." *NCF* 21(1967): 369-380.

19439. Thale, Jerome. "The Narrator as Hero." *TCL* 3(1957): 69-73.

19440. Thornton, Weldon. "An Episode from Anglo-Irish History in Conrad's *The Secret Agent*." *ELN* 10(1973): 286-289.

19441. Tick, Stanley. "The Gods of *Nostromo*." *MFS* 10(1964): 15-26.

19442. Tillyard, E. M. W. "*The Secret Agent* Reconsidered." *EIC* 11(1961): 309-318.

19443. Toliver, Harold E. "Conrad's *Arrow of Gold* and Pastoral Tradition." *MFS* 8(1962): 148-158.

19444. Tolley, A. T. "Conrad's 'Favorite' Story." *SSF* 3(1966): 314-320.

19445. Wagner, Geoffrey. "The Novel of Empire." *EIC* 20(1970): 229-242.

19446. Walsh, Dennis M. "Conrad's 'Typhoon' and the Book of Genesis." *SSF* 11(1974): 99-101.

19447. Walton, James. "Conrad and Naturalism: The Secret Agent." *TSLL* 9(1967): 289-301.

19448. ----------. "Mr. X's 'Little Joke': The Design of Conrad's 'The Informer.'" *SSF* 4 (1967): 322-333.

19449. ----------. "Conrad, Dickens, and the Detective Novel." *NCF* 23(1969): 446-462.

19450. Wasserman, Jerry. "Narrative Presence: The Illusion of Language in *Heart of Darkness*." *SN* 6(1974): 327-338.

19451. Watson, Wallace. "'The Shade of Old Flaubert' and Maupassant's Art Impeccable (Presque)': French Influences on the Development of Conrad's Marlowe." *JNT* 7(1977): 37-56.

19452. Watt, Ian. "Conrad Criticism and *The Nigger of the 'Narcissus*.'" *NCF* 12(1958): 257-283.

19453. ----------. "Conrad's Preface to *The Nigger of the 'Narcissus*.'" *Novel* 7(1974): 101-115.

19454. Watts, C. T. "Joseph Conrad and the Ranee of Sarawak." *RES* 15(1964): 404-407.

19455. ----------. "A Minor Source for *Nostromo*." *RES* 16(1965): 182-184.

19456. Weston, John Howard. "'Youth': Conrad's Irony and Time's Darkness." *SSF* 11(1974): 399-407.

19457. Whitehead, Lee M. "Alma Renamed Lena in Conrad's *Victory*." *ELN* 3(1965): 55-57.

19458. ----------. "*Nostromo*: The Tragic 'Idea.'" *NCF* 23(1969): 463-475.

19459. Vidan, Ivo. "One Source of Conrad's *Nostromo*." *RES* 7(1956): 287-293.

19460. ----------. "The Politics of *Nostromo*." *EIC* 17(1967): 392-398.

19461. Widmer, Kingsley. "Conrad's Pyrrhonistic Conservatism: Ideological Melodrama Around 'Simple Ideas.'" *Novel* 7(1974): 133-142.

19462. ----------. "Conrad's Pyrrhic *Victory*." *TCL* 5(1959): 123-130.

19463. Wiesenfarth, Joseph, F. S. C. "Stevie and the Structure of *The Secret Agent*." *MFS* 13(1967: 513-517.

19464. Wilcox, Stewart C. "Conrad's 'Complicated Presentations' of Symbolic Imagery in *Heart of Darkness*." *PQ* 39(1960): 1-17.

19465. Wilding, Michael. "The Politics of *Nostromo*." *EIC* 16(1966): 441-456.

19466. ----------. "The Politics of *Nostromo*." *EIC* 18(1968): 234-236.

19467. Williams, George Walton. "The Turn of the Tide in *Heart of Darkness*." *MFS* 9(1963): 171-173.

19468. Williams, Porter, Jr. "The Brand of Cain in 'The Secret Sharer.'" *MFS* 10(1964): 27-30.

19469. ----------. "The Matter of Conscience in Conrad's The Secret *Sharer*." *PMLA* 79 (1964): 626-630.

19470. ----------. "Story and Frame in Conrad's 'The Tale.'" *SSF* 5(1968): 179-185.

19471. Wills, John Howard. "Adam, Axel, and 'Il Conde.'" *MFS* 1,#1(1955): 22-25.

19472. ----------. "A Neglected Masterpiece: Conrad's *Youth*." *TSLL* 4(1963): 591-601.

19473. Worth, George J. "Conrad's Debt to Maupassant in the Preface to *The Nigger of the 'Narcissus*.'" *JEGP* 54(1955): 700-704.

19474. Wright, Walter F. "The Truth of My Own Sensations." *MFS* 1,#1(1955): 26-29.

19475. Yates, Norris W. "Social Comment in *The Nigger of the Narcissus*." *PMLA* 79(1964): 183-185.

19476. Zuckerman, Jerome. "Contrapuntal Structure in Conrad's *Chance*." *MFS* 10(1964): 49-54.

19477. ----------. "The Motif of Cannibalism in *The Secret Agent*." *TSLL* 10(1968): 295-299.

19478. ----------. "'A Smile of Fortune': Conrad's Interesting Failure." *SSF* 1(1964): 99-102.

See also 80, 84, 5123, 5190, 5556, 15335.
CROWTHERS, DAVID. 19479. Baylen, Joseph O. *"Some Memories of an Edwardian Childhood"* [introduction and Crowthers' text]. *SLI* 1,#1(1968): 67-71.

DAVIE, DONALD. 19480. Bergonzi, Bernard. "Davie, Larkin, and the State of England." *Con L* 18(1977): 343-360.

DE LA MARE, WALTER. 19481. Richey, Clarence W. "The Falling Portrait: A Note Upon Walter De La Mare's Use of Superstition in 'The Picture.'" *NCL* 2(May, 1972): 9-10.

DELANEY, SHELAGH. 19482. Oberg, Arthur K. "*A Taste of Honey* and the Popular Play." *Con L* 7(1966): 160-167.

DENNIS, NIGEL. 19483. Onley, James. "*Cards of Identity* and the Satiric Mode." *SN* 3(1971): 374-389.

DICKINSON, G. LOWES. See 19598, 19609.
DOUGHTY, CHARLES. 19484. Bishop, Jonathan. "The Heroic Ideal in Doughty's *Arabia Deserta*."

MLQ 21(1960): 59-68.

19485. Holloway, John. "Poetry and Plain Language: The Verse of C. M. Doughty." *EIC* 4 (1954): 58-70.

DOYLE, ARTHUR CONAN.   19486. Baylen, Joseph O. "A Letter from Conan Doyle on the 'Novelist Journalist.'" *NCF* 12(1958): 321-323.

19487. Kissane, John M. "Sherlock Holmes and the Ritual of Reason." *NCF* 17(1963): 353-362.

19488. Moore, John Robert. "Conan Doyle, Tennyson, and *Rasselas*." *NCF* 7(1952): 221-223.

DRABBLE, MARGARET.   19489. Hardin, Nancy S. "An Interview with Margaret Drabble." *Con L* 14 (1973): 273-295.

19490. Libby, Marion Vlastos. "Fate and Feminism in the Novels of Margaret Drabble." *Con L* 16(1975): 175-192.

DURRELL, LAWRENCE.   19491. Baldanza, Frank. "Lawrence Durrell's 'Word Continuum.'" *Crit* 4,#2 (1961): 3-17.

19492. Beebe, Maurice. "Criticism of Lawrence Durrell: A Selected Checklist." *MFS* 13 (1967): 417-421.

19493. Brown, Sharon Lee. "*The Black Book*: A Search for Method." *MFS* 13(1967): 319-328.

19494. Burns, J. Christopher. "Durrell's Heraldic Universe." *MFS* 13(1967): 375-388.

19495. Dare, Captain H. "The Quest for Durrell's Scobie." *MFS* 10(1964): 379-383.

19496. Friedman, Alan Warren. "A 'Key' to Lawrence Durrell." *Con L* 8(1967): 31-42.

19497. ----------. "Place and Durrell's Island Books." *MFS* 13(1967): 329-341.

19498. Godshalk, William Leigh. "Aspects of Lawrence Durrell." *JML* 1(1971): 439-445.

19499. ----------. "Some Sources of Durrell's *Alexandria Quartet*." *MFS* 13(1967): 361-374.

19500. Gossman, Ann. "Some Characters in Search of a Mirror." *Crit* 8,#3(1966): 79-84.

19501. Goulianos, Joan. "A Conversation with Lawrence Durrell about Art, Analysis, and Politics." *MFS* 17(1971): 159-166.

19502. Hagopian, John V. "The Resolution of the *Alexandria Quartet*." *Crit* 7,#1(1964): 97-106.

19503. Katope, Christopher. "Cavafy and Durrell's *The Alexandria Quartet*." *Comp L* 21 (1969): 125-137.

19504. Kruppa, Joseph E. "Durrell's *Alexandria Quartet* and the 'Implosion' of the Modern Consciousness." *MFS* 13(1967): 401-416.

19505. Lemon, Lee T. "*The Alexandria Quartet*: Form and Fiction." *Con L* 4(1963): 327-338.

19506. Levitt, Morton P. "Art and Correspondences: Durrell, Miller, and *The Alexandria Quartet*." *MFS* 13(1967): 299-318.

19507. Morcos, Mona Louis. "Elements of the Auto-biographical in *The Alexandria Quartet*." *MFS* 13(1967): 343-359.

19508. Proser, Matthew N. "Darley's Dilemma: The Problem of Structure in Durrell's *Alexandria Quartet*." *Crit* 4,#2(1961): 18-28.

19509. Read, Phyllis, J. "The Illusion of Personality: Cyclical Time in Durrell's *Alexandria Quartet*." *MFS* 13(1967): 389-399.

19510. Taylor, Chet. "Dissonance and Digression: The Ill-Fitting Fusion of Philosophy and Form in Lawrence Durrell's *Alexandria Quartet*." *MFS* 17(1971): 167-179.

19511. Trail, George Y. "Durrell's Io: A Note on *Tunc* and *Nunquam*." *NCL* 5(May, 1975): 9-12.

19512. Weatherhead, A. K. "Romantic Anachronism in *The Alexandria Quartet*." *MFS* 10 (1964): 128-136.

19513. Wedin, Warren. "The Artist as Narrator in *The Alexandria Quartet*." *TCL* 18(1972): 175-180.

19514. Weigel, John A. "Lawrence Durrell's First Novel." *TCL* 14(1968): 75-83.

See also 18927.

EMANUEL, VICTOR ROUSSEAU.   19515. Mullen, Richard D. "H. G. Wells and Victor Rousseau Emanuel: *When the Sleeper Wakes and the Messiah of the Cylinder*." *Ext* 8(1967): 31-63.

EMPSON, WILLIAM.   19516. Empson, William. "Answers to Comments." *EIC* 3(1953): 114-120.

19517. Ford, Newell F. "Empson's and Ransom's Mutilations of Texts." *PQ* 29(1950): 81-84.

19518. Jensen, James. "The Construction of *Seven Types of Ambiguity*." [with comments by Empson, Robert Graves and I. A. Richards] *MLQ* 27 (1966): 243-259.

19519. ----------. "Some Ambiguous Preliminaries." *Criticism* 8(1966): 349-361.

19520. Schutz, Fred. "Aparian Imagery in Empson's 'To An Old Lady.'" *NCL* 4(March, 1974): 5-7.

19521. Sleight, Richard. "Mr. Empson's Complex Words." *EIC* 2(1952): 325-337.

ENRIGHT, D. J.   19522. Gardner, Philip. "D. J. Enright Under the Cherry Tree." *Con L* 9 (1968): 100-111.

FLINT, F. S.   19523. Breunig, Le Roy C. "F. S. Flint, Imagism's '*Maître d'Ecole*'." *Comp L* 4(1952): 118-136.

See also 4969.

FORD, FORD MADOX.   19524. Ashwell, Duncan. "The Saddest Storyteller in Ford's *The Good Soldier*." *CLA* 14(1970): 187-196.

19525. Baernstein, Jo-Ann. "Image, Identity, and Insight in *The Good Solider*." *Crit* 9,#1(1966): 19-42.

19526. Barnes, Daniel R. "Ford and the 'Slaughtered Saints': A New Reading of *The Good Soldier*." *MFS* 14(1968): 157-170.

19527. Beebe, Maurice, and Robert G. Johnson. "Criticism of Ford Madox Ford: A Selected Checklist." *MFS* 9(1963): 94-100.

19528. Bender, Todd K. "The Sad Tale of Dowell: Ford Madox Ford's *The Good Solider*." *Criticism* 4(1962): 353-368.

19529. Borowitz, Helen Osterman. "The Paint Beneath the Prose: Ford Madox Ford's Pre-Raphaelite Ancestry." *MFS* 21(1975): 483-498.

19530. Bort, Barry D. "*The Good Soldier*: Comedy or Tragedy?" *TCL* 12(1967): 194-202.

19531. Brown, Christopher. "Marlow and Dowell." *PQ* 56(1977): 136-140.

19532. Cassell, Richard A. "The Two Sorrels of Ford Madox Ford." *MP* 59(1961): 114-121.

19533. Cohen, Mary. "*The Good Solider*: Outworn Codes." *SN* 5(1973): 284-297.

19534. Cox, James Trammell. "The Finest French Novel in the English Language." *MFS* 9(1963): 79-93.

19535. ----------. "Ford's 'Passion for Provence.'" *ELH* 28(1961): 383-398.

19536. Feaster, John. "Conrad and Ford: Criticism at the End of the Tether." *JML* 2(1971): 417-421.

19537. Gabbay, Lydia Rivlin. "The Four Square Coterie: A Comparison of Ford Madox Ford and Henry James." *SN* 6(1974): 439-453.

19538. Gordon, Ambrose. "At the Edge of Silence: *The Good Soldier* as 'War Novel.'" *MFS* 9(1963): 67-68.

19539. ----------. *Parade's End*: Where War Was Fairy Tale." *TSLL* 5(1963): 25-41.

19540. Gose, Elliott B., Jr. "The Strange Irregular Rhythm: An Analysis of *The Good Soldier*." *PMLA* 72(1957): 494-509.

19541. Griffith, Marlene. "A Double Meaning of *Parade's End*." *MFS* 9(1963): 25-38.

19542. Hafley, James. "The Moral Structure of *The Good Soldier*." *MFS* 5(1959): 121-128.

19543. Harvey, David D. *Pro Patria Mori*: The Neglect of Ford's Novels in England." *MFS* 9(1963): 3-16.

19544. Heldman, James M. "The Last Victorian Novel: Technique and Theme in *Parade's End*." *TCL* 18(1972): 271-284.

19545. Henigham, T. J. "*The Desirable Alien*: A Source for Ford Madox Ford's *The Good Soldier*." *TCL* 11(1965): 25-29.

19546. Howarth, Herbert. "Hewlett and Ford among Renaissance Women." *JML* 5(1976): 79-88.

19547. Hungiville, Maurice. "'The Last Happy Time': Ford Madox Ford in America." *JML* 6 (1977): 209-221.

19548. Huntley. H. Robert. "Flaubert and Ford: The Fallacy of 'Le Mot Juste.'" *ELN* 4 (1967): 283-287.

19549. ----------. "*The Good Soldier* and *Die Wahlverwandtschaften*." *Comp L* 19(1967): 133-141.

19550. Hynes, Samuel. "Ford and the Spirit of Romance." *MFS* 9(1963): 17-24.

19551. ----------. "Ford Madox Ford: 'Three Dedicatory Letters to *Parade's End*' with Commentary and Notes." *MFS* 16(1970): 515-528.

19552. Johnson, Ann S. "Narrative Form in *The Good Soldier*." *Crit* 11,#2(1969): 70-80.

19553. Kennedy, Alan. "Tietjens' Travels: *Parade's End* as Comedy." *TCL* 16(1970): 85-95.

19554. Lehan, Richard. "Ford Madox Ford and the Absurd: *The Good Soldier*." *TSLL* 5(1963): 219-231.

19555. Lentz, Vern B. "Ford's Good Narrator." *SN* 5(1973): 483-490.

19556. Levin, Gerald. "Character and Myth in Ford's *Parade's End*." *JML* 1(1970): 183-196.

19557. Ludwig, Richard M. "The Reputation of Ford Madox Ford." *PMLA* 76(1961): 544-551.

19558. McFate, Patricia, and Bruce Golden. "*The Good Soldier*: A Tragedy of Self-Deception." *MFS* 9(1963): 50-60.

19559. Moser, Thomas C. "From Olive Garnett's Diary: Impressions of Ford Madox Ford and His Friends, 1890-1906." *TSLL* 16(1974): 511-533.

19560. Ray, Robert J. "Style in *The Good Soldier*." *MFS* 9(1963): 61-66.

19561. Seiden, Melvin. "Persecution and Paranoia in *Parade's End*." *Criticism* 8(1966): 246-262.

19562. Stang, Sondra J. "A Reading of Ford's *The Good Soldier*." *MLQ* 30(1969): 545-563.

19563. Thornton, Lawrence. "Escaping the Impasse: Criticism and the Mitosis of *The Good Soldier*." *MFS* 21(1975): 237-241.

19564. Tytell, John. "The Jamesian Legacy in *The Good Soldier*." *SN* 3(1971): 365-373.

19565. Wagner, Geoffrey. "Ford Madox Ford: the Honest Edwardian." *EIC* 17(1967): 75-88.

19566. Webb, Igor. "Marriage and Sex in the Novels of Ford Madox Ford." *MFS* 23(1977): 586-592.

19567. Weisenfarth, Joseph F.S.C. "Criticism and the Semiosis of *The Good Solider*." *MFS* 9(1963): 39-49.

See also 5908, 18922.

FORSTER, E. M. 19568. Allen, Glen O. "Structure, Symbol, Theme in E. M. Forster's *A Passage to India*." *PMLA* 70(1955): 934-954.

19569. Austin, Don. "The Problem of Continuity in Three Novels by E. M. Forster." *MFS* 7(1961): 217-228.

19570. Beebe, Maurice, and Joseph Brogunier. "Criticism of E. M. Forster: A Selected Checklist." *MFS* 7(1961): 284-292.

19571. Benson, Alice R. "E. M. Forster's Dialectic: *Howard's End*." *MFS* 1,#4(1955): 17-22.

19572. Bolling, Douglas. "The Distanced Heart: Artistry in E. M. Forster's *Maurice*." *MFS* 20(1974): 157-167.

19573. Berman, Jeffrey. "Forster's Other Cave: The Platonic Structure of *The Machine Stops*." *Ext* 17(1976): 172-181.

19574. Churchill, Thomas. "Place and Personality in *Howard's End*." *Crit* 5,#1(1962): 61-73.

19575. Clubb, Roger L. "*A Passage to India*: The Meaning of the Marabar Caves." *CLA* 6 (1963): 184-193.

19576. Crews, Frederick C. "E. M. Forster: The Limitations of Mythology." *Comp L* 12(1960): 97-112.

19577. ----------. "*The Longest Journey* and the Perils of Humanism." *ELH* 26(1959): 575-596.

19578. Das, G. K. "The Genesis of Professor Godbole." *RES* 28(1977): 56-60.

19579. Dauner, Louise. "What Happened in the Cave? Reflections on *A Passage to India*." *MFS* 7(1961): 258-270.

19580. Donald, Miles. "*Howard's End*." *EIC* 20(1970): 108-109.

19581. Ellem, Elizabeth Wood. "E. M. Forster's Greenwood." *JML* 5(1976): 89-98.

19582. Fleishman, Avrom. "Being and Nothing in 'A Passage to India.'" *Criticism* 15(1973): 109-125.

19583. Friedman, Albert B. "Forster, Dostoyevsky, Akutagawa, and 'St. Peter and His Mother.'" *ELN* 1(1964): 286-291.

19584. Fussell, Paul, Jr. "E. M. Forster's Mrs. Moore: Some Suggestions." *PQ* 32(1953): 388-395.

19585. Gillen, Francis. "*Howard's End* and the Neglected Narrator." *Novel* 3(1970): 139-152.

19586. Goldman, Mark. "Virginia Woolf and E. M. Forster: A Critical Dialogue." *TSLL* 7(1966): 387-400.

19587. Green, R. J. "Messrs. Wilcox and Kurtz, Hollow Men." *TCL* 14(1969): 231-240.

19588. Hall, James. "Forster's Family Reunions." *ELH* 25(1958): 60-78.

19589. Hanquart, Evelyne. "The Manuscript of Forster's *The Longest Journey*." *RES* 25(1974):

152-162.

19590. Harvey, John. "Imagination and Moral Theme in E. M. Forster's *The Longest Journey*." *EIC* 6(1956): 418-433.

19591. Hoffman, Frederick J. "*Howard's End* and the Bogey of Progress." *MFS* 7(1961): 243-257.

19592. Hollingsworth, Keith. "*A Passage to India*: The Echoes in the Marabar Caves." *Criticism* 4(1962): 210-224.

19593. Horowitz, Ellin. "The Communal Ritual and the Dying God in E. M. Forster's *A Passage to India*." *Criticism* 6(1964): 70-88.

19594. Hotchkiss, Joyce. "Romance and Reality: The Dualistic Style of E. M. Forster's *Maurice*." *JNT* 4(1974): 163-175.

19595. Hoy Cyrus. "Forster's Metaphysical Novel." *PMLA* 75(1960): 126-136.

19596. Hunt, John Dixon. "Muddle and Mystery in *A Passage to India*." *ELH* 33(1966): 497-517.

19597. Italia, Paul G. "On Miss Quested's Given Name, in E. M. Forster's *A Passage to India*." *ELN* 11(1973): 118-120.

19598. Kennard, Jean E. "*A Passage to India* and Dickinson's Saint at Benares." *SN* 5 (1973): 417-427.

19599. Klingopulos, G. D. "E. M. Forster's Sense of History: and Cavafy." *EIC* 8(1958): 156-165.

19600. Lee, L. L. "Oedipus at Colonus: The Modern Vulgarizations of Forster and Kay Cicellis." *SSF* 8(1971): 561-567.

19601. Levine, June Perry. "An Analysis of the Manuscripts of *A Passage to India*." *PMLA* 85 (1970): 284-294.

19602. Lucas, John. "Wagner and Forster: *Parsifal* and *A Room with a View*." *ELH* 33(1966): 92-117.

19603. Magnus, John. "Ritual Aspects of Forster's *The Longest Journey*." *MFS* 13(1967): 195-210.

19604. Malek, James S. "Forster's 'Albergo Empedocle': A Precursor of *Maurice*." *SSF* 11(1974): 427-430.

19605. ----------. "Forster's 'The Classical Annex': The Triumph of Hellenism." *NCL* 5 (Nov. 1975): 4-6.

19606. ----------. "Persona, Shadow, and Society: A Reading of Forster's 'The Other Boat.'" *SSF* 14(1977): 21-27.

19607. Maskell, Duke. "Style and Symbolism in *Howard's End*." *EIC* 19(1969): 292-308.

19608. Martin, John S. "Mrs. Moore and the Marabar Caves: A Mythological Reading." *MFS* 11 (1965): 429-433.

19609. McDowell, Frederick P. W. "E. M. Forster and Goldsworthy Lower Dickinson." *SN* 5 (1973): 441-456.

19610. ----------. "E. M. Forster's Theory of Literature." *Criticism* 8(1966): 19-43.

19611. ----------. "Forster's Many-Faceted Universe: Idea and Paradox in *The Longest Journey*." *Crit* 4,#1(1960): 41-63.

19612. ----------. "Forster's 'Natural Supernaturalism': The Tales." *MFS* 7(1961): 271-283.

19613. ----------. "'The Mild, Intellectual Light': Idea and Theme in *Howard's End*." *PMLA* 74(1959): 453-463.

19614. Meyers, Jeffrey. "The Politics of *A Passage to India*." *JML* 1(1971): 329-338.

19615. Missey, James L. "Forster's Redemptive Siren." *MFS* 10(1964): 383-385.

19616. Müllenbrock, Heinz-Joachim. "Modes of Opening in the Work of E. M. Forster: A Contribution to the Poetics of His Novels." *MP* 70 (1973): 216-229.

19617. Naslund, Sena Jeter. "Fantasy, Prophecy, and Point of View in *A Passage to India*." *SN* 7(1975): 258-276.

19618. Nierenberg, Edwin. "The Withered Priestess: Mrs. Moore's Incomplete Passage to India." *MLQ* 25(1964): 198-204.

19619. Oliver, Harold J. "E. M. Forster: The Early Novels." *Crit* 1,#2(1957): 15-33.

19620. Roby, Kinley E. "Irony and Narrative Voice in *Howard's End*." *JNT* 2(1972): 116-124.

19621. Shaheen, M. Y. "Forster on Meredith." *RES* 24(1973): 185-191.

19622. Shusterman, David. "The Curious Case of Professor Godbole: *A Passage to India* Reexamined." *PMLA* 76(1961): 426-435.

19623. Stallybrass, Oliver. "Editing Forster." *EIC* 26(1976): 373-376.

19624. Stape, John H. "Myth, Allusion, and Symbol in E. M. Forester's 'The Other Side of the Hedge.'" *SSF* 14(1977): 375-378.

19625. Sullivan, Zorah, T. "Forster's Symbolism: *A Room with a View*, Fourth Chapter." *JNT* 6(1976): 217-223.

19626. Thomson, George H. "E. M. Forster and Howard Sturgis." *TSLL* 10(1968): 423-433.

19627. ----------. "Symbolism in E. M. Forster's Earlier Fiction." *Criticism* 3(1961): 304-320.

19628. ----------. "Thematic Symbols in *A Passage to India*." *TCL* 7(1961): 51-64.

19629. ----------. "Theme and Symbol in *Howard's End*." *MFS* 7(1961): 229-242.

19630. Turk, Jo M. "The Evolution of E. M. Forster's Narrator." *SN* 5(1973): 428-440.

19631. VanDe Vyvere, J. L. "The Mediatorial Voice of the Narrator in E. M. Forster's *Howard's End*." *JNT* 6(1976): 204-216.

19632. Wagner, C. Roland. "The Excremental and the Spiritual in *A Passage to India*." *MLQ* 31 (1970): 359-371.

19633. Wallace, Ronald. "The Inclusion of Merriment: Comedy in *A Passage to India*." *EL* 4 (1977): 37-48.

19634. Westburg, Barry R. "Forster's Fifth Symphony: Another Aspect of *Howard's End*." *MFS* 10 (1964): 359-365.

19635. White, Gertrude M. "*A Passage to India*: Analysis and Revaluation." *PMLA* 68(1953): 641-657.

19636. Wilde, Alan. "The Aesthetic View of Life: *Where Angels Fear to Tread*." *MFS* 7(1961): 207-216.

19637. ----------. "Desire and Consciousness: 'The Anironic Forster.'" *Novel* 9(1976): 114-129.

19638. Wilcox, Stewart C. "The Allegory of Forster's 'The Celestial Omnibus.'" *MFS* 2(1956): 191-196.

19639. Zwerdling, Alex. "The Novels of E. M. Forster." *TCL* 2(1957): 171-181.

See also 60, 207, 18922.

FOWLES, JOHN. 19640. Berets, Ralph. "*The Magus*: A Study in the Creation of a Personal Myth." *TCL* 19(1973): 89-97.

19641. Campbell, James. "An Interview with John Fowles." *Con L* 17(1976): 455-469.

19642. Churchill, Thomas. "Waterhouse, Storey, and Fowles: *Which Way Out of the Room?*" *Crit* 10,#3(1968): 72-87.

19643. Detweiler, Robert. "The Unity of John Fowles' Fiction." *NCL* 1(March, 1971): 3-4.

19644. DeVitis, A. A, and William J. Palmer. "*A Pair of Blue Eyes* Flash at *The French Lieutenant's Woman*." *Con L* 15(1974): 90-101.

19645. Dixon, Terrell F. "Expostulation and a Reply: the Character of Clegg in Fowles and Sillitoe." *NCL* 4(March, 1974): 7-9.

19646. Fleishman, Avrom. "*The Magus* of the Wizard of the West." *JML* 5(1976): 297-314.

19647. Eddins, Dwight. "John Fowles: Existence as Authorship." *Con L* 17(1976): 204-222.

19648. Kane, Patricia. "The Fallen Woman as Free-Thinker in *The French Lieutenant's Woman* and *The Scarlet Letter*." *NCL* 2(Jan., 1972): 8-10.

19649. Kaplan, Fred. "Victorian Modernists: Fowles and Nabokov." *JNT* 3(1978): 108-120.

19650. Mathews, James W. "Fowles's Artistic Freedom: Another Stone from James's House." *NCL* 4(March, 1974): 2-4.

19651. Rankin, Elizabeth D. "Cryptic Coloration in *The French Lietenant's Woman*." *JNT* 3(1973): 193-207.

19652. Rubenstein, Roberta. "Myth, Mystery, and Irony: John Fowles's *The Magus*." *Con L* 16 (1975): 328-339.

FRIEL, BRIAN. 19653. Coakley, James. "Chekov in Ireland: Brief Notes on Friel's *Philadelphia*." *CD* 7(1973): 191-197.

FRY, CHRISTOPHER. 19654. Carnell, Corbin S. "Creation's Lonely Flesh: T. S. Eliot and Christopher Fry on the Life of the Senses." *MD* 6(1963): 141-149.

19655. Donoghue, Denis. "Christopher Fry's Theatre of Words." *EIC* 9(1959): 37-49.

19656. Ferguson, John. "*The Boy With a Cart*." *MD* 8(1965): 284-292.

19657. Greene, Anne. "Fry's Comic Vision." *MD* 4(1962): 355-364.

19658. Knepler, Henry W. "*The Lark*: Translation vs. Adaptation: A Case History." *MD* 1(1958): 15-28.

19659. Louis, Dolores Gros. "Tragedy in Christopher Fry and in Shakespeare: A Comparison of *Curtmantle* and *Richard II*." *CLA* 9(1965): 151-158.

19660. Roy, Emil. "Archetypal Pattons in Fry." *CD* 1(1967): 93-104.

19661. ----------. "The Beckett Plays: Eliot, Fry, and Anouilh." *MD* 8(1965): 268-276.

19662. ----------. "Christopher Fry as Tragicomedian." *MD* 11(1968): 40-47.

19663. ----------. "Imagery in the Comedies of Christopher Fry." *MD* 7(1964): 79-88.

19664. Spanos, William V. "Christopher Fry's *A Sleep of Prisoners*: The Choreography of Comedy." *MD* 8(1965): 58-72.

19665. Stanford, Derek. "Comedy and Tragedy in Christopher Fry." *MD* 2(1959): 3-7.

19666. Wiersma, Stanley M. "Christopher Fry's *A Phoenix Too Frequent*: A Study in Source and Symbol." *MD* 8(1965): 293-302.

19667. ----------. "Spring and the Apocalypse, Law and Prophets: A Reading of Fry's *The Lady's Not for Burning*." *MD* 13(1970): 432-447.

19668. Woodfield, J. "Christopher Fry's *Curtmantle*: The Form of Unity." *MD* 17(1974): 307-318.

GALSWORTHY, JOHN. 19669. Bache, William B. "*Justice*: Galsworthy's Dramatic Tragedy." *MD* 3(1960): 138-142.

19670. Eaker, J. Gordon. "Galsworthy and the Modern Mind." *PQ* 29(1950): 31-48.

19671. Freeman, James C. "Whyte-Melville and Galsworthy's 'Bright Beings.'" *NCF* 5(1950): 85-100.

19672. Harkness, Bruce. "Conrad on Galsworthy: The Time Scheme in *Fraternity*." *MFS* 1,#2 (1955): 12-18.

19673. Pallette, Drew B. "Young Galsworthy: The Forging of a Satirist." *MP* 56(1959): 178-186.

19674. Scheick, William J. "Chance and Impartiality: A Study Based on the Manuscript of Galsworthy's *Loyalties*." *TSLL* 17(1975): 653-672.

19675. Scrimgeour, Gary J. "Naturalist Drama and Galsworthy." *MD* 7(1964): 65-78.

See also 18927.

GARNETT, EDWARD. See 19363.

GARNETT, DAVID. 19676. Irwin, William R. "The Metamorphoses of David Garnett." *PMLA* 73 (1958): 386-392.

19677. Johnson, Ann S. "Garnett's Amazon from Dahomey: Literary Debts in *The Sailor's Return*." *Con L* 14(1973): 169-185.

GASCOYNE, DAVID. 19678. Atkinson, Ann. "David Gascoyne: A Check-List." *TCL* 6(1961): 180-192.

19679. Jackaman, Rob. "View from the White Cliffs: A Close Look at One Manifestation of English Surrealism." *TCL* 21(1975): 72-80.

19680. Quinn, Sister Bernetta, O.S.F. "Symbolic Landscape in David Gascoyne." *Con L* 12 (1971): 466-494.

GAUNT, MARY. 19681. Miller, Carroll. "'Between Two Worlds': The Educated African in Three Novels by Mary Gaunt." *CLA* 18(1975): 521-531.

GIBBON, LEWIS G. See: JAMES L. MITCHELL

GILBERT, STUART. 19682. Sebba, Helen. "Stuart Gilbert's Meursault: A Strange 'Stranger.'" *Con L* 13(1972): 334-340.

GOLDING, WILLIAM. 19683. Babb, Howard. "On the Ending of *Pincher Martin*." *EIC* 14(1964): 106-108.

19684. Baker, James R. "Review Essay: Golding's Progress." *Novel* 7(1973): 62-70.

19685. Biles, Jack I. "Piggy: *Apologia Pro Vita Sua*." *SLI* 1,#2(1968): 83-109.

19686. ----------. "A William Golding Checklist." *TCL* 17(1971): 107-121.

19687. ----------., and Carl R. Kropf. "The Cleft Rock of Conversion: *Robinson Crusoe* and *Pincher Martin*." *SLI* 2,#2(1969): 17-43.

19688. Bufkin, E. C. "The Ironic Art of William Golding's *The Inheritors*." *TSLL* 9(1968): 567-578.

19689. ----------. "*Pincher Martin*: William Golding's Morality Play." *SLI* 2,#2(1969): 5-17.

19690. Crane, John Kenny. "Crossing the Bar

Twice: Post-Mortem Consciousness in Bierce, Hemingway, and Golding." *SSF* 6(1969): 361-376.

19691. Davis, W. Eugene. "Mr. Golding's Optical Delusion." *ELN* 3(1965): 125-126.

19692. Delbaere-Garant, Jeanne. "From the Cellar to the Rock: A Recurrent Pattern in William Golding's Novels." *MFS* 17(1971): 501-512.

19693. Dick, Bernard F. "*The Pyramid*: Mr. Golding's 'New' Novel." *SLI* 2,#2(1969): 83-95.

19694. Gindin, James. "'Gimick' and Metaphor in the Novels of William Golding." *MFS* 6 (1960): 145-152.

19695. Gordon, Robert C. "Classical Themes in *Lord of the Flies*." *MFS* 11(1965): 424-427.

19696. Hollahan, Eugene. "Running in Circles: A Major Motif in *Lord of the Flies*." *SN* 2(1970): 22-30.

19697. Hust, James R. "Grendel's Point of View: *Beowulf* and William Golding." *MFS* 13(1967): 264-265.

19698. O'Hara, J. D. "Mute Choirboys and Angelic Pigs: The Fable in *Lord of the Flies*." *TSLL* 7(1966): 411-420.

19699. Roper, Derek. "Allegory and Novel in Golding's *The Spire*." *Con L* 8(1967): 19-29.

19700. Skilton, David. "Golding's *The Spire*." *SLI* 2,#2(1969): 45-56.

19701. Sutherland, Raymond Carter. "Medieval Elements in *The Spire*." *SLI* 2,#2(1969): 57-65.

19702. Talon, Henri. "Irony in *Lord of the Flies*." *EIC* 18(1968): 296-309.

19703. Walker, Marshall. "William Golding: From Paradigm to Pyramid." *SLI* 2,#2(1969): 67-82.

19704. White, Robert J. "Butterfly and Beast in *The Lord of the Flies*." *MFS* 10(1964): 163-170.

19705. Whitehead, Lee M. "The Moment Out of Time: Golding's *Pincher Martin*." *Con L* 12 (1971): 18-41.

GRANVILLE-BARKER, HARLEY. See GRANVILLE BARKER.

GRAVES, ROBERT. 19706. Enright, D. J. "Robert Graves and the Decline of Modernism." *EIC* 11(1961): 319-337.

19707. Hayman, Ronald. "Robert Graves." *EIC* 5(1955): 32-43.

19708. Hollahan, Eugene. "Sir Kenneth Clark's *The Nude*: Catalyst for Robert Graves's 'The Naked and the Nude.'" *PMLA* 87(1972): 443-451.

19709. Kirklam, M. C. "Incertitude and the White Goddess." *EIC* 16(1966): 57-72.

GREEN, HENRY. 19710. Churchill, Thomas. "*Loving*: A Comic Novel." *Crit* 4,#2(1961): 29-38.

19711. Davidson, Barbara. "The World of *Loving*." *Con L* 2,#1(1961): 65-78.

19712. Labor, Earle. "Henry Green's Web of Loving." *Crit* 4,#1(1960): 29-40.

19713. Shapiro, S. A. "Henry Green's *Back*: The Presence of the Past." *Crit* 7,#1 (1964): 87-96.

19714. Taylor, Donald S. "Catalytic Rhetoric: Henry Green's Theory of the Modern Novel." *Criticism* 7(1965): 81-99.

19715. Turner, Myron. "The Imagery of Wallace Stevens and Henry Green." *Con L* 8(1967): 60-77.

GREENE, GRAHAM. 19716. Beebe, Maurice. "Checklist of Graham Greene: A Selected Checklist with an Index to Studies of Separate Works." *MFS* 3(1957): 281-288.

19717. Boyd, John D., S.J. "Earth Imagery in Graham Greene's *The Potting Shed*." *MD* 16(1973): 69-80.

19718. Cheney, Lynne. "Joseph Conrad's *The Secret Agent* and Graham Greene's *It's a Battlefield*: A Study in Structural Meaning." *MFS* 16(1970): 117-131.

19719. Cunningham, Lawrence. "The Alter Ego of Green's 'Whiskey Priest.'" *ELN* 8(1970): 50-52.

19720. Cottrell, Beekman W. "Second-Time Charm: The Theatre of Graham Greene." *MFS* 3 (1957): 249-255.

19721. Coulthard, A. R. "Graham Greene's 'The Hint of an Explanation': A Reinterpretation." *SSF* 8(1971): 601-605.

19722. Davis, Robert Murray. "Contributions to *Night and Day* by Elizabeth Bowen, Graham Greene and Anthony Powell." *SN* 3(1971): 401-404.

19724. ----------. "Review-Essay: From Standard to Classic: Graham Greene in Transit." *SN* 5(1973): 530-546.

19725. DeVitis, A. A. "Allegory in *Brighton Rock*." *MFS* 3(1957): 216-224.

19726. Evans, Robert D. "Existentialism in Greene's *The Quiet American*." *MFS* 3(1957): 241-248.

19727. Glicksberg, Charles I. "Graham Greene: Catholicism in Fiction." *Criticism* 1 (1959): 339-353.

19728. Grob, Alan. "*The Power and the Glory*: Graham Greene's Argument from Design." *Criticism* 11(1969): 1-30.

19729. Haber, Herbert. "The Two Worlds of Graham Greene." *MFS* 3(1957): 256-268.

19730. Hargreaves, Phylis. "Graham Greene: A Selected Bibliography." *MFS* 3(1957): 269-280.

19731. Hoggart, Richard. "The Force of Caricature: Aspects of the Art of Graham Greene, with particular reference to *The Power and the Glory*." *EIC* 3(1953): 447-462.

19732. Hortmann, Wilhelm. "Graham Greene: The Burnt-out Catholic." *TCL* 10(1964): 64-76.

19733. Hynes, Joseph. "The 'Facts' at *The Heart of the Matter*." *TSLL* 13(1972): 711-726.

19734. Jones, Grahame C. "Graham Green and the Legend of Péguy." *Comp L* 21(1969): 138-147.

19735. Lewis, R. W. B. "The 'Trilogy' of Graham Greene." *MFS* 3(1957): 195-215.

19736. Marković, Vida E. "Graham Greene in Search of God." *TSLL* 5(1963): 271-282.

19737. McCall, Dan. "*Brighton Rock*: The Price of Order." *ELN* 3(1966): 290-294.

19738. Patten, Karl. "The Structure of *The Power and the Glory*." *MFS* 3(1957): 225-234.

19739. Ruotolo, Lucio P. "*Brighton Rock's* Absurd Heroine." *MLQ* 26(1964): 425-433.

19740. Spier, Ursula. "Melodrama in Graham Greene's *The End of the Affair*." *MFS* 3(1957): 235-240.

19741. Stratford, Philip. "The Uncomplacent Dramatist: Some Aspects of Graham Greene's Theatre." *Con L* 2,#3(1961): 5-19.

See also 483, 18927.

GUNN, THOM. 19742. Stimpson, Catharine R. "Thom Gunn: The Redefinition of Place." *Con L* 18 (1977): 391-404.

HARTLEY, L. P. 19743. Athos, John. "L. P. Hartley and the Gothic Infatuation." *TCL* 7 (1962): 172-180.

19744. Gill, Richard. "A Letter from L. P. Hartley." *JML* 5(1976): 529-531.

19745. Webster, Harvey Curtis. "The Novels of L. P. Hartley." *Crit* 4,#2(1961): 39-51.

HEWLETT, MAURICE. 19746. Howarth, Herbert. "Hewlett and Ford among Renaissance Women." *JML* 5(1976): 79-88.

HILL, GEOFFREY. 19747. Martin, Wallace D. "Beyond Modernism: Christopher Middleton and Geoffrey Hill." *Con L* 12(1971): 420-436.

HILTON, JAMES. See 18922.

HOUSMAN, A. E. 19748. Brashear, William R. "The Trouble with Housman." *VP* 7(1969): 81-90.

19749. Brogunier, Joseph. "A Housman Source in *The Sound and the Fury*." *MFS* 18(1972): 220-225.

19750. Franklin, Ralph. "Housman's Shropshire." *MLQ* 24(1963): 164-171.

19751. Gray, Allan. "A Shakespearian Allusion in Housman, *Last Poems* XXIX." *ELN* 8 (1970): 36-39.

19752. Haber, Torn Burns. "A. E. Housman and *Ye Rounde Table*." *JEGP* 61(1962): 797-809.

19753. ----------. "A. E. Housman's Downward Eye." *JEGP* 53(1954): 306-318.

19754. ----------. "Housman's Poetic Method: His Lecture and His Notebooks." *PMLA* 69(1954): 1000-1016.

19755. -------. "The Poetic Antecedents of A. E. Housman's 'Hell Gate.'" *PQ* 31(1952): 433-436.

19756. Kowalczyk, R. L. "Horatian Tradition and Pastoral Mode in Housman's *A Shropshire Lad*." *VP* 4(1966): 223-235.

19757. Larkin, P. A. "Palgrave's Last Anthology: A. E. Housman's Copy." *RES* 22(1971): 312-316.

19758. Leggett, B. J. "The Limits of the Intellect: Housman's *Name and Nature of Poetry*." *MLQ* 32(1971): 58-72.

19759. ----------. "The Miltonic Allusions in Housman's 'Terence, This is Stupid Stuff.'" *ELN* 5(1968): 202-207.

19760. ----------. "The Poetry of Insight: Persona and Point of View in Housman." *VP* 14 (1976): 325-340.

19761. Marlow, A. N. "The Earliest Influences on *A Shropshire Lad*." *RES* 6(1955): 166-173.

19762. McFarland, Ronald E. "'The Tune the Old Cow Died Of': An Allusion in Housman." *VP* 11(1973): 60-61.

19763. Pearsall, Robert Brainard. "Housman's 'He Standing Hushed.'" *VP* 7(1969): 62-64.

19764. ----------. "Housman Versus Vaughan Williams: 'Is My Team Ploughing?'" *VP* 4(1966): 42-44.

19765. ----------. "The Vendible Values of Housman's Soldiery." *PMLA* 82(1967): 85-90.

19766. Perrine, Laurence. "Housman's 'The Olive.'" *VP* 11(1973): 340-341.

19767. Pitts, Gordon. "Housman's 'Be Still, My Soul.'" *VP* 3(1965): 137-138.

19768. Reedy, Gerard, S. J. "Housman's Use of Classical Convention." *VP* 6(1968): 51-62.

19769. Ricks, Christopher. "The Nature of Housman's Poetry." *EIC* 14(1964): 268-284.

19770. Seigel, Jules Paul. "A. E. Housman's Modification of the Pastoral Elegy." *VP* 2(1964): 47-50.

19771. Sparrow, John. "G. A. Simcox, Mr. T. Burns Haber, and Housman's *Hell Gate*." *PQ* 33 (1954): 437-442.

19772. ----------. "A Housman 'Reminiscence.'" *RES* 10(1959): 183-185.

19773. ----------. "A Housman 'Reminiscence.'" *RES* 11(1960): 190-191.

19774. Stevenson, John W. "The Ceremony of Housman's Style." *VP* 10(1972): 45-56.

19775. White, William. "'The Death of Socrates': A. E. Housman's First Published Poem." *PMLA* 68(1953): 913-916.

19776. Wight, John. "A Source of A. E. Housman's 'The Land of Biscay.'" *VP* 8(1970): 341-344.

HUDSON, W. H. 19777. Fairchild, Hoxie N. "Rima's Mother." *PMLA* 68(1953): 357-370.

HUGHES, RICHARD. 19778. Henighan, T. J. "Nature and Convention in *A High Wind in Jamaica*." *Crit* 9,#1(1966): 5-18.

HUGHES, TED. 19779. Hainsworth, J. D. "Ted Hughes and Violence." *EIC* 15(1965): 356-359.

19780. Libby, Anthony. "God's Lioness and the Priest of Sycorax: Plath and Hughes." *Con L* 15 (1974): 386-405.

19781. Rawson, C. J. "Ted Hughes and Violence." *EIC* 16(1966): 124-129.

19782. ----------. "Ted Hughes: A Reappraisal." *EIC* 15(1965): 77-94.

19783. Watt, Donald J. "Echoes of Hopkins in Ted Hughes's 'The Hawk in the Rain.'" *NCL* 2 (May, 1972): 10-12.

HULME, T. E. 19784. Primeau, Ronald. "On the Discrimination of Hulme: Toward a Theory of the 'Antiromantic': Romanticism of Modern Poetry." *JML* 3(1974): 1104-1122.

19785. Krieger, Murray. "The Ambiguous Anti-Romanticism." *ELH* 20(1953): 300-314.

19786. Martin, Wallace. "The Sources of the Imagist Aesthetic." *PMLA* 85(1970): 196-204.

19787. Schuchard, Ronald. "Eliot and Hulme in 1916: Toward a Revaluation of Eliot's Critical and Spiritual Development." *PMLA* 88(1973): 1083-1094.

HUNT, VIOLET. See 19545.

HUXLEY, ALDOUS. 19788. Allen, Walter. "*Point Counter Point* Revisited." *SN* 9(1977): 373-377.

19789. Baker, Robert S. "The Fire of Prometheus: Romanticism and the Baroque in Huxley's *Antic Hay* and *Those Barren Leaves*." *TSLL* 19 (1977): 60-82.

19790. ----------. "Spandrell's 'Lydian Heaven': Moral Masochism and the Centrality of Spandrell in Huxley's 'Point Counter Point.'" *Criticism* 16(1974): 120-135.

19791. ----------. "A Tour of Brighton Pavilion and Gog's Court: The Romantic Context of *Point Counter Point* and *Eyeless in Gaza*." *SN* 9 (1977): 537-563.

19792. Bentley, Joseph. "Aldous Huxley's Ambivalent Responses to the Ideas of D. H. Lawrence." *TCL* 13(1967): 139-153.

19793. ----------. "Semantic Gravitation: An Essay on Satiric Reduction." *MLQ* 30(1969): 3-19.

19794. Birnbaum, Milton. "Aldous Huxley's Animadversions upon Sexual Love." *TSLL* 8(1966): 285-296.

19795. ----------. "Politics and Character in *Point Counter Point*." *SN* 9(1977): 468-487.

19796. Bowen, Zack. "Allusion to Musical Works in *Point Counter Point*." *SN* 9(1977): 488-508.

19797. Bowering, Peter. "'The Source of Light': Pictorial Imagery and Symbolism in *Point Counter Point*." *SN* 9(1977): 389-405.

19798. Church, Margaret. "Concepts of Time in Novels of Virginia Woolf and Aldous Huxley." *MFS* 1,#2(1955): 19-24.

19799. Clareson, Thomas D. "The Classic: Aldous Huxley's *Brave New World*." *Ext* 2(1961): 33-40.

19800. ----------, and Carolyn S. Andrews. "Aldous Huxley: A Bibliography 1960-1964." *Ext* 6(1964): 2-21.

19801. Enroth, Clyde. "Mysticism in Two of Aldous Huxley's Early Novels." *TCL* 6(1960): 123-133.

19802. Firchow, Peter C. "The Brave New World of Huxley Studies." *JML* 1(1970): 278-283.

19803. ----------. "Mental Music: Huxley's *Point Counter Point* and Mann's *Magic Mountain* as Novels of Ideas." *SN* 9(1977): 518-536.

19804. ----------. "The Satire of Huxley's *Brave New World*." *MFS* 12(1966): 451-460.

19805. ----------. "Science and Conscience in Huxley's *Brave New World*." *Con L* 16(1975): 301-316.

19806. ----------. "Wells and Lawrence in Huxley's *Brave New World*." *JML* 5(1976): 260-278.

19807. Holmes, Charles M. "The Early Poetry of Aldous Huxley." *TSLL* 8(1966): 391-406.

19808. Huxley, Aldous. "Exhumations I. Huxley's 'Chaucer.'" *EIC* 15(1965): 6-21.

19809. Marovitz, Sanford E. "Aldous Huxley's Intellectual Zoo." *PQ* 48(1969): 495-507.

19810. May, Keith. "Accepting the Universe: The 'Rampion-Hypothesis' in *Point Counter Point* and *Island*." *SN* 9(1977): 418-427.

19811. McMichael, Charles T. "Aldous Huxley's *Island*: The Final Vision." *SLI* 1,#2 (1968): 73-82.

19812. Meckier, Jerome. "Aldous Huxley: Satire and Structure." *Con L* 7(1966): 284-294.

19813. ----------. "Fifty Years of Counterpoint." *SN* 9(1977): 367-372.

19814. ----------. "The Hippopotamian Question: A Note on Aldous Huxley's Unfinished Novel." *MFS* 16(1970): 505-514.

19815. ----------. "Philip Quarles's Passage to India: *Jesting Pilate, Point Counter Point*, and Bloomsbury." *SN* 9(1977): 445-467.

19816. ----------. "Quarles Among the Monkeys: Huxley's Zoological Novels." *MLR* 68(1973): 268-282.

19817. ----------. "Sir George Sitwell's Contributions to *Chrome Yellow*." *MFS* 23(1977): 235-239.

19818. Nagarajan, S. "Religion in Three Recent Novels of Aldous Huxley." *MFS* 5(1959): 153-165.

19819. Quina, James. "The Mathematical-Physical Universe: A Basis for Multiplicity and the Quest for Unity in *Point Counter Point*." *SN* 9(1977): 428-444.

19820. Roston, Murray. "The Technique of Counterpoint." *SN* 9(1977): 378-388.

19821. Schmerl, Rudolph B. "The Two Future Worlds of Aldous Huxley." *PMLA* 77(1962): 328-334.

19822. Vitoux, Pierre. "Aldous Huxley and D. H. Lawrence: An Attempt at Intellectual Sympathy." *MLR* 69(1974): 501-522.

19823. Watt, Donald K. "The Absurdity of the Hedonist in Huxley's 'The Gioconda Smile.'" *SSF* 7(1970): 328-330.

19824. ----------. "The Criminal-Victim Pattern in Huxley's *Point Counter Point*." *SN* 2 (1970): 42-51.

19825. ----------. "The Fugal Construction of *Point Counter Point*." *SN* 9(1977): 509-517.

19826. ----------. "Vision and Symbol in Aldous Huxley's Island." *TCL* 14(1968): 149-160.

19827. Watts, Harold H. "The Viability of *Point Counter Point*." *SN* 9(1977): 406-417.

See also 207, 210, 18922.

ISHERWOOD, CHRISTOPHER. 19828. Brogan, Hugh. "*Lions and Shadows*." *TCL* 22(1976): 303-311.

19829. Bruehl, William J. "*Polus Naufrangia*: A Key Symbol in *The Ascent of the F6*." *MD* 10 (1967): 161-164.

19830. Finney, Brian. "Laily, Mortmere and All That." *TCL* 22(1976): 286-302.

19831. Fryer, Jonathan H. "Sexuality in Isherwood." *TCL* 22(1976): 343-353.

19832. Geherin, David J. "An Interview with Christopher Isherwood." *JNT* 2(1972): 159-170.

19833. Gerstenberger, Donna. "Poetry and Politics: The Verse Drama of Auden and Isherwood." *MD* 5(1962): 123-132.

19834. Heilbrun, Carolyn G. "Christopher Isherwood: An Interview." *TCL* 22(1976): 253-263.

19835. ----------. "An Interview with Gavin Lambert." *TCL* 22(1976): 332-342.

19836. Lehman, John. "Two of the Conspirators." *TCL* 22(1976): 264-275.

19837. Mendelson, Edward. "The Auden-Isherwood Collaboration." *TCL* 22(1976): 276-285.

19838. Orphanos, Stathis. "Christopher Isherwood: A Checklist 1968-1975." *TCL* 22(1976): 354-361.

19839. Thomas, David P. "*Goodbye to Berlin*: Refocusing Isherwood's Camera." *Con L* 13(1972): 44-52.

19840. Thomas, Peter. "'Camp' and Politics in Isherwood's Berlin Fiction." *JML* 5(1976): 117-130.

19841. Wilde, Alan. "Irony and Style: The Example of Christopher Isherwood." *MFS* 16(1970): 475-489.

19842. ----------. "Language and Surface: Isherwood and the Thirties." *Con L* 16(1975): 478-491.

19843. Wilson, Colin. "An Integrity Born of Hope: Notes on Christopher Isherwood." *TCL* 22(1976): 312-331.

JACOBS, W. W. 19844. Harkey, Joseph H. "Foreshadowing in 'The Monkey's Paw.'" *SSF* 6 (1969): 653-654.

JONES, DAVID. 19845. Dilworth, Thomas R. "David Jones's Use of a Geology Text for *The Anathemata*." *ELN* 15(1977): 115-119.

19846. Gemmill, Janet Powers. "*In Parenthesis*: A Study of Narrative Technique." *JML* 1 (1971): 311-328.

19847. Manglaviti, Leo M. J. "The *Anathemata* of David Jones: Notes on Theme and Structure." *TCL* 15(1969): 105-114.

19848. Spears, Monroe K. "Shapes and Surfaces: David Jones, with a Glance at Charles Tomlinson." *Con L* 12(1971): 402-419.

JOYCE, JAMES. 19849. Adicks, Richard. "The Unconsecrated Eucharist in *Dubliners*." *SSF* 5(1968): 295-296.

19850. Aitken, D. J. F. "Dramatic Archetypes in Joyce's 'Exiles.'" *MFS* 4(1958): 42-52.

19851. Anderson, Chester G. "James Joyce's 'Tilly'." *PMLA* 73(1958): 285-298.

19852. Atherton, J. S. "Islam and the Koran in *Finnegans Wake*." *Comp L* 6(1954): 240-255.

19853. Baker, James R. "James Joyce: Affirmation after Exile." *MLQ* 18(1957): 275-281.

19854. Beards, Richard D. "'Ivy Day in the Committee Room': The Identity of Tierney." *SSF* 14(1977): 290-293.

19855. Beebe, Maurice. "James Joyce: Barnacle Goose and Lapwing." *PMLA* 71(1956): 302-320.

19856. ----------. "Joyce and Aquinas: The Theory of Aesthetics." *PQ* 36(1957): 20-35.

19857. Beebe, Maurice, Philip Herring, and Walton Litz. "Criticism of James Joyce: A Slected Checklist." *MFS* 15(1969): 105-182.

19858. Beebe, Maurice, and Walton Litz. "Criticism of James Joyce: A Selected Checklist with an Index to Studies of Separate Works." *MFS* 4(1958): 71-99.

19859. Begnal, Michael H. "The Mystery Man of *Ulysses*." *JML* 2(1972): 565-568.

19860. Benstock, Bernard. "Arthur Griffith in *Ulysses*: The Explosion of a Myth." *ELN* 4(1966): 123-128.

19861. ----------. "Every Telling has a Taling: A Reading of the Narrative of *Finnegans Wake*." *MFS* 15(1969): 3-25.

19862. ----------. "*Exiles*: 'Paradox Lust' and 'Lost Paladays.'" *ELH* 36(1969): 739-756.

19863. ----------. "The Final Apostacy: James Joyce and *Finnegans Wake*." *ELH* 28(1961): 417-437.

19864. ----------. "L. Boom as Dreamer in *Finnegans Wake*." *PMLA* 82(1967): 91-97.

19865. ----------. "On William Gaddis: In Recognition of James Joyce." *Con L* 6(1965): 177-189.

19866. ----------. "Persian in *Finnegans Wake*." *PQ* 44(1965): 100-109.

19867. ----------. "Review-Essay: Three Generations of *Finnegans Wake*." *SN* 9(1977): 333-338.

19868. Berrone, Louis. "Two James Joyce Essays Unveiled: 'The Centenary of Charles Dickens' and L'influenza latteria....'" *JML* 5(1976): 3-18.

19869. Bickerton, Derek. "James Joyce and the Development of Interior Monologue." *EIC* 18 (1968): 32-46.

19870. Bierman, Robert. "'Steameress Mastress to the Sea': A Note on *Finnegans Wake*." *MFS* 2(1956): 79-80.

19871. ----------. "'White and Pink Elephants': *Finnegans Wake* and the Tradition of 'Unintelligibility.'" *MFS* 4(1958): 62-70.

19872. Block, Haskell M. "James Joyce and Thomas Hardy." *MLQ* 19(1958): 337-342.

19873. Blum, Morgan. "The Shifting Point of View: Joyce's 'The Dead' and Gordon's 'Old Red.'" *Crit* 1,#1(1956): 45-66.

19874. Broes, Arthur T. "Swift the Man in *Finnegans Wake*." *ELH* 43(1976): 120-140.

19875. Campbell, Joseph. "Contransmagnificandjewbangtantiality." *SLM* 3,#2(1970): 3-18.

19876. Carlson, Marvin. "Henrik Ibsen and *Finnegans Wake*." *Comp L* 12(1960): 133-141.

19877. Church, Margaret. "The Theme of Return: The Nostos of *Ulysses*." *Coll L* 3(1976): 124-129.

19878. Clarke, John. "Joyce and the Blakean Vision." *Criticism* 5(1963): 173-180.

19879. Cohn, Alan M. "Rosenbach, Copinger, and Sylvia Beach in *Finnegans Wake*." *PMLA* 77 (1962): 342-344.

19880. Cohn, Ruby. "Absurdity in English: Joyce and O'Neill." *CD* 3(1969): 156-161.

19881. Cole, David W. "Fugal Structure in the Sirens Episode of *Ulysses*." *MFS* 19(1973): 221-226.

19882. Connolly, Thomas F. "Marriage Divination in Joyce's 'Clay.'" *SSF* 3(1966): 293-299.

19883. Cope, Jackson I. "James Joyce: Test Case for a Theory of Style." *ELH* 21(1954): 221-236.

19884. ----------. "The Rhythmic Gesture: Image and Aesthetic in Joyce's *Ulysses*." *ELH* 29 (1962): 67-89.

19885. Copland, R. A., and G. W. Turner. "The Nature of James Joyce's Parody in 'Ithaca.'" *MLR* 64(1969): 759-763.

19886. Cowan, S. A. "Celtic Folklore in 'Clay': Maria and the Irish Washerwoman." *SSF* 6 (1969): 213-215.

19887. Cunningham, Frank. "Joyce's *Exiles*: A Problem of Dramatic Stasis." *MD* 12(1970): 399-407.

19888. Davies, Phillip George. "Maria's Song in Joyce's 'Clay.'" *SSF* 1(1964): 153-154.

19888a. Davis, J. K. "The City as Radical Order: James Joyce's *Dubliners*." *SLI* 3,#2(1970): 79-96.

19889. Degnan, James P. "The Reluctant Indian in Joyce's 'Encounter.'" *SSF* 6(1969): 152-156.

19890. Deneau, Daniel P. "Joyce's 'Minute' Maria." *JNT* 2(1972): 26-45.

19891. Dibble, Jerry Allen. "Stephen's Esthetic and Joyce's Art: Theory and Practice of Genre in *A Portrait of the Artist as Young Man*." *JNT* 6(1976): 29-40.

19892. Doherty, James. "Joyce and *Hell Opened to Christians*: The Edition He Used for his 'Hell Sermons.'" *MP* 61(1963): 110-119.

19893. Dolmatch, Theodore B. "Notes and Queries Concerning the Revisions in *Finnegans Wake*." *MLQ* 16(1955): 232-236.

19894. Duncan, Joseph E. "The Modality of the Audible in Joyce's *Ulysses*." *PMLA* 72(1957):

286-295.

19895. Dundes, Alan. "Re: Joyce-No in the Womb." *MFS* 8(1962): 137-147.

19896. Duffy, John J. "The Painful Case of M'Intosh." *SSF* 2(1965): 183-185.

19897. Eckley, Grace. "Shem is a Sham but Shaun is a Ham, or Samuraising the Twins in *Finnegans Wake*." *MFS* 20(1974): 469-481.

19898. Edwards, Philip. "'Ulysses' and the Legends." *EIC* 5(1955): 118-128.

19899. Evans, William A. "Wordagglutinations in Joyce's *Ulysses*." *SLI* 3,#2(1970): 27-37.

19900. Fabian, David R. "Joyce's 'The Sisters': Gnomon, Gnomic, Gnome." *SSF* 5(1968): 187-189.

19901. Fackler, Herbert V. "Stephen Dedalus Rejects Forgotten Beauty: A Yeats Illusion in *A Portrait of the Artist as a Young Man*." *CLA* 12 (1968): 164-167.

19902. Fanger, Donald. "Joyce and Meredith: A Question of Influence and Tradition." *MFS* 6 (1960): 125-130.

19903. Feshbach, Sidney. "Hunting Epiphany-Hunters." *PMLA* 87(1972): 304-306.

19904. Fiedler, Leslie. "Bloom on Joyce; or, Jokey for Jacob." *JML* 1(1970): 19-29.

19905. Fleishman, Avrom. "Science in Ithaca." *Con L* 8(1967): 377-391.

19906. Foster, John W. "Passage Through 'The Dead.'" *Criticism* 15(1973): 91-108.

19907. Friedrich, Gerhard. "Brete Harte as a Source for James Joyce's 'The Dead.'" *PQ* 33 (1954): 442-444.

19908. Garrison, Joseph M., Jr. "The Adult Consciousness of the Narrator in Joyce's 'Araby.'" *SSF* 10(1973): 416-417.

19909. ----------. "*Dubliners*: Portraits of the Artist as a Narrator." *Novel* 8(1975): 226-240.

19910. Geckle, George L. "Stephen Daedalus and W. B. Yeats: The Making of the Villanelle." *MFS* 15(1969): 87-96.

19911. Gibbon, F. P. "The Truth of Fiction." *EIC* 10(1960): 480-483.

19912. Gill, Richard. "The 'Coporal Works of Mercy' as a Moral Pattern in Joyce's *Ulysses*." *TCL* 9(1963): 17-21.

19913. Goldberg, S. L. "The Aesthetic of *Ulysses*." *ELH* 24(1957): 44-64.

19914. Groden, Michael. "Criticism in New Composition: *Ulysses* and *The Sound and the Fury*." *TCL* 21(1975): 265-277.

19915. Hagopian, John V. "The Epiphany in Joyce's 'Counterparts.'" *SSF* 1(1964): 107-112.

19916. Hall, Vernon, Jr. "Joyce's Use of DaPonte and Mozart's *Don Giovanni*." *PMLA* 66(1951): 78-84.

19917. Hart, Clive. "James Joyce's Sentimentality." *PQ* 46(1957): 516-526.

19918. ----------. "Notes on the Text of *Finnegans Wake*." *JEGP* 59(1960): 229-239.

19919. Hartley, Lodwick. "'Swiftly-Stereward': The Question of Sterne's Influence on Joyce." *SLI* 3,#2(1970): 37-47.

19920. Hassan, Ihab. "Joyce-Beckett: A Scenario in Eight Scenes and a Voice." *JML* 1(1970): 7-18.

19921. Hayman, David. "Forms of Folly in Joyce: A Study of Clowning in *Ulysses*." *ELH* 34 (1967): 260-283.

19922. ----------. "From *Finnegans Wake*: A Sentence in Progress." *PMLA* 73(1958): 136-154.

19923. ----------. "Review Article: James Joyce's Critical Case, or 'Conscience' versus Conscience." *PQ* 48(1969): 116-129.

19924. Helsinger, Howard. "Joyce and Dante." *ELH* 35(1968): 591-605.

19925. Herring, Philip F. "The Bedstead-fastness of Molly Bloom." *MFS* 15(1969): 49-61.

19926. ----------. "Experimentation with a Landscape: Pornotopography in *Ulysses*—The Phallocy of Imitative Form." *MFS* 20(1974): 371-378.

19927. Higginson, Fred L. "Notes on the Text of *Finnegans Wake*." *JEGP* 55(1956): 451-456.

19928. ----------. "Two Letters from Dame Anna Earwicker." *Crit* 1,#2(1957): 3-14.

19929. Hirschberg, Stuart. "Bloom Revealed Through the Contents of His Secret Drawers." *NCL* 5(Nov., 1975): 2-3.

19930. Humma, John R. "Gabriel and the Bed-Sheets: Still Another Reading of the Ending of 'The Dead.'" *SSF* 10(1973): 207-209.

19931. Jack, Jane H. "Art and 'The Portrait of The Artist.'" *EIC* 5(1955): 354-364.

19932. Jarrell, Mackie L. "Joyce's Use of Swift's *Polite Conversation* in the 'Circe' Episode of Ulysses." *PMLA* 72(1957): 545-554.

19933. ----------. "Swiftiana in *Finnegans Wake*." *ELH* 26(1959): 271-294.

19934. Jenkins, Ralph. "Theosophy in 'Scylla and Charybdis'." *MFS* 15(1969): 35-48.

19935. Jenkins, William D. "It Seems There Were Two Irishmen." *MFS* 15(1969): 63-71

19936. Kain, Richard M. "James Joyce and the Game of Language." *SLI* 3,#2(1970): 19-25.

19937. ----------. "Two Book Reviews by James Joyce." *PMLA* 67(1952): 291-294.

19938. Kaplan, Fred. "Dickens' Flora Finching and Joyce's Molly Bloom." *NCF* 23(1968): 343-346.

19939. Kaye, Julian. "The Wings of Daedalus: Two Stories in *Dubliners*." *MFS* 4(1958): 31-41.

19940. Kelly, H. A., S.J. "Consciousness in the Monologues of *Ulysses*." *MLQ* 24(1963): 3-12.

19941. Kenner, Hugh. "Joyce's *Ulysses*: Homer and Hamlet." *EIC* 2(1952): 85-104.

19942. Kenny, Thomas J. "James Joyce's System of Marginal Markings in the Books of His Personal Library." *JML* 6(1977): 264-276.

19943. Kershner, R. B., Jr. "Time and Language in Joyce's *Portrait of the Artist*." *ELH* 43(1976): 604-619.

19944. Killeen, J. F. "James Joyce's Roman Prototype." *Comp L* 9(1957): 193-203.

19945. Kiralis, Karl. "Joyce and Blake: A Basic Source for *Finnegans Wake*." *MFS* 4(1958): 329-334.

19946. Kloss, Robert J. "The Function of Forgetting in Joyce's 'Clay.'" *HSL* 6(1974): 167-186.

19947. Knight, Douglas. "The Reading of *Ulysses*." *ELH* 19(1952): 64-80.

19948. Knight, G. Wilson. "Lawrence, Joyce and Powys." *EIC* 11(1961): 403-417.

19949. Kuehn, Robert. "Mr. Bloom and Mr. Joyce: A Note on 'Heroism' in *Ulysses*." *Con L* 4 (1963): 209-215.

19950. Kumar, Shiv K. "Joyce's Epiphany and Bergson's 'L'Intuition Philosophique.'" *MLQ* 20 (1959): 27-30.

19951. ----------. "Space-Time Polarity in *Finnegans Wake*." *MP* 54(1957): 230-233.

19952. Leatherwood, A. M. "Joyce's Mythic Method: Structure and Unity in 'An Encounter.'" *SSF* 13(1976): 71-78.

19953. Leithauser, Glayd Garner, and Paul Sporn. "Hypospadia: Linguistic Guidepost to the Themes of the 'Circe' Episode of Ulysses.'" *JML* 4 (1974): 109-114.

19954. Lemon, Lee T. "*A Portrait of the Artist as a Young Man*: Motif as Motivation and Structure." *MFS* 12(1966): 439-450.

19955. Lillyman, W. J. "The Interior Monologue in James Joyce and Otto Ludwig." *Comp L* 23 (1971): 45-54.

19956. Litz, A. Walton. "Early Vestiges of Joyce's *Ulysses*." *PMLA* 71(1956): 51-60.

19957. ----------. "The Evolution of Joyce's *Anna Livia Plurabelle*." *PQ* 36(1957): 36-48.

19958. ----------. "Joyce's Notes for the Last Episodes of *Ulysses*." *MFS* 4(1958): 3-20.

19959. Loomis, C. C., Jr. "Structure and Sympathy in Joyce's 'The Dead.'" *PMLA* 75(1960): 149-151.

19960. Lorch, Thomas M. "The Relationship between *Ulysses* and *The Waste Land*." *TSLL* 6(1964): 123-133.

19961. Loss, Archie K. "The Pre-Raphaelite Woman, the Symbolist *Femme - Enfant* and the Girl with the Long Flowing Hair in the Earlier Work of Joyce." *JML* 3(1973): 3-23.

19962. Lyons, John O. "James Joyce and Chaucer's Prioress." *ELN* 2(1964): 127-132.

19963. MacNicholas, John. "Joyce contra Wagner." *CD* 9(1975): 29-43.

19964. Maddox, James H., Jr. "'Eumaeus' and the Theme of Return in *Ulysses*." *TSLL* 16 (1974): 211-220.

19965. Madtes, Richard E. "Joyce and the Building of Ithaca." *ELH* 31(1964): 443-459.

19966. Magalaner, Marvin. "The Anti-Semitic Limerick Incidents and Joyce's 'Bloomsday.'" *PMLA* 68(1953): 1219-1223.

19967. ----------. "James Mangan and Joyce's Dedalus Family." *PQ* 31(1952): 363-371.

19968. ----------. "Joyce, Nietzsche, and Hauptmann in James Joyce's 'A Painful Case.'" *PMLA* 68(1953): 95-102.

19969. ----------. "Labyrinthine Motif: James Joyce and Leo Taxil." *MFS* 2(1956): 167-182.

19970. Manso, Peter. "The Metaphoric Style of Joyce's *Portrait*." *MFS* 13(1967): 221-236.

19971. Marre, K. E. "Experimentation with a Symbol from Mythology: The Courses of the Comets in the Ithaca Chapter of *Ulysses*." *MFS* 20(1974): 385-390.

19972. Mason, Ellsworth. "James Joyce: Moralist." *TCL* 1(1956): 196-206.

19973. ----------. "James Joyce's 'William Blake.'" [with text] *Criticism* 1(1959): 181-189.

19974. ----------. "James Joyce's Shrill Note— The *Piccolo Della Sera* Articles." *TCL* 2 (1956): 115-139.

19975. Mason, Michael York. "*Ulysses* The Sequel to *A Portrait*? Joyce's Plans for the Two Works." *ELN* 8(1971): 296-300.

19976. ----------. "Why is Leopold Bloom a Cuckold?" *ELH* 44(1977): 171-188.

19977. McCarthy, Patrick A. "The Riddle in Joyce's *Ulysses*." *TSLL* 17(1975): 193-205.

19978. ----------. "Three Approaches to Life's Robulous Rebus in the Quiz Section of *Finnegans Wake*." *JML* 5(1976): 407-435.

19979. McFate, Patricia Ann. "'A Letter to Rome' and 'Clay': Similarities in Character and Conclusion." *SSF* 9(1972): 277-279.

19980. McGuinness, Arthur E. "The Ambience of Space in Joyce's *Dubliners*." *SSF* 11(1974): 343-351.

19981. McLean, Andrew M. "Joyce's *Ulysses* and Döblin's *Alexanderplatz Berlin*." *Comp L* 25 (1973): 97-113.

19982. McMichael, Charles T., and Ted R. Spivey. "'Chaos-hurray!—is come again': Heroism in James Joyce and Conrad Aiken." *SLI* 3,#2(1970): 65-68.

19983. Metzger, Deena P. "Variations on a Theme: A Study of *Exiles* by James Joyce and *The Great God Brown* by Eugene O'Neill." *MD* 8(1965): 174-184.

19984. Miller, Milton. "Definition by Comparison: Chaucer, Lawrence and Joyce." *EIC* 3 (1953): 369-381.

19985. Mitchell, Breon. "Joyce and Döblin: At the Crossroads of *Berlin Alexanderplatz*." *Con L* 12(1971): 173-187.

19986. Morse, J. Mitchell. "Augustine, *Ayenbite*, and *Ulysses*." *PMLA* 70(1955): 1143-1159.

19987. ----------. "Augustine's Theodicy and Joyce's Aesthetics." *ELH* 24(1957): 30-43.

19988. ----------. "Cain, Abel, and Joyce." *ELH* 22(1955): 48-60.

19989. ----------. "The Disobedient Artist: Joyce and Loyola." *PMLA* 72(1957): 1018-1035.

19990. ----------. "Jacob and Esau in *Finnegans Wake*." *MP* 52(1954): 123-130.

19991. ----------. "More Early Vestiges of *Ulysses*." *PMLA* 71(1956): 1173.

19992. Moseley, Virginia Douglas. "Joyce's *Exiles* and the Prodigal Son." *MD* 1(1959): 218-227.

19993. Murphy, M. W. "Darkness in *Dubliners*." *MFS* 15(1969): 97-104.

19994. Newman, F. X. "The Land of Ooze: Joyce's 'Grace' and the *Book of Job*." *SSF* 4(1966): 70-79.

19995. Noon, William T., S.J. "James Joyce: Unfacts, Fiction, and Facts." *PMLA* 76(1961): 254-276.

19996. Norris, Margot C. "The Consequence of Deconstruction: A Technical Perspective of Joyce's *Finnegans Wake*." *ELH* 41(1974): 130-148.

19997. O'Brien, Darcy. "The Twins that Tick Homo Vulgaria: A Study of Shem and Shaun." *MFS* 12(1966): 183-199.

19998. O Hehir, Brandon P. "Structural Symbol in Joyce's 'The Dead.'" *TCL* 3(1957): 3-13.

19999. Pearce, Richard. "Experimentation with the Grotesque: Comic Collisions in the Grotesque World of *Ulysses*." *MFS* 20(1974): 378-384.

20000. Petroski, Henry. "What Are Pomes?" *JML* 3(1974): 1021-1026.

20001. Phillips, Norma. "Sillitoe's 'The Match' and Its Joycean Counterparts." *SSF* 12

(1975): 9-14.

20002. Pomerang, Victory. "The Modification of *Sweets of Sin*." MFS 23(1977): 245.

20003. Poss, Stanley. "A Portrait of the Artist as Hard-boiled Messiah." MLQ 27(1966): 68-79.

20004. ----------. "*Ulysses* and the Comedy of the Immobilized Act." ELH 24(1957): 65-83.

20005. Power, Mary. "The Naming of Kathleen Kearney." JML 5(1976): 532-534.

20006. Prescott, Joseph. "Concerning the Genesis of *Finnegan's Wake*." PMLA 69(1954): 1300-1302.

20007. ----------. "James Joyce's *Stephen Hero*." JEGP 53(1954): 214-276.

20008. ----------. "Local Allusions in Joyce's *Ulysses*." PMLA 68(1953): 1223-1228.

20009. ----------. "Notes on Joyce's Ulysses." MLQ 13(1952): 149-162.

20010. ----------. "Two Manuscripts by Paul Léon Concerning James Joyce." MFS 2(1956): 71-76.

20011. Radford, F. L. "'Christofox in Leather Trews': The Quaker in the Library in *Ulysses*." ELH 39(1972): 441-458.

20012. Raisor, Philip. "Grist for the Mill: James Joyce and the Naturalists." Con L 15(1974): 457-473.

20013. Redford, Grant H. "The Role of Structure in Joyce's *Portrait*." MFS 4(1958): 21-30.

20014. Reynolds, Mary T. "Joyce's Villanelle and D'Annunzio's Sonnet Sequence." JML 5(1976): 19-45.

20015. Reynolds, Michael S. "The Feast of the Most Precious Blood and Joyce's 'The Sisters.'" SSF 6(1969): 336.

20016. Richardson, Robert O. "Molly's Last Word." TCL 12(1967): 177-185.

20017. Rocco-Bergera, Niny. "Joyce and Svevo: A Note." MFS 18(1972): 116-117.

20018. Rodewald, Clark. "A Note on the Names in *Finnegan's Wake*." ELN 2(1965): 292-293.

20019. Rodway, Allan. "Gnosers to the Grindstone: Review Article." EIC 10(1960): 181-194.

20020. Rosenberg, Bruce A. "The Crucifixion in 'The Boarding House'." SSF 5(1967): 44-53.

20021. Rossman, Charles. "Review Essay: On Doing unto Joyce before He Does unto You: Modes of Critical Engagement in Some Recent Joyce Studies." SN 8(1976): 351-366.

20022. Russell, H. K. "The Incarnation in *Ulysses*." MFS 4(1958): 53-61.

20023. Rutherford, Andrew. "Joyce's Use of Correspondences." EIC 6(1956): 123-125.

20024. Ryf, Robert S. "Joyce's Visual Imagination." TSLL 1(1959): 30-43.

20025. Scarry, John. "'Poor Georgina Burns' in Joyce's 'The Dead'." ELN 10(1972): 123-126.

20026. ----------. "William Parkinson in Joyce's *The Dead*." JML 3(1973): 105-107.

20027. Scheverle, William H. "'Gabriel Hounds' and Joyce's *The Dead*." SSF 2(1965): 369-371.

20028. Schmidt, Hugo. "Hauptmann's *Michael Kramer* and Joyce's 'The Dead.'" PMLA 80(1965): 141-142.

20029. Schoenberg, E. I. "The Identity of the 'Cyclops' Narrator in James Joyce's *Ulysses*." JML 5(1976): 534-539.

20030. Scholes, Robert E. "Stephen Dedalus: Eiron and *Alazon*." TSLL 3(1961): 8-15.

20031. ----------. "Stephen Dedalus, Poet or Esthete?" PMLA 79(1964): 484-489.

20032. Scholes, Robert, and Florence L. Walzl. "The Epiphanies of Joyce." PMLA 82(1967): 152-154.

20033. Scholes, Robert, and William T. Noon, S.J. "James Joyce: An Unfact." PMLA 79(1964): 355.

20034. Schwartz, Lewis M. "Eccles Street and Canterbury: An Approach to Molly Bloom." TCL 15(1969): 155-166.

20035. Shapiro, Stephan A. "Leopold Bloom and Gulley Jimson: The Economics of Survival." TCL 10(1964): 3-11.

20036. Sharpe, Garold. "The Philosophy of James Joyce." MFS 9(1963): 120-126.

20037. Sherwood, John C. "Joyce and the Empire: Some Thoughts on *Finnegans Wake*." SN 1 (1969): 357-363.

20038. Simon, Elliott M. "James Joyce's *Exiles* and the Tradition of the Edwardian Problem-play." MD 20(1977): 21-36.

20039. Smith, Don Noel. "Musical Form and Principles in the Scheme of Ulysses." TCL 18 (1972): 79-92.

20040. Smith, Grover, Jr. "The Cryptogram in Joyce's *Ulysses*: A Misprint." PMLA 73(1958): 446-447.

20041. Solomon, A. J. "'The Celtic Note' in 'A Little Cloud.'" SSF 9(1972): 269-270.

20042. Somerville, Jane. "Money in *Dubliners*." SSF 12(1975): 109-116.

20043. Spivey, Ted R. "The Reintegration of Modern Man: An Essay on James Joyce and Hermann Hesse." SLI 3,#2(1970): 49-64.

20044. Staley, Thomas F. "Review Essay: Recent Joyce Criticism." SN 6(1974): 486-491.

20045. Stanford, W. B. "Ulyssean Qualities in Joyce's Leopold Bloom." Comp L 5(1953): 125-136.

20046. Steinberg, Erwin R. "'Lestrygonians', A Pale 'Proteus.'" MFS 15(1969): 73-86.

20047. Summerhayes, Don. "Joyce's Ulysses and Whitman's 'Self': A Query." Con L 4(1963): 216-224.

20048. Swinson, Ward. "Riddles in *Finnegan's Wake*." TCL 19(1973): 165-180.

20049. Tessitore, John. "A Joyce Annotation." ELN 14(1976): 50-51.

20050. Thrane, James R. "Joyce's Sermon on Hell: Its Source and Its Backgrounds." MP 57 (1960): 172-198.

20051. Turner, G. S. "Princess on a Rocking Horse." SSF 5(1967): 72.

20052. Von Abele, Rudolph. "*Ulysses*: The Myth of Myth." PMLA 69(1954): 358-364.

20053. Von Phul, Ruth. "The Boast of Heraldry in the 'Proteus' Episode of Ulysses." JML 1(1971): 399-405.

20054. Vickery, John B. "Finnegans Wake and Sexual Metamorphosis." Con L 13(1972): 213-242.

20055. Wallace, Ronald. "'Laughing in Your Sleeve': James Joyce's Comic *Portrait*." EL 3 (1976): 61-72.

20056. Walzl, Florence L. "A Date in Joyce's 'The Sisters.'" TSLL 4(1962): 183-187.

20057. ----------. "The Liturgy of the Epiphany Season and the Epiphanies of Joyce." PMLA 80(1965): 436-450.

20058. West, Michael. "Old Cotter and the Enigma of Joyce's 'The Sisters.'" MP 67(1970):

370-372.

20059. West, Michael, and William Hendricks. "The Genesis and Significance of Joyce's Irony in 'A Painful Case.'" *ELH* 44(1977): 701-727.

20060. Whaley, Helen R. "The Role of the Blind Piano Tuner in Joyce's *Ulysses*." *MFS* 16 (1970): 531-539.

20061. White, John. "*Ulysses*: The Metaphysical Foundations and Grand Design." *MFS* 15(1969): 27-34.

20062. Whitaker, Thomas R. "The Drinkers and History: Rabelais, Balzac, and Joyce." *Comp L* 11(1959): 157-164.

20063. Woodbery, Potter. "The Irrelevance of Stephan Dedalus: Some Reflections on Joyce and the Student Activist Movement." *SLI* 3,#2(1970): 69-78.

20064. Worthington, Mabel P. "American Folk Songs in Joyce's *Finnegan's Wake*." *AL* 28(1956): 197-210.

20065. ----------. "Irish Folk Songs in Joyce's *Ulysses*." *PMLA* 71(1956): 321-339.

20066. ----------. "Joyce's Use of Gilbert and Sullivan: Gilbert and Sullivan Songs in Joyce." *HSL* 1(1969): 209-218.

20067. Wykes, David. "*The Odyssey* in *Ulysses*." *TSLL* 10(1968): 301-316.

20068. Yannella, Philip R. "James Joyce to *The Little Review*: Ten Letters." [with text] *JML* 1(1971): 393-398.

20069. Young, Dorothy E., and Paul Delany. "Turgenev and the Genesis of 'A Painful Case.'" *MFS* 20(1974): 217-220.

20070. Zlotnick, Joan. "Dubliners in Winesburg, Ohio: A Note on Joyce's 'The Sisters' and Anderson's 'The Philosophers.'" *SSF* 12(1975): 405-407.

See also 55, 71, 80, 88, 94, 436, 455, 4341, 6799, 18930, 19057, 19172, 20103, 21150.

LAMBERT, GAVIN. 20071. Heilbrun, Carolyn G. "An Interview with Gavin Lambert." *TCL* 22 (1976): 332-342.

LARKIN, PHILIP. 20072. Bergonzi, Bernard. "Davie, Larkin, and the State of England." *Con L* 18(1977): 343-360.

20073. Cox, C. B. "Philip Larkin, Anti-Heroic Poet." *SLI* 9,#1(1976): 155-168.

20074. Naremore, James. "Philip Larkin's 'Lost World.'" *Con L* 15(1974): 331-344.

20075. Reibetanz, John. "'The Whitsun Weddings': Larkin's Reinterpretation of Time and Form in Keats." *Con L* 17(1976): 529-540.

20076. Weatherhead, A. Kingsley. "Philip Larkin of England." *ELH* 38(1971): 616-630.

LAWRENCE, D. H. 20077. Adam, Ian. "Lawrence's Anti-Symbol: The Ending of *The Rainbow*." *JNT* 3(1973): 77-84.

20078. Adleman, Gary. "Beyond the Pleasure Principle: An Analysis of D. H. Lawrence's 'The Prussian Officer.'" *SSF* 1(1963): 8-15.

20079. Appleman, Philip. "D. H. Lawrence and the Intrusive Knock." *MFS* 3(1957): 328-332.

20080. ----------. "One of D. H. Lawrence's 'Autobiographical' Characters." *MFS* 2(1956): 237-238.

20081. Arnold, Armin. "D. H. Lawrence's First Critical Essays: Two Anonymous Reviews Identified." *PMLA* 79(1964): 185-188.

20082. ----------. "D. H. Lawrence and Thomas Mann." *Comp L* 13(1961): 33-38.

20083. ----------. "In the Footsteps of D. H. Lawrence in Switzerland: Some New Biographical Material." *TSLL* 3(1961): 184-188.

20084. ----------. "The Transcendental Element in American Literature: A Study of Some Unpublished D. H. Lawrence Manuscripts." *MP* 60(1962): 41-46.

20085. Baim, Joseph. "Past and Present in D. H. Lawrence's 'A Fragment of Stained Glass.'" *SSF* 8(1971): 323-326.

20086. ----------. "The Second Coming of Pan: A Note on D. H. Lawrence's 'The Last Laugh.'" *SSF* 6(1968): 98-100.

20087. Baker, James R. "Lawrence as Prophetic Poet." *JML* 3(1974): 1219-1238.

20088. Baldanza, Frank. "D. H. Lawrence's Song of Songs." *MFS* 7(1961): 106-114.

20089. Barber, David S. "Community in *Women in Love*." *Novel* 5(1971): 32-41.

20090. Bartlett, Phyllis. "Lawrence's *Collected Poems*: The Demon Takes Over." *PMLA* 66(1951): 583-593.

20091. Beards, Richard. "Lawrence Now." *JML* 1(1971): 434-438.

20092. ----------. "*Sons and Lovers* as *Bildungsroman*." *Coll L* 1(1974): 204-217.

20093. Beebe, Maurice. "Lawrence's Sacred Fount: The Artist Theme of *Sons and Lovers*." *TSLL* 4(1963): 539-552.

20094. ---------- and Anthony Tommasi. "Criticism of D. H. Lawrence: A Selected Checklist with an Index to Studies of Separate Works." *MFS* 5(1959): 83-98.

20095. Blanchard, Lydia. "Love and Power: A Reconsideration of Sexual Politics in Lawrence." *MFS* 21(1975): 431-443.

20096. Blissett, H. William. "D. H. Lawrence, D'Annunzio, Wagner." *Con L* 7(1966): 21-46.

20097. Branda, Eldon S. "Textual Changes in *Woman in Love*." *TSLL* 6(1964): 306-321.

20098. Brotherston, J. G. "Revolution and the Ancient Literature of Mexico for D. H. Lawrence and Antonin Artaud." *TCL* 18(1972): 181-189.

20099. Daleski, H. M. "The Duality of Lawrence." *MFS* 5(1959): 3-18.

20100. Dataller, Roger. "Elements of D. H. Lawrence's Prose Style." *EIC* 3(1953): 413-424.

20101. ----------. "Mr. Lawrence and Mrs. Woolf." *EIC* 8(1958): 48-59.

20102. Davis, Patricia C. "Chicken's Queen's Delight: D. H. Lawrence's 'The Fox.'" *MFS* 19 (1973): 565-571.

20103. Deakin, William. "D. H. Lawrence's Attacks on Proust and Joyce." *EIC* 7(1957): 383-403.

20104. Draper, R. P. "D. H. Lawrence on Mother-Love." *EIC* 8(1958): 285-289.

20105. ----------. "The Defeat of Feminism: D. H. Lawrence's *The Fox* and 'The Woman Who Rode Away.'" *SSF* 3(1966): 186-198.

20106. Cecchetti Giovanni. "Verga and D. H. Lawrence's Translations." *Comp L* 9(1957): 333-344.

20107. Chamberlain, Robert L. "Pussum, Minette, and the Africo-Nordic Symbol in Lawrence's *Women in Love*." *PMLA* 78(1963): 407-416.

20108. Coombes, H. "A Word on 'The Fox.'" *EIC* 9(1959): 451-453.

20109. Cowan, James C. "D. H. Lawrence's *The Princess* as Ironic Romance." *SSF* 4(1967):

245-251.

20110. Craig, David. "Mr. Liddell and Dr. Levins." *EIC* 5(1955): 64-68.

20111. Cushman, Keith. "'A Bastard Begot': The Origins of D. H. Lawrence's 'The Christening.'" *MP* 70(1972): 146-148.

20112. ----------. "D. H. Lawrence at Work: The Making of 'Odour of Chrysanthemums.'" *JML* 2 (1971): 367-392.

20113. ----------. "D. H. Lawrence at Work: 'Vin Ordinaire' into 'The Thorn in the Flesh.'" *JML* 5(1976): 46-58.

20114. ----------. "Lawrence's Use of Hardy in 'The Shades of Spring.'" *SSF* 9(1972): 402-404.

20115. ----------. "The Making of D. H. Lawrence's 'The White Stocking.'" *SSF* 10(1973): 51-65.

20116. ----------. "A Note on Lawrence's 'Fly in the Ointment.'" *ELN* 15(1977): 47-51.

20117. ----------. "Some Varieties of D. H. Lawrence Criticism." *MP* 69(1971): 152-158.

20118. Elliott, John R., Jr., editor. "The Man who was Through with the World." *EIC* 9(1959): 213-221.

20119. Empson, William. "Lady Chatterly Again." *EIC* 13(1963): 101-104.

20120. Engelberg, Edward. "Escape from the Circles of Experience: D. H. Lawrence's *The Rainbow* as a Modern *Bildungsroman*." *PMLA* 78(1963): 103-113.

20121. Erlich, Richard D. "Catastrophism and Coition: Universal and Individual Development in *Women in Love*." *TSLL* 9(1967): 117-128.

20122. Fadiman, Regina. "The Poet as Choreographer: Lawrence's 'The Blind Man.'" *JNT* 2 (1972): 60-67.

20123. Farmer, David. "An Unpublished Version of D. H. Lawrence's Introduction to *Pansies*." *RES* 21(1970): 181-184.

20124. Finney, Brian H. "Two Missing Pages from 'The Ladybird.'" *RES* 24(1973): 191-192.

20125. Fitz, L. T. "The Rocking-Horse Winner' and the Golden Bough." *SSF* 11(1974): 199-200.

20126. Ford, George H. "Shelley or Schiller? A Note on D. H. Lawrence at Work." *TSLL* 4 (1962): 154-156.

20127. Ford, George H. "'The Wedding' Chapter of D. H. Lawrence's *Women in Love*." *TSLL* 6 (1964): 134-147.

20128. Fulmer, O. Bryan. "The Significance of the Death of the Fox in D. H. Lawrence's *The Fox*." *SSF* 5(1968): 275-282.

20129. Gill, Stephen. "The Composite World: Two Versions of *Lady Chatterly's Lover*." *EIC* 21 (1971): 347-364.

20130. ----------. "Lawrence and Gerald Crich." *EIC* 27(1977): 231-247.

20131. Goldberg, Michael. "Dickens and Lawrence: More on Rocking Horses." *MFS* 17(1971): 574.

20132. ----------. "Lawrence's 'The Rocking Horse Winner': A Dickensian Fable?" *MFS* 15(1969): 525-536.

20133. Goldberg, S. L. "*The Rainbow*: Fiddle-Bow and Sand." *EIC* 11(1961): 418-434.

20134. Gregor, Ian. "'The Fox': A Caveat." *EIC* 9(1959): 10-21.

20135. Gullason, Thomas A. "Revelation and Evolution: A Neglected Dimension of the Short Story." *SSF* 10(1973): 347-356.

20136. Gurko, Leo. "D. H. Lawrence's Greatest Collection of Short Stories—What Holds It Together." *MFS* 18(1972): 173-182.

20137. ----------. "*Kangaroo*: D. H. Lawrence in Transit." *MFS* 10(1964): 349-358.

20138. ----------. "*The Lost Girl*: D. H. Lawrence as a 'Dickens of the Midlands.'" *PMLA* 78 (1963): 601-605.

20139. Guttmann, Allen. "D. H. Lawrence: The Politics of Irrationality." *Con L* 5(1964): 151-163.

20140. Harris, Janice H. "Insight and Experiment in D. H. Lawrence's Early Short Fiction." *PQ* 55(1976): 418-435.

20141. Heywood, Christopher. "Oliver Schreiner's *The Story of an African Farm*: Prototype of Lawrence's Early Novels." *ELN* 14(1976): 44-50.

20142. Hinz, Evelyn J. "*The Rainbow*: Ursula's 'Liberation.'" *Con L* 17(1976): 24-43.

20143. ---------- and John J. Teunissen. "Savior and Cock: Allusion and Icon in Lawrence's *The Man Who Died*." *JML* 5(1976): 279-296.

20144. Hogan, Robert. "The Amorous Whale: A Study in the Symbolism of D. H. Lawrence." *MFS* 5(1954): 39-46.

20145. ----------. "D. H. Lawrence and His Critics." *EIC* 9(1959): 381-387.

20146. Hudspeth, Robert N. "Quality as Theme and Technique in D. H. Lawrence's 'The Border Line.'" *SSF* 4(1966): 51-56.

20147. ----------. "Lawrence's 'Odour of Chrysanthemums': Isolation and Paradox." *SSF* 6 (1969): 630-636.

20148. Humma, John B. "D. H. Lawrence as Friedrich Nietzsche." *PQ* 53(1974): 110-120.

20149. ----------. "Melville's *Billy Budd* and Lawrence's 'The Prussian Officer': Old Adams and New." *EL* 1(1974): 83-88.

20150. Jacobson, Sibyl. "The Paradox of Fulfillment: A Discussion of *Women in Love*." *JNT* 3(1973): 53-65.

20151. Janik, Del Ivan. "D. H. Lawrence's *Etruscan Places*: The Mystery of Touch." *EL* 3 (1976): 194-205.

20152. ----------. "D. H. Lawrence's 'Future Religion': The Unity of *Last Poems*." *TSLL* 16(1975): 739-754.

20153. ----------. "Toward 'Thingness': Cezanne's Painting, Lawrence's Poetry." *TCL* 19 (1973): 119-128.

20154. Junkins, Donald. "D. H. Lawrence's 'The Horse Dealer's Daughter.'" *SSF* 6(1969): 210-212.

20155. ----------. "'The Rocking-Horse Winner': A Modern Myth." *SSF* 2(1964): 87-89.

20156. Kalnins, Mara. "D. H. Lawrence's 'Odour of Chrysanthemums': The Three Endings." *SSF* 13(1976): 471-479.

20157. Kendle, Burton S. "D. H. Lawrence: The Man Who Misunderstood Gulliver." *ELN* 2(1964): 42-46.

20158. Kessler, Jascha. "D. H. Lawrence's Primitivism." *TSLL* 5(1964): 467-488.

20159. Kestner, Joseph. "Sculptural Character in Lawrence's *Women in Love*." *MFS* 21 (1975): 543-553.

20159a. Kinkead-Weekes, Mark. "This Old Maid: Jane Austen Replies to Charlotte Brontë and D. H. Lawrence." *NCF* 30(1975): 399-420.

20160. Kleinbard, David J. "D. H. Lawrence and Ontological Insecurity." *PMLA* 89(1974): 154-163.

20161. Knight, G. Wilson. "Lawrence, Joyce and Powys." *EIC* 11(1961): 403-417.

20162. Lainoff, Seymour. "*The Rainbow*: The Shaping of Modern Man." *MFS* 1,#4 (1955): 23-27.

20163. ----------. "The Wartime Setting of Lawrence's 'Tickets, Please.'" *SSF* 7(1970): 649-651.

20164. Langman, F. H. "*Woman in Love*." *EIC* 17(1967): 183-206.

20165. Levin, Gerald. "The Symbolism of Lawrence's *The Fox*." *CLA* 11(1967): 135-141.

20166. Liddell, Robert. "Lawrence and Dr. Leavis: The Case of 'St. Mawr.'" *EIC* 4(1954): 321-327.

20167. Mahnken, Harry E. "The Plays of D. H. Lawrence: Addenda." *MD* 7(1965): 431-432.

20168. Marks, W. S., III. "D. H. Lawrence and His Rabbit Adolph: Three Symbolic Permutations." *Criticism* 10(1968): 200-216.

20169. ----------. "The Psychology of the Uncanny in Lawrence's 'The Rocking-Horse Winner.'" *MFS* 11(1965): 381-392.

20170. McCabe, Thomas H. "Rhythm as Form in Lawrence: 'The Horse Dealer's Daughter.'" *PMLA* 87 (1972): 64-68.

20171. Merivale, Patricia. "D. H. Lawrence and the Modern Pan Myth." *TSLL* 6(1964): 297-305.

20172. Meyers, Jeffrey. "Katherine Mansfield, Gurdjieff, and Lawrence's 'Mother and Daughter.'" *TCL* 22(1976): 444-453.

20173. ----------. "*The Plumed Serpent* and the Mexican Revolution." *JML* 4(1974): 55-72.

20174. Miller, Milton. "Definition by Comparison: Chaucer, Lawrence and Joyce." *EIC* 3 (1953): 369-381.

20175. Mori, Haruhide. "Lawrence's Imagistic Development in *The Rainbow* and *Women in Love*." *ELH* 31(1964): 460-481.

20176. Mortland, Donald E. "The Conclusion of *Sons and Lovers*: A Reconsideration." *SN* 3(1971): 305-316.

20177. Moynahan, Julian. "Lady Chatterley's Lover: The Seed of Life." *ELH* 26(1959): 66-90.

20178. ----------. "Lawrence's 'The Man who Loved Islands': A Modern Fable." *MFS* 5(1959): 57-64.

20179. Myers, Neil. "Lawrence and the War." *Criticism* 4(1962): 44-58.

20180. Paniches, George A. "D. H. Lawrence's Biblical Play *David*." *MD* 6(1963): 164-176.

20181. ----------. "D. H. Lawrence's War.'" Letters." *TSLL* 5(1963): 398-409.

20182. Peter, John. "The Bottom of the Well: *Lady Chatterly's Lover*." *EIC* 12(1962): 226-227.

20183. ----------. "Lady Chatterly Again." *EIC* 12(1962): 445-447.

20184. ----------. "*Lady Chatterly* for the last time." *EIC* 13(1963): 301-302.

20185. Phillips, Steven R. "The Double Pattern of D. H. Lawrence's 'The Horse Dealer's Daughter.'" *SSF* 10(1973): 94-97.

20186. ----------. "The Monomyth and Literary Criticism." *Coll L* 2(1975): 1-16.

20187. Pollak, Paulina Salz. "The Letters of D. H. Lawrence to Sallie and Willie Hopkin." *JML* 3(1973): 24-34.

20188. Roberts, Mark. "Mr. Liddell and Dr. Leavis." *EIC* 5(1955): 68-75.

20189. Rose, Shirley. "Physical Trauma in D. H. Lawrence's Short Fiction." *Con L* 16(1975): 73-83.

20190. Ross, Charles I. "The Revisions of the Second Generation in *The Rainbow*." *RES* 27 (1976): 277-295.

20191. Rossi, Patrizo. "Lawrence's Two *Foxes*: a Comparison of the Text." *EIC* 22(1972): 265-278.

20192. Sagar, Keith. "'The Best I Have Known': D. H. Lawrence's 'A Modern Lover' and 'The Shades of Spring.'" *SSF* 4(1967): 143-151.

20193. Sale, Roger. "The Narrative Technique of *The Rainbow*." *MFS* 5(1959): 29-38.

20194. Secor, Robert. "Language and Movement in 'Fanny and Annie.'" *SSF* 6(1969): 395-400.

20195. Schwarz, Daniel R. "Speaking of Paul Morel: Voice, Unity, and Meaning in *Sons and Lovers*." *SN* 8(1976): 255-277.

20196. Sharpe, Michael C. "The Genesis of D. H. Lawrence's *The Trespasser*." *EIC* 11(1961): 34-39.

20197. Shields, E. F. "Broken Vision in Lawrence's 'The Fox.'" *SSF* 9(1972): 353-363.

20198. Smith, Constance. "St. Mawr." *EIC* 5(1955): 292-293.

20199. Smith, Grover, Jr. "The Doll-Burners: D. H. Lawrence and Louisa Alcott." *MLQ* 19(1958): 28-32.

20200. Solomon, Gerald. "The Banal, and the Poetry of D. H. Lawrence." *EIC* 23(1973): 254-267.

20201. Sparrow, John. "*Lady Chatterly* again." *EIC* 13(1963): 202-205.

20202. ----------. "*Lady Chatterly* for the last time." *EIC* 13(1963): 303.

20203. Spilka, Mark. "Lessing and Lawrence: The Battle of the Sexes." *Con L* 16(1975): 218-240.

20204. ----------. "Post-Leavis Lawrence Critics." *MLQ* 25(1964): 212-217.

20205. ----------. "The Shape of an Arch: A Study of Lawrence's *The Rainbow*." *MFS* 1,#2 (1955): 30-38.

20206. Squires, Michael. "Lawrence's *The White Peacock*: A Mutation of Pastoral." *TSLL* 12 (1970): 263-283.

20207. ----------. "Pastoral Patterns and Pastoral Variants in *Lady Chatterley's Lover*." *ELH* 39(1972): 129-146.

20208. ----------. "Recurrence as a Narrative Technique in *The Rainbow*." *MFS* 21(1975): 230-236.

20209. Stanford, Raney. "Thomas Hardy and Lawrence's *The White Peacock*." *MFS* 5(1959): 19-28.

20210. Stoehr, Taylor. "'Mentalized Sex' in D. H. Lawrence." *Novel* 8(1975): 101-122.

20211. Stewart, Garrett. "Lawrence, 'Being,' and the Allotropic Style." *Novel* 9(1976): 217-242.

20212. Taylor, John A. "The Greatness in *Sons and Lovers*." *MP* 71(1974): 380-387.

20213. Tedlock, E. W., Jr. "Lawrence's Annotation of Ouspensky's *Tertium Organum*." *TSLL* 2(1960): 206-218.

20214. Thomas, T. W. "Mr. Liddell and Dr. Leavis." *EIC* 5(1955): 75-80.

20215. Tracy, Billy T. "'Reading up the Ancient Etruscans': Lawrence's Debt to George Dennis." *TCL* 23(1977): 437-450.

20216. Waterman, Arthur E. "The Plays of D. H. Lawrence." *MD* 2(1960): 349-357.

20217. Waters, Frank. "Quetzalcoatl Versus D. H. Lawrence's *Plumed Serpent*." *WAL* 3(1968): 103-113.

20218. Wasson, Richard. "Comedy and History in *The Rainbow*." *MFS* 13(1967): 465-477.

20219. Whitaker, Thomas R. "Lawrence's Western Path: Mornings in Mexico." *Criticism* 3(1961): 219-236.

20220. Widmer, Kingsley. "D. H. Lawrence and Critical Mannerism." *JML* 3(1974): 1044-1050.

20221. ----------. "Lawrence and the Fall of Modern Woman." *MFS* 5(1959): 47-56.

20222. ----------. "Lawrentian Manias: A Review of Recent Studies of D. H. Lawrence." *SN* 5(1973): 547-566.

20223. ----------. "The Pertinence of Modern Pastoral: The Three Versions of *Lady Chatterley's Lover*." *SN* 5(1973): 298-313.

20224. ----------. "Review-Essay: Profiling an Erotic Prophet: Recent Lawrence Biographies." *SN* 8(1976): 234-244.

20225. ----------. "Review-Essay: Psychiatry and Piety on Lawrence." *SN* 9(1977): 195-200.

20226. Wilde, Alan. "The Illusion of St. Mawr: Technique and Vision in D. H. Lawrence's Novel." *PMLA* 79(1964): 164-170.

20227. Wolkenfeld, Suzanne. "'The Sleeping Beauty' Retold: D. H. Lawrence's 'The Fox.'" *SSF* 14(1977): 345-352.

20228. Vickery, John B. "Myth and Ritual in the Shorter Fiction of D. H. Lawrence." *MFS* 5 (1959): 65-82.

20229. ----------. *The Plumed Serpent* and the Eternal Paradox." *Criticism* 5(1963): 119-134.

20230. ----------. *The Plumed Serpent* and the Reviving God." *JML* 2(1972): 505-532.

20231. Vitoux, Pierre. "Alduous Huxley and D. H. Lawrence: An Attempt at Intellectual Sympathy." *MLR* 69(1974): 501-522.

20232. ----------. "The Chapter 'Excurse' in *Women in Love*: Its Genesis and the Critical Problem." *TSLL* 17(1976): 821-836.

See also 15327, 15771, 18922, 18927, 19792.

LAWRENCE, T. E.   20233. Boak, Denis. "Malraux and T. E. Lawrence." *MLR* 61(1966): 218-224.

20234. Meyers, Jeffrey. "The Revisions of Seven Pillars of Wisdom." *PMLA* 88(1973): 1066-1082.

20235. Weintraub, Rodelle and Stanley. *"Moby-Dick* and the *Seven Pillars of Wisdom*." *SAF* 2(1974): 238-240.

LEAVIS, F. R.   20236. Jarrett-Kerr, Martin. "The Literary Criticism of F. R. Leavis." *EIC* 2 (1952): 351-368.

20237. Leavis, F. R. "The State of Criticism: Representations to Fr. Martin Jarrett-Kerr." *EIC* 3(1953): 215-233.

See also 284, 304, 16618.

LEHMANN, JOHN. 20238. Fry, Phillip, and James W. Lee. "An Interview in Austin with John Lehmann." *SN* 3(1971): 80-96.

20239. Henig, Suzanne. "Conversation with John Lehmann." *JML* 3(1973): 91-99.

LEHMANN, ROSAMOND. 20240. Gindin, James. "Rosamund Lehmann: A Revaluation." *Con L* 15(1974): 203-211.

20241. Gustafson, Margaret T. "Rosamund Lehmann: A Bibliography." *TCL* 4(1959): 143-147.

LESSING, DORIS.   20242. Barnow, Dagmar. "Disorderly Company: From *The Golden Notebook* to *The Four-Gated City*." *Con L* 14(1973): 491-514.

20243. Burkom, Selma R. "A Doris Lessing Checklist." *Crit* 11, #1(1968): 69-81.

20244. ----------. "'Only Connect': Form and Content in the Works of Doris Lessing." *Crit* 11,#1 (1968): 51-68.

20245. Bolling, Douglass. "Structure and Theme in *Briefing for a Descent into Hell*." *Con L* 14(1973): 550-564.

20246. Carey, John L. "Art and Reality in *The Golden Notebook*." *Con L* 14(1973): 437-456.

20247. Graves, Nora Calhoun. "Doris Lessing's Two Antheaps." *NCL* 2(May, 1972): 6-8.

20248. Hardin, Nancy S. "Doris Lessing and the Sufi Way." *Con L* 14(1973): 565-581.

20249. ----------. "The Sufi Teaching Story and Doris Lessing." *TCL* 23(1977): 314-326.

20250. Hinz, Evelyn J., and John J. Teunissen. "The Pietà as Icon in *The Golden Notebook*." *Con L* 14(1973): 457-470.

20251. Howe, Florence. "A Conversation with Doris Lessing." *Con L* 14(1973): 418-436.

20252. Joyner, Nancy. "The Underside of the Butterfly: Lessing's Debt to Woolf." *JNT* 4(1974): 204-211.

20253. Kaplan, Sydney. "The Limits of Consciousness in the Novels of Doris Lessing." *Con L* 14(1973): 536-549.

20254. Karl, Frederick R. "Doris Lessing in the Sixties: The New Anatomy of Melancholy." *Con L* 13(1972): 15-33.

20255. Krouse, Agate Nesaule. "A Doris Lessing Checklist." *Con L* 14(1973): 590-597.

20256. Lightfoot, Marjorie J. "Breakthrough in *The Golden Notebook*." *SN* 7(1975): 277-284.

20257. Marchino, Lois A. "The Search for Self in the Novels of Doris Lessing." *SN* 4(1972): 252-261.

20258. Morgan, Ellen. "Alienation of the Woman Writer in *The Golden Notebook*." *Con L* 14 (1973): 471-480.

20259. Mulkeen, Anne M. "Twentieth-Century Realism: The 'Grid' Structure in *The Golden Notebook*." *SN* 4(1972): 262-274.

20260. Porter, Dennis. "Realism and Failure in *The Golden Notebook*." *MLQ* 35(1974): 56-65.

20261. Pratt, Annis. "[Doris Lessing] Introduction." *Con L* 14(1973): 413-417.

20262. Richey, Clarence W. "Professor Watkins' 'Sleep of Necessity': A Note on the Parallel Between Doris Lessing's *Briefing for a Descent Into Hell* and the G. T. Gurdjieff-P. D. Ouspensky System of Esoteric Psychology." *NCL* 2(March 1972): 9-11.

20263. Rose, Ellen Cronan. "The End of the Game: New Directions in Doris Lessing's Fiction." *JNT* 6(1976): 66-75.

20264. ----------. "The Eriksonian Bilungsroman: An Approach Through Doris Lessing." *HSL* 7 (1975): 1-17.

20265. Ryf, Robert S. "Beyond Ideology: Doris Lessing's Mature Vision." *MFS* 21(1975): 193-201.

20266. Spilka, Mark. "Lessing and Lawrence: The Battle of the Sexes." *Con L* 16(1975): 218-240.

20267. Sukenick, Lynn. "Feeling and Reason

in Doris Lessing's Fiction." *Con L* 14(1973): 515-535.

20268. Vlastos, Marion. "Doris Lessing and R. D. Laing: Psychopolitics and Prophecy." *PMLA* 91(1976): 245-258.

20269. Zak, Michele Wender. *"The Grass is Singing*: A Little Novel about the Emotions." *Con L* 14(1973): 481-490.

LEWIS, C. DAY. 20270. Repogle, Justin. "The Auden Group." *Con L* 5(1964): 133-150.

LEWIS, C. S. 20271. Hume, Kathryn. "C. S. Lewis' Trilogy: A Cosmic Romance." *MFS* 20(1974): 505-517.

20272. Lewis, C. S. "De Descriptione Temporum." *EIC* 6(1956): 247.

20273. Loomis, Roger Sherman. "Literary History and Literary Criticism: A Critique of C. S. Lewis." *MLR* 60(1965): 508-511.

20274. Neuleib, Janice. "Technology and Theocracy: The Cosmic Voyages of Wells and Lewis." *Ext* 16(1975): 130-136.

20275. Norwood, W. D. Jr., "Underlying Themes in C. S. Lewis's Trilogy." *Crit* 9,#2(1967): 67-80.

20276. Philmus, Robert M. "C. S. Lewis and the Fictions of 'Scientism.'" *Ext* 13(1972): 92-101. See also 62, 159, 163, 8872, 15771.

LEWIS, WYNDHAM. 20277. Chapman, Robert T. "Satire and Aesthetics in Wyndham Lewis' *Apes of God*." *Con L* 12(1971): 133-145.

20278. Materer, Timothy. "The Short Stories of Wyndham Lewis." *SSF* 7(1970): 615-624.

20279. Wagner, Geoffrey. "Wyndham Lewis' Inhuman Tetralogy: An Introduction to 'The Human Age.'" *MFS* 2(1956): 221-227. See also 6838.

LINDSAY, DAVID. 20280. Rabkin, Eric S. "Conflation of Genres and Myths in David Lindsay's *A Voyage to Arcturus*." *JNT* 7(1977): 149-155.

20281. Schofield, Jack. "Cosmic Imagery in *A Voyage to Arcturus*." *Ext* 13(1972): 146-151. See also 177.

LIVINGS, HENRY. 20282. Giannetti, Louis D. "Henry Livings: A Neglected Voice in the New Drama." *MD* 12(1969): 38-48.

LODGE, DAVID. 20283. Honan, Park. "David Lodge and the Cinematic Novel in England." *Novel* 5(1972): 167-173.

MACAULAY, ROSE. 20284. Irwin, W. R. "Permanence and Change in *The Edwardians* and *Told By an Idiot*." *MFS* 2(1956): 63-67.

MACDIARMID, HUGH. 20285. Boutelle, Ann E. "Language and Vision in the Early Poetry of Hugh MacDiarmid." *Con L* 12(1971): 495-509.

MACNEICE, LOUIS. 20286. Collins, P. A. W., and R. P. Draper. "Miss Barroff on 'Snow.'" *EIC* 9(1959): 209-211.

20287. Cragg, R. C. "Snow." *EIC* 4(1954): 231-236.

20288. ----------. *"Snow*, a Philosophical Poem: a Study in Critical Procedure." *EIC* 3(1953): 425-433.

20289. Dawson, S. W. "Snow." *EIC* 4(1954): 339-340.

20290. Barroff, Marie. "'Snow' and Poetic Theory." *EIC* 9(1959): 450-451.

20291. ----------. "What a pom is: for instance, *Snow*." *EIC* 8(1958): 393-404.

20292. Gitzen, Julian. "Louis MacNeice: The Last Decade." *TCL* 14(1968): 133-142

20293. Irwin, John T. "MacNeice, Auden, and the Art Ballad." *Con L* 11(1970): 58-79.

20294. McKinnon, William T. "The Cad with the Golden Tongue." *EIC* 20(1970): 109-115.

20295. ----------. "MacNeice's 'Pale Panther,' an Exercise in Dream Logic." *EIC* 23(1973): 388-398.

20296. Roberts, M. A. M. "'Snow': An Answer to Mr. Cragg." *EIC* 4(1954): 227-231.

MANSFIELD, KATHERINE. 20297. Baldeshwiler, Eileen. "Katherine Mansfield's Theory of Fiction." *SSF* 7(1970): 421-432.

20298. Bateson, F. W. "Katherine Mansfield's *The Fly*: A Sort of Answer." *EIC* 12(1962): 347-351.

20299. ----------. "More on *The Fly*." *EIC* 12(1962): 451-452.

20300. ----------, and B. Shahevitch. "Katherine Mansfield's *The Fly*: a Critical Exercise." *EIC* 12(1962): 39-53.

20301. Boyle, Ted E. "The Death of the Boss: Another Look at Katherine Mansfield's 'The Fly.'" *MFS* 11(1965): 183-185.

20302. Copland, R. A. "Katherine Mansfield's *The Fly*." *EIC* 12(1962): 338-341.

20303. Davis, Robert M. "The Unity of 'The Garden Party.'" *SSF* 2(1964): 61-65.

20304. Garlington, Jack. "Katherine Mansfield: The Critical Trend." *TCL* 2(1956): 51-61.

20305. Greenwood, E. B. "Katherine Mansfield's *The Fly*." *EIC* 12(1962): 341-347.

20306. ----------. "More on *The Fly*." *EIC* 12(1962): 448-450.

20307. Hagopian, John. "Capturing Mansfield's 'Fly.'" *MFS* 9(1963): 385-390.

20308. Hull, Robert L. "Alienation in 'Miss Brill.'" *SSF* 5(1967): 74-76.

20309. Jolly, R. A. "Katherine Mansfield's *The Fly*." *EIC* 12(1962): 335-338.

20310. Kleine, Don W. "The Chekhovian Source of 'Marriage à la Mode.'" *PQ* 42(1963): 284-288.

20311. ----------. "'The Garden Party'." A Portrait of the Artist." *Criticism* 5(1963): 360-371.

20312. ----------. "Katherine Mansfield and the Prisoner of Love." *Crit* 3,#2(1960): 20-33.

20313. Michel-Michot, Paulette. "Katherine Mansfield's 'The Fly': An Attempt to Capture the Boss." *SSF* 11(1974): 85-92.

20314. Nebeker, Helen E. "The Pear Tree: Sexual Implications in Katharine Mansfield's 'Bliss.'" *MFS* 18(1972): 545-551.

20315. Sutherland, Ronald. "Katherine Mansfield: Plagiarist, Disciple, or Ardent Admirer?" *Crit* 5,#2(1962): 58-76.

20316. Taylor, Donald S., and Daniel A. Weiss. "Crashing the Garden Party." *MFS* 4(1958): 361-364.

20317. Waldron, Philip. "Katherine Mansfield's *Journal*." *TCL* 20(1974): 11-18.

20318. Walker, Warren S. "The Unresolved Conflict in 'The Garden Party.'" *MFS* 3(1957): 354-358.

20319. Wright, Celeste Turner. "Darkness as a Symbol in Katherine Mansfield." *MP* 51(1954): 204-207.

20320. ----------. "Genesis of a Short Story." *PQ* 34(1955): 91-96.

20321. Wright, Celeste Turner. "Katherine Mansfield's Boat Image." *TCL* 1(1955): 128–132.
See also 20172.

MASEFIELD, JOHN. 20322. Drew, Fraser Bragg. "John Masefield and the *Manchester Guardian*." *PQ* 37(1958): 126–128.

MAUGHAM, SOMERSET. 20323. Cordell, Richard A. "The Theater of Somerset Maugham." *MD* 1(1959): 211–217.

20324. Fielden, John Steward. "The Ibsenite Maugham." *MD* 4(1961): 138–151.

20325. Heywood, C. "Two Printed Texts of Somerset Maugham's *Mrs. Craddock*." *ELN* 5(1967): 39–46.
See also 18927.

MIDDLETON, CHRISTOPHER. 20326. Carlin, M. M. "*Torse 3*." *EIC* 13(1963): 112–117.

20327. Martin, Wallace D. "Beyond Modernism: Christopher Middleton and Geoffrey Hill." *Con L* 12 (1971): 420–436.

MITCHELL, JOHN L. 20328. Campbell, Ian. "The Science Fiction of John Leslie Mitchell." *Ext* 16(1974): 53–63.

20329. Wagner, Geoffrey. "'The greatest since Galt': Lewis Grassic Gibbon." *EIC* 2(1952): 295–310.

MONTAGUE, C. E. 20330. Irwin, W. R. "Experiment in Irony: Montague's 'A Hind Let Loose.'" *MFS* 3(1957): 141–146.

MOORE, GEORGE. 20331. Burkhart, Charles. "The Short Stories of George Moore." *SSF* 6(1969): 165–174.

20332. Cary, Meredith. "Saint Biddy M'Hale." *SSF* 6(1969): 649–652.

20333. Cave, Richard. "George Moore's 'Stella.'" *RES* 28(1977): 181–188.

20334. Michie, Donald M. "A Man of Genius and a Man of Talent." *TSLL* 6(1964): 148–154.

MUIR, EDWIN. 20335. Garber, Frederick. "Edwin Muir's Heraldic Mode." *TCL* 12(1966): 96–103.

20336. Grice, Fred. "The Poetry of Edwin Muir." *EIC* 5(1955): 243–252.

20337. Huberman, Elizabeth. "Imitation and Tragedy: A New Look at Edwin Muir's 'The Gate.'" *PMLA* 87(1972): 75–79.

20338. Mellown, Elgin W. "Autobiographical Themes in the Novels of Edwin Muir." *Con L* 6 (1965): 228–242.

20339. ----------. "The Development of a Criticism Edwin Muir and Franz Kafka." *Comp L* 16 (1964): 310–321.

MUNRO, H. H. 20340. Beaty, Frederick L. "Mrs. Packletide and Tartarin." *NCF* 7(1952): 219–220.

20341. Drake, Robert. "Saki's Ironic Stories." *TSLL* 5(1963): 374–388.

20342. Thrane, James R. "Two New Stories by 'Saki' with an Introduction." *MFS* 19(1973): 139–152.

MURDOCH, IRIS. 20343. Baldanza, Frank. "Iris Murdoch and the Theory of Personality." *Criticism* 7(1965): 176–189.

20344. ----------. "The Manuscript of Iris Murdoch's *A Severed Head*." *JML* 3(1973): 75–90.

20345. ----------. "The Murdoch Manuscripts at the University of Iowa: An Addendum." *MFS* 16 (1970): 201–202.

20346. ----------. "*The Nice and the Good*."

MFS 15(1969): 417–428.

20347. Bellamy, Michael O. "An Interview with Iris Murdoch." *Con L* 18(1977): 129–140.

20348. Culley, Ann. "Theory and Practice: Characterization in the Novels of Iris Murdoch." *MFS* 15(1969): 335–345.

20349. ----------, with John Feaster. "Criticism of Iris Murdoch: A Selected Checklist." *MFS* 15(1969): 449–457.

20350. Felheim, Marvin. "Symbolic Characterization in the Novels of Iris Murdoch." *TSLL* 2 (1960): 189–197.

20351. German, Howard. "Allusions in the Early Novels of Iris Murdoch." *MFS* 15(1969): 361–377.

20352. ----------. "The Range of Allusions in the Novels of Iris Murdoch." *JML* 2(1971): 57–85.

20353. Gindin, James. "Images of Illusion in the Works of Iris Murdoch." *TSLL* 2(1960): 180–188.

20354. Hall, James. "Blurring the Will: The Growth of Iris Murdoch." *ELH* 32(1965): 256–273.

20355. Hall, William F. "*Bruno's Dream*: Technique and Meaning in the Novels of Iris Murdoch." *MFS* 15(1969): 429–443.

20356. Hoffman, Frederick J. "Iris Murdoch: The Reality of Persons." *Crit* 7,#1(1964): 48–57.

20357. Hoskins, Robert. "Iris Murdoch's Midsummer Nightmare." *TCL* 18(1972): 191–198.

20358. Kaehele, Sharon, and Howard German. "The Discovery of Reality in Iris Murdoch's *The Bell*." *PMLA* 82(1967): 554–563.

20359. Kane, Patricia. "The Furnishings of a Marriage: An Aspect of Characterization in Iris Murdoch's *A Severed Head*." *NCL* 2(Nov., 1972): 4–5.

20360. Kemp, Peter. "The Fight Against Fantasy: Iris Murdoch's *The Red and The Green*." *MFS* 15(1969): 403–415.

20361. Kenney, Alice P. "The Mythic History of *A Severed Head*." *MFS* 15(1969): 387–401.

20362. Kuehl, Linda. "Iris Murdoch: The Novelist as Magician/The Magician as Artist." *MFS* 15(1969): 347–360.

20363. Majdiak, Daniel. "Romanticism in the Aesthetics of Iris Murdoch." *TSLL* 14(1972): 359–375.

20364. Meidner, O. M. "Iris Murdoch's *The Flight* from the *Enchanter*." *EIC* 11(1961): 435–447.

20365. Murray, William M. "A Note on the Iris Murdoch Manuscripts in the University of Iowa Libraries." *MFS* 15(1969): 445–448.

20366. Obumsely, Ben. "Iris Murdoch and Satre." *ELH* 42(1975): 296–317.

20367. O'Connor, William Van. "Iris Murdoch: The Formal and the Contingent." *Crit* 3,#2 (1960): 34–46.

20368. Porter, Raymond J. "*Leitmotiv* in Iris Murdoch's *Under the Net*." *MFS* 15(1969): 379–385.

20369. Sullivan, Zohreh T. "The Contracting Universe of Iris Murdoch's Gothic Novels." *MFS* 23(1977): 557–569.

20370. Vickery, John B. "The Dilemmas of Language: Sartre's *La Nausée* and Iris Murdoch's *Under the Net*." *JNT* 1(1971): 69–76.

20371. Wall, Stephen. "The Bell in *The Bell*." *EIC* 13(1963): 265–273.

20372. Weatherhead, A. K. "Backgrounds with

Figures in Iris Murdoch." *TSLL* 10(1969): 635-648.

20373. Whiteside, George. "The Novels of Iris Murdoch." *Crit* 7,#1(1964): 27-47.

20374. Widmann, R. L. "An Iris Murdoch Checklist." *Crit* 10,#1(1967): 17-29.

20375. ----------. "Murdoch's *Under the Net*: Theory and Practice of Fiction." *Crit* 10,#1 (1967): 5-16.

See also 18925.

NEWBY, P. H. 20376. Bufkin, E. C. "Quest in the Novels of P. H. Newby." *Crit* 8,#1(1965): 51-62.

20377. Mathews, F. X. "Newby on the Nile: The Comic Trilogy." *TCL* 14(1968): 3-16.

20378. ----------. "Witness to Violence: The War Novels of P. H. Newby." *TSLL* 12(1970): 121-135.

O'BRIEN, CONOR CRUISE. 20379. Cohen, Michael. "Politics vs. Drama in O'Brien's *Murderous Angels*." *Con L* 16(1975): 340-352.

O'BRIEN. FLANN. 20380. Lee, L. L. "The Dublin Cowboys of Flann O'Brien." *WAL* 4(1964): 219-225.

O'CASEY, SEAN. 20381. Armstrong, William A. "History, Autobiography, and *The Shadow of a Gunman*." *MD* 2(1960): 417-424.

20382. ----------. "The Integrity of *Juno and the Paycock*." *MD* 17(1974): 1-10.

20383. ----------. "The Sources and Themes of *The Plough and The Stars*." *MD* 4(1961): 234-242.

20384. Ayling, Ronald. "Feathers Finely Aflutther." *MD* 7(1964): 135-147.

20385. ----------. "'Nannie's Night Out.'" *MD* 5(1962): 154-163.

20386. ----------. "Popular Tradition and Individual Talent in Sean O'Casey's Dublin Trilogy." *JML* 2(1972): 491-504.

20387. Blitch, Alice Fox. "O'Casey's Shakespeare." *MD* 15(1972): 283-290.

20388. Carpenter, Charles A. "Sean O'Casey Studies Through 1964." *MD* 10(1967): 17-23.

20389. Coakley, James and Marvin Felheim. "Thalia in Dublin: Some Suggestions about the Relationships between O'Casey and Classical Comedy." *CD* 4(1970): 265-271.

20390. Daniel, Walter C. "The False Paradise Pattern in Sean O'Casey's *Cock A Doodle Dandy*." *CLA* 13(1969): 137-143.

20391. DeBaun, Vincent C. "Sean O'Casey and the Road to Expressionism." *MD* 4(1961): 254-259.

20392. Durbach, Errol. "Peacocks and Mothers: Theme and Dramatic Metaphor in O'Casey's *Juno and the Paycock*." *MD* 15(1972): 15-25.

20393. Edwards, A. C. "The Lady Gregory Letters to Sean O'Casey." *MD* 8(1965): 95-111.

20394. Esslinger, Pat. "Sean O'Casey and the Lockout of 1913: *Materia Poetica* of the Two Red Plays." *MD* 6(1963): 53-63.

20395. Fallon, Gabriel. "The House on the North Circular Road." *MD* 4(1961): 223-233.

20396. Hogan, Robert. "O'Casey's Dramatic Apprenticeship." *MD* 4(1961): 243-253.

20397. Johnston, Denis. "Sean O'Casey: A Biography and an Appraisal." *MD* 4(1961): 324-328.

20398. Krause, David. "O'Casey and Yeats and the Druid." *MD* 11(1968): 252-262.

20399. ----------. "'The Rageous Ossean': Patron-Hero of Synge and O'Casey." *MD* 4(1961): 268-291.

20400. Malone, Maureen. "*Red Roses for Me*: Fact and Symbol." *MD* 9(1966): 147-152.

20401. McLaughlin, John J. "Political Allegory in O'Casey's *Purple Dust*." *MD* 13(1970): 47-53.

20402. Ritchie, Harry M. "The Influence of Melodrama on the Early Plays of Sean O'Casey." *MD* 5(1962): 164-173.

20403. Rollins, Ronald G. "Form and Content in Sean O'Casey's Dublin Trilogy." *MD* 8(1966): 419-425.

20404. ----------. "From Ritual to Romance in *Within the Gates* and *Cock-a-Doodle-Dandy*." *MD* 17(1974): 11-18.

20405. Schrank, Bernice. "Dialectical Configurations in *Juno and the Paycock*." *TCL* 21 (1975): 438-456.

20406. Snowden, J. A. "Dialect in the Plays of Sean O'Casey." *MD* 14(1972): 387-391.

20407. Templeton, John. "Sean O'Casey and Expressionism." *MD* 14(1971): 47-62.

20408. Todd, R. Mary. "The Two Published Versions of Sean O'Casey's *Within the Gates*." *MD* 10(1968): 346-355.

20409. Worth, Katharine J. "O'Casey's Dramatic Symbolism." *MD* 4(1961): 260-267.

O'CONNER, FRANK. 20410. Brenner, Gerry. "Frank O'Connor's Imprudent Hero." *TSLL* 10(1968): 457-469.

20411. Briden, Earl F. "'Guests of the Nation': A Final Irony." *SSF* 13(1976): 79-81

20412. Coen, Frank. "Frank O'Connor's 'First Confession,' One and Two." *SSF* 10(1973): 419-421.

20413. May, Charles E. "Frank O'Conner's 'Judas.'" *NCL* 2(Nov., 1972): 11-13.

O'FAOLIN, SEAN. 20414. Hopkins, Robert H. "The Pastoral Mode of Sean O'Faolain's 'The Silence of the Valley.'" *SSF* 1(1964): 93-98.

O'FLAHERTY, LIAM. 20415. Doyle, P. A. "A Liam O'Flaherty checklist." *TCL* 13(1967): 49-51.

20416. Murray, Michael H. "Liam O'Flaherty and the speaking Voice." *SSF* 5(1968): 154-162.

ORTON, JOE. 20417. Fraser, Keath. "Joe Orton: His Brief Career." *MD* 14(1972): 413-419.

ORWELL, GEORGE. 20418. Conners, James. "'Do It to Julia': Thoughts on Orwell's *1984*." *MFS* 16(1970): 463-473.

20419. ----------. "Zamyatin's *We* and the Genesis of *1984*." *MFS* 21(1975): 107-124.

20420. Cook, Richard. "Rudyard Kipling and George Orwell." *MFS* 7(1961): 125-135.

20422. Edrich, Emanuel. "George Orwell and the Satire of Horror." *TSLL* 4(1962): 96-108.

20423. Elsbree, Langdon. "The Structured Nightmare of *1984*." *TCL* 5(1959): 135-141.

20424. Fink, Howard. "*Coming Up for Air*: Orwell's Ambiguous Satire on the Wellsian Utopia." *SLI* 6,#2(1973): 51-60.

20425. Green, Martin. "Orwell as an Old Etonian." *MFS* 21(1975): 3-10.

20426. Guild, Nicholas. "In Dubious Battle: George Orwell and the Victory of the Money-God." *MFS* 21(1975): 49-56.

20427. Harris, Harold, J. "Orwell's Essays and *1984*." *TCL* 4(1959): 154-161.

20428. Knapp, John V. "Dance to a Creepy Minuet: Orwell's *Burmese Days*, Precursor of *Animal Farm*." *MFS* 21(1975): 11-29.

20429. Lee, Robert A. "Symbol and Structure in *Burmese Days*: A Revaluation." *TSLL* 11(1969): 819-835.

20430. ----------. "The Uses of Form: A Reading of *Animal Farm*." *SSF* 6(1969): 557-573.

20431. Lyons, John O. "George Orwell's Opaque Glass in *1984*." *Con L* 2,#3(1961): 39-46.

20432. Meyers, Jeffrey. "George Orwell: A Selected Checklist." *MFS* 21(1975): 133-136.

20433. ----------. "Orwell's Apocalypse: *Coming Up for Air*." *MFS* 21(1975): 69-80.

20434. ----------. "Review Article: George Orwell, the Honorary Proletarian." *PQ* 48(1969): 526-549.

20435. New, Melvyn. "Orwell and Anti-semitism: Toward *1984*." *MFS* 21(1975): 81-105.

20436. Philmus, Robert M. "The Language of Utopia." *SLI* 6,#2(1973): 61-78.

20437. Quintana, Ricardo. "George Orwell: The Satiric Resolution." *Con L* 2,#1(1961): 31-38.

20438. Rankin, David. "Orwell's Intention in *1984*." *ELN* 12(1975): 188-192.

20439. Smith, Marcus. "The Wall of Blackness: A Psychological Approach to *1984*." *MFS* 14 (1968): 423-433.

20440. Smyer, Richard I. "*Animal Farm*: The Burden of Consciousness." *ELN* 9(1971): 55-59.

20441. ----------. "Orwell's *A Clergyman's Daughter*: The Flight from History." *MFS* 21(1975): 31-48.

20442. Van Dellen, Robert J. "George Orwell's *Coming Up for Air*: The Politics of Power-lessness." *MFS* 21(1975): 57-68.

20443. Voorhees, Richard J. "Justice to George Orwell." *JML* 1(1970): 127-133.

20444. ----------. "Some Recent Books on Orwell: An Essay Review." *MFS* 21(1975): 125-131.

See also 207, 210, 18922.

OSBORNE, JOHN. 20445. Bailey, Shirley Jean. "John Osborne: A Bibliography." *TCL* 7(1961): 118-120.

20446. Bierhaus, E. G., Jr. "No World of Its Own: *Look Back in Anger* Twenty Years Later." *MD* 19(1976): 47-56.

20447. Faber, M. D. "The Character of Jimmy Porter: An Approach to *Look Back in Anger*." *MD* 13(1970): 67-77.

20448. Gersh, Gabriel. "The Theater of John Osborne." *MD* 10(1967): 137-143.

20449. Haltresht, Michael. "Sadomasochism in John Osborne's 'A Letter to my Fellow Countrymen.'" *NCL* 4(May, 1974): 10-12.

20450. Huss, Roy. "John Osborne's Backward Half-Way Look." *MD* 6(1963): 20-25.

20451. Karrfalt, David H. "The Social Theme in Osborne's Plays." *MD* 13(1970): 78-82.

20452. Spacks, Patricia Meyer. "Confrontation and Escape in Two Social Dramas." *MD* 11(1968): 61-72.

OWEN, WILFRED. 20453. Cohen, Joseph. "In Memory of W. R. Yeats—and Wilfred Owen." *JEGP* 58(1959): 637-649.

20454. Freeman, Rosemary. "Parody as a Literary Form: George Herbert and Wilfred Owen." *EIC* 13(1963): 307-322.

20455. ----------. "Wilfred Owen's 'Greater Love.'" *EIC* 16(1966): 132-133.

20456. Hill, James J., Jr. "Wilfred Owen's 'Greater Love.'" *EIC* 15(1965): 476-477.

20457. Posey, Horace G., Jr. "Muted Satire in 'Anthem for Doomed Youth.'" *EIC* 21(1971): 377-381.

20458. Wellend, D. S. R. "Half-Rhyme in Wilfred Owen: Its Derivation and Use." *RES* 1(1950): 226-241.

PINTER, HAROLD. 20459. Adler, Thomas P. "Pinter's *Night*: A Stroll down Memory Lane." *MD* 17(1974): 461-466.

20460. Amend, Victor E. "Harold Pinter—Some Credits and Debits." *MD* 10(1967): 165-174.

20461. Berkowitz, Gerald M. "Pinter's Revision of *The Caretaker*." *JML* 5(1976): 109-116.

20462. Bernhard, F. J. "Beyond Realism: The Plays of Harold Pinter." *MD* 8(1965): 185-191.

20463. Boulton, James T. "Harold Pinter: The *Caretaker* and Other Plays." *MD* 6(1963): 131-140.

20464. Brater, Enoch. "Pinter's *Homecoming* on Celluloid." *MD* 17(1974): 443-448.

20465. Brody, Alan. "The Gift of Realism: Hitchcock and Pinter." *JML* 3(1973): 149-172.

20466. Burghardt, Lorraine Hall. "Game Playing in Three by Pinter." *MD* 17(1974): 377-388.

20467. Burkman, Katherine H. "Pinter's *A Slight Ache* as Ritual." *MD* 11(1968): 326-335.

20468. Canady, Nicholas, Jr. "Harold Pinter's 'Tea Party': Seeing and Not-Seeing." *SSF* 6 (1969): 580-585.

20469. Carpenter, Charles A. "The Absurdity of Dread: Pinter's *The Dumb Waiter*." *MD* 16(1973): 279-286.

20470. ----------. "Symbolic Fallout in Pinter's *Birthday Party*." *MD* 17(1974): 389-402.

20471. Dawick, J. D. "'Punctuation' and Patterning in *The Homecoming*." *MD* 14(1971): 37-46.

20472. Eigo, James. "Pinter's *Landscape*." *MD* 16(1973): 179-184.

20473. Eilenberg, Lawrence I. "Rehearsal as Critical Method: Pinter's *Old Times*." *MD* 18 (1975): 385-392.

20474. Gale, Stephen. "McCann's Political and Religious Allusions in Pinter's *The Birthday Party*." *NCL* 7(May, 1977): 5-6.

20475. Gillen, Francis. "'All These Bits and Pieces': Fragmentation and Choice in Pinter's Plays." *MD* 17(1974): 477-488.

20476. Hinchliffe, Arnold P. "Mr. Pinter's Belinda." *MD* 11(1968): 173-179.

20477. Hirschberg, Stuart. "Pinter's Caricature of *Howard's End* in *The Homecoming*." *NCL* 4 (Sept., 1974): 14-15.

20478. Hoefer, Jacqueline. "Pinter and Whiting: Two Attitudes Toward the Alienated Artist." *MD* 4(1962): 402-408.

20479. Hughes, Alan. "Myth and Memory in Pinter's '*Old Times*.'" *MD* 17(1974): 467-476.

20480. Imhof, Rudiger. "Pinter's *Silence*: The Impossibility of Communication." *MD* 17(1974): 449-460.

20481. Jiji, Vera M. "Pinter's Four-Dimensional House: *The Homecoming*." *MD* 17(1974): 433-442.

20482. Jones, John Bush. "Stasis as Structure in Pinter's *No Man's Land*." *MD* 19(1976): 291-314.

20483. Kaufman, Michael W. "Actions that a Man Might Play: Pinter's *The Birthday Party*." *MD* 16(1973): 167-178.

20484. Lesser, Simon O. "Reflections on Pinter's *The Birthday Party*." *Con L* 13(1972): 34-43.

20485. Martineau, Stephen. "Pinter's *Old Times*: The Memory Game." *MD* 16(1973): 287-298.

20486. Miller, Mary Jane. "Pinter as a Radio Dramatist." *MD* 17(1974): 403-412.

20487. Osherow, Anita R. "Mother and Whore: The Role of Woman in *The Homecoming*." *MD* 17(1974): 423-432.

20488. Palmer, David S. "A Harold Pinter Checklist." *TCL* 16(1970): 287-296.

20489. Powlick, Leonard. "Temporality in Pinter's *The Dwarfs*." *MD* 20(1977): 67-76.

20490. Quigley, Austin E. "*The Dwarfs*: A Study in Linguistic Dwarfism." *MD* 17(1974): 413-422.

20491. Rosador, Kurt Tetzeli V. "Pinter's Dramatic Method: *Kullus, The Examination, The Basement*." *MD* 14(1971): 195-204.

20492. Salmon, Eric. "Harold Pinter's Ear." *MD* 17(1974): 363-376.

20493. Schitt, Ellen F. "Pancakes and Soap Suds: A Study of Childishness in Pinter's Plays." *MD* 16(1973): 91-102.

20494. Walker, Augusta. "Messages from Pinter." *MD* 10(1967): 1-10.

20495. Warner, John M. "The Epistemological Quest in Pinter's *The Homecoming*." *Con L* 11(1970): 340-353.

20496. Wray, Phoebe. "Pinter's Dialogue: The Play on Words." *MD* 13(1970): 418-422.

See also 5.

POWELL, ANOTHONY. 20497. Davis, Robert Murray. "Contributions to *Night and Day* by Elizabeth Bowen, Graham Greene, and Anthony Powell." *SN* 3(1971): 401-404.

20498. Hall, James. "The Uses of Polite Surprise: Anthony Powell." *EIC* 12(1962): 167-183.

20499. McLeod, Dan. "Anthony Powell: Some Notes on the Art of the Sequence Novel." *SN* 3 (1971): 44-63.

20500. Quesenbery, W. D. "Anthony Powell: The Anatomy of Decay." *Crit* 7,#1(1964): 5-26.

20501. Riley, John J. "Gentlemen at Arms: The Generative Process of Evelyn Waugh and Anthony Powell before World War II." *MFS* 22 (1976): 165-182.

20502. Ruoff, Gene. "Social Mobility and the Artist in *Manhatten Transfer* and *The Music of Time*." *Con L* 5(1964): 64-76.

20503. Wilcox, T. W. "Anthony Powell and the Illusion of Possibility." *Con L* 17(1976): 223-239.

20504. Zegerell, James J. "Anthony Powell's *Music of Time*: Chronicle of a Declining Establishment." *TCL* 12(1966): 138-146.

POWYS, JOHN COOPER. 20505. Blake, George. "The Eccentricity of John Cowper Powys." *MFS* 22 (1976): 201-211.

20506. Cook, David A. "The *Autobiography* of John Cowper Powys: A Portrait of the Artist as Other." *MP* 72(1974): 30-44.

20507. ----------. "John Cowper Powy's *A Glastonbury Romance*: A Modern Mystery Play." *Con L* 13(1972): 341-360.

20508. Knight, G. Wilson. "Lawrence, Joyce and Powys." *EIC* 11(1961): 403-417.

20509. Robilland, Douglas. "Landscapes with Figures: The Early Fiction of John Cowper Powys." *SLI* 1,#2(1968): 51-58.

POWYS, T. F. 20510. Steinmann, Martin, Jr. "The Symbolism of T. F. Powys." *Crit* 1,#2(1957): 49-63.

PRIESTLEY, J. B. 20511. Rogers, Ivor A. "The Time Plays of J. B. Priestley." *Ext* 10(1968): 9-16.

PRITCHETT, V. S. 20512. Hughes, Douglas A. "V. S. Pritchett: An Interview." *SSF* 13(1976): 423-432.

QUILLER-COUCH, ARTHUR. 20513. Atkinson, F. G. "Ezra Pound's Reply to an 'Old-World' Letter." *AL* 46(1974): 357-359.

READ, HERBERT. 20514. Wasson, Richard. "*The Green Child*: Herbert Read's Ironic Fantasy." *PMLA* 77(1962): 645-651.

See also 18922.

RENAULT, MARY. 20515. Burns, Landon C., Jr. "Men are Only Men: The Novels of Mary Renault." *Crit* 6,#3(1963): 102-121.

RHYS, JEAN. 20516. "Mellown, Elgin W. "Characters and Themes in the Novels of Jean Rhys." *Con L* 13(1972): 458-475.

RICHARDS, I. A. 20517. Cruttwell, Patrick. "Second Thoughts, IV; I. A. Richard's Practical Criticism." *EIC* 8(1958): 1-15.

20518. Foster, Richard. "The Romanticism of I. A. Richards." *ELH* 26(1959): 91-101.

20519. Graff, Gerald E. "The Later Richards and The New Criticism." *Criticism* 9(1967): 229-242.

20520. Maxwell, J. C. "Practical Criticism." *EIC* 9(1959): 211-212.

20521. Muir, Kenneth. "Practical Criticism." *EIC* 9(1959): 106.

20522. Roberts, Mark. "Practical Criticism." *EIC* 9(1959): 103-106.

RICHARDSON, DOROTHY. 20523. Edel, Leon. "Dorothy Richardson, 1882-1957." *MFS* 4(1958): 165-168.

20524. Glikin, Gloria. "Dorothy M. Richardson: The Personal 'Pilgrimage.'" *PMLA* 78(1963): 586-600.

20525. Rose, Shirley. "Dorothy Richardson's Theory of Literature: The Writer as Pilgrim." *Criticism* 12(1970): 20-37.

20526. Rose, Shirley. "The Unmoving Center: Consciousness in Dorothy Richardson's Pilgrimage." *Con L* 10(1969): 366-382.

RICKWORD, EDGELL. 20527. Holbrook, David. "The Poetic Mind of Edgell Rickword." *EIC* 12 (1962): 273-291.

ROBERTS, MICHAEL. 20528. Hynes, Samuel. "Michael Roberts' Tragic View." *Con L* 12(1971): 437-450.

ROBINSON, LENNOX. 20529. Everson, Ida G. "Lennox Robinson and Synge's *Playboy* (1911-1930): Two Decades of American Cultural Growth." *NEQ* 44(1971): 3-21.

20530. ----------. "Young Lennox Robinson and The Abbey Theatre's First American Tour (1911-1912)." *MD* 9(1966): 74-89.

RODGERS, W. R. 20531. Amis, Kingsley. "Ulster Bull: the Case of W. R. Rodgers." *EIC* 3 (1953): 470-475.

SACKVILLE-WEST, VICTORIA. 20532. Irwin, W.R.

"Permanence and Change in *The Edwardians* and *Told by an Idiot*." *MFS* 2(1956): 63-67.

SAKI.   See H. H. MUNRO.

SANSOM, WILLIAM.   20533. Neumeyer, Peter F. "Franz Kafka and William Sansom." *Con L* 7 (1966): 76-84.

SASSOON, SIEGFRIED.   20534. Moore, L. Hugh, Jr. "Siegfried Sassoon and Georgian Realism." *TCL* 14(1969): 199-210.

SHAW, GEORGE BERNARD.   20535. Adams, Elsie B. "Bernard Shaw's Pre-Raphaelite Drama." *PMLA* 81(1966): 428-438.

20536. Adler, Jacob H. "Ibsen, Shaw, and *Candida*." *JEGP* 59(1960): 50-58.

20537. Albert, Sidney P. "The Price of Salvation: Moral Economics in *Major Barbara*." *MD* 14(1971): 307-323.

20538. ----------. "Reflections on Shaw and Psychoanalysis." *MD* 14(1971): 169-194.

20539. Armstrong, William A. "George Bernard Shaw: The Playwright as Producer." *MD* 8(1966): 347-361.

20540. Barber, George S. "Shaw's Contributions to Music Criticism." *PMLA* 72(1957): 1005-1017.

20541. Barnet, Sylvan. "Bernard Shaw on Tragedy." *PMLA* 71(1956): 888-899.

20542. Baylen, Joseph O., and Patrick G. Hogan, Jr. "G. B. Shaw and W. T. Stead: An Unexplored Relationship." *SEL* 1,#4(1961): 123-147.

20543. Berst, Charles A. "The Anatomy of Greatness in *Caesar and Cleopatra*." *JEGP* 68(1969): 74-91.

20544. ----------. "The Craft of *Candida*." *Coll L* 1(1974): 157-173.

20545. ----------. "The Devil and *Major Barbara*." *PMLA* 83(1968): 71-79.

20546. ----------. "Propaganda and Art in *Mrs. Warren's Profession*." *ELH* 33(1966): 390-404.

20547. ----------. "Romance and Reality in *Arms and the Man*." *MLQ* 27(1966): 197-211.

20548. Bevan, Earl Dean. "A Shaw Concordance." *MD* 14(1971): 155-168.

20549. Block, Toni. "Shaw's Women." *MD* 2 (1959): 133-138.

20550. Brashear, William R. "O'Neill and Shaw: the Play as Will and Idea." *Criticism* 8 (1966): 155-169.

20551. Brecht, Bertolt (trans. by Gerhard H. W. Zuther). "Ovation for Shaw." *MD* 2(1959): 184-187.

20552. Bullough, Geoffrey. "Literary Relations of Shaw's Mrs. Warren." *PQ* 41(1962): 339-358.

20553. Carpenter, Charles A. "Shaw's Collected Letters." *MD* 9(1966): 190-194.

20554. Cohn, Ruby. "Hell on the Twentieth-Century Stage." *Con L* 5(1964): 48-53.

20555. Couchman, Gordon W. "Here Was a Caesar: Shaw's Comedy Today." *PMLA* 72(1957): 272-285.

20556. Crane, Milton. "Pygmalion: Bernard Shaw's Dramatic Theory and Practice." *PMLA* 66 (1951): 879-885.

20557. Dawick, John D. "Stagecraft and Structure in Shaw's Disquisitory Drama." *MD* 14 (1971): 276-287.

20558. Demaray, John G. "Bernard Shaw and C. E. M. Joad: The Adventures of Two Puritans in

their Search for God." *PMLA* 78(1963): 262-270.

20559. Duerksen, Roland A. "Shelley and Shaw." *PMLA* 78(1963): 114-127.

20560. Dukore, Bernard F. "Shaw Improves Shaw." *MD* 6(1963): 26-31.

20561. ----------. "The Undershaft Maxims." *MD* 9(1966): 90-100.

20562. ----------. "*Widower's Houses*: A Question of Genre." *MD* 17(1974): 27-32.

20563. Farley, Earl, and Marvin Carlson. "George Bernard Shaw: A Selected Bibliography (1945-1955): Part 1: Books." *MD* 2(1959): 188-202.

20564. ----------. "George Bernard Shaw: A Selected Bibliography (1945-1955) Part II: Periodicals." *MD* 2(1959): 295-325.

20565. Fielden, John. "Shaw's *Saint Joan* as Tragedy." *TCL* 3(1957): 59-67.

20566. Frank, Joseph. "*Major Barbara*— Shaw's 'Divine Comedy.'" *PMLA* 71(1956): 61-74.

20567. Ganz, Arthur. "The Ascent to Heaven: A Shavian Pattern (Early Plays, 1894-1898)." *MD* 14(1971): 253-263.

20568. Geduld, Harry M. "*Back to Methuselah* and The Birmingham Repertory Company." *MD* 2(1959): 115-129.

20569. Gerould, Daniel Charles. "George Bernard Shaw's Criticism of Ibsen." *Comp L* 15 (1963): 130-145.

20570. Gibbs, A. M. "Comedy and Philosophy in *Man and Superman*." *MD* 19(1976): 161-177.

20571. Griffith, Benjamin W. "Lydia and the Lady from Zurich: The Birth of a Shavian *Bon Mot*." *NCL* 1(May, 1971): 14-15.

20572. Hatcher, Joe B. "Shaw the Reviewer and James's *Guy Domville*." *MD* 14(1971): 331-334.

20573. Henderson, Archibald. "Shaw and America: The End of a Century." *MD* 2(1959): 173-177.

20574. Hill, Eldon C. "Shaw's 'Biographer-in-Chief.'" *MD* 2(1959): 164-172.

20575. Irvine, William. "Shaw and America." *MD* 2(1959): 160-161.

20576. Jordan, Robert J. "Theme and Character in *Major Barbara*." *TSLL* 12(1970): 471-480.

20577. Kalmar, Jack. "Shaw on Art." *MD* 2 (1959): 147-159.

20578. Kennedy, Andrew K. "The Absurd and the Hyper-Articulate in Shaw's Dramatic Language." *MD* 16(1973): 185-194.

20579. King, Walter N. "The Rhetoric of Candida." *MD* 2(1959): 71-83.

20580. Knepper, B. G. "Shaw's Debt to *The Coming Race*." *JML* 1(1971): 339-353.

20581. Laurence. Dan H. "Genesis of a Dramatic Critic." *MD* 2(1959): 178-183.

20582. Lawrence, Kenneth. "Bernard Shaw: The Career of the Life Force." *MD* 15(1972): 130-146.

20583. Lazenby, Walter. "Love and 'Vitality' in *Candida*." *MD* 20(1977): 1-20.

20584. Leary, D. J. "Shaw's Blakean Vision: A Dialectic Approach to *Heartbreak House*." *MD* 15 (1972): 89-103.

20585. ----------. "Shaw's Use of Stylized Characters and Speech in *Man and Superman*." *MD* 5 (1963): 477-490.

20586. Levin, Gerald. "Shaw, Butler, and Kant." *PQ* 52(1973): 142-156.

20587. Lowe, Robert Liddell. "Two Shaw

Letters." *MLR* 53(1958): 548-550.

20588. Matlaw, Myron. "The Denouement of *Pygmalion*." *MD* 1(1958): 29-34.

20589. Mayer, David. "The Case for Harlequin: A Footnote on Shaw's Dramatic Method." *MD* 3(1960): 60-74.

20590. McDowell, Fredrick P. W. "Bernard Shaw: Biographical and Textual Scholarship." *JML* 3(1973): 120-129.

20591. ----------. "Bernard Shaw the Artist." *JML* 4(1974): 145-154.

20592. ----------. "Bernard Shaw: Writer of 'The Grand School.'" *JML* 3(1974): 1039-1044.

20593. ----------. "'The External Against the Expedient': Structure and Theme in Shaw's *The Apple Cart*." *MD* 2(1959): 99-113.

20594. ----------. "Politics, Comedy, Character, and Dialectic: The Shavian World of *John Bull's Other Island*." *PMLA* 82(1967): 542-553.

20595. ----------. "Protean Wit and Wisdom: Shaw's Uncollected Essays and Speeches." *MD* 5 (1962): 187-193.

20596. ----------. "Spiritual and Political Reality: Shaw's *The Simpleton of the Unexpected Isles*." *MD* 3(1960): 196-210.

20597. ----------. "Technique, Symbol, and Theme in *Heartbreak House*." *PMLA* 68(1953): 335-356.

20598. McKee, Irving. "Bernard Shaw's Beginning on the London Stage." *PMLA* 74(1959): 470-481.

20599. ----------. "Influential Women in Bernard Shaw's Life." *PMLA* 76(1961): 156-157.

20600. Mills, Carl Henry. "*Man and Superman* and the Don Juan Legend." *Comp L* 19(1967): 216-225.

20601. Morgan, Margery M. "Bernard Shaw on the Tightrope." *MD* 4(1962): 343-354.

20602. Murphy, Daniel J. "Lady Gregory Letters to G. B. Shaw." *MD* 10(1968): 331-345.

20603. Nelson, Raymond S. "Blanco Posnet - Adversary of God." *MD* 13(1970): 1-9

20604. ----------. "*Mrs. Warren's Profession* and English Prostitution." *JML* 2(1971): 357-366.

20605. Nethercot, Arthur H. "Bernard Shaw and Psychoanalysis." *MD* 11(1969): 356-375.

20606. ----------. "Bernard Shaw, Ladies and Gentlemen." *MD* 2(1959): 84-98.

20607. ----------. "Bernard Shaw, Philosopher." *PMLA* 69(1954): 57-75.

20608. Nickson, Richard. "The Art of Shavian Political Drama." *MD* 14(1971): 324-330.

20609. Nickson, Richard, and Elsie B. Adams. "'Methinks It Is Like a Weasel': Shaw's Pre-Raphaelite Drama." *PMLA* 84(1969): 597-607.

20610. O'Donnell, Norbert F. "The Conflict of Wills in Shaw's Tragicomedy." *MD* 4(1962): 413-425.

20611. ----------. "Shaw, Bunyan, and Puritanism." *PMLA* 72(1957): 520-533.

20612. Pollock, Ellen. "The Lightness in Shaw." *MD* 2(1959): 130-132.

20613. Reinert, Otto. "Old History and New: Anachronism in *Caesar and Cleopatra*." *MD* 3(1960): 37-41.

20614. Rodriguez-Seda, Asela C. "Shaw and the Hispanic World: A Bibliography." *MD* 14(1971):

335-339.

20615. Rosador, Kurt Tetzelli v. "The Natural History of *Major Barbara*." *MD* 17(1974): 141-154.

20616. Rypins, Stanley. "Influential Women in Bernard Shaw's Life." *PMLA* 76(1961): 156-157.

20617. Salmon, Eric. "Shaw and the Passion of the Mind." *MD* 16(1973): 239-250.

20618. Shattuck, Charles H. "Bernard Shaw's 'Bad Quarto.'" *JEGP* 54(1955): 651-663.

20619. Sidnell, M. J. "John Bull's Other Island—Yeats and Shaw." *MD* 11(1968): 245-251.

20620. ----------. "*Misalliance*: Sex, Socialism and the Collectivist Poet." *MD* 17(1974): 125-140.

20621. Silverman, Albert H. "Bernard Shaw's Shakespeare Criticism." *PMLA* 72(1957): 722-736.

20622. Smoker, Barbara. "GBS and The ABC." *MD* 2(1959): 139-146.

20623. Solomon, Stanley J. "*Saint Joan* as Epic Tragedy." *MD* 6(1964): 437-449.

20624. Stanton, Stephen S. "Shaw's Debt to Scribe." *PMLA* 76(1961): 575-585.

20625. Stone, Susan C. "Biblical Myth Shavianized." *MD* 18(1975): 153-164.

20626. Timko, Michael. "*Entente Cordiale*: The Dramatic Criticism of Shaw and Wells." *MD* 8 (1965): 39-46.

20627. Turco, Alfred, Jr. "Shaw's Pragmatist Ethic: A New Look at The Quintessence of Ibsenism." *TSLL* 17(1976): 855-879.

20628. Tyson, Brian F. "One Man and His Dog: A Study of a Deleted Draft of Bernard Shaw's *The Philanderer*." *MD* 10(1967): 69-78.

20629. ----------. "Shaw Among the Actors: Theatrical Additions to *Plays Unpleasant*." *MD* 14 (1971): 264-275.

20630. Ure, Peter. "Master and Pupil in Bernard Shaw." *EIC* 19(1969): 118-139.

20631. Veilleux, Jere. "Shavian Drama: A Dialectical Convention for the Modern Theatre." *TCL* 3(1958): 170-176.

20632. Watson, Barbara Bellow. "Sainthood for Millionaires: *Major Barbara*." *MD* 11(1968): 227-244.

20633. Weintraub, Stanley. "The Embryo Playwright in Benard Shaw's Early Novels." *TSLL* 1(1959): 327-355.

20634. ----------. "Exploiting Art: The Pictures in Bernard Shaw's Plays." *MD* 18(1975): 215-238.

20635. ----------. G. B. S. Borrows from Sarah Grand: *The Heavenly Twins and You Never Can Tell*." *MD* 14(1971): 288-297.

20636. ----------. "*Heartbreak House*: Shaw's Lear." *MD* 15(1972): 255-266.

20637. ----------. "The Metamorphosés of The Shaw Review." *MD* 2(1959): 162-163.

20638. Wilkenfeld, Roger B. "Perpetual Motion in *Heartbreak House*." *TSLL* 13(1971): 321-335.

20639. Wisenthal, J. L. "The Cosmology of *Man and Superman*." *MD* 14(1971): 298-306.

SILKIN, JON. 20640. Brown, Merle. "Stress in Silkin's Poetry and the Healing Emptiness of America." *Con L* 18(1977): 361-390.

SILLITOE, ALAN. 20641. Byars, John A. "The Initiation of Alan Sillitoe's Long Distance Runner." *MFS* 22(1976): 584-591.

20642. Dixon, Terrell F. "Expostulation and a Reply: the Character of Clegg in Fowles and Sillitoe." *NCL* 4(March, 1974): 7-9.

20643. Gindin, James. "Alan Sillitoe's Jungle." *TSLL* 4(1962): 35-48.

20644. Hurrell, John Dennis. "Alan Sillitoe and the Serious Novel." *Crit* 4,#1(1960): 3-16.

20645. Isaacs, Neil D. "No Man in His Humour: A Note on Sillitoe." *SSF* 4(1967): 350-351.

20646. Nardella, Anna Ryan. "The Existential Dilemmas of Alan Sillitoe's Working-Class Heroes." *SN* 5(1973): 469-482.

20647. Penner, Allen R. "Human Dignity and Social Anarchy: Sillitoe's 'The Loneliness of the Long-Distance Runner.'" *Con L* 10(1969): 253-265.

20648. ----------. "Illusory Deluge: Alan Sillitoe's 'Noah's Ark.'" *CLA* 12(1968): 136-141.

20649. ----------. "'What are Yo' Looking So Bleddy Black For?' Survival and the Bitters in 'On Saturday Afternoon.'" *SSF* 4(1967): 300-307.

20650. Phillips, Norma. "Sillitoe's 'The Match' and Its Joycean Counterparts." *SSF* 12 (1975): 9-14.

20651. Staple, Hugh B. "*Saturday Night and Sunday Morning*: Alan Sillitoe and the White Goddess." *MFS* 10(1964): 171-181.

See also 18925.

SIMPSON, N. F.　20652. Fothergill, C. Z. "Echoes of *A Resounding Tinkle*: N. F. Simpson Reconsidered." *MD* 16(1973): 299-306.

STIWELL, EDITH.　20653. Amis, Kingsley. "'Emily-coloured primulas.'" *EIC* 2(1952): 342-345.

20654. Brophy, James D. "Edith Sitwell: The Primary of Poetry." *JML* 2(1971): 427-431.

20655. Harrington, David V. "The 'Metamorphosis' of Edith Sitwell." *Criticism* 9(1967): 80-91.

20656. Hassan, Ihab H. "Edith Sitwell and the Symbolist Tradition." *Comp L* 7(1955): 240-251.

20657. Nokes, Geoffrey. "'Emily-coloured primulas.'" *EIC* 2(1952): 338-342.

20658. Ower, John B. "Cosmic Austocracy and Cosmic Democracy in Edith Sitwell." *Con L* 12 (1971): 527-553.

20659. ----------. "Edith Sitwell: Metaphysical Medium and Metaphysical Message." *TCL* 16(1970): 253-267.

20660. Reid, Jane Davidson. "Eurydice Recovered?" *Comp L* 5(1953): 213-234.

See also 4341.

SNOW, C. P.　20661. Graves, Nora. "Literary Allusions in *Last Things*." *NCL* 1(Jan., 1971): 7-8.

20662. Hall, William F. "The Humanism of C. P. Snow." *Con L* 4(1963): 199-208.

20663. Stanford, Raney. "Personal Politics in the Novels of C. P. Snow." *Crit* 2,#1(1958): 16-28.

20664. Vogel, Albert W. "The Academic World of C. P. Snow." *TCL* 9(1963): 143-152.

SPARK, MURIEL.　20665. Baldanza, Frank. "Muriel Spark and the Occult." *Con L* 6,#2(1965): 190-203.

20666. Ohmann, Carol B. "Muriel Spark's *Robinson*." *Crit* 8,#1(1965): 70-84.

20667. Schneider, Harold W. "A Woman in Her Prime: The Fiction of Muriel Spark." *Crit*

5,#2(1962): 28-45.

SPENDER, STEPHEN.　20668. Herzman, Ronald B. "Stephen Spender: The Critic as Poet." *NCL* 3(Nov., 1973): 6-7.

20669. Repogle, Justin. "The Auden Group." *Con L* 5(1964): 133-150.

20670. Sellers, W. H. "Wordsworth and Spender: Some Speculations on the Use of Rhyme." *SEL* 5(1965): 641-650.

20671. Thompson, Leslie M. "Spender's 'Judas Iscariot.'" *ELN* 8(1970): 126-130.

20672. Weatherhead, A. K. "Stephen Spender: Lyric Impulse and Will." *Con L* 12(1971): 451-465.

See also 5145, 15367.

STAPLEDON, OLAF.　20673. Smith, Curtis C. "Olaf Stapledon: Saint and Revolutionary." *Ext* 13(1971): 5-15.

STEWART, MARY FLORENCE.　20674. Fries, Maureen. "The Rationalization of the Arthurian 'Matter' in T. H. White and Mary Stewart." *PQ* 56 (1977): 258-265.

STOPPARD, TOM.　20675. Babula, William. "The Play-Life Metaphor in Shakespeare and Stoppard." *MD* 15(1972): 279-282.

20676. Berlin, Normand. "*Rosencrantz and Guildenstern Are Dead*: Theatre of Criticism." *MD* 16(1973): 269-277.

20677. Crossley, Brian M. "An Investigation of Stoppard's 'Hound' and 'Foot.'" *MD* 20(1977): 77-86.

20678. Gabbard, Lucina P. "Stoppard's *Jumpers*: A Mystery Play." *MD* 20(1977): 87-95.

STOREY, DAVID.　20679. Churchill, Thomas. "Waterhouse, Storey and Fowles: *Which Way Out of the Room?*" *Crit* 10,#3(1968): 72-87.

20680. Free, William J. "The Ironic Anger of David Storey." *MD* 16(1973): 307-316.

20681. Kalson, Albert E. "Insanity and the Rational Man in the Plays of David Storey." *MD* 19(1976): 111-128.

20682. Stinson, John J. "Dualism and Paradox in the 'Puritan' Plays of David Storey." *MD* 20(1977): 131-144.

STRACHEY, LYTTON.　20683. Sanders, Charles Richard. "Lytton Strachey and the Victorians." *MLQ* 15(1954): 326-342.

20684. ----------. "Lytton Strachey as a Critic of Elizabethan Drama." *PQ* 30(1951): 1-21.

SYNGE, JOHN M.　Ayling, Ronald F. "Synge's First Love: Some South African Aspects." *MD* 6 (1964): 450-460.

20686. Bigley, Bruce M. "*The Playboy of the Western World*." *MD* 20(1977): 157-168.

20687. Cusack, Cyril. "A Player's Reflections on *Playboy*." *MD* 4(1961): 300-305.

20688. Durbach, Errol. "Synge's Tragic Vision of the Old Mother and the Sea." *MD* 14(1972): 363-372.

20689. Eckley, Grace. "Truth at the Bottom of a Well: Synge's *The Well of the Saints*." *MD* 16(1973): 193-198.

20690. Everson, Ida G. "Lennox Robinson and Synge's *Playboy* (1911-1930): Two Decades of American Cultural Growth." *NEQ* 44(1971): 3-21.

20691. Fackler, Herbert V. "J. M. Synge's *Deirdre of the Sorrows*: Beauty Only." *MD* 11(1969): 404-409.

20692. Farris, Jon R. "The Nature of the Tragic Experience in Deirdre of the Sorrows." *MD*

14(1971): 243-251.

20693. Ganz, Arthur. "J. M. Synge and the Drama of Art." *MD* 10(1967): 57-68.

20694. Gerstenberger, Donna. "Bonnie and Clyde and Christy Mahon: Playboys All." *MD* 14 (1971): 227-231.

20695. Greene, David H. "Synge and the Celtic Revival." *MD* 4(1961): 292-299.

20696. Grene, Nicholas. "Synge's *The Shadow of the Glen*: Repetition and Allusion." *MD* 17(1974): 19-26.

20697. Gutierrez, Donald. "Coming of Age in Mayo: Synge's *Playboy of the Western World*." *HSL* 6(1974): 159-166.

20698. Hogan, Robert. "John Synge and Jack Yeats." *JML* 3(1974): 1031-1038.

20699. Kilroy, James F. "The Playboy as Poet." *PMLA* 83(1968): 439-442.

20700. Krause, David. "'The Rageous Ossean': Patron-Hero of Synge and O'Casey." *MD* 4(1961): 268-291.

20701. Leech, Clifford. "John Synge and the Drama of His Time." *MD* 16(1973): 223-238.

20702. Leyburn, Ellen Douglas. "The Theme of Lonliness in the Plays of Synge." *MD* 1(1958): 84-90.

20703. Michie, Donald M. "Synge and his Critics." *MD* 15(1973): 427-432.

20704. Murphy, Brenda. "Stoicism, Asceticism, and Ecstacy: Synge's *Deirdre of the Sorrows*." *MD* 17(1974): 155-164.

20705. O'Neill, Michael I. "Holloway on Synge's Last Days." *MD* 6(1963): 126-130.

20706. Orel, Harold. "Synge's Last Play: 'And a Story Will Be Told For Ever.'" *MD* 4(1961): 306-313.

20707. Pierce, Howard D. "Synge's Playboy as Mock-Christ." *MD* 8(1965): 303-310.

20708. Podhoretz, Norman. "Synge's *Playboy*: Morality and the Hero." *EIC* 3(1953): 337-344.

20709. Price, Alan. "Synge's Prose Writings: A First View of the Whole." *MD* 11(1968): 221-226.

20710. Salmon, Eric. "J. M. Synge's *Playboy*: A Necessary Reassessment." *MD* 13(1970): 111-128.

20711. Spacks, Patricia Meyer. "The Making of the Playboy." *MD* 4(1961): 314-323.

20712. Slattery, Sister Margaret Patrice. "*Deirdre*: The 'Mingling of Contraries' in Plot and Symbolism." *MD* 11(1969): 400-403.

20713. Sullivan, Mary Rose. "Synge, Sophocles, and the Un-making of Myth." *MD* 12(1969): 242-253.

20714. Triesch, Manfred. "Some Unpublished J. M. Synge Papers." *ELN* 4(1966): 49-51.

TERSON, PETER. 20715. Elvgren, Gillette, Jr. "Peter Terson's Vale of Evesham." *MD* 18 (1975): 173-188.

THOMAS, DYLAN. 20716. Astley, Russell. "Stations of the Breath: End Rhyme in the Verse of Dylan Thomas." *PMLA* 84(1969): 1595-1605.

20717. Davies, James A. "Dylan Thomas' 'One Warm Saturday' and Tennyson's *Maud*." *SSF* 14(1977): 284-286.

20718. Davies, Walford. "Imitation and Invention: the Use of Borrowed Material in Dylan Thomas's Prose." *EIC* 18(1968): 275-295.

20719. Davis, Cynthia. "The Voices of 'Under Milk Wood.'" *Criticism* 17(1975): 74-89.

20720. Dawson, S. W. "Mr. Maud on Dylan Thomas." *EIC* 5(1955): 187-189.

20721. Empson, William. "Dylan Thomas." *EIC* 13(1963): 205-207.

20722. Gingerich, Martin E. "Rhetoric and Meaning in "A Refusal to Mourn.'" *NCL* 1(Jan., 1971): 5-6.

20723. Havard, Robert G. "The Symbolic Ambivalence of 'Green' in García Lorca and Dylan Thomas." *MLR* 67(1972): 810-819.

20724. Kelly, Richard. "The Lost Vision in Dylan Thomas's 'One Warm Saturday.'" *SSF* 6(1969): 205-209.

20725. Maud, Ralph. "A Clark Lecture Revisited." *EIC* 18(1968): 60-62.

20726. ----------. "Dylan Thomas' Collected Poems: Chronology of Composition." *PMLA* 76(1961): 292-297.

20727. ----------. "Dylan Thomas's Poetry." *EIC* 4(1954): 411-420.

20728. Mosher, Harold F., Jr. "The Structure of Dylan Thomas's 'The Peaches.'" *SSF* 6(1969): 536-547.

20729. Moynihan, William T. "Dylan Thomas and the 'Biblical Rhythm.'" *PMLA* 79(1964): 631-647.

20730. ----------. "Dylan Thomas' 'Hewn Voice.'" *TSLL* 1(1959): 313-326.

20731. Scherting, Jack. "Echoes of *Look Homeward Angel* in Dylan Thomas's 'A Child's Christmas in Wales.'" *SSF* 9(1972): 404-406.

20732. Tritschler, Donald. "The Stories in Dylan Thomas' Red Notebook." *JML* 2(1971): 33-56.

20733. Wittreich, Joseph Anthony, Jr. "Dylan Thomas' Conception of Poetry: A Debt to Blake." *ELN* 6(1969): 197-200.

See also 4341.

THOMAS, EDWARD. 20734. Coombes, H. "The Poetry of Edward Thomas." *EIC* 3(1953): 191-200.

20735. Underhill, Hugh. "The 'Poetical Character' of Edward Thomas." *EIC* 23(1973): 236-253.

THOMAS, R. S. 20736. Knapp, James F. "The Poetry of R. S. Thomas." *TCL* 17(1971): 1-9.

TOLKIEN, J. R. R. 20737. Epstein, E. L. "The Novels of J. R. R. Tolkien and the Ethnology of Medieval Christendom." *PQ* 48(1969): 517-525.

20738. Glover, Willis B. "The Christian Character of Tolkien's Invented World." *Criticism* 13(1971): 39-53.

20739. Green, William H. "Legendary and Historical Time in Tolkien's *Farmer Giles of Ham*." *NCL* 5(May, 1975): 14-15.

20740. Hayes, Noreen, and Robert Renshaw. "Of Hobbits: *The Lord of the Rings*." *Crit* 9,#2 (1967): 58-65.

20741. Kirk, Elizabeth D. "'I Would Rather Have Written in Elvish': Language, Fiction and *The Lord of the Rings*." *Novel* 5(1971): 5-8.

20742. O'Connor, Gerard. "Why Tolkien's *The Lord of the Rings* Should *Not* Be Popular Culture." *Ext* 13(1971): 48-55.

20743. O'Hare, Colman. "On Reading an 'Old Book.'" *Ext* 14(1972): 59-63.

20744. Spacks, Patricia M. "Ethical Pattern in *The Lord of the Rings*." *Crit* 3,#1(1959): 30-42.

20745. Thomson, George H. "*The Lord of the Rings*: The Novel as Traditional Romance." *Con L*

8(1967): 43-59.

20746. West, Richard. "An Annotated Bibliography of Tolkien Criticism." *Ext* 10(1968): 17-45.

TOYNBEE, ARNOLD J.   20747. Greeslade, Rush. "Arnold Joseph Toynbee: A Checklist." *TCL* 2(1956): 92-104.

TOMLINSON, CHARLES.   20748. Mariani, Paul. "Tomlinson's Use of the Williams Triad." *Con L* 18(1977): 405-415.

20749. Rasula, Jed, and Mike Erwin. "An Interview with Charles Tomlinson." *Con L* 16(1975): 405-416.

See also 19848.

TRESSALL, ROBERT.   20750. Mayne, Brian H. *The Ragged Trousered Philantropists*: An Appraisal of an Edwardian Novel of Social Protest." *TCL* 13 (1967): 73-83.

TREVELYAN, ROBERT.   20751. Collins, J. A. "R. C. Trevelyan and His Edwardian Sisyphus." *MD* 12(1970): 346-356.

VANSITTART, PETER.   20752. Howarth, Herbert. "Pieces of History." *Crit* 2,#1(1958): 54-64.

WAIN, JOHN.   20753. Dixon, Terrell F. "The Use of Literary History in *Hurry on Down*." *NCL* 2 (March, 1972): 6-7.

20754. O'Conner, William Van. "John Wain: The Will to Write." *Con L* 1,#1(1960): 35-49.

See also 18925.

WALEY, ARTHUR.   20755. Tatlow, Anthony. "Stalking the Dragon: Pound, Waley, and Brecht." *Comp L* 25(1973): 193-211.

WARNER, REX.   20756. Churchill, Thomas. "Rex Warner: Homage to Necessity." *Crit* 10,#1 (1967): 30-44.

20757. Devitis, A. A. "Rex Warner and the Cult of Power." *TCL* 6(1960): 107-116.

20758. Howarth, Herbert. "Pieces of History." *Crit* 2,#1(1958): 54-64.

See also 18922.

WATERHOUSE, KEITH.   20759. Churchill, Thomas. "Waterhouse, Storey, and Fowles: *Which Way Out of the Room*." *Crit* 10,#3(1968): 72-87.

See also 18925.

WAUGH, EVELYN.   20760. Churchill, Thomas. "The Trouble with *Brideshead Revisited*." *MLQ* 28 (1967): 213-228.

20761. Davis, Robert Murray. "Evelyn Waugh's Early Work: The Formation of a Method." *TSLL* 7(1965): 97-108.

20762. ----------. "*Harper's Bazaar* and *A Handful of Dust*." *PQ* 48(1969): 508-516.

20762a. ----------. "The Serial Version of *Brideshead Revisited*." *TCL* 15(1969): 35-44.

20763. Delasanta, Rodney, and Mario L. D'Avanzo. "Truth and Beauty in *Brideshead Revisited*." *MFS* 11(1965): 140-152.

20764. Edwards, A. S. G. "A Source for Waugh's *A Handful of Dust*." *MFS* 22(1976): 242-244.

20765. Farr, D. Paul. "Waugh's Conservative Stance: Defending 'The Standards of Civilization.'" *PQ* 51(1972): 471-484.

20766. Firchow, Peter E. "In Search of *A Handful of Dust*: The Literary Background of Evelyn Waugh's Novel." *JML* 2(1971): 406-416.

20767. Hall, James. "The Other Post-War Rebellion: Evelyn Waugh Twenty-Five Years After." *ELH* 28(1961): 187-202.

20768. Heath, Jeffrey M. "Waugh and the

Pinfold Manuscript." *JML* 5(1976): 331-336.

20769. Hynes, Joseph. "Varieties of Death Wish: Evelyn Waugh's Central Theme." *Criticism* 14(1972): 65-77.

20770. Kosok, Heinz. "Evelyn Waugh: A Checklist of Criticism." *TCL* 11(1966): 211-215.

20771. LaFrance, Marston. "Context and Structure of Evelyn Waugh's *Brideshead Revisited*." *TCL* 10(1964): 12-18.

20772. Linck, Charles E., Jr. "Works of Evelyn Waugh, 1910 to 1930." *TCL* 10(1964): 19-25.

20773. Lord, George. "Heroic Games: Homer to Waugh." *Coll L* 3(1976): 180-202.

20774. Mattingly, Joseph F. "Guy Crouchback's 'Children.'" *ELN* 6(1969): 200-201.

20775. Riley, John J. "Gentlemen at Arms: The Generative Process of Evelyn Waugh and Anthony Powell before World War II." *MFS* 22(1976): 165-182.

20776. Wasson, Richard. "*A Handful of Dust*: Critique of Victorianism." *MFS* 7(1961): 327-337.

WELCH, DENTON.   20777. Phillips, Robert. "*Brave and Cruel*: The Short Stores of Denton Welch." *SSF* 7(1970): 357-376.

WELLESLEY, DOROTHY.   20778. O'Shea, Edward. "Yeats as Editor: Dorothy Wellesley's *Selections*." *ELN* 11(1973): 112-118.

WELLS, H. G.   20779. Bailey, J. O. "Is Science-Fiction Art? A Look at H. G. Wells." *Ext* 2(1960): 17-19.

20780. Bergonzi, Bernard. "Another Early Wells Item." *NCF* 13(1958): 72-73.

20781. ----------. "The Publication of *The Time Machine* 1894-5." *RES* 11(1960): 42-51.

20782. Bowen, Roger. "Science, Myth, and Fiction in H. G. Well's *Island of Dr. Moreau*." *SN* 8(1976): 318-335.

20783. Donaghy, Henry J. "Love and Mr. Wells: A Shelleyan Search for the Epipsyche." *SLI* 1,#2(1968): 41-50.

20784. Eisenstein, Alex. "Origins of Some Major Physical Motifs in *The Time Machine* and *The War of the Worlds*." *Ext* 13(1972): 119-126.

20785. Herbert, Lucille. "*Tono-Bungay*: Tradition and Experiment." *MLQ* 33(1972): 140-155.

20786. Haight, Gordon. "H. G. Well's 'The Man of the Year Million.'" *NCF* 12(1958): 323-326.

20787. Hughes, David Y. "H. G. Wells and the Charge of Plagiarism." *NCF* 21(1966): 85-90.

20788. ----------. "H. G. Wells: Ironic Romancer." *Ext* 6(1965): 32-38.

20789. ----------. "The Mood of *A Modern Utopia*." *Ext* 19(1977): 59-67.

20790. Johnston, Dillon. "The Recreation of Self in Wells's 'Experiment in Autobiography.'" *Criticism* 14(1972): 345-360.

20791. Karl, Frederick, R. "Conrad, Wells, and the Two Voices." *PMLA* 88(1973): 1049-1065.

20792. Mullen, Richard D. "H. G. Wells and Victor Resseau Emanuel: *When the Sleeper Wakes* and *The Messiah of the Cylinder*." *Ext* 8(1967): 31-63.

20793. Neuleib, Janice. "Technology and Theocracy: The Cosmic Voyages of Wells and Lewis." *Ext* 16(1975): 130-136.

20794. Ower, John. "Theme and Technique in H. G. Well's 'The Star.'" *Ext* 18(1978): 167-175.

20795. Philmus, Robert M. "*The Time Machine*; or, the Fourth Dimension as Prophecy." *PMLA*

84(1969): 530-535.

20796. Steinmann, Theo. "The Second Death of Nunez in 'The Country of the Blind.'" *SSF* 9 (1972): 157-163.

20797. Storm, Melvin G., Jr. "Thematic Parallelism in *Tono-Bungay*: 'Night and the Open Sea' As Structural Device." *Ext* 18(1977): 181-185.

20798. Timko, Michael. "Entente Cordiale: The Dramatic Criticism of Shaw and Wells." *MD* 8 (1965): 39-46.

20799. ----------. "H. G. Wells and 'The Most Unholy Trade.'" *ELN* 1(1964): 280-284.

20800. Wayer, W. Warren. "H. G. Wells and the Radicalism of Despair." *SLI* 6,#2(1973): 1-10.

20801. Wilson, Harris. "The Death of Masterman: A Repressed Episode in H. G. Well's *Kipps*." *PMLA* 86(1971): 63-69.

See also 163, 20424.

WESKER, ARNOLD. 20802. Latham, Jacqueline. "*Roots*: A Reassessment." *MD* 8(1965): 192-197.

20803. Page, Malcolm. "Whatever Happened to Arnold Wesker?: His Recent Plays." *MD* 11(1968): 317-325.

20804. Stoll, Karl-Heinz. "Interviews with Edward Bond and Arnold Wesker." *TCL* 22(1976): 411-432.

WHITE, TERENCE HANBURY. 20805. Fries, Maureen. "The Rationalization of the Arthurian 'Matter' in T. H. White and Mary Stewart." *PQ* 56 (1977): 258-265.

WHITING, JOHN. 20806. Hoefer, Jacqueline. "Pinter and Whiting: Two Attitudes Toward the Alienated Artist." *MD* 4(1962): 402-408.

20807. Hurrell, John D. "John Whiting and the Theme of Self-Destruction." *MD* 8(1965): 134-141.

20808. Lyons, Charles R. "The Futile Encounter in the Plays of John Whiting." *MD* 11 (1968): 283-298.

20809. Page, Malcolm. "The Two Versions of John Whiting's 'A Penny for a Song.'" *NCL* 1(Jan., 1971): 8-9.

20810. Robinson, Gabriele Scott. "Beyond the Waste Land: An Interpretation of John Whiting's *Saint's Day*." *MD* 14(1972): 463-477.

20811. ----------. "A Private Mythology: The Manuscripts and Plays of John Whiting." *MD* 14(1971): 23-36.

WILLIAMS, CHARLES. 20812. Cockshut, A. O. J. "The Art of the Enemy." *EIC* 7(1957): 339-340.

20813. Conquest, Robert. "The Art of the Enemy." *EIC* 7(1957): 42-55, 341-343.

20814. Craig, Alec. "The Art of the Enemy." *EIC* 7(1957): 340-341.

20815. McMichael, Barbara. "Hell is Oneself: An Examination of the Concept of Damnation in Charles Williams' *Descent Into Hell*." *SLI* 1,#2 (1968): 59-71.

20816. Moorman, Charles. "Myth in the Novels of Charles Williams." *MFS* 3(1957): 321-327.

20817. Pitt, Valerie. "The Art of the Enemy." *EIC* 7(1957): 330-335.

20818. Spacks, Patricia Meyer. "The Art of the Enemy." *EIC* 7(1957): 335-339.

WILLIAMSON, ROBIN. 20819. Brivic, Sheldon. "The Incredible String Band and Robin Williamson's song 'Creation.'" *HSL* 4(1972): 123-134.

WILSON, ANGUS. 20820. Biles, Jack I. "An Interview in London with Angus Wilson." *SN* 2(1970):

76-87.

20821. Bradbury, Malcolm. "The Short Stories of Angus Wilson." *SSF* 3(1966): 117-125.

20822. Cockshut, A. O. J. "Favoured Sons. The Moral World of Angus Wilson." *EIC* 9(1959): 50-60.

20823. Halio, Jay L. "The Novels of Angus Wilson." *MFS* 8(1962): 171-181.

20824. Sudrann, Jean. "The Lion and the Unicorn: Angus Wilson's Triumphant Tragedy." *SN* 3(1971): 390-400.

See also 18925.

WOOLF, VIRGINIA. 20825. Ames, Kenneth J. "Elements of Mock-Heroic in Virginia Woolf's *Mrs. Dalloway*." *MFS* 18(1972): 363-374.

20826. Araujo, Victor de. "'A Haunted House'—The Shattered Glass." *SSF* 3(1966): 157-164.

20827. Baldanza, Frank. "Clarrisa Dalloway's 'Party Consciousness.'" *MFS* 2(1956): 24-30.

20828. ----------. "*Orlando* and the Sackvilles." *PMLA* 70(1955): 274-279.

20829. ----------. "*To the Lighthouse* Again." *PMLA* 70(1955): 548-552.

20830. ----------. "Virginia Woolf's 'Moments of Being.'" *MFS* 2(1956): 78.

20831. Bazin, Nancy Topping. "Virginia Woolf's Quest for Equilibrium." *MLQ* 32(1971): 305-319.

20832. Becker, Miroslav. "London as a Principle of Structure in *Mrs. Dalloway*." *MFS* 18 (1972): 375-385.

20833. Beebe, Maurice. "Criticism of Virginia Woolfe: A Selected Checklist with an Index to Studies of Separate Works." *MFS* 2(1956): 36-45.

20834. Benjamin, Anna S. "Towards an Understanding of the Meaning of Virginia Woolf's *Mrs. Dalloway*." *Con L* 6(1965): 214-227.

20835. Bevis, Dorothy. "*The Waves*: A Fusion of Symbol, Style and Thought in Virginia Woolfe." *TCL* 2(1956): 5-20.

20836. Bicknell, John W. "Virginia Woolf in Homage and Understanding." *JML* 3(1973): 108-115.

20837. Bloom, Lillian D. "Review Essay: They All Cried Woolf." *Novel* 7(1974): 255-266.

20838. Blotner, Joseph L. "Mythic Patterns in *To the Lighthouse*." *PMLA* 71(1956): 547-562.

20839. Brogan, Howard O. "Science and Narrative Structure in Austin, Hardy and Woolf." *NCF* 11(1957): 276-287.

20840. Chapman, R. T. "*The Lady in the Looking-Glass*: Modes of Perception in a Short Story by Virginia Woolf." *MFS* 18(1972): 331-337.

20841. Church, Margaret. "Concepts of Time in Novels of Virginia Woolf and Alduous Huxley." *MFS* 1,#2(1955): 19-24.

20842. Cohn, Ruby. "Art in *To the Light-House*." *MFS* 8(1962): 127-136.

20843. Collet, Georges-Paul. "Jacques-Emile Blanche and Virginia Woolf." *Comp L* 17(1965): 73-81.

20844. Cumings, Melinda Feldt. "*Night and Day*: Virginia Woolf's Visionary Synthesis of Reality." *MFS* 18(1972): 339-349.

20845. Dataller, Roger. "Mr. Lawrence and Mrs. Woolf." *EIC* 8(1958): 48-59.

20846. Deiman, Werner J. "History, Pattern, and Continuity in Virginia Woolf." *Con L* 15(1974):

49-66.

20847. Doner, Dean. "Virginia Woolf: The Service of Style." *MFS* 2(1956): 1-12.

20848. Farwell, Marilyn R. "Virginia Woolf and Androgyny." *Con L* 16(1975): 433-451.

20849. Fleishman, Avrom. "Woolf and McTaggart." *ELH* 36(1969): 719-738.

20850. Fox, Stephen D. "The Fish Pond as Symbolic Center in *Between the Acts*." *MFS* 18 (1972): 467-473.

20851. Friedman, Norman. "The Waters of Annihilation: Double Vision in *To The Lighthouse*." *ELH* 22(1955): 61-80.

20852. Gelfant, Blanche H. "Love and Conversion in *Mrs. Dalloway*." *Criticism* 8(1966): 229-245.

20853. Gillen, Francis. "'I am This, I am That': Shifting Distance and Movement in *Mrs. Dalloway*." *SN* 4(1972): 484-493.

20854. Gindin, James. "Review Essay: Bolts of Iron." *SN* 8(1976): 336-350.

20855. Goldman, Mark. "Virginia Woolf and E. M. Forster: A Critical Dialogue." *TSLL* 7 (1966): 387-400.

20856. ----------. "Virginia Woolf and the Critic as Reader." *PMLA* 80(1965): 275-284.

20857. Gorsky, Susan. "'The Central Shadow': Characterization in *The Waves*." *MFS* 18(1972): 449-465.

20858. Graham, J. W. "The Drafts of Virginia Woolf's 'The Searchlight.'" *TCL* 22(1976): 379-393.

20859. ----------. "A Negative Note on Bergson and Virginia Woolf." *EIC* 6(1956): 70-74.

20860. Green, David Bonnell. "*Orlando* and the Sackvilles: Addendum." *PMLA* 71(1956): 268-269.

20861. Hafley, James. "On One of Virginia Woolf's Short Stories." *MFS* 2(1956): 13-16.

20862. Havard-Williams, Peter and Margaret. "Mystical Experience in Virginia Woolf's 'The Waves.'" *EIC* 4(1954): 71-84.

20863. Hoffmann, A. C. "Subject and Object and the Nature of Reality: The Dialectic of *To the Lighthouse*." *TSLL* 13(1972): 691-703.

20864. Hoffmann, Charles G. "Fact and Fantasy in *Orlando*: Virginia Woolf's Manuscript Revisions." *TSLL* 10(1968): 435-444.

20865. ----------. "'From Lunch to Dinner': Virginia Woolf's Apprenticeship." *TSLL* 10(1969): 609-627.

20866. ----------. "From Short Story to Novel: The Manuscript Revisions of Virginia Woolf's *Mrs. Dalloway*." *MFS* 14(1967): 171-186.

20867. ----------. "Virginia Woolf's Manuscript Revision of *The Years*." *PMLA* 84(1969): 79-89.

20868. Hungerford, Edward A. "'My Tunnelling Process': The Method of *Mrs. Dalloway*." *MFS* 3(1957): 164-167.

20869. Hunting, Constance. "The Technique of Persuasion in *Orlando*." *MFS* 2(1956): 17-23.

20870. ----------. "Three More Hazards towards Virginia Woolf." *JML* 4(1974): 155-159.

20871. Hynes, Samuel. "The Whole Contention Between Mr. Bennett and Mrs. Woolf." *Novel* 1 (1967): 34-44.

20872. Kreutz, Irving. "Mr. Bennett and Mrs. Woolf." *MFS* 8(1962): 103-115.

20873. Latham, Jacqueline E. M. "The Manuscript Revisions of Virginia Woolf's *Mrs. Dalloway*: A Postscript." *MFS* 18(1972): 475-476.

20874. Leyburn, Ellen Douglas. "Virginia Woolf's Judgment of Henry James." *MFS* 5(1959): 166-168.

20875. Lilienfeld, Jane. "'The Deceptiveness of Beauty': Mother Love and Mother Hate in *To the Lighthouse*." *TCL* 23(1977): 377-389.

20876. Lyons, Richard S. "The Intellectual Structure of Virginia Woolf's *Between the Acts*." *MLQ* 38(1977): 149-166.

20877. Miller, David Neal. "Authorial Point of View in Virginia Woolf's *Mrs. Dalloway*." *JNT* 2(1972): 125-132.

20878. Morgenstern, Barry. "The Self-Conscious Narrator in *Jacob's Room*." *MFS* 18(1972): 351-361.

20879. Naremore, James. "World Without a Self: The Novels of Virginia Woolf." *Novel* 5(1972): 122-134.

20880. Ohmann, Carol. "Culture and Anarchy in *Jacob's Room*." *Con L* 18(1977): 160-172.

20881. Page, Alex. "A Dangerous Day: Mrs. Dalloway Discovers Her Double." *MFS* 7(1961): 115-124.

20882. Payne, Michael. "The Eclipse of Order: The Ironic Structure of *The Waves*." *MFS* 15 (1969): 209-218.

20883. Pedersen, Glenn M. "Vision in *To the Lighthouse*." *PMLA* 73(1958): 585-600.

20884. Pratt, Annis. "Sexual Imagery in *To the Lighthouse*: A New Feminist Approach." *MFS* 18 (1972): 417-431.

20885. Proudfit, Sharon L. "Virginia Woolf: Reluctant Feminist in 'The Years.'" *Criticism* 17 (1975): 59-73.

20886. ----------. "Lily Briscoe's Painting: A Key to Personal Relationships in *To the Lighthouse*." *Criticism* 13(1971): 26-38.

20887. Rachman, Shalorn. "Clarissa's Attic: Virginia Woolf's *Mrs. Dalloway* Reconsidered." *TCL* 18(1972): 3-18.

20888. Richardson, Robert O. "Point of View in Virginia Woolf's *The Waves*." *TSLL* 14(1973): 691-709.

20889. Rogat, Ellen Hawkes. "The Virgin in the Bell Biography." *TCL* 20(1974): 96-113.

20890. Rosenberg, Stuart. "The Match in the Crocus: Obtrusive Art in Virginia Woolf's *Mrs. Dalloway*." *MFS* 13(1967): 211-220.

20891. Sacks, Sheldon. "Novelists as Storytellers." *MP* 73(1976): S97-S109.

20892. Samuels, Marilyn Schauer. "The Symbolic Function of the Sun in *Mrs. Dalloway*." *MFS* 18(1972): 387-399.

20893. Schaefer, Josephine O'Brien. "Sterne's *Sentimental Journey* and Woolf's *Jacob's Room*." *MFS* 23(1977): 189-197.

20894. Shanahan, Mary Steussy. "The Artist and the Resolution of *The Waves*." *MLQ* 36(1975): 54-74.

20895. ----------. "*Between the Acts*: Virginia Woolf's Final Endeavor in Art." *TSLL* 14 (1972): 123-138.

20896. Shoukri, Doris Enright-Clark. "The Nature of Being in Woolf and Duras." *Con L* 12 (1971): 317-328.

20897. Smith, J. Oates. "Henry James and Virginia Woolf: The Art of Relationships." *TCL* 10 (1964): 119-129.

20898. Stewart, Jack F. "Existence and Symbol in *The Waves*." *MFS* 18(1972): 433–447.

20899. ──────────. "Historical Impressions in *Orlando*." *SN* 5(1973): 71–85.

20900. ──────────. "Light in *To the Lighthouse*." *TCL* 23(1977): 377–389.

20901. Summerhayes, Don. "Society, Morality, Analogy: Virginia Woolf's World Between the Acts." *MFS* 9(1963): 329–337.

20902. Temple, Ruth Z. "Three Approaches to Virginia Woolf." *JML* 2(1971): 421–427.

20903. Webb, Igor M. "'Things in Themselves': Virginia Woolf's *The Waves*." *MFS* 17(1971): 570–573.

20904. Weiser, Barbara. "Criticism of Virginia Woolf from 1956 to the Present: A Selected Checklist with an Index to Studies of Separate Works." *MFS* 18(1972): 477–486.

20905. Whitehead, Lee M. "The Shawl and the Skull: Virginia Woolf's 'Magic Mountain.'" *MFS* 18(1972): 401–415.

20906. Wilkinson, Ann Yanko. "A Principle of Unity in 'Between the Acts.'" *Criticism* 8 (1966): 53–63.

20907. Wyatt, Jean M. *Mrs. Dalloway*: Literary Allusion as Structural Metaphor." *PMLA* 88(1973): 440–451.

20908. Zorn, Marilyn. "The Pageant in *Between the Acts*." *MFS* 2(1956): 31–35.

20909. Zwerdling, Alex. "*Between the Acts* and the Coming of War." *Novel* 10(1977): 220–236.

20910. ──────────. "*Mrs. Dalloway* and the Social System." *PMLA* 92(1977): 69–82.

See also 60, 88, 18930, 20252.

YEATS, JACK. See 20698.

YEATS, WILLIAM BUTLER. 20911. Ackerman, Cara. "Yeat's Revisions of the Hanrahan Stories, 1897 and 1904." *TSLL* 17(1975): 505–524.

20912. Adams, Hazard. "Yeats, Dialectic and Criticism." *Criticism* 10(1968): 185–199.

20913. ──────────. "Yeats Scholarship and Criticism: A Review of Research." *TSLL* 3(1962): 439–451.

20914. ──────────. "Yeats's *Country of the Young*." *PMLA* 72(1957): 510–519.

20915. Allen, James Lovic. "Belief versus Faith in the Credo of Yeats." *JML* 4(1975): 692–716.

20916. ──────────. "Recent Yeatsiana: The Failed Quest for Unity of Being." *JML* 2(1971): 148–154.

20917. ──────────. "Unity of Archetype, Myth, and Religious Imagery in the Work of Yeats." *TCL* 20(1974): 91–95.

20918. ──────────. "Yeats' Bird-Soul Symbolism." *TCL* 6(1960): 117–122.

20919. Altieri, Charles. "From a Comic to a Tragic Sense of Language in Yeats's Mature Poetry." *MLQ* 33(1972): 156–171.

20920. Ayling, Ronald W. "W. B. Yeats on Plays and Players." *MD* 9(1966): 1–10.

20921. Baird, Sister Mary Julian, R. S. M. "A Play on the Death of God: The Irony of Yeats's *The Resurrection*." *MD* 10(1967): 79–86.

20922. Barnwell, William C. "The Blandness of Yeat's Rhadamanthus." *ELN* 14(1977): 206–210.

20923. ──────────. "A Possible Italian Influence on Yeat's 'Statues.'" *PQ* 56(1977): 140–143.

20924. Baumgarten, Murray. "'Body's Image': *Yerma, The Player Queen* and the Upright Posture." *CD* 8(1974): 290–299.

20925. ──────────. "Lyric as Performance: Lorca and Yeats." *Comp L* 29(1977): 328–350.

20926. Beja, Morris. "*2001*: Odyssey to Byzantium." *Ext* 10(1969): 67–68.

20927. Benson, Carl. "Yeats and Balzac's *Louis Lambert*." *MP* 49(1952): 242–247.

20928. Beum, Robert. "Yeats's Octaves." *TSLL* 3(1961): 89–96.

20929. Bizot, Richard. "Pater and Yeats." *ELH* 43(1976): 389–412.

20930. Block, Haskell M. "Yeats's *The King's Threshold*: The Poet and Society." *PQ* 34(1955): 206–218.

20931. Bornstein, George J., and Hugh H. Witemeyer. "From *Villain* to Visionary: Pound and Yeats on Villon." *Comp L* 19(1967): 308–320.

20932. Bradford, Curtis. "Yeats and Maude Gonne." *TSLL* 4(1962): 452–474.

20933. ──────────. "A Yeats Gathering." *MLQ* 28(1967): 96–101.

20934. ──────────. "Yeats's Byzantium Poems: A Study of their Development." *PMLA* 75(1960): 110–125.

20935. Brater, Enoch. "W. B. Yeats: The Poet as Critic." *JML* 4(1975): 651–676.

20936. Byars, John A. "Yeats's Introduction of the Heroic Type." *MD* 8(1966): 409–418.

20937. Callan, Edward. "W. B. Yeat's Learned Theban: Oswald Spengler." *JML* 4(1975): 593–609.

20938. Carpenter, William M. "The *Green Helmet* Poems and Yeat's Myth of the Renaissance." *MP* 67(1969): 50–59.

20939. Cohen, Joseph. "In Memory of W. B. Yeats—and Wilfred Owen." *JEGP* 58(1959): 637–649.

20940. Coleman, Antony. "A Calendar for the Production and Reception of *Cathleen Ni Houlihan*." *MD* 18(1975): 127–140.

20941. Clark, David R. "Aubrey Beardsley's Drawing of the 'Shadows' in Yeat's *The Shadowy Waters*." *MD* 7(1964): 267–272.

20942. ──────────. "*Nishikigi* and Yeats's *The Dreaming of the Bones*." *MD* 7(1964): 111–125.

20943. Davenport, A. "W. B. Yeats and the Upanishads." *RES* 3(1952): 55–62.

20944. Dawson, Leven Magruder. "'Among School Children': 'Labour' and 'Play.'" *PQ* 52(1973): 286–295.

20945. Desai, Rupin W. "A Note on 'Yeats on the Possibility of an English Poetic Drama.'" *MD* 11(1969): 396–399.

20946. Dunseath, T. K. "Yeats and the Genesis of Supernatural Song." *ELH* 28(1961): 399–416.

20947. Eagleton, Terry. "History and Myth in Yeats's Easter 1916.'" *EIC* 21(1971): 248–260.

20948. Eggenschwiler, David. "Nightingales and Byzantine Birds, Something Less Than Kind." *ELN* 8(1971): 186–191.

20949. Engelberg, Edward. "Picture and Gesture in the Yeatsian Aesthetic." *Criticism* 3 (1961): 101–120.

20950. Estrin, Barbara L. "Alternating Personae in Yeats' 'Lapis Lazuli' and 'Crazy Jane on the Mountain.'" *Criticism* 16(1974): 13-22.

20951. Fallis, Richard. "'I seek an image': The Method of Yeats's Criticism." *MLQ* 37(1976): 68-81.

20952. ----------. "Yeats and the Reinterpretation of Victorian Poetry." *VP* 14(1976): 89-100.

20953. Fallon, Gabriel. "Profiles of a Poet." *MD* 7(1964): 329-344.

20954. Faulkner, Peter. "Yeats as Critic." *Criticism* 4(1962): 328-339.

20955. Finneran, Richard J. "'Old lecher with a love on every wind.: A Study of Yeats' *Stories of Red Hanrahan*." *TSLL* 14(1972): 347-358.

20956. ----------. "On Editing Yeats: The Text of *A Vision* (1937)." *TSLL* 19(1977): 119-133.

20957. ----------. "Progress Report on the Yeats Industry." *JML* 3(1973): 129-133.

20958. Fixler, Michael. "The Affinities Between J.-K. Huysmans and the 'Rosicrucian' Stories of W. B. Yeats." *PMLA* 74(1959): 464-469.

20959. Fleissner, R. F. "The Second Coming of Guess Who?: The 'Rough Beast' as Africa in *The Second Coming*." *NCL* 6(Nov., 1976): 7-9.

20960. Friedman, Barton R. "*On Baile's Strand* to *At the Hawk's Well*: Staging the Deeps of the Mind." *JML* 4(1975): 625-650.

20961. Garab, Arra M. "Fabulous Artifice: Yeats' 'Three Bushes' Sequence." *Criticism* 7 (1965): 235-249.

20962. ----------. "The Legacy of Yeats." *JML* 1(1970): 137-140.

20963. ----------. "Yeats and *The Forged Casement Diaries*." *ELN* 2(1965): 289-292.

20964. ----------. "Yeats's 'Dark Betwixt the Polecat and the Owl.'" *ELN* 2(1965): 218-220.

20965. Gaskell, Ronald. "*Purgatory*." *MD* 4(1962): 397-401.

20966. Geckle, George L. "Stephen Daedalus and W. B. Yeats: The Making of the Villanelle." *MFS* 15(1969): 87-96.

20967. Gerstenberger, Donna. "Yeats and the Theater: A Selected Bibliography." *MD* 6(1963): 64-71.

20968. Gorsky, Susan R. "A Ritual Drama: Yeats' Plays for Dancers." *MD* 17(1974): 165-178.

20969. Gose, Elliott B., Jr. "The Lyric and the Philosophic in Yeats' *Calvary*." *MD* 2 (1960): 370-376.

20970. Grab, Frederic D. "Yeats' *King Oedipus*." *JEGP* 71(1972): 336-354.

20971. Greene, D. J. "Yeats's Byzantium and Johnson's Lichfield." *PQ* 33(1954): 433-435.

20972. Gwynn, Frederick L. "Yeats's Byzantium and Its Sources." *PQ* 32(1953): 9-21.

20973. Halloran, William F. "W. B. Yeats and William Sharp: The Archer Vision." *ELN* 6 (1969): 273-280.

20974. Hill, Archibald A. "Method in Source Study: Yeats' Golden Bird of Byzantium as a Test Case." *TSLL* 17(1975): 525-538.

20975. Hinden, Michael. "Yeats's Symbolic Farce: *The Player Queen*." *MD* 14(1972): 441-448.

20976. Hirschberg, Stuart. "The Influence of the Japanese Noh Play, *Nishikigi*, on Yeats's 'Crazy Jane' Poems." *NCL* 6(May, 1976): 2-3.

20977. ----------. "Masefield's Influence in Yeats' 'Under Ben Bulben.'" *NCL* 6(Sept., 1976): 8-12.

20978. ----------. "Why Yeats Saw Himself as a '*Daimonic* Man' of Phase 17: A Complementary View." *ELN* 11(1974): 202-205.

20979. ----------. "Yeats's 'Vision of Evil' in 'Meditations in Time of Civil War.'" *NCL* 4(May, 1974): 13-14.

20980. Hodges, Robert R. "The Irony of Yeats' 'Long Legged Fly.'" *TCL* 12(1966): 27-30.

20981. Holberg, Stanley M. "'Sailing to Byzantium': A New Source and a New Reading." *ELN* 12(1974): 111-116.

20982. Huberman, Elizabeth. "To Byzantium Once More: A Study of the Structure of Yeat's 'Byzantium.'" *EL* 1(1974): 193-205.

20983. Hurwitz, Harold M. "Yeats and Tagore." *Comp L* 16(1964): 55-64.

20984. Islam, Shamsul. "The Influence of Eastern Philosophy on Yeats' Later Poetry." *TCL* 19(1973): 283-290.

20985. Jeffares, A. Norman. "The Yeats Country." *MLQ* 25(1964): 218-222.

20986. Jochum, K. P. S. "Yeats's Last Play." *JEGP* 70(1971): 220-229.

20987. Keith, W. J. "Yeats's 'The Empty Cup.'" *ELN* 4(1967): 206-210.

20988. Kim, Myung Whan. "Dance and Rhythm: Their Meaning in Yeats and the Noh." *MD* 15(1972): 195-208.

20989. Kinsella, Thomas. "Literature and Politics in Ireland." *JML* 3(1973): 115-119.

20990. Krause, David. "O'Casey and Yeats and the Druid." *MD* 11(1968): 252-262.

20991. Lapisardi, Frederick S. "The Same Enemies: Notes on Certain Similarities Between Yeats and Strindberg." *MD* 12(1969): 146-154.

20992. Leamon, Warren. "Theatre as Dream: Yeats's Stagecraft." *MD* 20(1977): 145-156.

20993. Levin, Gerald. "The Yeats of the Autobiographies: A Man of Phase 17." *TSLL* 6 (1964): 398-405.

20994. Lightfoot, Marjorie J. "*Purgatory* and *The Family Reunion*: In Pursuit of Prosodic Description." *MD* 7(1964): 256-266.

20995. Martin, Graham. "Fine Manners, Liberal Speech; A Note on the Public Poetry of W. B. Yeats." *EIC* 11(1961): 40-59.

20996. Masson, David I. "Word and Sound in Yeats' 'Byzantium.'" *ELH* 20(1953): 136-160.

20997. Maxwell, D. E. S. "Time's Strange Excuse: W. B. Yeats and the Poets of the Thirties." *JML* 4(1975): 717-734.

20998. McAlindon, T. "The Idea of Byzantium in William Morris and W. B. Yeats." *MP* 64(1967): 307-319.

20999. ----------. "Yeats and the English Renaissance." *PMLA* 82(1967): 157-169.

21000. Mercier, Vivian. "Douglas Hyde's 'Share' in *The Unicorn from the Stars*." *MD* 7 (1965): 463-465.

21001. ----------. "In Defense of Yeats as a Dramatist." *MD* 8(1965): 161-166.

21002. Michie, Donald M. "A Man of Genius and a Man of Talent." *TSLL* 6(1964): 148-154.

21003. Moore, John R. "Cold Passion: A Study of *The Herne's Egg*." *MD* 7(1964): 287-298.

21004. Moore, John Rees. "An Old Man's Tragedy— Yeats' *Purgatory*." *MD* 5(1963): 440-450.

21005. Murphy, Daniel J. "Yeats and Lady Gregory: A Unique Dramatic Collaboration." *MD* 7

(1964): 322-328.

21006. Nelick, Frank C. "Yeats, Bullen, and the Irish Drama." *MD* 1(1958): 196-202.

21007. Newton, Norman. "Yeats as Dramatist: *The Player Queen*." *EIC* 8(1958): 269-284.

21008. Orel, Harold. "Dramatic Values, Yeats, and *The Countess Cathleen*." *MD* 2(1959): 8-16.

21009. O'Shea, Edward. "Yeats as Editor: Dorothy Wellesley's *Selections*." *ELN* 11(1973): 112-118.

21010. Parker, J. Stewart. "Yeats' *The Hour Glass*." *MD* 10(1968): 356-363.

21011. Parkin, Andrew. "Singular Voices: Monologue and Monodrama in the Plays of W. B. Yeats." *MD* 18(1975): 141-152.

21012. Parkinson, Thomas. "The Sun and the Moon in Yeats's Early Poetry." *MP* 50(1952): 50-58.

21013. ----------. "W. B. Yeats: A Poet's Stagecraft, 1899-1911." *ELH* 17(1950): 136-161.

21014. ----------. "Yeats and Pound: The Illusion of Influence." *Comp L* 6(1954): 256-264.

21015. Phillips, Steven R. "The Monomyth and Literary Criticism." *Coll L* 2(1975): 1-16.

21016. Pearce, Donald R. "Yeats' Last Plays: An Interpretation." *ELH* 18(1951): 67-76.

21017. Perloff, Marjorie. "'*Another* Emblem There': Theme and Convention in Yeats's 'Coole Park and Ballylee, 1931.'" *JEGP* 69(1970): 223-240.

21018. ----------. "The Consolation Theme in Yeats's 'In Memory of Major Robert Gregory.'" *MLQ* 27(1966): 306-322.

21019. ----------. "Heart Mysteries: The Later Love Lyrics of W. B. Yeats." *Con L* 10 (1969): 266-283.

21020. ----------. "Spatial Form in the Poetry of Yeats: The Two Lissadell Poems." *PMLA* 82(1967): 444-454.

21021. ----------. "'The Tradition of Myself': The Autobiographical Mode of Yeats." *JML* 4(1975): 529-573.

21022. ----------. "Yeats and Goethe." *Comp L* 23(1971): 125-140.

21023. Raines, Charles A. "Yeats' Metaphors of Permanence." *TCL* 5(1959): 12-19.

21024. Rayan, Krishna. "Yeats and the 'Little and Intense' Poems." *EIC* 25(1975): 407-418.

21025. Rees, Thomas. "Ezra Pound and the Modernization of Yeats." *JML* 4(1975): 574-592.

21026. Ritvo, Rosemary Puglia. "*A Vision B*: The Plotinian Metaphysical Basis." *RES* 26 (1975): 34-46.

21027. Rogal, Samuel J. "Keble's Hymn and Yeats' *The Words Upon the Window-Pane*." *MD* 16 (1973): 87-90.

21028. Rose, Marilyn Gaddis. "The Daughter of Heroidas in *Hérodiade*, *Salomé*, and *A Full Moon in March*." *CD* 1(1967): 172-181.

21029. ----------. "A Visit with Anne Yeats." *MD* 7(1964): 299-307.

21030. ----------. "Yeats' Use of *Axël*." *CD* 4(1970): 253-264.

21031. Rosenberg, Bruce A. "Irish Folklore and 'The Song of Wandering Aengus.'" *PQ* 46(1967): 527-535.

21032. Ryf, Robert S. "Yeats's Major Metaphysical Poems." *JML* 4(1975): 610-624.

21033. Salerno, Nicholas A. "A Note on Yeats and Leonardo da Vinci." *TCL* 5(1960): 197-198.

21034. Sandberg, Anna. "The Anti-Theater of W. B. Yeats." *MD* 4(1961): 131-137.

21035. Scanlon, Sister Aloyse. "The Sustained Metaphor in *The Only Jealousy of Emer*." *MD* 7(1964): 273-277.

21036. Schleifer, Ronald. "Narrative in Yeats's *In the Seven Woods*." *JNT* 6(1976): 155-174.

21037. Schmitt, Natalie Crohn. "Curing Oneself of the Work of Time: W. B. Yeats's *Purgatory*." *CD* 7(1973): 310-333.

21038. Schneidau, Herbert N. "Pound and Yeats: The Question of Symbolism." *ELH* 32(1965): 220-237.

21039. Schuler, Robert M. "W B. Yeats: Artist or Alchemist?" *RES* 22(1971): 37-55.

21040. Sena, Vinod. "Yeats on the Possibility of an English Poetic Drama." *MD* 9(1966): 195-205.

21041. Shanley, J. Lyndon. "Thoreau's Geese and Yeats's Swans." *AL* 30(1958): 361-364.

21042. Sharoni, Edna G. "*At the Hawk's Well*: Yeats Unresolved Conflict between Language and Silence." *CD* 7(1973): 150-173.

21043. Shmiefsky, Marvel. "Yeats and Browning: The Shock of Recognition." *SEL* 10(1970): 701-721.

21044. Sidnell, M. J. "John Bull's Other Island—Yeats and Shaw." *MD* 11(1968): 245-251.

21045. Southam, B. C. "Yeats: Life and the Creator in 'The Long Legged Fly.'" *TCL* 6(1961): 175-179.

21046. Spanos, William V. "Sacramental Imagery in the Middle and Late Poetry of W. R. Yeats." *TSLL* 4(1962): 214-227.

21047. Spitzer, Leo. "On Yeats's Poem 'Leda and the Swan.'" *MP* 51(1954): 271-276.

21048. Spivak, Gayatri Chakravorty. "Some Theoretical Aspects of Yeats's Prose." *JML* 4 (1975): 677-691.

21049. Stallworthy, Jon. "W. B. Yeats's 'Under Ben Bulben.'" *RES* 17(1966): 30-53.

21050. Storhoff, Gary and Linda. "'A Mind of Winter': Yeats's Early Vision of Old Age." *CLA* 21(1977): 90-97.

21051. Stucki, Yasuko. "Yeats's Drama and the No: A Comparative Study in Dramatic Theories." *MD* 9(1966): 101-122.

21052. Thatcher, David S. "Yeats' Repudiation of *Where There is Nothing*." *MD* 14(1971): 127-136.

21053. Torchiana, Donald T. "Review Article: Three Books on Yeats." *PQ* 46(1967): 536-556.

21054. ----------. "W. B. Yeats, Jonathan Swift, and Liberty." *MP* 61(1963): 26-39.

21055. Trowbridge, Hoyt. "'Leda and the Swan': A Longinian Analysis." *MP* 51(1953): 118-129.

21056. Unterecker, John. "The Shaping Force in Yeats's Plays." *MD* 7(1964): 345-356.

21057. Ure, Peter. "The Evolution of Yeats's 'The Countess Cathleen.'" *MLR* 57(1962): 12-24.

21058. ----------. "Yeats and the Two Harmonies." *MD* 7(1964): 237-255.

21059. ----------. "Yeats's Christian Mystery Plays." *RES* 11(1960): 171-182.

21060. ----------. "Yeats's Supernatural Songs." *RES* 7(1956): 38-51.

21061. Vendler, Helen Hennessey. "Yeats's Changing Metaphors for the Otherworld." *MD* 7 (1964): 308-321.

21062. Vogel, Joseph F. "Yeats's 'Nine-and-Fifty' Swans." *ELN* 5(1968): 297-300.

21063. Vogt, Kathleen M. "Counter-Components in Yeats's *At the Hawk's Well*." *MD* 17 (1974): 319-328.

21064. Walton, Geoffrey. "Yeats's 'Perne': Bobbin or Bird?" *EIC* 16(1966): 255-258.

21065. Warschausky, Sidney. "Yeats's Purgatorial Plays." *MD* 7(1964): 278-286.

21066. Watkins, Vernon. "W. B. Yeats—the Religious Poet." *TSLL* 3(1962): 475-488.

21067. Watson, Thomas L. "The French Reputation of Yeats." *Comp L* 12(1960): 256-262.

21068. Watts, C. T. "A Letter from W. B. Yeats to R. B. Cunninghame Graham." *RES* 18(1967): 292-293.

21069. Whitaker, Thomas R. "The Dialect of Yeats's Vision of History." *MP* 57(1959): 100-112.

21070. ----------. "The Early Yeats and the Pattern of History." *PMLA* 75(1960): 320-328.

21071. ----------. "Yeats's 'Dove or Swan.'" *PMLA* 76(1961): 121-132.

21072. Wilson, F. A. C. "Patterns in Yeats's Imagery: *The Herne's Egg*." *MP* 55(1957): 46-52.

21073. Winters, Yvor. "The Poetry of W. B. Yeats." *TCL* 6(1960): 3-24.

21074. Witt, Marion. "The Making of an Elegy: Yeats's 'In Memory of Major Robert Gregory.'" *MP* 48(1950): 112-121.

21075. ----------. "Yeats: 1865-1965." *PMLA* 80(1965): 311-320.

21076. ----------. "Yeats's 'The Song of the Happy Shepherd.'" *PQ* 32(1953): 1-8.

21077. Worth, Katharine J. "Yeats and the French Drama." *MD* 8(1966): 382-391.

21078. Youngblood, Sarah. "A Reading of *The Tower*." *TCL* 5(1959): 74-84.

21079. ----------. "The Structure of Yeats's Long Poems." *Criticism* 5(1963): 323-335.

See also 488, 514, 5145, 15717a, 19901.

GENERAL

21080. McDowell, Robert E., and Joseph J. Jones. "A Selected Checklist of Commonwealth English Novels." *SN* 4(1972): 321-332.

AFRICA

GENERAL. 21081. Killam, G. D. "Modern Black African Writing: A Selected Bibliography." *TCL* 17(1971): 37-64.

DRAMA. 21082. Baker, Donald. "African Theatre and the West." *CD* 11(1977): 209-226.

21083. Ferguson, John. "Nigerian Drama in English." *MD* 11(1968): 10-26.

FICTION. 21084. Berrian, Albert H. "Aspects of the West African Novel." *CLA* 14 (1970): 35-41.

21085. Larson, Charles R. "Things Fall Further Apart—New African Novels." *CLA* 10 (1966): 64-67.

21086. ----------. "Whither the African Novel?" *CLA* 13(1969): 144-152.

21087. Lindfors, Bernth. "African Vernacular Styles in Nigerian Fiction." *CLA* 9(1966): 265-273.

21088. ----------. "Oral Tradition and the Individual Literary Talent." *SN* 4(1972): 200-217.

21089. Palmer, Eustace. "Social Comment in the West African Novel." *SN* 4(1972): 218-230.

21090. Povey, John. "The English Language of the Contemporary African Novel." *Crit* 11,#3 (1969): 79-96.

ACHEBE, CHINUA. 21091. Champion, Earnest A. "The Story of a Man and His People: Chinua Achebe's *Things Fall Apart*." *BALF* 8(1974): 272-277.

21092. Meyers, Jeffrey. "Culture and History in *Things Fall Apart*." *Crit* 11,#1(1968): 25-32.

21093. Sarvan, Ponnuthrai. "The Mirror and the Image: Achebe's 'Girls at War.'" *SSF* 14 (1972): 277-279.

21094. Shelton, Austin J. "The 'Palm-Oil' of Language: Proverbs in Chinua Achebe's Novels. *MLQ* 30(1969): 86-111.

21095. Weinstock, Donald, and Cathy Ramadan. "Symbolic Structure in *Things Fall Apart*." *Crit* 11,#1(1968): 33-41.
See also 21087.

CLARK, J. P. 21096. Povey, John. "West African Drama in English." *CD* 1(1967): 110-121.

EASOM SHARIF. See 21096.

EKWENSI, CYPRIAN. 21098. Povey, John. "Cyprian Ekwensi and *Beautiful Feathers*." *Crit* 8, #1(1965): 63-69.

NKOSI, LEWIS. 21099. McCartney, Barney C. "Dramaturgical Movement in Lewis Nkosi's *The Rhythm of Violence*." *BALF* 8(1974): 268-270.

OKARA, GABRIEL. 21100. Goodley, Nancy C. "Two Levels of Meaning in Babriel Okara's *The Voice*." *CLA* 19(1975)" 312-317.
See also 21087.

SOYINKA, WOLE. 21101. Povey, John F. "Wole Soyinka: Two Nigerian Comedies." *CD* 3 (1969): 120-132.

21102. Hayden, Lucy K. "*The Man Died*, Prison Notes of Wole Soyinka: A Recorder and Visionary." *CLA* 18 (1975): 542-552.

TUTUOLA, AMOS. 21103. Collins, Harold R. "Founding a New National Literature: The Ghost Novels of Amos Tutuola." *Crit* 4,#1(1960): 17-28.

21104. Lindfors, Bernth. *The Palm-Wine Drinkard* and the Oral Tradition." *Crit* 11,#1(1968): 42-50.

AUSTRALIA

GENERAL. 21105. Meyer, Roy W. "The Outback and the West: Australian and American Frontier Fiction." *WAL* 6(1971): 3-19.

BOLDREWOOD, ROLF. See 21105.

FRANKLIN, MILES. See 21105.

FURPHY, JOSEPH. See 21105.

HOPE, A. D. 21106. Perrine, Laurence. "A. D. Hope's 'Agony Column.'" *NCL* 2(May,1972): 2-4.

PENTON, BRIAN. See 21105.

PRICHARD, KATHERINE S. See 21105.

RICHARDSON, H. H. 21107. Elliot, William D. "H. H. Richardson: The Education of an Australian Realist." *SN* 4(1972): 141-153.

STOW, RANDOLPH. 21108. New, William H. "Outsider Looking Out: The Novels of Randolph Stow." *Crit* 9,#1(1966): 90-99.

TUCKER, JAMES. See 21105.

WHITE, PATRICK. 21109. Carroll, Dennis. "Stage Conventions in the Plays of Patrick White." *MD* 19(1976): 11-24.

21110. Donaldson, Ian. "Return to Abyssinia." *EIC* 14(1964): 210-214.

21111. Dutton, Geoffrey. "The Novels of Patrick White." *Crit* 6,#3(1963): 7-28.

21112. Garebian, Keith. "The Desert and the Garden: The Theme of Completeness in *Voss*." *MFS* 22(1976): 557-569.

21113. Makenzie, Manfred. "The Consciousness of 'Twin Consciousness': Patrick White's *The Solid Mandala*." *Novel* 2(1969): 241-254.

21114. ----------. "Yes, Let's Return to Abyssinia." *EIC* 14(1964): 433-435.

CANADA

GENERAL. 21115. Green, Donald. "Western Canadian Literature." *WAL* 2(1968): 257-280.

21116. Moss, John. "Invisible Nation." *MFS* 22(1976): 341-345.

21117. Parker, George L. "Annotated Bibliography: Canadian Fiction and Poetry." *TCL* 16 (1970): 217-224.

21118. New, William H. "A Wellspring of Magma: *Modern Canadian Writing*." *TCL* 14(1968): 123-132.

DRAMA. 21119. Page, Malcom. "Three New Canadian Plays." *TCL* 16(1970): 203-206.

FICTION. 21120. Ferres, John H. "Criticism of Canadian Fiction Since 1945: A Selected Checklist." *TCL* 22(1976): 485-500.

21121. Harrison, Dick. "The American Adam and the Candian Christ." *TCL* 16(1970): 161-167.

21122. Wiebe, Rudy. "Western Canadian Fiction; Past and Future." *WAL* 6(1971): 21-30.

POETRY. 21123. Mandel, Eli. "Modern Canadian Poetry." *TCL* 16(1970): 175-183.

ATWOOD, MARGARET. 21124. Glicksohn, Susan Wood. "The Martian Point of View." *Ext* 15(1974):

161-173.

21125. Rubenstein, Roberta. "*Surfacing*: Margaret Atwood's Journey to the Interior." *MFS* 22(1976): 387-399.

AVISON, MARGARET. 21126. New, William H. "The Mind's Eyes [I's] [Ice]: The Poetry of Margaret Avison." *TCL* 16(1970): 185-202.

BONNER, MARGERIE. 21127. Grace, Sherrill. "Margerie Bonner's Three Forgotten Novels." *JML* 6(1977): 321-324.

DAVIES, ROBERTSON. 21128. Brown, Russell M., and Donna A. Bennett. "Magnus Eisengrim: The Shadow of the Trickster in the Novels of Robertson Davies." *MFS* 22(1976): 347-363.

GODFREY, DAVE. 21129. New, W. H. "Godfrey's Book of Changes." *MFS* 22(1976): 375-385.

GROVE, FREDERICK PHILIP. 21130. Margaret R. "'Frederick Philip Grove' and the Canadianism Movement." *SN* 4(1972): 173-185.

See also 21115.

HERBERT, JOHN. 21131. Carson, Neil. "Sexuality and Identity in *Fortune and Men's Eyes*." *TCL* 18(1972): 207-218.

LAURENCE, MARGARET. 21132. Thomas, Clara. "The Novels of Margaret Laurence." *SN* 4(1972): 154-164.

21133. ----------. "The Wild Garden and the Manawka World." *MFS* 22(1976): 401-411.

LOWRY, MALCOM. 21134. Arac, Jonathan. "The Form of Carnival in *Under the Volcano*." *PMLA* 92 (1977): 481-489.

21135. Barcham, Terence. "After the Volcano: An Assessment of Malcom Lowry's Posthumous Fiction." *SN* 6(1974): 349-362.

21136. Baxter, Charles. "The Escape from Irony: *Under the Volcano* and the Aesthetics of Arson." *Novel* 10(1977): 114-126.

21137. Costa, Richard Hauer. *Pieta*, *Pelado*, and 'The Ratification of Death': The Ten-Year Evolvement of Malcom Lowry's *Volcano*." *JML* 2(1971): 3-18.

21138. ----------. "The Northern Paradise" Malcom Lowry in Canada." *SN* 4(1972): 165-172.

21139. Cross, Richard K. "Malcom Lowry and the Columbian Eden." *Con L* 14(1973): 19-30.

21140. ----------. "*Moby-Dick* and *Under the Volcano*: Poetry from the Abyss." *MFS* 20(1974): 149-156.

21141. Edmonds, Dale. "Mescallusions or The Drinking Man's *Under the Volcano*." *JML* 6(1977): 277-288.

21142. ----------. "The Voyage Begins: Toward an Understanding of Malcom Lowry." *JML* 4(1974): 133-138.

21143. Richey, Clarence W. "'The Ill-Fated Mr. Bultitude': A Note Upon an Allusion in Malcom Lowry's *Under the Volcano*." *NCL* 3(May, 1973): 3-5.

21144. Richmond, Lee J. "The Pariah Dog Symbolism in Malcom Lowry's *Under the Volcano*." *NCL* 6(March, 1976): 7-9.

21145. Woodcock, George. "Malcom Lowry's *Under the Volcano*." *MFS* 4(1958): 151-156.

See also 21127.

MACKENZIE, ALEXANDER. 21146. Kime, Wayne R. "Poe's Use of Mackenzie's *Voyages* in 'The Journal of Julius Rodman.'" *WAL* 3(1968): 61-67.

MANDEL, ELI. See 21115.

MCLUHAN, MARSHALL. 21147. Watson, Wilfred. "Education in the Tribal/Global Village." *TCL* 16 (1970): 207-216.

21148. Milowicki, Edward J. "Some Medieval Light on Marshall McLuhan." *SLI* 4,#2(1971): 51-59.

MOORE, BRIAN. 21149. Kersnowski, Frank L. "Exit the Anti-Hero." *Crit* 10, #3(1968): 60-71.

21150. Ludwig, Jack. "Brian Moore: Ireland's Loss, Canada's Novelist." *Crit* 5,#1(1962): 5-13.

21151. Dahlie, Hallvard. "Brian Moore's Broader Vision: *The Emperor of Ice-Cream*." *Crit* 9,#1(1966): 43-55.

21152. Sale, Richard B. "An Interview in London with Brian Moore." *SN* 1(1969): 67-80.

MUNRO, ALICE. 21153. Macdonald, Rae McCarthy. "A Madman Loose in the World: The Vision of Alice Munro." *MFS* 22(1976): 365-374.

21154. Monaghan, David. "Confinement and Escape in Alice Munro's 'The Flats Road.'" *SSF* 14(1977): 165-168.

O'GRADY, ROHAN. See June O'Grady Skinner.

REANEY, JAMES. See 21119.

RICHLER, MODECAI. 21155. Ower, John. "Sociology, Psychology, and Satire in *The Apprenticeship of Duddy Kravitz*." *MFS* 22(1976): 413-428.

SKINNER, JUNE O'GRADY. 21156. Troost, Betty Todd. "O'Grady's Classic: *O'Houlihan's Jest*." *Crit* 10,#1(1967): 78-84.

RYGA, GEORGE. See 21119.

SIMONS, BEVERLEY. See 21119.

INDIA

GENERAL. 21157. McCutchion, David. "The Indian Novel in English." *SN* 4(1972): 304-320.

21158. Rao, K. S. Narayana. "The Indian Novel in English: A Search for Identity." *SN* 4(1972): 296-303.

21159. Williams, H. Moore. "English Writing in Free India (1947-1967): *TCL* 16(1970): 3-15.

JHABVALA, R. PRAWER. 21160. Williams, H. Moore. "The Yogi and the Babbitt: Themes and Characters of the New India in the Novels of R. Prawer Jhabvala." *TCL* 15(1969): 81-91.

TAGORE, RABINDRANATH. 21161. Murwitz, Harold M. "Ezra Pound and Rabindranath Tagore." *AL* 36 (1964): 53-63.

21162. Shahane, V. A. "Rabindraneth Tagore: A Study in Romanticism." *SR* 3(1963): 53-64.

21163. Sharma, Mohan Lal. "Rabindranath Tagore as Playwright." *MD* 13(1970): 83-92.

NEW ZEALAND

FRAME, JANET. 21164. Robertson, Robert T. "Bird, Hawk, Bogie: Janet Frame, 1952-62." *SN* 4 (1972): 186-199.

SOUTH AFRICA

GENERAL. 21165. Woodrow, Mervyn. "South African Drama in English." *CD* 4(1970): 132-148.

ABRAHAMS, PETER. 21166. Wade, Michael, "The Novels of Peter Abrahams." *Crit* 11,#1(1968): 82-95.

CAMPBELL, ROY. 21167. Povey, John F. "A

Lyre of Savage Thunder: A Study of the Poetry of
Roy Campbell." *Con L* 7(1966): 85-102.

FUGARD, ATHOL. 21168. Green, Robert J.
"Athol Fugard's *Hello and Goodbye*." *MD* 13(1970):
139-155.

21169. ----------. "South Africa's Plague:
One View of *The Blood Knot*." *MD* 12(1970): 311-
345.

SCHREINER, OLIVE. 21170. Heywood, Chris-
topher. "Olive Schreiner's *The Story of an
African Farm*: Prototype of Lawrence's Early
Novels." *ELN* 14(1976): 44-50.

21171. Rive, Richard M. "Olive Schreiner:
A Critical Study and Checklist." *SN* 4(1972): 231-
251.

WEST INDIES

GENERAL. 21172. Brown, Lloyd W. "The
Crisis of Black Identity in the West Indian Novel."
Crit 11,#3(1969): 97-112.

21173. Davies, Barrie, "The Personal Sense
of Society—Minority View: Aspects of the 'East
Indian' Novel in the West Indies." *SN* 4(1972):
284-295.

21174. Harris, L. J., and D. A. Ormerod.
"A Preliminary Checklist of West Indian Fiction
in English, 1949-1964." *TCL* 11(1965): 146-149.

21175. Page, Malcom. "West Indian Writers."
Novel 3(1970): 167-172.

HARRIS, WILSON. 21176. Boxill, Anthony.
"Wilson Harris's *Palace of the Peacock*: A New
Dimension in West Indian Fiction." *CLA* 14(1971):
380-386.

JAMES, C. L. R. See 6431.

MAIS, ROGER. Dathorne, Oscar R. "Roger
Mais: The Man on the Cross." *SN* 4(1972): 275-
283.

HODGE, MERLE. See 6431.

NAIPAUL, V. S. 21178. Ormerod, David.
"In a Derelict Land: The Novels of V. S. Naipaul."
Con L 9(1968): 74-90.

21179. ----------. "Theme and Image in V. S.
Naipaul's *A House for Mr. Biswas*." *TSLL* 8(1967):
589-602.